CW00503357

Betty's Diaries

Transcribed, unabridged, from the original diaries of
Elizabeth Hewes

by

Mary Julia Johns (née Hewes)
Mary Blue

This first edition published 11th May 2010
by
the collaboration of Fantastic State Company Limited, Paragon Publishing & Into Print

Address for all correspondence:
Fantastic State Limited
1 Burton Road,
Sileby
Loughborough
Leicestershire
LE12 7RU

Email: info@fantasticstate.co.uk

www.fantasticstate.co.uk

Production management
by
Into Print
www.intoprint.net

Printed and bound
In the United Kingdom
by
Lightning Source UK Ltd.
MK11 3LW

Betty's Diaries

The life & times of Elizabeth Hewes
of Ravenstone, Leicestershire
1944 to 2001

ISBN 978-1-899820-99-3

www.fantasticstate.co.uk

Contents

Brief summary of contents per year · vi
Foreword by Stephen Butt · xi
Introduction · xii

Photographs - *Betty's Album / 1* · xiii
Family Trees · xxx

Diary for 1944 · 3
Diary for 1945 · 21
Diary for 1947 · 36
Diary for 1948 · 46
Diary for 1949 · 56
Diary for 1950 · 63
Diary for 1951 · 71
Diary for 1952 · 74
Diary for 1953 · 75
Diary for 1954 · 77
Diary for 1955 · 81
Diary for 1956 · 85
Diary for 1957 · 89
Diary for 1958 · 95
Diary for 1959 · 99

Photographs -
people pomp & circumstances / 2 · 102

Diary for 1960 · 111
Diary for 1961 · 114
Diary for 1962 · 117
Diary for 1963 · 121
Diary for 1964 · 124
Diary for 1965 · 147
Diary for 1966 · 171
Diary for 1967 · 195
Diary for 1968 · 220
Diary for 1969 · 242

Photographs -
...at work, rest & play / 3 · 253

Diary for 1970 · 259
Diary for 1971 · 271
Diary for 1972 · 284
Diary for 1973 · 297
Diary for 1974 · 309
Diary for 1975 · 321

Contents

Diary for 1976   333
Diary for 1977   345
Diary for 1978   357

Handprints   368

Diary for 1979   371

Photographs -
homes, gardens, pets & places / 4   383

Diary for 1980   389
Diary for 1981   401
Diary for 1982   413
Diary for 1983   425
Diary for 1984   437
Diary for 1985   448
Diary for 1986   459
Diary for 1987   470
Diary for 1988   481
Diary for 1989   492

Photographs -
Coalville Amateur Operatic Society / 5   505

Diary for 1990   513
Diary for 1991   526
Diary for 1992   571
Diary for 1993   585
Diary for 1994   598
Diary for 1995   616
Diary for 1996   635
Diary for 1997   653
Diary for 1998   670
Diary for 1999   686
Diary for 2000   704
Diary for 2001   719

Afterword   727

Every effort has been made to acknowledge all copyright holders where Betty had inserted excerpts and extracts from various publications, newspapers and magazines. If any have been inadvertently overlooked, the publishers will be pleased to make the necessary arrangements at the first opportunity.

Brief summary of contents for each year

1944 - On 1st January 1944, when she was 12 years old, Betty started to keep a diary. England is at war; food is rationed; evacuees are living with Betty, her mother and her brother Robert (Robin) at 27 Leicester Road, Ravenstone in Leicestershire, where she was born and would live all her life. Betty attends Coalville Grammar School in Forms 3A and 4A

1945 - Betty aged 13 to 14 – the war comes to an end; Coalville Grammar School Forms 4A and 5A; camping with the Girl Guides; holidaying again at mother's cousins on the farm at Willoughby-on-the-Wolds

1946 - No diary for 1946 (the year Betty was bridesmaid for her half-sister Bunting)

1947 - Betty aged 15 to 16 in the Lower Sixth Form, Form 6B and Upper Sixth Form, Form 6A, at Coalville Grammar school - "worst blizzard ever" – "80 mph gale"- first boyfriends – Mum starts work as a nursing auxiliary at Ashby Cottage Hospital on night duty 8 p.m. to 8 a.m.

1948 - John Marsden (Cocky) comes into Betty's life – Betty leaves school – first permanent job in the Motor Licence Office in Friar Lane in Leicester – Betty joins Coalville Amateur Operatic Society

1949 - Cycling on a tandem with boyfriend "Chet" – Coalville Amateurs production of "Hit the Deck" – first kiss from Cocky

1950 - Continuing disapproval from relatives – many tears – Betty & Cocky try to say goodbye - Coalville Amateurs give "Maid of the Mountains" – John Dolman steps in – more tears

1951 - Cocky goes to work in Lancashire – Betty's brother Robin dies – Cocky comes back home

1952 - Betty turns 21 – still trying to say goodbye to Cocky – a lot of heartache

1953 - John Dolman takes Betty here there & everywhere to no avail

1954 - Revd. Dowling dies – final break with Cocky – singing lessons with Lilian Dunkley, Winston Churchill's 80th birthday

1955 - Like Betty, Princess Margaret chooses not to marry the man she loves; Betty's singing lessons continue

1956 - Reevsie's 21st – Cocky finds a new girlfriend and gets engaged - more tears – Bible

Reading Fellowship formed with Betty as secretary.

1957 - Cocky marries Joan – Coalville Amateurs give "Wild Violets"- Chet gets married - Betty's first aeroplane flight - Premium Bonds introduced - Reevsie gets engaged

1958 - Holidays in Clacton and the Isle of Man - Betty's first day as Sunday School teacher at St. Michael & All Angels Church, Ravenstone, Leicestershire

1959 - Coalville Amateurs give "White Horse Inn" – Gustav Aronsohn inducted at church

1960 - Coalville Amateurs give "Chu Chin Chow" – Princess Margaret marries – holiday in Dublin

1961 - Amateurs give "No No Nanette" – Cocky & Joan have baby daughter – holidays in Newquay and Guernsey

1962 - Betty buys a motor scooter – holiday in Isle of Wight – fails driving test on scooter!

1963 - Passes driving test on scooter – holiday in Ireland – Kennedy assassinated

1964 - Now Betty has her first "Five Year Diary" and achieves an entry every day for the next five years – Amateurs give "The Desert Song" - Betty learns shorthand & typing

1965 - Driving lessons in a car – death of Churchill – Amateurs give "Annie Get Your Gun" Mary Blue gets married – Betty passes driving test in a car – Gustav Aronsohn leaves Ravenstone Church

1966 - Betty meets the Provost of Leicester Cathedral – promotion at the Motor Licence Office– flower arranging – new Rector at Ravenstone, Revd. Matthew Rice-Lewis – another promotion at work to the Public Counter issuing Vehicle Excise Licences – Aberfan Disaster - the Sunday School grows – Betty becomes Editor for the Church Magazine - Bob Gerard

1967 - Donald Campbell killed – Amateurs give "White Horse Inn" – Brian Lamming is encountered - Betty learns to play the piano - a new Scooter – New County Hall being built - Alf Hall elected – accident on scooter – new car bought – Motor Licence Office moves from Friar Lane to County Hall, Glenfield

1968 - Amateurs give "Merry Widow" – Southgates underpass opens in Leicester – Betty has now been working 20 years in the Motor Licence Dept. of Leicestershire County Council

1969 - Amateurs give "Oliver!" which is Betty's 21st show - first Man on the Moon – Motor Licence work transfers to Ministry of Transport – Revd. Matthew Rice Lewis leaves Ravenstone Church – Betty takes elocution lessons

1970 - Age of majority down from 21 to 18 – Marshall & Snelgrove close down – Amateurs give "Kiss Me Kate" – Betty is now a Civil Servant – Revd. Leslie Buckroyd new Rector for Ravenstone - £20 notes issued for the first time – dustmen etc. on strike - decimalisation introduced stage by stage

1971 - Ibrox disaster – postal strike – farewell £-s-d – Amateurs give "Pink Champagne" – the great Census – Britain voted into Common Market – a telephone is installed

1972 - Miners strike – power cuts – Amateurs "Bless the Bride" postponed – Duke of Windsor dies – Idi Amin expels 8,000 Ugandan Asians – Olympic Games in Munich Expo '72

1973 - Amateurs give "My Fair Lady" - Betty's last appearance on stage as Mrs Higgins – new car for Betty – arm in plaster – Princess Anne marries

1974 - Three day week – Amateurs give "Maritza" – County Council shake-up – Watergate - guitar lessons – promotion to Executive Officer

1975 - Galloping inflation– redundancies – unemployment – Channel tunnel abandoned – Amateurs give "Fiddler on the Roof" – Betty visits Rome – D.V.L.C. Swansea takes over issuing of driver and vehicle licences

1976 - Huge gales – Concorde – Amateurs give "Viva Mexico!" – Olympic Games – Britain's worst drought for 250 years - new car for Betty

1977 - Amateurs give "Showboat" – Queen's Silver Jubilee – Elvis dies – Betty goes down Snibston Pit

1978 - L.T.O. closure – Betty joins Department of Energy at Wigston (Gas Standards) – Leicester city centre pedestrianised – death of two Popes – house for sale

1979 - Strikes – snow – "Hello Dolly" – Mountbatten dies – Mum goes into hospital, never to return

1980 - The Queen comes to Leicester – Joanne entertains Betty – 14 Friar Lane becomes "Isabella's" night club

1981 - Prince Charles visits Leicester – going metric – Census time again – Charles & Diana marry – barcodes – a fifty pound note! – Rubik's Cube – a white Christmas

1982 - Total eclipse of the Moon – Falklands conflict – 2nd London Marathon – Betty goes from Prompter to Treasurer at C.A.O.S. – Prince William born – Betty's Mum dies – Snibston School Diary

1983 - Seat belts become compulsory – burials discontinued at St. Mary's Snibston – Betty resigns as Sunday School Teacher - £1 coin replaces £1 note – "Tomlinson" by Rudyard Kipling

1984 - Gas Standards – stars – miners strike – Prince Harry born - Brighton bomb – St. Martin's shopping centre opens in Leicester

1985 - House of Lords televised live – fire at Bradford football ground – ban on English soccer clubs – Titanic found 2 ½ miles deep – Fox Cub bus outing – Dr Jeannon dies

1986 - Space shuttle disaster – Greater London Council scrapped - Duchess of Windsor dies - Prince Andrew marries – AIDS spreads – Human Genome Project

1987 - 3 million unemployed – John Marsden makes contact – Betty has a new car – C.A.O.S. Grand Reunion

1988 - Rev. Leslie Buckroyd dies – CFCs – Piper Alpha explosion – wheelie bins – cashless shopping

1989 - Air crash at Kegworth – new rector, Revd. Kerry Emmett – nuclear fusion – word processing – House of Commons televised – Downing Street out of bounds

1990 - Nelson Mandela freed – Poll Tax – M&S opened at Fosse Park – Ravenstone Darby & Joan closes – Saddam Hussein

1991 - Gulf War –Betty acts as Enumerator for the 1991 Census - Betty retires from Gas Standards – Les Miserables – Betty's car stolen – Terry Waite freed

1992 - Snibston Discovery Park opens – The Maze in Horsefair Street, Leicester – Euro Disney opens – Betty buys a new car – lots more travelling now she is retired

1993 - D.N.A. – Guys & Dolls – James Bulger – Grand National – Doris Scott (who nursed Lawrence of Arabia) – pit closures

1994 - "Cats" – Privatisation of British Rail – Hubble – 50th Anniversary of D-Day – Sunday Trading – Donor eggs and IVF – National Lottery launched – 'The Hollies' is sold

1995 - 50th Anniversary of VE Day – death of Peter Townsend – 1994 Marriage Act takes effect – 50th Anniversary VJ Day – Carlton Hayes close down – Fred West

1996 - British Gas loses monopoly – De Montfort University – IRA bomb London – Charles & Diana divorce – M.R.S.A. – Legoland – Andrew & Fergie divorce – Big Bang theory – New driving theory test – gene maps – Cable TV – Tony Blair

1997 - Camilla & Charles – 'Carousel' – New Labour victory - Britannia's last voyage – Hong Kong – Digital TV - Millennium Bug warnings – Rutland – Lesley Hale - Diana's dresses auctioned – Fosse Park South – Death of Diana and Mother Teresa

1998 - Countdown to Millennium begins – Talking Newspaper – Portcullis House – SORN - Princess Margaret ill – Angel of the North – Winter Fuel Payment – civil weddings increase - Miner's statue in Coalville – 'Cosmos' – The Times – new £2 coin – David Taylor, Labour MP, makes his presence felt

1999 - "The Card" – "The Croft" built in Wash Lane – Scott goes to Australia – traffic 'calming' comes to Coalville – Donald Dewar First Minister for Scotland – Manchester United triumph – Timothy Stevens new Bishop of Leicester – Cardinal Basil Hume dies – baby boy for the Linleys – John F. Kennedy Jr killed – SS Waratah found – total eclipse of the sun – Cousin Miles to Malta – Pay & Display metres – The Diana Report – Barry Branson – London's Wheel rises at last – Lord Lucan officially dead – Betty gets 'Webwise' – Millennium fever grows

2000 - Cocky's 70th birthday – Ravenstone's oldest resident dies at 103 – first woman provost – "Charlie Girl" – Diamond Wedding of Pat & Evelyn – Brian Land's death – C & A to close in Leicester – Queen Mother's 100th birthday – Concorde crash – James Hunt QC – the Kursk disaster – Betty learns 'Computing in Retirement'

2001 - Like Princess Margaret, Betty is 'unwell' – centenary of the death of Queen Victoria – Betty fills in some gaps in her family's history – she is admitted to hospital but still keeps writing notes for her diary

Betty died 10th March 2001

Foreword

A diary is a unique historical document, but it is much more than merely a readable glimpse into the past.

Arguably, no written history is truly and totally objective. Even the most scholarly research is written from a certain standpoint or to present a specific explanation as to why something happened when it did; but a diary is a personal record and the author is therefore free to be selective without having to provide a reason why one event may be included whilst another is ignored.

A diary is sometimes so personal that, as in the case of Francis Kilvert, people close to the author may feel that it should not be released into the public domain. Diarists may offer shrewd social comment as in the commentaries on contemporary events provided by Samuel Pepys; or they may show, as in the diary of the Revd James Woodforde, that in the past, when news travelled more slowly, the seemingly insignificant local event was the one most worth recording.

The development of speedier forms of communication in the 19th and 20th Centuries - from the telegraph and the telephone through to the ability to send information in audio, text and visual forms between handheld mobile devices - has meant that for most people life has also become faster and consequently more transient. Betty witnessed many of these changes. She records how, during the Second World War, the village of Ravenstone was invaded by 'Yanks', whom she saw arriving at the nearby crossroads and she observes Neil Armstrong's 'one small step' decades later. She writes about royalty, the Rubik's Cube craze, compulsory seat belts and the Kegworth air crash.

Betty began keeping her diary in 1944, yet she lived to be part of the internet age. However, her own means of communicating her thoughts and her observations of life did not alter. Apart from her childish early years, throughout that span of time and change we see the same neat handwriting, the same careful choice of word and phrase and the same attention to grammar.

The diary is a fascinating insight into Betty's world. For some readers it may seem a rather small and restricted existence, from the farming community of Ravenstone in north-west Leicestershire as far as her place of work in the centre of Leicester and, apart from holidays and day trips, nowhere else in over half a century of experience. Her life was centred on family, the church, her membership of Coalville Amateur Operatic Society and her job; her influences and friends were drawn from these elements of her day-to-day existence. Descriptions of her role as a Sunday School teacher and her work in the County's vehicle licensing department (in Greyfriars and later at the newly-constructed County Hall) are punctuated by thoughtful records of much broader news events such as the death of Winston Churchill or the assassination of President Kennedy.

Betty never married. When she fell in love, her family disapproved and so the relationship ended; but in the vein of a romantic novel, Betty and her 'only true love' were to get in touch again many years later.

She continued to keep her diary until, quite literally, she was too ill to lift her pen. Even then, she believed that her work could live on beyond her own lifetime. She committed her treasured writings to her niece Mary, asking her to take over the record at the point when Betty's health had forced her to stop.

This book is part of the ongoing commitment to Betty, made at that time. Her books are safe, and they are forming the basis of a new online enterprise through which many others will gain from her scrupulous work. Her thoughts and comments and her quiet perception of life are being read now, and appreciated perhaps, by more people than Betty ever met in her entire lifetime.

Stephen Butt

April 2010

Introduction

My Aunt Betty had kept a diary since News Years Day 1944, when she was twelve years old. She began because Mrs Cassell, a war time evacuee staying with the family, had given her a large desk diary for Christmas. What an amazing gift that turned out to be. The diaries were to run from January 1st 1944 up until her death at the age of sixty-nine in March 2001.

I was aware that Betty had kept a diary because my mum used to tease me and my dad about it, keeping us in line by saying, 'Watch out – or you'll be in the diary!' But no-one had ever seen them; not until Betty became ill in the early part of 2001 and entrusted me with her affairs. She told me where the diaries were and that she had bought an oak chest for them to be stored in safely. (See 18th July 2000)

She wanted me to complete the last diary for her; explaining that, in any event, she had planned to finish them at the end of 2001. She was in the habit of keeping rough notes before writing up the entries, and she had taken her notebook with her into hospital. I visited her most days in those last weeks and I was asked to pick out salient points from this rough book and write them up in the final diary. Told I could begin reading the rest of them, I was amazed at their neatness, attention to detail, and the depth and scope of the content. I remarked to Betty that they ought to be published. She looked at me and simply smiled; adding after a moment that they were to be passed on as far into the future as possible.

The diaries were mainly five-year diaries and each day had just six lines to be written on; each entry filled these lines exactly, leaving no space at the end. I mentioned this to Betty and she said that achieving this was 'a work of art' which she had perfected over many years. She was especially pleased if the six lines could be completely filled with just one sentence! She also insisted they had to be written with a fountain pen – her Parker pen – because ink from a ball-point fades over time. Feeling very nervous at being charged with this daunting task and not wanting to spoil the last diary with my not-so-neat handwriting, I decided to transcribe the whole lot and save them on a compact disc with a view to getting them published one day. It has been a labour of love that has taken me nine years on and off; but I think this will ensure they go on into the future as Betty wished - even if one of my descendants should decide to chuck the originals on a bonfire one day!

After reading the diaries over again, through transposing them into digital format, it is clear they were very precious to her; they tell of her life and indeed they are her life's work. Publishing them properly now, in book form, ensures that a copy will be lodged with the British Library - securing access for all as long as that great institution exists. Last of all in the realm of posterity, made possible by the digital age, this edition will be available as an eBook, creating global access for future generations. I believe Betty would be pleased to know that people can read for themselves who she really was; her thoughts, opinions, values, beliefs, her humour, the sadness she often felt and the genuine sincerity with which she lived her life.

It became clear that Betty sometimes made entries in advance; putting interesting items or thoughts which befitted some future date. Reading these after she had died almost felt like she was still talking to me. One of the last entries she had made ahead of time was written on the date of 26th December 2001 and reads:

So Farewell! For I am going
On a long and distant journey.
But my books I leave behind me.
Listen to their words of wisdom.
Listen to the truth they tell you...

Mary Julia Johns (née Hewes)

Sileby, Leicestershire, UK

April 2010

Betty's Photograph Album

July 1972
On holiday
with cousin Enid
at Ilfracombe.

NOTES

"THE HOLLIES"
built by Grandpa
George Harry Hewes
at Ravenstone on
land he purchased
on 25 Sept. 1897.

The old family home

NOTES

My dad, Reg
with his firstborn
'Bunting' born
7 July 1915
firstborn of Julia

My dad, Reg
with me (Betty)
born 14 July 1931

NOTES

My mum, born
23 August 1905
Mary Sketchley.
Her twin sister
Elizabeth (Cissie)
died of diphtheria
when she was
10 years old.

NOTES

My dad, Reg (seated) with 2 of his 5 brothers, Aubrey (left) ~ Cyril, during the First World War 1914 – 1918.

NOTES

My dad, Reg, in later years at work in the office of the family firm, G. H. Hewes ~ Sons, Marlborough Square Coalville.

NOTES

This was my
Mum as a young
woman. She was
born in 1905,
MARY SKETCHLEY.
Her twin sister
Elizabeth (Cissie)
died aged 10. Mum
died in 1982.

Bunting with
her mother Julia
(née Stacey)

Julia died in
1918, shortly
after the birth
of her second
child, Pat

Following the
death of his
first wife, Julia,
my dad went to
live with relatives
in Canada, where
he broke his leg.
He ~ my mum
married in 1929.

Brother Pat
now is a soldier
in World War 2.
On 16 March 1940
he married Evelyn
(née Roberts).
His cousin Norman
(son of Aubrey) was
Killed in the war

NOTES

The biggest gap in our lives come on 11 Jan 1939 when my dad died, aged 49. My mum become a widow, aged 33, with 2 young children. I was aged 7.

NOTES

1935
With my little brother Robin (Robert Arthur) born 21 Jan: 1934 slightly crippled, he died aged 17.

NOTES

Rob ~ I at Snibston School in war-time. The Second World War started on 3 Sept. 1939 and ended in 1945.

NOTES

From 1942 - 1948
I was at Coalville
Grammar School
(standing 3rd left)

NOTES

When I left
school, cousin Don
(son of Fred) &
his wife Phyl
were particularly
Kind & helpful,
taking me with
them on holiday
for several years.

NOTES

Holidays now
with cousin Enid
(Cyril's daughter)

This is 1955
at Butlin's Hotel
SALTDEAN
Near Brighton

NOTES

1959
Enid & I on
holiday at Portrush,
Northern Ireland.

NOTES

August 1964
Mum & I join
a coach-trip to
Devon & Cornwall
staying 2 nights at
Paignton, 2 nights
at Penzance and
2 nights at
Ilfracombe.

NOTES   *1965*
Joan Dillow,
Barry Edwards,
me & Frank Goddard
in Coalville Amateur
Operatic's production
"Annie get your gun".
I joined the society
when I left
school in 1948.

NOTES

From 1958
to 1983, I
was a Sunday
School Teacher
at Ravenstone
Church.
With Harold Moore
Superintendant, who
died in 1980.

NOTES

In May 1962
I bought a scooter.
Mum sometimes
rode pillion.

In March 1963
I passed my scooter
driving test.

NOTES

1 July 1963
Cong, Ireland.
Enid & I on
holiday in Galway
visit Cong, the
only place on
earth where I
experienced complete
natural silence.

NOTES 29 June 1963

President Kennedy, who was assassinated in November 1963, visited Galway on the very date we began our holiday ~ he received the Freedom of the city. We just missed seeing him.

NOTES

The Irish Flag ~ the American Flag welcome President Kennedy to Galway. After one week in Galway we spent the following week in Dublin.

NOTES

Dublin
July 1963

The 134 ft high Nelson Pillar, erected in 1808, was destroyed by a time bomb in March 1966.

NOTES

From 1948-1978
I worked in the
Motor Licence
Office of the
Leics. County Council.
I managed to
acquire KAY 7
for Auntie Cis, seen
here with Aunt Dos.

NOTES

In July 1965
I passed my
car driving test,
but could not
afford to buy
a car. This was
my first car
which I bought
second-hand in 19..

NOTES

July 1973
Aunt Dos & mum
beside my first
brand new car
which replaced
FBT 638 D.

On 24 April 1965
Pat ~ Evelyn's
daughter Mary
married Jerry
Jarman at
Ravenstone Church.
Mary is known
as Mary Blue.

On 4 June 1966,
cousin Don's
daughter Lesley
married cousin
Minna's son
John Sear at
Ravenstone Church.
Minna was Uncle
Aubrey's daughter.

Mary Blue ~ I
with Steven
her firstborn.
Born 28 Dec. 1967,
this was the day
he was Christened,
2 June 1968,
Whit Sunday.

NOTES

March 1970
and snow for
Coalville Amateurs
production of
'Kiss me Kate'.

NOTES

CHRISTMAS 1968
I am Geni of
the Ring in the
local Stage
Society's production
of "Aladdin"
at the Town Hall
Ashby-de-la-Zouch.

NOTES

With Bunting's
2 sons, Julian
(left) ~ Michael,
on Julian's
wedding day.
Julian ~ Shirley
were married at
Malvern on
31 May 1975.

NOTES

In October 1958 I became a Sunday School teacher at Ravenstone Church. Here I am in June 1976, as we prepare to take part in a Pageant for the Diocese of Leicester.

NOTES

Guitarist Hewsie mastered only a few simple chords. Our Sunday School was thriving in 1976 with several talented & enthusiastic teachers. I was a Sunday School teacher for 25 years.

NOTES

24 May 1992
Four generations:-
Evelyn, Mary Blue,
Karen (bride on
7 July 1990) ~
baby Suzannah,
born 21 Nov. 1991.

NOTES

6 July 1996
Mary Blue's
firstborn Steven,
born 28 Dec. 1967,
marries Jane at
the Register Office,
Coalville. I have
a new hat for the
occasion.

NOTES

6 July 1996
The baby at
Steven ~ Jane's
wedding is
Andrew, born
8 March 1996,
son of Karen,
who now has
three children.

NOTES

Katherine Sullivan
in Frogmore Gardens
Windsor in 1992.
I first met her
on Christmas Day
1980 at the home
of Pat & Evelyn,
when she was 76.
(born April 1904)

NOTES

10 May 1997
A beautiful
approach to our
village along the
Ashby Road.
My little green
Peugeot car on
the right K49 PUT.

NOTES

"THE HOLLIES"
built by Grandpa
George Harry Hewes
at Ravenstone on
land he purchased
on 25 Sept. 1897.

The old family home

NOTES

General Election
1 May 1997.
Landslide win
for LABOUR,
ending 18 years of
Tory domination.
Even "The Hollies"
the old family home
supported "LABOUR".

NOTES

7 July 1995.
Bunting celebrates
her 80th birthday.
Seated (from left)
Julian, Bunting
~ Michael.
Standing (from left)
Mary Blue, Pat,
Evelyn ~ me.

The Hewes Family Tree Appertaining to Betty's Diaries

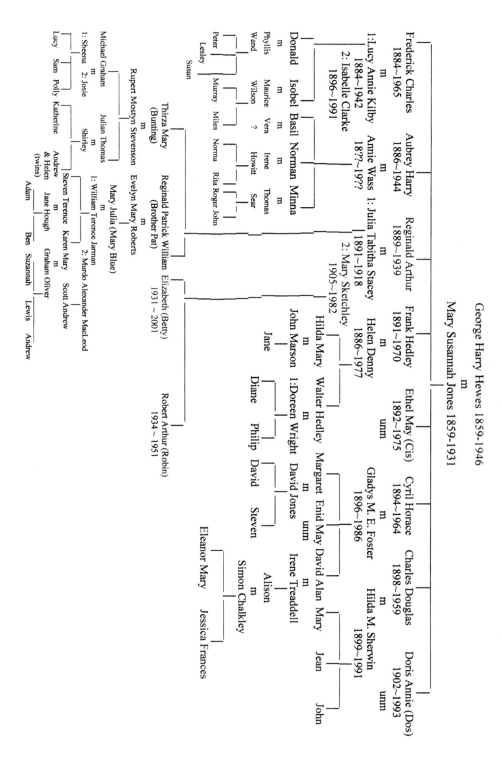

Part of the Sketchley Family Tree Appertaining to Betty's Diaries

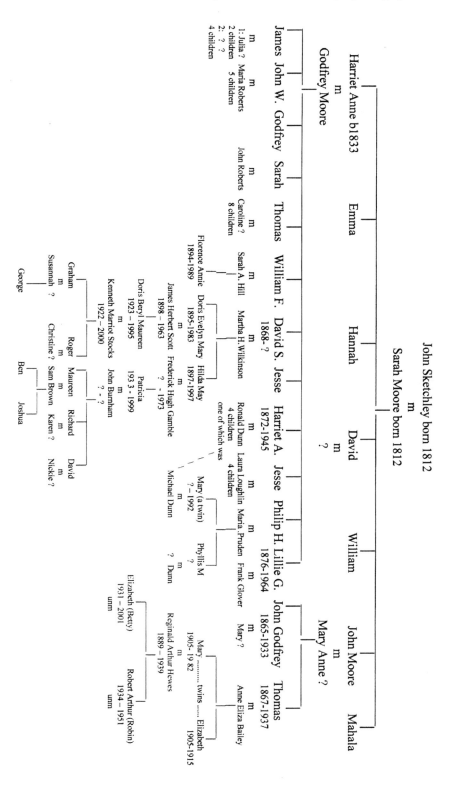

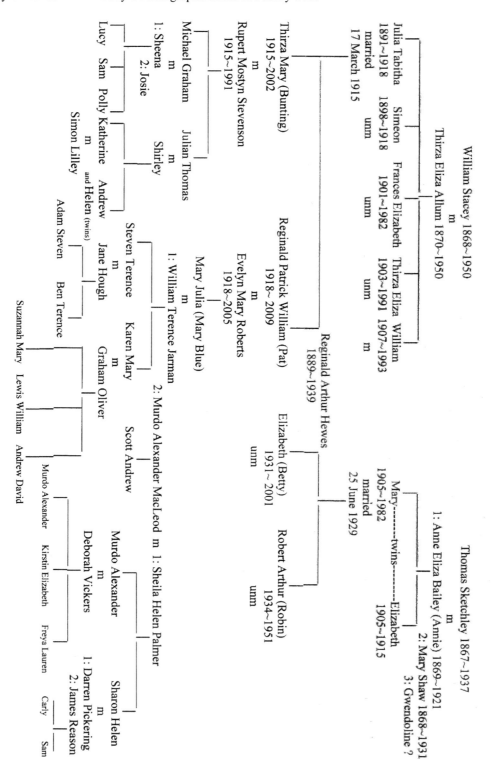

Betty's Father Reg Hewes (who married twice)

Betty's

Diaries

1944
to
2001

22nd December 1982 Wednesday

I seem to notice the changing pattern of life in the village more particularly because I have not followed the normal course of life.

I have not married & raised a family of my own, but seem to be more like an onlooker, a listener & a recorder, & do not notice how much I change myself...

1944

On 1st January 1944, when I was 12 years old and England was at war – the 2nd World War (1939 – 1945), I started to keep a diary.

1st January 1944 Saturday
Nurse came & cooked a good dinner. Mummy got up for first time. Auntie Dos in bed with flu. Grandpa acting babyish & mental. Margaret Hewes on leave, went out with her boy.

Note - Nurse = Nurse Leighton – friend of the family. Mummy had almost died with pneumonia.
Grandpa = George Harry Hewes.

2nd January 1944 Sunday
Had no dinner. Mummy helped wash up, after which she nearly fainted. Bunt came in evening. Auntie Dos still ill with flu. Practised racing. Rob fell down & hurt his bad knee.

Note – Rob = my younger brother – born 1934.

3rd January 1944 Monday
Very wet, cold & miserable. Auntie Cis came home from Peterborough. Mummy got up and helped wash up. Potty Emma came & helped with dinner. At night all finished up crying after a row.

Note – Potty Emma = Mrs Emma Congrave, neighbour.

4th January 1944 Tuesday
Enid came because she was fed up in the evening. Rob slept in the front bed because he had wet his own. I played with Rob. We went to see builders. We played "Guess What."

5th January 1944 Wednesday
Took my bike to Lamberts. Came home down Wash Lane with Jean Darlastone. Mrs Dalby sent up some Ovaltine by Mr Nield. Mrs Nield came to see Mummy in evening and brought three mince pies.

Note – Mrs Dalby – a good neighbour who looked after us while Mummy convalesced at Willoughby with relations. Mr Nield – the milkman. Mum got pneumonia through helping the milkman on his round.

6th January 1944 Thursday
I scrubbed the kitchen floor. Mummy made a boiled pudding, but had aches all day. I made some chips for the rest of dinner. Mr Nield brought Mummy some tomatoes, cress and vegetables in mayonaize.

7th January 1944 Friday
Yanks came in huge army lorries and gave us many things. Doctor came. Mrs Dalby came. Rob went to Auntie Gladys for dinner. Mummy & I had chips & I had corn flakes for pudding. Rob went to Coalville on Hicken's dray for some paraffin.

Note – American service men in huge army lorries came to Ravenstone, handing out goodies to the children.

8th January 1944 Saturday
Dorothy came with baby. Nurse came.
Keith Lambert brought my bike back after having a thorough overhaul by Mr Lambert. Robert & I cleaned out under the stairs.

Note – Dorothy = Dorothy Yates, at one time our maid.

9th January 1944 Sunday
Went to Sunday School in Church. Very drizzly. Went to see Dorothy. She came down to our house & brought some nice eatables. Went a walk with Marje & Rita & Doreen.

10th January 1944 Monday
Rob & I went to see "Bambi." Did some shopping & went to a café for tea. Only just caught the bus going & walked home. Uncle Sketch & Auntie Patty came in evening. Rob started school & had a holiday in afternoon especially to go to pictures.

Note – Uncle Sketch & Auntie Patty = Sketch Moore (parents of Auntie Doris & Hilda)

11th January 1944 Tuesday
I started school. *(Note - Coalville Grammar School)* Polly changed us so that I blinkin well sat by myself "SO HORRID" Had some good films at school. Only had French homework. Had an air-raid practice. Broke up last lot of coal at home.

12th January 1944 Wednesday
Had a nice school dinner. Had a gas mask inspection at school. *(Note – the children carried gas-masks with them to school)* Had a clothes inspection. Heard Welsh teacher speak for first time. Had all homework except biol. Stopped hockey practice.

13th January 1944 Thursday
Mr Brady pulled my hair for talking. Stopped for hockey practice although we had no hockey lesson owing to the rain. Had cake pudding for second time this year.

14th January 1944 Friday
Had a lovely school dinner. Had a French test but we marked our own. Got a new library ticket & a library for first time this year. Did my maths homework only.

15th January 1944 Saturday
Rob went to Snibby school party. I went to get some black stockings but got none. Rob forgot to bring home his dessert spoon from party.

16th January 1944 Sunday
Mummy went to Willoughby. I went with her. Rob & I slept at Vot's. Did not go to Sunday School, but Rob went in afternoon.

Note – Vot = Enid, who said once – " Vot did you say?"

17th January 1944 Monday
Rob & I slept at Vot's although we should have gone to Dalby's, but as it was dark we didn't. Rob went to

Preston's. I had no end of homework.
Had funny stew stuff for dinner.

18ᵗʰ January 1944 Tuesday
Rob & I went to Dalby's. I did not have much homework. I wrote to Mummy. I stopped hockey after which JM, JR, MM, MW, MD & I stopped talking to Arthur Hughes & Thomas (approx. 1 hour)

Note – JM = Jean Merchant, JR = Jean Roddis, MM = Margaret Middlebrook, MW = Margaret White.

19ᵗʰ January 1944 Wednesday
Dreadfully wet coming home from school. Rob had a bath at Dalby's. Miss Hoyle's birthday. Glass Eye blinkin well started teaching us analysis. Had a letter from Ma.

20ᵗʰ January 1944 Thursday
Had a French test. Had music books for first time. Had a lovely games lesson. Swindled a shower by saying I was going to stop playing longer.

21ˢᵗ January 1944 Friday
Had a rotten gym lesson 'cos Smiggy was in a bad temper. Got a book for special topic. Had French test back. MM & I got 10 (only ones). Jean Merchant not at all well – excused showers.

22ⁿᵈ January 1944 Saturday
Mummy sent me my super long black stockings. I wrote to her & sent it off for first time. Had Sunday School party. Goulding came to Dalby's – stopped till gone supper and walked home. John went part of way with him.

23ʳᵈ January 1944 Sunday
Had Sunday School leaflets distributed. Rob, Rob and I went for walk to woods. We got absolutely sopping drenched – we were up to the neck in slimy sludge. George Formby spoke on wireless – so funny!!!

24ᵗʰ January 1944 Monday
Stopped Junior Choir. Goulding came. Helped John with homework. Peter Swanwick came to be helped with his homework. Learnt Past Historic in French. Had the most horrible geog. lesson.

25ᵗʰ January 1944 Tuesday
Rained & blew dreadfully – worst I have ever known – wondered if ever get home from school. John went pictures with Goulding. Had forms to fill in to say which forms we were going in. Had history test.

26ᵗʰ January 1944 Wednesday
Mr Dalby came home unexpectedly. Stopped gym after school. Had history test back. I got 8/15. JM got 14/15. Miss Yates away. Had Brady first half – Smiggy second half. Had French test.

27ᵗʰ January 1944 Thursday
Seemed a very long morning for lessons. Had French test back. I got 7, MM and JM got 8, making a total of MM 18, me and JM 17. Betty Newbold played piano for prayers. Stopped hockey practice after school.

28ᵗʰ January 1944 Friday
Had no apparatus work in gym. Had a maths & physics test. Mummy sent back forms & wrote. I wrote to her. Junior team played Senior team & Juniors won 1-0.

29ᵗʰ January 1944 Saturday
Went to Ashby to play hockey. We won 2-1. First eleven played after us at Ashby but lost 9-0
Second eleven played at home & lost 7-0. I had a bath. Mrs Dalby & Robert Dalby went to see "Old Mother Riley"

30ᵗʰ January 1944 Sunday
Rob & I went to Sunday School morning & afternoon. Erma came home. Bunt came & brought Rob his birthday present. We got up rather late.

31ˢᵗ January 1944 Monday
Rob went to Preston's. Had fish mixed up with 'tatos for dinner & boiled pudding. Stopped Junior Choir. Had fair geog. lesson and lovely gym lesson. I borrowed some school gym shoes.

1ˢᵗ February 1944 Tuesday
Played goalie against Harley. Awful game – we lost 2-1. Highfields beat Charnwood with Hazel Hudson goalie by 7-0. Had a graph to do for homework. Had lovely dinner.

2ⁿᵈ February 1944 Wednesday
Fanny Yates came back. Had Tuesday night's French homework back. JM got 6, I got 4, and MM got 3. Had a French test. Saw Fluffy for first time since Mummy had gone away.

3ʳᵈ February 1944 Thursday
Had French test back. I got 5, JM got 8 & MM got 7. Dreadfully windy. I rode home with Miss Knight. I had a letter from Mummy. Wrote first poem for "My Hobbies"

4ᵗʰ February 1944 Friday
JM was away from school – a thousand million wonders. Colin Goulding came down and Peter Swanwick. Junior team played first eleven & drew 1-1. Smiggy made MM & I draw & mark the hockey pitch.

5ᵗʰ February 1944 Saturday
Played Loughborough School at Coalville. We won 1-0. Mummy came home in morning. Went to social at 'stute. I danced with Jerry Palmer. Jimmy Jones was there in his uniform. He looked lovely.

6ᵗʰ February 1944 Sunday
Rob & I went to Sunday School in après midi, mais ne pas au matin. J'ai écrivé à mon oncle Tom. Nous avons eu pilchards pour notre thé. J'ai mis mes cheveux in curlers que ma mere a apporte from Willoughby.
Note – Mon oncle Tom at Willoughby = Tom Bailey

7ᵗʰ February 1944 Monday
Stopped Junior choir. Senior hockey match. We beat Highfields 3-2. Charnwood beat Harley 3-0. Learnt conditional tense in French. JM away from school. SG away. JF away. Cadle and Boot away.

8th February 1944 Tuesday
Junior team playing hockey. Highfields beat Broughton 8-0. Charnwood beat Harley 1-0. Had a history test. JM still away. Had to draw a panther for art. I went out for a bit after tea.

9th February 1944 Wednesday
Had a lovely Domes' lesson and no end of fun. Had un Français test. JM no better – still away. JF away. Had history test back. I got 5 ½ out of 12. Had no writing homework. I went out to play a bit après thé.

Note – My behaviour at school was disgraceful. I was particularly bad during Domestic Science lessons & showed no respect to the teacher Miss Yates. I was eventually suspended from the class, being too disruptive. At the same time I was being nurtured at home in the Christian Faith & regularly attended Sunday School, where the good seeds began to take root.

10th February 1944 Thursday
Nous avons eu la test de Français back. J'ai got 8 & MM got 9. JM came back for biol. test. She & MM & I got 10. If she had not come back, it would have brought my maths down to 18, but now she beats me by 23.

11th February 1944 Friday
Had a geography test. Was no time for showers. We were weighed & measured in gym. I was 7 stone 6 lbs. and 5′ 2 ⅝″   Had lovely dinner. JM looking much better. Had my hair washed and curled.

12th February 1944 Saturday
I went to an old fashioned dance at the 'stute. Rob went to Dalbys for dinner & was at Hickens all morning & afternoon. Middlebrook came down. We went a bike ride to Kelham Bridge.

13th February 1944 Sunday
Rob & I went to Sunday School both morning et après midi. J'ai fait tout de mes devoirs. I saw Mabel's baby at Hayes. Had blanc-mange for tea. I went a walk with Marje et Rita.

14 February 1944 Monday Valentine's Day
Ivy Jordan fell off ribstalls & hurt her back. Cadle came back for first time since beginning of term. His voice had broken.
I played hockey for Broughton Seniors. We lost to Charnwood 2-1.

15th February 1944 Tuesday
I had to go to Glister to tell him of Ivy Jordan. Stopped hockey. We drew with Charnwood 1-1. Had to walk to school & back for second day following as I had got a puncture. Highfields beat Harley 3-0.

Note – Mr Glister was our Head Master at Coalville Grammar School.

16th February 1944 Wednesday
Nous avons eu un Français test. JM et MM ont eu dix. J'ai eu neuf. Nous avons eu beaucoup de devoir d'Anglais. J'ai vu ma soeur qui parlait au conjouror. Nous avons eu la maths test back.

17th February 1944 Thursday
Did not wake till 7-55a.m.
Stopped for films on **Town Planning** during dinner hour. Thomas gave a lecture on **Town Planning**. Had dancing instead of double games.

18th February 1944 Friday
Did not wake till 7-45a.m.
Had three inspectors at school. Broke up for half term. It snowed. Had good dinner. Did not do gym 'cos we were late. Clare Pacey came for money for Comforts Fund.

19th February 1944 Saturday
Went to play hockey at Burton. Had a lovely train ride but we lost 3-1.
Mr Lambert mended our wireless & we listened to it for the first time for months. Mummy & I listened to a murder story which finished at 11p.m.

20th February 1944 Sunday
Rob & I went to Sunday School in morning & afternoon. Had a lovely breakfast, dinner & tea. After Sunday School in morning I went a walk round the village by Wash Lane with Marje & Michael.

21st February 1944 Monday
I went to Altons with Marje on the bikes. I played marbles after tea & gained one. We listened to "Monday Night at 8" Mr Lambert came down.

22nd February 1944 Tuesday
It snowed. Rob & I went to dentists. Rob had got something to be done but I had not. Mummy did not go with us. We got 1d. each. Walked home to top of Wash Lane where Uncle Cyril picked us up.

23rd February 1944 Ash Wednesday
Started back to school après half term. Had grand Domes' lesson as usual. Owd Lizzy Yates had had her cheveux cut. I did my Thursday nights French homework. I saw Nurse in Hugglescote.

24th February 1944 Thursday
Bunt came at about 6 heures moin le quart et elle est restée à la maison for quite longtemps. Mummy went to monthly lecture at Mrs Wilsons. Mummy went to Hales. We had a French test. I got 9.

25th February 1944 Friday
Had Chemie half term marks. I got 19/50. Smiggy inspected our backs in gym
I had a bath & my hair washed. Marje brought us some sausage.
Enid fetched her pink frock.

26th February 1944 Saturday
I went to Coalville (walked there & back) intending to go to Elaine's party, but as Audrey Cooper was not at Coalville, I didn't go.
Mummy went to Maureen Scott's 21st birthday party.

Note – Maureen Scott = daughter of "Auntie Doris".

27th February 1944 Sunday
Snowed dreadfully. I went to Sunday School in morning

& afternoon after much difficulty. Uncle Norman's funeral service. We had blanc-mange for tea. Had a good dinner.

Note – Uncle Norman = my cousin Norman Hewes, killed in action in the war in Italy. (Old enough to be my uncle)

28th February 1944 Monday
It took me all my time to get out of our gate for snow – snow – snow. At last I got out & I walked to school & back with Vot. I read the lesson. Had a good dinner.

Note – The first time I ever read the lesson. Our class, Form 3A read the lessons at morning assembly each day for one week. I read – ISAIAH, Chapter 11, verses 1 – 5.

29th February 1944 Tuesday
Messenger read the lesson. Glister told us about Lizzie Green copying that song from a hymn book. MM, JR, JM & I didn't speak to AY. She looked miserable all day.

1st March 1944 Wednesday
Merchy read the lesson. Had history test back. I got 7/10. JM got 8/10. Had lovely Domes' lesson. Had a French test. Had corned beef, raw carrot, potatoes and milk pudding for dinner. I biked to school in snow.

2nd March 1944 Thursday
Rob had very bad ear–ache in both ears. He stopped in bed all day. I was examined at school by M. Wesson, who gave us a lecture. Had French test back. MM, JR & I got 6. JM got 7. Marie Findley got 9.

3rd March 1944 Friday
Had a geography test. I used JR's hand towel for shower. Had a lovely dinner. Did none of my homework. Stopped country dancing. MM & I fell out with JM & AY. Went out with Marje & Syb till gone 8p.m.

4th March 1944 Saturday
I got up at 5 – 30 p.m. Mummy went to a dance at 'stute. I read my library & finished it from Snibby. Rob got up 'cos his ear was a bit better. I did a jig–saw.

5th March 1944 Sunday
I went to Sunday School morning et après midi, in l'eglise both times. I had a duck egg for my supper. Rob got up after dinner. There were two girls baptised, Coral and Marlene Anne.

6th March 1944 Monday
Stopped Junior choir. Listened to "Monday Night at Eight"
Hayes had a fire at about 6 a.m. We heard the fire engine.
Had a good dinner. Had pilchards for tea. Mummy got up at 10 a.m.

7th March 1944 Tuesday
Had jolly good dinner. Had a lot of homework. Went in 2B at dinner time. Had a French essay for first time. Mummy went to Ashby. I found out Daddy's old white bed–socks.   M. Hatton read the lesson.

8th March 1944 Wednesday
Had a good dinner. Had English test with Glassy. Made rock buns in Domes'. We altered the recipe on the board. Marg came & did her homework avec moi. Broughton read the lesson.

9th March 1944 Thursday
Had a biol. test. Had bread & butter pudding & enough dinner. Mummy went to a meeting. Bunt came but did not stop long.
We had to sing **"Praise"** at dinner time to Bungard.

10th March 1944 Friday
Mummy & I went to see "Lord Richard in the Pantry". Enid went with us. Enid took prelims. We sang **"Praise"** in morning. Had a good dinner. I took a few of the class for gym.

11th March 1944 Saturday
I went to Leicester with Bunt. I saw Cadle at Leicester & I saw Smiggy at Leicester, who came home with us on bus & sat with us. I bought des crayons which were painted.
I heard of **Billy Barrow** Road.

12th March 1944 Sunday
Rob & I went to Sunday School morning & afternoon. We had sardines and a blanc-mange for tea. I washed my feet & Mummy washed hers. Dorothy came.

13th March 1944 Monday
We had no singing 'cos of prelims. Had fuzzy dinner. Stopped Junior choir. Mummy went to a **Rest Centre** practice & brought some 'stute blankets home to air. Norma brought the Billet.

Note – Norma Hewes, daughter of "Uncle" Norman. The Billet was a local war time magazine.

14th March 1944 Tuesday
Had no end of homework. Fell out with Middlebrook. Had lovely dinner. Mummy went to a dance at the Baths. Had physics test & a French test. Went in Chemistry lab. For single Chemie.

15th March 1944 Wednesday
I got 2 for histoire car la première temps, et je l'ai eu re-ecrir. Had good Domes' lesson et nous avons eu un bon diner.
Millions of bombers went over in evening.

(Note – Ravenstone was in direct line with Coventry, a prime target for the German bombs. We lived in fear of being blown up.)

16th March 1944 Thursday
Practised athletics for Sports Day. Had music in 3B 'cos of prelims. Had fairly good dinner. Mummy went to Hales. Bill was in bed. All form had a maths impot.

17th March 1944 Friday
Ma mère et moi avons eu nos cheveux washed. Nous avons stopped dans les showers pendant break et nous etions un peu en retard pour Maths qu'etait 4th leçon du matin. Je n'ai pas fait de de mes devoirs.

18th March 1944 Saturday
J'ai m'eu le dejeuner et le diner au lit. J'ai changé des stamps foreign avec Marg. Mummy went to scout's social & dance. I did not go because of my bad pied. J'ai fait mes devoirs.

19th March 1944 Sunday
Le bébé d'Evelyn était born.
Mon frère et moi, nous sommes allés à l'école de Dimanche au matin et après midi. J'ai fait des souliers rouges. Maman a écrit à des personnes.

Note – Mary Blue was born, a daughter for brother Pat & Evelyn.

20th March 1944 Monday
Some soldiers from Glenfield came to **Cross Roads** to have some practice for invading France. One soldier came in our house late in evening. Mummy went to a meeting at Ravenstone school.

21st March 1944 Tuesday
Had a history test. I did my French homework in 2B at dinner time. I did my maths homework on Monday 20th We had physics reading homework which I didn't do. Consequently I did no homework. Played netball for first time.

22nd March 1944 Wednesday
Miss Irons said **Good-bye** to C.G.S. More soldiers came to corner. Mummy went to 'stute dance. Had history test back. I got 12/15. Had French and Biology term results. I was 3rd and 16th.

23rd March 1944 Thursday
That man who had been German prisoner gave us a lecture. Had liver for dinner. Only had one games lesson instead of double games 'cos of lecture. Had awful geography homework – vegetation of Asia.

24th March 1944 Friday
The cast of **The Rivals** practised and we missed gym, so we went in Biol. lab. Had sausage-meat and steam pudding – a jolly good dinner. Had the most awful geog. lesson.

25th March 1944 Saturday
I went to Coalville avec ma mère to buy des nouveaux souliers. A blacky in an army lorry skidded at the corner and nearly killed me. We went to the pantomime au soir.

26th March 1944 Sunday
Je ne suis pas allé à l'école de Dimanche au matin, mais je suis allé après midi. Nous avons eu les Anniversary copies. We went a walk over **Fryer's** fields to Auntie Doris'. I saw O^2A.

Note – O^2A = Oliver Ambrose Owen – boy at school.

27th March 1944 Monday
We had early dinner as we watched "The Rivals" in the afternoon. I went selling raffle tickets with Marje. Rob went to Dickie Wobblers. I stopped net-ball. I had a very bad cold.
Note – Dickie Wobbler = Mr Dick Preston.

28th March 1944 Tuesday
I stopped net-ball. I went a walk with ma mère round The Recky. I thought I heard Mrs Morse coming and I got my truncheon ready, after which Mummy shouted and hit me.

29th March 1944 Wednesday
Had super Domes' leçon. Had tons of dinner. Drizzly day prevented us from playing net-ball. Had very little homework. Ma mère est allée to a meeting at Ravo school. Brought my sewing home.

30th March 1944 Thursday
Miss Bungard was away and in music lesson we practised for Sports Day, the result of which we had athletical lessons all afternoon. Had a good dinner. Did not have much homework. Mummy went to meeting.

Note – Miss Bungard = music mistress.

31st March 1944 Friday
Only had to pay 1/- dinner money. Had a staff meeting so we missed maths and did dancing. Had a good dinner. Went in the library for geography because Miss Silk was absent. JM had to stop in for E.P.3

Note – E.P.3 = nickname for lady teacher who read out instructions from the book – quoting E.P.3 in a deep voice and unfamiliar dialect.

1st April 1944 Saturday
Rob had a bath in the little bath. Maman et I went selling flags. Altered clocks. Films came to 'stute. I played on banks with Vot, Es, and M. Congrave. I had my hair washed. Ma had her hair washed.

2nd April 1944 Palm Sunday
Had Sunday School in church, Rob did not go. I went in afternoon. Wet and drizzly. I slept avec ma mère. Did all mes devoirs. Did some maths in my rough maths book. I had a blanc- mange.

3rd April 1944 Monday
SG gave a letter to Glister about home-work. Had no junior choir. Miss Silk and Miss Bungard came back. Broomhall gone to London. Had fair dinner. Practised for gym display.

4th April 1944 Tuesday
We broke up!!! Mummy went to a dance at the Baths. I was 4th on my report. Mummy went to Ashby and bought me some ankle socks. Had a film called "The Wandering Jew"

5th April 1944 Wednesday
I cleaned the bike. I cleaned out the shed. Mr Bagnall came to tie up the roses. I went to Ashby Castle and Church with JM and MM. A proper April showery day. Rob brought a library from S.C.S.

6th April 1944 Thursday
I cleaned out the cupboards. Mr Bagnall came and did the rose trees. Rob broke up. I had my hair cut very short, after which I had it curled. Groceries came. A big sack of potatoes came.

7ᵗ April 1944 Good Friday

We all went to Church au matin. Ma mère et mon frère sont allés voir Uncle Sketch. Had sausage for dinner. I filled my rough maths book in the evening.

8ᵗʰ April 1944 Saturday

Rob went to Auntie Pattie's by himself, on the 2 bus. Uncle Sketch and Auntie Pattie brought him home, with them came "Rough" the dog. I started decorating my pram for "Salute the Soldier Week"

9ᵗʰ April 1944 Easter Sunday

We all went to church in the morning. We had a fire in the front for first time for ages. Maman went to church in the evening. We had pilchards for tea. Did not have my hair curled.

10ᵗʰ April 1944 Easter Monday

We all went sticking to **Normanton Woods**. I went to a dance at the 'stute. Had sausage and bacon for dinner. Had a lot of toast for breakfast with dripping on it.

11ᵗʰ April 1944 Tuesday

I never washed my face. We all went sticking again and we got a big sack full.
We all went to see Pantomime at the 'stute.
Tom, Ann & Jane Wilson had a sister, Jill.

12ᵗʰ April 1944 Wednesday

The nail came off my toe I did not get up because I felt bad. Sybil came home from work bad also. Mummy went to a dance at 'stute. Brought us refreshments.

13ᵗʰ April 1944 Thursday

I went a ride with AY and Merchy but it rained so we went in Merchy's house, but Ruth was asleep, so we came to our house & they banged on t'piano.

14ᵗʰ April 1944 Friday

I went to Bradgate Park with Merchie. We saw some horses and some deer. We saw some marvellous water-falls. We bought some pop as we were dying with thirst.

15ᵗʰ April 1944 Saturday

We all walked to Coalville and back to get a bike but there wasn't one. We went to a café and had some pancakes. We all had a bath. We had tea on lawn. I went to Altons.

16ᵗʰ April 1944 Sunday

I went to Sunday School au matin et après midi. Rob only went après midi. Foggy and drizzly in the morning but cleared up in evening.
Rob & I went a walk & met two horrid lads.

17ᵗʰ April 1944 Monday

I went to the Monastery with Merchie and Middlebrook – on the way we met AY. We cleaned out the middle bedroom & also did the washing. Fairly nice day.

18ᵗʰ April 1944 Tuesday

Rob started school after Easter holiday. I went to Packington with Merchie after which we went to Merchie's house. We carried on cleaning out middle bedroom. Ma went to Ashby.

19ᵗ April Wednesday

I went to Leicester with Merchie and saw Elaine. We slept in the middle bedroom after Spring cleaning. Fine in morning then at nearly four it drizzled & was awful all night.

20ᵗʰ April 1944 Thursday

I went round Packington & Heather with Merchie & AY who bought 1lb of cake & some pop. Rob slept with us in middle bedroom 'cos his room was being Spring cleaned.

21ˢᵗ April 1944 Friday

Bunt came & told us that Evelyn had got to stay in bed for 19 weeks with phlebitis. We Spring cleaned out the back bedroom. I cleaned my teeth with salt. Mummy ordered the sweep.

22ⁿᵈ April 1944 Saturday

I heard the cuckoo for the first time. We went to the woods to get some sticks. I stayed in bed all morning & read the whole of my library "Yellow Eyes" from S.C.S.

23ʳᵈ April 1944 Sunday

We learned "Bells, bells, bells" and could not help laughing. Syd went to Scouts parade at Coalville. We went to Auntie Dos' to see Auntie Lizzie. Audrey Johnson was at Vots.

24ᵗʰ April 1944 Monday

I had a bath & I had my hair washed and curled. Uncle Bert came to mend front room door but Uncle Aub had mended it so he just took middle room door latch. I went to Cadeby avec Merchie.

25ᵗʰ April 1944 Tuesday

We started back to school after holidays. I played cricket on Hollies lawn in evening. Had films free. P Broomhall read the leçon. We had a fire practice during Physics.

26ᵗʰ April 1944 Wednesday

We had a name inspection in 4B and I had got all my things named. We stopped to practise for gym display. Mummy went to Police Dance at the Baths. I played cricket on Hollies lawn.

27ᵗʰ April 1944 Thursday

Glister went round for Oral so we had Smiggy for geom. Middlebrook didn't feel well. J Hooper fainted. We stopped to practise gym. Mummy went to meeting.

28ᵗʰ April 1944 Friday

We stopped to practise for gym display. We had a physics test. I got 5 out of 25. We had Barbara Morris for geography. Rob went to Recky till 9-30p.m. Maman went to Hugglescote.

29ᵗʰ April 1944 Saturday

I read **"White Fang"** all morning. Mummy went to see "Lord Richard in the Pantry" at 'stute, after which she stopped to a dance & she & I went to bed at 12-30p.m. I did some swat.

30ᵗʰ April 1944 Sunday

We went to Sunday School morning and afternoon. I

practised Anniversary hymns both times. A terribly low plane flew over. A lovely day.
Pat came with baby. Maman went to see Evelyn.

1st May 1944 Monday
Rob went to dentists to have his tooth repaired. Mummy & I went to Dickie Wobblers &
heard Rob sing. I thought I guessed deliberate mistake in "Monday Night at 8". We stopped for gym display practice.

2nd May 1944 Tuesday
We had an exceptionally good dinner. We stopped to practice for gym display. Had history test. Miss Willoughby took us for English as Miss Darby was away. She was also away hier.*(sic)*

3rd May 1944 Wednesday
We made vegetable soup in cookery. Had history test back. I got 6 out of 10. We had a French test. I got 5 out of 10. We had Miss Hoyle for English. We stopped to practise for gym display

4th May 1944 Thursday
Dreadfully rainy but we had to go out in it for Smiggy. Stopped for net-ball. Had sausage-meat and cauliflower for dinner. Had the gramophone in music. Had a geom. test. The rations came.

5th May 1944 Friday
John Dalby died. Marje came at night & stopped in our house till 9 o'clock 'cos it rained. Howard Wharmby came also. We had fish & potatoes for dinner and a good pud.

Note – John Dalby, a Ravenstone school-boy, was killed in a road accident.

6th May 1944 Saturday
Bus had a crash & knocked Dalby's fence down. Mummy went to parade at Coalville. We went to variety show at 'stute. Cec Tebbe (the conjurer) gave me a card. I was thrilled.

7th May 1944 Sunday
Marje, Rob & I went to Sunday School in the morning. We all went to Children's Service in après midi. I had a go on Vot's typewriter. We had tea on lawn. Couldn't forget **SSSSSSSS**

8th May 1944 Monday
We stopped to practise for gym display. We had Parker for English & Poll came in & found us sitting in wrong places. Dylis Ward took us for geog. Enid gave me many of her old exercise books.

9th May 1944 Tuesday
We practised for gym display from 2- 45p.m. until 5- 45p.m. John Dalby's funeral. Mummy & I went down when I came home from school to see grave. I practised play for Miss Hughes at dinner time.

10th May 1944 Wednesday
We had our gym display & so did the boys. We had no home-work due to this. We saw Leicester Band twice.

SG away. I practised at dinner time for a play for Miss Hughes. Had sausage-meat for dinner.

11th May 1944 Thursday
I went to Mr Hayes allotment with Marje & picked up dead Brussels sprouts stalks. I stopped in for Miss Bungard. I stopped Junior Dramatic Society. Had soupy vegetable stuff for dinner.

12th May 1944 Friday
Had French test back. I got 8. We had a Maths test. Had the most horrible geog. and phys. Lesson. 3C had Archimedes Principle to write out 100 times. I had a chem. book to almost fill.

13th May 1944 Saturday
I went down to Dalbys. Did the orange juice. Stayed for dinner and then sold Billets all afternoon. Our "Salute the Soldier" week started. Mummy went to a dance at 'stute.

14th May 1944 Sunday
Had a Parade in morning so we didn't go to Sunday School. We went to Sunday School in the afternoon. A very cold day. Rob fell down while watching parade. Hurt his face & knee.

15th May 1944 Monday
Had a geog. test. Had gym outside and practised for Sports Day. There was a Social & Dance at 'stute.

16th May 1944 Tuesday
Vot read the lesson. Should have practised for heats but it rained. Had a history test. I had a library. Middlebrook gave me some lovely liquorice. Had a good dinner. Mummy went to Whist Drive.

17th May 1944 Wednesday
We practised heats for hurdles and running. Had a Fancy Dress Parade. Had a French test. Had history test back. I got 7 out of 10. Had good dinner. Stopped to practise gym after 4 o'clock.

18th May 1944 Thursday
We went to 'stute at night & heard Rob & The Songsters sing. We saw Mr Grey the conjurer. We had heats all afternoon. We stopped for Junior Dramatic Society at 4 o'clock.

19th May 1944 Friday
We went to Sports in Waltho's field & saw a lovely little foal. I read A and E which belonged to **Wogga**. Did some reading in bed at night. Listened to Belgians talk at Sports.

20th May 1944 Saturday
I had a bath. Read my library all morning. Got up after 3 o'clock. I went to Old Tyme Dance at 'stute. Marje went & her Auntie, Uncle & cousin from Ellistown. Kilbys had a wedding.

21st May 1944 Sunday
Rob slept nearly all day & got up after tea. I did all my home-work. We practised Anniversary Hymns a.m. and p.m. We had a good dinner & tea.

I played dominoes after tea.

22nd May 1944 Monday
Had a French test but did not give it in. Not a very good dinner. Had fairly nice geog. lesson. Had gym outside. Talked about insects in biol., fairly nice lesson.

23rd May 1944 Tuesday
Had a fairly nice phys. Lesson. Stopped in phys. lab. all break. Stopped at dinner & after 4 to practise for relay. Stopped to practise rounders. Talked to Joyce Shaw for ages.

24th May 1944 Wednesday
Had a lovely lecture about paratroops & saw one fully equipped. We had blancmange for dinner. Had Sports Day. I was Junior Champion. Only did geometry home-work. Rob went to Recky and played.

25th May 1944 Thursday
In games MM, AY & I were naughty so we were sent in, where we met Miss Silk who gave us a map to draw of India for punishment. Glister told us off. We stopped Junior Drama. Had poor dinner.

26th May 1944 Friday
We broke up for Whit holidays. Had Maths test back. I was top with 18 out of 20. Had a geography test. Had French test back. JM and I got 8. MM got 9. Had a lot of paper from Gladys.

27th May 1944 Saturday
Mummy was very spiteful to me. I had my hair washed & curled. I washed up dinner pots. I read library all morning. Rob and Mummy went to grave-yard. I had duck egg for dinner.

28th May 1944 Whit Sunday
Marje, Rob & I took some flowers to grave-yard in morning & then went up Friar's fields. No Sunday School in a.m. We went in church in the afternoon & practised Anniversary Hymns. We all went to Church at night.

29th May 1944 Whit Monday
Mummy helped with milk round. Went to Sports on Waltho's field after which we watched a cricket match between girls and boys at recky. Gladys Bennett came down.

30th May 1944 Tuesday
We went to gymkhana at Ashby. Terribly hot. Saw Uncle Sketch & Pat Gamble. Rode a horse. Watched a Punch & Judy show. Doctor came when we had just gone upstairs.

Note – Doctor Forsythe, old friend of my dad.

31st May 1944 Wednesday
Mummy went to Ashby in morning. She went to Rest Centre, the other side of Leicester, in afternoon. Bunt came & slept the night. A woman came round about G.V.M.

1st June 1944 Thursday
Rob and I went to Coalville for fun on 3 o'clock bus. Marje also went 'cos Vivian came from Desford. Mummy came back from Rest Centre at Thurmaston. Marje helped to cook dinner.

2nd June 1944 Friday
Rob fell down a ladder while getting up the cherry tree. He went pale. His breath was short, but that was about all. Mummy cut my hair very short but I had it curled as best as possible.

3rd June 1944 Saturday
I went to Janet's for tea & found out where Weston lived & saw - - in his garden.
Went to hear The Sheringham Singers at Janet's chapel.
I came home on Bunt's bicycle.

4th June 1944 Sunday
Went to Sunday School in church morning & afternoon. Two babies were Christened.
I biked to Stanton-under-Bardon with Marje. Avery's baby was Christened.

5th June 1944 Monday
I took Bunt's bike back in morning. I went to Coalville with Rob on 3 o'clock bus and walked back. Listened to "Monday Night at 8". Went to bed at half past ten.
Went selling raffle tickets.

6th June 1944 Tuesday
We started back to school after Whit holiday. Mr Broomhall brought his wireless to school & we listened to the news at 1 o'clock 'cos we invaded France.

7th June 1944 Wednesday
Had a scripture test. Had a French test. Had excellent dinner except pudding. Had wireless on at dinner time. Middlebrook & I had a fine time avec Miss Yates. Terribly cold evening.

8th June 1944 Thursday
Had French test back. I got 7. JM got 8. MM got 9. Stopped Junior Drama. I got some ink on green frock. Got toy patterns off Kathleen. Had nice games lesson.

9th June 1944 Friday
Had ropes out for first time in gym. Phys. lesson not too bad. Geog. lesson not too bad. Spilt ink in geog. It went on Elaine's frock. A rainy morning. Stopped to practise for rounders.

10th June 1944 Saturday
I was on Cake Stall at 'stute for "Bring & Buy Sale". Went to dance at night. Yanks came in & frightened us. I had some brown ankle strapped shoes which hurt.

11th June 1944 Sunday
Mummy went to early morning church. Rob & I went to Sunday School in church morning & afternoon. I made a big map for **Pilgrim's Progress**. Rained after tea.

12th June 1944 Monday
Miss Bungard away. Had ropes out for second time in gym. Smiggy in a good humour. Me and Middlebrook

came home with Hazel Hudson. I finished **Pilgrim's Progress.**

13th June 1944 Tuesday
We played Charnwood rounders after 4 and lost 5-1. Had one awful maths sum for home-work. In French lesson Polly spent half the lesson talking on hobbies. Had a French test. Marked our own.

14th June 1944 Wednesday
Had history test back. I got 6 out of 15. Had a French test. I forgot to take my sewing to school. Had milk pudding. Showery day. Had to do plan for **Pilgrim's Progress** for English home-work.

15th June 1944 Thursday
Had French test back. I got 10. Merch. Got 7. Got rabbit pattern off Miss Yates. Miss Darby gave us impot for misbehaving in Double Domes'.

16th June 1944 Friday
Had a fair geog. lesson and had a geog. test. Had a fair phys. lesson. Stopped quite late for rounders practice. Fluffy had her first 2 kittens. I had my hair washed and a bath.

17th June 1944 Saturday
I went to Coalville in morning & cashed some of my money out of bank. Mummy Rob & I went to Ashby in afternoon & bought me an Anniversary rig-out. Mummy went to dance.

18th June 1944 Sunday
Had Anniversary. Mummy Rob & I went a lovely long walk after night Anniversary across woods and out Bennion's fields at Altons. One kitten died.

19th June 1944 Monday
Had fair geog. lesson. Had nice biol. lesson. I got to top of ropes for first time. Watched Senior rounders match & **Harley** beat **Broughton**. Doreen Wells was missing.

20th June 1944 Tuesday
Went to see George Formby in "Bell Bottom George". Had fair phys. lesson. George Fox showed us our Maths. Stayed for Junior Rounders Match. **Highfield** beat **Broughton.**

21st June 1944 Wednesday
Made salad in Domes. Science. Stopped rounders practice till 5-30p.m. Went to see George Formby for second time. Saw Bunt in Coalville. Had lovely pudding. Walked behind Yank at night.

22nd June 1944 Thursday
Had French test back. MM got 8. JM got 8. I got 7, making MM and I level in French altogether. Had super shower after games lesson. Stopped Junior Drama. Sold flags at night.

23rd June 1944 Friday
Higher School Cert. began. Had lovely big dinner. Rita came for interview. I stopped for rounders practice. I biked to school with Marjorie.

24th June 1944 Saturday
We all went a lovely pic-nic to somewhere near Ross Nob. I did mine and MM's Maths H.W. Rob and I sold flags in morning. 23 gliders went over. Had my hair curled.

25th June 1944 Sunday
Mummy & Rob went to Auntie Pattie's after tea. There were only 6 girls in Rector's class in morning. Had a missionary story in afternoon. Marje gave me a chip. I did nearly all my home-work.

26th June 1944 Monday
Had Maths test back. I got 16, Merchie got 14. Very rainy day.
Norma's photo was in paper for Leicester rounders tournament.
I gave Rita my black velour hat.

27th June 1944 Tuesday
Rob went to Scouts Meeting for first time. Annie Shaw came for tea. I stopped at 4 to practise COC. Stopped for School Choir for Bungard at 1-30p.m.

28th June 1944 Wednesday
Had history test. Had a good Domes. Science lesson with **Katy Greta.** I had two ice pies. Went to dance with Marje. Mummy went to parents' evening.

29th June 1944 Thursday
Middlebrook came down at night and we raided Hollies orchard. Had history test back. I got 6 out of 12. Had French test back. I got 9, MM got 10. JM got 8. I took prayers.

30th June 1944 Friday
We had **Daphne Hurr** for geography. We all did our homework in geography. Stopped for rounders practice. Bought 2 ice pies. Had nice fish cakes for dinner. Had a good dinner.

1st July 1944 Saturday
I stopped in bed all morning. Mummy and I had a hair-wash. Rob had a bath in the little bath. I tried to clean the bike. I had the seat of the bike highered.

2nd July 1944 Sunday
I went to Sunday School in morning. Rob & I went to Childrens' Service in afternoon.   Pat and Evelyn came with baby & I held the baby for quite a long time.

3rd July 1944 Monday
Mr Glassy took us for geog. 'cos Miss Silk was absent. Had nice biol. lesson. I did no real home-work. Listened to "Monday Night at 8" Rob went to Prestons.

4th July 1944 Tuesday
Did no physics in the lesson 'cos Mr Broomhall was making house. Had final French test. I got 6. Stopped for Rounders Match. We beat Charnwood.

5th July 1944 Wednesday
Glassy was absent so we had Sealey for English. Had super Domestic Science lesson. Nobody heard bell so we went up to dinner at 12-45 and sat on boys' table

6th July 1944 Thursday
Janet missed bus home so she borrowed my bike. I stopped for Junior Dramatic. Glassy watched play & criticized. Mummy went to Hales.

7th July 1944 Friday
Had a Double chem. in form room. Had "Z" for geog. 3A had a letter from Miss Silk. Stopped for rounders practice. Margaret came down & we swotted. Got a lot of cherries.

Note-Mr Williams, the chemistry teacher, was known as "Z" or "Zn" = Zinc – his favourite chemical

8th July 1944 Saturday
Mr Raith came. I swotted biol. and history all morning. Rob had a bath in the little bath.
Rob was at Hicken's all day. Had baked beans on toast for supper.

9th July 1944 Sunday
I went to Sunday School in morning and in afternoon with Marje and Freda Johanson.
We all three went to Church in morning. It rained hard.

10th July 1944 Monday
Exams started. I stopped for "Campbell of Kilmohr." Had English comp. and history & biol. exam. Rob went to Preston's. Marj went to school with Freda on bus, so I biked alone.

11th July 1944 Tuesday
Had steam pudding and stew & peas & potatoes for dinner. Smiggy made us stop rounders. Had geog. and physics and algebra exam. Mummy went collecting salvage afternoon and night.

12th July 1944 Wednesday
Had geom. alg. & English general exam. I stopped for "C of K." Marj came down at night. Had a letter from Cassells about bombs.

13th July 1944 Thursday
Had arith. and chemi. exam in morning. Had funny exam in afternoon like a group test. Stopped for choir. Marj stopped for dancing practice. She came down at night.

14th July 1944 Friday
I forgot my dinner money. Had Kath Bevin for chem. Had Glassy for physics & no-one for geog. Did French homework in geog. Stopped rounders. Had a nice birthday tea and five cards.

15th July 1944 Saturday
Went to watch rounders match but it was cancelled because it rained a bit. Went to practice of "C of K" in afternoon. Went to see **"The Mikado"** at night. Came home in a taxi.

16th July 1944 Sunday
Marj did not go to Sunday School at all. I went in morning. Went with Marj to see Freda back in afternoon & got a puncture. Went with Marj to church at night. Hot day.

17th July 1944 Monday
Stopped for "C of K". Stuck some pictures in my Hobbies book. Only did a bit of home-work. Hot day. Had tea on lawn. Mummy went voir Doug.

18th July 1944 Tuesday
Did no home-work. Stopped to watch "Bloaters." Had Chemistry exam result. Stuck some pictures in my Hobbies book.

19th July 1944 Wednesday
Had super domes. science lesson and had awful geog. HW. Had a bath & had my hair washed. Stopped for C of K in gym & Middlebrook waited for me. Had my hair curled.

20th July 1944 Thursday
Glister did not take in geom. HW. Had extra music lesson 2nd & 3rd lesson in morning for **Prize Day.** Stopped for C of K in 3A form room. Cleaned glass in Biol. lesson.

21st July 1944 Friday
Messed about in form room on our own from break until dinner.
Hobbies exhibition in afternoon. I got 2nd prize for my dog.
Had fuzzy dinner.

22nd July 1944 Saturday
Went to school all morning for practice of all 3 plays. Went to Bring and Buy sale in afternoon and got some sugar and cakes. Cut graves at night. Had hair curled.

23rd July 1944 Sunday
Went to church in morning to hear Bishop. Mr Harper took Sunday School a.m. and afternoon. I went both times. Went a walk with Rita and Marj à l'après midi. Went to see Dorothy at night.

24th July 1944 Monday
Had practice of C of K from break until dinner. Stopped till 7-30p.m. to practise C of K. Collected text books all afternoon. Had tea at school. Dorothy lent me a lot of clips for play.

25th July 1944 Tuesday
Did C of K to school. Went to recky at night. Got my feet soaking wet but had a good time. Practised C of K in morning. Had cake for pudding, but I couldn't eat much.

26th July 1944 Wednesday
Had two practices of C of K in morning. Had steam pudding with fruit on. Had singing all afternoon ready for Prize Day. Did C of K to audience in evening.

Note – End of term at school & I perform on stage in my first play "Campbell of Kilmohr". Mum & Rob, my younger brother, are in the audience for our school play.

27th July 1944 Thursday
We broke up. Had the film called "The White Spy" in afternoon. In morning 6th form played staff at rounders. Pritch left. Had about the best milk pudding for dinner.

Note – I have now been at Coalville Grammar School for 2 years, in Form 2A, & in Form 3A. It is now the School Summer holiday Rob, aged 10 is at Snibston Junior School, but is handicapped, & has missed a lot of schooling, having to attend Coalville clinic. He wears an iron on his right leg & cannot use his right hand properly. His chief delight is spending as much time as possible at the nearby farm.

28ᵗʰ July 1944 Friday
I went to sleep in afternoon. I started **"Jane Eyre."**
Had sweet ration at night. Went to recky at night and had a super time.
Deaf and dumb man came. Mummy was out.

29ᵗʰ July 1944 Saturday
It rained in morning. Rob went to Sinope in morning. Rob went to recky in afternoon. Watched a cricket match. It rained very hard at night.

30ᵗʰ July 1944 Sunday
I went to Sunday School morning and afternoon. Rob went in choir for first time. Went a walk to grave-yard late at night. Got some chocolate from Auntie Dos.

31ˢᵗ July 1944 Monday
I got Doreen a birthday card, which, together with a toy dog, took to her. I took her a walk at night. I had a sore throat. I did no knitting but read **"Jane Eyre."**

1ˢᵗ August 1944 Tuesday
I had a sore throat but I went to recky for a little while. Rob went to scouts. I had a rotten night because I could not sleep. I read **"Jane Eyre."**

2ⁿᵈ August 1944 Wednesday
I went to Snibby School in afternoon and played punch ball. Rob had his report and was bottom. Mummy, Rob & I went to **Beetle Drive** at 'stute in evening.
Note - On his latest school report, Rob was bottom of the class.

3ʳᵈ August 1944 Thursday
I went to Ashby in afternoon with ma mère. Rob went to choir practice for 2ⁿᵈ time since he started. I had my hair washed and I had it curled.

4ᵗʰ August 1944 Friday
I had doctor in morning and he brought me some medicine in afternoon. Uncle Bert came in morning. I played with Marje a bit at night and could not stop laughing. Nice day.

5ᵗʰ August 1944 Saturday
Rob went to Sinope in butcher's van with Howard. I had no breakfast and no supper 'cos rations were short. Had kam for dinner. Mummy made a lot of pastry in morning.

Note – War-time rationing means that we sometimes are short of food.

6ᵗʰ August 1944 Sunday
No Sunday School. Rob and I took some flowers to grave in afternoon. G.V.M. for first time. Doctor came.

Rob went to church in a.m., but not at night.
Had tea at 7 p.m.

7ᵗʰ August 1944 Monday
Had letter from Madge. Rob had a bath. Very hot day. I had my hair curled. Ken had a new straw hat. Jean Hewes went back to Bosworth and Auntie Dos, Grandpa and Pat & family went too.

8ᵗʰ August 1944 Tuesday
Went to Willoughby. It rained while we were in the float. Went in a taxi from Loughborough to Wymeswold & Rob was sick. Rob went to see Aunt Aggie who gave him some apples.

Note – for our Summer holidays Mum Rob & I go to Mum's cousins who run a farm at Willoughby-on-the-Wolds, where Mum was born in 1905, about 22 miles from Ravenstone. Rob is in his element, on the farm.

9ᵗʰ August 1944 Wednesday
Bertha took David to fair at Nottingham. Rex went to Loughborough. I went to sleep in afternoon. Peggy was shod at village blacksmiths. Aunt Aggie gave us some sweet coupons.

10ᵗʰ August 1944 Thursday
Rex went to buy a horse from Melton and walked all the way back with a big brown 4 year old. Rob & I went to fields in morning. Rob took **Bonzo** for a walk at dinner time.

11ᵗʰ August 1944 Friday
Bertha went fire watching. Rex caught 3 rabbits. They tried out new horse. Rob & I shelled some broad beans. I cut up some apples for a pie with Madge and Joan.

12ᵗʰ August 1944 Saturday
Rex went to Sheffield. We went to see the church at Willoughby. We went to see Aunt Aggie in morning. I podded some peas. I unravelled some silk for Mrs Skuse. Bertha went to play golf at Stanton.

13ᵗʰ August 1944 Sunday
Tony Wisher shaved for first time. Mummy, Rob and I went to Willoughby church in morning. There were 10 in congregation and 4 choir. Mummy, Madge & I went to **Egg and Flower Anniversary** at night.

14ᵗʰ August 1944 Monday
Mummy & I went a walk to the end of Occupation. Rex came back from Sheffield and Bertha went to Sheffield. Mummy & Madge went to Broughton. Nice day.

15ᵗʰ August 1944 Tuesday
I had a letter from Marje. Walter had his first day of his holiday. Mummy went to Melton with Madge. We watched Adam's pig be taken away.

16ᵗʰ August 1944 Wednesday
Rob & I went to sleep all afternoon. Mummy, Madge & I went to see Aunt Aggie & Madge and I each carried an old hen back. Bonzo got stuck in a pond up Broughton Lane field. Lovely day.

17th August 1944 Thursday
Walter took Rob & me to Widmerpool to have "Rob's" back feet shoed for first time. Mummy, Rob & I went a walk down Widmerpool Lane in morning.
Bertha came back from seeing Emily at Manchester.

18th August 1944 Friday
Battle of Normandy Won.
Rob & I watched the cows milked in morning for first time. We came home from Willoughby with 9/- each from friends.

19th August 1944 Saturday
Watts' left. A terrible rainy day. I did some jig-saws. We had some pudding left over from some school. Rob went a ride in butcher's van but got soaked and soon came home.

20th August 1944 Sunday
Neither Rob nor I went to Sunday School. Rob went to church in morning and at night. I went to church with Mummy at night. A rainy day. I did some jig-saws. Had good tea.

21st August 1944 Monday
I went fishing in Willar's pond with Marje, Doreen and Rita. We got some water beetles, frogs and newts. Uncle Bert came. Marje came at night and we did some of her jig-saws.

22nd August 1944 Tuesday
Rob & I went to Coalville to buy Mummy her birthday presents. From Coalville, we went to Ashby and Mummy got on bus at Ravenstone and came with us. A very miserable day.

23rd August 1944 Wednesday
Rob and I went to Hugglescote in morning to fetch some cartridges for Rex. Mummy & I went to Loughborough in afternoon and gave cartridges to Mrs Mackley to give to Rex.

24th August 1944 Thursday
I cleaned out shed. Rob went to Poynton's sale in afternoon. I had a bath and my hair washed. Marje went a bike ride with June Geary. A very wet evening.

25th August 1944 Friday
Mummy, Rob and I went to Coalville on the 3 o'clock bus and came back on the 5 bus. Mummy, Rob and I went to Hugglescote at night on 7 bus to Uncle Bert's and called at the fair.

26th August 1944 Saturday
We all went to a Garden Fête at Piggott's. The Duchess of Gloucester had a son. Rob went to Sinope in butcher's van. Ma mère did the flowers for church. A lovely day.

27th August 1944 Sunday
I read the whole of Red Lynx. Rob went to church a.m. and night. Mummy and I went at night. Sunday School was in church. I went in afternoon and had to teach the infants.

28th August 1944 Monday
At night I went black-berrying with Marje down Ibstock Lane. A windy day. Mummy polished middle room floor and made it shine lovely.
Rob ate some cake with a dead wasp in it.

29th August 1944 Tuesday
I went to Altons with Marje. We got about 5lbs of blackberries between us. We had some tea in the field and saw 2 Italian prisoners who were working there. Had blackberry pud.

30th August 1944 Wednesday
I went a ride round Ibstock and Ellistown with Marjorie. I started "Old Christie's Cabin." I saw Mu. Findley. Marjorie and I went to see Mrs Spares who was off colour.

31st August 1944 Thursday
Mummy, Rob & I went to Hales. We saw Bill's 2 rabbits and had a go on his bone shaker. Mummy went to meeting at Wilson's. Rob went to Choir practice.

1st September 1944 Friday
Mummy went to market in morning and got 4 cups. I got 2 in afternoon. Dorothy gave us some marge. I got three Christmas cards. Mummy & I went to grave-yard at night.

2nd September 1944 Saturday
I had a bath and Mummy had a bath. Cassell's came and Mrs Cassell's friend, a nurse. Mummy, Mrs Cassell & Nurse went to flower show at night. I slept with twins.

3rd September 1944 Sunday
There was a parade. It rained hard at night so Rob didn't go to church. Twins, Marjorie & I went a walk.
I played Rummy at night with Mrs Cassell, Nurse and Mummy. Lovely game.

4th September 1944 Monday
Rob started school after holidays. Michael started. Twins went to school. I went up to Dorothy's and got 1lb of tomatoes. I tumbled down in Wash Lane and my knee bled. Rainy day.

5th September 1944 Tuesday
Mrs Cassell and Nurse went to Leicester. Went to Recky with twins and Marje. Had kam for dinner. Had chips which Mrs Cassell and Nurse brought home for supper. I went to Ashby.

6th September 1944 Wednesday
I went to Leicester with Mummy and saw **"Pride and Prejudice"**. I had jelly and blanc-mange for pudding at Winn's café. I saw **Charlie Kunz** in Winn's café. GVM for 2nd time.

7th September 1944 Thursday
Mummy went to Mrs Hales. Mrs Cassell and Nurse went to Lamberts for supper. I read "Old Christmas Cabin" to twins. Marje came at night and played cards.

8th September 1944 Friday
I went to Marje's auntie's at Hugglescote with Marje on

bike. The twins and Rob had a bath. Marje came in our house at night. Ann had a jolly good hiding.

9th September 1944 Saturday
The twins & I went to scout rally. I went with twins, Mrs Cassell and Nurse to Coalville in morning. Mummy, Nurse & Mrs Cassell went to dance in the evening.

10th September 1944 Sunday
I went to Sunday School morning and afternoon. We all went to Bardon Hill at 5 o'clock and came back at 8. I went to Altons with Marje. A gorgeous day.

11th September 1944 Monday
Mrs Cassell went to Bradgate Park with Nurse. The twins played with Enid at night so I went a walk with Marje and Syb & got a few black-berries.

12th September 1944 Tuesday
Mrs Cassell went to Leicester with Nurse. The twins & I got 2lbs of blackberries at night round Piper Lane. We had batter pudding with apples and blackberries in it.

13th September 1944 Wednesday
Mummy & I went to Bardon Hill and were the only ones there. We walked all the way back, except from the **"Fox and Goose"** to Coalville. I had a bath and my hair washed.

14th September 1944 Thursday
I started school after holidays. *(Note – now in Form 4A)* Had films. I covered books at night and played cards with Mrs Cassell, Nurse and Mammy. Had a good dinner. Sat on Betty Newbold's table.

Note – War-time evacuees from London, who had returned home to London are now back in Ravenstone after renewed scares in London. As well as Mum, Rob & me in the house, we somehow manage to accommodate Mrs Cassell & her twin daughters Pam & Ann, plus Mrs Cassell's friend, a nurse, known as "Nurse".

15th September 1944 Friday
Had a service in the afternoon and choir went on stage. Miss Wells changed the seats so that I didn't sit opposite MM. I played cards at night with vacs and mummy. *(vacs = evacuees)*

16th September 1944 Saturday
The twins & I went blackberrying in the morning & got about 6 pounds. The twins and Rob went to pictures in afternoon and I covered some school books.

17th September 1944 Sunday
The twins and I went to Sunday School in morning. We all went to Bradgate in afternoon and had a lovely time. The street lights were lit for first time since blackout started.

Note – After years of "black-out", no lights to be seen anywhere after dark, the street lights are again lit.

18th September 1944 Monday
We had Miss Bursell for first time. We had Mr Wells for first time. I went to Auntie **Lizzy's** in Auntie Cis' car.

Had **Latin** for first time. Lovely day.

19th September 1944 Tuesday
It rained. Rob went to scouts. Mammy went to Ashby. Whitwick coal came. Had steam pudding and had beans for dinner. Played cards at night and won some doe.

20th September 1944 Wednesday
Had a nice double games lesson. Had a shower. Middlebrook biked to school for first time. Middlebrook came down at night and did homework.

21st September 1944 Thursday
I stopped for choir practice. Had awful maths homework. Middlebrook came down and did her homework. I didn't have a shower after gym. Did not have time to do any **Latin** homework.

22nd September 1944 Friday
Mr Bridges took dinner money. Mam, Rob and Ann went to see George Formby. Mrs Cassell and Nurse went to Lambert's. It rained at night. I had to stay behind at break for Miss Yates.

Note – Miss Yates = Domestic Science Teacher. I was the naughty girl.

23rd September 1944 Saturday
Mrs Cassell, Nurse, Pam and I went to see George Formby in afternoon. Fluff had 4 kittens, and one died. We all went to social and dance at night. I won musical arms prize.

24th September 1944 Sunday
I went to Sunday School in afternoon but not in morning. Pam did not go to Sunday School, but Ann did. I did my homework at night. Rob went to church at night.

25th September 1944 Monday
Had cake pudding. Had **Latin** test back and I got 15 out of 15.
Had awful maths homework. Did not do any French homework.
Sheila Dalby did our maths outside school gates.

26th September 1944 Tuesday
School dentist was at school and he saw my teeth. In art we painted our patterns. Stopped hockey practice after school and had a lovely game. I had Josephine Smalley's pads.

27th September 1944 Wednesday
Mrs Cassell, Nurse & Mammy went to Co-op pageant. It rained in afternoon so we couldn't have games but instead we had gym for 2 lessons. I did not have a shower.

28th September 1944 Thursday
MM, MF, JM, JF and I had to report to Miss Silk for bad behaviour in gym lesson. Mammy went to see "Rebecca" at Leicester and also went to see Annie Shaw. Had nice pud.

Note – Mum's father, Tom Sketchley, married a "Shaw"

for his 2nd wife. Annie Shaw was a relation of hers.

29th September 1944 Friday
I went to the pageant with **Ethel Ballard** and Marg Middlebrook. I came home with **Mrs Swanwick** and Michael, Marje and Syd, Esme and John, and had a few chips.

30th September 1944 Saturday
I went to AY's, with Middlebrook, in the morning and got some apples. I went to pageant in afternoon with Rob and twins. I went to dance and won spot prize.

1st October 1944 Sunday
There was no Sunday School in morning but there was Children's Service in afternoon. I didn't go to Sunday School in afternoon but went to **Harvest Festival** at night.

2nd October 1944 Monday
I went up to AY's with Middlebrook at night and got some apples. Had pastry and jam for pudding. Had carrots and stewed meat and potatoes.

3rd October 1944 Tuesday
I got home before School Bus. Marje had her hair washed.
The twins had their two new red coats. Mrs Cassell made a hand-bag. She went with Nurse to Leicester.

4th October 1944 Wednesday
My new hockey shoes came. It rained so that we couldn't have games but we had hockey after school. Had a geography test. Had nice dinner.

5th October 1944 Thursday
I stopped at school for choir practice. Middlebrook had to stop in for Miss Smith.
No-one had a shower after gym.

6th October 1944 Friday
Mr Bridges was absent so Miss Yates took dinner and milk money. We made a big scone. Middlebrook and I stopped hockey. Mr Glister announced death of F. Preston.

Note – Headmaster = Mr Glister (Headmistress = Miss Silk)

7th October 1944 Saturday
I went with twins blackberrying in the afternoon down Ibstock Lane and finished up at **Kelham Bridge**, jumping over H$_2$O. Pam fell in, and had to be carried home.

8th October 1944 Sunday
Nurse Heasman's birthday. I went with Marje and twins to Harvest Festival in afternoon at **St. Mary's**.
I went to Sunday School in morning – took some flowers to grave-yard.

9th October 1944 Monday
F. Preston was buried.
Some of school went potato picking. Rob went to fair.
I did Middlebrook's maths homework. It rained nearly

all day.

10th October 1944 Tuesday
I stopped for hockey practice. Tom went potato picking, so we had Miss Willoughby and Miss Smith for double art. Miss Wells went potato picking and so did Polly.

11th October 1944 Wednesday
A terrible gale blew in the evening. Mammy and Mrs Cassell went to Baths to see a **Variety** concert. The twins went to Lamberts. Mr Cockburn and Miss Wells went spud picking.

12th October 1944 Thursday
Miss Bursnell went potato picking, so we had **Polly** for history. I stopped choir. Had fairly good dinner. I came home with Uncle Len. Twins went to fair.

13th October 1944 Friday
Middlebrook made scones in cookery. Miss Yates said Middlebrook and I behaved well. I did no homework. Middlebrook and I went down Coalville for birthday present.

14th October 1944 Saturday
Mrs Cassell's birthday. Mammy went to Whist Drive at 'stute. Rob went to Sinope and to Dolman's farm in afternoon and in the evening.

15th October 1944 Sunday
I went to Sunday School in morning. I didn't go in afternoon 'cos I went to Coalville with Marje who was going on her hols to Groby at Freda Johanson's.

16th October 1944 Monday
Pat Rigby got hit on mouth with a hockey ball. We listened to "Monday Night at 8". It poured and poured with rain in morning. Ravenstone bus didn't run.

17th October 1944 Tuesday
We had a lecture on China by Wai Po Kan.
I went with Mummy to pictures at night to see **"This is the Army"**.
Marj and I painted 4 hockey balls at dinner time.

18th October 1944 Wednesday
Mummy went to dance at 'stute in evening. Mrs Cassell had a bath. Had fair geog lesson. I heard that I had got the French prize. Had nice pudding and dinner.

19th October 1944 Thursday
G.V.M. for third time. I stopped choir. Marg stopped hockey practice. Had a lovely milk pudding for dinner. Rob and Mammy went to Whitwick and Rob had a farm drawing book.

20th October 1944 Friday
We had **Prize Day** and the Bishop of Leicester presented prizes. Middlebrook had her photo taken. Had spam, beans and spuds for dinner. Had prunes for pudding.

21st October 1944 Saturday
We supposed to play Ashby at hockey but didn't because it was too wet. Margaret Middlebrook, Jean Roddis and I cleaned out canteen for Mrs Forsythe.

Mammy went to dance at 'stute.

22nd October 1944 Sunday
I did not go to Sunday School in morning but I went in afternoon with Marje. Twins and Mrs Cassell went to Lamberts at night. Mammy, Rob and I went to church.

23rd October 1944 Monday
I played in a Senior House match against Charnwood and we lost 1-0. Marg played in Senior House match against Harley. Marg had a shower but I didn't.

24th October 1944 Tuesday
I played in the Junior match against Charnwood and we lost 1-0. I had a bath before tea and Mammy had a bath and then went to the **Baths** with Bar, Clara and Mrs Wilson.

25th October 1944 Wednesday
We had a nice games lesson. Had a hockey game and drew 2-2. After school the 1st XI played the staff at hockey and staff won 3-0.

26th October 1944 Thursday
Mammy went to meeting at 'stute. Had steam pud with bread in it for pudding. I did a jig-saw of Grumpy's at night and did maths HW of Middlebrook. Twins went home.

Note – the evacuees went home to London.

27th October 1944 Friday
I had my hair washed and curled. Mr Lambert came and put new side and back in Kitchen fireplace. We made apple pie and custard in Domestic Science.

28th October 1944 Saturday
The twins and Mrs Cassell came back from London because of the rockets. Mummy, Rob and I went to dance at night. We had apple pie for pudding which I made Friday.

29th October 1944 Sunday
I didn't go to Sunday School in morning, but I went in afternoon with Marje. Dorothy came at night with baby. Rob didn't get up till afternoon.

30th October 1944 Monday
Charnwood played **Harley** and **Highfields** played **Broughton** seniors. Broughton lost 5-2. Had a Latin test. Boot read lesson. I was chosen to read poem.

Note – The 4 school houses. I was in Broughton (Yellow)

31st October 1944 Tuesday
I played goalie in Junior hockey team against Highfields and we lost 3-0. Marg and I swindled a shower. We had English and Latin half term marks.

1st November 1944 Wednesday
Middlebrook stopped at school for Form play.
Pat Colver came down at night to do physics and maths.
I had a bath and so did Mrs Cassell and ma mère.

2nd November 1944 Thursday
We broke up for half-term. Had films in afternoon. Had dancing practice at dinner.
Janet Cowlishaw read the lesson. Practised hockey after school.

3rd November 1944 Friday
I went with Doreen and Rita to Snibston School in afternoon. I got up at dinner time.
Had steam pud, spam and pickled onions for dinner.

4th November 1944 Saturday
Ma mère et je, nous sommes allés a la Ville de Coal et nous avons acheté des souliers pour moi, de Swanns. Mon frère est allé au cinéma avec twins et leur mère.

5th November 1944 Sunday
I went to Sunday School in morning and to Children's Service in afternoon. I went to church at night with Marj, M. Moore and J. Shaw. Twins and Mrs Cassell went to Dorothy's after tea.

6th November 1944 Monday
I had a bath and my hair washed. I went to Coalville on 2 o'clock bus and walked back across the fields. Rob and I started our secret league.

7th November 1944 Tuesday
Mammy & I went to Leicester and had tea at Annie Shaw's. I had my party frock material. I had a blouse, knickers and a pair of stockings from Graham Gardner's.

8th November 1944 Wednesday
I started school after half term. Mr Glister read out half term lists. Elaine was first and Marg and I second. Had steam pudding.

9th November 1944 Thursday
We could not have gym because the bars were being mended, so we had a game of hockey. Had a nice pudding but had fuzzy mince-meat.

10th November 1944 Friday
We had dinner money in afternoon for first time. I did no homework. Stopped hockey after school. Played badly and felt daft. Had Yorkshire pud.

11th November 1944 Saturday
We went to Pantomime at night. Should have played hockey at Burton but match was cancelled due to the rain.

12th November 1944 Sunday
I didn't go to Sunday School in morning but went in afternoon and only a few were there because it rained. Mammy and Mrs Cassell went to Ebenezer concert.

13th November 1944 Monday
Had jam roll for pudding. Joan Goddard absent with mumps. No-one had a shower after gym. Had all writing homework. Had Jean Roues French book for homework. Rob went clinic.

14th November 1944 Tuesday
Played **Harley** at hockey & lost 1-0. I had 9 out of 10 for

Latin test and Marg had 10. Shirley Gettings had **Diary** signed for work specially commended.

15th November 1944 Wednesday
I had to play goalie in games lesson. Only Marg and I had a shower. Had chocolate pudding. It snowed for first time but none settled on ground.

16th November 1944 Thursday
I had my pair of gym shoes from school. Mrs Cassell tacked my party frock together. Had baked apple for dinner. Stopped choir practice. Had horrid dinner.

17th November 1944 Friday
Maman et Mrs Cassell, elles sont allées au cinéma. Nous avons eu un beau dîner. Nous avons eu chesse avec les pommes de terre, et le chocolat pudding.

18th November 1944 Saturday
The twins and I went to Bunt's to fetch Bunt's coat. Pat, Evelyn and baby went to Coalville and bought a fireguard. Hilda came home from having a baby.

19th November 1944 Sunday
G.V.M. for fourth time. I went to Sunday School morning and afternoon. Mrs Cassell and twins went to Leicester to see Connie's relations.

20th November 1944 Monday
I did not do gym. Mrs Cassell went to Lamberts at night. 5A had their concert and it wasn't very good. Had batter pudding with currants in and stew with fat meat.

21st November 1944 Tuesday
We all went to pictures to see "**My Friend Flicka**"
I did Latin homework in school. Had horrid stewed apples for pudding. Had a job to avoid hockey practice.

22nd November 1944 Wednesday
Had fish and potato and steam pudding with dates in it. Had a big geog. test.
Had an awful accident at Snibston pit.

23rd November 1944 Thursday
I stopped choir and coughed nearly all the time. I did not do gym. Had a Grand Geography Test, consisting of 20 questions but marked some ourselves.

24th November 1944 Friday
Rob fell down in Wash Lane and broke a bit of his front teeth. In Domestic Science, had my material to make my summer frock.

25th November 1944 Saturday
I went to Coalville in afternoon with Marj and Esme Wallis. I went to dance at 'stute at night. I did a bit of French swot in morning.

26th November 1944 Sunday
My party frock was almost finished. I did not go to Sunday School in morning but went in afternoon and wore Bunt's blue coat. It snowed a bit.

27th November 1944 Monday
Nurse came back from London for her holidays. Had

steam pudding. Spent all English lesson rehearsing the play. Only had maths writing homework.

28th November 1944 Tuesday
Had bread and butter pudding with apples in it. Mammy went to meeting at Mrs Wilson's. Rob did not go to scouts. Had our art exam. No game because of rain.

29th November 1944 Wednesday
Exam seating lists were up. Did history revision only. Clara Pacey came collecting and stopped quite a long while. Rob had his hair cut at Dos's.

30th November 1944 Thursday
We went into our exam places and I sat in my own desk. Swotted history and a bit of French. Stopped for junior choir and had to stay until 5 o'clock.

1st December 1944 Friday
Started exams. Had **History, French, English Composition** and **Arithmetic**. I went to Auntie Doris' with Mammy. Had fish cakes for dinner. Played cards at night.

2nd December 1944 Saturday
Twins, Rob, Marj and I went to Pantomime. Rob and I went a lovely walk round Ibstock and Heather. Started at 11 o'clock and got back at 2 o'clock. Marj and Sybil went Christmas shopping.

3rd December 1944 Sunday
I went to Sunday School in morning in church. Went to Children's Service in afternoon. Did some geog swot and then played cards. Mummy went to church at night.

4th December 1944 Monday
Had **Geography, Latin** and **Geometry** exams.
Mrs Cassell and Nurse went to see "**Gone with the Wind**", and Mrs Cassell left her gold necklace under the cinema seat.

5th December 1944 Tuesday
Nurse ringed up Cinema and Mrs Cassell got her necklace back.
Finished exams. Had General Science, English PS and Algebra.
Mammy went to see "**Gone with the Wind**".

6th December 1944 Wednesday
Uncle Aubrey was found in Willars pond after being there all night.
Only had Latin, French and English lessons. Had Bradey for English. Practised for school concert.

Note – My dad's brother Aubrey committed suicide.
My poor distraught Uncle Aubrey, father of cousin Norman killed in action, drowned himself in a local pond.

7th December 1944 Thursday
I won recitation competition at school. Went to concert at 'stute, where Rob, Gig, Kendrick and David sang. "**Wings for Victory Week**". Certificates were presented. 'Twas free.

8th December 1944 Friday
We were in gym all day watching Senior plays and poems. Had no homework. Had steam pudding, sausage meat and beans. Uncle Aub was brought home.

9th December 1944 Saturday
I was in our concert at Coalville Grammar School. Victor Kendrick came home with us and we walked. Kath Bevin sang June after competing with Jean Essex & Joan Goddard.

10th December 1944 Sunday
It was Uncle Aubrey's funeral. It snowed hard but had all gone by evening. I took some flowers down to church-yard in morning and we did not go to Sunday School at all.

11th December 1944 Monday
Had little steamed pudding for first time. Mammy and I went to Auntie Annie's in the evening from 8-45pm to 10 o'clock. Miss Bursnell told me about my poem. I felt glad.

Note – Auntie Annie = wife of Uncle Aubrey.

12th December 1944 Tuesday
We didn't wake up until 20 past 8, and so I went to school eating my breakfast and got there about 8-35 a.m. Mr Sealy was decorating the gym, so we watched him during the French lesson.

13th December 1944 Wednesday
Mummy went to a dance at the 'stute and brought home some lovely refreshments. It was a foggy day and I had to walk to school - ugh - because my bike tyre had bust!

14th December 1944 Thursday
Had cake pudding. We voted for town council. Miss Silk was doing something for parties, so we had no-one for geography and played about. I missed General Science because of a singing practice.

15th December 1944 Friday
We had our school Christmas party and I danced with Mr Glister quite a lot. Mrs Cassell met me out and Elaine stayed at our house. Had chocolate pudding.

16th December 1944 Saturday
I went to a dance at the Institute. The twins and I went to Coalville with Elaine to see her home. Pam and I went home on bus. Ann walked.

17th December 1944 Sunday
I went to Sunday School in afternoon but did not wake up early enough to go in the morning. Syd Hayes read us a Missionary story instead of Rector, to save his voice.

18th December 1944 Monday
Miss Darby caught us under the desks in the form room and gave out impots.
4A's concert, only 2 items! Listened to "Monday Night at 8 o'clock"

19th December 1944 Tuesday
Had potato and cheese and peas and stewed apples for dinner. Had Term and Exam results.
I was 2nd in the combined list. Middlebrook was top of 2nd half-term.

20th December 1944 Wednesday
We had reports. Maman lost her purse. I received a letter from O²A and wrote to O²A.
Had a **Carol Service**. Had mince-meat pie for dinner. Goosey away in morning.

21st December 1944 Thursday
Rob and I went to a black man dentist and we also broke up.
We had super film called "The man who changed his name".
Had a lovely Christmas dinner. Had end of term service.

22nd December 1944 Friday
We put Christmas trimmings up. Mrs Cassell went to **Library**. The cockerel arrived. Had a letter from **Reta** and Madge. We put presents on Christmas tree.

23rd December 1944 Saturday
The twins went to bed before tea-time because Mrs Cassell was not in a happy mood. Mummy decorated the Church and helped Mamie Dowling. Brought home some holly.

24th December 1944 Sunday
I took the twins to a **Carol Service** at church.
Belle came at night and brought 5 shillings each for Rob and me. The Church choir sang hymns on Hayes' yard late at night.

25th December 1944 Monday
Fifth GVM. Had a lovely dinner & tea. We played pass the parcel, & Pam won.
All children had a jig-saw & a face cloth & a piece of soap. Had a lovely day.

26th December 1944 Tuesday
Middlebrook came and she went with me to a **Fancy Dress Dance** at the 'stute. She stopped the night. Donald and Pat were "Old Mother Riley and Kitty" and they won.

27th December 1944 Wednesday
Middlebrook and I went to AY's. We had 8 apples and had slides most of the time on a slide from the gate down the drive. Played Ludo with Alwin's game.

28th December 1944 Thursday
Middlebrook and I went with Marjorie and Michael to Dolman's pond in morning and went to lake opposite Moseley's in afternoon.
We went to pantomime party. Not very nice.

29th December 1944 Friday
Middlebrook went home. I took Rob to Coalville on 3 o'clock bus with Marjorie and Sydney. We had a bit to eat at Midland Café. Had plums for pudding.

30th December 1944 Saturday
Mummy went to Coalville with Mrs Cassell and bought a frock pattern and some material for a frock for herself.

Marjorie stopped with me and twins and played indoors.

31st December 1944 Sunday
I went a walk with Marje to graveyard.
Rob went to Evelyn's and fetched scissors for Mrs Cassell to make Mummy's frock.

* * *

I had an ice-cream for last time on 24-9-42.

Vera Dolman's 21st Birthday was on 23 Jan 1943.

1945

1ˢᵗ January 1945 Monday
Marjorie went with Rob & I to the dentists with black man. Mr Marks was there with his wife & baby, & gave us 1/- each. Mrs Cassell had a telegram from her husband to say he was in England & she nearly went crazy. I had a bath.

Note – Mrs Cassell's husband is home from the war; she is ecstatic and immediately returns with her children to London.

2ⁿᵈ January 1945 Tuesday
The twins & Mrs Cassell went home in a bustle & hurry & only just caught the train. We got up before 6-30 a.m. & Rob & I cleaned out under the stairs. Mummy did the milk round. We had parcel from Auntie Mary containing chocolate, powder puff and letter.

Note – Mum has a morning job helping the local milkman, Mr Neild, deliver milk door to door.

3ʳᵈ January 1945 Wednesday
Mummy went on milk round with Mr Nield. Had a letter from Mrs Cassell. The sirens went at about 7 p.m. We washed in the afternoon & started to get ready for making sack rug. It rained & was drizzly all day. Took Christmas trimmings down.

4ᵗʰ January 1945 Thursday
Mammy went on milk round again with Mr Nield. Mr Bullen came and mended kitchen light. I took Evelyn's scissors back. I had my hair washed. Marjorie and I fetched some vegetables from allotment.

5ᵗʰ January 1945 Friday
Mummy had to go on the milk round at short notice because Mrs Nield was ill. We all went to Hales in the afternoon. I went with Marj, Syd and Esme to Preston's to practise some dances for tomorrow. M hit me with coat-hanger.

6ᵗʰ January 1945 Saturday
We all went to a dance at the 'stute for chapel and Evelyn Powell was there and was engaged. I did **"Signing of Magna Carta"** jig-saw in morning and a bit of rug pegging in afternoon. I wore my pink party frock at dance & went to bed at gone midnight. Won spot prize – **cigarettes.**

7ᵗʰ January 1945 Sunday
It snowed a bit in morning. Went to Children's Service in afternoon. M made some tarts. It was Norman Collier's funeral service. We all played cards at night.

8ᵗʰ January 1945 Monday
Rob started back to school after Christmas holidays. It snowed a bit. We went to Coalville, M and I, to tell L.M.S. to fetch Cassell's trunk. I went to Willar's and slipped & felt daft. Very windy and a very cold day.

We started back to school. We had awful films in afternoon. It snowed quite hard. The two Siam girls started our school. We had history reading homework. Many Seniors went to Ashby with Glassy for a Debating Society or something.

10ᵗʰ January 1945 Wednesday
It snowed quite a lot and instead of games we had gym first lesson and played "A man and his object" in 3B, second lesson. We had steam pudding. Had all homework except General Science. I finished knitting my pencil case.

11ᵗʰ January 1945 Thursday
Had a Name Inspection in 2B form room. Stayed for choir. Missed Latin because of Name Inspection. Mr Wells told us that Miss Bate was going to teach us. I finished my pencil case except for 3 press studs.

12ᵗʰ January 1945 Friday
I started sewing my school frock and did the sleeves. Had fish for dinner. Marg & I bought some tarts & buns. I had a library book for the first time since I had been in the 4's. I did not set out for school until 8-30 a.m.

13ᵗʰ January 1945 Saturday
Mummy went to a dance at 'stute. Enid, Bunt and Monica were there. Monty brought the clock back and it stopped about ¼ hr. after he had gone. Grumpy came in morning & afternoon. We played marbles and I read my library to him and Rob.

Note – Grumpy = My brother Rob's pal.

14ᵗʰ January 1945 Sunday
Marj and I went to Sunday School in afternoon but not in morning. We went to church at night and sat with Joyce Shaw and Margaret Moore.

15ᵗʰ January 1945 Monday
We started having Morning Service at school in a different way, when Mr Glister chooses the subject for each day. Had a Maths test. Had a lot of homework. Lambert sat on our table for dinner.

16ᵗʰ January 1945 Tuesday
Rob went to scouts. M and I went to see **"Lassie Come Home"**. It was packed and we sat on the steps for a while. I got 6 out of 10 for art. Had analysis homework. Had steam pudding and Cave sat on our table.

17ᵗʰ January 1945 Wednesday
Miss Smith made Middlebrook and me play goalie (one each end) because we were late getting to the shower. We had two impositions. Cave sat on our table for 2ⁿᵈ time.

18ᵗʰ January 1945 Thursday
Cave again sat on our table. Mummy went to W.V.S. party and Marj and Syb stayed with Rob and me until nearly 10 o'clock. I stopped choir. It was terribly windy and rained nearly all day. Had cake pudding.

19th January 1945 Friday
I had a wretched cold. Had to stop for hockey practice. Mazzarella was outside school so we had an ice-cream before playing hockey. I was first in dinner queue.
I did some of my frock at night. It snowed.

20th January 1945 Saturday
My spots came & I had the measles. The doctor came in the morning
Rob went to choir supper at night. It snowed quite a lot.
I went to sleep almost all of the afternoon.

21st January 1945 Sunday
Rob went to church at night but not in morning. He did not go to Sunday School.
I went downstairs for a bit at night while Rob was out.

22nd January 1945 Monday
G.V.M. for 6th time. Doctor came to say I had not got measles. I got up at night and played cards with Rob and M. Clare Pacey came for **"Comforts"** money.
I read "Deerfoot in the Mountains" at night in bed.

23rd January 1945 Tuesday
The doctor brought my medicine. I got up after tea.
Ma went to 'stute for sale of house next door to Vot's. It made £925.
Rob went to scouts. Mr Guy did not go because of snow.

24th January 1945 Wednesday
I read "The Jungle Goddess". Did some Knitting of mittens.
I finished my medicine and got up just before tea. Papers full of murder by that girl. Rob went to bed at 7-30p.m. We listened to **Will Hay.**

25th January 1945 Thursday
I started my mittens with fur backs. Rob did not go to choir because of bad weather. Terribly snowy. I got up for tea. M went to Ashby and bought ¾ lb sweets which we ate all at once.

26th January 1945 Friday
I was Knitting most of the day. I got up for dinner but did not dress. Went back to bed & got up about 2-30 p.m. I went out a bit about 4 p.m. & met Marj off bus. Went to bed at 11 o'clock.

27th January 1945 Saturday
I wore stockings for the first whole day.
I went a walk with M down Heather Lane. I went round Mary's Lane with Rob on our old horse sledge and had a super time on the snow.

28th January 1945 Sunday
Rob was not very well. I finished my mittens.
I was at Hayes' all afternoon & stopped for tea. There was only Marj and Syb in.
Mr & Mrs Hayes and Syd went to George Watson's because he was on embarkation leave. We had a lovely time and played cards etc.

29th January 1945 Monday
I started back to school after being absent for a week. Betty Newbold was there for a wonder. Mr Williams & Joan Goddard were both absent with the measles. June Fern, Cave and Annable came on our table.

30th January 1945 Tuesday
The snow lay deep on the ground and the Ravenstone bus did not go. About 200 were absent and we had some extras on dinner table as yesterday – T. Turner and another lad out of the fives.

31st January 1945 Wednesday
I again walked to school and came home on 5 o'clock bus. Buckingham, Cave and Annable and June Fern were extras on dinner table. Miss Willoughby absent, so we had Glister for Latin.   **68 miles from Berlin.**

Note – Our soldiers are nearing Berlin.

1st February 1945 Thursday
Bunt came and helped me with my homework. She told us about E. E. P. I biked to school for first time this week because snow was not so bad. Miss Willoughby still absent so we had Miss Bursnell for Latin.

2nd February 1945 Friday
- 2 was absent in the morning but came in the afternoon. Middlebrook & I stayed for hockey practice (not so bad). Rob & I crayoned a Coalville Times competition at night. Stephanie's birthday.

3rd February 1945 Saturday
I played in Junior Eleven against Loughborough and Miss Hoyle took us. We won 6-3. It was the loveliest morning possible. All the country-side looked like a perfect picture as we travelled on the bus.

4th February 1945 Sunday
Sunday School was in church. I went morning & afternoon. It was Children's Service. I did essay on "**The New Horse**". A lovely day.

5th February 1945 Monday
I played Centre Half for Senior House match against Charnwood and we lost 3-0. M Hart, N Irons, O Hawtin & I had a shower. It rained a bit in the match & we had to take shelter in the middle of it.

6th February 1945 Tuesday
We had first précis. M almost finished her spotted frock. Had a geometry test, ugh! Astronomer spoke of G M T on wireless. It was a rainy day. In morning horrid stuff was left from soap flakes.

7th February 1945 Wednesday
Miss Smith came back after being absent for Monday & Tuesday. We had Glister for Latin (not so bad as expected). Seemed an awfully long morning for lessons. M went to Leicester to take Barbara Storer's books back and went to see Aunt Mary.

8th February 1945 Thursday
I stopped Junior Choir. Mr Hayes came round and blew bike tyres up. I cleaned bike. Had some chocolate & sweets from "Oak Tree Cottage" at night. Had Gen. Science test. No-one had showers after gym. Smiggy grumpy with Middlebrook and me.

9th February 1945 Friday
J'ai vu aujourd'hui ma tante qui s'appelle la soeur de Dos sur une bicyclette. Aussi, j'ai vue O^2A. Pour Latin nous avons eu H M. I listened to the play "Julius Cæsar" on wireless. We had **Annie** for an enjoyable domes lesson. Poo!

10 February 1945 Saturday
I read the biggest part of "The last war trail". I had my hair washed. M had hers washed.
I did 100 lines impot for **Annie**. We played Burton High School at C.G.S. and won 3-0. Had a shower. Poo!

11th February 1945 Sunday
Grumpy came for tea. Went Sunday School morning & afternoon. Had missionary story.
Did all homework. I ate no peppermints!!!

12 February 1945 Monday
No-one had shower. Middlebrook & I could not do apparatus.
Took "The last war trail" back. Had King on our table.
Old M^{ac}Donald had a farm où ah, où ah, où, went to pictures to see "Russia".

13th February 1945 Tuesday
It rained hard in the morning. Had steam pudding with orange juice jam on it. I had library with Yellow River in it. Came home round Coalville. I cleaned my hockey shoes.

14th February 1945 Wednesday
Had fish cakes. Missionary was my Good Bye.
I did no homework. Sold Billets for Mrs Swanwick.
Played hockey at dinner-time. Torked bewt Eberdesh & Asks et diny table. Lovely day.

15th February 1945 Thursday
I stopped choir. Had Gen. Science test back. Marg & I both top with 30 out of 45.
Marj came in at night. Merchy absent – a great wonder.
We had a geom test. Played hockey at dinner time.

16th February 1945 Friday
I stopped hockey. We broke up for half term. We had enjoyable films. Had Annie Bevan, Betty Newbold, Miss Hoyle and Miss Wells for Domes Science. We had a lecture by **Ogre.**
Sewed my school frock all night.

17th February 1945 Saturday
I went as reserve for Second Eleven at Burton.
Second Eleven lost 10-2 and First Eleven lost 6-1.
We had super feast & only just caught train home.
I went to Hayes. Doctor came to say Marj had got measles.
Margaret Hewes home on leave.

18th February 1945 Sunday
All went to church at night. David & Mr Carter sang "Story of Cross".
Went a walk with Syb & found a ball.

Note – During the season of Lent, we hear every Sunday night at Ravenstone Church the deeply moving "Story of

The Cross". This, as much as anything, makes me a regular Church attender. With its haunting music & exquisite solos, it can never be forgotten.

19th February 1945 Monday
M and I went to Rex to see "Rebecca".
We all went to Ashby with Alice but blacksmith was too busy and told us to go tomorrow because it was Market Day and he had about 6 horses then.

20th February 1945 Tuesday
We all went to Ashby and Alice was shod. While she was there, we went into town.
Had some lovely U S A red apples and went to Radford's café.
I walked back for considerable distance & got lovely pussy willow.

21st February 1945 Wednesday
Started back to school after half term. S.C.S. had school hot dinners for first time.
M went to Whist Drive at Mrs Davidson's for Belgium Fund.
Great commotion at St. Mary's church.

22nd February 1945 Thursday
We had miserable little jam roll. I stopped choir. I went selling raffle tickets with Marj and Mrs Swanwick down Main Street. Went in Swanwick's at night. Had super time. Doreen Carter was there.

23rd February 1945 Friday
It rained almost all day. We had quite big steam pudding with orange juice jam. I went selling raffle tickets with Marj round Alms Houses. Did only bit of homework. Got 7/- for raffle tickets.

24th February 1945 Saturday
Junior Eleven played Ashby but Dot Wood and Margaret Burton did not play, so we lost 3-0. Went to Mrs Swanwick's dance at night. Doreen Carter was there with her sailor. Lovely day.

25th February 1945 Sunday
I went to Sunday School morning and afternoon. Went to church at night.
Vera Brown and Mr Carter sang "Story of the Cross".

26th February 1945 Monday
GVM for 7th time. We listened to "Monday Night at 8". Annable and Omara came on our dinner table. I saw my picture in Coalville Times window. Paid dentist for bill and bought 6d of chips.

27th February 1945 Tuesday
Marj came in till 8 o'clock. M went to Farmers Dance at 'stute. Clare Pacey came for Comforts money. Had geog test. Had steam pudding with dried apricots in it.

28th February 1945 Wednesday
Smiggy sent Janet Cowlishaw and me inside for all games lesson for not listening to her.
I stopped for debate for competition between the 4th forms. A nice sunny day.

1st March 1945 Thursday
I stopped Junior Choir. No-one had shower after gym. Had -2 for Latin because Evil Eye was absent and she gave us no homework. We were in the front for first time since ages ago.

2nd March 1945 Friday
We all went to Pat's at night and played "Chase the Navy". Evelyn gave me her navy coat. We played 2 house matches. We beat Charnwood 1-0 and drew Highfields 1-1 – wonderful!

Note – What with war-time austerity & being fatherless (my dad died when I was aged 7), we are extremely poor. Evelyn gave me her navy winter coat to keep me warm.

3rd March 1945 Saturday
I did English essay and geog essay. Went to Scout social at night. Won one game and so had 6d worth of refreshments free. No grown ups were there hardly. Vot went.

4th March 1945 Sunday
I went to Sunday School in morning and Children's Service in afternoon.
I went to Altons with Marj.

5th March 1945 Monday
I did not take my L Cs to school and so I did gym in my outdoor shoes. I had very little homework and listened to "Monday Night at Eight". No-one had shower after gym.

6th March 1945 Tuesday
Had lots of homework. Had a 3d ice-cream. We went to Woodwork Room instead of Art and painted large parts of scenery. Had super time. Got in trouble with Miss Silk after noisy Monday.

7th March 1945 Wednesday
Had very little homework. Had 6d ice-cream. Went with Marj, Doreen and Rita to Willar's green-house and had super time. Had athletics for first time and also had gym which we purposely did not do and made an excuse that we were looking for Janet Whatnal's brooch.

8th March 1945 Thursday
I went to school specially early and was there quite a long while before any-one came. M went to Mrs Hales for dinner. I stopped for Junior Choir and it was in 5-2 room. Miss Smith said we would be reported for missing gym yesterday.

9th March 1945 Friday
We ragged Miss Yates pretty badly and we went in detention for Miss Silk & saw Belinda. I had a bath and had a hair wash. I stopped hockey. Bunt came for a bit.

10th March 1945 Saturday
Junior Eleven played a school at Leicester and we won 4-0. I went with Marj to Altons in afternoon and got some lovely pussy willow. Uncle Happy was there. Went to Scout social at night. Simmons was there. Vot won game.

11th March 1945 Sunday
Went to church at night. Doreen and Mr Carter sang "Story of Cross". Rector gave out Anniversary sheets and we practised a bit.

12 March 1945 Monday
Had quite a lot of homework. Harry Hemsley was on "Monday Night at Eight". Joan Goddard and Betty Newbold were both absent from dinner table so Marg was at head and Crabby at foot. B B Simmons was on our table.

13th March 1945 Tuesday
Had film in afternoon and War Savings. Old MacDonald had a farm, où ah, où ah, où. Went to Leicester to Newport Street. I got home ever so early. Theresa, Marie and Marg had to stay out of films.

14th March 1945 Wednesday
Got some frogs' spawn from Willar's pond. Merchy, Middlebrook, Marion Dean & Jean Roddis came down at night and gave me a surprise. Rob fell down twice and bashed himself up.

15th March 1945 Thursday
I stopped choir. We checked up a few of term marks with staff. No-one had showers. Had -2 for Latin. Had burnt cake pudding. Simmons came on our dinner table.

16th March 1945 Friday
Did no homework. Kate G put me in of decem thé sur. We made pancakes. Z took us for Latin. School play rehearsal all afternoon, so had no-one for English last lesson except giraffe occasionally coming in.

17th March 1945 Saturday
I finished library "Hunters of the Ozark". We played "Chase The Navy" a bit at night. Old MacDonald and Rob went round Mary's Lane and got some wood. Old MacDonald went on milk round and got home at 11.

18th March 1945 Sunday
Did not go to church. Dandy sang "Story of the Cross". Marj and I went to Altons & got some wood. Went to Sunday School a.m. and après midi.

19th March 1945 Monday
Je suis allé dans le of decem thé sur pour Madame Y. Pardon thé es.
Nous listened à Lundi nuit à huit heures. Had Thomas for Latin. Hugglescote School saw "Importance of being Ernest"

20th March 1945 Tuesday
Had Miss Hughes for Latin. Only had English (learning poetry) for HW. Marian Dean read lesson. Had geog test on South America. Had Art results, I was 7th.

21st March 1945 Wednesday
Only did Maths HW which took about 3 hours. First performance of "Importance of being Earnest". Marie played violin and stopped at Marg's until next Sunday. Had Thomas for Latin.

22nd March 1945 Thursday

No Choir Practice. Had ropes in gym. Mea mater (où Maman) (où ma mère) went to Whitwick all day, and to Hugglescote at night, to S.I.S. Marie Findley ill in school and had no dinner.

23rd March 1945 Friday

Went to see School Play. Je cassa un losadow au matin et j'alla à la button de notre tête. I did not curl my hair. Had Thomas for Latin. Jean Botterill and UU went to la button du tête.

24th March 1945 Saturday

Je pensa tout le jour de la button. À l'après midi ma mère went to Tea Dance at Hugglescote. Mon frère se tomba down les escaliers, mais, de bon fortune, ne hurt pas.

25th March 1945 Palm Sunday

Went to Church at night and Sunday School a.m. and après midi. Ma mère alla sur la circle du lait et au nuit alla à Hugglescote.

26th March 1945 Monday

We saw play at school. Went to see "Robin Hood". A staff meeting, so we missed gym. I felt approstantiocraticly abostliticalablified because Paedagoglinclivre who stopped dinner, did not walk up Standard Hill.

27th March 1945 Tuesday

Had reports. La Button me voyait quand j'àvais sur un fl-f-l et il pensa que j'àvais esticulose de 2. Clare Pacey came and stopped ages.
I learnt some Latin vocabs, quamquam necessary non.

28th March 1945 Wednesday

Had films "**Banana Ridge**", not partic nice. Jean Goddard had to sing solo "When I survey the wondrous cross" in prayers, and Jean Essex sang at end of term service. **Broke up.**

29th March 1945 Maundy Thursday

Rob and Broomleys broke up. Ma mère alla à la circum de lait. Grumpy came in our house till 8-15. We washed. I had egg for tea. A meeting at Mrs Wilson's house.

30th March 1945 Good Friday

I went to Coalville with **Marj**. A load of wood came and T Wardle helped to get it in. Ma mère went to church in morning and went to cut grass in afternoon with Rob at St. Mary's.

31st March 1945 Saturday

We finished little navy cap. Barbara et Clara venait et nous apportérent des oeufs (3). Miserable day. Ma mère made two cakes. Very sweet! Very tasty! Allâmes au lit a 10-30.

1st April 1945 Easter Sunday

Went to Church at night – very full. Marj came in morning, after noon and stayed for tea. Ma mère went to church at 11.

2nd April 1945 Easter Monday

I read most of "**My Lonely Lassie**" in morning. Had cold dinner. Listened to "**Monday Night at 8**".
Mea mater et Rob went a walk to Pat's in afternoon. Lovely day.

3rd April 1945 Tuesday

Went up Ross Nob with Uncle Len and Marj and got caught in a terrible thunder-storm.
Went to Aunt Sybil's for tea. Rainy all day. I finished "My Lonely Lassie". M went to Ashby.

4th April 1945 Wednesday

Went to allotment with Marj and got some rhubarb, and greens. Went to Aunt Sybil's to take some peels. Pantomime practice at Mrs Swanwick's. Stopped out late with Brenda Hewes.

5th April 1945 Thursday

The rations should have come but they did not. M and I went to Coalville at night & got some chips. We walked there and back. Marj went to Opera practice. I took "**My Lonely Lassie**" back. Grumpy was here nearly all day.

6th April 1945 Friday

I went to Marj's for tea and we went to Altons at night.
Maman went to Farmer's Dance at the Institute.
I was at Marj's all afternoon because ma mère went to Coalville.
Grumpy came to our house for tea. Rations came.

7th April 1945 Saturday

Sold a few flags in morning. Went to dance at night. Electricity was switched off until about 10 o'clock, so we had candles and lamps – quite **Olde Tymish**. I wore green summer frock – first time.

8th April 1945 Sunday

Went to church at night and saw Middlebrook when I came out. Leaflets of Diocese were given out. Did not go to Sunday School a.m.

9th April 1945 Monday

I cleaned bike in morning. Lovely gorgeous day. I went to Altons in afternoon with Marj and came back at 8. Took Margaret Woodings a walk and went walk with Linda. We all had a bath.

10th April 1945 Tuesday

Broomleys, Hugglescote and Snibston School started school after Easter Holiday. I did ironing all night after day's wash. Esmé took billets round. Pat got tickets for his play.

11th April 1945 Wednesday

I went with Marj, Doreen and Rita across Willar's field. It rained at night a bit. Rob ill in bed, hot and feverish. Michael went in field and was a perfect nuisance.

12 April 1945 Thursday

Rob a lot better. Played ball at night with Marj, Brenda, Norma, Rita and Doreen. Went a bike ride down Kelham Bridge and Gig was a nuisance. Spence also went.

13th April 1945 Friday

Nurse came because she had been to Bill's.

Rob well again & got up. Piggy and co. had a bike race round Mary's Lane.

Played ball at night with Marj, Norma, Rita and Doreen.

14th April 1945 Saturday

Went to concert at 'stute for Church Organ Fund (Pantomime children). I had a bath and hair washed. Felt quite ill at night. Rector was at concert and made a short speech.

15th April 1945 Sunday

I was ill in bed, hot and feverish. Headlines of Sunday Dispatch were:-

"VICTORY WEEK-END"

16th April 1945 Monday

Rob had a terrible shock in morning in his sleep and doctor came before 8 a.m. Mid and Jod came down at night and Marj came round. I was better except sore throat.

Note – Rob, my handicapped brother started having epileptic fits, which he was to suffer until the day he died in 1951. He died at the age of 17 after a night of terrible fits, which utterly exhausted him.

17th April 1945 Tuesday

C.G.S. started school. Only had one film and works conked out. Had Miss Horrocks for first time. Told our form was going swimming and had all English discussing it. Quite decent geog lesson.

18th April 1945 Wednesday

Marj washed her hair. I went to school in my blazer. Played hop-scotch at night. I had 6d ice-cream and came to Coalville with Olive Hawtin and home down Wash Lane. Wonderful day.

19th April 1945 Thursday

I went to the Baths with Middlebrook and "Chub Knuckle, chub dent chub". Smiggy was there. Got home at 9 o'clock. Had -2 for Latin. Stopped Choir, - very few there. Lovely day. Wore blazer.

20th April 1945 Friday

Went in Chemistry Lab for Latin for first time since I was in Form 3A. Terrible thunderstorm at night. I slept in back bed, same as yesterday. Bunt came. Evelyn brought tickets for "Barretts of Wimpole Street".

Note – I was at Coalville Grammar School from 1942 until 1948. In Forms 2A: 3A: 4A: 5A: 6B: 6A.

21st April 1945 Saturday

Hollies got eyes on our gooseberries, half out. Marj brought "The Lamplighter". Much cooler after thunderstorm. Terrible news filled paper about Concentration Camps. Seven miles from Berlin.

Note – As the war draws to a close, we learn of the suffering inside the Concentration Camps. Our soldiers are within reach of Berlin.

22nd April 1945 Sunday

Rob had 2 WWWWWs. I went to Sunday School only in afternoon. Rector in a good mood. Maman alla a Auntie Doris at night.

23rd April 1945 Monday

Margaret Choyce wanted me to stop rounders, but I didn't.

Had spam, beans and steam pudding with treacle on.

Mid and Jod came at night for French homework while I was at Recky playing football.

24th April 1945 Tuesday

I stopped rounders. Went to Kendrick's field (**The Plough Inn**) at night and played football. Had to write poem for homework on famous man of war.

Rob had no fit either today or yesterday.

25th April 1945 Wednesday

Tubby came and gave us super lecture and told us about school hymn – "**Jerusalem**". Had Theorem 49 for HW. Maman went to pictures pour voir "**Lady Let's Dance**" No writing HW

Note – Tubby Clayton, Toc H, explained the meaning line by line ---"And did those feet in ancient time walk upon England's mountains green" For the first time, I realised it referred to Christ.

26th April 1945 Thursday

Ma mère, Marj et I went to Progressive Hall to see "**Such Things Happen**" by Coalville Players. We had to stand in the Hall for ¼ hour after dinner for making a din instead of eating our din.

27th April 1945 Friday

I went to Altons with Marj.

Mr Sealy started Black Mark Table but it was not put into force.

Had a Latin test. The cat very ill. Bunt bought whip and top for Rob. A very cold day.

Note – Whip and Top was one of my favourite games as a child. We would whip this little top, shaped a bit like a mushroom, and keep it spinning as we whipped it along the road.

28th April 1945 Saturday

I went to AY's in the morning for wild flowers. I heard cuckoo for first time. **It snowed**. Went to Ashby in afternoon and got some new shoes. Had some ginger biscuits. Bought a new bike pump.

29th April 1945 Sunday

Fluff dangerously ill. Snowed again. Went to Sunday School morning and afternoon. Took some flowers to grave-yard.

30th April 1945 Monday

Fluff found dead.

We had chimney on fire OO.

Glass house school for first time. We did not listen to Monday Night at 8.

Did nothing but maths HW all night, because I had not done Thursdays.

1st May 1945 Tuesday

Had a précis only writing homework.
Ma mère got some TCP tooth-paste.
Stopped rounders practice! Had sausage meat for dinner.
Appro came on our table.

2nd May 1945 Wednesday

News of **Hitler's** death at 8 o'clock.
Went to see "**Barretts of Wimpole Street**". Rob went to Pat's. Mr Bagnall came.
Nearly all staff were at Progressive Hall. Rode home in dark without lights.

3rd May 1945 Thursday

Stayed choir. Went to the Baths.
Shirley Gettings ill in afternoon because she wore wet clothes after going to Baths.
Had XYZ from MTMK. I wore new white socks for first time.
Had a longer time at the Baths.

4th May 1945 Friday

Made baked sponge pudding in domi scio. Had Latin test.
I had to make a speech in English on films. It was awful.
Went to Altons at night with Marj. Had lovely time. Got cowslips.

5th May 1945 Saturday

It rained all day & so went nowhere. Went to bed before 9 o'clock.
South Germany, Holland & Sweden had surrendered at 8 o'clock. News getting exciting. Announcers stopped giving their names. A dance at the 'stute – 2/6d.

6th May 1945 Sunday

Dorothy came. Took some flowers to the church-yard.
Ma mère went to church at night and so Marj came round.

7th May 1945 Monday

Wonderful. Glorious Day. Last all clear. Bells ring. Flags out.
I stopped tennis for first time. I was nearly late for school. Did no HW. Cloak room end knocked out. Very hot. Rob went with Bangles and Mr Francis to Doctors.

Note – Bangles was the pony. Mr Francis had a pony & trap.

8th May 1945 Tuesday

V.E. Day. Rejoicing and thanks-giving. Flags everywhere.
Coalville clock tower beautifully lit up at night.
H. M. King George VI and Mr Churchill, Premier, both made speeches.

Note – Victory in Europe, the last "All Clear", bells ring, flags out, general rejoicing. The war is over, apart from continued fighting in the far east.

9th May 1945 Wednesday

Went to Stanton in afternoon. Ma mère went to milk round in morning.
Flags still out. Hot day. Did HW at night.

Maman went to Pat's for a little at night because they went to see Coalville lit up.

10th May 1945 Ascension Day

Started school after Victory holiday & wore frock for first time.
Heats day. Went to the Baths in morning. Went school in blazer.
Went to Anniversary practice at church.
Had prunes & custard for pud. I had none but had a lot of first course.

11th May 1945 Friday

Went to Girl Guides for first time. Nearly late for school.
Had jam roll for pudding.
Bought some asters seeds from Woolworth's. Had ice-cream.
Had Glister for English, because Glassy had gone to Manchester to see **Taffy**.

12 May 1945 Saturday

Went to see "**Iolanthe**". Had tea at 'stute.
Went with Marj to meet Freda Johanson from **Fox & Goose**. Came home from Broomleys School in Beadman's car & saw folks at Hugglescote with banners of fire. Fairy lights down Broughton St.

13th May 1945 Sunday

Went to Altons and Marj got a puncture.
Rob went to Hollies tea party.
Ma mere went to church at night, after which we went to Auntie Doris'.

14th May 1945 Monday

Rained at dinner time. Had steam pudding. Ma mère started to "Spring Clean" the pantry. Monday Night at Eight, a Victory one, quite jolly. Wore tunic again because it was cold. Had sour milk cheese for tea.

15th May 1945 Tuesday

Ma mère white-washed the pantry. Had a maths test which was marked on 17/5/45. Marg got 17: I got 16: Marie Findley got 15: Merchy got 20: Buckingham got 19. Wore tunic, and yesterday.

16th May 1945 Wednesday

Sports Day. Mr Glister went away because his father died. Ma mère went to see Iolanthe. Had hobbies book. I had a bath. Had Latin test. Mrs Clamp at Sports Day. Dot Wood was Sports Champion again.

17th May 1945 Thursday

Went to baths. Middlebrook absent so AY was my partner. **Betty Newbold** left. Mr Glister not at school. I went to Girl Guides and had belt & frock whatsit. Had Tenderfoot Card, and 10 tickets to sell for concert.

18th May 1945 Friday

Went to fair which was on for first time. Rob had 3 fits in night. Doctor came. Ma mère fetched medicine at night and called at Scott's for ages. I walked up to fetch her. Marj went to Groby for holiday.

19th May 1945 Saturday

Ma mère et mon frère sont allés to the Circus at Ravo. I

went with Syb to fair at night and went with Rob in afternoon. Piggy Collier there. Gave us about 6d all together with slot machines.

20th May Whit Sunday
Ma mere went to Church at night.
Terrible rainfall. Entry flowing.
I stopped in all day. Read plays. Slept in back bed.

21st May 1945 Whit Monday
Went Circus at night at **Plough**. Went fair after.
Ma mère went on milk round. Started writing S.T. in book. Had egg for dinner.
Went to Sports at Waltho's. It rained half way through and spoilt it.

22nd May 1945 Tuesday
Football match at recky between **Ibby** and **Ravo**. Ravo easily wiped out poor old **Ibby**.
I went to fair afternoon and night. Ma mère went to dance at 'stute. Last performance of circus at Ravo.

23rd May 1945 Wednesday
Parliament dissolved.
Marj came home. Syb, Marj and I went to fair at night. Circus went early in morning.
Ma mère went to Whist Drive at Mrs Wilson's and won prize for sitting in the lucky chair.

24th May 1945 Thursday
Went to Baths in afternoon with Pat Colver.
Ma mère et mon frère went to Whitwick in afternoon.
Had two 6d ice-creams – one from Ayres.
Mon frère commence des Bebes de L'eau, mais je le lisais.

25th May 1945 Friday
Nurse came. Ma mère had the ends of her hair permed in morning. Went Guides and only practised for concert.
Jean Roddis got full uniform off Mrs Biddle woman.
Rob slept upon la montagne premierement.

26th May 1945 Saturday
Went to football match at recky against Whitwick and we lost 6-5.
Rob went to Belles and Fred's who lent us game about Spaniards and Americans.
All had a bath. Fair on for last time.

27th May 1945 Trinity Sunday
Anniversary. AO[2] went at night. So full at night, had to fetch chairs from near houses.
Marj wore new blue costume for first time.

28th May 1945 Monday
Went to Guides concert practice at Progressive Hall.
Started to make Cuba & U.S.A. game. Ma mere went to Ashby for rations.
Did a bit of S.T. (**Special Topic**) in afternoon.
Ma mere did some collecting for **District Nurse**.

29th May 1945 Tuesday
Started school after Whit holiday. Had fuzzy stew stuff for dinner.
Miss Yates not at school. Had 8 for Art. Had no writing home-work.
I wore my brown frock that I made, for first time at school, but daren't take blazer off.

30th May 1945 Wednesday
Had Guides Concert. Did no homework. Had no writing. Got some chips. Had sausage meat for dinner. 222 did not stop dinner. Had 6d ice-cream.
Marg had impot from Miss Silk, which we did behind scenes.

31st May 1945 Thursday
Went baths. Stayed Choir. Had lecture from Smiggy for not staying rounders yesterday. Had history test out of 50. Ma mere went to Whitwick. Had orange juice jam on school pudding.

Note – We now go from school once a week to Coalville Swimming Baths and I learn to swim.

1st June 1945 Friday
Went to guides at Miss Orton's house for first time. Had ink from Rags and Yellow.
Had lots of cars on road. Petrol used for first time since ages.
Ma mère went with Mrs Wilson to Leicester, to see the Duchess of Kent.

Note – Motor cars return to our roads, as petrol is once more available for private motoring.

2nd June 1945 Saturday
I had my hair washed. Pat Colver came and we did some "Tenderfoot".
Ma mère et mon frère alla à le petit church et cut l'herbe.
Did a lot of cooking, cake and tarts.
Coke came yesterday. Grand-pop helped to get it in.

3rd June 1945 Sunday
Stayed at home all day. Ma mère went on milk round. Rain all day. Chapel Anniversary. My hair awful fuzzy fuzzy mess. Keith Woodings is born.

4th June 1945 Monday
Did BBC script nearly all night – what I should have done for weekend HW.
I ripped my blazer on balcony at school. Started frog in biology.
Started "We are cupid somewhat stupid" in music.
Joan stopped for dinner. Red cheeked lad on our table.

5th June 1945 Tuesday
Had Latin in 2A. Should have had it in 5-**two**.
Had spam for dinner. Last Sunday Mabel Poole had baby boy. Mrs George had baby girl. Should have played rounders house match but it rained. Only English writing homework.

6th June 1945 Wednesday
Had fine games lesson in the quadrangle. Had fish for dinner. Had no shower. Learned the date in Latin.
Marg, Marie et je devaunt aller a la salle de dix sur pour notre magister de la science de la cuisinarariment.

7th June 1945 Thursday
Stopped Choir. Had 6d ice-cream.
Merchy broke her tooth at the baths. Joan Goddard got hay fever.
Did Latin learning vocabs only for HW. Sang Merrie England at choir.
Margaret Pegg and Rita Newton stayed for dinner.

8th June 1945 Friday
Was very good in domie- scio (half class made bread and butter pudding).
Went to guides at Miss Orton's. I went from Primrose to Poppy. Pat Colver did not go. Middlebrook stopped games.
After guides, Middlebrook and I went to Coalville Fair for a bit.

9th June 1945 Saturday
Mabel's baby a week old tomorrow. Mrs Hayes went to see her at Ashby. I was at Hayes' all afternoon. Did map of France in morning. Stanley came to mend lights in morning. His mother died on last Monday morning early, just after midnight.

10th June 1945 Sunday
Marj went to Sunday School in morning. I didn't. There wasn't any in afternoon.
Had bigger supper than usual and a horrible dreamy night.

11th June 1945 Monday
Cadle's birthday. He came on our dinner table.
South African lad came to 4A, C.G.S. for first time. Had biology test.
Went to bed at 8-30p.m. for a change. Did not have much HW.
Fair at Hugglescote – that which was at Ravenstone.

12th June 1945 Tuesday
Cadle on our dinner table again. Had Art Exam. Had fat meat for dinner and orange juice jam. Played Charnwood at rounders and we won!!! Very rainy all day. Only had Latin writing HW. I had lost my Latin book.

13th June 1945 Wednesday
Had no writing HW. Had English essay back on "**Iron**". I only got 3. Stayed Rounders. Had pastry with jam in for dinner and corned beef – first time for ages. Ma mère went to Scotties & saw Maureen's house.

14th June 1945 Thursday
Told La tête de Button of Tractor of Bent Toes. No choir because both pianos being mended. Had physics test. Had lovely first dinner with pastry covering red meat. Ma mere went to Hales morning et du soir.

15th June 1945 Friday
Made 3 little puddings. Told La tête de Button of Tractor of To Vels.
Went to guides and passed "Tenderfoot". Had some chips from Allen's.
Rob in bed, hot and feverish. Weeded Orton's garden path.

16th June 1945 Saturday
Sold raffle tickets at gymkhana at Coalville. Got in free. Went on 2 o'clock bus and got home (walked) just before 8 o'clock. Did some biol revision in morning.
Florrie Moore (Uncle Will's daughter) came in morning. M went to Ashby.

17th June 1945 Sunday
Marj did not go to Sunday School at all. She went out in afternoon. I went both times. Rector in a good mood. Very jolly.

18th June 1945 Monday
I found my Latin book after having it lost for a week.
Had biol test. Middlebrook stopped for Senior rounders match. Clare Pacey came at night. Labour Candidate yelling through a megaphone. Nobody telling what he's on about. Middlebrook got all 3 rounders.

19th June 1945 Tuesday
Very hot. Hottest day this year, (so the papers say). Middlebrook came down and we scrumped Hollies. Stopped rounders and we beat Harley 2 ½ - 0. Highfields beat Charnwood 3-0.

20th June 1945 Wednesday
Stayed Rounders Practice. Very stifling at night. **Zum ze bum di da** at 'stute. Ma mere alla seulement de notre famille. Rained at tea-time.

21st June 1945 Thursday
Stopped Choir. Very rainy but cleared up at night. Rob had lots of falls and bad do's all day and a bad night. I went to butcher's at night from school to fetch some liver.

22nd June 1945 Friday
Went to Guides. Went to Coalville Park in the meantime and played rounders. Miss Yates absent. Had **Kathleen Annie Bevin**. Took some roses for **Polly**. I forgot my dinner and milk money.

23rd June 1945 Saturday
Lovely hot day. Maureen Scott's wedding. Rob & I went to St. Mary's Church and took some flowers. Two men with spying glasses were at gate. Rob and I had tea on the lawn. I went to Aunt Dos' in the morning.

Note – Maureen Scott married Ken Stocks.

24th June 1945 Sunday
Rector told us about **Stone Henge**. Went a walk at night. Rob had lots of do's tonight and 3 in the daytime.

25th June 1945 Monday
Stayed Tennis. Had steam roll with currants in for pudding. Drunkards went up road at night, causing much laughter. Senior rounders match. Highfields beat Broughton.

26th June 1945 Tuesday
Had geog test. Rob very ill all day. Bit better at night. Marj came for nearly all evening and brought some strawberries. No rounders because rain.

27th June 1945 Wednesday
Stayed Choir at dinner and rounders at night. Had impot on Common Sense from Sarkie Soo. Mrs Dalby, Auntie Gladys and Cis and Dos and Clare Pacey all came. Rob lots better. Hollies gone at last. Marj came till 8-30p.m.

28th June 1945 Thursday
Went baths. Stopped choir. Had Maths test. Stopped up till gone midnight, chiefly doing **Special Topic**. Rob a lot better. Ma mère went to fetch some medicine but got none. We had some of Maureen Scott's Wedding cake.

29th June 1945 Friday
Went to guides. It poured with rain so went into greenhouse. Went inside Middlebrook's church (Roman Catholic). Had steam pudding. Had corned beef in stew – ugh! Half class made ginger biscuits in domestic science.

30th June 1945 Saturday
Went to Altons in afternoon. Newitts were there. Saw Mabel's 2nd baby for first time.
Had bath & hair washed. M went to Ashby in morn for Ration Books.
Doctor called to bring Rob's medicine. Very rainy the whole of the day.

1st July 1945 Sunday
Very rainy. Went Sunday School in morning but not in afternoon.
David came and stopped for tea. Ice Cream man came.

2nd July 1945 Monday
Went with Belle, Fred and Mrs Clark all over The Hollies.
Had impot from Christine Bate for stealing paper.
Stopped gym display practice for first time. Practised constant hitting practice.

3rd July 1945 Tuesday
Stayed Rounders match against **Highfields** and wonder of wonders we won ½ - 0, thus getting the **Cup**. 4S went up **Bardon Hill** in afternoon with Miss Silk.
Had **Art** outside on the field.

4th July 1945 Wednesday
Stayed till gone 5-30p.m. for gym display practice. Had geog test. Read 4 Tales by Conrad for the whole of English. **Mina Hart** read the lesson. Stayed Choir practice at dinner. Had horrid yellow blanc-mange for dinner.

5th July 1945 Thursday
All our form went with Miss Silk up **Bardon Hill**. Went baths in morning and after school. Exam places up. I am in my own desk. I was first in dinner queue. Had **Latin** in 6th form. Irene Mason read the lesson.

6th July 1945 Friday
I was enrolled at guides.
Got into hot water in Domestic Science. 4P went up **Bardon Hill**. Rob went out in Fred's car. Bunt came to **Ravenstone**. Went to exam places.
Auntie Dos decided to give up pies.

7th July 1945 Saturday
Went to **Ashby Procession**. **Groby Guides** presented with The Shield.
Went to a service at Ashby Church and had a feast at **Town Hall**.
Maman et Belle went to C.G.S. to a Whist Drive.

8th July 1945 Sunday
I did not go to Sunday School at all.
Rob et Maman went for a walk at night. Marj went to Sunday School morning & afternoon. Maman went to Church p.m.

9th July 1945 Monday
Exams started. Stayed for gym display practice. Joan did not stay dinner.
Had **English Language**, **Latin** and **Geography**.
Had steam pudding, spam, tomatoes and new potatoes for dinner. Had Miss Bate & Smiggy for examinations.

10th July 1945 Tuesday
Had **Algebra**, **Geometry** and **General Science** exams. Mr Glister set the Algebra and it was ever so difficult. Auntie Annie from Leicester came. Very rainy all day. **Latin** and **German** exam results were received.

11th July 1945 Wednesday
Had **English Literature**, **History** and **French** exams. I did no home-work. Stayed gym display practice. Had **Geometry** results. **Lieut** came to see about camping. Had blanc-mange for dinner.

12th July 1945 Thursday
Stayed Choir. Went baths. Only had **Arithmetic** exam. Had mince-meat stuff in gravy for dinner. Played ball on front with Marj. Uncle Charlie & John came to Ravenstone.
Bunt came to see about taking me to **Bradgate**.

13th July 1945 Friday
Stayed gym display practice. Did not get home until nearly 6 p.m. and had to rush to guides. Had blanc-mange for dinner. Did not do Domestic Science. Bunt came. Had English Composition results. I was 2nd with 86%.

14th July 1945 Saturday
Went to Bradgate with Bunt. A lovely hot day and I got very brown. Thunderstorm at night. Had handbag from 69 Newport St. (Auntie Annie from Leicester). Went to Johnscliffe for tea. Went by Groby Pool. Had delicious ice-cream coming home.

15th July 1945 Sunday
Went to **Youth Parade** from Coalville **Marlborough Square** to Coalville Grammar School, for service. Glister not looking well. Going grey. Very hot. Went church at night.

16th July 1945 Monday
Had fishes for dinner – something like pilchards. Middlebrook and I set dinner table and so we had all nice knives, forks & spoons. Betty Baker's birthday. Had gym display practice first lesson in afternoon & after 4p.m.

17th July 1945 Tuesday
Had gym display practice first lesson in the afternoon and after 4p.m. Had Prize Day singing practice last lesson in morning. I had a free ice-cream by a bit of swizzling. I had my hair washed. Nice hot day.

18th July 1945 Wednesday
Had Choir Practice first lesson in afternoon. Had gym from **Break** until dinner and in **Games Lesson** from 4 – 5 o'clock. Had ice-cream. Took Chubby to school on bike and went with **N Blakemore**.

19th July 1945 Thursday
Had gym practice first two lessons in afternoon, and Choir last lesson. Stayed Choir practice after 4 o'clock. Did no HW. Played avec **Bin Bon** at marbles in glarny hole.

Note – Bin Bon = Robin, my brother. Glarny hole is a small hole in the hard soil, where the marble rolls.

20th July 1945 Friday
Had **Gym Display** and **Hobbies Day**. Had tomatoes and corned beef, spuds, lettuce and roly poly pudding. Mr & Mrs Clamp at school. Had exam results of positions. Joyce Preece back at guides after illness.

21st July 1945 Saturday
Went to Altons in afternoon and stayed for tea. Took some honey to Altons and had some honey ourselves. Watched bees at Preston's. Very rainy all day. Thunderstorm at night. A brick came down the chimney.

22nd July 1945 Sunday
Went Sunday School twice and church at night. Ma mère forgot about flowers on the Altar which should have been done today.

23rd July 1945 Monday
Did not go to school. Went with ma mère et mon frère to clinic in morning in Aunt Dos' car with Grandpop et ma tante Dos. Ma mere went to Ashby in afternoon. I went to Preston's and watched bees.

24th July 1945 Tuesday
Went to dentists but had nothing done. A new woman was there. Saw photo of guides parade at Stacey's, the photographers. Helped Pat clean car at office before I went. Lights being fitted up at **Rex**, **Regal** and **Grand** in Coalville.

25th July 1945 Wednesday
School played rounders all afternoon. The winners of the 8 girls teams played the winners of the 8 boys teams and the winners of those play tomorrow with the staff, all being well.

26th July 1945 Thursday
Broke up. Would have watched Cricket Match in afternoon but it rained and so I came home at just gone 2-30p.m. Election results, **Labour** got in with a majority. **Attlee** new **Prime Minister**. Ma mère went to dance at 'stute.

Note – General Election – Labour victory, Attlee is

Prime Minister, defeating war-time leader Winston Churchill.

At the end of my school year in Form 5A, I passed the Oxford School Certificate with credits in four subjects: - English Language, English Literature, French & Maths; and with passes in two subjects: - History & General Science.

27th July 1945 Friday
Went to Guides. Gave my 30/- for camp. Pat Colver not at guides because her father comes home from India tomorrow. Brenda Hewes had kitten from **Bardon**. Mostly arranging for camp at guides.

28th July 1945 Saturday
Archie Ford married. Pat Colver's dad came home. Ma mère cut grass at grave-yard.
Soft water stinking. Pat had slab up from over cistern. David came a bit at night. He and pop had a banana which Marg brought.

29th July 1945 Sunday
Went Sunday School morning & afternoon. Went church at night.
Wireless wavelengths altered.
Sydney Hayes went into long trousers.

30th July 1945 Monday
Marj went with me selling **District Nursing Day** flags up the road at night.
Frederick Christoph of **Prussia** tomorrow marries **Lady Brigid Katherine Rachel Guinness**.

31st July 1945 Tuesday
Went selling flags again down the road and took money in to **Mrs Wilson** who gave me an enamel mug to use at guides.
David Hewes goes to Mablethorpe tomorrow to stay for a week.

1st August 1945 Wednesday
Took ration books to Caps. Ann, Jill, Jane & Tom went to Wilson's. Ma mère went to Ashby in the morning and bought some things for camp.
My **Certificate Saving** money came to be cashed.

2nd August 1945 Thursday
I fetched my bathing costume from Bunts. Pat Colver came up and helped me pack.
Ma mère went to Whitwick on bike.
I had "Older Mousie" from Pat Colvers and I gave her "School Friend Annual".

3rd August 1945 Friday
I saw "Aunt" for first time on her "**Bessie**" (a three-wheeled cycle).
Went guides only came home very early because of camp tomorrow
Had a bath and so did all of us. Had hair washed yesterday. Luggage went to camp.

4th August 1945 Saturday
Went camping with the **Girl Guides**. (Did not take my diary)

Note – I went camping with the Girl Guides – roughing it for a week in the wilds of Charnwood Forest – not my scene. Give me all mod cons & running hot water. From what I can recall, many years later, the only thing I liked about camping with the Girl Guides, was sitting round the camp-fire at night, wrapped in a blanket, with a hot drink, and singing camp fire songs. I did however love sleeping beneath the stars – until it rained in the middle of the night. In the darkness it was difficult to see where our tent was pitched.

There were many things I did not like about camping – digging trenches which we used for toilets – fetching & carrying firewood & water – eating food which tasted of smoke – stung by stinging nettles in the woods – sleeping in a tent, etc.

6th August 1945 Sunday
Atomic Bomb destroyed Hiroshima, Japan.

9th August 1945 Thursday
Atomic Bomb dropped on Nagasaki, Japan, by U.S.A.

Note – This brought World War II to an end – Victory in Japan, V. J. Day.

25th August 1945 Saturday
Ma mère et moi nous allâmes voir les tantes qui s'appellant Marie et Martha.
Mon frère, il resta avec Madge.

Note – Now we are on the farm at Willoughby-on-the-Wolds, staying with Mum's cousins Madge & Bertha and their father, Uncle Tom.

26th August 1945 Sunday
Went with Uncle Tom round Willoughby church and had to yell at him writing on graves.
Ma & I went to church in morning. Lovely day.

28th August 1945 Tuesday
I rang up **Reta** & we all went there at night in the Fire Engine. (Bertha's car)
Hollingshead's horse Lorna went back with Mrs Cam & I went with Bertha in the Fire Engine to bring Mrs Cam back.
I took cows to field and fed fowls down street.

29th August 1945 Wednesday
I came home from Willoughby in Beadman's car, driven by Jack Willars. A rainy day.
Rob & I went up to Broughton Lane field & Rex & Walter made a fence round the stack.
The black cow which kicked me had a calf which was born too soon and dead.

30th August 1945 Thursday
Mrs Swanwick went out selling "Billets" at night, and left Michael alone in the house. He woke up and started yelling blue murder.

31st August 1945 Friday
Doreen Willars sick. I wrote to Elaine. Mrs Sherwin's funeral. Mrs Hayes and Aunt Sybil went in their black hats tomorrow because funeral is tomorrow.

1st September 1945 Saturday
Flower Show at Ravenstone Institute. Mr Jack Carter got cup. He got 51 points & J Colver got 47 points. **Bazaar** at St. James, Highfields. Rob, Marje & I went & had ice-cream. Mr Kendrick, Coalville Grammar School caretaker, was at Ravenstone Institute with lovely spaniel.

2nd September 1945 Sunday
I went to church at night with Marje. Infirmary Parade was in morning. I took the old doll's pram to pieces. Nice hot day. Started to empty water cistern.

3rd September 1945 Monday
Went to Elaine's. Went to Old Time Dance.

Note – Elaine Cooper, school friend who lived at Glenfield.

4th September 1945 Tuesday
Went to pictures in afternoon to see George Formby in "**I Didn't Do It**".

5th September 1945 Wednesday
Mrs Clayton came. Elaine & I went black-berrying.

6th September 1945 Thursday
Went to Palace Cinema at night to see "**One of our Aircraft is Missing**" and "**Escape to Happiness**".

7th September 1945 Friday
Came home from Elaine's. Went to Girl Guides.

8th September 1945 Saturday
Went to Wicksteed Park.

9th September 1945 Sunday
Went to church at night. Mrs Clark came for tea and dinner. I started my bootees.

10th September 1945 Monday
Went blackberrying & got about 4lbs from The Altons. Jerry working there. Ma mère went to a Whist Drive at Mrs Wilson's. I washed my hair. Left Altons about 5-30p.m. Went in Marjorie's Wellingtons.

11th September 1945 Tuesday
Had a bath & got ready for school. (New term – into Form 5A after the summer holidays) Ma mère had a bath.

12th September 1945 Wednesday
Started back to school. Had 1st dinner on Cad's table. Only Marie, Marg et moi. Covered nearly all my books.

13th September 1945 Thursday
Had Latin & Geography mistresses for first time and Mr Smith. First dinner again. I rang the school bell!
Mostyn came home Wednesday night and I saw him tonight.

Note – Mostyn Stevenson, betrothed to my sister Bunting, is home again in Ravenstone, after the long separation as a war-time soldier.

14th September 1945 Friday
Went to Girl Guides at night. Last time this year at Orton's. It was dark almost when I came home & I walked most of the way.

15th September 1945 Saturday
Ma mère went on milk round in morning, & I did my homework. Rob & I went blackberrying & got about 2 ½ lbs. Belle & Fred went to Mablethorpe for a week.

16th September 1945 Sunday
I went to The Altons with Marje & had some of Margaret Wooding's birthday cake. Her birthday is next Tuesday. Auntie Doris came & brought kitten.

Note – Life is slowly reverting to normal, but food is still rationed. At least we are enjoying ice-cream again. I had ice-cream 24th September 1942, and not again until 1st January 1945.

On September 19th 1945, in the Old Bailey, a man called William Joyce was sentenced to death for treason. He is better known to history as Lord Haw-Haw.

21st September 1945 Friday
Mr & Mrs **Jappy** came with 4 month old baby *(Susan)* to see if they could come as lodgers to our house.
Bunt came for ½ min. Cis & Dos came because L.M.S. brought chocolate to our house when Auntie Dos was out.

22nd September 1945 Saturday
I ran away!!! I had my hair cut at Shiffy's. Rainy day. Would have gone to pictures at 'stute, only man didn't come, so I went next Saturday & saw Paul Robeson.

23rd September 1945 Sunday
Getting ready for **Jappys**.
Went Sunday School morning & afternoon and to church at night.
Enid went with her hair up at back. I had a bath.

24th September 1945 Monday
Seniors played hockey match against **Highfield** and lost 10-0. Shame on them!!!

25th September 1945 Tuesday
Jappys came. I had a bath. Jappys got here about 10p.m. and Mr Jappy looked like a dust-bin man.

26th September 1945 Wednesday
Telegram for Mr Jappy to say they'd got to sail on 3rd October.
Been putting things straight all day so had to think about getting things out of drawers again.
I had a bath. Mr & Mrs Jappy rang up London to tell them news.

Note – Our new lodgers were only here one night when they received a telegram to say they could set sail for Australia on 3rd October.

27th September 1945 Thursday
Mr & Mrs Jappy went to Plough and brought Bin & me some pop back.

Saw "**The Tempest**" by Birmingham Rep. Company. Stayed choir at dinner.
Marg came down at night for homework & got Mr Jappy's autograph.

28th September 1945 Friday
Stayed hockey. Went to guides & passed a mile. Mr Orme here when I got back.
Went to Willars with TCTJ who rang up **Birmingham & London**.

29th September 1945 Saturday
Mr Jappy went to **Birmingham** to get a pram for Susan & after that went to London ready for going abroad from Liverpool.
I fetched 12 eggs from Robies & got Mr Beadman to take Mrs Jappy to Coalville station.

30th September 1945 Sunday
Sydney's birthday. Harvest Festival at church & at chapel. I went to **Joyca Preecas** & got some rose hips for guides.

1st October 1945 Monday
Got up Standard Hill without getting off my bike because I thought I was late because bus which was potato picker's bus which I thought was school bus passed me.

2nd October 1945 Tuesday
Junior Broughton beat Harley 5-0 !!!!

3rd October 1945 Wednesday
Stayed hockey. Had tests in following subjects: - **Latin**: **History**: **Geography**: **Maths**.
Oh Dear. I only got 10 out of 20 for history.

4th October 1945 Thursday
Stayed choir. Had my hair washed. Played hockey instead of gym because 5M was doing 5P's lessons because of potato pickers and thus made numbers too many to get in gym.

5th October 1945 Friday
Went to Girl Guides and somebody let my bike tyre down, so I had to walk home.
The doctor died. Nurse came.
Rob hit me on the head with a black wooden whatsit.

Note – Dr Forsyth, our doctor & family friend, died.

6th October 1945 Saturday
Played hockey at Loughborough for 2nd XI. Both 1st and 2nd XI went in Brown's Blue private bus and 2nd XI won 7-0 and 1st XI lost 5-0. Went to Scout's Social at 'stute at night. Doreen & Rita won the **Spot Prize**.

7th October 1945 Sunday
Went to Sunday School morning and afternoon. Ma mère went to church at night. We all went to Belle's at night and played **Lexicon** and **Rummy**.

8th October 1945 Monday
I had to walk to school and back because of my flat tyre. Took 1¼ lbs of rose hips to Lieuts. Stayed Senior

hockey and lost 4-1 to Charnwood.

9th October 1945 Tuesday
Auntie Annie came. Took my knitting slippers to school for domes. science. Pat brought tickets for his play.

10th October 1945 Wednesday
Stayed play practice for first time. Had it in gym. Had **Latin**, **Maths** and **History** test. I got to school about first. Mammy got a sore throat. Had steam pudding.

12th October 1945 Friday
Mostyn went back. I walked with Bunt and with my bike nearly all way to guides and she asked me to be her bridesmaid.

Note – Bunting & Mostyn plan their wedding for January 1946, with 5 bridesmaids.

13th October 1945 Saturday
Went 1st Class hike with Jean Cox. She and Joyce Preece and Lieut. were to pass and B. Broughton. I did all HW in morning.

15th October 1945 Monday
Stayed hockey. I read lesson badly.

16th October 1945 Tuesday
Did not stay for anything.

17th October 1945 Wednesday
Stayed play practice.

18th October 1945 Thursday
Stayed Choir.

19th October 1945 Friday
Ma mère et Monsieur Bagnall cleaned Well out.
Mummy went to Pat's play.
Stayed hockey. Went to guides & passed "Health".

20th October 1945 Saturday
Played hockey for 2nd XI at Barrow. Both 1st and 2nd XI went.
A school dance – first this term.
Ma mère went to Belle's at night & had hare pie.
Doreen Carter married.

21st October 1945 Sunday
Went to Belle's at night. Rainy day.

24th October 1945 Wednesday
Had General Science test out of 40.

25th October 1945 Thursday
Only had a short choir practice because of Prize **Day**.
Had a practice also at last lesson in morning.
Mrs Leadbetter died.

26th October 1945 Friday
Prize Day.

27th October 1945 Saturday
Belle and mother and husband came to our house from 8p.m. to 1a.m. and played cards and **"Who Knows"**.

28th October 1945 Sunday
We went to Belle's. Rainy nearly all day.

29th October 1945 Monday
Rained ALL day. Had ½ term list. I was 4th so sat on back row.

2nd November 1945 Friday
Went to Girl Guides.
Marg & I got a bobbies autograph for Simmons. I only just caught bus going.

3rd November 1945 Saturday
Went to school to practise for our form play – **Unnatural Scene**. Ma mère faisait le circle du lait parceque Mr Nield est à l'hospital. Mrs Worth had a baby.

4th November 1945 Sunday
Went to Belle's at night and she gave me her red skirt and coat.

Note – I am still receiving other's cast-offs for clothing.

6th November 1945 Tuesday
Had my hair washed.

8th November 1945 Thursday
Started back to school after half term.

9th November 1945 Friday
Went to Girl Guides and to Rangers Den where it was opened by Kettleban. (Or something similar)

10th November 1945 Saturday
Played hockey at school against Ashby Juniors and drew 2-2.
First Eleven played at C.G.S. against Ashby and lost 9-0.

12th November 1945 Monday
Went in Auntie Cis' car with her, Belle, Auntie Gladys & Mummy to see **"Jane Eyre"**.

13th November 1945 Tuesday
Mammy again went to see Jane Eyre.
Machined my skirt in Domestic Science and had to undo no end.

16th November 1945 Friday
Marg did not go to Guides because she was selling programmes at the Church School for **"Square Pegs"**.
Mammy went to see **"Square Pegs"**.

17th November 1945 Saturday
Played hockey for Second Eleven at Ashby.

18th November 1945 Sunday
Went to Church and an old man sat against us. Ken Collier sat behind us.

23rd November 1945 Friday
Went to Guides on bus.

24th November 1945 Saturday
Went to Scouts' Social at 'stute.
Went to hockey tournament in morning at Aylestone.

Won 2 matches. Drew 1. Lost 1.
Rita Hewes had her hair permed (ends) for first time at Glynns.
Syb had hers done also at Bootons.

27ᵗʰ November 1945 Tuesday
Half of our form made meat pie.

8 pints = 1 gallon
2 gallons = 1 peck
4 pecks = 1 bushel
8 bushels = 1 quarter

Ale & Beer Measure
4 gills = 1 pint
2 pints = 1 quart
4 quarts = 1 gallon
9 gallons = 1 firkin
2 firkins = 1 kilderkin
2 kilderkins = 1 barrel
1 ½ barrels = 1 hogshead
1 ½ hogsheads = 1 puncheon
1 ½ puncheons = 1 butt

Avoirdupois Weight
16 drams = 1 ounce
16 ounces (oz) = 1 pound
28 pounds (lbs) = 1 quarter
4 quarters = 1 hundredweight (cwt)
20 cwt = 1 ton

3ʳᵈ December 1945 Monday
EXAMS!

4ᵗʰ December 1945 Tuesday
EXAMS!

5ᵗʰ December 1945 Wednesday
EXAMS!

8ᵗʰ December 1945 Saturday
Played hockey at school against Market Bosworth. Won 5-2.
Margaret Burton chosen to play for the **County**.

10ᵗʰ December 1945 Monday
Music Festival

12ᵗʰ December 1945 Wednesday
Went to Guides Party at Ashby and had a grand time.
Speech Festival.

13ᵗʰ December 1945 Thursday
Second Forms had their **Christmas Party**.

18ᵗʰ December 1945 Tuesday
Had School Party. Elaine stopped at our house and left her pyjamas. Made toffee at school.

19ᵗʰ December 1945 Wednesday
Rob's School Party.

20ᵗʰ December 1945 Thursday
Broke up from school. Had super films – Laurel and Hardy.

Went **Carol Singing**. Had rotten time.

Motor Car (Private) Licences
Not exceeding 6 Horse Power £7 - 10s - 0d
Exceeding 6 H.P. – for each unit £1 - 5s - 0d
Motor Driver's Licence 5s - 0d

25ᵗʰ December 1945 Tuesday
We all went to Belle's for tea.
Ma mère nearly fainted & Rob was sick.
I stopped until nearly 2 a.m. (26ᵗʰ). Horace was there and taught us no end of tricks.

28ᵗʰ December 1945 Friday
No Guide meeting because of **Christmas**.

* * *

Note – Unless I am given a diary for Christmas, I have no money to buy one myself. Last Christmas Mrs Cassell bought me a lovely big desk diary which I completed in pencil & later transferred to a 5 year diary.
In 1946 I had no diary.

Note by Mary Blue - Betty had re-written the diaries for 1944 & 1945 into the 5 year diary which also records 1999, 2000 & 2001 – and destroyed the originals.
This had enabled her to intersperse various explanatory notes.

1947

Note – Now I am in the Lower Sixth Form at school, Form 6B, preparing for Higher School Certificate in three subjects only – English Literature, Geography & French: preparing also for another School Certificate Credit in Latin. Apart from geography, which I would not take by choice, I enjoy all the other subjects.

What is more, I have a diary! For Christmas, Bunting bought me a Girl Guides Diary, containing lots of interesting facts & figures that a Girl Guide ought to know.

1ˢᵗ January 1947 Wednesday
I went to see "Simple Simon" the panto, at Birmingham, with trip from Ravenstone, organised by Mrs J. Swanwick.

2ⁿᵈ January 1947 Thursday
Went with mother and Rob to see "**Wildfire**", a horse film. Stayed through 1ˢᵗ & 2ⁿᵈ house. Received 1ˢᵗ letter from Edith Richardson from New Zealand this being 4ᵗʰ from N.Z.

3ʳᵈ January 1947 Friday
Did some French homework. Mother not very well in evening – bilious. Wrote to Edith. Old scholars' dance at school. G.W.R. & L.N.E.R. announce that they must take some trains off because of fuel shortage.

4ᵗʰ January 1947 Saturday
We all went to fancy dress party at 'stute. Beadman's children were dressed as Jack Frost and a snowman. Marje won Port raffle.

5ᵗʰ January 1947 Sunday
I went to Church at night with Brenda. Bitterly cold therefore Marje did not go.

6ᵗʰ January 1947 Monday
1ˢᵗ day of School Parliament. 1ˢᵗ day snow settled this winter. I seconded Police & N.F.S. exempt from forces training.

7ᵗʰ January 1947 Tuesday
2ⁿᵈ day of Parliament. Mr Hale spoke to us in afternoon about Parliament. **More snow**.

8ᵗʰ January 1947 Wednesday
Started back to school after Xmas holiday. No films. No more snow. Blustery wind & hail in evening.

9ᵗʰ January 1947 Thursday
Much snow gone. Roads very slippery & icy. Mother went to party for W.V.S. at 'stute. Had 5ᵗʰ letter from New Zealand.

10ᵗʰ January 1947 Friday
Mr J. Swanwick finished putting cupboard in kitchen. Brian Nichols came in the evening and we played cards. Mother took M. Scott's party frock back.

Note – The large in-built cupboard was moved from the middle room to the kitchen.

11ᵗʰ January 1947 Saturday
Miserable rainy day. Read some more of "The Woodlanders".
Listened to a jolly good play in **Saturday Night Theatre** called "They Came by Night".

12ᵗʰ January 1947 Sunday
I went to church at night with Brenda.
Cleared the dining room, ready for Peggs the Painters.

13ᵗʰ January 1947 Monday
Painters and decorators here for 1ˢᵗ day to do the dining room.

14ᵗʰ January 1947 Tuesday
Had 2ⁿᵈ letters from Janet & Joy, N.Z. Janet told me to send her a list of foods we are short of. 1ˢᵗ cycle inspection by Police. **Did not** see mine.

15ᵗʰ January 1947 Wednesday
Mrs Clarke came in evening. Played games for 1ˢᵗ time for ages. Had a letter from Loot to tell me to go to a Guide lecture at Leicester. Very windy day. Finished "The Woodlanders".

16ᵗʰ January 1947 Thursday
Foot & mouth disease broke out at Walthos'. All paper now on wall. Should have had puppet show but it is postponed until 22ⁿᵈ due to break down.

17ᵗʰ January 1947 Friday
We all except Rob went to see "Robert's Wife" produced by Sydney Cockbain at the Baths. We sat on front row.

18ᵗʰ January 1947 Saturday
Played Broom Leys old scholars and won 9-0.
I got Birthday cards for Rob & Marj. Got a Valentine Card. Bought 2 water glasses from Woolworth's.
Foot & mouth broke out at Robinson's at Sinope.

19ᵗʰ January 1947 Sunday
Marjorie, Brenda and I went to church in evening. Wrote for 2ⁿᵈ time to Janet Richardson. Lovely Spring-like morning.

20ᵗʰ January 1947 Monday
Had Marionette Puppet Show at school, giving "**Faust**". Had 1ˢᵗ reading through of "**Quality Street**".

Note – At school, I have been given a part in the forthcoming school play "Quality Street".

21ˢᵗ January 1947 Tuesday
Had 2ⁿᵈ reading through of "**Quality Street**". Miss Willoughby absent with lumbago.

22ⁿᵈ January 1947 Wednesday
I went to a dance at 'stute. Auntie Cis was there & she payed 6ᵈ for a trifle for me. Played hockey. Got frozen.

23ʳᵈ January 1947 Thursday
Joan absent from school because yesterday she was hit on the head with a hockey ball.

24th January 1947 Friday
It snowed & settled. Jean Roddis & I went to Miss Simpson & Miss Jenkins at Ibstock to pass Readers' Badge. (Guides)

25th January 1947 Saturday
Could not play hockey because of snow on ground. I washed my hair in evening.

26th January 1947 Sunday
Did not go to church because of such cold snowy weather. Marj and Brenda did not go.

27th January 1947 Monday
I walked to school all this week except Friday because of bad roads.

28th January 1947 Tuesday
Tomorrow, 29th, Mother goes to Brum with Women's Guild to see "Goody 2-Shoes".

29th January 1947 Wednesday
Had dancing in gym instead of games. Mr Howry away this week and last week and expected to be so for a few weeks.

30th January 1947 Thursday
Had a lovely gym lesson. No exercises, no showers. Had all apparatus out & played Pirates etc.

31st January 1947 Friday
Mr Sealy away. Very snowy. Stayed for "Quality Street" practice. Went through Act III for first time.

1st February 1947 Saturday
Royal family set sail for S. Africa.
Went with Rita & Norma to dance at 'stute.

2nd February 1947 Sunday
Did not go to Church. Very windy & snowy.

3rd February 1947 Monday
Mr Sealy still away. Hail, sleet, snow & wind. I came home on school bus for 1st time in my life. (Without a Permit)

4th February 1947 Tuesday
Ravenstone bus did not get to school because of badly snowed roads.
I came home from school in Donald's car. Rather skiddy. As good as the fair.

5th February 1947 Wednesday
I did not go to school. Had a terrible cough. Sneezed all day.
Ravenstone school bus managed to get to school via Wash Lane.

6th February 1947 Thursday
Went to school. Still a lot absent. Though a few more than Tuesday's total of 107.
I did 3rd form absentees.

7th February 1947 Friday
Had last 2 lessons play rehearsal. Walked home with my bike which I had left at school all week. Broadcast of "Simple Simon" but we missed it.

8th February 1947 Saturday
Rob & I were clearing snow away from front & entry nearly all day. Did not snow at all. Warning that electricity would be off next week 9 a.m. -12 a.m. & 2 p.m. - 4 p.m.

9th February 1947 Sunday
More snow. Did not go to church again because of weather.

10th February 1947 Monday
Did not stay to play rehearsal because of weather. Standard Hill road to Coalville blocked. Came home on school bus via Wash Lane.

Note – An exceptionally severe winter, with roads completely snow-bound.

11th February 1947 Tuesday
Again did not stay for rehearsal. Came home on school bus.

12 February 1947 Wednesday
Had play rehearsal last 2 lessons in afternoon. Only just caught bus home. It had to stop down Forest Road for me.

13th February 1947 Thursday
Stayed for play rehearsal and walked home. Again had a grand gym lesson. Swinging on ropes etc.

14th February 1947 Friday
Stayed play rehearsal. I read lesson. Broke up for half term.

15th February 1947 Saturday
Mr Weaver brought our coal from colliery. Syd Hayes helped me get it in. I had a bath & my hair washed. Auntie Dos had heart attack 10hrs. long.

16th February 1947 Sunday
Marj & I went to church. Only 15 in congregation. Roads terribly slippery.

17th February 1947 Monday
I almost finished making my pink gauntlet mittens, trimmed with green.

18th February 1947 Tuesday
Had play rehearsal at school in morning and afternoon. Bought all my sweet ration from shop at Hugglescote.

19th February 1947 Wednesday
Had play rehearsal last two lessons instead of games. Back to school after half term.

20th February 1947 Thursday
Had another lovely gym lesson. Received some snaps from Joy Needham.

21st February 1947 Friday
Received a lovely parcel of soap from Winsome Peake.

Had play rehearsal all afternoon.

22nd February 1947 Saturday
Dance at 'stute but Marje & I did not go.

23rd February 1947 Sunday
No church in evening because of fuel shortage.

24th February 1947 Monday
Stayed play rehearsal.

25th February 1947 Tuesday
Stayed play rehearsal.

26th February 1947 Wednesday
Stayed play rehearsal. Had gym instead of games for 1st lesson.

27th February 1947 Thursday
Learning set books ready for exams tomorrow, when we get Eng.Lit. & French.

28th February 1947 Friday
Bunt had baby boy.
Mother went with Auntie Cis to Baths "Harry Davidson's Those were the days" band.

Note – Bunting gave birth to Michael.

1st March 1947 Saturday
Went to dance at stute.

2nd March 1947 Sunday
No church again because of shortage of coal.

3rd March 1947 Monday
Stayed play rehearsal. Had geog exam. More snow.

4th March 1947 Tuesday
Had Latin set books exam. Should have been grammar.

5th March 1947 Wednesday
No exams. I did play rehearsal nearly all day & after 4 o'clock.

6th March 1947 Thursday
Worst Blizzard ever. All Standard Hill blocked. Many away. Over 50%

Note – More than half the children never made it to school.

7th March 1947 Friday
Went to Coalville can make it & sell it exhibition from school, after which general exam.

8th March 1947 Saturday
Had play rehearsal in morning. Dance at stute but did not go.

9th March 1947 Sunday
Again no church because of fuel shortage. Got 6 buckets of snow from false roof.

Note – The snow found its way into our attic & we removed 6 bucketfuls from the roof space above our middle bedroom.

10th March 1947 Monday
Stayed play rehearsal after 4 o'clock.

11th March 1947 Tuesday
Had play rehearsal from 6-30p.m. to 9-30p.m. & stayed the night at Gwenfred Jarvis'.

12th March 1947 Wednesday
Stayed play rehearsal after 4 o'clock.

13th March 1947 Thursday
Did not feel well in school. Did not do gym.

14th March 1947 Friday
Had play rehearsal last 2 lessons in afternoon & until about 5 o'clock.

15th March 1947 Saturday
Marj came in, in evening. Started to read "The Mill on the Floss".

16th March 1947 Sunday
Terrible, 80 M.P.H. gale. The Hollies summer house blown over. Our chimney pot blown off. 11 people killed.

Note – On March 16th a roaring 50 m.p.h. gale swept over England. In Birmingham a shop window was forced down & men's suits were being whipped round the streets in water which was already high because of melting snow & overflowing rivers. One man was picked off his feet by the wind & was hurled through a shop window. I went a walk in the wind round Mary's Lane.

17th March 1947 Monday
Had holiday for Speech Day. Lovely Spring morning. Had dress rehearsal for play at night.

18th March 1947 Tuesday
Had photographers at school for play all morning and dress rehearsal after dinner.

19th March 1947 Wednesday
First production of play. Mother & Bin came. Slept at G. Jarvis'.

Note – From 19th March to 22nd March we presented our play "Quality Street".

20th March 1947 Thursday
Press at play in evening. I was ill in bed all day. Coey came to see me in bed.

21st March 1947 Friday
Mother & other Hewes' came to play.

22nd March 1947 Saturday
Last night of play. Went to Adult School after. Came home (to Jarvis') with Tammy.

23rd March 1947 Sunday
Church open again because had some fuel. Our 1st

"Story of Cross" service. Syd sang.

24th March 1947 Monday
Did play to school.

25th March 1947 Tuesday
Had a mock trial at school. Dr Newberry charged with stealing money from show.

26th March 1947 Wednesday
Went in library instead of doing games.

27th March 1947 Thursday
Had high jump in gym lesson & it made me terribly stiff.

28th March 1947 Friday
Broke up for Easter. Mr Glister's last day at school. VIth form & staff had a lovely party at night for Mr Glister.

29th March 1947 Saturday
I went to Coalville in afternoon with Marje.

30th March 1947 Sunday
Wet miserable day. I went to church with Brenda.

31st March 1947 Monday
Went to Mr Glister's house to take him some school letters.
Terrible rainy day.

1st April 1947 Tuesday
Went to pictures at Regal to see "Bedelia" with Tammy.

Note – Following my appearance on stage in "Quality Street", I attracted the attention of one of the boys at school, "Tammy" Turner.
As the prophet Ezekiel wrote, long, long ago: - "Behold, thy time was the time of love".

2nd April 1947 Wednesday
Went to Leicester in afternoon with Mother & bought new green coat.

3rd April 1947 Thursday
Snow forecast, but none came, although very cold day.

4th April 1947 Good Friday
We all went to church in morning.

5th April 1947 Saturday
Social & dance at 'stute but did not go.
Spent all day knitting navy blue gloves ready for wedding on Monday.

6th April 1947 Easter Sunday
Went to church at night. Marje did not go because she went to Altons. Brenda did not go because she had gone out.

7th April 1947 Easter Monday
Went to Jean & Maldwyn's wedding. Sun shone for 1st time for ages although quite windy. Saw Blue Man.

8th April 1947 Tuesday
Went to Rex to see "South Riding" with Tammy. "Nat" & Shaw went also. Windy rainy day.

9th April 1947 Wednesday
Really lovely day.

10th April 1947 Thursday
Lovely weather continues. Went walk with Rita.

11th April 1947 Friday
More fine weather. Went bike ride in afternoon & stayed in at night.

12 April 1947 Saturday
Lovely day. Went bike ride with Marje & Rita. Doreen on holiday.

13th April 1947 Sunday
Went to church with Marje, Norma & Rita. Went walk in afternoon with Tammy.

14th April 1947 Monday
Went bike ride with Tammy to Willesly Lake. Went bike ride with Marje & Rita at night.

15th April 1947 Tuesday
Went bike ride with Marje & Rita at night & walk with Rita in afternoon.

16th April 1947 Wednesday
Went bike ride in afternoon with Rob & with Norma & Rita at night.

17th April 1947 Thursday
Went walk with Tammy in afternoon & bike ride at night with Marje & Rita. Lovely day.

18th April 1947 Friday
Went to Roger & John's with Norma & Rita in evening & bought some chips from Ashby Road on way home.

19th April 1947 Saturday
Went to Rex to see "The Man that Dared" with Tammy. Went to Norma's bank in afternoon with Rita.

20th April 1947 Sunday
Went walk with Tammy in afternoon. Went to church at night. Rainy day.

21st April 1947 Monday
Started getting ready for school after hols.
Princess Elizabeth spoke on T.S.F. at night though in S. Africa.

22nd April 1947 Tuesday
New headmaster Mr Hodson started. Did work for last 6 periods. No films.

23rd April 1947 Wednesday
Had gym instead of games. Mostly high jump. Blustery, pouring with rain all day. Left my gym shoes on cloakroom window sill. Got them soaked.

24th April 1947 Thursday
Did high jump again in gym. Jumped 4′ 6″. Very stiff afterwards.

25th April 1947 Friday
Had Mr Hodson for 1st time. Played football on form room teacher's desk at dinner time. Played football in ench with Binus at night.

Note – ench = entry, along the side of the house.

26th April 1947 Saturday
Mr Hale spoke on wireless on "This week in parliament". Went bike ride in afternoon with Doreen, Rita, P. Horn, and J. Lambert to Broomleys Cemetery. Lovely day.

27th April 1947 Sunday
Had big scout & guide parade at Ravenstone.
I went with Marje at night to Sermons at Marlborough Square Chapel.

28th April 1947 Monday
Mother went to see "Dear Brutus" with Mrs Hale at Progressive Hall.
Had cheese & potato pie & peas for dinner.

29th April 1947 Tuesday
Had a name inspection.
Had awful dinner. Horrid blackish green cabbage & stew floating in fat, bones & gristle.

30th April 1947 Wednesday
Miss Smith away so we had Miss White for games. Played rounders. Dreadfully cold outside.

1st May 1947 Thursday
I went to the baths after 4 o'clock with Joan Holmes. Had to pay 7d!
Miss Silk visiting junior schools.

2nd May 1947 Friday
Marie & I fished things from under our form room floor at edge.
Played football in form room.

3rd May 1947 Saturday
Went a ride with Rita at night to Roger & John's. Went to Coalville in afternoon.
Helped mother get a ton of coal in, in morning.

4th May 1947 Sunday
Rainy day but lovely evening. Mother went to church.

5th May 1947 Monday
I washed my hair at night. Miss Williams, Miss Smith & Miss White away with laryngitis.

6th May 1947 Tuesday
Heats Day. Lovely weather. Miss Silk away this week going to junior schools.

7th May 1947 Wednesday
No-one took us for games so we sun bathed on fields. Lovely day.

8th May 1947 Thursday
Good programme on wireless all night. Miss Smith back for gym but could hardly speak.

9th May 1947 Friday
Went bike ride with Norma, Rita & Marje. Bought some chips each from Ashby Road.   No-one in shop so served quickly.

10th May 1947 Saturday
Went to Coalville in afternoon with Rita.
Olive Tovell married in rain.
Went to Doctor's for Bin's tablets at night.

11th May 1947 Sunday
Went to church in evening with Marje, Rita & Auntie Rene.
Went bike ride in afternoon with Marje, Rita & Norma. Lovely day.

12th May 1947 Monday
Mother & Rob went to see Circus at Coalville. Coronation 10th Anniversary. I listened to recordings of Coronation Day on T.S.F.

13th May 1947 Tuesday
Missed French because Mr Sealy out on field trying out loud speaker for sports day tomorrow.

14th May 1947 Wednesday
Lovely day for Sports Day. Broughton had least points as usual.

15th May 1947 Thursday
Marie stayed away because of Ascension Day.
Went to see play "Berkeley Square" at C.G.S. done by Charnwood Players.

16th May 1947 Friday
I biked to school. Joan Holmes came down at night & we went a walk. Drizzling with rain nearly all day.

17th May 1947 Saturday
Went to see "My Pal Trigger" at Rex with Tammy.

18th May 1947 Sunday
Rainy day. Stayed in. Did not go to church at night.

19th May 1947 Monday
Went to shop in Hugglescote & got sweet ration, ¼ lb of sweets & 4 mars bars, at dinner time.

20th May 1947 Tuesday
Played football on form room desk at dinner time.

21st May 1947 Wednesday
Did batting practice the whole of games. First time Arrow was shot, after had finished games.

22nd May 1947 Thursday
Arrow was shot again at dinner time but Rot's presence made it very brief.

23rd May 1947 Friday
Arrow shot again as we came out of Latin in Room 9.

24th May 1947 Saturday
Went bike ride with Rita. Marje had her hair permed.

25th May 1947 Sunday
Marje went to Aunt Sybil's for tea & after came to church with me. Florry & Mr Heward there too.

26th May 1947 Monday
Fair going at Ravenstone for 1st time. Went, & stayed until 11 o'clock. Had grand time.

27th May 1947 Tuesday
Went a walk at night to Swannington with Tammy. Car loads of Heweseses & Heweseses passed us. Phew!!

28th May 1947 Wednesday
Went to Marie's for a few days. Went to Bradgate in afternoon. Very hot day. My arms went brown for 1st time this year.

29th May 1947 Thursday
Went to Leicester in morning with Marie & Anne. Horace on bus. I bought white sandals. Went to Kirby Castle in afternoon.

30th May 1947 Friday
Went to Marie's auntie's in afternoon & cleaned her kitchen. Painted bathroom in morning. Terribly hot day. Came home from Marie's.

31st May 1947 Saturday
Garden Fête at institute in afternoon. Flannel Dance at night, but did not go.
I went down to fair with Syb.

1st June 1947 Sunday
Went to Church at night with Marje, without a coat. Went a walk after to her Uncle Phil's.

2nd June 1947 Monday
Started back to school after Whit hols. Lovely day.
Played Highfields at rounders at night & lost.

3rd June 1947 Tuesday
Went to baths last lesson in afternoon. Lovely day. Biked to school.

4th June 1947 Wednesday
Cooler, but still lovely weather. Went to school on bus, but got into prayers. Into prayers every day this week.

5th June 1947 Thursday
Marie stayed away from school & went to help her Auntie who can't walk.
Much colder & rainy. Biked to school. Came home on bus.

6th June 1947 Friday
Had fish & potato pie, beans & steam pudding for dinner. Still cold.
Went to Coalville with Joan. Bought chips.
Housewives of Britain attacked Minister of Food for more & better food.
Terrible disorder in House of Commons.

7th June 1947 Saturday
Area sports held on C.G.S. fields.
Dr. came with an appointment for Rob to go to Oxford

on June 18th to Dr. Cairns.

8th June 1947 Sunday
Anniversary at Ravenstone. Did not go. Very windy with several sharp showers during day.

9th June 1947 Monday
Party from school went to **Trent Bridge** to see cricket match between Middlesex & S. Africa.

10th June 1947 Tuesday
Did grammar all double French lesson. Had stew, cabbage & batter pudding for dinner.   Rob jumpy all evening.

11th June 1947 Wednesday
Lovely weather for Games. Had musical appreciation in morning for 2nd time. Continuing with Chopin.

12th June 1947 Thursday
Marj had her hair washed & set for 1st time after it had been permed.
6A French Section went for oral exam.

13th June 1947 Friday
Wrote to Winsome Peake for 2nd time. Went in U.S.A. for P.S. last lesson.
Went to Coalville after 4 with Joan & bought some chips.

14th June 1947 Saturday
Went to school for rounders match to be played away but it was cancelled because of rain.

15th June 1947 Sunday
Went with Marje to church. Washed my hair at night. Saw G. R. with his girl going walk.

16th June 1947 Monday
Went with Joan to Regal to see Cæsar & Cleopatra. Derby on news, at pictures.

17th June 1947 Tuesday
Went on different tables for 1st time to try to decrease noise & 6th former had to be on every table as far as possible.

18th June 1947 Wednesday
Went to Baths. Mr Sealy away with lumbago so Joan, Marie & I went to see him after 4 o'clock.

19th June 1947 Thursday
Mr Sealy still away. Had shower after gym. Yesterday Joan & I went to Rex to see "To each his own".

20th June 1947 Friday
Our outside pump conked. Mr Sealy came back. I forgot to take my dinner money.

21st June 1947 Saturday
Went down to Aunt Syb's with Marje. Gave us a sweet & strawberry each.

22nd June 1947 Sunday
Ravenstone Chapel Anniversary. Only 20 at Church at

night. Marje did not go. Mrs Swanwick sat with me.

23rd June 1947 Monday
Had stew, potatoes, cabbage for dinner. Shortage of potatoes. Novelty idea, with packet potatoes. Rob's school having bread instead of spuds.

24th June 1947 Tuesday
Pat Goulding & Eva Johnston stayed away to swot.

25th June 1947 Wednesday
Didn't go to school at all. Stayed at home to swot for exams. Miss Shaw and Mr Wardle came.

26th June 1947 Thursday
Did P.S. in Room 9 with Joan, Marie & Nat. Didn't have Gym because of Junior Plays.

27th June 1947 Friday
Sat on back row in Scripture. Mr Sealy didn't come to French, in morning.

28th June 1947 Saturday
Marje went to see Junior Plays at our school with Norma & Rita.

29th June 1947 Sunday
Didn't go to church at night. Miserable Day. Stopped in all day. S. Reynolds banns read 1st time.

30th June 1947 Monday
Didn't go to school in morning.
Had Eng. Lesson & Mr Taylor told us about when he was in Egypt.

1st July 1947 Tuesday
Had 3hr. English Lit. exam in morning. Played Tennis in afternoon on field.

2nd July 1947 Wednesday
Didn't go to school in morning. Had Latin Grammar exam in afternoon.

3rd July 1947 Thursday
Had French exam in morning. Did lessons in afternoon. Had new **pen!**

4th July 1947 Friday
Didn't go to school in morning. Did lessons in afternoon.

5th July 1947 Saturday
Yesterday went to Dentists to have teeth cleaned & after to Ravo Chapel with Auntie Cis & Dos to hear the **Trekkers.**

6th July 1947 Sunday
Went a walk with Marje & took "Bill" at night to Birch Tree & back.

7th July 1947 Monday
Mother went to Auntie Annie's in afternoon to take some gooseberries.

8th July 1947 Tuesday
Mummie goes tomorrow with Inner Wheel round Ashby

Church & to Royal Hotel for tea.

9th July 1947 Wednesday
Official announcement of Princess Elizabeth's Engagement.

10th July 1947 Thursday
Had geog exam 2-5 p.m. Last of exams!
Went a bike ride to Ibstock with J. Holmes.

Note – I attained the Higher School Certificate (subsidiary standard) in English Literature, Geography & French; plus School Certificate Credit in Latin. Staying on at school now I am 16, attempting the Higher School Certificate proper in the Upper Sixth Form, Form 6A.

11th July 1947 Friday
Went on bike to school in afternoon. Slept till 12-45 in morning.

12th July 1947 Saturday
Went with Sunday School Trip of 5 bus loads to Sutton Coldfield. Had a glorious time on fair & lake.

13th July 1947 Sunday
Went a walk at night with Marje round Altons & China Town.

14th July 1947 Monday
Betty Tracey started my birthday cake. Marie away from school.

15th July 1947 Tuesday
Bunt, Michael & Mostyn came for tea. My cake wasn't finished.

16th July 1947 Wednesday
Went with Norma to pictures to see "The Kid from Brooklyn".

17th July 1947 Thursday
Arrow was shot for 4th time on Monday last (Birthday)

18th July 1947 Friday
Went a bike ride at night with Rita, Marje & John Mosely.

19th July 1947 Saturday
Garden Party, Baby Show & Dance at stute. Poured & poured with rain in afternoon.

20th July 1947 Sunday
Bunt's baby Christened by Mr Smith. All had tea at Don & Phylis'.

21st July 1947 Monday
Miss Silk gone to Bardon Hill with 4th form so did nothing in double geog.

22nd July 1947 Tuesday
Watched cricket match between 1st XI & Ashby in afternoon. We lost!

23rd July 1947 Wednesday

All form except P. Fort & me went to Leicester to Historical things.
Watched Junior Cricket in afternoon.

24th July 1947 Thursday

Taking books in, carrying them to various cupboards all afternoon.

25th July 1947 Friday

Hobbies Day. Had Gym Display in gym because of wet. In morning stocking books.

26th July 1947 Saturday

Went to Leicester in morning & bought new blue gathered frock.

27th July 1947 Sunday

Went a picnic with Auntie Cis & Dos, Pat, Evelyn & Mary, Cyril & Glad & David to Kegworth.

28th July 1947 Monday

Was knitting my Pullover nearly all day at school which I began on Saturday 26th July.

29th July 1947 Tuesday

Taking in books & checking numbers for Mr Taylor. Did quite a lot of knitting.
School leaving **Dance**.

30th July 1947 Wednesday

Broke up. Polly left. Knitting all morning. Checking geog books in afternoon.

31st July 1947 Thursday

In morning cleaned out the shed. Did some knitting in afternoon.

1st August 1947 Friday

Went a bike ride in afternoon to Shackerstone with Rita. Lovely Day.

2nd August 1947 Saturday

Was knitting pullover nearly all day.

3rd August 1947 Sunday

Went to Church at night alone. Had tea on lawn. A lovely day.

4th August 1947 Monday

Wrote to Bunt & Jaques. Auntie Dos was "**Detective**" yesterday. She told Police of whereabouts of an escape man.

5th August 1947 Tuesday

Finished my pullover except for one pocket band which I finish tomorrow afternoon.

6th August 1947 Wednesday

Ashby Agricultural Show. All Hayes' went but Marje. I stayed with Marje in afternoon & for tea.

7th August 1947 Thursday

Went a long bike ride in evening to Ibstock via Heather, Shackerstone, Odstone, Nailstone.

8th August 1947 Friday

Had headache because went to bed in afternoon. Did French translation of El Verdugo at night.

10th August 1947 Sunday

Went to Church by myself. Marj had gone with Syb out.

13th August 1947 Wednesday

Went a bike ride with Mummy to Bradgate.

14th August 1947 Thursday

We all went to Willoughby in Billy Hollingshed's car.

Note – Again for our summer holidays, Mum, Rob & I go to the farm at Willoughby-on the-Wolds.

15th August 1947 Friday

India gained its independence from Britain.

16th August 1947 Saturday

Madge & Bertha went to Scarborough.

22nd August 1947 Friday

I went home from Willoughby to Ravo & stayed the night at Marj's.

23rd August 1947 Saturday

Went to Ludlow for 1st time on bus & got there at 6 o'clock.

Note – I also include a holiday with Bunting & family at their home in Ludlow.

24th August 1947 Sunday

Went to see Mostyn play tennis at courts.

25th August 1947 Monday

Took Michael to clinic.

28th August 1947 Thursday

Went round Ludlow Castle.

30th August 1947 Saturday

Went blackberrying. Got off with 3 lads. They gave me 1d & 3 fags.

31st August 1947 Sunday

Went to Henley to watch Mostyn play tennis.

1st September 1947 Monday

Didn't get ready in time to go to clinic because Michael filled his pants.

2nd September 1947 Tuesday

Went Blackberrying on Ludlow Hills

3rd September 1947 Wednesday

Sold Peachy 12 lbs of blackberries at Dinner Time.

4th September 1947 Thursday

Came home to Ravo from Bunt's & slept at Hayes'.

5th September 1947 Friday

Went to Willoughby & got there at dinner time.

Note – I re-join Mum & Rob at Willoughby & have another brief romantic fling with the young farm-hand there, Tony Wisher. He actually has a girl-friend already, & she soon sends me packing.

6th September 1947 Saturday
Went Water - carting for 1st time at Willoughby.

7th September 1947 Sunday
The bow crossed the arrow once for the 1st time.

8th September 1947 Monday
Lost count of the archers. Came home from Willoughby.

9th September 1947 Tuesday
Went a ride in afternoon & at night with Joan Holmes.

10th September 1947 Wednesday
Started school after holidays.

11th September 1947 Thursday
Went to Coalville at night & Joan & I got birthday card for Marie.

12th September 1947 Friday
Went to Willoughby at night to fetch things we'd left.

13th September 1947 Saturday
Went water carting. Saw 3 bows.
Went to first Whist Drive at night with Madge.

14th September 1947 Sunday
Lost count of Archers. Rainy Day. Came home from Willoughby.

15th September 1947 Monday
Wrote to Edith Richardson & Bunt.
Read lesson in morning at school.

18th September 1947 Thursday
Received first letter from Tone.

20th September 1947 Saturday
Played Hinckley hockey & won. Went to see Upturned Glass in Leicester with Joan & Marie.

21st September 1947 Sunday
Wrote to Tony for 1st time. Went to Ilis Newton's in afternoon to fetch bikes.

22nd September 1947 Monday
Played Harley at night & won 7-2.

26th September 1947 Friday
Went to Joan's at night & saw her sister Mary for 1st time.

27th September 1947 Saturday
Got an awful cold.

28th September 1947 Sunday
Rainy day. Went to Church at night with Marje. Had 2nd letter from Tony tomorrow.

29th September 1947 Monday
Played Highfields & lost 6-3.
Went with mother 2nd house to see "**Spellbound**".

30th September 1947 Tuesday
Oak Tree across road almost completely down!

Note – A large oak tree across the road from our house is felled, making the house shudder. Its stump is left for another 10 years.

1st October 1947 Wednesday
No petrol allowed from today for Private cars.
Mother went to Leicester to see Mrs Reading be elected for head of W.V.S.

2nd October 1947 Thursday
Mother went to Ashby hospital to do night duty as first try out practice.

Note – Mum starts work as a Nursing Auxiliary at Ashby Cottage Hospital – night duty 8 p.m. to 8 a.m. She is now aged 42 & continues working until she is 65.

3rd October 1947 Friday
Mother went to Ashby hospital again for night duty from 8 p.m. to 8 a.m.

4th October 1947 Saturday
Went with school party to see Bournville England hockey team. Mother went to Ashby again.

5th October 1947 Sunday
Wrote to Tony for 2nd time. Went walk at night with Marje instead of going to church.

6th October 1947 Monday
Saw Mary Wesson before dinner in Mistresses old staff room.

11th October 1947 Saturday
Went to tea dance & mannequin parade at Adult School for Inner Wheel.

12th October 1947 Sunday
Rob & I biked to Willoughby in afternoon.
Mother went to Ashby Hospital at night.

13th October 1947 Monday
Joan Holmes' sister Mary had baby girl at about 1 a.m. in Ashby.

14th October 1947 Tuesday
Joan & I went to pictures yesterday to see **The Outlaw**.

15th October 1947 Wednesday
Played Badminton for 1st time.

16th October 1947 Thursday
Had 3rd letter from Tony. Was hit on ankle in hockey.

18th October 1947 Saturday
Mummy went to Willoughby at night.
Marie & Syb came in until 10 p.m.

19th October 1947 Sunday
Did not go to church because waiting for mother to get back from Willoughby.

21st October 1947 Tuesday
Went to school on bus. Very late didn't arrive at school until 9 o'clock.

22nd October 1947 Wednesday
Umpired Junior house matches.

23rd October 1947 Thursday
Played staff at hockey & won 2-0.

24th October 1947 Friday
Went to Whist Drive at Coalville with Joan. Lost my head square.

25th October 1947 Saturday
Played Quorn & won 7-1. Went to Coalville in afternoon with Marje. Lovely day.

26th October 1947 Sunday
Wrote to Tony for 3rd time.

27th October 1947 Monday
Sybil Hayes had this week as a holiday.

31st October 1947 Friday
Speech Day. Alderman Allen M.P. presented prizes. Went to see "Pygmalion" at Baths.

2nd November 1947 Sunday
Rainy day. Didn't go to church. Marje gone to Stanton for weekend.

3rd November 1947 Monday
Had 4th letter from Tony. Half term. Really lovely clear day, though quite cold.

14th November 1947 Friday
Went to see Jean Essex as **Tilly** at the Baths.

15th November 1947 Saturday
Had 5th letter from Tone. Played Loughborough in morning & won 2-0.

16th November 1947 Sunday
Fred's birthday.

20th November 1947 Thursday
Royal Wedding of Princess Elizabeth and Lieutenant Philip Mountbatten.

28th November 1947 Friday
Mr Mattock's father died.

29th November 1947 Saturday
Went to Adult School to a dance with Joan. Played Market Bosworth hockey & won 7-2.

2nd December 1947 Tuesday
Jack Train's Birthday!
Mr Taylor told us about his blackie wives & children & showed us photos.

6th December 1947 Saturday
Went to Dance at Stute. Played Evington Convent & won 3-0.

7th December 1947 Sunday
Cat died at 9-30 p.m.

17th December 1947 Wednesday
Our school party. Went with Nixen to supper. Had grand time.

18th December 1947 Thursday
Broke up.

31st December 1947 Wednesday
Went to Mrs Forsyth's dance at Adult School.

* * *

Personal Measurements –

Height 5′ 6″ Weight 8 stones 8 lbs.

1948

1ˢᵗ January 1948 Thursday
Cocky Marsdon & Marje came at night.

Note – John Marsden (Cocky), a farm worker in Ravenstone, comes into my life. He takes my brother Rob under his wing & visits us most evenings. My Aunt Dos keeps an ever watchful eye on me, as does my Uncle Fred (her brother) who both live nearby.
Cocky therefore comes like "my beloved" in the Bible's Song of Solomon, Chapter 2, verse 9 – "behold, he standeth behind our wall, he looeth forth at the windows, showing himself through the lattice".
Cocky came over the garden wall, out of sight of my disapproving relatives.

2ⁿᵈ January 1948 Friday
Went to dance at baths for C.G.S. old scholars with Pat, Evelyn, Don, Phyl, J. Fort & E. Hall.

4ᵗʰ January 1948 Sunday
Burma became fully independent from the British Commonwealth.

6ᵗʰ January 1948 Tuesday
Cocky came in at night.

7ᵗʰ January 1948 Wednesday
Started school after holiday. Went to party for Inner Wheel family at Adult School.

8ᵗʰ January 1948 Thursday
Cocky came in at night.

9ᵗʰ January 1948 Friday
Cocky came in at night.

10ᵗʰ January 1948 Saturday
Went to Derby Panto to see Babes in Wood.

11ᵗʰ January 1948 Sunday
Went to Church with Marje. Cocky came in afternoon & night.

12ᵗʰ January 1948 Monday
Cocky came in. Brought some milk.

13ᵗʰ January 1948 Tuesday
Cocky came in. Mummy at Ashby in afternoon. Washed my hair.

14ᵗʰ January 1948 Wednesday
Cocky came in. Mummy at Ashby all night. Rob's leg hurt. Fetched Auntie Belle at 12 p.m.

15ᵗʰ January 1948 Thursday
Cocky came in. Mummy at Ashby all night.

17ᵗʰ January 1948 Saturday
Went to pictures with Joan to see "Beau Geste"

18ᵗʰ January 1948 Sunday
Went to church with Marje & Rita.

19ᵗʰ January 1948 Monday
Mummy went to Leicester to get things from Annie Shaw's.

24ᵗʰ January 1948 Saturday
Played Loughborough & lost 3-1.

25ᵗʰ January 1948 Sunday
Went to Leicester with Mummy to fetch last of things from Auntie Annie's.

26ᵗʰ January 1948 Monday
Washed my hair.

27ᵗʰ January 1948 Tuesday
Played Badminton at night.

30ᵗʰ January 1948 Friday
GHANDI DIED!!

31ˢᵗ January 1948 Saturday
Went to Panto "Humpty Dumpty" with Duggie Wakefield at Leicester. Rainy day.

1ˢᵗ February 1948 Sunday
Went bike ride in afternoon with Joan. Very windy. Saw 1st baby lamb down Heather Lane.

3ʳᵈ February 1948 Tuesday
Played Badminton at night.

5ᵗʰ February 1948 Thursday
Went to Van Gogh exhibition at Birmingham with school.

6ᵗʰ February 1948 Friday
Cocky came in at night. Mr Taylor told us that he was in circus.

7ᵗʰ February 1948 Saturday
Auntie Cis on holiday so I slept at Aunt Dosh's.

8ᵗʰ February 1948 Sunday
Went to church with Marje. Slept with Aunt Dosh.

9ᵗʰ February 1948 Monday
Slept again chez – Dosh. Washed my hair.

10ᵗʰ February 1948 Tuesday
Went to see "Sea of Grass". Made pancakes at night.

11ᵗʰ February 1948 Wednesday
Cocky came in 7-40 to 10-40. Marje came in 6 to 7-30. Mummy at Ashby 6 to 10-30.

12ᵗʰ February 1948 Thursday
Cocky came in. Went round to Hayes till 9 o'clock.

13ᵗʰ February 1948 Friday
Pictures at stute. Rob went, saw "Princess Ju Ju".

14ᵗʰ February 1948 Saturday
A dance at stute. Didn't go. Cocky came in at night.

15th February 1948 Sunday
Went to church with Marje. Mummy & Rob went to Don's at night. Cocky came in till 10-15.

16th February 1948 Monday
Cocky came in till 10 p.m. Bought navy suède shoes.

17th February 1948 Tuesday
Half term. Cocky came in. M. at Ashby all night.

18th February 1948 Wednesday
Cocky came in. Mother at Ashby all night.

19th February 1948 Thursday
Very cold. Snowed nearly all day. Mother at Ashby all night.

20th February 1948 Friday
Cocky came in at night. Snowed a lot. Mother at Ashby all night.

21st February 1948 Saturday
Very cold snowy weather. Mother at Ashby all night. Cocky came in. Frozen to death.

22nd February 1948 Sunday
Went to church with Marje. Very few there because of snow. Slept chez - Bar Wilson.

23 February 1948 Monday
Much of snow gone. Mother at Ashby 4 - 8.

25th February 1948 Wednesday
Cocky came in at night.

26th February 1948 Thursday
Cocky came in at night.

27th February 1948 Friday
Cocky came in at night.

28th February 1948 Saturday
Mother very late arriving home at night. Very worried. Played Barrow, lost!

29th February 1948 Sunday
Went to church at night with Marje.

1st March 1948 Monday
Had marvellous game of hockey against Highfield & drew 3-3.

2nd March 1948 Tuesday
Played Badminton at night.

3rd March 1948 Wednesday
Cocky came in. M. at Ashby all night.

4th March 1948 Thursday
Mother at Ashby all night. Cocky came in. Exams started.

5th March 1948 Friday
Cocky came at 9-15 till 10-20. Played Draughts.

6th March 1948 Saturday
Went to **Ice Show** at Coventry. Played hockey in morning at school & beat Hinckley 5-1. Indian came!

7th March 1948 Sunday
Asleep nearly all day. Got up at gone 6 p.m.

8th March 1948 Monday
Had Latin exams all day.

9th March 1948 Tuesday
Cocky came in at night. Lovely day.

10th March 1948 Wednesday
Cocky came in at night. Exams finished.

11th March 1948 Thursday
I fainted in Latin lesson at 3-30. Cocky came in at night.

12 March 1948 Friday
Rob & I stayed at Don's till 1 a.m. while Phil; Don & Mum went to dance at Ashby.

Note – Cousin Don is one of my most helpful relatives & I am happy to baby-sit for his two young children, Peter & Lesley, when Don & his wife Phyl have an evening out.

13th March 1948 Saturday
Went to Bradgate with Joan. Called in to see Marie.

14th March 1948 Sunday
Went long bike ride with Joan to Zouch – Castle Donington.

15th March 1948 Monday
Played Harley & won 2-1.

16th March 1948 Tuesday
Saw school play "Tobias & The Angel" in afternoon. Played Badminton.

17th March 1948 Wednesday
Played Badminton at night. Cocky came.

18th March 1948 Thursday
Umpired Junior hockey match. Cocky came.

19th March 1948 Friday
Rob & I went to pictures at night.

20th March 1948 Saturday
Mother at Ashby all night.
Rob & I stayed with Lesley & Peter while Don & Phil went to C.G.S. play.

21st March 1948 Sunday
Mummy at Ashby all night. I was pegging rug nearly all day.

22nd March 1948 Monday
Played staff at hockey. Drew 2-2. Hurt my hand badly. Pegging rug all night.

23rd March 1948 Tuesday
Broke up. Had very funny Will Hay film. Cocky came.

24th March 1948 Wednesday
Mummy went to Auntie Doris'. Cocky came.

25th March 1948 Thursday
Mummy at Ashby all night. Cocky came. Washed my hair.

26th March 1948 Friday
Mummy at Ashby all night. Cocky came.

27th March 1948 Saturday
Went to Prew's with Rob & fed cows. Georgie at Peterborough.

28th March 1948 Sunday
Mummy at Ashby in afternoon.
Rob & I went to woods in afternoon & to church at night.

29th March 1948 Monday
Went to Prew's again. Wore Rob's breeches. Went walk at night with Marje.

30th March 1948 Tuesday
Went to Prew's. Mummy at Ashby all night.
Rob & I stayed with Don's kids.

31st March 1948 Wednesday
Went to Prew's. Mummy at Ashby all night. Cocky came.

1st April 1948 Thursday
Went to see "Pink Strings & Ceiling Wax". Mummy at Ashby all night.
Cocky stayed with Rob.

2nd April 1948 Friday
Went to Prew's. Riddled potatoes. Milked a cow. M. at Ashby. Cocky came.

3rd April 1948 Saturday
Mummy at Ashby all night. Dance at Stute but did not go.

4th April 1948 Sunday
Snowed in morning. In bed until 4-30 p.m. Went a walk at night with Marje. M at Ashby.

5th April 1948 Monday
Went to Swannington blacksmiths with Rob & George. Marje, Syb & Cocky came in at night. M. at Ashby all night.

6th April 1948 Tuesday
Went to Leicester with Joan & saw **"Gone with the Wind"**.
Cocky came at night.

7th April 1948 Wednesday
Went to 1st Confirmation Class. Washed hair.

8th April 1948 Thursday
Joan came at night. Cocky came & mended puncture.

9th April 1948 Friday
Went to Prew's. Cocky came at night. Got locked in cowshed with Joan.

10th April 1948 Saturday
Went to farm muck spreading with George. Marje came at night. Mother at Ashby all night.

11th April 1948 Sunday
Went to Church at night. Went to Vera's in afternoon with Marje.
Had photos taken with Alan Boyles.

12th April 1948 Monday
Went to farm in morning. Went to pictures first house with Marje.
M at Ashby all night. Cocky came.

13th April 1948 Tuesday
Last day of holiday. Cocky came at night.

14th April 1948 Wednesday
Started back to school. Had films in afternoon. Went ride at night with Joan.

15th April 1948 Thursday
Went a ride with Joan at night.
M. at Ashby all night.

16th April 1948 Friday
M. not at Ashby at night. Went to football match at recky.

17th April 1948 Saturday
In bed till 2-30 p.m. Rainy day. M. not at Ashby.

18th April 1948 Sunday
Went to church at night. M. at Ashby all night.

19th April 1948 Monday
Marje & Syb came in at night. Had name inspection at school.

20th April 1948 Tuesday
Washed hair. Chain came off bike going to school. Used **Yeast-Pac**.

21st April 1948 Wednesday
Had athletics. Warm day. Made me very stiff.

22nd April 1948 Thursday
Went to Burton to hear lecture in French on 17th Century Literature.

23rd April 1948 Friday
M. at Ashby all night. Marje came in at night.

24th April 1948 Saturday
Went bike ride with Joan to Zouch. Cocky went to London: Cup Final Manchester beat Blackpool 4-2.

25th April 1948 Sunday
Went to church at night. Up at 7 a.m. Windy day.

26th April 1948 Monday
Went to baths 1st time this year at night with Pat.
Marje had tooth out.

27th April 1948 Tuesday
Syb came round at night. Used 2nd Yeast Pac. M. at
Ashby all night.

28th April 1948 Wednesday
Rainy day. Could not have games. M. at Ashby all night.

29th April 1948 Thursday
M at Ashby all night. Stayed at school for reading of
"Les Femmes Savantes".

30th April 1948 Friday
M. not at Ashby. Got awful cough & cold. So has Joan.

1st May 1948 Saturday
In bed until 6 – 30 p.m. Still got awful cold. No coal.
George had **Trix** on Thursday.

2nd May 1948 Sunday
Went to Church at night. Went to farm in afternoon.

3rd May 1948 Monday
Went to farm at night. Georgie passed test for driving
tractor.

4th May 1948 Tuesday
Should have had heats but too rainy. Marje & Syb came
at night. M. at Ashby.

5th May 1948 Wednesday
Had heats. Up till gone midnight doing geog essay. M at
Ashby.

6th May 1948 Thursday
Marie away nearly all this week because her mother
away. M. at Ashby. Washed my hair.

7th May 1948 Friday
Went walk at night with Marje. **Burke** proposes to run
away.

8th May 1948 Saturday
Glorious day. Went to cut grass at grave. Hayes' put new
stair carpet down that Mrs Hayes made.

9th May 1948 Sunday
Went to church at night & to grave in afternoon. Very
warm day.

10th May 1948 Monday
Burke gone on escape from school. Dull muggy day.

11th May 1948 Tuesday
Went to farm at night. M at Ashby. Burke captured.
Very close day.

12th May Wednesday
Sports Day. M. at Ashby. Warm day. Thundered in
night.

13th May Thursday
Went to farm at night. M. at Ashby.
Lovely day. Played Harley Rounders. Won 1 ½ - 1.

14th May 1948 Friday
Went selling flags for Sailors' Orphans. Broke up for
week's holiday.

15th May 1948 Saturday
Lovely day. Got very brown.
Selling flags again. Got £1 – 6s – 9d. M. at Ashby.
George mended my bike – shortened chain.

16th May 1948 Sunday
Went to church at night by myself. Marje at Stanton.
Very hot day. M. at Ashby.

17th May 1948 Monday
Very hot day. M. at Ashby all night. I got brown.

18th May 1948 Tuesday
Washed my hair. Sun bathing nearly all day on lawn.
Played croquet in afternoon. Got up at 5 – 30 a.m.

19th May 1948 Wednesday
Had bath yesterday. Went to Willoughby. Had a wiz
time.

20th May 1948 Thursday
Went to pictures by myself for 1st time to see "**A
Haunting We Will Go**".

21st May 1948 Friday
Hot day. Went to farm at night. Pegging rug.

22nd May 1948 Saturday
Rainy day. Stopped talking to Cocky & George in
Prew's garden. Heard about Ted Holland. M. at Ashby at
night.

23rd May 1948 Sunday
Miserable rainy day. Did not go to church. M. at Ashby.

24th May 1948 Monday
Started back to school after Whit hols. Joan away with
boil. M. at Ashby. Rainy day.

25th May 1948 Tuesday
Went to baths with school. Went to farm at night alone.
M. at Ashby all night.

26th May 1948 Wednesday
Pat bought new dog **Trixie**. Rainy day. M not at Ashby.

27th May 1948 Thursday
Hayes had electric lights on for 1st time. M. at Ashby.

*Note – Next door, 29 Leicester Road, Ravenstone, home
of the Hayes family, had electricity installed for the very
first time. They had always managed with an oil lamp
which hung from the ceiling over the living room table.*

28th May 1948 Friday
Played rounders at night against Charnwood & lost. M.
at Ashby.

29th May 1948 Saturday
Washed my hair. Rob in bed all day. Rainy. Went walk with Bill. M. at Ashby.

30th May 1948 Sunday
Anniversary at Ravo church. Rainy day. M. at Ashby. Made pink pyjama trousers.

31st May 1948 Monday
M at Ashby. Up till 11-30 doing French essay. Rob went to farm.

1st June 1948 Tuesday
M not at Ashby. Did geog swot at night. Dull day.

2nd June 1948 Wednesday
M at Ashby. Cocky came at night. Rainy day.

3rd June 1948 Thursday
Yesterday nearly set house on fire making pancakes. Today Cocky came. M. at Ashby.   Rainy day.

4th June 1948 Friday
Rainy day. Did type-writing at school. M. at Ashby.

5th June 1948 Saturday
Rainy day. M. at Ashby. Mummy bought new navy suede shoes.

6th June 1948 Sunday
Rainy day. Celebrated Syb's 21st birthday. Did not go to church. M. at Ashby.

7th June 1948 Monday
Marie took our photos at school. M. at Ashby.

8th June 1948 Tuesday
M. not at Ashby. Syb took Marje's & my photos – one in bathing costumes.

9th June 1948 Wednesday
Mummy went to London to see "Annie Get Your Gun". Cocky came in trilby.

10th June 1948 Thursday
Rainy day. M. not at Ashby. M. went to pictures.

11th June 1948 Friday
M. at Ashby. Sybil going to Marie's ready for week's holiday at Skegness.

12th June 1948 Saturday
In bed until dinner time. Went to Altons at night with Marje. M. at Ashby.

13th June 1948 Sunday
Very hot muggy day. Marje went to Stanton. I went to church by myself. M. at Ashby.

14th June 1948 Monday
Had bath. Some of our school went to 1st test match at Trent Bridge. Dull day. Bet Marsden married I reckon.

15th June 1948 Tuesday
Stayed at home to swot. M. at Ashby in afternoon.

Don Bradman out for duck.

16th June 1948 Wednesday
M at Ashby in afternoon. Played tennis at school.

17th June 1948 Thursday
M. at Ashby in afternoon. Played rounders at night. Went to Dorothy's & saw her baby for 1st time.

18th June 1948 Friday
Went to French Oral exam at Birmingham University. Alan Reed there.

19th June 1948 Saturday
Went to Leicester, bought 2 new frocks & white jumper.

20th June 1948 Sunday
Went to church at night. Mr Nield gave me credit ticket for Leicester Mercury.

21st June 1948 Monday
M. at Ashby in afternoon. M. went to pictures at night.

22nd June 1948 Tuesday
Some heavy showers during day. M at Ashby in afternoon.

23rd June 1948 Wednesday
Did not go have to go school because Higher starts on Friday. M at Ashby.

24th June 1948 Thursday
At home all day. M. at Ashby in morning & at Dinner at night. Cocky came.

25th June 1948 Friday
Had Eng. Exam. M at Ashby in afternoon. Sat in gutter with Brenda.

Note – Higher School Certificate examination. I reached the required standard in English Literature & French. I failed in Geography. Therefore I failed to qualify for University, which needed three subjects. I had the option of another year at school & try again, or leave school & set my sights lower. I chose to leave school in July this year.

26th June 1948 Saturday
Went to dance at stute. Jack Clarke there. Mr Nield pushed me in sink in morning & wet me.

27th June 1948 Sunday
Rainy day. Went to church, Norman Silver there. Mr Nield gave me Mercury thingy.

28th June 1948 Monday
Did not go to school. Poured with rain all day.

29th June 1948 Tuesday
Had French exam. Washed my hair.

30th June 1948 Wednesday
Did not go to school. Pat ill in bed. M at Ashby.

1st July 1948 Thursday
Confirmed at Heather. M. at Ashby all night.
Note – I was "Confirmed" as a member of the Church of England at Heather Church.

2nd July 1948 Friday
Geog exam in afternoon. M. at Ashby all night. Alan Stanley had new red auto.

3rd July 1948 Saturday
Went to Prew's to fetch a bucket of manure. Mr Nield gave me holey 3d. bit. M. at Ashby all night. Down at graveyard all afternoon, cutting grass etc.

4th July 1948 Sunday
Poured with rain in morning. Went to church. M. at Ashby all night. Cocky came.

5th July 1948 Monday
Had 2nd geog exam in morning. M. not at Ashby. Cut grave next to ours.

6th July 1948 Tuesday
Went to Marie's with Joan. M at Ashby in afternoon. New folks come to old Aunt's house. Marje had her hair permed.

7th July 1948 Wednesday
Not at school. M. at Ashby in morning.

8th July 1948 Thursday
M. at Ashby in morning. Played cricket at night in Wash Lane.

9th July 1948 Friday
M. at Ashby all night. Went to farm at night. Had Enid's skirt. Cut grave in morn.

10th July 1948 Saturday
Went haymaking till 7 p.m. Had tea in Prew's dairy. Earned 2/-. George away. M. at Ashby all night.

11th July 1948 Sunday
Went to first communion. Went church at night. Mrs Clarke came in. M. at Ashby all night.

12th July 1948 Monday
Had Latin exams in morn & afternoon. M. at Ashby all night. Rob ill in school.

13th July 1948 Tuesday
Doing nothing at school. M. at Ashby all night. Cried half the night. Joan away because mother ill.

14th July 1948 Wednesday
Went to parents' day at Rob's school. M. went to Stratford. Went selling flags for sailors.

15th July 1948 Thursday
Went to baths after school. Played cards in school. Went to farm at night. M. at Ashby all night.

16th July 1948 Friday
Played cards nearly all day at school. M. at Ashby all night. Grand day.

17th July 1948 Saturday
Asleep till dinner. Garden Fête in afternoon at Forsyth's. Went hay-making after. Came home in pouring rain in Mr Prew's S. Wester. Rob in Cocky's army coat. M. at Ashby all night.

18th July 1948 Sunday
Hot sultry night. Went to church at night. M at Ashby all night. Cocky came tomorrow.

19th July 1948 Monday
Went to 1st Amateur practice. Went to farm to take rain clothes back. Had tennis racket from school. M. at Ashby all night. Played tennis in morn.

Note – I joined Coalville Amateur Operatic Society.

20th July 1948 Tuesday
Joan and I went hay making. Went to Baths in afternoon. Stayed at home in morn.

21st July 1948 Wednesday
Numbering Geog books all day. Pegging rug at night.

22nd July 1948 Thursday
Did not go to school in morning. Pegged rug & finished it at night. Cocky came after 10 o'clock. M. at Ashby. Sorting library tickets all afternoon in Biology Lab.

23rd July 1948 Friday
Hobbies Day. M. at Ashby all night.

24th July 1948 Saturday
Went to Conservative garden fete at Ashby. Sunday School gone on trip to Cleethorpes. M at Ashby all night. Cried half the night.

25th July 1948 Sunday
Hottest day this year. Went to church. M. at Ashby all night. Laughed all night.

26th July 1948 Monday
Lovely hot day. Went to farm & fetched cows up. Cow had calf. Went to school leaving dance. Cocky came in with Rob after hay making.

27th July 1948 Tuesday
Left school. Had grand time hay making at night till 10-30. Cocky came in.

Note – My school days were over.

28th July 1948 Wednesday
Hottest day in 60 yrs. Started work at Don's. M. at Ashby all night.

Note – My cousin Don offered me a stop-gap job in his office at Barton-under-Needwood, near Burton-on-Trent, where I worked until I settled permanently in the Motor Licence Office at Leicester in October.

29th July 1948 Thursday
Another baking hot day. Mr Bowler started work at Don's. M at Ashby all night.
Wrote to Bunt.

30th July 1948 Friday
Brought my first pay packet home. Baking hot day. M not at Ashby. Slept Chez-Dosh.

31st July 1948 Saturday
Slept Chez-Dosh. Cooler day. Heard of Uncle Tom's death. Went to Farm. Had bath. M. at Ashby 26th & 27th. Rob & I slept Chez-Dosh 29th.

1st August 1948 Sunday
Marje went to Stanton so I went to Church alone & sat in front of Mr Bagnall. M at Ashby. Rob & I slept Chez-Dosh.

2nd August 1948 Monday
Joan, Rob & I went to Zouch in Dos' car & met Mr Bartram. Went on river. Had chips for supper. Rob & I slept Chez-Dosh. M. at Ashby.

3rd August 1948 Tuesday
Uncle Tom's funeral. M. went to Willoughby. Rob & I slept Chez-Dosh.

4th August 1948 Wednesday
Rob, Don & I went to pictures. Rob & I slept Chez-Dosh. Back to work. M at Ashby.

5th August 1948 Thursday
M. at Ashby all night. Washed my hair.

6th August 1948 Friday
Very rainy day. Crash at corner in morning. Cocky came. Super time. M. at Ashby all night.

7th August 1948 Saturday
Another rainy day. Dance at stute but did not go. M at Ashby. Went to sleep listening to Sat. night theatre.

8th August 1948 Sunday
Asleep on & off all day. Got up at 4 p.m. Went to Church. Cocky came. M. at Ashby.

9th August 1948 Monday
Uncle C. reduced nostra pecunia. Went to 2nd Operatic practice. Don not well. M at Ashby.

Note – Uncle Cyril, my dad's brother & partner in the family business (G.H.Hewes & Sons, Estate Agents, Marlborough Square, Coalville.) was committed to paying my Mum £1 per week for life, following the death of my dad in 1939. Now that both Mum & I were at work, he reduced this to ten shillings.

10th August 1948 Tuesday
Rob not well all day. M at Ashby. Did a lot of typing at work.

11th August 1948 Wednesday
Pouring with rain sort of day. Thunder & lightening. M at Ashby. Cocky came.

12th August 1948 Thursday
Not such a rainy day. M. at Ashby. I went to Thornborough at night.

13th August 1948 Friday
Washed my hair. Had a bath. M. at Ashby. Sat next to Freddy at dinner.

14th August 1948 Saturday
Arrived at Ludlow. M & Rob went to Willoughby. Lovely day.

Note – While Mum & Rob went to Willoughby-on-the-Wolds for their summer holiday, I again spent a week in Ludlow with Bunting, Mostyn & 18 month old Michael.

15th August 1948 Sunday
Went to 2 pubs at night with Mostyn & Bunt. Went to tennis courts after dinner.

16th August 1948 Monday
Went with Bunt to see "**Pinocchio**". Went to "Tally Ho" in afternoon.

17th August 1948 Tuesday
Took Michael walk in morning in rain. Went a walk at night.

18th August 1948 Wednesday
Took Michael walk. Fetched some lovely chips at night.

19th August 1948 Thursday
Went to pictures alone to see "This was a Woman". Mostyn not home till 7-30.

20th August 1948 Friday
Came home from Bunt's. Helped road man. Went to Willoughby. Rainy day.

21st August 1948 Saturday
Laughing at night playing David's bugle. Played cards & darts.

22nd August 1948 Sunday
Lovely day. Came home from Willoughby. Stayed at Auntie Bell's.

23rd August 1948 Monday
Went to work with Uncle Fred. Went to 3rd Amateurs, after which the fair & had a date.

24th August 1948 Tuesday
Again went with Uncle Fred. Washed hair. Cocky came in.

25th August 1948 Wednesday
Went & cut grave & took flowers with Marje.

26th August 1948 Thursday
Went to see "**The Best Years of Our Lives**". Came home with Mr Bullen.

27th August 1948 Friday
Took coffee beans to Whitwick. Cleaned silver. Cocky came. Left landing light on.

28th August 1948 Saturday
Don came home from Boscombe. Had Higher Results. Lovely day. I went to the farm.

Hilda Reynolds married.

29th August 1948 Sunday
Had a bath. Cocky came in at night & brought me down to Don's. Went to church.

30th August 1948 Monday
2nd night at Don's. Went to Amateurs & walked home with Pat.

31st August 1948 Tuesday
Went with Joan to see **Fiesta**. Lovely day.
Yesterday went to W.M.R. for dinner all alone.

1st September 1948 Wednesday
Uncle Fred didn't go to work. Went home at night. Cocky came in.

2nd September 1948 Thursday
Had parcel from E. Richardson. Had mushrooms for breakfast.

3rd September 1948 Friday
Mummy & Rob came home from Willoughby. Left Burton at 7. Don saw Mr Farmer.

4th September 1948 Saturday
Mr Prew gave me some apples. Mr Bowler went on trip to New Brighton. Washed my hair.

5th September 1948 Sunday
In bed nearly all day. Went to church at night. Mummy has a sty on her eye.

6th September 1948 Monday
Went to Amateurs & walked home. Had 6 in car at night.

7th September 1948 Tuesday
Went with Joan to see "**Black Swan**". Learned Earny was Grandpa.

8th September 1948 Wednesday
Poured with rain all night. M. at Ashby.

9th September 1948 Thursday
M at Ashby. Joan came down & we went walk. Rode Moseley's horse.

10th September 1948 Friday
M. at Ashby & witness in morning for gypsy case.
Mr Lea's wife collapsed.

11th September 1948 Saturday
Joan came down. Sister Hughes married. M. at Ashby. Did some embroidery at night.
Peter went to work. Mr Lea's wife ill again.

12th September 1948 Sunday
Poured with rain all day. Went to church alone. Very few there.

13th September 1948 Monday
Went to Amateurs. Brought home lovely seat. Ran over dog in car.

14th September 1948 Tuesday
Joan came down at night & we took Gillian a walk. M. at Ashby.

15th September 1948 Wednesday
Had lovely time at work. Marje got awful cold. M. at Ashby.

16th September 1948 Thursday
M. at Ashby. Had grand time at work. Lovely day.

17th September 1948 Friday
Went to 1st practice of Edwardians tomorrow.
Stayed with Peter & Lesley at night.

18th September 1948 Saturday
Don's, went to Statutes. Washed my hair. M. at Ashby.

19th September 1948 Sunday
M. at Ashby. Lovely day. Rose at 7-30 a.m.
Went blackberrying with Jack Hill over Ross Nobb. Fetched my bike from Willoughby.

20th September 1948 Monday
M. at Ashby. Biked to Amateurs with Enid. Gloria on holiday.

21st September 1948 Tuesday
Went to Statutes with Joan. M. at Ashby.

22nd September 1948 Wednesday
Rob went to see Dick Barton at Coalville pictures. M. at Ashby.

23rd September 1948 Thursday
M. at Ashby. Went blackberrying at night tomorrow for Don.

24th September 1948 Friday
M. not due at Ashby till 10. Amari Ernthere.

25th September 1948 Saturday
Played Alderman Newtons at school & won 2-0. Bought hockey stick.
Went to farm.

26th September 1948 Sunday
Went to Church at night. Nurse Thompson & Florence came.

27th September 1948 Monday
Went to Amateur practice. M. at Ashby.

28th September 1948 Tuesday
Went to see "The Yearling". M. at Ashby.

29th September 1948 Wednesday
M. at Ashby. Rob went to see The Yearling.

30th September 1948 Thursday
W.M.R. played Marley Tiles & lost 8-2. Stayed with Don's kids till 12 p.m. M. at Ashby.

1st October 1948 Friday
Washed my hair. Amari Ernthere. M. at Ashby.

2nd October 1948 Saturday

Went Potato Picking in morning. **Had my hair permed in afternoon**. Don went to car racing at Silverstone.

3rd October 1948 Sunday

Florence came in afternoon. Went to church at night.

4th October 1948 Monday

Went to Amateur Practice & came home with Enid. Went to work in BNU 22 after it had been away 2 months being re-done up.

5th October 1948 Tuesday

Joan came at night. Burton Statutes on. M. at Ashby.

6th October 1948 Wednesday

M. at Ashby. Lovely hot days this week. Marje went to **London**.

7th October 1948 Thursday

Heard from Lester. Marje came in at night. Earny did well at dinner. I sat next to him.

8th October 1948 Friday

Went for interview to E.C.Mason at Leicester. Lovely hot day. Cleaned front window & scrubbed front doorstep. Had bath.

9th October 1948 Saturday

Played Sileby at hockey & lost 3-2. Heard I'd been accepted at Lester. Went to grave yard with Peter & Lesley. M. went to Stratford to see "Winter's Tale".

10th October 1948 Sunday

Went to Dress Rehearsal in afternoon & to Church at night.

11th October 1948 Monday

Dress Rehearsal at night. M. at Ashby. Rainy night.

12th October 1948 Tuesday

First night of Variety Concert. Lovely day.

Note – Coalville Amateur Operatic Society gave a Variety Concert. This was my first time on stage with the Society.

13th October 1948 Wednesday

2nd & last night of Variety Concert. M. at Ashby.

14th October 1948 Thursday

Went to 1st Keep Fit Class & after took bike to Stevenson's & WELL!! M. at Ashby.

15th October 1948 Friday

Last day at W.M.R. Sobbed & sobbed at night. Don gave me 5/- extra.

16th October 1948 Saturday

Left Don's. Went to farm in afternoon for 1stone of spuds. Hosed out cowshed etc. Cocky broke brush handle.

17th October 1948 Sunday

Joan & I went to church at Ravo Harvest Festival. Cocky

there. Rob & I stayed with Don's kids till 11.

18th October 1948 Monday

Started work at Leicester. Mr Bowler ill & sent home. Went to Amateurs. Had dinner in bus station.

Note – On St. Luke's Day, 18th October, I started work in the Motor Licence Office, where I would be employed for the next 30 years!

19th October 1948 Tuesday

Had dinner for last time in Kath Aris' office. M. at Ashby.

20th October 1948 Wednesday

M. again at Ashby. Did some typing at work for 1st time.

21st October 1948 Thursday

Went to 2nd Keep Fit Class. Joan & Freda Lane went for 1st time. Went round Leicester with P. Rigby at dinner. Warm day.

22nd October 1948 Friday

Went to bed as soon as I got home because very tired. Slept with bed sideways.

23rd October 1948 Saturday

Caught 12-30 bus home. Home before 1-30. Went down to Don's at night. He'd got air in his pipes. Saw about applying for Coll.

24th October 1948 Sunday

In bed all morning. M. got a cold. Filling in College forms all night. Lovely evening. Rita had budgy last Thurs or Fri.

25th October 1948 Monday

Went to Amateurs but did nothing because the big nobs were holding a committee meeting all the time. Rainy. Had my dinner in Lewis' Basement.

26th October 1948 Tuesday

Joan & I went down to Don's at night & fetched him out of the bath. M. at Ashby.

27th October 1948 Wednesday

Started doing Driving Licences yesterday. M. at Ashby.

28th October 1948 Thursday

Went to 3rd Keep Fit Class. Don met me in Coalville yesterday for 1st time.

29th October 1948 Friday

Don brought me home. Picked me up from Forest Road Garage. Went to bed early.

30th October 1948 Saturday

Went to **Darwen** to see "Hit the Deck". Sat with Brenda Glithero & Mr Turner coming home. Put clocks back.

31st October 1948 Sunday

Went to Church alone. Woke up at 4-15 p.m. Went to bed 4 a.m.

1st November 1948 Monday
Had my slacks. Rainy Day.

3rd November 1948 Wednesday
Did repeat of Variety Show.

4th November 1948 Thursday
Did Variety Show & had tea at Glover's. Came home in **Davis'** van. Florence slept at our house.

5th November 1948 Friday
Barbara Bagnall's mother killed.

6th November 1948 Saturday
Caught 1 bus from Coalville & didn't get home till nearly 3.

7th November 1948 Sunday
Went to Church alone. Marj not well.

8th November 1948 Monday
Had a reading through of Hit the Deck.

11th November 1948 Thursday
Went to Keep Fit & then to stay with Don's kids.

12th November 1948 Friday
Played Darts at Pat's.
Florence came in afternoon.

13th November 1948 Saturday
Went to Hinckley to play hockey but didn't play because of rain.

14th November 1948 Sunday
Went to Church. Mrs Bagnall's funeral service.

15th November 1948 Monday
Went to Amateurs. Sang songs of Hit the Deck for first time.

17th November 1948 Wednesday
Went to Edwardian's Dance at Adult School.

18th November 1948 Thursday
Went to keep fit. Had my rear light stolen.

19th November 1948 Friday
M. at Ashby all night.

20th November 1948 Saturday
Cocky brought letter from Phyl. Jack & Phil gone to Leicester without him. Went to Don's birthday Party.

21st November 1948 Sunday
Went to Church. In bed all morning.

22nd November 1948 Monday
Extremely foggy. Came home on 4-45 bus. Went to practice Hit the Deck.

24th November 1948 Wednesday
Mummy went to Pictures. Cocky came.

25th November 1948 Thursday
Went to Keep Fit & later stayed with Don's kids.

27th November 1948 Saturday
Went to Don's until after 1-30 a.m. Played Loughborough Brush at school & lost 18-3.
Had kitten.

28th November 1948 Sunday
In bed nearly all day. M. at Ashby 4 - 8. Very foggy. Went to Church with Marje.

1st December 1948 Wednesday
Went for interview at Sheffield for Hereford.

5th December 1948 Sunday
Went to Church at night with M. Marje went to Rita's party.

12th December 1948 Sunday
Went to church at night & sat with Enid. Went round Hayes' later & played cards with Blades Googy etc.

25th December 1948 Saturday
Went to Auntie Belle's at night. Cried all morning.

26th December 1948 Sunday
Florence & King came – walked from Ashby – went to Church.

27th December 1948 Monday
Went to Don's at night. M. at Ashby.

28th December 1948 Tuesday
Went to Party at Ashby Hospital.

29th December 1948 Wednesday
Started back to work after holiday.

30th December 1948 Thursday
Mummy at Ashby. Cocky came in with Driving Licence.

31st December 1948 Friday
Went to Mrs Forsythe's Dance at Masonic Hall.

* * *

1949

1st January 1949 Saturday
Worked overtime until 5-40.

Note – All vehicle licences expired on 31st December each year. This meant that January was the busiest month of the year at work, & I worked overtime each evening, catching the 7-20 p.m .bus home from Leicester, arriving in Coalville at 8 p.m. On Saturdays we worked until 5 p.m.. & seemed to travel for ever in darkness.

2nd January 1949 Sunday
Went to Church alone. In bed all day.

3rd January 1949 Monday
Working till 7-30. Then went to Amateurs. M. at Ashby.

4th January 1949 Tuesday
Cocky came. Worked till 7-30. Rainy day. Bought crêpe shoes & wellos.

5th January 1949 Wednesday
Came home at 7-20 & went straight to bed.

6th January 1949 Thursday
Cocky came. Came home 7-20. M. at Ashby.

7th January 1949 Friday
Cocky came with Mr Prew's forms for tractor – had long Discussion.

8th January 1949 Saturday
Working till 5-15. M. at Ashby. Very cold at night. Walked from Coalville.

9th January 1949 Sunday
In bed all day. M. at Ashby. Went to church with Marje.

10th January 1949 Monday
Caught 7-20 bus home. Went Amateurs. **My Tea Week**.

11th January 1949 Tuesday
Cocky came with amended forms for Mr Prew.

12th January 1949 Wednesday
Took £71-15/- for Driving Licences. Cocky came for Licence. Amateur Rehearsal.

13th January 1949 Thursday
Cocky came in. Came home on 7-20 bus.

14th January 1949 Friday
Cocky Came Dressed up. Met Man in Leicester.

15th January 1949 Saturday
Left work at 4. M. Rob & I at Don's all night while Phyl & Don went to hear Robert Easton with Worths at Nottingham.

16th January 1949 Sunday
In bed till 2. Went walk alone in afternoon.

Florence came at night.

25th January 1949 Tuesday
Cocky came. M. at Ashby. Came home on 7-20 bus.

26th January 1949 Wednesday
Cocky came. I went to Amateur rehearsal straight from work, came home on 10 bus.

27th January 1949 Thursday
Joan went out with Colin Baker for 1st time to pictures.

29th January 1949 Saturday
Went to Coalville in afternoon. 1st afternoon this year not working overtime.
Went to W. I. party at 'stute at night. M. at Ashby.

2nd February 1949 Wednesday
Went to Amateur rehearsal.

3rd February 1949 Thursday
Last night of overtime.

4th February 1949 Friday
Came home on 5-15 p.m. bus 1st time this year. Slept Chez-Dosh.

5th February 1949 Saturday
Pam & Les married. Played Alderman Newton's Old Scholars away & drew 2-2. Slept Chez- Dosh.

6th February 1949 Sunday
Went ride in Mr J. Swanwick's car round Groby Pool, Woodhouse Eaves etc. Skating on Pool. Went to Church with Joyce Sharp & Marj.

13th February 1949 Sunday
Cocky came after I had gone to bed. M. at Ashby.

14th February 1949 Monday
Cocky came. Brought some milk. M. at Ashby.

15th February 1949 Tuesday
Had rehearsal for Amateurs.

16th February 1949 Wednesday
Another rehearsal.

17th February 1949 Thursday
Went to Keep Fit Class for 1st time this year.

18th February 1949 Friday
Talked to Mr Green on Ashby Road.

19th February 1949 Saturday
Had my new bike. Lovely day.

20th February 1949 Sunday
Washed my hair. Had rehearsal in afternoon.

26th February 1949 Saturday
Played Ashby at hockey in afternoon & won 2-0. Went to Leicester panto at night.

27th February 1949 Sunday
Went to church & rehearsal in afternoon. **Very windy**.

28th February 1949 Monday
Rehearsal at night. **Cocky** came. M. at Ashby all night.

2nd March 1949 Wednesday
Cocky stayed with Rob while I was at Amateurs. Pat came in about 10-30.

3rd March 1949 Thursday
Pat went for X-ray at Markfield. Cocky came with Phil's driving licence & 5/-. Moon Mad. Went about 9-15. Pat came about 9-30 in Sailor's outfit.

4th March 1949 Friday
Cocky came & took Phil's driving licence form for him to sign & brought it back about 9-45. I was at rehearsal all night. M. Moore came for tea.

5th March 1949 Saturday
Played hockey V. Leics. Dom. Sci. Coll. on Welford Road in snow storm without umpire & lost 3-1. Took a little girl to the rondy at work.

6th March 1949 Sunday
Had Dress Rehearsal of Act I on stage at Regal. Clearing snow away in morning.

7th March 1949 Monday
Cocky came. Had rehearsal for Hit the Deck.

8th March 1949 Tuesday
Today & rest of week off from work. Talked to Road Man down Rookery.

9th March 1949 Wednesday
Final rehearsal of **Hit the Deck**. Sat on balcony with Mr Green.

10th March 1949 Thursday
Gave "**Hit the Deck**".

11th March 1949 Friday
Hit the Deck. K. Hickman came over.

12th March 1949 Saturday
Hit the Deck. Had chocolates & flowers etc.

Note – "Hit the Deck" was my first full musical production with Coalville "Amateurs" & all the excitement & joy of being on stage.

13th March 1949 Sunday
Went to church alone. Rained after.

14th March 1949 Monday
Had fortune told by Mrs Rouse at Progressive Hall.

15th March 1949 Tuesday
Cocky came. Mr Green gave me purse. M. at Ashby.

16th March 1949 Wednesday
Went to see **Chu Chin Chow**. Cocky stayed with Rob. M. at Ashby.

17th March 1949 Thursday
Took some flowers to grave in morn. Went to keep fit – last this season. Meus Cocky came.

18th March 1949 Friday
M. at Ashby. Mr Pochin gave me choc bisc & cake. Meus Cocky came.

19th March 1949 Saturday
Had dinner in Leicester with Mrs Green. Played Texagon at Leicester & won 3-0. **Mr Prew's Sale**. Meus Cocky came.

20th March 1949 Sunday
Cocky came. Went to church with Marje & Enid. Had bath.
Went to graveyard in afternoon.

23rd March 1949 Wednesday
Went to see "**Iolanthe**" with Don & Phyl at Coventry Doyle Carte.

25th March 1949 Friday
Joan away with flu. Ate my dinner in town hall square.

26th March 1949 Saturday
Great excitement!!! **Leicester City Beat Portsmouth 3-1** in semi-finals of cup.
Cambridge won boat race.
Ruescan Hero won Grand National.
We beat Loughborough Tech at hockey 2-1.

27th March 1949 Sunday
Went bike ride alone in afternoon to Newton Burgoland & Swepstone. Went to church at night alone. **Mothering Sunday**.

2nd April 1949 Saturday
Had busy morning at work. Lots of folk in for tax. Went to see **Mikado**. Bought white shoes & bag. Put **clocks on**.

10th April 1949 Sunday
On this day in 1849 the safety pin was patented in America by Walter Hunt of New York. He later sold the rights for £250.

16th April 1949 Saturday
Went a ride to Bradgate, Cropston, Thurcaston, Anstey etc. alone. Went Ross Nob in morning to get rhododendrons. Florence came at night.

17th April 1949 Sunday
Heard Cuckoo 1st time. Went communion (3rd in my life) at 7. Went ride in afternoon with Joan. Church at night.

20th April 1949 Wednesday
Took £100-10/- for Driving Licences. 280 by post!

24th April 1949 Sunday
Joan & I went our 1st long ride to Matlock.

29th April 1949 Friday
Cocky came. Rainy evening. M. at Ashby.

1st May 1949 Sunday
Joan & I biked to Matlock. Came back with Reg Fletcher.

2nd May 1949 Monday
Joan & I waited in Leicester to cheer City Cup Team home.

3rd May 1949 Tuesday
Didn't balance. Caught 5-30 bus.

6th May 1949 Friday
Pam stayed away to get her ration books. Again didn't balance.

7th May 1949 Saturday
May Lander & Miss Wells came in. Working on our field all afternoon. Don got me a cyclometer. M. at Ashby all night.

8th May 1949 Sunday
Biked to Stratford with Joan, Reg & Chet. M. at Ashby.

Note – Ken Chettleburgh, a keen cyclist, becomes my boyfriend for a while.

11th May 1949 Wednesday
Siam changed its name to Thailand.

14th May 1949 Saturday
Went to Adult School with Chet. Sunbathing in afternoon.

15th May 1949 Sunday
Went to church at night with Marje.

17th May 1949 Tuesday
Chet came down & he, Rob & I stayed with Don's kids.

19th May 1949 Thursday
Joan & I went to Chet's & printed photos.

20th May 1949 Friday
Had Judy. Madge & Bertha came over with dog.

21st May 1949 Saturday
Went to Chet's for tea & stayed in their house all night.Galli oculi primi. Joan had new coat.

22nd May 1949 Sunday
Went bike ride with Joan, Fletch & Chet to Derby, C. Donington & Zouch.
Had dinner at C. D.   Went to church at night with Joan.

24th May 1949 Tuesday
Chet & I stayed with Don's kids.

25th May 1949 Wednesday
Went to the Baths for first time this year. Came back with Chet.

26th May 1949 Thursday
Went to Wainwright's at night to see about a tandem.

Note – Chettleburgh buys a tandem & together we cycle

for miles & miles.

28th May 1949 Saturday
Went ride on Alf Wainwright's tandem with Chet to Frank Holden's at Ashby. M. went to Chatsworth with B & P club.

29th May 1949 Sunday
Joan & I went to Belton in morning to see the Coalville Wheelers 25 mile cycle race. Went to Chet's for tea & with him to church at Ravo at night.

5th June 1949 Sunday
Went Youth Hostelling. Stayed the night at Overton Hall. Had dinner at Repton.

6th June 1949 Whit Monday
Biked up the **Snake** to Glossop. Came back through Buxton, Bakewell, Matlock. Joan & Horace nearly got locked out.

Note – Bank Holiday, Chettleburgh & I go on the tandem as far as Glossop, up the Snake Pass, staying overnight at a Youth Hostel.

7th June 1949 Tuesday
Arrived home about 6 from youth hostelling. Rob & M. went to Ibstock **Gymkhana**.

8th June 1949 Wednesday
Back to work after Whit hol. Came home on 5-45 bus with Chet.

9th June 1949 Thursday
Went to Leicester Fair out of work with Chet. Came home on 10 bus. M. at Ashby. Went on big wheel for 1st time in my life.

10th June 1949 Friday
Chet went to pay for his tandem. I went to bed early.

11th June 1949 Saturday
Went to Chet's house for tea & met his granny & granddad. Mr Rose's first day of holiday to Bournemouth. Chet played piano at night & went home after midnight.

12th June 1949 Sunday
Ravo Church Sermons. Chettleburgh, Beryl (from Hollies) & I went to Bradgate. Beryl & I went to Church.

19th June 1949 Sunday
Glorious hot weather all week. Cocky très brown.

Note – All through the summer, Chettleburgh & I go out together, while Cocky, the ever faithful farm worker, looking like Adonis, bare backed & brown as a berry, is my one true love.

26th June 1949 Sunday
Sun Bathing all afternoon. M. biked to Willoughby.

27th June 1949 Monday
Started re-issuing red Driving Licence covers again.

29th June 1949 Wednesday
Went to Land's hay making for 1st time. Steered tractor.

30th June 1949 Thursday
Went haymaking again at Land's.

1st July 1949 Friday
Had new coat.

2nd July 1949 Saturday
Mr Chettleburg's Birthday Party.
Had new Green Frock. Talked to Jack, Phyl & Cocky in Wash Lane at night. Phyl gave me his Driving Licence to renew.

3rd July 1949 Sunday
Went to Sutton Coldfield. Chet took Rob ride on tandem at night.

8th July 1949 Friday
Cocky came for Phyl's Driving Licence.

10th July 1949 Sunday
Went to Rearsby Air Display & to Pam & Les' for tea.

14th July 1949 Thursday
Chet bought me watch. Navy Gorey skirt came.
Note – My 18th Birthday.

28th July 1949 Thursday
Went to see Charlie in Leicester Royal Infirmary.

31st July 1949 Sunday
Went to see Charlie in Royal. He gave me letter of proposal.

1st August 1949 Monday
Biked to Dovedale with Frank Holden & family.

4th August 1949 Thursday
Had my hair permed.

6th August 1949 Saturday
Pam & Les away in morning because Pam's brother's wedding.

7th August 1949 Sunday
Went to see Charlie at Zachery Merton. Very windy & rainy. M. at Ashby.

8th August 1949 Monday
Cocky came after I had gone to bed to see if Rob had any cabbage plants for sale.

13th August 1949 Saturday
Went to Hugglescote Show. Lovely hot day.

20th August 1949 Saturday
Went to Goodrington.

Note – This year for my summer holiday, for the first time since the war, I went to the sea-side for a lovely holiday at Goodrington with cousin Don & family. Chettleburgh went on holiday with his pal to Wales. Cocky went with his pals, Jack Congrave & Philip

Burder, to Yarmouth.

24th August 1949 Wednesday
Went to Torquay Pier & watched fireworks.

25th August 1949 Thursday
Went to Buxham. Went from there to Torquay in boat.

26th August 1949 Friday
Went to Zoo. Rainy day.

27th August 1949 Saturday
Rainy tea time.

17th September 1949 Saturday
Cocky went to Yarmouth for week. Chettleburgh gone to Wales with Goulding.

22nd September 1949 Thursday
Had medical.

26th September 1949 Monday
Mr Rose had the afternoon off.

27th September 1949 Tuesday
Mr Rose had the day off.

28th September 1949 Wednesday
Joan came down & we went a walk with Judy. Mr Rose had the day off.

29th September 1949 Thursday
Les had the afternoon off to put slabs down at Birstall.

30th September 1949 Friday
Rob & I stayed with Don's kids. I started awful cold. Phyl & Don both got colds.

1st October 1949 Saturday
I went to Doctor's for Rob's prescription. Took Judy to Vet. Meus Cocky came to see about Mr Cliff's Driving Licence.

2nd October 1949 Sunday
Harvest Festival. I went with Joan. Judy got a bad neck.

3rd October 1949 Monday
Cocky came. Went to Amateurs.
Pam moved off counter. Maurice started work.

4th October 1949 Tuesday
Meus Cocky came.

5th October 1949 Wednesday
Joan came. Cocky came.

6th October 1949 Thursday
Mary Moore came. Chettleburgh came down.

8th October 1949 Saturday
Chettleburgh's birthday party. I gave him pen.

9th October 1949 Sunday
Went to church at night & sat by Cocky.

10th October 1949 Monday
Bought music for "Maid of the Mountains".

12th October 1949 Wednesday
PRIMAUS. Cocky & Joan came.

Note – A kiss from Cocky that decided once & for all that he & I were locked for ever in each others hearts. From that day onward, Cocky & I ventured out together hand in hand. Immediately Aunt Dos, Uncle Fred & all my proud relations voiced their objections. Cocky's family & my family could never, ever, fuse into one big happy family. "Don't invite me to your wedding" was the general cry.
Chettleburg found himself a new girlfriend.

13th October 1949 Thursday
Meus Cocky came.

15th October 1949 Saturday
Went to Circus in afternoon with Chettleburgh.

16th October 1949 Sunday
Cocky & Jack went to Church. I sat on back row with Syd, Gig & another lad.

19th October 1949 Wednesday
Joan, Rob & I stayed with Don's kids.
M. went to Coventry with B & P club.

20th October 1949 Thursday
Chet came at night.

21st October 1949 Friday
Went first walk with Cocky down Heather Lane. Had some chips from Ravo chip shop.

22nd October 1949 Saturday
Went walk with meus Cocky. Stayed in SCHWEPPERVESCENCES barn. Ate chocolate biscuits & pears.

23rd October 1949 Sunday
Cocky came to church at night & then to see Rob about Xmas cockerels. Rainy day.
Don came at night for me to stay with kids.

24th October 1949 Monday
Went to Amateurs. Saw Chet as coming out with Helen Tovell.
Howard Hicken there for 1st time.

25th October 1949 Tuesday
Went walk with Cocky. Went in SCHWEPPES' barn.

26th October 1949 Wednesday
Cocky came. Played draughts. M. at Ashby.

27th October 1949 Thursday
Cocky came. M. at Ashby.
Played Draughts.

28th October 1949 Friday
Cocky came. M. at Ashby.

29th October 1949 Saturday
Meus Cocky came. **Put clocks back**. Chet came in afternoon for tandem. M. at Ashby.

30th October 1949 Sunday
Cocky came. M. at Ashby.

31st October 1949 Monday
Went to Amateurs. **Pam left work**.

1st November 1949 Tuesday
Cocky came in for a bit – M. at B & P meeting.

2nd November 1949 Wednesday
M. & Rob at pictures. Meus Cocky came.

3rd November 1949 Thursday
Stayed with Don's kids. Monty Worth's Birthday Party.

4th November 1949 Friday
Went to baths with Mummy to see "Dear Evelyn".

5th November 1949 Saturday
Went & watched Don's fireworks then went walk with Cocky to SCHWEPPES barn.

6th November 1949 Sunday
Went to Church. Sat with Enid & ES.

7th November 1949 Monday
Went to Amateurs. Came home in Pat's car with H. Hicken & Sheila Bottrill.

8th November 1949 Tuesday
Started navy knitting.

9th November 1949 Wednesday
Stayed at home knitting.

10th November 1949 Thursday
Went walk with Cocky to Schweppes barn. **Saw the Aunt Dosh**.

11th November 1949 Friday
M. at Ashby. Meus Cocky came.

12th November 1949 Saturday
M. at Ashby. Meus Cocky came.

13th November 1949 Sunday
M. at Ashby. **Meorum** Cocky came.

14th November 1949 Monday
Went to Amateurs.

15th November 1949 Tuesday
Cocky came to see if we wanted spuds, tomorrow.

16th November 1949 Wednesday
Yesterday went to bed & sobbed. M. hit me.

17th November 1949 Thursday
Stayed with Don's kids & slept there while he & Phyl went to Mrs Waltho's dance at Stute.

18th November 1949 Friday
Went walk with Cocky to Friar's barn.

19th November 1949 Saturday
Went with Cocky walk in fog to Schweppes. Ill feelings at home.

20th November 1949 Sunday
Went walk with Cocky after Church down Rookery.

21st November 1949 Monday
Went to Amateurs on 8 bus with Pat & back on 10 bus.

22nd November 1949 Tuesday
Cocky came. M. at Ashby.

23rd November 1949 Wednesday
Chettleburgh came & brought Rob horse photo.

24th November 1949 Thursday
Cocky came. M. at Ashby.

25th November 1949 Friday
We all went to bed early.

26th November 1949 Saturday
Mr Stevenson died during last night. M. & I went to see "**Maid of the Mountains**".

27th November 1949 Sunday
Went to church then a walk with Cocky to Schweppes barn.

28th November 1949 Monday
Went to Amateurs in Pat's car. **Prew's window bricked up**.

29th November 1949 Tuesday
Went with Meorum Cocky to Friar's barn.

30th November 1949 Wednesday
Went with meorum Cocky to Schweppes.

1st December 1949 Thursday
Chettleburgh came down. Washed my hair.

2nd December 1949 Friday
Went walk with meorum Cocky to Schweppes.
Didn't balance.

3rd December 1949 Saturday
Bought dance frock & high heel shoes & choker.
Went to Coalville Wheelers Annual dinner & social.

4th December 1949 Sunday
Went to Church. Cocky met me out but came straight home.

5th December 1949 Monday
Went to Amateurs. Cocky went with trip to Coventry.

6th December 1949 Tuesday
M. at Ashby. Cocky came.

7th December 1949 Wednesday
M. at Ashby. Cocky came.

8th December 1949 Thursday
M. at Ashby. Meorum Cocky came.

9th December 1949 Friday
Went to Dance at Ashby Town Hall for Hospital. Met Gustav.

10th December 1949 Saturday
Went walk with Cocky to Friar's barn. Very cold day.

11th December 1949 Sunday
Started knitted Doll's clothes for Leslie. Went to Church at night.

12th December 1949 Monday
Did not go to Amateurs, felt too tired & cold. Freezing day.

13th December 1949 Tuesday
Cocky went to Young Farmers Meeting.
I stayed in & knitted. Chet came.

14th December 1949 Wednesday
Went walk with Cocky to Friar's.

15th December 1949 Thursday
Went walk with Cocky to Friar's.

16th December 1949 Friday
Stayed in & knitted.

17th December 1949 Saturday
Played hockey against School, won 3-0. It snowed.
Cocky came. Later Chet came.

18th December 1949 Sunday
Went to Church. Came out at 8-15 then came home across recky with Cocky.

19th December 1949 Monday
Went to Amateurs in Pat's car.

20th December 1949 Tuesday
Cocky came. M. at Ashby.

21st December 1949 Wednesday
Went to Inner Wheel Dance at Masonic Hall.

22nd December 1949 Thursday
Chet came down. Brought nylons. Joan came.

23rd December 1949 Friday
Cocky came & killed the cockerel. Went home at midnight. Rob went to party at stute.

24th December 1949 Saturday
Went walk with Cocky at night to Friar's then Snibby School.

25th December 1949 Sunday
Cocky went to Church, then we went to Moseley's & a walk.

26th December 1949 Monday

Went to Chet's for tea then to dance at Adult School.

27th December 1949 Tuesday

Went to Ashby hospital party & came home 1 a.m. on motor bike.

28th December 1949 Wednesday

Went to Dr. Barnardo's children's' party at Coalville Y.M.C.A. Cocky came at night.

29th December 1949 Thursday

Cocky came at night. M. at Ashby. Rob at Television. Mended puncture.

30th December 1949 Friday

Came home on 8-15 bus. Cocky met me at Coalville with bikes. Bought chips from Ravo.

31st December 1949 Saturday

Stayed with Don's kids while all went to Dance. Came home on 5-45 bus.

* * *

National Insurance No. ZA 192172D

1950

1st January 1950 Sunday
Mummy ill in morning. Could not go to Ashby.
Went to Church at night then with Cocky Over Recky.
Watched circus television.

2nd January 1950 Monday
Came home on 8-15 bus. Cocky met me at Coalville.
Rainy evening.

3rd January 1950 Tuesday
Came home on 8-15. Cocky met me at Coalville.

4th January 1950 Wednesday
Came home on 8-15. Cocky met me at Coalville.

5th January 1950 Thursday
Mummy & Rob went to Don's while Phyl & Don went to Old Scholars Dance.
Cocky & I went to Stock's fish shop then in Burder's.

6th January 1950 Friday
I fainted at work & came home in ambulance. Cocky came in at night.

7th January 1950 Saturday
Stayed away from work for first time. Fancy Dress Party at 'stute.

8th January 1950 Sunday
Did not go to Church. Cocky, Jack & Phyl went. Cocky came in after church.

9th January 1950 Monday
Went to Doctor's in morning & to National health place at Coalville. Cocky came at night.

10th January 1950 Tuesday
Went to Cliff's farm for first time after going down fields spreading lime with Cocky.   Cocky came at night.

11th January 1950 Wednesday
M. at Ashby. I went down to Don's with pink doll's dress for Lesley.

12th January 1950 Thursday
Truculent sunk. Still away from work. M. at Ashby. Chettleburgh came.

13th January 1950 Friday
Cocky came & plucked cockerel for Rob. M. at Ashby.

14th January 1950 Saturday
I started back to work yesterday & left at 6-15.
Today left at 5-15.

15th January 1950 Sunday
Went to church & sat with Enid. Cocky & Phil went. M. at Ashby. Cocky came in at night after church.

16th January 1950 Monday
Came home on 7-20 bus. M. at Ashby. Cocky came.
Brought some food for Mr Rose's quad chicks.

17th January 1950 Tuesday
Came home on 7-20. Cocky at Meeting. M. at meeting.
Rob at Television.

18th January 1950 Wednesday
Came home on 7-20 bus. Saw Cocky for a bit up the road. Ate some biscuits.

19th January 1950 Thursday
Came home on 7-20. M. Moore came for tea.   Saw Cocky for a bit in Hollies.

20th January 1950 Friday
Came home on 8-15.
Went across recky with Cocky, tomorrow after coming on 7-20.

21st January 1950 Saturday
Came home on 7-20, got off top of Wash Lane.
Yesterday walked home from Coalville with Cocky, then came in home till 11-30.
M. at Don's, while Don & Phyl at Masonic Dance till 2 a.m.

22nd January 1950 Sunday
In bed until 2-30 p.m. Went to Church at night.
Walked home with Cocky & Phyl. Had Lemonade at Plough.

23rd January 1950 Monday
Came home on 8-15 bus. Cocky met me at Coalville with bike. M. at Ashby.

24th January 1950 Tuesday
M. at Ashby. I came home on 8-15 bus. Cocky met me at Coalville.

25th January 1950 Wednesday
Cocky went to pictures.
I came home on 8-15 bus & biked home alone Standard Hill way.

26th January 1950 Thursday
Came home on 8-15.   M. at Ashby.   Cocky met me with bike at Coalville.

27th January 1950 Friday
Mummy & I went to see "Pirates of Penzance" at Coalville Grammar.

28th January 1950 Saturday
Went to Pantomime at Leicester "Little Red Riding Hood". Helen Tovell & I went on 9 o'clock bus to work, 10 to 8 didn't come.

29th January 1950 Sunday
I had a bath in afternoon. Washed my hair at night. M. at Ashby from 8 a.m. till 4 p.m. Rector ill so Chaplin took service. Went walk with Cocky after church.

30th January 1950 Monday

First fall of snow this year.
Came home on 8-15. Cocky met me at Coalville & we walked home.

31st January 1950 Tuesday

Very foggy at night. Came home on 8-15 & walked with Cocky from Coalville.

1st February 1950 Wednesday

Came home on 8-15. Walked home with Cocky.

2nd February 1950 Thursday

Rainy evening. Cocky went to Pictures 1st house & then we walked home from Coalville.

3rd February 1950 Friday

Lovely evening. Ann Causer on bus. Walked home from Coalville with Cocky.

4th February 1950 Saturday

First time this year came home at Dinner Time on 12-30 bus. Went with Cocky at night to Jack Hill's & Harry Sutton's.

5th February 1950 Sunday

Lovely morning. Took Judy walk down Friar's. Cocky & Phil at Church. Cocky & I went to Ashby to take Ashby Hospital Laundry key.

6th February 1950 Monday

Came home on 7-20 bus & went straight from work to Amateurs for 1st time this year. Came home in Pat's car. Cocky at home with Rob.

7th February 1950 Tuesday

Came home on 7-20 bus - M. got on - Night Duty. Cocky met me off bus & came in.

8th February 1950 Wednesday

Came home again on 7-20. M. at Ashby all night. Cocky met me off bus & came in.

9th February 1950 Thursday

Cocky again met me off bus & came in. M. at Ashby all night.

10th February 1950 Friday

I got some **Nylons** for first time from Leicester market for 3/9. Cocky came in at night.

11th February 1950 Saturday

Cocky came in at night till 11-30. I came home on 1-15 bus & biked from Coalville.

12th February 1950 Sunday

Rainy day. Went to church & sat with Enid. Jack, Phil & Cocky went. M. not very well - I went to bed when I got home from church.

13th February 1950 Monday

Went to Amateurs on 7-15 bus. Came home on 10 bus.

14th February 1950 Tuesday

Cocky, Phil, Joan, Rob & I went to Regal to see **Danny**

Kaye in "The Secret Lives of Walter Mitty". Walked there & back.

15th February 1950 Wednesday

Rob went to Rex with Lands. W. I. social at stute. Cocky & Phil went. I stayed in & had a bath.

16th February 1950 Thursday

Went a walk with Cocky round Mary's Lane et je pleurais beaucoup.

Note – All through the winter months, Cocky & I continued to "go out" together, but we could not be truly happy together, when others were not happy for us, or with us. Maybe I should look elsewhere for a different boy-friend who might be more acceptable. As I walked round Mary's Lane with Cocky "je pleurais beaucoup."

17th February 1950 Friday

I went down to Don's & stayed with children while Phyl & Don went to dance at Burton. I slept there. Did a big jig saw for Peter. Mrs Cassell died,

18th February 1950 Saturday

My Saturday morning off. Yesterday got paid 2nd half of over time & bought plaid skirt. Tonight Mummy went to Mary Moore's & Cocky came.

19th February 1950 Sunday

Went walk with Beryl Kerr in afternoon. She had tea at our house & then came to church with me. Went walk after church with Cocky.

20th February 1950 Monday

Went to Amateurs & back in Pat's car. Cocky went to pictures to see Last of Redskins.

21st February 1950 Tuesday

M. at Ashby all night. I washed my hair & Cocky dried it. Then we made pancakes. I had pancakes for dinner at Woolworth's.

22nd February 1950 Wednesday

M. at Ashby all night. Cocky came. Talked about suum patrem.

23rd February 1950 Thursday

Election Day. I was polling all day at Ravo school with Mr Curtis. Cocky woke me in morning & stayed with Rob at night till I got home.

24th February 1950 Friday

Got some nylons 7/4 no seam. Went with Cocky to see **Rebecca** at Rex.

25th February 1950 Saturday

Came home on 12-30 bus with Johnny Johnson. Cocky went to Mary Moseley's **Wedding**.

26th February 1950 Sunday

Went walk down Rookery in afternoon with Beryl Kerr & Lee Burder. Beryl had tea chez-nous. Went walk with Cocky after church. Cold day.

27th February 1950 Monday
Went to Amateurs on bus, sat with Cocky. He, Jack & Phyl went up to Coalville for Farmers Meeting.

28th February 1950 Tuesday
Stayed in at night.

1st March 1950 Wednesday
Went walk with Cocky down Friar's.

2nd March 1950 Thursday
Stayed in at night & went to bed early.

3rd March 1950 Friday
Stayed overtime for Mrs Nicholls & came home on 7-20 bus.

4th March 1950 Saturday
Glorious day. Went walk with Cocky at night across Grange.

5th March 1950 Sunday
Went to church at night & sat on back row with Beryl Kerr & Rob. After church went walk with Cocky.

6th March 1950 Monday
Went to Amateurs with Pat. Walked home with Cocky who'd been to Pictures.
Mr Cooper away from Amateurs because buried his **Daughter**.

7th March 1950 Tuesday
Came home at dinner time from work because not well in morning. M. at Ashby all night. Cocky came.

8th March 1950 Wednesday
Had the day off: in bed all morning. Went a walk over Grange in afternoon.
Cocky came in at night.

9th March 1950 Thursday
Went back to work. I went to bed early. M. on night duty.

10th March 1950 Friday
Stayed with Don's kids while Don & Phyl went to a dance.
Les' dog died.

11th March 1950 Saturday
Went to see Joan of Arc at the Princes in Leicester with Cocky & then had tea at Lewis's.   Je donnai le ronson au Jean. Cocky & I had dinner at Woolworth's.

12th March 1950 Sunday
Lovely day. I took some flowers to grave. Went to church at night with Rob & after a walk with Cocky. M. at Ashby all day.

13th March 1950 Monday
Went to Amateurs on bus with Cocky. Very cold day.

14th March 1950 Tuesday
Stayed in at night. Rainy, went to bed early.

15th March 1950 Wednesday
Went down Heather Lane with Cocky. Later Helen Tovell came & cut frock out for me.

16th March 1950 Thursday
Maurice from work **married**. I got tickets for Maid of the Mountains. Took some to Burders & then went with Cocky down to Don's.

17th March 1950 Friday
Stayed in at night & did some sewing of my dress.

18th March 1950 Saturday
Went to Dentists in morning & then down to the graveyard. First grass cut of the year. In the evening went walk with Cocky.

19th March 1950 Sunday
Went to church with Rob. Pat sat with us. Later went walk down Mary's Lane with Cocky.

20th March 1950 Monday
Went to Amateurs & back on the bus. **Mr Rose's** birthday.

21st March 1950 Tuesday
M. at Ashby all night. Cocky & Joan came. Rob bought some chicks. Bus conductor swore at Helen & me in morning.

22nd March 1950 Wednesday
Had Amateur rehearsal at Progressive Hall.

23rd March 1950 Thursday
Stayed in at night.

24th March 1950 Friday
Went walk with Cocky at night up Standard Hill. He bought some sweets from Hanford's.

25th March 1950 Saturday
Stayed in at night & mended stockings.
Cocky went to Pictures with Phil.

26th March 1950 Sunday
Went to Church. Sat with Cocky, Phil & Rob.
Cocky & I then went to Chapel to hear Male Voice Choir.

27th March 1950 Monday
Went to Amateurs on bus & back on bus.

28th March 1950 Tuesday
Went with Cocky to see **"The Third Man"** at Regal. **Diximus Vale.**

Note – "Diximus Vale". Within 5 months of walking out together, Cocky & I decided it was a hopeless venture. Sadly we said, "Goodbye".

29th March 1950 Wednesday
Had rehearsal of Maid of the Mountains at Regal till about 1 a.m. Afterwards went down to Don's & finally went to bed at 2-30 a.m.

30th March 1950 Thursday
Gave first production of Show. I had a day's holiday from work. In bed all morning, then went a walk down Heather Lane.

31st March 1950 Friday
Gave Maid of the Mountains. Came home in D. O. V. Enid drove us home. I went up on the 7-20 bus.

1st April 1950 Saturday
Cocky came to Show. Had Bouquet of pink carnations. Busy morning at work.

Note – For the 2nd time I appeared on stage in Coalville "Amateurs" production – this year "Maid of the Mountains". Cocky came to see the show & was enraptured by the romantic story.

2nd April 1950 Sunday
Went to Church with Rob. Choir sang Golden City. Met Cocky in afternoon at St. Mary's Church, and then went up Friar's field.

3rd April 1950 Monday
Cocky & Rob went to the pictures to see **The Red Pony**, and afterwards came in home for a drink. M. at Ashby all night.

4th April 1950 Tuesday
Stayed overtime. Caught 7-20 bus home. M. at Ashby all night. Yesterday bought **Brown & Yellow** wool.

5th April 1950 Wednesday
Again came home on 7-20 bus. Knitting cardigan at night. M. at Ashby.

6th April 1950 Thursday
Came home on 7-20 bus. Cocky came & helped wind some wool. M. at Ashby all night.

7th April 1950 Good Friday
Went to work in morning only. Went down woods in afternoon with Rob.
Went to church at night.

8th April 1950 Saturday
Went to work until 2 p.m. Office full of folk. Yesterday was the 14th day for taxing quarterly. Bad as January. Went on bus in morning with Sam Geary.

9th April 1950 Easter Sunday
Went to Communion at 7 with Cocky (4th in my life). Went to church at night. Walked home with Cocky.

Note – Easter Day & Cocky & I were together again at 7a.m. Holy Communion.
Our shaky relationship continued anew, but things went from bad to worse.

10th April 1950 Easter Monday
Very blowy, rainy day. M. at Ashby in afternoon. Cocky came in afternoon. Had tea chez-nous & then dug for Rob. I slept chez-dosh.

11th April 1950 Tuesday
Very rainy day. I stayed in & knitted.

12th April 1950 Wednesday
Cocky went to Leicester on our bus.
He went to pictures in afternoon & we went to see Peter **Casson**, hypnotist, at night.

13th April 1950 Thursday
Came home on 7-20 bus. M. at Ashby all night.
Cocky dug the field for Rob & then stayed in with us.

14th April 1950 Friday
I felt very ill at night. M. at Ashby. Cocky tout worried.

15th April 1950 Saturday
Should have been my Saturday morning off but I had to go.
M. at Ashby. Cocky came in till past midnight.
Put clocks on.

16th April 1950 Sunday
I stayed in bed till 3 p.m. Went to church at night. M. at Ashby. Cocky came in after church.

17th April 1950 Monday
M. at Ashby all night. Rainy day.
Cocky went to pictures, called in about 10. I went to bed just after 9.

18th April 1950 Tuesday
M. went to hear **Lady Nutting** talk on Russia. I came home on 6-20 bus. Cocky came in at night.

19th April 1950 Wednesday
Went to Harry Sutton's with Cocky for some cigarettes.

20th April 1950 Thursday
Went with Cocky to take **Frank Nicholls** some forms for taxing van. Then went to Nield's for some milk & then to **Wilf's** for cup of tea.

21st April 1950 Friday
M. at Ashby all night. I stayed in Knitting.
Rob went with Johnny Dolman to Plough.

22nd April 1950 Saturday
Went a walk with Cocky down dumbalows. We came across Doreen Willars. Then we went to Hanford's & stayed in our house till 11-30. M. at Ashby all night.

23rd April 1950 Sunday
Cocky & I went a walk in afternoon down dumbalows. M. on 4 to 8. Cocky came for tea. Then we went Church & Cocky came in till 10.

24th April 1950 Monday
Cocky went to pictures alone & we all went to bed early.

25th April 1950 Tuesday
Did some Knitting at night & went to bed about 10.

26th April 1950 Wednesday
Rob & I went & stayed with Peter & Lesley while Don & Phyl went to the pictures.

27th April 1950 Thursday
I stayed with Peter & Lesley till 8-30 & Mummy stayed with them till 12.
Cocky came till about 10.

28th April 1950 Friday
Went walk with Cocky down dumbalows, till 8 o'clock. Then came home & washed my hair.

29th April 1950 Saturday
Went with Cocky on Mrs Swanwick's trip to Coventry ice show, & after down Ibstock Lane. I bought pyjamas from Rowes wool shop. Had my dinner at Leicester.

30th April 1950 Sunday
Got up at 3-30 p.m. Went to church with Beryl Kerr & Rob, then walk with Cocky.   Cocky came in but M. in panch. *(Pantry)*

1st May 1950 Monday
Cocky went to the pictures. Je restai chez moi et multos lacrimos. Uncle Fred came about me.

Note – "Multos lacrimos" – many tears as Uncle Fred, my dad's eldest brother, acting in lieu of my father, came to discuss this unsuitable relationship of Cocky & me, with my poor old Mum, who struggled to keep house & home together, working all night.

2nd May 1950 Tuesday
De neaiveau multos lacrimos. I went walk with Judy down grave after crying in our field.
M. at Ashby all night.

3rd May 1950 Wednesday
I went down to the grave with Cocky. M. at Ashby all night.

4th May 1950 Thursday
Joan came down & we went a walk down Heather Lane. Cocky came in for drink about 9-30.

5th May 1950 Friday
I took some narcissi down to Granddad's grave. Called in at Don's & saw his French nude books. Cocky at farm till 10-15.

6th May 1950 Saturday
Rainy day. M. at Ashby until 8 o'clock.

7th May 1950 Sunday
M. at Ashby 2-6. I took some tulips down to Daddy's grave. Cocky there. Came home with Cocky. Had Bath. Went to church with Cocky.

8th May 1950 Monday
I went to the dentists in afternoon & had my first tooth out with gas.

9th May 1950 Tuesday
Pam came out of hospital so Les away today & rest of week. Joan came down at night & we went walk.

10th May 1950 Wednesday
M. 4-8. I went down to Heather Lane Bridge with Cocky. Marje came in about 8-30 & helped me with my frock.

11th May 1950 Thursday
Went to the Baths 1st time this year with Joan. We got in for nothing. Later saw Cocky & went walk up Wash Lane.

12th May 1950 Friday
A collision at corner between cycle & car. Went ride with John Dolman at night round Hinckley way in his car.

Note – To the rescue comes a new Lochinvar, John Dolman, son of another local farmer, only too willing to be my boy-friend. His family and mine blended perfectly together. Unlike Cocky, he owns a car, & whisks me off for a ride. So now I have two boy-friends at once.

13th May 1950 Saturday
My Saturday morning off. Stayed in bed all morning. Biked to Ashby in afternoon for cheese ration. Glenn Magna British Legion concert party at stute. Rob went. Cocky & I went up Fryer's field. Lovely hot day.

14th May 1950 Sunday
Went a walk in the afternoon & to church at night with Cocky.

15th May 1950 Monday
M. on nights. I stayed in & knitted.

16th May 1950 Tuesday
M. at Ashby all night. I stayed in & knitted & went walk alone.

17th May 1950 Wednesday
Cocky came on his new bike. M. at Ashby.

18th May 1950 Thursday
I went to Baths with Joan. Cocky met us out & bought some chips. Came home & Cocky stayed till 11-30.

19th May 1950 Friday
I stayed in & started knitting cardigan for Michael.

20th May 1950 Saturday
Had renovated mowing machine from **Stanley**. Rob & I went to the graveyard at night till nearly 10, cutting grass.

21st May 1950 Sunday
M. 2-6. Cocky came in afternoon & had tea. We went to church after. Came out in terrific storm.

22nd May 1950 Monday
Went to Amateur meeting at night. Cocky met me out & we biked round Hoo Ash.

23rd May 1950 Tuesday
Stayed in at night knitting Michael's cardigan. That'n came so felt bad.

24th May 1950 Wednesday
Called at Joan's to tell her I couldn't go baths.
Saw Cocky in Wash Lane, walked down with him.

25th May 1950 Thursday
Stayed in at night knitting Michael's cardigan.

26th May 1950 Friday
Stayed in at night knitting.

27th May 1950 Saturday
Went with Cocky to Brooksby Hall gymkhana.

28th May 1950 Sunday
Went with Cocky to Church.

29th May 1950 Whit Monday
Went down to the graveyard in the morning & cut grass.

30th May 1950 Tuesday
Went to Ibstock gymkhana in afternoon with Rob, Cocky, Jack & Phil.

31st May 1950 Wednesday
Started back to work. Had a record day of licences. Cocky came at night & put up wire netting.

1st June 1950 Thursday
Went to baths with Joan. Cocky met me out & we went & had some chips & went to Jay Bee. I bought green vase for grave.

2nd June 1950 Friday
Went to see Old Mother Riley at Rex with Cocky & Rob.

3rd June 1950 Saturday
Very hot day. Norma married. I cut grass in afternoon at graveyard.

Note – Cousin Norma Hewes married. I was not invited. Uncle Hedley was not invited. "Never mind," he said to me, "I will come to your wedding."

4th June 1950 Sunday
Scorching hot day. Cocky, Rob & I went ride down Heather Lane. Cocky & I went to church at night & later sat on lawn.

5th June 1950 Monday
M. on nights. Rob was out with John Dolman at night. Cocky came & left about 11-30.

6th June 1950 Tuesday
I stayed with Don's kids until 10-30. Cocky came in with Rob. Bruce Woodcock beaten.

7th June 1950 Wednesday
M. at Ashby all night. I went up to Ravo chip shop & came home with Cocky.

8th June 1950 Thursday
Cocky took Judy to the vets. Joan & I went cycle ride round Farm Town. Cocky came in later.

9th June 1950 Friday
Cocky hoeing for his uncle Joe until 9. I met him up Wash Lane & we came in & put ointment on Judy's moist eczema.

10th June 1950 Saturday
My Saturday morning off but I went to work because Mr Rose on holiday. Cocky & I took Judy to Vets (Mr Cockburn's) then came home & put ointment on her.

11th June 1950 Sunday
Cocky & I went bike ride over Mill Dam in afternoon & then to Ravo Church Anniversary at night.

12th June 1950 Monday
Went down to the grave at night & cut grass.
Pat went to fetch Bunt home for Little Garg's funeral.

(Note by Mary Blue – Little Garg = Grandma Stacey who died 11th June)

13th June 1950 Tuesday
Mummy on 2-6. I stayed in at night knitting Cocky's pullover.

14th June 1950 Wednesday
Did not balance! Saw Tony Wisher in Lewis's, came down lift with him. **Started Piano Teaching** myself. Listened to Jamaica Inn.

15th June 1950 Thursday
Went to Baths with Joan. Cocky met me out & we had some chips. Rainy day.

16th June 1950 Friday
Cocky & I took Judy to the vets.

17th June 1950 Saturday
M. on nights. Cocky, Jack & Phil working at Uncle Joe's until 9-30. I went up & had some crisps & pop with them at Wrights Kings Head. Came home & Cocky came in until 12.

18th June 1950 Sunday
Cocky & I went to church. Cocky came in at night.

19th June 1950 Monday
Joan & I went a bike ride round Heather & Ibstock. Elle venait de finu avec Don.

20th June 1950 Tuesday
Cocky working late at night all week. I stayed in & knitted pullover.

21st June 1950 Wednesday
Stayed in & knitted, then listened to Jamaica Inn.

22nd June 1950 Thursday
Went to baths with Joan & came straight home.

23rd June 1950 Friday
Cocky, Rob & I took Judy to Vets. Cocky got the funnies. Vet not very amicable.

24th June 1950 Saturday
Cocky came in at night till presque minuit. Rob watching television until nearly 11.   M. on nights.

25th June 1950 Sunday
I stayed in bed until 4. Went to church at night with

Cocky then we went a walk over Bennion's & Mill Dam & back Heather Lane.

26ᵗʰ June 1950 Monday
M. on nights. I stayed in knitting at night then took Judy to Steve's to get bike & came up with Cocky. Had ¼ return in morning.

27ᵗʰ June 1950 Tuesday
I stayed in at Knight Knitting Cocky's pullover, then went a walk down woods.

28ᵗʰ June 1950 Wednesday
Stayed in at Knight Knitting pullover.
Judy not at all well.

29ᵗʰ June 1950 Thursday
Went to baths with Joan. Bought blue wool at dinner & started knitting cardigan for M.

30ᵗʰ June 1950 Friday
Cocky took Judy to the vets & I went to meet him coming home. Came home across fields.

1ˢᵗ July 1950 Saturday
Cocky & I took Judy walk round Mary's Lane. Took some roses to grave & saw Snibby Vicar. Then we went on 8 bus to Coalville & had some chips at Parker's. Walked home across jitty & Grange.

2ⁿᵈ July 1950 Sunday
In bed until 2. Then went sun bathing on lawn & knitted Fair Isle. Went to church at night with Cocky. Cocky came in until about 11 p.m.

3ʳᵈ July 1950 Monday
Went to Amateur meeting & decided to do Desert Song. Came out at 9 & I biked home. Cocky went to pictures.

4ᵗʰ July 1950 Tuesday
I went to see **Pinky** at Rex with Rob. Cocky met us off bus.

5ᵗʰ July 1950 Wednesday
Judy Buried. Mummy went to Inner Wheel dinner with Phyl.

6ᵗʰ July 1950 Thursday
Stayed overtime to do the D. L. reminders. Came home on 7-20 bus. Poured with rain at 5. Came home with Vic Studly.

7ᵗʰ July 1950 Friday
Stayed overtime again & came home on 7-20. Went to bed early.

8ᵗʰ July 1950 Saturday
Finished work at 1. Only Mr Rose, Frank & I doing D. L's. Les' last day at Skeggy after his week's holiday. Went walk with Cocky at night down woods & through Land's hay field. I finished his yellow pullover in afternoon & gave it him at night.

9ᵗʰ July 1950 Sunday
Our office outing to Hunstanton. Got up at 5-45 a.m. &

biked with Cocky up to Coalville. Glorious hot day.

10ᵗʰ July 1950 Monday
Stayed overtime till 6-30. **Started digging up High St. in Leicester to remove tram rails.**

11ᵗʰ July 1950 Tuesday
Caught 6-30 bus home. Went walk with Cocky at night. He gave me £3 to get some shoes for my birthday. M. 2-6.

12ᵗʰ July 1950 Wednesday
Bought my white shoes. Stayed overtime.

13ᵗʰ July 1950 Thursday
Pam started back to work. Went to baths with Joan. Started trying to dive.

14ᵗʰ July 1950 Friday
Finished work at 5-30. Bought Birthday cake from Winn's. Went walk with Cocky & cut grave.

15ᵗʰ July 1950 Saturday
Did not finish work until 2. I was famished. Had dinner at 2-15 at Woolworth's.

16ᵗʰ July 1950 Sunday
Went to church at night & sat with Rob & Cocky. Then went walk down to Schweppes barn.

17ᵗʰ July 1950 Monday
Had 1ˢᵗ Amateur practice this season. Finished at 9-20 & walked home with Howard Hickin.

18ᵗʰ July 1950 Tuesday
Went to see "**Trottie True**" with Cocky & Rob & then walked home.

19ᵗʰ July 1950 Wednesday
Stayed in at night knitting. Felt ill in afternoon. Mrs Nicholls gave me Sal Volatale. Went to Don's later & watched television.

20ᵗʰ July 1950 Thursday
Joan went to baths seule. I stayed in and knitted blue cardigan.

21ˢᵗ July 1950 Friday
Stayed in at night knitting. Went to bed early.

22ⁿᵈ July 1950 Saturday
Went & took flowers to Ravo church with Cocky. Called in at Mrs Hancock's & had drink of her wine. M. 4-8.

23ʳᵈ July 1950 Sunday
Got up at 2. Went to church at night & then Cocky & I went over Mill Dam.

24ᵗʰ July 1950 Monday
Went to Amateur practice. Biked home with Enid. Then stopped talking to J. Dolman till 10. Met Cocky off 10 bus.

25ᵗʰ July 1950 Tuesday
Stayed in at night knitting blue cardigan. Cocky came in

about 9 & wound some wool.

26th July 1950 Wednesday
Stayed in knitting after going down to grave with Cocky & cutting down no end of stinging nettles.

27th July 1950 Thursday
Went to baths with Joan. Swam length for 1st time. Cocky cut hedge for Rob at night.

28th July 1950 Friday
Went with Cocky & Rob to see Don's *(next bit illegible)* at Coalville. Rob biked home & I walked with Cocky over Bridges.

29th July 1950 Saturday
Had my hair permed at night by Phyl. Yesterday bought iron for Mummy.

30th July 1950 Sunday
Rainy evening. Went to Church with Cocky then Rob & I went to Don's & watched Alexander play on television.

31st July 1950 Monday
Went to Amateurs. Cocky went to pictures & we biked home together after having some chips at Stock's.

6th August 1950 Sunday
Went to church with Cocky, then walk over Mill Dam fields.

12th August 1950 Saturday
Went to Devon. Set out at 6 a.m. Pouring with rain at night.

Note – Don & family take me with them on holiday again to Goodrington.

13th August 1950 Sunday
Went on the beach all day. I went in sea in morning.

20th August 1950 Sunday
I nearly fainted in morning at Paignton Church Communion.

22nd August 1950 Tuesday
Rainy evening so went to see play "Paragon" in Paignton.

23rd August 1959 Wednesday
Went to Hall Sands past Blackpool Bay to see Phyl & Eric's Cousin Alice. Had photos taken on his fishing boat.

12th October 1950 Thursday
Went with Cocky to Leicester Palace to see **Anton Karas, Max Wall** & Robert Moreton.

21st October 1950 Saturday
Put clocks back.

22nd October 1950 Sunday
Cocky & Rob put wire netting in field.

23rd October 1950 Monday
Went to Amateurs on 7-20 bus & home in taxi with Cocky.

24th October 1950 Tuesday
M. at Ashby all night. Rob & I went to bed early.

25th October 1950 Wednesday
Charlie Parrock came into our office at 11 a.m. Then we went to Acaris for Ainmen. M. at Ashby all night. Cocky came.

28th October 1950 Saturday
Cocky & I went to Ebenezer to see Ingrid Hageman & Alfred Swain. Rob stayed chez dosh. M. at Ashby.

4th November 1950 Saturday
Uncle Cyril arresta complet nostra pecunia.

Note – Uncle Cyril, who reduced my Mum's £1 a week for life to ten shillings in August 1948, has now cancelled payment altogether.

9th November 1950 Thursday
Our set of pots came. Cocky & I went to see Old Mother Riley.

26th November 1950 Sunday
Went to Don's for tea. Mr & Mrs Ryley, Christopher & John there.

28th November 1950 Tuesday
Had dinner with Charlie.

29th November 1950 Wednesday
Cocky came at night. M. at Ashby.

10th December 1950 Sunday
Jack Botterill burned. Funeral service at night.

13th December 1950 Wednesday
Cocky came & we read Billy Bunter.

14th December 1950 Thursday
Heavy fall of snow. M. at Ashby all night. Cocky came. Rob did not come in till 11-30 p.m.

* * *

E.G. Monthly Pay Gross £12-13s-4d.
Net Pay £11-4s-5d.
Bicycle bought 19-2-49
1403 miles 19-2-50

1951

19th January 1951 Friday
Went for first rehearsal this year at Fox & Goose straight from work at 9 o'clock.

24th January 1951 Wednesday
Barbara & Frank engaged. Barbara's birthday.

28th January 1951 Sunday
Had a bath at Pat's.

30th January 1951 Tuesday
Washed my hair.

31st January 1951 Wednesday
Went to rehearsal at Fox & Goose.

8th February 1951 Thursday
Gave Desert Song.

9th February 1951 Friday
Desert Song.

10th February 1951 Saturday
Desert Song.

16th February 1951 Friday
Had Amateur Dinner Dance.

21st February 1951 Wednesday
Bought hockey boots.

24th February 1951 Saturday
Played hockey for 1st time in ages against Leicester & lost 4-1.

26th February 1951 Monday
Saw 107 at 5-30 by Woolworth's.

27th February 1951 Tuesday
Went with Cocky to see "**Danny Kaye**" as the Inspector General.

1st March 1951 Thursday
Went with Mammy to De Mont to see the ballet. Saw 107.

6th March 1951 Tuesday
Ivor Novello died.

10th March 1951 Saturday
Saw 107 but for 4th consecutive time Nullos "Vales".

15th March 1951 Thursday
Went with Cocky to see "The Countess of Monte Christo" (Sonia Henie)

17th March 1950 Saturday
Went with Cocky to the Baths to concert,

19th March 1951 Monday
Went with Cocky to see "Gone to Earth".

26th March 1951 Easter Monday
Marie engaged to Neville Hewes.

4th April 1951 Wednesday
Found 2/- at Woolworth's. Came to work in Don's car. Went walk with Cocky at night.

10th April 1951 Tuesday
Cocky & I went to Leicester Opera House to see "**Who on Earth**".

11th April 1951 Wednesday
We had our chimney on fire.

12th April 1951 Thursday
Cocky & I went to see "Old Mother Ryley".

14th April 1951 Saturday
Mr Ernest Bevin Died.
<u>**Cocky went to Lancashire.**</u>
Hockey Tournament at Leicester. Clocks put on 1 hour.

Note – Cocky & I try living apart from each other. Cocky goes to work on a farm in Lancashire.

15th April 1951 Sunday
I went to church with Jack & Phil. Came home with Enid.

16th April 1951 Monday
Submarine "**Affray**" went down. We had Amateur meeting.

17th April 1951 Tuesday
Mummy, Rob & I all had a bath.

18th April 1951 Wednesday
Rob & I went to see "Over the Garden Wall" at The Rex.

19th April 1951 Thursday
Mary Moore came for tea.

20th April 1951 Friday
Mummy went to London to stay at Hale's. I had the day off. Lovely sunny day.

21st April 1951 Saturday
I had poly foto taken. Very funny play on Saturday Night Theatre - "Half a Loaf"

3rd May 1951 Thursday
Auntie Lizzie died. The King opened Festival.

12th May 1951 Saturday
I went to **Cark** in **Cartmel**, met Cocky at 9 p.m. in **Manchester**.

Note – Whitsuntide Bank Holiday & I join Cocky for a long week-end together at Cark in Cartmel. He meets me off the train at Manchester & we are happy to be re-united.

13th May 1951 Whit Sunday
Went to church in Flookburgh.

14th May 1951 Whit Monday
Went to Morecambe & to Heysham Head.

15th May 1951 Tuesday
Came home from Lancs. Cocky had his hair cut in Manchester.

23rd May 1951 Wednesday
Duchess of Kent came to Leicester.

26th May 1951 Saturday
Les fell down rubble in his back yard into empty cavern.

27th May 1951 Sunday
Ravo Sermons.

2nd June 1951 Saturday
I had my hair permed at Glynn's.

3rd June 1951 Sunday
Went pic nic in afternoon with Don & family up the forest.

6th June 1951 Wednesday
Mummy on nights.

7th June 1951 Thursday
Rob in bed all day.
Came down at night to hear Paul Temple.

8th June 1951 Friday
Rob in bed all day.
Came down at night to hear "Adventures in Wonderland" with W. Pickles.

10th June 1951 Sunday
My Dear Brother Binus Died. 5-30 p.m.

Note – My 17 year old brother Rob dies after suffering a non-stop attack of epileptic fits. I am devastated, but Mum is relieved to know that all his suffering is over. Her great worry was how he would cope in later years. Now, more than ever, I want Cocky with me, & Cocky comes home briefly to help me through this sad time.

12th June 1951 Tuesday
Cocky came home. Arrived 9-30 p.m.

14th June 1951 Thursday
Cocky went back. He & I called at 14 Friar Lane in afternoon.

15th June 1951 Friday
Mummy & I went to Ashby for dinner & then to see Jo.

16th June 1951 Saturday
Barbara & Frank married.

14th July 1951 Saturday
Went with Auntie Doris & Mummy to Wigston to Hilda's for tea. Then to Cropston to fetch Micky.

15th July 1951 Sunday
Went ride in car with Don & family. Went to Traveller's Joy for tea.

19th July 1951 Thursday
Went with Muriel to see Miss Roberts & took her some flowers.

21st July 1951 Saturday
Went to Mablethorpe with Helen on the Sunday School outing.

22nd July 1951 Sunday
I gave Micky a bath. Went to church at night with Mummy.

24th July 1951 Tuesday
Mummy & I took Micky a walk through Normanton Woods.

4th August 1951 Saturday
Cocky came home from Lancs. for week's holiday. I met him at Leicester station.

12th August 1951 Sunday
Cocky went back to Lancs. Don took him in car to Leicester.

16th August 1951 Thursday
Cocky came home from Lancashire to stop.

Note – After 4 months in Lancashire, Cocky is home to stay.

18th August 1951 Saturday
Went with Cocky to Theatre Royal to see "The Breadwinner".

20th August 1951 Monday
Went with Cocky to Theatre Royal to see "When we are Married".

25th August 1951 Saturday
We went to Devon. Set off at 6-30 a.m. Got up at 4 a.m. I slept at Don's last night.

Note – Again, Don & family include me on their summer holiday to Goodrington.

29th August 1951 Wednesday
Went to pictures to see Bing Crosby in "Here Comes the Groom".

31st August 1951 Friday
Went to the Nile Bar & came across Segerdals.

1st September 1951 Saturday
Eric & Rene Wilkinson left Goodrington to go to Ilfracombe. We saw **Randon family**.

6th September 1951 Thursday
On 6th September 1651 Charles II spent the night in an oak tree at Boscobel following defeat at the Battle of Worcester.

30th November 1951 Friday
Aunt Sarah (Mrs Fairbrother next door to Plough) died.

4th December 1951 Tuesday
Chatham Marine Cadets killed by bus.

* * *

1952

1st January 1952 Tuesday
First fall of snow this winter.

3rd January 1952 Thursday
Saw the new 107 for first time.

20th January 1952 Sunday
I cut my hair.

31st January 1952 Thursday
The end of overtime.

6th February 1952 Wednesday
My Dear King Died. *(King George VI)*

8th February 1952 Friday
Went to Leicester Castle to hear Elizabeth II proclaimed
"**Queen of England**".

9th February 1952 Saturday
Went to Nottingham to see Panto: - **Puss in Boots**.

21st February 1952 Thursday
Cocky & I went to see **Frankie Howerd** at **The Palace**.
Got a puncture en route.

26th February 1952 Shrove Tuesday
Mummy went to Hale's.

27th February 1952 Ash Wednesday
Cocky & I went to see **Peter Brough** & **Archie
Andrews** at The Palace.

1st March 1952 Saturday
I had my hair permed. Mummy came back from London.

11th March 1952 Tuesday
Budget Day.

21st April 1952 Monday
Took Micky to the Vet with Eczema.

1st May 1952 Thursday
Went with Pat to see "The Greatest Show on Earth".

21st May 1952 Wednesday
Marie married.

31st May 1952 Saturday
Went to see "Kings Rhapsody" at Coventry.

1st June 1952 Sunday
Went to Ludlow with Pat, Evelyn & Mary.

2nd June 1952 Monday
Margaret White married.

4th June 1952 Wednesday
Made a record issue of D. L.s 456!

6th June 1952 Friday
Betsy's 21st Birthday. Betsy Engaged.

25th June 1952 Wednesday
Cocky & I went to Regal to see "Painting the Clouds
with Sunshine".

26th June 1952 Thursday
Diximus Vale. *Note – "Diximus Vale" - Here we go
again, trying to say "Goodbye".*

28th June 1952 Saturday
Ron Burder married.

14th July 1952 Monday
*Note – I reach the age of 21, but my diary records
nothing. "Will you be getting engaged on your 21st
birthday?" "No" I reply to my colleagues at work. Betsy
at work proudly displayed her new engagement ring on
her 21st birthday on June 6th . I simply escaped with
Mum for a few days away in the Lake District.*

15th August 1952 Friday
The worst flash-flood in British history struck the town
of Lynmouth, at the foot of Exmoor in Devon. A
massive 229mm of rain fell on Exmoor in just two days,
resulting in a surge of water and debris smashing
through Lynmouth. Thirty four people lost their lives.

23rd August 1952 Saturday
I went by bus to Bournemouth.

3rd September 1952 Wednesday
In 1752 what should have been September 3rd became
September 14th with the introduction of the Gregorian
calendar and crowds flocked through the streets crying:
"Give us back our 11 days". Documents, registers and
records of the time are chaotic.

25th September 1952 Thursday
I had the day off from work to go to the dentists. 2 teeth
filled.

29th September 1952 Monday
John Cobb killed on Loch Ness.

1st October 1952 Wednesday
I bought pink slippers.

2nd October 1952 Thursday
We had the tables covered at work down below.

8th October 1952 Wednesday
Harrow triple train disaster.

14th November 1952 Friday
Had first libretto practice.

25th November 1952 Tuesday
"**The Mousetrap**" opened at the Ambassadors Theatre,
London.

5th December 1952 Friday
New Queen stamps came out. Went to see Jimmy Jewel.

6th December 1952 Saturday
Smog enveloped London and killed more than 4,000
people in less than a week.

1953

16th January 1953 Friday
Stephen Anthony Hewes born.

17th January 1953 Saturday
My Saturday off. Micky died.

1st February 1953 Sunday
East Coast Flood Devastation.

14th February 1953 Saturday
End of overtime.

20th February 1953 Friday
Arthur Turner died.

21st February 1953 Saturday
Went to see "Waltz Time" at Coventry.

28th February 1953 Saturday
Pam left work. Went to see Mikado at Ashby.

5th March 1953 Thursday
Stalin Died.

7th March 1953 Saturday
Betsy married.

14th March 1953 Saturday
Jill Lambert married Gig.

24th March 1953 Tuesday
Queen Mary Died.

26th March 1953 Thursday
Gave "Waltz Time".

8th April 1953 Wednesday
Kathleen started work.

14th April 1953 Tuesday
Bought grey short coat.

12th June 1953 Friday
Went to London with Auntie Cis.

13th June 1953 Saturday
Saw The Queen.

14th June 1953 Sunday
Went to Epping Forest.

15th June 1953 Monday
Went ride up forest with J.D.

Note – John Dolman does his best to capture my heart, taking me in his car here, there & everywhere. We go for moonlight rides to the choicest parts of Charnwood Forest. He takes me to see Leicester City football matches, to the cinema & even to Wembley to see Hungary beat England 6-3, but all to no avail. I cannot fall in love with him.

16th June 1953 Tuesday
Overslept. Caught 9 a.m. bus from Coalville to work.

20th June 1953 Saturday
Had a Toni Home Perm.

30th June 1953 Tuesday
Bought white blouse.

1st July 1953 Wednesday
Bought dress.

4th July 1953 Saturday
Audrey Clarke married.
Worked overtime for the whole of July.

2nd August 1953 Sunday
Went to Newbold Verdon to see Marie. Saw Stephen for first time.

15th August 1953 Saturday
Jill Wallis had baby.

17th August 1953 Monday
Mrs Deeming died.

19th August 1953 Wednesday
We beat Australia & won The Ashes after 19 years.

22nd August 1953 Saturday
Pat Gamble married.

28th August 1953 Friday
Had a Eugène Perm.

29th August 1953 Saturday
Went to Newquay.

Note – Don & family take me on holiday to a different resort this year – to Newquay, & we manage to see Lands End.

4th September 1953 Friday
Went to Land's End.

19th September 1953 Saturday
Went to Scampton with J. D. Tony Wisher married. Aunt Aggie buried.

22nd September 1953 Tuesday
Went to Statutes with Cocky. Received cheque for £5 ″ 13s ″1d. for 2nd Dividend football sweep.

7th November 1953 Saturday
Went to see my first football match, Leicester v. Hull at Leicester. Leicester lost after 14 previous consecutive wins.

8th November 1953 Sunday
Yesterday Sylvia left.

14th November 1953 Saturday
Went with J.D. to Nottingham to football match & pictures.

25th November 1953 Wednesday
Went to Wembley to see Hungary beat England 6-3.

5th December 1953 Saturday
Oxygen. Went to see Leicester City beat Brentford 6-0.

6th December 1953 Sunday
Went to Marie's.

8th December 1953 Tuesday
5/- short at work.

* * *

1954

4th January 1954 Monday
Alterations begun chez-nous.

Note – At home, we have the back bedroom converted into a bathroom.

28th January 1954 Thursday
Went to N.F.U. dance at De Mont.

30th January 1954 Saturday
Had first bath & shower in new bathroom. My Saturday off from work.

31st January 1954 Sunday
Had photos taken for "Good Night Vienna".

2nd February 1954 Tuesday
Received cheque for £15 "11s "10d. for 3rd Dividend football sweep.

6th February 1954 Saturday
End of overtime.

13th February 1954 Saturday
Pat went to Panto at Coventry & had second attack of illness.

19th February 1954 Friday
Mr Roberts called in to Amateurs to take part on account of Pat falling out.

20th February 1954 Saturday
Joe died.

23rd February 1954 Tuesday
Miss Rippon's birthday. Had cakes at work at Happy's expense.

1st March 1954 Monday
The United States destroyed the Pacific island of Bikini Atoll with a hydrogen bomb hundreds or times more powerful than the weapons that devastated Hiroshima and Nagasaki in 1945.

4th March 1954 Thursday
Our dear Rector died.

Note – The Revd. Dowling, Rector of Ravenstone, died after a life-time nurturing not only my generation, but my Mum before me , in the Christian religion. All his long years of accumulated learning & wisdom now ceased to be.

25th March 1954 Thursday
Gave "Good Night Vienna".

31st March 1954 Wednesday
Petulengro took old fear off chest parmi multos lacrimos.

3rd April 1954 Saturday
Charlie came into the office.

4th April 1954 Sunday
Had long talk with Cocky after church parmi multos lacrimos.

Note – Cocky made one final effort to offer me a future as his wife. We could go away together & live happily ever after. But I could not live happily ever after, estranged from my family, & with children who could not share the love of both families.

5th April 1954 Monday
Dixi Vale Ad J.D.

Note - I chose to make a complete break. At one & the same time I stopped going out with either Cocky or John Dolman.

6th April 1954 Tuesday
I had audition with Lillian Dunkley. Cocky came at night. Pat came too for a while. Mummy on night duty. Rurous multos lacrimos.

Note - The decision was final.

7th April 1954 Wednesday
Had letter from J.D. I wrote letter to Mummy. Had my hair cut at Gaunt's.

Note – I wrote a letter to my Mum confirming my intentions: "Cocky & I have decided not to marry, but we will always love one another. In the knowledge of that love, we will be happy."
Needless to say, it was all very sad, but at least we all knew exactly where we now stood. The dithering was over.

10th April 1954 Saturday
Went with Pat & family to Worcestershire. Called to see Bunting. Auntie Cis bought caravan.

13th April 1954 Tuesday
Had first singing lesson.

Note – Maybe I shall become a famous singer. I take up singing lessons with Lilian Dunkley.
Maybe I shall marry some-one rich & famous.
I never see any-one remotely appealing.

21st April 1954 Wednesday
Issued 630 D.Ls.

22nd April 1954 Thursday
David on 5-45.

23rd April 1954 Friday
Stayed 2hrs. O.T. filing at work.

24th April 1954 Saturday
2nd singing lesson. Had part perm at Gaunt's. Went with Enid to Grammar School at night.

30th April 1954 Friday
3rd singing lesson (paid). Kathleen left work.

2nd May 1954 Sunday
Mr Raith came. Paul. E. L. Timson born.

6th May 1954 Thursday
Had the afternoon off for H. H. interview.

8th May 1954 Saturday
4th singing lesson. Leicester College Rag Day.

15th May 1954 Saturday
5th singing lesson. Queen arrived home.

16th May 1954 Sunday
Went to Margaret Hewes' at Lichfield.

19th May 1954 Wednesday
Went to Reg's funeral service at Kildare St.

21st May 1954 Friday
Enid had letter from Butlin's to say we were in at Clacton for August 21st.

22nd May 1954 Saturday
6th singing lesson

27th May 1954 Thursday
Went to dentist's in Halford St. & had teeth cleaned.

28th May 1954 Friday
7th singing lesson. My 1st Friday afternoon off with Saturday morning.

2nd June 1954 Wednesday
8th singing lesson.

18th June 1954 Friday
9th singing lesson.

25th June 1954 Friday
10th singing lesson.

26th June 1954 Saturday
Went to Worcester with Pat, Evelyn & Mary. Went to Bunt's at night.

30th June 1954 Wednesday
Received bus tickets for Clacton.

3rd July 1954 Saturday
Singing lesson. 2nd term - No 1.

9th July 1954 Friday
Induction of new Rector - Maurice Atterbury Thomas.

Note – Ravenstone has a new Rector.

10th July 1954 Saturday
Singing lesson. 2nd term - No 2.

11th July 1954 Sunday
New Rector's first Sunday at church.

17th July 1954 Saturday
Singing lesson. 2nd term – No 3.

23rd July 1954 Friday
Singing lesson. 2nd term – No 4.

24th July 1954 Saturday
Went with Enid to C. G. S. Gala.
Dance at night. Hm Hm.

27th July 1954 Tuesday
Mr Rose left "The Laurels".

28th July 1954 Wednesday
Started D. L. post after 4-30 because of pressure of counter applicants.

29th July 1954 Thursday
Singing lesson. 2nd term – No5.

31st July 1954 Saturday
Bought black bathing suit & black wool.

6th August 1954 Friday
Brenda Sally & Dabble Duck left work.

7th August 1954 Saturday
Bought Revelation suit case.

12th August 1954 Thursday
Storm hit Coalville, electricity off all evening at Ravo.

13th August 1954 Friday
Singing lesson. 2nd term – No 6.
Quote from Daily Mail Friday 13th August -
"Coalville, Leics. saw what it is like when it rains at the rate of 105 tons to the acre in 20 minutes. On the town, half-stilled by the local mining holiday, 1.05in of rain was jettisoned by a vast black cloud between 5-10 and 5-30 p.m."

20th August 1954 Friday
Singing lesson. 2nd term – No 7.

21st August 1954 Saturday
Went to Butlin's, Clacton with Enid.

Note – My first holiday with cousin Enid.

28th August 1954 Saturday
Came home from Clacton.

4th September 1954 Saturday
Singing lesson. 2nd term No 8.

6th September 1954 Monday
First rehearsal of Countess Maritza.

10th September 1954 Friday
Went to Whist Drive at Stute.

11th September 1954 Saturday
Mr Rose's daughter married. Brenda Hewes married.

17th September 1954 Friday
Singing lesson. 2nd term – No 9.

18th September 1954 Saturday
Played hockey at Loughborough Brush & lost 16-1.   1st match of season.

20th September 1954 Monday
Went to doctors & had a week off on account of my knee.

24th September 1954 Friday
Went to Coalville to see **Benny Hill**.

25th September 1954 Saturday
Singing lesson. 2nd term – No 10.
Saw **Benny Hill** at Palace.

26th September 1954 Sunday
Benny Hill was celebrity on "What's My Line?"

29th September 1954 Wednesday
Went to Whitwick to see "**Genevieve**" & "**Mandy**".

30th September 1954 Thursday
Thought I sang très bien
during practice at home. ← (Big 'ed)
Bought green shoes.

1st October 1954 Friday
Singing lesson. 3rd term – No 1.

6th October 1954 Wednesday
Had 1st Church Social at the 'stute. I went with Helen.

8th October 1954 Friday
Singing lesson cancelled because Lilian Dunkley's mother dies.

11th October 1954 Monday
Parts for "Countess Maritza" given out.

13th October 1954 Wednesday
I went with Helen to The Grand for the 1st time.

16th October 1954 Saturday
Singing lesson. 3rd term – No 2.

20th October 1954 Wednesday
Went to dance at The Grand.

22nd October 1954 Friday
Went to Pegson's social & dance with Enid at Fox & Goose.

23rd October 1954 Saturday
Singing lesson. 3rd term – No 3.

25th October 1954 Monday
Had day off for a Sat. Morning.

26th October 1954 Tuesday
Stayed O. T.

27th October 1954 Wednesday
Stayed O. T.

28th October 1954 Thursday
Stayed O. T.

29th October 1954 Friday
Had first reading through of "Countess Maritza".

30th October 1954 Saturday
David Hewes arrived home. Eric Winstone at Coalville.

3rd November 1954 Wednesday
Singing lesson. 3rd term No 4.

6th November 1954 Saturday
Went with Mummy to see **Chu Chin Chow** at Leicester Palace.

12th November 1954 Friday
Singing lesson. 3rd term No 5. Had my tooth out.

20th November 1954 Saturday
Singing lesson. 3rd term – No 6.

25th November 1954 Thursday
Singing lesson. 3rd term – No 7.

27th November 1954 Saturday
Went to see bike at Checketts Rd.

30th November 1954 Tuesday
80th birthday of Sir Winston Churchill.

1st December 1954 Wednesday
Birthday presentations to Sir Winston Churchill.
It is no easy thing for a British statesman to have a statue raised to his honour posthumously in the Palace of Westminster.....

But to Winston Churchill yesterday a singular mark of honour was paid. Under the medieval roof of Westminster Hall the rank and file of contemporary political life, men and women of all parties gathered in a vast company to hail him on his 80th birthday, as the greatest man of his time and to admit him, without delay, as a Freeman of British history.

For the birthday, and the gifts of his own portrait and a volume in which nearly all members of the House of Commons have honoured themselves by inscribing their names to honour him, were not the whole of it. The birthday itself served as the occasion, the gifts justified the ceremony....

The occasion, as Sir Winston Churchill himself said, was unique: "There has never been anything like it in British history, and, indeed, I doubt whether any of the modern democracies abroad have shown such a degree of kindness and generosity to a party politician who has not yet retired and may at any time be involved in controversy."

About him, left and right, sat Cabinet Ministers and Opposition leaders, with their wives. Before him, stretching far back through the gaunt spaces of the hall of history, were drawn up rows of those – 2,500 in number – who had come to pay him tribute....

"I have never accepted," he said, "what many people have kindly said, namely, that I inspired the nation. Their will was resolute and remorseless, and as

it proved, unconquerable. It fell to me to express it, and if I found the right words you must remember that I have always earned my living by my pen and by my tongue. It was the nation and the race dwelling all round the globe that had the lion's heart. I had the luck to be called upon to give"-the manner of his delivery now admirably suited the matter – "the roar."

Mr Attlee, to whom it fell to present Sir Winston Churchill with Mr Graham Sutherland's portrait, struck his sprightliest and wittiest humour in what the recipient fairly described as "a magnanimous appraisal of my variegated career."

The audience burst into laughter when Mr Attlee remarked that he had not come to bury Caesar but to praise him – Caesar indeed –"for you have not only carried on war but have written your own commentaries. We greet you today," ended Mr Attlee, "especially as a great Parliamentarian, the last of the great orators who can touch the heights." His last words were a quotation: "Old age hath yet his honour and his toil……some work of noble note may yet be done."

(newspaper cutting)

2nd December 1954 Thursday
Singing lesson. 3rd term – No 8.

4th December 1954 Saturday
Reeves bridesmaid to Jeff & Shirley.
Happy forecast 9 correct results & won £500 !!!!!

8th December 1954 Wednesday
Raleigh bicycle arrived chez-nous from Leicester.

9th December 1954 Thursday
Singing lesson. 3rd term – No 9.

10th December 1954 Friday
Dr Chick brought Mummy from Ashby at night.

Note – Mum is taken ill. Her face drops on one side, almost like a stroke, & she is seen by a specialist who advises complete rest. She spends a few weeks in hospital.

11th December 1954 Saturday
Specialist came with Dr Chick.

14th December 1954 Tuesday
Went to dentist's for teeth clean & paid him £1. Went to Coalville Tech. for interview.

15th December 1954 Wednesday
Went with Mummy in Don's car to Burton Infirmary.
Leslie Cato (Cuz) killed.

21st December 1954 Tuesday
Singing lesson. 3rd term – No 10.

23rd December 1954 Thursday
Mummy went from Burton to Ashby.

* * *

1955

5th January 1955 Wednesday
Singing lesson. 4th term No 1.

10th January 1955 Monday
Annette Mills died. (Muffin the Mule).

11th January 1955 Tuesday
Tomorrow Mummy comes home from Ashby.

12th January 1955 Wednesday
Singing lesson. 4th term No 2.

19th January 1955 Wednesday
Singing lesson. 4th term No 3.

24th January 1955 Monday
Had day off from work after painful foot.

25th January 1955 Tuesday
O. T. £5 "10/-

26th January 1955 Wednesday
Singing lesson. 4th term No 4.

2nd February 1955 Wednesday
Singing lesson. 4th term No 5.

8th February 1955 Tuesday
O. T. £3 "16s "5d.

9th February 1955 Wednesday
Singing lesson. 4th term No 6.

11th February 1955 Friday
Had £3 "3/- perm for £2.

12th February 1955 Saturday
Went to Worcester.
Mary Moore stayed night with Mummy.

15th February 1955 Tuesday
Peter Martyn died.

16th February 1955 Wednesday
Singing lesson. 4th term No 7.

18th February 1955 Friday
Went for X-Ray.

22nd February 1955 Tuesday
Mummy started back to work.

Note – Mum is well enough to return to work, but she is not 100% fit. Her face is almost back to normal.

23rd February 1955 Wednesday
Singing lesson. 4th term No 8.

24th February 1955 Thursday
Yesterday went to see **Mikado** at B. U.

25th February 1955 Friday
O. T. £3-8-1

2nd March 1955 Wednesday
Singing lesson. 4th term No 9.

5th March 1955 Saturday
Had gift coupon from Stocking Bar. Bought umbrella & cash box.

9th March 1955 Wednesday
Singing lesson. 4th term No 10.

11th March 1955 Friday
Received report from X-Ray = Normal chest.

16th March 1955 Wednesday
Singing lesson. 5th term No 1.

19th March 1955 Saturday
Reg Nadin left work.

24th March 1955 Thursday
Singing lesson. 5th term No 2. Gave Maritza.

25th March 1955 Friday
Maritza.

26th March 155 Saturday
Maritza.

30th March 1955 Wednesday
Singing lesson. 5th term No 3.

2nd April 1955 Saturday
Bought pyjamas & costume.

5th April 1955 Tuesday
Sir Winston Churchill finished as Prime Minister. Auntie Cis had false teeth.

6th April 1955 Wednesday
Singing lesson. 5th term No 4.

8th April 1955 Good Friday
Bunting & Family came to Pat's for Easter Holiday.

9th April 1955 Saturday
Bought photo album, blue plaid.

11th April 1955 Monday
Letter from Butlin's to say we were in at Ocean Hotel.

13th April 1955 Wednesday
Singing lesson. 5th term No 5.

18th April 1955 Monday
Had 2 teeth filled & nearly fainted.

20th April 1955 Wednesday
Singing lesson. 5th term No 6.

21st April 1955 Thursday
Little Theatre fire.

27th April 1955 Wednesday
Singing lesson/ 5th term No 7.

29th April 1955 Friday
Little Mary Blue Passed Scholarship.

4th May 1955 Wednesday
Singing lesson. 5th term No 8. Charlie came into the office.

11th May 1955 Wednesday
Singing lesson. 5th term No 9.

14th May 1955 Saturday
Went to see "**The Dancing Years**" on ice at Coventry. Slept in Auntie Dos' house all alone.

17th May 1955 Tuesday
Up at 4 a.m. to listen to fight on wireless. **It snowed**.

18th May 1955 Wednesday
Singing lesson. 5th term No 10.

21st May 1955 Saturday
Slept at Don's with Harriet. **Mrs Forsyth** had Uncle Cyril & Gladys "**At Home**".

22nd May 1955 Sunday
Slept with little Mary because Auntie Dos at Skegness. I felt very feverish & bad.
Mrs Nightingale at Pat's.

23rd May 1955 Monday
Felt quite bad all day but gradual improvement from yesterday.

24th May 1955 Tuesday
Felt almost 100% again.

25th May 1955 Wednesday
Singing lesson. 6th term No 1.

26th May 1955 Thursday
Election Day.
Went to De Mont at night.

27th May 1955 Friday
Went to De Mont in morning for Count of Melton Division.

28th May 1955 Saturday
Tony Hicks married.

2nd June 1955 Thursday
Mummy went to Skegness with Auntie Cis, Dos & Elizabeth.

3rd June 1955 Friday
Auntie Cis, Dos and Elizabeth came over in evening & played cards until after midnight.

4th June 1955 Saturday
Eileen Holmes married.

5th June 1955 Sunday
Peter Mould came alone for the day.

8th June 1955 Wednesday
Singing lesson. 6th term No 2.

10th June 1955 Friday
Went to Confirmation Service at Hugglescote.

13th June 1955 Monday
Bebe Daniels' Silver Wedding.

14th June 1955 Tuesday
Peter Mould came for the day.

15th June 1955 Wednesday
Singing lesson. 6th term No 3.

29th June 1955 Wednesday
Singing lesson. 6th term No 4.

2nd July 1955 Saturday
Went to Worcester.

6th July 1955 Wednesday
Singing lesson. 6th term No 5.

9th July 1955 Saturday
Princess Margaret came to Leicester. I bought my watch.

13th July 1955 Wednesday
Singing lesson. 6th term No 6.

14th July 1955 Thursday
Lightening struck Ascot. Percy Cooper's wife died.

16th July 1955 Saturday
Reeves went with Tony to Yarmouth.
Disneyland opened in California.

19th July 1955 Tuesday
Mr Raith called at Pat's.

20th July 1955 Wednesday
Singing lesson. 6th term No 7.

6th August 1955 Saturday
Enid & I went to Butlin's Saltdean.

Note - Enid & I have our second holiday.

7th August 1955 Sunday
We met Tony and Mike at evening meal.

8th August 1955 Monday
Enid & I walked into Brighton.

10th August 1955 Wednesday
Tony took us in his Jaguar AVG 788 to Brighton for coffee.

11th August 1955 Thursday
Went with AVG 788 to Brighton. Enid & I sat on the beach all morning.

12th August 1955 Friday
Enid & I went to Newhaven.

13th August 1955 Saturday
Came home from Butlin's.

15th August 1955 Monday
Went by bus to Upton on Severn.

Note – I also spend a few days at Bunting's new home in Upton-on-Severn.

16th August 1955 Tuesday
Climbed the Worcestershire Beacon - 1395ft.

17th August 1955 Wednesday
Dr Baker died.

18th August 1955 Thursday
Came home from Upton on Severn.

19th August 1955 Friday
Started back to work.

20th August 1955 Saturday
Funeral of Dr Baker.

22nd August 1955 Monday
Mummy went to Willoughby for holiday.

24th August 1955 Wednesday
Singing lesson. 6th term No 8.

26th August 1955 Friday
Philip Waltho died.

27th August 1955 Saturday
Peggy Kerr died at Newcastle.

28th August 1955 Sunday
David Christopher Timson born.

31st August 1955 Wednesday
Singing lesson. 6th term No 9.

7th September 1955 Wednesday
Singing lesson. 6th term No 10.

11th September 1955 Sunday
Peter Mould came for the day.

14th September 1955 Wednesday
Singing lesson. 7th term No 1.

21st September 1955 Wednesday
Singing lesson. 7th term No 2.
Cigarette.

22nd September 1955 Thursday
Report at work of stolen money.

28th September 1955 Wednesday
Singing lesson. 7th term No 3.

29th September 1955 Thursday
Dedication of altar cross in memory of Rev. Dowling.

3rd October 1955 Monday
Mummy goes to Hales' October 5-8.

5th October 1955 Wednesday
Singing lesson. 7th term No 4.

6th October 1955 Thursday
Had audition for Carmen in **Rio Rita**.

15th October 1955 Saturday
Went to see **Rio Rita** at Darlaston.

17th October 1955 Monday
Went to Dentists. Nothing doing.

19th October 1955 Wednesday
Singing lesson. 7th term No 5.

21st October 1955 Friday
Had first libretto practice for **Rio Rita**.

22nd October 1955 Saturday
Uncle Cyril not well. In tears.

26th October 1955 Wednesday
Went with Reeves to "**Donald's**" for tea & house warming.

28th October 1955 Friday
Went to Woodhouse to see **Ray Forsyth** in "When We are Married".

31st October 1955 Monday
Sang "Spanish Shawl" for 1st time at rehearsal – Terrible.

Note – Like me Princess Margaret chose not to marry the man she loved & confirmed her intentions in writing

Princess Margaret's personal message was issued from Clarence House at 7-21 p.m.
"I would like it to be known that I have decided not to marry Group Captain Peter Townsend. I have been aware that, subject to my renouncing my rights of succession, it might be possible for me to contract a civil marriage. But, mindful of the church's teaching that Christian marriage is indissoluble, and conscious of my duty to the Commonwealth, I have resolved to put these considerations before any others. I have reached this decision entirely alone, and in doing so I have been strengthened by the unfailing support and devotion of Group Captain Townsend. I am deeply grateful for the concern of all those who have constantly prayed for my happiness."

Margaret.

2nd November 1955 Wednesday
Singing lesson. 7th term No 7.

9th November 1955 Wednesday
Singing lesson. 7th term No 8.

12th November 1955 Saturday
Went to see **Virginia** at Hinckley. Roll Away Clouds!!

14th November 1955 Monday
Sang "Spanish Shawl" for 2nd time at rehearsal – improved.

16th November 1955 Wednesday
Singing lesson. 7th term No 9.

22nd November 1955 Tuesday
Frankie Wilson (caretaker) died.

23rd November 1955 Wednesday
Pat fell at work from stepladder.

7th December 1955 Wednesday
Singing lesson. 7th term No 10.   **Mr Attlee** resigned as leader of Opposition.

14th December 1955 Wednesday
Singing lesson. 8th term No 1.

18th December 1955 Sunday
Peter Mould came for the day.

19th December 1955 Monday
Sang "Spanish Shawl" with improvement.
Vanessa Lee's husband died.

21st December 1955 Wednesday
Singing lesson. 8th term No 2.

23rd December 1955 Friday
Had my hair cold permed.

28th December 1955 Wednesday
Singing lesson. 8th term No 3.

* * *

1956

1st January 1956 Sunday
Peter Mould came for the day.

4th January 1956 Wednesday
Singing lesson. 8th term No 4.

5th January 1956 Thursday
Fog very thick in Leicester, ¾ hr to get from Leicester to Groby. Bought green boots.

11th January 1956 Wednesday
Singing lesson. 8th term No 5.

16th January 1956 Monday
Singing lesson. 8th term No 6.

21st January 1956 Saturday
Sticky left for Kent.

8th February 1956 Wednesday
Singing lesson. 8th term No 7.

15th February 1956 Wednesday
Singing lesson. 8th term No 8.

22nd February 1956 Wednesday
Singing lesson. 8th term No 9.

29th February 1956 Wednesday
Singing lesson. 8th term No 10.

7th March 1956 Wednesday
Singing lesson. 9th term No 1.

10th March 1956 Saturday
Mummy & I in at Skegness.

14th March 1956 Wednesday
Singing lesson. 9th term No 2. Came home from Leicester on 5-45p.m. double decker. Went to sleep & woke up 6-35p.m. in Coalville Garage.

20th March 1956 Tuesday
Rio Rita.

21st March 1956 Wednesday
Phyl had baby.

Note – Don & Phyl have a third baby, Susan, a sister for Peter & Lesley.

21st March 1556
Thomas Cranmer, Archbishop of Canterbury 1533-56, burnt at the stake, Oxford,

28th March 1956 Wednesday
Singing lesson. 9th term No 3.

31st March 1956 Saturday
Bought Mac.

4th April 1956 Wednesday
Singing lesson. 9th term No 4. Barbara Lyon engaged to Mr Russell Turner.

6th April 1956 Friday
Had 2 new summer dresses. Our Dinner Dance.

11th April 1956 Wednesday
Singing lesson. 9th term No 5.

14th April 1956 Saturday
Peter Mould came & slept with me.

18th April 1956 Wednesday
Singing lesson. 9th term No 6.

19th April 1956 Thursday
Grace Kelly married.
Prince Rainier of Monaco married his dream princess, film star Grace Kelly.

21st April 1956 Saturday
Mummy & I went for early morning bike ride.

25th April 1956 Wednesday
Singing lesson. 9th term No 7.

27th April 1956 Friday
Ba Wilson died.

2nd May 1956 Wednesday
Singing lesson. 9th term No 8.

3rd May 1956 Thursday
Saw "**Rose Marie**" at De Mont.

7th May 1956 Monday
Mr Rose became Grandad to Andrew Mark Cunningham.

9th May 1956 Wednesday
Singing lesson. 9th term No 9.

12th May 1956 Saturday
Had my hair permed.

16th May 1956 Wednesday
Singing lesson. 9th term No 10.

17th May 1956 Thursday
Went to the dentists.

19th May 1956 Saturday
Mummy & I went to Butlin's Clacton on Sea.

Note – Mum & I have a holiday together at Butlin's.

24th May 1956 Thursday
Went a ride at night with Alec. i.e. A.G.Shinn.

26th May 1956 Saturday
Came home from Clacton. Mick Turner died.

30th May 1956 Wednesday
Singing lesson. 10th term No 1.

6th June 1956 Wednesday
Singing lesson. 10th term No 2.

9th June 1956 Saturday
John Hewes and Miss Roberts married.

13th June 1956 Wednesday
Singing lesson. 10th term No 3.

20th June 1956 Wednesday
Singing lesson. 10th term No 4.

23rd June 1956 Saturday
Went with Cocky to Reeves' 21st.

Note – My friend Reevsie at the Motor Licence Office celebrates her 21st birthday.
Cocky & I go together, although strictly speaking, he is no longer mine.

24th June 1956 Sunday
Carl Vodke born.

27th June 1956 Wednesday
Singing lesson. 10th term No 5.

4th July 1956 Wednesday
Singing lesson. 10th term No 6.

7th July 1956 Saturday
Bought 17/11 hat.

8th July 1956 Sunday
Cocky brought Joan to church & afterwards they both came chez-moi for coffee.

Note – Cocky has found a new girl-friend, Joan Lottey whom he met when on holiday in Morecambe. He stayed at her parents' guest house; & today she came to Ravenstone, including calling at my house for coffee after evensong at Ravenstone Church.

11th July 1956 Wednesday
Singing lesson. 10th term No 7.

14th July 1956 Saturday
Cocky & Joan chose engagement ring. Me? I stayed at home.

Note – My 25th birthday.

18th July 1956 Wednesday
Singing lesson. 10th term No 8.

21st July 1956 Saturday
Barbara Lyon married.

22nd July 1956 Sunday
Cocky came in after church: multos lacrimos.

25th July 1956 Wednesday
Singing lesson. 10th term No 9.

29th July 1956 Sunday
Cocky came in after church, nullos lacrimos.

31st July 1956 Tuesday
Saw **Victor Borge** on television "Comedy in Music"

2nd August 1956 Thursday
Dined at the **Forum** for the first time.

5th August 1956 Sunday
David, Pam, Enid & I went to Mablethorpe.

6th August 1956 Monday
Enid & I saw **Carousel** at Mablethorpe.

7th August 1956 Tuesday
Enid & I came home by bus from Skegness.

8th August 1956 Wednesday
The Prime Minister spoke to the nation about the **Suez**.

15th August 1956 Wednesday
Singing lesson. 10th term No 10.

17th August 1956 Friday
Cocky's engagement in the Coalville Times.
Cocky passed driving test Group "A". *(on a car)*

Marsden – Lottey. The engagement is announced between John, the youngest son of Mrs T. Marsden and the late Mr Marsden, of Ravenstone, Coalville, and Joan, eldest daughter of Mr and Mrs J. A. Lottey, of "Allonby", 42 Clarence Street, Morecambe.

22nd August 1956 Wednesday
Singing lesson. 11th term No 1.

27th August 1956 Monday
Bought scarlet umbrella.

29th August 1956 Wednesday
Singing lesson. 11th term No 2.

30th August 1956 Thursday
Saw **Danny Kaye** in "The Court Jester"

3rd September 1956 Monday
First Amateur rehearsal this season.

4th September 1956 Tuesday
Enid & I went to Coalville pictures.

5th September 1956 Wednesday
Singing lesson. 11th term No 3.

6th September 1956 Thursday
Bought Sirdar Tweedex wool.

7th September 1956 Friday
Had a perm at Glynn's. Alex Raymond (Rip Kirby) killed in car crash.

8th September 1956 Saturday
Went to Blackpool.

Note – Enid & I have a holiday in Blackpool.

10th September 1956 Monday
Went by bus for a tour of illuminations. Went to **Stanley Park**.

11th September 1956 Tuesday
Went to the top of Blackpool Tower. Saw **Albert Modley Show**.

12th September 1956 Wednesday
Went to **Derby Baths**. Went to Opera House.

13th September 1956 Thursday
Went to Tower Circus. Went by Landau to see the illuminations.

14th September 1956 Friday
Went to hairdressers. Saw Sabrina there. Went to Winter Gardens. Sat with **Kurt Eichwald**.

15th September 1956 Saturday
Came home from Blackpool.

16th September 1956 Sunday
Went to church & afterwards to Rector's Room. Became secretary of Bible Readers.

17th September 1956 Monday
Mummy & I went to Malvern.

19th September 1956 Wednesday
Mummy & I climbed Worcester Beacon.

20th September 1956 Thursday
Came home from Malvern.

23rd Sept 1956 Sunday
Went to Pat's for tea.

26th September 1956 Wednesday
Singing lesson. 11th term No 4. Had Amateur audition.

27th September 1956 Thursday
Went to church service followed by eats at Rectory & then to Don's.

1st October 1956 Monday
Ten year limit for Driving Licences began. Frank Newman resigned.

2nd October 1956 Tuesday
Mr Bentley gave me 20 Players for taxing his bus. First B.R.F. literature arrived.

3rd October 1956 Wednesday
Singing lesson. 11th term No 5.

7th October 1956 Sunday
Susan's Christening. First B. R. Meeting. Cocky came in evening.

Note – Susan, daughter of Don & Phyl is Christened & I am godmother.

8th October 1956 Monday
Parts given out for "Wild Violets".

10th October 1956 Wednesday
Singing lesson. 11th term No 6.

11th October 1956 Thursday
Our first issue of 9 lives.

12th October 1956 Friday
Saw "**Reach for the Sky**".

17th October 1956 Wednesday
Singing lesson. 11th term No 7. Anne Crawford died.

20th October 1956 Saturday
Enid & I sorted out tickets for Wild Violets at **Birmingham**.

21st October 1956 Sunday
Went to Auntie Doris' tea party.

24th October 1956 Wednesday
Singing lesson. 11th term No 8.

26th October 1956 Friday
Puskas died. (afterwards denied)

Ravenstone Parish Magazine
Oct.1956
<u>Bible Reading Fellowship</u>
A branch has now been formed, the secretary being Miss Betty Hewes of 27 Leicester Road, Ravenstone. The group is to meet after church on Sunday evenings for ½ hr of discussion. There is no limit to the numbers that can join.

27th October 1956 Saturday
Went to Willoughby for the week-end. Treated by **Mr Carr** to dinner.

31st October 1956 Wednesday
Singing lesson. 11th term No 9. Saw "Wild Violets" at Birmingham.

1st November 1956 Thursday
The first Premium Bonds went on sale in Britain.

3rd November 1956 Saturday
Went to Worcester.

4th November 1956 Sunday
Had tea at Bunting's.

5th November 1956 Monday
Went to Worcester Cattle Market.
Mary Spencer gave up her part as Liesel.

6th November 1956 Tuesday
Went to Upton on Severn in trailer behind tractor.

7th November 1956 Wednesday
Singing lesson. 11th term No 10. "End of my Course".

10th November 1956 Saturday
Went to Hinckley to see "**A Country Girl**" & afterwards to Snowdon's for a cup of tea.
Sticky's mother died.

14th November 1956 Wednesday
Came home from Leicester in lorry FJF 636.

15th November 1956 Thursday
Came home from Leicester on 667 bus at 5-45 with back window out (broken by passenger).

22nd November 1956 Thursday
All Driving Tests suspended until further notice.

24th November 1956 Saturday
Worked all afternoon: open for the issue of petrol coupons.

5th December 1956 Wednesday
Came home in lorry.

7th December 1956 Friday
Gwladys Carter engaged.

9th December 1956 Sunday
Had a film at church by the Church Missionary Society. **Hayes' had Television this week**. David Nixon's wife Paula died in car smash.

22nd December 1956 Saturday
Mummy & I went to Blackpool.

Note – Mum & I spend Christmas in Butlin's Hotel at Blackpool.

25th December 1956 Tuesday
A lovely day with snow to complete the Xmas scene.

27th December 1956 Thursday
Came home from Blackpool.

28th December 1956 Friday
Came home from work in lorry.

31st December 1956 Monday
Received letter & flowers from **Harry of Liverpool**.

* * *

"There is one broad sky over all the world, and whether it be blue or cloudy, the same heaven beyond"

n
s
.

"The Lord searcheth all hearts, and understandeth all the imaginations of thoughts; if thou seek Him, He will be found of thee."

King David

1957

The joy and happiness of Christmas still glows in our hearts.

1st January 1957 Tuesday
Salary = £436-17s-1d p.a.

3rd January 1957 Thursday
Leicester County Cricket Club Competition Card Code No.5-8-33.

4th January 1957 Friday
Daily Mail Quote – Bandleader Eric Winstone is wondering exactly which town he will be in when his law-suit with film-star Diana Dors begins. For Mr Winstone, this is a bad time of the year to have a lawsuit. He tours about 20 towns in January and doesn't know where he is likely to be. Mr Winstone became engaged on Christmas Day to 24 year old Myrtle Shepherd, of Belfast, who is a top Worth model.
(Eric Winstone born 1915)

5th January 1957 Saturday
Saw the Coalville pantomime "**Red Riding Hood**".
Tonight's Smile - If a man has his nose broken in two places, he ought to keep it out of those places.

9th January 1957 Wednesday
Sir Anthony Eden resigned as Prime Minister. Baby daughter born to Maurice (Hanker).

10th January 1957 Thursday
The Queen received The Right Hon. Harold Macmillan, M. P., in audience this afternoon and offered him the post of Prime Minister & First Lord of The Treasury. Mr Macmillan accepted Her Majesty's offer and kissed hands on appointment.

14th January 1957 Monday
Had a shampoo & set at Peat's, during dinner hour. Result? A shocking cold! Tch'Shoo!

15th January 1957 Tuesday
Brought Johnnie Dolman's Vehicle Licences & rode from Coalville home in his car.

23rd January 1957 Wednesday
Caroline Louise Marguerite (8lb 3ozs) baby for Princess Grace of Monaco.
Went with Pat & Evelyn to N.A.L.G.O. dinner & social at Fox.

28th January 1957 Monday
Happy Birthday to **My Ain Wee Darling!** ♥

4th February 1957 Monday
Came home from Leicester on Bill's motor bike.

5th February 1957 Tuesday
Had photographs taken for "Wild Violets".

6th February 1957 Wednesday
Went to see "Rock & Roll" film at Regal with Bill.

7th February 1957 Thursday
Came home from Leicester in Bill's lorry.

10th February 1957 Sunday
I spoke at B.R.F. on the meaning of The Cross of Christ.

11th February 1957 Monday
Earth tremor shook Leicestershire 3-44 p.m. Britain's severest earthquake for 200 years.

19th February 1957 Tuesday
Because of snow, I arrived at work at 9-35.
5-15 p.m. J'ai acheté C.W.P.

<u>Driving Snowstorm Hit Leicestershire</u> – Leicestershire was hardest hit of all the Midlands counties, with 18 inches to two feet of snow in some parts, compared with four inches in Nottinghamshire, and only a sprinkling in Northamptonshire. Not since the Towers weather station was established in 1874 has one foot of snow been recorded previously after a fall of four to five hours. This was the depth recorded at 9 a.m. today.

22nd February 1957 Friday
Mummy & I went to Sheffield.

23rd February 1957 Saturday
Saw "The Moon is Blue".

25th February 1957 Monday
Came home from Sheffield.

26th February 1957 Tuesday
Mr Wallis died.

28th February 1957 Thursday
Saw "A Country Girl" at B.U.

1st March 1957 Friday
Came home from Leicester in Jim's lorry.

3rd March 1957 Sunday
Amavimus.
The breathing in unison of lovers who think the same thoughts without need of speech.

4th March 1957 Monday
A letter from the "Hotel de France" accepting our booking in Jersey for September 21st.

9th March 1957 Saturday
I bought £6-6/- sun dress. "Luvley".
Chettleburgh married.

10th March 1957 Sunday
Amavimus.

11th March 1957 Monday
A letter from "Cook's" confirming 2 seats on aeroplane.

12th March 1957 Tuesday
I slept at home all alone. I sure was Oliver Dither!!

13th March 1957 Wednesday
Our settee went to be re-covered.

17th March 1957 Sunday
"A house with love in it"

21st March 1957 Thursday
Last Thursday I was really miserable! Did I cry?

23rd March 1957 Saturday
Joan Watson married to Dennis Pickering.

24th March 1957 Sunday
X xxxxxxx NO TEARS xxxxxxx X

25th March 1957 Monday
Painters and Decorators began work on the middle room.

28th March 1957 Thursday
Middle room finished.

29th March 1957 Friday
Swanwick – Dunn. Congratulations and best wishes, Phyllis and Geoff, on your silver wedding anniversary, 29th March. Len and Rhoda.

30th March 1957 Saturday

♥ ♥ COCKY MARRIED ♥ ♥

Well Done Hewsie!!

1st April 1957 Monday
Dress rehearsal for **Wild Violets.**

5th April 1957 Friday
Had day's holiday. Giving "**Wild Violets**".

Note – Coalville Amateurs' production of "Wild Violets" provided me with probably my best character part, the stately & commanding head-mistress of a school, which I thoroughly enjoyed playing.

6th April 1957 Saturday
E. S. A. M.   X

7th April 1957 Sunday
Went to Leicester Station with Kurt.

10th April 1957 Wednesday
Charlie came into our office. Our Amateurs Dinner.

13th April 1957 Saturday
I went to the Charnwood Ladies' Choir concert at the Marlborough Square Chapel. Rex, May & Madge came.

14th April 1957 Sunday
I cycled to Newbold Verdon & spent the day at Marie's.

15th April 1957 Monday
First Driving Tests since 22nd November 1956.

16th April 1957 Tuesday
I went to Leicester in Ice Cream Van.

18th April 1957 Thursday
Went over to Willoughby in Don's new Zodiac.

19th April 1957 Good Friday
Went in Pat's car to Kirby Muxloe to see Daphne Hull's auntie.

20th April 1957 Saturday
Heard the Cuckoo for the first time this year.   Played croquet till it was quite dark.   Slept at Pat's.

21st April 1957 Easter Sunday
Saw Cocky for the first time since March 24th. Had tea at Enid's.

22nd April 1957 Easter Monday
Went with Pat, Evelyn & Mary to **Trentham Gardens.**

25th April 1957 Thursday
Saw "**The King & I**" at The Rex with Enid.

26th April 1957 Friday
Saw "**Brothers in Law**" at Odeon. "Donald" joined us for dinner.

27th April 1957 Saturday
Saw "**Three Men in a Boat**" at Regal with Enid & Mary Blue.

30th April 1957 Tuesday
Frank Newman sat with me on the bus to Leicester.

3rd May 1957 Friday
Mummy went to Willoughby for a week.

4th May 1957 Saturday
I bought my short coat from C & A.

5th May 1957 Sunday
♥ We smiled at each other ♥

9th May 1957 Thursday
Prince Charles, Duke of Cornwall, had his tonsils and adenoids out. Prince Charles was vaccinated in March 1949, immunised against diphtheria in October 1949, and inoculated against poliomyelitis in January this year.

11th May 1957 Saturday
Saw "**Brothers in Law**" at The Regal.

12th May 1957 Sunday
Mary Blue sat between Enid & me at church.
Joan & I smiled at each other.

13th May 1957 Monday
Saw a total eclipse of the Moon.

14th May 1957 Tuesday
Dick Bentley 50 yrs old today. Ooh Ron!
Petrol rationed from 17th December 1956 to 14th May 1957.

23rd May 1957 Thursday
In Copenhagen there were deep, deep blushes when Prince Philip , walking round a needlework class, picked up a pair of butcher-blue "unmentionables" a girl had made.   "Ah," he said, as he draped them round himself, "I don't think they would fit me."

24ᵗʰ May 1957 Friday
Saw Carl Vodke for the first time. He was 11 months old.

25ᵗʰ May Saturday
Went to Butlin's Clacton.

Note – Mum & I had booked a holiday at Clacton, but Mum was not well enough to go & I went to this Butlin's camp on my own. I was pestered by undesirable men & told them I had a boy-friend at home, & was not interested.

26ᵗʰ May 1957 Sunday
Saw Billy Butlin.

27ᵗʰ May 1957 Monday
Met Andreas & Nicholas Beheris from sunny Spain.

28ᵗʰ May 1957 Tuesday
Saw the play "Gaslight" with my Senors.
In bed by 3 a.m.

29ᵗʰ May 1957 Wednesday
Went to Frinton & Walton on bus.

30ᵗʰ May 1957 Thursday
Met Bill & Percy from The Grovenor. Eric Winstone smiled at me. *(See 4ᵗʰ January 1957)*

1ˢᵗ June 1957 Saturday
Came home from Clacton.

2ⁿᵈ June 1957 Sunday
Glorious day – sunbathed!

3ʳᵈ June 1957 Monday
Reevsie had the day off from work because Tony had broken his nose.

6ᵗʰ June 1957 Thursday
Had letter from Douglas.

8ᵗʰ June 1957 Saturday
Electricity cut off until 11-15 p.m. after thunderstorm. Cocky gave me Wedding Photo.

9ᵗʰ June 1957 Sunday
Spent the day with Marg & Helmut.

10ᵗʰ June 1957 Monday
The Duke of Edinburgh, who is 36 today, is spending his birthday at Windsor Castle with the Queen, the Duke of Cornwall, Princess Anne, and Princess Andrew of Greece, his mother, who is staying at the castle.

11ᵗʰ June 1957 Tuesday
Went to Belvoir Castle with Enid, David & Pam.

12ᵗʰ June 1957 Wednesday
Saw Charlie. He arranged to have dinner with me Friday. But by Friday I was the Charlie.

14ᵗʰ June 1957 Friday
Amateur committee meeting re- Resignation of Ron Smith.

15ᵗʰ June 1957 Saturday
Hottest day this year. Played croquet & sun bathed.

16ᵗʰ June 1957 Sunday
Had our evening church service in the Institute.

17ᵗʰ June 1957 Monday
First rehearsal for Amateur's concert. I was asked to sing "Poor John!".

18ᵗʰ June 1957 Tuesday
Pat brought Daphne Hull over to our house during the evening.

19ᵗʰ June 1957 Wednesday
Pat elected Secretary of Coalville Amateur Operatic Society.(C.A.O.S.)
Mummy went to Skegness.

20ᵗʰ June 1957 Thursday
Last day we issued Provisional Licences stamped "Passed Test".

21ˢᵗ June 1957 Friday
Played croquet with Nunkie v. Auntie Gladys & Peter.

22ⁿᵈ June 1957 Saturday
Mummy went on night duty for the first time since March.

26ᵗʰ June 1957 Wednesday
Reevsie flew home from Jersey. Neb Down phoned for me.

27ᵗʰ June 1957 Thursday
Mummy & Auntie Cis went to Market Bosworth.

29ᵗʰ June 1957 Saturday
Had raspberries for tea – delicious – first this year.
At Darlington-street,Wolverhampton, spectators saw an egg fall from a housewife's basket, break, and **fry on the pavement.**

6ᵗʰ July 1957 Saturday
Bought our first Gramophone Record "Ronnie" "We Will Make Love"

7ᵗʰ July 1957 Sunday
Our church re-hallowed by The Venerable The Archdeacon of Loughborough.
Silver Wedding Greeting- As your future years unfold: may your silver turn to gold.

10ᵗʰ July 1957 Wednesday
Went to Leicester from Ravenstone in Ice Cream Van.

11ᵗʰ July 1957 Thursday
Aga Khan died.

13ᵗʰ July 1957 Saturday
David's friend "Oz" Gordon & Joyce over for the week end.

16th July 1957 Tuesday
Had a lift to Coalville in pouring rain with ARY 637.

18th July 1957 Thursday
Met Raymond Van Looke at Marianne's home.

19th July 1957 Friday
Saw the pageant "Charnwood Cavalcade" at South Charnwood School.

20th July 1957 Saturday
Went to the Rally of Old Broomleysians for Mr Hill's retirement.

22nd July 1957 Monday
My first journey to work by train because of Bus Strike.

25th July 1957 Thursday
I was cautioned by Police at 7-20 a.m. for failing to **Halt** on my bike.

26th July 1957 Friday
Went with Brian Land, Don & Lesley to meet Jean Guillaume & Jean Greinenberger.

27th July 1957 Saturday
Peter Mould slept with me.

29th July 1957 Monday
Kib caused a stir at work by arriving complete with her new **Engagement Ring**.

30th July 1957 Tuesday
Our record issue of Driving Licences today – 777

1st August 1957 Thursday
World Scout Jubilee Jamboree opened today.

5th August 1957 Monday
Went to **Woburn Abbey** with Enid, David and Pam.

7th August 1957 Wednesday
New regulation re- "Visitor to G.B." Driving Licences.

14th August 1957 Wednesday
Spent the evening at Don's. Said Goodbye to Jean Guillaume.

18th August 1957 Sunday
Saw Ian Carmichael in his first T.V. play.

20th August 1957 Tuesday
Played croquet.

21st August 1957 Wednesday
Played croquet.

23rd August 1957 Friday
Spent the evening at Uncle Fred's. Sat with Mrs Clarke for a while upstairs.

24th August 1957 Saturday
Nunkie very ill. I met Douglas & Dorothy at Auntie Dos'.

28th August 1957 Wednesday
Nunkie went into hospital.

31st August 1957 Saturday
Played croquet with Enid, Marg., & Auntie Gladys.

4th September 1957 Wednesday
Reevsie had the day off to attend a Wedding.

5th September 1957 Thursday
Saw "Ronnie" on I. T. V. at Anne's.

7th September 1957 Saturday
I walked up Friar's field in a dazzling setting sun. Jes' me, surrounded by glory.

8th September 1957 Sunday
Auntie Gladys went to Mablethorpe for holiday.
Hollies trees laid bare in preparation for Auntie Dos' bungalow.

Note – Auntie Dos has decided to build a bungalow right next door to our house – on the Hollies lawn.

13th September 1957 Friday
Had a Clynal "Perm" at Lewis's.

14th September 1957 Saturday
Went with Enid to see Nunkie in hospital.

15th September 1957 Sunday
Went with Enid to see "Ronnie" at De Mont.

21st September 1957 Saturday
Went with Enid to Jersey. Our first aeroplane flight.

Note – Enid & I fly to Jersey for our holiday – our first aeroplane flight. I subsequently suffer with breathing problems & for years avoid climbing hills.
I wonder whether I will live to see 30.

22nd September 1957 Sunday
Visited the German underground hospital.

24th September 1957 Tuesday
Lovely sunny afternoon.
Lay on the beach at Grève de Lecq.

25th September 1957 Wednesday
Went to community hymn singing in the glass church – St. Matthews.

26th September 1957 Thursday
Saw Corey Castle floodlit. Visited Rev. Granger.

27th September 1957 Friday
Went on afternoon bus tour to Devil's Hole. Went to the pictures at night.

28th Sept 1957 Saturday
Flew home from Jersey to Birmingham. Came from Tamworth by taxi, 30/-

4th October 1957 Friday
Mankind took the first real step into space when

Russia launched her No.1 Satellite.
Twinkle, twinkle satellite! How d'you do it day and night?

7th October 1957 Monday
Reevsie away from work all this week with the flu.

9th October 1957 Wednesday
First night of our Amateur's concert at Progressive Hall.

10th October 1957 Thursday
Auntie Dos & Mummy dissented over water for the builders of her bungalow.
A fire in No 1 Atomic Pile at Windscale on the West Cumbrian coast sent plumes of radioactivity soaring over Britain & Western Europe. It was the world's first nuclear accident, & the Windscale works never fully recovered from this disaster. The name of Windscale later changed to Sellafield.

17th October 1957 Thursday
Met Sammy Martin at The Gate, Osgathorpe.

19th October 1957 Saturday
Went to Bradgate Park in the afternoon & to "The Gate" at night with Sammy.

Note – Met a tall young man, Sammy Martin, at a local dance & he arranged to see me again. However, he did not turn up, & that was the end of that.

20th October 1957 Sunday
Jack Buchanan died.

22nd October 1957 Tuesday
H. M. The Queen & Prince Philip arrived home from their N. American tour.

31st October 1957 Thursday
Harriet 88 today.

1st November 1957 Friday
Saw "**Bitter Sweet**" at The Palace, Leicester.

2nd November 1957 Saturday
Saw "**Rose Marie**" at Kettering. I bought new black skirt and winter gloves.

3rd November 1957 Sunday
Russia launched her 2nd Satellite (carrying a dog)

9th November 1957 Saturday
Saw "**High Society**" starring **Grace Kelly** at The Rex.

11th November 1957 Monday
"Donald" joined us for dinner. **Over-alls provided at work.**

13th November 1957 Wednesday
Started knitting my fawn cardigan.

14th November 1957 Thursday
Had audition for part in "**Rose Marie**".

15th November 1957 Friday
Reevsie & I watched the pelvic pyrotechnics of **Elvis Presley** at The Gaumont "Loving You".

17th November 1957 Sunday
Peter & Lesley confirmed, after which we all with the Bishop of Leicester had Holy Communion at Ravenstone.

18th November 1957 Monday
Pat's first day at work in Market Bosworth.

Note – Brother Pat, who had worked with my dad & with Uncle Cyril in the family business, & latterly with Uncle Cyril only, was now so impoverished that he finally found himself another job in the Council Offices at Market Bosworth.

22nd November 1957 Friday
Had our first libretto read through of "Rose Marie" at Peter Jacques' home.

23rd November 1957 Saturday
Saw Ian Carmichael in "**Lucky Jim**" at The Gaumont, Leicester.

27th November 1957 Wednesday
Saw **Jack Hulbert** on the stage at "**The Palace**" in The Reluctant Debutante.

1st December 1957 Sunday
The rocket carrier of Sputnik I, Russia's first Satellite, reported to have landed today in Alaska.

4th December 1957 Wednesday
Lewisham train disaster.

6th December 1957 Friday
America launched her first Satellite. It rose 4ft. then crashed – Puffnik.

11th December 1957 Wednesday
Enid & I saw "The Odds & Ends" concert at Ellistown.

14th December 1957 Saturday
First snow this winter.

15th December 1957 Sunday
Went to hear Marianne sing in "The Messiah" at Coalville.

19th December 1957 Thursday
Watched the Lady Mayoress of Leicester switch on the Christmas lights in the Town Hall Square, saw Rudolph & Santa.

21st December 1957 Saturday
Enid & I went to **Gladys & Jack's**. The car wouldn't start home.

23rd December 1957 Monday
Amateur's Christmas Party. John Saunders brought Enid & me home in his car.

25th December 1957 Wednesday

Had dinner & tea at Pat's.

28th December 1957 Saturday

Enid & I were baby sitters at Don's & broke **2 Gramophone Records**

31st December 1957 Tuesday

Walsom – Reeves.   Mr and Mrs W. Reeves, 5, The Crescent, Blaby, are pleased to announce the engagement of their eldest daughter Patricia, to Anthony, youngest son of Mrs Saunders (formerly Walsom), 39, Charnwood Ave., Thurmaston.

Note – My friend Reevsie at the Motor Licence Office & her boy-friend Tony Walsom announce their engagement.

* * *

1958

The Rectory, Ravenstone, Jan 1958
Once more we go forward into another year, but the awe, reverence, and humility of Christmas remains. Should we not, as the shepherds did, glorify and praise God for all those things which we have heard and seen?

The Seven Gifts of the Spirit
Wisdom
Understanding
Counsel
Fortitude
Knowledge
Righteousness
Godly Fear

4th January 1958 Saturday
Went with Helen to the Coalville pantomime "Jack & The Beanstalk".

6th January 1958 Monday
David fetched the new car. PNR 400

8th January 1958 Wednesday
Had rehearsal at Vin Hardy's home. Came home in Vin's car.

11th January 1958 Saturday
Nunkie came home from hospital where he went 28th August 1957.

15th January 1958 Wednesday
Had rehearsal at Vin Hardy's home. Cycled home in fog.

17th January 1958 Friday
Had photograph taken for "Rose Marie".

18th January 1958 Saturday
Auntie Cis, Dos & I went to Nunkie's 35th Wedding Anniversary celebration.

20th January 1958 Monday
Dr. Fuchs arrived at the South Pole. Mr Reeves joined us for dinner.

24th January 1958 Friday
Billy Butlin's wife died.

26th January 1958 Sunday
I came out of church at 6-45 p.m. because I was not well.

28th January 1958 Tuesday
In bed with flu.

5th February 1958 Wednesday
I started back to work after having the flu.

6th February 1958 Thursday
Manchester United Football Team in Air Disaster.

7th February 1958 Friday
I bought new coat.

8th February 1958 Saturday
Went to the Butlin's annual festival of reunion at the Royal Albert Hall.

9th February 1958 Sunday
Went to a Baptist Chapel in S. Croydon & saw 3 baptisms.

18th February 1958 Tuesday
Mummy went to Willoughby till Friday.

21st February 1958 Friday
Duncan Edwards, Manchester United & England Left Half died at 1-16 a.m. G.M.T. in the Rechts der Isar Hospital, Munich.

25th February 1958 Tuesday
Woke to a winter wonderland of snow. Arrived at work at 9-30 a.m.

26th February 1958 Wednesday
Walked to Coalville through the snow, Standard Hill way.

27th February 1958 Thursday
Saw the ice show at Granby Halls "Winter Wonderland".

28th February 1958 Friday
Nous parlions inter nos!!

1st March 1958 Saturday
Enid & I went with bus load to see **"Maritza"** at the B. U.

8th March 1958 Saturday
Went on booking at The Regal for the Amateurs. Walked home in snow storm.

14th March 1958 Friday
Prince Albert Alexandre Louis Pierre (8lb 12oz) baby for Princess Grace of Monaco.

15th March 1958 Saturday
Bought Dolcis shoes – genuine silksheen velour calf !!

16th March 1958 Sunday
Charlie Kunz died.

22nd March 1958 Saturday
Mike Todd died in air crash.

23rd March 1958 Sunday
Had photographs in costumes for "Rose Marie".

24th March 1958 Monday
Full dress rehearsal for "Rose Marie".

27th March 1958 Thursday
Auntie Cis moved to High Tor.

29th March 1958 Saturday
Don took my photo in evening dress.

5th April 1958 Saturday
Auntie Dos moved into bungalow.

Note – Aunt Dos moved into her newly built bungalow.

18th April 1958 Friday
Amateur's dinner dance.

19th April 1958 Saturday
Princess Margaret left London Airport at 8-30 p.m. for her West Indies tour.

20th April 1958 Sunday
Auntie Cis called. Secret - Re: Bank Manager.

24th April 1958 Thursday
Saw "**The Bridge on The River Kwai**" at Coalville with Enid.

27th April 1958 Sunday
Pam, David, Enid & I went to Proctor's Pleasure Park, Barrow-on-Soar.

30th April 1958 Wednesday
Bought my black shoes from Lotus.

1st May 1958 Thursday
Saw "**Happy is the Bride**" at Coalville with Enid.

2nd May 1958 Friday
Had my hair permed at Lewis's.

3rd May 1958 Saturday
Played croquet for the first time this year.
I washed all my dresses.

5th May 1958 Monday
Princess Anne had her tonsils out.

8th May 1958 Thursday
Reevsie & I walked through The Town Hall to see the flowers.

9th May 1958 Friday
The Queen came to Leicester.

11th May 1958 Sunday
I washed 2 sheets.

13th May 1958 Tuesday
I walked into Charlie Parrock near The Savoy.

14th May 1958 Wednesday
Johnnie Dolman gave me a lift down Wash Lane.

15th May 1958 Thursday
The Duke of Rutland married Miss Sweeny.

22nd May 1958 Thursday
Electricity Pylon erected in Wash Lane.

26th May 1958 Whit Monday
Went to Malvern & to Worcester Cathedral with Pat, Evelyn, Mary & Auntie Dos.

27th May 1958 Tuesday
Started knitting blue cardigan.

28th May 1958 Wednesday
Pochin – Hammond. The engagement is announced between John Henry Illife, only son of Mr and Mrs H. L. Pochin, "Somerville", Houghton-on-the-Hill, Leicestershire, and Barbara Kay, elder daughter of Mr and Mrs B. Hammond, 45, Sybil Road, Leicester.

29th May 1958 Thursday
Bought camera.

31st May 1958 Saturday
Mummy & I went to Clacton.

Note – Mum & I spend a week at Butlin's holiday camp, Clacton, but I am far from well. I feel very weak & suffer now from claustrophobia. I cannot endure being inside a crowded theatre & need to get outside into the fresh air. One day I pass out completely, & am probably at my lowest ebb.

1st June 1958 Sunday
Saw variety show presented by The Grand Order of Water Rats.

2nd June 1958 Monday
Had terrific thunder storm. Watched Ben Warriss leave in the morning.

3rd June 1958 Tuesday
Went by bus into Clacton. Went on pier. Walked back along the front.

4th June 1958 Wednesday
Sick in the morning. In bed till 4-30 p.m. Passed out at 6-30 p.m. In bed all evening.

5th June 1958 Thursday
Eric Winstone & I smiled at each other.

(Note by Mary Blue – See 4th January 1957.)

11th June 1958 Wednesday
Mummy shook hands with a black man – the Assistant Bishop of **Sierra Leone**.

14th June 1958 Saturday
Went to Reevsie's wedding.

16th June 1958 Monday
Watched Victor Borge on television.

19th June 1958 Thursday
Mummy & Madge went to The Wye Valley. Uncle Bert came down.

25th June 1958 Wednesday
Uncle Bert spent the evening with us.
Auntie Dos C. I. D. was about to set the police on him.

26th June 1958 Thursday
Played croquet till 10 p.m. Peter played.

29th June 1958 Sunday
Sunday School Anniversary. Lesley went with me.
Hello - ☺

2nd July 1958 Wednesday
Market Harborough four feet under water. I rode home
from Leicester in Tom Land's car.

16th July 1958 Wednesday
Had dinner with Brash Hall.

26th July 1958 Saturday
Ravenstone Boy Scouts' new Hall opened by Lord
Crawshaw.

At the closing of the British Empire and Commonwealth
Games, this historic announcement was made in a tape-
recorded message from the Queen: "I intend to create
my son Charles, **Prince of Wales** today. When he is
grown up I will present him to you at Caernarvon" The
announcement was made at Cardiff. Charles was born on
14th November 1948.

4th August 1958 Monday
Went to Mablethorpe & Ingoldmells with Uncle Cyril,
Auntie Gladys & Enid.

10th August 1958 Sunday
We had a terrific thunderstorm. 2-in-1.

13th August 1958 Wednesday
Don gave me colour photos which he took 29th March
1958.

17th August 1958 Sunday
Visited Auntie Annie, Minnie & Maud. Americans sent
rocket to The Moon.(It did not arrive)

23rd August 1958 Saturday
Enid & I went to The Isle of Man.

Note - Enid & I have our holiday in the Isle of Man.

24th August 1958 Sunday
Went to open air church service at **Kirk Braddan**. Saw
Rawicz & Landauer.

25th August 1958 Monday
Went by ferry boat to The Tower of Refuge. Went to
Rushen Abbey & had peaches & cream out of doors.

26th August 1958 Tuesday
Went by coach all round the T. T. track. Watched
floodlit tattoo.

27th August 1958 Wednesday
Watched The Burtonwood Bullets – American football
match.

28th August 1958 Thursday
Went to Laxey Wheel. Carnival night with procession &
fireworks.

29th August 1958 Friday
Went by coach to The Calf of Man.

30th August 1958 Saturday
Came home from I. O. M.

3rd September 1958 Wednesday
Had tea with the 3 aunts: Maud, Minnie & Annie.

6th September 1958 Saturday
Auntie Dos' lodger Judy London arrived.

7th September 1958 Sunday
Went to church with Pat, Mary, Enid & Judy. Then went
car ride over forest.

9th September 1958 Tuesday
Had lift home at 7 p.m. in BVG 230.

10th September 1958 Wednesday
Bought Helena Rubinstein deep cleanser & foundation
cream.

12th September 1958 Friday
Golden Wedding Day of Sir Winston Churchill.

15th September 1958 Monday
Judy joined the Amateurs.

18th September 1958 Thursday
Took a driving licence from its folder & was my face
red!!!!?

19th September 1958 Friday
Saw Danny Kaye in "Merry Andrew".
Helen & I had a lift home from Leicester with G.
Wesson.

20th September 1958 Saturday
Our oak tree felled. I scrubbed line props.

22nd September 1958 Monday
Judy's sister Wendy stayed with Auntie Dos for the
night.

23rd September 1958 Tuesday
I spent the evening at Glenholm.

*(Note – Glenholm was Uncle Fred & Auntie Bell's
house, No. 46 Leicester Road - across the road on the
corner. Mary Blue.)*

24th September 1958 Wednesday
Saw Dorothy & Douglas at Auntie Dos'.

27th September 1958 Saturday
Enid & I spent the evening at Don's. Met his Auntie
Ethel from Canada.

4th October 1958 Saturday
Mummy & I saw "The King & I" at the Little Theatre.

9th October 1958 Thursday
The Pope died. Pope Pius XII

12th October 1958 Sunday
Our Harvest Festival. **My first day as Sunday School
Teacher.**

Note – I was to be Sunday School teacher from 1958 to 1983.

19ᵗʰ October 1958 Sunday
Helen Alderman & Pamela Kendrick paid me an unexpected visit.

23ʳᵈ October 1958 Thursday
Judy's 21ˢᵗ birthday & Auntie Dos' house warming party.

24ᵗʰ October 1958 Friday
Auntie Dos' house warming party No.2.

26ᵗʰ October 1958 Sunday
I took the infants' Sunday School in Rector's Room. Mary Blue brought her record player over in afternoon.

27ᵗʰ October 1958 Monday
Parts given out for "White Horse Inn".

28ᵗʰ October 1958 Tuesday
Saw the state opening of parliament televised for first time. New Pope chosen – John XXIII

1ˢᵗ November 1958 Saturday
I bought new hat & winter dress.

5ᵗʰ November 1958 Wednesday
Jimmy Edwards married.

7ᵗʰ November 1958 Friday
Auntie Dos had new television.

9ᵗʰ November 1958 Sunday
I spoke to the children at church for the first time.

15ᵗʰ November 1958 Saturday
I went by bus to Malvern. Saw Bunting in "Die Fledermaus".

16ᵗʰ November 1958 Sunday
Sealy – Frank L. 38, Greenhill Road, Coalville, passed away in hospital, November 16, aged 69 years. Funeral service at St. David's Church, Broom Leys, on Wednesday at 1 p.m. followed by cremation at Gilroes, 2 p.m.

6ᵗʰ December 1958 Saturday
Went to Stratford to see "The White Horse Inn".

18ᵗʰ December 1958 Thursday
Empire Day was re-named Commonwealth Day.
Nield – Eric William, on December 18, at 17, Main St., Ravenstone, aged 55, dearly loved husband of Connie, and father of Tony and Guy.

20ᵗʰ December 1958 Saturday
Went with Helen & Enid to dance at Ravenstone Institute. 39 12ᵗʰ Bruntingthorpe Band.

22ⁿᵈ December 1958 Monday
Margaret Wooding's first day at work. Amateurs' Christmas Party.

28ᵗʰ December 1958 Sunday
Sunday School children presented Nativity Play in church.

* * *

David Daniel Kominski = Danny Kaye

1959

11th January 1959 Sunday
I spoke to for the 2nd time to children: "The Feast of the Passover."

14th January 1959 Wednesday
Fog, frost & snow. Arrived at work 9-50 a.m.

15th January 1959 Thursday
Beryl & I had a lift from Coalville to Leicester with John Farmer.

21st January 1959 Wednesday
Cecil B. de Mille died aged 77. He was "a sentimental man, a loyal friend & deeply religious"
Quote: De Mille was King of the Paramount Lot, & no-one challenged his throne. De Mille was a titan of the film industry. Truly there has never been anyone like him & equally truly there never will be again. He made the biggest, if not the greatest, films. The evangelist Billy Graham said: "Mr De Mille was a prophet in celluloid."

22nd January 1959 Thursday
Had photographs taken for programme "White Horse Inn" **Mike Hawthorn died.**
Quote: - 29 year old genius of world motor racing, he had mastered the most hair-raising of sports and had survived all its perils. That he should have retired as world motor-racing champion only to be killed a month later in a road accident in Surrey is, indeed, grimly ironical. He was one of Britain's best – a fine fearless member of the younger generation.

25th January 1959 Sunday
Sunday School Prize Giving Day.

21st February 1959 Saturday
Had Polyfoto taken.

28th February 1959 Saturday
Bought "Ravenstone" flower bowl. Bought light blue handbag.

5th March 1959 Thursday
Mummy went to Willoughby & took navy blue cardigan for Dobbie.

17th March 1959 Tuesday
White Horse Inn.

23rd March 1959 Monday
The man who pioneered a new deal for old people in Leicestershire, Mr Harold John Tillson, died at his home in Westminister Road yesterday in his 67th year. Mr Tillson, who had been a council official for nearly 30 years, retired on New Year's Eve, 1957 after 9 years as County Homes Officer. Mr Tillson came to Leicester in 1929 as director of public assistance, a position he retained until the homes service which he had developed for the care of old folk, came under the control of the Health Service. He then took the title of County Homes Officer. His work was recognised by the King in 1949,

when he was awarded the C. B. E.

30th March 1959 Monday
Mummy & I saw "The Captain's Table" at The Rex.

31st March 1959 Tuesday
Enid & I saw "Cry from the Streets" at The Regal.

2nd April 1959 Thursday
Enid & I saw "Sailor Beware" at the Adult School.

10th April 1959 Friday
Amateur's Dinner Dance.

11th April 1959 Saturday
Marianne wrote her letter of resignation from the Amateurs.

13th April 1959 Monday
Mr Pochin formally presented with portable wireless by E. C. Mason. Drinks all round.

15th April 1959 Wednesday
Mr & Mrs Pochin entertained the motor licence office staff to dinner at Le Gourmet.

23rd April 1959 Thursday
Council's Housing Man Dies – The death has occurred after a long illness of Mr Charles Douglas Hewes (61), Church Cottage, Market Bosworth, Housing Officer of Market Bosworth Rural Council. Mr Hewes joined the staff of the council's Housing Department in 1937 and has been Housing Officer for some years. He leaves a wife, a son and two daughters. A member of a well-known Ravenstone family associated with the firm of G. H. Hewes and Sons, Estate Agents, Coalville, Mr Hewes was known throughout North West Leicestershire. The son, John, with his wife and child, is on his way home by plane from Nigeria, where he took up an appointment some time ago. He is expected to arrive tomorrow.

Note – My dad was one of 6 brothers. His first brother to die was my Uncle Aubrey in December 1944. Now another brother has died, my Uncle Charlie, leaving now only Fred, Hedley & Cyril, plus their 2 sisters, "Cis" and "Dos".
Uncle Charlie died of cancer, aged 61

2nd May 1959 Saturday
I played croquet for the first time this year.

3rd May 1959 Rogation Sunday
I read the lesson at church in the afternoon for the 1st time.

4th May 1959 Monday
Mr David Howie gave me a 4 leaf clover & a 5 leaf clover.

6th May 1959 Wednesday
Mr Charles K. Deeming aged 69 married Mrs Martin.

8th May 1959 Friday
Son born to the Duke & Duchess of Rutland. He will be known as the Marquis of Granby.

9th May 1959 Saturday
I went to Bradgate Park in the morning.

14th May 1959 Thursday
I had the day of from work. Mummy & I went to Bradgate Park.

18th May 1959 Monday
Auntie Dos & Cis went to Ingoldmels until Saturday.

19th Mat 1959 Tuesday
I slept at Pat's.

30th May 1959 Saturday
I bought white shoes.

2nd June 1959 Tuesday
Had our first ride to Leicester & back in NJJ 141.

4th June 1959 Thursday
Had the day off from work.

6th June 1959 Saturday
Mummy & I went to Llandudno.

Note – Mum & I have a holiday at Llandudno.

7th June 1959 Sunday
Went to St. Paul's church in morning. To Swallow Falls in afternoon.

8th June 1959 Monday
Went to Colwyn Bay in morning. To Ogwen Falls after dinner.

9th June 1959 Tuesday
Went on whole day bus tour to Barmouth, had lunch at Harlech.

10th June 1959 Wednesday
Went to Conway in the afternoon.

11th June 1959 Thursday
Went round the Great Orme in morning. Went to Beaumaris, Anglesy in afternoon.

12th June 1959 Friday
Ascended the Heights of Nebo on the Alpine Tour.

13th June 1959 Saturday
Ann & Steve had their first date. Went to London.

16th June 1959 Tuesday
Looked straight into a man's eyes from hedge bottom.

20th June 1959 Saturday
Played croquet by moonlight until 10-45 p.m.

23rd June 1959 Tuesday
Nunkie went to hospital. "Dosh v. Mary Blue" saga begins.

24th June 1959 Wednesday
Went to Ibstock church at night. Mary Blue confirmed.
On 24th June 1859, French and Austrian casualties on the battlefield at Solferino, Italy, inspired Swiss businessman Jean Henri Dunant to found the International Red Cross.

29th June 1959 Monday
Began to take a keen interest in **Freckles**.

7th July 1959 Tuesday
Very hot weather. I bought an electric fan (tomorrow).

12th July 1959 Sunday
Our Sunday School Anniversary. I read the lesson.

21st July 1959 Tuesday
. . . . . and a long look into the eyes of a good – looking man.

23rd July 1959 Thursday
Barbara Lyon filed a divorce petition. Barbara Lyon told Bromley Abbott: - "I have done everything possible to save our marriage. I have had the best religious and legal advice. Reluctantly, I have decided that the only course open to me is to institute legal proceedings"

24th July 1959 Friday
Judy's last day with Auntie Dos.

25th July 1959 Saturday
Went to Drayton Manor Park on Sunday School Outing.

28th July 1959 Tuesday
Post codes were introduced into Britain.

3rd August 1959 Monday
Went with Helen, Janet & Mrs Tovell to Skegness on Jacques' bus.

5th August 1959 Wednesday
I bought leather bag for Mummy.

6th August 1959 Thursday
Auntie Gladys went to Grace's for holiday.

7th August 1959 Friday
The news flashed round the world that our Queen is expecting a baby.

8th August 1959 Saturday
Enid & I spent the afternoon with Nunkie at Carlton Hayes Hospital.

9th August 1959 Sunday
The Rector, Rev. Maurice Atterbury Thomas, told us he was leaving.

15th August 1959 Saturday
Enid & I spent the afternoon with Nunkie again.

29th August 1959 Saturday
Enid & I went to Portrush.

Note – Enid & I have a holiday at Portrush, Northern Ireland.

30th August 1959 Sunday
Went to Giant's Causeway.

5th September 1959 Saturday
Enid & I came home from Portrush.

12th September 1959 Saturday
Ron, whom we met at Portrush, called to see Enid & me.

13th September 1959 Sunday
The first rocket reached the Moon. Sent from Russia.

19th September 1959 Saturday
Nunkie had his 1st weekend at home since June 23rd.

26th September 1959 Saturday
Mary Blue's 1st day working at Woolworth's
(Saturday job)

30th September 1959 Wednesday
The Rector formally presented with £42 cheque at institute.

Note – The Rector of Ravenstone, Maurice Atterbury Thomas, leaves.

17th October 1959 Saturday
Saw "The Merry Widow" at the De Mont.

21st October 1959 Wednesday
Last ride to Leicester in NJJ 141.

23rd October 1959 Friday
Went to Malvern.

26th October 1959 Monday
Parts given out for Chu Chin Chow. Went to P. Greenwood's house.

30th October 1959 Friday
Margaret Prescott & Margaret Woodings left work.

31st October 1959 Saturday
Had a lift to Leicester with Ladyman.

2nd November 1959 Monday
Bought turquoise blouse & girdle.

3rd November 1959 Tuesday
Bought black patent shoes.

4th November 1959 Wednesday
We had a chat in Wash Lane, re - Registration Books.

12th November 1959 Thursday
Mr Ford gave us farewell drinks & light refreshment.

13th November 1959 Friday
Had 1st Libretto Practice. Peter Jacques gave me a lift home.

14th November 1959 Saturday
Had my first ride to Leicester in MOX 746.

15th November 1959 Sunday
Auntie Dos, Ladyman & I had slap up dinner – chicken.

2nd December 1959 Wednesday
I bought black umbrella.

4th December 1959 Friday
We had television. Induction of Gustav.

Note – We had our first television – black & white. Induction of Ravenstone's new Rector, Gustav Aronsohn.

5th December 1959 Saturday
David broke a bone in his leg.

6th December 1959 Sunday
Rev. Aronsohn's first Sunday with us.

19th December 1959 Saturday
I went to see Dr Chick but he wasn't there.

20th December 1959 Sunday
We had Sunday School without an organist.

* * *

People, Pomp & Circumstances

How the diaries began…

This photograph, taken in September 1946 at Bembridge on the Isle of Wight,
shows Mrs Cassell with her twin daughters Pamela and Ann.
These three had lived with Betty's family in Ravenstone as evacuees from
London during the Second World War. It was Mrs Cassell who gave 12 year-
old Betty her first diary.
*"Last Christmas Mrs Cassell bought me a lovely big desk diary which I
completed in pencil & later transferred to a 5 year diary."*

Betty's father, Reg, died January 11th 1939, at the age of 49.
This was the day of his funeral, 16th January 1939, when relatives and friends assembled in Leicester Road, Ravenstone, prior to the coffin being brought from the house to make its way to St Mary's Church, Snibston.
Reg's eldest brother Fred, daughter Bunting and son Pat stand in line ready to follow it; Reg's brother Hedley (centre of photo) and brother Charlie (with moustache) are among the mourners.

Leslie Hale, Reg's best friend, who later became Lord Hale

13th May 1981 Wednesday
"Leslie Hale wrote of my dad, 'I never remember an unkind word. To his advice & guidance & help I owe much. It was Reg who helped to found my practice, Reg who introduced me to my wife, Reg who helped me to build my first house & to provide me with an office. I am not a man who makes friends readily & Reg was one of the few that I had – and certainly the closest & the finest & the best. Reg has left behind him the most that any man can hope to leave – the affection of his friends, the respect of all who knew him & the gratitude of hundreds'."

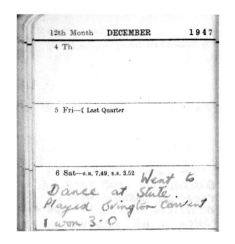

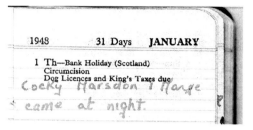

The first mention of John (Cocky) Marsden
January 1st 1948*: "Cocky Marsden & Marge*
came at night"
Many years later, on the occasion of her half-
sister Bunting's 45th wedding anniversary,
Betty reminisces:
10th January 1991 *"As I fell in love with Cocky*
at Ravenstone Institute, so Bunting fell in love
with Mostyn at Ravenstone Institute. As Cocky
& I have loved each other since first we met, so
Bunting & Mostyn's love has continued to this
day – they are united in Holy Matrimony, while
Cocky and I tried & failed to say goodbye."

Can we presume they met at the 'Stute' on 6th
December 1947? (above left)
Cocky (left) is mentioned many, many times
throughout the following few years. He offered
his hand in marriage, but she couldn't accept.

12ᵗʰ October 1949 Wednesday
"PRIMAUS"
"A kiss from Cocky that decided once & for all
that he & I were locked for ever in each others
hearts. From that day onward, Cocky & I
ventured out together hand in hand.
Immediately Aunt Dos, Uncle Fred & all my
proud relations voiced their objections. Cocky's
family & my family could never, ever, fuse into
one big happy family. "Don't invite me to your
wedding!" was the general cry."

26th August 1988 Friday
"And Old Maid Hewsie wept again when she
received in the post from Cocky a photograph
of Yvonne in her bridal outfit, looking lovingly
into the eyes of her father. Cocky is the only one
whose eyes I have ever looked into close
enough to see myself reflected there."

Thirza Mary Hewes - nicknamed
'Bunting' by her father Reg

Betty's half-brother Pat, father Reg and her
half-sister Bunting

Bunting with Betty's mother Mary and Betty who was only
seven years old when her father Reg died.

1956

5th August 1956: Mablethorpe
Back: Enid's Auntie Marge, Pam Bagnall,
Front: Enid and Betty

Leslie Hale's wife, Dorothy, with their
children Lesley & Bill

Bunting's sons Michael & Julian Stevenson
outside 27 Leicester Road, Easter 1961

25th April 1965 - Aunt Cis & Julian share a
joke while Michael attends to the car

Miss Katherine Sullivan who befriended
Betty in 1982 at the age of 78. She outlived
Betty, living to be over one hundred

Betty with Aunt Dos on her 80th Birthday
March 13th 1982

Betty had a penchant for leopard skin - be it a handbag, slippers, scarf or this jacket;
something she shared in common with another Bet - the landlady of this famous Inn.
She visited Granada Studios on **9th December 1991** with Mary Blue.

Pat, Evelyn, Karen, Graham, Betty, Scott, Mary Blue and Darren.
14th July 1991: Betty's 60th Birthday
Having hired a 'fox cub' mini-bus, to meet up with other members of the
family for a day out at Alton Towers on her 'Diamond Day', Betty wrote:
*"I am delighted to say that every single one of my dad's progeny have now
agreed to come."*

Outside number 27, Leicester Road; the white house opposite is Oak Tree Cottage.
6th May 1993 Thursday: "County Council Election & Cousin Miles was well & truly beaten by the Labour candidate."

Cousin Enid Hewes, Betty, Mary Danaher and Jacqui at Ravenstone Institute
8th May 1995 Monday: "A nostalgic evening to commemorate the 50th Anniversary of V.E. Day"

Nothing is known about this photograph.
It was found in the oak chest in which Betty kept her diaries and other keepsakes.
The diaries tell us that she and Cocky had only one brief holiday together.

12th May 1951 Saturday: *"I went to Cark in Cartmel, met Cocky at 9 p.m. in Manchester."*

Occasionally Betty added various explanatory notes at some later date and below this entry she had written:

Note: Whitsuntide Bank Holiday & I join Cocky for a long week-end together at Cark in Cartmel. He meets me off the train at Manchester & we are happy to be re-united...

1960

3rd January 1960 Sunday
Gustav said: - Resolve to greet the New Year with truth, freedom, faith & love.

10th January 1960 Sunday
Sylvia Cramphorn's first day as Sunday School Organist.

17th January 1960 Sunday
Rode to church with Enid & David.
"Where's Pamela?" said I.
"It's off" said Enid.
"Oh," said I.
Rode home with Irene.

21st January 1960 Thursday
Enid told me about Harold.

29th January 1960 Friday
"The cobbler" in Chu Chin Chow came from Leicester.

31st January 1960 Sunday
Sunday School badges given out.

6th February 1960 Saturday
Bought nylon dressing gown.

17th February 1960 Wednesday
We had our Sunday School party.

**19th February 1960 Friday
A prince is born – Prince Andrew.**

Note – The Queen has a baby – her second son, Prince Andrew Albert Christian Edward.

**26th February 1960 Friday
Princess Margaret engaged.**

1st March 1960 Tuesday
Went with Helen to the Institute for the Parish Family Party.

18th March 1960 Friday
I had my hair permed – La Croix. Met Mrs Ladyman.

**29th 30th 31st March Tuesday Wednesday Thursday
Chu Chin Chow.**

Note – Coalville "Amateurs" present Chu Chin Chow (one of my favourites)

10th April 1960 Sunday
I saw Pauline Aronsohn for the 1st time.

18th April 1960 Easter Monday
Went to Skegness & Mablethorpe with Enid, David & Irene.

26th April 1960 Tuesday
Enid & I saw concert at Progressive Hall given by Roy Johnson & Co.

27th April 1960 Wednesday
Mrs Nicholls retired from work.

29th April 1960 Friday
Amateur's Dinner Dance.

30th April 1960 Saturday
Miss Ladyman left Chez Dosh.

**6th May 1960 Friday
Princess Margaret married.**

Note – Princess Margaret married Antony Armstrong Jones.

7th May 1960 Saturday
I bought my blue suit.

8th May 1960 Sunday
Practice started for Sunday School Anniversary.

11th May 1960 Wednesday
Enid & I saw "A Country Girl" at Thringstone.

25th May 1960 Wednesday
I played croquet for the 1st time this year.

26th May 1960 Thursday
Communion Service at church 7-45 p.m.

27th May 1960 Friday
I bought my duster coat.

28th May 1960 Saturday
Brian Wardle took Enid & me to see a play at Staunton Harold.

31st May 1960 Tuesday
Snowdon. – Charles Stableforth, 258, Whitehill Road, Ellistown, the beloved husband of Ethel, passed away in hospital aged 55 years. Funeral service: St. Christopher's Church Ellistown, on Friday, 2-15 p.m. followed by cremation Gilroes 3 p.m. No flowers by request, but donations in lieu to Staunton Harold Home.

8th June 1960 Wednesday
In the rush hour traffic of Leicester, 6 p.m., an American Hudson car drew up beside our car & Helen said "If that's not the Duke of Bedford I'll eat my hat."
GJB 571.

18th June 1960 Saturday
Mummy & I went to Folkestone.

Note – Mum & I have a holiday in Folkstone.

21st June 1960 Tuesday
Went to Hythe & rode on the smallest public railway as far as **Dymchurch**.

22nd June 1960 Wednesday
We went to **Canterbury**. Went to the pictures at night, "School for Scoundrels".

23rd June 1960 Thursday
We went to Dover & got caught in a thunderstorm.

24th June 1960 Friday
Rainy day. We went to the pictures in the afternoon to see "**Gigi**".

25th June 1960 Saturday
Came home from Folkestone. Minnie of "Annie Minnie Maude" died.

26th June 1960 Sunday
Went to Marianne's house to hear a tape recording of Chu Chin Chow.

28th June 1960 Tuesday
Pat & Evelyn confirmed at St. James, Highfields.
Tony Stephens of Earl Shilton found, having been missing for fifteen months.

2nd July 1960 Saturday
I bought my dress from C & A.

3rd July 1960 Sunday
Auntie Belle & Uncle Fred brought home "**Skippy**" (skip along).

10th July 1960 Sunday
Our Sunday School Anniversary. I read the lesson at night

15th July 1960 Friday
Mummy went to Wysall for the day to see Reta.

17th July 1960 Sunday
Rodney Stacey wept at Sunday School because he thought he would not be able to go on the outing.

19th July 1960 Tuesday
I bought flower vase to use at work.

20th July 1960 Wednesday
Came home from Leicester via N. P. E. for the 1st time.

23rd July 1960 Saturday
Went to garden fête at Mrs Dunn's. (The Old Rectory)

24th July 1960 Sunday
Re-dedication of Ravenstone War Memorial.

30th July 1960 Saturday
Auntie Dos received a note from Auntie Nellie telling her not to visit Uncle Hedley.

8th August 1960 Monday
Mary Blue's first day at work. *(at Clutsom & Kemp, as a costing clerk)*
Uncle Hedley went into hospital.

17th August 1960 Wednesday
Cyprus Independence A midnight ceremony in the Assembly Hall of the new Republic ended 82 years of British rule in the island.

19th August 1960 Friday
Had my hair permed.

20th August 1960 Saturday
Enid & I flew from **Birmingham Airport** to **Dublin** 8-30 p.m.

21st August 1960 Sunday
Went to St. Paul's Church, Bray, for morning service. Tribute paid to Canon Campbell, who was buried yesterday, after being Rector in Bray for 17 years. Eamonn Andrews says of Bray in County Wicklow – "The little town tucked around the sea & ready to take you by the hand & lead you into the golden country it adorns."

22nd August 1960 Monday
Saw Dun Laoghaire for the first time at 8-40 p.m., & fell in love with it.

23rd August 1960 Tuesday
Went to Greystones & saw 2 fishermen mending their nets by their boats. I slept on a grassy slope.

24th August 1960 Wednesday
Went in Don's car to "The Hunter's Moon" & to Brittas Bay.

25th August 1960 Thursday
Went to Dalkey Island in the morning, to Greystones in afternoon & to Howth at night.

26th August 1960 Friday
Spent the morning shopping in Dun Loaghaire.
Went to Glendalough after dinner & coach tour along the coast to Wicklow at night.

27th August 1960 Saturday
Came home from Ireland & had tea at Enid's.

9th September 1960 Friday
Marlow. – Mary, of 52, Leicester Road, Ravenstone, the loving wife of Winson and mother of Dorothy, Jean, Pauline, loving grandma of Pat, Jean and Janet, passed peacefully away. Service at Ravenstone Church on Tuesday, 11a.m., followed by cremation, Gilroes.

10th September 1960 Saturday
Our Sunday School outing to **Mablethorpe**.

13th September 1960 Tuesday
Prince Aly Khan's will published today.
He died in a road crash in France in May.
Prince Aly directed that the remainder of his property be divided into three parts – two parts being divided among his heirs and the remaining third to pay legacies and duties. Yasmin's share is to be held on trust until she is 21. He added: "I solemnly request my two sons to treat my daughter Yasmin with affection, to give her good advice and to give her their protection,"

16th September 1960 Friday
Yesterday our entry wall was taken down.

22ⁿᵈ September 1960 Thursday
Geoffrey Chaucer was married in St. Mary De Castro Church, Leicester 22ⁿᵈ September 1360

27ᵗʰ September 1960 Tuesday
Dorothy & Douglas came to see Aunt Dos.

28ᵗʰ September 1960 Wednesday
Eve of our **Patronal Festival**. Went to church service at 8p.m. Preacher: The Archdeacon of Loughborough, The Venerable R. B. Cole.

2ⁿᵈ October 1960 Sunday
I read the lesson at the lectern for the first time at our Family Service at 2-30p.m.

3ʳᵈ October 1960 Monday
Rehearsals started for **"No No Nanette."**

6ᵗʰ October 1960 Thursday
Enid & I saw the comedy **"Friends and Neighbours"** at the Adult School.

12ᵗʰ October 1960 Wednesday
JAY 153 brought to be taxed.

14ᵗʰ October 1960 Friday
Went to Harvest Festival at The Plough.

In October 1935 – A bell presented to "Little St. Mary's" Church, Snibston, by Mr. Reg. A. Hewes and Mr. Cyril Hewes, of Ravenstone, was dedicated in memory of their mother, Mrs Mary Hewes.

15ᵗʰ October 1960 Saturday
Went to Harvest Supper at the Institute.

17ᵗʰ October 1960 Monday
Clarke.-Harriet formerly of Ravenstone Road, Coalville, widow of the late Arthur Clarke, passed peacefully away at the home of her daughter, "Glenholme," Leicester Road Ravenstone, in her 91ˢᵗ year. Service, Ravenstone Church Wednesday 1-45. Interment, London Road Cemetery.

18ᵗʰ October 1960 Tuesday
Harold & I went to the Rectory & discussed the Sunday School play with Gustav.

31ˢᵗ October 1960 Monday
Betsy left work.
A son was born to 22 year old **Queen Farah of Persia** today, giving the **Shah of Persia** an heir to the **Peacock Throne**. The Prince weighed four kilogrammes (about 8lb 12oz), the Queen & baby doing well. All the Royal Family gave thanks to Allah. A 3 day national holiday to celebrate the birth.

4ᵗʰ November 1960 Friday
We had a flat tyre going to work. Father Christmas crossed our path at night.

11ᵗʰ November 1960 Friday
I went by train to **Malvern**.

16ᵗʰ November 1960 Wednesday
Gilbert Harding died aged 53.

18ᵗʰ November 1960 Friday
First Libretto practice for "No No Nanette".

8ᵗʰ December 1960 Thursday
Mr Rose's daughter set sail for Australia.

10ᵗʰ December 1960 Saturday
Aunt Dos bought her car.

18ᵗʰ December 1960 Sunday
Our Sunday School play.

25ᵗʰ December 1960 Sunday
I read the lesson at 11a.m. service. Anne & Steve engaged this Christmas.

30ᵗʰ December 1960 Friday
Sheila Stacey married.

* * *

1961

Another one for the records. Has anybody realised that the year 1961 is an inverted palindrome? The last time this occurred was in 1881 and the next will be the year 6009.

D.W.Smith, Cranham, Essex.

1st January 1961 Sunday
Gustav said: - Most of us who were in their teens or over, twenty years ago, will remember King George VI's Christmas message as we were all moved by the words he spoke: "I said to the man who stood at the gate of the year 'Give me a light that I may tread safely into the unknown' and he replied 'Go out into the darkness and put your hand into the hand of God. That shall be to you better than light, and safer than a known way.'

The British farthing ceased to be legal tender.

4th January 1961 Wednesday
I cut my hair short, and made a fringe.

6th January 1961 Friday
Gustav came in the car with us to Leicester.

10th January 1961 Tuesday
Enid & I went to The Plough to watch Vic's pictures.

5th February 1961 Sunday
We welcomed the Rector back to church with flowers, after his illness.

8th February 1961 Wednesday
Went to Mary Spencer's flat at the Fosse Road Garage for rehearsal.

14th February 1961 Tuesday
Went to a concert at the Institute. Gustav gave me his chair.

15th February 1961 Wednesday
M.A.W.D. came into our office & gave me 10/- for tickets for the Amateurs.

18th February 1961 Saturday
Went with Brian Wardle on a bus trip from Griffydam (Church Choir) to Leicester Ice Show.

21st February 1961 Tuesday
Went to Vin Hardy's for tea & then had photos taken for the Amateurs.

24th February 1961 Friday
I had my hair permed at **Dany's** & saw **Francko** from the Hotel De France, Jersey.

25th February 1961 Saturday
Went to the De Montfort Hall to see the ballet "**Coppelia**".

27th February 1961 Monday
X-Ray

5th March 1961 Sunday
I sun bathed in the warm afternoon sun.

6th March 1961 Monday
George Formby died.

9th March 1961 Thursday
We had our new fence put up.

11th March 1961 Saturday
Went to **Nottingham** to see the film "**Ben Hur**".

13th March 1961 Monday
No No Nanette.

15th March 1961 Wednesday
Auntie Dos took Mummy & me in the car to Beacon Hill.

16th March 1961 Thursday
Went to Holy Communion at 10a.m. & to Anne's for elevenses.

21st March 1961 Tuesday
Pat became a member of the Parochial Church Council.

23rd March 1961 Thursday
Went with Enid & Aunt Dos to see "The Arcadians" at Thringstone.

24th March 1961 Friday
Amateurs' Dinner Dance.

25th March 1961 Saturday
Helen went into The Infirmary.

27th March 1961 Monday
Ladyman called to see Aunt Dos.

30th March 1961 Thursday
Bunting & family arrived at Pat's for the Easter Holiday.

31st March 1961 Good Friday
Michael, Julian, Aunt Dos & I went train spotting near Zouch. Had a film at night in church. Cocky came at dinner time.

1st April 1961 Saturday
Went train spotting at Burton on Trent.

4th April 1961 Tuesday
Went with Enid to see Roy Johnson's show at the Progressive Hall.

6th April 1961 Thursday
Enid & I went to see the play at the Adult School "**A Policeman's Lot**".

7th April 1961 Friday
Went to see Helen after her operation. I bought 2 sheets.

9th April 1961 Sunday
Practice started for Sunday School Anniversary.

11th April 1961 Tuesday
Eichmann trial begins today.

12th April 1961 Wednesday
Russia sent the first man into space. **Yuri Gagarin** was launched in **Vostok I** for a single orbit of the Earth. Went to Circus at Coalville.

13th April 1961 Thursday
I went to Snarestone for the County Council Election.

17th April 1961 Monday
Budget Day. Car Tax £15 from £12-10/-   Enid & I saw the film "South Pacific" at Coalville.

24th April 1961 Monday
Saw coloured slides of Vin's holiday in France.
A pebble off the beach from Capernaum (The Sea of Galilee) was brought to me.

28th April 1961 Friday
Went to the Rector's Room for a film show – Mission to Seamen.

29th April 1961 Saturday
I Colour-Glo'ed my hair for the first time.

13th May 1961 Saturday
First game of croquet this year.

22nd May 1961 Monday
Irene, David, Enid & I went to Mablethorpe for the day.

23rd May 1961 Tuesday
Went with Mummy in Aunt Dos' car to Howard Road, Glen Hills to take Audrey home.

7th June 1961 Wednesday
Note - Cocky & Joan have a baby daughter Yvonne. Although they live locally, I rarely see them.

11th June 1961 Sunday
Our Sunday School Anniversary.

17th June 1961 Saturday
Spent the afternoon at the Garden Fête at Ravenstone Hall.

18th June 1961 Sunday
Went to Coalville Park with Beverly & Christine Hill & Lynda Tivey.

19th June 1961 Monday
Went with the Amateurs to a barbecue on Beacon Hill.

23rd June 1961 Friday
Helen started to travel by bus instead of by car to Leicester.

3rd July 1961 Monday
Went playing bowls on The Scotlands with the Amateurs.

10th July 1961 Monday
Went to the Rectory for Sunday School Teachers'

meeting with Miss Fletcher.

18th July 1961 Tuesday
Mrs Wilde from Bardon Road started to travel with us to Leicester.

30th July 1961 Sunday
Had a Road Safety Service at church at 11a.m. Service relayed outside – lovely.

7th August 1961 Monday
David, Irene, Enid & I went to Mablethorpe for the day.

10th August 1961 Thursday
Enid & I went to see **Rita & John Tart** at "Greystones".

12th August 1961 Saturday
Enid & I flew from **Birmingham** to **Newquay, Cornwall**. Went to the pictures at night & saw "Tammy" & "Pyjama Game".

Note – Enid & I flew to Newquay for our summer holiday. We spent one day of the holiday with Enid's boss, Mr Clemerson & his family. Enid is his typist at Pegson's, Coalville. I am still unwilling to walk up hills. It upsets my breathing for a long time afterwards.

13th August 1961 Sunday
Went to **Tintagel**.

14th August 1961 Monday
Went to **Mevagissey**.

15th August 1961 Tuesday
Spent the day with Enid's Boss, Mr Clemerson & his family.

16th August 1961 Wednesday
Went across the ferry in a bus to **St. Mawes**.

17th August 1961 Thursday
Glorious hot day. Went in the swimming pool at our hotel "The Edgecumbe".

18th August 1961 Friday
Walked miles. Went to **Porth** in the morning & to **Pentire** in the afternoon & saw the River **Gannel**.

19th August 1961 Saturday
Came home from Newquay. Mummy came home from a week at Willoughby.

20th August 1961 Sunday
Learned that St. Bartholomew was Nathanial who was introduced to Jesus by Philip.

29th August 1961 Tuesday
New issue of red Driving Licence holders. Enid & I went down to Don's for the evening.

2nd September 1961 Saturday
Enid & I went to **Guernsey**.

Note – Enid & I take a second holiday, going by air to

Guernsey, the beautiful island forming part of the Channel Islands.

3rd September 1961 Sunday
Went by speed boat to **Herm**.

7th September 1961 Thursday
I met a Guernsey farmer at the dance.

8th September 1961 Friday
Jeff & Shirley had a baby girl **Tracy**.

9th September 1961 Saturday
Enid & I came home from Guernsey.

10th September 1961 Sunday
Arrival of Auntie Dos' new lodger K. Davies.

28th September 1961 Thursday
The Bishop came to bless our choir's new robes.

30th September 1961 Saturday
Enid & I went to the Adult School to see "The 10-5 Never Stops".

1st October 1961 Sunday
Gustav chose hymn 776, just for me.

7th October 1961 Saturday
Kibble left work.

9th October 1961 Monday
John Saunders asked me who owned car No. KUT 563.

25th October 1961 Wednesday
Electric heater installed in our bathroom. I went to Missionary Exhibition at Institute.

4th November 1961 Saturday
I went to Nottingham & bought a new coat.

8th November 1961 Wednesday
Marianne's Wedding.

24th November 1961 Friday
Enid & I went to **Malvern**.

9th December 1961 Saturday
Enid & I went to the Adult School to see the comedy **"Strike Happy"**.

13th December 1961 Wednesday
Went to "Any Questions?" at the Institute.

28th December 1961 Thursday
I bought our "Sole Mio" blanket.

30th December 1961 Saturday
I arrived at work at 10-30a.m. because of snow.

* * *

1962

20th January 1962 Saturday
I bought my beige shoes. Cocky came at night.

2nd February 1962 Friday
I came officially off the tea-making rota at work.

6th February 1962 Tuesday
I had an X-ray at Leicester Royal, for my impacted wisdom tooth.

26th February 1962 Monday
Margaret Dearden's baby daughter died.

28th February 1962 Wednesday
Treaddell – Hewes. – Mr and Mrs H. S. Treaddell, 385 Ashby Road, Coalville, wish to announce the engagement of their youngest daughter, Irene, on her 21st birthday, February 28th, to David, only son of Mr and Mrs C. H. Hewes, 50 Leicester Road, Ravenstone.

19th March 1962 Monday
South Pacific week. . . .

27th March 1962 Tuesday
Went to "**Fielding & Johnson**" to have my tooth out, but didn't because of my cold.

31st March 1962 Saturday
Went down to Harold's & made up sprays for Mothering Sunday.

2nd April 1962 Monday
Started "File As You Go" at work.

5th April 1962 Thursday
Auntie Dos gave me money in an envelope.

6th April 1962 Friday
Went to Amateurs' dinner dance.

7th April 1962 Saturday
Enid & I went to see "Wild Violets" at Thringstone.

13th April 1962 Friday
Went with Maurice Brooks to Social & Dance at The Fox & Goose.

16th April 1962 Monday
Played Table Tennis for the first time with the Amateurs.

17th April 1962 Tuesday
Terry & Mary Blue permed my hair at Pat's house.
20th April 1962 Good Friday
I went to an open air service in the Town Hall Square.

24th April 1962 Tuesday
I went into the Fielding Johnson hospital.

25th April 1962 Wednesday
I had my wisdom tooth out.

27th April 1962 Friday
I came home from hospital.

11th May 1962 Friday
Hewes – Dorman. – The engagement is announced between Theresa Ann, daughter of Mrs Patricia Dorman, Ridgway, Ashby-de-la-Zouch, and Peter Martin, son of Mr and Mrs Donald A. Hewes, "Littlecroft," Ravenstone.

14th May 1962 Monday
Played bowls with the Amateurs.

15th May 1962 Tuesday
Had X-Ray at Coalville.

19th May 1962 Saturday
I went to see a man about a scooter.

22nd May 1962 Tuesday
I went inside the Town Hall, & saw the masses of flowers ready for the new Lord Mayor.

23rd May 1962 Wednesday
Went with Enid in the Bluebell Car Rally organised by the Men's Fellowship.

27th May 1962 Sunday
Went by bus with the Rector & the choir to **3 farms & blessed the animals** etc.

2nd June 1962 Saturday
I had my first practice on my scooter in the yard behind Auto Supplies.

Note – I buy a motor scooter & have lessons with other learner drivers, mostly youths with motor cycles, on how to drive properly.

5th June 1962 Tuesday
Delivery of scooter. Pat went with me for practice down Mary's Lane.

6th June 1962 Wednesday
I went to Whitwick brickyard & had my first practice on a motor bike.

7th June 1962 Thursday
Practiced on my own & kangarooed round Institute corner.

11th June 1962 Monday
David, Irene, Enid & I went to Mablethorpe.

12th June 1962 Tuesday
Got up at 5-30 a.m. & went for scooter practice to Heather & Normanton. Still stalling.

13th June 1962 Wednesday
2nd scooter lesson. Fell off the practice scooter trying to turn. Then learned how to move slowly.

20th June 1962 Wednesday
Took my scooter to Whitwick brickyard for the first time. Mr Copestake rode pillion home.

23rd June 1962 Saturday
Pam Beadman married. I went to Measham on scooter.

24th June 1962 Sunday
Our Sunday School Anniversary.

27th June 1962 Wednesday
Went ride to Swannington, & back to Whitwick brickyard with Mr Copestake pillion.

30th June 1962 Saturday
Enid & I flew to **Sandown, Isle of Wight**.

1st July 1962 Sunday
Went to **Shanklin** along the sands & in a speed boat. Went to **Blackgang Chine** in the evening.

2nd July 1962 Monday
Blue Lagoon in morning. Boat ride in afternoon, & got sun-burned. Evening coach tour to St. Catherine's Lighthouse.

3rd July 1962 Tuesday
Morning walk to Culver Point & back through sheep fields. Bingo in hotel at night.

4th July 1962 Wednesday
Afternoon coach tour to Osborne House. Belles of St. Trinian-evening.

5th July 1962 Thursday
Went to East Cowes in afternoon to see **The Queen Mary** sail.

7th July 1962 Saturday
Up at 7-15 to walk along beach. Morning at Blue Lagoon. Sunshine all day. Watched television with manager. Later went with Roy to T.V. room.

8th July 1962 Sunday
Morning service at Parish Church. Afternoon coach tour to Needles. Saw baby sea-gulls & gathered wild flowers. 8p.m. sang hymns out of doors by the sea-shore.

9th July 1962 Monday
Sunshine all day. Sea very choppy. Swimming in blue lagoon.

10th July 1962 Tuesday
Wet morning. Afternoon went to Ryde & got a silver spoon. Had a drink with Roy in the bar.

11th July 1962 Wednesday
Afternoon putting. Evening fancy dress. Roy & I stayed in ballroom after dance.

12th July 1962 Thursday
Went to the Pier Ballroom to a concert. Saw Sandown from Pier Head, bathed in moonlight across the water.

13th July 1962 Friday
Boat trip to Culver Point. Swimming in Blue Lagoon. Stayed with Roy till 5.

14th July 1962 Saturday
Went with Roy to Ryde, for the afternoon. Flew home at 8-15p.m.

15th July 1962 Sunday
Went with Cocky to Hinckley in the morning & for a ride round the forest in the afternoon.

Note – Cocky & his pal were going by car to Hinckley & gave me a lift in the back of the car.

18th July 1962 Wednesday
Enid, Aunt Dos & I went on car rally which finished at Staunton Harold.

19th July 1962 Thursday
Uncle Cyril went into hospital.

20th July 1962 Friday
I went with Don & Phyl to Barbecue at Ashby. Met Vera & Russell Robinson.

21st July 1962 Saturday
Peter broke off his engagement with Theresa.

22nd July 1962 Sunday
Road Safety Service in morning. Pegson's Car Rally in afternoon, ending at Alvaston Park, Derby. We then called to see Walter & family.

25th July 1962 Wednesday
Went for scooter practice. Stayed at the Brickyard with Son & fell off doing figure 8.

1st August 1962 Wednesday
Spent scooter practice indoors at Whitwick colliery. Rode home with lights for 1st time.

4th August 1962 Saturday
Marilyn Monroe died.

5th August 1962 Sunday
Pat, Evelyn, Mum & I went a ride in the evening to Willoughby. **Nelson Mandela** sentenced to life imprisonment in South Africa.

6th August 1962 Monday
Peter's 21st birthday party at Masonic Hall. Had a perm.

8th August 1962 Wednesday
Went for ride on scooter to Beacon Hill. Auntie Dos led the way in her car.

12th August 1962 Sunday
I went a ride on scooter to Groby Pool & Old John.

16th August 1962 Thursday
Aunt Dos went with me to Coleorton, then Mr Copestake took me on scooter to Melbourne.

17th August 1962 Friday
Went scooter ride with Mr Copestake to Breedon & Shepshed.

18ᵗʰ August 1962 Saturday
Went on scooter to Loughborough & Barrow-on-Soar.

19ᵗʰ August 1962 Sunday
Went with Mr Copestake for afternoon scooter practice. Church at night with no parson.

22ⁿᵈ August 1962 Wednesday
Went to scooter practice & tried to do figure eight all night without success.

29ᵗʰ August 1962 Wednesday
Went out in ones round by Hugglescote church at practice. I took Mr Copestake to Coleorton.

30ᵗʰ August 1962 Thursday
Mr Copestake rode pillion with me to Willoughby. Mrs Copestake wasn't very pleased.

5ᵗʰ September 1962 Wednesday
Went out in ones round test circuit. I took Mr Copestake home.

8ᵗʰ September 1962 Saturday
Sunday School outing to Whipsnade Zoo & ride on the M. I.

12ᵗʰ September 1962 Wednesday
Had Highway Code Test practice.

13ᵗʰ September 1962 Thursday
Went ride with Mr Copestake. Practiced starting on hill etc. Came home by moonlight.

14ᵗʰ September 1962 Friday
I sent off application for Driving Test.

15ᵗʰ September 1962 Saturday
Pat, Enid, Mum & I went to the football match at **Leicester**.

19ᵗʰ September 1962 Wednesday
Practiced riding in & out of bricks, etc. Needed lights on.

21ˢᵗ September 1962 Friday
Aunt Dos bought Black Toy Poodle.

22ⁿᵈ September 1962 Saturday
Mr Copestake adjusted my clutch cable, at his house. Had the battery re-charged.

23ʳᵈ September 1962 Sunday
Pat & I went to see Fanny & Thirza. Pat rode pillion on scooter.

26ᵗʰ September 1962 Wednesday
Practiced figure 8's. Then went indoors for instruction from Son.

27ᵗʰ September 1962 Thursday
Went to coffee evening at "Littlecroft".

28ᵗʰ September 1962 Friday
Enid & I went to see "The Amorous Goldfish" at the Adult School.

29ᵗʰ September 1962 Saturday
Enid & I went with Pegson's outing to Matlock Bath illuminations.

30ᵗʰ September 1962 Sunday
Enid & I went on Pegson's car rally finishing at Drayton Manor.

3ʳᵈ October 1962 Wednesday
Practiced Right Hand Turn into Whitwick Colliery, then went indoors for simple maintenance instruction.

6ᵗʰ October 1962 Saturday
Scooter had 600 miles service. I bought green coat.

7ᵗʰ October 1962 Sunday
Mr Copestake rode pillion with me to Leicester for practice round the test course.

9ᵗʰ October 1962 Tuesday
"Nankie Poo" put to sleep. *(Aunt Dos's Pekinese dog)*

10ᵗʰ October 1962 Wednesday
Had Highway Code with Son.

11ᵗʰ October 1962 Thursday
Harvest Festival. Pat read lesson.

12ᵗʰ October 1962 Friday
Harvest Festival at The Plough.

13ᵗʰ October 1962 Saturday
Harvest Supper at the 'stute. **Ena Sharples** at Coalville.

14ᵗʰ October 1962 Sunday
Harvest Festival at church.

17ᵗʰ October 1962 Wednesday
Had instruction from Son on the workings of an engine

20ᵗʰ October 1962 Saturday
Enid & I went to Ellistown to see a play. Bought winter dress. Black & orange.

21ˢᵗ October 1962 Sunday
Went to Lount colliery for scooter practice.

24ᵗʰ October 1962 Wednesday
Had a mock test on Highway Code & simple maintenance one by one with Son.

26ᵗʰ October 1962 Friday
Auditions for "**Oklahoma**".

31ˢᵗ October 1962 Wednesday
Last practice at Whitwick colliery. I took Mr Copestake home.

1ˢᵗ November 1962 Thursday
Saw the film "**Oklahoma**".

3ʳᵈ November 1962 Saturday
Pete of "Auto Supplies" cleaned my spark plug & C.B.

points, ready for test tomorrow.

4th November 1962 Sunday
Went for the test & it was cancelled.

8th November 1962 Thursday
Terry bought his record player & we had a session at Pat's.

11th November 1962 Sunday
Mr Copestake & I went to Leicester via the forest. Our church altered to side door entrance instead of belfry door.

Note – Ravenstone Church changed its entrance from the belfry door to the side-door, facing the front gate.

15th November 1962 Thursday
Went to Confirmation service at Ravo.

18th November 1962 Sunday
Went for the R.A.C. test & failed.

25th November 1962 Sunday
Went to see Mr Copestake who was at home with a broken leg.

1st December 1962 Saturday
Went to Coalville to watch Enid play hockey & ended up playing goalie.

6th December 1962 Thursday
Stan Burder died.

8th December 1962 Saturday
Failed my Driving Test in Leicester.
Note – Took my driving test on scooter in Leicester & failed.

9th December 1962 Sunday
Went to see Mr Copestake in the morning.

28th December 1962 Friday
Did not go to work, because I'd been up all night with sickness & diarrhoea.

31st December 1962 Monday
Mr Kennard had the Driving Licence section into his office & blew his top because they were not "filing as you go".

* * *

1963

24th January 1963 Thursday
Had a Sunday School Teacher's meeting at Ravenstone School.

26th January 1963 Saturday
Mary Blue had a bath at our house, because their water supply was frozen.

2nd February 1963 Saturday
Went with Amateurs to see "**Oklahoma**" at Hanley.

9th February 1963 Saturday
Enid & I went to Ellistown to see the comedy "**Flat Spin**".

23rd February 1963 Saturday
Marion & I went to the Progressive Hall to watch a programme of children dancing.

2nd March 1963 Saturday
I went on booking for the Amateurs at the Gas Show Rooms.

3rd March 1963 Sunday
I went to see Susan in bed, after having her tonsils out.

6th March 1963 Wednesday
Had an interview with Mr Blackburn for 2nd clerk in Driving Licences.

8th March 1963 Friday
"**Oklahoma**" started.

16th March 1963 Saturday
Passed test Group "G".

Note – At my second attempt, I passed my scooter driving test.

28th March 1963 Thursday
Mr Rose retired.

29th March 1963 Friday
Went to **Launde Abbey**.

5th April 1963 Friday
Amateurs Dinner Dance.

6th April 1963 Saturday
Enid & I went to see "**The Quaker Girl**" at Thringstone.

7th April 1963 Sunday
I talked to the children about **Launde Abbey**.

9th April 1963 Tuesday
Sir Winston Churchill made Honorary Citizen of the U.S.A.

15th April 1963 Monday
Bunting, Mostyn, Michael & Julian at Ravenstone. We had tea at Pat's.

16th April 1963 Tuesday
Went to see "**Oklahoma**", given by **Melton Operatic Society**.

18th April 1963 Thursday
Mr Kennard went into hospital.

20th April 1963 Saturday
Mum & I had a shopping spree in Leicester.
Enid & I went to see the Adult School play "Curious Savage".

23rd April 1963 Tuesday
Went to Snarestone to see Uncle Frank & Aunt Lil. Mary Moore there.

27th April 1963 Saturday
David & Irene married at 2 p.m. I went to the Bell Hotel at night.

Note – Enid's brother David married Irene Treaddell.

4th May 1963 Saturday
Went to the Town Hall, Ashby-de-la-Zouch to see "The Mikado".

5th May 1963 Sunday
Started giving out "Adventurers" at Sunday School. Mr Bagnall made Church Warden Emeritus.

6th May 1963 Monday
I went to The Rex to see "The Royal Wedding" & "The Counterfeit Spy".

11th May 1963 Saturday
Kennard. – Donald, of 116, Lutterworth Road, younger son of the late William and Ada Kennard, husband of Gwen and father of Nan and Jane, brother of Colin and Edna, passed peacefully away, aged 53 years. At rest. No flowers or letters, by request. Funeral service at Aylestone Parish Church Wednesday at 11a.m. Cremation following at Gilroes Crematorium.

12th May 1963 Sunday
I went to the Anniversary at Ravenstone Chapel.

20th May 1963 Monday
Went to the annual meeting of the Ivanhoe Group of W. I. at Ravo.

21st May 1963 Tuesday
(Letter in paper – can you guess who the poet is?)

While Leicester thrills with prospects of "City for the Cup!" the price of final tickets is going up and up. Please tell me where is the man who'll say to me, "This ticket is worth three guineas. It's yours for three pounds three!"
   O. WARE, 27, Leicester Road, Snibston.

22nd May 1963 Wednesday
Went in 2nd Bluebell Car Rally.

23rd May 1963 Thursday
Mayor-Making Day in Leicester.

25th May 1963 Saturday
Watched the Cup Final on Television. **Manchester United** beat **Leicester** 3-1.

16th June 1963 Sunday
Sunday School Anniversary. I read the first lesson at night.

18th June 1963 Tuesday
Enid & I went to Normanton on the scooter.

23rd June 1963 Sunday
David, Irene, Enid & I went on Pegson's Car Rally to Stapleford Park.

24th June 1963 Monday
Enid & I went on the scooter to Beacon Hill for the Amateurs barbecue.

29th June 1963 Saturday
Enid & I flew to Dublin (President Kennedy there). Then by train to Galway.

Note – Enid & I chose Galway, on the far west coast of Ireland for a fortnight's holiday. First we flew to Dublin, but could not land until President Kennedy of America had left the airport. We travelled by train across Ireland from Dublin to Galway to find that there too, we had just missed seeing President Kennedy. The weather was atrocious – rain, rain, rain, every day, & so little of interest to do, we packed our bags & spent the 2nd week in Dublin.

1st July 1963 Monday
Went on an afternoon coach tour to Cong & walked round lovely Ashford Castle.

2nd July 1963 Tuesday
Went to the pictures & saw "The Miracle Worker", about a young girl who was blind, deaf and dumb.

3rd July 1963 Wednesday
Went to Galway. Walked to Salmon Bridge Weir. Evening tour.

4th July 1963 Thursday
All day tour of Connemara.

5th July 1963 Friday
Lovely afternoon motor launch cruise to Lough Corrib. Evening pictures to see "Pollyanna."

6th July 1963 Saturday
Left the west of Ireland & came to The Salthill Hotel, Monkstown, Co. Dublin.

8th July 1963 Monday
Explored Dun Laoghaire. Walked at night out to the lighthouse.

9th July 1963 Tuesday
Went to a comedy called "**Say it in French**"- very good.

10th July 1963 Wednesday
Went on a tour of Dublin City- South Dublin. Some of Dublin's finest buildings are seen on this tour. The library of Trinity College is visited to inspect the book of Kells. Also the Irish Hospitals' Sweepstakes Headquarters to see the sweep drum. (Given a Zodiac tumbler) Also a visit inside St. Patrick's Cathedral.

11th July 1963 Thursday
Watched part of the 78th Lawn Tennis Championships of Ireland in Dublin.

12th July 1963 Friday
Went on another City sightseeing tour of Dublin- North Dublin & coast. Included in this tour of Dublin is a drive through Phoenix Park (The biggest Park in the world except for a natural one in America). Round by the Dublin Zoo- from the bus you could see lions, bears, giraffes, an elephant, seals, etc. On to Corpus Christi Church Dublin, finished in 1940 (Eamonn Andrews married there). We stopped there & went inside. A big climb in the bus up the hill in Howth where from the top is a vast view of Dublin Bay.

20th July 1963 Saturday
Went to Snarestone after tea.

5th August 1963 Monday
Went to Barrow-on-Soar to see Marie & family.

6th August 1963 Tuesday
Mum & I went to New Brighton via The Mersey Tunnel.

10th August 1963 Saturday
Played croquet. Sent off 800 clue Crossword!

28th August 1963 Wednesday
Mr Johnson had his new Vauxhall WKV 101.
Martin Luther King made his "I have a dream" speech, which he wrote at night in a Washington hotel overlooking the Mall before delivering it on August 28th to 200,000 people in front of the Lincoln Memorial. He called on everyone to share his vision of a country where the colour of someone's skin did not determine his future.

31st August 1963 Saturday
Scott. - Bert, dearly loved husband of Doris, father of Maureen and Ken, granddad of Graham and Roger, on August 31. Service at Hugglescote Church, Wednesday, September 4th at 10-30a.m., followed by cremation at Loughborough Crematorium at 11-30a.m.

2nd September 1963 Monday
Went to Amateurs in Enid's car for the first time.

7th September 1963 Saturday
Went to Skegness on Sunday School outing.

10th September 1963 Tuesday
Rector gave me teeny cross. Mum on the jury.

Note – Mum was called for service on the Jury.

13th September 1963 Friday
I went to the De Montfort Hall to watch wrestling.

14th September 1963 Saturday
I went to Glenfield to see Reevsie's house & also Ann & Steve's.

15th September 1963 Sunday
Our new system of Sunday School started.

17th September 1963 Tuesday
WKV 101 conked out – no petrol.
We were home 1hr. late.

20th September 1963 Friday
Reevsie moved into new home at Glenfield.
The Coalville Times reported a snippet under the heading "**25 Years Ago**".
"Mr Reg A. Hewes' witty remarks between items were a highlight of the young people's harvest demonstration organised by Coalville Salvation Army." The **Times** recalls they "added spice to an excellent programme rendered by the young people."

Note – This was my fun-loving dad who, amongst other things, was the wittiest auctioneer in the district. People flocked to his auctions just for entertainment.

22nd September 1963 Sunday
Went with Enid, David & Irene on Pegson's Car Rally finishing at Market Bosworth. Had a flat tyre.

23rd September 1963 Monday
I arrived at work at 9-20a.m. because of traffic hold up.

26th September 1963 Thursday
Enid brought me 10/-. Share of 2nd Prize from Car Rally.

3rd October 1963 Thursday
Victor Kendrick married.

4th October 1963 Friday
Aunt Dos, Enid & I went to see "Doctor in the House" at the Adult School.

25th October 1963 Friday
Went with Amateurs to see "**Song of Norway**" at Burton-on-Trent.

27th October 1963 Sunday
George Reynolds had a ride as pillion on my scooter.

7th November 1963 Thursday
11 miners brought up after being trapped for a fortnight at Lengede in Germany.

22nd November 1963 Friday
President Kennedy died.
Note – President Kennedy was assassinated, in Dallas, Texas.

24th November 1963 Sunday
Lee Harvey Oswald, charged with the assassination of **US President John F. Kennedy,** was shot by nightclub owner **Jack Ruby**. **Epithet** - "Fate carved out a unique ordeal for Jacqueline Kennedy and history will recall her magnificent response." **Lilham**.

27th November 1963 Wednesday
Went to the Cathedral for a service in memory of **President Kennedy**.

29th November 1963 Friday
Mum & I went to see the Adult School play:-"When we are Married".

1st December 1963 Sunday
Went to Holy Communion at little St. Mary's for the first time.

3rd December 1963 Tuesday
Morgan & Squires new restaurant opened. Each customer given a red rose buttonhole.

6th December 1963 Friday
Mum & I went to Snarestone on the scooter. Mary Moore there.

16th December 1963 Monday
Glover. – Frank, dear husband of Lily Gertrude, passed away, aged 88 years. Funeral Snarestone Church, 3 p.m., Friday 20th.

* * *

1964

Note – Now I have my first "Five Year Diary", & achieve an entry for every day for the next five years.

1st January 1964 Wednesday
After a service in Ravenstone Church, saw the New Year in beneath the moon – very high in the sky. Dennis Collier rang the 3 bells all by himself and we had light refreshments in the Rector's Room followed by "Auld Lang Syne".

2nd January 1964 Thursday
Lovely Spring-like day. Reevsie up in arms because Mr Colderic ordered her to work until 8 p.m., & then not enough work to last us all until then. I left at 6-45 p.m.

3rd January 1964 Friday
Went to work on the 7 a.m. bus. Came home on the 8-20 p.m. from St. Margaret's – the church bells pealing out into the clear night air.
First mention at work of opening all dinner time.

4th January 1964 Saturday
The first visit to the Holy Land by a successor to St. Peter began with the visit of Pope Paul dressed in a long white cloak. The people of Jerusalem cheered wildly & waved palm branches. Leyton Orient knocked out Leicester City for the Cup.

5th January 1964 Sunday
Pope Paul visited Nazareth, Cana of Galilee & Capernaum & then returned to Jerusalem.
We had Sunday School in the Rector's Room minus electric light and heat because of power failure.

6th January 1964 Monday
The Pope took Epiphany gifts of gold, frankincense & myrrh to Bethlehem.
Then from Amman Airport he boarded a plane to fly back to Rome at the end of his 3 day "pilgrimage of peace".

7th January 1964 Tuesday
Lovely Spring-like day. Reevsie & I expected to work until 8-45 p.m. so we went in to see Mr Sharpe. Fortunately I was given permission to leave at 8 p.m.
Uncle Cyril went to Leicester for X-Ray.

8th January 1964 Wednesday
Mr Sharpe said he wanted to kill once & for all, the "MYTH" that D. Ls had to work too hard during the summer. Statistics showed that they worked no more than anybody else in the office.

9th January 1964 Thursday
I came home from work in a huff because I was made to stay until 7 p.m. with nothing to do but Driving Licence reminders. I there-upon decided to brush up my short hand. An advertisement in shorthand in the Leicester Mercury, also spurred me on.

10th January 1964 Friday
The Coalville Times again mentioned my dad who died

11th January 1939, under the heading-
<u>25 YEARS AGO</u>
The funeral took place of Mr Reg Hewes, the well-known auctioneer. There was a large congregation at St. Mary's Church, Snibston – so large that many people had to stand outside.

11th January 1964 Saturday
President Johnson in America is faced with his first big crisis since coming into office last November 22nd (when Kennedy died). Riots in Panama over the ownership of the 50 mile canal. The Republic of Panama objects to the 10 mile wide Canal Zone belonging to U. S. and not to them.

12th January 1964 Sunday
The first Sunday after Epiphany & also Plough Sunday. The Rector blessed the plough at evensong service. The plough was pushed up the aisle by Mr Cliff & Mr Waltho. Mrs H. Bennion & Mrs Brearley read the lessons.

13th January 1964 Monday
Got up in the morning to find snow everywhere. Snowed all the way to Leicester & we did quite a bit of skidding. Our new filing cabinets all being used for the first time today, at work.

14th January 1964 Tuesday
I stayed overtime until 8 p.m. helping with the out of orders which I quite enjoyed.
Our television away being mended. I bought a mother-of-pearl handled letter opener. Thought it might do for a <u>Christmas</u> present!

15th January 1964 Wednesday
Eamonn Andrews quits BBC after 12 years & goes to ITV. The bus home from Leicester took me for the very first time under the new bridge (ready for the M I) near The Flying Horse.

16th January 1964 Thursday
Mum went to Mountsorrel for the day to see Auntie Doris. Bitterly cold day. I bought silver spoon with Leicester City crest. Bus shelter being erected near to Ravenslea entrance.

17th January 1964 Friday
I bought ½ dozen fruit spoons. Caught the 6-20 bus home. Our television back home again – went to be mended on Monday! Two new extra-long single decker buses for Leicester's Outer Circle route - £5,000 each, 36 ft. long. Carry 53 people, two more also on order.

18th January 1964 Saturday
Uncle Cyril was up from 4 p.m. until 10 p.m. He looked very ill. Today is his wedding anniversary – 41 years. That which makes the roses grow was sighted outside our house, so I was out with the dust-pan!

19th January 1964 Sunday
The Rector gave me literature concerning religious drama, so I wrote to Mrs Smith, St. Martin's East, Leicester, offering my services for a speaking part.
Our television just back from being mended is worse

than ever it was before it went!

20th January 1964 Monday
Mum spent the day with Hilda at South Wigston. I caught the 7-20 p.m. bus home. Terribly foggy so I did not go to Amateurs rehearsal – in fact I have not been at all yet this year because of overtime.

21st January 1964 Tuesday
Because of exceptionally bad fog, I was allowed to catch the 5-20 p.m. bus home. A most interesting journey – finally reached home at 7 p.m. Part of the M I was closed by the police because of so many pile-ups.
I saw a Leicester City policeman wearing a "smog mask"; I had never seen one before.

22nd January 1964 Wednesday
Caught the 7 a.m. bus to work. Mr Johnson had left his car in Leicester for the night because of the fog. I bought a dozen 6″ rulers for the Sunday School children & also some Mothering Sunday cards for them from S.P.C.K.

23rd January 1964 Thursday
Went to the Amateurs after my long absence through working overtime. Made very welcome – did the whole of Act I (Desert Song). Came home & saw the latter part of Offenbach's sparkling operetta "La Belle Hóélène"- really great! (Hélène is Helen of Troy)

Note – January continues to be a very busy month at work & we work long into the evening. Even so, I manage to maintain my interest in Coalville Amateurs, & attend rehearsals whenever possible.

24th January 1964 Friday
Bought a book – **Teach Yourself Typewriting** – so for the first time in 16 years I typed the letter "A" with the correct finger. Then of course I got the urge to buy a type-writer!
Auntie Dos under the Doctor with laryngitis.

25th January 1964 Saturday
Went into Elmo's at Coalville for the very first time.
Learned that Dr. Hamilton had been made President of our Amateur Operatic Society.
Alan Pettitt put a new washer on our hot tap.

26th January 1964 Sunday
Ruth Jones & Rosemary Green in the choir for the first time. I had a ride down to church at night with Margery Slatter. I am very busy struggling along with my shorthand. Have been since January 9th, but am slowly but surely improving.

27th January 1964 Monday
I went to Imperial Typewriters for some literature, and then decided I would like to buy their Good Companion 7, £32-10/-. Reevsie away from work. Charles went to the Opticians to see about getting some reading glasses.

28th January 1964 Tuesday
I went to Morgan & Squires for dinner, because it was a rainy day & I did not fancy walking to Lewis's & back. Reevsie still not at work & so I spent ½ hr. at dinner time practicing type-writing in the office.

29th January 1964 Wednesday
The Leicester Mercury launched a scheme to help the old lonely people via The Welfare Department, 3, Pocklingtons Walk, Leicester. Envelopes to be marked- "The Lonely Ones".
Dunton Bassett Parish Church was full today for the funeral of Major Robertson-Aikman -97.

30th January 1964 Thursday
I ordered my type-writer, & was informed I should have to wait probably a fortnight for delivery. Glorious day- we had the doors open at work! Invitation came round the office to attend the unveiling of the bronze bust of Sir Robert Martin in the County Rooms.

31st January 1964 Friday
The Mercury gave the startling news that 64 year old Miss Walker of A. M. Walker Ltd. At Cosby, had married 82 year old Lord Hall of Germains Lodge, Amersham, Bucks. They were married on Wednesday. Miss Walker said, "It has nothing to do with Leap Year!"

1st February 1964 Saturday
Lovely day. I went for a scooter ride to Snarestone to see my Uncle Frank's grave. He died December 16th last year, aged 88. Auntie Gladys birthday. Uncle Cyril very ill. I spent much of the day practicing short hand.

2nd February 1964 Sunday
Enid & I called in to see Auntie Rene on the way home from church at night. We stayed until 9 p.m. She gave us each a glass of sherry & we looked at photos of Rita's wedding, & also of Shirley's.(Shirley Hinds who works with Auntie Rene)

3rd February 1964 Monday
Arnold Walker at the Amateur's rehearsal. He bought me a sherry. The Driving Licence Section had its own telephone installed – great excitement when it rang for the first time – it was only the switchboard testing whether or not we were connected.

4th February 1964 Tuesday
Philip Bancroft brought a wall-paper book for us to choose something for the front bed-room. Alma Ford home again after living for a while in Coventry. Her husband just won £100 & so they bought a car.

5th February 1964 Wednesday
We had wooden blocks laid at work to hold the new filing cabinets in place. Mr Rose came into the office & told us that yesterday was his 38th Wedding Anniversary. Clear blue sky & sunshine all day but very cold.

6th February 1964 Thursday
Cold & frosty morning. Reevsie away from work with a temperature. I had dinner with Steve. A list came round the office for those who would like to go on the County Council elections, to be held April 9th.

7th February 1964 Friday
The Queen Mother making good progress in hospital after her appendicitis operation last Tuesday. Photograph in the Coalville Times today of the oldest man in

Ravenstone, Mr Charles Colver – 92 last Wednesday!

8th February 1964 Saturday
"Friendly" Midland Red on strike, so I went by train to Leicester for an audition with the County Drama Adviser for his proposed autumn production.
Came home by car with Mrs Brabin-Smith.

9th February 1964 Sunday
The last day of the Winter Olympic Games at Innsbruck. Jacqueline Hull-Perry in the choir for the first time. Mum changed her night duty to be at home tonight, specially to see Nureyev dance!

10th February 1964 Monday
Mr Johnson came home from work at 4-30 p.m. in order to call at the Doctor's. I therefore came home on the 6-20 bus. Philip Bancroft & his mates started work re-decorating our front bedroom.

11th February 1964 Tuesday
I had a tooth filled. Nothing to pay until May as I have a 6 monthly check-up arranged for then – so I celebrate by buying a pair of shoes to wear in the office. Auntie Cis arrived in Ravenstone yesterday to stay for a week with Aunt Dos.

12th February 1964 Ash Wednesday!
We had a church service at 8 p.m. I went with Pat & Evelyn. The church was in the process of being painted & decorated.
The "**Beatles**" in America are a great success. Watched them on TV.

13th February 1964 Thursday
I had a phone call from Imperial Type-writers to say my type writer was ready & could be delivered tomorrow.
I made an appointment for a "**Bargain**" perm at Lewis's for February 29 th!
Special offer 3 guinea perm for 2 guineas!

14th February 1964 Friday
I had a phone call from Imperial Type-writers to say very sorry they'd not managed to get out to Ravenstone today. They would come on Monday at 9-30 a.m. to bring my new type-writer.
Our front bedroom being papered, now has all its new paper on –"Very nice too".

15th February 1964 Saturday
I took my scooter to have its 1,800 mile service. My type-writer arrived! Enid & I went to see John Saunders in his play "Time & The Conways" at the Little Theatre, Dover Street, Leicester. Fred Burton & his wife came with us. We all enjoyed it thoroughly.

Note I buy my first typewriter, & am delighted to have such a treasure.

16th February 1964 Sunday
Sleet and snow nearly all day long. The Queen Mother returned home after a fortnight in hospital following an operation for appendicitis.
I am very thrilled with my new type-writer – keep having another little "go" on it.

17th February 1964 Monday
Woke to find snow everywhere.
The "Mercury" headlines read:- "**Bulldozer Digs up Bomb on M I Workings**"
A live high explosive bomb – a German 100 pounder dropped 20 years ago uncovered yesterday at 11-40 a.m. near Lockington.

18th February 1964 Tuesday
I replied to this advertisement in the "Mercury"-
Ladies with own typewriters wanted with good knowledge of local and surrounding districts for addressing envelopes from local directories. For details, please send sample self addressed envelope to Barson Advertising Co., 97, Cromford House, Cromford Court, Manchester 4.

19th February 1964 Wednesday
Neither Mr Sharp nor Mr Colderic at work – so – while the cat is away the mice do play. Lots of frivolity & high jinks at work. Mum reading her first book from the travelling County Library "The Heart has its Reasons" – Memoirs of the Duchess of Windsor.

20th February 1964 Thursday
Ten Pound notes become legal tender today for the first time in nearly 19 years, and the Bank of England has printed ten million ready for issue. £10 notes were last issued in April 1943 & ceased to be legal tender in May 1945. I have never even seen one at all. The number of motor licences issued by Leicestershire County Council last year was more than double that of 10 years ago. Last year 119,690 were in force compared with 51,555 in 1954. Of the latest number, 79,830 were for private cars, 18,990 for motor cycles and 13,040 for goods vehicles.

21st February 1964 Friday
I paid for my type-writer. I spent the whole evening composing a poem which I sent to the Editor of the Leicester Mercury. It was a poem about how much I enjoy hearing the church bells ring (inspired by a poem on similar lines by somewhat of a non-lover of bells).

22nd February 1964 Saturday
Unprecedented scenes at London Airport when the "**Beatles**" arrived home after a most successful fortnight in America. Enid & I decided to write to "Clarehaven" Bognor, & also to the "Esplanade", Scarborough as possible hotels for our August holiday.

23rd February 1964 Sunday
Our church looking all spick & span having been freshly decorated all through. Six of my Sunday School children now in the choir – Carole Harrison, Zena Bennett, Ruth Jones, Rosemary Green, Jacqueline Hull-Perry & Lesley Hurst.

24th February 1964 Monday
I received a reply from Barson Advertising Co. saying I might be considered for typing envelopes for them (4/- per 100 envelopes). Would I please send ten shillings registration fee! (I think I might)

25th February 1964 Tuesday
Enid & I received replies from both Bognor Regis &

Scarborough & decided to accept the offer of the "Clarehaven" at Bognor for August 8th.
Uncle Cyril seriously ill in bed. I sat with him for about half an hour. He told me some of his inner fears & secret thoughts.

26th February 1964 Wednesday
Cassius Clay defeated **Sonny Liston**, thus winning the World Heavy-weight Championship. I watched 9 Leicester College students walk to the Town Hall Square carrying a 20ft. long "**Crocodile**" to publicise **Rag Week**.

27th February 1964 Thursday
I went to book for a Barton's Blue Bus Tour of Devon & Cornwall for Mum & me –Aug.29th
The Leicester Mercury printed my poem which I wrote last Friday. They found a title –

"Hooray for Bells!"
Ding
Ding Dong
Ding Dong Ding
What joy they bring
The city bells at night;
They fill us with delight.
When overtime has made us late
And we have worked 'til after eight,
We leave the office in a daze,
And then the bells our spirits raise.
Although the birds have ceased to sing,
We feel once more our hearts take wing.
The new born babes have surely timed
A perfect entrance – bells have chimed!
Like Whittington in days of old
We see the city paved with gold.
For when the moon is looking down
She casts her spell upon the town.
Then all our tribulation
Is lost in admiration
For all those worthy ringers;
Those ding dong ding dong dingers.
May all these men
Again and again
Ring Ding Dong
Ding Dong
Ding.

(Written for Page Four by Ravenna Stone, in reply to D.G., Lutterworth).

28th February 1964 Friday
"Bible Story", the weekly magazine out for the very first time this week. I bought the No 1 issue.
A new machine arrived at our office to act as a cash sheet for all vehicle licences issued over the counter.

29th February 1964 Saturday
The first of the four royal babies expected early this year- Princess Alexandra gave birth to her first son 9 ½ lbs. Mum & I went to Leicester at 8 a.m. with Mr Johnson. We ordered green fitted carpet for the front bedroom. I had my hair permed & Mum bought curtain material.

1st March 1964 Sunday
A four engined Britannia Turbo-prop belonging to British Eagle International was found completely wrecked in the mountains, 6 miles from its destination, Innsbruck, Austria. It left London Airport yesterday with a crew of 8 and 75 passengers aboard.

2nd March 1964 Monday
Uncle Cyril had his bed moved downstairs into the front room. I went in to see him for a few minutes. Mum very busy all day long making new curtains for the front bedroom.
I had my very first £10 note!

3rd March 1964 Tuesday
Pat & Evelyn arrived home from a long week-end (half-term) in Malvern staying with Bunting. Charles on holiday today & tomorrow. A couple of men in our office all afternoon explaining the whys & wherefores of the new cash register to be used by Miss Gazzard.

4th March 1964 Wednesday
Went to rehearsal on scooter. (Rehearsing Monday, Wednesday, Thursday & Friday this week ready for production of "Desert Song" starting next Monday) Tina brought the coloured slides of her wedding & honeymoon in Switzerland.

5th March 1964 Thursday
Costumes arrived for "Desert Song". I brought mine home on the back of my scooter – one Spanish dress – very nice – one evening dress – not quite so nice & one "old peasant woman dress". I shall also be wearing one of my own – "afternoon dress".

6th March 1964 Friday
Leicester Mercury photographer at the Amateurs to take photos of us in costume. He had neither patience nor manners & was in such a hurry to get away I went right off him altogether. A letter in the paper which started: - I get tired of reading about people who love the sound of church bells . . . .

7th March 1964 Saturday
Absolutely freezing cold day. Wendy Johnson married at 3 p.m. Mum went down to Don's to "baby-sit" with Susan. I spent quite a lot of time practising type-writing. Anne Causer called for about ½ hr. She admired the new curtains & wall paper in our front bed-room.

8th March 1964 Mothering Sunday
Full Dress Rehearsal for "Desert Song". The Bishop of Leicester at our church (floodlit for the occasion) to dedicate the choir vestry screen, the new stained glass window in memory of Cicely Fosbrooke & the Remembrance Garden.

9th March 1964 Monday
Opening night of "Desert Song". I have a week's holiday from work. I spent much of the day practising type-writing & then caught the 5 o'clock bus to be early for make-up. Pat is not taking part this year, but he is officer in charge of chocolates and ice-cream.

10th March 1964 Tuesday

8-20 p.m. H. M. The Queen gave birth to her 3rd son Prince Edward Anthony Richard Louis.
A beautiful day, I went for a scooter ride to Mountsorrel to see Auntie Doris. Staunton Harold patients at "Desert Song". I talked afterwards to one – Ron, and put his scarf on for him.

11th March 1964 Wednesday

Another beautiful day! I went out on my scooter in the afternoon & got some pussy willow which I gave to Auntie Gladys.
Mum & I fitted the front bedroom carpet in the morning. Mrs Roberts gave a bottle of sherry to our dressing room. I toasted the new-born prince.

12th March 1964 Thursday

Not such a nice day. I had my photograph taken in varying costumes & poses. I went out on my scooter to get some pussy willow for Maurice Gaunt (special request). A letter in the Mercury to the effect that the "**tortured verse**" which they print has "**no delight**".

13th March 1964 Friday

I did some type-writing practice – only 25 words per minute & that consisting of many mistakes! I then went to see how Uncle Cyril was & found him sitting by the side of his bed having his hair cut by Aunt Dos. I had 4 o'clockses with him & did a bit of his crossword.

14th March 1964 Saturday

Last night of "Desert Song". Our new President, Dr. Hamilton came on to the stage & the bouquets of flowers were presented by Mrs Hamilton. Ivy Hardy sat in the audience. It was her first time out since her recent operation. Mum went with Auntie Gladys.

15th March 1964 Passion Sunday

It snowed all day long. The trees at night outside our church were a perfect picture. We had only 6 at Sunday School; the least since we started last August using the Rector's Room. I called in at Don's to thank them for sending me a bouquet of flowers.

16th March 1964 Monday

Joan Walkerdine 21 today. Thirteen from the office dined at "Le Gourmet". **Ralph, Martin, Ray, Geoff, Tom, Len, Steve, Anne, Joan, Lynda, Enid, Reevsie & Me!** We came home from work at night over the forest. The snow made it look absolutely wonderful: & then I saw the new moon.

17th March 1964 Tuesday

Caught the 7 a.m. bus to work because Mr Johnson's car in dock for a day or two. I started work ½ hr early in the morning & then got on the late sheet for a couple of minutes in the afternoon. Reason? – "Somebody stopped to ask me something" – namely Beryl who is to be married next Saturday.

18th March 1964 Wednesday

I lost 2/- in the office sweep for "The Lincoln". I had 2 horses "Military Cross" 30-1, and "Rosary Lodge" 50-1. At night Mum & I went to the Belvoir Road Chapel in Coalville to hear "The Crucifixion". Soloists were Barrie Edwards & Brian Gadsby.

19th March 1964 Thursday

Mum & I went on the scooter to Hoo Ash & proceeded to distribute "**An Easter Message from the Rector**" to all the houses in our parish as far as Ravenstone turn. We rode home via "The Altons" & got caught up in the thickest fog I have yet driven through.

20th March 1964 Friday

Our Amateurs' Dinner Dance. Dr. & Mrs Hamilton there for the first time. 100 there altogether – a record number. I bought a stole and a gold evening bag for the occasion. The stole cost 32/6 from Morgan & Squires & the bag cost 21/- from Benefit shoe shop in Belvoir Street, Leicester.

21st March 1964 Saturday

Beryl White married at 11-30 a.m. Writer and broadcaster Nancy Spain was killed in an air crash half a mile from Aintree racecourse, Liverpool, a few hours before the Grand National. Enid and I went to see "Rio Rita" at Thringstone. Clocks put forward one hour tonight.

22nd March 1964 Palm Sunday

All the Sunday School children in church this morning for Palm Sunday. We walked round inside the church singing: - "Ride on, ride on in majesty". I led the way and the Rector brought up the rear. It was most moving, and the first time we had ever done anything like that.

23rd March 1964 Monday

I caught the 7a.m. bus to work because Mr Johnson's car in dock. I caught the 5-30p.m. home to Coalville & saw my first lambs of the year at Groby. I inadvertently left my make up all at home, so I did not look particularly glamorous throughout the day.

24th March 1964 Tuesday

Princess Alexandra chose her baby's name – James Robert Bruce.
I went to work on the 7a.m. bus. I stayed 2 hours overtime & caught the 7-20p.m. home. Our office being painted and decorated upstairs and downstairs and in my "ladies" chamber.

25th March 1964 Wednesday

Charles had the day off for the funeral of Helma's mother. Terribly windy – my scooter parked in the yard with its cover flapping like mad, was blown right over. I watched on television "Murder in the Cathedral", being the murder of Thomas Becket 29th Dec. 1170.

26th March 1964 Thursday

Very busy counter all afternoon at work because of our close down until next Wednesday.
I went to a devotional service and sermon for Maundy Thursday at 8 p.m., after which I was invited by Marjorie Slatter to join the ladies of the "Thursday Club" for a cup of tea in the Rector's Room.

27th March 1964 Good Friday

I am hoping to do a couple of flower arrangements for Easter in church. Today I have done my first flower arrangement, using a "floral candlecup" in a candlestick. The result is beautiful – my best arrangement ever. Puzzle – how to get it to church just as it looks now!

28th March 1964 Saturday
I dismantled my beautiful flower arrangement, and did it all over again in church. I did another one to match; and they had a window each, one behind the Rector and one right near to the altar. I sat with Uncle Cyril for about an hour. He had had both the Ravenstone & Snibston parsons to see him.

29th March 1964 Easter Sunday
Alaska is today a "Major Disaster Area", after a ten minute long earthquake during yesterday evening's rush hour. I read a story in church at the children's service – "The Red Anemones". A very cold and drizzly day for Easter Sunday.

Flowers in Church on Easter Day

I saw the flowers on Easter Day,
In beautiful and glad array;
And all around and everywhere
Their lovely fragrance filled the air.

On every ledge, and by the door,
Around each pillar, on the floor;
The font – the pulpit – all were gay
With freshest flowers for Easter Day.

And some their lovely faces bowed,
While others stood erect and proud,
And told again their favourite story:
"Solomon in all his glory . . . ."

Above them rose the window tall,
Ablaze with splendour, bringing all
The joyful tidings from death's prison:
"HE IS NOT HERE: FOR HE IS RISEN."

30th March 1964 Monday
Easter Monday, and statistics show that it is colder than it was at Christmas, with rain and sleet. A day for stopping by the fire – so I concentrated on my shorthand and typing practice. Typing now is 35 w.p.m. (with lots of mistakes). At last I translated the shorthand advert which was in the Leicester Mercury on January 9th.

31st March 1964 Tuesday
The Eiffel Tower is 75 years old today.
I spent a couple of hours in church creating a flower arrangement. I also spent a couple of hours at Pat's reading the minutes of the vestry meetings since 1897. They included tributes to Queen Victoria on her death – also to my Dad on his death.

1st April 1964 Wednesday
First day back to work after the Easter holiday – consequently a monstrous post and also an exceptionally busy counter all day long. We took over £100 on Driving Licences alone. I caught the 7-20p.m. bus home. A party of 12, led by Nan Fletcher & the Reverend Daybell, vicar of Old Dalby, left for the Holy Land – back on 17th.

2nd April 1964 Thursday
Don called to invite me to go (with his compliments) to a performance of "The Gondoliers" to be given on April 25th, in Ashby's Town Hall.
Mum reading her second book from the Travelling County Library & thoroughly enjoying it – "Bishop's Wife – but still Myself" by Cicely Williams.

3rd April 1964 Friday
I went over to see Uncle Cyril and sat with him for just over an hour. He was in great pain and very weak. I treated myself to a 21/- bottle of Eau de Toilette No 5 Chanel. "Ladies Night" tonight where Phyl has to make a speech because Don is W.M. until October.

Note – Don was a Freemason. W.M. = Worshipful Master.

4th April 1964 Saturday
Enid & I went to the Adult School to see "To Kill a Cat". The most shocking weather for April – sleet, snow & high winds. The Queen left Buckingham Palace today to spend a few weeks at Windsor Castle. She travelled by car, carrying the new baby prince, born on March 10th. Our first glimpse of him.

5th April 1964 Sunday
A definite improvement in the weather – I went for a morning ride on the scooter after Sunday School, to Farm Town, and watched the lambs in the fields. We agreed not to practice for the Sunday School Anniversary this year, during Sunday School time. Our first practice then is to be on Tuesday at 7p.m.

6th April 1964 Monday
Statistics showed that in the year ending March 31st 1964 we issued 75,000 Driving Licences. Total income from all licences was £1 ½ million. Mr Colderic decreed that we sign all receipts in future for duplicate licences, in our own name.

B
7th April 1964 Tuesday
We had our first practice for the Sunday School Anniversary, under the direction of Mr Biggs. Harold played the piano (in the Rector's Room) Janice Congrave, Margaret Woodings & I were there together with 20 children.
Margaret Hewes arrived from Wales to see her father (Uncle Cyril).

8th April 1964 Wednesday
Woolworth heiress Barbara Hutton married Vietnamese Prince Doan Vinh, last night. He is Miss Hutton's seventh husband. She is 51. He is 47.
Mr Johnson stayed in Leicester for wrestling, so I came home on the 5-30 bus to Coalville & then walked to Ravenstone. Phew! What a trek.

9th April 1964 Thursday
Hewes. – Cyril H., 50, Leicester Road, Ravenstone, passed away April 9th, aged 69. Funeral service at Ravenstone Parish Church on Wednesday, 10-10a.m., followed by cremation at Loughborough, 11a.m.

"Nunkie" - Uncle Cyril.

Note – Uncle Cyril, my dad's brother, father of Margaret, Enid & David, died of cancer, 69.

10th April 1964 Friday
I spent practically the whole of my dinner hour trying on hats both in "British Home Stores" and in Leas". (I didn't buy one however)
Aunt Dos & I went to inspect the broken card tables in the Rector's Room. There are 4 which require nut & bolting. We gave Mr Bagnall a lift home.

11th April 1964 Saturday
Mum & I caught the 8 a.m. bus to Leicester. We bought a hat & a raincoat for Mum.
Aunt Dos & I repaired the tables in the Rector's Room & then went to Brooks the florists at Coleorton to order 3 sprays for Uncle Cyril's funeral. I spent the evening with Enid, Margaret & Auntie Gladys.

12 April 1964 Sunday
I had a bumper bundle "Sunday School", 24 altogether – 14 of my own, 8 boys belonging to Margaret Woodings & 2 tiny tots with Diane Woodward.
Pat, Terry, Mary & I went to Coalville intending to see Uncle Cyril in the Chapel of Rest at Berrisford House, but it was all locked up.

13th April 1964 Monday
A strike by hand-fillers at Snibston Colliery, Coalville, which started last Wednesday, led to the pit becoming completely idle today. About 700 men are out of work, and it is spreading to New Lount Colliery.
All the postmen, too, are ready to go on strike. They want their strike on Thursday.

14th April 1964 Tuesday
I spent the evening in church all by myself, doing a flower arrangement for the window in the church porch ready for Uncle Cyril's funeral tomorrow. I did an all white arrangement (lilies, carnations, iris and freesias) in a candle cup. I then locked up with a monstrous key.

15th April 1964 Wednesday
Uncle Cyril's funeral. In the car following the hearse was Auntie Gladys with Enid, Margaret, David, Irene & Bunting. I went in the car behind them with Mum, Aunt Dos, Aunt Cis, Pat, Evelyn & Auntie Gladys' sister Grace. We went to Loughborough Crematorium where I was most impressed by the masses of flowers.

16th April 1964 Thursday
The Postmen, who decided to strike today, changed their minds.
On the 8th day of the 8th month – last August (8 months & 8 days ago) was the great Mail Train Robbery – Glasgow to London train, at Cheddington, Bucks.
Today at the Assizes at Aylesbury sentence is passed, including 30 years each for 7 of the men.

17th April 1964 Friday
The Soviet leader Nikita S. Kruschev is 70 years old today.
Margaret Hewes, who arrived at her mothers 10 days ago – April 7th, returned to Wales.
Patrick Anthony William Beresford Everard was on the Midland news with his helicopter,
(Mum saw him, but I didn't). He is now High Sheriff of Leicestershire.

18th April 1964 Saturday
Ravenstone Church was filled to capacity for the wedding of Brian Land & Jean Kendrick. Mum & I went to Snarestone for a scooter ride. I spent an hour in the Rector's Room, setting out my "stall" for Sunday School tomorrow.
I had fish & chips supper with Auntie Gladys, Enid, David & Irene.

19th April 1964 Sunday
The first Sunday after Uncle Cyril's funeral, so I sat at the front in church with Aunt Cis, Pat, Evelyn, David, Irene, Enid & Auntie Gladys. Afterwards we all went into Auntie Gladys' house & had sherry & mince-pies.
£400 was given to our church in the will of the late Mrs Sid Francis.

20th April 1964 Monday
Prince Edward, born on March 10th, is officially registered:- Edward Anthony Richard Louis.
On 14th November 1948 was born: - Charles Philip Arthur George.
On 15th August 1950 was born: - Anne Elizabeth Alice Louise.
On 19th February 1960 was born: - Andrew Albert Christian Edward.
Prince Edward will be christened on May 2nd.

21st April 1964 Tuesday
Our third practice for the Sunday School Anniversary (June 21st). Because there were 17 children only attended, we agreed to have the next practice on Sunday morning at 10 a.m. instead of the normal Sunday School. Mr Biggs told me that he had been with Ravenstone church choir for 56 years!

22nd April 1964 Wednesday
Greville Wynne, the British businessman sentenced to 8 years imprisonment by the Russians for alleged spying, arrived home today – a free man. He was exchanged for the master Russian spy Gordon Lonsdale, sentenced to 25 years imprisonment at the Old Bailey in March 1961.

23rd April 1964 Thursday
Today we celebrate the 400th anniversary of the birth of William Shakespeare.
I joined the ladies of the Thursday Club to listen to a talk given by the Rector, on the history of the Church of England.

24th April 1964 Friday
I went over to see Jean Kendrick's wedding presents & was given a glass of sherry by Langham. I also popped in to see Auntie Gladys, who was sitting at the table reading the deeds of various properties in Coalville connected with G. H. Hewes & Sons, & dating back to 1881, almost before Coalville existed at all.

25th April 1964 Saturday

I had my ears pierced!

I went with Don, Phyl, Susan & Enid to the Town Hall, Ashby-de-la-Zouch to see "The Gondoliers". This afternoon I did my first cutting of the year down at "St. Mary's".

A blackbird is sitting on a nest inside our coal-house!

26th April 1964 Sunday

I went on the scooter to Ashby at 8 a.m. to fetch Mum home from night duty. Instead of the usual Sunday School we had Anniversary practice. My poor ears are not altogether happy about being pierced. I keep trying to offer them encouragement with T. C. P.

27th April 1964 Monday

Mum went to Colchester to spend a week with Mary Moore. I am therefore head cook & bottle washer. In the Snibston Parish Magazine, delivered today, the Rev. Gerald Richardson announces his intention to discontinue services at little St. Mary's, which has stood for "Twice four hundred years."

28th April 1964 Tuesday

Being officer in charge of household duties, I came home from work & had to set about lighting a fire. Then I made myself a mushroom omelette for my tea.

A message through the letter box from Alf Hall – Vote for Alf Hall – your Independent Candidate, Ashby R. D. C. Polling Day May 4th.

29th April 1964 Wednesday

At 10-30 p.m. last night the 3rd Royal Baby of the year was born. A 7lb 8oz daughter for the Duke & Duchess of Kent.

The 24 year old Princess Irene of Holland married 34 year old Prince Hugo of Bourbon Parma. The bride's parents were not at the wedding.

30th April 1964 Thursday

Aunt Dos bought her cine camera and projector this week (Tuesday). I came home from work laden with potatoes, lettuce, beetroot, liver, ham, bread etc., being cook in charge this week. My ears, which were pierced last Saturday, have begun to skin slightly & are still a wee bit tender.

1st May 1964 Friday

The fourth Royal Baby of the year was born this morning. A baby daughter for Princess Margaret. Lesley Hewes & John Sear became engaged. I spent practically the whole evening doing a flower arrangement with 16/- worth of flowers, which I bought in Leicester.

2nd May 1964 Saturday

The F. A. Cup Final at Wembley. West Ham United beat Preston North End 3-2.

While the mother blackbird was off to get some dinner, I peeped into her nest (in our coalhouse). There I spied 4 of the tiniest birds I have ever seen.

3rd May 1964 Rogation Sunday

All the Sunday School children and teachers, church wardens, choir master, choir & Rector, went to Cliff's farm & to Tom Land's farm, where the animals were

blessed & we sang hymns. Mum came home from Nayland and brought Mary Moore back with her to stay for a few days.

4th May 1964 Monday

I voiced a complaint at work about sitting under the glass dome in direct line with the afternoon sun. Mr Sharp said he would endeavour to get something done – like white washing the dome. At 7 p.m. Mum & I, Aunt Dos & Auntie Belle were taken by car (Mr Reed's) in the pouring rain to vote for Alf Hall!

5th May 1964 Tuesday

In spite of the fact that I voted for Alf Hall, he did not get in on the R. D. C.

Prince Andrew who was four in February and is second in line of succession to the throne began his school lessons at Buckingham Palace this morning.

6th May 1964 Wednesday

Mary Moore returned home. Terry & Mary bought their new Ford car.

I purchased a Provisional Driving Licence for Mum to be able to ride my scooter, but she is rather hesitant to start learning at 58.

7th May 1964 Thursday, Ascension Day

The Lord Mayor of London has launched an appeal for a memorial to President Kennedy who was shot dead last November 22nd. The memorial will be at Runnymede where Magna Carta was signed in 1215. This is because Runnymede symbolises freedom.

The target is £1 million.

8th May 1964 Friday

I sent £5 to the Lord Mayor of London for "The Kennedy Memorial Appeal". The £1 million, which it is hoped will be given, is to be divided between a memorial plinth and steps, and scholarships in the U. S. for British students.

9th May 1964 Saturday

"Momma Blackbird" has a full time job satisfying the appetites of her quads in our coalhouse. They have grown tremendously in one week and now completely fill the nest. I gave Mum her first lesson on how to start the scooter. She got it moving, but just walked along with it.

10th May 1964 Commonwealth Youth Sunday

Susan Jarvis asked the Rector if there could be a dramatic group of young girls in Ravenstone. The Rector immediately appointed me as their leader.

Auntie Gladys, Enid & I went to Ravenstone Chapel Anniversary.

Our blackbird quads are absolutely adorable.

11th May 1964 Monday

I watched one of our blackbird quads taking a little flight around the garden – very clever! Poppa kept his beady eye on him from the apple tree, while Momma flitted to & fro along the top of the fence.

Princess Alexandra's 10 week old baby son was christened at Buckingham Palace.

12th May 1964 Tuesday

The hottest May day since 1959. I was sweltered at work underneath the dome.

I was left with most of the postal driving licences to finish after we had closed & I was consequently in a right old mood.

All our baby blackbirds have now left the nest.

13th May 1964 Wednesday

I went to the Midland Education Co. for a book of monologues for our proposed Drama Group in Ravenstone. From there I was referred to the Reference Library who in turn referred me to the British Drama League, 9 Fitzroy Sq. W I. Whereupon I wrote them a letter enquiring about monologues, sketches & one act plays.

14th May 1964 Thursday

Our office has begun its new "improved" system of checking & issuing vehicle licences; incorporating the use of the new £2,500 Burroughs machine, as done in Wiltshire & North Riding.

I ventured to remove one "sleeper" from one ear & very carefully try on my first ear-ring for pierced ears.

15th May 1964 Friday

Pat informed me that our next Amateurs production will be "Annie Get Your Gun", starting March 8th – 13th next year.

The River Nile is having its course changed. A gigantic project costing millions, it is receiving much support from Russia & Mr Kruschev is now in Egypt for the occasion.

16th May 1964 Saturday

Pat, Evelyn & Aunt Dos went to Weymouth for a week's holiday.

We had our first croquet game of the year. Enid & I played against David & Irene. All the time we were playing we could hear the cuckoo. Mum had another little go at starting the scooter & rode on it for a few yards on our back yard.

17th May 1964 Whit Sunday

Glorious hot day. I spent the afternoon sun-bathing.

David, Irene & Enid took Auntie Gladys to Mablethorpe where she is to stay with her sister Margery for a fortnight's holiday.

Because Aunt Dos is on holiday & Mum is on night duty I shall be sleeping 4 nights this week at Auntie Belle's.

18th May 1964 Whit Monday

I had a marathon grass cutting session down at St. Mary's. I cleared a complete area all round the grave of Grandma & Grandpa Hewes.

I started to write my poem "Ravenstone" to be learned by my proposed Drama Group.

19th May 1964 Whit Tuesday

I spent much of the morning in Ravenstone church, studying the detail of the stained glass windows, to describe them in my poem on Ravenstone Church.

Mum & I went after tea, a scooter ride to Willoughby-on-the-Wolds 20 miles away, to see Mum's cousins, Madge & Bertha Bailey.

20th May 1964 Wednesday

Today I am 12,000 days old! (Sorry, - wrong calculation – must be tomorrow)

I was born July 14th 1931.

I took some lilies of the valley to work & did a flower arrangement which a lady admired. She then quoted part of Omar Khayyam to me, about flowers.

21st May 1964 Thursday

Reevsie & I went in the dinner hour to Leicester Town Hall to see the masses of flowers ready for the mayor-making ceremony this evening. Leicester's first Roman Catholic Lord Mayor & Lady Mayoress, Alderman & Mrs A. H. W. Kimberlain, begin their term of office tonight with a banquet at the De Montfort Hall.

22nd May 1964 Friday

Alderman Kimberlin, the new Lord Mayor of Leicester, says that like the last two Lord Mayors, he will be launching an appeal during his year in office. His will be in aid of the President Kennedy Memorial Fund, which was launched on May 7th by the Lord Mayor of London.

23rd May 1964 Saturday

Pat, Evelyn & Aunt Dos returned from their week's holiday in Weymouth.

Aunt Dos gave her very first film show at about midnight. Films taken with her cine camera were viewed with great excitement by Pat, Evelyn, Terry & Mary, Langham & Annie Kendrick, Aunt Dos, Enid & me.

24th May 1964 Trinity Sunday

Aunt Dos gave a repeat performance of her film show for the benefit of Mum, David & Irene. (Enid & I also went along) I did quite a lot of shorthand practice today. I asked the Rector if he had a book on the history of our church at Ravenstone & he said he would lend me one.

25th May 1964 Monday

I wrote to Samuel French Ltd., and ordered –

1. "Speaking Well" – A First Book of Elocution 6/-
2. "Speech Training" – Teach Yourself Books series **7/6**
3. "Thomas the Mouse and Other 'Tails' in Rhyme" 2/-
4. "Come Out to Play" by Mabel Constanduros 3/6

26th May 1964 Tuesday

I broke one of my "sleepers" for my pierced ears. I was having a spot of trouble with the hole in my right ear. It was rather tender all day long, so at night I took the sleeper out & bathed it with T. C. P. Then big panic when I couldn't get the sleeper back in. Finally Mum attacked it from the rear & hey-presto success!

27th May 1964 Wednesday

I bought myself some new "sleepers" for my ears – 17/6 a pair. Mum put them in for me while I made all the appropriate facial expressions.

Jawaharlal Nehru, aged 74, Prime Minister of India since 1947, died today.

28th May 1964 Thursday

Nehru's funeral and cremation. Once he said: - "I would like people to say of me after I am gone - 'This was a man who, with all his mind and heart, loved India and the Indian people. And they, in turn, were indulgent to him and gave him of their love most abundantly and extravagantly.'"

29th May 1964 Friday
The Lord Mayor of London now has £50,000 towards his £1 million target for a memorial to President Kennedy. Today President Kennedy would have been 47 years old.

He once wrote a book – "Why England Slept" and said he hoped no-one would ever write a book –"Why America Slept" while he was in command.

30th May 1964 Saturday
The gear cable on my scooter snapped completely when I was at the bottom of Standard Hill. A passing lorry driver came to my rescue & managed to fix it in 3rd gear. I then went to Coalville in 3rd gear all the way & had it mended for £1-7s-0d.

31st May 1964 Sunday
Funeral service for Charlie Colver, Ravenstone's oldest man, who was 92 last February. The oldest man now in Ravenstone is Mr Bagnall, who will be 91 in July. Dorothy & Douglas called at Aunt Dos's on their way home to Somerset after a holiday in Norway.

1st June 1964 Monday
Aberdeen is suffering from an outbreak of Typhoid, believed to have started from a tin of corned beef. 227 people are in hospital. 30,000 children have been kept at home because the schools are closed. Dance halls also are closed, and thousands of people have cancelled holidays there.

2nd June 1964 Tuesday
I went to a "Dorothy Perkins" fashion show at Ravenstone Institute. Mr Johnson went to Windsor for the day on his office outing, so I came home on the bus. Geoff brought me to Glenfield turn in his car & then chased my bus round the island & raced it to the next bus stop.

3rd June 1964 Wednesday
Derby Day & the winning horse was "Santa Claus". 17 horses altogether. 30 in our office went in the office sweep & I managed to draw a blank.

I went to Snarestone at night on my scooter to fetch a dress for Aunt Lil to be posted to her at Nayland. My scooter conked out & I left it at David's at Normanton.

4th June 1964 Thursday
Today I saw the result of a fire which yesterday gutted Cowling's television & record shop on the corner of Belvoir Street & Stamford Street, Leicester. 13,000 records in the shop have been written off, but the staff managed to save much of the valuable stock, including radiograms & radios on the ground floor.

5th June 1964 Friday
"Homeward Bound" was today the winner in the Epsom Oaks. The Test Series have begun – England v. Australia. The England side consists of – Boycott, Titmus, Dexter, Cowdrey, Barrington, Sharpe, Parks, Trueman, Allen, Coldwell, Flavell .
The score to date is England 216 for 8.

6th June 1964 Saturday
I went to work from 9 a.m. until 12 noon. This was "voluntary" overtime, helping with the backlog of transfers. Ravenstone Garden Fete opened by D. Byford, C. B. E. A terribly wet & windy day. I had my fortune told by Madame Kantellum, who said that one day I should have my own business & that I should marry twice!

7th June 1964 Sunday
Yesterday I collected my scooter from Auto Supplies. They had fetched it from Normanton-le-Heath & put a new sparking plug in for me – 10/-. This morning I met Mum from Ashby after her night duty & the scooter conked out on the way home. Fortunately however, it started after a while. Later in the day it conked out altogether near Snibston School.

8th June 1964 Monday
I went to the Coalville Amateur's A. G. M. Mr Hamilton, our new President was there, & we had some really lively discussions. It was agreed to reduce the number of Saturday night tickets allowed to patrons & members from 6 each to 4 each. It was also agreed to play "God Save The Queen" at the end, & not at the beginning of each performance.

9th June 1964 Tuesday
Our television has broken down altogether and we have been advised to get a new one.
I had my first proper full introduction to Longfellow's poems, through a book which Mum borrowed from the travelling library. It is said that "Longfellow is the gentle poet whom all have loved." This now includes me.

Note – Having been introduced to the wonderful poetry of Longfellow, I have loved him ever since.

10th June 1964 Wednesday
The Leicester Mercury tonight reports that Ravenstone Hall, the 260 year old mansion, which has stood vacant since the death of the Squire of Ravenstone, Miss M. C. Fosbrooke, is to be occupied again. Mr Ernest Ottewell has bought the hall and expects to move in next August.

11th June 1964 Thursday
Beryl came in the evening with her wedding photographs. Walter Beniston came and brought me some music which he had written, and then Pat came & brought me a written invitation to a meeting of all the various bodies connected with Ravenstone Church to be held on June 23rd & to discuss "Planned Giving."

12th June 1964 Friday
I had a letter from Aunt Lil, who is in Nayland, Near Colchester, Essex, thanking me for sending a dress to her from her home in Snarestone, where she has not been living since Uncle Frank died last December. Aunt Lil is now 88, & she told me in her letter that she is miserable, & although she ought to "be grateful" she says "I'm **not**."

13th June 1964 Saturday
In the Queen's birthday honours today Mr Billy Butlin, 64 year old holiday camp King became **Sir** Billy Butlin!

Mum & I went with a bus load from Ravenstone to Great Glen to a flower festival in the church. We then had tea on the vicarage lawn.

14th June 1964 Sunday
In his sermon tonight, the Rector, the Reverend Gustav Aronsohn, said that in all the religions of the world, man was seeking God; but in the Christian religion alone, God was seeking man.
His text was St. Luke XV v. 4 & 5.

Note – An inspiring sermon at church.

15th June 1964 Monday
I read the whole of Longfellow's poem "**The Song of Hiawatha**", all 75 pages of it. I wept with Hiawatha, at the death of **Minnehaha**, when he rushed into the wigwam, saw his lovely Minnehaha, lying dead & cold before him, and he sat down still and speechless, on the bed of Minnehaha, at the feet of Laughing Water.

16th June 1964 Tuesday
Northern & Central Japan today suffered from a severe earthquake. In the city of Niigata, a gas tank exploded causing great fires. Also the river there, the River Shinano, burst its banks & caused heavy flooding. Reports say that at least 21 people were killed and more than 150 have been injured.

17th June 1964 Wednesday
Mr Johnson not well, so I had to travel to & from work by bus. Gordon Banks, Leicester's England goal-keeper, is on the transfer list. Leicester is asking £45,000 a record for a goal-keeper. Up to now there has been neither an enquiry nor a bid for him.

18th June 1964 Thursday
First day of the Second Test Match between England & Australia. This is at Lord's. No play today because of rain. The England side is –Edrich, Titmus, Dexter, Cowdrey, Barrington, Parfitt, Parks, Truman, Gifford, Coldwell, Flavell.
(The First Test Match ended with rain)

19th June 1964 Friday
My brother Pat & his wife Evelyn took my Aunt Dos to Skegness, where she hopes to stay for a fortnight with my Aunt Cis, who lives there. Pat & Evelyn will stay for the week-end only. Today is the 2nd day of the 2nd Test Match. Still no play because of rain.
I bought myself a pretty lilac hat, price £2- 2s- 6d.

20th June 1964 Saturday
President Kennedy's youngest brother, 32 year old Senator Edward M. Kennedy, received a broken back in a plane crash last night in which two people died. However, it is believed that he will be able to walk again.
I ran over a blackbird with my scooter, and the blackbird died within half an hour.

21st June 1964 Sunday
Ravenstone Sunday School Anniversary. Susan Jarvis sang a solo. In the afternoon the lessons were read by Ruth Jones and by Rosemary Green. In the evening I read the first lesson (Joshua Chapter I v. 1-7) and Harold read the second lesson.

22nd June 1964 Monday
The dome at work was white-washed (green). Mr Williams borrowed a book from the County Library 'specially for me. It was "The Ingoldsby Legends" containing a poem I wanted particularly "The Jackdaw of Rheims." A poem which I wrote about President Kennedy in Galway was published in the County Office's monthly magazine – "Spotlight".

23rd June 1964 Tuesday
We had our first meeting for "Planned Giving" at Church. There were 38 there. Mr Burne was elected Chairman, Marjorie Pickering – Secretary, Enid Hewes & Dennis Collier – joint Treasurers. A committee was formed, consisting of Mr Biggs, Mrs Woodings, Evelyn Hewes, Jean Land, Harold Moore, Mr Rolleston and Horace Johnson.

24th June 1964 Wednesday
A perfect summer evening, such as must have inspired Longfellow to write – "O Gift of God! O perfect day: whereon shall no man work, but play; whereon it is enough for me, not to be doing, but to be!" Nevertheless I chose to be out & "doing", namely collecting a barrow-load of weeds from Aunt Dos' front shrubbery.

25th June 1964 Thursday
Stirling Moss was married today to Elaine Barbarino, an American girl, aged 24.
We had a post card from Aunt Dos, who is staying at Skegness with Aunt Cis. She informed us that on Monday evening she walked into a lamp post, but it hasn't given her a black eye!!!

26th June 1964 Friday
One year ago today President Kennedy was making a triumphant visit to Western Berlin. Today, his brother Robert, Attorney General, was in West Berlin to unveil a memorial to the late President Kennedy.
Another lovely day "**Where through the sapphire sea, (i.e. the sky) the sun sailed like a golden galleon**"

27th June 1964 Saturday
Coleorton Hall Gala Day. We watched the procession of decorated floats as they came through Ravenstone about 12 noon.
We had our first meeting for our proposed Drama Group. Those who attended were – Ruth Jones, Rosemary Green, Diane Woodward and Zena Bennett. Ruth Jones said she would like to write a play for us.

28th June 1964 Sunday
Aberdeen is now back to normal after the typhoid epidemic. The Queen is at the moment touring Scotland. Yesterday she altered her planned route specially to visit Aberdeen & she received a tumultuous welcome there.
50 years ago today, the **First World War** saw its **beginning, with an assassination.**

29th June 1964 Monday
One year ago today, Enid & I went to Ireland for a fortnight's holiday. We arrived at Dublin Airport just as

President Kennedy's plane was ready to take off. President Kennedy went to Galway later in the day, & we followed in his wake; through Galway City bedecked with flags. We spent a week there at Galway Bay.

30th June 1964 Tuesday

Mr Sharp asked me whether I would like to leave Driving Licence work, & go on to Vehicle Licences, where there might be more chance of promotion. I said yes, so I expect to move round about August. I have worked with Driving Licences since October 1948!!

Mum went to Skegness to spend a couple of nights with Aunt Cis.

1st July 1964 Wednesday

Auntie Belle & I did several flower arrangements in Aunt Dos' bungalow, for a "Welcome Home" for her tomorrow, from Skegness. Aunt Cis will be bringing her & Mum home by car. While Aunt Dos has been away, I have been sleeping at Aunt Belle's, on the nights when Mum hasn't been at home.

2nd July 1964 Thursday

First day of the Third Test Match between England & Australia. This is at Headingley, Leeds. Because of rain the first 2 test matches counted as draws. But now the weather is glorious. The England side is :- **Dexter, Barrington, Boycott, Edrich, Parfitt, Taylor, Flavell, Gifford, Parks, Titmus, Trueman.**

3rd July 1964 Friday

President Johnson last night signed the **Civil Rights Bill**, to give black people the same rights as white people, throughout the whole of America.

I. T. V. is on strike, & so we missed seeing the presentation of a new colour to the R. A. F. by the Queen in the grounds of Buckingham Palace.

(T. V. cameras never been there before)

4th July 1964 Saturday

Aunt Dos read my poem about President Kennedy in Galway, and asked me to type her a copy. We had our 2nd meeting of the Ravenstone Children's Drama Group. Those who attended were – Ruth Jones, Rosemary Green, Susan Jarvis & Pamela Mason.

Australia are showing every sign of beating us in the 3rd Test Match.

5th July 1964 Sunday

Today, in the American of state **Georgia**, there have been terrible scenes of race violence brought about by the **Civil Rights Bill**, which President Johnson signed on July 2nd.

I fetched Mum home from night duty & we went for a ride round Farm Town. We could smell the newly mown hay.

6th July 1964 Monday

Australia today won the Third Test Match by 7 wickets. In their first innings the other day, one of their players named Burge scored **160**!!!

Quads have been born in Leicestershire! Mrs White, 51 Launde Road, Oadby, has 2 boys & 2 girls. Clinton (3lb 10oz), Catriona (3lb 6 ¾ oz), John (3lb 1 ½ oz), Theresa (3lb).

7th July 1964 Tuesday

Aunt Lil returned to her home at Snareston, having lived with Mary Moore in Essex since last December. Mum & I scootered over to see her in the evening & Mum slept the night there.

One of the newly born Leicestershire quads, Theresa, has died.

A terribly blustery day after a long spell of glorious weather.

8th July 1964 Wednesday

Today, at work, our new £2,500 Burroughs machine arrived. This is our 2nd one. We have been using one ever since May 14th this year.

Another of our Leicestershire baby quads, John, has died. The Australians today have been playing Leicestershire. Leicestershire won the toss & batted first.

9th July 1964 Thursday

I went to the Post Office to get a form of application for Repayment of Premium Savings Bonds. I intend to draw out £60 (i.e. from Jan. 1st 1959 to Dec. 1963 @ one per month) and I hope to buy a Grundig Tape Recorder after my holidays – that should be about Sept.7th.

10th July 1964 Friday

Last day of play between Australia & Leicester. The match ended in a draw. Our post at work did not arrive until 10a.m., consequently we had a hectic time later on in the day.

The postmen once more have decided to go on strike (see April 16th). It will be on July 16th.

11th July 1964 Saturday

We had the 3rd meeting of our Ravenstone Drama Group. Those who attended were – Susan Jarvis, Diane Woodward, Pamela Kendrick, Rosemary Green and Barbara Bath. We all had a very jolly time, & they all contributed some very good ideas for a production which we would like to put on just before Christmas.

12th July 1964 Sunday

I had a very poor attendance at Sunday School; only six out of a possible sixteen.

We had a phone-call from Snarestone to say Aunt Lil was not at all well, so Mum will be going over there first thing tomorrow morning, straight from work. She is on night duty tonight at Ashby hospital.

13th July 1964 Monday

Mum & I went to Snarestone on the scooter in the evening. Aunt Lil was in bed. Edith Copestake was there staying with her for a week. Mum stayed there all night. It was made public that our office would be open throughout the dinner hour, starting on August 5th.

14th July 1964 Tuesday

Today is my birthday. I was born on a Tuesday, 14-7-31. "Tuesday's child is full of grace!" Aunt Dos gave me a tin of Coty "L'Aimant" talc. Pat & Evelyn gave me Innoxa Paris Mist perfumed talc. Enid gave me "Yardley" Red Roses perfumed talc, & Reevsie gave me a white goblet-shaped flower vase.

15th July 1964 Wednesday

Gordon Banks, Leicester City's England international goal-keeper, re-signed this morning with Leicester on a monthly contract, i.e. until the end of July. Having been on the transfer list for a month, there is still no offer for him.

St. Swithin's day today- sunshine all day long & the further outlook is sunshine everywhere!!

16th July 1964 Thursday

Today, the postmen are on strike. That means no collections & no deliveries. With no post at work we spent most of the time clearing out the old expired Driving Licence record cards.

An old lady customer gave me a bunch of flowers. Mr Sharpe had a word with me about the possibilities of a promotion.

17th July 1964 Friday

After yesterday's postal strike, I received by post this morning, form R. P. F. 30, notice of allowance to vote by post in the General Election, to be held later this year. This is because I am hoping to be a poll clerk on Election Day.

I received also a belated birthday card & a letter from my sister Bunting.

18th July 1964 Saturday

I went down to St. Mary's church-yard to cut the grass & my leg went down a deep hole. Whereupon I wrote a letter to the vicar. Mum & I went to Snarestone where Aunt Lil lay dying. Fourth meeting of our Drama Group, which we had in the middle of a thunderstorm.

19th July 1964 Sunday

Glover, Lillie Gertrude, widow of Frank, passed away July 19th 1964, aged 88 years. Funeral, Snarestone Church, 3 p.m., Tuesday, 21st.

"Aunt Lil"

20th July 1964 Monday

I waited & waited & waited for Mr Johnson to pick me up in the morning at 7-50a.m., as usual, to take me to work. Eventually, in a right old frenzy, I contacted John Tart, who leaves for Leicester at 8-20a.m. each morning, & I rode in with him. Consequently I was half an hour late.

21st July 1964 Tuesday

I had the day off from work for Auntie Lil's funeral. Mum & I went over to Snarestone on the scooter. Auntie Lil before her marriage was Miss Moore, & when she was a very little girl, & was asked what her name was, she said: - "**Dirty Rude Lillie Moore.**"

22nd July 1964 Wednesday

I wrote to the Chief Constable, Leics. And Rutland County Police, London Rd., Leicester, for permission to have a concert on December 12th, given by our Ravenstone Drama Group in Ravenstone Institute. The postmen, still not satisfied with their pay offer, are threatening to stop work again at the week-end.

23rd July 1964 Thursday

First day of the fourth Test Match between England & Australia at Old Trafford. For the first time this series, Australia won the toss & went in to bat first. Their score at the end of the day was 253 for 2!! (Dexter, Boycott, Edrich, Barrington, Parfitt, Parks, Mortimore, Titmus, Cartwright, Romsey & Price)

24th July 1964 Friday

Mary Moore arrived last night, having been staying at Snarestone since Auntie Lil's funeral. She is staying with us now until Sunday.

The postman's strike, arranged for this coming week-end, has been called off.

In the Test Match Australia now have 570 for 4!! Simpson has 265!!

25th July 1964 Saturday

I had a letter from the Reverend Gerald Richardson which said, "**Thank you** for informing me about this hole – it shall be seen to. I hope you are none the worse for your frightening experience." (See July 18th)

Mary Moore, Mum & I spent the morning at Snarestone sorting out Aunt Lil's belongings.

26th July 1964 Sunday

On May 24th, the Rector said he would lend me some literature on Ravenstone Church. I reminded him today & he then produced same; asking me to take very great care of it. It was all hand written. Mary Moore returned home. Pat took her in his car to Leicester to catch the 9-30a.m. train to London.

27th July 1964 Monday

The advertisement which I answered on February 18th has proved to be an absolute fraud, i.e. a confidence trick.

Today I received a belated birthday present by post from my sister Bunting, namely a gaily striped towel. The post office have not been delivering any parcels at all for over a week, but now all is well.

28th July 1964 Tuesday

Mr Blackburn, the Local Taxation Officer & County Treasurer for Leicestershire – i.e. my boss at work, whom I see very rarely, made my day by smiling at me in Leicester market & saying a friendly "Hello!"

The 4th Test Match ended in a draw. Australia – 1st Innings 656 – 8 (declared) England 1st Innings 611 all out.

29th July 1964 Wednesday

We were provided with a beautiful electric fan at work. I wrote a verse for the Editor of the Leicester Mercury: - "Twinkle, twinkle, little star; Tell us what our fortunes are; Born towards the end of June, we are subjects of the Moon!" This was because in the horoscope in the paper on Saturday, "**Cancer**" was accidentally missed out.

30th July 1964 Thursday

On July 22nd, I wrote to the Chief Constable for permission to give our concert on December 12th. Today a Police Woman from Coalville called to see me on his behalf. As I was out at work, Mum entertained her. She was here for over ½ hr & was much impressed with all our gorgeous flower arrangements. I am to go & see her on Saturday!

31st July 1964 Friday

Last day at work before the August Bank Holiday – consequently a really hectic counter all day long. We took £144-7s-6d over the counter for Driving Licences. Ranger VII, the American spacecraft, reached the Moon, giving us the first real close up pictures ever taken. 12 previous lunar probes, over the last 6 years, all failed.

1st August 1964 Saturday

I went to Coalville Police Station & I was there for over ½ hr in connection with our proposed concert for December 12th. From there I was sent to the Fire Station to arrange for Fire Precautions!
The Rector's Room at 7p.m. was all locked up, so we had a rehearsal at our house.

2nd August 1964 Sunday

I walked across the Grange fields to see the pit ponies. The ponies are there for only a fortnight out of the whole year. The rest of the time they live down the coal-mine. I saw 6 of them. After a prolonged spell of glorious summer weather; yesterday & today, being bank holiday, have been very dull.

3rd August 1964 Monday

The Leicester Mercury printed the verse which I wrote last Wednesday. They found a title – "Moonstruck." A lovely day today for the bank holiday. I went a scooter ride to Packington, Normanton & Heather. I also went into Ravenstone church, where I talked to a man named Mr Kingdon – a friend of the Rector.

4th August 1964 Tuesday

50 years ago today, when the ultimatum expired at 11p.m., we were at war.
40 years ago today, Mr & Mrs Hayes, our next door neighbours, were married. They gave us today a big chunk of anniversary cake.
Aunt Dos in bed all day poorly. I fetched her some medicine.

5th August 1964 Wednesday

Our first day at work of keeping open throughout the dinner hour. I went to see Freddie Franks in the Leics. County Clerk's department to enquire about a licence for our Christmas concert. He gave me a form of application with so many formidable questions, I finished up in quite a deep depression.

6th August 1964 Thursday

Today's Wills. **Mr. Cyril Horace Hewes,** 50, Leicester Road, Ravenstone, left £9,098-8s, gross, £9,035-9s, net value. (Duty paid £362).

7th August 1964 Friday

I spent the evening at my brother Pat's house, having my hair permed by his daughter Mary. Mary works in a hair dressers shop in Ashby-de-la-Zouch. Her boy friend Terry is also a hair dresser. He has just launched out on his own –"For your hair dressing appointment in your own home, ring or write to **Terry.**"

8th August 1964 Saturday

Enid & I on the first day of our week's holiday at Bognor Regis, Sussex. We came in Enid's car, having our elevenses at Fortes, on the M I, & lunch in Windsor, where we walked all around outside the castle & then went for a ½ hr boat trip on the River Thames.
Enid is my cousin, daughter of Cyril.

9th August 1964 Sunday

Enid & I went to Holy Communion at 10-30a.m., at St John the Baptist Church, Bognor.
A scorching hot morning, so I bought myself a big straw sun hat, navy blue & white striped, for 15/11d. In the afternoon we went to Littlehampton about 7 miles away where the River Arun flows right into the sea.

10th August 1964 Monday

Enid & I spent the morning in Bognor. We sat on the pier & watched people fishing. In the afternoon we went by car to Chichester. We looked through the cathedral there, & were much impressed by the butter market in the city centre.
At night we went to the pictures to see "A Hard Day's Night" starring "The Beatles."

11th August 1964 Tuesday

Lovely day. Spent the morning on the beach in Bognor watching a sand castle competition for the children. In the afternoon we went by car to Littlehampton & while there, went for a boat trip. In the evening went to an excellent variety show in Bognor at the Esplanade Theatre.

12th August 1964 Wednesday

Enid & I went by car from Bognor to Portsmouth. While there we went for a ¾ hr boat trip & saw Nelson's Flagship, H. M. S. Victory, & also the Royal Yacht **Britannia.** On the way home to Bognor we called at a little seaside place called **Bosham.** There we saw the oldest church I have ever seen – a **Saxon Church.**

13th August 1964 Thursday

First day of the fifth and final Test Match between England & Australia at The Oval.
Enid & I spent the afternoon in Old Bosham, the quaint little place we found first of all yesterday. We were there at high tide when the sea floods the whole street, & swans sail down the road, which is used by cars at low tide.

14th August 1964 Friday

Enid & I went to Arundel in the afternoon. I did not like Arundel because of its very hilly roads. The river there was very dirty. No boat trips & only one swan! I much preferred Old Bosham. In the evening we went to another excellent variety show in Bognor given by the same company which we saw on Tuesday.

15th August 1964 Saturday

Enid & I returned home from our week's holiday in Bognor Regis.
We stopped at Windsor for lunch, & while there we went into the Parish Church. There we saw the "**One Only**" copy of the Bible printed in **Gold**, & also a picture 15ft x 14ft of **The Last Supper**, a national

treasure given to this church by **George III**.

16th August 1964 Sunday

Mary gave me a dark brown hair do for 25/-. This was to cover up my dozen or so pure white hairs.

Julian (aged 14) arrived from Malvern for a week's holiday staying at Pat's house. My father married a girl named **Julia Stacey** & they had 2 children Pat & Bunting. Bunting is now 49. She is Julian's mother. My father married twice.

17th August 1964 Monday

On April 16th this year, 7 men were each sentenced to 30 years imprisonment for their part in robbing a mail train of some £2,600,000 last August. Last Wednesday, in the early hours of the morning, one of them named Charles Wilson, was snatched from jail, in a brilliantly planned escape plot. The Police cannot find him.

18th August 1964 Tuesday

The fifth Test ended in a draw, with Australia winning the series 1 – 0, & thus retaining The Ashes. During this final Test, **Freddie Truman** reached and passed his 300th wicket in Test cricket. (Bowling, not batting) Others who played were:- Boycott, Barber, Dexter, Cowdrey, Barrington, Parfitt, Parks, Titmus, Cartwright & Price.

19th August 1964 Wednesday

The Leicester Mercury tonight reports the extent of damage caused by a severe thunderstorm which we had about 6 p.m. yesterday. At Ravenstone, two valuable in-calf Friesian heifers were killed by lightening in a field on the farm of Mr J. R. Cliff.

We went to this farm on May 3rd, to pray for the animals.

20th August 1964 Thursday

Julian, aged 14, has been playing croquet nearly all the while since he arrived for his week's holiday here in Ravenstone. Tonight Julian & I played against Pat & Auntie Gladys. We lost. Then Julian & Auntie Gladys played against Don & me. We won.

Don is my cousin, son of Fred, & father of Peter, Lesley & Susan.

21st August 1964 Friday

The Coalville Times today spotlights John Sear. (See May 1st) John Sear is the son of Minna, my cousin, who is the daughter of Uncle Aubrey. John Sear's fiancée, Lesley, is the daughter of my cousin Donald who is the son of Uncle Fred. John Sear is going to the 1964 Manx Grand Prix Motor Cycle Races, where it is expected he will do well.

22nd August 1964 Saturday

The Soccer season starts today. For their first match of the season Leicester City played at Sunderland (Gordon Banks in goal). Score 3 – 3.

Julian returned home to Malvern after his week's holiday in Ravenstone. His brother Michael came by train to escort him home. Michael is now 16.

23rd August 1964 Sunday

Mum is 59 today. Mum had a twin sister Elizabeth (I was named after her). She was always known as Sis &

she died of diphtheria at the age of 10, when there was an epidemic in Ravenstone. They came to Ravenstone from Willoughby-on-the-Wolds when they were 7. They were born there.

24th August 1964 Monday

Yesterday was Terry's 20th birthday, when he and Mary became engaged.

Aunt Dos is at Kegworth this week, staying with her friend Mary Dolman, so I am sleeping at Pat's house for 3 nights while Mum is on night duty.

Today, Christine Hughes started working in our office.

25th August 1964 Tuesday

My last day in the Driving Licence Section. A glorious hot sunny day. The temperature in Leicester at 3 p.m. was 25°c = 77°f , in the shade.

Have you ever heard of a hinny? In the Leicester Mercury tonight there is a lovely picture of mother donkey & 2 hour old baby hinny (son of a horse) born at Breedon.

26th August 1964 Wednesday

A real scorcher today. The temperature this afternoon was 28°c = 82°f.

Reevsie in the Driving Licence Section was on holiday Monday & Tuesday & due back today. She rang up to ask if she might have today off as well; so I worked with Driving Licences all day.

27th August 1964 Thursday

My first day at work in our "**Transfer**" section, under the direction of "**Lammy**."

Leicester's worst bottle-neck area, the junction of Fosse Rd. & Groby Rd., has been re-designed. A huge traffic island has been removed & traffic lights galore erected. This morning for the first time, we went through very easily.

Note – Having worked in the Driving Licence section at work for the last 16 years, I have now transferred to the Vehicle Licence section, commencing behind the scenes, instead of on the public counter, dealing with driving licences.

28th August 1964 Friday

It's all aboard for holidays! Tomorrow Mum & I set off for our tour of Devon & Cornwall. Pat & Evelyn are off for a week at Butlin's, Clacton. Enid & Auntie Gladys are off for a week at Mablethorpe to stay with Auntie Gladys' sister Marjorie.

Tomorrow is Pat's birthday. He will be 46.

29th August 1964 Saturday

Mum & I, on the first day of our tour of Devon & Cornwall. A beautiful sunny day. We had elevenses just before Warwick at "**The Saxon Mill**", a most delightful place. Lunch in Cirencester. Tea in Taunton, & evening dinner at **The Hydro Hotel**, Paignton. This is our hotel for 2 nights. We have a lovely front bedroom.

30th August 1964 Sunday

Blue skies & sunshine all day long. Mum & I went to 8 a.m. communion at St Andrews **Paignton**. During the morning we went by boat to **Brixham**. In the afternoon we went to Torquay & back on an open top double decker bus. In the evening, we walked to Goodrington. Our hotel, The Hydro, is terrific!

31st August 1964 Monday

On August 31st last year, my Uncle Bert died. He was husband to Auntie Doris who lives at Mountsorrel. His name was Bert Scott (he married Doris Moore).

Today Mum & I moved on from our lovely Hydro Hotel in **Paignton,** to the Hotel Royale, **Penzance.** We had lunch at **Looe,** & afternoon tea at **Truro.** Lovely sunny day.

1st September 1964 Tuesday

Mum & I went to Land's End, calling at Sennen where at the "**First and Last Inn**" we bought several souvenirs, & were entertained hilariously by the landlord. We spent the whole afternoon in St. Ives where the wind blew as hard as it possibly could. Afterwards I paid a brief visit to "**St. Michael's Mount.**"

2nd September 1964 Wednesday

Left Penzance & moved on to The Grosvenor at Ilfracombe, to a horrible back bedroom right at the top of the hotel & **no lift!** Highlight of today was lunch at King Arthur's Castle Hotel, from where we had the most wonderful coastline view of **Tintagel.** We called for tea at Clovelly, but I didn't like it there.

Note – Needless to say "I didn't like it there". Clovelly lies at the foot of a great hill.

3rd September 1964 Thursday

Had a wonderful day exploring the rugged coastline of Ilfracombe. We walked up to St. Nicholas Chapel on Lantern Hill & also watched a big boat leaving the harbour in the morning. In the afternoon we visited Woolacombe, where I had a swim in the sea. Watched the sunset over the sea at Ilfracombe.

4th September 1964 Friday

Mum & I returned home from our week's tour of Devon & Cornwall. We had sunshine all day & every day. This was a tour organised by Barton's bus company from Nottingham.

Today the Queen opened the £20 million new **Forth Suspension Bridge,** & was the first person to use it.

5th September 1964 Saturday

I went to Leicester on the 8 a.m. bus (2/8d single fare) & back on the 10-20 a.m.

I bought some items for Sunday School which starts again tomorrow after a break for the whole of August.

Jenny Coleman & Jacqueline Hull Perry joined our Drama Group. We now have 12 members.

6th September 1964 Sunday

Pat & Evelyn came in for an hour or two after church in the evening. We were telling them all about our holiday & they were telling us about theirs.

Auntie Dos, who has been staying at Kegworth for almost a month, paid a flying visit home with Bob & Mary Dolman. She said she will be coming home to stay tomorrow.

7th September 1964 Monday

I bought my tape recorder (65 guineas).

Tonight we had our first rehearsal for "**Annie Get Your Gun**" which will be produced next March.

Aunt Dos returned home & Mary Dolman came with her to stay until the week-end.

Mary Dolman has spent many years nursing in **Africa.**

8th September 1964 Tuesday

I spent the whole evening with my new tape recorder – getting really acquainted with it. For my first recording I read the first Chapter of the Gospel according to St. John. I would like if possible to record whole books of the Bible, starting with my favourite – The Gospel according to St. John.

9th September 1964 Wednesday

Mary Dolman gave a viewing of some of her many coloured film slides, in Aunt Dos' lounge. I went to see them with Mum, Ann Causer, Enid, Auntie Gladys & Aunt Dos. We saw views of Table Mountain – Mary Dolman going up by cable car & walking down (a 3 hour walk) & many other fascinating scenes.

10th September 1964 Thursday

Had tea & the evening at Mrs Hasler's in Blaby. Mrs Hasler works in our office & she invited Reevsie & her husband Tony & me to spend the evening with her. We played clock golf on the lawn after tea & then watched coloured film slides of N. Africa, of Scotland & of the Isles of Scilly. Mr & Mrs Hasler brought me home.

11th September 1964 Friday

For the first time at work I had a "go" on one of our £2,500 Burroughs machines.

Mary Dolman & Aunt Dos spent the evening with Mum & me. We listened to music on my tape recorder & had a drink of "Mead" which Mum & I brought home with us from Cornwall.

12th September 1964 Saturday

Spent the morning at Mary Dolman's lovely home in Kegworth, where we gathered lots of damsons. In the afternoon went to Wicksteed Park with the Sunday School Anniversary outing. Harold took me on a boat, on the train & on the water chute. The Rector treated me to tea with Harold, Mr Bagnall & Mr Lovett.

13th September 1964 Sunday

I had more children than I expected at the start of our new "Sunday School Year". Today there were eleven turned up & I had ordered only for ten – Susan Smith, Susan Parker, Zena Bennett, Pamela Kendrick, Sandra Lord, Jo Heap, Brenda Hill, Cordelia & Nicola Wallis, B. Hurst & L. Broadhurst.

14th September 1964 Monday

Miss Rippon & Muriel both away from work, so I helped Ann to do their work. I enjoyed this very much as I was able to do a lot of typing.

We had our 2nd rehearsal for "Annie Get Your Gun". Frank Newman, our former musical director, was there. Enid & I took him home in Enid's car.

15th September 1964 Tuesday

We purchased a new electric fire from a traveller who arrived about 7 p.m. The fire was   £16-10/-. The travelling salesman then took Mum in his car to Ashby for night duty.

I had the job which I do not like of delivering envelopes from our church to every house in our parish, from Hoo Ash to Ravenslea turn.

16th September 1964 Wednesday

I bought my first tape record for my new tape recorder – "On Tour with The George Mitchell Minstrels from The Black & White Minstrel Show". I then sat up till midnight recording from the wireless – "Music to Midnight".

Reevsie has invited Mrs Hasler & me for tea tomorrow, & I said I would take my tape recorder.

17th September 1964 Thursday

I had a most interesting afternoon at work – typing Miss Rippon's police reports.

Spent the evening with Mrs Hasler at Reevsie's house. We listened to my tape recorder & played cards. Pat & Tony brought me home in the car, (Pat is Reevsie) & they came into our house for a while.

18th September 1964 Friday

King Constantine of The Helenes and Princess Anne-Marie of Denmark were married in Athens. There were 6 brides-maids, one being Princess Anne. The bride was only just 18 years of age. She rode to church with the bridegroom. She was in an open landau, drawn by 6 white horses. He was in another open landau.

19th September 1964 Saturday

We decided at our Drama Group to have rehearsals during October, November, & December on Saturday afternoons, rather than at night.

The residents of Cresswell Drive, Ravenstone, had their road officially "opened" today, after which they all had dinner together in the village institute.

20th September 1964 Sunday

For the first time at Sunday School we sang a hymn to my tape recorder.

I asked Auntie Gladys if she would help with our concert by playing the piano for us, and she said she would love to. I spent many hours with my tape recorder, recording myself reading poetry.

21st September 1964 Monday

Frank Newman was again at Amateurs' rehearsal & Enid & I took him home in the car.

I was up till after midnight recording a selection of Longfellow's poems.

A definite hint of winter in the air. We were all very cold in the office, & bought a thermometer.

22nd September 1964 Tuesday

I took my portable type writer down to the Rector's Room & helped with the addressing of envelopes for every house in our parish in preparation for our church's planned giving scheme

Afterwards, I came home & spent an hour or so recording part of my favourite "**Hiawatha**" poem.

23rd September 1964 Wednesday

I did 3 hours overtime at work & caught the 8-20 p.m. bus home. I spent the whole time filing away application forms for vehicle licences in their respective folders. A beautiful day. I sat upstairs at work most of the day, with all the windows flung wide open, until after night had fallen.

24th September 1964 Thursday

A very warm sunny day. I was able to go out during the dinner hour, wearing neither coat nor cardigan, with a sleeveless summer dress on.

I spent the evening with Auntie Gladys at her house, going through the music for our Christmas concert. I was there from 7-30 p.m. to 11 p.m.

25th September 1964 Friday

I spent the whole day at work "booking out" a great batch of "home number" vehicle registrations.

Diane Woodward spent about an hour in the evening with me, sorting out some dance movements for the songs in our concert. I took her home & went into her house for a while.

26th September 1964 Saturday

Auntie Gladys came to our rehearsal for our Christmas concert for the first time.

We sang for the first time – "**All in the April Evening**", which the children picked up very well in two parts. After tonight we shall be rehearsing on Saturday afternoons, because of the cold dark nights.

27th September 1964 Sunday

I went to 8 a.m. Holy Communion & then scootered to Ashby to meet Mum off night duty. After morning Sunday School, Diane Woodward came to our house for about an hour to sort out some more dance movements for our concert.

In the evening I wrote 20 of my Christmas cards.

28th September 1964 Monday

Again it was warm enough for me to go out in the dinner-hour without coat or cardigan & a sleeveless summer dress on.

Frank Newman, our former musical director of the Coalville Amateur Operatic Society, who had to retire through ill health, was at rehearsal again.

29th September 1964 Tuesday

I purchased for our concert – one tambourine, one pair of cymbals, two triangles & half a dozen little sleigh bells.

I asked Pat if he would be Santa Claus in the concert and he said he would.

I spent all day at work doing "**Book-ins**" which I quite enjoyed.

30th September 1964 Wednesday

I received written notification that I had been appointed full time **Poll Clerk** at the **Parliamentary Election** on Thursday 15th October, at **Polling Station No 40** at **Ravenstone School**.

I had a most enjoyable day at work, "**Booking In**" again & answering the phone quite a lot.

1st October 1964 Thursday
I was given my first lesson at work on how to check applications for Vehicle Licences. I also had a long session on our Burroughs £2,500 machine, doing only the simpler operations – making out licences for Private Cars only, both 4 monthly & 12 monthly. I came home by bus. Geoff brought me to Groby in his car.

2nd October 1964 Friday
I bought 30 yards of lilac gingham at 2/11½ d per yard, to make dresses for the children in our concert. I made one late at night. Enid & I went to the Adult School to see "Poet & Pheasant" in which Ursula, from our Amateurs, excelled as an old woman.

3rd October 1964 Saturday
I made another dress for the concert. We had our first afternoon rehearsal, 2 p.m. – 5 p.m. We read through 3 plays **"Emma's Country Holiday"**, **"Freckles"** & **"Cinderella"**. We then learned the dance movements to the first 3 songs of our show: - **"When You're Smiling"**, **"Itsie Bitsy"** & **"Ain't We Got Fun"**.

4th October 1964 Sunday
Pat & I went on the scooter to Thornborough to see **Fanny & Thirza**. We had elevenses there. Tonight on the BBC Home Service, in the 4th of 13 programmes "Stories in Verse", Mum & I heard Charlton Hobbs reading **"The Jackdaw of Rheims"** from **The Ingoldsby Legends** & I taped it.

5th October 1964 Monday
We have 6 girls in our office who operate our Burroughs machines: - Enid, Anne, Linda, the two Joans & me. Today we were each given an over-all to wear while operating the machines. Mr Johnson has a week's holiday from work this week, so it's up with the lark for me, & on the bus.

6th October 1964 Tuesday
I made my third dress for our concert. Enid, my cousin, is 37 today. I gave her a **"Morris"** car key ring & a novelty lantern shaped ornament containing sherry, which I bought on holiday from "The First and Last Inn" in England, on September 1st.

7th October 1964 Wednesday
Reevsie & I went to "Swear" to secrecy for the General Election when we each will be **Poll Clerks** on October 15th. Ann spent ½ hr after we finished work at 5-15 p.m., showing Miss Gazzard & me how to issue the more complicated licences on our Burroughs sensimatic.

8th October 1964 Thursday
Went to Ravenstone Church Harvest Festival service, where the preacher was The Right Reverend H. A. Maxwell M. A., Assistant Bishop of Leicester. He preached on "The General Thanksgiving" prayer, stressing our **"Creation"** and our **"Preservation"** & finally our **"Redemption"**, with the **"Hope of Glory"**.

9th October 1964 Friday
When Aunt Lil died on July 19th, I was given a beautiful picture of hers which I had always liked. The frame was very old fashioned & dropping to bits, so I had it re-framed at Boots. Today it was collected from Boots – costing £3-11s-3d & was duly hung, in pride of place, on our wall.

10th October 1964 Saturday
We had our church harvest supper in Ravenstone Institute. For the entertainment afterwards we had a conjurer, an accordionist, a piano solo by Barbara Bath, a song by Susan Jarvis & a recitation by me:- "The Jackdaw of Rheims". I had to be prompted twice by Enid.

11th October 1964 Sunday
Harvest Festival Sunday in Ravenstone. In the evening, different couples walked up the aisle carrying varying items to the Rector, who stood waiting at the altar rails. Harold & I walked up with the Holy Communion bread & wine.
Today I made my fourth dress for our concert.

12th October 1964 Monday
Because of the General Election this week, the Labour Club at Coalville is not available for our Amateur's rehearsal. We therefore have no rehearsal this week. I posted my vote today. At work, I wore my over-all for the first time, & also I learned how to make out registration books for new vehicles.

13th October 1964 Tuesday
On August 5th I was given a form of application for a licence to perform our Christmas concert. Last Sunday I took this form to my cousin Rita who is secretary of the Ravenstone Institute committee. Tonight I spent the whole evening at her house, where I went to collect the form. Don, as Trustee, signed the form.

14th October 1964 Wednesday
I recorded **"King Robert of Sicily"** the Sicilian's Tale from "Tales of a Wayside Inn" by Longfellow.
I washed my hair ready for Election Day tomorrow when I shall be Poll Clerk at Ravenstone. We are in Loughborough Division. We have four divisions in our county: - Loughborough, Bosworth, Melton & Harborough.

15th October 1964 Thursday
Election Day! I had a most enjoyable day as Poll Clerk at Ravenstone School with Mr Taylor, Presiding Officer. We had 928 on our list of voters. (In the country as a whole there were 36 million who could vote.)
We had the school wireless on all day long, from 7 a.m. to 9 p.m.

16th October 1964 Friday
The election has been won by Labour, & our new Prime Minister is Mr Harold Wilson.
The four Leicestershire divisions retain their M Ps –
    Bosworth = Woodrow Wyatt (Labour)
    Harborough = J. Farr (Conservative)
    Loughborough = J. D. Cronin (Labour)
    Melton = Miss M. Pike (Conservative)
In Russia, Brezhnev takes over from Kruschev.

17th October 1964 Saturday
After this week's General Election, Labour have 317

seats, Conservatives 304, and Liberals 9. With only a majority of 4, it is expected that there will be another General Election within a year or two. Our new Minister of Transport is Thomas Fraser, who replaces Ernest Marples.

18th October 1964 Sunday

After Sunday School, I went to see Linda & Barbara Bath to decide exactly what they could do in our concert. They agreed to be in "**Santa Claus Comes Down the Chimney**". They are not able to come to rehearsals on Saturday afternoons.

Today I made my fifth dress for our concert.

19th October 1964 Monday

I went to the music shop & bought a couple of songs for our concert – "Jolly Good Company" & "California Here I Come".

I shall try & write my own words for our finale to the "California" tune. Something like – "Now we all say Cheerio, This is where we end our show" etc. etc.

20th October 1964 Tuesday

Mr Blackburn, whom I last saw on July 28th, was in our office today & smiled at me. He had come to see Mr Sharp about various promotions imminent amongst our staff. Anne was put up from the General Division to Clerical I, Ralph likewise. Lammy & Les were also upgraded

21st October 1964 Wednesday

For the first time at work, I used our Burroughs sensimatic for making out "Open" licences, & also did some for people waiting at the counter.

Last Sunday, my brother Pat went to a Deanery Conference held at Whitwick. He had to report on his Group's discussions, & tonight I typed his report out for him.

22nd October 1964 Thursday

I made my sixth dress for our concert.

A quiet day at work. I was on the machine for much of the morning. In the afternoon, I did "**scrapping**" of obsolete documents.

The Olympic Games are now in their second week in Tokyo. Britain to date has 4 gold medals, 12 silver & 1 bronze.

23rd October 1964 Friday

At work I had my first introduction to the work which Ralph does – "**Ministry Returns**". That means listing all our newly registered vehicles for a weekly return to the Ministry of Transport.

In the evening Diane Woodward, aged 11, and I went to Auntie Gladys' & worked out a dance for our concert.

24th October 1964 Saturday

Summertime ends at 2 a.m. tomorrow, when clocks go back one hour. This year there have been seven weeks more summertime than last year – 4 weeks in Spring & 3 in Autumn, after clocks were put forward on March 22nd.

I made my seventh dress for our concert.

25th October 1964 Sunday

A beautiful Autumn day. I scootered to Ashby before 8

a.m. to bring Mum home from night duty. While the village was still asleep, I saw a convoy of circus vehicles on the move. When they had passed, the world still slept on.

I made two more dresses for our concert – total now 9.

26th October 1964 Monday

Enid did not go to Amateurs tonight because she had a "Church Advancement" meeting. I therefore went on my scooter & I gave Joan Dillow a pillion ride home. We read through the libretto tonight for half the rehearsal, & had singing for the second half. I applied in writing for the part of "Dolly Tate".

27th October 1964 Tuesday

The 1964 Olympic Games, which were held in Tokyo, finished at the weekend.

Early this morning the British competitors in the first half of the home-coming team arrived at London Airport to a tumultuous reception. After a champagne breakfast they all had lunch with the Queen.

28th October 1964 Wednesday

Census time at work. We are doing a "**One in Ten**" census of every vehicle licenced in Leicestershire. This is being done by 4 teams of 3, & we hope to finish by November 6th.

Tonight I made my tenth dress for our concert.

The USA is all set for the election of a new President on November 3rd.

29th October 1964 Thursday

Census time at work means we get very dirty & covered in dust. The dust today got all in my throat & I felt I needed a good "breather" in the evening – so Mum & I went for a scooter ride – up Standard Hill, on to the Birch Tree – to Hoo Ash – to The Altons & then home.

30th October 1964 Friday

Diane Woodward & I went to Auntie Gladys' from 7 p.m. until 8-30 p.m. & worked out a few dance routines for our concert.

I was on the Census at work all day long, working with Joan & Mrs Gotheridge in the morning, & with Anne & Mrs Gotheridge in the afternoon.

31st October 1964 Saturday

I finished my eleventh & final dress for our concert. We rehearsed from 2p.m. to 7 p.m. taking a pic-nic tea. The rehearsal was somewhat of a shambles, but we also tried out various costumes.

In the evening Aunt Dos played 4 hymns on the piano for me to record for Sunday School.

1st November 1964 Sunday

After Sunday School I went for a ride in the morning sunlight with many trees still sporting their blazing autumn colours. I went to The Altons – on to Hoo Ash & back down Wash Lane. During the afternoon swirling fog enveloped the landscape & by evening it was very dense.

2nd November 1964 Monday

On November 2nd 1956, began the sale of Premium Bonds. I have been buying one each month since

January 1st 1959. Having drawn out 60, to pay for my tape recorder, I now have only 11. Today I cashed a cheque for £4, being my payment for my services as Poll Clerk on October 15th.

3rd November 1964 Tuesday
Last year on the 22nd day of the 11th month President Kennedy was shot dead. Immediately the new President was President Johnson; who now, eleven months & eleven days later, has thanked the people of America for supporting him so well, as he waits for the result of the American election, held today.

4th November 1964 Wednesday
President Lyndon Johnson has retained his office at The White House. He had 41 million votes as opposed to Senator Goldwater's 26 million. This was the biggest popular vote in US history. Prior to that, the record was Roosevelt's 60·8% of the popular vote, 28 years ago.

5th November 1964 Thursday
We finished our Census at work which we started on 28th October. We had 4 teams on the job & our team counted over 3,000 vehicles. Being a 1 in 10 census, we went through well over 30,000 dusty files.
Leicester has a plan to deal with the increase of motor vehicles over the next 30 years. It will cost £135 million.

6th November 1964 Friday
A letter from Mr Blackburn was passed round our office – "At its last meeting, the Finance Sub-Committee placed on record its appreciation of the way in which the Licences Section is keeping pace with the ever increasing volume of work, & offering a speedy service to the public . . . ."

7th November 1964 Saturday
Aunt Dos & I went for a morning car ride up to The Altons, & took various cine-shots of the Autumn trees.
We had a rehearsal for our Christmas concert from 2 p.m. to 7 p.m. Pat came from 4-30 p.m. until 5 p.m. & we did our first run through of "Santa Claus Comes Down the Chimney."

8th November 1964 Sunday
Peter Hewes, my cousin aged 23, is today lying in Leicester Royal Infirmary, after a car accident he had last night, when his head went through the windscreen & his face was cut very badly.
I walked to church with Mr Len Andrews who recited to me the whole of "Paul Revere's Ride" by Longfellow.

9th November 1964 Monday
We had auditions for parts in "Annie Get Your Gun".
Afterwards I went to enquire how Peter was, who was in a car accident on Saturday night. He was in bed at home. Apparently his face had been cut badly by the car mirror which shattered. He just needs rest & nourishment now.

10th November 1964 Tuesday
I bought a new hat! – a turban-style snug fitting imitation fur, beige colour, edged in brown.
I switched on the television in the evening, for the news, and it went snap, crackle pop!! This was followed by a smell of burning; so it looks as though a valve has burned out.
BBC 2 starts next week.

11th November 1964 Wednesday
Went to Ravenstone Institute to a supper in preparation for our church stewardship campaign. All in the middle of it, a Police-man came in to see me about the form I filled in a month ago for a licence to perform our concert. Mr Swanwick, who was sitting next to me, said he thought I had been arrested!

12th November 1964 Thursday
The Lord Mayor of Leicester, Alderman Archibald Kimberlin, is today launching his appeal for his own fund for the Kennedy Memorial Appeal, which was formed in May, & launched by the Lord Mayor of London. Leicester's contribution is for a Leicester Kennedy Scholarship to enable a Leicestershire student to be sent to America.

13th November 1964 Friday
Last Wednesday, Mr James Callaghan, the new Chancellor of the Exchequer, stunned the nation in his budget by putting up the price of petrol by 6d a gallon. Today, Mr Johnson, who gives me a lift in his car to & from work, stunned me, by putting up the price of my fare from 2/9d per day to 3/6d !!!

14th November 1964 Saturday
I went with a bus load of our Amateur's to the Grand Theatre, Wolverhampton, where the Bilston Operatic Company were presenting "Annie Get Your Gun". We had a good old sing-song on the way home, as the bus rattled along after midnight in the moonlight. We sang all the rip-roaring choruses of several of our previous shows.

15th November 1964 Sunday
I went for a walk in the afternoon sun-shine & met Don & Susan at the old farm-house where Mum used to live. It was empty & derelict with no windows, no doors & the ceilings caving in. We wandered all through, & went upstairs; reminiscing back to the days when I used to visit Grandad, when I was only 6.

16th November 1964 Monday
The parts were given out at the Amateurs for "Annie Get Your Gun". I received a letter which read:- "Dear Betty, Following your recent audition, the Committee have pleasure in advising you that you have been selected to play the part of **Dolly Tate**, in the Society's forthcoming production, Monday 8th March – 13th March."

17th November 1964 Tuesday
Mr Johnson's daughter Christine, passed her driving test today, & she drove us home from Leicester. I passed my driving test on my scooter on March 16th 1963, & I would like very much to take lessons in a car, starting next Spring. Mum decided not to use her one & only licence for my scooter.

18th November 1964 Wednesday
"The Wit of President Kennedy" listed by the New York Times as one of the top ten best selling non-fiction books, is to be published in Britain. It will be made

available on November 22nd , the first anniversary of President Kennedy's assassination. A ninety minute film tribute will be shown in Dublin on Friday.

19th November 1964 Thursday
We had our first libretto practice for "Annie Get Your Gun".
Mum & I watched an old film "**Wuthering Heights**" on television from 9-40 p.m. until   11-50 p.m. Laurence Olivier was Heathcliffe, Merle Oberon was Cathy, David Niven was Edgar Linton & Flora Robson was Ellen Dean. - a really dramatic film.

20th November 1964 Friday
Mr Blackburn, whom I last saw on October 20th, said "Hello" to me in Market Street, Leicester. Cor! He really sends me!
Tommy & I at work, had the dreary job of "**Filing**" all day long.
This week we have caught four mice in the house (Under the stairs).

21st November 1964 Saturday
We had a hilarious rehearsal for our concert. The play "Emma's Country Holiday" by Mabel Constanduros had us all doubled up with laughter when Jacqueline Hull Perry put a basket over her head. Mr Swanwick showed me the fireplace he will be making for us. I was very much impressed.

22nd November 1964 Sunday
On October 31st, I made my eleventh dress for our concert. Well, today I made another. Pamela Kendrick has asked for one to wear in the finale. We are hoping to have 12 girls in the finale:- Tina, Diane, Jacqueline, Susan Smith, Susan Jarvis, Carole, Jenny, Ruth, Rosemary, Linda, Pamela Mason & Pamela Kendrick.

23rd November 1964 Monday
Dawn Henn, at our Amateur's rehearsal was worried over her scripture home-work. She had to say what Job's three comforters said, to comfort Job. In an attempt to help her out, I sat up till after 1 a.m. trying to do a précis of the Book of Job, which has 42 chapters! I managed to get only half way, to Chapter 21.

24th November 1964 Tuesday
At work today, we each were told what to write down for our work sheet referendum.
Mine was worded thus –
"General Division"
Opening & checking vehicle excise licence applications 20%
Making out licences/Burroughs machine & checking for despatch 65%
Filing 15% of the time.

25th November 1964 Wednesday
Marjorie Hayes, aged 33 from next door, came in for a couple of hours. She has started work this week in the offices at Coalville Tech., after working for 18 years in a little private office. Enid, my cousin aged 37, will be starting work at Coalville Police Station on Monday after 14 years at Pegson's office.

26th November 1964 Thursday
We have provisionally sold all our tickets for our Christmas Concert for December 12th at 7-30 p.m. We are now considering a matinee for the same day. The premises are most inadequate. We are borrowing curtains from Pegson's, stage flooring from Coalville Amateur's, & a portable toilet for the changing room from Don.

27th November 1964 Friday
This week, Belgian paratroops freed a community of white people from Stanleyville, where they were being kept as hostages in the Congolese rebel stronghold, in Africa. Armed rebels had brutally tortured to death some of them. Nuns had been stripped naked, beaten, jeered at, and raped. Children too were tortured.

28th November 1964 Saturday
The latest news tells of more mass killing by rebels in the Congo. Since last Tuesday when Belgian paratroops landed at Stanleyville, about 80 white people have been killed around Paulis, 160 miles north. Four Spanish nuns had their throats cut, & bodies mutilated beyond recognition.

29th November 1964 Sunday
Yesterday was our church Christmas Fair held in Ravenstone Institute.
Because of our rehearsal, I was not able to go.
This morning, the Rector told me he was very annoyed that I'd had a rehearsal, keeping away so many children from the Christmas Fair. He said others too, were very cross about it!

30th November 1964 Monday
Sir Winston Churchill is 90 today! He himself has said, "When I get to Heaven I propose to spend a considerable portion of my first million years in painting."
During the last war 1939-1945 when England knew her darkest hour, the people had the heart of a lion, but Churchill gave the roar.
(See 1st December 1954)

1st December 1964 Tuesday
Sir Winston Churchill's birthday yesterday brought him more than 30,000 messages & telegrams. The flood of tributes was headed by a message from the Queen, with a bouquet of lilies. There were messages from the Pope, President de Gaulle (France), President Johnson (U. S.) & other Heads of State.

2nd December 1964 Wednesday
At the beginning of January this year, the Pope made a "Pilgrimage of Peace" to the Holy Land. Today he has gone to India, to the Eucharistic Congress in Bombay. He says this too, is a "Pilgrimage of Peace". This 4,000 mile journey by air is the longest ever made by any Pope.

3rd December 1964 Thursday
Pope Paul in Bombay was presented today with a copy of the Moslem Holy Koran. He is being acclaimed as the "Pilgrim of Peace". In the lounge of a convent being used as a press centre, he met Hindus, Moslems, Parsees,

Sikhs, Jews & Jains, who greeted with outstretched arms the "Holy Man" from Rome.

4th December 1964 Friday

Senator Edward Kennedy who received a broken back in a plane crash last June, walked again last night. He wore a back brace as he carefully walked about 10 feet across his room at New England Baptist Hospital, Boston, Massachusetts. The Senator was re-elected last month. (November 3rd)

5th December 1964 Saturday

Pope Paul left Bombay today by air for home after his 3 day visit. He returned home in a non stop jet airliner.

We had our dress rehearsal for our concert in Ravenstone Institute. The children had 12 photos taken in various costumes. They looked lovely.

6th December 1964 Sunday

Our first day at church for "Planned Giving". The collection plate was covered with small envelopes containing money. The Rector in his announcements for the coming week mentioned our concert to be given next Saturday. The Rector gave an excellent sermon on:-"A sword shall pierce through thy own soul also."

7th December 1964 Monday

Today I booked 2 seats for Mum & me to see "**Cleopatra**" at Leicester's new Odeon Cinema on Christmas Eve at 2 p.m. This is definitely THE film of the year, starring Elizabeth Taylor as Cleopatra, Richard Burton as Mark Antony & Rex Harrison as Julius Cæsar. Our seats are 10/6d each.

8th December 1964 Tuesday

Gale force winds are blowing today.

Our office staff are having Christmas dinner tonight at The County Arms, Blaby, but I am one of the few who chose not to go. I find it rather awkward living 20 miles away, & not having transport of my own. I would not venture there on my scooter!

9th December 1964 Wednesday

The millionth ton of coal to be brought to the surface through the new drift mine at Snibston Colliery, Coalville, was chalked up last night. The emergence of Snibston Colliery as a million ton a year coal producing unit follows a reconstruction scheme which has cost £1,500,000.

10th December 1964 Thursday

I spent the evening in Ravenstone Institute, sorting out the seating arrangement, etc. for our concert on Saturday. Alfie Bath, Stan Taylor, Stuart Reynolds & Keith Reynolds were there to help. We set out 100 chairs (the maximum allowed) & fitted up the curtains & the back cloth (a bed-spread).

11th December 1964 Friday

Little Tommy from work took me during the dinner hour on his scooter to a dress shop near Fosse Corner, where I had seen a dress I rather fancied in the window. I tried on the dress & decided it wasn't quite as nice as I expected, so I didn't buy it.

12th December 1964 Saturday

Our concert in Ravenstone Institute. We had an afternoon performance, to which about 80 people came. The children did extremely well. The evening performance was particularly good. I was presented with a lovely bouquet.

Note – The concert in Ravenstone Institute, which I have organised. Twelve girls from Sunday School present a mixed medley of turns. It has been a marathon effort to produce, with untold complications. We just do not possess sufficient talent or amenities, but we do our best.

13th December 1964 Sunday

Spent much of the morning in Ravenstone Institute, cleaning up after yesterday's concert. There were 100 chairs to be untied & stacked, the floor to be swept & various other items to attend to. Alfie Bath, Pat, Enid & Mum helped. We hope to realize a profit of about £10.

14th December 1964 Monday

I spent the day at work with the Driving Licence section, because Reevsie was away from work. I issued myself with a learner licence for a car, from January 1st to 30th June next year. I then contacted The Lansdowne School of Motoring & arranged my first lesson for Jan 5th 1965

15th December 1964 Tuesday

Pat, my brother aged 46, today had the last of his teeth out & a complete set of false teeth straight in.

I spent all day at work on our Burroughs machine, making out all the counter licences.

Having cleared our house of all the mice, last month, we now have a rat to contend with!

16th December 1964 Wednesday

We received our first Christmas cards today – one from Auntie Doris at Mountsorrel, one from Marie at Barrow-on-Soar, one from Clamps at Coalville & one from St. James Church, Snibston.

It was so foggy in Leicester this afternoon; we were allowed to finish work half an hour early.

17th December 1964 Thursday

Our Amateurs' Christmas party. I bought a new dark blue winter dress, 6 guineas. I went on my scooter to the party & came home at 10-45 p.m. I have to be up at crack of dawn tomorrow to catch the 7 a.m. bus, because Mr Johnson is taking his wife into hospital.

18th December 1964 Friday

We had rehearsal for the Amateurs' in a room at Coalville Marlborough Square Chapel.

After rehearsal I had a session at home of wrapping up Christmas parcels.

Today, I bought a pair of new shoes, Brevitt bouncers – flat, sensible shoes, ready for my driving lessons.

19th December 1964 Saturday

Nine members of The Ravenstone Drama Group & I went to see the Rector, to give him £1-1s-9d which we had collected towards the use of heating & lighting in the Rector's Room, which we had used regularly for rehearsals during the past 6 months. We have adjourned now, until next July.

20th December 1964 Sunday

I walked to church with Mr Len Andrews who recited to me the whole of "**The Spanish Armada**" by McCaulay.

This morning I took £10 worth of small change (proceeds from our concert) to Dennis Collier, treasurer for Ravenstone Church, to be put in safe keeping for some future use.

21st December 1964 Monday

We arrived at work this morning to find that the office had been burgled during the week-end. Nothing of value seems to be missing. There is one smashed window; & blood on the floor indicated that somebody had probably cut his fist. The incident occurred late on Friday night.

22nd December 1964 Tuesday

I was on the machine all day long at work, dealing with all the counter licences.

We had some cigarettes & chocolates given to our office for Christmas. These were raffled – Charles won the cigarettes & Lammy won the chocolates.

Mr Sharp gave us a big tin of biscuits for tea break!

23rd December 1964 Wednesday

I booked a holiday in Guernsey for Mum & me, starting September 5th next year, for 8 days. Mrs Swanwick, who lives next door but one, came in during the evening & kept us well entertained, talking non-stop until 10 p.m. Anne Causer also came in, & so did Pat.

24th December 1964 Thursday

We finished work today at 12-30 for the Christmas holiday. We start again next Tuesday. Mum & I spent the afternoon watching the film "**Cleopatra**" which we thoroughly enjoyed. We stayed in Leicester until 7 p.m. to see "Rudolph" & "Santa" touring through the city centre.

25th December 1964 Friday

A lovely sunny cold crisp day. Went to Holy Communion at 7 a.m. Went down to my dad's grave & saw that Mum's old farmhouse had been knocked down completely.

Mum & I spent the day at Auntie Gladys & Enid's. David & Irene, & Aunt Dos also there.

26th December 1964 Saturday

Bitterly cold day. During the evening it snowed quite heavily. I had dinner & tea at Pat's. Besides Pat, Evelyn & Mary, there was Aunt Dos, Auntie Gladys, Enid, Terry Jarman, his brother, his mum & dad, his grand-dad, who had recently lost his wife, & Stuart from Somerset.

27th December 1964 Sunday

A real winter's day – snow everywhere & bitterly cold. I spent many hours recording part of the Gospel according to St. Matthew. After church at night, I went with Alfie Bath to his house & sat & watched a very good film called "The Heiress" with all the Bath family.

28th December 1964 Monday

I went for a morning walk in the bright sunshine which made the snow everywhere look really beautiful. I took a couple of snap-shots of the birds eating in our garden.

To do this, I used my scooter cover as a "hide" & was thus able to get within a few feet of the birds.

29th December 1964 Tuesday

First day back to work after the Christmas holiday. I have got a shocking cold, so I've been sneezing & blowing most of the time. Today I received a belated Christmas present from Reevsie – Magie Mist, Lancôme Paris perfume. The bitterly cold weather is giving way to milder weather with rain.

30th December 1964 Wednesday

A new liner is to be built. It will be Cunard's new transatlantic express liner, the Q4, costing £23,000,000, & will be built on the Clyde. The contract was signed today in London. Delivery is expected in May 1968. This will be a 58,000 ton liner!

31st December 1964 Thursday

Just before dawn today, a car was travelling along the unopened section of the M I at Markfield, & crashed at about 60 m.p.h. A cyclist on the A50 rang the police, but when they arrived on the scene the car & driver had gone.

Tyre marks in the white hoar frost told the story.

* * *

**Motor Licences are
Doubled Since 1954**

The number of motor licences issued by Leicestershire County Council last year was more than double that of ten years ago. Last year 119,690 were in force compared with 51,555 in 1954. Of the latest number, 79,830 were for private cars, 18,990 for motor cycles and 13,040 for goods vehicles.

(Leicester Mercury 20-02-1965)

1965

1st January 1965 Friday
The Prime Minister, Mr Harold Wilson, today celebrates his silver wedding anniversary.
In the New Year's Honours List, Stanley Matthews, 50 year old soccer star, becomes **Sir Stanley Matthews.**
At work we had our first day's overtime for the January peak period. I worked until 8 p.m.

2nd January 1965 Saturday
A lovely sunny frosty day. I walked to Coalville & back across the fields. Today I bought a **Morphy Richards** hair dryer for £3-12-6d. Also I sent off £8 to Pitman's, Godalming, Surrey, for a correspondence course of **"Shorthand Writing".**

3rd January 1965 Sunday
We had the whole Sunday School in the Rector's Room this morning because the heating system in church was not working properly. Ravenstone School was still closed for the holiday. Terry & Mary announced today that they hope to get married on 30th August, bank holiday Monday.

4th January 1965 Monday
I worked until 8 p.m. doing nothing but check incoming applications for vehicle licences through-out the whole day. It was a steady & pleasant enough job midst all the hustle & bustle of the office. Mum went to see Roy Johnson's pantomime **"Little Miss Muffet."**

5th January 1965 Tuesday
I had my first driving lesson in a Hillman Imp car, number 587 HJF. I learned how to give signals properly & what to check. 1. Check the position of seat. 2. Check the position of mirror. 3. Check the hand brake. 4. Check that the gear is in neutral. 5. Check the door. I also steered.

6th January 1965 Wednesday
Reevsie & I booked a table for two at Lewis's & had lunch de luxe in the restaurant, instead of the usual cafeteria. Today I bought a white jumper & a thermometer.
I stayed at work until 8 p.m. – a very pleasant day's work, mostly checking & machine operating.

7th January 1965 Thursday
We all left work today on time. This is the first time I can remember such a thing happening at the beginning of January. I came home with little Tommy on his scooter.
I had a letter from Pitman Correspondence College to say that study material & full instructions would be coming.

8th January 1965 Friday
Again we finished work on time. Little Tommy gave me a lift on his scooter as far as Fosse Road corner, where I decided to catch the 5-20 p.m. bus home. However, I was too late. I caught the 5-30 p.m. to Coalville & then visited the **Hong Kong Restaurant** for mushroom omelette.

9th January 1965 Saturday
I took my scooter to be serviced. I have now done 2,575 miles. Yesterday I bought a new pen – an **Esterbrook** fountain pen with a special "shorthand" nib, so today I have been writing some shorthand, in readiness for my lessons by post which will shortly be starting.

10th January 1965 Sunday
I spent many hours perfecting my poem on "Ravenstone Church".
Mr Maurice Taylor surprised me by giving me 4/- towards our Drama Group funds. He said he was not able to come & see our concert but he had heard about it. This all took place in church after the evening service.

11th January 1965 Monday
I worked until 8 p.m., so did not go to Amateur's rehearsal.
About a fortnight ago, I developed a heavy cold. It was just clearing up nicely when I rode all the way home from Leicester on Tommy's scooter: & the result is now another cold. I've been sneezing & blowing well today.

12th January 1965 Tuesday
Had my second driving lesson, in which I learned how to engage first, second, third and fourth gears. Once, however, I managed to get into reverse gear by mistake! Today I received by post all my necessary study material from Pitman's. Again I worked until 8 p.m.

13th January 1965 Wednesday
Reevsie & I again had lunch in Lewis's restaurant, where we had reserved a table. I worked until 8 p.m., & sat with Ann Causer on the bus home. Today it is her birthday. A wet & windy day, but arrived in Ravenstone at 9-15 p.m. to find all the stars & the moon shining brightly.

14th January 1965 Thursday
I worked until 8 p.m. Tomorrow morning I have to be up very early & catch the bus to work because Mr Johnson will not be taking me by car. Mr Johnson will be going later than usual because he is taking his wife into hospital for an operation.
Beryl called in during the evening. She has neuralgia.

15th January 1965 Friday
I worked only until 7 p.m. because I wanted to go to rehearsal. (Annie Get Your Gun). I caught a bus to Coalville & walked over the bridges to the Labour Club. No rehearsal being held there so I walked to Marlborough Square Chapel. No rehearsal being held there, so I caught the 9 p.m. bus home.

16th January 1965 Saturday
Ravenstone W. I. have a competition in which you have to put as many items as possible into a match box. I have been helping Mum with hers, & up to now we have 63, with space to spare. Aunt Dos has over 100 in hers.
Tonight Aunt Dos entertained Auntie Gladys, Enid & me from 8 p.m. to 1 a.m.

17th January 1965 Sunday
Gale force winds have swept the whole country today, reaching hurricane force at times. My scooter, parked on

the yard, was blown over.

Sir Winston Churchill is dying. Today's wind with its colossal force seems to epitomise the very character & personality of this great man.

18th January 1965 Monday

I worked until 8 p.m. & then went to Amateur's rehearsal. I learned that the Friday night rehearsals have been switched to Wednesday for a few weeks. Starting this week we are rehearsing on Thursdays as well.

Aunt Dos with 112 articles in a match box won the W. I. competition.

19th January 1965 Tuesday

I worked until 8 p.m. All the licences have now been issued. Thousands of application forms are just waiting to be filed away. Filing is one job I do not like!

This time last year, the County Drama Advisor was planning a big religious production for Autumn, but nothing ever came of it.

20th January 1965 Wednesday

Got up this morning to find snow everywhere & no electricity. The electricity was off from
4-30 a.m. until about noon.

I was on the counter machine all afternoon & then I came home on time.

Because of the snow, I went to Amateur's rehearsal on the bus, instead of my scooter.

21st January 1965 Thursday

My third driving lesson. I had my first "go" at starting on a hill; & also did a lot of "turn right" "turn right again" "turn left" "turn right" "turn left" in quick succession.

At work, for the very first time, I took in some vehicle licence applications over the counter.

22nd January 1965 Friday

We have finished working over-time! At work this morning I was on "filing" which I do not like, but this afternoon I was on the counter machine, which I really enjoyed.

The new 18 mile long stretch of the **M 1** reaching up as far as **Markfield, Leicestershire**, was opened today.

23rd January 1965 Saturday

Enid & I discussed "summer holidays". We decided to write to Hastings & to Eastbourne for their holiday guides.

Today I have been practising shorthand. Last Sunday I sent by post my first test paper to be marked. I expected some reply before now, but I've heard nothing from my tutor.

24th January 1965 Sunday

Sir Winston Churchill died, at 8 a.m.

25th January 1965 Monday

The world today looks back on the life of Sir Winston Churchill, who on April 9th 1963 was made an honorary citizen of the United States. President Kennedy said then, **"In the dark days & darker nights when Britain stood alone - & most men, save Englishmen,**

despaired of England's life, he mobilised the English language & sent it into battle."

26th January 1965 Tuesday

My fourth driving lesson. I had my first introduction to reversing – just straight back. I also did some hill starts & I was shown the different ways to hold the gear lever for various gear changes. It snowed a little during the lesson.

Roy & Doreen Powers spent the evening with us.

27th January 1965 Wednesday

Reevsie & I dined in Lewis's restaurant, where as a special treat, I chose grilled fillet steak with chips, mushrooms, bacon & tomato. This course alone cost 10/-
.

Went to Amateur's rehearsal at night on the bus, because the weather was inclined to be wintry. I had a letter from Michael & one from Julian.

28th January 1965 Thursday

Yesterday, today & tomorrow, Sir Winston Churchill, whose funeral is on Saturday, lies in state in Westminster Hall, London. A constant flow of ordinary men, women & children of all ages passes the catafalque, where he lies beneath the Union Jack. The queue of waiting people spans the River Thames.

29th January 1965 Friday

After waiting nearly a fortnight, I have now heard from my shorthand tutor.

There are 20 lessons which I must attempt, & today I have the result of my first lesson. I have been given 75%.

Today at work, Beverly was a "learner" on the machine, while I sat beside her as "instructor".

30th January 1965 Saturday

The Queen led the nation's mourning in a vast congregation of 3,000 at St. Paul's Cathedral. From over a hundred nations representatives had come for the state funeral of Sir Winston Churchill, who **"was raised up in our days of desperate need to be a leader & inspirer of the nation"** & who **"lit the lamps of hope."**

31st January 1965 Sunday

After his state funeral yesterday, Sir Winston Churchill now lies buried in Bladon churchyard, outside the walls of Blenheim Palace where he was born, not far from Oxford. A wreath from the Queen bears the message –
"From the Nation & the Commonwealth, in grateful remembrance, Elizabeth R."

1st February 1965 Monday

The launching of a Winston Churchill Memorial Trust was announced today. The aim is to establish travelling fellowships, enabling men and women in all parts of the Commonwealth & the U. S. to further their knowledge, experience & education in another part of the Commonwealth or America.

2nd February 1965 Tuesday

Philip Bancroft brought a wall-paper book for us to choose something for the middle room.

The Queen is now on the second day of her state visit to

Ethiopia, where she had the most wonderful reception. She will be there for a week.

St. George is the patron saint of Ethiopia & of Britain.

3rd February 1965 Wednesday
My fifth driving lesson. I drove to Wigston & back. I reversed round a corner, with the help of my instructor. My instructor is Mr L. Smith; ex-Leicester City Police Sergeant – former member of the Leicester City Police Traffic Department – passed the Lancashire Police Advanced Driving Course.

4th February 1965 Thursday
Today I ordered a mirror from Lewis's. It is 44 inches by 15 inches & costs £4-19s-11d. It will be delivered on Tuesday morning.

This morning Uncle Fred was taken ill & tonight Mum is sleeping at his house to keep Auntie Belle company. Uncle Fred is my dad's eldest brother, aged 80.

5th February 1965 Friday
Mr Blackburn was in our office for half an hour this morning. He stood talking to Mr Sharp, only a few yards away from the Burroughs machine which I was operating. My heart just went "**Doyng!**"

Les Rayner's birthday today, so he bought everyone in the office a **Kit-Kat** chocolate.

6th February 1965 Saturday
"Friendly" **Midland Red** on strike, so I fetched Mum home from work at 8 a.m. on the scooter. I also took her to work at 8 p.m. on the scooter.

Uncle Fred has been advised to stay in bed for a week, although he feels well enough to get up now. I sat with him for an hour this afternoon.

7th February 1965 Sunday
I fetched Mum home from night duty. The scooter developed a bad attack of back firing, so Stan Colclough is going to try & cure it tomorrow.

Our middle room has been cleared of carpets, furniture, etc. in preparation for the painters & decorators who are expected tomorrow morning.

8th February 1965 Monday
I sent off a Postal Order value 37/6d for some black fishnet theatrical tights.

The walls in our middle room are now completely stripped, all ready for papering. We have chosen a perfectly plain paper, a delicate shade of green.

My scooter is spending the night at Stan Colclough's, in his garage.

9th February 1965 Tuesday
The new wall-paper is now all on in our middle room & looks smashing.

Today I had my 6th driving lesson. I did not make any particular progress, just a repetition of what I'd done before – hill starts & reversing round a corner, still with a lot of help from my instructor. He took me today into his office.

10th February 1965 Wednesday
Mary Blue & Terry, who decided to have their wedding in August, now have the chance of a flat at The Hollies,

so they will have a Spring wedding.

Uncle Fred had his bed moved downstairs today.

Stan Colclough has diagnosed my scooter back-firing trouble as a hole burned into the exhaust pipe.

11th February 1965 Thursday
Auntie Cis from Skegness called in on a flying visit. Tonight she is sleeping at Uncle Fred's house & then tomorrow she leaves for London.

The painters & decorators have finished working in our middle room, but have now set about the kitchen.

"**Ringo**" one of the famous "**Beatles**" was married today, 8-15 a.m.

12th February 1965 Friday
Enid & Auntie Gladys went to Mablethorpe for "Uncle Merton's" funeral.

The painters and decorators finished painting our kitchen. I collected my scooter from Stan Colclough's. He had patched up the hole in the silencer – 14/6d.

Sir Winston Churchill's will was published today. He left £300,000.

13th February 1965 Saturday
Bitterly cold day with gale force winds. Philip Bancroft put our new mirror up in the front room. Aunt Dos & I went to Coalville to see Arthur Haynes & Dermot Kelly, stars of radio & television, who were signing autographs from 10-30 a.m. until 12-30 p.m. We got their autographs & filmed them on the cine-camera.

14th February 1965 Sunday
Part of the windscreen on my scooter snapped right off this morning, when I caught it on the gate post.

I sent off my third shorthand lesson. The second one, which I sent off a fortnight ago, has not yet been returned.

Auntie Gladys & Enid came home from Mablethorpe, after Uncle Merton's funeral.

15th February 1965 Monday
The Queen is to hold a garden party in April for members of the Women's Institute throughout the whole country. Great excitement in Ravenstone tonight as our representative was chosen by popular vote. The winner was Mrs Hatton. Every women's institute is allowed to send one member.

16th February 1965 Tuesday
My 7th driving lesson. Today I had my first attempt at a "**three point turn**". The instructor chose a wide road for me where there was no other traffic. When I'd finished the turn, he said, "Quite good." I did a hill start however, which was quite bad; but I improved my slowing down to a "smooth" stop manipulation.

17th February 1965 Wednesday
Had a very pleasant morning at work on the machine. Had a very unpleasant afternoon at work on the filing. Mr Bill Bagnall called in during the evening to enquire about a "refund" for vehicle licence which he applied for last month & has not yet heard anything from our office.

18th February 1965 Thursday
I received by post the result of my 2nd shorthand lesson. I

have been given 89%. The tutor's comment was - "Well done". My chief fault is "not phrasing". E.g. But we have no way. The tutor underlined it with red ink. My tutor is Miss P. Broatch, F.S.C.T.

19th February 1965 Friday

Had a lovely day at work – on the counter machine all day long. Tonight we went to the Labour Club for our usual Friday night rehearsal, to find the hall was being used for a dance. We eventually were accommodated in the Belvoir Road School rooms. I'd never been there before.

20th February 1965 Saturday

A bitterly cold day. This morning it snowed quite heavily. Mum went to London with the Ravenstone Women's Institute outing. They went to Drury Lane to see the matinee performance of "Camelot", a dazzling musical, directed by Robert Helpmann. British Railways organised the outing.

21st February 1965 Sunday

Yesterday, America's rocket **Ranger Eight** reached The Moon & took 7,000 photographs which were flashed back to Earth. It is hoped to land a man on the moon by the year 1970. The Rector, in his sermon tonight, spoke about "**Holy Communion**" & said we should attend more regularly.

22nd February 1965 Monday

Enid & I have now written to the Hydro Hotel, **Paignton**, as a possibility for our summer holiday which we would like to have in June, this year.
It has been suggested today, that there might be a nation wide collection for a magnificent statue of Sir Winston Churchill, to stand above the white cliffs of **Dover**.

23rd February 1965 Tuesday

My eighth driving lesson. Today I practised clutch control. I did some things quite well & others not very well at all. I stalled the engine several times.
Les Rayner, Ralph, Geoff, Reevsie & I joined forces to send off 60 attempts at "Find the Ball" competition in the Mercury. First prize is £500.

24th February 1965 Wednesday

Ann Causer came for tea & spent the evening with us.
Langham Kendrick called in about 9-30 p.m. to ask me to get his car licence for him.
I asked Mr Johnson today if he would try to get me to work a bit earlier in the mornings. I am supposed to be there for 8-30 a.m., but am not always.

25th February 1965 Thursday

I spent several hours at work today on the counter, taking in vehicle licence applications.
I received, by post, the result of my third shorthand lesson. I have been given 86%. The tutor's comment was, "Very good progress".
I heard from the Hydro Hotel, Paignton – Fully booked for June.

26th February 1965 Friday

"Coco", the world famous clown, has been in Coalville all this week. Coalville's new shopping precinct is entertaining several celebrities just lately, in an attempt to boost trade & draw the shoppers.
Next Tuesday – **Pancake Day** – there will be a pancake race in **The Precinct** at 4 p.m.
Television & big prizes.

27th February 1965 Saturday

Mary Blue bought her wedding dress today. She is to be married on April 24th at 11-30 a.m. She celebrates her 21st birthday on March 19th.
Once again, the "Friendly" Midland Red are on strike; so I fetched Mum home from work this morning on the scooter, & took her again this evening.

28th February 1965 Sunday

I fetched Mum home from work this morning on the scooter. When I arrived at the Rector's Room this **morning** for Sunday School, I found the door locked, & a new message to say the key was with D. Collier. There were about 70 people at church tonight for the funeral service of Len Nicholls. (more than average)

1st March 1965 Monday

A heavy fall of snow this morning. Mr Johnson's car conked out underneath the M I bridge at Markfield. A passing motorist in car No. RRY 595, whom I later identified as Roger Colver from Whitwick, took me to Leicester in his car.
A very busy counter all day at work. I was on the counter machine all afternoon.

2nd March 1965 Shrove Tuesday

My ninth driving lesson – not very good at all. I drove into the kerb during a three-point turn; I drove up the kerb during a reverse round a corner; I stalled at the traffic lights & a driver behind started honking his horn. I pressed the foot brake down & it jammed; & once, I even lost the gear lever.

3rd March 1965 Ash Wednesday

Freezing cold weather. I put our thermometer outside & it registered 22^0 Fahrenheit.
Costumes arrived for "**Annie Get Your Gun**". I have a cow-girl outfit, complete with white boots & hat, an evening dress (Victorian style), an outdoor outfit, ditto; a dressing gown & night cap, & a Red Indian costume.

4th March 1965 Thursday

Auntie Cis from Skegness is spending this week in Ravenstone, staying with Aunt Dos.
We are rehearsing every day this week except Tuesday, ready for our show next week.
Enid & I have written to the Belvedere Hotel, Paignton, & they say we can get in there for one week at Whitsuntide.

5th March 1965 Friday

The state funeral of Sir Winston Churchill cost £48,000. This was disclosed today in Supplementary Civil Estimates for 1964 – 65.
We had some photos taken in costume during rehearsal tonight. The Leicester Mercury photographer was certainly a great improvement on last year. (6-3-64)

6th March 1965 Saturday
Once again, the "Friendly" Midland Red buses are on strike, so I took Mum to work on the scooter. A beautiful sunny day. Mum took my photo in the garden, as I wore the various costumes I have for "Annie Get Your Gun". I felt just like Hiawatha in my Red Indian outfit, as I stood with hands lifted toward the sun.

7th March 1965 Sunday
Full dress rehearsal for "Annie Get Your Gun".
I walked to church tonight with Mr Len Andrews, who recited to me "William Tell".
I have now completed my recording of the Gospel according to St. Matthew.
This morning I scootered to Ashby in dense fog to fetch Mum home from night duty. The fog cleared very quickly.

8th March 1965 Monday
Opening night of "Annie Get Your Gun". I have been to work today, but have the rest of the week holiday.
I bought a wedding present for Mary Blue - a shining silver stainless steel cake dish - £2 - 4/- A golden eagle has escaped from London Zoo & is having a wonderful time over London.

9th March 1965 Tuesday
A beautiful sunny day. I went for an afternoon walk to the Altons & back, and collected some pussy willow. I watched the sheep with their adorable little lambs, gambolling & bleating.
I then visited Uncle Fred & stayed an hour with him. He was in a gay mood & told me he once lived at "Lansdowne Villa".

10th March 1965 Wednesday
My tenth driving lesson. I did much better today than I did last week. My instructor also gave me words of encouragement, saying I was getting on very well.
I scootered to Snarestone this afternoon & talked to Dora who was cleaning inside the church there. I gave Maurice Gaunt some pussy willow.

11th March 1965 Thursday
Mum & I scootered to Newton Burgoland this morning to see Doreen Powers, who on Tuesday gave birth to a three months premature baby, born dead. She was up & dressed & looked quite well but naturally was very upset.
Last night, Leicester City football team was knocked out of the F. A. Cup by Liverpool.

12th March 1965 Friday
Today I kept Uncle Fred company for an hour while Auntie Belle went to Coalville shopping.
London Zoo's golden eagle was re-captured on Wednesday morning after 12 days of perfect freedom.
Colonel Robert Andrew St. George Martin is to succeed Lord Cromwell as Lord Lieutenant of Leicestershire.

13th March 1965 Saturday
I received by post the result of my fourth shorthand lesson. I was given 91% with this remark: - "**Excellent Progress.**"
This morning I went with Aunt Dos & Mary Dolman to Staunton Harold Hall where the Quorn hunt met. I have never been to a meet before. We took snap-shots & cine-films.

14th March 1965 Sunday
Mary Blue permed my hair for 30/-. She & Terry were given the key to their flat at "The Hollies" where Grandma & Grandpa Hewes brought up their eight children. We went & inspected the premises. I called in to see Don this evening, to thank them for a lovely bouquet of flowers which they sent me.

15th March 1965 Monday
Today I have been relief cashier on the vehicle licences counter in place of Len who was absent.
Tonight we had a get-together at the Amateur's to rehearse a concerted rendering of the musical numbers from "Annie Get Your Gun", which we are hoping to give to the patients at Staunton Harold on Wednesday.

16th March 1965 Tuesday
Pat & Evelyn today celebrate their Silver Wedding.
My eleventh driving lesson. My instructor told me today that he will be leaving in a month's time to take up a post as Driving Examiner in Derby.
At work today I had my first introduction to checking applications for refunds.
We had a new kitchen table delivered today.

17th March 1965 Wednesday
Went to Staunton Harold with the Amateurs' to sing the songs from our show "Annie Get Your Gun". We sang from about 7 p.m. until 8 p.m. We were then given tea & refreshments, & we talked to the patients until about 9 p.m. Most of the patients were in wheel chairs – Staunton Harold is one of the Cheshire Homes.

18th March 1965 Thursday
Mum went to Willoughby today to see Madge. I stayed at work tonight for 2 hours over-time. We were clearing the files of obsolete application forms. This is in preparation for extensive alterations in our office. The counter is to be moved to make more room for our ever increasing number of files. Tonight Mum & I watched Nureyev dance.

19th March 1965 Friday
Mary Blue is 21 today. Terry, her fiancé, bought her a gold watch. Mum & I bought her a dressing table set in pink & silver – mirror, hair brush, clothes brush & comb - £3-19s-6d. Tonight we had our Amateurs' Annual Dinner Dance – 16/-, held for the first time at The Fox & Goose, Coalville.

20th March 1965 Saturday
Harold, Janice & I represented the parish of Ravenstone in a deanery conference for laymen held at Ibstock this afternoon from 2-30 to 7 p.m.
Tonight I went to Pat's where 26 of us gathered to celebrate Pat & Evelyn's 25th Wedding Anniversary & at the same time Mary's 21st Birthday. Clocks put forward 1hour tonight.

21st March 1965 Sunday
The first day of Spring, & this morning we woke to find

there had been a considerable fall of snow during the night. This was most unexpected.

Susan Hewes, who is my god-daughter, is 9 today.

This morning Mr Billy Lambert of Ravenstone died.

Mary Blue gave my hair a brown colour rinse for £1.

22nd March 1965 Monday

I spent part of this morning working on the Driving Licence counter because Reevsie went to the dentist's. Miss Rippon is in hospital for an operation & Muriel has a few days holiday, so Ann and I are endeavouring to cope with their work. We are not however quite so expert at their job as they are.

23rd March 1965 Tuesday

Today I had 2 driving lessons, my 12th and my 13th – one at 1 p.m. & the other at 6 p.m.

At 6 p.m. the rain was coming down in torrents, but it stopped before 7 p.m. I enjoyed driving through the heart of Leicester, where the evening lights were already lit. This was my first experience of night driving.

24th March 1965 Wednesday

Evelyn has asked me to do the flower arrangements in church for Mary's wedding, in a month's time. Today I bought some green plastic-covered wire mesh from the florist's, & experimented at home with an arrangement of artificial flowers.

"The Lincoln" horse race was run today, but we had no office sweep.

25th March 1965 Thursday

The post office is expecting to get £37 million per year from its new postal charges which are due to come into force on May 17th. Ordinary letters which now go for 3d will be 4d, and post cards which now go for 2 ½d, will be 3d.

Statistics show that the average family income is now £22 a week.

26th March 1965 Friday

Miss Gazzard was not at work today, so I was relief cashier on the vehicle licence counter. Len was chief cashier & I took over while he went to dinner, & during his tea breaks. During that short time I took in over £200 cash & over £400 in cheques, & I quite enjoyed it.

27th March 1965 Saturday

A beautiful sunny day. I scootered to Staunton Harold, where I stayed for a couple of hours with Peter Mould. Peter will be 21 on June 30th this year. He is hoping to have a party in Packington village hall, to which I am invited. Peter's mother is a Sister at Ashby hospital – she works with Mum.

28th March 1965 Sunday

After last Sunday's unexpected fall of snow; today, for Mothering Sunday, we had an unexpected heat wave – the hottest March day for 25 years. It really has been a **Zippity Doo Dah Day**. "Zippity doo dah, zippity ay, my oh my what a wonderful day." Every-one you met responded & the blackbirds sang.

29th March 1965 Monday

Today has been the hottest day for March ever recorded.

All over this country & on the continent people have been enjoying the sunshine. In Leicester, the temperature at 1 p.m. was 72° in the shade.

Britain today mourns the Princess Royal, who died suddenly yesterday, aged 67. She was our Queen's aunt.

30th March 1965 Tuesday

My 14th driving lesson. My hill starts were good. Reversing round a corner was a bit wide, but passable. My 3-point turn became a 5-point turn. I negotiated a very tricky turn under West Bridge, but stalled in the Newarkes. My instructor, ever patient & encouraging, said I was improving.

31st March 1965 Wednesday

Reevsie & I today tried out the newly opened cafeteria at Woolworth's in Leicester. We were quite favourably impressed. It was certainly an improvement on the cafeteria which we used to visit there several years ago.

Six men at Snibston Colliery produced 3,008 tons of coal in a week, i.e. 100 tons per man per shift – a record.

1st April 1965 Thursday

I received by post the result of my fifth short-hand lesson. I was given 91% with this remark: - "Well displayed outlines."

Tonight I went to The Hollies where Mary Blue already has her bedroom papered & decorated, carpeted & furnished very tastefully.

2nd April 1965 Friday

My 15th driving lesson, which I had from 6 p.m. until 7 p.m. For the first time I drove from the Lansdowne Garage, down London Road & Granby Street, to the clock tower & then up High Street, on to Wigston & back. I felt like a real motorist when I raised my hand to another driver.

3rd April 1965 Saturday

This afternoon I had my first grass cutting session at "St. Mary's", Snibston. Tonight Mum & I scootered to Thringstone to see "**Carissima**", a lively & entertaining musical comedy. It was the Boat Race today – Oxford won.

We have had 8 days of glorious weather, but rain is now forecast.

4th April 1965 Sunday

Harold asked me today whether the Sunday School children could be taught something for the Garden Fête in June – singing or dancing. I thought it would be rather nice if they could do some movements to music, like a keep-fit team. I asked Enid if she could help & she agreed.

5th April 1965 Monday

Mum & I are reading a newly published book – "**The Yellow Earl**", the life of Hugh Lowther, 5th Earl of Lonsdale 1857-1944. Mum once went to a dinner which he attended. We are particularly interested in him because- "**Leicestershire was his real love**". Life for him was "**Lovely fun.**"

6th April 1965 Tuesday

My 16th driving lesson. The instructor said he would try

not to help me & see how well I fared, for consideration of putting in for a driving test. Within 5 minutes I had "failed" & got into some right predicaments. Fortunately he came to my rescue, but I came home feeling very dejected.

7th April 1965 Wednesday
Yesterday was Budget Day. Our office has been inundated today with phone enquiries regarding rise in price of vehicle licences. Private car licences have gone up to £17-10/- per year from £15. Goods vehicle licences have gone up 50%. Farm tractors up to £3-15/- from £2-10/-. Bikes up to £8.

8th April 1965 Thursday
Today at work we felt the full impact of this week's Budget. Yesterday we accepted by post, applications for vehicle licences with the old rates of duty. Today we did not. Consequently nearly every application received was returned out of order. Ann & I were doing that all day.

9th April 1965 Friday
My 17th driving lesson, which I had from 6 p.m. until 7 p.m. The instructor said I might put in for a test for about July, by which time he thought I should be up to test standard. My biggest fault now is "not looking right, left & right **before** emerging at cross roads".

10th April 1965 Saturday
Today I had my eyes tested & ordered a pair of specs which cost me £1-17s-2d, to enable me to read better at a distance. I took my scooter to Auto Supplies to have the wheels changed over, to be de-carbonized & general overhaul.
Enid & I worked out some movements to music for the Garden Fête.

11th April 1965 Palm Sunday
Diane Woodward came in the morning & helped sort out some more dance & P. T. movements to music, ready for the Garden Fête which will be on June 12th – the day Enid & I hope to be returning from holiday.
Enid & Auntie Gladys are going to Wales on Friday to spend Easter with Margaret.

12th April 1965 Monday
I received by post the result of my 6th shorthand lesson. I was given 83%, with the remark: - "Well done". I had done 5 pages. One only was absolutely free of errors; so that had a special message: - "A delightful page". One of my chief faults is "not phrasing".

13th April 1965 Tuesday
My 18th driving lesson. The instructor gave me an application form for driving test. He said that no-one had yet been appointed to take his place, so I am now instructor-less.
Today at work the partition dividing the public part of the office from the rest was removed completely.

14th April 1965 Wednesday
How about a few statistics?
The year ending March 31st 1965 our office issued the following: - 188,471 vehicle licences = £1,743,682.
  83,722 driving licences = £52,186.

Dogs, game, gun, hawker, refreshment house, pawn broker and money lender licences totalled £15,736. Arrears = £1,000.

15th April 1965 Thursday
We worked today to the accompaniment of hammering and sawing, as a solid counter at the back of our office was removed, & also a new door was fitted to replace double doors.
We are expecting, when we return to work next Wednesday, to see a complete transformation with the driving licence counter moved forward.

16th April 1965 Good Friday
Went to 11 a.m. church service & sat with Don, Phyl & Susan. I then called at their house for morning coffee. Went with Aunt Dos this evening to an outdoor service, held in Coalville's shopping precinct.
I sent off my application for a driving test. Although I am still instructor-less, I am hoping to be ready by July.

17th April 1965 Saturday
This morning I collected from Coalville my new pair of specs, & my scooter which had been repaired at a cost of £9. That was rather more than I had expected!
6 children & I did some movements to music, but decided not to pursue the idea as I shall be on holiday for the Garden Fête. Terrible squally weather.

18th April Easter Sunday
For no reason at all, I have written up my diary for today in the wrong place – please see over. This then, in retrospect, is what happened tomorrow – It hailed & snowed. There was sleet & gale force winds. In between times there were short spells of sunshine, but the wind howled all day long. A really depressing holiday.

19th April 1965 Easter Monday
Three little children & I battled to Sunday School this morning in a terrible hail storm.
I went to 7 a.m. Holy Communion & sat with Don.
Pat & I called in to see our church organist Mr Biggs, who was at home suffering from the after effects of falling off his bike; he had fallen on his face.

20th April 1965 Easter Tuesday
I wrote to the Lansdowne School of Motoring: - "Kindly advise me whether my driving lessons in your Hillman Imp may be continued."
Wedding presents for Mary Blue keep arriving at Pat's house. I took the cake dish from Mum & me. There are more pillow cases than anything else – about 10 pairs.

21st April 1965 Wednesday
Back to work after the Easter holiday to find great changes in the set out of our office. The work was not quite complete so we had plenty of bashing, banging and hammering all day long. Len was away, so I was relief cashier to Miss Gazzard.
Mr Blackburn came into the office today.

22nd April 1965 Thursday
I had a letter from the Lansdowne Garage: - "Dear Miss Hewes, Thank you for your letter dated the 20th April, & we have pleasure in advising you that driving lessons

can still be given on the Hillman Imp.....The writer is your new Driving Instructor. Yours Sincerely, A Mullins.

23rd April 1965 Friday

Mum & I spent the whole evening in Ravenstone Church, doing flower arrangements ready for Mary's wedding tomorrow. Bunting & family came from Malvern. Bunting, Mostyn & Julian slept at Auntie Belle's & Michael slept at our house. Auntie Cis arrived from Skegness & stayed with Aunt Dos.

24th April 1965 Saturday

Mary Blue's Wedding Day! Mum & I were very pleased with our flower arrangements in church. The Rector said he had never seen any better at any other wedding in our church. After the reception Roy & Doreen Powers stayed with us until 9 p.m.
Michael slept at our house.

25th April 1965 Sunday

We had our first practice for the Sunday School Anniversary. Mr Biggs, who should have taken it, is still not well enough after falling off his bike, so Harold & I did our best – Harold played the organ & I led the singing.
Bunting & family returned home. Aunt Cis returns home tomorrow.

26th April 1965 Monday

I received by post the result of my 7th shorthand lesson. I was given 88%, with the remark: - "Showing a thorough mastery of the principles".
Mary Blue's wedding was reported in the Leicester Mercury, under the heading: - "**Bridal Party went on to Hospital**" – to **Hillcrest**, to visit Mrs Lowe.

27th April 1965 Tuesday

I had my first driving lesson with Mr Mullins. I enjoyed it very much. He tried to teach me how to change from 2nd gear, quickly to first gear & be ready for off, at cross roads.
Mary Blue & Terry arrived home after their 3-day honeymoon in London. Aunt Dos & I carried to The Hollies some of their presents.

28th April 1965 Wednesday

As relief cashier to Miss Gazzard today, I took over £1,000 in cash & cheques.
Tonight Mum & I spent an hour or two in Ravenstone Church, resuscitating & re-arranging our floral decorations. Two great vases of lilies, left over from Easter, had just reached their lives' end.

29th April 1965 Thursday

As relief cashier to Miss Gazzard today, I took over £1,500 in cash & cheques.
Sir Malcolm Sargent is 70 years old today. He has definite connections with Leicestershire, as had Lonsdale, The Yellow Earl, whom he remembers well. He helped to form Melton Operatic Society & Leicester Symphony Orchestra.

30th April 1965 Friday

My super-annuation this month topped the £350 mark.

This evening Auntie Gladys & I went to a Whist Drive in the Rector's Room, Ravenstone, organised by the Men's Fellowship. We had a very pleasant time. I scored only 156 in 24 games, but that did include one at eleven & one at twelve.

1st May 1965 Saturday

The F. A. Cup Final at Wembley. Liverpool, who knocked out Leicester City on March 11th, were playing against Leeds United. I spent all afternoon watching the game on television. At the end of the game there was no score, but they played ½ hour extra time & Liverpool then won 2-1.

2nd May 1965 Sunday

This evening we saw history in the making as Europe & America were joined for the first time in a 2-way live television programme. This was made possible by the communications satellite known as "**Early Bird**" which was launched from Cape Kennedy on April 6th, & now hangs in space 22,300 miles above the Atlantic.

3rd May 1965 Monday

A very busy day at work. We had a real bumper bundle post & left much of it for tomorrow. We are also inundated with applications for refunds at the moment, so I spent all afternoon on them. This evening, I spent about 3 hours recording part of the Gospel according to St. John – Chapters 5, 6, 7 & 8.

4th May 1965 Tuesday

My second driving lesson with Mr Mullins. Again he concentrated on cross road procedure. He also gave me a most difficult three point turn, on a road which sloped considerably, one side to the other. Needless to say, I got in a bit of a mess trying to do this, & decided I would certainly have failed on a test.

5th May 1965 Wednesday

I went for a scooter ride after tea, up to the Birch Tree, Coalville & then on to Ravenstone Church, where I sorted out the last remains of our floral decorations. Only 4 carnations were still sufficiently respectable to be left on show, & I put them in with 2 dozen narcissi which I bought in Leicester.

6th May 1965 Thursday

Members of Parliament crowded into the Commons today to vote either for or against Steel Nationalisation. The Labour Government won in a "photo-finish", 310 for – 306 against.
M. P.s came home for this, from as far away as Australia, Fiji, France & America, & one came even by ambulance.

7th May 1965 Friday

Today I was relief cashier to Miss Gazzard with a hectic counter all day long. Fortunately I had no bulk applications from any garage, but even with single applications, mostly £17-10/- & £6-8/- I took altogether more than £1,500.
Don called to invite Enid & me to go & see the "Yeomen of The Guard" tomorrow.

8th May 1965 Saturday
I received by post an appointment for my Driving Test, for July 16th at 9-45 a.m. in Leicester.
Enid & I went with Don, Phyl, Susan, Peter & Peter's girl friend Christine, to the Town Hall, Ashby to see "The Yeomen of the Guard" which we enjoyed thoroughly.
Twenty years ago today was V. E. Day, the end of the war.

9th May 1965 Sunday
Mr Biggs was with us this morning for Sunday School Anniversary practice. After Sunday School, I went for a scooter ride up to the Altons & on to Hoo Ash, then home. I spent the afternoon doing shorthand. I am now up to my tenth shorthand lesson, which is halfway through the course.

10th May 1965 Monday
I received by post the result of my 8th shorthand lesson. I was given 88%, with the remark: - "Beautiful work. Transcription Excellent".
Mum & I had a letter from Michael, thanking us for sleeping him during the weekend of Mary's wedding. He said: - "I am longing to pass my driving test & come & see you all".

11th May 1965 Tuesday
My third driving lesson with Mr Mullins. He took me to the King Richard Road area, as my driving test is arranged for there. We had an interesting interlude when a huge bumble-bee flew into the car & settled on the windscreen. We stopped. The instructor got out & ushered out the intruder.

12th May 1965 Wednesday
A lovely sunny day. The temperature in Leicester at noon was 70^0f i.e. $21 \cdot 1$c
"The Kennedy Memorial Appeal" launched a year ago will reach fruition this week. On Friday the Queen will unveil the national memorial at Runnymede. Mrs Jacqueline Kennedy will be at the ceremony.

13th May 1965 Thursday
A very hot day. By 2 p.m. the temperature in Leicester was 76 degrees F = $24 \cdot 44^o$c.
Reevsie & I went to see Miss Rippon, at home after her recent operation. We went from 8 p.m. – 9 p.m. I scootered to Reevsie's in the morning & left my scooter there all day. I had tea with Reevsie & Tony.

14th May 1965 Friday
A perfect Summer's day. At Runnymede, where 750 years ago, Magna Carta was signed, the Kennedy Memorial was inaugurated by the Queen. Paying homage to President Kennedy, were his children John, aged 4, Caroline, aged 7, his wife Jacqueline, his brother Robert & his brother Edward, now walking again.

15th May 1965 Saturday
I received a letter from the Provost of Leicester: - . . . .
"As a subscription to the original Cathedral Appeal, may we look forward to your joining the **Friends of Leicester Cathedral**? . . . .We hope to arrange visits to the Cathedral to hear some aspect of its architecture &

history" etc. etc. Whereupon I joined.

16th May 1965 Sunday
Today, after 8 years, is the last day a letter may go for 3d. Tomorrow it will be 4d. For my last 3pennyworth I became a "Friend of Leicester Cathedral".
Pat, Evelyn & Aunt Dos spent the day visiting Bunting & family in Malvern. At 1 a.m. this morning I found I had locked myself out. Aunt Dos let me in.

17th May 1965 Monday
We have been asked to work over-time this week & I "volunteered" to work Monday, Tuesday & Wednesday. Tonight I stayed for 3 hours, acknowledging the receipt of documents from other authorities. A pleasant enough job – the time went quite quickly. All day long I was checking in-coming applications.

18th May 1965 Tuesday
My fourth driving lesson with Mr Mullins. My driving is still not up to test standard. Today I would have "failed" for about 6 different things. I managed, however, to drive along High Street, round the clock tower, up Granby Street & along Belvoir Street during the busy lunch hour, without "failing" on anything.

19th May 1965 Wednesday
Yesterday the Queen began her 11day state visit to Germany. She arrived at Cologne. Today in Bonn she was greeted enthusiastically by the crowds. Students tore branches off lilac trees & waved them at the Queen. She will be going to Munich on Friday & touring on to Berlin by 27th May, on to Hanover & Hamburg.

20th May 1965 Thursday
The Government is considering raising the cost of vehicle licences, but probably not until next year. It is expected that the bigger motor cars will have to pay more than the smaller ones; as indeed they did, when I first started work. After last month's budget, many people now are not sure what to pay.

21st May 1965 Friday
Today for the first time ever, I saw car number U.R.A. 1. It was on a beautiful Bentley which passed us at dangerous speed as we approached the "Flying Horse" round-about on our way home from Leicester, at about 6-30 p.m. I had seen this number plenty of times on humorous drawings.

22nd May 1965 Saturday
This morning, I wheeled my wheel-barrow, thro' streets broad & narrow to St. Mary's Church-yard, where with lawn mower & clippers, I keep an area round my dad's grave looking like an oasis in a wilderness of overgrown grass. Imagine my surprise when I found the whole of the wilderness beautifully cut, & a new path.

23rd May 1965 Sunday
I fetched Mum home from night duty. As it was such a delightful morning, we went for a scooter ride up to the Birch Tree, on to Hoo Ash & home. After Sunday School I went for a ride to Packington, Normanton & Heather. Allan Pettitt called in for a couple of hours this morning.

24th May 1965 Monday
Today's news is that Britain is to go **Metric**! To start with this will be only in weights & measures – not in money. It is estimated that it will take about 10 years to complete the change-over; & is primarily to facilitate export trade.
Leicester's new Lord Mayor is Alderman Sidney Bridges.

25th May 1965 Tuesday
My fifth driving lesson with Mr Mullins. I drove with him to his home in Leicester because he wanted to call in there. I was therefore left for a few minutes sitting in the driving seat entirely alone. I imagined myself as a qualified driver & had a secret longing to drive away, but I didn't move one inch.

26th May 1965 Wednesday
Mrs Jacqueline Kennedy & her children flew home from England today, having spent a fortnight here. The Queen, in Germany on an 11day tour, is dining this evening with the British Army of the Rhine. Last night Cassius Clay, alias Muhammad Ali of the Muslim faith, retained the Heavyweight Championship of the World.

27th May 1965 Thursday Ascension Day
I went to Holy Communion at 8 p.m. Don drove me down in his new Zodiac, & I sat with Pat & Evelyn.
I received by post the result of my 9th shorthand lesson. I was given 93%, with the remark: - "Beautiful work & **Excellent** progress". I also had a message written in shorthand.

28th May 1965 Friday
This evening we watched on television the Queen set sail from Hamburg in the Royal Yacht Britannia, after her state visit to Germany. Britannia sailed slowly & silently down the festive torch lit Elbe, escorted by German & British ships, all bedecked with flags. The Queen stood on the floodlit upper deck.

29th May 1965 Saturday
Lesley Hewes will be 21 on June 8th, during the week when Enid & I will be on holiday. Today I bought her the most beautiful birthday card, showing sunset over the sea, & the silhouettes of different boats anchored on quietly rippling waters. For her present I have a stainless steel holder for 3 candles.

30th May 1965 Sunday
This morning I fetched Mum home from night duty. We scootered to St. Mary's Church to admire its recent transformation from a wilderness of a church-yard into something highly respectable. The birds which fly non-stop in and out of Ravenstone church have made a terrible mess on the pews & on one wall.

31st May 1965 Monday
We had our Amateur's Annual General Meeting. The Treasurer's report on our last production of "Annie Get Your Gun" showed that we had made a total loss of £26. Our next production is to be "Carousel" which will be given from March 7th - March 12th next year.

1st June 1965 Tuesday
My sixth driving lesson with Mr Mullins. I did not drive as well as I might. After 24 lessons altogether, I am still not up to test standard.
Our office has set on a new man today named **Ben**. He is a black man!
Yesterday 8,717 women, one from each W. I. branch in the country, went to Buckingham Palace Garden Party.

2nd June 1965 Wednesday
Derby Day & the winning horse was **Sea Bird II**. 22 horses altogether. 34 in our office went in the office sweep & flip me if I didn't draw a blank again – same as last year.
The new county offices being built at Glenfield have been causing road hold ups because the road has been up for pipes.

3rd June 1965 Thursday
Today I had a very interesting phone call at work from Belvoir Estate, owned by the Duke of Rutland. For about ¼ hr, I was dealing with queries concerning vehicles to be taxed as "Goods Farmers" for the kitchen garden produce & for the Head Game Keeper: & "His Lordship" Roger's lost R. B.

4th June 1965 Friday
I spent the evening at The Hollies having my hair permed by Mary Blue. She & Terry have just acquired a kitten (a Siamese-Persian cross) & also a puppy (a corgi & something else cross). The antics of these two kept us well entertained for the whole of the evening.

5th June 1965 Saturday
Enid & I came in Enid's car to the **Belvedere Hotel, Paignton**, for a week's holiday. The weather was just right for our 226 mile journey through some delightful scenery. We set out at 9 a.m. & arrived at 6 p.m. In the evening we went for a boat trip round **Torbay**.

6th June 1965 Whit Sunday
Enid & I went to Holy Communion at 10 a.m. to St. Paul's church, **Paignton**. This afternoon we walked to **Goodrington** & lay on the cliff tops for about an hour in the sun, this evening we went by car to **Teignmouth**, where we joined in the hymn singing on the sea-shore.

7th June 1965 Whit Monday
Enid & I spent the morning in **Brixham**. This afternoon we took a ride on an open top bus, through **Torquay** to **Babbacombe**. There we walked round the model village & also sun-bathed on the grass high up above the sea. Tonight we went to **Brixham** again & walked out to the light-house.

8th June 1965 Whit Tuesday
This morning we walked along the water's edge to Paignton Harbour. This afternoon we motored in the rain to **Kingswear** & across the ferry to **Dartmouth** – to **Kingsbridge** – home via **Totnes**. This evening we went from **Brixham** to **Babbacombe** by boat – ¾ hour at **Babbacombe** & return by boat **singing all the way**.

9th June 1965 Wednesday
This afternoon Enid & I went in a horse drawn

brougham to **Cockington** where we walked through the most delightful grounds, with the sun shining most of the time. This evening we went on an open top bus to **Torquay** where we walked all round the harbour & along the seashore.

10th June 1965 Thursday
Went on a morning boat trip round **Torbay** on "The Pride of Paignton". Spent the whole afternoon on "The Pride of Paignton" on a 10/- boat trip from Paignton past Brixham to Dartmouth & up the river to **Dittisham** & back. In the evening we motored to **Dawlish** & strolled all around there.

11th June 1965 Friday
This morning I went by boat to **Brixham**. Because the tide was out we had to be rowed out to the boat in a smaller boat.
This afternoon Enid & I went to **Babbacombe** by boat. "Sam" the boatman allowed us to sit on top of the cabin & so we had the most wonderful ride we had ever had.

12th June 1965 Saturday
Enid & I returned home from our **Paignton** holiday. We left **Paignton** at 10-30 a.m. & arrived home at 10-30 p.m. We got held up in a monstrous queue of traffic between **Paignton** & **Exeter** & it was 5 p.m. before we crossed the **Devon - Somerset** border.
The Beatles today got the M. B. E.

13th June 1965 Trinity Sunday
Mum & Auntie Doris from Mountsorrel spent last week with Mary Moore in **Nayland**. Auntie Doris returned with Mum to spend this week-end with us. Tonight she went with me to church. Afterwards I went with Enid, Auntie Gladys and Auntie Marjorie (from Mablethorpe) To Beacon Hill & Bradgate.

14th June 1965 Monday
This morning at work I opened an application for vehicle licence which contained a Ministry of Transport Test Cert. No. M 403396. This was a stolen certificate which we had been on the look out for, for over a month.
This evening Auntie Gladys, Marjorie, Enid & I played croquet.

15th June 1965 Tuesday
Driving lesson No 25. I have arranged to have 2 driving lessons a week now until my test which is July 16th. That should make 34 in all. I shall then be 34 years old & it is estimated that a learner driver requires one lesson for every year of his life, before he is ready for the test.

16th June 1965 Wednesday
I received by post the result of my 10th shorthand lesson. I was given 80%, with the remark: - "Good work – Excellent transcription".
Mr Sharp today, in his report to Mr Blackburn, the County Treasurer & Local Taxation Officer, mentioned the "**needle in a haystack**" stolen Test Certificate which was found.

17th June 1965 Thursday
Mr Johnson is not at work this week, so Christine is driving the car, with Richard & me as passengers.

Had a post-card today from Reevsie who is on holiday, staying at **Looe**.
I have received my first "**Cathedral News Letter**" since becoming a "Friend of Leicester Cathedral".

18th June 1965 Friday
Driving lesson No 26.
In the Leicester Mercury tonight the death is reported of Mr John Pochin aged 39, only son of Mr & Mrs H. I. Pochin, Houghton-on-the-Hill. He was killed in a road accident yesterday.
Mr H. I. Pochin was the boss in our office until 1959.

19th June 1965 Saturday
I scootered to Coalville this morning & bought Reevsie a birthday present – a 16/6 bottle of Miss Americana perfume. This afternoon I had a marathon grass cutting session at St Mary's church, where I cleared an area almost as far as Doctor Forsyth's grave.
Enid took Auntie Marjorie to Mablethorpe.

20th June 1965 Sunday
This morning I went to 8a.m. Holy Communion.
I scootered to church with Mrs Swanwick pillion.
Afterwards I scootered to Ashby to meet Mum from night duty. We went into St. Helen's Ashby & admired the gorgeous flower arrangements for their flower festival.
Tonight at church we had no parson, so we just had hymns.

21st June 1965 Monday
From today we are to use proper registered letters, issued by the Post Office, when we return applications, containing money, out of order at work. This has resulted because one of our customers had £6 - 8/- returned by us, but received only £1 - 8/-
In the past we have always used our own envelopes marked "Registered".

22nd June 1965 Tuesday
Driving Lesson No 27. Today we concentrated on hill driving. My driving is now pretty good on the level, but not so good up & down hills. I need more practice with that.
Reevsie's birthday today. She is **thirty!**
She has worked in our office ever since she left school.

23rd June 1965 Wednesday
I received by post the result of my 11th shorthand lesson. I was given 85% with the remark: - "Good work throughout."
This week at work we have 4 or 5 "Time & Study" men watching us all day long.
"The Hollies" next door is to have new tenants at the top flat & they are really setting about the garden.

24th June 1965 Thursday
Fifty years ago today, during World War I, flags were flown for the Prince of Wales 21st birthday. The Prince (now the Duke of Windsor who gave up his throne to marry Mrs Simpson) was serving as an Army officer in France.
This week in Leicester, at the Odeon Cinema, "A King's Story", being his story, is on.

25th June 1965 Friday

Driving Lesson No 28.

Tonight when I got home from work I realised I had left my best black umbrella in an archway in Castle Street, Leicester.

At 7 p.m. I scootered to Leicester in quest of same.

The umbrella was no longer there, but I thoroughly enjoyed my 25 mile ride.

26th June 1965 Saturday

Mum & I went to Leicester on the 11 a.m. bus & back on the 3-20 p.m.

We visited St. Margaret's Church, where there was a Flower Festival.

We had lunch at Lewis's, where Mum bought a new coat.

Then we went to the Odeon Cinema to see "**A King's Story**" which moved me to tears.

27th June 1965 Sunday

This morning I scootered to Peter Mould's house, 2, Abbey Drive, Ashby-de-la-Zouch to take him a 21st birthday card & £2 from Mum & me. His birthday is next Tuesday.

Ravenstone Sunday School Anniversary today. The weather was fine.

The lessons were read by Diane Woodward, Pamela Kendrick & C. Lambert.

28th June 1965 Monday

For the first time in my life I received a salary cheque for more than £50.

This was because I had worked overtime to the value of £6-16/-. Before there were any

deductions it was £65-2s-8d. (Less tax £8-17/-) (Less Superannuation £3-4s-7d) (Less National Health Insurance payment £2-11s-8d)

29th June 1965 Tuesday

Driving Lesson No 29. My driving instructor will be on holiday next week, taking the car with him, so there will be no lessons for any of his pupils.

Ravenstone "Darby & Joan" today had their annual day's outing. They went to Mablethorpe.

Our house is now "**breathing with perfume**" – the perfume of June roses.

30th June 1965 Wednesday

I bought a new umbrella (£3) to replace the one I lost last week.

Tonight Mum & I scootered to Packington Village Hall where Peter Mould was having his 21st birthday party. We arrived home about 1 a.m. We drank to Peter, in champagne! & had a very enjoyable evening.

1st July 1965 Thursday

A perfectly beautiful summer's day. I walked up the garden to admire the sun-set & as I gazed at the sky I saw the sheerest outline of a new moon.

Our village Drama Group is due to have its first meeting on Saturday after a 6 month break. We are considering an attempt at "**Alice in Wonderland.**"

2nd July 1965 Friday

Driving Lesson No 30.

Because of exceptionally heavy traffic in Leicester at dinner time, my instructor was ¼ hr late meeting me. I therefore had a ¾ hr lesson. We practised driving round islands; & also I had my first introduction to driving in a traffic jam!

3rd July 1965 Saturday

We had our first read through of "Alice in Wonderland". Lena Bennett said she would like to play the Mad Hatter – Susan Jarvis the Duchess & Diane Stacey the Dormouse. There is provision for about fifty in the cast, but we shall have to manage with about fifteen. The play lasts 1 ¼ hours.

4th July 1965 Sunday

This morning I scootered to Ashby to bring Mum home from night duty.

Later I scootered again to Ashby to visit Peter Mould. I saw his new radiogram & his 21st birthday cards which totalled about 75 in number. He told me he had been given more than £100 in money altogether.

5th July 1965 Monday

The Leicester Mercury tonight reports that "After only three months on the site, contractors for the new £1 ½ million County Council Offices at Anstey Frith are already ahead of schedule. An official of the firm, William Moss & Sons Ltd. of Loughborough said: - "We have 2 winters to get through before completion date."

6th July 1965 Tuesday

Tonight I completed my recording of the Gospel according to St. John.

Today at work I sorted out the dog licence carbon copies which we receive weekly from Post Offices throughout the county. This was the first time I'd ever had anything to do with the dog licence section. I had "**one**" from Ravenstone.

7th July 1965 Wednesday

My sister Bunting (i.e. my half sister) is 50 years old today. She was born on the seventh day of the seventh month & I was born on the fourteenth day of the seventh month.

When I was seven years old, my dad died aged 7 x 7 = 49. Bunting was only a very little girl when her mother died.

8th July 1965 Thursday

On August 12th last year, Charles Wilson was snatched from jail, & has never been seen since. He was one of the Great Train Robbery gang.

Today, Ronald Biggs was snatched from Wandsworth jail. He was another one of the gang.

In broad day-light, outside help got him over the wall.

9th July 1965 Friday

A bison's bone, thought to be more than 50,000 years old has been found by workmen on the banks of the stream in Bradgate Park.

Bison lived in the Leicester region during the Ice Age, from about one million years ago, & died out at the end of the Palaeolithic Age - 10,000 years ago.

10th July 1965 Saturday
We had our 2nd read through of "Alice in Wonderland." Ruth Jones wanted to be the Mock Turtle & also the Queen. Susan Jarvis wanted to be the Duchess & the Knave. Jacqueline Hull Perry chose to be the March Hare & the Mouse; & Diane Woodward makes a perfect "Alice."

11th July 1965 Sunday
This afternoon Mum & I scootered to Market Bosworth to the Horsemen's Service, at which the Lord Bishop of Leicester gave the address. The Bishop spoke of Richard III who said: - "**A horse, a horse, my kingdom for a horse**", before he died, practically on that very spot at Bosworth.

12th July 1965 Monday
I received by post the result of my 12th shorthand lesson. I was given 83% with the remark: - "Achieving a masterly & flowing style of shorthand."
I still don't "phrase" properly. E.g. "which some people" should be not
Lesson 12 was particularly long & took some wading through.

13th July 1965 Tuesday
Driving Lesson No 31. Today we concentrated on driving up & down "them thar hills." Under driving test conditions the car must not be allowed to move back even one inch when you stop on a hill. Today, mine did; but otherwise my driving was not too bad; test on Friday.

14th July 1965 Wednesday
My Birthday! Today I am 34 years old. Mum & I had raspberries for tea. This is a "regular" tea time speciality for my birthday. A beautiful bouquet of flowers was delivered to me at work. They were from Reevsie.
Exactly one hundred years ago today, the Matterhorn was first climbed.

15th July 1965 Thursday
Dentist Day today! Fortunately after the inspection, there was nothing to be done. With £1 to spare, I therefore bought myself a new pair of tartan slacks – 35/- . I have arranged to have a day's holiday tomorrow because of my driving test. If I pass I shall be too elated to work. If I fail, I shall be too dejected.

16th July 1965 Friday

I Passed My Driving Test!

17th July 1965 Saturday
We had our third reading of "**Alice in Wonderland**" putting in some of the movements & action. A delightful summer's day. Auntie Gladys, Aunt Dos, Enid & I played croquet from
7 p.m. until 10 p.m. I have really been on top of the world today, thinking all day long about my driving test, & so glad that I've passed.

18th July 1965 Sunday
I scootered to Ashby this morning to meet Mum from night duty. We then went a 20 mile ride before breakfast.

We went to Coleorton, on to Staunton Harold, over the border into Derbyshire, to Melbourne, Breedon-on-the-Hill & back home through Swannington. We arrived home for breakfast at 9-30 a.m.

19th July 1965 Monday
Mr Johnson & Richard are on holiday this week, so Christine & I are travelling to & from work in Mr Johnson's car – Christine driver – me passenger. I find it rather frustrating having just passed my driving test, not having a car to drive. I have a message from the Minister of Transport: "I wish you many years of safe & happy motoring."

20th July 1965 Tuesday
We had a thunderstorm in Leicester at lunch time, so Reevsie & I dined close to the office – at Morgan & Squires. By evening however, the weather was so beautiful that I went for a 25 mile scooter ride through Swannington, Osgathorpe, Hathern, Loughborough, Shepshed, Swannington & home.

21st July 1965 Wednesday
Tonight I drove Mr Johnson's car home from Leicester, with Christine passenger. This was the first time I had ever driven without "L" plates. I stayed with Uncle Fred from 7 p.m. until 10 p.m. while Auntie Belle went to an "**at home**" at Ravenstone Hall, in aid of the Conservative funds.

22nd July 1965 Thursday
Again I drove Mr Johnson's car home from Leicester, with Christine passenger. Mum is preparing for a week's holiday next week. She & Madge (from Willoughby) are going on a Barton's bus tour, starting from Nottingham, up to the Isle of Skye & also visiting Inverness.

23rd July 1965 Friday
And yet again I drove Mr Johnson's car home from Leicester, with Christine passenger. Mum is sleeping at Willoughby tonight. She & Madge have to be at Nottingham by 8 a.m. tomorrow morning ready for the first day of their Scottish tour. By tomorrow evening they should be at Loch Lomond.

24th July 1965 Saturday
Margaret & Dai, with their 2 children David & Steven are staying with Auntie Gladys for a few days. Margaret is Auntie Gladys' eldest daughter, aged 42. She lives in Wales. With Mum away on holiday, I have had a "housewife" day – washing, ironing & getting meals.

25th July 1965 Sunday
This morning I went to 8 a.m. Holy Communion. We have no Sunday School until August 29th. Because Mum is on holiday, Pat & Evelyn asked me to have dinner with them. As my dinner was already prepared, I took it with me. I have arranged, however, to have dinner with them next Sunday – not taking my own with me.

26th July 1965 Monday
Mum should now have reached the Isle of Skye. She is spending tonight & tomorrow night at the White Heather Hotel, Kyleakin, Isle of Skye. Christine & Richard are both on holiday this week, so I am Mr Johnson's sole

passenger. I am longing for the time when I can have my own car.

27th July 1965 Tuesday
I was up until midnight making a tape recording of "**My Driving Test**" starting from my first lesson on January 5th, when I couldn't even steer; through all the various stages, until I received the coveted Test Certificate – thanks to the "Lansdowne School of Motoring!"

28th July 1965 Wednesday
Today, Mr Edward Heath became the new leader of the Conservative Party. This followed the resignation of the former leader, Sir Alec Douglas-Home. I received 2 picture postcards today from Mum, one sent on Sunday from Loch Lomond, after her 350 mile journey, & one on Monday showing Inveraray Castle.

29th July 1965 Thursday
Mr Johnson arranged to work late tonight & tomorrow night & so I decided to venture to work on my scooter. Today was the very first time that I had ever been all the way to work on my scooter. Riding my scooter through Leicester during the peak hours – 8-30 a.m. & 5-30 p.m., I used always to avoid.

30th July 1965 Friday
Again I scootered all the way to work. I actually enjoyed riding through Leicester, where there was much more traffic today than yesterday. (Thursday is half-day closing). I had another P.C. from Mum. This one showed The Ferry, Kyleakin, Isle of Skye. Mum is thoroughly enjoying her holiday – has been over a fairy bridge.

31st July 1965 Saturday
This evening Aunt Dos, Enid & I went in Aunt Dos' car to Kegworth to spend an hour or two with Mary Dolman. Aunt Dos allowed me to drive there & back, & I loved it. We came by the newly opened airport at Castle Donington & stopped to watch an aeroplane just taking off.

1st August 1965 Sunday
Mum arrived home this evening after her 1,500 mile tour of Scotland. Madge & Bertha from Willoughby brought her in their car.
This afternoon I drove Pat's car. I drove to Coalville, through Thornborough, Thringstone, to Belton & back through Osgathorpe. Before breakfast I went for a scooter ride over the forest

2nd August 1965 Monday
Mum has been recounting the many & varied experiences of her Scottish holiday. We are expecting Mary Moore to arrive here tomorrow to spend a few days with us. She is spending today with Auntie Doris at Mountsorrel. Today, the first Monday in August has always been bank holiday before; but this year it has changed.

3rd August 1965 Tuesday
Mary Moore arrived for a few days holiday. She arrived on a bus at 7-10 p.m. As she got off the bus, Mum got on it to go to work. Mum was not expecting to be at work until Friday, but one of the nurses has gone off sick.

I slept as usual at Aunt Dos', so Mary Moore slept all alone.

4th August 1965 Wednesday
I received by post the result of my 13th shorthand lesson. I was given 90% with the remark: - "Excellent progress is being maintained."
Tonight I met Mary Moore's friend Molly Donaldson who lives at Donington-le-Heath, near Coalville. She came to our house to see Mary, & stayed from 8 p.m. – 10 p.m.

5th August 1965 Thursday
Christine Johnson has been away from work sick this week. I have been travelling to & from work with Mr Johnson & Richard, aged 17. Richard drove the car home last night & tonight. He is still a learner, but is getting on very well. I just sit in the back, wishing & longing for my own car.

6th August 1965 Friday
I wrote to Mr Tom Fraser, Minister of Transport, London W. 1. I just told him how much I appreciated my "Message from the Minister of Transport" which was given to me on July 16th. It is quite possible that he will never read my letter, but you never know, he might be pleased to receive it.

7th August 1965 Saturday
Mary Moore went with me this morning to St. Mary's Churchyard where I had a quick grass-cutting session. She had dinner & tea at Donaldson's returning at 10 p.m. She & I then went round to Aunt Dos's, & stayed up till after midnight watching Aunt Dos's cine-films. We eventually got to bed at 1-30 a.m.

8th August 1965 Sunday
Aunt Dos took some cine-film of Mary Moore & me in our garden this morning.
This evening Mum was on night duty. Mary Moore & I listened to my tape recorder – to me reading the Sermon on the Mount. Half way through this, Aunt Dos came in, & she also listened to it with us.

9th August 1965 Monday
Mary Moore returned home today after staying with us for a week. She has invited Mum & me to spend Christmas with her & her husband Mick at their home in Nayland, Near Colchester, Essex. I have not yet met Mick, & they have been married now for about 7 years. Mick is Mary's husband & also her cousin.

10th August 1965 Tuesday
Ann at work announced that she is expecting a baby next February. The doctor confirmed this today & Ann was absolutely thrilled to bits. Her excitement really bubbled over, & we were all thrilled with her. She & Steve (her husband) have been married 4 years. They both work in our office - it was an office romance.

11th August 1965 Wednesday
I had a really hectic day at work today. Muriel was away on holiday. Miss Rippon is still away on the sick, after her big operation earlier this year. Ann did all the letters etc., which is Miss Rippon's job, & I was inundated with

"Remissions", "Out of Order Returns", "Refunds" & phone answering.

12th August 1965 Thursday
A beautiful summer's day. Mum & I went for a scooter ride this evening – through Heather, Swepstone, Snarestone, Twycross, out of Leicestershire into Warwickshire, to Atherstone, for a mile or two on the main A5 road, to Market Bosworth, Ibstock & home. It was a 37 mile ride & we arrived home at 9 p.m.

13th August 1965 Friday
Mr Johnson has been on holiday this week & I have been to work each day on my scooter. Today has been very warm & I was able to scooter home from work in my summer slacks & sleeveless jumper. Pat, Evelyn & Aunt Dos are off tomorrow for a week's holiday in Somerset. They will be staying in a caravan.

14th August 1965 Saturday
Enid & I stayed up until 1-30 a.m. doing shorthand. Enid can do shorthand at about 100 words a minute, & I can do about 25 words a minute, but I am improving steadily. I have chosen to sleep in the house all alone tonight. Auntie Gladys said I was welcome to stay at her house, but I am staying at home.

15th August 1965 Sunday
This morning I scootered to Ashby at 8 a.m. to meet Mum home from night duty. Last night, you remember, I braved sleeping in the house all by myself. I have always fought shy of this before, but I am pleased to say I was alright. The moon offered a friendly light, & I am alone again tonight.

16th August 1965 Monday
I received by post the result of my 14th shorthand lesson. I was given 85% with the remark: - "Praiseworthy outlines. Excellent transcription." I thought this was very generous of my tutor, considering I had made more than 20 mistakes. E.g. "Dearest" I put   instead of (dressed)

17th August 1965 Tuesday
A reader's letter in the Leicester Mercury tonight, read: - "I have driven a car, accident free, every day for the past 2 ½ years. I have done reverses, hill starts, three point turns until I'm dizzy, but in spite of all this, Leicester Test Examiners have failed me 7 times."
Signed, L (pless) Driver. Whereupon I wrote to L (pless).

18th August 1965 Wednesday
This evening Mum & I scootered to Mountsorrel to see Auntie Doris. Auntie Doris will be 70 tomorrow. The lights on my scooter were not as good as they ought to be, but we arrived home safely by 10-30 p.m. I must take my scooter to be serviced this week-end, & have the battery attended to. I have now done 3,500 miles.

19th August 1965 Thursday
Mr Frederick Vincent Brewin, aged 56, the principal of the "Safety First School of Motoring" has been fined £10 for aiding and abetting one of his pupils to drive carelessly. The pupil was also fined £10. At the junction of Park Road, Loughborough, with Ling Road, their car had its left hand indicator flashing, but went straight on.

20th August 1965 Friday
Aunt Dos, Pat & Evelyn returned home after their week's holiday in Somerset. We were not expecting them until tomorrow, but they came home a day early to avoid Saturday's heavy traffic. I have spent 3 nights this week sleeping in the house all alone, & have actually enjoyed it. A street light helps.

21st August 1965 Saturday
Bunting, Mostyn, Michael & Julian, having spent a week in Scarborough, called at Ravenstone on their way home. They arrived at 7 p.m. & stayed all night. Mostyn & Bunting slept at Pat's house. Michael & Julian slept at our house. I slept at Aunt Dos's as usual, while Mum was at Ashby on night duty.

22nd August 1965 Sunday
This morning I went to Ashby at 8 a.m. to meet Mum from night duty. I was requested to stop, as I scootered into Ashby, for a traffic census. Mum & I then scootered over the forest, through Woodhouse Eaves to "Old John", where we had a picnic breakfast. This afternoon I was "instructor" to Michael as we went for a drive.

23rd August 1965 Monday
Today Mum is 60. Today Terry is 21. Last night we had a get together at The Hollies in honour of Terry's 21st birthday. There were 23 people there. Terry had the most beautiful card you can imagine, from Mary Blue, with a £10 note inside. He also had £10 in each of three other birthday cards.

24th August 1965 Tuesday
Next Saturday is our Sunday School outing to Alton Towers. I joined Harold in the Rector's Room where the bookings were being taken. I walked down there, because the weather was so terrible. Howling winds & sleeting rain made it seem like mid-winter. I was given a lift home by Dennis Collier. About 60 have booked.

25th August 1965 Wednesday
Ann at work is 25 today. Ben, at work (our black man) who started with us on June 1st, has left this week. Mr Sharp informed us this morning that he has put in for a rise for 10 members of our staff (including me). His recommendations are now awaiting final approval by the Ministry.

26th August 1965 Thursday
I wrote to the Leicester School of Typewriting who advertised in the Leicester mercury: - "We are now able to accept bookings for our next course beginning September 6th full time, part time & evening classes. Write or phone for details to 171, London Road, Leicester."
I enquired about evening classes.

27th August 1965 Friday
Today I received my "Cathedral Newsletter" for September 1965. These news letters are written by the Provost, John C. Hughes & are most interesting. Today he tells us that he has recently been talking to Her

Majesty the Queen, who sent her best wishes to the Association of the friends of Leicester Cathedral. (That includes me!)

28th August 1965 Saturday

Mum & I went for an early morning scooter ride & arrived at Willoughby-on-the-Wolds by
9 a.m. We stayed there with Madge for a couple of hours. This afternoon I went with our Sunday School outing to Alton Towers in Staffordshire, where I experienced the thrill of riding in a chair lift.

29th August 1965 Sunday

This morning, after Sunday School, I called in at Don's. Lesley, aged 21, was at home & told me she has arranged her wedding for next year – June 4th. Afterwards I called in at Pat's, (it is his birthday today, he is 47), and he informed me that we shall be giving "**Carousel**" at the new "**Community Centre.**"

30th August 1965 Monday

Today is August Bank Holiday. The weather has been generally rather dull. I scootered to Ashby this morning to meet Mum home from night duty & again this evening to take her to duty. Pat & Evelyn called in about 8 p.m. & stayed until after 10 p.m. Evelyn is at work tomorrow, but Pat & I will both be on holiday.

31st August 1965 Tuesday

Bank Holiday Tuesday brought heavy rain & great black clouds for most of the day. Pat let me drive his car this morning to take Evelyn to school. This afternoon Pat & I went to the pictures in Leicester to see "**Mary Poppins**", a most delightful film. Pat let me drive his car again & I loved driving.

1st September 1965 Wednesday

I had a letter from the Leicester School of Typewriting: - "Dear Madam, ------ upon receipt of £1-1s-0d. deposit, we shall be pleased to book a typewriter for you for our evening classes commencing 21st September. We look forward to seeing you on that date and hope that you will gain the maximum benefit from the course."

2nd September 1965 Thursday

I worked 2 ½ hours overtime, leaving the office at 7-50 p.m. Little Tommy gave me a ride home on the back of his scooter. Dr. Albert Schweitzer, aged 90, the great medical missionary, is seriously ill in the jungle hospital which he helped to build. Having lived for Africa, it is his wish to die there.

3rd September 1965 Friday

Tonight I worked 3 hours overtime & caught the 8-20 p.m. bus home. I had a circular from Fred Burton, Secretary of our Coalville Amateur Operatic Society, saying that rehearsals for "**Carousel**" will commence on 20th September, in the "music room at the new centre, North Leicestershire Miners Welfare, Snibston."

4th September 1965 Saturday

Mum & I have been packing our cases today, ready for a week's holiday in Guernsey. We are going on a Barton's tour, leaving Leicester tomorrow morning at 8 a.m. & returning Sunday 12th September. Mum has never been

to the Channel Islands. Enid & I went to Jersey in 1957 & to Guernsey in 1961.

5th September 1965 Sunday

Mum & I on the first day of our holiday in Guernsey. We flew from Birmingham airport in a Viscount, arriving in Guernsey at 2-15 p.m. We are staying at the Dolphin Hotel where we have a very nice bedroom. Our chief complaint is that the Hotel is too far inland. We would like to have a sea-view, but that is a 5d. bus ride.

6th September 1965 Monday

Yesterday **Dr. Albert Schweitzer** died. Today Mum & I sailed to the lovely island of **Sark**. We arrived at 11 a.m. & left at 5 p.m. We had a horse-drawn carriage to take us to all the places of interest & wait for us while we wandered at leisure hither & thither. In spite of the weather which was not too good, we thoroughly enjoyed it.

7th September 1965 Tuesday

Went for a morning coach tour, visiting the tiny chapel which had been badly smashed up by a man who had gone berserk on June 21st this year. It is hoped to repair the damage after the tourist season ends this year. This afternoon we visited the tiny island of Jethou. We enquired about a boat trip to Alderney, but there isn't one on our free day.

8th September 1965 Wednesday

A wet & windy day. We drove from our hotel to Guernsey airport in torrential rain. We had a flight to Jersey already booked, but the plane was an hour late because of adverse weather conditions. We had a very bumpy ride over to Jersey, buffeted by gale force winds, but the return flight was delightful, with the wind behind us all the way.

9th September 1965 Thursday

Today was a "free day" on our holiday. Mum & I spent the morning in St Peter Port wandering through the shopping area & round the harbour. This afternoon we went a 9d. bus ride to the rugged south coast, to **Icart**, where we walked along the cliff tops. The sun shone, & the view was perfectly beautiful.

10th September 1965 Friday

Had a most interesting morning coach tour along the lovely rugged south coast of Guernsey. We went inside the church of St Peter in the Wood, where we literally walked "**up**" the aisle.
At night we went to Community Hymn Singing at my favourite St Peter's in St Peter Port, massed with flowers in preparation for the wedding tomorrow of the Governor's daughter.

11th September 1965 Saturday

Mum & I spent the morning walking through Candie Gardens, St Peterport & then visiting the underground German hospital. This afternoon I went to the island of Herm with another lady from our hotel, while Mum stayed in St Peterport & saw the bride (the Governor's daughter). This evening Mum & I went for a walk along by the harbour.

12th September 1965 Sunday
Mum & I returned home from our week's holiday in Guernsey. We had a good flight, & afterwards Barton's Transport brought us right home to our own door. Waiting for me at home was the result of my 15th shorthand lesson. I was given 91% with the remark: - "Maintaining a high standard." Now I want to save up for a car!

13th September 1965 Monday
Miss Rippon returned to work today after being away sick for 6 months. Miss Rippon's salary is on the Clerical II scale. Muriel, on Clerical I scale, has been doing Miss Rippon's work, & because of this Mr Sharp has applied for an "**Honorarium**" for Muriel. Likewise, I have been doing higher salaried work, & Mr Sharp has applied also for me.

14th September 1965 Tuesday
Beatle Ringo Starr's wife, Maureen, gave birth to a son in Queen Charlotte's Hospital, London. Ringo & Maureen were married at 8-15 a.m. on February 11th. The British stamp with a swastika on it became a best seller when it went on sale yesterday. M. P.s called for a withdrawal of this stamp when its design was published.

15th September 1965 Wednesday
I received by post the result of my 16th shorthand lesson. I was given 93% with the remark: - "Excellent progress." Auntie Belle has been having some very bad nights just lately because Uncle Fred is getting very old, & difficult to look after. Mum has therefore offered to stay with her all night tonight.

16th September 1965 Thursday
Mum & I went envelope delivering for our church, from Hoo Ash to Ravenstone turn.
On July 15th I bought some tartan slacks 35/-. They turned out to be faulty, & were subsequently returned. Today I chose another pair to replace them. I now have a very **good quality** pair, just plain green, costing £3-19s-11d.

17th September 1965 Friday
Tomorrow afternoon is the official opening of the North Leicestershire Miner's Welfare Scheme Community & Youth Centre at Coalville. It cost £125,000. We have our first rehearsal for "**Carousel**" there next Monday.
I cut in half a pink hyacinth bulb & a blue hyacinth bulb, crossed the pink with the blue, & hope to get variegated hyacinths.

18th September 1965 Saturday
We had our first read through of "**Through the Looking Glass**", a one hour play which may be given with "**Alice in Wonderland**" making a full length programme. The Rector's Room was in the process of being decorated. This evening Enid & I sat up until 1-30 a.m. doing shorthand. I have my first official typing lesson next Tuesday.

19th September 1965 Sunday
Her Majesty the Queen, & H. R. H. The Duke of Edinburgh, this morning attended the Battle of Britain memorial service in Westminster Abbey, which we saw on television. The Duke of Edinburgh read the lesson: St. Luke, Chapter 6, verses 43 to 49. During this service, the Queen unveiled the memorial stone to **Sir Winston Churchill**.

20th September 1965 Monday
We had our first rehearsal for "Carousel", in the music room of the new "Miner's Community Centre". As this was our first visit to the place, we went peeping into all the rooms, took a careful résumé of the vast size of the stage, & were disappointed in the very inadequate number of dressing rooms, back stage.

21st September 1965 Tuesday
I had my first typing lesson with the "**Leicester School of Typewriting**". There were 6 ladies in our class, all about my age. Imagine my great amazement when I found that one of the ladies is somebody from our office. We did typing to music, which I really did enjoy. I have never typed to music before.

22nd September 1965 Wednesday
A French author named Gilbert Cesbron has received a letter from Dr. Albert Schweitzer, who died on September 5th. Written shortly before his death, it said: "My dear friend, when you receive these words I shall be no more. Do not be sorry about me, for I have been privileged in being able to make of my life what I wanted it to be."

23rd September 1965 Thursday
I received by post the result of my 17th shorthand lesson. I was given 88% with the remark: - "Progressing very well with doubling. Excellent transcription."
This evening I went for my 2nd typing lesson.
Mr Sharp informed me today that I should get a salary rise from £725 p.a. to £750, commencing December 1st.

24th September 1965 Friday
Today at work, I was instructed in the art of doing the grand final balance. This includes counting the whole of the day's takings from both cashiers on vehicle licences, plus all the driving licence cash, plus all the cash received through our letter box. Today was a very slack day – suitable for such instruction.

25th September 1965 Saturday
This morning I spent 2 ½ hours at St. Mary's, having a marathon grass cutting session.
This afternoon we had our drama group meeting, during which the rain came down in torrents. It rained non-stop until well after midnight, which was hard luck for Ashby Statutes which started last night & are on until Tuesday night.

26th September 1965 Sunday
After yesterday's down-pour, we had a beautiful sunny morning. After Sunday School, Mum & I went for a 27 mile scooter ride, to Groby Pool where we stopped to watch people feeding the ducks; through Newtown Linford, Quorn, Loughborough & back home. I then left my scooter with Stan to attend to the lights.

27th September 1965 Monday
The price of the good old Leicester Mercury is increased

from 3d to 4d as from today.

I was late for work today. Just lately I have been late more often than not. I therefore asked Mr Johnson if he would endeavour to get me to work on time or else I shall seek alternative transport.

28th September 1965 Tuesday

After my complaint to Mr Johnson yesterday about being repeatedly late for work, he got me there on time this morning. Tonight I went for my 3rd typing lesson. Because of my previous self-teaching, I am the best in the class. Tonight I forged ahead of the others, advancing to the comma & full stop, which I've never done properly.

29th September 1965 Wednesday

Today is St. Michael & All Angels Day. I went to our Patronal Festival Service of Holy Communion at 8 p.m. During this service the Rector gave a 10 minute sermon, in which he emphasised the presence of unseen angels ever with us. He mentioned his favourite story of **Elisha**, quoting II Kings, Chapter 6, verses 15, 16 & 17, where **Elisha** said, **"Fear not."**

30th September 1965 Thursday

Tonight I went for my 4th typing lesson. I struggled along trying to sort out "C", "V", "B", "M" & "N". I typed: "The five cats were asleep; the mat was cosy", again & again & again, before I could do it correctly.

Pat, my brother, informed me tonight that our Rector, the Reverend Gustav Aronsohn, is to retire at Christmas.

1st October 1965 Friday

Another one of our office romances reaches fruition tomorrow when Len & Joan get married. Len had the day off today, & so I was relief cashier to Miss Gazzard. Being the first day of the month, & also being Friday, we had a hectic counter. I took £800 in cash & £1,200 in cheques.

2nd October 1965 Saturday

A lovely day today, after several weeks of heavy rain. Last month was the wettest September in Leicester on record. Rainfall records go back to 1885.

During the 6 years our Rector has been with us in Ravenstone, I have written down some of his best sermons. Today I have been typing them out, to have them printed,

3rd October 1965 Sunday

The Rector tonight gave an excellent sermon on Job, Chapter 2, verse 4, where Satan says: - "All that a man hath will he give for his life." He emphasised what it meant to Jesus to die for the ungodly. (Romans 5, verses 6, 7 & 8) "For a good man some would even dare to die, but while we were yet sinners, Christ died for us."

4th October 1965 Monday

Pope Paul today made his 3rd visit abroad. In January 1964 he flew to the Holy Land. In December 1964 he flew to Bombay, to the International Eucharistic Congress. And today marked the first ever visit of any Pope to the Western hemisphere. He left Rome at dawn, & will return tomorrow. He has gone to New York to address the United Nations, on a peace mission.

5th October 1965 Tuesday

Pope Paul returned safely to Rome today after his triumphant history making peace mission to the United Nations in New York, where he also met President Johnson.

Tonight I went for a typing lesson & there were definite signs of improvement. Gradually, I am getting the keys on the bottom row into the right perspective.

6th October 1965 Wednesday

Enid is 38 today. I gave her a "souvenir" letter opener which I bought in the Channel Islands. Today at work I have been relief cashier to Miss Gazzard & took a cheque from Murphy Bros., for £1,341 for 7 of their lorries. This is the biggest cheque I've ever taken over the counter.

7th October 1965 Thursday

This afternoon at 3-30 p.m., when Miss Gazzard was having her tea break, & I was left in charge of the counter, I had a most interesting customer, who was licensing a car from Northants to Northants. As a special favour I did it for him at Leicester. He thanked me very much & then said, "Will you marry me!"

8th October 1965 Friday

Tonight I sat up till after midnight, typing out some of the Revd' Aronsohn's sermons, which I have collected over the years. What I am hoping to do is type out about a dozen, & have them properly printed & bound in a beautiful cover. Then I want to give it to him as a very special sort of Christmas Card.

9th October 1965 Saturday

The lights on my scooter are not as good as they should be & I have been informed today by Auto Supplies that I need a new flywheel magneto. I have left my scooter with them. I walked home from Coalville across the fields & for the first time in my life I found a 4-leaf clover. In fact, I found two!

10th October 1965 Sunday

Last night we had our church harvest supper in Ravenstone Institute & today is our Harvest Festival. This evening at church, Harold & I walked up the aisle carrying the Holy Communion bread & wine. This morning I went with Pat to Measham & he allowed me to drive his car. Uncle Fred is very ill.

11th October 1965 Monday

Mum & Auntie Gladys went to the Rector's Room where the Harvest festival produce was being auctioned off by Pat. Enid & I went to Amateur's. Mum is sleeping every night (except when she's at work) at Auntie Belle's, while Uncle Fred is so very ill. Miss Gazzard is on holiday this week, so I am relief cashier to Len.

12th October 1965 Tuesday

I received by post the result of my 18th shorthand lesson. I was given 87% with the remark: - "Well done with the prefixes & suffixes." This afternoon at work, Miss Gazzard, Len & Mr Colderick were all away. Ann & I were left in charge of the grand final balance. We got in a bit of a mess, but all was well in the end.

13th October 1965 Wednesday
Today at work, both of the driving licence cashiers were away; & also Miss Gazzard the vehicle licence counter cashier was away. I therefore had the unique role of being relief cashier to Len on the vehicle licence counter & the rest of the day I was in charge of the driving licence counter.

14th October 1965 Thursday
Mr Johnson worked overtime tonight until 8-15 p.m. I went to my evening typing lesson & then I rode home with him in his car. My typing is still very inaccurate. The teacher has advised me to slow down & concentrate fully on typing **accurately**. I have almost mastered the art of knowing where the keys are.

15th October 1965 Friday
Today I have had a mystery toothache. In April 1962, I had my left lower impacted wisdom tooth removed under an operation in hospital. My mystery toothache today is in a double tooth, also lower left. I managed to see the dentist on an "emergency" appointment, but he said he could see nothing whatever that needed doing.

16th October 1965 Saturday
Uncle Fred is 81 years old today. I sat by his bedside this morning for about an hour, but he did not know I was there. Auntie Cis from Skegness has been staying in Ravenstone this week & has been keeping long vigils with Uncle Fred. Today has been really beautiful. Blue sky & sunshine all day long.

17th October 1965 Sunday
This morning we had a very dense fog, which cleared about 11 a.m. to give a beautiful sunny day. Auntie Cis offered to fetch Mum home from night duty in her car. I went with her in the fog. I spent many hours today typing out the Rector's sermons. I have now done eight. I hope to do ten.

18th October 1965 Monday
It was on October 18th 1948, that I started work in our office. That was 17 years ago, when I was 17 years of age.
Mr Johnson worked overtime tonight so I caught the 5-20 p.m. bus home.
This evening I went to Amateur's rehearsal for "**Carousel**" & while waiting for the 9-05 p.m. bus home, Mr Johnson picked me up in his car.

19th October 1965 Tuesday
Tonight I went for my 9th typing lesson. You will be pleased to hear that since last week my typing is showing great signs of improvement. Now that my typing is more accurate, I have been allowed to type out a proper letter, instead of sentence repetition, such as: - "he may pump the muck from the cellar with luck at five!"

20th October 1965 Wednesday
Mr Johnson worked overtime tonight, so I decided to catch the 5-20 p.m. bus home. I stood at the bus stop opposite St. Margaret's Church. The bus came, I stuck out my hand for it to stop, & it went sailing straight by, full! I therefore caught the next bus to Coalville &

walked all the way from Coalville to Ravenstone.

21st October 1965 Thursday
Tonight at our typing class, we progressed to the top row of keys, & learned what sign is with which number: - e.g. Inverted commas, over the 2 – just remember 2 ticks. @ sign, over the 4 – just remember 4 apples @ 4d. £ sign, over the 5 – just remember £5. _ over the 6, just remember draw the line at 6, etc. etc.

22nd October 1965 Friday
I was amazed to hear today that Mr Len Andrews died yesterday. He used to recite poetry to me, when we walked down the village together to church. He has been in the choir for many years. I always enjoyed listening to him recite poetry. He could go on and on, non-stop, from one end of the village to the other.

23rd October 1965 Saturday
It is announced today that as from next February, Premium Bonds are to have a top prize of £25,000 every 3 months. The odds of winning this are **five hundred million to one**!! The chances of winning any prize with Premium Bonds are 9,600 to one. With 24 bonds I should have just about a 400 – 1 chance.

24th October 1965 Sunday
Last night the clocks were put back 1 hour. This morning I went to 8 a.m. Holy Communion. At 5 p.m. Mum & I went for a walk round Mary's Lane. We went into St. Mary's churchyard, & found a newly placed bowl of flowers on my "**lawn**". This patch of grass has been adopted for cremations.

25th October 1965 Monday
At the Amateur's rehearsal tonight, we had a read-through of the libretto. I have made an application for the part of Mrs Mullins, the owner of the "carousel". (Amazing don't you think, that my driving instructor was named Mr Mullins!) Frank Newman, our dear old musical director came to rehearsal tonight & was given a big welcome.

26th October 1965 Tuesday
The Beatles today went to Buckingham Palace to receive their M.B.E.s from the Queen. Screaming teenagers swarmed up to the palace railings.
Mrs Jennifer Sleath, 32, Fairfield Road, Oadby, gave birth to twins last Sunday morning when we altered the clocks. The older twin became the younger. The older twin was born at 1-40 a.m. BST, the other at 1-10 a.m. GMT.

27th October 1965 Wednesday
Once again it is **Census** time at work, when we get dust all over our clothes & in our throats. This year we have a "**one in ten**" Census & have 5 teams of 3 on the job. I am with Steve & Ian. Tonight I spent 2 hours doing my typing homework. Tomorrow night will be our 12th lesson, exactly halfway through the course.

28th October 1965 Thursday
Auntie Cis went home on October 18th, but returned to Ravenstone after a few days, to help look after Uncle Fred who is dying. She & Mum sometimes sit up all

night together with him, so that Auntie Belle can have a night's sleep. They did so last night, but tonight Mum has sickness & diarrhoea, so is at home with me.

29th October 1965 Friday
I received by post the result of my 19th shorthand lesson. I was given 87% with the remark: - "Praiseworthy work throughout." Mum has felt much better today than she did yesterday, & has gone to work tonight. We have decided to have our office Christmas dinner this year at **The Firs**, Oadby, on December 22nd.

30th October 1965 Saturday
This morning I called in to see my poor old Uncle Fred, who looked so very ill, & was not expected to live until tomorrow. Sometimes he tried to speak, but it was very difficult to understand what he said. Our village drama group, rehearsing for "Alice in Wonderland", has gone into such a decline, that we are giving it up altogether.

31st October 1965 Sunday
The Bishop of Leicester came to Ravenstone Church tonight to dedicate our new Lych Gate. I had the unique honour of shaking hands with him twice! The Rector introduced me to him as one of his Sunday School teachers. We had the church floodlit. The Bishop was last at our church on March 8th last year.

1st November 1965 Monday
Today it has been bitterly cold with gale force winds blowing. I went to Amateur's from 7-30 p.m. until 9 p.m. Afterwards I went with Mum to stay with Auntie Belle for a while. We sat in the lounge with Auntie Belle, Auntie Cis, Dos, Fred Clark & his wife Grace. In the next room Uncle Fred lay breathing his last. I peeped in to see him.

2nd November 1965 Tuesday
My poor old Uncle Fred is still struggling on with his life. I called in this evening from 9-30 p.m. to 10-30 p.m. Auntie Cis & Aunt Dos were there with Auntie Belle. They said they had just all been gathered round my Uncle Fred's bed, really expecting him to die, but now he was breathing regularly again. Auntie Belle took me in to see him.

3rd November 1965 Wednesday
Uncle Fred continues his great effort to die. Auntie Belle's sister Dot, Auntie Belle, Auntie Cis, Aunt Dos & I, stayed all night with him. I sat up until 2-30 a.m., & then went to bed at Auntie Belle's. I hardly slept at all. The night seemed very long, & I was very glad to see the welcome light of morning.

4th November 1965 Thursday
Hewes,-Frederick Charles, Glenholm, Leicester Road, Ravenstone, beloved husband of Isabel and father of Donald & Isobel, passed away at his home, November 4th, aged 81 years. Service at Ravenstone Parish Church, 11 a.m. Monday, prior to cremation at Loughborough at 12 noon.

Uncle Fred

5th November 1965 Friday
We finished our Census at work. Princess Margaret &

her husband the Earl of Snowdon have just begun a three week tour of America. Events in the royal programme include a 50 mph hovercraft trip across **San Francisco Bay**, a ranch style barbecue & a dinner party at the **White House**.

6th November 1965 Saturday
This morning Mum & I went with Don & Auntie Belle to Coalville, to see Uncle Fred who was lying in the Chapel of Rest at Beresford House. Today my scooter was ready for collection after being 4 weeks having the fly wheel magneto re-magnetised. That cost me £5-10/-; & I have also been advised to have a new battery.

7th November 1965 Sunday
Members of our family have been arriving from far & near, ready for Uncle Fred's funeral tomorrow. Uncle Fred's daughter Isobel arrived with her family & is spending the night at Auntie Belle's. Bunting & Mostyn are spending the night at Pat's. They did not arrive until 10 p.m., & I joined them for supper at Pat's.

8th November 1965 Monday
We all went to Ravenstone Church this morning for Uncle Fred's funeral. A beautiful day, with sunshine all day long.
Grandma Hewes had 6 sons & 2 daughters. Now 5 of her sons have died. Uncle Hedley only is left, together with his 2 sisters Dos & Cis. Uncle Hedley is 76.

9th November 1965 Tuesday
On January 29th last year, 64 year old Miss Walker of A. M. Walker Ltd. at Cosby, married 82 year old Lord Hall, former Lord of the Admiralty. Last night Lord Hall died in Fielding Johnson Hospital. Today I had a **"Guerlain"** face cleanse & make-up at Marshall & Snelgrove's. I bought some Crème de Nettoyage – 18/-.

10th November 1965 Wednesday
This evening we had a get-together at Aunt Dos's – Aunt Dos, Auntie Cis, Auntie Belle, Auntie Gladys, Enid, Peter & his girl friend Christine, Mum & me. Peter showed us beautiful coloured slides of his recent holiday in Germany & Austria. Afterwards we looked at very old family photographs which really were most interesting.

11th November 1965 Thursday
Auntie Cis returned home to Skegness, after her month's stay in Ravenstone. Rhodesia today hit the headlines. Rhodesia today broke away from Britain & declared itself independent. This is the first rebellion of the kind since America broke away as a colony in 1776. It has come after 2 years of argument.

12th November 1965 Friday
This evening we had auditions for **"Carousel"**.
I received a letter today from Mr Blackburn – Dear Miss Hewes, I am pleased to be able to inform you that the Establishment Committee has approved a recommendation of the Finance Committee that you should be granted an honorarium of £12-10/- etc. etc...... in the December salary cheque.

13th November 1965 Saturday
This morning I received by post the following: -
The Lady Mayoress of Leicester (Mrs S. A. Bridges) invites you & your friends to a Coffee Morning & Bring & Buy, in aid of the Royal Commonwealth Society for the Blind, in the Tea Room at the De Montfort Hall, Leicester, 8th December, 10-30 a.m. & to meet the Society's Director Mr J. F. Wilson, C. B. E. who will speak.

14th November 1965 Sunday
I finished typing the 10 sermons which I hope to present to the Rector at Christmas. Having spent many, many hours getting them as perfect as possible, I proudly took them to Mr Northcott at Coalville to ask if they might be printed. He said: - "For what it is – it's not worth it." But he would bind them.

15th November 1965 Monday
Today I booked for Mum & me to go & see "**Sound of Music**" at the New Odeon Cinema, Leicester on the afternoon of December 8th. I have arranged to have a day's holiday from work that day. We are hoping to go to the Coffee Morning at the De Mont. first, to see Mr John Wilson, the blind man who travels all over the world.

16th November 1965 Tuesday
For the past 3 days we have been having a bit of Arctic weather. As there is not enough electric power to supply the millions of extra electric fires & appliances which have been switched on, there have been electricity cuts all over England. Our office was suddenly plunged into darkness at 4-45 p.m. today.

17th November 1965 Wednesday
Princess Margaret, on her 3 week tour of America is guest of honour this evening at "The White House". Earlier today she visited President Kennedy's grave.
We received a post card today from Mary Moore in Essex, to say that her husband Mick's mother died on November 15th. She was aged 93, & sister to Aunt Lil, who died last year.

18th November 1965 Thursday
I received by post the result of my 20th shorthand lesson. I was given 88% with the remark: - "A high standard has been achieved & maintained throughout the course." I told Mr Sharp at work today that February 4th 1966 will be Mr Rose's 40th Wedding Anniversary. Mr Rose is emigrating to Australia this month.

19th November 1965 Friday
I met Mary Moore's husband Mick. He & Mary came to Coalville today for his mother's funeral, & then stayed all night at our house. On September 27th I asked Mr Johnson if he would endeavour to get me to work on time. For the past month I have been late repeatedly. I shall finish with him at Christmas.

20th November 1965 Saturday
Mary Moore & her husband Mick returned home today after their one night stay at our house. Mr Northcott has returned my ten sermons in the most beautifully bound cover – dark blue with the letters G. A. embedded in

gold. I am delighted with it. Today I had a new battery for my scooter £2 -17s- 6d.

21st November 1965 Sunday
Mrs Jim Fletcher gave me a programme of events for the Mother's Union Carol Service which is to be held in the Rector's Room on December 2nd. There are 12 items, including one which says: - "Miss Betty Hewes". Evelyn, who also belongs to the Mother's Union, asked me to read a Christmas poem or story for them.

22nd November 1965 Monday
Ravenstone W. I. was formed 17 years ago, on the day Prince Charles was born. Every November the members gather together for a "Birthday Party", usually at Ravenstone Institute. This year they have launched out & gone for a dinner this evening at the Fox & Goose, Coalville. Mum went with Auntie Belle & Aunt Dos.

23rd November 1965 Tuesday
Cassius Clay retained his world heavyweight championship at Las Vegas, Nevada, last night, by beating Floyd Patterson. The referee stopped the fight in the 12th round.
Tonight at typing class I did a 2 hour examination paper at Intermediate Standard, requiring being able to type at 35 words per minute. The teacher said I should pass.

24th November 1965 Wednesday
Princess Margaret & Lord Snowdon last night attended a lavish farewell supper party in New York. Prior to the party, Princess Margaret went out for a final shopping spree. She bought a formal evening gown, two sweaters & a white shark skin tennis suit. The bill came to around £107. Today they are flying home.

25th November 1965 Thursday
Bakery workers are now on strike. The strike started this morning & goes on until Sunday. There was not a loaf to be seen in any of the shops in Leicester today. As a substitute I bought 6 little scones. This evening I walked from our office up to the typing school. It snowed for a little while.

26th November 1965 Friday
Because of the strike of bakery workers I was again unable to buy any bread today.
Every member of the Council's staff today received a "questionnaire" to complete in connection with moving the offices from Leicester to Glenfield. The new offices should be ready for occupation in the summer of 1967.

27th November 1965 Saturday
This afternoon I went to our church Christmas Fair held in Ravenstone Institute. It was opened at 3 p.m. by Miss Mary Bevin. Last year, you may remember, I did not go because we had a rehearsal for our drama group, & I was subsequently told off by the Rector, for keeping the children away from the Fair.

28th November 1965 Advent Sunday
Harold, Margaret, Janice & I (our four Sunday School teachers) discussed what to give the Rector as a leaving present from the Sunday School. We thought it would be rather nice if we could get him a black flower vase made

of "**Raven Stone**".

I went to Holy Communion this morning & had a special Blessing.

29th November 1965 Monday

The parts were given out at the Amateur's for "**Carousel**". I received a letter which read: - Dear Betty, Following your recent audition the Committee have pleasure in advising you that you have been selected to play the part of **Mrs Mullin**, in the Society's forthcoming production of "**Carousel**", Tuesday 8th March – 12th March.

30th November 1965 Tuesday

This past week we have been having some real wintry weather. This morning the roads were so icy that I was ½ hour late for work. This evening I went to my typing lesson & then had a lift home with Mr Johnson, who had been working overtime. When we reached our house the car refused to start again.

1st December 1965 Wednesday

I scootered to work today. I scootered home with little Tommy as my pillion passenger & took him to Whitwick. This evening I joined the members of Ravenstone Mother's Union for their Carol Service. I read to them "The Story of the Christmas Guest" by Helen Steiner Rice, from a German legend & poem.

2nd December 1965 Thursday

Mr Johnson's car was back in working order today, so I went in to Leicester with him. After my evening typing class, I caught the 8-20 p.m. bus home.

Steve at work showed me the final figures for the outcome of our recent **Census**.

It was a 1 in 10 **Census** & we counted 12,872 vehicles. Last year it was 11,969.

3rd December 1965 Friday

Mum bought a "**Grundig**" portable wireless. We had our first libretto practice for "**Carousel**"

In our Parish Magazine this month, the Rector writes his final letter, & the Churchwardens pay a farewell tribute to "Our Dear Rector" …….. no parish could have enjoyed the services of a more Godly man – a learned & well read scholar."

4th December 1965 Saturday

Yesterday the section of the M I from Markfield to Kegworth was opened.

Tomorrow & next Sunday it is the turn of Mum & me to do the flowers at Church. Today however, because of Rosemary Beadman's wedding, the flowers are already done. I called in church this afternoon to see 14 dozen white flowers.

5th December 1965 Sunday

I was moved to tears at church tonight by the words of the lesson – the end of The Sermon on the Mount, St Matthew, Chapter 7. I was moved to tears by the prayers & also by the words of the hymns. The Rector, the Reverend Gustav Aronsohn, who will be leaving us at Christmas, can stir me to the very depths of my soul.

6th December 1965 Monday

Mum & I had a "Christmas Card writing session" this evening.

Mum went into the Co-op at Coalville today & met Father Christmas himself, just preparing to go on duty. He said, "Hello! Are you still working at Ashby?" Mum was so mystified, she just stood there & laughed, & couldn't answer him.

7th December 1965 Tuesday

Today we received Barton's holiday brochure for 1966. We studied all the marvellous tours, dreaming of such fantastic adventures as seven nights at Rimini, on the Adriatic Riviera – through the Mont Blanc Tunnel, or seeing the wonders of Morocco; & settled finally for a Travel Film Show at Coalville, 8th February.

8th December 1965 Wednesday

This morning Mum & I went to the Coffee Morning in aid of the Royal Commonwealth Society for the Blind, at the De Montfort Hall, Leicester, where we met the society's director, Mr J. F. Wilson, C. B. E.

This afternoon we went to the Odeon Cinema to se "**The Sound of Music.**"

One hundred years ago today **Sibelius** was born.

9th December 19965 Thursday

This evening I went for my last typing lesson, thus completing my 12 week course. When a suitable opportunity occurs for me to take a typing exam, the school will write & let me know. They are waiting at the moment for the necessary licence, & estimate that it might be some time in the spring when I hear.

10th December 1965 Friday

Reevsie has had an operation today, to increase her chances of having a baby.

As it is mine & Mum's turn to do the flowers in church this week-end, & as it will be our last turn with the Revd. Gustav Aronsohn as Rector, I have gone all out & spent £4-6s-6d on flowers today, plus a vase - £2-7s-6d.

11th December 1965 Saturday

Mum & I spent the afternoon in Ravenstone Church. Mum cleaned the brasses & I did the flower arrangements. At 4-30 p.m., after Mum had gone home & I was in the lighted chancel of a dark church, the Rector came in. He & I looked long at the lovely flowers & talked of Christmas, of Jesus & of tomorrow's sermon.

12th December 1965 Sunday

Pat tonight showed me the minutes of the Parochial Church Council meeting, held this week, when Dennis Collier, as Rector's warden, informed the members that the Rector has requested that after the death of himself & his wife their ashes be put under a flagstone in the Sanctuary of Ravenstone Church, with a suitable inscription.

13th December 1965 Monday

Today we had a type-written letter from Mary Moore. (Mick has bought her a type-writer for her Christmas present). She says she is looking forward to seeing us both at Christmas. We are hoping to go to her home in

Essex on December 24th & return on December 27th. It will be my very first visit to her home.

14th December 1965 Tuesday

This morning I had a letter from Reevsie who is now home again, after her recent operation. This evening I scootered to Glenfield to see her. She was downstairs & dressed, & looked very well.

Mum was told today that Mrs Bennion had been moved to tears by the flower arrangements in church on Sunday.

15th December 1965 Wednesday

I called in church this evening to give the flowers some more water & see that they were alright for tomorrow – there will be Holy Communion in the morning & choir practice in the evening.

I have won a prize in the in the Ravenstone Derby & Joan Christmas raffle, a box of 100 "Players", valued at 27/1d.

16th December 1965 Thursday

This morning I scootered to Glenfield – left my scooter at Reevsie's house – went to work with Ann & Steve in their car. Came from work to Reevsie's with Ann & Steve, also bringing Mrs Mason. Mrs Mason & I had tea at Reevsie's & spent a very pleasant evening there.

I then scootered home at 10 p.m.

17th December 1965 Friday

The "Coalville Times" today reports the outcome of our Rector's sale, which was held at the Rectory last Wednesday. A pair of handsome Japanese china vases, 20″ high in royal blue & gilt & richly decorated - £40. A pair of 10″ Satsuma vases with covers - £15. Six paintings went to London art dealers - £850.

18th December 1965 Saturday

This morning I went to Coalville with Pat in his car to get their weekly supply of groceries. Pat let me drive. Pat had been bilious during the night & was not feeling at all well.

On March 12th this year London Zoo's golden eagle "Goldie" was recaptured after 12 days of freedom. Now it has escaped again.

19th December 1965 Sunday

This morning was our last Sunday School Children's Service in church, with the Reverend Gustav Aronsohn as our Rector. The children all went up to the altar rails & each one received a very special individual blessing. We were all moved to tears, including the Rector. We gave him our presents.

Note – We bid a fond farewell to our Rector, the Revd. Gustav Aronsohn, who is retiring to the south coast. He certainly left a lasting impression on me.

20th December 1965 Monday

"Goldie", the golden eagle from London Zoo, was recaptured yesterday. He escaped last Wednesday.

Today at work we received a Christmas Card from Mr & Mrs Rose, aboard the P. & O. Orient Liner "**Oriana**", as they sail to Australia.

This evening I had my hair permed by Terry at the Hollies.

21st December 1965 Tuesday

This evening we had our office Christmas dinner at The Firs, Oadby. (Les Rayner, who lives very near there, invited me home for tea & I met his wife Freda).

We had 2 long tables in a very cosy room. I sat at the same table as Mr Blackburn, the big chief who "sends" me. Afterwards Mr Colderick brought me home in his car.

22nd December 1965 Wednesday

Richard Dimbleby, the master commentator, aged 52, died this evening, after 2 months in hospital with cancer. In the Prime Minister's cabinet re-shuffle announced tonight, **Mr Tom Fraser** is no longer Minister of Transport. After being Minister of Transport for 14 months, he has now resigned. His place is taken by **Mrs Barbara Castle.**

23rd December 1965 Thursday

Although Mum was at work all night last night, she made a special effort to go to 10 a.m. Holy Communion – her last with the Revd. Gustav Aronsohn. He told her how pleased he was with the 10 sermons I had written out & given to him. He sent me a Christmas card & said: - "I write you soon. What you did for me was tremendous."

24th December 1965 Friday

Mum & I today travelled by bus from Ravenstone to Leicester – from Leicester to Colchester – from Colchester to Nayland, arriving at 5 p.m. to spend Christmas with Mary Moore & Mick & their dozen or so cats & kittens. A dear little kitten spent most of the evening snuggled up close in my arms.

25th December 1965 Saturday

Christmas Day in Nayland. Mum & I went to 8 a.m. Holy Communion at St James Church. It was a twenty minute walk through the completely deserted village street. To our amazement a man from church gave us a lift home in his car. We had our Christmas dinner at 6-30 p.m., at Mary Moore's.

26th December 1965 Sunday

A lovely sunny winter's day. This morning Mum & I went for a walk through the village of Nayland – out of Suffolk & over the border to Essex. Nayland lies right on the county boundary of Suffolk. This afternoon, Mary's husband Mick took me for a delightful 4 mile walk. This evening we went to a carol service.

27th December 1965 Monday

Mum & I returned home from Nayland. This morning there was a very heavy frost, but all day long there was brilliant sunshine & clear blue skies. We therefore saw the countryside for mile after mile as a veritable winter wonderland. We arrived home at 3-30 p.m.

I had tea & the whole evening at Pat's.

28th December 1965 Tuesday

This morning I walked to Ravenstone Church where Evelyn had informed me I should find on the notice board in the porch, our Rector's new address at Eastbourne. I then wandered round to the deserted Rectory & looked through the windows. I wandered down the fields, moved to tears by my thoughts.

29th December 1965 Wednesday

Today I bought a picture frame 8 ½ ″x 6 ½ ″ for the Christmas card which I received from the Rector. The card is designed by Strev, & is of "**Lucinda**", the dear little girl who wears a big bow on her hat, & an even bigger bow under her chin. She has rosy cheeks, dark brown eyes & a wonderful smile.

30th December 1965 Thursday

At last I have received my **honorarium** of £12 – 10/-, promised since last September. Also this evening Harold called to make out a cheque for me for £7 – 13s – 6d, being the amount I have spent recently for Sunday School books, etc.

Mum & I have re-arranged all the furniture ready for a New Year's Eve party tomorrow.

31st December 1965 Friday

This evening Mum & I had a New Year's Eve party at our house. There were 10 of us altogether, Pat & Evelyn, Terry & Mary, Auntie Gladys & Enid, Auntie Belle, Aunt Dos, Mum and me. We had a very jolly evening & finally dispersed at 1 a.m. Friday night is certainly the best night possible for a late night party.

* * *

1966

1st January 1966 Saturday
The Provost of Leicester, John C. Hughes, in his Cathedral news-letter to me this month, says, "What a wonderful resolution for this New Year –'I won't be good, I'll have fun.' You might be closer to the will of God than you think. Life is meant to be fun; to be more than just good; to be joyous."

2nd January 1966 Sunday
My poem on "Ravenstone Church" which has been in the making for well over a year, is now good enough for publication. (At least, that is my own opinion). I have decided to ask Dennis Collier if it might be printed in our next parish magazine, in view of the fact that we are now Rector-less.

3rd January 1966 Monday
This evening Mum & I scootered to Ashby to see Roy Johnson's pantomime "**Puss in Boots**". We just went "on spec", but were fortunate to get 2 very good seats from tickets which had been handed in. I quite thought we should be working overtime tonight. We had a monstrous post, but just left a lot for tomorrow.

4th January 1966 Tuesday
This morning I intended to catch the 7 a.m. bus to work, but I just missed it.
This evening I intended to catch the 5-20 p.m. bus home. I stood opposite St Margaret's Church, Leicester & watched the bus sail straight by – **full**.
Today I have been on the counter in the great January rush.

5th January 1966 Wednesday
This morning I scootered to work. Again I was on the counter all day long with a non-stop queue, but I enjoyed it very much. Tonight I worked 3 hours overtime. It was a pleasure to scooter home with the roads clear of all the peak hour traffic. It was quite warm for January.

6th January 1966 Thursday
Len was back at work today after being away on the sick for 2 days. I therefore was not on the counter today. I scootered to work this morning. Tonight I worked 3 hours overtime & when I collected my scooter to come home, a full moon & all the stars shone down on me, & the Cathedral bells rang out.

7th January 1966 Friday
Today I have been checking vehicle licence applications all day long. I did several large batches, including Murphy Bros. of Thurmaston, who had 32 vehicles. They paid by cheque - £6,820. Forty members of our staff (this includes 6 temporaries) have paid 1/- each & we have 2 Irish Sweep-stake tickets!

8th January 1966 Saturday
Today I started recording on a new tape, which should be long enough to hold the whole of the Gospel according to St Luke. I have also been composing an extra verse for my poem on Ravenstone Church. Today I took my scooter to Auto Supplies, as it had developed a terrible squeak. They cured it.

9th January 1966 Sunday
This evening I scootered to Leicester & went to Evensong at the Cathedral. I went 'specially to hear the Provost preach on the "**Comfortable Words**" from the Holy Communion. "Come unto me all that travail & are heavy laden, & I will refresh you." This was my first meeting with the Provost.

10th January 1966 Monday
This morning I scootered to work in a biting cold easterly wind. My hands were so cold that I got hot-aches. At dinner time therefore I bought myself a pair of lambswool lined mittens – 45/-, and was able to enjoy scootering home – I left the office at 8-15 p.m. Muriel went home sick & I had a trying time, doing her job.

11th January 1966 Tuesday
A bitterly cold day with occasional flurries of snow. I went to work on the 7 a.m. bus & caught the 5-20 p.m. bus home. Len was at tech. this afternoon, so I was with Miss Gazzard on the counter. I enjoyed that much more than doing Muriel's work. Fortunately Muriel was back at work today.

12th January 1966 Wednesday
Lal Bahadur Shastri, aged 61, Prime Minister of India since Nehru died in May 1964, died suddenly after a heart attack at 7 p.m. British time on Monday (1a.m. Indian time on Tuesday). Today he was cremated on the banks of the Jumna River. "Shastri" is a university academic title he won in Benares.

13th January 1966 Thursday
Tonight I stayed at work until after half past 8, checking vehicle licence applications. Then I scootered home, arriving at 9-30 p.m.
We had a letter from Mary Moore – type-written on her new type-writer. She said she enjoyed having Mum & me for Christmas – "Just the sort of company we like!"

14th January 1966 Friday
I received a letter from Mr Blackburn – Dear Miss Hewes, Mr Sharp informs me that following the resignation of Mrs Sharpe he allocated you to the duties on which she was engaged………In consequence I am pleased to inform you that I have decided to promote you to Clerical I Grade at a salary of £750 per annum.

15th January 1966 Saturday
This morning I took my scooter to Coalville to be serviced. I have now done 4,000 miles.
I walked home in the snow across the fields. It was really beautiful.
It is announced in the Leicester Mercury tonight that the Rev. Matthew Rice Lewis, Rector of St Mary Magdalene, Colchester, is to be Rector of Ravenstone.

16th January 1966 Sunday
It has snowed nearly all day long today. Our church & the trees in the church-yard looked perfectly beautiful this evening when all the lights were lit.
The Reverend Martin, a retired Rector who now lives at Whitwick, is taking the services while we are Rector-

less. Oh, we do miss our Rector!

17th January 1966 Monday
Having paid a shilling a week at work since can't remember when, to Regional Pool Promotions Ltd., I decided to give it up altogether at the end of last month. Flip me if I didn't go & win a "Goodwill Gift", value approx. 30/- this month; just too late to claim it. Was I glad it wasn't a car or a £1,000, which it might have been.

18th January 1966 Tuesday
Freezing cold day. I caught the 5-20 p.m. bus home from work & was glad to spend the evening at home with a lovely fire. I recorded the lines I have to learn for my part as Mrs Mullins in "Carousel", & then tried to learn them. I have about 90 lines altogether in this part.

19th January 1966 Wednesday
Another freezing cold day with temperatures well below zero. I caught the bus home from Leicester to Coalville & then walked to Ravenstone on hard packed snow & ice, & with a biting East wind. Enid & I are considering **Hastings** this year for our holidays.
"1066 and all that". "1966 and all this!"

20th January 1966 Thursday
Today I opened a bank account! I received a cheque from work for £5 – 3s – 6d for overtime worked this month. On the spur of the moment I opened my bank account at the Westminster Bank, Leicester, with £5. That is the first £5 towards my car I hope to have one day.

21st January 1966 Friday
George Harrison, one of the "**Beatles**" was married today. Paul McCartney is now the only bachelor Beatle. John Lennon & Ringo Starr are both married.
A dreary, dirty, foggy day with melting snow under foot. I went direct from Leicester to rehearsal of "**Carousel**". I was able to do about half my lines without the book!

22nd January 1966 Saturday
I had a marathon recording day today. Mum was on night duty last night, so spent all day in bed asleep. I recorded seven whole chapters from St. Luke.
Mum can't understand why I want to do this recording. Auntie Gladys & Enid too, tended to consider it quite unnecessary.

23rd January 1966 Sunday
The Reverend Martin who is doing his very best to keep our church going while we await the arrival of a new Rector & still weep for our old Rector, tonight held us all completely spellbound during his sermon, as he recalled his own life story in which he had met the Queen & travelled the world.

24th January 1966 Monday
An Indian airliner with 117 people on board crashed into Mont Blanc early today. The aircraft was bound from Bombay to New York.
In the Daily Mail today, it says: "Of the eleven First Division clubs through to the F. A. Cup 4th round, none can feel more hopeful if reaching Wembley than Leicester City!"

25th January 1966 Tuesday
I had "Christmas thank you" letters from Bunting – Michael & Julian, and also a letter from Hastings, which said in its postage slogan "Hastings – popular with visitors since 1066." This letter was from the Stafford Hotel offering us "a very nice twin-bedded room" for the week commencing June 4th.

26th January 1966 Wednesday
I wrote to Hastings sending £4 deposit for our "very nice front twin-bedded room" at the Stafford Hotel. With £5 in the bank I was very tempted to write out my first cheque, but my cheque book is not ready yet. I had written asking for a room with sea view, as we live "in the very middle of England."

27th January 1966 Thursday
Next Tuesday, Auntie Gladys will be 70. To mark this auspicious occasion, I managed to get for her today a beautiful birthday card & 2 gold numbers, 7 and 0, which I stuck on.
We had in our office today a Policeman & a Police Dog which barked at Christine at a given command.

28th January 1966 Friday
Today I received from our old Rector the letter he promised before Christmas to send to me, thanking me for the ten sermons of his which I wrote down. "……. I feel that the hours given to them for their construction have been worth every minute of it & words still fail me to thank you adequately for this most wonderful gift."

29th January 1966 Saturday
On Thursday next at 6-30 p.m. in the County Rooms, Leicester, certain members of the W.V.S. are to be presented with long term service medals. These include Auntie Belle and Auntie Dos. Auntie Dos has invited me to go along with them.
Prince Charles today arrived in Australia where he will be going to school.

30th January 1966 Sunday
Our church magazine for February is out today containing my poem on "St. Michael & All Angels, Ravenstone." In it also, there is a lovely poem called "Winter" by Longfellow. The last verse reads: - "O God! Who give'st the winter's cold, As well as summer's joyous rays, Us warmly in thy love enfold, And keep us through life's wintry days."

31st January 1966 Monday
Today I bought a book called "**The Poems of Longfellow**" price 18/-. Longfellow, my favourite poet, was born 27th February 1807 & died 24th March 1882. I feel very proud to have my poem in our church magazine printed on the very same page with Longfellow.
Our dear old musical director Frank Newman was at rehearsal tonight.

1st February 1966 Tuesday
Today I took £15 to the bank, bringing my total now in the bank to £20! When I got there they had no

electricity, & each bank cashier worked by the light of a solitary candle. It was most interesting to see – a perfect setting for a hold-up. It was mid-day. The sun was shining, but it was dark in the bank.

2nd February 1966 Wednesday

The Queen & the Duke of Edinburgh have just started a five week Caribbean tour. They will visit Jamaica, Trinidad & Tobago & 12 British dependent territories in the area. In Barbados, they will embark in the Royal Yacht Britannia to sail to British Guiana. The tour ends at Jamaica on March 6th.

3rd February 1966 Thursday

This evening I went to the County Rooms in Leicester to see Aunt Dos & Phyl receive their W.V.S. medals for 15 years service. Auntie Belle was not well enough to go & receive hers, but she hopes to go in the summer to the next presentation. We met the Duchess of Rutland who stood & chatted with us.

4th February 1966 Friday

"Cathedral News-letter" day! The more I know the Provost, the more I love him. His news-letters are really great. He comments this month on the recent criticism there has been in the Leicester Mercury about Leicester's Cathedral not being grand enough; & he says "Perhaps we can take heart that our Lord was born in a stable."

5th February 1966 Saturday

Harold has received a letter from our dear old Rector the Reverend Gustav Aronsohn, which is to the whole Sunday School & will be read out tomorrow morning to the children in church. I have chosen "The Epistle of Paul to the Ephesians" as a parallel, & today have made a précis of it in simple language.

6th February 1966 Sunday

This morning, at our children's service in church, I spoke to the children telling them about St. Paul – how he travelled thousands of miles to teach people about Jesus, & how the people of Ephesus loved him so very dearly & wept when he said goodbye. I read my version of his letter to them, & then read our Rector's letter.

7th February 1966 Monday

The Leicester Mercury tonight has devoted a large space to report on our Cathedral news-letter. Under a large heading reading "Cathedral Critics Urged 'Join Us & Help'," it goes on to say –The Provost, the Very Reverend John C. Hughes, invites the critics to join the Friends of the Cathedral & "share some of our planning & some of the cost."

8th February 1966 Tuesday

This evening Mum & I went to the Progressive Hall, Coalville, to see a film show given by Barton's Transport for their 1966 British & Continental tours, We did a thorough tour of Scotland – then to the lovely island of Jersey – from there to the Isle of Man & finally the most wonderful glimpse of Norway's glory.

9th February 1966 Wednesday

Auntie Dos is compiling a Jubilee Year scrap book for Ravenstone and Snibston W.I. She has newspaper cuttings of all the village events during last year. She has photographs of St. Michael's Church Ravenstone, & St. Mary's Church Snibston & she is including my poem on St. Michael's & the Rev. Wallace's on St. Mary's.

10th February 1966 Thursday

It has been snowing practically all day long today – wet snow causing plenty of slush. Mum went by bus to Leicester intending to go on from there to Willoughby, but because of the blizzard she about turned & came home.

I am now trying to compile a crossword for a competition, & find it very difficult.

11th February 1966 Friday

Mum tonight went to the De Montfort Hall, Leicester to see "**Coppelia**" given by The Royal Ballet. We had our rehearsal for "Carousel" tonight at the Primitive Chapel in Marlborough Square. Usually we get up a bus load to go & see whatever show we are giving, but no other society is doing Carousel right now.

12th February 1966 Saturday

This week I have had my first puncture – the back wheel of my scooter was quite flat when I went to start it on Wednesday morning. Today I asked Stan Colclough if he could mend it & he said he didn't know when he'd find time for that. Auto Supplies, however, did it for me & Stan was quite huffy.

13th February 1966 Sunday

Having gone for 3 weeks without so much as one tear for our old Rector, I decided that I had finished weeping for him. However, tonight when I went into church, Dennis told me that he had had a letter from him & he had said he thought my poem was excellent. That brought back my tears.

14th February 1966 Monday

Little Tommy at work is 21 today. Thirteen from the office dined at the Annabelle: - Little Tommy, Ralph, Ian, Mrs Hasler, Mrs Mason, Maureen, Jane, Marilyn, Carolyn, Christine, Dawn, Reevsie & me.

I have had a trying day at work doing Muriel's job. One continual fight against time.

15th February 1966 Tuesday

The crossword which I am compiling for a competition is shaping very well. I now have all the answers & most of the clues. The competition is purely for Local Government workers and I have one clue: - "Clog men travel on" (5.10. anagram) Answer: - "Local Government." First prize is £3 – 3/-

16th February 1966 Wednesday

This evening a whole crowd of us from Coalville Amateur's went to Leicester to see "**The Pyjama Game**" given by H.T.H. Peck Limited, Amateur Choral & Dramatic Society, in their works canteen. It was a really great production – much better than we expected. This afternoon Mum saw the film "**Mary Poppins.**"

17th February 1966 Thursday

I spent the whole evening reading chapter after chapter

of "**Dame of Sark**", a most interesting book which Mum has just obtained from the library. The Dame of Sark, who is now in her eighties, recalls the highlights of her fantastic life, particularly under German occupation. Mum & I went to Sark last September.

18th February 1966 Friday
There is quite an epidemic of flu about at the moment. One by one the members of our staff are going sick, & those of us who are managing to keep going are all wheezing & coughing & feeling terrible.
February, the shortest month, seems to be so long & dreary, so cold & wet & dismal.

19th February 1966 Saturday
Prince Andrew is 6 years old today.
This afternoon I went to Loughborough Town Hall to see "The Pied Piper" presented by the Bannister Academy. This was a production by Miss Bannister who has dancing classes for children in Coalville, Loughborough & Nuneaton. There were about 100 in the cast.

20th February 1966 Sunday
Today is **Quinquagesima Sunday**, which means next Wednesday will be Ash Wednesday. It is usual to have a church service on Ash Wednesday & read through the whole of the **Litany**. However, we had the **Litany** tonight at church instead of a sermon. The sermon will be on Wednesday.

21st February 1966 Monday
Steve arrived at work today with the news that his wife Ann had her baby yesterday – **a boy** – Colin Geoffrey.
Miss Gazzard & Ralph were both away with the flu & so I was **Cashier No 1** for the day on the counter, with Steve Cashier No.2.
During the day I had one millionaire licencing his Rolls Royce!

22nd February 1966 Tuesday
Again I was counter Cashier No 1 at work today with Little Tommy as counter Cashier No.2. This evening I was on booking for "**Carousel**" from 7-30 p.m. to 9-30 p.m. with Norman Bodicoat. He had been for his driving test for a car this afternoon & failed, so we had a long discussion on tests.

23rd February 1966 Wednesday
Ash Wednesday! We had a short church service this evening. We are expecting our new Rector to be inducted on March 18th.
Mrs Mason, who started work in our office a few months ago, came to work yesterday morning - went for lunch in a huff - & has never been seen since. She has now left.

Note – The beginning of the season of Lent, when at Church we usually read through the whole of "The Litany" praying for everything & everyone you could think of, & "in the world to come life everlasting."

24th February 1966 Thursday
It is announced today that there will be a **General Election** on 31st March.
The Bishop of Leicester, Dr. R. R. Williams, is very proud of the latest car number he has managed to acquire – RRW 680.
R.R.W. are his initials. 680 A. D. was the year that Leicester had its first Bishop.

25th February 1966 Friday
I have now completed the **crossword** which I have compiled for a competition. Closing date is March 14th.
Barry Edwards, at rehearsal tonight, informed me that he and Freda are to be married on April 9th.
Today I read "**Evangeline**" by Longfellow – the very sad love story of Evangeline & Gabriel.

26th February 1966 Saturday
Philip Bancroft, 29 year old painter and decorator who does our painting & decorating, is this week's winner of £500 in the Leicester Mercury's "Where's the Ball?" Only a few months ago he won £400 on a football pool!
Me? I have £20 in the bank, but am hoping to increase this to £50 on pay day.

27th February 1966 Sunday
This morning I went to 8 a.m. Holy Communion. This evening Mum & I caught the 5 p.m. bus to Leicester where we went to evensong at the Cathedral. We went 'specially to hear the Provost preach on "**There is a green hill far away**", the hymn written by Mrs Alexander who lived 1823 – 1895 in Londonderry.

28th February 1966 Monday
Today I was relief cashier to Miss Gazzard with the busiest counter I have yet encountered. I took £1,130-5/- in cash & £2,461-19/- in cheques.
John Saunders at rehearsal tonight informed me that he is to be married on May 7th.
Princess Margaret today left London airport to visit **Hong Kong**.

1st March 1966 Tuesday
I had intended to put £30 in the bank today to boost my bank account to £50. However I put in £15, making my total now £35. The other £15 went to Marshall & Snelgrove & bought me a beautiful new coat for Spring. The coat is called "**Mornessa**" – pastel green - £13-13/-.

2nd March 1966 Wednesday
Our driving licence section was short – staffed today, so I spent the whole day at work writing out **Driving Licences** – I did one hundred & eleven!
I had a post card from London – The Editor of "Public Service" thanks you for your entry for the current competition to compile a crossword.......

3rd March 1966 Thursday
Brian Wardle in our Amateur's, reminded me tonight that he is to be married March 12th.
Our new Rector has taken up residence in Ravenstone, but I have not seen him yet.
Our poor old village institute, in a sorry state of dilapidation, is to be improved. There is to be a house to house collection.

4th March 1966 Friday
Cathedral News-Letter Day! The Provost says: "I have just been talking to a man whose occupation takes him

round many of the English Cathedrals & he has gladdened my heart by telling me that we had the loveliest Cathedral he had seen, **"because I felt at home, I felt wanted, it's so friendly & homely."**

5th March 1966 Saturday
Spring Has Come Today! As my old friend Longfellow says: - "Gentle Spring! In sunshine clad, Well dost thou thy power display......." After the long dreary months of winter, how lovely to feel the warmth of the sun & to hear the birds singing all day long. The garden is gay with golden crocuses & snowdrops.

6th March 1966 Sunday
This afternoon we had dress rehearsal for "Carousel". I have only one costume in this show – a striking full length dress complete with bustle. The dress is beautifully styled in bright green with maroon layers of frills & a hat to match. We had a very good photographer who did his best.

7th March 1966 Monday
Tonight we had our final rehearsal for "Carousel". Opening night tomorrow. I sat & watched quite a lot of it tonight with Dr. Hamilton our President, who kept me well entertained. He has a very lively wit.
The Queen arrived home today after her five week tour of the Caribbean.

8th March 1966 Tuesday
Opening night of "Carousel". I am on holiday today until the end of the week.
In Dublin's fair city – in O'Connell Street, I have seen the 134 foot high Nelson Pillar which was erected in 1808. Today at 1-30 a.m. it was destroyed by a time bomb. Six men are being questioned.

Note – The Nelson Pillar, which I saw in June 1963, blown up by terrorists.

9th March 1966 Wednesday
Leicester City Football team was tonight knocked out of the F. A. Cup by Manchester City.
Our church at Ravenstone is in debt. With no money in the bank we owe over £100 for printing of the Parish Magazines, apart from maintenance costs. This evening there has been an urgent meeting called.

10th March 1966 Thursday
Today's Wills. **Mr Frederick Charles Hewes**, 46, Leicester Road, Ravenstone,
left £15,636 - 11s gross, £15,446 - 2s net (duty £939).

11th March 1966 Friday
This afternoon I went out on my scooter to get some pussy willow. The sky looked somewhat threatening. While I was out it thundered and lightened & I scootered home in a violent hailstorm. Dawn Henn at the amateur's is 16 years old today. She was presented on stage tonight with birthday flowers.

12th March 1966 Saturday
Aunt Dos & I went to **Staunton Harold** Cheshire Home this morning to see the hounds meet. Afterwards we went indoors there & talked with Peter Mould. We had a

drink of hot "punch".
Last night of "**Carousel**". Pat, Evelyn, Auntie Gladys, Enid & Aunt Dos came in afterwards. We went to bed at 2-30 a.m.

13th March 1966 Sunday
This evening as we walked to church all the blackbirds were singing their very utmost.
We had a film show at church for the "Mission to Seamen".
This was the last Sunday for the Revd. Martin to be with us. Next Sunday we are expecting to have our new Rector the Revd. Lewis.

14th March 1966 Monday
I received by post notification that I had been appointed **Poll Clerk** for the General Election (£4) at Coalville.
I arrive at work to be informed – **hard luck mate – you can't go.** Due to an unexpected By-Election at Melton we cannot spare those originally booked for the General.

15th March 1966 Tuesday
Tonight I went to see "**The Pyjama Game**" at Loughborough Town Hall, done by
Loughborough Amateur's. I had a lift from Leicester to Loughborough with Maurice Gaunt who does their make up. Then I joined up with a party of Coalville Inner Wheel & came home with Mum in Price's car.

16th March 1966 Wednesday
Mr Sharp at work told me about a job he had seen advertised which he thought would suit me – so I applied.
"Administrative County of Leicester: Health Department: Area Officer required in the Home Help Area Office, Coalville. Salary within Grade A.P.T. I £750 - £960 p.a."

17th March 1966 Thursday
I listened on the wireless to "**The Anger of Achilles**" an epic from the translation of Homer's "**Iliad**", written down in about the 9th century B.C. The Greeks were at war with the Trojans. The anger of Achilles who was a Greek occurred when his best friend was killed by Hector of Troy. Achilles in revenge killed Hector.

18th March 1966 Friday
The Bishop of Leicester & the Archdeacon of Loughborough were at Ravenstone tonight for the Induction of our new Rector, the Revd. Lewis. Afterwards we assembled at the Institute for refreshments. Everybody came, including the Bishop! I then wrote to our old Rector to tell him all about it.

19th March 1966 Saturday
British Summer Time begins at 2 a.m. G.M.T. tomorrow, so tonight we put the clocks forward one hour. A sure sign of spring is the awful smell of bonfires which I have suffered all evening from the Hollies.
Mr Hayes next door lies dying with pneumonia. I feel so sorry for him.

20th March 1966 Sunday
Mothering Sunday! And our first Sunday with our new Rector, the Revd. M. Rice Lewis.

I went to 8 a.m. Holy Communion.

We then had a service at 2-30 p.m. during which the children gave flowers to their mothers. Then we had evensong 6-30 p.m.

21st March 1966 Monday

We rehearse for our Amateur's every Monday from September to March.

From March to September we often have social get-togethers; & tonight we had a hilarious time watching coloured slides of our latest show "**Carousel**" & several previous shows.

We also saw Brian Wardle's wedding photos.

22nd March 1966 Tuesday

We had a new lawn mower delivered today.

I received a letter from the County Medical Officer, 17, Friar Lane, Leicester: - Dear Madam, Appointment of Area Officer (Coalville). Thank you for your completed application form for the above post. I will be in touch with you again in due course.

23rd March 1966 Wednesday

History was made today when **Pope Paul VI received the Archbishop of Canterbury** in Rome – the first time such an event has occurred since the Reformation.

I organised our office sweep for the "**Lincoln**". We had 36 people for 49 horses – some people having 2 horses. The winner was "**Riot Act**".

24th March 1966 Thursday

We received by post today five envelopes all marked **Election Communication** – 2 for Mum, 2 for me - & one between us. We had one each from Dr. John Cronin – vote Cronin….. Vote Labour. We had one each from the Conservative man – vote Conservative for Elton: & one from Dr. Brian Stratford – vote Liberal.

25th March 1966 Friday

This week-end & next, Mum & I are on the rota for flower arrangements in church. As it is **Lent**, there will be no flowers on the **altar**, but we shall do an arrangement on a pedestal in the sanctuary. Today I bought flowers in Leicester - £1-5/- & brought them home on my scooter (**stuffed up my jumper**).

26th March 1966 Saturday

This afternoon I spent 4 hours in Ravenstone Church all by myself. I did a gorgeous flower arrangement for the sanctuary using about thirty daffodils, 6 blue iris, 4 sprigs of white lilac,

6 pink tulips, 2 lilies, flowering currant, laurel & fern.

Oxford won the boat race today. "**Anglo**" won the Grand National.

27th March 1966 Sunday

The wind today has been colossal. Winds gale force nine & storm force ten have been battering the whole country relentlessly all day long. I brought my scooter indoors to save it being blown over. This morning at Sunday School I had 19 children – the most I think I have ever had. It was most rewarding.

28th March 1966 Monday

Although I shall not be a Poll Clerk on Thursday at the General Election, I have still been accepted as a "**postal voter**". I therefore voted today. As the Election Day draws nearer, so the threats and promises of prospective M.P.s continue to hit the headline news. Our labour candidate is now suing for slander the conservative.

29th March 1966 Tuesday

Mr Hayes, our next door neighbour, died in the early hours of this morning. He has been my next door neighbour since the day I was born. His funeral will be on Thursday – Election Day. Like Hiawatha he "Learned of every bird its language, learned their names & all their secrets, how they built their nests."

30th March 1966 Wednesday

I called in Ravenstone Church this evening to see how my flower arrangement was getting on. After topping up with water & removing one or two drooping flowers, it looked as good as new & perfectly in order for Mr Hayes' funeral service tomorrow, with its 2 lilies.

31st March 1966 Thursday

Election Day and Labour win easily. Out of 630 seats Labour = 363. Conservatives = 253. Liberals = 12 & others = 2 …..Today was the funeral of our next door neighbour Mr Hayes. This evening Mum & I went round & sat with Mrs Hayes, Marj & Sybil from 8p.m.to 10p.m.

1st April 1966 Friday

I have received a letter asking me to attend for interview at 8, St. Martins, Leicester at 10-50a.m. on 5th April. (Appointment of Home Help Area Officer – Coalville)

This prompted me today to buy a new black leather handbag £5-5/- & a new pair of black leather shoes £4-10/-

2nd April 1966 Saturday

Again it is the turn of Mum & myself for flowers at church. I spent much of the afternoon in church, trying to create an arrangement with a cross of white iris as the central theme.

This morning Mrs Mould brought Peter to see us & he stayed for dinner.

It has been snowing nearly all day.

3rd April 1966 Palm Sunday

Today we had a children's service in church without the Rector, so I spoke to the children. I spent the whole evening yesterday preparing my speech & told them a lot about Bethany – about Mary, Martha & Lazarus – about Palm Sunday & the days following – what Jesus did & what He said.

4th April 1966 Monday

I spent a very pleasant evening by the fireside with my old friend Longfellow.

I read his "**Travels by the Fire-side**" – let others traverse sea & land, & toil through various climes, I turn the world round with my hand, reading these poet's rhymes.

I also found a poem called "**Elizabeth**" – my name.

5th April 1966 Tuesday

I had a letter to say: "The judging of our 1966 crossword

compiling competition has now been completed, & I am writing to let you know that your own entry has not been successful."

I went for an interview for "Home Help Officer" & was told I was not altogether suitable. – Not my day.

6th April 1966 Wednesday

Today my scooter mileage reached 5,000. I had a very foggy ride into Leicester this morning, but the ride home was delightful. The sky was so beautiful with long shafts of sunlight reaching out from behind the clouds to the very ends of the earth & embracing everything.

7th April 1966 Thursday

Mum & I have been invited to the Hollies on April 9th for the Silver Wedding Anniversary of Ted & Janie Jarman. Their son married Mary Blue. Mary Blue lives at the Hollies – not Ted & Janie. Today after much searching of the shops I bought them a present – 6 wine glasses with black stems – 32/6d.

8th April 1966 Good Friday

A very foggy day – just like mid November.

This morning I went to church at 9-45a.m. On the way home I called in at Auntie Belle's for about an hour, & then at Pat's, where I also had fish & chips for dinner.

Tonight Pat & I went to church for an evening service at 7-30p.m.

9th April 1966 Saturday

This morning I scootered in torrential rain to St. James the Greater, Oaks in Charnwood, to the wedding of Barrie Edwards & Freda.

This afternoon I went to Ravenstone Church to see the flower arrangements for Easter & had never seen the church look more beautiful.

Tonight Mum & I went to Janie's party.

10th April 1966 Easter Sunday

This morning I went in torrential rain to Holy Communion at 7a.m. All afternoon the sun shone bravely & Mum & I set out in all our finery & went to evensong at Leicester Cathedral. During the service in the Cathedral it thundered heavily, & once again the rain came down in torrents.

11th April 1966 Easter Monday

This morning our new Rector called to see us.

This afternoon I went with Pat & Evelyn to the pictures at Coalville, where I thoroughly enjoyed the film "**The Sword of Ali Baba**".

I spent the whole evening writing a poem "**Flowers in Church on Easter Day**", inspired by this year's lovely arrangements.

Flowers in Church on Easter Day

I saw the flowers on Easter Day,
In beautiful and glad array;
And all around and everywhere
Their lovely fragrance filled the air.

On every ledge, and by the door,
Around each pillar, on the floor;
The font – the pulpit – all were gay

With freshest flowers for Easter Day.

And some their lovely faces bowed,
While others stood erect and proud,
And told again their favourite story:
"Solomon in all his glory . . . ."

Above them rose the window tall,
Ablaze with splendour, bringing all
The joyful tidings from death's prison:
"HE IS NOT HERE: FOR HE IS RISEN."

B

12th April 1966 Easter Tuesday

The last day of the Easter holiday and as cold as Christmas. Dismal grey skies all day long & a biting cold wind. I walked down to Ravenstone Church to water the flowers. Much of their Easter glory had faded. The rest of the day I was glad to be at home by the fire, typing & writing.

13th April 1966 Wednesday

Today I bought myself a new pair of ear-rings – little pearl stud ear-rings - £2.

Another very cold day with a biting east wind.

We now have another black man at work. His name is Peter. Our other black man – Ben – has left. We already have a Peter – so it's Black Peter & White Peter.

14th April 1966 Thursday

The whole of Britain has been in an Arctic grip today. Worst hit areas were Wales & the south of England, with five foot drifts on Exmoor. It was not too bad here.

I scootered to work this morning. It was very cold but dry. Tonight, however, I scootered home in sleet and snow.

15th April 1966 Friday

Woke this morning to find snow everywhere – the worst April fall for 16 years. It was strange to see daffodils bowed beneath the weight of snow. I therefore went to work on the bus. Today I became better acquainted with our black man at work. He calls himself **Peter** in this country, but his real name is **Bhupendra**.

16th April 1966 Saturday

This morning I took my scooter to be serviced.

This evening Enid & I went to the Adult School, Coalville, to see a hilarious comedy "**Too Soon for Daisies**". We laughed & laughed. I received by post today an unexpected envelope from Ireland containing 6 sweepstake tickets.

17th April 1966 Sunday

Christopher Collier (son of Dennis) is 7 years old today. I met him this morning dressed up like a big game hunter – white tropical hat, binoculars & ferocious looking rifle.

Our new Rector tonight gave a really excellent sermon, about Jesus always being there on the beach after our night of toil & failure.

18th April 1966 Monday

I posted my poem "**Flowers in Church on Easter Day**" to Dennis, for possible publication in the May parish magazine.

Auntie Dos made a wonderful "**Easter Bonnet**" for the W.I. competition tonight, but she did not win. A customer at work offered to sell me his red MG!

19th April 1966 Tuesday
This evening I completed my reading of "**Tales of a Wayside Inn**" by - guess who – Longfellow. 114 pages – packed with stories which were told by the fireside in "**The Red Horse**" by half a dozen guests – there for a couple of nights. Tales of adventure – tales of love – merry tales – sad tales - & legends of old.

20th April 1966 Wednesday
Just lately it has done nothing but rain, so imagine our surprise this morning to find snow everywhere. I scootered to Leicester in sleet & snow. The roads were mostly just plain wet – very wet. A bus passed me & I was covered from head to foot in wet slush, & my face was smarting with the sleet.

21st April 1966 Thursday
H.M. The Queen is 40 years old today. This morning she drove in the state coach to Westminster for the State Opening of the new Parliament; & for the first time T V cameras were allowed into the Commons Chamber to screen the official ceremony.
A definite improvement in the weather – a sunny day!

22nd April 1966 Friday
Today I made out my first cheque - £20 for the "Friends of Leicester Cathedral." I am hoping to become a life member. My bank balance now stands at the princely sum of £15!! That is £15 towards a car which costs £700. I haven't even got enough to buy the licence!

23rd April 1966 Saturday
I stayed up till after 1 a.m., recording tale after tale from "**Tales of a Wayside Inn**".
"Paul Revere's Ride", "The Falcon of Ser Federigo", "The Legend of Rabbi Ben Levi", "Torquemada", "The Birds of Killingworth", "The Bell of Atri", "The Cobbler of Hagenau", "The Ballad of Carmilhan".

24th April 1966 Sunday
Auntie Belle, Aunt Dos & I went to Coalville Marlborough Square Sunday School Anniversary, where we were deeply moved to hear sung some of the beautiful hymns written 50 years ago by Auntie Belle's father, **Arthur Clark**. I liked best, one called: "**The Beautiful Harbour**", the beautiful harbour of heaven.

25th April 1966 Monday
I had a busy day at work doing Ralph's job – Muriel's job - & my own job. I have decided it's high time I made some attempt to learn how to play the piano. I have therefore bought "**A Child's First Piano Book**" and this evening gave myself my first lesson – 1 hour.

26th April 1966 Tuesday
Today we had a note pushed through our letter box, which said: **Ravenstone with Snibston Village Institute**. "We wish to thank you for your excellent response to the recent door to door collection. Together with proceeds from other efforts, our balance now stands at £110."

27th April 1966 Wednesday
On Monday I had a piano lesson – 1 hour. On Tuesday I had a piano lesson – 1 hour. Today I had a piano lesson – 1 hour, and I can now play a few very simple tunes like "Baa Baa Black Sheep." Mum & I have had an invitation to the wedding of **Lesley Hewes & John Sear** on June 4th, at 11-30 a.m.

28th April 1966 Thursday
A really beautiful day. I thoroughly enjoyed scootering to & from work. This morning in the city traffic hold up, a **Friendly Midland Red Bus** was side by side with me. The driver knew me & we had quite a chat. Spring in full beauty can certainly be seen properly, travelling by scooter.

29th April 1966 Friday
Mum had her ears pierced!!
It is announced in the Leicester Mercury tonight that the Bishop of Leicester, Dr. R. R. Williams, is to lead a pilgrimage cruise to the Mediterranean & the Holy Land next spring, visiting Gibraltar, Malta, Patmos & Ephesus – 145 guineas. I should love to go.

30th April 1966 Saturday
April has gone out in a blaze of glory after starting off as one of the worst Aprils on record. Today we have had blue skies & sunshine all day long, making the blossom on the Hollies' pear tree look a perfect picture. I had my first grass cutting session down at St. Mary's.

1st May 1966 Sunday
A glorious hot sunny day with the temperature reaching 77°f.
This afternoon I went with Enid, Aunt Dos, Pat, Evelyn, Terry & Mary to the open-air swimming pool at Ashby-de-la-Zouch.
Our parish magazine for May is out today, containing my poem: "**Flowers in Church on Easter Day**."

2nd May 1966 Monday
Budget Day tomorrow! With everyone expecting a further rise in the cost of vehicle licences, we have been absolutely overwhelmed at work with post, & public, in a last minute "**Beat the Budget**" spree. With the temperature well up in the seventies again, we all felt just about exhausted.

3rd May 1966 Tuesday
Budget Day, & the headlines on the front page of the Leicester Mercury were: - "**Beat the Budget**" **Rush on Car Licences.** This was accompanied by a photograph of the queue waiting outside our office - "**The Long, Long Tax Trail.**"
Final verdict – **no increase on licences!!**

4th May 1966 Wednesday
I am still persevering with my piano lessons & have now progressed from my first book "**Jibbidy – F**" to my second book "**Sugar and Spice**." I am now able to play (with a struggle) "**Silent Night**".
Evelyn has asked me to help her this week-end with her flower arrangements in church for Sunday.

5th May 1966 Thursday
I joined up with a bus load from Ashby Hospital staff to see "**My Fair Lady**" starring Audrey Hepburn & Rex Harrison at the ABC Cinema in Leicester. Mum went & Pat & Evelyn & Mary Blue. We all thoroughly enjoyed the film – packed with beauty & action & deeply moving.

6th May 1966 Friday
We had a letter at work today from Mr Blackburn, Local Taxation Officer: - Dear Mr Sharp, I shall be glad if you will convey to the members of your section my appreciation for the way in which they responded to the tremendous pressure of the last few days, when forebodings as to the Budget ……..

7th May 1966 Saturday
Mum & I went to Leicester for the Annual General meeting of the Association of Friends of Leicester Cathedral, held in Church House. First we saw a selection of coloured slides of the Cathedral & its life; afterwards we were invited to evensong in the Cathedral & allowed to sit in the Choir.

8th May 1966 Sunday
Last December I bought a large white vase for church flower arrangements in the sanctuary. Today it had pride of place with a massive arrangement which really did look beautiful. My previous attempts at using it have all failed, so I was delighted with its success today.

9th May 1966 Monday
I called at Hall Bros., Motor Dealers, Ravenstone, to take a supply of licence application forms. I was invited into the house & given a glass of sherry. Afterwards I went into church to see how my flowers were getting on & topped them up with water. They still were looking very beautiful.

10th May 1966 Tuesday
I have received an invitation from the Shaftesbury Society, to spend a fortnight at the Shaftesbury Society holiday camp, Dovercourt, Essex, where they give holidays for the physically handicapped. I have been invited to go as a helper – to be responsible for one person in a wheelchair & look after him.

11th May 1966 Wednesday
I decided this morning to accept the invitation from the Shaftesbury Society, but after discussing the details with Muriel & Reevsie, I finally decided that I was not altogether suitable for such a job, & was not prepared to commit myself for a fortnight for "light domestic duties" etc.

12th May 1966 Thursday
Still persevering with my piano lessons, I am now on my 3rd book – "**The Easiest Tune Book of Hymns**", & quite enjoy being able to play with both hands – a thing I have never done before. Mind you, each hand consists of all single notes! Sometimes I cope with 3 notes all at once for a dramatic end piece.

13th May 1966 Friday
Funds for the renovation of our poor old village institute are gradually rising. Today the Coalville Times reports: - "A rummage sale for Ravenstone with Snibston village hall funds in Coalville precinct on Saturday raised £74. This brings the total raised to £185." We need £250 for renovation.

14th May 1966 Saturday
Cup Final Day! Everton beat Sheffield Wednesday 3-2. The Queen was not there to present the cup. Princess Margaret acted on her behalf. The Queen & the Duke of Edinburgh have been on a state visit to Belgium this last week, starting on Monday & finishing yesterday.

15th May 1966 Sunday
A beautiful day. I scootered to Ashby this morning to bring Mum home from night duty. We went for a ride as far as Normanton. We met a herd of cows unattended – then a ferocious looking bull walking down the road - then we got a flat tyre. Hall Brothers came to our rescue

16th May 1966 Monday
This evening I went to Ravenstone W.I. meeting where there was a competition for the best flower arrangement in a 6″ saucer. I did an arrangement for Evelyn, but we did not win. The winner was Aunt Dos. Today the seamen of Britain have gone on strike.

17th May 1966 Tuesday
I had tea with Muriel at her flat in Leicester.
On March 18th I wrote to our old Rector & told him that Enid & I hope to visit his church on June 5th, while we are on holiday. Today Pat received a letter from him. He thinks Pat is going! (**Not** Enid & me). I therefore wrote to him again to explain.

18th May 1966 Wednesday
Went to a Coffee Evening given by Auntie Belle for the Ravenstone "**Darby and Joan**".
I had a letter from Bunting in Malvern – "How about coming over with a car load to the matinee of "**The Gipsy Princess**" next Saturday – very light gay music. You could picnic in the park.
Ask Dos – Enid – Pat …….."

19th May 1966 Thursday, Ascension Day
I went to Holy Communion at 7-30p.m. I then called in at Pat's. We discussed the pros & cons of going to Malvern on Saturday and decided not to bother.
Reevsie is away from work this week with **lumbago**. Miss Rippon is on holiday, so I've been extra busy. Today I worked late & started early.

20th May 1966 Friday
This evening I had my hair permed, 37/6d. Afterwards I completed my recording of the Gospel according to **St. Luke**.
Evelyn, who has been a teacher at **Heather School** for the past 18 years, has applied for the vacancy at **Snibston School**. Today she heard that she has been accepted, to start August 31st.

21st May 1966 Saturday
I received a letter from our old Rector: "My Dear Betty,

Thank you for your letter. Delighted to hear from you and see you on June 5th, after the service & both of you must come home with me for a chat. As ever, your old Rector,   Gustav Aronsohn."

22nd May 1966 Sunday
Cassius Clay retained his world heavy-weight championship last night against Britain's **Henry Cooper**. The referee stopped the fight in the 6th round. It was the first world heavy-weight fight to be staged in Britain for nearly 60 years.

Today gale force winds blew my scooter over.

23rd May 1966 Monday
I scootered to work very early this morning & started work all by myself at 7-45 a.m. Most of the day I was working on "**Refunds**". At the moment we have a terrific back-log of Refunds, accentuated by the Budget scare. This evening I had a recording session – part of **St. Mark**.

24th May 1966 Tuesday
Leicester's new Lord Mayor is Councillor Monica Trotter (elected yesterday). She has chosen that her husband might be her companion instead of having a "Lady Mayoress".

Lewis's today had suddenly grown to twice its original size, with its new extension finally completed.

25th May 1966 Wednesday
Derby Day! I organised our office sweep. We had 32 people for 25 horses & I managed to draw the winner! "**Charlottown**" – 18/-.

I left my scooter overnight at the **Cresta Garage**, Groby Road, Leicester, because I had a leaking valve in the front tyre.

26th May 1966 Thursday
I collected my scooter this evening from **Cresta Garage,** where I was informed that they don't usually mend scooters, but they had fitted my front wheel with a new tube, & gave me the bill £1-8s-6d.

Aunt Dos, Pat & Evelyn are preparing to spend the Whit holiday at Skegness – staying with Auntie Cis.

27th May 1966 Friday
This evening I had my hair coloured dark brown – 30/-, by **Mary Blue** at the Hollies. This was to cover up my 2 dozen or so pure white hairs. The result was stronger than I anticipated – a very obvious looking dye. I am hoping it will improve – a bit too dark for my liking.

28th May 1966 Saturday
A glorious day of wind & sunshine. I spent 3 hours this morning down at St. Mary's Church & I finished clearing the grass which runs the length of the west wall of the church.

This afternoon I went for a scooter ride in the sun & wind without a hat on – hoping to lighten my hair!

29th May 1966 Whit Sunday
Scootered to church this morning to 8 a.m. Holy Communion – scootered to Ashby to meet Mum home from night duty. Scootered to Glenfield to take a photograph of the County Offices being built. This afternoon, scootered to Willesley to see the Duke of Rutland at a scout gathering. This evening scootered to the Cathedral.

30th May 1966 Whit Monday
Perfect holiday weather. Clear blue skies all day & every day with the moon ever eager to take her turn, stationed in the sky by mid-day. As I am sleeping in the house alone this week, I appreciate the moon's efforts. - Full moon next Friday.

This afternoon I scootered to Leicester & back.

31st May 1966 Whit Tuesday
The last of our 4 day Whit holiday. Four days of sunshine & wind – a gorgeous fresh air holiday.

This morning I cleared the whole length of the ditch on the north wall of St. Mary's Church. This afternoon I went for a 20 mile scooter ride, & have acquired a goodly tan.

1st June 1966 Wednesday
The Seamen's strike which started on 16th May is having far-reaching effects. The T.T. races in the Isle of Man originally planned for June 13th 15th and 17th have been postponed until late August or early September.

Aunt Dos today is literally black & blue after falling off her steps last night.

2nd June 1966 Thursday
America today landed a space-craft on the moon. This space-craft is expected to have a life of 14 days on the moon, during which it is expected to send back a stream of pictures invaluable for the preparation for the first manned landing – a race between America & Russia.

3rd June 1966 Friday
Lesley's wedding day tomorrow. This evening we had a family gathering down at her house – Aunt Cis – Aunt Dos – Auntie Belle – Auntie Gladys – Enid – Pat – Evelyn – Mum & me. Afterwards we went into Ravenstone Church to admire the wonderful flower arrangements done by Mrs. Worth – really beautiful.

4th June 1966 Saturday
This morning we went to Ravenstone Church for the wedding of **Lesley Hewes** and **John Sear**. Enid & I did not go to the reception but set out at 1-30 p.m. for our 185 mile journey to St. Leonards-on-Sea, Sussex, arriving at 7-30 p.m. We have a gorgeous bedroom.

Note – Cousin Don's daughter Lesley marries John Sear, who is the son of my cousin Minna, Uncle Aubrey's daughter.

5th June 1966 Trinity Sunday
This morning Enid & I went to 11 a.m. Holy Communion at **Friston**, the dear little 11th Century church where our beloved ex-Rector is now Hon. Assistant priest. We were delighted to see him again. He took us home to his gorgeous house where we met his wife & daughter & stayed for lunch.

6th June 1966 Monday
Today, being the 6th day of the 6th month of 1966, I bought a Premium Bond in **Hastings** which this year is

celebrating 1066 & all that.

A lovely day! This morning we explored the ruined castle & this evening we motored to **Battle** & went into the church to see the beautiful **Te Deum** window.

7th June 1966 Tuesday

I forgot to tell you that we are staying at the **Stafford Hotel** – No. 50 on the sea front.

This afternoon we went into **Eastbourne** & from there we took an open top bus to the top of **Beachy Head** which was shrouded in mist.

I had a little go at driving, but got stuck on a hill start.

8th June 1966 Wednesday

A day of sunshine! This morning we sat on the beach & this afternoon we sat high on the cliff tops to get a little more breeze.

This evening we motored to **Eastbourne** & up to **Beachy Head**. We saw Beachy Head in all its beauty with the evening sun setting over the distant downs by **Friston**.

9th June 1966 Thursday

Another day of sunshine! This morning we sat on the grassy slopes by the ruined castle high up above the sea & town.

This afternoon it was so hot we sat for a while in the shade, & then went to the end of the pier, where the strong breeze counter-balanced the fierce heat of the sun.

10th June 1966 Friday

A scorching hot day which ended in a thunderstorm. This morning we sat up on the cliff tops near the castle. This afternoon we visited **Battle Abbey** where **Harold** died in 1066. Today being 10-6-66, I bought a Premium Bond at **Battle Post Office** & also one at **Hastings**.

11th June 1966 Saturday

Enid & I returned home from our holiday in **Hastings**, leaving at 2 p.m. & arriving home at 8-15 p.m. A lovely sunny morning. We went for a tour of **Hastings** on an open top bus & then visited the **Fishermen's** museum in the old fishermen's church. We had afternoon tea at **Kew**.

12th June 1966 Sunday

Mum & I went to 8 a.m. Holy Communion. Dennis was interested to hear all about my visit last week to see our old Rector. Our new Rector was interested to hear all about Mum's visit last week to **Colchester**. This evening Mum & I visited Auntie Belle who was 70 on Friday.

13th June 1966 Monday

Having bought a spare wheel for my scooter, I scootered to work this morning for the first time with a spare wheel. Guess what! I got a puncture.

I wrote to our old Rector today to tell him how pleased we were to see him, & to tell him to expect more visitors next week from Ravenstone.

14th June 1966 Tuesday

This evening I called round at **Hall Bros.** Motor Dealers, who had very kindly mended my puncture & charged me nothing. Afterwards I went for a little ride with Pat in his new car, which he bought from Hall Bros.

Then I went down to St. Mary's where the grass was 6 inches high.

15th June 1966 Wednesday

I spent the whole evening grass cutting down at St. Mary's Church. I left it highly respectable before I went on holiday. One week's neglect & it looked like a wilderness. However, it now looks quite respectable again. i.e. the small area I care for. The rest is worse than ever.

16th June 1966 Thursday

Leicester Prison made head-line news today. Three desperate prisoners including Tommy Wisbey, one of the Great Train Robbers sentenced to 30 years in jail, managed to climb 40 feet up on to the roof of a boiler house at 3-44 p.m. yesterday & stayed there until 7-54 p.m., calling over the 40 ft. walls.

17th June 1966 Friday

This evening we gathered at Aunt Dos's to see her cine film of Lesley's wedding, - Mum & I, Pat & Evelyn, Enid & Auntie Gladys and Auntie Belle. Aunt Dos had some really excellent shots & we all thoroughly enjoyed viewing.

Lesley's brother Peter is to be married later this year.

18th June 1966 Saturday

Tomorrow is Father's Day, so I made my dad's grave especially respectable today & also took him some sweet peas. Now that there is never a service at St. Mary's Church, the church door was beginning to get choked with grass, so I cleared it completely & then polished it.

19th June 1966 Sunday

Sunday School Anniversary today. We also had Sunday School this morning & I spoke to the children about **St. Peter** – from the day he first met Jesus to the day Jesus ascended into heaven. Next Sunday I hope to tell them all I can about **St. Peter** after Jesus ascended into heaven.

20th June 1966 Monday

Billy Graham, the American Evangelist, is at present in London relaying his message from **Earls Court**. Mum, this evening, went to the **Granby Halls**, Leicester, to see & hear him on closed circuit television. There are television relays to ten major cities of **Great Britain**.

21st June 1966 Tuesday

Princess Margaret today received the Freedom of the **City of London** – at 12 o'clock at Guildhall.

The "**Friendly**" Midland Red are now partly on strike, with the result that a bus might come & it might not. It is a strike against overtime.

The **Seamen** who went on strike on 16th May are still on strike.

22nd June 1966 Wednesday

This evening I completed my recording of the Gospel according to **St. Mark**. This completes my recording of the **4 Gospels**.

Today, because of the bus strike, I scootered home with Tommy riding pillion, & took him home to Whitwick.

Thousands were stranded today because of the strike.

23rd June 1966 Thursday

Leicester Traffic Committee, in its first report to the City Council since it was formed in 1959, reports a £9 million programme for the 1970's to ease the congestion of Leicester roads & streets. The Southgates underpass will be an important feature designed with the utmost care by the City Engineer & City Architect.

24th June 1966 Friday

The **Halt Sign** near our house has been replaced by a modern "**Stop**" sign.

This evening I took Mum to work on the scooter because of the buses being so unreliable. **Midland Red** bus crews attached to Coalville Garage have now decided to go on strike every Saturday till dispute settled.

25th June 1966 Saturday

This morning I cleared the ditch on the east wall of St. Mary's Church. I have now cleared along every wall of the church, so that the church is no longer lost under the debris. Also this week a huge area of overgrown grass has been cut.

I had dinner in Coalville's Chinese restaurant.

26th June 1966 Sunday

I spoke to the children this morning at Sunday School. I spent a long time trying to prepare a speech about **St. Peter** as an Apostle, but without success. I therefore talked about the **Feast of the Passover** & how it originated.

Rosemary Green told me about her visit to our old Rector.

27th June 1966 Monday

Today we had a gay new hearth rug – orange & brown.

I am now doing a brief outline of "**The Children of Israel**", so tonight I got as far as the end of **Genesis**. I once did a very interesting précis of the whole of the Old Testament, but I never found anybody to appreciate it.

28th June 1966 Tuesday

Today's news is that **Marjorie Hayes** has a boy friend. She is my life-long next door neighbour, born 29-1-31.

I read today the most amazing story of a ship which apparently sailed off the earth. In 1909, the 16,000 ton liner **Waratah** left Australia for England & just vanished.

29th June 1966 Wednesday

A perfect summer's evening – "O gift of God, O perfect day – where-on shall no man work but play" – and what happens? Bonfires! Bonfires!! Aunt Dos's bonfire puthered smoke all through our house & I complained in no uncertain terms.

After 45 days, peace has come in the Seamen's strike.

30th June 1966 Thursday

Pay day today brings my superannuation up to £400. A survey out today shows that in 1965 the income per household for an average family was £24-12s-9d per week. In 1964 it was £23-12s-1d.

Today's entry in this diary completes the half-way mark – exactly 2 ½ years.

i.e. – Halfway through the 5 year diary started January 1964.

1st July 1966 Friday

Put your L.S.D. in the T.S.B. So says the advertisement for the Trustee Savings Bank. On a sudden impulse today I opened a Savings Bank account with £10.

Cathedral News-letter day! The Provost wants a Cathedral Secretary - with the qualifications of an archangel.

2nd July 1966 Saturday

Aunt Dos, Pat & Evelyn set out today for a week's holiday in Wales. I am therefore sleeping alone tonight because Mum is on night duty.

Our next show (Coalville Amateur Operatic Society) is to be "**White Horse Inn**" which will be given March 7th – 11th 1967. I joined in September 1948.

3rd July 1966 Sunday

Harold spoke to the children at Sunday School today.

While we yearn for our old Rector, the Revd. Gustav Aronsohn, the people of Colchester yearn for their old Rector, the Revd. Matthew Rice Lewis. An 84 year old lady from Colchester was at our church today. She wept for her Rector.

4th July 1966 Monday

Reevsie arrived back at work today after a fortnight's holiday with the great news that she is expecting a baby. She has been married eight years.

Today is the first day for the Leicester Mercury in the new premises at St. George Street, after being at Albion Street since 1890.

5th July 1966 Tuesday

Ravenstone Darby & Joan went to Mablethorpe for the day. Mum went. Auntie Gladys went & brought her sister Margery back with her. Auntie Belle went & stayed for a holiday with Aunt Cis at Skegness.

Today I scootered home in torrential rain – in thunder and lightning.

6th July 1966 Wednesday

Today at work I wept for one of our customers whose application was rejected after he phoned to say his insurance company had gone into liquidation. Until he phoned his application was being accepted, & I answered the phone assuring him his licence was being issued. It seemed gross injustice.

7th July 1966 Thursday

I spent the whole evening sorting out **Who's Who** in the Bible, from the days of **King Solomon** to the days of the prophet **Jeremiah**. This period spanning about 400 years, brought in **Elijah** – **Elisha** – **Jonah** – **Isaiah** – **Jeremiah**, apart from all the **Kings** (both of **Judah** & of **Israel**).

8th July 1966 Friday

This evening I concluded my sorting out of **Who's Who** in the Bible from the days of **Daniel** to **Malachi** where the Old Testament ends. As the books of the Bible are most confusing over this period, I have found invaluable help in "**Hurlbut's Story of the Bible**", being one continuous story.

9th July 1966 Saturday
Played croquet until 10-30 p.m. with Enid, David & Irene. After supper at Enid's we stayed up until 2 a.m. playing cards with Auntie Gladys & Auntie Margery.
Auntie Dos returned home from her week's holiday in Wales. I did three flower arrangements for her "**Welcome Home**".

10th July 1966 Sunday
I spoke to the children this morning at Sunday School, giving them a brief outline of the Old Testament from the days of Moses, on to Joshua – the 15 Judges ending with Samuel – the 3 Kings, Saul – David – Solomon – the division of the Kingdom – the prophets – captivity in Babylon – Jerusalem rebuilt.

11th July 1966 Monday
A perfect summer's evening – "Whereon shall no man work but play". Auntie Margery & I played croquet until 10 p.m.
Footballers from every part of the world are now in Britain for the **World Cup**. This championship is held once every four years. **Sweden** (1958) **Chile** (1962) **Mexico** (1970).

12th July 1966 Tuesday
This morning I had almost reached North Bridge, Leicester, when my clutch cable snapped on the scooter. Mr Sharp at work went to great lengths to get it mended for me. Murphy Bros. Thurmaston, collected it, mended it, & Mr Sharp took me in his car to Thurmaston to fetch it.

13th July 1966 Wednesday
This evening I compiled 60 questions for our Sunday School children, to wind up the end of the Summer Term on 24th July. I worked out 20 on the Old Testament, 20 on the New Testament & 20 on such things as "What Sunday is it today?" – a contest between girls & boys.

14th July 1966 Thursday
35 today! As my old friend Longfellow said – "**Half way up the hill**".
This evening Auntie Margery & I played croquet until 10 p.m. Then Auntie Margery, Auntie Gladys, Pat, Evelyn and Aunt Dos joined Mum & me at home for a birthday get-together. We all had a real good time!

15th July 1966 Friday
Today my scooter mileage reached 7,000.
There is a job advertised in the Coalville Times & in the Leicester Mercury which I am very tempted to apply for – "Coalville Mining & Tech. College – Clerical Assistant (female) for P.B.X. switchboard & general office duties. Ability to type an advantage."

16th July 1966 Saturday
"Alice in Wonderland" is to be shown as a television film on Christmas Day. The production, which will cost £25,000 is now in the making. Two sequences for the film – the Caucus Race & the scene at the Pool of Tears are being filmed at Donington Hall, Castle Donington, in Leicestershire.

17th July 1966 Sunday
This evening I scootered to Leicester to evensong at the Cathedral. I sat with one of the ushers who always looks after me very well. I was also introduced to **Canon Cray & Mrs Cray**. The **Provost** gave a wonderful sermon on the whole of Chapter 19, **I Kings** – God appearing to **Elijah**.

18th July 1966 Monday
I was informed last night, by my friend at the Cathedral that the **Provost** is still looking for a secretary. How would I like the job? You know how much I love the **Provost**, but I am not a qualified secretary. Even so, this decided me not to apply for the job at Coalville Tech.

19th July 1966 Tuesday
Our television picture has packed in. A man from **Alex Owen** came this evening & stayed for over an hour testing this – that & the other. He finally gave his verdict – a **new transformer** needed!
With rain lashing the windows & howling winds all round the house, it sounds just like mid-winter tonight.

20th July 1966 Wednesday
Stringent economic measures were announced today by the **Prime Minister**, the **Rt. Hon. Harold Wilson**. What with our exports not keeping pace with our imports & the recent Seamen's strike, it is a time of crisis. In a broadcast to the nation the **Prime Minister** said – "**A time of crisis is a time for greatness.**"

21st July 1966 Thursday
I have now started to read the **Apocrypha**. Never before have I read the Apocrypha, & I am agreeably surprised at the depth of wisdom it contains. So far I have read only the 2 Books of Esdras. Esdras a descendant of Aaron in the days of Artaxerxes was shown clearly the end of the world.

22nd July 1966 Friday
Today at work I typed my very first letter on quarto sized paper giving as a reference TVS/BH. The lessons I had last year with the Leicester School of Typewriting proved a tremendous help to me. I knew exactly how to space the paragraphs & it looked beautiful.

23rd July 1966 Saturday
England today reached the semi-final of the football **World Cup** for the first time. We watched the game on television – the most fantastic game ever seen at **Wembley**. England were playing against Argentine & won 1-0. There was absolute pandemonium at one stage & play stopped for 8 minutes.

24th July 1966 Sunday
All the newspapers today are full of **World Cup** news. There are now 4 teams left in. **West Germany** will play **Russia** tomorrow. **England** will play **Portugal** on Tuesday. Then next Saturday will be the **Final**. The fiery tempered **Argentine** team who almost caused a riot yesterday have been severely cautioned.

25th July 1966 Monday
West Germany tonight beat **Russia** 2-1 thus taking them to the **World Cup Final**. Tomorrow night

England play **Portugal** to decide the other finalist.
Last Saturday **Portugal** played **North Korea**. **North Korea** were winning 3-0, when Portugal's **Eusabio** scored 4, & finally they lost 5-3.

26th July 1966 Tuesday

England tonight beat **Portugal** 2-1 & thus qualify for the **World Cup Final**.
We watched the whole of the game on television – a game packed with thrills – **Leicester City Goal-keeper Gordon Banks** in goal making some terrific saves.
Eusabio, Portugal's ace player, left the field in tears.

27th July 1966 Wednesday

Last night's **World Cup** semi-final at **Wembley** between **England** & **Portugal** has been hailed as one of the greatest matches of all time.
Bobby Charlton who scored both our goals is the hero of the day. A Swedish newspaper says it is the Queen's duty now to give him a knighthood.

28th July 1966 Thursday

Portugal tonight beat **Russia** 2-1 in the "**Loser's Final**" at **Wembley** to gain 3rd place. Russia's goalie **Yashin** is a firm favourite as also are Portugal's skilful **Eusebio** & towering **Torres**.
Bunting & Mostyn called in this evening. They are spending a few days at Coalville with Fanny & Thirza.

29th July 1966 Friday

Cathedral News-letter day! ......at this present time our Cathedral is besieged by craftsmen of all kinds. The interior stonework is all being scrubbed & the walls are being lime-washed. Outside, a solitary craftsman is installing the very fine garden seats that the **Friends of the Cathedral** commissioned & gave ......

30th July 1966 Saturday

The World Cup Final! England beat **West Germany** 4-2.
We watched the game on television. It was estimated that 400 million people altogether watched the game on television. The £200,000 gate money taken today at Wembley is an all time record for any football match.

31st July 1966 Sunday

England today is "**on top of the world**" after yesterday's World Cup Final. Sunday papers have such headlines as "**How the Lion Roared**", "**The Game of the Century**", "**England's Glory 4-2**", "**Wembley has Never Seen Such a Game**". Hero of the game is **Geoff Hurst** who scored 3 of our 4 goals.

1st August 1966 Monday

Leicester's Lord Mayor – Mrs **Monica Trotter** – has organised a civic reception for England's Leicester City goal-keeper **Gordon Banks**. It is to be on Wednesday evening.
The Postmaster General has also ordered a special issue of a 4d. stamp to celebrate England's victory in the World Cup –"**England – Winners**".

2nd August 1966 Tuesday

A reader's letter in the "Mercury" tonight says: - **We have now proved that we have the world's finest footballers and Britain also has the world's finest campanologists** – and Leicester has specimens of both. Why not celebrate with a special peal of, say, **Wembley Victory Maximus on the 12 bells of Leicester Cathedral**?

3rd August 1966 Wednesday

This evening I stayed in Leicester for the civic reception of **England's Leicester City Goal Keeper – Gordon Banks**. I sat on one of the seats in the Town Hall Square & saw very little but heard all the din. I did however see **Gordon Banks** at close quarters as he drove away in his car.

4th August 1966 Thursday

I told you about England's economic crisis on July 20th. Although we are on top of the world, as regards football, the fact remains that Britain's National Debt is £31,327,000,000.
One lady aged 64 has sent the Chancellor £64 to help, but it would cost £577 each to wipe out the debt.

5th August 1966 Friday

I spent the whole evening trying to write a poem about **Bob Gerard's Christmas Tree**.
This tree which stands all year round in the front garden at **Tudor House, Groby**, is certainly the most impressive each Christmas. It seems to stand there all the year round just longing for Christmas.

6th August 1966 Saturday

This morning, during my weekly grass-cutting session down at St. Mary's, I met a man named **Mr. W.H.Sawbridge** of Weston Rushes, Clay Lane, Ellistown. He and his son spent the whole morning laying a gravestone for Mrs. Platts & I arranged for him to straighten my dad's grave-stone.

7th August 1966 Sunday

Muhammad Ali (formerly **Cassius Clay**) last night knocked out **Brian London** in the 3rd round of a 15 round fight, to retain his world heavy-weight title. His maxim – "**I am the greatest**".
Marjorie Hayes today borrowed my type-writer to do the balance sheet for **Ravenstone Institute** – over £200.

8th August 1966 Monday

I am still working on my "**Christmas Tree**" poem for Bob Gerard. It starts something like this: - Dear Mr Gerard, let us cheer, for Christmas once again is here: and we the passers by expect – to see your tree so gaily decked, 'though when the Christmas season ends, this well loved tree has fewer friends ....

9th August 1966 Tuesday

The Leicester Mercury tonight reports on "**Clean-up for the Cathedral**".
"Leicester Cathedral is currently having its biggest face-lift for years with workmen busy cleaning, washing & scrubbing. By the end of the month, says the Provost, the Cathedral will once more be thoroughly clean & beautiful."

10th August 1966 Wednesday

"**Public Service**" the monthly N.A.L.G.O. paper out

today gives full details of the new Local Government salaries agreement, which was due to come into force on August 1st. There is some delay however, due to the country's economic crisis. I am now on Clerical Division I – maximum £835. This goes up to £900.

11th August 1966 Thursday

Today at work I made my longest distance phone call yet when I phoned London County Council – Motor Licence Department.

This evening I started translating the Epistle to the Romans – trying to make it more like our Cathedral News-letter, with the address **Corinth A.D. 58.**

12th August 1966 Friday

Three London policemen, wearing plain clothes, were today shot dead.

Travelling in a Triumph 2000 "Q" car, they stopped to make a routine check on a "suspicious" car. Two men got out of the "suspicious" car. One by one the three policemen – all unarmed – were shot down.

13th August 1966 Saturday

Today I bought a new pair of white shoes in Coalville – 49/-.

I am suffering at the moment from something like insect bites. I have a swollen right hand & 2 more very inflamed swellings above my left knee. There are definite signs of another bite on my left hand, so I'm beginning to wonder if I've got a flea or something.

14th August 1966 Sunday

My insect bites kept me awake during the night, but Auntie Belle has now given me some "Insect Bite Cream".

This morning at Sunday School we had some of the questions I compiled last month – boys versus girls - & they were greeted with enthusiasm & interest. Being holiday time, there were only 5 at Sunday School.

15th August 1966 Monday

Princess Anne is 16 years old today. She is spending her birthday with her father the Duke of Edinburgh in **Jamaica**, where they arrived a few days ago to open the **British Empire & Commonwealth Games.** Today I bought a lovely "**Antler**" 21″ suitcase ready for Mum's birthday present – August 23rd.

16th August 1966 Tuesday

Ann came into the office this afternoon with her 6 month old baby son who was a firm favourite with everyone. I held him for a while.

Mr Smith is on holiday this week, so I spent most of the day doing his work – Post Office weekly returns of **Dog Licences – Game Licences – Gun Licences**, etc.

17th August 1966 Wednesday

This evening I completed "**The Epistle to the Romans**" in the form of our Cathedral News Letter. I have made it easy to understand without losing any of its finer passages. It takes up three pages of foolscap paper – type written.

At the moment we are having a spell of really lovely weather.

18th August 1966 Thursday

The lovely summer weather continues. There are however serious floods in some parts of the world, including Northern Italy, where our new Rector & his wife are at present on holiday. Today the Queen Mother opened the new **Tay Bridge**.

Two men have been caught & charged with killing the 3 policemen.

19th August 1966 Friday

England is still enjoying a heat wave while sunny Italy is flooded with torrential rain.

After 2 months of continual rain & really dismal weather, the present sunny spell is very welcome.

This evening I went down to St. Mary's Church and polished the door again. I first polished it 18-6-66.

20th August 1966 Saturday

A scorching hot day. I went grass cutting wearing slacks & bra sun top. It was really too hot to work & I kept seeking the shade of the Church.

This morning I scootered to Coalville where I bought some gold ear-rings shaped like a rose. They look beautiful on Mum's ears, but not so good on mine.

21st August 1966 Sunday

This morning at Sunday School with a good attendance of both boys & girls we had a contest – boys versus girls answering questions I had sorted out for them, & I was delighted with the enthusiastic response.

One almighty thunderstorm very late last night brought our recent heat wave to an end.

22nd August 1966 Monday

It was quite a work of art today getting Mum's birthday present home. A suit-case 21″long was rather awkward to get on the scooter, but with the help of a lot of office string I managed to secure it, & finally smuggle it into Pat & Evelyn's house until Mum went to work.

23rd August 1966 Tuesday

Mum's birthday! 61 today. The type-writer man called at our house this morning (as requested) & cleaned my type-writer. He told Mum that he visits **Sandringham** to clean the type-writers used in the Royal family offices there!

Today I bought a white handbag 29/11d to go with my new white shoes.

24th August 1966 Wednesday

Last Friday there was a major earthquake in **Turkey** in which 3,000 people died, countless thousands were injured & 110,000 were left homeless. After a radio appeal tonight for money, I made out my 2nd cheque - £5.

This is the first chance in Britain to help our "**Disasters Emergency Committee.**"

25th August 1966 Thursday

This evening Mum & I went to the **De Montfort Hall** to see "**Iolanthe**" presented by the **D'Oyly Carte Opera Company**. I had never seen "**Iolanthe**" before. We enjoyed it so much we would like to go on Saturday afternoon to see "**The Gondoliers**" if we can manage to get tickets.

26th August 1966 Friday

This morning the exhaust pipe on my scooter parted company with the silencer. I left the scooter near Bardon Chapel & went to work from there on the bus. Mr Colderick very kindly took me in his car & patched up the exhaust for me.

Today I bought the most beautiful white pedestal vase.

27th August 1966 Saturday

This afternoon Mum & I went to Leicester to see "**The Gondoliers**" given by the **D'Oyly Carte Opera Company**. We sat right at the front & saw every detail. The opening number was so beautifully portrayed, I almost cried. The costumes were immaculately splendid.

28th August 1966 Sunday

This evening I went to Leicester Cathedral & heard the **Provost** preach on: St. John, Chap. 9. Why must people be born blind? Why must people suffer? The Provost said, "Where there is suffering there is love: & where there is love there is suffering." He chose Romans Chap. 8 to "**wrestle with this problem.**"

29th August 1966 Monday

August Bank Holiday. The weather was quite good this morning. I spent a couple of hours grass cutting at St. Mary's Church. But this afternoon we had a terrible thunderstorm, the house literally shook with the violent claps of thunder. And the rain came down just like the monsoon season.

30th August 1966 Tuesday

Bank Holiday Tuesday, with a steady drizzle practically all day long. I spent most of the day transposing the **First Epistle of Paul to the Corinthians**, again in the form of our Cathedral Newsletter, with the address **Ephesus A.D. 57**, & starting: "My Dear Friends in **Corinth**."

31st August 1966 Wednesday

This evening I completed my "**Epistle to the Corinthians**", breaking down the more confusing passages into simpler language, but retaining all the great & splendid passages in their entirety.

Today was Evelyn's first day as teacher at Snibston School. She kept us highly entertained relating the day's happenings.

1st September 1966 Thursday

Auntie Belle & Aunt Dos, who belong to Ibstock flower lover's guild, today did their first masterpiece in the form of a huge pedestal arrangement in Ibstock Church, as part of a flower festival being held this week.

Mum & I scootered to the church this evening to admire the wonderful display.

2nd September 1966 Friday

My scooter mileage has now reached 8,000.

Bhupendra, who came to work in our office last April, left last week.

This week there has been a serious air disaster. A **Britannia** airliner carrying 117 passengers & crew from England to Yugoslavia crashed near the Yugoslav airport killing 95 (6 from Leicester).

3rd September 1966 Saturday

This afternoon I scootered to **Staunton Harold Cheshire Home** where they were holding their 12th annual fete. I saw inside the church & later went inside the Hall where I spent a very pleasant evening in the company of **Bill**, whom I met there 17th March 1965. We shared a bag of hot chips!

4th September 1966 Sunday

This evening I scootered to Ibstock for evensong at Ibstock parish church, where my beloved Provost was preaching. The church was packed with people & massed with flowers. In this delightful setting the Provost spoke of "The lilies of the field - & Solomon in all his glory."

5th September 1966 Monday

The Leicester Mercury tonight reports that Saturday's Staunton Harold garden fete raised £3,500 - a record.

I have been thinking a lot about **Bill** confined to his wheel-chair. I did enjoy being with him. Before his tragic illness he was a happily married man & he has 4 children from 7 to 17.

6th September 1966 Tuesday

The South African Prime Minister, Dr. Hendrik Verwoerd aged 64, was today assassinated. While seated in Parliament, a Parliamentary messenger walked up to him as if to speak to him, but instead, stabbed him to death. Dr. Verwoerd was the architect of South Africa's apartheid doctrine of complete racial segregation.

7th September 1966 Wednesday

Aunt Dos has a lodger. She is a school teacher at Ashby Grammar School – just started this term. Her name is **Lesley**. Aunt Dos has had school teacher lodgers before – they come & go – like ships that pass in the night.

The **St. Leger** today was won by **Sodium**. Only 9 horses were running.

8th September 1966 Thursday

The Queen today opened the new £8 million **Severn Bridge**, Britain's second longest suspension bridge. This evening on television we watched the story of its construction in a documentary film, which spanned the 5 years since it was first started. An engineering triumph! Our next big bridge will be over the Humber.

9th September 1966 Friday

A lovely sunny day. During the dinner hour I sat for a while on the Cathedral wall & the sun poured down on the Cathedral & on me. I do like being "**A Friend of the Cathedral**" & also a friend of the smallest church in our diocese – little **St. Mary's, Snibston**. Last night I found a human bone there!

10th September 1966 Saturday

Mum & I today went to **Cleethorpes** with our Sunday School outing. A really beautiful day! We were able to settle on the grass by the boating lake & have a long siesta. We then caught a bus to **Grimsby** but saw very little there, & were glad to return to Cleethorpes.

We came home (like Hiawatha) into the fiery portals of the sunset.

11th September 1966 Sunday

Our Rector – the Revd. Matthew Rice-Lewis, gave a very good sermon this evening on St. Matthew, Chap. 10, verse 39 "**He that findeth his life shall lose it: and he that loseth his life for my sake shall find it**." He spoke of all the things you can give away to make yourself richer – e.g. knowledge, happiness, etc.

12th September 1966 Monday

Today & tomorrow the industries of Leicester are having their Bank Holiday, so that getting in and out of Leicester during the "rush" hour is quite a rare treat. This is part of the Leicester Holiday Committee's effort to spread out the holidays – an experiment started last year, but proving to be most unpopular.

13th September 1966 Tuesday

While Pat went to a church meeting this evening, Evelyn spent an hour or two at our house telling us all about the latest escapades of her children at school. She has now completed her first two weeks at Snibston School, where she has to cope with the infants, & she has not been used to this.

14th September 1966 Wednesday

This evening Mum & I listened to the **Third Programme** on the wireless to "The Fall of Troy". This was an opera by **Berlioz** (pronounced **barely owes**) based on the narrative of **Vergil's Aeneid**, **Book Two**, it contains the magnificent choruses with brass bands widely separated (as **Berlioz** directed) for full effect of the Trojan March.

15th September 1966 Thursday

Queen Elizabeth the Queen Mother today launched Britain's first ballistic missile submarine H.M.S. Resolution at **Barrow in Furness**. On the approach road to the shipyard, while the Queen Mother drove by, demonstrators stood with placards carrying such messages as: "**Work for Peace, not War**."

16th September 1966 Friday

This evening I started to transpose the 2nd **Epistle to the Corinthians** putting it into simple language. I found Chapter I so difficult to understand myself, that I got no further than that. Alan Pettitt called this evening & mended our tap. He told me it is his birthday on 26th September. He will be 28.

17th September 1966 Saturday

A really beautiful day. Blue skies & sunshine & all the birds chirruping non-stop all day long in the Hollies orchard. This evening Auntie Belle, Enid, Auntie Gladys & I played cards until after midnight at Auntie Gladys's. Today I progressed further with the 2nd Epistle to the Corinthians, getting a clearer over-all picture.

18th September 1966 Sunday

This morning I scootered to Ashby to meet Mum home from night duty.

Spent the afternoon typing my transposition of the Epistles.

Our Rector this evening gave a sermon on: "Keep right on to the end of the road." Then what? Have we reached the terminus; or the junction for the great main line?

19th September 1966 Monday

Enid & I tonight went to our first rehearsal for "**White Horse Inn**". Rehearsals started a fortnight ago but we did not know. It was announced at the Annual General Meeting held at the beginning of June, but we were away on holiday. We have given "**White Horse Inn**" before – in 1959.

20th September 1966 Tuesday

I was dealing at work with Driving Licence applications received out of order, when all of a sudden I saw one received from **Friston, Eastbourne**. It was from none other than **Mrs. Pauline Aronsohn**. I sent her a letter to say we were forwarding her application to East Sussex: & added "**Greetings to you all from Ravenstone & Leicester**."

21st September 1966 Wednesday

Ronald "Buster" Edwards, sought by the police for 3 years, in connection with the Great Train Robbery which took place 8th August 1963, gave himself up this week. £2,600,000 was stolen. Only £343,000 has been recovered. Bruce Reynolds, believed to be one of the master minds behind the plot, is still wanted.

22nd September 1966 Thursday

I spent the whole evening with the 2nd Epistle to the Corinthians, getting as far as Chap. 7. This represents 2 ½ pages of foolscap typing in my: "**The Epistles of St. Paul – re-told in simple language**." "**The First Epistle to the Corinthians**" took up 5 ½ pages, ending with - Signed by my own hand – **Paul**.

23rd September 1966 Friday

My hair looked such a mess when I got up I decided to wash it at 7 a.m.! A quick 5 minutes with the hair dryer – a few pins at the bottom – and off to work at 7-45 a.m. The result was beautiful. Christine Hughes at work does this quite regularly, so I really got the idea from her. This was my first time.

24th September 1966 Saturday

A day of fog. Spent the morning grass cutting at St. Mary's Church.

I learned today that Marjorie Hayes is leaving Coalville Tech. & is to work in Leicester. She will live at Wigston Fields with her brother Sidney, his wife & 2 young sons. Auntie Gladys, Enid & I tonight played a new card game, learned recently at Mablethorpe.

25th September 1966 Sunday

This afternoon I went with Aunt Dos to Ravenstone Methodist Chapel harvest festival.

This evening I went on the bus to Leicester Cathedral. I sat with Mr. Tindall, the usher who looks after me. (Not on the bus – in the Cathedral) Last time I went, I sat all alone & didn't like that very much at all.

26th September 1966 Monday

I learned today, with the help of the telephone directory, that my friend at the Cathedral, who takes such good care of me, is Mr. Kenneth Tindall, Architect, 36, Holmfield Avenue, Stoneygate, Leicester. He is white-haired, with a North Country accent – an excellent bass singer. I enjoy singing at the side of him.

27th September 1966 Tuesday
This evening Mum went with a bus load from Ashby hospital to the Coventry Theatre to see a performance of "**Swan Lake**" given by the Royal Ballet. One of Mum's chief delights in life is ballet. She also loves to watch horse jumping.
My delight is writing, reading aloud, & being welcomed like the Queen at the Cathedral.

28th September 1966 Wednesday
The most surprising news of the day is that **Dennis Collier**, our stalwart church warden, bred & born in Ravenstone, solid as a rock, & seemingly established here for life, is to leave. He is going to keep a pub at Coleorton!
This evening Mr Woolley the plumber, called to discuss with us **Central Heating**!

29th September 1966 Thursday
Lilian Dunkley – producer of Leicester Amateur Operatic Society – great soprano singer - & teacher of singing (when I was aged 22 I spent £50 on singing lessons with her) was married today in **Leicester**. This was her 2nd marriage. She was a widow.
Today I bought a new dressing gown – turquoise – wool - £4-9s-11d.

30th September 1966 Friday
Cathedral News Letter day! The Provost now has his new secretary, **Mrs. Olwen Walden**. Today he asks for another sort of help – a guild of embroiderers to make a set of 50 cushions for the Canons' & Lay Canons' stalls in the Cathedral choir. This will be done on Tuesday afternoons, so it leaves me out.

1st October 1966 Saturday
Terry (Mary Blue's husband) is giving up being a hairdresser to become a **Prison Warder!**
It is now 20 years since 2 Germans were sentenced to 20 years in **Spandau Prison** in West Berlin, & they were released last night at midnight.
1. **Von Schirach** aged 59, former Hitler Youth leader, & 2. **Speer** aged 61, Nazi armaments minister.

2nd October 1966 Sunday
This afternoon I took eleven of our senior Sunday School children with me to Leicester Cathedral for the **Harvest Festival** service. We heard the Provost preach on Galatians 5. 22 (N.E.B.) "But the harvest of the spirit is love, joy, peace, patience, kindness, goodness, fidelity, gentleness and self-control." We sat with Mr. Tindall.

3rd October 1966 Monday
This morning as I scootered to work the rain came down in torrents. Apart from a few seconds in the dry, under the M I bridge, it was head down all the way. At one point a passing motorist showered me with so much water, my face was completely submerged - **SPLOSH!!**
The ride home tonight was delightful – dry & sunny.

4th October 1966 Tuesday
This evening it feels like winter & it sounds like winter with the wind howling all round the house. Reevsie, now half-way through her pregnancy, like June, is busting out all over. Les Rayner at work is now in hospital having had his appendix out, & Muriel is due to go into hospital next week for a minor operation.

5th October 1966 Wednesday
Mr Colderick is leaving our office to become Local Taxation Officer in Hampshire. Les Timson will have his job. Geoff will have Les's job. Ralph will have Geoff's job & I am to have Ralph's job on the counter with Miss Gazzard. This means I shall go from **Clerical I** salary to **Clerical II** which rises to a maximum of £1,020 p.a.

Note – I am promoted to Cashier No. 2, full time on the public counter issuing Vehicle Excise Licences.

6th October 1966 Thursday
Enid is 39 today. Christine at work is 19 today. This evening I went to Ravenstone Church for our Harvest Festival service. In the Leicester Mercury tonight there is a photograph of the oldest house in Leicester, Manor Farm, Donington-le-Heath, 1280. Also mentioned is St. Mary's Church Snibston, early English style, 24 feet by 12 feet.

7th October 1966 Friday
Today I bought a gorgeous winter suit from Joan Barrie in Leicester – a **Daphne Raven** model, winter weight, dark green, trimmed with black fox fur collar & cuffs - £12-19s-6d.
I saw it in the shop window & liked it immediately. There was no definite indication what size it was, so I was delighted to find it my size.

8th October 1966 Saturday
This afternoon Mary Blue gave me a trim shampoo & set – 6 shillings, & made me look rather glamorous for the Church Harvest Supper which we had in our newly decorated village institute. Mrs. Fletcher asked me if I would take the part of the Virgin Mary on 7th December at the Mothers' Union carol service.

9th October 1966 Sunday
Ravenstone Church Harvest Festival. I went to Holy Communion at 8 a.m., to Children's Church at 10 a.m., to the Children's Fruit & Flower Gift Service at 2-30 p.m., where I read the lesson; & to Evensong at 6-30 p.m. with Mum & Auntie Belle.
A foggy morning, so I was glad to wear my beautiful new winter suit!

10th October 1966 Monday
The tenth day of the tenth month of the year '66 – 10-10-66. I nearly bought a Premium Bond! But I resisted the temptation, having spent £13 on a suit & £4-10/- on a dressing gown. My holiday bank is down to rock bottom, but I have £15 in the Westminster Bank & the princely sum of £40 in the T. S. B.

11th October 1966 Tuesday
Reevsie, now having abandoned her ordinary work-a-day attire, is looking extremely pretty in her new maternity wear. She is hoping to stay at work for another 2 months. Her baby is expected about 1st March.
Today I bought a very smart green hat 36/- , to wear with my new suit: "**Each by the other's presence**

lovelier made."

12ᵗʰ October 1966 Wednesday
Muriel at work had her operation today. She had a bigger operation than originally expected, & instead of being away from work for a few weeks she will most likely be away for a few months.
Mum spent the day at Willoughby with Madge.
I remember Wednesday 12 October 1949 – my first love.

13ᵗʰ October 1966 Thursday
Once again our Cathedral News Letter has found a place in the Leicester Mercury. The Provost says: - "I find that I have grown very fond of Daisy Belle. She has a lovely daisy chain round her neck & a roguish look in her eye." Daisy Belle's photo is in the paper. She is actually a bull on the Cathedral's Herrick memorials.

14ᵗʰ October 1966 Friday
Today is the 900ᵗʰ anniversary of the **Battle of Hastings**. The Post Office have issued 8 different stamps to commemorate this. I spent a long time in the Post Office queuing for stamps, sticking them on envelopes to send to Aunt Dos, David & Peter who are all keen collectors.
Peter is getting married tomorrow.

15ᵗʰ October 1966 Saturday
Today I went by bus to Leicester to the Odeon Cinema in Queen Street, to see **"The Greatest Story Ever Told."** This was the story of Jesus. We saw the nativity – the baptism of Jesus – his temptation – the calling of his disciples – his ministry – his crucifixion – the resurrection. An excellent film, but it did not satisfy me completely.
Note – Cousin Don's son Peter Hewes marries Christine Hill.

16ᵗʰ October 1966 Sunday
Uncle Fred's birthday, so Aunt Dos & I called to see Auntie Belle this evening.
We heard a detailed account of Peter's wedding which Auntie Belle attended yesterday. Auntie Belle is to meet the Duchess of Rutland on Tuesday, & will receive the W. V. S. long service medal which she missed on 3ʳᵈ February.

17ᵗʰ October 1966 Monday
Leicester Amateur Operatic Society are giving "King's Rhapsody" this week at the De Montfort Hall. We are going in a party from our Amateur's to see this on Friday.
We would like to go & see **"White Horse Inn"** which we are rehearsing for at present, but it would mean going either to **Croydon** or to **Oldham!**

18ᵗʰ October 1966 Tuesday
On the anniversary of my starting work in our office, this letter was passed round from Mr. Sharp: - "It always gives me great pleasure to improve staff salaries wherever & whenever possible, & to a large degree my efforts to do so are successful because of the hard work, loyalty & support of all members of the staff, & I shall still endeavour to improve staff gradings ......"

19ᵗʰ October 1966 Wednesday
This evening Mum & I went to Ravenstone Hall, the home of Mr & Mrs Ottewell, where a fashion show was being held in aid of "The Friends of Market Bosworth". There were also the most fabulous flower arrangements on display, looking even more wonderful in the setting of the Hall with its gorgeous furniture & fittings.

20ᵗʰ October 1966 Thursday
A reader's letter in the Leicester Mercury today complains of the service received from the **city** motor licence office, Charles Street, Leicester. This letter takes up 3 columns & has a large heading: "**Trouble over a Driving Licence**", with sub headings "We just do it" and "Petty bureaucracy".
My scooter mileage has now reached 9,000. (28 daily).

21ˢᵗ October 1966 Friday
Went to the De Montfort Hall to see the Leicester Amateur Operatic Society's production of "**King's Rhapsody**". A really great performance with excellent leads & fine chorus singing. "Some day my heart will awake" was a moving solo. The "National Anthem of Murania" unaccompanied was grand, & the ending was superb.

22ⁿᵈ October 1966 Saturday
In a will published this week, a bequest of about £2,000 is made to our Rector, the Revd. Matthew Rice Lewis & his wife. Mrs. Cripwell of Colchester left this "**as a mark of the high esteem in which I hold the Revd. Lewis as a parish priest & in gratitude for many kindnesses shown to me by him & his wife in my lonely old age**".

23ʳᵈ October 1966 Sunday
On Friday morning, 21ˢᵗ October, a two million ton coal tip moved half a mile at **Aberfan** near **Merthyr Tydfil, Glamorgan** & engulfed three classrooms of the Tantglas County Infants School. Houses nearby were completely buried & today as bodies are being dug out it is estimated that the death toll will be 200.

24ᵗʰ October 1966 Monday
A reader's letter in the Leicester Mercury today is headed "**No trouble in getting his new full licence**" ...."without any fuss whatsoever the issuing officer at the Leicestershire County Council Offices issued me my full licence ......" signed **County Dweller**.
Yesterday the clocks were put back 1 hour, so now it is dark when we finish work.

25ᵗʰ October 1966 Tuesday
Census time once more at work! This year it is a complete census for our office, & we have 6 teams of 3 on the job. Because I am doing Muriel's work, I am not on the census.
Margaret Prescott, who used to work in our office, called into the office today with her 2 sons, Mark (4) & Richard (2). They "helped" me type!

26ᵗʰ October 1966 Wednesday
Alma Cogan, Britain's highest paid woman singing variety star, & most fabulously gowned star in British show business, died this morning, aged 34.

The Leicester Mercury has launched an appeal for the "**Aberfan Disaster Fund**", & already it has reached £10,000. The Queen & Prince Philip will visit **Aberfan** on Saturday.

27th October 1966 Thursday

Flags today flew at half mast because of last Friday's disaster at Aberfan. Today in Aberfan hearses stood in every street as 80 people, mostly children, were taken for mass burial. There still remain about 40 bodies not yet found under the avalanche from the slag heap.
Tonight Mum & I went to see the film "**Born Free**".

28th October 1966 Friday

Mum today went to Colchester to spend a long week-end with Mary Moore.
Mrs. Barbara Castle, Minister of Transport, said today it was hoped to have the Channel Tunnel, between England & France, completed by the end of 1975. The estimated cost is between £155 million & £170 million, by private capital, & public money.

29th October 1966 Saturday

H.M. The Queen & the Duke of Edinburgh today visited the Welsh village of **Aberfan**, scene of last Friday's disaster in which about a hundred children at school were buried alive by a sliding 2 million ton coal tip. The "Leicester Mercury" Aberfan Disaster Fund has reached £25,000 & closes today.

30th October 1966 Sunday

This morning I had 21 children in my class at Sunday School – most encouraging.
On 3rd July an 84 year old lady from Colchester came to our church & wept for her former Rector. Tonight she came again.
I have now completed my transposition of the second Epistle to the Corinthians – 7 pages of foolscap paper – typewritten.

31st October 1966 Monday

The "Leicester Mercury's" **Aberfan Disaster Fund** has now topped £30,000. The response has been absolutely wonderful, from all sorts of people – "The Indian Community of Leicester" "The Hebrew Community" "The Salvation Army" "Church Collections" "Office Collections" "The Provost & Chapter of Leicester Cathedral" etc. etc. etc.

1st November 1966 Tuesday

We have received from Mr. Woolley a quotation for our central heating – One Crane Cavendish No. 3 boiler in the kitchen – one Primatic Cylinder in the bathroom – one circulating pump – 5 radiators – total cost £247.
Mr. Pochin, who used to be boss of our office, called into the office this morning, together with Mrs. Pochin.

2nd November 1966 Wednesday

The Queen Mother came to Leicester today. She opened extensions at the Leicester Colleges of Art & Technology & later visited **Oadby** to open officially the Royal Masonic Benevolent Institution's old people's home. The Queen Mother last visited Leicester 20 years ago. At that time she was the Queen & came with the King.

3rd November 1966 Thursday

Today I bought a new winter hat – a **Jacoll** dark brown nylon fur with its own built in woollen scarf – 29/11d.
The Editor of the Leicester Mercury, **Mr. Fortune**, has received a letter from the Mayor of Merthyr Tydfil in connection with the **Aberfan Disaster Fund** ………"I am deeply touched by the generosity of the inhabitants of Leicester."

4th November 1966 Friday

Cathedral News Letter day! (A bit late) The Provost's letters always remind me of St. Paul's letters. Today he quotes from a letter written by a doctor to the national press in defence of "reason, understanding & love", & says: "I thought there was a touch of St. Paul in his masterly summary of the situation."

5th November 1966 Saturday

This afternoon I went to Coalville pictures to see "The Greatest Story Ever Told", which I saw in Leicester 3 weeks ago. I enjoyed it more than I did the first time. Two Sunday School girls went with me.
Money is still being sent to the Leicester Mercury Aberfan Disaster Fund, & the total now received is £40,684.

6th November 1966 Sunday

Dennis Collier who will be leaving Ravenstone on 8th November to go to Coleorton, asked me this morning if I would like to take over from him as "**Editor**" of the Ravenstone Parish Magazine. I gladly accepted. This morning at Children's Church I read two stories to the children. 1. **St. Martin**. 2. **St. Wenceslas**.

7th November 1966 Monday

The city of **Florence** in Northern Italy, known as "La Bella" (the beautiful) & "The City of Flowers", beloved to the poet Robert Browning, is now suffering from its worst flooding in history. Buildings are coated with reeking mud, & the streets are clogged with wreckage. The **River Arno** has overflowed into the streets but since receded, leaving all its havoc.

8th November 1966 Tuesday

Although the city of Florence was worst hit by the floods of Northern Italy, Venice too has suffered. The unprecedented onrush of the Adriatic sea water has smashed nearly 70 of the elaborate gondolas which cost about £3,500 each. Many priceless paintings in Florence have been destroyed, & treasures from the Middle Ages & the Renaissance.

9th November 1966 Wednesday

Today I went inside the **Provost's** house, **7, St. Martins East, Leicester**. I went to the Cathedral Office where Christmas cards are sold, & found it was actually inside the Provost's house! I met the Provost's new secretary, **Mrs. Olwen Walden**, who was young & gay, & I thought she was just the right secretary for the Provost.

10th November 1966 Thursday

Yesterday at 11-30 a.m. when I walked along New Street towards the Cathedral in the morning sunshine, the Cathedral looked absolutely gorgeous surrounded completely by pale blue sky. This morning before 8-30 as I approached Leicester, I saw the distant Cathedral spire beneath the glory of the early morning sun & was moved to tears.

11th November 1966 Friday

Today was Mr Colderick's last day at work in our office. Over the past eighteen years I have said goodbye to many different members of our staff, but I have never been so upset as I was today saying goodbye to Mr Colderick. He is such a live wire – absolutely genuine, & has been extremely kind to me.

12th November 1966 Saturday

I have just learned that last Monday, 7th November, my next door neighbour, Marjorie Hayes was married at a register office!

This week we have had a lovely new light fitted outside our house, at the top of the entry. Today I have spent practically the whole day composing my first letter for the Parish Magazine.

Note – Marjorie, my neighbour & friend since early childhood, married Maurice Preston.

13th November 1966 Sunday

This was our first Sunday without Dennis Collier & his family living in the village. His empty house next to the Rector's Room looked strangely desolate. Harold, his close friend & right hand man, was too busy helping him at Coleorton even to be at Sunday School. The church stood stark & lonely as though it felt deserted.

14th November 1966 Monday

Prince Charles today is 18 years old. He is Charles Philip Arthur George, Prince of Wales, Earl of Chester, Duke of Cornwall, Duke of Rothesay, Earl of Carrick, Lord of Renfrew, Lord of the Isles, and Great Steward of Scotland. He owns 4 castles, the Oval cricket ground, & is landlord of Dartmoor Prison!

15th November 1966 Tuesday

Cassius Clay (Muhammad Ali) once more defended his world heavyweight championship, and battered challenger Cleveland "**Big Cat**" Williams to defeat in the 3rd round in **Texas** last night. **Harry Roberts**, wanted by the police since 12-8-66, when 3 London policemen were shot dead, was caught today.

16th November 1966 Wednesday

Today I went for the first time to **Holy Communion** in Leicester Cathedral. It was in St. Dunstan's Chapel at 1-10 p.m. with **Canon Pratt**.

All day long the wind has been gale force, or severe gale force. I did not even attempt to go to work on the scooter.

This evening went to "**Planned Giving**" social.

17th November 1966 Thursday

Tonight we watched on television the 16th Miss World Contest. There were 51 contestants & the winner was Miss India, a beautiful girl who was training to be a Doctor & Gynaecologist. India is suffering badly at the moment from drought. Premier Mrs. Indira Gandhi said yesterday: "**Let every Indian eat a little less rather than let one Indian die of hunger.**"

18th November 1966 Friday

Having completed the census (full census) this week in our office, the next marathon task is re-organising the whole system of filing. This work began yesterday. Instead of having AY 1, AY 2, AY 3, JU 1, JU 2, JU 3, NR 1, NR2, NR 3, UT 1, UT 2, UT 3, we are now going to have AY 1, JU 1, NR 1, UT 1, AY 2, JU 2, etc.

19th November 1966 Saturday

Arthur Haynes, star of Radio & Television who came to Coalville 13-2-65, died today, aged 52. Today I received a letter from Mr. John Wilson, C.B.E., director of the Royal Commonwealth Society for the Blind, whom we met in Leicester last December. I wrote to him earlier this month.

Harold brought me all the items for next month's Parish Magazine.

20th November 1966 Sunday

This morning I went to 8 a.m. **Holy Communion**. I was in tears. I remembered our old Rector & the special blessing he gave me last November. I had no special blessing today, just "**Take this and be thankful.**" This usually reduces me to tears. Dennis Collier saw me in tears & asked most gently "Are you alright?"

21st November 1966 Monday

Today I received a letter from Mr. Blackburn – Dear Miss Hewes, As part of the staff changes following the resignation of Mr. Colderick, & acting on recommendations of Mr. T.V.Sharp, I have decided to promote you to the post in Clerical 2 previously occupied by Mr Widdowson. As from 14th November 1966, your salary will be at the rate of £800 p.a.

22nd November 1966 Tuesday

Three years ago today, President Kennedy was assassinated. He was shot by a man named Lee Harvey Oswald. Before Lee Harvey Oswald had a chance to be sentenced, he too was assassinated. It is now thought that more than one assassin fired at President Kennedy, & today there is talk of re-opening the inquiry.

23rd November 1966 Wednesday

Tonight as I left Leicester for home, I saw the Cathedral with its spire floodlit. Lights inside the Cathedral lit up the stained glass windows & it looked really beautiful.

The Leicester Mercury's **Aberfan Disaster Fund**, now £43,407 is the largest single gift to Aberfan, & the cheque will be taken to Aberfan next week.

24th November 1966 Thursday

It is reported in the Leicester Mercury tonight that the Provost of Leicester would like to have a Festival of Flowers in the Cathedral during its Ruby Year 1967. The proposed date is mid-June. Because the Cathedral is the Mother Church of the Leicester Diocese, every parish will be asked to participate.

25th November 1966 Friday

Pat brought me a "Ravenstone Parish Magazine" only just delivered by the printers, as this contained "**A message from the new editor**". This was my first effort as the new editor & Dennis had given me all the necessary extras – a poem – a prayer – a hymn – the

Rector's letter – the Calendar for December – the flower rota – Baptisms – Sidesmen, etc.

26th November 1966 Saturday

I spent today composing a poem for "Ruby Year Celebrations". The Diocese of Leicester was re-formed as such in 1927, & next year we celebrate – with different events throughout the whole year. Our Cathedral became a Cathedral in 1927. Prior to that it was an ordinary church dating back to 1220 A.D.

27th November 1966 Advent Sunday

Advent Sunday! I went to 8 a.m. Holy Communion at Ravenstone, & to an Advent Sunday Carol Service this evening at the Cathedral. I heard a Cathedral Choir boy sing solo "Once in Royal David's City", first verse. I saw the Cathedral in the light of a full moon & I took the poem I wrote yesterday, "Our Mother Church".

28th November 1966 Monday

"White Horse Inn" has now been cast. I am mostly in the chorus this year, but have been given a tiny part – **The Courier**.

Mum had her name in the Leicester Mercury tonight – **Mrs. M. Hewes** – winner of competition prize at the meeting of Ravenstone Derby & Joan Club. This was the weekly raffle last Tuesday.

29th November 1966 Tuesday

This morning I fell off my scooter on the icy road at Hugglescote. Fortunately I did not hurt myself very much. I tried to ride a bit further but the road was so icy I eventually walked along pushing my scooter. Along comes Mr. Anker in his car & very kindly took me in his car to Leicester & back to my scooter.

30th November 1966 Wednesday

The final total of the Leicester Mercury Aberfan Disaster Fund is £43,544-9s-7d. A cheque for this sum was taken to South Wales today & was handed to the Mayor of Merthyr Tydfil by the Lord Mayor of Leicester, Councillor Mrs. Monica Trotter who was accompanied by Leicester Mercury Editor, Mr. John Fortune.

1st December 1966 Thursday

I received a letter from the Provost: "Thank you so much for sending me your Ruby Year poem "Our Mother Church." I am so pleased that you have obviously given so much thought to our Cathedral & to its Ruby Year. It is most heartening to read this & to see that it means so much to you, & as you may imagine, this is a great encouragement to me. With every good wish etc.

2nd December 1966 Friday

Cathedral News-letter No.35. The Provost says: ...... I just had to rejoice the other day that a writer to the Leicester Mercury listed our Cathedral as the only place in the city worth a visit. Even that was grudging – "St. Martin's might merit a visit." However grudging, it was nice to be even remembered! ....

3rd December 1966 Saturday

This afternoon I went to our Church Christmas Fair held in **Ravenstone Institute**. It was opened at 3 p.m. by **Mrs. Curtois** of Donisthorpe. This evening Dorothy

Taylor called to inform me that I had sold a winning ticket for the raffle – one sack of potatoes for Mr. John Dexter, 14, Friar Lane, Leicester.

4th December 1966 Sunday

The Rector, the Revd. Matthew Rice Lewis this evening gave an excellent sermon for the 2nd Sunday in Advent incorporating the Collect & the Epistle for today – **whatsoever things were written aforetime, were written for our learning; that we through patience & comfort of the scriptures, might have hope.** Like all treasure, it is well hidden.

5th December 1966 Monday

This evening I missed Amateur's rehearsal to go to a rehearsal for the Ravenstone Mothers' Union Nativity Play, which is on Wednesday this week.

Our house at the moment is all in the middle of having central heating installed. We have 5 radiators which are now in place & waiting to be connected up.

Note – We have central heating installed. In the kitchen we have a Crane Cavendish solid fuel (coke) boiler installed, & five radiators overall. No radiator in the middle room, where we spend most time, as Mum prefers an open coal fire.

6th December 1966 Tuesday

The Prime Minister, Mr. **Harold Wilson**, spoke to the nation tonight on television concerning **Rhodesia**. You remember how Rhodesia broke away from Britain on 11th November 1965 & declared itself independent? This week Rhodesia has been given a last chance to co-operate with Britain & has rejected the offer.

7th December 1966 Wednesday

Today for the first time at home we have our central heating working.

This evening I joined the Ravenstone Mothers' Union for their Carol Service and Nativity Play. I read a poem which **Mrs. Fletcher** provided – "**No Room at the Inn**", & then took the part of the **Virgin Mary** in the play with **Mrs. Moseley** as **Joseph**.

8th December 1966 Thursday

Today I decided I would like a new scooter. I studied the book of new Registration Numbers at work & chose **KAY 7E** which should be available early next year. Auntie Cis owns car number **KAY 7**. My present scooter is **2 BAY**.

The Lord Mayor of Leicester has **ABC 1** and also **1 ABC**.

9th December 1966 Friday

"**Spotlight**", the County Offices' monthly magazine, ceased to exist in the summer of 1964 for want of an Editor. Today an excellent new magazine has emerged, called "**Impact**", printed & published by the Leicestershire branch of N.A.L.G.O.

Its slogan: "**Don't let us carry all the weight! Ring extension 2.2.8.**"

10th December 1966 Saturday

The Vatican announced today that **Pope Paul** will celebrate Christmas midnight mass in the Cathedral of

Florence to bring comfort to its flood stricken people. The Florentine Cathedral of Santa Maria de Fiore was, like most of the city's churches, submerged in the flood of November 4th.

This year we have a Christmas midnight service at Ravenstone.

11th December 1966 Sunday

This morning I went to 8 a.m. Holy Communion.

Yesterday 18 girls were confirmed at Ravenstone Church, so today there were about 50 at Holy Communion – much more than usual.

This evening I went to the Cathedral to hear the Provost preach on the coming of Christ as Judge at the end of the world – a Judge with **compassion, sympathy & understanding.**

12th December 1966 Monday

The poem which I started at the beginning of August about Bob Gerard's beautiful Christmas tree is now complete, & today I posted it to him.

We had a collection at work for Reevsie's leaving present - £5-3/-. She has bought a really lovely gold bangle, less than ½ " wide, which cost £7- 15/- !

Christmas 1966
Dear Mr Gerard, Let us cheer
For Christmas once again is here
And all the passers by expect
A Christmas Tree so gaily decked.

But when the Festive Season ends
Your well loved tree with fewer friends
Will stand unnoticed in the Spring
When other trees their blossom bring.

And then again in Summer time
When scented roses in their prime
Great galaxies of blooms display
How many think to look her way?

She waits 'til Summer fades at last
And others quake at Autumn's blast
Then she alone can bravely stand
And welcome Winter by the hand.

Yes, only she with noble mien
Can laugh to scorn the frost so keen
And take the backcloth of the night
To give to all her joyful light.

Our thanks to you we now extend
And greetings we would like to send
Your Christmas Tree, we all agree
Is quite the best we ever see.
A Passer By.

13th December 1966 Tuesday

This evening Mary Blue permed my hair, 37/6d.

Today I bought a new hat – cream jersey wool, ruched into turban style, 42/-

This week is Reevsie's last week at work after 15 ½ years. She & I have lunched together all that time. For our last lunch hour on Friday we are going to the Cathedral.

14th December 1966 Wednesday

A letter was passed round the office today from Mr. Sharp "To All Members of the Staff", which ended ......
I am always conscious of & appreciative of your efforts at my behest, & I cannot let the occasion pass without tendering my sincere thanks & appreciation for your efforts during the past year. (We have 40 on the staff)

15th December 1966 Thursday

Walt Disney died today, aged 65. Walt Disney was the greatest of all film cartoonists – creator of **Mickey Mouse, Donald Duck,** etc.

Today I bought a new dress to match my new hat. The dress is cream courtelle, sparkling with silver thread – 79/11d. I have just finished knitting some adorable bootees for Reevsie's baby.

16th December 1966 Friday

Reevsie, my best friend, left work today. She has been my constant companion at work for
15 ½ years.

Reevsie has twin sisters, Phyllis & Sherry, who were born just over 15 ½ years ago. They are hoping to leave school next week, & then after Christmas start to work – Guess where! Our office!

Note – My friend Reevsie leaves work, expecting her first baby.

17th December 1966 Saturday

Today I wrote a poem **"On Leaving Grey Friars"** for the new County Offices magazine **"Impact".**

This afternoon I called in at Auto Supplies to order a new scooter, a **Vespa 150cc Super,** costing £165-6s-11d. I am hoping to get about £50 for my old scooter, borrow £50 from Mum, & spend £65 which I have saved in the T.S.B.

18th December 1966 Sunday

This evening we had our Carol Service at Church – 9 lessons & carols preceded by a very short Nativity play by the children, under the able direction of 14 year old Susan Jarvis, now a Sunday School Teacher. Today I visited the Rectory, Mr. Biddle & Dorothy Taylor for items of news for the Parish Magazine.

19th December 1966 Monday

Muriel has now been away from work for 10 weeks. This evening I wrote her a letter & put it inside a Christmas Card. While she is away, I do her work which I really enjoy – refunds, remissions, & out of order licence applications. Today I posted the bulk of our Christmas Cards – 40 at 3d.

20th December 1966 Tuesday

I spent the whole evening compiling the Parish Magazine for **January.** I had excellent response from Mr. Biddle (**Men's Fellowship**). He wrote out a most interesting newsy item for me. I had no response at all from the Young Wives (programme not yet arranged), & I managed a couple of my own quotations.

21st December 1966 Wednesday

Today I received a Christmas Card, signed Joan & Bob Gerard which said: "Very many thanks indeed for the excellent verse. I'm afraid the tree was late this year &,

due to moving our business, it was touch & go as to whether it could be done in time, nonetheless, it represents a special effort by our electrician and gardener."

22ⁿᵈ December 1966 Thursday

Our office Christmas Dinner & Party which we had at "**The Foxhunter**", **Narborough**. Thirty of us went, including **Big Chief** Mr. Blackburn, & also Mr. Colderick who left 6 weeks ago. It was one of the loveliest parties we have ever had, including an official photographer. Reevsie came, & afterwards I spent the night at her house.

23ʳᵈ December 1966 Friday

My scooter mileage today reached 10,000.
I spent a very comfortable night last night at Reevsie's. I weighed myself this morning on her bathroom scales – 9 ½ stone. I am 5′ 8″ tall, 38″ bust & 40″ hip, with brown hair & hazel eyes – teeth a little crooked, with 2 missing – Roman nose – stockings 10 ½ ″ & shoes size 6.

24ᵗʰ December 1966 Saturday

Went to the Cathedral for the Service of Nine Lessons & Carols at 5-15 p.m. I then stayed in town to see "Rudolph" & "Santa" ride down to the Clock Tower from London Road Station. This evening I went carol singing in the village with a small contingent from church, & finally went to midnight Communion, & the church was full.

25ᵗʰ December 1966 Sunday

Went to 11 a.m. service at Ravenstone Church & sat with Auntie Belle, Auntie Ethel from Canada & Don.
Went to 3 p.m. Carol Service at Ravenstone Chapel with Aunt Dos, where I was invited to read the lesson.
Went to Janie Jarman's for tea, & then later went to Auntie Gladys', where we played party games 'til after midnight.

26ᵗʰ December 1966 Monday

Bunting, Mostyn, Michael & Julian arrived in Ravenstone unexpectedly today & joined the family gathering we were holding at Pat's house. This was one of the very rare occasions when all my dad's children & grandchildren were together – Bunting & her 2 sons Michael & Julian, Pat & his daughter Mary, Mum & me.

27ᵗʰ December 1966 Tuesday

This afternoon I went to the Town Hall Theatre at Ashby-de-la-Zouch to see Roy Johnson's seventeenth annual Christmas Pantomime "**Dick Whittington**". For 16 years Roy Johnson's wife Brenda has played leading boy, but for the first time this year she was behind scenes as Production Assistant. Roy Johnson has always been the Dame.

28ᵗʰ December 1966 Wednesday

This evening I read Longfellow's sixty page long story of **Michael Angelo**. Michael Angelo lived from 1475 – 1564. He lived to be an old man. He admired the bronze gate to the baptistery at Florence designed in the year 1400, & through the pen of Longfellow said that these gates were worthy to be the gates of Paradise.

29ᵗʰ December 1966 Thursday

I received the proof of the **January** Parish Magazine from the printers. I found I had omitted one day completely from the "Calendar of Events". I had made one spelling error – **recurrence**, & there were one or two other minor adjustments to be made. I asked Pat to phone for me tomorrow, as he is on holiday.

30ᵗʰ December 1966 Friday

The sky this morning at 8 o'clock as I scootered to work was one of the most beautiful I have ever seen, with all the trees silhouetted in their leafless beauty – and then when I reached the bleak heights of Markfield I encountered black ice on the road & had a nasty fall from my scooter.

31ˢᵗ December 1966 Saturday

This evening Mum & I had a New Year's Eve party at our house. There were 6 of us, including Aunt Dos, Auntie Gladys, Auntie Belle & Auntie Ethel from Canada. We had a most enjoyable evening & played cards (including "**Cheat**", which went very well).
Today I sold my scooter, **2 BAY,** to Auto Supplies, Coalville.

* * *

Quotation

**Time goes, you say? Ah no!
Alas, Time stays, we go.**

(Austin Dobson: The Paradox of Time.)

1967

1ˢᵗ January 1967 Sunday

This is Ruby Year! The fortieth anniversary of the re-hallowing of our Diocese & Cathedral. The exact day is 21ˢᵗ February. Our Ruby Year begins on a Sunday & ends on a Sunday.

This morning I went to 8 a.m. Holy Communion at Ravenstone & this evening I went to the Cathedral to hear the Provost preach.

2ⁿᵈ January 1967 Monday

When I came off my scooter on the icy road last week, a passing motorist very kindly took me to Leicester in his car. I took careful note of his car number & afterwards I wrote & thanked him. Today I had a lovely letter from him in reply which ended: - "Please mind how you go. I may not be there!"

3ʳᵈ January 1967 Tuesday

Today I have been wearing my "Ruby Year" badge which I obtained yesterday from the Provost's secretary. I bought 20 altogether, 1/6d each, to give to my Sunday School children. The Provost says he would like **everyone** to wear this badge during 1967.

The man who assassinated the man, who assassinated President Kennedy, died today.

4ᵗʰ January 1967 Wednesday

Donald Campbell, aged 45, was killed today at Lake Coniston when his jet speedboat – **Bluebird** – somersaulted 50 feet into the air & then sank. The boat had reached a speed of about 300 M.P.H. Campbell was attempting a speed of 300 M.P.H. on water. He already held the record of 400 M.P.H. on land.

5ᵗʰ January 1967 Thursday

Divers have searched all day without success, attempting to recover the body of Donald Campbell, 120 feet below the waters of Lake Coniston. Today he has been hailed as one of the world's pioneers & path-finders, without whom the human race would be standing still – "**They show us all the way to live, & occasionally the way to die**".

6ᵗʰ January 1967 Friday

Did not get to bed until 2-30 a.m. after a late night party given by Auntie Belle. There were 8 of us there – Auntie Belle, Auntie Ethel from Canada, Aunt Dos, Auntie Gladys, Enid, Don, Mum & me. Don showed us coloured slides of his holiday in **Majorca** & also of Peter's wedding; & Aunt Dos showed some of her films.

7ᵗʰ January 1967 Saturday

Last week-end & this week-end it is the turn of Mum & me to do the flowers at Ravenstone Church. I spent £3 on flowers last week & £2 this week. This afternoon I did a very beautiful arrangement for the Sanctuary, using my white pedestal flower vase.

I have written an acrostic for the Parish Magazine – Ravenstone.

Acrostic

Ravenstone - home of the good people here,
Always the place they hold specially dear,
Visitors, friends and relations declare
Everything here is so peaceful and fair.
Nothing is hurried, and when work is done,
Still there is time for enjoyment and fun.
This is a village where people are true,
Open and forthright in all that they do;
Never forgetting the one place alone
Ever they keep in their heart – Ravenstone.

8ᵗʰ January 1967 Sunday

This morning at Sunday School I gave out "Ruby Year" badges to eleven children – Zena Bennett, Carole Harrison, Susan Smith, Susan Parker, Rosemary Green, Ruth Jones, Rhoderick Jones, Stephen Cross, Michael & John Needham & Pat Jarvis.

I am hoping to take the children to the Cathedral during Ruby Year.

9ᵗʰ January 1967 Monday

Today, on the spur of the moment, I bought a new suit – double jersey – a mixture of turquoise & black, with its own turquoise all wool blouse, £7-10/-

This is the first suit I have ever had which is suitable for indoor wear. It should be alright for the office. And it goes very well with my Ruby Year badge!

10ᵗʰ January 1967 Tuesday

Terry has now started his training to be a **Prison Warder**. Yesterday was his first day, & he now has to report to Leicester Prison each morning at 7 a.m.

The prisoners call him "**Mini-Screw**", meaning a small prison warder.

Pat called in this evening & told us of the ambitious proposals for our village institute – library – bar, etc.

11ᵗʰ January 1967 Wednesday

Princess Alexandra came to Leicester today. She opened the new Princess Alexandra wing (£7,000) at the Leicester Red Cross headquarters. She visited blind people at Prebend House & she formally opened the new £2,500,000 Leicester Mercury building in St. George Street, Leicester. The Editor said ......"**A great city & a flourishing county**."

12ᵗʰ January 1967 Thursday

Mr. Sharp today mentioned how impressed he was by the way I had done Muriel's work, & he only wished he could give me another rise! Today also we all received congratulations on our good team-work from Mr. Blackburn, plus a message from the Ministry of Transport thanking our staff for "their fine effort".

13ᵗʰ January 1967 Friday

The Dame of Sark, Dame Sibyl Hathaway, is 83 today. Also Ann Causer's birthday today.

I have worked 1hr. overtime each night this week, but this has been entirely by my own choice. Generally speaking there has been no overtime at all this January, which is a great achievement & the first time in all my 19 Januarys at work.

14th January 1967 Saturday
Today I renewed my acquaintance with Alfred Lord Tennyson, by reading again "**The Holy Grail**", a most beautifully inspired poem, which I first read & studied over 20 years ago when at school. The Holy Grail is "**the cup itself from which our Lord drank at the last sad supper**" & seen in glory by King Arthur's Knights.

15th January 1967 Sunday
Tonight at church, Mabel Woodings gave me a nice newsy letter for the February Parish Magazine from the Mothers' Union, plus a little note which said: "Dear Betty, The Mothers' Union members invite you to their birthday party in the Rector's Room on Wednesday 1st February at 7-30 p.m." It is their 12th birthday.

16th January 1967 Monday
It is now thought possible that Donald Campbell will never be found. He died on the 4th January, & police now say that the chance that his body is trapped on the bottom of Coniston Water after the crash of Bluebird cannot be discounted. Divers have found widely scattered fragments of the speedboat, but that is all.

17th January 1967 Tuesday
The Prime Minister has been to Rome for talks concerning Britain's proposed entry into the Common Market. Today he had audience with the **Pope**.
I arrived in Leicester well before 8 a.m. this morning & would have liked to have gone to
8 a.m. Holy Communion at the Cathedral, but I didn't have the courage to venture in.

18th January 1967 Wednesday
Today I went to the Cathedral for Holy Communion at 1-10 p.m. with Canon Pratt in St. Dunstan's Chapel. I much prefer Holy Communion with Canon Pratt, to Holy Communion with our Rector, because Canon Pratt breaks the bread really audibly & includes everybody fully in the promise of everlasting life.

19th January 1967 Thursday
This evening I recorded "**Mazeppa's Ride**" by Lord Byron – a most impressive poem, which I had the opportunity to read first of all at school.
Today at work, I answered a phone enquiry to be told – "**What a lovely voice!**" I was speaking to a garage proprietor who said he would come & "**See that voice**".

20th January 1967 Friday
Today I obtained 20 tickets for "**Holiday on Ice**", the fabulous world famous ice show which includes **Leicester** in its world wide travels. We are hoping to take a party from Sunday School on 11th February. This year "**Holiday on Ice**" celebrates its 21st birthday. The present show has toured America & Europe.

21st January 1967 Saturday
Diane Woodward called today & brought me a ticket for "**Humpty Dumpty**", to be given by the Bannister dancing academy at the Town Hall, Loughborough on 18th February.
Today I called on Mrs. Pulford, Mrs. Robertson, Mrs. Gage & Mr. Biddle for some Parish Magazine news, but didn't have much success.

22nd January 1967 Sunday
I had a wonderfully rewarding morning with full response from everybody I met. The children were thrilled with the prospect of the Ice Show.
Mr Biddle gave me the Men's Fellowship programme up to 16th May, which to my delight included "**conducted tour of Leicester Cathedral**" 4th April.

23rd January 1967 Monday
This evening we had photographs taken for "**White Horse Inn**". I am in the chorus for this show, so was taken in a large chorus group. Five people have booked through our office for the Saturday night performance – Mrs Hasler, her friend & her husband & Mr & Mrs Dunnett. Today I booked 12 more seats for the Ice Show.

24th January 1967 Tuesday
The Prime Minister, Mr Harold Wilson, & the Foreign Secretary Mr George Brown, have been in **Paris** today for talks with General de Gaulle on Britain's proposed entry into the Common Market. A gorgeous cartoon in the paper today bears the caption "….. **and remind him who won the World Cup**".

25th January 1967 Wednesday - Conversion of St. Paul
Today I went to the Cathedral for Holy Communion at 1-10 p.m. to find that it was being held at the **High Altar** by the Provost himself; so you can imagine what a tremendous effect it had on me. This was the first time I had ever been given Communion by the Provost, & it was good to be on the "Conversion of St. Paul".

Note – Sometimes during the dinner hour I go to Leicester Cathedral for Holy Communion. The Cathedral is quite near to our office.

26th January 1967 Thursday
This evening I was pleased to see again & hear once more the voice of **President Kennedy** in a television "**Portrait of John F. Kennedy**".
It was on January 20th 1961, at the age of 43 (the youngest President ever elected) when he first became President, & he was President for 1,000 days.

27th January 1967 Friday
The **Coalville Times** this week celebrates its 75th birthday, the first issue having appeared on January 22nd 1892. Today 14,000 people buy the paper each week.
The good old **Leicester Mercury** sells 175,000 copies every day, & our Ravenstone Parish magazine 300 each month.

28th January 1967 Saturday
Three American astronauts were burned to death last night in their highly inflammable space-craft at **Cape Kennedy**. They were preparing for a 14 day orbital flight, to start 21st February.
President Kennedy once said: "**We choose to go to the moon in this decade & do the other things, not because they are easy, but because they are hard.**"

29th January 1967 Sunday
The Rector this evening gave a very good sermon on the Epistle of St. Paul to the Philippians, Chap. I, verse 21. **"For to me to live is Christ."** He said that we, like St. Paul, might have Christ as Master, Friend & Saviour – a Master to inspire us, a Friend to love us – a Saviour to deliver us.

30th January 1967 Monday
The **Archbishop of Canterbury** will be preaching at Leicester Cathedral on Tuesday 21st February for the 40th birthday of our Cathedral & Diocese. The Provost, in his newsletter for February, stresses that this will be **"by ticket only"**. "We try to be as fair as possible on these occasions, but some are inevitably disappointed." Maybe me.

31st January 1967 Tuesday
The **Aberfan** disaster fund closes officially today. The fund which was launched last October, has reached £1,570,000 breaking all records. The largest single donation, £43,000, resulted from the appeal fund launched by the Lord Mayor of Leicester. The mammoth task now is spending the money to best advantage.

1st February 1967 Wednesday
Went to the Cathedral at 1-10 p.m. to Holy Communion, which was in St. Dunstan's Chapel with the Succentor. I felt that the Succentor failed to weigh each word sufficiently in the balance, and consequently I was unmoved.
This evening I joined the Ravenstone Mother's Union for a very jolly birthday party.

2nd February 1967 Thursday
The February Parish Magazine is now out containing my acrostic **"Ravenstone"**, plus an invitation to **"Holiday on Ice"** ….."If there are any adults who would like to pay for a ticket & travel with us, please contact Miss Hewes before 5th February." Up to now I have 38 seats booked. I have also been asked at work for 2 more seats for our Amateurs.

3rd February 1967 Friday
This evening Auntie Gladys & I joined the Men's Fellowship for a most interesting talk given by Mr. J. Jones on the history of **Ravenstone**.
Tonight in the Leicester Mercury there is the most wonderful write-up for the Ice Show ……"**Only rarely is a critic enraptured, but I can say, unhesitatingly, here's a show in a thousand."**

4th February 1967 Saturday
Today I bought my new scooter, **KAY 7E**.
I also bought a pair of golden ear-rings in the shape of an anchor for myself, & a pair of golden ear-rings in the shape of a shamrock for Mum.
I wrote a long letter to Bunting, having recently received letters from Bunting, Michael & Julian, replying for Christmas.

Note – I now have a new scooter, KAY 7E. This replaces the scooter I bought in 1962, 2 BAY, which I sold after 10,000 miles. Working in the Motor Licence Office, I can choose a good Registration Number.

5th February 1967 Sunday
Tonight at church the Rector read a long letter from the Bishop in connection with our Ruby Year. This letter was read today in all the 348 churches of our Diocese.
The Rector himself gave one of his best sermons on I Corinthians, Chapter 13 ….."**Faith, Hope, Charity, these three; but the greatest of these is Charity."**

6th February 1967 Monday
I was very upset today at work when I answered the phone to receive a tirade of abuse directed straight at me by one very irate lady who refused to be comforted. There was no such thing as **"What a lovely voice!"** (As on 19th January) This was a full blooded farmer's wife, defending her husband, & demanding a written apology.

7th February 1967 Tuesday
Cassius Clay, who prefers to be known as **Muhammad Ali**, last night retained his title of world heavyweight boxing champion by beating **Ernie Terrell** at the Houston Astrodome, Texas. There was a record crowd there of 37,321 & the fight went the full 15 rounds. This was Clay's 8th successful defence.

8th February 1967 Ash Wednesday
Went to Holy Communion at the Cathedral at 1-10 p.m. with the Provost. The Provost's wife sat at my side in the Canon's stalls.
This evening went to evensong at Ravenstone Church.
Afterwards, Pat, Evelyn & I were invited to the Rectory where we saw coloured slides of Italy, & I fell in love with **Milan** Cathedral.

9th February 1967 Thursday
The beautiful Cathedral of **Milan** has set me off today studying all the inviting holiday brochures. I have set my heart on the Cosmos **"Two Weeks Holiday in Sunny Italy"** – by air from **London** to **Milan** & then visiting **Florence, Rome, Capri, Pompeii, Naples, Assisi, Rimini, Ravenna, Venice** & back to **Milan**.

10th February 1967 Friday
Sylvia (from work) & I today went to Reevsie's for tea. Reevsie expects her baby in about 3 weeks time. All the house spoke of a warm & loving welcome to the new arrival – one bedroom contained the most delightful crib, nappies lay heaped on the bed, & Tony was making a really excellent wardrobe.

11th February 1967 Saturday
This afternoon we went to the **Granby Halls**, Leicester, to see **"Holiday on Ice"**. This was my bus load outing from Sunday School – 24 children & 16 adults. It cost us £9 for the bus & £9 for tickets @ 7/6d for the children. Adults paid 10/- each for their tickets & 5/- bus fare.
I enjoyed organising this outing.

12th February 1967 Sunday
Went to 8 a.m. Holy Communion at Ravenstone & to evensong at the Cathedral. The Provost preached on the temptations of the devil – always there was goodness underneath – e.g. power which gets out of control – healthy love which turns to lust – politics – education – unity turning to division.

13th February 1967 Monday
I cry no more for our old Rector. I miss his beautiful prayers & blessings, but I appreciate the sincere & cheeky ways of our new Rector, & of course I am most influenced by the Provost. Last night in the Cathedral, the Provost looked straight at me with such a look, I almost melted into tears.

14th February 1967 Tuesday
This evening I helped Mr. Saunders with the member's bookings for "**White Horse Inn**". This usually is Enid's job, but I did it this year in her place, as she now takes a **Keep Fit** class every Tuesday. I was not so efficient as Enid, & we finished 18/6d short, which was most discouraging.

15th February 1967 Wednesday
Today I am 13,000 days old!!!
Went to the Cathedral for Holy Communion at 1-10 p.m. with Canon Gundry in St. Dunstan's Chapel. Went to Lent evensong at Ravenstone, where the Rector is giving a series of talks on the "Divine Invitations". Today it was "**Come ye yourselves apart** …….. **and rest awhile.**"

16th February 1967 Thursday
John Saunders, who was married last May, had a baby daughter today. He was not at Amateur's rehearsal tonight, but the news came through his Mum, who heard at 9-45p.m.
We had a most enjoyable rehearsal tonight & managed to go all through the whole show – "**White Horse Inn**", which starts 7th March.

17th February 1967 Friday
My self appointed piano lessons last April & May eventually came to nothing, but today I have found a very tempting offer in the paper : "**Now you can play good rhythm piano in just 30 days!**" ….. the cost of the whole course is just 30/- complete. If you cannot play popular tunes in 30 days, money refunded.

18th February 1967 Saturday
This afternoon I went to Loughborough Town Hall to see "**Humpty Dumpty**" presented by the **Bannister Academy**. I went mainly to see Diane Woodward dance, but who should I come across in the audience but my old school pal **Marie Findley**. It was good to see her again.

19th February 1967 Sunday
This evening we had a most unexpected visit from a long lost cousin of Mum's – **John Bailey** & his wife. They have recently bought a bungalow at Markfield & invited us to visit them some time. This evening I had planned to prepare the March Parish Magazine so this unexpected visitor kept me up till 1 a.m.

Note – Mum's long lost cousin - Johnty.

20th February 1967 Monday
Tomorrow is the "**Great Service of Thanksgiving in the Cathedral**" at 7-45 p.m., at which the **Archbishop of Canterbury** will preside. I have looked forward to this for months. I so gladly & readily accepted the invitation to be a "**Life Member**", but for this great occasion, I am not invited, & I feel very hurt indeed.

21st February 1967 Tuesday
The Bishop of Leicester has requested that all the church bells in our Diocese shall be rung this evening, while the Archbishop of Canterbury is here for our **Ruby Year**. I heard the bells of Leicester Cathedral, & wept because I was not invited. I came to Ravenstone & heard our bells doing their best.

22nd February 1967 Wednesday
I read in the paper that there were **1300** in the congregation at the Cathedral last night. Today I was one of **13** in the congregation at the Cathedral for Holy Communion at 1-10 p.m., with my beloved Provost.
This evening I saw "**How to Succeed in Business without really Trying**", a most enjoyable modern musical at "**Pex**".

23rd February 1967 Thursday
This morning I had a lift into work with Mr. Whitmore. Muriel returned to work today after her operation which was 12th October last year.
(Miss Rippon's birthday).
This evening we had a most enjoyable rehearsal for "**White Horse Inn**" – a show which has everything – humour – pathos – rich music etc.
(Miss Rippon's birthday today – not October!)

24th February 1967 Friday
Today at work I took up residence on the counter as Cashier No.2. I had exactly 77 customers & took over £1,000.
Mr. Sharp showed us the drawing board plans of our new office which promises to be really super. This is thanks to Mr. Sharp who likes nothing but the best – a man after my own heart!

25th February 1967 Saturday
For the March Parish Magazine I wrote an article "**For the Children**", incorporating the special family service for Mothering Sunday – March 5th, and quoting from the Bible how Jesus cared for his mother while he was dying on the Cross, mentioning also the meaning of Maundy Thursday. I now wonder whether I was authorised to do so!

26th February 1967 Sunday
The Rector tonight in his sermon spoke of the gentleness of Christ: not the gentleness of weakness, but true gentleness where there was power to crush. It reminded me of the gentleness of a lion when all its mighty strength was under perfect control – as Robert Browning wrote: - "**So the all great were the all loving too.**"

27th February 1967 Monday
My millionaire who licensed his **Rolls Royce** on February 21st last year was in the office again today. I quite enjoy handing him his licence! He treats all women with great suspicion, but I gave him a very special look. I also took a particular fancy to a certain garage man, but he remained quite aloof.

Note – I encounter Brian Lamming, a car-salesman who comes regularly to license new cars. Unlike John

Dolman, he captures my heart completely, without even trying. In fact, I fall for him hook, line & sinker, while he remains completely unmoved.

28th February 1967 Tuesday

You will remember that this time last year I was relief cashier to Miss Gazzard with the busiest counter I had yet encountered. Well today we had another such counter. It was much too busy for my liking. The queue seemed endless all day long.

Tonight I joined the **Men's Fellowship** for "**Journey to New Zealand.**"

O.K. = "Orl Korrect" (American)
1st March 1967 Wednesday

I am on holiday from work from today until 13th March. I had lunch today at the Chinese Restaurant in Coalville. This evening went to Lent evensong in Ravenstone Church where the Rector continued with his addresses on the "**Divine Invitations**". Today: "**Come – follow me.**" Last week I missed "**Come and see.**"

2nd March 1967 Thursday

Today we had our costumes for "**White Horse Inn**". I have 2 different national costume dresses which are very pretty, plus a costume for "**Mayor's Secretary**", a very small comedy part calling for Red Bloomers, plus a costume for "**Courier**", another small part where I am in uniform. (Formerly Herts. Constabulary).

3rd March 1967 Friday

Cathedral News Letter – No. 38. The Provost announces that he is to lead a pilgrimage to the Holy Land in 1968 ….. "We start on April 17th 1968, & the tour lasts 15 days. My wife hopes to accompany me, & we hope that there are 35 of you who will join us. The cost will be something like 115 guineas." You know how much I would like to go!

4th March 1967 Saturday

Today I began my piano lessons under the "Sutra System of Metric Music". I will let you know how I progress!

Also today I launched out on a course of Postal Instruction for the Local Government Clerical Exam - £9-5/- This exam automatically gives a salary increase of £80 if I pass.

5th March 1967 Sunday

Mothering Sunday! Went to 8 a.m. Holy Communion, then we had our family service at
11 a.m. Ruth Jones read the first lesson & I read the second.

This afternoon we had our full dress rehearsal for "White Horse Inn" & were there 'til nearly 7 p.m. Having such a variety of parts I found it most interesting.

6th March 1967 Monday

Final rehearsal for "**White Horse Inn**". We did not finish until 11-30 p.m.! Our dear old Musical Director Frank Newman came to watch. He stayed right to the end & we watched him make his sad journey home. He had great difficulty getting his breath & he told me sometimes he wishes he might die.

7th March 1967 Tuesday

Walsom. *To Pat and Tony, a daughter, March 7th. Thanking all at Bond Street.*

To Reevsie a baby daughter! She did so want a girl in preference to a boy.

I learned the great news only from the Leicester Mercury this evening, so I wrote post haste to wish this baby "**A Very Happy Birth Day.**"

8th March 1967 Wednesday

Went to Leicester this morning for a dentist appointment at 10-15 a.m.

I then called at the office for elevenses, & was informed that Reevsie had an 8 lb baby, to be named **Joanne**. I stayed in Leicester for Holy Communion at the Cathedral at 1-10 p.m. with Canon Pratt in St. Dunstan's Chapel.

9th March 1967 Thursday

Today I bought a new dress for our Amateur's Dinner Dance on 17th March. It was from Coalville Co-op - £5-2s-11d, plain navy with a very pretty neckline trimmed with spotted white.

Leicester City football team, this year as well as last, have been knocked out of the F. A. Cup by Manchester City.

10th March 1967 Friday

Aunt Dos has been so impressed by our central heating system, that she now has had central heating installed in her bungalow – in use today for the first time.

This morning I spent an hour or so at Ravenstone Rectory where I met the Rector of Coleorton. This afternoon I gathered pussy willow in lovely sunshine & wind.

11th March 1967 Saturday

Last night of "**White Horse Inn**" & for me the end of a really wonderful week.

The show has gone so well & we all have enjoyed it thoroughly. After a joyful carefree week, I now have the dreary prospect of studying for the Local Government Clerical Exam, which I have chosen to undertake!

12th March 1967 Sunday

To **Marjorie Hayes** a son! (Born yesterday)   *Note – A baby son named Ian.*

Today I started my studies for the Clerical Exam. I have 3 subjects – Local Government – Central Government – English Language. I am beginning with Local Government, & I am constantly reminded of our hilarious mock council meeting on stage this last week.

13th March 1967 Monday

Tonight we had a very pleasant get-together at the Amateur's, where we arranged to visit **Staunton Harold** on 4th April to sing songs from "**White Horse Inn**". Much as I would love to go, I prefer to keep my prior engagement for that date: "**Conducted Tour of Leicester Cathedral**", arranged since 22nd January.

14th March 1967 Tuesday

Auntie Ethel will be flying home to Canada on Thursday this week. Tomorrow there is to be a farewell party at Don's, to which we are all invited.

Mum & I have been kept well entertained this evening by a hilarious book from the library called: "**The Hills is Lonely**", by **Lillian Beckwith**, telling of life in the Hebrides.

15th March 1967 Wednesday
Went to the Cathedral for Holy Communion at 1-10 p.m. with the Succentor.
This evening 24 of us assembled at Don's for Auntie Ethel's farewell party. I wore my smart new dress which I bought last week.
As well as studying "Local Government", I am now studying "**English Language**", which is a favourite subject of mine.

16th March 1967 Thursday
This evening Mum & I went with Aunt Dos & her lodger – **Lesley** – to the pictures at Coalville to see the epic film, by **Cecil B. de Mille**, "**The Ten Commandments**". It lasted nearly 4 hours, but we enjoyed it very much. The scene where the Children of Israel moved out of Egypt was really great, & full of lively detail.

17th March 1967 Friday
St. Patrick's Day! And my dad's birthday. Had he lived he would be 78 years old today.
We had our Amateur's Annual Dinner Dance tonight. While I was dancing with Don, we came side by side with the Chairman, **Mr. Clamp**, an old friend of my dad's & he said: "Your dad's birthday today!"

18th March 1967 Saturday
Clocks are put forward 1 hour tonight! Clocks are due to be put back 1 hour on 29th October, but there is talk of keeping our time 1 hour forward as British Summer Time all the year round, to agree with the continent.
Today I completed a competition stating what I name my cat & why. My cat's name? **Puskas!**

19th March 1967 Palm Sunday
I spent most of the day preparing the Parish Magazine for April. As I received no complaints about last month's Editorial, I wrote a further article – **for the children** – and described the work of **Mrs. Alexander**, who wrote "**All Things Bright and Beautiful**", "**Once in Royal David's City**" etc.

20th March 1967 Monday
Today at work we each received a detailed account of the **New County Hall**, which is now in the process of being built. It is expected to be ready by **November** this year. We had a questionnaire to complete in connection with travelling, mid-day meals etc. & were asked what shop we would like.

21st March 1967 Tuesday
Today I met Joanne, Reevsie's adorable baby daughter – 2 weeks old today!
Today I also met the Reverend **Best**, Rector of Sibson, who designed the Ruby Year Badge which I was proudly wearing. He came into our office to renew his car licence but he remained completely apart & apparently un-moved.

22nd March 1967 Wednesday
Went to Holy Communion at the Cathedral at 1-10 p.m. with **Canon Gundry**. Being the Wednesday before **Easter**, the Gospel for the day was exceptionally long, & it was a joy to hear it read by **Canon Gundry**, who has an excellent voice, & a perfect understanding of the scriptures. This gospel was **Holy Communion** itself expounded.

23rd March 1967 Thursday
Today I met the Garage Proprietor who thought I had a lovely voice (see January 19th). However, my favourite customer remains "a certain garage man" (see February 27th).
He brings licences regularly from "**Federated Garages, Market Harborough**." He neither speaks to me, nor even smiles, but I like him.

24th March 1967 Good Friday
Today I wrote to **Scarborough**, as our choice for this year's summer holiday.
This evening we had a church service at 7-30 p.m.
Last Saturday the tanker **Torrey Canyon**, carrying 25 million gallons of crude oil ripped into the Seven Stones reef off the **Scilly Isles**, & now the marathon task is keeping Cornish beaches oil-free.

25th March 1967 Saturday
I spent much of the day trying to write a poem for our church magazine. Our church at the moment is in the process of having its spire restored: - "**Sliced & severed – like an oast house, stood our church with uncapped spire, when the soaring bells of Easter thrilled to send their message higher ....**"

26th March 1967 Easter Sunday
This evening I went to the Cathedral where the Provost preached on "**Go to work on an egg!**" a well known national advertisement. He "grappled" with the subject of the resurrection, and likened the empty tomb to an empty eggshell. He felt that the gospel for today falls very short in showing only the empty tomb.

27th March 1967 Easter Monday
The 61,263 ton tanker **Torrey Canyon**, fast on Seven Stones reef for more than a week, last night split in two. Millions more gallons of oil poured out, & it is feared the beaches of Cornwall may be polluted for at least 2 years. Sea birds are dying & detergents in great quantities are threatening fish etc.

28th March 1967 Tuesday
As a climax for the Easter holiday today we had **snow – sleet – hail – thunder & lightening!** It has not been fit to go out either yesterday or today.
This afternoon at 4 p.m., the stricken tanker, **Torrey Canyon**, still partly afloat with oil continuously pouring from her, was completely blown up by forty-two 1,000 lb bombs.

29th March 1967 Wednesday
Went to the Cathedral for Holy Communion at 1-10 p.m. with **Canon Pratt**. There were only 7 of us in the congregation. Afterwards I had a good look round at the really beautiful flower arrangements there since **Easter**

Sunday. It was almost like a miniature flower festival. I was much impressed.

30th March 1967 Thursday
Pay day today, & with a bag full of money I could not resist the temptation to buy a book I happened to come across in Smith's book shop. Price 50/- it was called "**Benham's Book of Quotations**" containing thousands of proverbs, phrases, maxims & sayings from all sources: - so look out for one or two now in this diary!

31st March 1967 Friday
Today we had a colossal counter at work, but I thoroughly enjoyed it.
I balanced perfectly at the end of it all – cheques £2,795 & cash £1,106.
I had over 200 customers, including one man who said: "**Thank you for being so patient**", & also my favourite customer from "Federated Garages".

1st April 1967 Saturday
Today I spent many hours with my new book: - "**Benham's Book of Quotations**". Do you like this one? "**That's what I want – ready wit. I must get some ready.**"
It is now 4 weeks exactly since I began my piano lessons (play the piano in 30 days), I do not practise sufficiently, so am not a Ready Pianist!

2nd April 1967 Sunday
As on 18th April 1965 I have again written up my diary for today in the wrong place. (Please see over). This then in retrospect is for tomorrow.
We try out our new lawn-mower, £16-5/- & find it rather heavy going. It is a "**Flexa**" – supposed to cut grass either ½" or 12" long; with super blades.

3rd April 1967 Monday
I learned this evening, from a lay reader at our church, the origin of the word "**sincere**". Dating back to the days of the Roman Villa, the man engaged in the building of so fine a marble edifice, must sign a certificate that all was indeed unadulterated marble – without wax – "**sine cerus**".

4th April 1967 Tuesday
Cathedral News-letter No. 39. The chief message this month is "**Ride forth Singing**".
It was with great joy that we went this evening for our conducted tour of Leicester Cathedral. There were 21 of us from Ravenstone & we were escorted & conducted entirely by my beloved **Provost**.

5th April 1967 Wednesday
Went to Holy Communion at 1-10 p.m. at the Cathedral in **St. Dunstan's Chapel** with the **Provost**.
Mary Moore arrived yesterday & is staying with Mum & me until next Monday. Her friend Edith Whittaker from Derby came for tea today.
The Lincoln Handicap was won by **Ben Novus**.

6th April 1967 Thursday
Next Thursday we have the County Council elections & I have been appointed **Poll Clerk** at Ravenstone School with a **Mr. Hodges** whom I have never met.

Today a whole tribe of us from the County Offices trooped to the **County Rooms** to be "sworn" before a Justice of the Peace.

7th April 1967 Friday
Mr. Lammiman at work retired yesterday.
Today several friends & acquaintants of Mary Moore's called at our house – her old school pal **Molly Taylor** – her sister-in-law **Veronica** – **Aunt Dos**. Mary also visited **Mrs. Inwood** – **Florrie Moore** – **Mary Causton** & tomorrow is lunching with **Mrs. Lesley**.

8th April 1967 Saturday
This afternoon on television I watched **Foinavon**, 100-1, win the **Grand National**. **Foinavon** was so far behind at the 23rd fence (third from last), that when all those in front became involved in a gigantic pile up, he alone was able to find a clear jump & make a 200 yard lead!

9th April 1967 Sunday
Our Rector is on holiday at the moment, staying with his daughter & family in **Germany**.
Mary Moore who is on holiday with us returns home tomorrow. Today she had lunch & tea with **Molly** who afterwards brought her home.
We had a phone call from Willoughby to say Mum's Aunt Mary had had a fall.

10th April 1967 Monday
Today it has been like mid-winter. I went to work on the bus.
Enid & I have tried without success to book our holiday this year at **Scarborough**. We have now written to the N.A.L.G.O. holiday camp at **Cayton Bay**, which lies about 3 miles south of Scarborough. We both belong to N.A.L.G.O.

11th April 1967 Tuesday
Budget Day, but nothing of consequence to report.
This evening Mum went with a bus load from Ashby to see the Black & White Minstrels at Coventry. I sat up until well after midnight writing an account of our visit to the Cathedral for the May Parish Magazine. Another cold wintry day.

12th April 1967 Wednesday
Went to the Cathedral for Holy Communion at 1-10 p.m. with Canon Pratt in St. Dunstan's Chapel.
My favourite customer was in the office today, & from his signature I worked out that he is **Brian Lamming**, 90, St. Mary's Road, Market Harborough, & he lives with **Lawrence Webb** & **Eileen Webb**.

13th April 1967 Thursday
County Council Election Day! I was **Poll Clerk** at **Ravenstone** with **Mr. Hodges** as **Presiding Officer**. This was my first meeting with Mr. Hodges & I liked him well.
We had 950 on our list of voters, but less than half voted.
We were No. 5 of the 8 Polling Stations in the Heather division.

14th April 1967 Friday
I had a day's holiday from work today & had my first

grass cutting session of the year at **St. Mary's Church**, Snibston. My new **"Flexa"** lawn mower proved its worth & did a really grand job.

Results of yesterday's elections show a nation-wide swing to Conservatives – even Heather had a Conservative win.

15th April 1967 Saturday
Today I received a printed letter from the Provost dated March 1967 ....At the Great Service of Thanksgiving on 21st February we celebrated the Fortieth Anniversary of the hallowing of the Cathedral. It would, however, be a pleasant addition to our Ruby Year if all closely connected with the Cathedral met for a Cathedral Dinner 2nd May ......

16th April 1967 Sunday
A really lovely day. I scootered to Ashby this morning to meet Mum from night duty.

I spent many hours with my Book of Quotations. **"A thing of beauty is a joy for ever: its loveliness increases; it will never pass into nothingness; but still will keep a bower quiet for us, & a sleep full of sweet dreams." Keats.**

17th April 1967 Monday
Reevsie came into the office this morning carrying her beautiful sleeping baby – 6 weeks old. I sat & held the beautiful sleeping baby for about 10 minutes. Reevsie, too, looked radiantly beautiful.

England Goal-Keeper Gordon Banks today signed a £55,000 transfer from Leicester City to **Stoke**.

18th April 1967 Tuesday
Brian Lamming, my favourite customer, came into the office today. Though he spoke never a word, my heart melted.

This morning, I was telling Miss Gazzard that **Coalville Post Office** was surely the worst at sending their forms to us in any order, when a customer volunteered to put this matter right.

19th April 1967 Wednesday
Went to the Cathedral for Holy Communion at 1-10 p.m. with the Succentor in St. Dunstan's Chapel. I appreciated the Succentor more than I did before, because he did deal with each communicant as a complete person, & did not leave anybody with half a message, as happens so often.

20th April 1967 Thursday
We had a circular at work today from the **Computer Licensing Organisation Branch**, Minister of Transport, St. Christopher House, S.E. 1, to the effect that all motor licence work is to be concentrated in one office to be built at **Swansea**, staffed by 2,500, & this will be ready by 1972.

21st April 1967 Friday
Brian Lamming came into the office today & as usual chose to ignore me completely. You would really wonder why I care for him at all, but I do. (And I know that on 2nd November 1965 he was fined £40, or 3 months imprisonment, for driving under the influence of drink, & £10 for dangerous driving.)

22nd April 1967 Saturday
On March 4th I launched out on a course of Postal Instruction for the Clerical Exam. Today I wrote to say: **"It has now been established that I do not require this examination ....."** which means the dreary mundane subjects of **Local** and **Central Government** cannot compare with love & literature.

23rd April 1967 Sunday
Ruth Jones & **Rosemary Green** today officially left Sunday School. My poor old Sunday School class is now reduced to about 6 children. The whole Sunday School is not much more than 20 & it used to be well over 100. Due to the lack of support we are having no Sunday School Anniversary this year.

24th April 1967 Monday
Vladimir Komarov, 40 year old Soviet Cosmonaut, was killed today – the first astronaut to die in flight. He was returning to Earth when his parachute failed to open properly. He has been awarded the **Gold Star of Hero of the Soviet Union**, the country's highest award, & a statue of him will be built.

25th April 1967 Tuesday
President Johnson has sent this telegram to Moscow: "The death of Komarov is a tragedy in which all nations share. Like three American astronauts who lost their lives recently, this distinguished space pioneer died in the cause of science, & in the eternal spirit of human adventure ...." The American astronauts died 27th January 1967.

26th April 1967 Wednesday
Today I had a letter from the **Rapid Results College** saying "I am prepared to make an allowance towards any alternative tuition you may wish to undertake ....."
In my Book of Quotations it says: "**Love needs no teaching**" - (Raleigh 1618).
It is, however, most frustrating loving my favourite customer.

27th April 1967 Thursday
Miss Gazzard is on holiday this week, so I have changed my dinner hour. This meant I could not go to the Cathedral yesterday for Holy Communion at 1-10 p.m.
Today, while I was out at dinner, in came a licence application from **Federated Garages**, brought presumably by my beloved.

28th April 1967 Friday
We had a monstrous counter today at work. I had over 200 customers (including my beloved)
I took over £1,000 in cash & over £4,000 in cheques. With Miss Gazzard on holiday I was in charge of the grand final balance, which came to well over £3,000 to be put up for the bank.

29th April 1967 Saturday
Today I did a competition which I found in the W.I. monthly magazine "Home & Country" Sussex comes on the scene this month, with the opening of the **Brighton Festival**, so let us have some pleasant Sussex Memories in not more than 150 words. I told of my visit to Battle on the 6th day of the 6th month '66.

30th April 1967 Sunday

Tonight I went to **Leicester Cathedral** for the **Leicester Christian Industrial Council Annual Service**, where the preacher was **The Right Reverend Mervyn Armstrong** (former **Provost** of Leicester). He could not compare with my beloved Provost.

As **Samuel Pepys** once wrote: **A good, honest & painful sermon.**

1st May 1967 Monday

I am on holiday for a couple of days.

This morning I scootered to Leicester & went on a shopping spree. I bought a pair of new shoes – flat brown leather - £5-9s-9d from Joshua Robson & a pair of lilac sheets & pillow cases - £3-1s-9d from Lewis's.

2nd May 1967 Tuesday

Much as I would love to have gone to the **Cathedral Ruby Year Dinner** at the **Grand Hotel**, Leicester; having no partner, I went instead with the **Ravenstone Men's Fellowship** to Staunton Harold reservoir, & afterwards to **Dennis Collier's** pub at Coleorton, where we had a grand time.

3rd May 1967 Wednesday

Went to the Cathedral for Holy Communion at 1-10 p.m. with **Canon Pratt**.

This evening with the help of my Book of Quotations, I wrote a letter to the Leicester Mercury, prompted by: "An American pays £190,000 for a picture, while people starve & **Oxfam** calls out for money. Would someone explain?"

4th May 1967 Thursday

My beloved was in the office today. He did not speak to me, but he did not ignore me completely.

I had a letter from Bunting which began: - "**Sister Dear**" ….& proceeded to invite me to spend a few days with her in **Malvern** from June 9th, but I have booked my holiday with Enid for then.

5th May 1967 Friday

"Impact", the County Offices monthly magazine which came into being 9th December 1966, has come to an abrupt end. Because of some of the articles which were published, certain members of the council were most offended, & it has therefore "**been found necessary to stop further publication of Impact.**"

6th May 1967 Saturday

Cathedral News-letter No. 40! It starts: "I wonder if you've heard of **Walter Wynkeburne**? Probably not. He was, of course, before your time. In fact he was hanged in Leicester in 1363 for some crime or other, so he probably wasn't your sort ….." and ends "Every blessing to you in this merry, merry month of May!"

7th May 1967 Sunday

The time has come round again to "**Vote for Alf Hall - your Independent Candidate**" (see 28th April 1964) Polling day is tomorrow. Today I visited **Hall Brothers** in connection with a duplicate Registration Book they require, & was given a glass of sherry by **Alf**.

This morning at Sunday School we had no key & had to force the door open.

8th May 1967 Monday

The Leicester Mercury printed my letter – put a frill round it - & gave it a heading: -

"Enough to go round, but...

An American pays £190,000 for a picture, while people starve and Oxfam calls out for money. Would someone explain, a reader asks.

The explanation is very simple. There is more than enough money in this world to feed all the hungry and still have bread enough and to spare. What then should be neglected? Art? Never! Science? Never! Sport? Cigarettes? Gambling? Wine, women and song? Name what you will. We, who have been given heads to make money, and hearts to spend money, are free to choose. The American Ella Wilcox best described the World's Needs as follows:

So many gods, so many creeds,
So many paths, that wind and wind,
While just the art of being kind
Is all the sad world needs."

ART LOVER

Tonight the 16 churches of our Deanery gathered at Coalville Park for a Ruby Year celebration of open air Holy Communion. The Bishop was there and my beloved Provost, but I didn't like Holy Communion mass produced.

9th May 1967 Tuesday

Yesterday I voted for **Alf Hall** in the Ashby Rural Council election & I am pleased to say he was successful. **Mr Fern** topped the poll with 464 votes – then **Alf Hall** 316 votes.

They defeated **Ray Hextall** 311 votes & **Valerie Pulford** 90 votes.

10th May 1967 Wednesday

A perfectly beautiful day. I was woken by the **Dawn Chorus** & the sun shone all day long. Went to the Cathedral for Holy Communion at 1-10 p.m. with my beloved Provost.

I saw my favourite customer for a few seconds, but he chose to ignore me, & as I love him so very dearly, I was reduced to tears.

11th May 1967 Thursday

My favourite customer was in the office today, & although I love him & love him & love him, his love for me appears to be non-existent. I will therefore trouble you no further with details of my encounters with him, unless he returns my love.

You may like to know: "**The love which is fostered by despair is long-lasting.**" Ovid.

12th May 1967 Friday

Tomorrow there is to be a sale of old furniture – books – clothing etc. gathered from our village in aid of Ravenstone Institute. Mum & I have had a terrific clear out of old pictures & old books which we have harboured for years. As a matter of fact the Bible I now use says: "**Elizabeth Bailey, December 22nd 1867.**"

13th May 1967 Saturday

Last month (11th April) I wrote an account of our visit to

Leicester Cathedral for the May Parish Magazine. As there was so much other material for the May Magazine it did not get included. Today I have written another article, for the June Magazine, dealing with the history of our diocese – "**This is Ruby Year.**"

14ᵗʰ May 1967 Whit Sunday

Went to the Cathedral for **Evensong** where the preacher was the **Bishop** – a most uplifting service, with so many beautifully spoken words which sank deep into my heart. Best of all I enjoyed hearing **Canon Gundry** read the 2ⁿᵈ lesson – **Romans, Chapter 8**, containing verse 28, my dad's favourite verse.

15ᵗʰ May 1967 Monday

Although yesterday was **Whit Sunday**, we are not having the official **Whit Monday & Tuesday** holiday for another fortnight. However, I have a couple of day's holiday now, just to finish up my holiday for the year.
This evening Aunt Dos, Auntie Belle, Lesley the lodger & I went to **St. David's Broomleys** flower festival.

16ᵗʰ May 1967 Tuesday

This evening I went with Dennis Collier & his wife to the Induction of the Reverend Alan Thomas Green at **Oaks in Charnwood**. This lovely church, in the heart of **Charnwood Forest**, where Barrie Edwards was married 9ᵗʰ April 1966, was filled to capacity & we sat in the belfry. The Bishop of Leicester excelled himself in his Address.

17ᵗʰ May 1967 Wednesday

Went to the Cathedral for Holy Communion at 1-10 p.m. with **Canon Pratt**. This evening went to a coffee evening given by Auntie Belle for the Ravenstone **Darby & Joan**.
The new **Littlewood's** store in the centre of Leicester was officially opened today. It cost £450,000 to build.

18ᵗʰ May 1967 Thursday

Enid & I, having been accepted at N.A.L.G.O.'s **Cayton Bay Holiday Centre**, Scarborough, today received further details. Most of all I liked: "**Camp fire is in a wonderful fairy-lit glade, in a beautiful woodland setting, where you all can let yourselves go in the good old camp-fire songs.**"

19ᵗʰ May 1967 Friday

Miss Gazzard is on holiday at present, so I am enjoying being in charge of the counter. Being the middle of the month the counter is not too busy. I was on the **Driving Licence** counter for 14 years, but prefer the **Vehicle Licence** counter, even though at the moment it entails great emotional strain.

20ᵗʰ May 1967 Saturday

Cup Final Day! Spurs beat **Chelsea 2-1**. The Cup was presented this year by **H.R.H. the Duke of Kent**.
I spent 3 hours this morning grass cutting all round little St. Mary's Church, Snibston.
This evening we played cards until after 1 a.m. – Auntie Gladys – Enid – David – Irene & me.
To **Lesley Hewes** a baby daughter.

21ˢᵗ May 1967 Trinity Sunday

Our Rector this evening gave the best **Trinity Sunday** sermon I have ever heard. He told of the 3 in one God who stamped everything he made with his 3 in one trade mark. **Heaven, Earth & Sea – Animal, Vegetable & Mineral – Body, Mind & Spirit – Faith, Hope & Love, etc. etc.**

22ⁿᵈ May 1967 Monday

I spent the whole evening typing out the contents of our June Parish Magazine to send to the **printers**. Our magazine takes 4 foolscap pages of typing. Page 1 = Poem, Calendar for the month & little verse. Page 2 = Prayer & Rector's letter. Page 3 = Article by Editress, Mother's Union News, flower rota. Page 4 = Baptisms etc. Sidesmen's rota & hymn.

23ʳᵈ May 1967 Tuesday

I had a really wonderful day at work today. I thoroughly enjoyed being in full command of the counter – not too busy, & time to give each customer extra special attention.
So it was today, after 3 months of silent loving, my own beloved **Brian Lamming** & I spoke to each other.

24ᵗʰ May 1967 Wednesday

Went to the Cathedral for Holy Communion at 1-10p.m. with the Succentor. Throughout the service there were great claps of thunder & the rain beat down on the roof like a cloud-burst. It was 2 weeks ago that we had such a perfectly beautiful day & the Provost gave thanks for "**This glorious day.**"

25ᵗʰ May 1967 Thursday

Ralph at work, who is relief cashier at the moment while Miss Gazzard is on holiday, told me today of the unspoken love which passes between him & the girl from "**Central Garages**". Our office at **14, Friar Lane, Leicester** has certainly played its full part in bringing lovers together.

26ᵗʰ May 1967 Friday

Leicester's new Lord Mayor is Alderman Sir Mark Henig (elected yesterday). He is "**a gay conversationalist, dominant in character, forceful in debate, versatile in talents & unselfish in service to this city.**" In the New Year's Honours List of 1965 he was knighted for his political & public services to the city.

27ᵗʰ May 1967 Saturday

Today is the beginning of the "**Spring Bank Holiday 1967**".
Pat, Evelyn & Aunt Dos have made their annual pilgrimage to see Auntie Cis at Skegness, so I am sleeping in the house alone tonight.
This evening Auntie Gladys, Enid & I went to the Little Theatre, Leicester, to see John Saunders in "**The Gazebo**".

28ᵗʰ May 1967 Sunday

On August 27ᵗʰ 1966, **Sir Francis Chichester** left **Plymouth** in **Gipsy Moth IV** to sail alone round the world. He arrived in **Sydney** in 107 days – December 12ᵗʰ. On January 29ᵗʰ this year he sailed from **Sydney**, &

after 119 days, arrived this evening at **Plymouth**.

It was in August 1573 when **Sir Francis Drake** returned.

29ᵗʰ May 1967 Monday

On March 14ᵗʰ Mum & I enjoyed reading "**The Hills is Lonely**" by **Lillian Beckwith**. Today we have equally enjoyed reading her second book "**The Sea for Breakfast**" another hilarious story of life in the wild **Hebrides**.

Today is the birthday of our Rector, the Revd. Matthew Rice Lewis.

30ᵗʰ May 1967 Tuesday

The book of quotations I bought on March 30ᵗʰ has given me many hours of pleasure. I think perhaps the quotations of **Ovid** have impressed me most. Today I have compiled a list of my favourite quotations by **Ovid**, including – "**Live righteously; you shall die righteously. Cherish religion.**"

31ˢᵗ May 1967 Wednesday

Went to the Cathedral for Holy Communion at 1-10 p.m. with **Canon Gundry**, & who better than Canon Gundry could have read that wonderful **Epistle for the 1ˢᵗ Sunday after Trinity**, whose main theme is "**Love**" - Beloved, let us love one another: for love is of God ...... God is love ......

1ˢᵗ June 1967 Thursday

Enid & I are looking forward to our holiday which begins 3ʳᵈ June, but now Enid has quite unexpectedly developed **Shingles**! However, she has no pain & feels perfectly fit, so the Doctor says she may go on holiday, but may neither swim nor sun-bathe! And Enid does enjoy swimming.

2ⁿᵈ June 1967 Friday

Ralph & I had a monstrous counter today, but each of us had the satisfaction of serving our own dearest loved customer.

Romance continues to thrive in our office. **Geoff & Jane** are now firmly established in their courtship. **Little Tommy** goes out with **Maz**, & **Eric & Sherry** have fallen for each other.

3ʳᵈ June 1967 Saturday

Enid & I arrived at **Cayton Bay**, Scarborough, for our holiday at the N.A.L.G.O. holiday centre. We stopped for lunch on the way at **York** & were much impressed with this lovely ancient city. We visited **York Minster** & were greatly inspired by its very height.

(It took 250 years to build!)

4ᵗʰ June 1967 Sunday

This morning Enid & I went to the Parish Church in Scarborough (St. Martin on the Hill) for Matins & Holy Communion.

This afternoon I walked into Scarborough – a 40 minute walk, & this evening we motored 20 miles to **Whitby**. Best of all from 10-30 to 11-30p.m. we enjoyed "**Twilight Hour**" non-stop community hymns.

5ᵗʰ June 1967 Monday

The day started with Camp group photos, followed by

"**Cayton Olympics**" at which I thoroughly enjoyed being "**Clerk of the Course**" writing down the names of all the winners. This evening we had a jolly session of Folk Dancing, followed by dancing for all, & "**Captain's Capers**" where I fell for the Captain!

6ᵗʰ June 1967 Tuesday

The Captain "**Ricky**" & I continue to regard each other with fond admiration – but nothing more serious than that.

This evening we all enjoyed "**A night at the races**" in the ball-room, followed by "**Camp-fire sing song**" in the fairy-lit glade. Visited **Filey** this afternoon & sun-bathed.

7ᵗʰ June 1967 Wednesday

This morning we visited **Flamborough Head** & **Bridlington**.

All this week it is the Scarborough Benelux Festival, & this afternoon we watched the most excellent carnival procession.

This evening we went to the impressive & vast open-air theatre where there was community singing followed by Festival Gala.

8ᵗʰ June 1967 Thursday

This morning I not only heard the **Dawn Chorus**, but I saw the full glory of dawn break across this beautiful bay, just south of **Scarborough**.

This evening we had our camp concert, & I thoroughly enjoyed singing in the opening number "On a wonderful day like today", standing in the middle.

9ᵗʰ June 1967 Friday

Dave, the night guard here, who reminds me so much of my first love of long ago, sat with me at 4 a.m. & while all the camp slept we watched day break over the sea.

This evening I won 1ˢᵗ Prize in a fancy hat contest & also won a folding chair in the camp raffle.

10ᵗʰ June 1967 Saturday

Enid & I returned home after our week's wonderful holiday.

We had elevenses in **York** & then made a break for lunch at Fortes on the A.1. motorway, arriving home at 3-30 p.m. This evening we sat up until 1 a.m. playing cards – Auntie Gladys, David and Irene – Enid & me.

11ᵗʰ June 1967 Sunday

Our Rector this evening preached on one of the quotations in my "Book of Quotations".

Two men look out through the same bars; one sees the mud, the other sees stars.

As we sang the closing hymn No. 477, the words "the dawn leads on another day" had a very deep & extra special meaning for me.

12ᵗʰ June 1967 Monday

I returned to work after my week's holiday to find Little Tommy & Maz have become engaged! (June 10ᵗʰ)

Mr Sharp was most interested to hear all about my N.A.L.G.O. holiday at Cayton Bay as he has been going there regularly for the past 12 years. He will be going in July.

13th June 1967 Tuesday

A lovely sunny day. It was a joy to scooter to work & smell the newly mown hay & to have the doors flung wide open at the office.

"And what is so rare as a day in June? Then, if ever, come perfect days. Then heaven tries earth if it be in tune, and over it softly her warm ear lays." – Lowell.

14th June 1967 Wednesday

Another lovely sunny day. Went to the Cathedral at 1-10 p.m. for Holy Communion with **Canon Pratt**. The great west door was flung wide open & people were sprawled over the Cathedral lawn – sun-bathing.

A delightful summer's evening - spoilt by the persistent stink of bon-fires.

15th June 1967 Thursday

And yet another lovely day, made more lovely for me by the fact that my favourite customer came into the office, & chose to be served by me. This gladdened my heart as I had not seen him for almost a fortnight. Now that we are on speaking terms it is much more satisfactory & more rewarding.

16th June 1967 Friday

The delightful summer weather continues. Today is the first day of Leicester Cathedral's **Ruby Year Flower Festival**. I went during the dinner hour to see the flowers, described in the Leicester Mercury this evening as **"a once-in-a-life-time sight"**. I am hoping to go again on Sunday afternoon.

17th June 1967 Saturday

Another glorious day of sunshine. I spent the afternoon sun-bathing & acquired a goodly tan.

I also spent some time absorbing the unrivalled quotations of **Shakespeare** –

"Who ever loved that loved not at first sight?"

"Night's candles are burnt out, & jocund day stands tiptoe on the misty mountain tops."

18th June 1967 Sunday

For months I looked forward to the great Cathedral Service on 21st February, only to be disappointed by not even being invited.

Likewise for months I have looked forward to the great Cathedral Flower Festival today, hoping to take my Sunday School children, but not one child chose to go.

I therefore stayed at home & sun-bathed.

19th June 1967 Monday

It is reported in the Leicester Mercury this evening that 20,000 people are estimated to have passed through Leicester Cathedral during the 3 day flower festival – "one of the most successful events ever staged in the Cathedral."

This evening I went to Ravenstone W.I. where Auntie Belle was flower arranging.

20th June 1967 Tuesday

This evening I had my hair permed by **Mary Blue** – 37/6d. Mary Blue is at present a most attractive mother-to-be. She expects her baby early in January.

David & Irene are also expecting their first baby early in December.

Peter Hewes & Chris had their baby this month, 2 months premature.

21st June 1967 Wednesday

Went to the Cathedral for Holy Communion at 1-10 p.m. with the Succentor.

As on May 10th I was in tears – all for the love of Brian Lamming. He came into the office at 12-30 p.m., stood in front of me like Prince Charming & **"Oh, all my heart how it loved him"** & how I yearned for him.

22nd June 1967 Thursday

Reevsie is 32 today. I sent her some flowers for her birthday & she came into the office to thank me. Tony & baby Joanne came too & stayed for afternoon tea.

Do you remember the competition I did on 29th April? The results are now out. I did not win but was highly commended.

23rd June 1967 Friday

Guess what! I have written to Brian Lamming. My love for him is such that, instead of smiling sweetly & chatting merrily to him in the office, I practically ignore him. So today he walked out & looked as though he did not want to come again. I have invited him to meet me on Sunday evening.

Note – I wrote to Brian Lamming, inviting him to visit the Cathedral with me.

24th June 1967 Saturday

Brian Lamming received my letter today. Like the Queen, he **"was not amused."** In fact he rang up Pat & asked to speak to me. He told me in no uncertain terms that he was not at all in love with me, that he just could not understand why I had written, & that he would not meet me tomorrow.

Note – Brian Lamming rang me at home & absolutely blew his top. After that he kept well away from me when he came to our office. I could not believe that he & I were not made for each other.

25th June 1967 Sunday

Went to 11 a.m. **"Civic Service"** at Ravenstone Church. The church was full & we sang one hymn accompanied by Snibston Colliery Band.

This evening went to Leicester Cathedral where for the first time I heard **Canon Gundry** preach. He spoke of yesterday's "turbulent" mid-summer day.

26th June 1967 Monday

"Qui nimium multis, non amo, dicit; amat."

He who protests overmuch to many, "I do not love", he is in love. – **Ovid.**

Bearing this in mind I spent the whole evening writing a beautiful letter to give to **Brian Lamming**. Whether I shall ever give it to him depends entirely on how he next greets me.

27th June 1967 Tuesday

Aunt Dos this evening took Lesley (the lodger) & me to **St. Peter's Church**, Market Bosworth to the Flower Festival there.

Having been to Flower Festivals at St. Margaret's,

Leicester – Leicester Cathedral – Ashby – Ibstock – Great Glen & Broomleys, there is still a new wonder in every festival.

28th June 1967 Wednesday
Went to the Cathedral for Holy Communion at 1-10 p.m. with **Canon Pratt**.
A lovely warm day. We had the doors open all day long at work, & I wore my best turquoise cotton coat to go to the Cathedral.
Mum spent the evening at the **Hollies** having her hair permed by **Mary Blue** – 37/6d like mine.

29th June 1967 Thursday
Mum spent the day with **Madge** at Willoughby.
Evelyn has just had a new **Singer Sewing Machine**, the very latest & best - £107. We went to admire it this evening.
Evelyn asked me to help at the **Snibston School** garden fete on July 1st. I am to be in charge of "**Pegs on the line at 30 seconds a go.**"

30th June 1967 Friday
Today I had my first encounter with **Brian Lamming** since last weekend's incident. We had the office absolutely milling with customers & he took great care to avoid my look. I did not therefore, give him the beautiful letter I had for him, instead I just loved him silently from a safe distance.

1st July 1967 Saturday
Took my scooter for its 1200 mile service.
Spent the whole afternoon at **Snibston School** garden fete. A perfect summer's afternoon with the **Hewes** family out in full force. The fete was opened by **Don Hewes**. Enid was in charge of the darts, Aunt Dos had a bran tub, & I had "**Pegs on the line.**"

2nd July 1967 Sunday
Our church today looked rather like the Town Hall at **Mayor Making** time. This was because Jacqueline Brooks, daughter of the florists, was married on Thursday, & the masses of potted plants were still there.
I spent much of the day writing an article for the August Parish Magazine "For the Children".

3rd July 1967 Monday
My dearest **Brian Lamming** came into the office & deliberately chose to go to **Miss Gazzard** rather than to me. However, Miss Gazzard was called away for some considerable time, so I had great pleasure in going & serving him. Not a glimmer of love passed between us - & this is the man I love!

4th July 1967 Tuesday
Today I bought a gorgeous new dress from **Marshall & Snelgrove** – **White Tricel** with navy spots, reduced from 75/- to 59/11d.
Mum went to Hunstanton for the day with Ravenstone Darby & Joan.
In the July Cathedral News-letter out today, the **Provost** mentions love – weak & vulnerable & yet invincible.

5th July 1967 Wednesday
Went to the Cathedral for Holy Communion at 1-10 p.m. with **Canon Pratt**.
I enjoyed wearing my new gorgeous dress – long white gloves, white high heeled shoes & white Breton hat trimmed with navy. A beautiful day for being all dressed up, & my counter at work breathing with the perfume of roses.

6th July 1967 Thursday
Because of holidays & a somewhat depleted staff, I was on the Driving Licence counter today when my love came into the office. Though he spurns me as he does, my heart still thrills for him, & I left my roses to convey my love to him.
Auntie Dos's lodger leaves today. Her wedding is 29th July.

7th July 1967 Friday
We had a fine display of **Brian Lamming's** impatience & impulsiveness, when he arrived at our office today a few seconds before we closed, with a cheque for too much money.
I thoroughly enjoyed dealing with him & getting through to his heart.
Miss Gazzard & Ralph both agreed I am a good match for him.

8th July 1967 Saturday
In the Wimbledon finals today, we watched on television 23 year old American Billie-Jean King win the women's singles title, the women's doubles title & also the mixed doubles title. This triple victory was last achieved in 1951 by Doris Hart.
Actress Vivien Leigh died today aged 53.

9th July 1967 Sunday
Today we had our Sunday School Anniversary in spite of the fact I told you on April 23rd we had decided against it. A really beautiful day & I did so enjoy reading the 1st lesson this afternoon, I Samuel, Chapter 3.
It made my day this morning when I saw **Cocky** (my first love). I had not seen him for 5 years.
Note – Still smarting from rejection by Brian Lamming it made my day when I saw Cocky.

10th July 1967 Monday
A very hot day. I was dressed in my beautiful palm tree sun dress when my dearest love came into the office this morning. He came while I was alone on the counter & patiently waited his turn. I gave him my very best attention.
We were told today that our new offices will be ready by November.

11th July 1967 Tuesday
This is the second week of Leicester's Industrial Annual Holiday, which means the roads are almost perfectly clear at the normal "**rush hour**". The glorious summer weather makes it a pleasure to scooter to & from work.
This week traffic lights have been introduced at Sanvey Gate – a big improvement.

12th July Wednesday
Went to the Cathedral for Holy Communion at 1-10 p.m. with my beloved **Provost**.
Today it has been so hot we have all been wilting.

Mr Tom Fraser, Labour M.P. for Hamilton, who was Minister of Transport 2 years ago, has now been appointed chairman of the North of Scotland Hydro-Electric Board & quits as M.P.

13th July 1967 Thursday

With a heart as hard as iron & as cold as steel, Brian Lamming stood before me today to be served, while I literally trembled. It seems that he is impenetrable, but because I love him, I wept for him. I now repeat 11th May: - I will trouble you no further with details – unless he ever returns my love.

14th July 1967 Friday

I am now 36.
To celebrate my birthday I had a gorgeous display of roses on the counter at work. I had tea at Reevsie's, arriving home at 9-30 p.m. to find an unexpected bouquet of 36 carnations from **Alf Hall**. I thereupon went straight down to **Hall Bros**. & stayed until midnight.

15th July 1967 Saturday

A hot sunny day. Sun bathed this afternoon.
Continued to celebrate my birthday with a belated card from Bunting & a box of chocolates from Pat.
My most appropriate card was from Reevsie "You have reached another of the 7 ages of woman. 1. Baby 2.Child 3.Adolescent 4.Young Woman 5. Young Woman 6.Young Woman 7.Young Woman."

16th July 1967 Sunday

This morning I found I had to cope with the whole Sunday School from 3 years old to 13 years old, but with the help of 2 of the older girls, we managed remarkably well.
Tonight our Rector gave an excellent sermon on "**The Least, the Last & the Lost.**" The least can be the greatest, the last can be first, & the lost can be found.

17th July 1967 Monday

I sat up till after midnight doing another competition in the W.I. monthly magazine "**Home and Country**" – An address in your own words to a **horse** famous in history or literature. With the help of my old friend Longfellow I wrote an address to the horse "**Kyrat**" in "**The Leap of Roushan Beg.**"

18th July 1967 Tuesday

I received a belated birthday letter & present from Bunting – a very useful towel. She has asked me to visit her sometime next month, so I will make an earnest endeavour to do so. Today has been another scorcher. It is grand at work having the doors flung wide open.

19th July 1967 Wednesday

Today I received a letter from Colgate-Palmolive Ltd., in reply to a competition I entered: - "**Dear Prize-winner, Congratulations on winning a share of the First Prize in the House of Ajax £30,000 competition. There were 191,347 successful entrants & your share of the £17,000 First Prize is 1/9d.**"

20th July 1967 Thursday

I was delighted to hear from Pat today that my beloved

Provost is coming to **Ravenstone** Church to preach on Sunday evening 22nd October, which is 22nd Sunday after Trinity.
Today when I was strolling along in Leicester during the dinner hour I saw the Provost!
He does not even recognise me.

21st July 1967 Friday

This morning, as I scootered to Leicester, I met a baby rabbit running along the main road & coming straight towards me. I only just missed it as it shot into the hedge-side.
As the time draws nearer for our move from 14, Friar Lane, Leicester, my affection grows for the place which has shared my sorrow & joy.

22nd July 1967 Saturday

Auntie Gladys & Enid today went to Mablethorpe to spend a week with Auntie Margery, so I missed my usual Saturday night visit to their house.
For about 10 years now, I have had a regular Saturday night out from 9 p.m. till after midnight, playing cards & watching television etc.

Note – For the past 10 years I have played cards with Enid & at one time with her parents also – Uncle Cyril & Auntie Gladys. Now we play as a three-some, following the death of Uncle Cyril. This practice will continue until the death of Auntie Gladys, (1986).

23rd July 1967 Sunday

I sat up till midnight compiling the Parish Magazine for August. I included one of my favourite poems – "A Day of Sunshine" by my old friend Longfellow & one of my favourite Sunday School Anniversary hymns "The Beautiful Harbour of Heaven" (See 24th April 1966) & my own article for the children about the 3 King Herods.

24th July 1967 Monday

To commemorate Sir Francis Chichester's lone voyage round the world in Gipsy Moth IV, the Post Office today issued a special stamp – 1/9d. I was therefore at Leicester Post Office today, despatching "**First Day Issue**" envelopes to Aunt Dos, David & Peter. This particular stamp is especially popular.

25th July 1967 Tuesday

I had a phone call at work today to the effect that the salary increase I received last April was a clerical error! Would I therefore like the necessary deductions made gradually or all at once? It was a great relief when I had a further phone call to say it was alright after all.

26th July 1967 Wednesday

Went to the Cathedral for Holy Communion at 1-10 p.m. with **Canon Gundry**.
Today in Leicester, for the first time, we had the new crossing areas at main junctions with the road criss-crossed in bright yellow painted lines. Such an area is called a "**Sin-Bin**" for traffic lights.

27th July 1967 Thursday

It is announced today that the 81,000 ton liner **Queen Mary** is to be sold to the port of **Long Beach, California**, for use as a tourist attraction. She will be moored in the harbour & converted into a hotel, museum & conference centre, with arcades of high class shops, restaurants & offices - £850,000.

28th July 1967 Friday
Today I bought a book of Christian Verse 25/- This contained an old favourite of mine – "**Saul**" by Robert Browning, a poem I studied while at school; "**The Hound of Heaven**" by Francis Thompson; "**The World**" by Henry Vaughan, etc., etc.
I bought it primarily as material for our Parish Magazine.

29th July 1967 Saturday
After 2 whole months of uninterrupted glorious summer weather, today was dismal, dreary & rainy. I took my scooter for its 1800 mile service & scootered home in a down-pour.
Aunt Dos went to **Lesley's** wedding. (Her lodger for the past year). She has arranged to have another lodger in September.

30th July 1967 Sunday
Our last Sunday School for this school year. We have a holiday for the whole of August & resume on 3rd September.
For the best attendance during the year, Michael & John Needham were presented with a pocket sized chess set each, & Susan Smith with a Longfellow Birthday Book.

31st July 1967 Monday
Being the last day of the month we had our usual busy counter today. I enjoyed all the hubbub of activity after a fortnight of exceptional quiet.
I bought another book of poems "**The Oxford Book of English Verse**", 25/- , but found nothing in it to reach the very depths of my soul.

1st August 1967 Tuesday
My recently acquired book of poems led me today to study in detail the **Phoenix** rising out of the flames, which I must have seen a thousand times, at the corner of Friar Lane.
I learned that the **Phoenix** was a fabulous bird which cremated itself every 500 years & rose rejuvenated.

2nd August 1967 Wednesday
Tonight I was scootering home from Leicester when I was knocked off my scooter by a motorist. I had reached **Markfield Service Station**, & was on the inside lane of 2 or 3 cars which were about to turn right, & as I emerged past the front car another car cut right across my path.

Note – I am knocked off my scooter on the way home from work & very badly shaken.
This brings to an end my days of travel by scooter. I am advised to buy a car, although I can hardly afford to do so. Mum helps me as much as she can & together we manage to buy a second-hand car.
With no parking facilities at home I park in Aunt Dos's drive.

3rd August 1967 Thursday
Today I am well bruised & very stiff after yesterday's fall from my scooter.
I went to work on the 7 a.m. bus & had a slow & laborious walk from the bus to the office.
I managed pretty well all day on the counter & I appreciated all the concern & sympathy which I received.

4th August 1967 Friday
Our neighbour Mr Marlow, aged 67, died today.
Queen Elizabeth the Queen Mother is 67 years old today.
After falling from my scooter, I have been advised by so many people to buy a car, that I have decided to do so. Mum has offered me £200 to put towards it.

5th August 1967 Saturday
After 12,000 miles of scooter riding I have now ordered a car. This morning I went to see **Hall Brothers, Ravenstone**, & chose a **Morris-Mini de Luxe** 1966 model, FBT 638D - £435. (Grey).
This evening I met Enid's Auntie Grace & Uncle Billy. (Known as **Auntie Gracious** & **Uncle Billious**).

6th August 1967 Sunday
This evening I went with Aunt Dos to **Ravenstone Chapel**, where I was invited to read the lesson. We sang lots of the rip-roaring "**Cliff College Choruses**".
Afterwards we called to see **Alf Hall** who gave me a cover note of Insurance & the Registration Book for my new car.

7th August 1967 Monday
Tonight I took delivery of my new **Mini** car – named **Minnehaha** – which has done exactly 15,127 miles. Enid's Uncle Billy went with me & drove the car from **Hall Brothers** to Heather Lane. I then drove to Heather – Ibstock & home to **Ravenstone,** parking in Aunt Dos's drive.

8th August 1967 Tuesday
I came home from work by bus & was met at Coalville by Aunt Dos & **Minnehaha**. I drove home from Coalville & afterwards drove for the very first time unaccompanied. I went to Hall Bros. & left the car to have wing mirrors fitted. **Reg Hall** brought me home in his super jag.

9th August 1967 Wednesday
Again I came home from work by bus & was met at Coalville by Aunt Dos & **Minnehaha**. After tea **Pat**, Mum & I went for a most delightful evening drive along country lanes with **Pat** as navigator. We went 30 miles & arrived home by moonlight. Pat bought me some petrol.

10th August 1967 Thursday
Tonight I went to **Hall Bros**. & paid £200 deposit on my car (provided by Mum out of her £500 capital, left to us by my **Dad**.) Afterwards I called to see Don to enquire about a garage. He is hoping to erect several garages, next door to our house, in the grounds of the **Hollies**.

11th August 1967 Friday
This evening for the first time I took Mum to work by car. Aunt Dos came with us, & afterwards Aunt Dos & I went to **Hall Bros.**, where I learned of **Reg Hall's** interest in poetry. He lent me 4 books of poems, & thus introduced me to **Robert Service**, his favourite poet.

12th August 1967 Saturday
Reg Hall went with me this morning to see **Ron Hunt**, the Coalville Solicitor, in connection with my recent fall from my scooter.
This evening I drove to Ashby to take Mum to work. I have considerable difficulty trying to reverse through Aunt Dos's gates, but am hoping to improve with practice.

13th August 1967 Sunday
Drove to Ashby at 8 a.m. to meet Mum from night duty. Spent most of the day with the poems of **Robert Service**. I enjoyed his style of writing & his subject – his tremendous love for the frozen wilds of North America, & his excellent descriptive power & alliteration.

14th August 1967 Monday
Miss Gazzard is on holiday this week so I am enjoying being in charge of the counter.
Beryl offered me a ride home from Leicester to Coalville in her mini van, but we had great difficulty getting the engine to start, & eventually I was given a lift by somebody else coming our way home.

15th August 1967 Tuesday
Mum & I this evening went for a short ride in our new car. We went to Snarestone. Afterwards Aunt Dos gave me a concentrated lesson on how to reverse through her gates.
Mr Sharp went to see our new office today & came back with a very favourable report.
It sounds very grand.

16th August 1967 Wednesday
I finished reading **Reg Hall's Book of Poems** by Robert Service & I can well understand why he is his favourite poet. I sat up till nearly midnight recording poem after poem on a tape which I hope to give to **Reg. Hall**. It is poetry which is packed with drama & action.

17th August 1967 Thursday
This morning I had an unexpected lift to Leicester with **Ivy Coombes** in her car.
This evening I drove Mum to Ashby for night duty & then came home to a long session of recording. I completed the second side of my tape for **Reg Hall** with "**Rough Rhymes of a Padre**" (Woodbine Willie).

18th August 1967 Friday
One of the most attractive girls I was at school with, **Margaret White**, came into our office today. I was amazed at the transformation. She looked slovenly & unkempt & had no front teeth! I see quite a few of my old school mates in our office. Some are quite grey now & look middle aged.

19th August 1967 Saturday
This morning I went to see **Hall Bros.** & gave **Reg** my

recording of his favourite poems. While I was there, **Alf** rang up **Auto Supplies** for me. They said my scooter would cost £31 to be repaired. I have to pay £15 & my Insurance Company £16. My solicitor will then endeavour to claim £15 for me.

20th August 1967 Sunday
The 13th Sunday after Trinity & the Gospel for today tells the story of the Good Samaritan. Our Rector this evening, after being absent for the past 3 Sundays for a holiday in **Majorca**, held the congregation completely spellbound as he told of the part he played in Majorca's coach disaster.

21st August 1967 Monday
Today I received a letter from Coalville Police Station – **Dear Sir**, I have considered the report concerning the accident in which you were involved, on the 2nd August 1967 at Ashby Road, Markfield, & inform you that no further action will be taken – **Superintendent**.

22nd August 1967 Tuesday
Today is the anniversary of the Battle of Bosworth Field. In today's national papers the following In Memoriam was published:
Plantagenet, Richard. - **Richard III**, who fell at the Battle of Bosworth Field, 22nd August 1485.
"This day was our good King Richard piteously slain & murdered."

23rd August 1967 Wednesday
Last December I wrote a poem "**On Leaving Grey Friars**" & sent it to the new magazine "**Impact**". However in **May** this year the new magazine "**Impact**" came to an abrupt end. Today I had a phone call to say a magazine will be printed in October featuring my poem on the front cover!

24th August 1967 Thursday
Aunt Dos has gone to **Cannock** today to spend a few days with her friend, so I am sleeping alone in the house tonight.
This evening I took Mum to Ashby in the car & afterwards did my **Parish Magazine** for September, including a poem I wrote for **St. Michael's** day. (Our church is St. Michael's).

25th August 1967 Friday
Today we broke up for the **Bank Holiday** & return to work next Wednesday.
I have arranged to spend the week-end with Bunting & family at **Malvern**, travelling by bus tomorrow morning & returning home on Monday. There is a daily bus service from Leicester to **Hereford** via Malvern.

26th August 1967 Saturday
Today I came to Malvern on the 9-15 a.m. bus from Leicester arriving at 1-45 p.m.
Julian aged 17, tall & bubbling over with the joy of youth, met me off the bus.
Michael aged 19, champion tennis player of the whole county, tall & handsome, was very sad after a broken romance.

27th August 1967 Sunday
Went to **Malvern Priory,** to 11 a.m. morning service, which moved me very deeply.
While Julian continues to enjoy life to the full, Michael looks so very sad, & talks seriously of going to Africa. This is a great worry to Bunting who suffers as a parent having a "**Prodigal Son**".

28th August 1967 Monday
Bank Holiday Monday! I returned home from **Malvern**. The holiday has been one of warm sunshine. It was very pleasant today travelling from Malvern through Worcester, Evesham, Stratford-on-Avon, Warwick, Leamington Spa & Coventry to Leicester.
This evening took Mum to Ashby in the car.

29th August 1967 Tuesday
Bank Holiday Tuesday! A lovely sunny day.
Mum & I went in the car this evening to **Twycross Zoo** where a baby giraffe 5 feet tall was born this week. However we were too late to get in.
Aunt Dos's new lodger, **Mary**, arrived today in a grey Morris Mini just like **Minnehaha**.

30th August 1967 Wednesday
Went to the Cathedral for Holy Communion at 1-10 p.m. with **Canon Gundry**.
Canon Gray from the Cathedral died this week (See 17th July 1966)
We had a very busy counter all day long, & such a monstrous post after the holiday, we have been asked to work overtime tomorrow and also Friday.

31st August 1967 Thursday
The balance due for payment of my car is £185-1/- which I have arranged to pay by 17 instalments of £10-4s-6d & a final instalment of £11-4s-6d. This is to be paid to C.D.M. Motor Trust Ltd., 1A, Salisbury Road, Leicester. Today I arranged with **Westminster Bank** to do this for me.

1st September 1967 Friday
Yesterday & today I worked overtime until 8 p.m. The holiday on Monday & Tuesday resulted in a tremendous post on Wednesday. The beginning of the month naturally brings a heavy counter & a shoal of refunds, & on top of that we have staff on holiday. I spent the whole day with Driving Licences.

2nd September 1967 Saturday
Today in Sweden all traffic changed from driving on the left to the right. The changeover of all road signs etc. cost £40 million.
Mum went to **Colchester** today to spend a week with **Mary Moore**. Aunt Dos & I motored to **Kegworth** this afternoon to see **Mary Dolman**.

3rd September 1967 Sunday
A wet & windy day. I enjoyed going to Sunday school by car for the first time & also to church this evening by car for the first time.
I spent practically the whole day writing an article for the **October Parish Magazine** about the origin of our calendar from ancient Greece & Rome.

4th September 1967 Monday
The Leicester Mercury tonight reports that Saturday's Staunton Harold's 13th garden fete raised £4,000 – a new record.
Tonight we had our first rehearsal for "**The Merry Widow**" which we are giving next **March**.
The result of the competition I did on July 17th is now out. "**Kyrat**" got a mention.

5th September 1967 Tuesday
Today we were advised by the **Post Office** that Postal Coding is to be introduced in Leicester & the surrounding area, including Ashby-de-la-Zouch & Coalville.
I sent off another competition to the W.I. magazine "Home & Country". This time I wrote a little verse about the giant "**Enceladus**".

6th September 1967 Wednesday
Today I am writing my diary by candle-light. Why? Because I've just managed to fuse all the lights in the house! Went to the Cathedral at 1-10 p.m. for Holy Communion with my beloved **Provost**. There were only 4 people there so I felt very much included. Not like 8th May 1967.

7th September 1967 Thursday
I arrived home from Leicester to find all the lights in the house working again – thanks to Herbert the electrician, who came in while I was at Leicester. Aunt Dos took **Minnehaha** to Coalville to meet me off the bus, but we managed to miss each other, & I walked from Coalville to Ravenstone.

8th September 1967 Friday
Tomorrow I expect mum home from her week's holiday with **Mary Moore**, so this evening I have been doing "**Welcome Home**" flower arrangements, Also, tomorrow Auntie Cis is expected, to stay for a short while with Aunt Dos.
Today I bought a pair of new shoes, light brown court, 59/11d.

9th September 1967 Saturday
Our Sunday School outing! Left at 7-30 a.m. for **Hunstanton**, arriving just before mid-day.
A lovely sunny day. Lay on the grass on the cliff tops & then walked back along the beach. Although we went to the East Coast, Hunstanton actually faces **West**, so we saw the sun across the sea.

10th September 1967 Sunday
The Rector tonight spoke of the raising to life of the son of the widow of **Nain**. He spoke of tears of love & said that love needs rain as well as sunshine.
I gave Auntie Gladys & Enid a lift home from church, but being very much a "**novice**" driver, I stalled twice at the cross roads.

11th September 1967 Monday
There is to be a sale of much of our old office furniture when we move to new premises. Members of the office have first choice & may apply for any item they choose.
Today I applied for a desk which should be rather useful, with a roomy cupboard one side & drawers the other.

12 September 1967 Tuesday
This evening I went with **Mary Wild**, who is Aunt Dos's new lodger, to **Coalville Tech.**, where we both enrolled for a course of 12 lessons for **Lady Car Owners** – simple maintenance, etc. We paid 22/6d each & our first lesson will be on **Thursday 21st September – St. Matthew's Day.**

13th September 1967 Wednesday
Went to the Cathedral for Holy Communion at 1-10 p.m. Much to my surprise it was with the **Provost** again – 2 consecutive weeks!
I had a letter from the Guardian Assurance Group to say that insurance for my car will be £33-13/-. If however, my solicitor can claim for my scooter, it will be reduced.

14th September 1967 Thursday
Twenty-seven years ago today the **Battle of Britain** was at its height.
On September 15th 1940, the R.A.F. claimed its greatest victory, & 2 days later Hitler postponed his plans for the invasion of **England**.
Tonight on television we watched a most remarkable film: "**The Battle of Britain**".

15th September 1967 Friday
We now have only 9 more weeks in our office at dear old Friar Lane. We shall be visiting the new **County Hall** on 27th September for a conducted tour of the building.
Next week there will be several of our senior staff away from work so I have been asked to help with their work.

16th September 1967 Saturday
The 81,000 ton Cunard liner **Queen Mary** was given a tremendous send off today as she left **Southhampton** for her last east-west transatlantic crossing to **New York**. There were cheers & there were tears. She is due back at Southhampton on 27th September & leaves on 31st October for **California**.

17th September 1967 Sunday
This evening I ventured for the first time in my car to Leicester. I went to evensong at the **Cathedral**, where the **Provost** was preaching, The Provost spoke of man's responsibility in **Creation**. Made in the image of God – allowed to name every living creature – having dominion over them – a challenge & a privilege.

18th September 1967 Monday
We have now been informed by the **Post Office** that the **Postal Code** for our address is
LE6 2AR.
Langham Kendrick invited me this evening to receive the baskets of fruit & flowers from the children at **Ravenstone Chapel** next Sunday afternoon when they will be holding their **Harvest Festival**.

19th September 1967 Tuesday
Had a lift to Leicester this morning with **Tom Whitmore** in his **Volkswagen**. This saved me my bus fare – 9d to Coalville, & then 3/2d to Leicester.
Today it was "**New Stamp Special Issue**" at the Post Office, so I was in the merry throng at Leicester Post Office, sending stamps to Aunt Dos, David & Peter.

20th September 1967 Wednesday
Her Majesty the Queen today launched the new £25,500,000 fifty-eight thousand ton Cunard liner & named her "**Queen Elizabeth the Second**" (See 30th December 1964)
I went to the Cathedral at 1-10 p.m. for Holy Communion. Again it was with the **Provost**! There were 7 of us in the congregation.

21st September 1967 Thursday
Mary, the lodger, & I went to **Coalville Tech**. this evening for our first lesson in car maintenance. The class consisted of 13 ladies, all about my age, & we enjoyed our lesson very much. Mr Pattle, the teacher, explained in very simple terms the function of a 4 stroke engine & we all understood.

22nd September 1967 Friday
Enid, Mum & I went to **Ashby Statutes**. We parked the car in Ashby Hospital car park, & called in the hospital to see the newly born babies, all in their cots in the nursery.
We had a go at **Bingo** & darts, ate brandy snaps & marvelled at the workings of the major attractions. Music blared away & the din was terrific.

23rd September 1967 Saturday
Mum & I went to Leicester this afternoon to see the film called "**The Bible**". It was a 3 hour film which started with the Creation. We saw the building of the ark – the entrance of all the animals – living in the ark – the tower of Babel – Lot & his wife – Abraham - & finally Isaac saved from sacrifice.

24th September 1967 Sunday
This afternoon I went with Aunt Dos to Ravenstone Methodist Chapel harvest festival where I received the baskets of fruit etc. from the children.
I spent the whole evening on the **October Parish Magazine**. Having 5 Sundays in the month I had a very full calendar.

25th September 1967 Monday
Enid will be 40 next month, so I have gone to great lengths to get her a suitable birthday card, & have found one which says on it –"Ah – just the right age", & I have pinned to it one of my **Ruby Year** badges.
Terry & Mary Blue are leaving this week to go & live in **Market Harborough**.

Note – Mary Blue & Terry move to live in Market Harborough & we offer to take in their beautiful cat "Tosca".

26th September 1967 Tuesday
A beautiful autumn day – the most charming period of the year – "Formosissimus Annus" (According to **Ovid**, the autumn; according to **Virgil**, the spring) I invariably agree with **Ovid**, whose wisdom I greatly admire. Today I read of an ancient civilisation - the Lemurians, destroyed by earthquake 12,000 years ago.

27th September 1967 Wednesday
This evening we went in a party from work to see the **New County Hall**. It reminded me very much of the

unfinished **German** underground hospital in **Guernsey**. Some of the rooms had a delightful outlook. Our office was not too bad – but the ceiling was not high enough.

28th September 1967 Thursday
We had our 2nd lesson on car maintenance. We went into the "motor room" & saw a cross section of an engine. We watched in slow motion what happens when the engine is going.
We handled various parts and saw badly worn items compared with new; and located different things.

29th September 1967 Friday
Seven more weeks in our dear old office!
Terry & Mary have now settled in their new home in **Market Harborough**. We now therefore have taken possession of "Tosca", probably the most beautiful cat in the world, who belonged officially to **Mary**, but who wanders freely around all the family.

30th September 1967 Saturday
This morning I went to see Mr. R. Hunt, my solicitor, who is having some difficulty in getting the £15 for me in connection with my scooter accident.
This afternoon Mum & I went in the car to **Willoughby** to see Madge & Bertha.
Spent the evening compiling a "Quiz" for Sunday School tomorrow.

1st October 1967 Sunday
Mum & I went to Leicester Cathedral this afternoon for the **Harvest Festival**.
This evening we had the Revd. Edwards from Broom Leys at Ravenstone Church for our **Patronal Festival**, & I was much impressed by his sermon. He spoke of angels & spirits & things invisible.

2nd October 1967 Monday
This evening I went to the **Edward Wood Hall**, Leicester, to see a religious film "I Beheld His Glory". It was a coloured film of the crucifixion as witnessed by **Cornelius**, the Roman Centurion. The hall was absolutely packed solid. A silver collection was taken & all the stewards were black men.

3rd October 1967 Tuesday
Today I bought a "Prestige wall can opener" – 42/9d.
A wild, wet & windy day. I had a lift to Leicester this morning with **Tom Whitmore**, but walked home from Coalville this evening.
This week our usual Monday night rehearsal for "Merry Widow" was changed to Tuesday, just for tonight.

4th October 1967 Wednesday
Sir Malcolm Sargent, aged 72, chief conductor for the past 21 years of the Promenade concerts, died yesterday. We last saw him on television on 16th September at the last night of the Proms. He could control that wild, enthusiastic audience in a moment, and hold them spellbound.

5th October 1967 Thursday
We had our 3rd lesson on car maintenance, concentrating mainly on lubrication.
We saw clearly where the oil lies in the oil sump – 6

pints in a big pie dish container, & how it goes merrily all round the works, when in action. We now know the pistons, crankshaft, camshaft, etc. etc.

6th October 1967 Friday
Enid is 40 today! Like our cathedral & diocese of Leicester this is her **Ruby Year**.
She celebrates appropriately by having a new car, MJU 15F, which was registered today. Minnehaha, our little Mini, today took Mum & Aunt Dos to Mountsorrel. They called to see Auntie Doris who was out.

7th October 1967 Saturday
Went to **Sheffield** this evening with a bus load from our Amateur's to see "The Merry Widow". We went through **Chesterfield** & saw the church there with the crooked spire. We all thoroughly enjoyed "The Merry Widow", & the sing-song in the bus home, stopping at midnight for coffee.

8th October 1967 Sunday
Lord Attlee, aged 84, former **Prime Minister**, died today.
Ravenstone Church Harvest Festival. I read the lesson this afternoon at the children's fruit & flower gift service. Later in the afternoon Mum & I went for a ride in the car to **Mount St. Bernard's Abbey**, Whitwick.

9th October 1967 Monday
At midnight last night the new law came into force using the breathalyser for drunken drivers. It is now an offence to drive if the alcohol-blood level is over 80 milligrammes per 100 millilitres of blood.
Prince Charles, aged 18, starts today at Trinity College, Cambridge, reading **Anthropology** & **Archaeology**.

10th October 1967 Tuesday
The new drink & driving laws brought out by **Mrs. Barbara Castle, Minister of Transport,** have had an immediate dramatic effect. Public houses have reported a slump in sales, & the paper tonight is full of car hire & taxi services: - "You Drink, We Drive", "Why Take a Risk?", "Don't Take Chances" etc. etc.

11th October 1967 Wednesday
Today I sent off another competition to the W.I. magazine "Home & Country". Given certain names in a little verse we had to suggest gifts in rhyme. "I would give Flavia a ….., I would give Fritz a ….." etc. etc. I did a complete theme on hairstyles – for Flavia, a home perm much wavier, for Fritz a toupee that fits.

12th October 1967 Thursday
We had our 4th lesson on car maintenance & were introduced to the **Carburettor**.
This is the part of the mechanism where air is mixed with petrol & works like a scent spray. We saw one taken all to bits, & learned what happens inside it when you accelerate, or when you use the choke.

13th October 1967 Friday
Five more weeks in our office in Leicester!
Today is Friday the thirteenth. We had a busy counter today, which I thoroughly enjoyed.
It is now 3 months since I last mentioned **Brian**

Lamming. You may like to know that I still love him, just as much as ever, but he never so much as even looks at me.

14th October 1967 Saturday
Mum & I went again to **Mount St. Bernard's Abbey**, hoping this time to find their book shop open, but again it was closed. I thought I might get a book there about **St. Catherine**, (Who was tortured on the **Catherine Wheel**), for our **November** magazine.
St. Catherine's Day is November 25th.

15th October 1967 Sunday
My Sunday School class has now reverted to the encouraging number of 15. I lost 6 of my best children in one fell swoop earlier this year but now I have several promising new younger ones. My most promising child of all is Michael Needham, who attends church regularly, & really does know his Bible.

16th October 1967 Monday
Christine Hughes, from our office, today had a baby daughter. A day of torrential rain.
We had our Amateur's rehearsal for "**Merry Widow**" in the table tennis room at the **Community Centre** as no other room was available.
We are now arranging a bus load to see "**South Pacific**" in Leicester on 22nd November.

17th October 1967 Tuesday
On November 19th 1964, Mum & I watched "**Wuthering Heights**" on television. This same film was shown again tonight & we were able to enjoy it all over again. - "Set amid the stormy Yorkshire moors, this immortal story of passion, hatred & revenge is presented with relentless vigour & brooding violence."

18th October 1967 Wednesday
St. Luke's Day, so we had Holy Communion today at the High Altar in the Cathedral, instead of the usual "**St. Dunstan's Chapel**".
The Russians today landed their 1st spacecraft on **Venus**, 50 million miles distant, which sent back signals to **Earth** indicating that **Venus** could not support earthly life.

19th October 1967 Thursday
We had our 5th lesson on car maintenance. Tonight we were introduced to the **ignition** system. We learned what happens when you "switch on" the engine. We followed the course of electric current, from the battery through the distributor to the spark plugs, & we all handled the distributor.

20th October 1967 Friday
Enid, Mum & I tonight went to the Adult School to see their 25th production "**If Four Walls Told**".
Today I bought a white nylon overall 30/- ready for our annual dusty census at work, which will be starting on Monday. I shall be on the counter all morning & on the census each afternoon.

21st October 1967 Saturday
Pat & Evelyn took me to spend the day with **Mary Blue** in her new home on the **Gartree Prison** estate.

In the afternoon Pat & I went into **Market Harborough**, & we saw the house where my dearest **Brian Lamming** lives – **90, St. Mary's Road**, and also "**Federated Garage**" where he works on **Farndon Road**.

22nd October 1967 Sunday
The **Provost** came to Ravenstone & spoke on St. Matthew, Chap.16, verses 13-19. "Whom do men say that I the Son of man am? ...... But whom say ye that I am? ...... As Peter could recognise the Christ, the Son of the living God, may Ravenstone too know Christ, & be a rock & a lively stone.

23rd October 1967 Monday
Came home from Leicester to Coalville on the bus with **Helen Tovell**. Aunt Dos was there to meet the bus with **Minnehaha** & I was able to give Helen a lift home.
This evening I took Enid to Amateur's rehearsal, & afterwards gave **Joan Dillow** & Enid a lift home.

24th October 1967 Tuesday
I sat up till midnight typing out the **Ravenstone Parish Magazine** for **November**.
I rang up **Dennis Collier** for the list of lesson readers, & the written list was later delivered to me personally by **Alf Hall**, who invited me to accompany him tomorrow night at 9-30 to Dennis's pub.

25th October 1967 Wednesday
Went to the Cathedral for Holy Communion at 1-10 p.m. with **Canon Gundry**, who introduced us to the new form of service, which is part of a 4 year experiment. I thought the new service had much to commend it.
Tonight I went with **Alf Hall** to Dennis's pub at Coleorton.

26th October 1967 Thursday
We had our 6th lesson on car maintenance. We continued last week's lesson on the ignition system, & had a model board which operated winking lights, etc. We checked the contact breaker points in the distributor, & learned how to readjust them, by unscrewing the right screws.

27th October 1967 Friday
Three more weeks in our office in Leicester!
The Leicester Mercury tonight has devoted half a page to our move to Glenfield – "The invasion of Glenfield is about to be launched, & a new gleaming white landmark on the skyline of Leicestershire will have had life breathed into it ....."
Today, for the first time, I motored to work.

28th October 1967 Saturday
Tonight we put the clocks back for the last time. Clocks will go forward again on February 18th 1968, & from then on Britain will live by Summertime all year round, & be in line with **Central European Time**.
British Summer Time was first introduced in 1916 to conserve fuel & light.

29th October 1967 Sunday
Continuing last week's theme by the **Provost**, our Rector this evening gave a sermon on a house built on a rock. He said it was more important to know Christ, than merely to know about Christ, more important to know

the Shepherd than to know the 23rd Psalm, & to live rather than say **The Creed**.

30th October 1967 Monday
Pat has now acquired another car from **Hall Bros**. He has chosen a 1965 **Hillman Minx** de luxe, 1725cc, number **DBF 773C**.
Today we had our first pay slips bearing the address of **County Hall, Glenfield**. Our office is now stacked high with boxes ready for the big move.

31st October 1967 Tuesday
The County Office magazine "**Impact**" is out today, with my poem "**On Leaving Grey Friars**" printed boldly on the front cover. Imagine my delight when I received a phone call this morning, from "**Mr. Leicester**" of the **Leicester Mercury,** saying he would like to print my poem in the Mercury.

1st November 1967 Wednesday
All Saints Day! So today we had Holy Communion in the Cathedral at the High Altar.
This evening I took Mum to Ashby in the car for night duty.
Mum has recently become eligible for a pension - £4-18s-6d, which means her night duty is now limited to 2 nights a week.

2nd November 1967 Thursday
I had the day off from work today. I motored into Leicester for a dentist appointment at 11-15 a.m., an appointment for a perm at 1-30, & then called to see Reevsie for an hour.
Tonight we had our 7th lesson on car maintenance, & learned about the cooling system, & also how the petrol tank functions.

3rd November 1967 Friday
This morning I had a phone call from Mr. Hunt, my solicitor, who is still endeavouring to get £15 for me in connection with my fall from my scooter on 2nd August. He assured me that he had not forgotten me, & after much correspondence, he was now to meet our opposing team.

4th November 1967 Saturday
Cathedral News-Letter No.46. It was in **November 1517** (450 years ago) that **Martin Luther** challenged the mediaeval Church by nailing his 95 theses to the door of the Castle Church at **Wittenberg, East Germany**. Quoting in length, the Provost says, "**You can say that Martin Luther wrote to you this month!**"

5th November 1967 Sunday
The "**Radio Times**" this week contains a special pull-out supplement "**Welcome to BBC Radio Leicester**". There are to be 8 local radio stations opened in different parts of the country, but good old **Leicester** will be the first. The Postmaster-General is to open BBC Radio Leicester next **Wednesday**.

6th November 1967 Monday
Today I bought a new winter dress to wear at our office Christmas party. It is a turquoise woollen dress, with very short sleeves, & attractive low, wide neckline - £5-19s-11d.
This evening at Amateur's, we all applied for parts, & I chose "**Olga**", a very minor part – auditions next Monday.

7th November 1967 Tuesday
Today the Soviet Union celebrates the 50th Anniversary of the **Communist Party's** access to power in the 1917 Revolution. Russia has 3 days holiday to celebrate, & today Moscow's Red Square has been jubilant with brass bands, parades, fireworks & elaborate festivities to mark the occasion.

8th November 1967 Wednesday
My poem "**On Leaving Grey Friars**" which I wrote 17th December 1966 was printed tonight in the Leicester Mercury.

On Leaving Grey Friars
Dearest Leicester, we are leaving,
Now it seems so hard to say,
For we know we all will miss you
When we move so far away.
We will miss the morning market,
(Dodging round the crates and stock)
Miss the hub-bub of the city
And the ever chiming clock.
We will even miss the puddles,
And the pavements badly cracked,
Miss the old familiar streets
Which with history are packed.
We have been so long in Leicester,
Seen it knocked around and down;
Now that all is looking better,
Sadly we are leaving town.

This poem, by Miss Betty Hewes, 27 Leicester Road, Ravenstone, who works in the County Motor Taxation Department, Friar Lane, Leicester, appears on the front cover of "Impact", journal of Leicestershire branch of NALGO.
Today also marked the last Leicestershire County Council meeting to be held in the County Rooms, Leicester, after 79 years, & described as a "**historic occasion**".

9th November 1967 Thursday
This morning I went with many other County Council employees to the gorgeous **Council Chamber** in the County Rooms, Hotel Street, Leicester, where we were instructed in the art of our new telephone system, now installed in the New County Hall, - **P.A.B.X.** – Private Automatic Branch Exchange with 530 lines.

10th November 1967 Friday
One more week to go in our dear old office. It is now "**All Systems Go**".
The Clerk of the County Council goes on Thursday. The County Architect & the County Treasurer go on Friday. The County Engineer & Surveyor, the Local Taxation & Motor Licences go on Saturday, & all the rest move during Sunday & Monday. (20th)

11th November 1967 Saturday
On September 11th I applied to the County Council for one of the old desks in our office.

This week I had a letter stating that this desk was required elsewhere by the County Council and therefore was not for sale.

Perhaps this was just as well, being 4′ 6″ by 2′ 6″, we hardly had room for it.

12ᵗʰ November 1967 Sunday

Went to Ravenstone Church for a **Remembrance Day Service** at 10-45 a.m. & also to **Evensong** at 6-30 p.m. At both services the main theme of the sermon was the fact that we enjoy so many benefits which we have contributed absolutely nothing towards, & yet everything had to be paid for.

13ᵗʰ November 1967 Monday

The £13,000 traffic light scheme at Leicester's clock tower came into operation today. Being my last Monday working in Leicester, I was there to see them.

Tonight we had auditions for "The Merry Widow". I enjoyed reading in for **Anna**, the widow, but my singing cannot compare with my speaking.

14ᵗʰ November 1967 Tuesday

This morning I had another phone call from Mr. Hunt, my solicitor, who informed me that he had been successful in claiming £15 for damage to my scooter, and a further £35 to compensate for all my bumps & bruises! I was amazed!! Furthermore he would claim his expenses from them as well.

15ᵗʰ November 1967 Wednesday

Went for the last time to Holy Communion at 1-10 p.m. in Leicester Cathedral with my beloved Provost, who prayed for the County Council & their "great move. **Brian Lamming**, the man I love so dearly, dealt one final blow today by saying he would get licences by post in future. My heart sank completely.

16ᵗʰ November 1967 Thursday

For our 9ᵗʰ lesson in "car maintenance" we had an Insurance man to tell us all about "Car Insurance". (Last week we learned about the gears & the clutch) **Miss Peru** tonight won the 17ᵗʰ Miss World contest. I sent off another entry to "Home & Country" competition.

Enceladus (5ᵗʰ September) did not win.

17ᵗʰ November 1967 Friday

Our last day at work in 14, Friar Lane, Leicester, where I have worked since 1948.

By the light of the full moon we finally left after a day of great activity. All week we have been packing files, records etc. etc. into a thousand boxes which today were chain ganged into the great removal vans.

18ᵗʰ November 1967 Saturday

Spent the whole day at **New County Hall** moving in & unpacking our thousand boxes. What a transformation since 27ᵗʰ September when we saw the building as an empty shell. Today, bright with sunshine after morning frost, the whole building looked absolutely wonderful, & fitted with delightful new furnishings.

19ᵗʰ November 1967 Sunday

Sat up till after midnight writing a poem "**Ode to New County Hall**".

This morning I called to see **Alf Hall**, who put me a new thermostat in the car, & for the first time was able to have the heat on. Also, he put me some methylated spirits in my window washing water, to stop it freezing.

20ᵗʰ November 1967 Monday

Our first day at work in **New County Hall**. I am quite sure we have the loveliest part of the whole building. With vast expanses of views, we look immediately on to the large low sun roof & pool, beneath the county coat of arms. We were all enchanted with our new office & the customers shared our delight.

21ˢᵗ November 1967 Tuesday

Mr Sharp took me this afternoon to our old office in 14, Friar Lane, Leicester, for a last sentimental look round. The letter box was boarded up & a huge message announced our new address. Inside, in the semi darkness, everything was bare & desolate. We returned to the welcoming lights of New County Hall.

22ⁿᵈ November 1967 Wednesday

Went this evening to the De Montfort Hall, Leicester, to see "**South Pacific**", given by Leicester Amateur's. We went in a bus load from Coalville Amateur's.

After **New County Hall,** in all its grandeur & splendour, the De Montfort Hall was strangely small & unimpressive. We gave "South Pacific" in 1962.

23ʳᵈ November 1967 Thursday

Our 10ᵗʰ lesson in car maintenance. We learned about the rear axle – how wheels take corners etc., & all about tyres.

In the Leicester Mercury tonight there is a detailed outline of **New County Hall - £1,800,000.**

Our old boss Mr. Pochin, & his wife, came to look round today.

24ᵗʰ November 1967 Friday

We have now completed one week aboard our luxury liner – **New County Hall.**

Of the 800 crew, we on the counter of the Motor Licence office surely have the best view, right at the helm. This morning, to complete the picture, I watched a seagull in flight across the length of our windows.

25ᵗʰ November 1967 Saturday

This morning I called to see **Mr. Hunt**, my solicitor, who gave me a cheque for £50 from the Royal Exchange Assurance Group, following my accident on 2ⁿᵈ August. I then called to see **Hall Brothers**, & ordered a fog lamp & a wireless for my car, which I hope to have fitted next Tuesday.

26ᵗʰ November 1967 Sunday

On 10ᵗʰ August I asked Don about the possibility of a garage at the **Hollies**. It would now appear that such a possibility is very remote. Poor **Minnehaha** was absolutely frosted up this morning & had to be de-iced before I fetched Mum home from night duty.

I keep the car in Aunt Dos's drive.

27ᵗʰ November 1967 Monday

Had a day's holiday today. This morning Alf Hall & I

went to Burton-on-Trent to take my car to have a wireless & fog lamps fitted. I drove all the way behind Alf, in his **Mercedes**, & we both came back in Alf's car. This afternoon I went to Leicester for a dentist appointment, & bought some shoes - £5-5/-.

28th November 1967 Tuesday
This evening I collected my car from **Hall Bros**. I was delighted with the new wireless which had been fitted, & the first music I heard was, remarkably enough, "**Vilia**" from "The Merry Widow". Mum & I went for a little ride especially to enjoy driving to music. Two excellent fog lamps had also been fitted.

29th November 1967 Wednesday
Mr James Callaghan today resigned as **Chancellor of the Exchequer**. He is now Home Secretary in place of **Mr. Roy Jenkins**, who has swopped places to become Chancellor of the Exchequer.
Our country is suffering at present from a serious epidemic of foot & mouth disease – 1,241 cases in the past 5 weeks.

30th November 1967 Thursday
Our 11th lesson in car maintenance. We learned about the brakes & also about the steering. We were shown the difference between drum brakes & disc brakes, & learned why the brakes may not work after driving through floods. We were advised not to leave the hand brake on after a very long hot journey.

1st December 1967 Friday
"**La Terrasse a Sainte-Adresse**", a picture painted in 1867 – the Monet masterpiece – was sold today at Christies for 560,000 guineas = £588,000.
Today I had a letter from the Guardian Assurance Group to say I may now be allowed a no claim discount, £8-8/-, on my car insurance. (See September 13th)

2nd December 1967 Saturday
Went to Leicester today on a grand shopping spree. I bought a licence for our wireless & television - £5, a licence for my car radio – 25/-, a **Premium Bond** - £1, postage stamps ready for Christmas - £1, 2 **Berlei** foundation girdles £5 each, £5 worth of Postal Orders for 5 different charities, etc., etc.

3rd December 1967 Advent Sunday
Our Rector tonight gave an inspiring sermon on **St. Andrew** – the disciple who brought others to **Jesus**.
On television this evening we watched Shakespeare's "**Romeo & Juliet**". It was a joy to me to hear the great quotations, not only of Shakespeare, but of my old friend **Ovid**, brought to life.

4th December 1967 Monday
Miss Gazzard was not at work today so I had the pleasure of being in full command of the counter. A beautiful day with the sun streaming through the office windows, & then a glorious sunset which we can enjoy to the full, being on the west wing of the building. After the sunset a four day old moon.

5th December 1967 Tuesday
Again Miss Gazzard was not at work, so I manned the

counter alone, & did the grand final balance. We have now reached our Index Mark **MUT**, & today I licensed **MUT 1F** – a new £4,000 Mercedes Benz. We number from 1 to 999 & every 999 number is taken by the man I love – **Brian Lamming**.

6th December 1967 Wednesday
Winter arrived today in full force. Quite unexpectedly this afternoon we had a heavy fall of snow. I gave little Tommy a lift home to **Whitwick**.
This evening Mum & I went to the **Mothers' Union Carol Service** in **Ravenstone Church**, where **Barrie Edwards** was guest soloist.

7th December 1967 Thursday
Our 12th lesson in car maintenance & the most interesting one of all. We did not go to Coalville Tech. but to Mr. Pattle's big garage at **Bardon Quarries**. I drove **Minnehaha** on to a ramp (very dodgy), & we saw underneath the car, under the bonnet etc., & learned how to change a wheel.

8th December 1967 Friday
The foot & mouth disease at present in our country is the worst epidemic on record. So far there have been 1,659 cases confirmed, & a total of 273,216 animals destroyed. Sylvia & I yesterday went for a lunch time drive to see "**Old John**", & the gates of Bradgate Park, closed completely to protect the deer.

9th December 1967 Saturday
This morning we had a heavy fall of snow. With howling winds & more snow forecast, poor **Minnehaha** does not like being out in the cold all night. I have done my best to keep snow from sneaking in through the radiator by placing a blanket, a waterproof, & finally a pair of steps right up to the bonnet.

10th December 1967 Sunday
Although some parts of the country have been badly hit by blizzards, it has not been too bad here, & this morning I was able to motor to Ashby to fetch Mum home from night duty. Today being the 2nd Sunday in Advent, it is **Bible Sunday**, so like 4th December 1966 we had a good sermon on the scriptures.

11th December 1967 Monday
Rehearsals are now well on the way for "**Merry Widow**". I am in the chorus altogether. I did not even get the very minor role of **Olga** which I auditioned for. Ursula is proving a very capable "**Merry Widow**" & the whole show promises to be very good. The costumes are expected to be lavish.

12th December 1967 Tuesday
Today I explored the nether regions of **New County Hall** – great long subterranean passages with rooms leading off – used primarily for stores, but designed also as a refuge in atomic warfare. It was good to emerge into daylight – into a land of peace, with fresh air, & freedom to wander at will.

13th December 1967 Wednesday
I was encouraged this evening by a report in the Leicester Mercury about a newly published book "**The

Myth of the Machine" by the American Lewis Mumford. "Although man & always has been a tool making animal, he also dreamed, played & prayed, & recited. He invented above all & first of all the art of language."

14th December 1967 Thursday

Our 13th & final lesson in car maintenance. For this we learned about the legal obligations affecting the motorist. Mr. Pattle was joined by **Sgt. Ward** of Coalville Police who helped make our last lesson most enjoyable. "**Safety**" was the keynote, & Sgt. Ward's chief concern is Road Safety.

15th December 1967 Friday

Bob Gerard's beautiful Christmas tree was lit up tonight when I motored home from work, & I thought to myself: "Dear Mr Gerard, let us cheer, for Christmas once again is here ….."
We have arranged our office dinner this year for Wednesday 20th December, at **The Star**, **Thrussington**.

16th December 1967 Saturday

Had another pre-Christmas shopping spree in Leicester this morning. As well as buying gifts for friends & relations I bought myself a new leather purse-cum-wallet - £2.
Last Wednesday, the Reverend John D. Adey, aged 35, was inducted into St. James Church & little St. Mary's Church, **Snibston**.

17th December 1967 Sunday

Went to **Leicester** Cathedral this evening to hear the **Provost** preach.
The Provost has written a jolly article for "**Tally Ho**", the journal of Leicester & Rutland Constabulary, which Enid showed me. He likens the good policeman to a good camel – sure footed, steady & utterly reliable.

18th December 1967 Monday

Mr Hollier, in our office, is an expert sign writer. Today I took my 100 year old Bible for him to write in. It bears the inscription – **Elizabeth Bailey, 22nd December 1867**.
He will now add – **Elizabeth Hewes, 22nd December 1967**. **Elizabeth Bailey** was my mother's mother's mother.

19th December 1967 Tuesday

This morning I went with others from our office to the **Abbey Motor Hotel**, Leicester, to hear a talk given by the staff of **Burroughs Sensimatic Machines** on converting to **Decimalisation**. **D-Day** will be a Monday in February 1971. Our office has but 2 of the 2 million machines to be converted.

20th December 1967 Wednesday

I wept today when we received by post licence applications signed by B. Lamming from Federated Garages, Market Harborough. He is the man of my dreams & I cannot simply dismiss him from my thoughts.
Had tea today at Reevsie's & then Reevsie & I & her 16 year old twin sisters went to our office party.

Hewes. – To Irene (nee Treadell) and David, a daughter Alison, born December 20th at Bond Street.

21st December 1967 Thursday

Amongst our Christmas cards received today was one from Irene & David & Alison.
Alison is 1 day old today!
We are now waiting for Mary Blue to have her baby expected very soon.

22nd December 1967 Friday

Today we broke up for our Christmas holiday & return to work next **Thursday**.
This evening I took Mum to Ashby for night duty. I went into **Ashby Hospital** to see the Christmas decorations, & also peeped at the newly born babies all sleeping peacefully, & tucked up in the nursery.

23rd December 1967 Saturday

This morning I motored to **Barrow-on-Soar** to visit my old school pal **Marie Findley** who is now **Mrs. Neville Hewes**. By a most remarkable coincidence she married one of my distant relations. I stayed for dinner & afterwards came home via the Monastery where I took photographs.

24th December 1967 Sunday

This evening Enid & I joined members of Ravenstone Chapel, together with Mr. Essex & his 4 champion trumpeters, on a tour of the village carol singing. We began at **Hall Brothers**, where for the first time ever, we saw coloured television, & finished at **Don's** before leaving for midnight Communion.

25th December 1967 Monday

Went to 11 a.m. service at **Leicester Cathedral**.
Anne Causer had Christmas dinner & tea with Mum & me, & then afterwards I spent the evening with Auntie Gladys, Enid & David.
Aunt Dos & Auntie Belle spent the day at Don's, & Pat & Evelyn are at Mary Blue's for a fortnight.

26th December 1967 Tuesday

On September 3rd I wrote an article for the October Parish Magazine about the origin of our calendar. As there was sufficient material for the magazine without that it was not included. Today I have re-arranged it as an introduction to the New Year for the **January** magazine, which is still not completed.

27th December 1967 Wednesday

Today I finished compiling all the items for our **January Parish Magazine**. Being so very late in the month, I went to **Burton-on-Trent** this evening 'specially to deliver same to **Parkers** the printers.
The Rector, in his letter, expressed "sincere thanks & gratitude to Miss Betty Hewes, editress of our Magazine".

28th December 1967 Thursday

To Mary Blue, a son – **Steven**, born today.
This means **Pat** is now Grandpa Hewes! Pat is my half brother, so it has been decided that I am now a great half aunt! And Aunt Dos of course is great, great Aunt Dos.

Although my dad has dozens of relations my mum has very few.

29th December 1967 Friday

Our last day at work for this year. A very busy counter which I thoroughly enjoyed.

This has been the year when I met the man of my dreams. However, my dreams seem to have been in vain, & so, as in all good musical comedies, the curtain closes on **Act II**, with the heroine in tears.

30th December 1967 Saturday

This afternoon Mum & I motored to **Gartree Prison** estate, to see **Pat & Evelyn**, who are staying at **Mary Blue's** house until next week-end. We did not see **Mary Blue**, as she is in **Market Harborough Hospital**, with her 2 day old baby. **Terry** was overjoyed to have a son.

31st December 1967 Sunday

New Year's Eve! Mum & I stayed up till well after midnight watching television. Our year ended by listening to a wonderful poem, timed perfectly to finish on the stroke of 12, & inviting us to drink to **1968** & to make our toast that some-one somewhere may love us!

* * *

1968

1ˢᵗ January 1968 Monday
This is Leap Year!
Today it was the beginning of our great **January** peak period at work. I enjoyed being on the counter. It is the first time I have ever been on the counter during **January**. I did my best to look my most glamorous!

2ⁿᵈ January 1968 Tuesday
Today I received from **Hall Brothers** the bill for my car radio & fog lamps fitted last November. Radio - £20-15/-, lamps £12-5/-, Total, including speaker, aerial, switch panel, fitting etc. £46-5s-2d. I really do appreciate my car radio.

3ʳᵈ January 1968 Wednesday
Today at work we started on the **NAY** registrations, following the **MUT** series. There were some people who refused to have **MUT** on their new car!
While Pat is staying at Market Harborough I am very pleased to use his garage.

4ᵗʰ January 1968 Thursday
My Editorial in the January Magazine ends: "….. and we have now reached the Year of Our Lord 1968." The bishop, in his letter, mentions "….. in the Year of Our Lord one thousand nine hundred and sixty eight, and of my consecration the fifteenth."

5ᵗʰ January 1968 Friday
The Bishop, in his letter, says, "Each one of our lives not only occupies a certain span among the years of Our Lord, but makes a contribution to the Lordship of Christ in the midst of the years.
If you are looking for a motto for 1968 may I give you this one – **'More than conquerors'**."

6ᵗʰ January 1968 Saturday
Yesterday I joined the library at County Hall, & now I am enjoying my very first library book: "**Daily Life in Greece at the Time of Pericles**" (400 B.C.)
Last night Mum & I saw **Roy Johnson & Brenda** in "Goody Two Shoes".

7ᵗʰ January 1968 Sunday
I am now fairly well acquainted with Athens as it was in the **5ᵗʰ Century B.C.** –"A Golden Age & the birthplace of ideas which still stir the hearts of men". However, I still prefer to benefit from such ideas, in the luxury of the 20ᵗʰ Century.

8ᵗʰ January 1968 Monday
Tosca, the most beautiful cat in the world, which we acquired last **September**, now has a winter coat rather like a polar bear, & is admired by everyone who comes to the house.
Tosca has blue eyes & is fawn coloured with chocolate face, tail & legs.

9ᵗʰ September 1968 Tuesday
Snow – Snow – Snow –"buried **Minnehaha** – covered her with snow, like ermine".
I caught the 7 a.m. bus to Coalville, which ploughed

manfully through deep drifts, but eventually stopped altogether on Standard Hill. Everybody at work had a tale of adventure.

10ᵗʰ January 1968 Wednesday
The **Winter's Tale** continues. With sub-zero temperatures, & hazardous road conditions, I again went to work on the bus.
Our great **January** "rush" is non-existent & the counter has been remarkably slack.
Mr. Hollier, at work, retired today.

11ᵗʰ January 1968 Thursday
The foot & mouth epidemic, which hit our country last October, is still with us but is now very much on the decline. There have been 2,255 cases confirmed in these past 3 months. As restocking begins the Queen has offered livestock of her own.

12ᵗʰ January 1968 Friday
Today at work I had a cheque from **Murphy Bros.** for £4,588 & one for £2,187, which helped to boost my cheque total to a record **£9,222.**
County Hall looks beautiful in her Alpine winter setting & her decks iced with snow.

13ᵗʰ January 1968 Saturday
Continuing with my book "**Daily Life in Greece at the Time of Pericles**", I have become much better acquainted with **Socrates**, the Greek Philosopher, 470-399 B.C. "The best & wisest & most upright in his generation, yet condemned to death for impiety".

14ᵗʰ January 1968 Sunday
Heard an excellent sermon today on "**Christ in the midst**", whose light reaches all …. in the midst of wise men as a baby – as a twelve year old … in the midst of doubt & suffering – between 2 others at **Calvary**, after his resurrection in the upper room & final glory in **Revelation**.

15ᵗʰ January 1968 Monday
Mother Nature waved her magic wand & all the snow, which came last week, has now disappeared. Today we have had gale force winds, which have been so fierce in Scotland, that falling masonry has killed 15 people & injured hundreds.

16ᵗʰ January 1968 Tuesday
Poor old England, no longer <u>Great</u> Britain, is in such financial difficulties, that drastic economy cuts by the Government have been announced today. Ministry spending has been axed by millions of pounds & we have been told to expect a severe Budget in **March**.

17ᵗʰ January 1968 Wednesday
With our country in such a sorry economic plight, the latest craze is a campaign called "**I'm Backing Britain**". All sorts of people are coming up with generous offers & novel ideas to try & help.
I'M BACKING BRITAIN

18ᵗʰ January 1968 Thursday
We have now started rehearsing on Thursdays as well as Mondays for "Merry Widow" which we shall be giving

from 5ᵗʰ – 9ᵗʰ March.

We learned tonight that **Barrie Edwards**, who was to take the lead as "**Danilo**", cannot continue for health reasons.

19ᵗʰ January 1968 Friday

With summer holidays in mind, I have sent for a holiday guide to **Whitby**, Yorks. This year, **Whitby** celebrates the bi-centenary of **Captain James Cook**, who on 26ᵗʰ August 1768, set sail in his **Whitby**-built ship "**Endeavour**" for **Australia & New Zealand**.

20ᵀᴴ January 1968 Saturday

A reader's letter in the **Leicester Mercury** tonight, complains bitterly about our office closing as early as 4 p.m., & ends: - "….. we could do with a bit of that **Backing Britain** spirit in certain quarters."

Don't you think the "**I'm Backing Britain**" stickers are nice!

21ˢᵗ January 1968 Sunday

Today I wrote a poem "**County Hall at Glenfield**" & sent it to the **Leicester Mercury** in reply to yesterday's reader's letter about our office.

Our choir at Church improved considerably tonight with the addition of Doreen Carter, Sally Springthorpe & Kath Nicholls.

22ⁿᵈ January 1968 Monday

This evening we had photographs taken for "**Merry Widow**". With 6 weeks to go to the show, **Derek Capel** has taken over from **Barrie Edwards** as **Danilo**, the male lead. Patron subscriptions are up this year to £1-1/- & seats also are up to 7/-.

23ʳᵈ January 1968 Tuesday

Spent the evening preparing the February Parish Magazine. This included a trip to the Church yard with paper, pencil & torch to copy the instructions concerning care & respect for the Churchyard. I had to compose a diplomatic article on this subject.

24ᵗʰ January 1968 Wednesday

There are 2 letters in the Leicester Mercury tonight in reply to Saturday's letter. One is headed "**Work goes on after 4 o'clock**", from **Mrs. Cartwright, 84, Park Road, Birstall**, & the other signed **E**, starts: - "I am a member of the motor taxation staff."

25ᵗʰ January 1968 Thursday

A letter from **Mr. Sharp** was passed round at work today, which mentioned the letter from "**E**" in last night's **Leicester Mercury**, & said " … I should point out that <u>MY</u> superiors may not look kindly on anonymous staff replies to anonymous letters."

26ᵗʰ January 1968 Friday

Another letter in the Mercury tonight …. "**I called at the New County Hall on January 16ᵗʰ to pay my husband's car tax, due on January 31ˢᵗ, & was told I could not pay it until January 18ᵗʰ since it was payable only 2 weeks beforehand, or 2 weeks afterwards ….. the public, who have paid for that luxurious building ……**"

Signed: - Irritated Customer.

27ᵗʰ January 1968 Saturday

Pat, Evelyn, Aunt Dos & I, today went to see **Mary Blue** & her month old baby **Steven**.

Mary Blue made a lovely young mother & her baby watched her with such alert interest.

Mum today went to London, & to the Prince of Wales Theatre, with the W.I. outing.

28ᵗʰ January 1968 Sunday

On 16ᵗʰ April 1964, **Charles Wilson** was sentenced to 30 years imprisonment for his part in the £2 ½ million **Mail Train Robbery**, 8ᵗʰ August 1963. On 12ᵗʰ August 1964 he escaped. This week he has been found, living in **Canada**, & has now returned to jail.

29ᵗʰ January 1968 Monday

From the **Whitby** holiday guide, Enid & I have chosen the **Oxford Private Hotel**, where we have been offered a twin bedded room, on the floor above the lounge, with sea view, for week commencing 8ᵗʰ June. We have accepted the offer.

30ᵗʰ January 1968 Tuesday

My poem "**County Hall at Glenfield**" 21/1/68, was not printed. However, a letter signed "**County Driver**" is printed tonight in the Leicester Mercury, under the heading: "**County Hall visit a pleasant occasion**", & mentions "a most excellent service" we always give.

31ˢᵗ January 1968 Wednesday

Today we had the busiest counter we have yet encountered at **New County Hall**. With non-stop queues for most of the day it was almost impossible to get our afternoon tea-break. However, it was most enjoyable, & a pleasure to be on the counter.

1ˢᵗ February 1968 Thursday

Again I have been invited to the Mothers' Union birthday party, which is arranged for next **Wednesday**. Our **Ravenstone "Young Wives"** at one time decided to call themselves "**The Thursday Club**", but now they are "**St. Michael & All Angels Ladies Guild.**"

2ⁿᵈ February 1968 Friday

Tonight on television we saw again the impressive state funeral of **Sir Winston Churchill**, (30-1-65), & heard again his voice declaring those now famous words which we always associate with him – words which are a beacon of light beyond dark & troubled waters.

3ʳᵈ February 1968 Saturday

Spent the morning shopping in **Leicester**. I took Minnehaha for a car wash 7/6d.

This afternoon Auntie Belle, Mum & I went to see Auntie Doris at Mountsorrel, where I bought a Shetland wool pale blue cardigan, £3. We stayed at Mountsorrel 'til 9 p.m.

4ᵗʰ February 1968 Sunday

Whitby, where we have booked our summer holiday for this year, is today completely cut off by heavy falls of snow. Blizzards have ranged from Scotland down as far as Derbyshire, but I am very pleased to say that here we had only winds and rain.

5th February 1968 Monday

It is announced today that silver decimal coins will be in circulation later this year – the first stage of **Britain's** switch to decimal currency. 1. Five new pence = the present shilling. 2. Ten new pence = the present 2 shilling. 3. Fifty new pence = the present 10/- note.

6th February 1968 Tuesday

I will tell you what our money is like in 1968.
Twelve pence = 1/-. Twenty shillings = £1.
Our silver coins today are 6d, 1/-, 2/-, 2/6. We call our 6d a tanner, our shilling a bob, our 2/- a florin, & our 2/6d half a crown. Eight half crowns = £1.

7th February 1968 Wednesday

This evening I joined the **Mothers' Union** for their 13th Birthday Party, which was held at **Snibston School**. Evelyn, being a staunch member of the M.U. & a teacher at **Snibston School**, was able to arrange this, & we all had a most enjoyable evening.

8th February 1968 Thursday

From 400 B.C. I have now reached 600 A.D. with my latest book from County Hall Library, called "Augustine of Canterbury". St. Augustine was chosen by Pope Gregory the Great to go to darkest England where he brought the Christian religion to the pagan Anglo-Saxons.

9th February 1968 Friday

On 24th August 1966 our "**Disasters Emergency Committee**" made its first appeal.
Today, in response to the latest appeal, I sent £5 for war-torn **Vietnam**. This is intended for the thousands of homeless civilians whose homes & possessions have been destroyed by **Viet-Cong**.

10th February 1968 Saturday

This evening I met **Alison Hewes**, seven week old baby daughter of **David** & **Irene**, who were spending the evening with Enid & Auntie Gladys. Alison was as good as gold. She lay contentedly cradled in my arms, & gradually fell fast asleep.

11th February 1968 Sunday

Septuagesima! Mum & I went to the Cathedral where the Provost preached on God's continual creation – a creation in which man can partake. He quoted St. Augustine: "Where there is love, consider not the gift of the lover, but the love of the giver."

12th February 1968 Monday

Louie at work is to be relief cashier on the counter when either Miss Gazzard or I am on holiday. I shall be on holiday for a week commencing 4th March for "**Merry Widow**" & Louie is to take my place tomorrow on the counter for practice.

13th February 1968 Tuesday

Mum & I watched on television tonight a film made of the sinking of the **Titanic** in 1912. Long before this Longfellow wrote: - "And they all knew their doom was sealed; they knew that death was near; some prayed who never prayed before, & some they wept, & some they swore, & some were mute with fear." - Tales of a Wayside Inn.

14th February 1968 Wednesday

Out of the archives of **County Hall** library they have managed to find for me, on special request, a book called "**Socrates and his Friends**".
Apparently the library service in **Leicestershire** is the best in the country, & they gladly find any book.

15th February 1968 Thursday

Three years to go to D-day. It is announced today that decimalisation of our money will become fully operative on 15th February 1971.
Britannia, who has been on the reverse side of our coins since the reign of **Charles II**, will not appear on the new coins.

16th February 1968 Friday

Had a letter from Bunting inviting me to take a trip with her to London some time when Michael has a flat there.
It seems he has been persuaded not to go to Africa. (See 27th August 1967)
Michael is now working in London. He will be 21 on February 28th.

17th February 1968 Saturday

Tonight for the very last time, we put our clocks forward one hour. Gone is our **G.M.T.** (Greenwich Mean Time) & we now have **British Standard Time**, or as the news reader said on T.V. this evening, it is now summer time for ever & ever.

Note – Put clocks forward (supposedly for the last time). This new year-long time will be British Standard Time, to be in line with Central European Time.

18th February 1968 Sunday

I have now finished my book "**Socrates and his Friends**". I admire **Socrates** for his great wisdom & his love of truth & justice. He reminds me much of **Jesus** in his gathering of disciples, in his teaching, in his primary concern for the soul, & his brave acceptance of death.

19th February 1968 Monday

Up the City! In tonight's fourth round F.A. Cup replay, **Leicester City** beat **Manchester City** 4-3. The fifth round will be on March 9th when **Leicester City** meets **Rotherham**. Rotherham are fighting fit & have already beaten Wolves & Aston Villa.

20th February 1968 Tuesday

Dense fog this morning made motoring to work at day-break very hazardous. I almost drove into a parked car & could only just discern the traffic lights at the Fox & Goose crossroads. My £12 fog lamps did not seem to be particularly helpful.

21st February 1968 Wednesday

Sat up till after midnight preparing the **March Parish Magazine**. I wrote a delightful article for the children on **St. David** (March 1st), **St. Gregory** (March 12th) & **St. Patrick** (March 17th). I don't know, however, whether there will be room for it.

22nd February 1968 Thursday

With the prospect of a severe Budget next month many

people are buying their new car now. Garages everywhere are doing a bumper trade & we are giving out new car numbers at a fantastic rate. **NAY 1F** to **NAY 999F**, **NJU 1F** to **NJU 999F** etc.

23rd February 1968 Friday

I have now completed one year at work on the vehicle licence counter. I began by taking a particular fancy to a certain garage man (27th February 1967) & have wept much for him since then. As we have 100,000 customers per year you can see he is one in 100,000.

24th February 1968 Saturday

Auntie Cis, aged 75, from Skegness, is in **Ravenstone** for the weekend. She motored here in her car **KAY 7**. (See 8th December 1966) I kept my scooter **KAY 7E** only six months, so I never had the pleasure of photographing this unique pair together.

25th February 1968 Sunday

Mrs Moore informed me tonight that she has managed to get tickets for Mum & me to go with a party from the village to **London** on 4th May to see **Harry Secombe** in "The Four Musketeers" at **Drury Lane**. This is a W.I. outing.

26th February 1968 Monday

Mum today went to **Derby** with the **Ashby Hospital Sports & Social Club**, where they visited the **Crown Derby China** works.
Sylvia & I went for a lunch time drive to **Newtown Linford**.
Bradgate Park re-opens this week after the foot & mouth epidemic.

27th February 1968 Tuesday

One year ago today began my association with "a certain garage man". We now receive their licence applications by post (see 15th November 1967), which lately have borne another signature. I do not know where he is, or whether we shall meet again, but I hope so.

28th February 1968 Wednesday

Today was the quarterly council meeting held for the very first time in **New County Hall** Council Chamber. The **Bishop of Leicester** came & blessed the new building & Council Chamber; & to mark this auspicious occasion, we had the flag flying!

29th February 1968 Thursday

A hectic counter today, which was most enjoyable, but tiring. Garages brought many bulk applications. One of the licences we renewed today was **LAY 1**, a gorgeous number held by **Midland Eggs Ltd., Syston. Dr. Drury** of Blaby has **SAY 99**.

1st March 1968 Friday

Cathedral News-Letter No.50! The Provost says "I'll leave you this **Lent** with a word from old **Bishop Walsham How**. 'You will never lead souls heavenward unless you are climbing yourself. You need not be very far up – but you must be climbing.' Good climbing!"

2nd March 1968 Saturday

My latest book from **County Hall Library** is "Anglo-Saxon England" by Sir Frank Stenton. Covering a period from 500 A.D. to 1066 and all that, it describes in detail the chief phases of the early church, including St. Augustine & the **Venerable Bede**.

3rd March 1968 Sunday

This afternoon we had our full dress rehearsal for "Merry Widow", finishing at 7 p.m.
I met Ursula's 2 year old bundle of mischief – **Christopher**; I met Peter Jacques' most delightful baby daughter **Lisa**, & Margaret Lillyman was there, expecting her baby next week.

4th March 1968 Monday

One year later! (See 4th March 1967) Piano lessons – failure! Clerical Exam – abandoned! Romance – shattered!
Today I went to **Market Harborough** – a thirty mile car ride.
Mary Blue cut my hair & I stayed in **Market Harborough** for lunch & afternoon shopping.

5th March 1968 Tuesday

Opening night of "**Merry Widow**". I am on holiday this week.
Went to Leicester this morning & had my hair permed.
Mum & I went gathering pussy willow this afternoon & met a tame magpie which ate from our hands & stayed long with us.

6th March 1968 Wednesday

A day of gale force winds & little sunshine. "**Merry Widow**" tonight went extremely well. Sylvia, Louie & Frank Dunnett from work came to the show tonight. Tickets are selling well, & it is proving to be one of our most popular shows.

7th March 1968 Thursday

"Merry, but not Memorable".
So reads the heading in the **Leicester Mercury** tonight reporting on our show. "**The Merry Widow**".....
"Achieved a reasonable standard, but could have made it a memorable show with just a little more attention to the niceties."

8th March 1968 Friday

Mum & I went for a morning ride to **Groby Pool & Old John**, where I had my photograph taken in my "**Merry Widow**" **National Costume**. Maurice Gaunt has brought along one of his hair dressers each evening & she has given me some gorgeous hair dos.

9th March 1968 Saturday

Last night of "Merry Widow". Seats have sold so well for this show that we did not have enough programmes to last out until tonight. Our society gave its first production in 1919 with "**Ben Hur**" so next year is to be a special 50 year celebration.

10th March 1968 Sunday

The Rector asked me tonight if I would give the Children's Address at the Mothering Sunday Service a fortnight today. I have in the past spoken to children only, but never to children accompanied by parents; & with others there too.

11th March 1968 Monday

Searched long in County Hall library for some guidance for a talk to the children on Mothering Sunday but without success. Searched long through all my own literature at home, & planned a foundation on "Mothers of the Bible" & "Mothers of great men".

12th March 1968 Tuesday

Went on a dinner hour jaunt into **Leicester** where I enjoyed lunch time shopping once more in the big stores. I experienced for the first time driving through the market place, buzzing with shoppers, who wandered freely all over the road.

13th March 1968 Wednesday

Up the City! In tonight's fifth round F.A. Cup replay, **Leicester City** beat **Rotherham** 2-0. The sixth round will be on March 30th when **Leicester City** meets **Everton**.

Mr Sharp informed Miss Gazzard & me that we are to have name plates made.

14th March 1968 Thursday

Mum & I went to Loughborough Town Hall this evening to see Loughborough Amateurs' production "**South Pacific**". Acclaimed in the Leicester Mercury as a really marvellous show, we were of the opinion that it was rather second rate.

15th March 1968 Friday

Our Amateurs' Annual Dinner Dance at the **Fox & Goose Hotel, Coalville**.

Mr Cherry, the **Leicester Mercury** photographer, was there before we started dinner & took a photograph of Mr & Mrs Saunders, Mr & Mrs Fred Burton & me in a group.

16th March 1968 Saturday

Our poor old Government seems virtually on the point of collapse. **Mr George Brown**, the Foreign Secretary, has now resigned. He is also the deputy leader of the Labour Party & during the past 3 ½ years has threatened to resign at least nine times!

17th March 1968 Sunday

Spent much of the day preparing my talk for "**Mothering Sunday**" which is next Sunday. Having read dozens & dozens of stories, anecdotes & facts, illustrating the church's teaching, I now have a clear outline of what I hope to say.

18th March 1968 Monday

Beat the Budget Day! A monstrous queue at work, non-stop, all day long. I dealt with a record number of customers, over 250.

This evening we went in a party from the Amateurs' to **Staunton Harold Cheshire Home** to sing "**Merry Widow**".

19th March 1968 Tuesday

Budget Day! Car licences up to £25 from £17-10/-
This evening Mum & I saw "**The Taming of the Shrew**" starring **Elizabeth Taylor** & **Richard Burton**. Absolutely great!
I'M BACKING BRITAIN

20th March 1968 Wednesday

Budget Day reactions! As predicted we had a severe budget. Extra taxation totals £923 million a year. The present Government came into office on 15th October 1964, & since then the extra taxation has totalled altogether £2,216 million a year.

21st March 1968 Thursday

An army of workmen descended on **New County Hall** & the inner quadrangles were transformed into verdant pastures from mounds of muck & rubble. Freshly cut turf was laid row after row & flattened with long planks. The whole job was done in record time.

22nd March 1968 Friday

Sylvia & I went to Reevsie's for tea, & stayed until 10-30 p.m. Joanne, now twelve months old, was full of high spirits & bubbling over with all the joy of early childhood. Already she has a vocabulary of single words & easily said, "**Betty**".

23rd March 1968 Saturday

Terry's brother **Teddy** was married today. A day of gale force winds, but the bride managed to look radiantly beautiful with a perfect hair style created by **Mary Blue**, and held so firmly with lacquer, that not a hair was out of place.

24th March 1968 Sunday

Mothering Sunday! I gave the address at our Family Service this morning & I am very pleased to say it was a great success. This afternoon Mum & I went to a **Mothering Sunday Service** at the Cathedral taken entirely by the **Provost**.

25th March 1968 Monday

Mr Brian Shaw, headmaster of **Ravenstone School**, has been publicly criticised by the **Bishop of Leicester** for encouraging children not to be given religious instruction ….. "A shot from the humanists' fleet has been fired across our bows. Christian England expects every Christian parent to do his duty & to support all efforts to maintain Christian standards."

26th March 1968 Tuesday

MY LATEST BOOK FROM COUNTY LIBRARY TEACHES PEN LETTERING.

27th March 1968 Wednesday

Spent the whole evening typing out the **April Parish Magazine** for the printers & then motored to **Burton on Trent** at 10 p.m. to deliver same.

The Rector in his letter mentioned my "Mothering Sunday" address – "stirring and challenging" "most appropriate & refreshing".

28th March 1968 Thursday

A day of sunshine. Motored home with all the car windows open & completely bare armed. Guess what! The **Bonfire Brigade** were out in full force.

I spent the evening with the Ladies Guild, where Auntie Belle demonstrated flower arranging.

29th March 1968 Friday

Enid & I went this evening to Coalville Adult School to

see **"Sky's the Limit"**, a hilarious comedy, in which Tom Whitmore excelled as a drunk.

Today I paid £3-7s-6d for a new tyre, to conform with the new tyre regulations, which operate from 1st April.

30th March 1968 Saturday
Leicester City were knocked out of the F.A. Cup by Everton who won 3-1. Red Alligator won the Grand National, and Cambridge won the 114th Boat Race.

As you can see, I am practising the art and craft of writing. We bought a lawn mower £8-3s-6d.

31st March 1968 Sunday
Mr David Tribe, President of the National Secular Society, defending the Headmaster of Ravenstone School, says: "The majority of parents have effectively abandoned Christianity and wish their children to know about it as history."

1st April 1968 Monday
Miss Gazzard was on holiday today, so I was in charge of the Grand Final Balance, which, being the first day of the month, exceeded £3,500. With 4 monthly car licences now £9-3/- we need a fantastic amount of change. Every other customer wants 17/-.

2nd April 1968 Tuesday
2-4-68 – Two, four, six eight, being quite a special date, I bought a Premium Bond.

This evening Mum & I went with the Rector & his wife to see **"Iolanthe"** at Ashby Town Hall, & afterwards we went to the Rectory for coffee.

3rd April 1968 Wednesday
The chief topic in the readers' letters in the **Leicester Mercury** this evening is "Religious instruction in schools", prompted by the **Ravenstone Head Master**, who does not wish to give such instruction. There are several heated letters, both for & against.

4th April 1968 Thursday
Cathedral News-Letter No.51. The Provost with his "little band of pilgrims" will be going to the **Holy Land** on 17th April, & he has been invited to preach in the **Cathedral Church** of St. George in **Jerusalem** on Sunday April 21st at **Matins**.

5th April 1968 Friday
Dr. Martin Luther King, the most eloquent Negro Baptist minister, who worked unceasingly for the rights of the Negro, has been assassinated in **Memphis, U.S.A.**, by a white sniper. This has sparked off an immediate wave of race rioting, so contrary to his way of peace.

6th April 1968 Saturday
In a big Cabinet re-shuffle last night, **Mrs Barbara Castle** was promoted to First Secretary of State. We now, therefore, have yet another **Minister of Transport – Mr. Richard Marsh**.

Geoff & Jane, both from our office, became engaged today.

7th April 1968 Palm Sunday
Holy Week began at **Ravenstone** with the unveiling of a picture of the **Last Supper** in Ravenstone Church, worked in tapestry.

The church was well filled for this occasion & the Rector gave an excellent sermon on "One of **you** shall betray me" & the response "**Lord, is it I**?"

8th April 1968 Monday
This evening I spanned the reign of **King George III, 1760 – 1820**, with my latest library book. A generous King with a tender heart, I watched him suffer the torment of insanity in his later years, while his wife Queen Charlotte wept & wept.

9th April 1968 Tuesday
Today I met **Mr. J. Arnold Kirby**, Senior Director of **Federated Garages**. He now signs all the application forms for vehicle licences which were once signed **B. Lamming**.

I longed to ask him where my darling was, but I remained sadly silent.

10th April 1968 Wednesday
The Lord Mayor of Leicester, **Sir Mark Henig**, & all his merry men, came to County Hall last night & were presented with a silver water jug in appreciation of 78 years of accommodation for the County Council in **Leicester**.

".... the sojourning of the children of the County in the land of the **Semper Eademites**."

11th April 1968 Thursday
The name plates I mentioned on 13th March arrived today, & so I sat at the counter duly identified as **Miss E. Hewes**. My name is **Elizabeth**, but I am always known as **Betty**.

Hiding therefore, behind the name **E. Hewes**, I can travel incognito.

12th April 1968 Good Friday
Mum & I went to 11 a.m. **Matins** at **Ravenstone Church** & then drove to **County Hall** for Mum to see the splendid surroundings of our gorgeous new offices.

Under a clear blue sky **County Hall** looked absolutely magnificent & palatial.

13th April 1968 Saturday
How about a few more statistics? (See 14th April 1965)
The year ending 31st March 1968 our office issued the following: -
230,384 vehicle licences = £2,732,135
  89,255 driving licences = £57,001
Other licences = £13,000   Arrears = £1,000   Refunds = £88,000

14th April 1968 Easter Sunday
Went to the Cathedral this evening where the **Provost** spoke of the resurrection as **Good** overcoming **Evil, Truth** overcoming **Falsehood, Love** overcoming **Hate**, & **Life** overcoming **Death**. In the final analysis all these finest qualities win through.

15th April 1968 Monday
For the first time in 5 years we have had a glorious sunny day for **Easter Monday**.

As you may expect this called for many bonfires. I spent

all day clearing & digging our unruly garden & actually joined the **Bonfire Brigade** with a real stinker.

16th April 1968 Tuesday
I finished my library book which took me from **William the Conqueror** through every succeeding monarch to our present Queen, **Elizabeth II**. I saw them all from Windsor Castle, where in turn they lived & loved, & laughed & cried, and died.

17th April 1968 Wednesday
In order to introduce decimal currency as smoothly as possible, we shall start next Tuesday by having 2 new coins, the 10p & the 5p. These two have an exact equivalent in size & use now. The 10p = a two shilling piece, now 24 pennies, & the 5p = a shilling, now 12 pennies.

18th April 1968 Thursday
Brian Lamming, whose name is engraved on my heart, is constantly in my thoughts, although I never see him at all these days.
"The love which is fostered by despair is long-lasting"- **Ovid**. (See 11th may 1967)
I would however prefer mutual love to our unfinished symphony.

19th April 1968 Friday
Tomorrow evening there is to be an **Olde Tyme Music Hall** in **Ravenstone Institute – Dress Optional**, but old time costume preferred.
The Matron from Ashby Hospital has provided me with a splendid black cape, long dress, & a fine feathered hat.

20th April 1968 Saturday
Ravenstone Village Institute was packed solid this evening for the Olde Tyme Music Hall. From all directions villagers arrived in their old time costume. **Mr. Cherry**, the Leicester Mercury photographer, came & took lots of photos, including me in my borrowed plumage.

21st April 1968 Sunday
Our Rector gave a very good sermon this evening on Jesus appearing to the 2 disciples on the road to **Emmaus**. At the height of the Passover, we saw the road jostling with crowds, as opposed to the popular more tranquil scene, but always Christ in the midst.

22nd April 1968 Monday
On May 16th our Amateurs' have been booked to give a concert at Groby for the Groby Women's' Institute. Tonight we had our first rehearsal, singing all the rousing numbers from our recent shows – Oklahoma – South Pacific – Desert Song, etc.

23rd April 1968 Tuesday
The new five penny & ten penny pieces – the first of Britain's decimal coins – are out today.
Welcomed by the go-aheads, treated with a great deal of suspicion by the over-cautious, & completely rejected by the stubborn stalwart stick-in-the-muds.

24th April 1968 Wednesday
Spent all evening compiling the **Parish Magazine** for

May. May 26th is **St. Augustine** of **Canterbury**'s day. Thanks to **County Hall Library** (see 8th February 1968), I had ample material to compile an article "For the Children" on "**Augustine of Canterbury**".

25th April 1968 Thursday
Mum & I motored to Burton on Trent this evening to deliver the **May Parish Magazine** contents to **Parkers** the printers. You never saw such a back alley set up. It amazes me that such craftsmanship is housed in such poor quarters, like something from Dickens.

26th April 1968 Friday
My Favourite Customer! Are you tired of hearing about him? Like the father of the Prodigal Son I never cease to look for him. I have decided he is a coward – a liar – a drunkard - & dare not trust anybody, but I love him and long for his return.

27th April 1968 Saturday
This evening I met **Andrew**, 5 week old baby of **Roy & Doreen Powers**. Doreen became a **Mother** on **Mothering Sunday**. Andrew is a tiny baby with dark hair. As with Alison (see 10th February 1968), I endeavoured to rock him to sleep in my arms, but not so successfully.

28th April 1968 Sunday
By request from my 8 Sunday School children we now have "**Bible Study**". We are now working systematically through "The Acts of the Apostles" one chapter per week – reading the whole chapter, writing a brief outline, & drawing a suitable drawing.

29th April 1968 Monday
My annual salary increase takes me this month from £900 p.a. to £940 p.a., & my superannuation has now reached £483-18s-6d. My latest expedition is to the **South Pole** with my latest book from County Library – **Scott's Last Antarctic Expedition 1910 – 1913**.

30th April 1968 Tuesday
Came home from work exhausted after one of the busiest counters we have had at **New County Hall**. I took £9,418 – 8/- in cheques & cash. Customers queued 50 deep & remained remarkably cheerful & patient. It was a real pleasure to serve them.

1st May 1968 Wednesday
The latest law for motorists is compulsory seat belts. Every new car is now fitted with seat belts, but "**If your car was registered after January 1st 1966, & has no seat belts, they must be fitted by 30th June 1968**." **Minnehaha** is in this category.

2nd May 1968 Thursday
Leicester's £2 million Southgates underpass was officially opened today by the Lord Mayor, Alderman Sir Mark Henig.
The Provost arrived home in Leicester today, after his pilgrimage to the Holy Land, which he described as the event of a life-time.

3rd May 1968 Friday
The Rector & Mrs. Lewis called in for an hour this

evening. On 5th May they begin a 15 day holiday in Spain, with the compliments of "**Sky Tours**" in appreciation for all that they did in connection with the **Majorca Coach** disaster. (See 20th August 1967)

4th May 1968 Saturday
A day in **London**, packed with interest. Visited Trafalgar Square, Horse Guards Parade, boat trip from Westminster Bridge to Tower Bridge, & an afternoon visit to Drury Lane, where we saw the most magnificent comedy musical "**The Four Musketeers**".

5th May 1968 Sunday
My collection of crested silver spoons now includes **Westminster Abbey, York Minster, Windsor, Hastings, Isle of Wight, Jersey, Guernsey, Sark, Dublin, Londonderry, Tintagel & Good Old Leicester**. Yesterday I also bought a Premium Bond in **London**.

6th May 1968 Monday
Made a quick dash into Leicester in the dinner hour to get Mum a coach ticket to **Colchester**. She is hoping to spend a week with **Mary Moore** starting 11th May.
I have one day's holiday May 9th & one week's holiday starting May 27th.

7th May 1968 Tuesday
Travelling with Scott on his last Antarctic Expedition (see 29th April 1968), I have met a party of really fine men – **Wilson** – **Bowers** – **Dates** – **Cherry** – **Garrard**, etc. & have seen the splendours of Nature, in her most opulent **Winter Wonderland**.

8th May 1968 Wednesday
The Rector asked me to write his letter for him for the **June** magazine, so I was up till after midnight tonight reconstructing the outline of his **Trinity Sunday Sermon** last year (see 21st May 1967) as a climax to **Whit Sunday**, & a mention of St. Peter's Day 29th June 1968.

9th May 1968 Thursday
Spent the morning shopping in Leicester. Being Thursday, it was half-day closing, but I was surprised to find several shops were closed all day. Went & investigated the new £2 million Southgates underpass, but much of Leicester is still re-shaping.

10th May 1968 Friday
Worked overtime until 8-30 p.m. & then came home to join **Wilson, Bowers & Cherry** in their winter journey to **Cape Crozier** in quest of **Emperor Penguin** eggs. In temperatures minus 77° & literally frozen stiff, face to face with death, they made it.

11th May 1968 Saturday
Took Mum to Leicester to catch her bus to **Colchester**. Mum is spending a week with **Mary Moore**. Meanwhile, I continue my quest of the Antarctic & have reached the mountain ranges, indescribably beautiful in the splendours of snow & ice.

12th May 1968 Sunday
"Then they buried **Minnehaha**: in the snow a grave they made her." Having wept for **Hiawatha** (see 15th June 1964), today I saw how Scott, Wilson & Bowers died & were buried in the snow, beneath a dark Cross against a sky of golden glory, 12th November 1912.

13th May 1968 Monday
Had our final rehearsal tonight for our concert next Thursday at **Groby**.
"**Songs from the Shows by Coalville Amateur Operatic Society.**" My star part is "**Aunt Eller**" in "**Oklahoma**" where I have a little solo work in "**The Farmer & the Cowman.**"

14th May 1968 Tuesday
Leicester has been chosen to become the top security gaol in **Great Britain**. **Leicester** holds the zero post-war escape record – dog patrols are on duty inside the grounds 24 hours a day – it has closed-circuit television & the highest walls in the country. Good old Leicester!

15th May 1968 Wednesday
Continuing with my letter for the magazine (see 8th May 1968), I have managed to incorporate gems of wisdom from the Reverend Gustav Aronsohn (see 14th June 1964) & also: "The Son of God became the son of man that the sons of men might become the sons of God,"

16th May 1968 Thursday
Tonight we went to **Groby** to sing "Songs from our Shows". The audience was most appreciative & clapped loud & long. Afterwards a bouquet was presented to **Ivy Hardy**, as yesterday she and **Vin** celebrated their **Silver Wedding Anniversary**.

17th May 1968 Friday
Another quick dash into Leicester in the dinner hour to get music for "Olde Tyme Music Hall" at Coalville West End Club tomorrow night. Aunt Dos is the pianist.
Among those taking part are **Brian Land**, **Brian Gadsby**, **Michael Swanwick**, **Jack Carter** & **Walter Beniston**.

18th May 1968 Saturday
Walter Beniston collapsed & died while singing on stage tonight at Coalville West End Club. He was 63.
Cup Final Day. West Bromwich Albion beat **Everton 1-0.**
I negotiated with Langham Kendrick to make me a drive-in for **Minnehaha**.

19th May 1968 Sunday
After hours of work on the June Parish Magazine, I rounded it off this evening with one of my favourite quotations: "**And what is so rare as a day in June? Then, if ever, come perfect days. Then heaven tries earth if it be in tune, & over it softly her warm ear lays.**"

20th May 1968 Monday
Today Mr. J. Arnold Kirby paid a second visit to our office (see 9th April 1968). Licence applications from Federated Garages are now few & far between. We had a little chat. Naturally, I gave him extra special attention, because he must know my darling as well as anybody.

21st May 1968 Tuesday

Everybody in **France** has gone on strike! There are no trains, planes, buses, postal services or street cleaners. No teachers – factories closed – complete turmoil, in rebellion against the 5th Republic. 77 year old President de Gaulle says he will bend, but not yield.

22nd May 1968 Wednesday

We have now completed 6 months in our new offices. Customers continue to marvel at our delightful outlook. We look out on to our sun deck, now adorned by the most beautiful flowering shrubs, & fountains playing – the loveliest office you could wish for.

23rd May 1968 Thursday, Ascension Day

My own beloved Brian Lamming! Can you imagine how I wept for him today?

It was on May 23rd 1967 that he said to me, "I'll see you again, & we'll discuss this further."

"This" being the question of removal of endorsements. It seems to me but yesterday.

24th May 1968 Friday

Leicester's new Lord Mayor (elected yesterday) is **Alderman Kenneth Bowder**. The Lord Mayor's chaplain for the year is to be the Provost of Leicester Cathedral, the **Very Reverend J.C. Hughes**. I am on holiday from work now until 5th June.

25th May 1968 Saturday

Bunting, Mostyn & Michael are spending the week-end with Fanny & Thirza. (These are 2 sisters of **Julia**, Bunting's mother – i.e. my dad's first wife.) Bunting, Mostyn & Michael were at **Pat's** for the evening & Aunt Dos & I joined the family gathering.

26th May 1968 Sunday

Mum & I went to the Cathedral this evening. The Cathedral looked like the Town Hall on **Mayor Making** day. Masses of potted flowers, banked in tiers, both outside & on the chancel steps. This was for the Annual Civic Service held at 11 a.m.

27th May 1968 Monday

Got up this morning with the Dawn Chorus to take Mum to work for 5 a.m.! The birds sang non-stop all day long until 10 p.m. Had a grass cutting session this afternoon at little St. Mary's & a garden digging session this evening in our overgrown garden.

28th May 1968 Tuesday

A day of sunshine! This morning I had the seat belts fitted into my car.

This afternoon Mum & I went to **Twycross Zoo**. We saw the smallest elephant you could imagine, great giraffes, etc., but my favourites were 2 penguins who posed for a photograph.

29th May 1968 Wednesday

Spent the morning in Leicester. Being "first day issue of new stamps", I joined the merry throng at the Post Office, & then went on a shopping spree. Remember **Eusabio?** (See 26th July 1966) We saw him distinguish himself again tonight on TV in the **European Cup**.

30th May 1968 Thursday

A day of leisure! Enjoying lazing in the sun – a drive in the car – a little gardening & hour after hour with my latest library book "Stevenson's Book of Quotations" – 70,000 quotations, "the most comprehensive dictionary of quotations ever published".

31st May 1968 Friday

Pay Day! Went to County Hall to collect my salary cheque. Took Mum to see inside County Hall. We then motored to Woodhouse Eaves, for an exclusive lunch at The Tudor House, & afterwards settled at the top of Beacon Hill with cushions etc. for sun-bathing.

1st June 1968 Saturday

Cleared a mountain of rubbish out of our shed, & then had one almighty bonfire, which served very nicely to burn up all the garden rubbish as well. I finished up looking like a cross between a chimney sweep & a bloater – never been quite so dirty.

2nd June 1968 Whit Sunday

Transformation today into a sun-tanned beauty, complete with full glamour & summer attire, for the Christening of **Mary Blue's** baby, **Steven**.

Felt the full impact of **Whit Sunday**, with Holy Communion at 8 a.m. & an excellent sermon tonight on "another comforter."

3rd June 1968 Monday

Finished my book of 70,000 quotations & added richly to my store of the world's wisdom. "Tears, too, are useful; with tears you can melt iron." – **Ovid**. "A flood of thoughts came o'er me, that filled my eyes with tears." – **Longfellow**. I thought of Brian.

4th June 1968 Tuesday

The last day of my eleven day holiday. Sunshine every day!

On Saturday I begin another eleven day holiday. Enid & I will be spending a week at **Whitby**, **Yorks**; & on June 18th Mum & I are hoping to go with a village outing to **Windsor**.

5th June 1968 Wednesday

On November 22nd 1963 **President John Fitzgerald Kennedy** was assassinated.

Today, his brother **Senator Robert Kennedy** was shot in an assassination attempt, & is now critically ill, after an operation to remove a bullet lodged in his brain.

6th June 1968 Thursday

Senator Robert Francis Kennedy, aged 42, died today. President Johnson said: "This is a moment for all Americans to join hands & walk together through the dark night of common anguish into a new dawn of healing unity." Senator Kennedy lived 25 hours after yesterday's shooting.

7th June 1968 Friday

Following the **Whitsuntide** holiday, we have been absolutely overwhelmed with post at work. I have worked 10 hours overtime this week. Today we started on the **ONR** numbers – next will be **OUT** – then **PAY**, **PJU**, **PNR**, **PUT**, & then a jump to **RAY**.

8th June 1968 Saturday
Enid & I arrived at The Oxford Hotel, **Whitby**, at the start of our week's holiday. We had the most delightful ride across the Yorkshire moors from **Pickering** to **Whitby** – bathed in sunshine. This evening at 9-15 p.m. we saw the life-boat launched.

9th June 1968 Sunday
After morning service at **St. Oswald's Church, Lythe**, settled at **Sandsend** till lunch time. Spent the whole afternoon exploring the quaint old fishing port of Whitby, including a ½ hour boat trip. **Whitby**, on a sunny day, is beautiful; & we have a very comfortable hotel.

10th June 1968 Monday
Perfect holiday weather. This morning we lay on the cliff tops, overlooking the beautiful harbour, where **Captain Cook** stands so magnificently looking out to sea.
This afternoon we went a most delightful coach tour to Runswick Bay via Guisborough Moors – wonderful scenery.

11th June 1968 Tuesday
A day of drizzle & swirling sea-mist. No sun-bathing today! Watched the fishermen unload their crabs & fish. Visited **Raven Hall**, **Ravenscar**, with its view of **Robin Hoods Bay**, very like Tintagel, & went to bed to the accompaniment of fog horns.

12th June 1968 Wednesday
A morning walk along the sands to **Sandsend** where we had elevenses.
This afternoon we motored 40 miles inland to **Rievaulx Abbey** & home across the Cleveland hills. The setting sun across the sea tonight tinged all the water with a pinkish glow – really beautiful.

13th June 1968 Thursday
A day of perfect holiday weather, apart from swirling mist, which came for an hour just before lunch.
Spent the afternoon at **Runswick Bay** – absolutely enchanting. **Whitby**, this evening, was a joy to behold – kissed by the sun & bells across the harbour.

14th June 1968 Friday
Watched the sun rise over the sea at 4-30 a.m. Last night we saw the sun go down over the sea at 9-30 p.m. From our hotel bedroom we can see both sun-rise & sunset.
Spent the morning at **Robin Hood's Bay** & this afternoon we sun-bathed at **Redcar**.

15th June 1968 Saturday
Came home from **Whitby** via **York**, where we stopped for elevenses, & went into **York Minster**. With the central tower in danger of collapse, the whole building was a mass of scaffolding – inside & out. An appeal for £2 million was launched 7th April 1967 & £1 ½ million has been raised.

16th June 1968 Sunday
A most rewarding Sunday School this morning with 9 children all full of enthusiasm for the lesson – **Acts of the Apostles, Chapter 8**. They listened most attentively

while I read the Chapter to them & then wrote it in their own words extremely well.

17th June 1968 Monday
This afternoon Mum & I motored to **Willoughby-on-the-Wolds** to see **Madge**.
This evening I had a grass cutting session at **St. Mary's Snibston**, where I was helped considerably by 4 young members of St. James.
Prince Charles today was made a **Knight of the Garter**.

18th June 1968 Tuesday
Mum & I went with a village outing to **Windsor Castle** – agog with activity & sightseers, as the Queen had just left for **Ascot**. Later we visited London Airport where we had to dash for shelter in a sudden thunderstorm. Planes continued to take off.

19th June 1968 Wednesday
Went to a coffee evening at Ravenstone Rectory & afterwards prepared the Parish Magazine for July. My sole contribution – **"Not she with trait'rous kiss her Saviour stung: not she denied Him with unholy tongue; she while apostles shrank could danger brave; last at his Cross & earliest at His grave"** – **"Woman"** by **Eaton Stannard Barrett**.

20th June 1968 Thursday
"The Management Committee of the Leicestershire County Council Staff Social & Sports Club invite Miss B. Hewes and Partner to the **Official Opening** by Col. P. H. Lloyd and a Dance to be held at **County Hall** on 25th June."
The only trouble is – I have no partner, so I shall not be going.

21st June 1968 Friday
Sylvia left work today. **Christine** leaves next Friday.
President Kennedy's youngest brother, Senator Edward Moore Kennedy, last survivor of 4 brothers, may now be a candidate – and target – for the 1972 Presidential campaign. Robert Kennedy was such a candidate this year.

22nd June 1968 Saturday
A day of rain – all day long. I took my car this morning for its 21,000 mile service.
Spent much of the day writing a poem for the August Parish Magazine: - **"Holidays"** -Holidays are here again. Shall we sail to sunny Spain? Fly away to lands unknown? Or stay at home in **Ravenstone**!

23rd June 1968 Sunday
My Sunday School class totalled 10 this morning – most encouraging! Next Sunday is our Sunday School Anniversary, & on the following Friday, the Rector is giving a party on the Rectory lawn for all the Sunday School children.
On 12th October I complete 10 years as a Sunday School teacher.

24th June 1968 Monday
A letter from Mr Sharp to the staff today thanked us for our efforts in the recent hectic periods at work …. "It is

a tremendous relief to me to have the support of a loyal staff in these all too frequent periods of emergency & my sincere thanks are due to all members for their support."

25th June 1968 Tuesday
At last our country is completely free from foot & mouth restrictions after the worst ever epidemic when ½ million animals had to be slaughtered. Tony Hancock, who twice won the award as best British TV comedian of the year; after recent failure & heartbreak, died today.

26th June 1968 Wednesday
It is estimated that the foot & mouth epidemic cost £150 million!
The epidemic began 25th October 1967 and ended exactly 8 months later 25th June 1968.
The epidemic cost the lives of 210,500 cattle 104,300 sheep & 114,800 pigs. Altogether 2,364 farms were hit by this epidemic.

27th June 1968 Thursday
The railway men of this country are at the moment on a go slow strike, & have decided to stop altogether on Sunday. There will be no trains from 10 p.m. on Saturday until 6 a.m. on Monday. This will be the longest complete shut-down since the 1926 General Strike.

28th June 1968 Friday
This afternoon we had a thunderstorm. It rained so hard that County Hall was flooded!
Across the quadrangle from our office we could see them bailing out. Water by the bucketful was being poured out of the windows & tonight it was operation mop-up.

29th June 1968 Saturday
Today I bought a clock - £10-15/-. Mum gave me £5 for my birthday, and with £5-10/- from recent overtime at work, I chose a clock, which I just happened to see in a shop at Coalville this morning – such a beautiful clock!

30th June 1968 Sunday
Perfect weather for our Sunday School Anniversary. There were 21 Sunday School children. I read the lesson this afternoon & Ruth Jones read the lesson this evening. This morning Mum & I went for a car ride along the leafy lanes of the forest.

1st July 1968 Monday
Just imagine today is July 15th. I just got my lines crossed. I wrote to Ashby R.D.C. for an application form to erect a garage. Pat says I can have a garage next to his if I can get planning permission. The chances of that, however, are rather remote.

2nd July 1968 Tuesday
Cathedral News-Letter No.54. The Provost sadly reports the resignation of **Lay Canon George Gray**, who will retire at the end of this year as Cathedral organist. He is the last of the old long-serving Cathedral staff, & the Provost, like Elijah "only am left".

3rd July 1968 Wednesday
This evening **Pat**, Mum & I went in Pat's car to Leicester – to Mountsorrel, where we stayed for an hour with Auntie Doris; & to **Castle Donington** airport, where we admired the most attractive entrance bedecked with 5 coats of arms, and bordered with roses.

4th July 1968 Thursday
Lone yachtsman **Alec Rose**, aged 59, arrived home at Portsmouth today, after his round the world voyage in "**Lively Lady**". Cheered by a crowd of 250,000 people, the Lord Mayor gave him a telegram from the Queen: "**Warmest congratulations on your magnificent voyage.**"

5th July 1968 Friday
The Rector & his wife today had a party on the Rectory lawn for children of the Sunday School. After tea at 5 p.m. in the Rector's Room, we played games on the Rectory lawn until 7-30 p.m. I enjoyed teaching them **croquet**.

6th July 1968 Saturday
One of God's truly beautiful days. Sunshine & gentle cloud, while the whole of Nature hardly stirred – an air of sweet content. Just the right sort of day for Snibston School's 2nd Summer Fair, opened by Mrs. Bennion. Once more I had "**Pegs on a Line**".

7th July 1968 Sunday
Another still summer's day. My Sunday School class totalled 11 this morning – even more encouraging - & I do so like encouragement. Concluding **Acts, Chapter 9**, they were impressed most of all by one **Simon**, a tanner. They called him Simon Sixpence & drew him.

8th July 1968 Monday
Work started today on the reconstruction of London Road, Coalville. This is necessary because of deterioration of the road foundations & will cost over £30,000.
Work has also started on the Markfield by-pass – a formidable task, blasting through solid volcanic rock.

9th July 1968 Tuesday
Cocky my first love! I wept for him much as I wept for Brian Lamming. Much as I loved him I chose not to marry him. For my 21st birthday in 1952, he bought me a gold topped Parker "51" pen – the very best - & with that I have written this diary.

Note – I recall Cocky my first love. "I wept for him much as I now weep for Brian Lamming" whom I long to see, but who seems to have gone away. He certainly does not come to County Hall these days.

10th July 1968 Wednesday
I last saw Brian Lamming on 24th January, exactly 24 weeks ago. You would think by now I may be getting over him. True, I no longer sob & sob for him – rather as my old friend **Ovid** observed, in my tears "there is a certain pleasure in weeping". "Truly it is allowed us to weep: by weeping we disperse our wrath, & tears go through the heart, even like a stream."
I weep therefore without effort & am ever hopeful.

11th July 1968 Thursday

Like me, the heavens poured out their heart, & from 9 a.m. yesterday until 9 a.m. this morning, it rained & rained & rained. Consequently the floods were out everywhere today. I about-turned at the bottom of Standard Hill, going to work this morning, & went up **Wash Lane**, to avoid flood water.

12th July 1968 Friday

After we had closed our office at 4 p.m. today, we had so many customers standing outside, insisting on attention, that we unlocked the doors & dealt with them! They arrived in somewhat of an aggressive mood, but one man said: "**Forgive us our trespasses.**"

13th July 1968 Saturday

Ravenstone Darby & Joan Garden Fete held at the Chaplain's House, was opened by the Rector, the **Reverend Matthew Rice-Lewis**. The weather was fine, & I enjoyed being in charge of the **Spinning Jenny** – 3d a go, I made £3-13s-6d.

14th July 1968 Sunday

Today I am 37. An uninteresting number, divisible neither by 2, 3, 5 nor 7.

My saddest birthdays were when I was 25 (weeping much for Cocky) and when I was 36 (weeping much for Brian Lamming).

Cocky became engaged on my 25th birthday. I would love to become engaged.

15th July 1968 Monday

Phew! Today we all literally wilted in the heat. Every window & every door at County Hall was flung wide open, & with scarcely a breath of air, we were wiping the sweat from our brows. And now I find I'm on the wrong page! Oh dear. Should be July 1st.

16th July 1968 Tuesday

Got a mention in the July "Home and Country", & my limerick in print. In a competition given "There was a young girl called May Day, who cried "Help!" once too often they say" …. I added, "When she yelled grab my lug-hole, I've slipped down the plug-hole, 'twas only the chain that saved May." My latest effort is a variation on **Omar Khayyam.**

17th July 1968 Wednesday

Omar Khayyam wrote: - "A book of verses underneath the bough, a jug of wine, a loaf of bread and thou …." In my variation for the latest competition I wrote: "Above the night clouds, underneath Orion, a wonderland, a world of white, and Brian …" Guess who!

18th July 1968 Thursday

The Government is now making plans to go metric on the roads, replacing miles with kilometres on all road signs. Can you imagine the confusion?

A **kilometre** is ⅝ mile. One hundred kilometres = 62 miles. Altering sign posts & speed limit signs will cost millions of pounds.

19th July 1968 Friday

My choice for the **August Parish Magazine**: - "Tis easy enough to be pleasant when life flows along like a song.

But the man worth while is the one who will smile when everything goes dead wrong. For the test of the heart is trouble, & it always comes with the years; but the smile that is worth the praise of earth, is the smile that comes through tears."

20th July 1968 Saturday

It is announced today that Britain hopes to be fully metric by 1975. By 1975 preferably, & by 1978 definitely, measuring or buying anything in lbs and ozs, inches & miles, pints & gallons, square feet or acres will be out. It will be beer by the half litre, sugar by the kilo.

21st July 1968 Sunday

Today I wrote an article "**For the Children**" for the **August Parish Magazine**. Starting: "I wonder how many of you have seen the new decimal coins now in circulation" it continued to explain £ - s - d, the Roman denarius, Jesus & the tribute money & ended with a writing contest.

22nd July 1968 Monday

Spent most of the day helping the Driving Licence section, doing Charles' work, as he is on holiday. This consists of sending back every "out of order" application, dealing with applications for duplicates, change of address & various other oddments of correspondence – quite interesting.

23rd July 1968 Tuesday

The Government is to spend £20 million on improving conditions in towns & cities facing serious immigrant troubles. There is a list of 23 areas which qualify, including **Leicester**. Already £860 million is being spent in priority areas where there is a large immigrant population.

24th July 1968 Wednesday

"**Leicester** – that's the place with the slag heaps isn't it?" So said Prince Charles at a Buckingham Palace garden party for 8,000 guests yesterday, to a Leicester woman, who added insult to injury by saying today: "I think he must have got confused with **Coalville.**"

25th July 1968 Thursday

Having received by post, a catalogue and price list of **Batley** garages, I am now "raring to go" to have one erected. I have chosen one the same as **Pat's**, 16′ 4″ long outside, 15′ 8″ long inside, 8′ 3″ wide, 6′ 3″ high, with "up & over" door - £74-19s-6d.

26th July 1968 Friday

The latest addition to **County Hall** is **Colour Television** in the "Quiet Room".

Already we have table tennis & darts, cinema & lecture theatre, sick room – so very much like a de luxe hotel that a customer asked if we had a room vacant!

27th July 1968 Saturday

The 83,000 ton liner Queen Elizabeth, the largest liner in the world, has been sold to a group of business men at **Philadelphia, Pennsylvania**, for £3,230,000. She will be moored in Delaware River in **Philadelphia** & used as a hotel & tourist attraction. The 81,000 ton liner Queen Mary was sold for £1,230,000.

28th July 1968 Sunday

The Lambeth Conference, held once every 10 years, has just begun & lasts for the next 4 weeks. Assembled in London are 500 Bishops from all over the world. We are hoping to meet Bishop Crowley of Michigan, U.S.A., at Oaks in Charnwood on August 18th.

29th July 1968 Monday

Enid's Auntie Grace & Uncle Billy arrived today for a few days holiday, staying at Enid's.

Mary Moore has written to Mum, saying she will be coming to stay with us for 10 days, from 9th August to 19th August.

Pat is on holiday this week, so I am pleased to have the use of his garage.

30th July 1968 Tuesday

400 million people watched the **World Cup Final** on television 30th July 1966. About 400 million people are also expected to see on TV the investiture of **Prince Charles** as **Prince of Wales** next year.

Our Rector set off today for another long holiday, so he has asked me to write his September letter.

31st July 1968 Wednesday

A delightful day at work, with lots of customers.

August 1st is the change-over date-line for new car numbers to end "**G**" instead of "**F**". Most people have held back for the past few weeks, to wait for a "**G**" number, & all the garages have been busy.

1st August 1968 Thursday

Lammas Day, so you may well imagine – "**A flood of thoughts came o'er me, that filled my eyes with tears**." Like Longfellow's Evangeline, I know "All the aching of heart, the restless, unsatisfied longing …"

And the world goes by, while my heart seems to lie dormant.

2nd August 1968 Friday

All Local Government Officers are to have a salary increase, dating from August 1st.

This means my present salary of £940 per annum is increased to £975. Next year, I should reach £1,000. In fact, next April I should reach £1,015 per annum.

3rd August 1968 Saturday

Today, at 22,000 miles, I had a set of 5 new tyres for **Minnehaha.** Alf Hall chose them – **Cinturato**, by Pirelli, good strong radial tyres. My car insurance is due this month. I received a renewal notice "**Amount payable £29**", which is more than I expected.

4th August 1968 Sunday

Mum & I went to Leicester Cathedral at 11 a.m., where the preacher was **Bishop West** of **Florida, U.S.A.,** here for the Lambeth Conference.

This evening I went to **Ravenstone Chapel**, where I had been invited to read the lesson – John 14, v. 1 – 21.

5th August 1968 Monday

Had a day's holiday from work. Spent the morning in Leicester, where I had my hair permed – Eugene 30/-.

Today I completed the marathon task of clearing & digging our top garden. It has taken me all summer. We are hoping to have it lawned.

6th August 1968 Tuesday

Reevsie phoned me today & invited me to tea on Thursday.

I motored into Leicester during the dinner hour for a quick dash into Marshall & Snelgrove. In the market there were raspberries for sale – my favourite – so I bought some.

7th August 1968 Wednesday

After a summer of toil, sweat & tears on the garden, I now have a beautiful area measuring 6 yards square, ready for turfing. Apart from all the natural overgrowth, I have cleared 6 bucketfuls of stones & untold pieces of broken pottery.

8th August 1968 Thursday

Spent the evening with Reevsie, Tony & Joanne, now 17 months old. Joanne is bubbling over with vitality and quite talkative.

I weighed myself on Reevsie's bathroom scales – over 10 stone. It's no use – I must try & cut down on cream cakes, etc.

9th August 1968 Friday

Mary Moore arrived to spend a 10 day holiday with Mum & me.

Mr Sharp – our boss at work, has just had a hernia operation & will be away for a few weeks. Les Timson & Frank are on holiday for the next fortnight, so I shall be with Driving Licences.

10th August 1968 Saturday

Mary Moore, Mum & I motored 20 miles to Plumtree, Nottinghamshire to see Jean Dunlevy, one of Mary Moore's many, many friends. We sat in the garden in the lovely summer sunshine, had tea there, & stayed until 8 p.m. Jean is now 53.

11th August 1968 Sunday

Got caught up in a whirlwind of activities, taking Mary Moore to visit Auntie Doris.

As Auntie Doris was out, we went down to the river, up to the "Mount", searched for Maureen at Quorn, back to Mountsorrel, found Auntie Doris – cautioned for parking.

12th August 1968 Monday

Spent the day doing Frank's work – head of Driving Licence section – answering phone, checking licence applications, extracting postal orders and cheques & doing the final balance. Stayed up till after midnight with our very loquacious visitor.

13th August 1968 Tuesday

This evening Mary Moore, Mum & I went to **Snarestone**, where we called to see **John, Edward & Margaret Glover** – 2 brothers & sister at "**The Shrubberies**" – a gorgeous spacious farm-house, where we were highly entertained with jovial chat.

14th August 1968 Wednesday

Took Mary Moore to County Hall this morning to meet 2 of her old work-mates.

Took her to Snarestone again this evening, & afterwards Molly Donaldson, Aunt Dos, Pat & Evelyn joined Mary, Mum & me at home. Mary talks & talks & talks.

15th August 1968 Thursday
This week's Leicester Illustrated Chronicle features **County Hall, Glenfield**, with a whole page of pictures – "**Meet the Workers**", including one of our office, & a four column write up, in full praise of our efficiency, which ends …. "going to work is a pleasure".

16th August 1968 Friday
Had a letter from Fred Burton to say rehearsals for "**Coalville Amateur Operatic Society**" will commence 19th August: We are hoping to give a concert, possibly in November, as well as our usual show next March, which will be "**Oliver**".

17th August 1968 Saturday
Took Mum to Ashby for night duty & then entertained Mary More, Aunt Dos, Enid & Auntie Gladys. We played cards until midnight.
Spent much of the morning inside Ravenstone church doing flower arrangements – our flower Sunday this week.

18th August 1968 Sunday
Took **Mary Moore** to Donington to have lunch with **Molly Donaldson**. I was then invited to stay for lunch, too. I met Molly's father, husband, daughter, son & girl friend & Swedish boy **Ulf**. Spent the evening on the **September Magazine**.

19th August 1968 Monday
This evening I went with Mum, Aunt Dos, Auntie Belle etc. with the **Ravenstone W.I.** annual outing to **Toton Grange**, near **Nottingham**, where we had the most excellent meal, served perfectly, in the most delightful surroundings – most impressive.

20th August 1968 Tuesday
Spent the whole evening compiling an article for the **September Parish Magazine**. Under the heading "St. Michael & All Angels" I referred to **Rebecca Wilkins**, who gave the price-less Communion Plate to our Church in 1715, & her other lasting gifts.

21st August 1968 Wednesday
I was well pleased today to hear from the Guardian Assurance Group that …. "We regret to learn that the renewal papers for policy 5500269 – Miss E. Hewes, were incorrectly prepared. The no claim discount should be £11-4s-6d." I therefore pay £22-8s-6d.

22nd August 1968 Thursday
Completed the **September Magazine**. This was a marathon effort, because I had nothing from the Rector this month. I wrote an article for the children on "**Holy Cross Day**" & several other smaller items. The poem I chose was: "**Say not the struggle nought availeth**".

23rd August 1968 Friday
Completed my 2 weeks in the Driving Licence section doing Frank's work while he was away on holiday. My efforts were well & truly appreciated by the whole section – **Ruby, Annette, Frances, Margaret, Jane & Charles,** who much preferred my system to Frank's.

24th August 1968 Saturday
Went to Leicester on a shopping spree. Bought a dark brown gossamer light cocktail dress £4. For 5 books full of Green Shield Stamps I obtained some very nice bathroom scales. I now weigh 9stone 10lbs – reducing weight by cutting out all stodgy food.

25th August 1968 Sunday
Pat, my brother, is not well. He has been away from work for several months & tomorrow he is going into Leicester Royal Infirmary for treatment. He has "**Simmonds Disease**", which means the balance of salt in his system is incorrect, & needs to be adjusted.

26th August 1968 Monday
For our concert in November, given by **Coalville Amateur Operatic Society**, we have decided half the programme will be "**Trial by Jury**". Tonight we enjoyed learning some of the rich chorus numbers.
We are hoping to see "**Oliver**", our main show, on 19th October in Manchester.

27th August 1968 Tuesday
Eighteen months ago, on 27th February 1967, I met **Brian Lamming**. Now, I never see him at all, but he continues to dominate my thoughts. I weep silently for him, & wonder where he is, & how he is, & what he's doing, & wish so much that I could find him again.

28th August 1968 Wednesday
Mum today went with a party from Ravenstone to **Chatsworth**, where they have a 2 day flower festival. Although the flower arrangements were truly beautiful, Mum was more impressed by the house itself, its pictures, furniture, carpets, art treasures etc.

29th August 1968 Thursday
Pat is 50 today. He is expected to be away from work for at least another month. His thyroid gland is under-active, which makes him weary & worn & sad. He feels miserable & listless, cannot enjoy his meals, & looks forward to the day when he feels better.

30th August 1968 Friday
My Superannuation has now reached £500.
The flag today flew at half mast on County Hall for the funeral of Princess Marina, Duchess of Kent, who died this week, aged 61. It was the wish of the Queen that flags should fly at half mast on all public buildings.

31st August 1968 Saturday
Spent the afternoon in Leicester, enjoying once more the "**hub-bub of the city**" – the crowded market, the colour, the variety, the noise & the bustle. Bought a new tape £2-10/-, for my tape recorder, & this evening recorded the whole of "Trial by Jury" from the wireless.

1st September 1968 Sunday
Auntie Belle & I went to **Heather** Church this evening, where they were holding a flower festival. The preacher was my beloved **Provost**. We lingered long in the church afterwards, admiring the gorgeous flower

arrangements – one by Auntie Belle.

2nd September 1968 Monday

Today is **Bank Holiday Monday**, so we are not at work this week until Wednesday.

This sad world weeps tonight. **Persia** is suffering from a severe earthquake – 20,000 dead, 50,000 injured, 100,000 homeless.

Czechoslovakia is suffering from Russian tyranny.

3rd September 1968 Tuesday

Mum & I went to Mrs Smedley's garden in Ashby-de-la-Zouch this morning, where we bought flowers, ordered plants for October, & rose bushes for November. We chose 6 assorted small rose bushes – 38/-, and 2 standard rose trees, "**Elizabeth of Glamis**" - £1 each.

4th September 1968 Wednesday

Mr Smith at work, & I, both received a mysterious picture postcard this morning, signed "**Guess Who**", from Skegness, & addressed to **County Hall**. We guess it must be a customer who got our name from our name plates; but not my own dearest customer.

5th September 1968 Thursday

"**Mowmacre Turf Supplies** – fresh, precision-cut, weed free lawn turf – 2/- per square yard. Lawns laid at 3/- per sq. yd. – Phone Leicester 61113."

Following this advertisement in the Leicester Mercury, I phoned for a lawn, 6yds by 6yds, & was promised one for Saturday.

6th September 1968 Friday

County Hall is advertising for a new manager £1,370 - £1,625 salary, within grades miscellaneous X/XI – caretaking, security, cleaning, 250,000 sq. ft. floor area – the direction & supervision of caretaking staff & recruitment & supervision of 50 part time cleaners.

7th September 1968 Saturday

On March 21st this year, I witnessed the transformation of **County Hall**, when the lawns were laid. Today our poor old garden was similarly transformed. Turf was laid row by row & my long & arduous efforts were crowned with success. The cost of the lawn was £8-8/-

8th September 1968 Sunday

The Acts of the Apostles, Chapter 12 – a wonderful chapter for holding the children spell-bound this morning at Sunday School – most rewarding! No Sunday School next Sunday because it is the Sunday School outing to Skegness on Saturday.

9th September 1968 Monday

Autumn's glory is just beginning to tinge the trees. I watched the first autumn leaves fall almost imperceptibly at County Hall today. When the last leaves of autumn are falling we shall have completed a year's full cycle in our new surroundings.

10th September 1968 Tuesday

My newly laid lawn needs plenty of water, so it is a joy to me to be writing now, & hear the rain doing its best. As my old friend Longfellow says: "How beautiful is the rain! ….. The rain, the welcome rain ….. To the dry grass & the drier grain, how welcome is the rain!"

11th September 1968 Wednesday

The fountains at County Hall splashed happily all day long – a most enjoyable day at work. Mr Smith is on holiday, so I kept an eye on his work   issued a dog licence, & my first "Moneylenders licence £50". Helped Driving Licences, checked Post Office returns, & served on the counter.

12th September 1968 Thursday

Our new-look garden would now like a new path to set it off. Today, therefore, I phoned **Oldham Bros**. of Wigston, who advertised in the good old Leicester Mercury – slabbing, concreting, tarmacing, etc., estimates free. I should know their estimate by tomorrow.

13th September 1968 Friday

The estimate for a path for our top garden was £56!! I declined the offer. (Today is Friday the thirteenth.) Had a very busy counter at work today – enjoyable, but quite exhausting. I then came home & with the sweat of my brow, cut down a laurel bush.

14th September 1968 Saturday

Our Sunday School outing to **Skegness**. Browsed round all the shops & bought a "Smiths" alarm clock – 35/-

Went to the pictures to see "**Thoroughly Modern Millie**" starring Julie Andrews.

Had tea right at the end of the pier. Arrived home 10 p.m.

15th September 1968 Sunday

In the **Coalville Times** this week, there is an advertisement – "The Stage Society urgently require a girl with good speaking voice & good appearance for the spectacular pantomime "**Aladdin**" at the Town Hall, Ashby-de-la-Zouch, commencing 28-12-68. I applied.

16th September 1968 Monday

The Post Office today starts a speed service.

First class letters bearing a 5d stamp will be delivered the day after posting.

Second class letters bearing a 4d stamp will take about a day longer.

There will no longer be a cheaper rate for postcards.

17th September 1968 Tuesday

Mum & I went to the De Montfort Hall, Leicester, this evening, to see **Victor Borge**. He is a brilliant pianist who delights in burlesque & comedy. We sat on the front row & watched his every move & expression. He is billed as "World's funniest entertainer".

18th September 1968 Wednesday

Mum & I went with a bus load from Ashby Hospital, to the **Odeon Cinema**, Nottingham, to see the latest great film, "**Star**" – the story of Gertrude Lawrence (played by Julie Andrews). This truly was the story of a great star, who died in 1952.

19th September 1968 Thursday

Had a reply from the Stage Society ….. "…..we would be pleased to have you join us as a fairy. We know what you can do, so we would not have to see you for an audition, & needless to say, you would not be in a tu-tu for the part!" I start tomorrow.

20th September 1968 Friday
Went to my first rehearsal of Roy Johnson's pantomime "Aladdin", where I have been accepted for the small part of "**Geni of the Ring**". Set in the mystic East, this is a part I can really enjoy, with full dramatic dignity & splendour, (no ordinary fairy!)

21st September 1968 Saturday
Mum & I went with Ravenstone Church Choir outing to the **Cotswolds**. We called at **Stratford-upon-Avon**, which we enjoyed best of all, & then to **Bourton on the Water** for tea. I searched in vain for Brian Lamming through **Warks**.

22nd September 1968 Sunday
Spent most of the day preparing the **October Parish Magazine**. I chose my dad's favourite quotation – "… we know that all things work together for good to them that love God". Romans 8. V.28. I also reported on yesterday's choir outing.

23rd September 1968 Monday
Being "**Geni of the Ring**", I requested to have a week's holiday from work immediately following the Christmas holiday – our peak period, when nobody dreams of having time off. I used all the charm I had, & what do you think! The answer was "**No**".

24th September 1968 Tuesday
Went to my second rehearsal for "**Aladdin**". I was made very welcome, & enjoyed singing all the lively chorus numbers. We rehearse every Tuesday & Friday, & certainly make tremendous progress. Rehearsals started on 3rd September, so I have quite a lot to catch up on!

25th September 1968 Wednesday
Next Sunday, it is St. Michael & All Angels Day, & Saturday will be our church's annual gift day. Harold arrived at our house tonight with 50 envelopes for distribution some time before Saturday. As you know, this is a job I don't like very much, but regularly accept.

26th September 1968 Thursday
Mum & I duly delivered our 50 envelopes, & then we joined the Ladies Guild in the Rector's Room, where the Rector was showing coloured slides of his recent holidays in Spain & Scotland. We saw sunset over Skye & a full moon over the Mediterranean.

27th September 1968 Friday
Mum went with a party from Ashby Hospital to see **Margot Fonteyn** dance in "**Swan Lake**" at **Coventry**.
For the past 3 weeks we have had quite torrential rain, so our new lawn is positively thriving. Stan Colclough said today that he may soon have a spare garage!

28th September 1968 Saturday
In the Coalville Times this week, there is an advertisement: "**Leicestershire – Coalville King Edward VII Upper School.**" Applications are invited from suitable qualified men & women for the post of senior clerk. This is a new post … Salary £895 - £1,265.

29th September 1968 Sunday
St. Michael & All Angels Day! Went to Holy Communion at 8 a.m.
Called to see Don this afternoon & ordered 13 concrete slabs 2′ by 2′ and 9 slabs 1½′ by 2′ for making paths on our top garden. Alan Pettit has agreed to lay them for us.

30th September 1968 Monday
Today I applied for the advertised post of Senior Clerk at Coalville King Edward VII School. It says "This is a new post which by 1970 will achieve the status of Administrative Assistant." The slabs I ordered yesterday for the garden were delivered today.

1st October 1968 Tuesday
Like the restless, westward wind, the wayward wind, I seek new ventures, ever searching, (but floating like driftwood). With a heavy heart, I long for a kindred spirit to communicate with freely, & find at the end of a perfect day "the soul of a friend".

2nd October 1968 Wednesday
Mrs. Sheila Ann Thorns, aged 30, made history today by giving birth to sextuplets at Birmingham. Four girls & two boys were delivered alive by caesarean operation. One girl died soon after birth. Mrs. Thorns had been taking the fertility drug gonodrophin.

3rd October 1968 Thursday
Ian, Roger, Lynne, Julie & Susan, the five living sextuplets, are headline news today. They have a 50-50 chance of survival. All born within 3 minutes, Lynne is the eldest, Ian – Julie – Susan & Roger the 5th & youngest survivor. The 6th baby died.

4th October 1968 Friday
With the utmost sincerity, Mr. Sharp said to me: "I do so hope you don't get the job at Coalville." I was moved to tears. I belong so very much to the Motor Licence Office; I can hardly bear to sever myself completely from all that it means to me.

5th October 1968 Saturday
Today I wept for Brian Lamming for the last time. It occurred to me that he will never love me. With the dawning of such a realisation, I no longer feel kicked into the mire & trodden underfoot, but feel liberated, & like the Phoenix, can come up smiling again.

6th October 1968 Sunday
Born on July 14th, I am very much a subject of the moon, & have all the qualities of the sea – sometimes under dark clouds, sometimes very upset, but with unfathomable depths of calm. Tonight, with a full moon, I went to the top of the Beacon.

7th October 1968 Monday
Stan Colclough today offered me the choice of a lock up garage at 10/- per week, or a doorless garage at 4/- per week. I chose the lock up garage. With the approach of winter, I am well pleased to have a garage, & so is Minnehaha.

8th October 1968 Tuesday
On 7th October 1956, Susan Hewes was Christened at Ravenstone Church & I was her God-mother. Tomorrow, almost exactly twelve years later, Susan will be confirmed at Ravenstone Church, & I have been invited to her house afterwards.

9th October 1968 Wednesday
Ravenstone Church was filled this evening for the **Confirmation Service** at 8 p.m. It was a moving experience to see my own God-daughter confirmed, & really quite a relief to know that those life-long vows of **Baptism** had now been confirmed.

10th October 1968 Thursday
A most delightful day at work. I arrived at 8 a.m., with the moon watching me through the trees. The fountains played merrily, & the sun shone all day long. All the customers seemed to be in the best of spirits. A joy to serve them.

11th October 1968 Friday
All is now set for the Olympic Games which start tomorrow in **Mexico**, & last for the next two weeks …. High Jump, Long Jump & all other Athletics; Boxing, Canoeing, Cycling, Equestrian events, Fencing, Gymnastics, Hockey, Rowing, Shooting, Soccer, Swimming, Weight-lifting, Wrestling, etc., etc.

12th October 1968 Saturday
Took my car to **Hall Brothers** for its 24,000 mile service.
Having chosen a lock-up garage from Stan Colclough, he told me today that it is not now available. Did you ever know such a man! He is just about as reliable as the weather.

13th October 1968 Sunday
Harvest Thanksgiving at Ravenstone. Went to Holy Communion at 8 a.m., Children's Harvest Service at 2-30 p.m., where I read the lesson & Harvest Festival this evening. Had an unexpected gift (a potted plant) from Stephen Cross, ("With many thanks for your guidance"). He is one of my newly confirmed Sunday School children.

14th October 1968 Monday
Our top garden is now looking very smart, with its newly laid lawn, & now with the slabs laid into two paths. The slabs cost £4-10/- & Alan put them down in 3 hours. He charged us £5. The next thing we would like is a pretty garden fence.

15th October 1968 Tuesday
Betty Hewes found *her* joy **"above the clouds with the one you love"** So it said in the W.I. Magazine "Home & Country", following the competition I did on 17th July. If only they knew how I had searched & searched with breaking heart, for the one I love, they would hardly have thought so.

16th October 1968 Wednesday
Auntie Belle, Mum & I went to see **"A Man for all Seasons"**, voted best picture of the year, at the **Rex Cinema**, Coalville. Set in the days of **Henry VIII**, it portrayed the sterling qualities of **Sir Thomas More**, against treacherous opposition.

17th October 1968 Thursday
I have now completed exactly 20 years at work in the **Motor Licence Department** of the **Leicestershire County Council**. My starting salary was £152 per annum, which was something like 1/6d per hour. Now at £975 per annum, I have 10/- per hour.

18th October 1968 Friday
The final section of the London – Leeds **M 1** motorway was opened at Dodworth, West Riding, today, by Mr. **Richard Marsh**, Minister of Transport.
It is announced today that **Jackie Kennedy**, 39 year old widow of President Kennedy, is to marry **Aristotle Onassis**.

19th October 1968 Saturday
I am writing this at 3 a.m.!! We have just returned from Manchester, where we went in a coach load from Coalville Amateurs to see "Oliver", given by the **Urmston Amateur Operatic Society**. We went at 4-30 p.m., for the 8 p.m. performance, & stopped for a meal at midnight on the **M 6** motorway.

20th October 1968 Sunday
Aristotle Socrates Onassis, Greek multi-millionaire, aged 69, today married Jackie Kennedy, aged 39. They were married on his beautiful private island, **Scorpios**, & will spend their honeymoon on his beautiful private luxury yacht, **Christina**.

21st October 1968 Monday
Three weeks ago, I applied for another job. I never heard another word – not so much as an acknowledgement!
A beautiful day today – warm enough to be out of doors bare armed, and a delightful sunset, which we could enjoy from the windows of our office.

22nd October 1968 Tuesday
After yesterday's beautiful weather, today was a day of fog.
Mum & I were well entertained this evening by the Rector, & Don, who both decided to pay us a visit. Don is Grandpa Hewes again to Lesley's new baby Clare. He now has three grand-daughters.

23rd October 1968 Wednesday
Spent the evening compiling the **November Parish Magazine**. I chose "No" by Thomas Hood. "No park, no ring, no afternoon gentility: no company, no nobility; no warmth, no cheerfulness, no healthful ease, no shade, no shine, no butterflies, no bees, no fruits, no flowers, no leaves, no birds – **November!**"

24th October 1968 Thursday
It was my pleasure & privilege to escort "Councillor" Alf Hall & his wife, on a conducted tour of **County Hall**. I took them through the marble hall, up the grand staircase, into the Council Chamber, the quiet room, the dining hall, & back again.

25th October 1968 Friday
Stan Colclough offered me the shelter of his newly

erected doorless garage. The floor was so rough & irregular I declined his offer. He made loud protestations, that the floor was perfectly alright, but eventually agreed to level it up somehow.

26th October 1968 Saturday
Lynne, the eldest sextuplet, born 2nd October 1968, has died. **Ian**, the second sextuplet, has died. **Julie**, **Susan** and **Roger** are making excellent progress. The 6th baby died shortly after birth.

Giving a pre-view of **Aladdin**, it says in this week's **Coalville Times**: - "A newcomer is Betty Hewes, who will be playing the Geni of the Ring."

27th October 1968 Sunday
In this month's **Parish Magazine**, I received a special word of thanks from the Rector, for my efforts as **Magazine Editress**: - "Editress, Miss Betty Hewes, whose letter with timely reference to the Church was so appropriate at this time, and delightfully written."

In print 3 times this month for 3 different occasions!

28th October 1968 Monday
The XIX Olympiad, held in **Mexico**, has now finished. **Great Britain** won only 5 of the 174 gold medals. We watched most of the highlights on television, sharing the tension, the excitement, the honour & glory, & also disastrous failure.

29th October 1968 Tuesday
Census time is here again! Much to my delight, I am in charge of the counter & not on the census at all.

This year, being the first year we are not putting the clocks back to G.M.T., it is getting progressively darker & darker every morning.

30th October 1968 Wednesday
We have booked our office Christmas Dinner this year at the **Bracken Hill Hotel**, Newtown Linford, which suits me fine, being this side of Leicester in familiar territory. Only 8 weeks to Christmas, & then this dear old diary will near its end.

31st October 1968 Thursday
A typical end of the month day at work. We had a monstrous queue which stretched out of the door & across the sun roof towards the pool. I was in charge of the grand final cash balance – some £3,000 – a wonderful feeling of achievement.

1st November 1968 Friday
Another £3,000 cash balance today. I had well over 250 customers, & by 3 o'clock I was beginning to wilt. We had the roughs and scruffs, & those demanding to "**see the manager**", but never a "Prince Charming" among the whole lot of them.

2nd November 1968 Saturday
Mum & I went to Leicester this morning in torrential rain (through floods).

I had my hair permed at Lewis's - £3-3s-0d. I bought some super, lambs-wool lined, leather gloves £4-12s-6d, a pair of leopard skin slippers 22/6d, & sent for a brown suit.

3rd November 1968 Sunday
I "**moved**" into my new ramshackle garage. It is built at an almost impossible angle, so that the effort of getting either in or out is more than it's worth. And when the car is in the garage there is barely enough room to open the car door.

4th November 1968 Monday
After morning frost, we had the most beautiful sunny November day you could imagine. At work we had the doors & windows flung wide open – just like a day in June.

I made a second attempt at garaging my car, & from another angle managed better.

5th November 1968 Tuesday
On 5th November 1605, **Guy Fawkes** & his fellow conspirators tried to blow up Parliament. Today it is the American Presidential Election Day. **Richard Nixon** – Republican candidate: **Hubert Humphrey** - Democratic candidate: **George Wallace** – Independent.

6th November 1968 Wednesday
Richard Milhous Nixon – Republican candidate, aged 55, has been elected as the 37th President of America. This was one of America's closest, hardest fought & tensest election battles, with Hubert Humphrey a very, very close second.

7th November 1968 Thursday
Tomorrow we give our concert, including "**Trial by Jury**". After this, we shall be concentrating on "**Oliver**", to be given in March.

Rehearsals are now well on the way for "**Aladdin**", & I'm sure "**Geni of the Ring**" is one of the best parts I've ever had.

8th November 1968 Friday
Cathedral News-Letter No. 58.
As on 1st July 1966, the **Provost** once more wants a **Cathedral Secretary** – this time he says: "If any-one knows of someone with the qualities of an angel, willing to work with me, I should be delighted to hear of her." Not a mention of shorthand or typing!

9th November 1968 Saturday
Bruce Richard Reynolds, aged 37, last of the Great Train Robbers, wanted by the Police, was arrested in **Torquay** yesterday, & is now in the top security wing of **Leicester Prison**. Train Robber **Ronald Biggs**, who escaped 8th July 1965, is still free.

10th November 1968 Sunday
I was very tempted to write to the **Provost**, offering my services as **Cathedral Secretary**, especially as tomorrow is **St. Martin's Day**. I decided, however, not to do so. He did not altogether welcome the poem I gave him 27th November 1966, & I hardly think he would choose me.

11th November 1968 Monday
As you may well imagine, my thoughts today have centred mostly on the **Provost**, & the possibilities of being "**Cathedral Secretary**". I doubt whether there is any-one else who merits the job, more than I do, so do

you wonder that I feel restless & unsettled.

12th November 1968 Tuesday

At our Pantomime rehearsal tonight, Roy Johnson gave out the names of the understudies. He said he would like all the understudies to learn their parts thoroughly. Brenda is Principal Boy – Aladdin, & for her understudy he chose – Guess Who! **Me**.

13th November 1968 Wednesday

Today we had the flag flying for the County Council meeting. Congratulations were given to Mr. Stewart Mason, Director of Education, for his recent C.B.E. The new County Hall manager (see 6th September 1968), is expected to be taking over very shortly.

14th November 1968 Thursday

Quote from the Leicester Mercury tonight: The Provost of Leicester requires a full-time secretary. This is an important & interesting post, part of the team-work in the life of our Cathedral. The applicant should be of a cheerful personality ….. in complete charge of the Cathedral office ….. receptionist, etc.

15th November 1968 Friday

Spent all day weighing up the pros & cons of being Cathedral Secretary – coping with rush hour city traffic – a small city office compared with our gorgeous palace at County Hall – a formal "**Miss Hewes**" as opposed to "**Bet**" – yet I still would like to apply.

16th November 1968 Saturday

Having spent all day, writing the most beautiful letter to the Provost, I decided not to send it. Knowing what heart-break it caused me when I opened my heart to Brian Lamming, I have decided to keep my distance, & worship him from afar.

17th November 1968 Sunday

I was told rather bluntly this morning that **Michael Needham**, **John Needham** & **Pat Jarvis**, 3 of my most promising children at Sunday School, don't wish to come again. Once more my spirits sank, & I longed to see some reward for all my labours.

18th November 1968 Monday

After a week of dithering, doubting and deliberating, I finally wrote to the Provost, offering my services as **Cathedral Secretary**. I knew I could not settle until I had at least returned the ball from my court. It is now entirely up to the Provost.

19th November 1968 Tuesday

Feeling sad & weary, I read: -
"Not to the swift, the race: Not to the strong, the fight: Not to the righteous, perfect grace: Not to the wise, the light. But often faltering feet come surest to the goal; & they who walk in darkness meet the sunrise of the soul." Henry Van Dyke, "**Reliance**".

20th November 1968 Wednesday

Spent all evening preparing the **December Parish Magazine**.
This is one quotation I like, but never include: - "King David & King Solomon led merry, merry lives, with many, many lady friends & many, many wives. But when old age crept over them, with many, many qualms, King Solomon wrote Proverbs, & King David wrote the Psalms." – James Ball Naylor.

21st November 1968 Thursday

With the help of my tape recorder, I set about the task of learning Aladdin's part.
Today, I saw my old mate, Reevsie. She came into the office for a licence, & informed me that her father has left home, & gone to live with another woman.

22nd November 1968 Friday

And yet again our country is faced with a financial crisis. This follows the devaluation of the franc in **France**. The government requires a further £250 million, so it's another 10% increase on Purchase Tax. Petrol up from 5/11d to 6/4d. Cigarettes etc. etc. all up.

23rd November 1968 Saturday
New Tax Office Will Be "Based On Leicester"

Both Leicester city and county motor taxation offices will close when vehicle licensing is taken out of the hands of local authorities in the early 1970s.

But local people need not worry, for one of the 60 new licensing offices is to be "based on Leicester".

The exact location of the office, or the area it will have to cover, has not been decided. But it will probably cater for the whole county.

The change-over will start in the early 1970s, and the new system should be in operation by about 1974.

Based on a computer in a central office, the new system is designed to minimise the evasion of vehicle duty, and help the public by providing a better service.

The Provost has replied: - "I regret to have to tell you that the position is already filled, so alas, to the best of my knowledge we shall not have a poet on the premises ….. However, unlike other candidates for the post, I am quite certain that in your case we shall retain a firm "friend" with both a capital & a small F."

24th November 1968 Sunday

So now you know – the Provost did not choose me to be his secretary, but I can be his friend! No doubt that will be much more satisfactory; & much easier just to read his letters, instead of having to take them down in shorthand! He said: "I must confess your memory of them surpasses my own."

25th November 1968 Monday

The parts for "**Oliver**" were announced this evening. I applied for nothing, so I got nothing. This show gives great opportunities to members of our society who have always been in the chorus – unusual character studies – while the recognised stars cannot shine.

26th November 1968 Tuesday

It is now quite dark in the mornings when we arrive at work.
County Hall, this morning, looked like a fairy castle from the distance; & at close quarters the coat of arms was spot-lighted with flood-lighting from the pool below.

27th November 1968 Wednesday
Mum & I went on another envelope delivering mission – **Ravenstone Church** planned giving scheme. The scheme certainly brings in a regular source of income which we might not otherwise have – sometimes £30 a month – sometimes £40, as well as similar general collections.

28th November 1968 Thursday
Geoff & Jane, who work in our office & are engaged to be married, have come up on the football pools this week. They have won £141.
Don. My cousin, has given me an unexpected present for Christmas – a book entitled "Bible Stories" by David Kossoff, 30/-

29th November 1968 Friday
With the help of County Hall Library, I have now been introduced to the poetical works of **John Greenleaf Whittier**, American poet, 1807 – 1892. Though not up to the standard of my old pal, Longfellow, his poetry is full of loving kindness & perfect trust in **God**.

30th November 1968 Saturday
Spent the morning in Leicester, spending a lot of money - £5 for Television Licence - £1-5/- for car wireless licence - £5 worth of Postal Orders for 5 charities - £1-10/- for a tapestry for Susan's Christmas present - £1-1/- for a lovely picture for Aunt Dos.

1st December 1968 Sunday
Highlight of today was teaching the whole Sunday School "**The Twelve Days of Christmas**", ready for a **Carol Service** on 20th December. Divided into 4 groups they sang in turn "5 gold rings – 4 colly birds – 3 French hens – 2 turtle doves & a partridge in a pear tree."
It sounded grand.

2nd December 1968 Monday
Tonight we met "Oliver", "The Artful Dodger", & the rest of the boys taking part in our show this year. We have some very fine talent & collectively they are really impressive. It would appear that we have the makings of a first rate production for our 50th Anniversary.

3rd December 1968 Tuesday
The **Reverend John Adey, Vicar of Snibston**, in his **Parish Magazine** this month, complains of Christmas celebrations starting before Christmas, & says: "I must say I am disappointed to find a **Carol Service** being held in our own Cathedral Church in the middle of the season of Advent."

4th December 1968 Wednesday
Spent most of the evening with John Whittier, American poet, 1807 – 1892. From his writings, I managed to collect some beautiful quotations suitable for the Parish Magazine – for Trinity etc., & one called "**Centennial Hymn**", ideal for the start of the 1970's.

5th December 1968 Thursday
Cathedral News-Letter No. 59. The Provost says: - "I am delighted to be able to tell you that I have managed to obtain the services of another excellent secretary. **Miss Cumberland** will take over as my secretary at the

end of this year." "So", he says, "my guardian angel continues to look after me!"

6th December 1968 Friday
I am now working on another poem, which I would like to put in next month's Parish Magazine.
"Farewell to 1968. The New Year opens wide her gate, And cradled in the breaking dawn, she gently holds her newly born."
"Come let us greet this infant dear, …etc."

7th December 1968 Saturday
My New Year's poem took quite a different turn today: "Carried on the wings of morning, comes the infant, glad new year, born of countless thousand ages, bringing hope & joy & cheer." My poems take so long to evolve they never finish quite as they start.

8th December 1968 Sunday
I am now progressing very well in the learning of my part as understudy to Aladdin.
As one of my quotations says: "I started to sing as I tackled the thing that couldn't be done, & I did it."
I cannot sing as well as Brenda, but I can manage the speaking part.

9th December 1968 Monday
As well as our pantomime, **Aladdin** at the Town Hall, Ashby-de-la-Zouch, there is also the professional pantomime, Aladdin, at the De Montfort Hall, Leicester, ending 18th January 1969. Mum & I have booked seats for this. It will be interesting to compare the two.

10th December 1968 Tuesday
Our own **Pantomime**, **Aladdin**, which starts officially on Saturday 28th December, is already up to presentation standard. This is due entirely to the excellent production of Roy Johnson & his wife, Brenda. Nothing is left to chance, & everything is orderly.

11th December 1968 Wednesday
My New Year poem is now finished. It took me hours & hours to perfect it. It has four verses & ends: "Mother Nature has assembled all her children in a line, And she whispers to her new-born, "Welcome 1969." There is a procession of the seasons.

12th December 1968 Thursday
Mum & I today received our first Christmas Card – "**With kindest thoughts and happy memories – the Revd & Mrs. Gustav Aronsohn.**"
Pat, my brother, after being on the sick for almost a year, started on a new job this week at Grieve's factory.

13th December 1968 Friday
At our rehearsal of Aladdin tonight, I was so intent on following Brenda – watching her every move, & wondering how I would get on in her role of "Aladdin", that I forgot to come in for my own dramatic entrance as "Geni", heralding the grand procession.

14th December 1968 Saturday
On 2nd November I ordered by post a brown suit, which was advertised in the newspaper. It has never arrived. Nevertheless, I ordered today a car cover & reflective

number plates – also through a newspaper advertisement. This one says: "**Sent by return**"!

15th December 1968 Sunday

Today, being the 3rd Sunday in Advent, we had an excellent sermon on St. Luke, Chap.7 v.20. John the Baptist, who had once announced so confidently the coming of Christ; John the Baptist, the man of the great outdoors; from the narrow confines of Herod's prison cell, in total despair, asked, "Art thou he that should come? Or look we for another?"

16th December 1968 Monday

At our Amateur's rehearsal of "**Oliver**", this evening, I was invited to play the part of "Old Sally". This is a part that nobody applied for – a dying woman in the workhouse. I accepted. You could hardly find two more opposite roles than "**Geni**" & "**Old Sally**".

17th December 1968 Tuesday

Reevsie phoned me today & invited me to have tea with her on Thursday.

This is the evening of our office Christmas party, & Reevsie will also be coming to the party. I have been asked to take Christine home to Groby, & Jackie to Coalville, after the party.

18th December 1968 Wednesday

Sat up till after midnight doing the **January Parish Magazine**. The Rector, in his letter, says, "I would like to take this opportunity to thank our Editress, Miss Hewes, for the time & effort she has given each month to producing our Magazine."

19th December 1968 Thursday

Our office Christmas party at the Bracken Hill Hotel, Newtown Linford – a very jolly evening. Had tea with Reevsie. Joanne, who will be 2 next March, has a wonderful vocabulary, & recites one nursery rhyme after another, just like a 4 year old.

20th December 1968 Friday

Minnehaha now looks much smarter with her new reflective number plates which were fitted today. Also I have at last received the brown suit which I sent for on 2nd November.

The costumes arrived today for Aladdin – Dress rehearsal on Sunday.

21st December 1968 Saturday

Spent the morning in Leicester. Bought a Black Watch tartan car rug (made in Connemara). Went to Mrs. Smedley's & collected the rose bushes we ordered. Mum & I set the rose bushes quite easily. The weather was warm & sunny – just like spring.

22nd December 1968 Sunday

Spent practically the whole day at the Town Hall, Ashby-de-la-Zouch, where we went through the whole of **Aladdin**, complete with costumes, scenery, lighting, sound effects & the lot. Brenda & Roy, last Tuesday, adopted a 2 month old baby son – **Ian**.

23rd December 1968 Monday

200,000 miles away, 3 American spacemen are heading for the Moon. Apollo 8, a 30 foot moonship, is hoping to make 10 orbits of the Moon, & then return to Earth.

Tonight on television, for the first time ever, I saw the Earth from outer space – fantastic!

24th December 1968 Tuesday

The 3 American astronauts, Frank Borman, James Lovell & William Anders, are at this very moment orbiting the Moon. It has been so exciting following their progress – sharing the adventure with them, hearing them speak from outer space & getting their pictures.

25th December 1968 Wednesday

Christmas Day 1968. Went to the Cathedral at 11 a.m. with Anne Causer. The Bishop spoke of the 3 astronauts who this Christmas went up to the Moon. He admired their courage, their faith & their cheerfulness & said: "God came down at Christmas."

26th December 1968 Thursday

"I, singularly moved to love the lovely that are not beloved, of all the seasons, most love Winter." – C.K.D. Patmore, 1877. A perfectly beautiful winter's day. Blue skies & sunshine on a world of white, & our garden looking better than ever before.

27th December 1968 Friday

The world's first lunarnauts arrived safely home on Earth today. Their speed of 24,530 m.p.h. was the fastest speed that man has yet travelled. The Queen sent her congratulations & said,

"……. we have all followed with greatest admiration this thrilling & historic journey."

28th December 1968 Saturday

Opening night of "**Aladdin**". We had a matinee as well as the evening performance; & this will be so for the next two Saturdays also. This means that we have 16 performances altogether. I have never been in such a long standing show.

29th December 1968 Sunday

Once upon a time there was a girl who dreamed – me! She wrote her 5 year diary every single day & thought how lovely it would be if she could close her diary by marrying her Prince Charming, & living happily ever after, but it was not so.

30th December 1968 Monday

May I leave you now with the words of Dinah Maria Mulock Craik – "**The New Year**" – "Who comes dancing over the snow: his soft little feet all bare & rosy? Open the door, though the wild winds blow. Take the child in & make him cosy. Take him in & hold him dear. He is the wonderful glad **New Year**."

31st December 1968 Tuesday

Having been with me every day, for the past five years, I am sure you will be interested to know the highlights of the next five years (next page). I do not intend to keep another detailed five year diary, so I will close now. It's been a pleasure writing to you! Love, Betty.

* * *

1969

21st July - Neil Armstrong – first man on the Moon.

1970

25th January – Uncle Hedley died – aged 78.
4th May – Aunt Mary died – aged 99.
26th June – Karen born, daughter of Mary Blue.

1971

10th January – Bunting's Silver Wedding.
30th January – Julian's 21st birthday.
15th February – D. Day – Decimal money.
25th April – The Great Census.
31st July – Michael & Sheena's wedding.
28th October – Britain voted into the Common Market.

1972

3rd May – Leslie Hale is now Lord Hale.
6th May – Centenary Cup Final at Wembley.
28th May – The Duke of Windsor died.
August – Olympic Games at Munich.
20th November – The Queen's Silver Wedding.
December – Apollo 17 – final Moon mission.

1973

1st January – Britain joined the Common Market.
14th February – Mary Blue married Murdo.
24th March – Retired after 25 years with the Amateurs.
9th July – Bought new car KAY 7L
14th November – Royal Wedding – H.R.H. Princess
Anne.

*****

1969

1st January 1969 Wednesday
Here I am – **Elizabeth Hewes**, aged 37 – unmarried, living with my Mum, & ever waiting for my Prince Charming! In the world of Pantomime, where dreams come true, I am appearing in "**Aladdin**" as "**Geni of the Ring**".

3rd January 1969 Friday
We have now given 7 of our 16 performances of Aladdin. We started on 28th December & finish on 11th January. I am **Scheherazade**, Geni of the Ring – an absolutely gorgeous part – dressed in dazzling splendour – dramatic, & a joy to play.

5th January 1969 Sunday
The Ravenstone Parish Magazine for January is now out, containing my latest poem "**1969**". One of the advantages of being Parish Magazine Editress, I can get all my literary efforts in print, if only for a few hundred possible readers.

1969

Carried on the wings of morning,
Comes the Infant Glad New Year,
Filling every heart with wonder,
Bringing hope and joy and cheer.

What a cavalcade for escort!
Winter wearing armour white;
Spring bedecked with apple blossom;
Summer, gay as noonday bright.

Autumn, laden with her treasure,
All for this one child alone.
Come and see the great procession!
It will pass through Ravenstone.

Mother Nature has assembled
All her children in a line,
And she whispers to her new born:
"Welcome 1969"

7th January 1969 Tuesday
We are at present enjoying a spell of remarkably mild weather, which is most fortunate for all of us in our Pantomime, Aladdin. Every seat is now sold for our 5 remaining performances. The scenery & costumes cost £1,200 which we are hoping to cover.

9th January 1969 Thursday
"Aladdin" is now nearing its final performance. Brenda this evening was suffering from a terrible cold & almost lost her voice. I was therefore a most gentle "Geni" & looked after her with special affection. Fortunately she kept going.

11th January 1969 Saturday
On 11th January 1939 my dad died. I was then 7 years old. Today, at 37 years old, I enjoyed the completion of our 16 performances of Aladdin. As my speaking voice is my greatest asset, it was a delight to me to be "Geni of the Ring".

13th January 1969 Monday
Yesterday, Miss Gazzard's father died, so with Miss Gazzard away from work today, I was in charge of the counter & the grand final balance.
We had detailed instructions from the Ministry of Transport concerning the reorganisation of Motor Licensing.

15th January 1969 Wednesday
For 20 years – that is all my working life, I have been employed by the Leicestershire County Council, in the Motor Licence Department, where we have worked indirectly for the Ministry of Transport. However, it has been decided to remove the work from County Councils.

17th January 1969 Friday
On 27th February 1967, I fell hopelessly in love with one of my customers at work. However, my Prince Charming did not return my love, and disappeared completely a year ago. Can you imagine how I felt then, yesterday, when he came back again!

19th January 1969 Sunday
Spent most of the day preparing the **Ravenstone Parish Magazine** for **February**. I wrote an article "For the Children" about **St. Matthias**, whose day is February 24th. I told them how he was chosen to replace Judas Iscariot, & referred to **Acts, Chapter 1**.

21st January 1969 Tuesday
This evening all the members of our Pantomime, "**Aladdin**", gathered at the **British Legion**, Ashby-de-la-Zouch, where we saw ourselves on closed-circuit television. The whole show had been video-taped & we did enjoy watching it all again.

23rd January 1969 Thursday
Love's battle continues!
The man of my dreams has returned only to spurn me – to turn away from me, or deliberately walk straight past me. I feel humiliated, hurt, & wonder when, oh when shall I ever penetrate that rock like countenance.

25th January 1969 Saturday
2,000 years ago – 43 B.C. to 17 A.D. – lived my very old friend, Publius Ovidius Naso, a Roman poet, better known as **Ovid**. His wisdom is profound & knowing that "**Love is a kind of warfare**" he gives me tremendous encouragement as I battle on.

27th January 1969 Monday
The weather is quite remarkable. Today the sun was really warm & you would never have thought it was mid-winter. Apparently we are enjoying a prolonged spell of air drawn up from the **Canary Islands** – much better than the Arctic breezes.

29th January 1969 Wednesday
For the past 15 years, my cousin Enid & I have been on holiday together – **Clacton, Saltdean, Blackpool, Jersey, Isle of Man, Portrush, Bray, Newquay, Isle of Wight, Galway, Bognor Regis, Paignton, St. Leonards, Scarborough, Whitby,** & this year, **Brighton.**

31ˢᵗ January 1969 Friday
Sorely wounded on Love's Battlefield, I entered the W.I. latest competition – compiling a "**Gold Poem**", in praise of my "**Beau**" of burning **Gold**. "Gold is irresistible", "Gold is fair", "Gold is a deep persuading orator", "Gold can do much", etc. etc.

2ⁿᵈ February 1969 Septuagesima Sunday
In the February Cathedral News-letter, my beloved **Provost**, the **Very Reverend John C. Hughes**, concludes: "**May I wish you a victorious Lent**. God Bless!" Like **Ovid**, & my favourite poet, Longfellow, the Provost gives me constant encouragement.

4ᵗʰ February 1969 Tuesday
My latest competition effort is writing Limericks with an Irish flavour to win a free holiday in Ireland. I have written 5, including: -
"**I thought I might fly to the prairies; Cross deserts whose mood never varies; But now I can see, 'tis Ireland for me, for this is the home of the fairies.**"
The winner also gets £100 spending money.

6ᵗʰ February 1969 Thursday
This letter in tonight's Leicester Mercury refers to our office in general & to **me** in particular!

Smile, Please
Visiting the County Hall, to pay my road fund tax, I was agreeably surprised by the modern, clean lines of the building, both inside and out. But the people who work there! Couldn't they be trained to smile and say "Thank you", or is the professional mourner's look adopted for the customer's benefit when he pays out his fivers?
        St. Christopher
Note – I am accused of serving customers with a "professional mourner's look". All because Brian Lamming does not wish to know me.

8ᵗʰ February 1969 Saturday
God's army of little snowflakes yesterday immobilised all the mighty mechanical forces of man. I left Minnehaha at County Hall safely under cover & came home by bus. Every hill in the county was blocked by stranded vehicles. I arrived home at 10 p.m.!

10ᵗʰ February 1969 Monday
Rehearsals are now well on the way for "**Oliver**", which we shall be giving in four weeks time. I am "**Old Sally**", a dying pauper in the work-house. It is only a very small part, but highly dramatic, calling for absolute silence & attention.

12ᵗʰ February 1969 Wednesday
I have now completed the payments on Minnehaha – my very first car, which I bought in August 1967 for £435. Mum gave me £200. I provided £75, & paid the rest in monthly instalments, at the rate of £10 a month.

14ᵗʰ February 1969 Friday
St. Valentine's Day! My heart overflowed with love for Brian Lamming, but like the waters of a fountain, never ending, but getting nowhere, my tears fell in vain, while he remained oblivious to the fact that he was my **Valentine**.

16ᵗʰ February 1969 Quinquagesima Sunday
For the March Parish Magazine, with **Mothers Day** on 16ᵗʰ March, I have chosen to include:
"Lord of the pots & pipkins, since I have no time to be
A Saint by doing lovely things, & vigilling with thee,
By watching in the twilight dawn & storming Heaven's gates, Make me a Saint by getting meals & washing up the plates." – Cecily Hallack.

18ᵗʰ February 1969 Shrove Tuesday
Had an exciting interlude on the way home from work, when I was flagged down by a Prison Warder. His car had broken down, while he & his mate were escorting a prisoner, & I had to get help from the nearest garage.

20ᵗʰ February 1969 Thursday
Another mighty blizzard struck today. You will be pleased to know that Minnehaha is safely tucked up for the night under the Coat of Arms at County Hall – not only under cover, but securely guarded within the inner courts.

22ⁿᵈ February 1969 Saturday
Wrote an article for the March Parish Magazine, under the heading "**A Winter's Tale**".
….. Like Chaucer's pilgrims on their way to Canterbury we walked ….. Not a car in sight as the wintry landscape enfolded us, & we told our tales.

24ᵗʰ February 1969 Monday
Barrie Edwards – leading male singer of our Amateur Operatic Society, died yesterday at the early age of 30, after a year's illness of **Hodgkin's Disease**.
I went to his wedding 9ᵗʰ April 1966, & shall be going to his funeral at Coalville on Thursday.

26ᵗʰ February 1969 Wednesday
I am now on holiday – Wednesday, Thursday, & Friday this week, & all next week when we shall be giving "Oliver". Most people choose to have all their holiday during the summer months, but it suits me fine to have my holiday just when I fancy.

28ᵗʰ February 1969 Friday
"Oliver" is my 21ˢᵗ show!

1. Hit the Deck	11. White Horse Inn
2. Maid of the Mountains	12. Chu Chin Chow
3. Desert Song	13. No, No, Nanette
4. Lilac Domino	14. South Pacific
5. Waltz Time	15. Oklahoma
6. Good Night Vienna	16. Desert Song
7. Maritza	17. Annie
8. Rio Rita	18. Carousel
9 Wild Violets	19. White Horse Inn
10. Rose Marie	20. Merry Widow

1ˢᵗ March 1969 Saturday
While I celebrate my 21ˢᵗ show with **Coalville Amateur Operatic Society**, the society itself celebrates its 50ᵗʰ anniversary, for it was founded in 1919. There is to be a Grand Golden Jubilee Dinner & Dance on Friday 21ˢᵗ March, 27/6d.

3rd March 1969 Monday

Minnehaha is now exactly 3 years old, & for her birthday she had her 27,000 mile service, M.O.T. test, new windscreen wipers, a smart new mirror, wheels changed over, a new spare fan belt, a good clean under the wings & paint touch up - £11.

5th March 1969 Wednesday

This week we are giving "**Oliver**". The show tonight went extremely well. I enjoyed doing my "**Old Sally**" act. I lie on a make-shift bed with a brown cushion pillow, & old grey blanket, wearing a long bedraggled grey wig. I say my bit & die.

7th March 1969 Friday

"**Oliver**", our Golden Jubilee show, has been widely acclaimed & hailed as one of our greatest productions. It appeals to the deeper emotions, being full of pathos, & yet wildly gay with rousing chorus numbers – tremendous contrasts.

9th March 1969 Third Sunday in Lent

Mum & I went to Leicester Cathedral this evening to hear the Provost preach. To a handful of people he delivered a powerful sermon on the great humility of Almighty God. He spoke of perfect love, & the perfect example of Jesus.

11th March 1969 Tuesday

Four patients died in a fire at **Carlton Hayes Hospital, Narborough**, at 2-30 a.m. today. The hospital has 760 mental patients, some old & infirm, & some young – both men & women. Built in 1907, it is a very go ahead modern hospital.

13th March 1969 Thursday

Aunt Dos is 67 today! She is, however, young at heart & always ready for fun. In fact all the **Hewes** family love to play. We are all deeply religious – all enjoy singing – all very emotional – all rather noisy, but extremely loyal.

15th March 1969 Saturday

Today is the 2,013th anniversary of the murder of **Julius Cæsar**, in the Roman Senate on the Ides of March. In today's paper "**In Memoriam**", it said: "**Cæsar**, husband of **Calpurnia**, conqueror of Gaul, etc., we remember you."

17th March 1969 Monday

In tonight's Leicester Mercury, "Mr. Leicester" reports on his visit to County Hall to renew his car licence. After queuing – a cold sweat – slipping surreptitiously back to the car – another long wait, the clerk "**with suitable admin. aplomb**" revealed that licences are no longer recorded in the Registration Book.

19th March 1969 Wednesday

The W.I. magazine "Home & Country" celebrates its 50th birthday this month.
In its grand jubilee edition, the result of the "**Gold Poem**" competition includes "**Highly Commended** .... **Betty Hewes**." There are now 9,005 Institutes with 456,230 members.

21st March 1969 Friday

For the first time ever, my name was mentioned on the wireless! My letter to "**Motoring & the Motorist**" was chosen from listeners' letters, & was called ... "**very short brief letter – a model if I may say so Miss Hewes of Leicester – interesting.**"

23rd March 1969 Passion Sunday

All our regular **Lesson Readers** were absent from church tonight, so I was very pleased when the **Rector** asked me to read both the lessons. Although I am one of the world's worst conversationalists, I command instant attention when I read.

25th March 1969 Tuesday

I am currently engrossed in trying to compile a **crossword** for a competition. After many hours of trial & error, I have at last fitted all the necessary words together in the right pattern. The great thing now is to work out clues for them.

27th March 1969 Thursday

From good old **County Hall Library**, I have found the very book I want at the moment: -"**Ximenes on the Art of the Crossword**". The author, **D. S. MacNutt**, gives me wonderful help & guidance on the art of making the perfect clue.

29th March 1969 Saturday

Great excitement today when **Leicester City** beat **West Bromwich Albion** 1- 0 in the F.A. Cup Semi-Final. The Final will be on April 26th against **Manchester City**.
Four times in the last 20 years we've reached **Wembley**, but never won.

31st March 1969 Monday

A bumper day at work today, being the last day of the month, & also the possibility of car tax increase with next month's budget. One of my customers took offence to the way I told him certain facts, & said: "You must think you are all omnipotent."

2nd April 1969 Wednesday

Motor Licence staff from far & near assembled this evening in the grand Council Chamber of good old County Hall, Glenfield, where 2 men from the Ministry of Transport spent a most uncomfortable 2 hours being bombarded by awkward questions.

4th April 1969 Good Friday

The new system for licensing motor vehicles means that **Motor Licence** staff in the future will be **Civil Servants**, instead of **Local Government Officers**. I have therefore applied for an interview to become a civil servant.

6th April 1969 Easter Sunday

Went to 11 a.m. service at **Leicester Cathedral** & little **Rowlie Jarvis**, aged 11, came with me. He attends Ravenstone Church regularly & was quite familiar with the service. It was a pleasure to have such a model child with me.

8th April 1969 Easter Tuesday

What delightful holiday weather. We have just had 5

wonderful sunny days – the best **Easter** holiday weather for over **20 years**. Apart from enjoying the sunshine, I have also completed & sent off my crossword competition – my best clues ever.

10th April 1969 Thursday
A good clue should always give the answer twice within itself. I therefore have clued "Scarlet" – "Red **mark allowed**". Red = scarlet, mark = scar, let = allowed. "**Numerates**" means true numbers. The word itself means numbers, & the letters are in "**means true**", etc.

12th April 1969 Saturday
Following an advertisement in this week's **Coalville Times**, Mum & I booked a holiday for August Bank Holiday – V. & M. Coaches Ltd., 4 days **Edinburgh**, **Forth Bridge** & **Military Tattoo**, depart Ashby 29th August. Inclusive fare £17 each.

14th April 1969 Monday
Tomorrow is Budget Day. With rumours of a possible increase in car tax, we had a bumper day at work today, & worked 2 hours overtime. We had a letter at work complimenting us on our excellent efficiency, speed & cheerful courtesy.

16th April 1969 Wednesday
Watched on television "Son of Man", the Wednesday play by **Dennis Potter**. This was the story of **Jesus**, the story of a man – a man burning with convictions – not the usual gentle Jesus, but wild, rough, & very much down to earth.

18th April 1969 Friday
Well, the Budget did not bring any rise in **Motor Tax**. There was another 2d on petrol, making my petrol now 6/6d per gallon. I usually do about 150 miles each week in the car, and have about 4 gallons of petrol, which makes it 26/-. Twenty six shillings being interpreted is one pound and 30 new pence.

20th April 1969 Sunday
My poor old Sunday School class which dwindled almost completely away has suddenly grown to a most encouraging size, with an influx of children from the younger school. Last week I had 14, & this week another 3 children came along.

22nd April 1969 Tuesday
In a sheltered nook, on a corner window ledge, within the inner quadrangles of County Hall, a blackbird has built her home. We watched the nest take shape & then we saw one speckled egg appear, & today another one.

24th April 1969 Thursday
Yesterday, our County Hall blackbird laid a third egg in her nest, & today she laid her fourth. She sits on her nest in full view to us all, & we know more or less exactly what time to expect another egg. We look forward to meeting the family.

26th April 1969 Saturday
Shared in all the excitement of **Cup Final Day**, & watched on television poor old **Leicester City** beaten 1-0 by **Manchester City**. The Cup was presented this year by **Princess Anne**, now 18 years old & just starting out on her public engagements.

28th April 1969 Monday
Leicester City's homecoming after losing the **Cup** for the 4th time in 20 years, & facing relegation if we don't win our last vital league games, was absolutely stupendous. The band played, a hundred thousand people cheered & the players were moved to tears.

30th April 1969 Wednesday
My salary now exceeds £1,000 per year! This month's annual increment raises my salary from £975 to £1,015. This is **Local Government Clerical 2** grade, which reaches a maximum £1,055. **Clerical 3** grade starts £1,055 & **Clerical 4** starts £1,215.

2nd May 1969 Friday
I had a letter to say: "The judging of our recent crossword competition has now been completed & I am sure you will be pleased to hear that you are among the runners-up, who will each receive a prize of two guineas, payable when the puzzle is printed.

4th May 1969 Sunday
Our **Parish Magazine**, this month, is not printed but simply duplicated copies of my typing. This is an attempt to cut down expenses & means that I now have to submit my work in its final state of perfection, always covering 4 pages exactly.

6th May 1969 Tuesday
With this month's **Cathedral News-letter**, I received a 12 page booklet "The Friends of Leicester Cathedral – List of Members 1969." Bishop, Provost, Assistant Bishops, Archdeacons & Canons, Lay Canons, 25 Life Members (including me), 250 members & various bodies.

8th May 1969 Thursday
The blackbird who built her nest and laid 4 eggs at County Hall has now abandoned house & home. We are all very disappointed. No doubt the bird chose her site at the week-end, when the building was empty, & did not appreciate our return to work.

10th May 1969 Saturday
Knowing that I have won £2-2/- for my recent Crossword, I chose to buy for my prize a new **Dictionary**. My present dictionary is literally dropping to bits, so today I bought a lovely new "**Chambers' Twentieth Century Dictionary**" 27/6d.

12th May 1969 Monday
Today I rang up **Imperial Typewriters**, Leicester, to enquire the price of an electric typewriter. I was informed that the cheapest would be £180. I asked if there was any chance of a 2nd hand one about £100. They will let me know.

14th May 1969 Wednesday
Leicester City football's future now hangs by a single thread. Tonight they gained one point when they drew 1-1 against **Everton**.
On Saturday they will be playing **Manchester United** &

they must win to avoid relegation.

16th May 1969 Friday
I had a letter from the Ministry of Transport, St. Christopher House, Southwark Street, London SE 1, inviting me to an interview for a post in the Ministry of Transport, in connection with Centralisation of Motor Licensing, on 6th June.

18th May 1969 Sunday
Manchester United yesterday beat Leicester City 3-2, and so we go out of **Division I** into **Division II**. Today we watched on television, **Apollo X** set out for the Moon. **Apollo XI** in July will land the first man on the Moon.

20th May 1969 Tuesday
I had a phone call to say that Imperial Typewriters could get me an electric type-writer for £100. This would be one which had been used for demonstration, & almost as good as new, with a 12 month guarantee. I said I would like to see it.

22nd May 1969 Thursday
In front of County Hall, in the noon-day sunlight, I was introduced to my beautiful new stream-lined electric type-writer, which was later delivered at home. I shall draw out £50 from my Premium Bonds & pay another £50 over 3 months.

24th May 1969 Saturday
Apollo X, now on its 600,000 mile round trip of the Moon, today sent back our closest ever views of the Moon's surface. We saw great craters & mountain ranges, & the proposed landing site for the 1st man on the Moon in July.

26th May 1969 Whit Monday
Astronauts Thomas Stafford, Eugene Cernan & John Young arrived safely back on Earth today after their trip round the Moon. We watched the splash down in the **Pacific** this afternoon on television. It was dawn in the Pacific.

28th May 1969 Wednesday
While astronauts prepare for the first ever man on the Moon, Enid & I look forward to our more down to Earth holiday – a week in **Brighton** starting June 14th. We have booked at the Arnold House Hotel, which organises a whole variety of entertainment.

30th May 1969 Friday
I received further details for my interview next Friday – 2 p.m. The Albert Hall Institute, Derby Road, Nottingham (3rd Floor – Room 7).
Alf Hall has agreed to take me in his Mercedes.
We have a whole day's holiday, so I shall have my hair set.

31st May 1969 Saturday
On this day in 1669 - Samuel Pepys stopped writing his diary because of failing eyesight.

1st June 1969 Trinity Sunday
Here we are again in June – "And what is so rare as a day in June. Then, if ever, come perfect days. Then heaven tries earth if it be in tune, & over it softly her warm ear lays." J. R. Lowell.
It was good to start June with Trinity Sunday.

3rd June 1969 Tuesday
The Decimal Currency Board announces today that our old familiar coin the ½d (ha'penny) will go altogether on 1st August: our very good friend the half crown will go on 1st January next year. Coming in on 14th October this year will be the new 50 penny.

5th June 1969 Thursday
On the eve of my very important interview, I am busy compiling facts & figures – listening to top men talking on television, reading the newspaper more than usual, looking up details in the **Encyclopaedia**, & generally doing my **homework**.

7th June 1969 Saturday
I am well pleased to tell you that I felt perfectly at ease during my half hour interview yesterday, & was asked only questions which I was capable of answering. I was interviewed by 3 men – all very clever & important, but they did not try to belittle me.

9th June 1969 Monday
Coalville Amateur Operatic Society's Annual General Meeting. I was chosen to be on the **Selection Committee**, which will include listening to auditions for parts in our next show – "**Kiss Me Kate**", which we give 2nd – 7th March 1970.

11th June 1969 Wednesday
At 11 a.m. today the **Fire Alarm** rang loud & long & the whole building was vacated in 2 minutes flat. This was our first organised fire drill at County Hall & all our customers joined in the exercise. The sun shone & it was fun.

13th June 1969 Friday
The June issue of "**Public Service**", our **Local Government** newspaper which does the **Crossword Compiling** competition is now out giving the names of the winners. H. J. Pilling (Dundee Health Services) is the 1st Prize Winner. Ten runners up include **Elizabeth Hewes**.

15th June 1969 Sunday
The great excitement of yesterday, before starting out for our week's holiday in **Brighton**, was that I had won £25. This was **1st Prize** given by the **Daily Express**, for my clue to "Stumps" – **Stupid M.P.s with no heart may be caught out by them.**
This will help towards my typewriter.

17th June 1969 Tuesday
Brighton unfolds her treasures to us. We gazed in wonder at the inner magnificence of the Royal Pavilion – watched the dolphins in the Dolphinarium – visited Devil's Dyke & saw the wonderful view from there: & saw in a bird museum at Bramber, the full story of **"Who Killed Cock Robin."**

19th June 1969 Thursday

Getting to know **Brighton** more intimately. Took a ride on **Brighton's** sea front railway – the first electric railway in this country; strolled leisurely through "**The Lanes**", where old fisher folk's bow-windowed cottages of long ago, are now transformed into antique & curio shops of world renown.

21st June 1969 Saturday

Arrived home from **Brighton**, much more learned & knowledgeable in the meaning of the word "**Regency**". In 1811, King George III was old, & his mental powers were failing, so his son (later George IV) became Prince Regent. His architect, John Nash, transformed his Brighton home into the Royal Pavilion & built Regent Street.

23rd June 1969 Monday

Spent all evening typing out the **July Parish Magazine** on my new electric typewriter.

On July 5th we have our Sunday School outing to Mablethorpe – not very exciting.

All the really interesting sea-side places are too far away for a single day's outing.

25th June 1969 Wednesday

On March 18th 1966, the Reverend **Matthew Rice Lewis** became **Rector of Ravenstone**.

He has now decided to retire to **Swansea**, & will be leaving at the end of September. We have enjoyed his brief stay with us, as he is a holy man full of fun.

27th June 1969 Friday

After my week's holiday at health giving **Brighton**, I have developed one of the worst colds I have ever had. So now it is out with the smelling salts, the brandy bottle, handkerchiefs by the dozen, sneezing & blowing, & jolly glad to have a free day tomorrow.

29th June 1969 Sunday

On July 1st is the Investiture of **Prince Charles** as **Prince of Wales** at **Caernarvon Castle**. At 3 p.m. he will declare publicly to the Queen: "I, Charles, Prince of Wales, do become your liege man of life & limb & earthly worship, & faith and truth I will bear unto you to live and die against all manner of folks." He is now 20.

1st July 1969 Tuesday

The Investiture of H.R.H. the Prince of Wales. We saw on coloured television the whole ceremony, & watched H.M. the Queen present "her dear son" Charles to the people of Wales as "their Prince". It seemed that no bride for Charles could possibly ever match his mother. She was an absolute inspiration.

3rd July 1969 Thursday

Following yet another complaint from a customer who could not get a licence after we had closed, Mr. Sharp wrote to him – a school teacher : -

"If on any occasion during the holidays you are in a position to come to County Hall, I should be pleased to show you some of the problems in this section, which handles thousands of applications expeditiously …."

5th July 1969 Saturday

Spent many hours puzzling out the **Daily Express** weekly crossword puzzle. This is a puzzle with no clues – just a prepared square with the blank spaces marked out, & you put any words you like which fit together, & clue just one.

7th July 1969 Monday

Have just finished a most interesting book from County Hall Library, "**An Island to Oneself**" by Tom Neale, who chose to live alone for **6 years** on a desert island. The island was "**Anchorage**", part of the atoll "**Suvarov**", in the Cook Islands of the Pacific.

9th July 1969 Wednesday

With the prospect of the first man on the Moon later this month, I wrote an article for the **August Parish Magazine**, "**Man on the Moon**". I traced man's concept of the universe from the days of **Genesis**, culminating with the Book of **Revelation**.

11th July 1969 Friday

It is Leicester's **Holiday Fortnight** this week & next, so I have been going into town most days during the lunch hour. There is plenty of room to park & it is nice to have all the shops more or less to yourself …. like a deserted city.

13th July 1969 Sunday

Tomorrow is my birthday – aged 38.

What a lovely number – twice nineteen. I have now completed 2 **Metonic Cycles** of 19 years. In the 86th **Olympiad**, **Meton** the Greek astronomer discovered that the great planets move in a set pattern lasting 19 years, & so it is that 19 is a "Golden Number".

P. S. The first Olympiad = 776 B.C.

15th July 1969 Tuesday

Man prepares to land on the Moon & so my latest books from County Hall Library are : - "**Man Probes the Universe**" and "**The Flammarian Book of Astronomy**".

I am amazed at the vastness of the universe. Landing on the Moon seems nothing.

17th July 1969 Thursday

Learning more & more about our solar system.

Imagine the sun in the middle with Venus going round, outside of that the Earth & then Mars. This is a minute section of the universe & the Moon just goes round the Earth.

19th July Saturday

Reg Hall has loaned me a massive book "**Splendour of the Heavens**". With a wider concept & fuller understanding of the planets & stars I gazed at the night sky. I also read the Gospel of **St. John, Chapter 17**, & gave it deeper meaning.

21st July 1969 Monday

Man took his first step on the Moon today. Neil Armstrong & Edwin Aldrin unveiled a plaque : - "Here men from the Planet Earth first set foot upon the Moon, July 1969 A.D. We came in peace for all mankind."

23rd July 1969 Wednesday
Being fully engrossed with "**Man on the Moon**", I have acquired a much more intelligent concept of the Universe. And to think I am a personal friend of the Lord & Creator of all.
It adds even greater momentum to the fact that I was made an inheritor of the **Kingdom of Heaven**.

25th July 1969 Friday
The first men on the Moon have arrived safely back on Earth. They landed in the **Pacific** & were taken aboard the carrier **Hornet**, where the President of the U.S.A. President **Nixon** was there to give them a personal welcome. He said the past week was the most important since Creation – a gross over-statement.

27th July 1969 Sunday
We have just completed 2 months of glorious summer sunshine. It has been virtually like the **French Riviera**, with sun tanned beauties everywhere – customers at work bare chested & bare legged. The best summer weather we've had for years.

29th July 1969 Tuesday
I now have a regular passenger who travels with me daily to & from County Hall. His name is **Malcolm**, an eighteen year old boy straight from school, who lives just down the road. He is a clever lad, training to be an accountant, & pleasant company.

31st July 1969 Thursday
All Local Government Officers are to have a 7 % pay rise. This is to operate in 2 stages. The first rise will be 3½ % starting 1st August 1969 & a further rise 1st August 1970 to bring all salaries in line with decimal currency. My £1,015 now goes to £1,055 making Clerical II maximum eventually reaching £1,134.

2nd August 1969 Saturday
America plans a journey to **Mars**!
Twelve astronauts would leave Earth for **Mars** on 12th November 1981. They would arrive
9 months later on 9th August 1982 – stay in orbit until 28th October 1982, returning via **Venus**! They would arrive home on Earth the following year, 18th August 1983.

4th August 1969 Monday
Mercury, Venus, Earth, Mars, Jupiter, Saturn, Uranus, Neptune, Pluto.
These are the 9 major planets of our solar system & we now want to do a "grand tour" in the mid-1970s while they are all in a suitable position. Such an opportunity will not recur for another 180 years! (It will be unmanned).

6th August 1969 Wednesday
Feeling very subdued this evening after being £5 short in cash when I came to balance after the day's takings at work. We counted and re-counted, but the fact remained – I was £5 short.
This set up a chain reaction of depression, & how I longed for a loving shoulder to rest against for comfort.

8th August 1969 Friday
Guarded all my money at work today as I have never guarded it before. Locked the drawer every time I moved any distance away, kept the key, & decided that if my money had been deliberately stolen, the thief would probably strike again.

10th August 1969 Sunday
Mum & I went to **Leicester Cathedral** this morning & heard the Chancellor in Residence, the Rev. **Canon Gundry** give the most excellent sermon on **Job**: Chap. 38, V.4.
God, by His mighty works, from the vastness of the universe speaks to one little man, on this planet **Earth**.

12th August 1969 Tuesday
At **Leicester Cathedral** last Sunday I was introduced by **Mr. Tindall** to **Mr. C. Saunders** who is 93, and is getting married on 6th September. A former director of the **John Bull Rubber Company**, he has been appointed lay canon emeritus of Leicester Cathedral. He is a wonderful old man – not a bit crotchety.

14th August 1969 Thursday
Enid's Auntie Grace & Uncle Billy (known as Gracious & Billious) are staying in Ravenstone for a few days. This evening we all enjoyed a rare game of croquet.
Today at work we have had alarm bells fitted under the counter, to give direct contact with Leicester Police Headquarters in case of attack.

15th August 1969 Friday
The Army went on duty in the streets of Northern Ireland.

16th August 1969 Saturday
Winner of the £25 prize in the 3,068th Daily Express Crossword Contest was Miss Elizabeth Hewes, Leicester Road, Ravenstone, Leicester.
*Her cryptic clue to "**Loud**" was "**Roaring Fortes!**"*

Mum set out for a week's holiday with Mary Moore with the good news that we have again won £25 – 1st Prize given weekly by the Express.

18th August 1969 Monday
As an aid to **Crossword Compiling**, I am now making my own list of 9, 10, 11, & 12 letter words & phrases. Going systematically through the dictionary I came across this word: - **Honorificabilitudinity**. It comes from the Latin **Honorificabilitudinitatibus**.

20th August 1969 Wednesday
Mum & I have now received all the details for our Scottish holiday. We leave Ravenstone at
2 p.m. on Friday 29th August & stay for one night at the County Hotel, **Carlisle** – then on to **Edinburgh**, where we stay for 2 nights, returning home on Monday.

22nd August 1969 Friday
I now have a most useful collection of words & phrases suitable for **Crossword** compiling. Nine letter words such as **Pizzicato**, 10 letters such as **Up a Gum Tree**, 11 letters such as **Schottische**, & 12 letters such as **Raise the Roof** & **Jack in the Box**.

24th August 1969 Sunday

Had an interesting interlude yesterday when Mum & Auntie Belle missed their bus home from **Colchester** to **Leicester**. They eventually caught a bus to Northampton & I motored fifty miles to Northampton (my longest journey yet) to meet them. Their relief & joy at seeing me was a reward in itself.

26th August 1969 Tuesday

Mrs. Hayes, my life long next door neighbour, died yesterday. She died without effort, quite unexpectedly, although she had not been too well of late. She was a typical Leicestershire character, & spoke the local dialect perfectly. Her expression: "**Ghee awe, Sid**" was one of my favourites.

28th August 1969 Thursday

Scotland! Here we come. Tomorrow Mum & I travel to **Carlisle** by coach & then on Saturday continue north to **Edinburgh**. Mum has been to Scotland before, but this will be the very first time I have gone north of the border.

30th August 1969 Saturday

Today I made my first acquaintance with **Edinburgh** & was absolutely enchanted. It far surpassed anything I had ever imagined. The sun shone all day long, & this evening we went to the **Tattoo**, which was a most moving experience.

1st September 1969 Monday

Returned home from **Edinburgh** with a wealth of wonderful memories – morning service yesterday at **St. Giles Cathedral**, where we sang with the Band of the **1st Battalion Black Watch** – a trip to the magnificent **Forth Bridge** – a visit to the Palace of **Holyroodhouse** – a city indeed to return to again.

3rd September 1969 Wednesday

Minnehaha, my little car, now 3 ½ years old, has just been done up to face the wintry blasts. All the rust lurking in the crevices has been properly dealt with, the roof has been painted a pretty Old English White, & Reg Hall has attended to a variety of minor defects lurking under the bonnet quite unbeknown to me.

5th September 1969 Friday

A most enjoyable busy day at work today. I dealt with a non stop queue all day long – over 250 customers, without getting overwhelmed at all. It was good to feel in perfect command of the situation – poised & confident – calm & efficient!

7th September 1969 Sunday

I have now gone all the way through my **New Dictionary**, & have reaped a bumper harvest of words useful for **Crossword** compiling – especially those ending with a vowel, like **cornucopia, nostalgia, spaghetti, portfolio, incognito, portmanteau, and trousseau.**

9th September 1969 Tuesday

B, F and **X** are tricky endings to find words for. For these I have found "**smash and grab**" "Jockey Club" "handkerchief" "coral reef" "anticlimax" "sealing

wax" "Income Tax" "powder puff" "treble clef" "damp squib" "waterproof" etc.

11th September 1969 Thursday

Had a day's holiday from work yesterday for the funeral of **Frank Newman**, former musical director of **Coalville Amateur Operatic Society**, who died last Saturday, after years of suffering & struggling & fighting for breath.

13th September 1969 Saturday

Sat up till long after midnight struggling with this week's **Prize Crossword**. It was certainly the hardest I have known them to set. Instead of the usual 12 letter square, it was a 15 letter square, & it took me till Sunday tea-time to finish it! I was able to use my word "Spaghetti."

15th September 1969 Monday

Last night at Church, our appointed **Lesson Readers** were not there, so I was very pleased when the Rector invited me to read both lessons. What a joy to read from **I Peter**.... "You are a chosen generation, a royal priesthood, a holy nation, called out of darkness into His marvellous light."

17th September 1969 Wednesday

Derek Buxton, former **Precentor** of **Leicester Cathedral**, was last night inducted as **Rector** of **Ibstock**. The Church was packed to capacity. I was there – Mr. Tindall was there – my beloved **Provost** was there, & the Bishop likened his relationship with **Derek** to **St. Paul** & **Timothy**.

19th September 1969 Friday

Received a letter from the **Ministry of Transport** … following your interview before the Civil Service Commission, you have been recommended for appointment as a Clerical Officer. Further details, including the station (i.e. Swansea or a local office) will be forwarded later this year.

Note – Motor Licence work is to transfer from the Leicestershire County Council (Local Government) to Central Government – the Ministry of Transport. We are to become Civil Servants rather than Local Government Officers. We have to be interviewed to determine our new Civil Service grade. I am recommended for appointment as Clerical Officer.

21st September 1969 Sunday

All of a sudden this week, without any pre-meditation, I signed on for the Winter Session (24 weeks – 48/-) **at Leicester City Adult Education Centre** for **Elocution** on Wednesday evenings 7 p.m. – 9 p.m. This covers voice production, articulation, enunciation & pronunciation, tone, colour etc.

23rd September 1969 Tuesday

The Rector & I combined our talents & spent a long time together perfecting his last **Parish Magazine**. We went to great lengths to find the most appropriate poem & prayer, & went through his letter in great detail – re-phrasing & correcting.

25th September 1969 Thursday

Last night I went to my first elocution class & was favourably impressed. We had 13 in the class, & we each had the opportunity to read aloud. As you know, I love reading aloud!

It seems that the course of lessons covers all the subjects that I like best – **Poetry** – **Drama** & **Pure English**.

27th September 1969 Saturday

Our retiring Rector, the Revd. **Matthew Rice Lewis**, as a parting gift to me, gave me £2 & a letter suggesting I buy "**Treasures of English Words & Phrases**" … you will find it most useful. I hope I've given enough to purchase same. **Many thanks and blessings galore.**
Your friend & Rector, M. Rice Lewis.

29th September 1969 Monday

I have been stung on my leg by a wasp. The swelling got worse & worse & more painful, so eventually I went to Ashby hospital. I now have my leg bandaged from knee to toes & advised not to go to work tomorrow.

I have an appointment to see the Doctor tomorrow morning at 11 a.m.

1st October 1969 Wednesday

Because of my wasp sting I have had 2 days off work. I was given **Piriton** tablets (tiny yellow pills marked a/h) which give you a relaxed drowsy feeling. Consequently I slept much of yesterday. I am hoping to return to work tomorrow.

3rd October 1969 Friday

What a lot of discomfort my wasp sting has given me! And what a lot of supposedly soothing appliances it has been given – first raw onion, then the blue bag – Anthisan cream galore – vinegar – cold water & talcum powder – dequalinium gauze, but itch, itch, itch & burning hot. I hope it's nearly finished.

5th October 1969 Sunday

Enid's birthday tomorrow! She will be 42! Twice 21, & half way to 84.

She has boundless energy – plays hockey & runs as fast as ever – takes a keep fit class; & goes from one thing to another non-stop – gardening – mowing the lawn – hedge-cutting – washing – ironing; & never tires.

7th October 1969 Tuesday

Mr. Richard Marsh, Minister of Transport, has been removed from office.

Mr. Anthony Crosland is now head of the Ministry of Transport as well as Housing & Local Government, with Mr. Fred Mulley under him as the new Transport Minister.

So our poor old Ministry of Transport has been down graded.

9th October 1969 Thursday

Motored into Leicester during the dinner hour, & while negotiating one of the big traffic islands, I knocked down a scooter rider. He was **Mike Glover**, 191, Dominion Road, Leicester, on **FXE 33C**. He said he was not hurt, his bike seemed alright & my car was slightly marked, for which he offered to pay.

11th October 1969 Saturday

The October issue of "**Public Service**", the Local Government news-paper, is now out & contains the **Crossword** which I compiled earlier this year. I received a cheque for £2-2/- for this marathon effort.

There is also a prize offered to those who do it, which should be easier.

13th October 1969 Monday

Tomorrow, the new 50 pence piece comes into circulation. Equivalent in value to half a pound note, it will gradually replace our present 10 shilling note.

This will be our third decimal coin, the others being 5p & 10p.

Our present pennies are called d. = denarii   240 in a £.

15th October 1969 Wednesday

We have now had 4 elocution lessons. We read a few exercises all together for vowel sounds etc. & then we read individually – anything we fancy – poetry – prose – speeches by Churchill, Queen Elizabeth I, or II or extracts from a play. Then we comment   encourage, & gradually all improve.

17th October 1969 Friday

The competition in the W.I. magazine "Home & Country" this month is a 4 line verse to a cat. I wrote:
"There never was seen a queen so serene, Nor eyes so exquisitely bright; You have your own way, & sleep all the day, Then out every night for a fight."
Dogs come later.

19th October 1969 Sunday

As with all my poems, "**Ode to a Cat**" now is quite different from its original composition & reads: - "There never was seen a queen so serene, Whose charm everybody beguiles. You have your own way & you sleep all the day, then at night you go out on the tiles."
I thought that better.

21st October 1969 Tuesday

"**Kiss Me Kate**" has now been cast, & for the first time in 20 years I was chosen to voice my opinion in the casting.

I chose Janice for Kate, & Ursula got the part. I chose Derek for Petruchio, & Frank got the part. I chose Peter for Baptista, & John got the part – so much for my valued opinion!

23rd October 1969 Thursday

Spent all evening typing out the **November Parish Magazine**. We are now **Rectorless**, & for the prayer I chose a favourite of our previous Rector, the Revd. Gustav Aronsohn – "May the love of the Lord Jesus draw us to Himself, may the power of the Lord Jesus strengthen us in His service, may the joy of the Lord Jesus fill our souls …"

25th October 1969 Saturday

Tonight there is a full moon, & the stars are literally sparkling – perfectly beautiful. Mum was on night duty last night at Ashby hospital & they had more new babies than they'd had for a week or two. Matron is firmly convinced that the full moon is totally responsible for this.

27ᵗʰ October 1969 Monday
"You are more welcome than the flowers in May," said a member of our staff to me at work today, when I joined the Driving Licence section, while their section head was fully engrossed in preparing new records for Driving Licence Centralisation.

29ᵗʰ October 1969 Wednesday
We have had a wonderful summer this year, & the sunny days have lasted until now. Today at work we had the fountains splashing away – blue sky & brilliant sunshine, & the trees looking an absolute picture of autumn splendour. My poem "**1969**" seems to describe it well.

31ˢᵗ October 1969 Friday
Minnehaha, my faithful little car, conked out yesterday morning when we stopped at **Bardon** level crossing. Malcolm, my worthy passenger, got out & pushed but to no avail. Then a gallant passer by came to the rescue with a tow rope, & for the first time ever, I experienced driving a dead car, which then came to life.

2ⁿᵈ November 1969 Sunday
Last Tuesday I went to **Kirby Muxloe** to see their portrayal of "**Kiss Me Kate**", & then last night we went in a bus load from our Amateurs to Burslem, Stoke on Trent, to see another presentation – very spectacular, & on a grandiose scale. Even so, I much prefer the original "**Taming of the Shrew**".

4ᵗʰ November 1969 Tuesday
Through County Hall Library I have now made the acquaintance of **Peter Pook** – one of the funniest writers I have ever known. He has written 7 books, covering different phases of his life, & I am now on my third. He gets himself into all manner of predicaments, but like Brer Rabbit, gets out.

6ᵗʰ November 1969 Thursday
At our elocution classes, we have now advanced to reading Shakespeare. We have two foreigners in the class & it is interesting to hear their opinions & problems. Trying to understand our complex language, when you have not been born into it, is almost beyond the bounds of possibility.

8ᵗʰ November 1969 Saturday
After 14 years of faithful service my fur lined winter boots have now been relegated to gardening boots. Today I bought a new pair – brown leather, with inside zip fastening,
9″ high, fleecy lined, stout soled, & yet managing to combine elegance with warmth, £7.

10ᵗʰ November 1969 Monday
"**Public Service**" is now out for **November** giving the solution to the crossword I compiled & the names of the 2 winners – Miss C. J. Allen, (Hammersmith) & G. Ryan (Durham C. C.). It is nice to know that people took the trouble to do it.
P.S. I forgot to tell you – I am 14,000 days old today.

12ᵗʰ November 1969 Wednesday
Minnehaha is spending the night in the car park at

County Hall – not from choice, but because when I tried to start the engine this evening it could manage no more than a click. I rang Alf, & he said it would be the starter motor at fault, & he would come tomorrow morning to put it right.

14ᵗʰ November 1969 Friday
Minnehaha is now home again, safe and sound, thanks to Alf who went 'specially to County Hall & revived her with a push & a tap with the hammer, a tightening up of this & that, an adjustment here & there, a revving up as if about to go into orbit, & a general once-over.

16ᵗʰ November 1969 Sunday
Went to the Cathedral for Evensong, where the cream of the Church seemed almost wasted on a microscopic fragment of the populace. The Bishop preached – Canon Gundry & the Provost read the lessons – the Choir sang an Anthem, but there were less than 50 people in the 1,300 seats.

18ᵗʰ November 1969 Tuesday
The fashion for young ladies today is to wear their skirts as short as possible, showing the whole of their leg & sometimes more. From one extreme to the other, comes the very latest full length coat, down to the ankle. I tried one on today & liked it very much.

20ᵗʰ November 1969 Thursday
Brian Lamming, the man of my dreams, who chooses to remain a man of mystery, has not been into our office since last **January**. He then came from Colmore's Garage – Loughborough. Today I accepted a **Certificate of Insurance** from Dick Protheroe's Garage – Husbands Bosworth, including B. Lamming.

22ⁿᵈ November 1969 Saturday
Born under the sign of the moon, with all its watery influences, makes me super sensitive, & interested in fathoming the mysteries of Crossword Puzzles; makes me a creative writer; & makes me love **Brian Lamming**, who must surely be the most impossible man to love. He certainly makes himself unfathomable.

24ᵗʰ November 1969 Monday
If you could see me now, wondering what on earth to put in my diary, you would hardly call me a **creative writer**! Monday night is rehearsal night for "**Kiss Me Kate**", & tonight we have had a first class rehearsal, with our new choreographer, who taught us the first moves.

26ᵗʰ November 1969 Wednesday
Motoring home alone from elocution class, I was flagged down by a policeman on a dark lonely stretch of road. There were 3 police cars & other policemen around.
"Good evening, Sir – Sorry! Good evening, Madam. Just a routine check. Where have you come from & where are you going?"

28ᵗʰ November 1969 Friday
In a further effort to safeguard all our money at work, from a possible smash & grab, we now have a new automatic lock on the swing doors immediately behind

the counter. This is put into operation when we think it advisable.

30th November 1969 Advent Sunday

Three months ago we returned from Scotland & picked some Scottish heather from the roadside. That same heather still looks as fresh as ever sitting on the mantelpiece in a vase of water. It drinks quite a lot & we are quite surprised that it has lasted so long without drooping.

2nd December 1969 Tuesday

Tosca, our beautiful cat – a cross between a **Persian** & a **Siamese**, now has his full winter coat & looks gorgeous. Sometimes he looks like a sheep – a fox – a lion – the Sphinx & even a swan, when sitting broad beamed. He lies like a dead rabbit or all curled up & cuddly.

4th December 1969 Thursday

My latest effort at trying to win a fortune is the **Daily Express "Fairy Godmother"** contest – **Win a Golden 1970**. The prize is £20 a week for a year, £500 on your birthday, £200 for your holiday, plus £250 for Christmas 1970. (Or £1970 lump sum). Just the thing for 1970.

6th December 1969 Saturday

Cathedral Newsletter No. 71. The Provost says, "…. Just so long as Jesus is born in us & borne by us, we need have no fear, but rather expectation & excitement. He will shock us & shake us, & possibly shatter us, but He will also share with us His joy & peace everlasting … God bless you all, & the happiest of Christmases. As ever, John C. Hughes, Provost.

8th December 1969 Monday

One of my regular customers – a car salesman from **Market Harborough**, told me today of the heart break he has suffered, since his wife left home & went to live with her **Prince Charming**, in **Kettering**.
The thought occurred to me – **could that possibly be Brian Lamming!**

10th December 1969 Wednesday

Motor Licence centralisation seems to be more of a complex proposition than anticipated.
The Ministry of Transport starts some marathon scheme which does not seem to go according to plan. We get detailed instructions what to do, & then we get further instructions to abandon that idea.

12th December 1969 Friday

The great Christmas shopping spree is now in full swing. This week I bought presents for **Pat & Evelyn**, **Auntie Gladys & Enid**, & also bought myself a gorgeous new leather purse, 7 inches wide, with nice roomy compartments for 3 sorts of coins, & 3 pockets for notes etc. £2-15/-

14th December 1969 Sunday

According to my handwriting – the size of it shows I am ambitious, optimistic & adventurous!
The height of it shows I am spiritual, idealistic, imaginative or intellectual.
The slant of it shows I am extrovert, progressive & sympathetic, & the disconnected letters shows I think

intuitively & have creative & inspiring ideas.

16th December 1969 Tuesday

Received a Christmas card from our old Rector, the Reverend Gustav Aronsohn, & also a Christmas card & letter from our last Rector, the Reverend Matthew Rice Lewis. Both now have lovely homes overlooking the sea – one near **Eastbourne** & the other near **Swansea**.
Nice to hear from them both together!

18th December 1969 Thursday

The man I love, **Brian Lamming**, stood before me today, & my heart melted. I had not seen him since last **January,** so can you imagine how I felt? I looked at him long & lovingly, while he did his best to remain unmoved.

20th December 1969 Saturday

The book I now have from the library, "**The Young & Lonely King**", tells the story of **King Charles I**. First published only this year, it is priced in the old familiar style at 30/- & also in the new decimal style £1-50p.

22nd December 1969 Monday

Mum & I have now dispatched our 40 Christmas cards – 20 for relations, & 20 for friends & acquaintances. We iced the Christmas cake tonight.
Last night at Church we had our service of 9 Lessons & Carols by candle-light. I enjoyed helping light the many night lights before we started.

24th December 1969 Wednesday

Christmas Eve! We finished work at 12 noon today, so I spent the afternoon in Leicester, doing the last minute Christmas shopping.
Watched on television this evening "**The Merry Widow**", & how Count Danilo Danilovitch reminded me of my own beloved, who likewise behaves towards me.

26th December 1969 Friday

Had a long lazy lie-in this morning, after a very late night last night. We were playing cards until 2 a.m. – Auntie Gladys, Enid, Aunt Dos, Anne Causer, Mum & I. Today the sun has shone as bright as mid-summer. Went for a car ride over the forest, & then to the pictures.

28th December 1969 Sunday

Spent practically the whole day preparing the **January Parish Magazine**. I wrote a short article on "**The Epiphany**", & Dennis wrote the main letter to the **Parish**. This is rather a unique issue, because it is the start, not only of a new year, but of a new decade – the 70s.

30th December 1969 Tuesday

And so we come to the end of the sixties. I am 38 years old & have of late changed my image – chiefly through hair style. With an entirely different hair style, & a regular weekly hairdressing appointment, including cutting & colouring at regular intervals, I now feel & look better.

* * *

At Work, Rest & Play

Aerial photograph of Snibston Primary School in the
1970s. Betty attended this school from 1936 to 1942.
At date of publication (May 2010) the school is closed,
the weeds are growing and its fate appears undecided.

A few hundred yards away along
Leicester Road is No 27, the
house where Betty lived for her
entire life.

Here is Mary's Lane leading
to little St Mary's Church,
one of the three churches
which Betty regularly visited.
Her father and mother lie
buried there, together with
many other relatives.
Betty's ashes are among
several which, over the
years, have been placed into
her dad's grave in the
Churchyard.

Right - Betty in Mary's Lane.

Betty, far right, with friends from Coalville Grammar School, circa
1944 when she began to keep a diary

Sunday 27th July 1947 - Picnic at Kegworth
Going clockwise from Betty - Aunt Cis, Evelyn,
Mary Blue aged 3, David Hewes (standing) Aunt
Gladys (with cup) brother Pat and Uncle Cyril

Croquet on Uncle Cyril's lawn at No.
50, Leicester Road, Ravenstone

Betty at her desk in the Motor Licence Office

Betty with the friend she called
'Reevsie'at work in the 1950's. Her
name was Pat Reeves (now Walsom)
Here they are issuing licences

Motor Vehicle Licence Office Staff 1959
In those days licences for Leicestershire were issued from 14 Friar lane, Leicester

1966 Motor Licence Office party
Betty is seated far right

1988

29th March 1988 Tuesday: *"What a lovely day for G.O.M.B.'s Branch Liaison Officer today, organising for the whole Branch a photographic session. First we all assembled on the front steps of the building for a big group photograph & then..."*

Above - **22nd January 1959 Thursday**
*"Had photographs taken for programme
'White Horse Inn' "*

Left - Butlins, Clacton 1954

12th July 1991 Friday: *"My last day at work and a wonderful "send off" from the office."*
Betty - seen here with Derek Moody

On holiday with Phyllis & Donald Hewes and their
two children Peter & Lesley in the early 1950s

Above - Peter & Lesley Hewes
August 28th 1949

The photo on the left was taken in
the early 1960s at the Ravenstone
Conservative Party Fete.
Mary Blue is having her fortune
told. Looking on, in the centre at
the back, is Betty's mother. Mary
Blue's mother, Evelyn, is between
her and Betty.

Betty was a Sunday School
Teacher at St Michael and All
Angels Church, Ravenstone,
from 1958 until 1983.

23rd August 1975 Saturday:
Sunday School outing to
Gloucester Cathedral,
Slimbridge Wildfowl Trust and
Berkeley Castle...

1970

1ˢᵗ January 1970 Thursday
15,000 Instant Adults
About 15,000 young people in Leicester came of age at midnight as a result of the Family Law Reform Act 1969 which lowers the age of majority from 21 to 18. From now on young people will be treated as responsible adults from their 18ᵗʰ birthday. They will be able to: -
Own and dispose of houses, land and all other kinds of property.
Act as an executor or administrator of an estate or trustee.
Marry without consent and make wills.
Bring and defend legal actions in a court of law.
Apply for a passport on their own.
Buying and selling goods should also be easier for them. Hire purchase companies will no longer need to insist on an older person acting as guarantor.
Eighteen-year-olds will also be able to vote at Parliamentary and local elections provided their names are on the electoral register.
In Leicester it is estimated that about 15,000 18-year-olds will have the vote as this is the extra number on the roll since the Representation of the People Act, 1969, extended the right to them.

2ⁿᵈ January 1970 Friday
Greeted the New Year at 5-20 a.m. yesterday morning, by being nearly tipped out of bed, when the leg of the bed collapsed under my 10 stone weight (65 kilogrammes?) It was what you might call "**Plunging into the Seventies**".

4ᵗʰ January 1970 Sunday
How about **Plymouth** for a holiday this year? According to the official guide it looks very promising. I wrote off to a couple of hotels today for their brochures. There are lots of lovely shops, lots of lovely boats, & lots of lovely wide open spaces – magnificent sea, city & moor land vistas.

6ᵗʰ January 1970 Tuesday
Had a letter from Michael, introducing me to "Sheena"
"... I expect you know I got engaged on Halloween night .... Sheena is lovely & arrived just in time – I thought I was on the shelf!"
And Michael will be 23 next month!!

8ᵗʰ January 1970 Thursday
Had tea with Reevsie, Tony & Joanne. Joanne will be 3 next month, & is full of the joys of childhood – not a care in the world. It was a delight to be with her. She showed me all her toys she had had for Christmas, & is a proper little chatterbox. Reevsie is most attractive & a lovely mother.

10ᵗʰ January 1970 Saturday
Cathedral News-Letter No. 72.
The Provost tells the legend of **King Leir**, adapted later by Shakespeare into "**King Lear**".
According to the ancient legend, Cordelia buried her father **Leir**, in a certain underground chamber, beneath the River Soar, near Leicester. This underground chamber was dedicated to the 2 faced **Janus**.

12ᵗʰ January 1970 Monday
The Provost concludes ... "But our God, thanks be, is not two-faced, He is revealed to us in the face of Jesus Christ, a God of Love. So as we go forward into another decade, I make no prophecies & no recriminations. Jesus said: "**Be of good cheer. I have overcome the world. And this is the victory, even our faith.**"

14ᵗʰ January 1970 Wednesday
Through our elocution classes, I have now become much better acquainted with some of Shakespeare's famous lines, seeing them in their true setting & giving added meaning to them. – "**Ay me! For aught that I could ever read, could ever hear by tale or history, the course of true love never did run smooth.**"

16ᵗʰ January 1970 Friday
"**Marshall & Snelgrove**", Leicester's top quality store in the heart of town, is closing down next week. Today I bought some "**Charles of the Ritz**" perfume, & was pleased to hear that the "**Charles of the Ritz**" counter is to be transferred to **Lewis's**. You can't get it anywhere in Coalville.

18ᵗʰ January 1970 Sunday
Read a thousand poems, hymns & prayers, to find the most appropriate for next month's **Parish Magazine**. As we have no Rector, I have free rein to choose just what I like. The wealth of the world's literature is there for the asking. It's just a question of searching & sounding the unfathomable depths.

20ᵗʰ January 1970 Tuesday
Wrote an article "For the Children", for the **February Parish Magazine**. I wrote about the family tree of Jesus ... "And there shall come forth a rod out of the stem of Jesse, & a branch shall grow out of his roots." Isaiah. Chap.XI. Concluding "**The Son of God became the Son of Man, that the sons of men might become the sons of God.**"

22ⁿᵈ January 1970 Thursday
Went with a coach load from Snibston School to see the Pantomime "**Ali Baba**" at Leicester. Thoroughly enjoyed it. The Principal Boy was relating to his mother, the Dame, how the Robber Pirates got into their cave with "Open Sesame". What do you think was inside? "Snibston School bus?" she asked.

24ᵗʰ January 1970 Saturday
Had a letter from Bunting, mentioning Michael's recent engagement to Sheena ... "We are delighted with his choice ....", as though Sheena is a slave girl, or objet d'art. I know from personal experience, that love must be mutual to be effective – you know my choice, & how far that got me.

25ᵗʰ January 1970 Sunday
Hewes, on January 25ᵗʰ, 1970, at Kingsway Hospital, Derby, Frank Hedley Hewes, aged 78 years, of 26, Melton Avenue, Littleover, Derby.
The beloved husband of Helen, dear father of Hilda and Walter and a very dear grandfather.

Funeral Friday, service and cremation Markeaton Crematorium, at 2-45 p.m.

26th January 1970 Monday
Uncle Hedley, my dad's last remaining brother, died yesterday. Only their 2 sisters remain alive now – Aunt Dos & Cis.

28th January 1970 Wednesday
Markfield by-pass opened this week, one way only. We go to work on the by pass & we come home from work on the old **A50**. Work has still to be completed on the merging of the 2 roads, & it is rather like competing in an obstacle race – in & out, & roundabout.

30th January 1970 Friday
Received my long awaited letter from the Ministry of Transport (**interview last June!**)
"… an appointment could be offered to you at **Leicester** ….. It is open to you to consider whether you wish to receive a formal offer of appointment … Clerical Officer Salary, reaching a maximum £1,155."

1st February 1970 Sunday
"Visit the Pilgrim City in Mayflower Year, when Plymouth celebrates the 350th Anniversary of the sailing of the Pilgrim Fathers for America …. See Plymouth as it was in 1620."
So reads the holiday advertisement, but so far Enid & I have not found a likely hotel. "Be a 20th century pilgrim."

3rd February 1970 Tuesday
Malcolm, my regular passenger to & from work, has a couple of mates who travel daily to County Hall by scooter. Both their scooters are out of action at the moment, so I have had three young men with me in the car this week. They are all about 6 feet tall – lanky youths, who squeeze into the back seat.

5th February 1970 Thursday
You will be pleased to know I am now smiling more than I was this time last year. Not that I have any more to smile about, but the healing hand of time eases the heart break I suffered for **Brian Lamming**. I no longer sit at work, fighting back tears, nor sob myself to sleep.

7th February 1970 Saturday
Plymouth prepares a great welcome for visitors this year. The **Mayflower '70** celebrations start on May 2nd & go on to Sept 30th. Every week there are different highlights, & Enid & I would like to go June 20th – 27th – Army Week – Devonport Carnival Week – Spectacular military tattoos, with V.I.P.s.

9th February 1970 Monday
This is one of my rare "**Out Every Night**" weeks – **Sunday** – Church, **Monday** – Amateurs rehearsal "Kiss Me Kate", **Tuesday** – Booking Office, giving out members tickets for Kiss Me Kate, **Wednesday** – night school, elocution, **Thursday** – rehearsal, **Friday** – Aqua show in Leicester, & **Saturday** – regular visit to Enid's house.

11th February 1970 Ash Wednesday
Poor old Leicester City! And yet again, we are knocked out of the F.A.Cup. In tonight's fifth round replay between Leicester City and Liverpool, we lost 2-0.
The eight teams now left in the running are Liverpool v. Watford, Middlesbrough v. Manchester United, Q.P.R. v. Chelsea, and Swindon Town v. Leeds United.

13th February 1970 Friday
On the Eve of St. Valentine, my best beloved – **Brian Lamming** – came twice to our office today. First time for Mrs. Judith Edwina Lamming, Bramble Cottage, Bringhurst, Market Harborough, & secondly for S. Leics. Garages Ltd.
Supposing Judith to be his wife, all my tears returned.

Note – Brian Lamming licenses a car for Mrs Judith Edwina Lamming, & I suspect he has now married. Nevertheless, I still adore him.

15th February 1970 Sunday
A notice on the church door at Ravenstone announces that the Bishop of Leicester hereby signifies that he proposes to institute the Reverend **Leslie Buckroyd** B.A. to the Benefice of Ravenstone. He was Curate of Tamworth 1950 – 53, Vicar of Dordon 1953 – 61, & now Vicar of St. Barnabas, Leicester.

17th February 1970 Tuesday
Spent all evening composing an article for the **Parish Magazine** on the theme of **Easter**. "**Resurgam**", I shall rise again. This, I learned, was in the old St. Paul's, destroyed by the Fire of London in 1666, & incorporated by Sir Christopher Wren in the new St. Paul's. Like the Phoenix, rose through fire.

19th February 1970 Thursday
Enid & I chose Plymouth for our holiday this year, but none of the accommodation offered was to our liking. We have therefore transferred our affections to **Exmouth**, & from the holiday guide we have written today to the Grand Hotel, which looks most delightful, & has this boast – the beach is on our doorstep.

21st February 1970 Saturday
Bought a hair piece from the hair dressers. (Ravina Wigs 100% Human Hair £7-10/-)
I hope with this to have a variety of hairstyles – long hair – hair piled high – ringlets, etc. etc. There should be plenty of scope for it next month on stage in "**Kiss Me Kate**", & also our Dinner Dance.

23rd February 1970 Monday
Had a day's holiday today. Got the March Parish Magazine off, & having written an article including the macabre story of the Phoenix, wondered whether that was suitable material for children. My imagination ran wild, & I wondered what the children might burn, just as an experiment.

25th February 1970 Wednesday
The Grand Hotel, Exmouth, certainly wins our vote for this year's holiday. The letter we have received from Mr. Taylor, Resident Proprietor, deserves full marks. He could not have been more helpful, efficient or friendly.

27ᵗʰ February 1970 Friday

Three years ago today, Brian Lamming came into my life. Do you recall how I described him? – "He neither speaks to me, nor even smiles, but I like him." No-one has ever hurt me more than he has done, & today he neither speaks to me, nor even smiles, but I still adore him.

2ⁿᵈ March 1970 Monday

Minnehaha is now 4 years old & going rusty. I drove behind **Reg Hall** to Loughborough where Minnehaha stayed for a day or two to be de-rusted. I then came back with **Reg**, & we ran out of petrol!

I am on holiday from work all this week for "**Kiss Me Kate**" which starts tomorrow.

4ᵗʰ March 1970 Wednesday

A heavy fall of snow this morning brought things to a standstill. It took us hours to clear the paths & the drive. Tosca found it impossible to reach the garden, but eventually we effected a clearway. The snow scene then made a delightful setting for photographs in my "**Kiss Me Kate**" colourful costume.

6ᵗʰ March 1970 Friday

"Kiss Me Kate" is going very well, & we are all enjoying playing it. I have been most pleased with my hair piece, which has done wonders for me. I have 3 different outfits in this show –

Slacks & casual loose top.

Full length grey velvet dress & hat – carnival style.

Red velvet Elizabethan dress & hat.

8ᵗʰ March 1970 Sunday

Enid is a keep fit enthusiast. **Eileen Fowler**, a famous keep fit instructress, now aged 62, but as graceful as ever, came to Leicester today, & all keep fit enthusiasts flocked to her for an afternoon session of keep fit. I went as a spectator & was delighted with the warmth of her personality.

10ᵗʰ March 1970 Tuesday

Prince Edward is 6 years old today, so we had the Union Jack hoisted at County Hall today. We have the Union Jack flying for royal birthdays, & the County Council flag flying for council meetings, but we have not yet had a council meeting on a royal birthday. We have 2 flag poles.

12ᵗʰ March 1970 Thursday

Mum & I will be doing the flowers on the Altar at **Ravenstone Church** on **Easter Day**. It is customary to have white flowers only, so we have ordered £5 worth of white flowers & greenery for the occasion. This will include arum lilies, carnations, white iris, etc. to make 2 matching arrangements.

14ᵗʰ March 1970 Saturday

There is a rummage sale next Saturday, so I have had one almighty clear out. The result is that all our drawers are highly respectable for a change, instead of being cluttered up with rubbish galore, that nobody ever uses. Also, on the credit side, I unearthed some useful items, long since forgotten.

16ᵗʰ March 1970 Monday

The **New English Bible** – complete with Old Testament, Apocrypha, & New Testament, is on sale today.

This mammoth work of re-translation is the biggest landmark in Bible publishing history since the familiar Authorised Version (**King James's Bible**) appeared in 1611.

18ᵗʰ March 1970 Wednesday

On my way home from elocution class, at 9-30 p.m., I was flagged down by a man waving frantically at the side of the road. There had just been a road accident, & a motor cyclist lay by the roadside. I went poste haste to the nearest police car, which I had just seen, & got help.

20ᵗʰ March 1970 Friday

Having accepted my appointment as a **Civil Servant**, under the new centralisation of vehicle licensing, I am very pleased to tell you that all civil servants have been given a pay rise of 8%. The Clerical Officer salary, reaching a maximum of £1,155 is now £1,260.

22ⁿᵈ March 1970 Palm Sunday

Spent all day preparing the **April Parish Magazine**. I wrote an article for the children on the **New English Bible**, tracing the origin of the Bible back to the beginning. Ancient Hebrew & Greek first of all being translated into Latin - & then from Latin to English.

24ᵗʰ March 1970 Tuesday

"Public Service", the N.A.L.G.O. monthly magazine, is now offering its 11ᵗʰ annual **Crossword** compiling competition. As I am a crossword compiling enthusiast, I am having my final fling with N.A.L.G.O. in this manner. On 1ˢᵗ April I leave N.A.L.G.O. for C.P.S.A. (Civil Service).

26ᵗʰ March 1970 Thursday

Spent my last day at work as a **Local Government Officer**, employed by the Leicestershire County Council. When we return to work on **Wednesday**, after the **Easter** holiday, I shall be a Civil Servant, i.e. a **Servant** of the Queen, (not military), but a civilian.

28ᵗʰ March 1970 Saturday

Today we met Sheena. Michael and his new fiancée arrived unexpectedly on a brief visit. We all liked Sheena & thought she and Michael were well matched. They informed us that they have fixed their wedding for 21ˢᵗ August 1971.

30ᵗʰ March 1970 Easter Monday

Mum & I have had Mary Moore staying with us for the Easter Holiday. The weather has not been very good – lots of rain & black clouds, & even thunder & lightening.

I managed to complete my crossword for the N.A.L.G.O. competition & get it in the post while I still qualify as a member.

1ˢᵗ April 1970 Wednesday

Meet Elizabeth Hewes, aged 38, 409795 member of C.P.S.A. Civil and Public Services Association.

From "Public Service", our old familiar N.A.L.G.O. journal, we now go to "**Red Tape**", the official journal of C.P.S.A. We have now joined the **Services**, & are servants of the Crown.

3rd April 1970 Friday

After 20 years of contributing towards the Superannuation Scheme of the County Council, I now transfer my dowry of £598 to the Civil Service.

Civil Service hours are ½ hour per week less than the County Council, so we are now paid ½ hour overtime for each week we work.

5th April 1970 Sunday

The Civil Service handbook says: - "**An established woman civil servant, who resigns on marriage, may be granted a marriage gratuity of one month's pay for each complete year of service, subject to a maximum of 12 month's pay.**"

Here I am then – an unclaimed treasure, & most likely don't qualify.

7th April 1970 Tuesday

As a member of the selection committee for choosing next year's show for Coalville Amateur Operatic Society, went to a meeting where we eventually decided on 2 which we liked best – 1. **Pink Champagne**. 2. **Orpheus in the Underworld**.

My own personal choice "**King's Rhapsody**" was 3rd choice.

9th April 1970 Thursday

County Council Elections today. They are held once every 3 years. We are in the Heather Electoral division & had to choose between **Kathleen Dingley**, Appleby House, Appleby Parva - "Your Conservative Candidate", and **Harold Fern**, 135, Church Lane, Ravenstone – "Your Labour Candidate".

11th April 1970 Saturday

Cup Final Day – but no cup was presented. The result after half an hour's extra play was a draw: Chelsea 2 Leeds 2. The replay will be on April 29th at Old Trafford. Not since 1912 has the result been a draw, when Barnsley played West Bromwich at Crystal Palace.

13th April 1970 Monday

Last night Mum & I went to Evensong at **St. Barnabas**, **Leicester**, for the last service there of our new Rector, the **Reverend Leslie Buckroyd**. The prayers spanned over to Ravenstone, & we were later welcomed very warmly, by several members of the church, as well as by the Rector.

15th April 1970 Wednesday

Apollo XIII, America's 3rd manned flight, for man to walk on the Moon, is now returning home from the Moon without accomplishing its object.

A mystery explosion damaged part of the space ship, & the world waits with bated breath, for the safe return of astronauts **Haise, Lovell & Swigert**.

17th April 1970 Friday

Jim Lovell, **Fred Haise** and **Jack Swigert** are safely home.

The Astronauts' Prayer

The Iwo Jima's chaplain read this prayer to the astronauts as they stepped aboard the carrier:

"O Lord, joyfully welcome back to Earth astronauts Lovell, Haise and Swigert who, by Your grace, their skill and the skill of many men, survived the dangers encountered in their mission and returned to us safe and whole. We offer our humble thanksgiving for this successful recovery. Amen."

19th April 1970 Sunday

Ravenstone Church was filled to over-flowing for yesterday's Induction of our new **Rector**, the **Revd. Leslie Buckroyd**.

He brought 2 bus loads of people from his previous parish, & even brought the choir in their robes, to join with ours. He has left the big city for a quieter life.

21st April 1970 Tuesday

Spent the evening with Reevsie & family. Tony has been away from work for the past seven weeks with a form of nervous breakdown. Both he & Reevsie have been in tears, while Joanne, 3 years old, has kept as lively as a cricket, full of the joys of spring, & as happy as Larry.

23rd April 1970 Thursday

The Leicester Mercury has recently been providing a "**Prize**" Crossword each Saturday.

Enid & I combine our talents & do the Crossword between us, & this week we have won first prize – a book token, value £3.

25th April 1970 Saturday

Had an out of the blue visit from Marie Findley, who was at school with me. She & her husband Neville spent the evening with Mum & me – Pat & Evelyn & Aunt Dos. They have 4 children, aged 10, 12, 15 and 17.

27th April 1970 Monday

Received my first salary cheque from the **Ministry of Transport** (to be cashed on the last day of the month). **H.M. Paymaster General** .... Issuing department: Ministry of Transport, Albion Court, Marlowes, Hemel Hempstead, Herts.

29th April 1970 Wednesday

Chelsea won the F.A.Cup tonight in their re-play against Leeds. The score was Chelsea 2 – Leeds United 1 (after extra time).

Also tonight the European Cup Winners' Cup was won by Manchester City, who beat Gornik, Poland 2 – 1.

1st May 1970 Friday

Here we are again in the merry month of **May**. The fountains at work splashed merrily all day long, the birds sang merrily until it was almost dark at 9 p.m. & all the trees & bushes & flowers are bursting with the joy of spring. Our garden has never looked so good before.

3rd May 1970 Sunday

The merry month of **May** suddenly turned into mid-summer today. It was out with the sun lounger for a prolonged spell of sunbathing, & then off for a three mile cycle ride for the sheer joy & freedom of sun & fresh air.

4th May 1970 Monday

Sketchley, Mary, of The Grange, Willoughby-on the-Wolds, widow of John Godfrey Sketchley, passed peacefully away on May 4th 1970 in her 100th year. Funeral service at St. James the Greater, London Road, Leicester, Friday at 2 p.m., prior to cremation at Gilroes Crematorium. Flowers to Loughborough and District Funeral Service, 12 Leicester Road, Loughborough. Tel: 5331.

5th May 1970 Tuesday

Mum received a letter from solicitors at Loughborough:- "We write to inform you of the death of Mrs. Mary Sketchley, formerly of The Grange, Willoughby-on-the-Wolds... Mrs. Sketchley has mentioned you in her Will …" She was an Aunt of Mum's whom we rarely saw.

7th May 1970 Ascension Day Thursday
Ashby Rural District Council Election
Ravenstone with Snibston Ward

H. Fern = 481
Alf Hall = 413
R. Hextall = 274
Mrs. Pulford = 157

Alf (Independent) & H. Fern (Labour) retained their seats on the Council – now 13 Labour & 12 Independent.

9th May 1970 Saturday

Mum received a copy of Aunt Mary's Will.
Samuel Bryans & W.J.B. Beardsley as Executors and Trustees £50 each.
St. James the Greater, London Road, Leicester £400. Willoughby Church £100. Mary Hewes £300. John Palmer £300. Sydney Marriot & Royston Marriot £100 each. Frank & Elsie Starbuck £100 each.

11th May 1970 Monday

Aunt Mary gives us £300, and our immediate reaction is to thank her – but how do you thank some-one who is dead? Mum & I went to her funeral on Friday. Live to be a hundred, & you belong to another age. The world hardly knows you. Die in the bloom of youth & the world weeps.

13th May 1970 Wednesday

Get mentioned in a **Will**, & suddenly - wham! Folks you haven't seen or heard of since can't remember when suddenly take a great interest in you. Long lost distant relations come to life, & want to know every detail of who gets what, & ancient family feuds come to light.

15th May 1970 Friday

You'd be surprised what a web of intrigue & life-long conspiracy lurks in Aunt Mary's **Will**. So long as she lived in her house, she kept out others who would instantly stake their claim. "She'll live to be a hundred," said malicious tongues long, long ago; & just for spite, she did!

17th May 1970 Whit Sunday

The new Rector of Ravenstone, the Rev. Leslie Buckroyd, gave me his letter for the June Magazine – Phew! Our cosy little 4 page magazine suddenly doubled its size. It really was too much for me to cope with on a spare evening. He is much too revolutionary for my liking.

19th May 1970 Tuesday

Ravenstone's Annual Garden Fete, is to be opened this year on June 13th, by the Honourable Jonathan Guinness. He asked for a brief picture of the local set up – personalities he should mention, etc.; & it was my pleasure to write him a light hearted account of our village life.

21st May 1970 Thursday

My own lamb – my best beloved – **Brian Lamming**, stood before me, like one in a daze. He looked like a lost lamb, as though he had never met me before. He looked weary & worn & sad. Gone was his sporty air, & his **Prince Charming** look, but oh – how I loved him.

23rd May 1970 Saturday

Everybody is now on holiday – next Monday & Tuesday are the official "**Spring Holiday**", & I happen to have Wednesday as well, so I am not back to work until next Thursday. The weather is perfect holiday weather, & I have enjoyed a good long session of sun bathing in the garden.

25th May 1970 Monday

Mum, I & Anne Causer went into Leicester this afternoon, to see the film "**Anne of a Thousand Days**" – a historical film set in the days of **Henry VIII**. I was moved to tears. It made you appreciate living in the 20th century, where we enjoy justice, & marry only for love.

27th May 1970 Wednesday

Added considerably to my collection of quotations & little poems suitable for use in the Parish Magazine, through "**Stevenson's Book of Quotations**", that most comprehensive dictionary of quotations ever published, which I am privileged to obtain from good old County Hall library.

29th May 1970 Friday

A bumper end of the month day at work today. I took over £11,000 & felt quite exhausted at the end of the day.
Today is the birthday of our former **Rector**, the Revd. Matthew Rice Lewis. We sent him a card to Swansea, & this very day received a card from him in Germany.

31st May 1970 Sunday

Remember last summer, Mum & I went to Scotland & brought home some Scottish heather? Well! It has lasted until now in a vase of water on the mantle-piece – that is **nine months!** Although it still has a few last lingering signs of colour, it is rather thread-bare now.

2nd June 1970 Tuesday

The June issue of "**Public Service**" is now out, giving the result of the recent **Crossword** compiling competition. Winner (for the 4th time) is John Masters of Swindon. There were 147 entries this year, & in the top ten there is H.J. Pilling (last year's winner) & Elizabeth Hewes.

4th June 1970 Thursday
Malcolm, my travelling companion for the past year, has now bought himself a car, & no longer requires my services.
The summer weather is so delightful at the moment; I have rebelled against sleeping in Aunt Dos's bedroom with closed curtains, where I feel like a prisoner.

6th June 1970 Saturday
Geoff & Jane from our office were married today – another office romance which led to wedding bells.
Another romance has sprung up lately between another Jane & Brian – not my Brian – the one & only Brian Lamming, but Brian Phillips.
Neither he nor Geoff would be my choice.

8th June 1970 Monday
Coalville Amateur Operatic Society's Annual General Meeting.
Mr Clamp, our chairman for the past 25 years, handed over the chair to **Mr Roberts**.
Our next show "**Pink Champagne**" is arranged for the first week in March 1971 & rehearsals start on 7th September.

10th June 1970 Wednesday
Out of our 40 strong staff, we have at the moment 3 pregnant women – Louie, Ann & Maz. Remember Little Tommy & Maz were engaged on June 10th 1967, 3 years ago today?
Louie & Ann expect their babies in December & Maz in November, so that will mean 3 vacancies in our office.

12th June 1970 Friday
Received an application for renewal of car tax for **Judith Edwina Lamming**.
On 13th February she paid by cheque – **J.E. Lamming**.
Today her cheque was **B. and J.E. Lamming**.
This more or less convinced me that she & Brian Lamming are man & wife.
So ends my great heart-breaking romance – the romance that never was.

14th June 1970 Sunday
Who said: "With tears you can melt iron." **Ovid**.
Who said: "Love conquers all." **Virgil**.
"Who ever loved that loved not at first sight?" **Shakespeare**.
"And this I set down as a positive truth. A woman with fair opportunities may marry whom she likes." **Thackeray**.
"From what a height of hope have I fallen." **Terence**.

16th June 1970 Tuesday
On Thursday it is the General Election. There are 630 constituencies, & at the moment **Labour** is in power, with **Harold Wilson** Prime Minister. They have 347 seats.
The Conservatives have 263 – the Liberals 13 – The Speaker = 1, & there are 6 others.
Edward Heath is the Conservative leader.

18th June 1970 Thursday
General Election – and a devastating defeat for the **Labour Government**, who were quite confident of victory. And so we now have a new **Prime Minister** – **Edward Heath**, leader of the Conservative Party – a new **Home Secretary** – **Reginald Maudling**, & **Chancellor of the Exchequer** – **Iain MacLeod**.

20th June 1970 Saturday
Mum & I popped over to **Willoughby** this evening to see Madge. We learned the latest village news of Aunt Mary's Will. Apparently the **Executor**, who is to sell the house & land, & distribute the money to others, is likely to buy it for himself, & sell it at great profit – so the rumours go.

22nd June 1970 Monday
On June 1st, new Driving Licence Regulations came into force. Three yearly licences went up to £1 from 15/- but have the added advantage now of incorporating **Provisional** use, if required. Six monthly Provisional licences at 10/- (i.e. 50p) changed to 12 monthly licences, & are now £1.

24th June 1970 Wednesday
Midsummer Day! Now that we have a new Government, we have yet another Minister of Transport – **Mr. John Peyton** – my new boss. We are paid actually by H.M. Paymaster General, & the new Paymaster General is **Lord Eccles**. Foreign Secretary is Sir Alec Douglas-Home, & Education Minister is Margaret Thatcher.

26th June 1970 Friday
To **Mary Blue** a baby daughter – her second child, born at **Market Harborough**.
For the past 2 weeks, I have been helping out at work in the Driving Licence section, because Charles has been on holiday. We were inundated with applications for licences – all out of order, due to the change of price.

28th June 1970 Sunday
Prince Charles, 21 year old **Prince of Wales**, this week became the first heir to the throne to get a degree, when he gained his B.A. (Hon.) in history at Cambridge University.
Yesterday he also received the honorary freedom of **Windsor**, where he swore to be "subject & obedient to the good custom" of the Borough of New Windsor.

30th June 1970 Tuesday
Today I wrote to **Karen**, 4 day old daughter of **Mary Blue**, born, like me, under the moon.
I have now decided to slim! Weighing in at ten stones, I have cut down on potatoes, bread, pastry, cakes & chocolate biscuits; & am concentrating on salads, fresh fruit, cheese & biscuits, & other food for slimmers.

2nd July 1970 Thursday
Cliff College, Calver, Sheffield. This Methodist College in the Peak District of Derbyshire, trains men & women for lay leadership & evangelism.
This week, 6 of their members are staying in Ravenstone, & at a gathering at **Ravenstone Chapel**, I bought a lovely new "**Red Letter Bible**", with index, 30/-

4th July 1970 Saturday

The Bishop of Leicester, in the Diocesan leaflet this month, says: - ".... When we have done all, of course we are unprofitable servants. We have done no more than what was our duty to do, & not always that. But over the years, God has helped us. In due time we shall reap, if we faint not."

6th July 1970 Monday

Uncle Hedley, who died in January this year, has a son named **Walter**.

Walter has a daughter named **Diane**, who is 21 years old. Diane went to work as usual one morning recently, & came home married, without any of the family knowing a thing about it!

She did not even bring her husband home for tea.

8th July 1970 Wednesday

Mum will be 65 on 23rd August, & she is considering finishing work at Ashby on that date. She has worked there for 25 years, as an assistant nurse at the Cottage Hospital, doing night duty from 8 p.m. until 8 a.m. At present she works just one or two nights each week, & enjoys the extra money it brings.

10th July 1970 Friday

This in retrospect is tomorrow – Enid & I started our holiday in **Exmouth**. A perfectly beautiful day for our 200 mile journey. We had lunch in **Bath**, & afternoon tea in **Honiton**. We are staying at the Grand hotel, right on the sea front; & our first impression of Exmouth is very favourable.

12th July 1970 Sunday

Perfect holiday weather. Went to morning service at Holy Trinity Church, Exmouth.

This afternoon we gained a goodly tan on a delightful boat trip up the **River Exe**.

This evening we motored to **Sidmouth**, where we sat in the most beautiful cliff gardens, & listened to the music of **Sidmouth Town Band**.

14th July 1970 Tuesday

39 today! Made my first acquaintance with **Exeter**, & visited the Cathedral.

Enid & I spent our £3 book voucher which we won recently. Enid chose a 30/- book called "**The Forsyte Saga**" by John Galsworthy, & I chose **Esso's Road Atlas of Great Britain & Ireland** – a superb book of maps.

16th July 1970 Thursday

Having a lovely holiday in glorious Devon. Exmouth is much more beautiful than ever we expected. As Keats wrote of South Devon: "Here all the summer could I stay." The coastline is most picturesque; & the River Exe & the River Teign being so near means lots of boating activity on the sea.

18th July 1970 Saturday

So ends our 1970 summer holiday. Exmouth gave us everything you could wish for on holiday. Moonlight over the sea at night & sunshine by day. Lots of interesting places to visit, by land or by sea, beautiful walks, & many pleasant memories.

One of the loveliest holidays Enid and I have had.

20th July 1970 Monday

Had a good old spending spree on holiday. Bought a very smart leather bag - £5-10/- to replace my old tattered bag, which had given 16 years valued service. Bought a very nice beige skirt, & a couple of summer jumpers. Bought a pair of pillow cases, two pairs of stockings, two vests, and a spoon marked "**Exeter**", etc.

22nd July 1970 Wednesday

Iain MacLeod, aged 56, appointed only last month as our new Chancellor of the Exchequer, died unexpectedly this week, after a heart attack.

And so we now have a new Chancellor of the Exchequer, **Anthony Barber**, aged 50.

Two gas bombs were thrown from the public gallery this week at M.P.s in the House of Commons.

24th July 1970 Friday

Received a post card from Reader's Digest Ass. Ltd. – "Congratulations! Next week is Lucky Number week in your district, & **you** have been selected to receive a Lucky Number ..."

This was addressed to 65211, **M/S E. Hewes**.

Aunt Dos had one, & I don't know how many others.

26th July 1970 Sunday

Rebel Hewsie, who chose to sleep at home, in a spacious bed & airy bedroom, rather than in a small divan in Aunt Dos's stuffy room, is about to return to Aunt Dos – to her guest room. (Special request on my part, graciously granted by Aunt Dos).

We have **Mary Moore** coming to stay for a week.

28th July 1970 Tuesday

My latest subject is **Numismatics** – the study of coins.

As we shall all be going metric next year, our old coins are fast becoming collectors' pieces. Working with money all day long, I have a great advantage, & have saved some very interesting shillings & florins, & rare old sixpences.

30th July 1970 Thursday

Mr. Sharp told me today that he would like me to take over Louie's job when she leaves.

This will of course mean coming off the counter, where for the past 3 ½ years, so much of my life's drama has been enacted. He offered the promise of an eventual rise in salary, but not before next April.

1st August 1970 Saturday

Mary Moore, Mum & I went to **Castle Donington Airport** to see Pat & Evelyn leave for their holiday in the **Isle of Man**. The plane should have left at 2 p.m. but because of delays earlier at Ostend, did not leave until 4-30 p.m. We all had lunch at the Airport.

3rd August 1970 Monday

Today I have handled my very first £20 note. This is a new note, only brought out very recently.

The World Cycling Championships are being held this week in Leicester, & have attracted 37 nations – a record number. It is the greatest sporting event ever held in the city and county of Leicester.

5th August 1970 Wednesday
Excitement grows as the 1970 World Cycling Championships make their presence felt in Leicester. The official opening is tomorrow, by Edward Heath, Prime minister, & the events continue for 10 days, culminating in a 7 hour **road race** on Sunday 16th August finishing at **Kirkby Mallory**. Eddy Merckx of Belgium is tops.

7th August 1970 Friday
Mum & I have 2 tickets for next Wednesday 12th August at 6-30 p.m. **"World Cycling Championships" Leicester Sports Centre, Saffron Lane, Leicester.** We chose tickets at £3 each, from a choice of £1, £2, £3, £4, £5. This is for the professional sprint semi-finals & finals, tandem finals, & motor paced final.

9th August 1970 Sunday
After a month of gentle dieting, I have now reduced my weight from 10 stone to 9 ½ stone. (60 kilogrammes). Nobody in this country thinks metric, & now that we have the World Cycling Champions racing 3,000, 4,000, 5,000 metres; 100 kilometres, 200 & 300 kilometres, we have to puzzle out what it means.

11th August 1970 Tuesday
A man with a measuring rod came to our office today, in preparation for the counter to be fitted with **"Anti-Bandit Glass Screens"**.
All banks & Post Offices have recently been barricaded fight up to the ceiling, in an attempt to safeguard their money & their staff from any possible attack.

13th August 1970 Thursday
Shared with the World Champion cyclists their absolute joy in victory: - Gordon Johnson, the Australian sprint champion, riding to within inches of us with arms flung high in jubilation: tandem riders Barth & Muller from West Germany equally jubilant in victory; & West Germany also winners in the team pursuit.

15th August 1970 Saturday
The world cycling champions were out in full force today on a 9 mile circuit of Leicester roads. Twelve times round they went & we could see them at 20 minute intervals. What a thrilling sight! 150 cyclists racing along together with motor cycle outriders, a retinue of special cars, & a helicopter.

17th August 1970 Monday
I have been attacked – there I was in bed at Aunt Dos's, when my assailant struck in the silence & darkness of the night. I jumped out of bed in a flash & killed him – **dead**.
One poor little wasp who stung me on the face, has left me looking like a prize fighter, with one eye almost closed.

19th August 1970 Wednesday
As a result of the wasp sting on my face, I now have an unexpected week's holiday from work. The doctor gave me a Medical Certificate for **"Oedema"**, & I have to go every day to Ashby Hospital for penicillin injections. Happily, I am now over the worst, & look much better now.

21st August 1970 Friday
I am pleased to tell you, my wasp sting has almost faded away. Unlike last year (3rd October) when I had to put up with itch, itch, itch, etc., it seems that my 5 injections this week have prevented that irritation.
So I have really had a lovely lazy holiday; & did my magazine at leisure!

23rd August 1970 Sunday
Sunday at my 3 churches – the **3 M's.**
Holy Communion at 8 a.m. **St. Michael's** Ravenstone. 3 p.m. Family gathering at **St. Mary's** – Snibston for the burial of Uncle Hedley's ashes at the foot of my dad's grave. Evensong at 6-30 p.m. at **St. Martin's** – Leicester Cathedral. **Mum 65 today!**

25th August 1970 Tuesday
Mum decided to retire at 65, but has now decided to carry on for a bit longer. Her night duty brings in a useful £5 per week, & she also gets £5-8/- Old Age Pension.
My salary at the moment is £1,134 per annum, & this makes up our combined income. I hope to have a rise in September.

27th August 1970 Thursday
After we left **Local Government**, to become **Civil Servants**, Local Government had a 12 ½ % increase in salaries. So, if we had stayed in Local Government, do you know what my salary would be now? £1,227 per annum! This of course requires superannuation deduction, but I hope to catch up.

29th August 1970 Saturday
After only 5 weeks, sleeping in Aunt Dos's spare bedroom, I am about to move out to make room for her latest lodger – **Valerie**; who is starting out in her career as a Biology teacher at Coalville Grammar School.
This means that every week-end – half term & school holiday, I'm back to the stuffy room.

31st August 1970 Monday
Bank Holiday Monday. Spent the day clearing up the garden – grass cutting – weeding etc.
Now that we are **Civil Servants**, we do not have **Tuesday** holiday, so tomorrow we are at work. County Hall generally will be empty – only 20 out of the 800 staff are Civil Servants, so it should be an interesting day.

2nd September 1970 Wednesday
Mum & I have launched out this week on a new **television**. We have chosen H.M.V., the same as our last set, which gave us long faithful service. At the moment, we have the set on trial, so we can still change our minds – have a different one – pay for it outright – or have it on a rental system.

4th September 1970 Friday
Mrs. Mary Sketchley, of 48, Main Street, Willoughby-on-the-Wolds, who died on May 4th, left £3,061-15s-1d, gross, £2,894-10s-3d, net. She left £400 for religious purposes in the parish of St. James the Greater, London Road, Leicester, and £100 for religious purposes in the parish of Willoughby-on-the-Wolds.

Aunt Mary's will appeared in the Leicester Mercury tonight, four months exactly after she died. She left Mum £300, plus a further share in the sale of her land. It seems the land is now sold.

Note – Mum's Aunt Mary at Willoughby died, aged 99, and left Mum in her will £1,389-14s.

6th September 1970 Sunday

Pat, Evelyn & I spent the afternoon & evening yesterday with Cousin Walter & family at **Derby**. Walter keeps a Chemist's shop, & manages to make over £6,000 income. Consequently he has everything money can buy – a **Jaguar** car for himself & a car each for his family; & every modern convenience inside the house.

8th September 1970 Tuesday

A man named **James Anderson** was given a violin by a friend. He had it valued & was told that as a musical instrument it was worth £25. He offered it for sale last week in the **Leicester Mercury** – "270 year old 'Stradivarius' violin, Dresden made with fine old walnut case."

10th September 1970 Thursday

Mr. James Anderson sold his 'Stradivarius' violin for £30. After he had sold it, his phone never stopped ringing, with people offering more money each time. Finally, he was offered £300 by an antique dealer, & then he really knew what he had lost – so much for trusting a valuer.

12th September 1970 Saturday

Minnehaha, my little car, for which I paid £460, plus £100 in extras, for such things as wireless, fog lamps, new exhaust pipes, a set of 5 new tyres, etc., is now suffering so badly from body rot that I must consider buying another. Alf has a nice one for sale at £595 – deposit required £240.

14th September 1970 Monday

Poor old Minnehaha – first the exhaust pipe drops to bits, & the next thing you know – steam erupting from under the bonnet. I filled up with water at County Hall, & limped home with a leaking radiator lead.
I arrived with a sizzle & a hiss & a knocking engine.

16th September 1970 Wednesday

A day of absorbing interest. Two men from Swansea spent all day giving us a detailed account of the work covered by the Ministry of Transport.
We saw a plan of the new building now under construction at Swansea, & were instructed in the general workings of our country, showing exactly our privileges as **Civil Servants**.

18th September 1970 Friday

Minnehaha is having a lot of trouble under the bonnet. As soon as the engine gets warm, all the water gurgles & splutters, & then erupts like a volcano. And the noise as she belches forth is most unladylike. But, with only £3-6s-7d in the bank, we can't buy another just yet.

20th September 1970 Sunday

A day of sunshine! It was warm enough to sun-bathe in the garden, where all the birds chirruped & twittered for joy throughout the day.
I left Minnehaha with **Reg Hall**, who said he would deal with the trouble personally, & have her right by tomorrow – a new gasket required.

22nd September 1970 Tuesday

Had a day's holiday 'specially to do the **October Parish Magazine**. The Rector provides more than ample material to cover 8 pages, & it is the editing & fitting exactly into those 8 pages that is the work of art. Fortunately, I can choose my own incidental extras – quotations etc., & cut where necessary.

24th September 1970 Thursday

Nothing but trouble with poor Minnehaha. It was decided not to give her a new gasket, but a new thermostat & then a new element – this all resulted in the gauge registering wrongly.
As for Reg giving it his personal attention – he passed it all on to over-worked **Charlie**, who wanted nothing more to do with it.

26th September 1970 Saturday

Today I met **Karen**, baby daughter of **Mary Blue** – 3 months old today. She is a little darling. I "crossed her palm with silver" & gave her a pretty silver serviette ring, decorated with leaves & engraved "**Karen**".
Terry, her father, is soon to move from Gartree Prison, as warder, to Leicester Prison.

28th September 1970 Monday

I have now acquired a new regular passenger to County Hall – **Martin**, 18 year old son of the **Revd. Buckroyd**, our newly appointed **Rector**. Today was **Martin**'s first day at work. He is a quiet, sad boy, extremely sensitive & easily hurt; but very polite, & grateful to ride with Minnehaha, evoking my protective instinct.

30th September 1970 Wednesday

My salary has now increased to £1,167 p.a. which is enough to save £25 per month for a new car. I now therefore have £25 towards one new car.
At the moment, we are having the house painted and decorated - £60, & we would really like a new carpet, but liking nothing but the best, we have to wait.

2nd October 1970 Friday

I came – I saw – I conked out. There I was alone with Minnehaha at Glenfield roundabout, when a passing motor cyclist gallantly came to my rescue. He stayed for an hour, doing his very best to get me started, & finally a motorist came along & managed to start the engine. They diagnosed worn points.

4th October 1970 Sunday

Yesterday I took Minnehaha to a new garage – **Parkin & Jones**, Thornborough Road, Coalville, who advertise "Mechanical Repairs" "Body Repairs" "Painting Repairs".
I was completely satisfied with the thorough check they made - pin-pointing the cause of all the trouble – a thoroughly clogged up air filter.

6th October 1970 Tuesday

An out of the blue visit from **Bunting**, who spent the

evening with Mum & me – Pat, Evelyn & Aunt Dos joined the gathering.

Bunting's husband, Mostyn, has just started a new job in **Hitchin, Herts**. & until they find a new home Bunting is free to wander.

8th October 1970 Thursday

Spent the evening with Reevsie & family. Tony is now looking much better again after his nervous breakdown earlier this year.

Joanne is now 3 ½ years old & such delightful company. Her chief interest at the moment is writing – she can write any word, if you spell it out to her, knowing all the alphabet.

10th October 1970 Saturday

Took Minnehaha to **Parkin & Jones** for a 6,000 mile service, including oil change.

Total mileage now is 42,000.

On Monday October 19th Minnehaha has a further booking for "Body Repairs" which will take several days. This includes one new wing on the recommendation of Cyril & Co. at the garage.

12th October 1970 Monday

Rehearsals are now coming on very well for "**Pink Champagne**".

Next Monday is Audition Night, when I shall be one of the judges. To prepare for this I am currently engaged in studying the script in detail – determining exactly what each part entails, knowing how much singing, speaking, dancing, etc. is required.

14th October 1970 Wednesday

Louie, who is now very much pregnant, hopes to finish work in our office on 13th November; **Maz & Ann** have already left & this means a big re-shuffle in the office.

Having been launched with County Hall, at its very helm – on the front row – I expect shortly to take up an uninspiring rear position.

16th October 1970 Friday

I learned today that **Brian Lamming** married **Miss Judith Edwina Lewis** of Market Harborough in 1968. For a year they lived at Woolley's Farm, Naseby, in Northhamptonshire, & then moved to Bramble Cottage, Bringhurst, in Leicestershire. This was revealed in the records of Car Number 442 PKO.

18th October 1970 Sunday

As you will see, my heart has not broken completely – just sunk to unfathomable depths. And yet it is a buoyant heart, capable of surfacing swiftly & silently, but not while it is being pressed down. I feel like a lovely tree trying to grow underneath a steam roller; or a flower under hard ground.

19th October 1970 Monday

On this day **BP** announced the first oil find in the North Sea.

20th October 1970 Tuesday

Last night I was on the panel of judges listening to auditions for "**Pink Champagne**". A learned panel consisting of Mr. Roberts, Musical Director; John Saunders, Producer; Angela, the Dancing Mistress; & 2 ordinary members of the society – Peter Jacques & me. We meet again on Thursday to voice our opinions.

22nd October 1970 Thursday

"**Pink Champagne**" is now cast, with Margaret Dearden & Jack Lee taking the lead.

We had a most successful meeting to decide this, and had virtually a unanimous decision right the way through. The preparation I did – knowing exactly how many lines each character had, etc., proved to be of great value.

24th October 1970 Saturday

Welcome home to Minnehaha! How good she looks after a week at **Parkin & Jones**.

No more rust lurking in every nook & cranny, but one new wing, & the other wing looking just as good. It was **Alf & Co**. who implied that Minnehaha was more trouble than she was worth, but now she seems fine.

26th October 1970 Monday

Mum went to **Willoughby** today to spend a few days with **Madge**. I am therefore o/c of feeding the cat – putting the milk bottles out – winding up the clock – washing up – making the fire – emptying the ashes – locking up, etc. & then going to bed all by myself in an empty house – "all by my own alone self".

28th October 1970 Wednesday

Tosca, our beautiful cat, who spends most nights out of doors, graciously condescended to keep me company all night long. It was much nicer than being quite alone. Tosca loves to be out in the night air; but once the wintry blizzards strike, & the snow lies thick & deep, then Tosca just will not go out.

30th October 1970 Friday

Received my bill from **Parkin & Jones**.

"Fitting new wing to offside: lead fill nearside front wing, & paint as required:"

Labour = £19-11s-3d.

1 wing = £7.

¾ lb. body solder = 16s-10d.

1 badge = 4s-6d.

1 pint paint = 17s-7d.

½ pint primer = 3s-3d.

1 pint thinners = 4s-4d.

6 pop rivets = 1/-

This makes the grand total £28-18s-9d.

1st November 1970 Sunday

Yesterday, had a £15 shopping spree in Leicester, buying all sorts of little necessities, such as towels, hot water bottle, bed socks, underskirt, books for the children at Sunday School, etc.

Leicester looked terrible – all the litter bins overflowing, & the streets lined with litter, because the dustmen have gone on strike.

3rd November 1970 Tuesday

Premium Savings Bonds were introduced on the 2nd November 1956.

Since then, I have bought them regularly at the rate of one a month. Every now & then I cash a whole bundle of them; & having just cashed the whole lot, I now have none at all.

And every bond has the chance of a £25,000 win!

5th November 1970 Thursday

Ravenstone Darby & Joan Club this week celebrated their 21st anniversary. The Duchess of Rutland, who is head of the Women's Royal Voluntary Service in Leicestershire, was special guest of honour at a party in Ravenstone Institute. There are about 70 members, who meet once a week, under the leadership of Auntie Belle.

7th November 1970 Saturday

This year marks the 50th anniversary of the unveiling of the **Cenotaph** in Whitehall, & the laying to rest of the **Unknown Soldier** in Westminster Abbey.

Also, this year commemorates the 25th anniversary of the end of the **2nd World War**. Tomorrow is **Remembrance Sunday**, with rather special services of Remembrance.

9th November 1970 Monday

Two delightful books from County Hall Library "Siamese Cats" & "Persian Cats" have enlightened me greatly on our own beautiful **Tosca**.

"A Persian cat with Siamese colouring! That is your Colourpoint, or Himalayan cat, as it is known in the U.S.A." And that is **Tosca** – first bred in 1924 as Malayan Persians.

11th November 1970 Wednesday

Martinmas – the feast of St. Martin. Leicester Cathedral is **St. Martin's**, & the November Cathedral News-letter brings a message from **Canon Jacques Sadoux**, Rector of the Basilica of St. Martin of Tours, where St. Martin is buried. He gives a most interesting account of the Basilica, & its checkered history.

13th November 1970 Friday

The Department of the Environment came into being yesterday.

That is the integration of the Ministry of Housing & Local Government, the Ministry of Public Building & Works, and the **Ministry of Transport**.

The approved abbreviated title is to be **DOE**; so I start my new job under **DOE**.

15th November 1970 Sunday

Tomorrow I start my new job. It will be virtually the same as my old job, except that I shall be dealing with applications for vehicle licences by post, instead of personal applications. In addition, I shall have several side-lines, such as Police enquiries to answer regarding unlicensed vehicles, etc.

17th November 1970 Tuesday

Started my new job by being overwhelmed with work – exchange licences galore (they always reach their peak on the 17th of the month), licences out of suspense – police enquiries by the dozen – incessant phone queries, plus a smattering of Ralph's work.

Tomorrow Ralph is on holiday, so I shall have his job too!

19th November 1970 Thursday

Siamese cats belonged originally only to persons of royal blood in Siam. They were considered sacred, & were used as guard cats in the temples & shrines. They can sit up & "say prayers", & can hold a conversation with you.

Persian cats are the most beautiful of all cats, with great dignity & unwavering affection, purring all the time you comb or fuss them.

Tosca is all this rolled into one.

21st November 1970 Saturday

Went to Leicester this morning, for my 6 monthly dental check up. The dentist told me that I have now passed the age of regular dental decay, & with all my double teeth firmly "filled", should need little more attention – Hurray! As Thackeray observed: "Forty times over let **Michaelmas** pass."

23rd November 1970 Monday

Mr Sharp confirmed that my new job has now been passed for upgrading by the council to **Clerical III**. As I am a **Civil Servant** working for the council, this has to be approved by the Civil Service, to give me the equivalent rise. This rise is operative from 1st April 1971. In Local Government it is £1,272 p.a.

25th November 1970 Wednesday

There are several distinct advantages with my new job – a different dinner hour (going now from 12 – 1 p.m., instead of 1 – 2 p.m., there is much more choice of menu) – more freedom of movement (able to leave my post at any chosen moment, at any hour of the day) - & quite a variety of interesting work.

27th November 1970 Friday

Mum & I went to Leicester to see the film "**Cromwell**" – a wonderful history lesson, set in the days of **King Charles I**. As with "Anne of a Thousand Days" which we saw 6 months ago, it made you appreciate living in the 20th century, with all the opportunity of free education, & enjoying the benefits men of old fought for.

29th November 1970 Advent Sunday

Advent Sunday – and a special Advent Carol Service at church, with Bible readings alternating with carols. I had the pleasure of reading the first lesson – Isaiah, Chap. 6. v. 1-11. Other readers were **Dennis**, **Harold**, **Mrs Buckroyd**, the **Rector** & **Mrs Woodings**.

A very enjoyable service.

1st December 1970 Tuesday

In February 1968 (for the very last time!) we put our clocks forward one hour. Gone was G.M.T. – Greenwich Mean Time, & instead we were to have **British Standard Time**. However – after only 2 winters of exceptionally dark mornings, Parliament voted this week by 366 to 81 to revert to G.M.T. next October 31st.

3rd December 1970 Thursday

Martin, my recently acquired regular passenger, finishes work at County Hall tomorrow, after 10 weeks. Being so sad & withdrawn, he was not readily accepted in the office where he worked, & was told that he was not suitable for the post. He now has to look elsewhere for a job, where I hope he may be happier.

5th December 1970 Saturday
Had a gorgeous day shopping – all morning in Leicester & all afternoon in Ashby - & bought all my Christmas presents: - Fur lined winter boots for **Mum** £9-9/-, 100 cigarettes for Auntie Gladys, & 50 for Enid, perfume for Auntie Belle & Evelyn, handkerchiefs for **Pat**, de luxe coat hanger for Anne, etc. etc.

7th December 1970 Monday
To **Maz & Little Tommy** – a son, **David Richard**.
While sharing the joy of Maz & Little Tommy, we have all, this week, been sharing the sorrow of another member of our staff – **Charles**, whose wife died last Thursday. This was doubly sad, insomuch that Charles married in turn, 2 sisters, & both of them have now died.

9th December 1970 Wednesday
Widened my experience at work today with the monthly record of refunds. In the bank we can allow £10,200 provided each month for us to give out in refunds, & we have to keep a
monthly account of how many people have actually cashed their refunds, & credit back to ourselves any more than 6 months old.

11th December 1970 Friday
County Hall by candlelight! It is now the electricity workers who are demanding more money, & to make their point felt, it's "**lights out**" anywhere, anytime. It was really quite exciting seeing County Hall working by the light of little candles.
The whole country is affected – the Queen, Parliament & the lot.

13th December 1970 Sunday
Minnehaha is all dressed up for Christmas with spanking new car seat covers - £7-15/- in warm ocelot.
With only 2 months to go to D. Day – Decimalisation day, we shall soon be thinking of money in £ - p. instead of £ - s - d. Next Friday I shall be going on a whole day course of instruction.

15th December 1970 Tuesday
Mr Pochin, former boss of our office, died last Tuesday, aged 76. Yesterday was his funeral at **St. Catherine's, Houghton on the Hill**. Mr Sharp, the present boss, took Miss Gazzard, Muriel & me in his car from the office to the funeral service – a well attended, homely little village church ceremony.

17th December 1970 Thursday
Today we had our decimalisation course, which was originally designated for tomorrow.
In one of the rooms at County Hall, 16 of us played shops. We were given £5 each to spend on various items of our own choice, priced in the new decimal currency. We handled the new ½ p, 1p, & 2p, not yet in circulation, & had great fun.

19th December 1970 Saturday
Both Louie & Ann have had a baby daughter this week – Louie on Thursday, & Ann on Friday.
Aunt Dos's lodger Valerie has broken up for a fortnight's Christmas holiday, so I am back sleeping with Aunt Dos. Aunt Dos has a nasty cough at the moment, & her bedroom is worse than ever.

21st December 1970 Monday
Today is the shortest day of the year, but as we are still enjoying "**British Standard Time**", we can come home from work in the daylight, & it does not seem so much like the depths of winter. Today has been really lovely – blue skies & sunshine. I enjoyed a lunch-time walk round the fields.

23rd December 1970 Wednesday
Mum has now taken the plunge after much deliberation, & written to the **Matron**, saying she would like to finish work at the end of the year. This means that we shall have to live solely on my salary & Mum's pension, which we could manage quite comfortably, if we didn't want to save up for a car.

25th December 1970 Friday
Christmas Day! And snow. How lovely it was to see Ravenstone Church in the snow at 8 a.m. Holy Communion.
At 11 a.m., Anne Causer & I went to Leicester Cathedral to a most uplifting and inspiring service. After the recent electricity power cuts, the Bishop chose most appropriately – Isaiah Chapter 60. v. 2.

27th December 1970 Sunday
Spent the whole morning clearing snow, & the rest of the time puzzling out the latest "Home & Country" competition – one colossal anagram: - "**The Seven Deadly Sins – Gluttony, Avarice, Sloth, Wrath, Pride, Envy, Lust.**" This had to be changed into lively virtues.
The result was: - "**Gosh! Every lady understands lively virtues – constant help with tea.**"

29th December 1970 Tuesday
1970 draws to its close, with none of the dramatic closing down such as we had last year, when a whole new decade began. In fact, we all have a new date line at the moment. D-Day February 15th 1971. This will be the most dramatic change-over we have known for about a thousand years.

31st December 1970 Thursday
Today I bought my first **£10 Premium Savings Bond**. Starting from rock bottom, I am hoping to buy a £10 Premium Savings Bond each month, in my determined effort to save up for a new car. The trouble is, as fast as I save, poor old Minnehaha needs more & more spending on repairs.

* * *

1971

1st January 1971 Friday
Well, here I am – **Elizabeth Hewes**, aged 39 – unmarried, living with my Mum …..
Enid & I have chosen **Tenby** – South Wales – for our summer holiday this year –
"An historic walled town, in the Pembrokeshire National Park with 4 golden sandy beaches."
Official Guide 2/- (10p)

3rd January 1971 Sunday
Yesterday at **Ibrox Park**, **Glasgow Rangers** played **Celtic**. The score was 1-1, with Rangers scoring in the last seconds of the match. A barrier collapsed on an exit stairway, causing the worst spectator disaster in the history of British football. **66** people died & many were injured.

5th January 1971 Tuesday
Every tree round County Hall was coated with thick frost today – a veritable winter wonderland. This week we have had freezing fog to contend with – de-ice the windscreen of the car every 5 minutes. I have now acquired a new regular passenger – **Margaret**, a young girl from County Hall.

7th January 1971 Thursday
Another bill this week for Minnehaha – To checking heater unit, battery & ignition; clean out heater system, fit new hose, check battery and tune engine £3-16s-6d.
To supplying 1 bulb, 3 hose clips, 1 hose, 14s-11d.
Total £4-11s-5d.
Having no thermostat, there is no heat; but with a thermostat, the water boils over.

9th January 1971 Saturday
Tomorrow Bunting & Mostyn celebrate their Silver Wedding Anniversary.
Twenty-five years ago they were married at **Ravenstone Church**, & for the only time in my life – I was a bridesmaid. I had the day off from school without permission, & the Headmaster said: - "**Next time**, you ask for permission."

11th January 1971 Monday
Last September, Minnehaha boiled over repeatedly, & the only solution seemed to be – remove the thermostat. This is all very well in the warm weather, but in mid-winter it means a very cold car. Cyril, at **Parkin & Jones**, has advised me to have a new radiator, as there is an obvious blockage there.

13th January 1971 Wednesday
Enid & I have chosen "The Esplanade Hotel", **Tenby**, for our summer holiday. We had a letter this week from **Mrs Pat Dart**, Resident Proprietress: - "We have pleasure in offering you one twin-bedded room, facing sea, first floor, £20 each weekly, for one week commencing 12th June. Deposit £2 each.

15th January 1971 Friday
The January issue of "**Public Service**", the **Local Government** news-paper, is now out, & amongst all the dreary news, and long-winded arguments, how refreshing to see the Crossword – compiled by **Miss Elizabeth Hewes (Leicestershire)**, for which I have received **Two Guineas**. (£2-2/-) i.e. £2-10p.

17th January 1971 Sunday
England has become a **Nation of Strikers**. Next Wednesday the Postal Workers are to begin their strike for more money. That means no letter boxes will be emptied, & no-body will receive any mail. Our office depends entirely on the post. Every day we receive, & also send out, mail by the sackful.

19th January 1971 Tuesday
Mum & I watched on television a superb production of "The Tragedy of King Richard II", by William Shakespeare, with those magnificent famous lines, such as: - "**For God's sake let us sit upon the ground, & tell sad stories of the death of kings …**" or "**This royal throne of kings, this sceptred isle …..**"

21st January 1971 Thursday
Had a couple of days holiday from work, & spent all day today typing out the **February Parish Magazine**, while **Tosca** the beautiful, **Tosca** the faithful, lay as close as possible to the typewriter.
This evening Mum & I went to the Little Theatre, Leicester, to see "**Toad of Toad Hall**".

23rd January 1971 Saturday
Minnehaha's latest bill is: -
1 thermostat £1, 1 gasket 1/-, 1 radiator £8-10/-, 1 fan belt 11/-, 1 pint antifreeze 5/-,
To checking heater, remove thermostat housing, fit new thermostat, radiator & fan belt, etc. £5-1/- Grand Total = £15-8s-0d.
With all the postal workers on strike, this was hand delivered.

25th January 1971 Monday
"**The Six Wives of Henry VIII**" is being shown for 6 weeks, as a series on television.
Henry VIII lived from 1491-1547, & so far, we have seen 3 excellent programmes: -
1. **Catherine of Aragon**. 2. **Anne Boleyn**. 3. **Jane Seymour**. Next comes 4. **Anne of Cleves**.
5. **Catherine Howard**. 6. **Catherine Parr**.

27th January 1971 Wednesday
My latest book from County Hall Library is: - "**Greeks & Trojans**" by **Rex Warner**. This is a fascinating translation of **Homer's Iliad**, in simple English. All those well-known names come to life in correct sequence – Zeus, Apollo, Priam & Hecuba, Hector, Aeneas son of Aphrodite, Paris & Helen of Troy.

29th January 1971 Friday
The Post Office strike continues – the **Last Post** having been sounded on January 20th.
All our salary cheques from **Hemel Hempstead** are still "somewhere in transit", & the County Council very kindly paid all of us from the County coffers.
With no Post Offices open & no postal service, our office was overwhelmed with customers.

31ˢᵗ January 1971 Sunday
Apollo 14 today set off for the Moon with 3 astronauts –
Alan Shepard, Edgar Mitchell & Stuart Roosa.
Touchdown on the Moon is scheduled for Friday
February 5ᵗʰ. Lift off from the moon is scheduled for
Saturday February 6ᵗʰ, & splashdown home Tuesday
February 9ᵗʰ
(P.S. **Apollo** built the walls of **Troy!**)

2ⁿᵈ February 1971 Tuesday
The **Apollo 14** mission is hoping to accomplish what
Apollo 13 failed to do last April, when a mystery
explosion damaged the space-ship. The mission is to the
lunar foothills, known as **Fra Mauro**, littered with rocks
of outstanding geological interest. The **Fra Mauro**
formation is one of the oldest parts of the Moon.

4ᵗʰ February 1971 Thursday
The postal strike continues, making life very interesting
at work. No post means every application for licence is
brought by hand – many applications are left for delivery
later, or collection, & a wonderful net-work of courier
service has evolved.
No bills arrive - & at work all the out-of-date records
had time to be cleared.

6ᵗʰ February 1971 Saturday
Spent many hours fascinated by the "live" TV pictures
of Alan Shepard & Edgar Mitchell on the Moon. They
walked over boulders & rocks pulling a cart full of tools
& cameras; & gathering up interesting specimens.
Shepard produced 2 golf balls & a golf club & had 2
shots. "There we go", he said, "It goes miles & miles."

8ᵗʰ February 1971 Monday
When man first stepped on the Moon in July 1969, Reg
Hall loaned me his book "Splendour of the Heavens" – a
massive book of 976 pages, & hundreds of pictures;
showing real & imaginary views from Earth, from the
Moon, from the planets & from the stars.
Reg Hall has now given me this book.

10ᵗʰ February 1971 Wednesday
With **Apollo 14** safely home from the Moon, it is now
all systems go, for our next big blast off next Monday -
D-Day. This is when our country changes it's £-s-d
money into decimal currency.
All the banks closed today, for the marathon change-
over, & re-open on Monday; while still the Post Office
strikes.

12ᵗʰ February 1971 Friday
The winners of my **Crossword**, published just before the
great **Postal Strike**, were Mrs B. Bolton (Durham) and
Christopher Green (Carlisle).
Because of the Postal Strike, fewer greetings cards have
been sold in the shops. I bought a card for Julian's 21ˢᵗ
birthday on January 30ᵗʰ, but could not send it.

14ᵗʰ February 1971 Sunday
St. Valentine's Day! – "Talk not of wasted affection.
Affection never was wasted: If it enrich not the heart of
another, its waters returning back to their springs, like
the rain, shall fill them full of refreshment." **Longfellow**
"**Evangeline**".

16ᵗʰ February 1971 Tuesday
And so we say farewell to our old £-s-d. (Pounds,
shillings & pence).
The story began in the late 8ᵗʰ century A.D., when the
pennies of **Offa**, **King of Mercia**, weighed 22 ½ grains,
240 being made out of a pound weight of silver.
In 1503 **Henry VII** standardised the shilling – a silver
coin worth 12d.

18ᵗʰ February 1971 Thursday
And yet again **Leicester City** football team has reached
the Quarter Finals of the F.A. Cup –the 6ᵗʰ time in 10
years. The 8 teams now left in the running are **Liverpool**
v. **Spurs**, **Hull** v. **Stoke**, **Everton** v. **Colchester**, and
Leicester v. **Arsenal**.
Everton are favourites, & Arsenal 2ⁿᵈ.

20ᵗʰ February 1971 Saturday
Spent nearly all weekend typing out eight pages for the
March Parish Magazine.
Dennis, pillar of our church for many years, is now
moving to become landlord of a pub in **Burton-on-
Trent**. He is currently "**Rector's Warden**". Also the
Rector's Room, where we have our Sunday School, is
now up for sale.

*Note – The Rector's Room, beside Ravenstone Church,
becomes an extension of the tiny house at its far end.*

22ⁿᵈ February 1971 Monday
The Leicester Mercury this week has published a superb
16 page supplement "Looking Back – Number One –
1700-1870" "The Developing Years". This is the story
of **Leicester**, which suddenly grew from a small sleepy
town, into the most prosperous city in Europe, when
"Leicester clothed the world".

24ᵗʰ February 1971 Ash Wednesday
The Postal Strike means I have the pleasure of
answering the phone much more at work. With no daily
post to cope with, I can relax more, & never get harassed
by too much work. An idyllic way of earning your living
– drive to work into the beauty of daybreak, enjoy the
dawn chorus, & even **sun bathe** at midday.

26ᵗʰ February 1971 Friday
Costumes have now arrived for "**Pink Champagne**". I
have one "house-maid's" long grey dress, with apron &
cap; & one elegant mauve satin evening dress.
Went on my first big "decimal" shopping expedition to
Leicester for accessories, such as shimmering silver long
gloves, silver shoes, a pretty fan, & white stockings.

28ᵗʰ February 1971 Sunday
Ronald Ralph, Bishop of Leicester, came to Ravenstone
Church to preach at evensong. This was the first Sunday
in Lent but no great special occasion. There was just the
usual congregation, about 30, with a choir of 4 young
boys, 4 men & a dozen women.
The Bishop said he enjoyed coming to an ordinary
service – something he rarely did - & for his text he
chose Genesis 9. 14. "And it shall come to pass, when I
bring a cloud over the earth, that the bow shall be seen in
the cloud." This was a most inspiring sermon – to see the
rainbow in the clouds of uncertainty, the clouds of

sorrow & suffering, & in the clouds of sin.

1ˢᵗ March 1971 Monday
I am just one of the chorus in "Pink Champagne", but all of a sudden – due to Marlene taking ill, I have acquired a very small part, "**Frau Trauber**", proprietress of a coffee house.
"**Pink Champagne**" is actually an adaptation of "**Die Fledermaus**", produced in **Vienna** in 1874, with **Johann Strauss** music, including "The Blue Danube".

3ʳᵈ March 1971 Wednesday
Minnehaha is now exactly 5 years old, & today she had her 45,000 mile service, MOT Test, new rear bumper, new tyre, 1 TL valve, cleaning fluid, bushes, 2 pairs brake shoes, nuts, bolts, washers, contact set, bracket, filter, oil, clean under wings, clean the engine, puncture mended & wheels changed round - £24.

5ᵗʰ March 1971 Friday
According to the write-up in the Leicester Mercury our "**Pink Champagne**" was rather flat – "The greatest weakness was in the singing of male principals & some of the chorus could have looked more cheerful."
But according to the Coalville Times "**Pink Champagne** bubbles into life in a colourful galaxy of gay costumes & sweet music".

7ᵗʰ March 1971 Sunday
Throughout **Lent**, we are having at Church different Lay people of various occupations, to speak about their faith & their jobs. Tonight the preacher was Selwyn H. Bate, L.L.M. – a Tamworth Solicitor. He spoke of his life as a lawyer. Having studied the law for the past 35 years, he said it had trebled itself in that time.

9ᵗʰ March 1971 Tuesday
The Postal strike, Britain's longest **national** stoppage for 45 years, ended on Sunday night. This 47 day strike lost the Post Office £27 million.
Tonight Mum & I watched on television "**The Fight of the Century**", **Muhammad Ali**,
(Née **Cassius Clay**), beaten by **Joe Frazier** after 15 rounds.

11ᵗʰ March 1971 Thursday
County Hall at the moment stands well back from the main road, with a belt of beautiful trees stretching along the roadside. A dual carriageway is planned, with a 40 foot wide central reservation, 'specially to retain the trees. This means the new road will come much nearer to County Hall. Total cost: - £273,913.

13ᵗʰ March 1971 Saturday
Aunt Dos is 69 today.
Spring has arrived, with all the birds singing merrily away from morn 'til night.
Spent a long time in the garden, clearing up dead leaves etc.; with the "**help**" of little **Ian** next door, just turned 4. He brought his little barrow & his spade, & then everybody made a bonfire – 4 bonfires all in a row.

15ᵗʰ March 1971 Monday
Leicester is now out of the F.A. Cup, knocked out by **Arsenal** in tonight's replay. The 4 teams left in the semi-final are Arsenal – Stoke, Liverpool – Everton.
Dennis, pillar of our church, has relinquished his duties as Rector's Warden and Church Treasurer; & we are staggered to hear his wife has left.

17ᵗʰ March 1971 Wednesday
St. Patrick's Day! My dad's birthday.
I now have a very interesting book from County Hall Library called "**Dear & Glorious Physician**" – the life story of **St. Luke**. The only **Apostle** who was not a **Jew**, he was fortunate to have studied medicine at Alexandria; & reference is made to the great medical advances of those days.

19ᵗʰ March 1971 Friday
Had a day's holiday from work today. Mum & I visited **Madge & Bertha** at **Willoughby** this morning. This afternoon I went to the hairdressers for an elegant hair style, & this evening went to the **Coalville Amateur Operatic Society Annual Dinner & Dance** – my 23ʳᵈ year with the society.

21ˢᵗ March 1971 Sunday
The 4ᵗʰ Sunday in Lent – Mothering Sunday.
Our guest preacher at church tonight was Mr J. H. Fisher, a farmer & Diocesan Lay Reader, of Grendon, Warks. He was most interesting, & told us of his mother's favourite quotation – Proverbs 3. 6. "In all thy ways acknowledge Him, and He shall direct thy paths".

23ʳᵈ March 1971 Tuesday
All our local Amateur Operatic Societies seem to choose **March** for their productions – so we have been off to the De Montfort Hall, Leicester, for "Sound of Music" – Loughborough Town Hall for "Waltzes from Vienna"- the Little Theatre, Leicester for "The Gondoliers" & Ashby Town Hall for "Trial by Jury" and "H. M. S. Pinafore".

25ᵗʰ March 1971 Thursday
The Moon rocks, weighing 96 lbs, which were brought back by the "Apollo 14" astronauts last month, are proving to be of great interest to the scientists. Some fragments of the rock may date back to the formation of the Moon's crust 4,600 million years ago. They contain 23 minerals, 10 of which have not been identified.

27ᵗʰ March 1971 Saturday
This morning Aunt Dos, Mum & I went to **Staunton Harold Cheshire Home**, to see the **Quorn Hunt** meet. We met **Cecil Hewes** (on horse-back) – one of our distant relations we rarely see. The horses & huntsmen made a splendid sight as they set off with all the hounds, in that truly delightful setting.

29ᵗʰ March 1971 Monday
Following the great **Postal Strike**, received a Christmas "Thank You" letter from Bunting. "Michael & Sheena are busy with their wedding plans. The great day is July 31ˢᵗ at Padmore Church, Stourbridge ..... Julian leads a most hectic life, & is never in. His little girl friend is **Eleanor**."

31ˢᵗ March 1971 Wednesday
Budget Day yesterday, & the Chancellor, **Mr Anthony**

Barber, cut down taxes by £680 million. **Pensioners**, who now get £5 a week, will get £6 a week from next **September**. The money is to come from higher **National Insurance** contributions. At the moment I pay £20 a month tax, & £4 National Insurance.

2nd April 1971 Friday
Mum received a letter from "Woolley, Beardsleys & Bosworth", Solicitors, Rectory Place, Loughborough: - "Dear Mrs Hewes, We now have the pleasure to enclose herewith our firm's cheque for £300 in payment of the pecuniary legacy of that amount bequeathed to you by the Will of Mrs Mary Sketchley."

4th April 1971 Sunday
Apart from the pecuniary legacies (all free of death duties) bequeathed in Aunt Mary's Will, she also owned half a share in property at **Willoughby**. When this was sold, & all debts, expenses & death duties paid, Aunt Mary willed that her share should be divided equally between S. & R. Marriott, J. Palmer & Mum.

6th April 1971 Tuesday
My latest book from County Hall Library is "The Space around Us" by A. Edward Tyler. It explains how man is so very limited by his physical make up, as to where he can venture into space. Either he would freeze to death, or be burned to death. Our sun is but one of 100 billion stars in one galaxy, & there are billions of galaxies.

8th April 1971 Thursday
So – why not communicate with other beings in outer space by radio or television? Within our own solar system we could reach **Mars** by radio in 3 minutes. (Mars comes within 30 million miles at its closest approach to Earth) Outside our own solar system, our next neighbour is 4 light years away (4 years by radio). Our galaxy is 120,000 light years across.

10th April 1971 Saturday
So – it would take 120,000 years to contact the other side of our own galaxy by radio (and that would be one way only). One simple question, such as "**Anybody there?**" & you would have to wait for another 120,000 years just to get the answer.
At our Good Friday Service, we saw Christ on the Cross, looking down at our world.

12th April 1971 Easter Monday
Mary Moore arrived yesterday to spend a week with Mum & me. She now lives at **Wivenhoe**, near Colchester, & has invited us to spend a few days with her in August.
Mum & I are hoping also to spend a long weekend in October visiting the Lakes & Blackpool Illuminations, staying one night at Patterdale & one at Fleetwood.

14th April 1971 Wednesday
This month – on Sunday April 25th – we are having the biggest, most comprehensive **Census** ever held in **Britain**. Every household will have a form to fill in, comprising 134 questions. The forms will be delivered & collected by 105,000 enumerators, each covering an average of 180 homes, & being paid £48 each.

16th April 1971 Friday
As a prelude to the mighty **Census**, we have received a small pamphlet E.8, signed by **Michael Reed**, Registrar General, Somerset House, London ".... The Census will involve us all .... it must count everyone ... give details of ages, occupations, education, housing conditions, etc. .... without you, the Census would be incomplete."

18th April 1971 Sunday
We have now completed our **Census** form. "**Elizabeth Hewes**, born 14-7-31 (Female) daughter of the household – single – in a job as Civil Servant, issuing licences, travelling to work by car – in the same job one year ago – born in England – Father & Mother born in England – my address the same 5 years ago – no advanced qualifications, etc."

20th April 1971 Tuesday
After the facts of all the **Census** forms have been fed into a computer, the **Census** forms will be locked away for 100 years! Mum's signature will bear witness that she – **Mary Hewes**, born 23rd August 1905, was head of her household in 1971 with a cooker, kitchen sink, fixed bath, 2 toilets, hot water supply, etc.

22nd April 1971 Thursday
Dennis Collier – pillar of our church for so long – has now left our church completely, taking **Harold** with him. **Harold** has been Sunday School Superintendent for many years, & now I find myself in this doubtful rôle. Over the past 12 years I have watched the numbers diminish from 100 to 20.

24th April 1971 Saturday
Road-work in front of **County Hall** to make a dual carriage-way is now in full swing. Great earth-moving vehicles, like science-fiction monsters, devour the ground, & tremendous progress is made in a short time. One track laying "monster" got itself stuck, & had to be rescued by another.

26th April 1971 Monday
In October 1968 (2 ½ years ago) I wrote in my diary "....the next thing we would like is a pretty garden fence." Tonight I ordered from Don, my cousin, who is a "builders' merchant", fencing, and materials for a concrete base. Mr. Swanwick, our near neighbour, has agreed to lay the concrete & fence for us.

28th April 1971 Wednesday
Received an unexpected letter from "Department of the Environment", Lambeth Bridge House, London, S.E.1. – **Personal** – Miss E. Hewes, L.T.O., Leics.C.C. – "You are invited to attend for interview by a Board which is considering officers for promotion to the grade of Executive Officer. Will you please report to St. Christopher House, 4th May 1971.

30th April 1971 Friday
"Please report to Room 8/ 122, St. Christopher House, London S.E.1 on 4th May 1971 at 11-25 a.m." Puzzle – find this one house in London! I hope to motor to Leicester – train to London (St. Pancras) – London Underground to Blackfriars – walk over the River Thames, & settle somewhere in Southwark Street.

2nd May 1971 Sunday

You will not be in the least surprised that my latest book from County Hall Library is "**In Search of London**" by H. V. Morton. He is a writer who shows you everything, not only as it is today, but as it was in Shakespeare's day, as it was in Roman times, & really makes an ideal travelling companion.

4th May 1971 Tuesday

Not a very satisfactory interview in London, but afterwards I spent a most enjoyable afternoon visiting Southwark Cathedral – the Monument – the Bank of England – St. Paul's – a most delightful stroll by the river-side, past Cleopatra's Needle, finishing at Big Ben, with sunshine all day long.

6th May 1971 Thursday

The "**Board**" who interviewed me on Tuesday comprised 2 ladies & one gentleman. They implied that it was rather "**stick in the mud**" to spend 20 years in the same office, as I have done. They were looking for progressive up & coming young people with plenty of drive & wide interests. They were merely coolly polite.

8th May 1971 Saturday

Cup Final Day! Arsenal became the 2nd club this century to win the League Championship & the Cup in the same season. They beat Liverpool 2-1 after extra time. Known as the "**Gunners**" they are now called the double barrelled Gunners. (Spurs were the double champions in 1961). The Cup was presented today by the Duke of Kent.

10th May 1971 Monday

On 14th November 1966, I was promoted from Local Government Clerical I to Clerical II. Although I am now a Civil Servant – Clerical Officer – I have been allowed the status of Local Government, Clerical III. A letter from Swansea confirms that an allowance of £71 per annum is payable from 1st April 1971. Total salary now £1,238 p.a.

12th May 1971 Wednesday

Britain is making great progress in her latest bid to join the **Common Market**. This was formed by a treaty signed in **Rome** 25th March 1957. At that time, Britain chose not to join, because of her desire to maintain a policy of imperial preference. The 6 who did join were France, Italy, Germany, & the Benelux countries.

14th May 1971 Friday

Up the City! Two years ago we were relegated to Division II. "It's been two hard years of slogging to get back, but now that we are up, it's been very worthwhile," said Leicester City manager Frank O'Farrell, when we stepped proudly back into Division I, from Second Division championship.

16th May 1971 Sunday

Mum received a further letter & cheque yesterday from the solicitors dealing with Aunt Mary's will.

"Pending the settlement of the outstanding **Capital Gains Tax** liability on the net proceeds of sale of the properties at Willoughby-on-the-Wolds, which we fear may take a little time to resolve, we enclose herewith our firm's cheque for £500."

18th May 1971 Tuesday

The 1971 Annual Conference for the C. P. S. A. takes place this week at the Villa Marina, Douglas, Isle of Man. Every item on the agenda spells discontent. This conference rejects … deplores … regrets … instructs the N. E. C. to press for higher salaries, longer holidays, earlier retirement, shorter working week, increase in retirement pension, etc.

20th May 1971 Thursday

A week of glorious weather has enabled Mr. Swanwick to spend each evening on the erection of our "pretty garden fence" – it really does look super.

Also in the course of erection at the moment, is a de-luxe bungalow for **Peter Hewes**, in the spacious grounds of the **Hollies**, next door. Peter is Don's son.

22nd May 1971 Saturday

The "**Midland Red**" are running a day trip to London next Saturday, as one of their Whitsuntide holiday attractions, & Mum & I have booked a seat. The coach leaves Coalville at 8-15 a.m., & the fare is £1-50p each.

In 40 years, this will be my 4th trip to London! – Twice this month.

24th May 1971 Monday

Yesterday, Mum & I went to **Leicester Cathedral**, where the choir from **Krefeld** (Leicester's twin town in West Germany) were singing. The address was given by Pastor Karl F. Schneider, who said that in Germany you could well imagine that God was dead. It was good to be in Leicester, with so many worshippers.

26th May 1971 Wednesday

Quote from yesterday's "**Daily Mail**": - *****Hayden Hewes**, of **Oklahoma City**, says he's identified three types of alien from Outer Space. One is about 3′ 6″ & has a pointed head, another is a hairy non-human "which is probably trained for reconnaissance operations" & the 3rd could easily be taken for the guy next door. ***Cousin Hayden?**

28th May 1971 Friday

For the past 2 years I have typed our Parish Magazine in its final state of perfection, on the best glossy paper, which Parkers the Printers, of Burton-on-Trent, have simply duplicated. Rising costs have now made us turn to Mr. Broughton of Blaby, who produces a cheaper magazine – not so good – but much easier for me.

30th May 1971 Whit Sunday

Mum & I just missed seeing the rehearsal for the Trooping of the Colour on the Queen's Birthday, on Horse Guards Parade yesterday. We arrived in time to see only the sweep-up which followed the horses.

In the afternoon, we went by boat from **Westminster Pier** to **Greenwich** – to the very centre of time, & the Prime Meridian.

1st June 1971 Tuesday

Mum & I hope to make a return visit to London next Saturday, to see the 2nd rehearsal for the Troop. Also we hope to take a 2 hour **Sightseeing Tour** by bus from

Piccadilly to Marble Arch – South Kensington – over the River Thames at Lambeth Bridge, back across Waterloo Bridge – St. Paul's – over London Bridge to Southwark.

3rd June 1971 Thursday

The 2 hour **Sightseeing Tour** of London continues from Southwark, back over the River Thames at Tower Bridge – round the Tower of London, past the Monument, & along the Embankment to Big Ben – past Horse Guards – Trafalgar Square, down the Mall to Buckingham Palace & back to Piccadilly via Hyde Park.

5th June 1971 Saturday

There we were – walking past the famous **Number 10 Downing Street**, when we heard a passer by say he had 2 spare tickets for the troop. Mum & I therefore watched this most splendid of ceremonies from a Grand Stand seat – **Price: - nothing**.

Later we went on the sightseeing coach tour, & were introduced to the full beauty of Hyde Park.

7th June 1971 Monday

Coalville Amateur Operatic Society's Annual General Meeting. The show which has been chosen for next year is "**Bless the Bride**", starting March 6th, & ending March 11th.

Mr Roberts resigned as Musical Director, after many years in that rôle, & our new musical director is Peter Jacques.

9th June 1971 Wednesday

As a result of negotiations which have proceeded non-stop since the meeting with **Earl Jellicoe** on 24th May, the C. P. S. A. has achieved a pay rise of £15 million a year for 200,000 **Clerical Officers & Clerical Assistants**. This is to be back-dated to January 1st 1971. My salary now = £1,290.

11th June 1971 Friday

On the eve of our summer holiday in **Tenby**, South Wales, the weather is more like mid-winter. For the past week we have had torrential rain; & with no heat on at all, in County Hall, the staff have been really cold. So we are packing all our winter woollies – the car rug – hot water bottle – winter gloves – umbrella, etc.

13th June 1971 Sunday

Well! Here we are in **Tenby**, in the beautiful county of **Pembrokeshire**. This afternoon we went by coach to the southernmost headland, **St. Govan's Head**, & further along the coastline, to **Stack Rocks**, with its impressive natural arch lying beneath the massive rocky coastline. Some of the extensive views were really magnificent.

15th June 1971 Tuesday

Spent this morning on **Caldey Island** – 20 minutes from **Tenby** by boat: & this afternoon we went on the **Tenby Queen** – a lovely big boat – for a ride all round **Caldey Island**, & back to **Tenby**. This evening we went on a very pleasant coach trip through **Pembroke** with its splendid castle, as far as **Milford Haven**.

17th June 1971 Thursday

The coast-line of Pembrokeshire is really magnificent. Yesterday we visited the lovely **Cathedral of St.**

David's on the westernmost tip, & explored the coastline of **St. Justinian** – Do go if ever you have the opportunity.

Today we enjoyed a visit to **Manorbier Castle**, with more superb coastal scenery, & interesting churches in every village.

19th June 1971 Saturday

Arrived home from **Tenby** after a day of torrential rain yesterday from morning 'til night. Last Monday also was such a day, but the rest of the week was nice enough to be out & about seeing all the places of interest. Nice to come home to a warm welcome – a fire in mid-June, to **Tosca**; & to find our newly installed telephone – **Coalville 3583**.

Note – With money left to Mum from her Aunt Mary, we have a telephone installed.

21st June 1971 Monday

Spent the afternoon & evening with Reevsie & family. Met Reevsie's 86 year old grand-dad, staying for a fortnight with Reevsie's mum. Mr. and Mrs. Reeves are now divorced. Tomorrow is Reevsie's birthday – she will be 36. Joanne, now 4 years old, is as delightful as ever, & looking forward to starting school.

23rd June 1971 Wednesday

Received the bill for our new fence £28-87p. This was made up of : –

Nine 3′ x 6′ interwoven fence panels with trellis top @ £1-85p = £16-65p. Ten oak posts with caps plus fittings = £7-48p. Ballast = £3-20p. Cement = £1-54p. Mr. Swanwick charged only £6-80p for about 10 hours sweat & toil to erect the fence, but we gladly gave him £10.

25th June 1971 Friday

Mum is spending a few days at Willoughby with her cousin Madge, so I am in charge of the house & Tosca.

My latest book of absorbing interest from County Hall Library is "**Bosworth Field & the Wars of the Roses**" by Dr. A. L. Rowse. From **Richard II** to **Richard III** it sorts them all out, with lots of help from Shakespeare.

27th June 1971 Sunday

Spent much of the day with Henry IV, V & VI. This House of Lancaster fought & won not only the Crown of England, but also that of France. Henry IV snatched the Crown of England from Richard II, having been sorely provoked. His son Henry V made a fine King, & won a great battle at Agincourt, but Henry VI is my favourite – so good & holy.

29th June 1971 Tuesday

After Henry IV, V & VI, the Crown of England was snatched back by the House of York, (War of the Roses), when Edward IV became King. He died in 1483, when his 12 year old son became Edward V, only to be murdered by his uncle, Richard III (The murder of the Princes in the Tower).

1483 – The only year since 1066 in which there have been 3 English Kings.

1st July 1971 Thursday

Richard III, the tyrant King, was not worthy of the

crown. Having murdered everybody in line for the crown, he himself was killed at last in 1485 – the Battle of Bosworth. The next in line for the House of Lancaster was the almost unknown Henry Tudor. He became the next King – Henry VII, married the heiress of York, & together they produced Henry VIII.

3ʳᵈ July 1971 Saturday

Three Russian astronauts returned to Earth on Wednesday this week, after man's longest trip – 23 ½ days, since blast off on June 6ᵗʰ. But when the hatch of Soyuz II was prised open, the 3 men lay dead. They were Lt. Col. Georgi Dobrovolsky (43), Flight Engineer Vladislaw Volkov (37), & Test Engineer Viktor Patsayev (38).

5ᵗʰ July 1971 Monday

Man has now been probing outer space for 10 years. Yuri Gagarin (Russian) was the first man to go into orbit. The longer a man stays in space (beyond the force of gravity) his weightless condition causes his heart to become lazy, & the sudden plunge back into the force of gravity becomes more than the heart can take.

7ᵗʰ July 1971 Wednesday

Ah well, back to the mundane things of this life. Received a letter from Department of the Environment, Lambeth Bridge House, London, S. E. 1. "Following your appearance before the recent Promotion Board to Executive Officer, I regret to inform you that you have not been recommended for promotion."

9ᵗʰ July 1971 Friday

Dear, oh dear! Now **Mary Blue** has run away. **Mary Blue**, who married **Terry** in April 1965, has left home. She caught the night train to **Scotland**, & is now in **Inverness**, with a man who lives there with his father & mother. He used to live next door to **Mary Blue** at **Gartree**, & is now parted from his wife.

11ᵗʰ July 1971 Sunday

Terry caught the next train to Inverness, in an attempt to bring home the Prodigal **Mary Blue**. **Pat** spoke to her on the phone – but all to no avail. **Terry** returned home – utterly exhausted – without her. Meanwhile, there are the children to consider. Tonight, **Steven** aged 3 is with **Terry**'s mother, & **Karen** aged 1, with **Evelyn**.

13ᵗʰ July 1971 Tuesday

Tomorrow is my birthday – aged 40.
"**The Age of Wisdom**" – "…. Wait till you come to 40 year." (Thackeray).
St. Augustine being asked, "What is the first thing in religion?" replied, "**Humility**". "And what is the second?" "**Humility**". "And what is the third?" "**Humility**".
Do you think my lack of success, one way & another, might help?

15ᵗʰ July 1971 Thursday

St. Swithin's Day! Poor old St. Swithin. He was Bishop of Winchester, & yet he requested not to be buried in a place of honour, as befitted his rank.
But 1,000 years ago today, in 971 A.D. his body was moved, to be placed more honourably, inside the

Cathedral. As if in protest, the heavens opened, & it rained for 40 days.

17ᵗʰ July 1971 Saturday

Not only St. Swithin. Poor old Henry VI – he had a similar story. He was murdered by Edward IV & did not receive a burial fit for a King. It was the tyrant usurper Richard III who finally arranged for him to be moved to a place of honour. After many evil deeds, this was a vain attempt to impress – no-one was moved – except **Henry!**

19ᵗʰ July 1971 Monday

Apollo XV is scheduled for blast off to the Moon next Monday for a 12 day mission, including 67 hours on the Moon.
The **Apollo 14** astronauts walked 2 miles on the surface of the Moon, but the **Apollo 15** astronauts are hoping to drive 22 miles in the Moon buggy **Rover 1**. They will land 465 miles north of the equator near the Moon's highest mountains.

21ˢᵗ July 1971 Wednesday

Having reached the "**Age of Wisdom**", it is appropriate that my latest book from County Hall Library is "The Evolution of Man & Society", by C. D. Darlington. From ape-men, it traces man's progress through every age, throughout the whole world, covering a detailed survey of the cause & effects of different religions.

23ʳᵈ July 1971 Friday

Excitement grows as **Apollo 15** prepares for blast off with its 3 man crew, Col. David Scott, Lt. Col. James Irwin & Major Alfred Worden.
This is the first expedition to the mountains of the Moon, making it the most difficult & dangerous Moon landing so far attempted. Also nearby is a deep canyon **Hadley Rille**.

25ᵗʰ July 1971 Sunday

How wonderfully uplifting to go to Leicester Cathedral this evening & hear **Canon Gundry** preach on **Psalm 139** – the **Crown** of all the Psalms.
Comparing man's quest for outer space with his inner quest for God, he chose for his text: "If I climb up into heaven, Thou art there: if I go down into hell, Thou art there also." – verse 7.

27ᵗʰ July 1971 Tuesday

Man is due to take his first ride on the Moon next Saturday – the day Michael & Sheena get married.
Pat & Evelyn are going to the wedding – feeling rather uncomfortable, now that their only daughter's wedding vows have been broken.
Terry & Mary should have been going, but **Mary Blue** is up in Scotland with another man.

29ᵗʰ July 1971 Thursday

Mary Blue is in contact with her Mum & Dad, & writes home regularly. Evelyn showed me the letters she has written to date. Not a word about her children – but most interesting accounts of her impressions of Inverness – hilarious character studies, especially her mean old landlady, & details of her new hairdressing job.

31st July 1971 Saturday
The wedding of Michael & Sheena at St. Peter's Church, Pedmore, Near Stourbridge.
A lovely wedding, which we all enjoyed. The vicar gave the newly-weds a text for life – Proverbs 3. 6. "In all thy ways acknowledge Him, & He shall direct thy paths." (See March 21st). Julian, aged 21 was Best Man.

2nd August 1971 Monday
Have you ever seen the Moon's Post Office? Moon-men **Scott & Irwin**, staying for the past 3 days at the foot of the Moon's 15,000 ft. high **Apennine Mountains**, today stamped an envelope on the Moon, with an official date stamp, & then in the rôle of postmen, left for home. We saw this on television.

4th August 1971 Wednesday
On August 4th 1966, **Britain's National Debt** was £31,327,000,000. That was £577 per head. This debt is now £33,425,000,000. That is £600 per head.
The American Space programme costs America so much money that only 2 more flights remain – Apollo 16 & 17, for at least another 10 years. Apollo 15 has cost £190 million.

6th August 1971 Friday
An interesting demonstration was given to us by **Scott** on the Moon. Holding a feather in one hand, & his 14 inch aluminium rock hammer in the other, he let them both go. Both landed into the Moon dust at exactly the same time, just over a second later.
It was a happening predicted over 350 years ago by **Galileo**.

8th August 1971 Sunday
Watched on television a superb production of Shakespeare's "**Hamlet**".
All those famous lines were brought to life, & given their full interpretation: - "To be, or not to be: that is the question". "Alas! Poor Yorick: I knew him well". Poor Yorick was now only a skull, who once had been such a lively & jolly King's jester.

10th August 1971 Tuesday
Mum & I went with a bus load from Ravenstone to **Burghley House, Stamford,** - home of the **Marquess of Exeter**. Here we gazed upon riches untold – in gold – silver – marble – ivory & finest Chippendale furniture. Highlight was undoubtedly "**The Heaven Room**", **Verrio's** masterpiece, completed in 1694.

12th August 1971 Thursday
Mum & I will be going by bus tomorrow to Colchester for a short holiday with **Mary Moore** at her home in **Wivenhoe**. I shall be staying only for the week-end, returning on Monday, but Mum will be staying until the following week-end.
Our proposed visit to Blackpool Illuminations (12th April 1971) fell through.

14th August 1971 Saturday
Again – not very good weather when I continue my summer holiday. Spent the day in **Colchester** & bought a large man-size umbrella - £4.
Spent Sunday (tomorrow) visiting the island of Mersea.

This is where Mary Moore's husband Mick grew up. His father was for many years the Rector of East Mersea.

16th August 1971 Monday
Home again from my brief stay with Mary Moore.
Tosca, having been left under the care of Aunt Dos for the past few days, is at the moment snuggled up on my lap, purring loudly. Mary & Mick have ten cats!
This evening we had a run through of the music for "**Bless the Bride**" & acquired the libretti.

18th August 1971 Wednesday
April 25th 1971 was **Census Day** – the biggest, most comprehensive census ever held in Britain. The first provisional figures show that the population of the United Kingdom is 55,346,661. The population of Leicester City is 283,549 & the population of Leicester County is 487,664 – Total 771,213.

20th August 1971 Friday
The 1971 Census puts **Leicester** in 13th place in a table of size headed by Greater London.
The population of Greater London – 7,379,014. Birmingham = 1,013,365. Coalville = 28,334. Ashby-de-la-Zouch = 8,291. Hinckley = 47,982. Loughborough = 45,863. Market Harborough = 14,527.

22nd August 1971 Sunday
Our Sunday School outing yesterday to Hunstanton, calling to see **Sandringham Church**, with its dazzlingly beautiful interior – the pulpit panelled in solid silver & ornate in design – the altar & reredos again in solid silver, with angels bearing the Royal Coat of Arms; & a jewelled bible covered with over 500 precious stones.

24th August 1971 Tuesday
Enjoyed our Sunday School outing to Hunstanton as much as any I had ever been on.
My companion for the day was 9 year old Louise Green – a most delightful child. Highly independent – intelligent – full of fun & trust, as willing to tour all the shops with me as to sample all the fun of the fair – including a ride on the Ghost Train.

26th August 1971 Thursday
Not only the **Civil Service**, but **Local Government** also, has had tremendous salary increases recently. If I were still in Local Government, I should be on **Clerical III** which now spans from £1,395 - £1,599. **Clerical IV** is £1,599 - £1,812.
For an idea of the sort of increase, see 30th April 1969.

28th August 1971 Saturday
Civil Service however has different scales altogether from **Local Government**. I am classed as a **Clerical Officer**, currently on £1,290 p.a. rising next month (by annual increment) to £1,330, & finally to £1,385.
Only by successful interview can you rise from **Clerical Officer** to **Executive Officer**.

30th August 1971 Monday
So – guess what my latest book from the library is called?
"**The Skills of Interviewing**" by Elizabeth Sidney & Margaret Brown. This includes a very good chapter on

"How to be interviewed". It gives lots of detailed examples of different people being interviewed – both good & bad.

1st Sept 1971 Wednesday
This week Mum & I visited Leicester's Annual **Abbey Park Show** – the first time I have ever been. We went chiefly to see **Harvey Smith**, champion horse jumper, & were delighted to see him at such close quarters – in the main ring & also out of the ring, for about ¼ of an hour on the horse exercise ground.

3rd Sept 1971 Friday
Ravenstone Church will be holding its first **Flower Festival** this month – for 3 days September 17th 18th & 19th. I have been asked to do a flower arrangement on the **Font**, & organise flower decorations round the base of the **Font** by the Sunday School children – cut flowers & potted plants.

5th September 1971 Sunday
"**Have Your Handwriting Analysed**" – this is the latest offer in "**Woman's Own**" magazine – "A Personal Handwriting Analysis by one of Britain's leading graphologists … send a minimum of 10 lines of your handwriting (pen, not pencil) on unruled paper, & state your age & sex." I will let you know the result!

7th September 1971 Tuesday
Princess Anne, who was 21 years old last month, has now joined the ranks of horse-jumping champions. Riding her chestnut gelding "**Doublet**" in the 3 day European Championships, held at **Burghley Park** over the week-end, she led the British team to victory & was the best individual.

9th September 1971 Thursday
Opposite **Ravenstone Church** is a large house – **Church Farm**, with farm buildings & a large muddy yard where Mr & Mrs Tom Land live. This has now been sold, & the whole lot is coming down, to become a select residential area. **David Hewes** (Enid's brother) is hoping to build there.

11th September 1971 Saturday
Mum & I went with her cousin Cyril Bailey & his wife Elsie (formerly of Willoughby – now living in Loughborough) to **Stapleford Lion Reserve**, near **Melton Mowbray**. Driving through the park, with all the car windows safely closed, we saw the most beautiful lions at really close quarters – very much like **Tosca**!

13th September 1971 Monday
Civil Service, which specialises in reports, Select Committees of enquiry, analysis, surveys etc. gives details of the 233 successful candidates recently promoted from Clerical Officer to Executive Officer. Age under 25 = 40. Age 25-40 = 102. Age 41-50 = 46. Age 51-65 = 45. 650 people were interviewed; 417 (including me) **not** recommended.

15th September 1971 Wednesday
The Rector of Ravenstone, the Revd. Leslie Buckroyd, who was inducted April 1970, has now included me on the list of Lesson readers. I begin this month, on September 26th at Evensong, reading both lessons 1. Daniel 10 (4-end), and 2. Revelation 5.
It will be our **Patronal Festival**.

17th September 1971 Friday
Ravenstone Church is now decked in its fullest glory for the 3 day **Flower Festival** which starts today. The Sunday School children responded wonderfully well, & helped to create a "**Carpet of Flowers**", in low tiny containers, around the base of the **Font**; & the weather is absolutely perfect.

19th September 1971 Sunday
Ton up! That is £100, saved since 31st December 1970, at the rate of £10 per month in the form of **Premium Bonds**, in my determined effort to save up for a new car. Still no more than £3 in the bank, but I am hoping Minnehaha (now at 50,000 miles) will last a bit longer.

21st September 1971 Tuesday
Our lovely Flower Festival, which was due to be dismantled yesterday, still looks so good that no-one has had the heart to remove any of the flowers.
I was delighted to learn that the "**Coalville Times**" photographer had been, & chosen a photograph of the Sunday School children's "**Carpet of Flowers**".

23rd September 1971 Thursday
Mrs Swanwick – our neighbour – is 60 today.
Auntie Belle is in **Canada** at the moment, having the time of her life.
Auntie Belle is the widow of Uncle Fred, whose daughter Isobel seems to have come into money from all directions; & it is she who invited Auntie Belle to join her & her husband on this trip to **Canada**.

25th September 1971 Saturday
The headlines in the paper this morning are: - **Spy Purge – Britain Kicks Out 105 Russian Diplomats**.
This follows the defection of a Soviet agent, & intense investigation by **British Intelligence** into spying & sabotage – industrial disputes - & the **Ulster Crisis** where the I. R. A. are continually planting bombs in public buildings.

27th September 1971 Monday
Watched on television "**A Midsummer Night's Dream**" by William Shakespeare – absolutely super. This classic comedy – this dream – this fairy fantasy, interspersed with typical amateur dramatic activities, was entertainment at its very best. To think that Shakespeare could write this & bloody murder too.

29th September 1971 Wednesday
My latest book from good old County Hall Library is "**The Battle of Trafalgar**" – "**Lord Nelson Sweeps the Sea**" by Alan Villiers. **Horatio Nelson**, born September 29th 1758, died on board "**The Victory**" at the **Battle of Trafalgar**, on 21st October 1805, near the Strait of Gibraltar.

1st October 1971 Friday
Being in the **Civil Service**, with the privileges of a Local Government Officer on the Clerical 3 grade, means that

instead of rising to a maximum of Civil Service £1,385 as a Clerical Officer, I am entitled to an additional responsibility allowance (ARA) to follow the Local Government scale to £1,599.

3ʳᵈ October 1971 Sunday
A letter from the Department of the Environment, Welcombe House, 90/91 The Strand, Swansea, advises me of my latest position, following Civil Service pay award – 1ˢᵗ January 1971, Local Government pay award 1ˢᵗ July 1971, & my increment date 14ᵗʰ September 1971, & Local Government increment 1ˢᵗ April each year. Now £1,330 + £26.

5ᵗʰ October 1971 Tuesday
Enid's birthday tomorrow! She will be 44, & still she has the same boundless energy – playing hockey – keeping fit - & smoking 20 cigarettes a day.
I smoked for 12 years, from age 18 to age 30, but then I was persuaded – chiefly by my good friend Reevsie – to give it up, & I must say, I'm glad I did.

7ᵗʰ October 1971 Thursday
Mr Richard Marsh, ex-Minister of Transport, is now doing very well for himself as the newly appointed chairman of British Rail, at £20,000 p.a.
Meanwhile, **Mr John Peyton**, currently enjoying the rôle of **Transport Minister**, has announced his intention to make Driving Licences valid for life, starting in 1974.

9ᵗʰ October 1971 Saturday
The twins – Reevsie's sisters – both got engaged today, & had identical rings.
Peter Hewes & family moved into their new home in the grounds of the **Hollies** – our old ancestral home.
Enid & I went with a bus load of singing Amateurs to **Warrington, Lancashire,** to see "**Bless the Bride**".

11ᵗʰ October 1971 Monday
Read in the paper today about "**The Biggest Beano Since Babylon** …"
At a cost of £5 million, the **Shah of Persia** is celebrating the founding of the **Persian Empire** by **Cyrus the Great** 2,500 years ago. Guests of honour include our Princess Anne & her father, Prince Philip, & many other royals.

13ᵗʰ October 1971 Wednesday
The Shah's great party will be under canvas, a tented Xanadu, a city of pyramidical pavilions, richly carpeted & quilted against the cool night desert air. Each tent has silver wall-paper. After the feast, the Iranian Army will parade on camelback, dressed in splendour, to recall the days of Xerxes & Darius.

15ᵗʰ October 1971 Friday
Three months after **Mary Blue's** dramatic get-away from her husband & 2 young children, she has now returned to Leicestershire, complete with her lover – **Murdo**. This week we met **Murdo**, a handsome young Scot, aged 25. Meanwhile the 2 children are being cared for by **Terry's** family.

17ᵗʰ October 1971 Sunday
Murdo, from Inverness, is an authority on the **Loch Ness**

Monster. He told us that **Loch Ness** is deep & dark & connected by subterranean caves to the sea. The sea-monster comes & goes by way of these caves. No diver is ever prepared to penetrate the dark & dangerous depths of the **Loch**.

19ᵗʰ October 1971 Tuesday
We watched on television the great parade which passed before the Shah of Persia & his wealthy guests. Rather like Trooping the Colour, which we saw in June, contingent after contingent of soldiers depicting every age in Persia's 2,500 years of history. Correct in every detail from beard to the correct footwear; even the change in music over the years.

21ˢᵗ October 1971 Thursday
21ˢᵗ October 1805 – **The Battle of Trafalgar** fought off the coast of **Spain**, when **Lord Horatio Nelson**, with 27 ships including his famous "**Victory**" defeated the Franco-Spanish fleet of 33. Nelson had waited 84 sea-weary weeks for **Napoleon's** Franco-Spanish fleet to sail where he wanted them, & then he struck.

23ʳᵈ October 1971 Saturday
Every day brings more news of the troubles in **Northern Ireland**. Trouble makers from the south sneak over the border with guns & bombs. **British** troops, in a vain attempt to restore law and order, have stones thrown at them by gangs of youths; buses are set on fire, & civilians are killed daily.

25ᵗʰ October 1971 Monday
Now then – the big decision for this week is "**Do we, or do we not, join the Common Market?**" Mr Edward Heath, the Prime Minister, & all his merry men think we should; while opposition leader Harold Wilson & company think we should not. They sit up all night arguing, & will make their final vote on Thursday.

27ᵗʰ October 1971 Wednesday
What is the voice of **Britain** generally? The Daily Express, "For eleven years has steadfastly opposed the idea of Britain joining the Common Market", while the Daily Mail, "Calls upon every wavering M.P. who is torn between conscience & calculation, to gather his courage & vote for **Britain's entry into Europe**."

28ᵗʰ October 1971 Thursday
The Republic of Congo changed its name to Zaire. (See 18ᵗʰ May 1997)

29ᵗʰ October 1971 Friday
M.Ps voted last night to take **Britain** into the **Common Market** – 356 voted for the motion, and 244 voted against it. In the House of Lords, 451 voted for the motion & 58 against.
What do we do next? Sign the **Treaty of Accession** in Brussels later this year.
When do we become a member of the **Common Market**? 1ˢᵗ January 1973.

31ˢᵗ October 1971 Sunday
British Standard Time ends today. At 3 a.m. clocks are put back an hour to 2 a.m. They will be advanced an hour on March 19ᵗʰ 1972 for **British Summer Time**.

British Standard Time was introduced as an experiment for 3 years in 1968, but last December, **Parliament** agreed to end the experiment.

2nd November 1971 Tuesday

Premium Bonds were introduced 2nd November 1956, & this year the top monthly first prize has been raised to £50,000. With £800 million held in bonds, the chance of winning this is 800 million to one. **Ernie** picks the winners – **Ernie** is actually two machines – **Electronic Random Number Indicator Equipment**.

4th November 1971 Thursday

The Local Government Bill, published today, gives details of the changing face of England. Instead of County Councils, Rural District Councils, Parish Councils; Borough Councils & Urban District Councils, which we have had since 1888, we are to have a 2 tier system of counties & districts – to start April 1974.

6th November 1971 Saturday

Today is the day that **Santa Claus** comes to town. In Leicester this morning, we saw **Santa Claus** in his vintage yellow Rolls, escorted to his **Grotto** in Lewis's, with Police out-riders & brass band.
Outside the Co-op, another Santa Claus arrived by stage-coach & 4 fine horses.

8th November 1971 Monday

Last night at church, it was my privilege to read the lesson from the book of the prophet Jeremiah – Chapter 10, verses 1-16, including "… when He uttereth His voice, there is a multitude of waters in the heavens …. He maketh lightnings with rain …" while torrential rain beat on the roof.

10th November 1971 Wednesday

Mum is spending this week at Willoughby with her cousin Madge.
I met Margaret Middlebrook & Dilys Grewcock in County Hall canteen today. We all were in the same class at school, a quarter of a century ago, & compared notes. "Do you ever see …? He's old & fat …. Married into money …. Moved up north" etc.

12th November 1971 Friday

Department of the Environment is one year old today, & in spite of the hurtful letter I received on July 7th, I am well pleased to belong to this great department, & to the Civil Service as a whole. While the Civil Service neither speaks to me nor even smiles, I daily search further into its hidden depths.

14th November 1971 Sunday

The fascinating hidden depths of the **Civil Service** led me right back to the Roman Empire with its efficient system of organisation.
Napoleon based his empire on virtually the same pattern of administrative organisation, providing his administrative generals & his military generals with the same basic training.

16th November 1971 Tuesday

Spain was the first European country since the fall of the Roman Empire, to establish an efficient Empire, founded on efficient administration Europe re-awakened in the 16th & 17th centuries. Napoleon marched into the early 19th century, while inefficiency & corruption reigned in England until 1854.

18th November 1971 Thursday

What happened in 1854? Sir Charles Trevelyan & Sir Stafford Northcote were appointed by Gladstone (then Chancellor of the Exchequer) to iron out the **British Civil Service**.
And so we advanced through the **Playfair Commission** 1874, the Ridley, MacDonnell, Tomlin, Priestley, & Fulton, to today.

20th November 1971 Saturday

But even the mighty **Napoleon** met his **Waterloo**, defeated on the 18th June 1815, & then exiled on **Saint Helena** in the South Atlantic. **Napoleon** had insisted that Europe should render to him, as to Caesar, what belonged to Caesar, but failed to allow her to render to God what belonged to God.

22nd November 1971 Monday

Yesterday was the last Sunday in the Church year, before we start off again next Sunday with Advent Sunday.
Mum & I went to Leicester Cathedral last night, where the Bishop was preaching, & the lessons were read by the Provost & Canon Gundry. The Bishop called it "**Stir up Sunday**."

24th November 1971 Wednesday

Poor old Minnehaha now is having difficulty changing from top gear to a lower gear. This suggests clutch trouble, so I am having a day's holiday on Friday, for her to be attended to.
I read in the paper today, that the world's known supplies of petrol cannot be expected to last more than 20 years.

26th November 1971 Friday

Let me introduce you to **Cousin Audrey**. She is actually my dad's cousin, & she was 70 last Monday. She is now a widow, & has recently come to live in Ravenstone, where in fact she was born. Four months older than Aunt Dos, she is a similar type, with a great sense of humour – a definite character.

Note – Cousin Audrey celebrated her 70th birthday on 22nd November. She moved into the Alms Houses at Ravenstone. She & Aunt Dos played together as children.

28th November 1971 Advent Sunday

My latest book from good old County Hall Library is "**The French Revolution**".
Gosh! If ever a book made you thankful to live in the 20th century, this does. The number of people who were sent to the guillotine in order to give birth to the Republic was dreadful – "**The King is dead; long live the Republic**."

30th November 1971 Tuesday

What a funny pay slip, this month! There has now been a payroll merger of "Road Research Laboratory, Central

Licensing Directorate, Swansea (including those out stationed at Local Government offices)" – that's where I come in – "Heavy Goods Vehicle Testing Centre", etc. 73,000 altogether. Payslip now comes from Ashdown House, Hastings.

2nd December 1971 Thursday
Everybody these days is pressing for more & more money, to keep pace with the ever rising cost of living. The latest pay rise is for the Royal family. The Queen is to have a 106% increase over the £475,000 p.a. established in 1952, making it now £980,000 for her, & rises for all the family.

4th December 1971 Saturday
The Queen Mother's allowance goes from £70,000 to £95,000, & the Duke of Edinburgh's (the Queen's husband) from £40,000 to £65,000. Princess Anne – from £6,000 to £15,000 rising on marriage to £35,000. Prince Andrew & Prince Edward are to get £20,000 each when they are 18, & £50,000 when married.

6th December 1971 Monday
The Queen's £980,000 annual allowance, paid by the Treasury, is known as the **Civil List**. The Civil List originated in 1761, when George III made over the Crown Lands to the nation in return for a fixed allowance. The agricultural land produces revenue in excess of £1 million per annum, & the town property over £3 ½ million.

8th December 1971 Wednesday
Who next for a pay rise? Members of Parliament! It is proposed to raise M.P.s salaries from £3,250 p.a. to £4,500. The Prime Minister's salary from £14,000 to £20,000, & Cabinet Ministers from £8,500 to £13,000. M.P.s secretarial allowances from £500 to £1,000 plus travel expenses & food etc.

10th December 1971 Friday
"**The Story of China**" by **Lo Hui-Min**, a Senior Fellow in the Department of Far Eastern History at the Australian National University – this has been to me like Aladdin's lamp, whisking me off into more than 2,000 years of the wonders of China, through every dynasty. No wonder Marco Polo in 1275 was so enraptured.

12th December 1971 Sunday
Last year it was County Hall by candlelight. Last Sunday it was Ravenstone Church, lit only by the light of the candles on the Altar. Plunged suddenly into darkness in the middle of the service, the Rector coped admirably. He gave his address in the dark, & concluded with prayers, without faltering at all.

14th December 1971 Tuesday
Minnehaha is all dressed up for Christmas this year with spanking new clutch plate £2-50p, Ring £1-60p, Seal 60p, Lever £1-58p, Cover £2-20p, & 2 bushes 12p. Dismantle, overhaul clutch & fit new fly-wheel ring gear, fit new joining gear seal & new stabilising bushes (labour) £8-21p. Total £16-81p.

15th December 1971 Wednesday
Minimum age for motor cycle, scooter & 3 wheeled car drivers raised from 16 to 17 from midnight tonight.

16th December 1971 Thursday
On December 16th 1968, I was asked to play the part of "**Old Sally**" in our Amateurs' production of **Oliver** – a part nobody applied for. Now I have been offered the part of **Harriet** (Grandmama) in our latest show "**Bless the Bride**". Nobody applied for this part either, & I am the 3rd offer.

18th December 1971 Saturday
I have accepted the part of **Harriet**, who together with Grandpapa is celebrating her Golden Wedding Anniversary, in the midst of a great family gathering. She has 4 short lines to say, & is on stage for quite a long while, sitting comfortably by the fire with Grandpa, on their big day.

20th December 1971 Monday
Mum received a letter today from **Lesley Hale**, 92 College Road, London, SE 21. "I am very sorry to tell you my mother died very suddenly yesterday ..... a cerebral haemorrhage." The letter was dated 15th December. The **Hale** family were very good friends to my mother in her darkest hour, when my dad died.

Note – Mrs Dorothy Hale died suddenly. Her husband, Leslie Hale was my dad's best friend & they both supported my mum wonderfully over the years.

22nd December 1971 Wednesday
Mr Leslie Hale was my dad's best friend. He prospered in life – became a lawyer & then a Member of Parliament. When my dad died, he arranged for my mother to be given £1 a week for the next ten years – until I left school & went to work. That alone was a gift of £500.

24th December 1971 Friday
Another friend of my dad's was somebody named John Read of Coalville. Amongst the treasures handed down to me from my dad, is a volume of rare old books called "**An Exposition of the Old & New Testament**" by **Matthew Henry**, dated 1721. Every verse in the Bible is explained in great detail. Given to my dad by John Read in 1925.

26th December 1971 Sunday
At Leicester Cathedral yesterday, the Bishop of Leicester – **Ronald Ralph Williams**, chose for his text – St. Luke 2. 15. .... "as the angels were gone away from them into heaven." Quoting from good old **Matthew Henry**, who is a source of great help to the Bishop, he said the Christmas message should leave us with the same absolute faith that the shepherds were given.

28th December 1971 Tuesday
The last day of the Christmas holiday, with weather almost like spring. Mum & I & Ann Causer went to see the **Boxing Day Meet** of the **Quorn** at **Loughborough**; & to the latest film "**Nicholas & Alexandra**" – the last of the Romanovs, yesterday afternoon in Leicester. This was the story of the last Tsar of Russia. (Tsar meaning Caesar).

30th December 1971 Thursday

Harold Fern, prominent member of our village (see 7-5-70) died on Monday, aged 61, & was buried today. Yesterday, there was another local personality buried – **Jimmy Jones**, aged 51.

"Time, like an ever-rolling stream, bears all its sons away; they fly forgotten, as a dream dies at the opening day."

1972

2nd January 1972 Sunday
Leap year! And one of those rare years where there are 53 Sundays.
Our house at the moment is about to lose all the privacy which we have enjoyed here over the years. Yet another house is being squeezed into the grounds of the **Hollies**, & the more it grows, the worse it gets.

4th January 1972 Tuesday
"When Britannia ruled the waves" …. The world has no greater story to tell.
And beginning next Tuesday, this epic is to unfold in a 13 part series of 1 hour documentary films on television. This historic series is to be a detailed account of the **British Empire's** rise to its peak & decline.

6th January 1972 Thursday
"The Shadow of the Tower" – another 13 part series began tonight on television. This is the way to learn history – the story of **Henry VII** began today with the **Battle of Bosworth** 1485. (See 1st July 1971) We saw the wedding of **Henry VII** & **Elizabeth of York** – **Edward IV's** eldest daughter.

8th January 1972 Saturday
In my pursuit of wisdom (having reached 40 years), I have now got back to my old friend **Socrates** via "The Republic of Plato." **Plato** was born 428/7 B.C. & died at the age of 80 or 81 in 348/7 B.C. **Plato** was born in the year of the revolution, & was 23 when Athens lost her empire to **Sparta**.

10th January 1972 Monday
A letter written by **Plato** near the end of his long life recalls, "When I was young, a revolution took place in Athens. Some of the leaders were relatives & friends of mine, & I imagined they would give us a new & wonderful world. But when they brought Socrates to trial & executed him (in 399), all my trust in them was gone."

12th January 1972 Wednesday
Cathedral News-Letter 96.
The Provost concludes … "I do wish you a truly exciting & happy New Year."
God bless you, as ever,
John C. Hughes.

14th January 1972 Friday
From **Plato** to **Aristotle** to **Alexander**. **Aristotle** was born in 384 B.C., & in 367 B.C. went to **Athens** to study under **Plato**. He left Athens in 347 B.C. (the year **Plato** died) & went to Macedonia as Alexander's tutor. He died in 322 B.C.
They all learned from **Socrates** the one great truth – "**Know thyself.**"

16th January 1972 Sunday
Who are the latest folk on strike? The Miners. They have now been on strike for a week, but of course their strike does not have immediate effect. Most people have several weeks' supply of coal, but if the strike goes on

for very long, we shall all know about it.

18th January 1972 Tuesday
Apart from my role as **Granny** in "**Bless the Bride**" (Granny appears in Act I only), I emerge in Act II in the chorus, first as a bathing belle (1870 A.D.) & then as a waitress (also 1870 vintage) in a French café. We have 6 waitresses who have a most delightful number with the leading man.

20th January 1972 Thursday
What a lovely summer's day. Went with Jane (who was married 6th June 1970) to **Groby Pool** in the dinner hour, where we watched the ducks & the swans; & walked by the lovely water's edge. **Groby Pool** is about 5 minutes away (by car) from **County Hall**, & we spent half an hour there.

22nd January 1972 Saturday
On 28th October 1971 M.P.s voted to take **Britain** into the Common Market. This afternoon on television we watched **Britain's Prime Minister Edward Heath**, sign the **Treaty of Accession** at the **Egmont Palace** in **Brussels**.
The signing was delayed for 1 hour, because a woman threw ink at Mr. Heath.

24th January 1972 Monday
In addition to Britain, Ireland Denmark & Norway also signed the Treaty of accession on Saturday, making a total of 10 nations now involved.
Is this then the prophecy of the Bible? Are these 10 nations the **Beast with 10 Horns**? (Revelation 17. 3.) Shall a Dictator beast devour the whole Roman Catholic Church?

26th January 1972 Wednesday
The "**Beast with 7 heads & 10 horns**" portrayed in the Book of Revelation is a frightening character. His reign of terror lasts for 3 ½ years (Revelation 13. 5.) & his number is **666** (Revelation, Chapter 19). It is a comfort to know that **Righteousness** has the final victory.

28th January 1972 Friday
Well, now that we are all Europeans, & not just **Englishmen**, we hear tell of "The European Anthem" viz. **The Ode to Joy** from Beethoven's 9th Symphony. I don't really know when it is likely to be heard, because it seems to me that each member country of the "**Big 10**" likes to retain its own nationality.

30th January 1972 Sunday
This evening I was lesson reader at church. The lessons were **Genesis 2** and **Mark 10**. These lessons dwelt solely on God creating **Man** and **Woman** – one man & one woman – one man & one wife … "**What therefore God hath joined together, let not man put asunder.**"

1st February 1972 Tuesday
The troubles in Northern Ireland get worse & worse (see 23rd October 1971). Watched on TV a panel of eminent men questioning the hot-blooded Irish chief spokesman in an attempt to understand all aspects of the problem. I was most impressed by **Lord Caradon** – a man of infinite wisdom & compassion.

3rd February 1972 Thursday
Lord Caradon – formerly **Sir Hugh Foot**, spent 30 years in the **British Colonial Service**. His experience of riot & rebellion stretched from Palestine – Arabs & Jews – through Africa, Jamaica & Cyprus. I now have from the library his book written in 1964 "A Start in Freedom"

5th February 1972 Saturday
Travelling with **Lord Caradon** through his book, I have become much better acquainted with the Arabs – what a magnificent people they are: - "At their best, their manners are superb, their endurance almost superhuman, their hospitality spectacular, their courage romantic, and their dignity unequalled."

7th February 1972 Monday
But, the Arabs have their weaknesses. "They are quick & sensitive to take offence. They are individualists & dislike discipline. They quarrel easily & cherish enmities. For long past they have been lacking in an urge either to co-operate with others or to construct, to create. Their cry is - **'The religion of Mohamed was founded on the sword'.**"

9th February 1972 Wednesday
Lord Caradon as Governor of Cyprus from 1957 – 1960 sorted out the most explosive situation possible between **Greeks** & **Turks**. Far, far worse than the present troubles in Northern Ireland. He helped Cyprus, made up of Greeks outnumbering Turks, to think for themselves & sort out their own problems.

11th February 1972 Friday
Poor old Leicester City! Knocked out this year by Orient in the 4th round.
Leicester 0, Orient 2. Top scorers in the 4th round were Derby, who beat Notts. County 6 – 0. Greatest heroes at the moment are little Hereford, who knocked out Newcastle (6 times winners) in a 2 – 1 victory.

13th February 1972 Sunday
On the Eve of St. Valentine, nothing more romantic to report than all the miners are still on strike. This is affecting the electricity power stations, & we are all on a rota for 4 hour power cuts. Last night we were plunged into darkness until 9 p.m. How wonderful to see the stars, just as bright as ever.

15th February 1972 Tuesday
An unexpected pay rise! The Civil Service has been given yet another salary increase to operate from 1st January 1972.
I am currently on £1,330 (with a £26 ARA – see 1st October 1971). This is increased by £100 to £1,430 rising with my next September increment 14th September 1972, to £1,489.
(See also 30th April 1969).

17th February 1972 Thursday
"Highway Statistics" published by D.O.E. (H.M.S.O. 85p) gives the latest facts & figures.
Population of Leicestershire = 487,664 – number of cars registered = 130,430.
Population of Leicester = 283,549 – number of cars

registered = 56,840
With 12 million cars in the U.K. the car tax revenue = £1,863 million.
Rutland has only 7,590 cars. (See 18th August 1971)

19th February 1972 Saturday
If you wonder how 12 million cars paying £25 tax per year can bring in £1,863 million, the answer is that there are 15 million vehicles altogether, & of the other 3 million there are many heavy lorries which pay very high tax – the heavier the lorry, the more they pay.
A lorry weighing 10 tons pays £459 tax per year.

21st February 1972 Monday
The Department of the Environment Section of C.P.S.A. (See 1st April 1970) is holding a Section Weekend School at Scarborough next weekend, & I am one of the 33 "students" hoping to attend. We all meet at Leeds at 4-30p.m. on Friday, & leave there by coach for the St. Nicholas Hotel, St. Nicholas Cliff, Scarborough.

23rd February 1972 Wednesday
I am writing now by the light of our old oil lamp, because Wednesday night is our night for the electric power cut. Every-one is still on a strict rota of rationing, but fortunately, good old County Hall has its own generator, which provides an excellent light for me when we have the power cuts at work.

Note –The Miner's strike is now beginning to affect us all. The electricity power stations are fuelled by coal, & we are on a rota for 4 hour power cuts. At home we use our old oil lamp – this was a wedding present to my mum & dad from Leslie Hale.

25th February 1972 Friday
Well, here I am at St. Nicholas Hotel, Scarborough - & what a hotel! I have a gorgeous bedroom with sea-view – a wireless – a telephone – a hot radiator – a double bed & a single bed, & the hotel itself is beautiful. We arrived at 7p.m. when it was dark, & tomorrow is our day for power cuts!

27th February 1972 Sunday
Came home from Scarborough, through the beautiful city of York, after a most interesting week-end. I met some fascinating characters who had many tales to tell, from visits to the Grand Canyon to being lost on the mountains of Scotland. My journey ended in the company of an Indian, who sat by me in the train.

29th February 1972 Tuesday
The miners have all been granted the big pay rises they went on strike for & resumed work yesterday. So coal is on the move again, the electric power stations are being fed, & industry is on the move again. We all enjoyed the power cuts really, especially in the hotel, where it was dinner by candle-light last Saturday.

2nd March 1972 Thursday
Minnehaha is now 6 years old, & not only going rusty, but **gone** rusty.
Today she had her 54,000 mile service & M.O.T. test. Cyril said she was literally dropping to bits underneath, but patched her up enough to keep her going for a little

while. Don, the car salesman, let me drive one of their new "1300s".

4th March 1972 Saturday

As a direct result of the power cuts during the past weeks, & not knowing for sure how long they would continue, **Coalville Amateur Operatic Society** postponed the date of this year's show "**Bless the Bride**".

The show was arranged originally for next week, but now it has been changed to the first week in **May**.

6th March 1972 Monday

For our summer holiday this year Enid & I have chosen "Moonta Hotel" Capstone Crescent, Ilfracombe, for one week commencing July 8th.

The hardest hit place for summer holidays is Ireland. Because of continued bomb planting by the I.R.A. & daily accounts of terrible explosions, nobody chooses Ireland for a holiday.

8th March 1972 Wednesday

Plans are now well under way for Leicester's **Expo '72**, a 10 day festival to be held in September on Leicester's Abbey Park. The idea is to make people take notice of Leicester's achievements. Instead of ordinary canvas tents, there are to be specially made orange canopies – one huge one, and six smaller ones.

10th March 1972 Friday

"**The Best Laid Schemes?**" – **A cool look at Local Government reform**. This is my latest educational book from the library, & very enlightening it is, too. The Local Government Bill, published last November, was not achieved by any easy means. To try & alter anything, once it is firmly established, is a marathon effort.

12th March 1972 Sunday

Mothering Sunday! Several Sunday School children went with Susan & me to Ravenstone Rectory after Sunday School this morning, where we tied up little bunches of daffodils for the afternoon Mother's Day Service. At the afternoon service, Stephen & Jessica Willars took the collection, & the lesson reader was Angela Brown.

14th March 1972 Tuesday

Tonight was the Easter Vestry & Annual Church Meeting held at **Ravenstone**.

Just one year ago, **Dennis Collier** relinquished his duties as **Rector's Warden**. **Sam Land** was elected **Rector's Warden** & **Pat** (my brother) was elected **People's Warden**. After one year in office, with **Mary Blue's** divorce imminent, **Pat** has now resigned.

16th March 1972 Thursday

Mum & I went with a party, organised by the **Ravenstone Mothers' Union,** on a conducted tour of the Belvoir Bacon Co. Coalville. We saw a pig chopped up into its various "**cuts**"; saw the sausage making process – the pork pie department – the hams at their different stages & tongues in their initial state.

18th March 1972 Saturday

Britain has struck oil. **Sir John Eden**, Minister at the Department of Trade, predicts that by 1980 up to 75% of our present oil needs will be met from the North Sea. This is as good as striking gold & sea drilling is getting full government support. (See 24th November 1971) This week the number of telephones in Britain reached 10 million.

20th March 1972 Monday

"**Work when you like**" – **Civil Servants to start new scheme of office hours**. This is the startling headline in today's **Daily Mail**. Following an experiment in **Germany**, British Civil Servants are to be encouraged to switch from fixed to flexible hours. "**Gleitzeit**" they call it in Germany - "**Gliding Time**" with only a fixed "**core**" time.

22nd March 1972 Wednesday

Here we go again! The Amateur Operatic Society Season.

We started our rounds this year with "**Passion Flower**" an adaptation of "**Carmen**", the famous opera by **Georges Bizet**, presented this week at the **Little Theatre, Leicester**. The music is really great – vibrant gypsy music – Spanish and gay.

24th March 1972 Friday

With the explosive situation in N. Ireland likely to lead to **Civil War**, **Mr Edward Heath**, **British Conservative Prime Minister**, today announced its last but one resort. **Westminster** is to rule **Ulster**, instead of **Stormont**. That means we are to be responsible for law & order there under Mr Whitelaw.

26th March 1972 Sunday

Mr William Whitelaw, aged 53, **Lord President & Leader of the Commons**, has been chosen by **Mr Heath** (P.M.) to be **Secretary of State for Northern Ireland**. The takeover becomes law next Thursday.

If this fails, we have only one card left – **the total withdrawal of all British Forces**.

28th March 1972 Tuesday

Following the announcement that **Stormont** is to be suspended for one year, to see if **Whitehall** can do any better, all the loyal **Ulster** men have gone on strike. **Mr Faulkner**, the **Ulster Prime Minister**, said that this move merely proves that violence **does** pay – to bow down to the violent I.R.A.

30th March 1972 Thursday

In the Budget this month, the Chancellor of the Exchequer, **Mr Anthony Barber**, has made even more dramatic cuts in taxation than last year. Personal allowances are to be increased at a cost of £960 million in 1972-73, & £1,200 million in a full year.

Personal allowances up by £135 to £460 means an extra £1 per week.

1st April 1972 Saturday

Leslie Hale, friend of my dad, (see 22nd December 1971) once said, "**When I am Prime Minister, I will make you Lord Ravenstone**."

Mr Hale was **Labour M.P.** for Oldham West from 1945 to 1968; & now at the age of 69, he has been made a **Life Peer** – one of eight announced this week.

3rd April 1972 Easter Monday
Mum & I and Anne Causer went to Leicester this afternoon to see the latest film, "**Mary Queen of Scots**". **Mary Stuart**, daughter of **James V of Scotland**, had a very sad life which ended in 1587 A.D. with execution. Her son however became in time **James VI of Scotland & James I of England**.

5th April 1972 Wednesday
Long, long ago there lived in **Egypt**, a **King** named **Tutankhamun** (circa 1370-1352 B.C.) Fifty years ago, in November 1922, his fabulous tomb was discovered & all the treasures of the tomb are now on display in London, at the British Museum. The exhibition opened last week & closes in September.

7th April 1972 Friday
Britain has struck oil (see 18th March 1972) & the next thing we hear is that it will cost over £1,500 million in the next 10 years to get it into the pipe-line.
So, to finance this new-found oil in the North Sea, & other offshore explorations around Britain, up goes the cost of petrol & oil – a "**highly speculative venture**".

9th April 1972 Sunday
Last night, Auntie Gladys, Enid, Mum & I went to the De Montfort Hall, Leicester, to hear the **Halle Orchestra**. We were introduced to **Haydn**, **Rachmaninoff** & **Beethoven**, of which I liked Beethoven best. (Symphony No. 5 in C minor). The Hall was packed to capacity & the applause was thunderous.

11th April 1972 Tuesday
The new house in the grounds of the **Hollies** is now almost ready for use. (See 2nd January 1972).
Although it invades the privacy of our house & garden, it has developed from an ugly duckling into a veritable swan, with a delightful balcony, & altogether most attractive.
I would love to live there.

13th April 1972 Thursday
Reevsie's twin sisters, **Phyllis & Sherry**, who are now nearly 21 years old, both finished working in our office yesterday. They have been in our office over five years, but have not been very satisfied lately. The Civil Service gave them only C.A. pay, which is not very good.

15th April 1972 Saturday
Apollo 16 (See 4th August 1971) is due to blast off tomorrow & land on the Moon on Thursday. Lift off from the Moon is scheduled for 23rd April 1972, arriving home Friday 28th April. There will be a 3 man crew, led by **John Young**, who will land with **Charlie Duke**, while **Ken Mattingly** stays in the command ship.

17th April 1972 Monday
Watched on television "**The Merchant of Venice**" by William Shakespeare, in which **Portia** tries to persuade the hard-hearted **Shylock** to show mercy; exhorting the qualities of mercy: -
"The quality of mercy is not strained; it droppeth as the gentle rain from heaven …. It blesseth him that gives & him that takes."

19th April 1972 Wednesday
Mum & I went to the **De Montfort Hall**, Leicester, to see & hear a concert by the Massed Bands, Corps of Drums & Pipes & Drums of the Guards Division – The Life Guards, Grenadier Guards, Coldstream Guards, Scots Guards & the State Trumpeters. They marched up & down the aisles – absolutely super.

21st April 1972 Friday
Ever fascinated by "**Man on the Moon**" spent many hours watching **John Young** & **Charlie Duke** enjoying themselves in the **Descartes Highlands** of the Moon.
This is man's 5th landing on the Moon, & the television pictures which come through "live" from the Moon are the best ever.

23rd April 1972 Sunday
Saw the Earth from the Moon's camera, looking like a half moon in the sky, then went out into the moonlight & gazed in wonder at the heavens, knowing that 2 men were actually there on the Moon.
Apollo 16 has been one of the most successful missions, bringing home 245lbs of lunar rocks. The value of these rocks is £600,000 per lb.

25th April 1972 Tuesday
On May 1st there is to be a display at Coalville with all the local Sunday Schools contributing some sort of project on Missionary work. I have chosen for **Ravenstone's** effort "Christianity Comes to Darkest Britain", with writing & drawings covering 1,000 years up to 1066 A.D.

27th April 1972 Thursday
The man who helped me most with my project "Christianity Comes to Darkest Britain" is a monk, named **The Venerable Bede**, whose book "The History of the Church of our Island & Race" was written over 1,200 years ago, & is now in good old County Hall Library, having been translated from Latin.

29th April 1972 Saturday
I have had my horoscope prepared by computer from my hour & exact date of birth ….. "Your ascendant is Scorpio ….. Scorpian thoroughness combined with Cancerian shrewdness & tenacity make you a desirable colleague & a formidable adversary. Serious, reserved & quiet, your strength comes from within."

Note – "Born under the 4th sign of the Zodiac gives you the Crab as your symbol. Like the crab you possess tenacity – you hold on – you are a clinger. Only when cornered do you nip. Like the crab you love the sea. You have lots of charm & grow old gracefully, & should not therefore be an old crab. Your birth flower is the fuchsia, your birthstone the ruby, your lucky number is 9, & colours, grey & green. You have a retentive memory, & would make a good teacher, or public speaker. You are imaginative & rather romantic, though often too shy or proud to admit it. Like the sea, you have hidden depths of great calm, but on the surface are given to a variety of moods. You can be difficult to understand, especially by people who do not know you well. You do have weak points. You can be very lazy & you have a habit of ignoring people who are trying to help you.

Overall, you mix a feeling for convention with a good imaginative sense – strong enough to label you a romantic."

Cancer (June21-July21) Ruling planet: the Moon. Symbol: the Crab. Born 14th July.
The Cancer-born are emotional and imaginative, long-sighted, highly intuitive. They protect themselves with a shell of reserve. Underneath they are sensitive, shy, kindly, easily upset. They're not easy to know, but once you know them they are loyal friends, lovers, partners. They inspire confidence and trust – and can be trusted with a secret. Security is important to them; they are deeply attached to home and family, yet they are driven at times to explore new ground. They're inclined to be over-cautious and get depressed over trifles. They are jealous, but seldom without cause.

1st May 1972 Monday
This week I am on holiday for our show "**Bless the Bride**" which starts tomorrow night. I am 3 different characters -
1. Granny, celebrating her Golden Wedding, dressed in a rich purple & gold dress.
2. On the beach in orange bathing costume – 1871 vintage.
3. French Waitress in very short black dress & black tights.

3rd May 1972 Wednesday
Leslie Hale, friend of my dad, was today sworn into the House of Lords as **Baron Hale of Oldham**. Born on July 13th 1902, he became Labour M.P. for Oldham in 1945, & was a Labour back-bencher until 1968, when he resigned. In 1969, he was given the freedom of Oldham. (See 1st April 1972 and 22nd December 1971).

5th May 1972 Friday
Have thoroughly enjoyed my week's holiday for "**Bless the Bride**". The show has gone well & we had a good write-up in the Leicester Mercury. No mention was made of Granny or the bathing belle scene, but - "**the café scene was most effective in a show which excelled in costume**". Signed D.D.

Show Enjoyed
I went to the Miners' Welfare Club at Coalville to see "Bless the Bride" produced by Coalville Amateur Operatic Society, and found it absolutely outstanding, with marvellous costumes, perfect music, and a superb cast. It was a wonderful evening which gave me great happiness and pleasure to be there.
                    ***Tony Hudson**, Markfield Hospital.*

7th May 1972 Sunday
Yesterday was the **Centenary Cup Final**, when Leeds beat Arsenal 1-0, & the Cup was presented by **Her Majesty the Queen**. The first winners – a hundred years ago in 1872 were the **Wanderers** who beat the **Royal Engineers of Chatham** 1-0 at **Kennington Oval**. Wembley Stadium opened in 1923.

9th May 1972 Tuesday
Cathedral News-Letter No.100. The Provost – **John C. Hughes** – says: - "With this letter I score my century!"

He then relates the story of an incident on Boxing Day in the year 1300 when some man was attacked in the lane by St. Martin's; comparing the incident with something very similar just lately.

11th May 1972 Thursday Ascension Day
£600 million is to be spent on a network of new roads, to widen bottle-necks & ease
congestion, in many towns & villages.
The new dual carriageway in front of County Hall opened this week (See 11th March 1971). Also the new greatly improved road down Standard Hill is now open.

13th May 1972 Saturday
Had a shopping spree in Leicester this morning.
Bought a very expensive summer suit, £29 – with a further interview in mind.
A list of about 800 names (including mine), was sent to the office this week, of those to be interviewed this summer for the chance of promotion to E. O.

15th May 1972 Monday
Received a letter: - "**Promotion Board for Executive Officer Vacancies**" …. "You are invited to attend before a Promotion Board to be held in Room 521, Auchinleck House, Islington Row, Edgbaston, Birmingham 15, on Wednesday 24th May 1972 at 12-05 p.m. Addressed to Miss E. Hewes, L.T.O. Leicester.

17th May 1972 Wednesday
You'll never guess who have gone on strike now! School children. This is the outcome of the S.A.U. the **Marxist-Leninist** backed "**Schools Action Union**". Leader of the S.A.U. is Steve Finch, an 18 year-old Marxist from Rutherford School in Paddington. The S.A.U. is affiliated to adult adherents of **Maoism**.

19th May 1972 Friday
The Queen & the Duke of Edinburgh have spent this week on a state visit to **Paris**.
President Pompidou was a most charming host & the Queen wore the most beautiful clothes. While in Paris, the Queen called to see the Duke & Duchess of Windsor, but the 77 year old Duke is very ill.

21st May 1972 Whit Sunday
The 2nd Lesson appointed for reading in Church tonight was from Romans, Chapter 8, including my dad's favourite verse 28 –
"**And we know that all things work together for good to them that love God.**"

23rd May 1972 Tuesday
Had a day's holiday in preparation for my interview tomorrow in **Birmingham**.
A most remarkable thing is that tomorrow **Peter Walker**, the head of the Department of the Environment, will be in **Birmingham** to open the Gravelly Hill interchange, which has been nicknamed **Spaghetti Junction**.

25th May 1972 Thursday
The "**Board**" who interviewed me yesterday treated me more gently than those a year ago (see 6th May 1971). The Chairman was a man from the **Motor Licence**

Headquarters at Swansea, & I was asked "**Motor Licence**" questions for a good half of the interview, which was much better.

27th May 1972 Saturday
A day in London. Walked from Big Ben via Downing Street to Horse Guards Parade & watched the rehearsal for "The Troop".
Walked through St. James Park to Buckingham Palace & back down The Mall to Trafalgar Square – up Charing Cross Road to the British Museum for the **Tutankhamen Exhibition** (see 5th April 1972) & then to St. Pancras.

1352 BC: **Tutankhamun**, the young Egyptian pharaoh, is buried in the **Valley of Kings**. His face mask is solid gold.

Note – I visit the Tutankhamen Exhibition, & am over-awed by the golden face mask of this young Egyptian King. I look into his eyes, but he looks right through me & beyond, with his piercing yet infinite gaze. He just will not look at me.

28th May 1972 Trinity Sunday
"HRH the Prince Edward Albert Christian George Andrew Patrick David, Duke of Windsor. Born 1894. Died 1972.
King Edward VIII 20th January – 11th December, 1936.

29th May 1972 Monday Spring Bank Holiday
The Duke of Windsor died yesterday morning at 2-25 a.m. Born 23rd June 1894, he was christened Edward Albert George (for England) Andrew (for Scotland) Patrick (for Ireland) & David (for Wales).
In 1936 when his father died, he became King Edward VIII but was never crowned, choosing rather to marry Mrs. Simpson.

31st May 1972 Wednesday
The flag at County Hall is at half mast this week for the Duke of Windsor, whose body was brought "**home**" to England today, after living in **France** for 36 years.
His body will lie in state at Windsor chapel on Friday & Saturday, & his funeral will be on Monday.

2nd June 1972 Friday
The Duchess of Windsor, formerly **Mrs. Wallis Simpson**, who married the uncrowned **King of England** on June 3rd 1937, came to England today & was received for the first time as guest of the **Queen** at **Buckingham Palace**. Twice divorced, she was not allowed to be wife of a King, & so the King abdicated.

4th June 1972 Sunday
Another day in London! Yesterday, I watched the Queen ride on horseback down the Mall to the Troop. Then I watched the Household Cavalry go back home to their headquarters near Hyde Park. Walked along Piccadilly & then visited the Planetarium & Madame Tussaud's. All the flags flew at half mast.

5th June 1972 Monday
The Duke of Windsor died in Paris on May 28th, aged 77. The long obituary recalled the days of adulation when he was the Prince of Wales and contrasted them with his exile.

Duke Buried in Simplicity after Funeral Pomp
The Duke of Windsor was buried today in the grounds of the castle from which he derived his title after he abdicated the crown of England and with the solemn, truncated ceremonial due at the death of a former king. After the private funeral service in St. George's Chapel, the Duke was buried in the royal burial ground, Frogmore, near the mausoleum like an Italian campanile that his great-grandmother had built for herself and Prince Albert. About 20 descendants of Queen Victoria are buried there in a secluded plot thickly hedged round with tall trees, azaleas, rhododendrons and sombre cypresses.

Big, silent, funereal limousines, with passes of a printed black crown stuck to their windscreens, brought the Prime Minister and Mr Harold Wilson, Mr Jeremy Thorpe, senior members of the Government, and other eminent guests to the King Henry VIII gate and the lower ward.

At 11 the Duchess of Windsor and the party of five accompanying her arrived from Buckingham Palace at the Deanery. The Queen, the Queen Mother, the Duchess of Windsor, and other members of the Royal Family who were not walking in the procession were conducted to their seats in the choir by the Dean and Canons of Windsor. The Duchess sat between the Queen and the Duke of Edinburgh in the pews in front of the Garter stalls on the south side of the choir. She was heavily veiled and leaned forward in her seat with her head bowed.

The bearer party of eight men of the Prince of Wales Company 1st Battalion, Welsh Guards, carried the coffin in procession from the Albert Memorial Chapel. Garter King of Arms and the Lord Chamberlain walked immediately in front of the coffin, followed by a double column of family mourners: King Olav of Norway, the Duke of Edinburgh, the Prince of Wales, Prince William and Prince Richard of Gloucester, the Duke of Kent, Prince Michael of Kent, Lord Mountbatten of Burma and the Duke of Beaufort.

After brief funeral prayers and the last hymn, "Lead us heavenly Father", Garter Principal King of Arms proclaimed the styles and titles of the Duke of Windsor in the choir, as he does by ancient custom at the death of kings. The lengthy catalogue ... contained a bald summary in bland ceremonial terms of the brief and unfortunate reign of the Duke of Windsor: "And sometime most high, most mighty and most excellent monarch, King Edward VIII, Emperor of India, Defender of the Faith and uncle of the most high, most mighty and most excellent monarch, Queen Elizabeth, whom God bless".

The Archbishop of Canterbury gave the blessing. Then four state trumpeters of the Household Cavalry, standing at the west door of the chapel, splintered the silence by sounding the Last Post and Reveille. The Royal Family left the choir, each member pausing to bow to the coffin.

6th June 1972 Tuesday
A mid-14th century Chinese red & blue wine jar – one of only 3 known to exist, fetched £220,500 at **Christie's** in London yesterday. This was a world record for a work of

art apart from paintings. The jar belongs to a rare group of porcelains made at the factories of Ch'ing te chen. (See later – 18th September 1988)

8th June 1972 Thursday
We heard that Aunt Cis, who lives in Skegness, was very ill & likely to die. Therefore Aunt Dos, Auntie Belle, Pat & I arranged to all go to Skegness on Saturday – Auntie Belle & Aunt Dos to stay for a few days to help Auntie Hilda (who lives next door to Aunt Cis) & Pat & I return the same day.

10th June 1972 Saturday
Arrived at Skegness to find Aunt Cis in Skegness hospital, looking remarkably cheerful. She sat up in bed & laughed with us, while Auntie Hilda (Uncle Charlie's widow) gave us a very cool reception.
Auntie Belle & Aunt Dos decided they were not wanted, & came home with Pat & me.

12th June 1972 Monday
Yesterday was **St. Barnabas Day**, & we had the best sermon I have yet heard on "**St. Barnabas**" by our Rector, the Revd. Buckroyd.
His former parish was "St. Barnabas" (see 13th April 1970). Without **St. Barnabas** we may well have never known **St. Paul**. (See Acts 9. 27.) Like Andrew & Peter (John 1. 42.)

14th June 1972 Wednesday
The film "**Cromwell**" is showing at Coalville this week (See 27th November 1970) & Mum & I went again to see it. As we watched **King Charles I** brought to trial, sentenced to death & finally executed, I thought of poor **Louis XVI** whose story was so similar.
I saw them both at Madame Tussaud's 4th June 1972.

16th June 1972 Friday
My latest book from good old County Hall library is "**The Story of Surnames**", a custom we copied from France, where they started about the year 1000 A.D.
The Romans had surnames, e.g. **Gaius Julius Caesar**, but after the fall of the Roman Empire it took us nearly 1000 years to get back to surnames.

18th June 1972 Sunday
This has been a month of terrible disasters all over the world – a mining disaster in Rhodesia, a burst dam in America, a train crash in France, and today – Britain's worst air disaster, when a B.E.A. Trident £1 million "Papa India" crashed shortly after take-off from Heathrow Airport, London to Brussels, killing 119 aboard.

20th June 1972 Tuesday
Sunday's plane crash was caused by the aircraft beginning to stall at 1,750 feet & 174 m.p.h., never reaching its full height & speed. It was a case of unrecoverable stall; & it appears that the stalling began when a lever, used to return the wings' leading edges from "droop" position to level, was operated too soon.

22nd June 1972 Thursday
Next Sunday is our Sunday School Anniversary, & our numbers have now swelled to 20 in my class, & 12 in

Susan's. This is more than we have had for several years & they are quite a talented lot. Jessica Willars is playing the piano, Andrea Dickinson is singing solo & they are all singing the latest lively hit songs.

24th June 1972 Saturday
It is now exactly 3 months since Mr. William Whitelaw was made Secretary of State for Northern Ireland. He has been nicknamed **Wary Willie** by some but his "masterly inactivity" now seems to be bearing fruit. The Provisional I.R.A. – toughest & most ruthless of the terrorists – have offered a cease-fire starting Monday.

26th June 1972 Monday
Coalville Amateur Operatic Society Annual General Meeting. Our next show "My Fair Lady" is arranged for 19th March 1973 to 24th March 1973, with rehearsals starting 2nd October.
We start with £250 in the bank - £600 in the Building Society, and £100 worth of equipment. Our last show made a loss of £75.

28th June 1972 Wednesday
Minnehaha has sprung a leak. Every time it rains, water seeps through the rusty sills underneath the doors, & then I have to bail out. So my latest bill is £18 "to supply & fit inner & outer body sills to offside & nearside".
Also just lately I have had 2 new tyres which amounted to £12.

30th June 1972 Friday
Meet the new slim-line Hewsie! In the last 2 years I have reduced from 10 stones to 9 stones. Auntie Belle & Aunt Dos today went to Skegness to care for Auntie Cis, aged 80, who is now home from hospital.
Pat & Evelyn are off this week to Inverness to stay with Murdo's family.

2nd July 1972 Sunday
It was a truly exciting & happy occasion for me tonight when the **Provost of Leicester** came to preach at **Ravenstone Church**. (See 12th January 1972)
I was chosen to read the lessons – two beautiful lessons, I Kings 18. 17-39, and John 15. 1-16, which included the Provost's text: "I have called you friends."

4th July 1972 Tuesday
July 4th – America's Independence Day (1776) and with 15 American visitors at County Hall Glenfield today, we had for the first time the **Stars & Stripes** flying on one flag pole, & the **County of Leicestershire** flag alongside. The visitors were in Britain to see how our local government system works.

6th July 1972 Thursday
President Pompidou of France yesterday sacked his Prime Minister, 57 year old Jacques Chaban-Delmas, following one of the greatest tax scandals Europe has known, when he managed to use his position to avoid paying any tax at all.
The new Prime Minister is a great De Gaulle man – Pierre Messmer.

8th July 1972 Saturday
Enid & I arrived at Ilfracombe, after a very interesting

journey of 234 miles, including lunch at Bath, & afternoon tea in Wells, where we called into the Cathedral: then on to the notorious 1 in 4 Porlock Hill, which we only just managed to get up with a struggle - & the weather was terrible.

Note – Enid & I have our summer holiday in Ilfracombe. Family commitments & other financial outlays will restrict our holidays for the next 20 years.

10th July 1972 Monday

Our bedroom at the Moonta Hotel, Capstone Crescent, Ilfracombe is nearer to the sea than any we have ever had before – only 5 yards.

The sea at high tide is a splendid sight, lashing up & over & round the rocks in cascades of foam; & nearby is the shining red light up on Lantern Hill.

12th July 1972 Wednesday

Visited the lovely house & grounds called Arlington Court in North Devon. Home of the famous Chichester family for many centuries, it was finally bequeathed to the National Trust in 1949. So there stand 3,471 acres of England – peace & tranquillity – with green fields stretching to the far horizon on every side.

14th July 1972 Friday

July 14th – My Birthday & a great day for the French. This is **Bastille Day** – the day when the Bastille – a mighty fortress in Paris, which was used as the state prison, was captured in 1789 by a mass rising of hungry and militant people. This was the **French Revolution** – the fall of despotism, & the beginning of liberation.

16th July 1972 Sunday

Home again from glorious Devon, and a most interesting sermon at church tonight, based on the 1st lesson, 1 Kings, Chapter 21. This was a character study of **Jezebel**, the scheming wife of **King Ahab**, who found her palace in Samaria too small, & stooped to any depths to get what she wanted.

18th July 1972 Tuesday

Peace in Northern Ireland (see 24th June 1972) did not last long. This week the death toll of British soldiers trying to maintain law & order reached 100; & every day we hear of more & more bombs, blasts & absolute devastation.

The Catholics want Ireland for the Irish, & this is their way of saying so.

20th July 1972 Thursday

Received a letter from Department of the Environment, Lambeth Bridge House, S.E.1

(See 7th July 1971) "I am sorry to have to tell you that you have not been selected for promotion following your recent appearance before a board."

Ah well! Local Government salaries are to be raised, so that helps.

22nd July 1972 Saturday

At the moment I am a **Civil Servant** of the **Clerical Officer** grade, reaching £1,489 maximum in September this year. But I am still allowed the benefits of the Local Government **Clerical III** grade, which I would have

been on (see 1st October 1971), & this now reaches a maximum of £1,746.

24th July 1972 Monday

Went last night to Ellistown Church where they had an impressive flower service, with **Noah** in his ark at the back of the church – a dove in flight over the aisle, & a huge rainbow in the chancel.

The preacher was the Bishop, who took the opportunity to preach on the rainbow.

(See 28th February 1971).

26th July 1972 Wednesday

Mum & Auntie Doris from Mountsorrel are spending the week with Mary Moore at her home in Wivenhoe, Colchester.

Aunt Dos & Auntie Belle hope to return home on Saturday, after spending a month in Skegness looking after Aunt Cis.

They will be bringing Auntie Cis home to Ravenstone with them.

28th July 1972 Friday

Auntie Cis is much improved after her recent illness, & is now having the time of her life, getting everybody to do just as she wishes. Twice during the last few months she has changed her will. Do anything to offend & you stand to lose anything up to £1,000 so now she has many "friends".

30th July 1972 Sunday

Another ton up! (See 19th Sept 1971) That is £200 towards buying a new car.

The latest Local Government Pay Award makes my salary now exceed £1,500 p.a. (See 30th April 1969) Civil Service salary = £1,430 plus £104 A.R.A., with effect from 1st July 1972, rising to £1,489 plus £45 in September.

1st August 1972 Tuesday

Today the new cars have their suffix "L" & the demand has been "**fantastic**".

After 7 years of sales averaging 1,100,000 a year, it has suddenly jumped to 1,600,000.

The car makers cannot keep up with the demand. Anybody now wanting a new Mini has to wait at least 12 weeks for delivery.

3rd August 1972 Thursday

Auntie Cis, born June 19th 1892, is now in Ravenstone, & is literally turning the whole place upside down. She has fallen out with Aunt Dos, fallen out with Cousin Audrey, utterly exhausted Auntie Belle now aged 76, & threatened to go back to Skegness, where she could not possibly cope on her own.

5th August 1972 Saturday

Auntie Cis was taken by ambulance this evening (very much against her will) to the **Wilfred Keene Clinic, Carlton Hayes Hospital**.

It was very sad to see her – an ex-headmistress – in such a confused state. Intermingled with her wild rambling was her old familiar intelligent self.

7th August 1972 Monday
Yesterday I was 15,000 days old. (Or is it today? – the older I get the longer the sum)
Pat, Evelyn, Aunt Dos & I visited Aunt Cis in hospital. She was utterly broken hearted & sobbed & sobbed. Then gradually she accepted us – ate chocolates with us, even made us laugh; & when we left, waved enthusiastically.

9th August 1972 Wednesday
The thoughts & prayers of our family this week have all centred on Aunt Cis. How wonderful then to see her slowly improving.
It reminds me of **St. Paul**, who started by "**breathing out threatenings & slaughter** ...." (Acts 9. 1.) until suddenly "**there shined round about him a light from heaven.**"

11th August 1972 Friday
Visited the church of **St. Laurence, Measham**, to see this year's prize winning "**Best Kept Churchyard in Leicestershire**".
There were 55 entries for this competition (including **Ravenstone**) & the 2nd prize went to **Thurcaston**.
Measham churchyard was a massive lawn edged with flowers & paved with gravestones.

13th August 1972 Sunday
Mum & I visited the Manor House, Donington-le-Heath (2 miles from Ravenstone) which opened to the public only last month, after a massive restoration programme, carried out by Leicestershire County Council. It is reputed to be one of the oldest houses in England, dating back to 1280 A.D.

15th August 1972 Tuesday
Our Sunday School outing this year is to be London Zoo – August 26th. This is proving to be a most popular choice, & we have booked 3 bus loads. The outing includes a visit to Buckingham Palace to see the changing of the guard - & then on to Regents Park, for the whole afternoon at the Zoo.

17th August 1972 Thursday
Our latest national problem is the threat of being flooded by **Indians** from **Uganda**. Thousands of Indians went to Africa some 70 years ago to work on railways. When Kenya & Uganda were granted independence about 10 years ago, the Asian minorities were given British passports, & now Uganda is telling them to go.

19th August 1972 Saturday
50,000 British Asians, at present living in **Uganda**, have been given 3 months notice to quit. And the most popular city of refuge is **Leicester**. Already we have quite a large Indian community, because in Leicester they can find plenty of employment, but this latest threatened avalanche is causing great concern.

Note – Idi Amin gave 8,000 Ugandan Asians 48 hours to leave the country.

21st August 1972 Monday
Mum & I visited Auntie Cis at the **Wilfred Keene Clinic**, & you would never believe she was the same person we visited a fortnight ago. Today she was a real "lady", charming & dignified. We sat with her in the television lounge, & met several other patients, who were equally calm & confident.

23rd August 1972 Wednesday
The 1972 Olympic Games are due to begin at Munich on Sunday 27th August, lasting a fortnight. But there is so much disagreement over Rhodesia, the rebels who refused to be ruled by Britain, that everybody is threatening to walk out.
The Games which began in 776 B.C. were revived 76 years ago.

1. 1896 Athens	XV. 1952 Helsinki, Finland
11. 1900 Paris	XVI. 1956 Melbourne, Australia
111. 1904 St. Louis	XVII. 1960 Rome, Italy
1V. 1908 London	XVIII.1964 Tokyo, Japan
V. 1912 Stockholm	XIX. 1968 Mexico City, Mexico
V1. WW I	XX. 1972 Munich, West Germany
V11. 1920 Antwerp	XXI 1976 Montreal, Canada
V111. 1924 Paris	XXII 1980 Moscow, USSR
1X. 1928 Amsterdam	XXIII 1984 Los Angeles, USA
X. 1932 Los Angeles	XXIV 1988 Seoul, South Korea
X1. 1936 Berlin	XXV 1992 Barcelona, Spain
X11. WW II	XXVI 1996 Atlanta, Georgia, USA
X111. WW II	XXVII 2000 Sydney, Australia
X1V. 1948 London, England	

25th August 1972 Friday
The people making the biggest shout over Rhodesia at the Olympic Games are the black people of Africa. It was Mr. Ekangaki, the new Secretary General of the Organisation of African Unity, who called on all African countries to boycott the Games, unless Rhodesia withdrew, so the Rhodesians have been asked to go.

27th August 1972 Sunday
Our Sunday School outing yesterday to London Zoo included a most interesting drive round London to see the major places of interest.
We saw some splendid animals at the Zoo, but were disappointed at the lack of space provided in the Lion House for the big cats – leopards, cheetahs, etc.

29th August 1972 Tuesday
Prince William of Gloucester, elder son of the Duke & Duchess of Gloucester, a dashing 30 year-old bachelor, cousin of the Queen, and ninth in line to the throne, died yesterday afternoon when his plane crashed shortly after take-off in the "Goodyear International Trophy Race" in Staffordshire.

31st August 1972 Thursday
The 1972 Olympic Games in Munich are now in full swing. We spend hours watching all the drama of the different events on television.
Underwater cameras give fantastic pictures of the diving & swimming – the Russian girl gymnasts are a delight to watch, they absolutely steal the whole show.

2nd September 1972 Saturday
It's just one expense after another at the moment with Minnehaha. New tyres – new exhaust – new water pump – new plugs – new battery carrier, etc. - total £70.

The car broke down altogether when the water pump packed up, & I was towed into Coalville – quite an experience, especially when the rope broke over a bridge.

4th September 1972 Monday

The result of my handwriting analysis – see 5th Sept 1971: -

"… you expect other people to agree with your ideas, & are often dismayed when met by any opposition to them … you have the capacity to concentrate intensely for short spans of time & to produce instant conclusions … extremely sensitive – easily hurt, often when no unkindness on the part of other people is intended."

6th September 1972 Wednesday

"The Religion of Mohamed was founded on the sword" (see 7th February 1972).

This was brought home forcibly to the whole world today, when news of Arab Terrorists at the Olympic Games in Munich shocked us all. The Games were brought to a complete standstill, after 17 people had died, including eleven Israeli athletes.

8th September 1972 Friday

Opposite Ravenstone Church the new houses are now going up. An advertisement in the Coalville Times reads – "Choice homes by Macoll Builders … a small select development of 24 detached houses of character to be built to an excellent specification, £10,400 to £12,750."

10th September 1972 Sunday

The 1972 Olympic Games draw to a close in Munich – a mixture of joy & sorrow. These are the most expensive Games ever staged, costing £300 million. These are the Games in which one man alone won a record of 7 Gold Medals, **Mark Spitz**, the great American swimmer; & Britain won only 4.

12th September 1972 Tuesday

Watched last night on television the Olympic Flame flicker & die; saw the five ringed Olympic Flag (representing the five continents) lowered & carried ceremoniously away, for use next time in Montreal 1976.

And everyone stood in silence in memory of the athletes slain in the Arab massacre.

14th September 1972 Thursday

One of the funniest things at the Olympic Games was the Marathon. This was once round the track, & then out on the roads for a 25 mile run, finishing once round the track again. Into the stadium came running the supposed winner, fresh as a daisy; it was a student having a joke.

16th September 1972 Saturday

D.O.E. World – Newspaper of the Department of the Environment, which we receive once a month, is inviting people to compile a crossword, preferably with a D.O.E. flavour. For each crossword published in D.O.E. World, a book or record token value £2 will be paid to the compiler.

18th September 1972 Monday

Fully engrossed compiling a crossword for D.O.E.

World. What a challenge! Managed to include "**Interview**" – doing your best with people who sound bored. "**Red Tape**" – ties up just about everything. "**Tea-time**" – breaking point for Civil Servants. "**Transport**", "**Diplomacy**", "**Whitehall**", "**Elector**", etc.

20th September 1972 Wednesday

Mum received a cheque for £589-14p from the solicitors Woolley, Beardsleys & Bosworth, being the balance due from Aunt Mary's will. This means that altogether Aunt Mary left Mum £1,389-14p. £300 received 2nd April 1971, £500 received 16th May 1971, & the balance today. Aunt Mary died 4th May 1970, aged 99.

22nd September 1972 Friday

The troubles of Northern Ireland are at the moment overshadowed by the troubles of Africa. Here again, everybody is in fighting mood. Arab v. African: the Arab Moslem north, versus black Sub-Sahara, with General Idi Amin Dada, the vicious dictator who calls himself President of Uganda, creating untold havoc; & he is a black Moslem.

24th September 1972 Sunday

Harvest Festival this afternoon at little St. Mary's – incidentally, one of the smallest churches in England.

Afterwards the harvest produce was taken in baskets to the sick & elderly. One of the delighted recipients was Auntie Cis, now in residence with Aunt Dos, & much improved after her recent illness.

26th September 1972 Tuesday

Norway today voted against joining the European Common Market – the European Economic Community – the E.E.C.

The Irish, ever blowing up all the buildings in Northern Ireland, have threatened a day of bomb terror throughout Britain on October 18th, the eve of the E.E.C. summit conference being held in Paris.

28th September 1972 Thursday

"Own a complete proof set of the last £. s. d. coins **ever** for £3"- this is the latest tempting offer from the Royal Mint, & I have decided to have £3 worth, although the coins are no more than 37p in actual value.

But what a history! The story of £. s. d. spans 12 centuries.

30th September 1972 Saturday

"Liking nothing but the best, we have to wait" – see 30th September 1970. Mum is now hoping to buy a new carpet with the money Aunt Mary gave her.

Today we bought a very elegant table lamp for £15, & we have arranged to have the bathroom & middle bedroom papered & decorated.

2nd October 1972 Monday

Denmark today voted overwhelmingly to join the European Common Market, so now we are 9 – France, West Germany, Italy, Belgium, The Netherlands, Luxembourg, Britain, Ireland & Denmark.

After the last war, **Winston Churchill** said, "We must build a kind of United States of Europe."

4th October 1972 Wednesday

It is to be hoped that the Common Market may help the problem of Northern Ireland.

When the original 6 countries joined forces, they said they were "resolved to substitute for historic rivalries a fusion of their essential interests … the foundation of a wider & deeper community among peoples long divided by bloody conflicts."

6th October 1972 Friday

D.O.E. World this month has another tempting offer "ODE for £25". The Civil Service Council for Further Education are again organising their annual poetry competition. And they are offering a first prize of at least £25. Entries should be sent to CSCFE by December 31st.

8th October 1972 Sunday

An ODE for DOE – I have chosen for my ode "Flight of Apollo XIII" (see 17th April 1970).

Starting with Apollo himself, building the walls of Troy, & mentioning Icarus, it proceeds to the ancient wise astronomers & the final Apollo Moon missions, highlighting the homecoming of Apollo 13.

10th October 1972 Tuesday

Auntie Cis returned this evening by ambulance to the Wilfred Keene Clinic, happily much more gladly than she first went on August 5th; but again because she became more than the family could cope with – full of hare brained schemes, like an over wound piece of clockwork, utterly exhausting everybody.

12th October 1972 Thursday

Auntie Cis, in her state of confusion, is a rare mixture of high intelligence – dominating head mistress – excessive generosity – absolute thrift – love & hate.

She bought herself 2 very expensive mink hats this week & offered to buy mink hats for all & sundry – a Rolls Royce for Aunt Dos & her bungalow for Pat.

14th October 1972 Saturday

Went to Leicester on a grand old shopping spree for our stall at the Christmas Fair. This year,

for the first time, the Sunday School have been asked to provide a stall & we have been given £8 to start with. I bought books to read, books to colour, a picture of a pony, beads to thread, embroidery, etc. etc.

16th October 1972 Monday

Leicestershire car numbers are a combination of 4 basic double letters: - AY, JU, NR, UT, then we go AAY, AJU, ANR, AUT, then we go BAY, BJU, BNR, BUT. We have numbers 1 to 999 followed by a single letter which denotes the year of the car.

We have just reached GAY 123L. How lovely to have a new car with a GAY number.

18th October 1972 Wednesday

The I.R.A. dedicated to "Ireland for the Irish" are not the only force to be reckoned with in Northern Ireland. The latest trouble is from the U.D.A. – the Ulster Defence Association. They are fighting to remain British; but who are they fighting? The poor old British army, torn between the two.

20th October 1972 Friday

Made my first acquaintance with the interior of "White Lodge", the newly built house in the grounds of the "Hollies".

Cor! It is really beautiful. A kitchen with everything in you could wish for, plus another room for washing, complete with deep freeze, etc., archways, steps, dais – most artistic.

22nd October 1972 Sunday

Mum & I had tea with Cousin Audrey (my dad's cousin, who will be 71 years old next month)

During the evening we looked through her old photographs which were most interesting. We saw the village as it looked 70 years ago   a group of Ravenstone school children in 1910 & her mother's wedding group.

24th October 1972 Tuesday

Last night we had auditions for "My Fair Lady". With 8 applications for the part of Eliza it was a late night session & then we have more for next Monday. I enjoyed my audition for "Mrs. Higgins" which I did 4 times with 4 different Elizas. Mrs. Higgins is a rich elegant lady.

26th October 1972 Thursday

Had one day's holiday while Minnehaha went for her 60,000 mile service. Spent much of the day in the garden clearing up the autumn leaves.

The Mini car came on to the market 13 years ago & this week, at the London Motor Show, Mini number 3 million was unveiled. A record for British cars.

28th October 1972 Saturday

Auntie Dos & I visited Auntie Cis in hospital. She really did look a frail old lady. The doctor has signed her medical certificate to the effect that she is suffering from "mental illness" & will be so for 12 months.

Another patient who moved me deeply was a sad, silent, beautiful Indian girl.

30th October 1972 Monday

Yesterday Mum & I had tea with her cousin Cyril & his wife Elsie at Loughborough (it was Cyril's birthday). Cyril's name is Cyril Bailey, & his father & Mum's mother were brother & sister. Mum's mother married Tom Sketchley, & also had a brother Tom Bailey, father of Madge, Bertha, Rex, Eric & John.

1st November 1972 Wednesday

This afternoon we had our second fire drill at County Hall (see 11th June 1969). Being the first day of the month we had lots of customers to join in the exercise. When the alarm bell rang, a fire officer came into our office & stood looking at his watch, while all we like sheep vacated the building.

3rd November 1972 Friday

Thanks to Aunt Mary, we have now been able to spend £50 having our old (40 years old) black fire grate removed from the middle room, & replaced by a very attractive fire-place. This really transforms the room, & as I sit now by the fire I think of Hiawatha …. "Very pleasant is the firelight."

5ᵗʰ November 1972 Sunday

"Please to remember the fifth of November – gunpowder treason & plot."

It was on 5ᵗʰ November 1605 that **Guy Fawkes**, in league with a dozen other Roman Catholic conspirators, planned to blow up King James I who had recently come from Scotland to succeed Queen Elizabeth. The persecution of Catholics, which began with Henry VIII, was the cause of the plot.

7ᵗʰ November 1972 Tuesday

The longest, loudest political show in the western world – the election of the **President of the United States** – which hit the road 9 months ago, culminated in the poll today when **Richard Milhous Nixon** was re-elected for another 4 years.

No-one may be in office for more than 10 years.

9ᵗʰ November 1972 Thursday

The skull of a man (or woman) was found in **Kenya** this week, which was at least 2,600,000 years old. Until now the earliest evidence of man's existence has gone back only a million & a half years.

The big question now is: - "**What was man doing for the best part of 2 million years?**"

11ᵗʰ November 1972 Saturday

Drama at 1-00a.m. with a little mouse. Auntie Belle, who has just had a new central heating system installed in her home, arrived long after the midnight hour to seek assistance. Fortunately, it was my late night for playing cards with Enid & family, so I went with Auntie Belle to catch the mouse.

13ᵗʰ November 1972 Monday

Parts were announced tonight at our rehearsal for "My Fair Lady" which will be given next March. **Eliza** – the leading lady, is **Margaret Lilleyman**; **Professor Higgins** – the leading man, is **Hughie Adcock**; **Colonel Pickering** is **Frank Goddard** & amongst the other roles I am 60 year old **Mrs Higgins**.

15ᵗʰ November 1972 Wednesday

While I perform on the stage in light musical comedy, **Bunting** (my father's first-born) performs in grand opera. This week she is singing in Verdi's **Aida**, & I am hoping to visit her at the week-end & go to the Saturday night performance.

Today she sent me the story to peruse.

17ᵗʰ November 1972 Friday

The story of **Aida** is set in the Court of the Pharaohs at a time when **Egypt** was at constant strife with the neighbouring land of **Ethiopia**. The reigning Pharaoh has a daughter, **Amneris**, who has an **Ethiopian** slave girl named **Aida**. These two girls both love the same man, **Radames**, & **Aida** wins.

19ᵗʰ November 1972 Sunday

Returned home from Bunting's very impressed with **Aida**. The highlight of the show was the triumphant return of the Egyptian war leader, Radames, with all the spoils of Ethiopia. What a magnificent choral number!

I moved in such grand opera circles that I was shown pictures of the open air theatre at Verona with its 30,000 audience watching **Aida**.

21ˢᵗ November 1972 Tuesday

Yesterday was the Silver Wedding of the Queen & the Duke of Edinburgh.

I had a day's holiday & spent much of the time watching television. First there was a Service of Thanksgiving in Westminster Abbey, & then the state drive to Guildhall for lunch with the Lord Mayor.

23ʳᵈ November 1972 Thursday

Very busy at the moment preparing for our Sunday School stall at the Christmas Fair to be held on Saturday.

I have embroidered a tray cloth & cushion cover, Mum has made a pretty silver collar with matching cuffs; & it has been a whole evening's job pricing our many varied items.

25ᵗʰ November 1972 Saturday

Our stall was laden this afternoon with goodly produce at the Christmas Fair held in the village institute. Susan & I stood behind the stall & sold about half that there was for sale.

All the rest was left unwanted, including my tray cloth & cushion, & Mum's handiwork.

Our total profit was £9.

27ᵗʰ November 1972 Monday

Apollo 17, America's final Apollo mission to the Moon, is due to blast off December 6ᵗʰ, but a strike is threatening to block the launching. A militant group of 60 men employed on the project at **Cape Kennedy, Florida**, plan to walk out well before zero hour of the £180 million last journey to the Moon.

29ᵗʰ November 1972 Wednesday

An evening with **Reevsie, Tony & Joanne**.

Joanne, now aged 5 ½, is still bubbling over with the joys of childhood. Her chief delight in life is reading, & she can read almost every word in the children's books. The words which stumped her today were "cupboard" and "laughter".

1ˢᵗ December 1972 Friday

Oh, I do hope Apollo 17 can be launched successfully on December 6ᵗʰ. For the first time ever there is to be a geologist landing on the Moon – **Dr. Harrison Schmidt** – so he should really know what Moon rocks he is picking up.

The other two astronauts are Eugene Cernan (commander) & Ronald Evans.

3ʳᵈ December 1972 Advent Sunday

Advent Sunday – the beginning of a new church year - & my turn on our lesson reading rota to read the Advent lessons 1. Isaiah Chap. 2, & 2. First Epistle to the Thessalonians, Chapter 5

The Rector, in his sermon, then spoke in detail on the 2 lessons which made reading them mean so much more.

5ᵗʰ December 1972 Tuesday

£10 for Christmas for every old age pensioner in the country!

7,600,000 pensioners (including Mum) have been given an extra £10 this week by the Government, costing £76 million. Mum usually has £7-18p each week. Because she worked until she was 65 she gets more than the usual £6-75p.

7th December 1972 Thursday

I am pleased to tell you **Apollo 17** has been successfully launched, & is due to land the astronauts on the Moon on Monday. The landing is to be near the **Taurus** mountain range, close by the crater **Camelot**. During 75 hours on the Moon there will be 3 seven hour excursions, arriving home 19th December 1972.

9th December 1972 Saturday

Ravenstone's oldest resident died this week – **Mr Bagnall,** aged 99.

Mr Bagnall was churchwarden at Ravenstone for many years, & in 1961 he was made Churchwarden Emeritus. This unique honour was bestowed upon him by the Reverend Gustav Aronsohn when he was Rector here.

11th December 1972 Monday

The Rector yesterday referred to the only words of Jesus recorded outside the bounds of the four gospels – Matthew, Mark, Luke & John. These were the words of St. Paul in the Acts of the Apostles Chap. 20 v. 35 "…. Remember the words of the Lord Jesus, how He said, **it is more blessed to give than to receive."**

13th December 1972 Wednesday

December 13th 1577 – when Spain ruled the seas, **Francis Drake**, a brilliantly daring pirate & explorer, set out from **Plymouth**, & with his ship the **Golden Hind**, sailed round the world, returning 3rd November 1580, laden with booty & gold.

Queen Elizabeth I came on board & knighted him "**Sir Francis Drake**".

15th December 1972 Friday

Apollo 17 has successfully completed its Moon excursions, & the astronauts are now on their way home – due for splash down on Tuesday.

People generally have lost interest in the Moon missions, but I never cease to marvel at men on the Moon, & thoroughly enjoy watching in close-up the TV pictures.

17th December 1972 Sunday

On 17th December 1603, in Prague, **Johannes Kepler**, Astronomer Royal, watched the conjunction of 2 planets, **Saturn & Jupiter**, looking like a huge single bright star. He calculated backwards to the **Star of Bethlehem. Yes!** There would have been just such a conjunction in 6 or 7 B.C.

19th December 1972 Tuesday

Oh, dear! **Patrick Moore** – great astrologer of our time, says the **Star of Bethlehem** was not **Saturn & Jupiter** in conjunction. More likely a **supernova** (exploding star), or possibly **Halley's Comet**, which appears every 76 years – (**next** time 1986); or 2 meteors – but quite likely the **Star of Bethlehem** was divine.

21st December 1972 Thursday

A day in London! Caught the 7-30 train in the morning from Leicester, arriving in London shortly after 9 a.m. Went by underground to Liverpool Street to see **Petticoat Lane**, & then to Holborn to find **Dickens's Old Curiosity Shop** (London's oldest & most famous shop, built 1567).

23rd December 1972 Saturday

Samuel Johnson (1709-1784) once said: - "**When a man is tired of London, he is tired of life; for there is in London all that life can afford."**

The more I know London, the more I want to know. Went on an evening bus ride yesterday all through London to see the lights. Learned such a lot from the driver.

25th December 1972 Monday

Christmas Day & the Bishop of Leicester spoke on "What Christmas means to me".

1. Memories of childhood. 2. The circle of family & friends. 3. The message of the angels, which is the whole of Christianity in a nutshell.

He also said that "A man who is wrapped up in himself makes a very small parcel."

27th December 1972 Wednesday

And so we say farewell to Christmas 1972.

My holiday began with a day in London on Friday, a day in Coalville on Saturday, Ravenstone Church on Sunday, (including a midnight service), Christmas Day with Enid, Auntie Gladys, David, Irene & Alison, & yesterday Mum & I spent the whole day with Cyril & Elsie at Loughborough.

29th December 1972 Friday

We are currently enjoying on television one of the greatest epics of all time – **Count Leo Tolstoy's** masterpiece "**War & Peace".**

In 20 weekly episodes it tells the story of the **Rostov** family from the year 1805 to the coming of **Napoleon** to **Moscow** in 1812, his retreat, & how they rise again from the ashes of war.

31st December 1972 Sunday

As we come to the end of another year we find ourselves getting older & slower. Poor old Auntie Cis in hospital, poor old Auntie Gladys collapsing in the village shop yesterday, & poor old Mum finding it increasingly difficult to walk about. This week her legs will hardly support her as she struggles along.

* * *

1973

1st January 1973 Monday
And here I am again! **Elizabeth Hewes** aged 41 – unmarried, living with my Mum …….
Today **Britain** joins the European Community. On this historic day, **Edward Heath**, our **Prime Minister**, wishes us "A Happy, Prosperous, and Peaceful Community New Year."

3rd January 1973 Wednesday
Europe could be the world's most prosperous major area by the end of the century. The enlarged Common Market (from 6 countries to 9) is larger in population than America or Russia. 253 million Europeans outnumbering 244 million Russians & 205 million Americans. We have 5 years to adjust.

5th January 1973 Friday
D.O.E. World, the newspaper of the Department of the Environment, this month contains my crossword. (See 18th September 1972). But, much to my amazement, more than half my clues have been completely altered. Most of them have been improved but one or two are not as good as the original.

7th January 1973 Sunday
My poor old Mum has had such a trying week – hardly able to walk at all, & the doctor says he can do nothing to help.
All the family have been wonderfully kind, visiting her regularly & offering to give what help they can. But Mum feels so hopeless & helpless she is reduced to rears.

9th January 1973 Tuesday
Poor old Mum, in the depths of despair, is now in Ashby Hospital. They have agreed to look after her for a fortnight, but she is not at all contented there. The place is too hot; she does not like the doctor; she does not like the nurses; & she is utterly miserable, with nothing to look forward to.

11th January 1973 Thursday
Found Mum a little more cheerful this evening. Sybil Hayes (from next door) & I visited her, & she just managed to walk between us, supported on either arm. **Matron** says Mum may be able to manage at home with a bed downstairs, but thinks she will become more helpless.

13th January 1973 Saturday
Anne Causer & I visited Mum this evening. It is Anne's birthday today – aged 70.
Mum, aged 67, wished she could get about as well as Anne. Poor old Mum could not even get to a standing position from a sitting position without assistance; & so we go into the unknown future.

15th January 1973 Monday
Auntie Doris (from Mountsorrel) & I visited Mum in hospital this afternoon. It is certainly easier for Mum to cope in hospital, than ever it would be at home. They have so many gadgets to help the disabled, & **Matron** is

extremely kind to Mum having known her for many years.

17th January 1973 Wednesday
Watched on television poor old Leicester City beaten 2-1 by Arsenal in only their first game towards the Cup Final. This was a re-play following their game on Saturday which was a draw. But Leicester played magnificently, & the papers report: - "By all that is just in football, Leicester should have won."

19th January 1973 Friday
Mum is coming home tomorrow after spending 10 days in Ashby Hospital. She will have a bed downstairs, so I have been busy furniture removing. The most difficult manoeuvre was getting the settee through the hall doorway from the middle room to the front room, but at last I managed it.

21st January 1973 Sunday
How lovely to have Mum home by her own fire-side. She has on loan a "Zimmer" which is a 4 legged walking aid. This enables her to walk from the middle room to the kitchen. She can just manage to wash up the dishes, but cannot walk unaided to carry them back to the cupboard.

23rd January 1973 Tuesday
Spent all evening fitting our new carpet in the bathroom. **Pat** did most of the hard work – cutting to size & negotiating round all the protruding pipes, etc. while I offered the necessary encouragement. **Lady Barnett**, when asked "What do you give a man who has everything?" said, "**Encouragement.**"

25th January 1973 Thursday
Mum & I watched on TV Napoleon's retreat from Moscow in **Count Leo Tolstoy's "War & Peace"**. The French withdrawal began on 19th October 1812, & on 6th November snow began to fall. That was when God's army of little snowflakes defeated the **Grand Army of Napoleon** – an expression I borrowed from the Revd. Aronsohn. (See 8th February 1969).

27th January 1973 Saturday
A new vicar for Snibston! Former prison chaplain the **Revd. John Millyard** is to be inducted on 7th February. Straight from Wandsworth, he has also been at prisons in Exeter, Leeds & Pentonville. Aged 43, a bachelor, he is interested in music & art, & can play the organ.

29th January 1973 Monday
Booked 40 seats for "**My Fair Lady**". 25 for people at County Hall, & 15 for friends & neighbours. This is my 25th show, & for 25 years service we get a medal. This year **Coalville Amateur Operatic Society** is to present 3 medals – one to **Pat** – one to **Enid** - & one to me.

31st January 1973 Wednesday
With 8 books full of **Green Shield** stamps (which are given with the sale of **Esso** petrol) I went to the **Green Shield** shop in Leicester & chose a game of **Scrabble** – a word game which gives hours of pleasure; and a very useful bathroom stool / linen bin with cork covered seat. Our bathroom scales were from Green Shield stamps.

2nd February 1973 Friday
The troubles in Northern Ireland are no better than last year. When a 4,000 gallon petrol tanker, with bomb attached, was parked in the centre of **Belfast**, only the bravery of an army bomb disposal expert averted disaster.

4th February 1973 Sunday
Mum continues to struggle along with the help of her Zimmer. She gets very fed up & wishes she could move herself around without such effort.

We watch other people walking about with no effort at all – people much older than Mum, & Mum longs to be able to walk like them.

6th February 1973 Tuesday
Received a letter from my dear old Aunt Cis, aged 80, in **Carlton Hayes Hospital**. The message was written outside the envelope with the address & stamp on the back, & another name & address used earlier on the front. Inside were 6 used envelopes & a letter to somebody else.

8th February 1973 Thursday
The most fantastic pictures on the television news this week have been from **Iceland**, where a long dormant volcano suddenly erupted & a never ending flow of lava makes its way down to the harbour, creating great rising waves of steam while all the icy water is brought to the boil.

10th February 1973 Saturday
It really is most remarkable that the lesson set for reading in church this Sunday is from Isaiah Chap. 64 – "Oh, that thou wouldest rend the heavens, that thou wouldest come down, that the mountains might flow down at thy presence, as when the melting fire burneth, the fire causeth the waters to boil."

12th February 1973 Monday
Auntie Doris (aged 77) who lives at Mountsorrel came for tea yesterday, & then she & I went to Leicester Cathedral, where the Bishop was preaching. His text most appropriately was from Isaiah Chap. 64 & he said that God would surely "come down" & make his own presence felt.

14th February 1973 Wednesday
St. Valentine's Day & **Mary Blue's wedding**. Mary Blue married Terry in 1965. They had 2 children & then Mary Blue ran away to Murdo in Inverness. Murdo also had been married with 2 children. Murdo subsequently was divorced; then Mary was divorced; & today Murdo & Mary married.

16th February 1973 Friday
Ravenstone Church – where people have worshipped since 1323 – this year celebrates its 650th Anniversary, & the Rector, the Revd. Buckroyd, has arranged a whole range of interesting activities to support this. Nearly every month there is something special – either an outing or some-one to visit us.

18th February 1973 Sunday
Tosca, Mum & I are now (10 p.m.) all sitting by a lovely cosy fire, with gentle background music on the radio.

Mum is enjoying a good book from **County Hall** library; & I am delighted to tell you that Mum is managing remarkably well, even though she cannot move around very easily.

20th February 1973 Tuesday
England is still a nation of strikers (see 17th January 1971).

The gas men are now on strike, & the latest body of workers eager to strike are the Civil Servants. A one day strike has been called for February 27th & this will affect our office where we have 18 Civil Servants.

22nd February 1973 Thursday
With everybody for ever demanding higher wages it means that everything you buy goes up & up in price. In an effort to stop this escalation the government have created a "**freeze**" whereby prices and wages must stay where they are for a while. Any-one therefore due for a rise at the moment is asked to wait.

24th February 1973 Saturday
Now it just so happens that the **Civil Service** were due for a rise from January 1st this year. This, they consider, as their due right. They do not feel responsible for the inflation in Britain, & yet they are now denied their rise. That is why the **Civil Servants** are now about to strike.

26th February 1973 Monday
Oh, the power of the **Trade Unions**! It really is quite frightening. In an effort to protect the workers they rule with a rod of iron. Their whole doctrine is so opposed to the law of love – joy – peace – patience – kindness – goodness – fidelity – gentleness & self-control. (Gal.5.22)

28th February 1973 Wednesday
Yesterday, (my old friend Longfellow's birthday) & a day when I had thoughts other than going on strike, I was so disgusted with the methods adopted by **Trade Unions**, & the way our office was under the control of irresponsible young upstarts, I resigned from C.P.S.A. (See 1st April 1970).

1st March 1973 Thursday
My latest book from **County Hall Library** is "**Pepy's Diary**". This is only an abridged version, as he wrote enough to fill ten books. But how I enjoy his writing. Born in 1633, & dying in 1703, he began to keep his great diary 1st January 1660 (in shorthand), but finished in 1669 because of his eye-sight.

3rd March 1973 Saturday
Minnehaha is now exactly 7 years old & today she had her 63,000 mile service & M.O.T. Test. The total bill was £17-38p, which included £6-65p labour; £9-25p parts; £1-48p for the oil. How I would love a new car, but I really cannot afford one, & poor old Minnehaha keeps chugging along.

5th March 1973 Monday
I am very pleased to learn that the general secretary of N.A.L.G.O. has quit his job because (like me) he has had enough of **Trade Unions**. As he says, "I prefer the force

of argument to the argument of force." Every day more & more people are going on strike for more money.

7th March 1973 Wednesday

Ash Wednesday! The Rector gave a sermon this evening on the three creeds. 1. The Apostles Creed – "I believe in God …" 2. The Creed in the service of Holy Communion, the Nicene Creed – "I believe in one God …" and 3. The Creed of Saint Athanasius, "Quicunque Vult" in the prayer book before the Litany.

9th March 1973 Friday

The troubles of Northern Ireland have now come to England. Yesterday 4 bombs were planted in the heart of London causing considerable damage & alarm. Meanwhile the people of Northern Ireland have been voting whether to remain part of the United Kingdom or join the Irish Republic. The vast majority chose the United Kingdom.

11th March 1973 Sunday

Mum & I enjoyed listening to the radio this evening, to a programme called "**Sunday Half-Hour**", which is a programme of hymn singing. The hymns we heard tonight were recorded in Leicester Cathedral & the singing was superb. The programme ended with prayers & blessing by my beloved Provost.

13th March 1973 Tuesday

Marjorie Hayes, my life-long neighbour who married **Maurice Preston** in November 1966, is now divorced & lives with her young son **Ian** & her sister **Sybil**. She has recently become engaged to a widower, **George Merrill**, & plans to marry him shortly. That means Mum & I will soon have new neighbours.

15th March 1973 Thursday

Costumes arrived today for Coalville Amateur Operatic Society's 50th show "**My Fair Lady**". As **Mrs Higgins**, I have 3 beautiful long slim-line elegant dresses – turquoise ensemble for Ascot – gold for the Embassy Ball - & lilac when at home. Opening night is next Tuesday.
Note – This is my 25th show with the Society & I decide to make this my last show, actually appearing on stage; I still wish to belong to the Society.

17th March 1973 Saturday

Having such exquisite costumes for "**My Fair Lady**", this called for exquisite accessories. So it was off to Leicester today for turquoise shoes – gold evening gloves – and diamond & pearl ear-rings. (Do you wonder why I cannot afford a new car?) It is because I have such extravagant tastes.

19th March 1973 Monday

Apart from extravagant tastes for myself, I have equally extravagant tastes for others. So – I have chosen for Hughie Adcock, who is playing **Professor Higgins** in My Fair Lady, a lovely gift – a silver plated ash-tray, which I have had engraved "**My Fair Lady**" C.A.O.S. 1973.

21st March 1973 Wednesday

Thoroughly enjoying my part as **Mrs Higgins**. In my 25

years with the Coalville Amateurs, this is one of the loveliest characters I have played. And it is certainly the most beautifully dressed. It is a real pleasure to play with **Hughie Adcock** (my son) & with **Margaret Lilleyman** – "**Eliza Doolittle**".

23rd March 1973 Friday

Mum is so disappointed that she is not well enough to see our show "**My Fair Lady**". Always in the past she has been once, twice, or even three times to see a show, but now she dare not sit for 3 hours on a seat which is not particularly comfortable. So she stays at home in her old arm-chair.

25th March 1973 Sunday

Did a new kind of crossword puzzle today – called "**The Monkey Puzzle**". This was a crossword grid with all the answers listed in alphabetical order. You have to sort out which word fits where & then write a clue for one particular word.

27th March 1973 Tuesday

Mum has agreed to lend me £500 towards a new car. So thanks to Aunt Mary, who kindly gave the money in the first place, we are now hoping to have a new **Mini**. In 1967 I bought a new scooter **KAY 7E** (as Auntie Cis already had a car number **KAY 7**). Now of course we would like **KAY 7L**.

29th March 1973 Thursday

Saw "**The Yeomen of the Guard**" at the Little Theatre, Leicester. This was first performed in 1888, & was also given by Coalville Amateurs in 1925, when my dad played the part of the headsman (an executioner in black stockings, black tunic & black mask). But this was the first time I had seen it. (Sorry – 2nd)

31st March 1973 Saturday

Yesterday we had our Annual Dinner Dance for Coalville Amateurs, when I was presented with my Long Service medal from **N.O.D.A.** – the National Operatic & Dramatic Association. Altogether we have 18 members who over the years have completed 25 years service & one has 45 years service.

2nd April 1973 Monday

Mary Moore is spending the week with Mum & me. This evening we visited Hilda at Wigston. Hilda is Auntie Doris's sister, aged 75, & her husband **Fred** died a few weeks ago. Hilda was cheerful, but naturally very sad. She has only the happiest memories of Fred, as he was always so kind.

4th April 1973 Wednesday

Mighty **Jupiter** is the target for America's next spacecraft. Already one spacecraft is well on the way there. Launched more than a year ago, it is due to arrive on December 1st, & this 2nd one will arrive the following year. The journey is 365 million miles. Both spacecraft will give the first close up pictures of **Jupiter**.

6th April 1973 Friday

New hours for Local Government begin this week. Our new hours are 8-30 a.m. to 5 p.m. Monday, Tuesday, Wednesday & Thursday; & 8-30 a.m. to 4-30 p.m. on

Friday. This is ½ an hour per week less than previously, & brings Local Government into line with the Civil Service. (See 3rd April 1970).

8th April 1973 Sunday
My latest library book is "**A History of Inland Transport & Communication**". This is the fascinating story of how people & produce have been conveyed over the years – first by river, or by land over the poorest of roads – then by canal – then by railways & finally by motorways, by air & underground.

10th April 1973 Tuesday
According to what period of history we find ourselves born into, we live accordingly. I have just followed in detail the "**Canal Mania**" from 1791 – 1794, & the even greater "**Railway Mania**" from 1845 – 1846. You'd be surprised how everybody jumped on the bandwagon to get rich quick at other's expense.

12th April 1973 Thursday
Don't Forget to Vote Today
Elections being held today for the new powerful county authorities are the most important in local government for 100 years. Use your vote!
Mum & I voted for the new Leicestershire County Council which will become fully operative next April.

14th April 1973 Saturday
Our new Leicestershire County Council consisting of the former County of Rutland, the former County of Leicestershire, plus the City of Leicester, begins its 4 year term of office with 41 conservative councillors, 37 labour, 8 independent & 7 liberal. Our man is Mr Didcot.

16th April 1973 Monday
Went with the Amateurs to **Staunton Harold Cheshire Home** for a concert version of our recent show "My Fair Lady". As I was in none of the musical numbers I sat with the audience & enjoyed watching & hearing the excellent singing, which sounded grand in their big room.

18th April 1973 Wednesday
I have now signed on the dotted line to order a new car for July 1st – a birthday present for my 42nd birthday. I have chosen the new **Mini Clubman** with a 998cc engine.
Colour – Teal Blue, complete with radio, wing mirrors & a special pre-delivery treatment of rust proofing – **Zeibart**.

20th April 1973 Good Friday
At our Good Friday service today, the Rector emphasised "And a superscription was written over Him in letters of **Greek** & **Latin** & **Hebrew** – '**This is the King of the Jews**'." As our old friend **Matthew Henry** says – In 3 languages is Jesus Christ proclaimed King. It was written in these 3 languages to be read & known of all men.

22nd April 1973 Easter Sunday
Remember the Trinity Sunday sermon May 21st 1967? The 3 in one trade mark of God? Well, we not only saw

more of this on Good Friday this year, but today we saw the threefold guard of watch & stone & seal. The watch was the guard in the tower of Antonia, the seal no doubt of the Sanhedrim.

24th April 1973 Tuesday
The rate at which this earth is using up its natural resources is quite alarming. I was amazed to read how much water we in this country use every day. 2,000 million gallons a day & by the end of the century our requirements will have trebled. And apparently no country is really getting to grips with this major problem.

26th April 1973 Thursday
Ever since **Jason** sailed in search of his **Golden Fleece** it has been man's dream to bridge the Bosporus. This dream will soon be fulfilled as a six lane highway opens linking **Europe** with **Asia**. From Istanbul in Europe the main span will be 1,175 yards – the 4th longest suspension bridge in the world.

28th April 1973 Saturday
My latest book "**The World of Water**" is a great enlightenment on our water supply problems. I am very relieved to learn that the supply of water is not the problem – only its management & distribution. **What goes up must come down**. Water evaporates & then comes down as rain in a perfectly balanced hydrologic cycle.

30th April 1973 Monday
Tomorrow marks the centenary of the death of **David Livingstone** (1813-1873).
Mum & I watched this evening on television a programme called "**The Search for the Nile**" in which young **Henry Stanley** went in search of the elderly **Dr. Livingstone** & greeted him "**Dr. Livingstone I presume?**"

1st May 1973 Tuesday
In 1973 the May Day Bank Holiday was celebrated in Britain for the first time.

2nd May 1973 Wednesday
Went with a bus load from Coalville to see the Linwood Amateurs (Leicester) presentation of "**Fiddler on the Roof**" – a most enjoyable show, telling the story of a Jewish family in Russia in 1905. The simple faith, humanity & humour of "**Poppa**" stole the show as he tried to reason & make suggestions to God.

4th May 1973 Friday
Mum & I went with a bus load from Ravenstone Church to **Lichfield Cathedral**. After a conducted tour of the Cathedral, & tea at the Tudor Café, we had reserved seats in the choir for evensong. This Cathedral, which suffered more than any other in the Civil War, now has the most beautiful windows of all.

6th May 1973 Sunday
Yesterday was **Cup Final Day** when **2nd Division Sunderland** beat the mighty champions **Leeds** (last year's winners) 1 - 0.
Not since 1931, (the year I was born) when West

Bromwich Albion defeated Birmingham, has a 2nd Division side won the Cup.

8th May 1973 Tuesday
Received a letter from Department of the Environment, Swansea. "Dear Miss E. Hewes, I am writing to advise you that resulting from L.A. increment you are entitled to an additional responsibility allowance (A.R.A.). Your pay is accordingly assessed at £1,489 p.a. plus £99 p.a. A.R.A. with effect from 1st April 1973."

10th May 1973 Thursday
How lovely to see Mum so much improved over the past four months. No longer in the depths of despair, she is walking quite well now, although she dare not venture alone across the road. It seems that her illness is much affected by eating & we now endeavour to have the very best nutritious meals.

12th May 1973 Saturday
Yesterday we had **Fire Drill Number 3**. (See 11th June 1969 and 1st November 1972).
So soon after the last one! It really is quite impressive to see the whole of **County Hall** vacated in 2 minutes (customers included). I was relief cashier on the counter when the fire bell rang at 3 p.m., & being Friday we had quite an office full.

14th May 1973 Monday
Yesterday Cousin Audrey, Mum & I visited Auntie Cis in the **Wilfred Keene Clinic**. Although Auntie Cis was remarkably cheerful & made us all laugh, she said she was tired of living in an "**institution**" & would like to be discharged. But she cannot live alone & after a few weeks with the family nobody can cope with her.

16th May 1973 Wednesday
Found a magnificent book in the County Hall library – "The Tower of London in the History of the Nation". Filled with pictures, it tells the story of this three in one – this trinity of **fortress, palace & prison**, from the days of William the Conqueror, throughout all its turbulent history up to today.

18th May 1973 Friday
St. Michael & All Angels' Parish Church Ravenstone – 650th Anniversary Celebrations. The old walls of the Church heard music, the likes of which they had never heard before, when the **British College of Accordionists' Orchestra** gave a most impressive selection of lively marches & light music.

20th May 1973 Sunday
Aunt Dos, Mum & I were merrily motoring along to visit Auntie Cis when all of a sudden steam started erupting from the bonnet. With the help of a "Good Samaritan", who happened to be at hand, the trouble was soon diagnosed, & Minnehaha is now quite literally tied up with **red tape** on a leaking hose.

22nd May 1973 Tuesday
St. Michael & All Angels' Parish Church Ravenstone – 650th Anniversary Celebrations. More unusual music for the old walls to absorb, when the Salvation Army brought their own particular style of programme,

including lively tambourines; & we all joined in their singing & clapping "I want to live right ....."

24th May 1973 Thursday
Lord Jellicoe, who appeared in my diary 2 years ago (see 9th June 1971), today resigned as leader of the **House of Lords**, & **Lord Privy Seal**, whereby he was responsible for the **Civil Service**. Lord Jellicoe, aged 55, has been involved with certain call-girls whom the police have lately been watching.

26th May 1973 Saturday
Scotland Yard men were in pursuit of a major criminal gang involved in vice, pornography & such like, when by chance they learned that the most beautiful girls – models by day & prostitutes by night - lured the most eminent of men into their arms – men such as **Lord Lambton** & **Lord Jellicoe**.

28th May 1973 Bank Holiday Monday
Yesterday was Rogation Sunday, when the Bishop of Leicester led us in procession through the village to an open-air service in the fields. A most impressive service, & for his text the Bishop chose Psalm 115 v. 16 "The heaven, even the heavens, are the Lord's; but the earth hath He given to the children of men."

30th May 1973 Wednesday
A court circular dated yesterday from Buckingham Palace said, "It is with the greatest pleasure that the Queen & the Duke of Edinburgh announce the betrothal of their beloved daughter the **Princess Anne** to **Lieutenant Mark Phillips**, the Queen's Dragoon Guards, son of Mr. & Mrs. Peter Phillips.

1st June 1973 Friday
Tomorrow marks the 20th Anniversary of the Queen's Coronation. It is also the day appointed this year for "**Trooping the Colour**". The colour this year is that of the 1st Battalion Welsh Guards. So I am hoping to be off to London to see the Queen, & also the latest show "Joseph & the Amazing Technicolor Dreamcoat."

3rd June 1973 Sunday
What a glorious day yesterday for "**The Troop**". Starting from Hyde Park corner, I walked with all the Queen's horses & all the Queen's men to Buckingham Palace. Later, in the Mall, I had my best ever view of the whole procession.
Visited Westminster Abbey, then by river to the **Tower**.

5th June 1973 Tuesday
Coalville Amateur Operatic Society's Annual General Meeting.
Having completed 25 years with the society, I announced my decision not to be in the next production "**Maritza**". Rehearsals start in September & the show commences 5th March 1974.

7th June 1973 Thursday
Election Day for our new "District" councils. The new **Leicestershire** is divided into 9 new districts & we are in District Number One called North West Leicestershire. This covers the former Ashby-de-la-Zouch Urban District & Rural District, Coalville Urban

District, Castle Donington Rural District & Ibstock. Population 70,898.

9th June 1973 Saturday

Today I bought a new clock – a very smart "Metamec" battery clock, which now has pride of place over our new fireplace. (See 3rd November 1972).

Having ordered a new car this year, I am not planning a summer holiday. However, Enid & I have arranged to have one day's holiday in **London** on 20th July.

11th June 1973 Monday

Yesterday was Whit Sunday & at church in the evening we had a service of 9 lessons on the theme of the Holy Spirit. I was very pleased to read the 7th lesson which was about the "harvest" of the spirit, words which I learned from the Provost of Leicester at the 1966 Harvest Festival. (See also 26th February 1973).

13th June 1973 Wednesday

It was announced from Buckingham Palace today that Princess Anne & Lt. Mark Phillips will be married at Westminster Abbey on the morning of Wednesday November 14th. The service will be conducted by the Archbishop of Canterbury, Dr. Michael Ramsey, who will be 69 that day. Prince Charles also will be 25 that very day.

15th June 1973 Friday

St. Michael & All Angels' Parish Church Ravenstone – 650th Anniversary Celebrations. Tomorrow we have a bus load from church going to Southwell Minster & Lincoln Cathedral. At 10 a.m. we have a conducted tour of Southwell Minster – then to Lincoln for lunch, & at 2-30 p.m. a conducted tour of Lincoln Cathedral.

17th June 1973 Sunday

Mum & I went to Leicester Cathedral this morning to a "**county**" service attended by the Lord Lieutenant of Leicestershire Col. Martin, the chairman of the Leicestershire County Council Col. Lloyd, Mr Blackburn the County Treasurer & many others.

Mr Sharp (my boss) while taking the collection lost the plate!

Note – Mum managed to go with me to Leicester Cathedral to the "County" service. Mr Sharp, my boss, was one of several taking the collection. He lost the plate as it made its own way along the rows of people.

19th June 1973 Tuesday

Auntie Cis's birthday, 81 today. Pat & Evelyn, Aunt Dos & I visited Auntie Cis at the Wilfred Keene Clinic. Auntie Cis, in a little bedroom of her own, was able to entertain her guests privately. It was very sad to see her surrounded by birthday cards & gifts & yet too old & frail to have a really happy birthday.

21st June 1973 Thursday

Poor old Auntie Cis has tumbled out of bed, broken her leg, & is now in Leicester Royal Infirmary. Poor old Auntie Belle is just recovering from shingles. Poor old Anne Causer has just returned from hospital, having had a gland removed, but is far from well. And oh, how ill the Bishop of Leicester now looks.

23rd June 1973 Saturday

Last Saturday at Lincoln Cathedral, I bought an authentic replica on antiqued parchment of "**Magna Carta**", an English translation of the Magna Carta of King John, A.D. 1215. Twelve copies were originally sealed, but today only 4 remain. The best one & most clearly legible is now in Lincoln Cathedral.

25th June 1973 Monday

Yesterday was our Sunday School Anniversary. A beautiful day, bright with sunshine, & the children looking like little angels – 12 of mine & 20 of Susan's. The children sang well – more of the latest hit songs. Jessica played the piano, 3 little girls played recorders, 2 little boys read prayers, & the children took the collection.

27th June 1973 Wednesday

Aunt Dos & I visited Auntie Cis in the Leicester Royal Infirmary. She was in the Fielding Johnson Ward, where most of the patients lay in bed with one leg hoisted up, or the bed itself hoisted up. How sad it is to be old & ill. I felt so sorry for Auntie Cis – so utterly alone, & with so little joy left on earth for her.

29th June 1973 Friday

1966 Mini deluxe with radio, lady owner, £250. – Phone Coalville 3582.

The advertisement for Minnehaha brought forth 8 phone calls. Seven were from local Leicestershire men, & one was from an Indian living in Leicester. Naturally, I was most interested in the Indian – after all, was not Longfellow's Minnehaha a Dacotah Indian?

1st July 1973 Sunday

Mum & I took Minnehaha to Leicester to meet the Indian who was interested in buying her. He was a shopkeeper, aged about 50, & was enquiring for his son, aged 23, who was in London. He had a brother, who was a mechanic, & he inspected the car, declaring it a worthy car; but the son really wanted a newer car.

3rd July 1973 Tuesday

Swanwick, Phyllis Mary, 31 Leicester Road, Ravenstone, dearly loved wife of Geoffrey, loving mother of Michael and Gill, dear Nana of Deana, Debbie and Joanne, passed peacefully away on July 3rd. Funeral service at St. Michael's Church, Ravenstone, on Monday July 9th at 10 a.m. followed by cremation at Loughborough.

5th July 1973 Thursday

Aunt Dos & I visited Auntie Cis in Leicester City General Hospital. She has just been moved there for intensive observation, & is in such a luxurious new wing, in a room of her own. She has so many things wrong with her, including thrombosis, diabetes, weak heart, but they are giving her every care.

7th July 1973 Saturday

Sold Minnehaha, at 66,666 miles for £200 cash to Hasmukh H. Thakerar, aged 23.

He was the perfect match for **Minnehaha**, a veritable **Hiawatha**, with long jet black hair, & the most beautiful dark eyes – "Wayward as the Minnehaha, with her moods of shade & sunshine, eyes that smiled & frowned alternate."

9th July 1973 Monday
Took delivery of my beautiful new car **KAY 7L** – total £963-11p.
This was thanks entirely to Mum providing £800, & Poppa Indian giving me £200 cash for dear old Minnehaha. The car salesman shook my hand & wished me "Happy motoring", & a little booklet inside the car wished me "Safe & happy motoring."

11th July 1973 Wednesday
Went with 8 Sunday School children – Lynn Brooks, Jessica Willars, Diane Kendrick, Andrea & Adrian Dickinson, Karen & Ian Groocock & Ian Hawkins, to the Rex Cinema at Coalville to see Cecil B. De Mille's epic 4 hour film "**The Ten Commandments**", showing Moses the conquering hero bringing home the spoils of Ethiopia, just like **Radames**.(See 19th Nov 1972)

13th July 1973 Friday
Tomorrow is my birthday – aged 42. So, it is 21 years since my first love – **Cocky** – gave me my **Parker 51** fountain pen, which faithfully records my diary.
Cocky now lives in Lancashire, so I never see him, & rarely give him a thought.
Brian Lamming, however, is still in my thoughts.

15th July 1973 Sunday
Auntie Belle, Aunt Dos & I visited Auntie Cis in the City General Hospital, Leicester.
We found her in bed, with a doctor & a male nurse attending to her. She looked very, very ill & could hardly speak, but oh, how kind they were to her – called her "Darling", & gave her every possible loving attention.

17th July 1973 Tuesday
Diameter of Moon = 6 x 6 x 60 miles
Diameter of Sun = 12 x 12 x 6000 miles
Diameter of Earth = 12 x 660 miles
Speed of Earth round Sun = 66,600 m.p.h.
Distance between Earth & Moon
= 6 x 60 x 660 miles
On the 6th day, God's creation was complete.

19th July 1973 Thursday
A day in London! Enid & I caught the 7-35 a.m. train from Leicester to London. Visited the Old Curiosity Shop, then to Buckingham Palace for a grand stand view of the changing of the guard. Lunch in the park, listening to the band – a river trip – a 2 hour bus ride, & finally "The Black & White Minstrel Show".

21st July 1973 Saturday
Having reached the age of 6 x 7, it is appropriate that my latest book from County Hall Library is "**City of Revelation**" by John Michell.
In it he explains the mysteries of all numbers, & interprets the meaning of all measurements quoted in the Bible. Mortal things compare with 6, the happy & blessed things with 7.

23rd July 1973 Monday
Ever fascinated by the meaning of numbers, I am pleased to learn that my number 7 is the number of things sacred & mysterious. There are 7 stars in the **Great Bear**, 7 notes in music, 7 colours of the rainbow, 7 petals on the temple flower the pomegranate, 7 veils of initiation, & God rested on the 7th day. (Genesis 2. 2.)

25th July 1973 Wednesday
Guess what's coming next! The biggest & brightest comet ever recorded is heading towards **Earth**. Named **Kohoutek**, after Lubos Kohoutek, a German astronomer who first spotted it last December, it is expected to arrive in full glory next Christmas. It should be ten times brighter than any previous comet.

27th July 1973 Friday
Comet Kohoutek is a total stranger, & it will probably be thousands of years before it reappears. The most famous comet known to man is **Halley's Comet**, which is due to return in 1986 after a 77 year orbit round the **Sun**. The Leicester Mercury now has a special feature called "Mercury Nightview".

29th July 1973 Sunday
At church tonight we were given the text from Isaiah, Chap. 41, verse 10.
Divided into 7 – one part for each day of the coming week: 1.Fear thou not 2. For I am with thee 3. Be not dismayed 4. For I am thy God 5. I will strengthen thee 6. Yea, I will help thee 7. Yea, I will uphold thee with the right hand of my righteousness.

31st July 1973 Tuesday
Hasmukh phoned to say he would be coming to see me because he wanted me to get a new car tax for Minnehaha.
How lovely then, at 9 p.m. to see Minnehaha, complete with Hasmukh & his married friend, & his married friend's little 4 year old son. He was an absolute little darling.

2nd August 1973 Thursday
Mum & I went to Hasmukh's house to take the new car tax for Minnehaha. We were well entertained by Hasmukh & his vivacious 18 year old sister. While Poppa served in the shop, we drank Indian tea, ate Indian savouries, & looked at lots & lots of photos. Momma was out for the day, but we met their old granny.

4th August 1973 Saturday
Hasmukh has 2 married sisters who live in East Africa; & it was photographs of their weddings which we saw this week. Bedecked & garlanded, with jewels, coloured paint, & in their finest array, we saw Poppa & Momma showering them with gifts & blessings; & bride & bridegroom joined together in one entwined garland.

6th August 1973 Monday
Minnehaha is being well cared for by her Hiawatha. She has a new mirror – a new petrol cap – new red mats – a new cover for the steering wheel, & is about to be fitted out with a stereo tape recorder. There is no doubt about it – if I were 20 years younger I would most certainly fall for this handsome Hiawatha myself.

8th August 1973 Wednesday

Remember all the Indians who arrived in Leicester from Uganda last year? (See 17-8-1972) Well, Hasmukh came to England about 3 years ago; but we have in our office one named Jasvant, who is a Ugandan Asian, & he is very interested to hear all about Hasmukh.

Now Jasvant has invited me to his home next week.

10th August 1973 Friday

When Enid & I visited London last month, I bought a chart "**Kings & Queens of England**". This chart of absorbing interest was on sale at the shop belonging to the Department of the Environment – 7 ½ p. I have now paid £5-35p to have this 7 ½ p chart framed, & the picture looks very impressive hanging on a plain wall.

12th August 1973 Sunday

Aunt Dos & I visited Auntie Cis at Leicester City General Hospital & found her much improved.

We then called at Markfield, on Aunt Dos's life-long friends "**Bomb**" & "**Doll**", now almost 80. "Bomb" was a soldier in the 1914-18 war & has a wealth of wonderful memories. As a child he met Queen Victoria.

14th August 1973 Tuesday

From good old County Hall library I now have a most enlightening book on **Kenya**. Once described as "**God's own country with the Devil's own problems**" this paradise, which lies astride the equator on the east coast of Africa, attracts many tourists with its wild life, scenery & climate. **Nairobi**, the capital, is 4000 miles from London.

16th August 1973 Thursday

Our Sunday School outing this year is to be **Windsor**, on August 25th. We leave Ravenstone by coach at 7-30 a.m. & travel as far as **Maidenhead**. Then by river – dear old Father Thames – down to the mighty sea, sailing as far as Windsor, hoping to arrive in time for lunch. We then leave Windsor at 5-30 p.m.

18th August 1973 Saturday

Little did I think a year ago that I would be taking afternoon tea with a family of Ugandan Asians in their own home. Jasvant, from our office, invited me to meet his mother & father, his wife, & his teenage brothers – Kishor, Kaushik & Hitesh. Jasvant also has a married sister living in Kenya.

20th August 1973 Monday

Figures show that during the last 10 years Britain has admitted 750,000 coloured immigrants & many more are expected.

The Kenya Government right now is speeding up the compulsory Africanisation of Asian businesses & throwing more & more Asians out of work. All these Asians are likely to come to Britain.

22nd August 1973 Wednesday

You would never believe it! I have been stung again by a wasp!

1969 on my leg. 1970 on my face. And now on the index finger of my right hand. All I did was go to the shop – pick up a loaf of bread - & there lurking on the loaf was a wasp.

How well I know those words – "**The sting is in the tail**".

24th August 1973 Friday

Went to **Skegness** with Pat, Evelyn & Aunt Dos. Auntie Cis's bungalow in Skegness is about to be sold, & Pat is in charge of affairs. While the estate agent spent the afternoon talking business with Pat, Evelyn & Aunt Dos, I had a lovely time sitting in a deck-chair on the pier, enjoying the sea & sun.

26th August 1973 Sunday

How very fortunate we were with weather for our Sunday School outing yesterday – sunshine all day long. My companion for the day was Helen Tovell (who is my age), & we chose to spend the afternoon at the **Royal Windsor Safari Park**. How lovely to see lions, tigers, cheetahs etc. with acres & acres of space.

28th August 1973 Tuesday

All the treasures from Aunt Cis's bungalow in Skegness arrived in a furniture van & were unloaded at Ravenstone – half into Pat's house & half into Aunt Dos's bungalow.

I was given the very nice bird-bath from the garden, & also a silver dish presented to Aunt Cis by the boys at school in Form 4B.

30th August 1973 Thursday

I am currently engrossed in writing a poem in Leicestershire dialect for an open competition promoted by the **East Midlands Arts Association**. The poem is to consist of approximately 50 lines, & there is a prize of £30 for the winner. Closing date is 31st October, so I have another 2 months.

1st September 1973 Saturday

Had a super shopping spree in Leicester. Bought a very smart brown leather hand-bag – a very smart pair of matching shoes & a pair of brown gloves. That is all I can afford for the time being. Next item on the agenda is a mink hat – then I would like a record player, & an office desk for my type-writer.

3rd September 1973 Monday

Samuel Pepys wrote of the "**Great Fire of London**" in September 1666, how it started on September 2nd (Lord's Day) & raged for 4 days ..... "But Lord! What a sad sight it was by moonlight, to see the whole City almost, on fire, that you might see it as plain at Woolwich as if you were by it."

5th September 1973 Wednesday

£1,700 per year! How about that? Received a most welcome letter from the Department of the Environment addressed to Miss E. Hewes on loan to Leics. C.C. ".... Resulting from L.A. pay award your A.R.A. has been revised. Your pay is accordingly £1,601 plus £99 A.R.A. with effect from 1st July 1973.

Note – I am at present a Civil Servant "on loan to Leics. C.C." Gradually, over the next few years, our work-load will change dramatically as the Government takes over control of all Driving Licence & Vehicle Licence records in one huge centre at Swansea.

7th September 1973 Friday
St. Michael & All Angels' Parish Church Ravenstone – 650th Anniversary Celebrations.
Rose Festival, September 7th, 8th, & 9th. How very beautiful the church looks today with roses roses everywhere. Also nearby is an exhibition of old local items of interest (plus my "Kings & Queens of England").

9th September 1973 Sunday
Auntie Cis has given me her new Bible, first published 1970. This is an up to date translation "**The New English Bible**", & was a gift to her "**With love and best wishes from Mark, Christmas 1970.**"
I have "**The New English Bible**" – **New Testament** only, which was first published 1961, so I am delighted to have it complete.

11th September 1973 Tuesday
"**An Armchair Voyage Round the World**". This is a series of 10 talks, illustrated with colour slides, by Mr. J.A.Brooks, & is offered as one of the night-school projects at Glenfield Junior School. So I have paid £1-30p to enrol as a member of the class. We shall set sail on our voyage next Monday.

13th September 1973 Thursday
Marjorie Hayes, aged 42, my life-long neighbour, today married **George Merrill**, so we are now living next door to an empty house. Then we have Mr. Swanwick, living all alone; & then another empty house. Also our magnificent house in the grounds of the Hollies is up for sale. So it's new neighbours all round.

15th September 1973 Saturday
The Crown Jewels! A display of replicas of the Crown Jewels was shown at Stoughton church with their flower festival. The whole theme was the Majesty of the King of Heaven – truly regal splendour. Saw the priceless royal crowns – the sceptre and orb, the magnificent swords, & the ampulla & spoon for anointing.

17th September 1973 Monday
Our voyage round the world began this evening at **Durban**, **South Africa**, where we had sailed to from Southampton. We motored inland & spent most of our time "**on safari**" looking at delightful animals in their own natural surroundings. Our journey took us inland as far as **Johannesburg**.

19th September 1973 Wednesday
Our voyage round the world will obviously omit far more of the world than ever it will cover. We hope to see a little more of South Africa, then off to the far East – across the Indian Ocean: then down to Australia – to New Zealand & across the Pacific to the west coast of North America: through the Panama Canal & home.

21st September 1973 Friday
Having begun our voyage round the world at South Africa, I now have a book from the library "**Let's Visit South Africa**". From this book I learn that the province of **Natal**, facing the Indian Ocean, was named by the Portuguese navigator **Vasco da Gama** who first sighted it on Christmas day 1497. "**Terra Natalis**".

23rd September 1973 Sunday
Have now completed the outline of my latest poem (in Leicestershire dialect).
Prince Charles once said of Leicester "Oh, that's the place with slag heaps!" In my poem therefore, I escort him personally round all the beauty spots between Leicester & Coalville, giving him a history lesson at the same time.

25th September 1973 Tuesday
Visited every town in South Africa going from Johannesburg to **Pretoria** where we saw the enormous memorial to the original Dutch settlers who made the **Great Trek** inland with ox-wagons. Saw the biggest hole in the world at Kimberley diamond mine, & finished up at **Cape Town** & **Table Mountain**.

27th September 1973 Thursday
Samuel Pepys went to the King's Theatre on September 29th 1662 & saw "Midsummer Night's Dream". His opinion of the play was this: - "To the King's Theatre, where we saw Midsummer's Night's Dream, which I had never seen before, nor shall ever again, for it is the most insipid ridiculous play that ever I saw in my life."

29th September 1973 Saturday
Next year on April 19th a party from Coalville Church (Young Wives Group) are hoping to spend a 6 day holiday in Rome. Enid & I have been asked if we would like to join them.
So now I am looking forward to seeing **Rome**! I have never been any further than the Channel Islands.

1st October 1973 Monday
Crossed the Indian Ocean from South Africa to **Malaya** & **Singapore**. Saw a mixture of Victorian – Gothic – Chinese buildings. Saw bananas growing – rubber trees & dense, dense jungle. Penetrated by river, deep into the heart of the forest, to find a real safari hide-out.

3rd October 1973 Wednesday
Mr. Brooks, who is taking us on our "Armchair Voyage Round the World", makes a most interesting guide. He talks non-stop for 2 hours (with a 15 minute break for coffee). The 2 places in the whole world which impressed him most were Cambodia & the Grand Canyon. Next week we go to Cambodia.

5th October 1973 Friday
Three American astronauts have recently returned to Earth after a record 60 days in space. (See July 3rd & July 5th 1971). Doctors say the astronauts lost 12% of their red blood cells & 20% of their blood plasma. Medical findings may affect long distance space plans.

7th October 1973 Sunday
The gilt-edged invitations to next month's royal wedding have now been dispatched. Beneath the royal crown, beneath E II R, "The Lord Chamberlain is Commanded by the Queen & the Duke of Edinburgh to invite …… to the Marriage of Her Royal Highness the Princess Anne with Captain Mark Phillips, 1st Dragoon Guards."

9th October 1973 Tuesday
Visited **Cambodia**! Why did this rate with the **Grand**

Canyon as the most impressive place in the world? Answer: - The colossal temples & shrines, both Hindu & Buddist. Having learned the mystery of all numbers & measurements (See 21st July 1973), I was intrigued to see these ancient temples of perfect symmetry.

11th October 1973 Thursday
Confirmation Service at Ravenstone Church. We had 9 candidates including 4 from my Sunday School class – Karen Groocock, Diane Kendrick, Andrea Dickinson & Joanne Hibbitt. An inspiring service & the Bishop chose for his address the 9-fold fruit of the spirit. 1.Love, 2.Joy, 3.Peace, 4.Patience, 5.Kindness, 6.Goodness, 7.Fidelity, 8.Gentleness, 9.Self-control.

13th October 1973 Saturday
Enid does not wish to visit Rome, but I have accepted the invitation.
The tour begins with a drive down the Appian Way into the heart of Rome. Then see the Roman Forum & the Colosseum. Day 2, visit the Vatican City. Day 3, free. Day 4, drive south. Day 5, visit Hadrian's Villa. Day 6, home.

15th October 1973 Monday
Our journey this evening took us to **Hong Kong** & then by boat for 11 days through all the islands down to Australia, where we landed at Sydney.
We have 23 people in the class, including a couple named Mr & Mrs Polkey, who told me they have been to **Rome**. They loaned me lots of slides & pictures of **Rome**.

17th October 1973 Wednesday
I have now completed 25 years in the **Motor Licence Office**. Much has improved in a quarter of a century. Shorter working hours (we used to work every Saturday morning). To work now in my own car (instead of by bus). The office moved nearer home; & much more money, from £150 p.a. in 1948 to £1,700 p.a. now.

19th October 1973 Friday
Keir Handford, brilliant pianist, who has played for **Coalville Amateur Operatic Society** for the past 20 years, died suddenly this evening while at a friend's house for tea. He was 64 years of age, & due to retire next February. A shattering blow for Coalville Amateurs.

21st October 1973 Sunday
Formosissimus Annus – The most charming period of the year. (According to Ovid, the autumn; according to Virgil, the spring). As I motored through all the loveliest lanes of Charnwood Forest, ablaze with autumn glory, I knew that my old friend Ovid was right.
(See 25th January 1969).

23rd October 1973 Tuesday
From Sydney, S.E. Australia, we took the coast road up to N.E. Australia, where all kinds of parrots lived wild in the trees. Sailed across the clear Coral Sea, visited a coral island & through a glass bottomed boat saw the treasures under the sea; & then returned by land to Sydney.

25th October 1973 Thursday
In case you are wondering what has happened to my writing, let me hasten to explain. I now have my right arm in plaster. In fact, I can hardly write properly at all. What did I do?
Fell over the garden fork & landed wallop on the concrete slabs in the garden.

27th October 1973 Saturday
Walk through the village with your arm in plaster, & all who are nodding acquaintances suddenly become big buddies, wanting to know what you have done; & then proceeding to give a detailed account of when they broke an arm or a leg. So it makes life much more matey, & a nice holiday.

29th October 1973 Monday
From Sydney, S.E. Australia, we took the coast road south, through Melbourne as far as Adelaide. We saw dear little koala bears asleep in the trees, & went inland to the top of the snow capped mountains. Adelaide was beautifully symmetric, exactly one mile square. Saw the new Sydney Opera House, opened very recently.

31st October 1973 Wednesday
The plaster on my right arm was put on at Burton-on-Trent Hospital, & I have my next appointment with the doctor there on November 12th. So I am away from work all this week & next. Actually my left arm hurts more than my right & I have not been able to drive the car all week.

2nd November 1973 Friday
Aunt Dos, aged 71, has been my valued chauffeur all week. She has taken me to Burton-on-Trent, to Loughborough & Leicester. Today in Leicester I bought a biscuit barrel, £3-49p.
What I cannot do at the moment is fasten my bra, carry weighty bags, or unscrew jar lids.

4th November 1973 Sunday
Our proposed holiday in Rome next April is off – cancelled through lack of support.
But not to worry. I have seen enough pictures & read enough literature on Rome, that it is almost as though I have actually been. Perhaps one day I shall go. At the moment, I cannot really afford to go in proper style.

6th November 1973 Tuesday
Ventured, driving the car, to Bradgate Park, where Mum & I enjoyed watching the swans on the water & the deer scampering about up & down the craggy slopes, where the ancient oaks still looked a picture of autumnal beauty. Our latest threat is the possibility of petrol rationing as a result of conflict in the Middle East.

8th November 1973 Thursday
Margaret, who has travelled with me to County Hall since January 1971, today celebrated her 21st birthday & on Saturday is to be married. She will then be living at Ashby-de-la-Zouch.
But of course THE wedding of the year is to be next Wednesday – the wedding of Princess Anne.

10th November 1973 Saturday
I am now writing with my arm out of plaster & hope to return to work next week after a most enjoyable fortnight's "holiday".
Remember the bird bath which we acquired in August from Aunt Cis's bungalow in Skegness? Well, it is really lovely to see the bigger birds literally queuing up for a good old splash.

12th November 1973 Monday
Last Monday we had a break from our journey round the world so tonight was Episode No. 8. Sailing from Sydney we crossed to New Zealand.
Visited "Glow Worm Cave", into the depths of a cave by boat to see the glow worms shining as the stars in heaven. Saw a volcanic mountain erupting, & went trout fishing.

14th November 1973 Wednesday
The Wedding of the Year!!
Her Royal Highness Anne Elizabeth Alice Louise aged 23, married Mark Anthony Peter Phillips, aged 25.
A day of brilliant sunshine, & a real fairy tale wedding with the lovely bride in a glass coach drawn by 4 white horses, & a right royal procession.

16th November 1973 Friday
Princess Anne is now on honeymoon in the Caribbean. She & Captain Mark Phillips flew from London 3,750 miles to Barbados, where they boarded the Royal Yacht Britannia.
On 4th December after 3 days at the Galapagos Islands, they officially visit Ecuador, Colombia, Jamaica, Montserrat & Antigua.

18th November 1973 Sunday
Our Armchair Voyage round the World is supposed to take 10 evenings to complete, but as we have already had 8 evenings & are still only halfway round the world we have been granted an extension.
We now have one extra evening, but even so, it will be "Full Steam Ahead."

20th November 1973 Tuesday
How beautiful is the South Island of New Zealand! Arrived in winter to a veritable Winter Wonderland – mountains & fiords, a mixture of Norway & Switzerland, all reflected in lakes like mirrors, & the world's most amazing glaciers, Fox Glacier & Franz Josef Glacier, & wonderful sunsets.

22nd November 1973 Thursday
From New Zealand made a quick 7,000 mile dash by boat across the Pacific, as far north as Vancouver, calling at Tonga in the Friendly Islands, & Hawaiian Islands, where we left the big ship "Canberra" at anchor & sailed ashore in the lifeboats, as if shipwrecked.

24th November 1973 Saturday
Our annual Christmas Fair in Ravenstone Village Institute, & our second effort with a stall for the Sunday School. This year we bought nothing. We had lots left from last year, plus various items brought by the children, & managed to produce a goodly display. The children manned the stall & took over £12.

26th November 1973 Monday
Sailed under the Golden Gate suspension bridge into San Francisco.
Visited California's groves of redwoods, & saw the tallest trees in the world. More than 2,700 years old, these conifers reached 367 feet.
Visited smog-bound Los Angeles & gaudy Las Vegas lit up all through the night & buzzing with casinos & gambling.

28th November 1973 Wednesday
Stood on the brink of the Grand Canyon.
"Whoever stands upon the brink of the Grand Canyon beholds a spectacle unrivalled on this earth." This was the high-light of our armchair voyage round the world. This was a spectacle of majesty, of ornate sculpture, & such vastness – the Grand Canyon of the Colorado.

30th November 1973 Friday
Four Russian space-craft are now heading for the planet Mars, hoping to get our first television pictures in close-up. Two will arrive in February & two in April.
Pictures taken 2 years ago by the circling American Mariner 9 showed huge chasms three times the size of the Grand Canyon!
Mariner 10 is off to Venus & Mercury.

2nd December 1973 Sunday
Mariner 10 hopes to be within camera range of Venus on February 5th 1974. All previous probes have been frizzled up by the planet's sizzling heat.
The longest space journey attempted so far is to the planet Jupiter, & space-craft Pioneer 10 is due to arrive tomorrow, after a journey lasting 21 months.

4th December 1973 Tuesday
Our voyage round the world finished with a journey through Mexico. Here we saw the remains of that great empire founded by the Aztecs, with colossal pyramids, & everywhere a mixture of Indian & Spanish influence.
Spain conquered this land in 1519 A.D. – the conquistadors!

6th December 1973 Thursday
Feisal Abdul Aziz al-Saud, King of Kings, ruler of Saudi Arabia, aged 67, has sent Sheik Ahmed Yamani, the Saudi Arabian Minister for oil, to London to explain their situation. Either we assist the Arabs, in getting the Israelis to withdraw from occupied Arab territory, or we in Britain get no oil.

8th December 1973 Saturday
Not only King Feisal, but all the oil sheiks of the Middle East have decided to cut their supplies of oil to the mighty western lands, whose wheels of fortune depend entirely on oil. Our country is now in a state of emergency. As the wheels of industry grind to a halt we must economise on petrol & cut down electricity.

10th December 1973 Monday
Mum & I went to the De Montfort Hall Leicester, & for the 2nd time saw & heard an absolutely super performance by the massed bands, corps of drums, & pipes & drums of the Guards Division. (See 19th April 1972) We sang Christmas carols with them, &

thoroughly enjoyed their musical fantasy "The Battle of Waterloo".

12th December 1973 Wednesday

Deep inside a mountain, north of Bogota in Colombia, South America, Princess Anne this week saw the "Cathedral of Salt" built in a huge cavern. Her husband Mark missed this highlight of the visit as he had gastro-enteritis. Princess Anne described this salt mine as one of the most impressive sights she had ever seen.

14th December 1973 Friday

Mr William Whitelaw, Secretary of State for Northern Ireland, (see 26th March 1972), has now handed over his hot seat to Mr Francis Pym.

The hot blooded Irish continue to plant bombs, & refuse to agree to any sort of compromise, but now we have other troubles of our own, & Mr Whitelaw is needed as Employment Minister.

16th December 1973 Sunday

Apart from the oil sheiks cutting our supplies of oil, we have industrial unrest amongst the miners, the railwaymen & the engineers.

As fuel stocks dwindle, drastic economies have been ordered by the government. The Prime Minister, Mr Edward Heath, spoke gravely to the nation, & warned us to **BEWARE**.

18th December 1973 Tuesday

In this country there are 94,000 registered charities, & about this time of the year, just before Christmas, they invite you to give them some money. It is impossible to support them all, so we select our top ten. Mum's number one is "The Donkey Sanctuary" & my number one is "The Shaftsbury Society" founded in 1844.

20th December 1973 Thursday

Because of the oil crisis, & men forever demanding more & more money, we have now toppled over the brink of inflation. Drastic cuts everywhere are now being enforced.

Next year £1,200 million is to be knocked off government spending, & we must work only 3 days a week to minimise the use of electricity.

22nd December 1973 Saturday

An evening with Reevsie, Tony & Joanne. Joanne, now aged 6, has recently learned to swim. She has lessons once a week at the swimming baths in Leicester & I went to see her at her lesson. She is a big girl for her age, & quite a handful, being very strong willed.

Reevsie's brother Ken married earlier this month.

24th December 1973 Monday

Anne Causer cannot spend Christmas with Mum & me this year because she is very ill.

She was taken to Leicester Royal Infirmary today because she is too sick to be left in her flat all alone.

Auntie Cis has recently transferred from Leicester City General Hospital to the Ava Private Nursing Home in Leicester.

26th December 1973 Wednesday

Mum & I went to Leicester Cathedral yesterday where the Bishop introduced us to Tennyson's moving poem "In Memoriam", written in memory of his dear friend Arthur Hallam, who died in Vienna in 1833. In these dark days he quoted: "O Father, touch the east, and light the light that shone when hope was born."

28th December 1973 Friday

The Bishop also cheered us on our way with words from Psalm 112 (New English Bible version) "Happy is the man who fears the Lord, & finds great joy in His commandments …. Nothing shall ever shake him ….. Bad news shall have no terrors for him, because his heart is steadfast, trusting in the Lord."

30th December 1973 Sunday

And so ends our first year as members of the European Community.

Not altogether "A Happy, Prosperous, & Peaceful Year". The Irish are anything but peaceful; & the conflict between Arabs & Jews has given us our oil crisis, with the price of oil & petrol likely to be doubled.

And poor Anne Causer is dying.

* * *

1974

1st January 1974 Tuesday
Starting this year, January 1st is now a Bank Holiday. So many people stay up late to see the New Year in that they have been absent without leave on January 1st. It has been decided therefore to make this leave official, & have a public holiday, rather than trying to cope with massive absenteeism.

3rd January 1974 Thursday
Anne Causer, friend of our family for many years, died yesterday in the Leicester Royal Infirmary. Her funeral is to be next Wednesday, just 4 days before her birthday. Anne had already bought Christmas presents for Mum & me, & it was very sad to receive them this week – **after** she had died.

5th January 1974 Saturday
Mum & I had quite an adventure today when our new car **KAY 7L** conked out halfway up Bradgate Hill, Markfield, outside the magnificent residence of **Dr. Small**. We were welcomed into the house, given a cup of tea, & eventually rescued by my good friend **Alf**, who came to us from Ravenstone.

7th January 1974 Monday
Received by post a copy of the 27th Shaftsbury Lecture, given recently by Dr. F. D. Coggan, Archbishop of York. A most inspiring lecture, dealing with Earth's problems today – population explosion & pollution; & reminding us of Psalm 115 v.16 "The Heaven, even the heavens, are the Lord's; but the earth he hath given to the children of men."

9th January 1974 Wednesday
Mum & I motored in convoy behind Anne's funeral procession to Loughborough Crematorium.
The funeral was at 3p.m., & the setting sun over the wintry landscape reminded me of **Hiawatha**. "Thus departed Hiawatha, in the glory of the sunset, to the Islands of the Blessed, to the land of the Hereafter."

11th January 1974 Friday
All industry – factories, shops & offices are working a 3 day week. This is not from choice, but because the country is desperately short of fuel – oil, coal & electricity. This is the result of political unrest in the Middle East, & our own miners continually on strike. We are therefore at work Thursdays & Fridays without lighting.

13th January 1974 Sunday
If the 3 day week lasts until the spring, it could mean **National Bankruptcy**. We have now reached the stage in this country where the government can hardly govern, because of lack of co-operation from those being governed – especially the all-powerful **Trade Unions** – a real & serious threat to Britain's heritage.

15th January 1974 Tuesday
Abraham Lincoln said: - (16th October 1854) "No man is good enough to govern another man without that other's consent." And that is the position we find our country in today. We face the prospects of a "Who governs the country?" election. It all rests now with the Union leaders. Will they be governed or not?

17th January 1974 Thursday
What entertainment does television offer during these gloomy months of national & economic crisis? Answer – **Othello**. Mum & I watched a superb performance of this Shakespearean tragedy, starring Laurence Olivier in the title role. What a story! Poor **Othello** driven to distraction, & smothering his wife **Desdemona**.

19th January 1974 Saturday
Comet Kohoutek, first spotted a year ago & scheduled to arrive in full glory this month, has been & gone without so much as much twinkle as a star. What an anticlimax.
This was supposed to be the biggest & brightest comet ever recorded, & expected to be ten times brighter than any previous comet.

21st January 1974 Monday
Poor old **Great Britain** is not feeling very great at the moment. Last year we had an adverse balance of trade of £2,348 million. That means in 1973, for each household, we exported from Britain £610, & we imported from abroad £735 worth of goods. Now we must **Bridge That Gap**.

23rd January 1974 Wednesday
Peter Walker, our trade & industry secretary, has told us how to bridge that gap: 1. Work harder.
2. Concentrate on exports. 3. Give priority to those investments which make our production more efficient & more competitive. 4. Try to reduce our need for expensive imports. 5. Replace imports with home produce.

25th January 1974 Friday
So what have the Union leaders to say in our days of economic crisis? Mr A. Scargill, president of the National Union of Miners says: - "I call on the whole of the trade union movement for a general strike." The miners are planning to strike with the train drivers & grind the country to a halt.

27th January 1974 Sunday
If we think **England** is in trouble, how about poor old **Brisbane**, the capital of **Queensland**, **Australia**? Yesterday a state of emergency was declared in **Brisbane**, Australia's third largest city, when floods followed a cyclone. The Premier of Queensland says, "The devastation is beyond comprehension."

29th January 1974 Tuesday
The good old Leicester Mercury is 100 years old today.
And good old Leicester has its own slogan in the present crisis, "Leicester will make it."

31st January 1974 Thursday
How very, very interesting to read the Centenary Souvenir Issue Leicester Mercury 1874-1974. From Gladstone to Heath. From Victoria to Elizabeth II. Looked at from further away, today's news is lost in all

the struggles and mighty achievements of other days.

2nd February 1974 Saturday
"**Biggs Arrested**". These are the headlines in today's morning paper. **Train Robber Ronald Arthur Biggs** was re-captured yesterday in **Rio de Janeiro**, following his dramatic escape from London's **Wandsworth** prison in July 1965. The Great Train Robbery £2 ½ million was in 1963.

4th February 1974 Monday
Scott MacLeod. Born January 29th 1974.
Scott is the latest addition to our family. A baby boy for **Mary Blue & Murdo**, & for the 3rd time I am a great-half-Aunt. As Auntie Cis (aged 81) declared when she heard the news, "**Great Scott!**"
He certainly belongs to a great clan, the MacLeods.

6th February 1974 Wednesday
With the miners now threatening an all-out strike, we are to have a General Election on 28th February. The present Parliament, whose full 5 year term was not due to expire until the middle of next year, is to be dissolved this week. The new Parliament will be opened on March 12th. This is a crisis election.

8th February 1974 Friday
And so the politicians prepare for battle. Each side continually belittles the other. The angry scenes inside the Houses of Parliament are disgraceful. Supposedly intelligent men behave more like children. One feels that they are not worthy of the magnificent building which houses them.

10th February 1974 Sunday
Church Army Mission Week at Ravenstone. This is intended to bring the children of the parish into church. At the moment I have 20 children in my class – aged 8 plus, & Susan has 20 children under 8 years. Two Church Army Sisters however, with the art of the Pied Piper, are bringing in the children by the dozens.

12th February 1974 Tuesday
Petrol goes up today from 42p to 50p per gallon. Our government taxes petrol so much (22p of the 42p is taxation) that the Middle East oil producers have decided that they might just as well charge more in the first place for their own oil.
Taxation on petrol alone brings our government £1,000 million per year.

14th February 1974 Thursday
Valentine's Day brought Cathedral News Letter No. 121, with news of the Provost's recent visit to Northern Nigeria: - "It was quite an experience to have the opportunity of meeting the Islamic Provost, the Imam of the old city of Zaria. To go to his mud house, & sit on a goat skin, surrounded by his Muslim elders."

16th February 1974 Saturday
The Provost continues: "Who could have believed that on a January evening I should be squatting there in an Arabian Nights' setting, expounding the Lord's Prayer to an Islamic audience, and part on good terms, hearing as once Paul heard of old at Athens, "We will hear thee

again of this matter."

18th February 1974 Monday
Next month at Olympia is the 51st Daily Mail Ideal Home Exhibition incorporating as part of its spectacle a re-creation of the **Hanging Gardens of Babylon** – one of the 7 wonders of the world. The hanging gardens soar to 75 feet in the Grand Hall – the height of the original. I shall endeavour to go & see them.

20th February 1974 Wednesday
A letter from **J. A. Chatterton**: -
"Parliamentary Election 1974, Loughborough Constituency. I have appointed you to act as a full-time Poll Clerk at this Election on Thursday 28th February 1974, at Polling Station No. 41, County School, Church Lane, Ravenstone. A fee of £7-50p will be paid." 7-00 a.m. – 10-00 p.m.

22nd February 1974 Friday
An amazing slip-up in statistics, revealed last night, is having untold effects today on the election campaign. Pay Board officials have proved that incorrect comparisons have inadvertently been quoted between wages of miners & of workers in other industries.
It all revolves round holiday pay, etc.

24th February 1974 Sunday
After months of being told that they were asking for too much, the miners have now been given the astonishing news that they have been asking for too little.
Because the miners could not have as much money as they felt they deserved, they went on strike, & a crisis election was called – next Thursday.

26th February 1974 Tuesday
January's trade figures plunged Britain another £383 million into the red. Our worst ever trade deficit, brought about chiefly by the rocketing cost of oil. This is the size of the problem facing our next government. Britain is already borrowing heavily in the Eurodollar market, & now goes to the International Monetary Fund.

28th February 1974 Thursday
Election Day! Spent a very pleasant 15 hours (from 7 a.m. to 10 p.m.) at Ravenstone School where the Presiding Officer – Mr K. Dobson from Loughborough, & I issued 971 ballot papers to the voters of Ravenstone. We had 1,110 on our list – many former Sunday School children, now of age – I hardly knew them.

1st March 1974 Friday
The election result has now created more problems than it has solved – almost a dead heat.
Labour 301, Conservative 296, Liberals 14, and 24 others including 10 United Ulster Unionists and 7 Scottish Nationalists. All now rests with the Liberals & the others. Will they support Labour, or the Conservatives?

3rd March 1974 Sunday
Today we have had the world's worst air disaster.
A giant DC 10 holiday jet, belonging to Turkish Airlines, flying from Istanbul to London via Paris, dived from a clear sky into Ermenonville Forest, 25 miles

north of Paris, just 9 minutes after take-off from Orly airport, killing all 345 people on board.

5th March 1974 Tuesday
The Conservatives are out, & we now have a Labour Government.
Prime Minister = Harold Wilson, Chancellor of the Exchequer = Denis Healey, Secretary for the Environment (my boss) = Anthony Crosland, Foreign Secretary = James Callaghan, Home Secretary = Roy Jenkins, top job of Employment Secretary = Michael Foot (to settle the miners).

6th March 1974 Wednesday
On this day in 1475, Michelangelo, Italian painter and sculptor, was born in Tuscany.

7th March 1974 Thursday
Maritza! Coalville Amateur Operatic Society's production is now in full swing.
This is the first year I have not been on stage after 25 consecutive years. However, I enjoyed selling programmes, wearing my smart orange coloured suit (bought May 1972 for interview) complete with 25 year medal.

9th March 1974 Saturday
Such excitement when I received the following letter –
"The Brigade Major Household Division refers to your application for tickets for the Queen's Birthday Parade and has pleasure in informing you that you have been allocated 2 tickets @ £2-20p each." These are for June 15th, Trooping the Colour.

11th March 1974 Monday
A day in London!
Visited the Daily Mail Ideal Home Exhibition at Olympia, where the Hanging Gardens of Babylon were little more than a painted backcloth – hardly one of the 7 wonders of the world.
So, back to Buckingham Palace, where I was in time to see the Queen returning from opening our new Parliament.

13th March 1974 Wednesday
While in London I went on an afternoon coach tour, which included a conducted tour inside St. Paul's Cathedral, & also inside the Tower of London. Saw so much detail I had never seen before & learned such a lot from a most knowledgeable guide.
And oh, how lovely to see St. James Park about to burst into spring.

15th March 1974 Friday
What impressed me most of all in London this week was Holman Hunt's picture of Christ, "The Light of the World" seen in St. Paul's Cathedral.
"Behold, I stand at the door, & knock; if any man hear my voice, & open the door, I will come in to him, & will sup with him, & he with me." Revelation 3. v 20.

17th March 1974 Sunday
St. Patrick's Day - & my dad's birthday. Born 85 years ago, & died at the age of 49.
What St. Patrick would think of the troubles in Ireland today, I do not know. Every day we hear of someone or another being shot dead, & this week the 968th person died – including 210 soldiers from England.

19th March 1974 Tuesday
Mary Blue's birthday. Today she is 30.
Mum & I visited Mrs Mould in the Private Ward at Ashby Hospital. Grace Mottram, the sister on night duty, took us on a conducted tour of the hospital, & showed us all the latest equipment, & also took us into the nursery to see the new-born babies.

21st March 1974 Thursday
"Bid to Kidnap Princess Anne"
These are the headlines in today's newspaper, following an attack on Princess Anne's car **NGN 1**, during which 4 people were shot – 1. The Princess's personal detective. 2. The chauffeur.
3. A uniformed policeman. 4. A passing taxi driver.
Princess Anne & Mark escaped unhurt.

23rd March 1974 Saturday
Mr Swanwick, our neighbour, today married his 2nd wife. His first wife died last July. So we shall be having more new neighbours. Mr Swanwick will be leaving to live at Whitwick. Our immediate next door neighbours will shortly be moving in – Mr & Mrs Keith Carter & 9 year old son Simon, to replace the Hayes family.

25th March 1974 Monday
Mum & I went to **Staunton Harold Cheshire Home** to hear the **Coalville Amateur Operatic Society** singing a selection from their latest show "**Maritza**". As always, the singing sounded rich & splendid in their lovely big room, & the dancing girls also did some lively dancing to the Hungarian gipsy music.

27th March 1974 Wednesday
Soon the dear little **County of Rutland** will be no more. With a population of only 27,000 it is to be swallowed up into Leicestershire.
On April 1st this year the great shake-up in Local Government becomes effective. 45 counties become 44 & 1,200 councils in England will be reduced to under 400.

29th March 1974 Friday
A letter from Department of the Environment, Vehicle Licensing Centre, Swansea, to Miss E. Hewes, on loan to Leicestershire County Council, "Dear Miss Hewes, I am writing to advise you that resulting from L.A.Increment, your additional responsibility allowance (A.R.A.) has been revised. Your pay is accordingly assessed at £1883 plus nil A.R.A. with effect from 1st April 1974.

31st March 1974 Sunday
To mark the re-organisation of Local Government in Leicestershire & Rutland, Mum & I went to Leicester Cathedral, to a "County Service" attended by all the county & city dignitaries. The first lesson, Isaiah 12, was read by the Chairman of Leicestershire County Council & the 2nd lesson, Romans 12, by the Chairman of the New Leicestershire County Council.

2nd April 1974 Tuesday
The New Leicestershire County Council, which came into force yesterday, replaces the one founded in 1888. The Bishop of Leicester, who launched us on our way, reminded us of Psalm 127 –
"Except the Lord build the house, they labour in vain that build it; except the Lord keep the city, the watchman waketh but in vain."

4th April 1974 Thursday
"Except the Lord keep the city ……."
Our city is Leicester; & now a marriage has taken place between the County of Leicester & the City of Leicester to include also dear little Rutland. Mum & I visited Oakham, in the County of Rutland, in its last days of belonging to Rutland, & how sad it was feeling.

6th April 1974 Saturday
"Leicester Will Make It"
Sadly, our slogan was lowered to half-mast & changed to "Leicester Didn't Quite Make It" when Liverpool beat Leicester 3-1 in the F.A. semi-final.
The F.A. Cup Final on May 4th will now be between Newcastle & Liverpool.
But we were gallant losers.

8th April 1974 Monday
A week's holiday, & what a glorious start! Not a cloud in the sky, & warm enough to sun-bathe.
Am hoping to cut all the grass, both at home & in the church-yard, ready for Easter.
Also having a good old Spring Clean – clearing out the garden shed, & clearing out the coal-house.

10th April 1974 Wednesday
The delightful holiday weather continues – **"Oh, to be in England, now that April's there"**
I have chosen these lines of Robert Browning for the Ravenstone Parish Magazine this month & the month is doing them full justice.
My favourite poem by Robert Browning is **"Saul"**.

12th April 1974 Good Friday
Today we made our **"Easter Garden"** at Sunday School. Previously, we have made the garden in a large rectangular flower box, but now we have a specially made water-tight metal container, in which we put soil & stones, & build up a moss-covered **"Green Hill"**, open tomb & flower beds.

14th April 1974 Easter Sunday
Aunt Dos & I visited Auntie Cis at the Ava Nursing Home in Leicester, & she was able to come out with us for a little drive in **KAY 7L** in the lovely spring sunshine. We went to Groby Pool & back through Newtown Linford. Auntie Cis is a frail old lady, but enjoyed the outing.

16th April 1974 Tuesday
In Leicestershire, we have the field where the **Battle of Bosworth** was fought in 1485. **Leicestershire County Council** are now providing £8,500 to make **Bosworth Field** a tourist attraction. An official opening to be performed by **Prince Richard of Gloucester** is planned for 2nd September.

18th April 1974 Thursday
One thousand dead. This is the sad story of strife torn Northern Ireland.
Joseph Neill, the 1,000th terror victim, blew himself up while making his own bomb. So far 215 British soldiers have been killed, 50 policemen & many terrorists among ordinary civilians.

20th April 1974 Saturday
Today, I might have been in **Rome**. But our proposed trip to Rome was cancelled last November, so instead of a morning visit to the splendours of the **Vatican City**, it was a morning visit to that other city founded by the Romans – **Ratae Coritanorum**, now known as **Leicester**.

22nd April 1974 Monday
How glad I was that I was not in Rome yesterday, because I heard the Abbot of Mount St. Bernard Abbey – the Rt. Rev. Dom Ambrose Southey OCR, preach at the Festival Evensong at the Church of St. James the Greater – Oaks in Charnwood. Truly this was a man of God – a man of God going to Rome today!

24th April 1974 Wednesday
The Abbot spoke about "Doubting Thomas" & said he was no more a doubter than any of the other apostles. Until they saw the Risen Lord in person, they all were doubters. "Blessed are they that have not seen & yet have believed." This, said the Abbot, was a continuation of the beatitudes of Jesus – Our Way, Truth & Our Life.

26th April 1974 Friday
"Once more unto the breach, dear friends, once more..."
For the 3rd time I have been invited to attend for interview before the Promotion Board for Executive Officer vacancies. This time it is at the Embankment Suite, 4th Floor, Lambeth Bridge House, London S.E.1 on Wednesday 1st May.

28th April 1974 Sunday
Mr Swanwick, our neighbour, who married his 2nd wife last month, died suddenly on Thursday 25th April. What a shock. He was 63, & it seems only yesterday that we were in his house with him & his first wife. His funeral service will be at Ravenstone on May 1st, followed by cremation at Loughborough.

30th April 1974 Tuesday
Remembering what Samuel Pepys wrote in his diary in March 1668, I decided to go for my interview tomorrow armed with a "Dram of Whisky"
"But I, full of thoughts & trouble touching the issue of the day, did drink a dram of brandy & with the warmth of this did find myself in better order as to courage."

2nd May 1974 Thursday
A day in London yesterday. Visited "The Old Curiosity Shop".
Then to my interview at midday, where I was treated with respect, & asked very reasonable & fair questions. And then to an afternoon conducted coach tour (a repeat of my earlier visit in March) to St. Paul's & the Tower, where I saw the Crown Jewels.

4th May 1974 Saturday

Liverpool, who knocked out Leicester City in the F. A. semi-final, today won the Cup, by beating Newcastle 3-0. The Cup was presented by Princess Anne. Attendance was 100,000. Receipts = £233,600. All 3 goals were scored in the 2nd half – 2 by Kevin Keegan & 1 by Steve Heighway.

6th May 1974 Monday

Our "Armchair Voyage Round the World" last year finished with a journey through Mexico.

Mr Brooks recommended to us then a book called "The Conquest of New Spain" by Bernal Diaz.

I now have the English translation of this book & find it absolutely fascinating. New Spain is Mexico & Diaz saw it all happen.

8th May 1974 Wednesday

"The Conquest of New Spain" is the story of Hernan Cortes & his small band of adventurers including Bernal Diaz. The story tells of the defeat of the Aztecs, of Montezuma's death, & the massacre of the conquering Spaniards, who eventually captured the capital of Mexico, & brought

to it their Christian religion.

10th May 1974 Friday

"Ballet for All"

Started in 1964, the Royal Ballet's third company tours the length & breadth of Britain, introducing the great ballets to ordinary people in their own home towns.

So Mum & I found ourselves on the front row at Coalville watching dancers from Covent Garden portraying "The World of Giselle".

12th May 1974 Sunday

Dom Ambrose Southey, Abbot of Mount St. Bernard Abbey, near Coalville, who said to us last month, "Jesus is our way, our truth & our life", is leaving to live in Rome, where he has been appointed to the highest office in his Order, Abbot General, responsible for 80 monasteries & 40 convents.

14th May 1974 Tuesday

"Ballet for All" appeared not only in Coalville but subsequently in Leicester. So Mum & I found ourselves on the front row at the Phoenix Theatre, Leicester, watching those same dancers from Covent Garden portraying this time "The World of Harlequin".

The Royal Ballet founded in 1931 – the year I was born.

16th May 1974 Thursday

Mum & I have acquired a very tame young blackbird. He is a big baby – comes fearlessly into the kitchen every day looking for food; at times gets perilously close to Tosca. He is so gentle & good mannered, he gets bullied by the cheeky little sparrows who pinch food out of doors from under his very nose.

18th May 1974 Saturday

Went with a bus load from Ravenstone Church to **Cambridge**.

We arrived at 10-30 a.m. & were taken on a conducted tour – including the beautiful King's College Chapel, &

all the magnificent buildings where once men learned the 7 liberal arts : - Grammar, Logic, Rhetoric, Arithmetic, Geometry, Music & Astronomy.

20th May 1974 Monday

At **Cambridge** we walked through the gates which symbolize academic progress. We entered through the Gate of Humility, then later the Gate of Virtue & finally the Gate of Honour. From **Cambridge** we travelled to the ancient tiny **City of Ely** & walked through the golden gates

of its **Cathedral**.

22nd May 1974 Wednesday

Ely Cathedral was founded as a double monastery of monks & nuns in the year 673, when **Etheldreda** was first made Abbess. The building today is mostly Norman architecture & has an

old very ornate **"Prior's Door"** & a unique **Octagonal Lantern** dome spanning 74 feet.

24th May 1974 Friday

Yesterday was **Ascension Day**, which is the great day for **Well-Dressing** at **Tissington**, the "loveliest village in Derbyshire". Went with a bus load from Ravenstone to Tissington & saw their

5 wells bedecked with flower petal pictures; & into the dear little Norman Church, which proclaimed, "Oh ye Wells, bless ye the Lord."

26th May 1974 Sunday

"Circumspice, si monumentum requiris"

These words are on the floor underneath the great dome of St. Paul's, & refer to its designer & architect **Sir Christopher Wren**. They mean, if you are looking for his monument, look all around

at the Cathedral. When I visited St. Paul's, I was shown these words.

28th May 1974 Tuesday

The Revd. Richard H. Barham (1788 – 1845) said, "**And talking of epitaphs, much I admire his 'Circumspice, si monumentum requiris'**, which an erudite verger translated to me, "**If you ask for his monument, Sir-come-spy-see.**"

I thought of this as another erudite verger escorted us round Ely Cathedral.

30th May 1974 Thursday

The verger of Ely Cathedral was a veritable wit. Ely Cathedral has so much to see high up on the roof. We gazed up at the painted ceiling & the exquisitely carved bosses in the roof. As we stood in awe looking at the carving of Christ looking down at us, the verger said, "There you see the Boss."

1st June 1974 Saturday

Do you know – the cost of living has gone up so much lately, that I could hardly afford to go on holiday at the moment.

Petrol is now 55p per gallon. Food costs me about £10 per week. Mum pays for fuel – electricity – telephone & rates. I save £10 per month (towards a new car), & still owe Mum £600 for my present car.

3rd June 1974 Monday

Our new next-door neighbours moved in today – **Keith Carter**, his wife **Margaret**, son **Simon**,
one cat & 2 dear little white Scottie dogs. The dogs romp around & come exploring into our garden, but oh what a commotion when Tosca sees them! It's not a question of dog chasing cat – it's Tosca doing all the chasing.

5th June 1974 Wednesday

This week I have acquired a new regular passenger to & from County Hall. Her name is Edna – a married woman, my age; & she has 3 children. She started work at County Hall last week & asked me if I could take her in the car. I agreed to do so & she offered me £1-50p per week.

7th June 1974 Friday

Why is every room in our house as clean as a new pin? Answer – we have just purchased a beautiful new Electrolux cleaner - £37, to replace our old Hoover. Talk about "a new broom sweeps clean", I have swept clean every carpet in every room & have never seen the house quite so smart.

9th June 1974 Trinity Sunday

Trinity Sunday brought further evidence of God's 3 in 1 trademark. The First Epistle General of John, Chapter 5, verses 7 & 8. "For there are Three that bear record in heaven, the Father, the Word & the Holy Ghost, & these 3 are 1. And there are Three that bear witness in earth, The Spirit & the Water & the Blood, & these 3 agree in One."

11th June 1974 Tuesday

Prince Richard Alexander Walter George of Gloucester, aged 29, yesterday became the new Duke of Gloucester, when his father died, aged 74. His father was the son of King George V, & as the son of a King, was granted £45,000 a year from the Civil List. The new Duke is entitled to – **nothing**.

13th June 1974 Thursday

Trooping the Colour this year is by the 1st Battalion Irish Guards.
This means the Queen will be dressed in her uniform of Colonel-in-Chief of the Irish Guards.
As Colonel-in –Chief of all seven regiments of the Household Division, the Queen wears the uniform of whichever regiment is actually trooping its colour. This year – the blue plume.

15th June 1974 Saturday

Went to London to see the Queen. Enid & I had grandstand seats for the Queen's Birthday Parade. The weather was perfect – blue skies & a welcome breeze. Trooping the Colour was a sight to behold & a joy to listen to. Never have I seen a more spectacular ceremony. Well done the Irish.

17th June 1974 Monday

Following "Trooping the Colour" on Saturday, Enid & I took a boat from Westminster Pier to Greenwich, where we visited the Painted Hall & the Chapel of the Royal Naval College. The buildings of the Royal Naval College are a "Baroque Masterpiece" designed by Sir Christopher Wren in a magnificent symmetrical design.

19th June 1974 Wednesday

Auntie Cis's birthday, 82 today.
I had a day's holiday so that Auntie Cis, Aunt Dos & I could have afternoon tea together. We took a picnic tea by car & sat in a country lane at Stoughton. Auntie Cis had lots of birthday cards, but was careful not to let anyone know how old she was – a secret we had to guard.

21st June 1974 Friday

Hurrah, hurray, success today!
A letter from Department of the Environment, to Miss E. Hewes, L.T.O. "Following your recent appearance before the Promotion Board, I am pleased to tell you that you have been selected for promotion to Executive Officer." That means more money & longer holidays.

23rd June 1974 Sunday

Our Sunday School Anniversary this year was helped considerably by Helen from Leicester who played guitar; & Chris & Adrian, 2 modern young men who introduced Helen to us, & have recently joined our ranks as Sunday School teachers. Susan leaves today as she is expecting her first baby.

25th June 1974 Tuesday

"Cleopatra" by Ernle Bradford. This is my latest book of absorbing interest. This is the story of Cleopatra, as seen from the point of view of the conquered, rather than the all conquering Romans. Cleopatra was a queen. She was a Macedonian Greek. Sadly, she was the last sovereign ruler of ancient Egypt.

27th June 1974 Thursday

Cleopatra VII was 18 when she ascended the throne of Egypt in 51 B.C. She was a brilliant linguist & very intelligent. Plutarch said, "Her voice was like a lyre." Had she succeeded in uniting the Roman Empire with the more cultured & civilised Greeks, (with a Greco-Roman monarchy), history would have been very different.

29th June 1974 Saturday

Julius Caesar & Cleopatra had a son & heir named Caesarion. He might well have brought together the East & the West. But – Julius Caesar was murdered & his successor Octavian, better known as Caesar Augustus, not only subdued Egypt but made sure that the young Ceasarion was put to death.

1st July 1974 Monday

Thousands of Asians gathered in Leicester at the weekend for the dedication of 2 statues at the Shree Sanaton Madir Temple, Catherine Street. The statues, given by an Indian millionaire Mr G. Biria, were the centre of the Krishna celebrations & were of Lord Krishna and Radha, worshipped by Hindus throughout the world.

3rd July 1974 Wednesday

Who is the Indian Lord Krishna? He is the Jesus Christ of the Hindu religion. The Hindu Trinity is 1. Vishnu, the preserver & protector of the world. 2. Shiva, the destroyer, and 3. Brahman, the creator. And these 3 are one – the supreme God, Brahman. Vishnu was made incarnate more than once, but once he was Krishna.

5th July 1974 Friday

Krishna was the 8th incarnation of Vishnu. Krishna was brought up as a cow-herd, & Radha was his sweetheart & consort. The 10th incarnation, Kalkin, has yet to come. To escape the cycle of birth & death the Hindu seeks 1. The Path of Good Works. 2. The Way of Spiritual Knowledge. 3. Unwavering Devotion to God – his ultimate goal.

7th July 1974 Sunday

At the Annual Regimental Parade Service of the Royal Leicestershire Regiment, held in Leicester Cathedral, the Address was given this year by the Revd. Peter Mallet, who spoke of the Christian's role as a bridge builder – bridging the gaps of misunderstandings. He told us that the word "Pontiff" meant a bridge builder.

9th July 1974 Tuesday

The Revd Peter Mallet, QHC, ACK, CF, said in his Address that we owe so much to the past.

The future, he said, is not ours. Unlike the agreement made in our working lives, that we are given a month's notice to quit, we might leave this world without any notice at all. We should always remember that the future belongs to God.

11th July 1974 Thursday

What I like about the Hindu religion, they accept others point of view; whereas Christianity insists that all the world should be Christians. The Hindu says, "As one can ascend to the top of a house by means of a ladder, or a bamboo, or a staircase, or a rope, so divers are the ways to God, or Allah, or Brahman."

13th July 1974 Saturday

Tosca the beautiful, Tosca the beloved, our colour point Persian cat, who has been with us for the past 7 years, is now suffering from arthritis & rheumatism in both front legs. The vet came the other day & diagnosed the complaint. He said he could not cure the trouble, but prescribed tablets to help.

15th July 1974 Monday

How uplifting to have my birthday yesterday on a Sunday – the 5th Sunday after Trinity.

Began the day with 8 a.m. Holy Communion, with its inspiring Collect, Epistle & Gospel; & ended the day with Evening Prayer at 6-30p.m. where I read the lesson from I Kings 18. v 17-39 – the powerful story of Ahab & Elijah.

17th July 1974 Wednesday

Dame Sibyl Hathaway, 90 year old Dame of Sark, died on Sunday 14th July (my birthday) at her home, La Seigneurie, where she had held dominion over the tiny Channel Island since 1927.

The heir to La Seigneurie is her grandson, aged 45, Michael Beaumont. Mum & I visited Sark in 1965.

19th July 1974 Friday

A day in the beautiful city of Chester. Visited the Cathedral – walked the length of the mighty city walls, & stood where Charles I once stood & watched his men defeated by Parliamentary troops. Went for a delightful boat trip on the River Dee; & enjoyed meandering round all the shops.

21st July 1974 Sunday

Spent the afternoon at Twycross Zoo with Mr & Mrs Green of Coalville & Helen Tovell.

A sunny afternoon - & we were able to picnic on the grass with strawberries & cream.

The animals at Twycross Zoo are seasoned performers. Watched the chimp's tea party, & also saw a very talented elephant.

23rd July 1974 Tuesday

Mum has been spending a few days on holiday at her cousin Madge's at Willoughby. I have taken 2 day's holiday for a marathon "spring clean" at home. Had a monster bonfire, washed & ironed all the curtains, & finished up doing carpentry! Made a super ledge for the kitchen.

25th July 1974 Thursday

Watched on television the most beautiful film taken recently in the Antarctic – all about penguins – their courtship & breeding habits, their trials & tribulations; & their great skill in the storm tossed arctic waters. Learned that the petrel was named after St. Peter, from its seeming to walk on the water. (Matthew 14. v 29)

27th July 1974 Saturday

Tomorrow we are expecting Mary Moore, (Mum's cousin from Essex) to spend a few days with us. So we have been busy preparing a suitable "guest room". We have cleared the middle bedroom, transferred Mum's little bed from downstairs, bought a pretty bedside lamp, & made it look very presentable.

29th July 1974 Monday

Having so recently enjoyed reading the book "Cleopatra", how wonderful to watch on television Shakespeare's "Antony & Cleopatra". As it is written, "There is no more superb tragedy in the history of literature. Cleopatra, in her own right, is by far the greatest in stature among Shakespeare's women."

31st July 1974 Wednesday

The most moving part of the story of Cleopatra is her magnificent death, in all its regal dignity.

First Guard, "What work is here Charmian, is this well done?"

Charmian (Cleopatra's hand maiden), "It is well done & fitting for a Princess descended of so many royal kings." Cleopatra's death was a great triumph.

2nd August 1974 Friday

An article on inflation in the Leicester Mercury, by Roy Blackburn, says it is an age old problem & quotes from the prophet Haggai Chapter 1, verse 6. "He that earneth wages earneth wages to put into a bag with holes."

These words were spoken 18 years after captivity in Babylon, during the reign of Darius.

4th August 1974 Sunday

The prophet Haggai said very little, but what he said is well worth reading, "I am with you, saith the Lord." "Be strong, all ye people of the land, saith the Lord, and work; for I am with you."

"The silver is mine, & the gold is mine." "I will make thee as a signet; for I have chosen thee, saith the Lord."

6th August 1974 Tuesday

A letter from Department of the Environment to "Dear Miss Hewes" confirming that the date of my promotion is 1st July 1974. "Your salary as an Executive Officer is £1,985 per annum on the National Scale £1,387 - £2,782. Your leave allowance will be 25 days rising to 30 days after twenty seven years service."

8th August 1974 Thursday

On 7th November 1972 Richard Milhous Nixon was re-elected for another 4 years as 37th President of America. But ….. his downfall is now imminent. His over-enthusiasm as a "Republican" versus the "Democratics" prompted a break-in by his merry men into the Democratic National Headquarters in Watergate.

Note – The Watergate building in Washington DC contained the headquarters of the Democratic Party in the presidential election. Hence the burglary.

10th August 1974 Saturday

The Watergate break-in, in the Watergate complex in Washington, took place as long ago as June 1972, but all is now being revealed.

Apart from dodging income tax, President Nixon spent £7 million from public funds on his own luxury homes in San Clemente, California & in Florida.

12th August 1974 Monday

When too many questions started being asked President Nixon sealed his own doom on 20th October 1973 "The Saturday Night Massacre". He ordered Attorney-General Elliott Richardson to fire Watergate prosecutor Archibald Cox. This turned the nation against the President & they decided to consider articles of impeachment.

14th August 1974 Wednesday

President Nixon fought to the end. In May this year he defied subpoenas from courts & Congress for more evidence (which he had on tape). The prosecutor was obliged to go to the Supreme Court to uphold his authority to procure evidence. But at last Justice took its course & Mr Nixon bravely refused to resign.

16th August 1974 Friday

President Nixon was finally obliged to resign against all his innermost convictions.

"I have never been a quitter" he said.

Sadly he left the White House & was replaced last Friday 9th August 1974 by Gerald Ford.

He made a farewell speech which ended "May God's grace be with you in all the days ahead."

18th August 1974 Sunday

Our Sunday School outing this year will be to Woburn Abbey Park & the Woburn Wild Animal Kingdom next Saturday 24th August. We have 2 coach loads & will be taken in the coaches through the animal safari park, & then on to the Abbey, where we shall spend the afternoon.

20th August 1974 Tuesday

Having a marathon clear out of the garden.

Pulling up this, that & the other, including great pieces of dead wood from the lilacs, uprooting the old forsythia bush & several old rose bushes, overgrown flowers & shrubs, pruning the rambler roses, & preparing another mighty bonfire.

22nd August 1974 Thursday

Mum's birthday tomorrow. She will be 69. Mum is keeping very well at the moment considering how helpless she was at the beginning of last year. She is limited in what she can do but can potter about the house & garden. She enjoys reading & car riding but is wary of travelling alone.

24th August 1974 Saturday

A lovely day for our outing to Woburn. Enjoyed a ride on the "Safari Jungle Cabin Lift" to the lake for a "Safari Boat Trip". Watched sea lions leaping for food from the boat. Saw dear little baby lions lying on the rocks, & found the mischievous monkeys most delightful jumping all over the cars.

26th August 1974 Bank Holiday Monday

Yesterday was the 11th Sunday after Trinity. And the collect for the 11th Sunday after Trinity was mentioned most particularly by Dr. Coggan, Archbishop of York, in his Shaftesbury Lecture.

(See 7th January 1974) God declares his almighty Power most chiefly in showing Mercy & Pity.

To be – matters more than **to have**.

28th August 1974 Wednesday

A week's holiday! Employing my talents as a landscape gardener. Having cleared out all the old overgrown flower beds & shrubs, have set out a very attractive centre-piece edged with diamond shaped lawn, to be surrounded by spring flowers. Also prepared a slabbed base ready for a garden seat.

30th August 1974 Friday

Our new landscaped garden is to include a small rose garden. Today I ordered new roses. Five standard roses at £1-50p each and a collection of 10 bush hybrid teas for £3-65p.

For our beautiful new-look garden, Mum has chosen a magnolia bush, so we are hoping anon to lead everybody up the garden path.

1st September 1974 Sunday

Auntie Belle, Aunt Dos & I went to Coalville Methodist Church, Marlborough Square, to a "**Sankey Evening**". This was an evening of hymn singing – all the old chapel favourites – hymns written by **Sankey**. Most of us were moved to tears by the beautiful words & the stirring music in the packed chapel.

3rd September 1974 Tuesday

This is my favourite **Sankey** hymn: - **Beulah Land**. And this is its chorus: -

"O Beulah Land, sweet Beulah Land,
As on thy highest mount I stand,
I look away across the sea,
Where mansions are prepared for me,
And view the shining glory shore;
My heaven, my home, for evermore."

We do not have this hymn at church.

5th September 1974 Thursday
"Beginner's Guide to Rose Growing." This is my latest book from good old County Hall library.
It tells you how to plant – feed – prune, etc. & suggests the best rose gardens to go & see are Kew Gardens & such like, but the most exquisite of all, Bagatelle & Roseraie de l'Hay in France.
Must try & go.

7th September 1974 Saturday
Visited Fowkes Garden Centre at Syston & bought stakes for the standard roses. Looked at their selection of garden seats – average price £40!
Having recently decided I would like to have a guitar, looked at the selection of guitars in town. Guess what? Average price £40! Guitar playing is very popular just now.

9th September 1974 Monday
Motored 10 miles through slush & puddles & torrents of rain to Bosworth College, Desford, to enrol for night school – **Guitar** "The class will be mainly for beginners, to set you on the right course, learning tuning, chords, etc."
When I got there, the list was complete – **full up**, so I went on a reserve list.

11th September 1974 Wednesday
My first visit to Leicester's new **Haymarket Theatre**, where with Frances (from the office) I saw "**Joseph & the Amazing Technicolour Dreamcoat**". This is the show I saw in London last year, but an entirely different production. The Leicester production has been a box office sell-out.

13th September 1974 Friday
Bought bulbs for the garden. 16 daffodils, 25 tulips, 6 hyacinths, 160 crocus. Lifted all my newly laid turf – the diamond shape – inserted all the crocus bulbs & covered them again with the turf. Then surrounded the diamond lawn with the other bulbs – daffodils, tulips and hyacinths.

15th September 1974 Sunday
The Annual Ashe Lecture at St. Helen's Church, Ashby-de-la-Zouch, is to be given this year on October 1st by The Most Rev. & Right Hon. The Lord Archbishop of York, Dr. Donald Coggan.
The title of his lecture is "Two Score Years – and Then?" Dr. Coggan will have been ordained exactly two score years.

17th September 1974 Tuesday
"Two Score Years – and Then?" For Dr. Coggan "and

then" means he will be Archbishop of Canterbury. He is due to take over the Archbishopric of Canterbury in November when Dr. Michael Ramsey retires. The new Archbishop of York is to be The Rt. Rev. Stuart Yarworth Blanch, present Bishop of Liverpool.

19th September 1974 Thursday
The Cathedral Tower is Falling Down.
So reads the Leicester Cathedral Tower appeal. We need £30,000 for the restoration of the tower & spire, & so far donations total £13,000.

21st September 1974 Saturday
This is the year of two General Elections. We had a General Election on February 28th, & we are to have another on October 10th. The reason being that no party had a big enough majority to achieve anything. Every time the government tries to make a new Act of Parliament too many oppose it.

23rd September 1974 Monday
Bought a cheap new guitar for £16-50p (plus £2-50p for a waterproof cover). The guitar is called "Espana" & was made in Spain. So now of course I am raring to go to play it. I have a useful book, "Play Guitar" by Ulf Goran, who gives a guitar lesson every Saturday on television.

25th September 1974 Wednesday
I'm in the Guitar Class! Lessons are on Wednesday evenings, & up to now we have learned the names of the 6 open strings E A D G B E, & we have tried playing a few chords, 1. C major,
2. G major, 3. D major & the difficult F major. I am reminded of David, who played to King Saul.

27th September 1974 Friday
In my bedroom, I have the prayer of St. Francis of Assisi, which starts, "Lord, make me an instrument of thy peace ......" And now I have the very thing – my guitar. An instrument indeed
of "Thy peace". No wonder my favourite poem is "**Saul**" by Robert Browning. It says it all.

29th September 1974 Sunday
St. Michael's Day. And today we learn that Michael (my nephew) & his wife Sheena, who married July 31st 1971, have parted company.
Dear, oh dear! First Mary Blue ran away (in July 1971), & now Sheena has gone.
Pat, my brother said to me, "Don't get married Bet." My best beloved married another.

1st October 1974 Tuesday
Heard Dr. Coggan, present Archbishop of York, give the Ashe Lecture at Ashby-de-la-Zouch.
He spoke of his life & experiences over the past 40 years, since he was first ordained, & told of his hopes for Christ's church in the years ahead.
"Remember" he said, "the words of Christ – feed my sheep." Never mind about the goats.

3rd October 1974 Thursday
During Dr. Coggan's 45 minute lecture the light on the pulpit suddenly went out. Without batting an eye-lid, Dr.

Coggan continued his theme on the "Joy" which the Africans express in their worship, as compared with the form of worship we have here, "The trouble with us is – our light has gone out!"

5th October 1974 Saturday

For the first time since Local Government re-organisation on April 1st this year, the General Election is being handled by the new District Councils instead of the County Council. I have been appointed Poll Clerk at Ravenstone (fee £10). Being in the Loughborough Constituency, this was through the Borough of Charnwood.

7th October 1974 Monday

Again I have accepted Betty Henn's invitation to join her party to Rome. They are hoping to go next April on a 5 day holiday from London by air to Rimini & San Marino. Then on to Florence, then to the leaning Tower of Pisa, then follow the coast to Rome, to Assisi & back to Rimini.

8th October 1974 Tuesday

Mould, Nellie, of 2 Pithiviers Close, Ashby-de-la-Zouch, passed peacefully away in Ashby and District Hospital on October 8th 1974. Dear mother of Peter and loving sister of Kath and Glad. Funeral service on Saturday October 12th at Holy Trinity Church, Ashby, at 10 a.m., followed by interment in Ashby Cemetery.

No flowers by request please, but if desired donations may be sent to the Staunton Harold Cheshire Home.

9th October 1974 Wednesday

At our guitar lessons, we have now been given 5 songs to play chord accompaniment.

"The Last Thing on my Mind" "Blowing in the Wind" "Five Hundred Miles" "I Know Where I'm Going" and "Morning has Broken".

These are for chord practice covering A, B, C, D, E, F, G, Am, Bm, Em, B7 and D7.

11th October 1974 Friday

General Election Number 2 this year has given the Labour Party the majority they need to outnumber all the rest put together – but only just.

Labour, who at the beginning of the year gained 301 seats, now have 319 against 316. This includes 276 Conservatives, 11 Liberals & 11 Scottish Nationalists.

13th October 1974 Sunday

Harvest Festival at Ravenstone. At the Children's Gift Service this afternoon, the children sang a "Song of Harvest", which I had written. We had guitar accompaniment from Ruth – another friend of Chris & Adrian. Chris & Adrian finish today as Sunday School teachers & go to university. Our new teacher is Diane.

15th October 1974 Tuesday

Went to the De Montfort Hall, Leicester, to "**Sing Sankey**", with my beloved Provost in the chair. The most moving item was the 23rd Psalm. The Provost spoke of the 3 Psalms – Psalm 22, 23 & 24. These, he said, were the 3 "C's" & also the 3 "P's". The Cross, the Crook & the Crown. Christ Past, Present & in Prospect.

17th October 1974 Thursday

Saw "**Aida**" at Leicester's new Haymarket Theatre. This was a great production, with almost 150 people on stage, & a professional orchestra. Even so, there were certain aspects which were not so spectacular as the Malvern production. (See 19th November 1972)

19th October 1974 Saturday

As an E.O. in the Civil Service, I am to go to Nottingham for the day on Tuesday, and then to Leeds for a day's course on November 21st. This will mean travelling to Leeds the previous day & stopping there overnight. (All expenses paid) This will be the first time I have had overnight expenses.

21st October 1974 Monday

The Rector of Ravenstone, the Revd. Buckroyd, is in Leicester Royal Infirmary after a slight coronary, & has been unable to write his usual letter for the November issue of the Parish Magazine. I have therefore written an account of our recent services – including the prophet Haggai.

23rd October 1974 Wednesday

What a lovely day we had yesterday at County Hall, Nottingham. About 30 people from Motor Licence Offices, far & near gathered together. From Nottingham, Leicester, Cambridge, Peterborough, Derby & Oakham. We were instructed in the art of transferring records to Swansea, due shortly.

25th October 1974 Friday

County Hall, Nottingham, overlooks the River Trent. Had lunch in the cafeteria with a lovely view of the river. After lunch, walked in the autumn sunshine along the banks of the river, crossed over the bridge, & sat in the beautiful gardens by the impressive War Memorial's "Arc de Triomphe".

27th October 1974 Sunday

Our guest preacher at church this evening chose for his sermon the first miracle of Jesus – turning water into wine. He emphasised the necessary work of man first – filling the water pots with water. God performs miracles with the help of man, & man performs miracles with the help of God.

(As in a garden).

29th October 1974 Tuesday

The story is told of a beautiful garden. One who admired this garden said to the gardener, "What a beautiful garden you & God have created." The gardener had to agree. "But", he added, "You just should have seen it when God had it on his own."

31st October 1974 Thursday

Watched on television the pomp & pageantry of the State Opening of Parliament. The Queen wearing the Imperial State Crown, & seated on her throne, read the words outlining the Government's programme for the coming session of Parliament.

My Government will …. My Ministers will …… etc.

2nd November 1974 Saturday

The State Opening of Parliament showed that the Queen

reigns – that the House of Commons rules. It was interesting to see Black Rod going from the Lords to the Commons to fetch the M.P.s, but good to hear the Queen end with these words, "I pray that the blessing of Almighty God may rest upon your counsels."

4th November 1974 Monday

Brother Pat is hoping to move from his home in Ravenstone to a new bungalow 2 miles away in Coalville. His house is now up "For Sale".
We have always lived at **Hewes' Corner**. Grandpa Hewes built the big corner house, & one by one his sons built side by side. But one by one they are going.

6th November 1974 Wednesday

There was Uncle Fred – Uncle Aubrey – and Uncle Cyril across the road (with Uncle Fred at the corner). Then there was Reg (my dad) next door to the Hollies itself.
Pat now lives where Uncle Aubrey lived, & Aunt Dos has built on the Hollies lawn. Uncle Fred's widow (Belle) Cyril's widow (Gladys) & Mum still live there.

8th November 1974 Friday

On 8th November in the year of our Lord 1519, those brave conquistadors from sunny Spain first entered the city of **Mexico**, & were welcomed by the great **Montezuma** himself, mighty ruler of the Aztecs.
Like all true Indians he had "eyes that smiled & frowned alternate" - he was about 40 years old.

10th November 1974 Sunday

Five hundred million people in the world today are suffering from famine & malnutrition. This week in Rome 1,000 delegates from 100 countries have assembled for the United Nations World Food Conference to try to find means of expanding food production "in magnitudes never before undertaken or even planned".

12th November 1974 Tuesday

The United Nations World Food Conference was the brain-child of America.
America's Secretary of State, Dr. Henry Kissinger (like Joseph – see Genesis, Chapter 41) is in charge. He said, "Will we pool our strengths & progress together, or test our strengths & sink together?" His plan was 5-fold.

14th November 1974 Thursday

This is the 5-fold plan of Dr. Henry Kissinger –
1. Increase the production of food exporters.
2. Accelerate production in developing countries.
3. Improve means of food distribution & financing.
4. Enhance food quality – and most important
5. Ensure security against food emergencies.

16th November 1974 Saturday

November 14th was the Hindu New Year's Day & the beginning of Vikram Avant Year 2031.
In Leicester the Hindu New Year had its biggest ever welcome when over 3,000 Asians gathered at Granby Halls to celebrate. Children in fancy dress were Lord Krishna & Radha.

18th November 1974 Monday

£20,400 "And still climbing". The Provost reports –

"The response has been truly wonderful. Old Contemptibles, International Companies, Parochial Church Councils, Salvation Army, Working Men's Clubs, Peers of the Realm, all have rallied to our support."

20th November 1974 Wednesday

Travelled by train from Leicester to Leeds for "Annual Staff Report Writing Course", to be held tomorrow at The Wool Industries Research Association, Headingly Lane, Leeds.
Well impressed with Leeds city centre. Spent the night at The Moorlands Hotel, 126 Otley Road, Leeds 6 – a very comfortable warm hotel.

22nd November 1974 Friday

There were 15 E.O.s for our one day course held yesterday in Leeds. All were Motor Licence staff from such places as Hull, Warrington, Kesteven. Every member of Civil Service staff is reported on **in detail** once every year. E.O.s may be called upon to report on C.O.s & this is what we were taught how to do.

24th November 1974 Sunday

This week has seen the bloodiest attack ever by the I.R.A. – the Irish terrorists bent on destroying the British Government's control of Northern Ireland. The attack was not in Belfast or Londonderry – scenes of so much bloodshed – but in Birmingham, where 2 bombs killed 19 & injured 184.

26th November 1974 Tuesday

The latest idea in the Civil Service is that we each have an interview with our own boss "to discuss your performance in your job during the past year, your work plan for the next year, & how your potential may be developed to your & the department's best advantage." My interview is on Friday.

27th November 1974 Wednesday

Doughty, Ruby. In fondest memory of our friend and colleague Ruby. Deepest sympathy to Eddie and family – From Staff of County Motor Taxation Dept.

28th November 1974 Thursday

Ruby, a member of our staff at County Hall, Motor Taxation Dept., Glenfield, Leicestershire, died of cancer yesterday. She had worked until she could work no more, & spent her last day at work on the counter by my side. She had one married daughter & a devoted husband Eddie.
1983 – Bennett, Pat (nee Doughty). Only daughter of Eddie and the late Ruby, died tragically in a parachuting accident, Adelaide, Australia, October 23rd. We are too stunned to find those beautiful words. We loved you, Pat. – From your loving Grandma, Nanny, Helen and Eddie.

30th November 1974 Saturday

Our Annual Christmas Fair in Ravenstone Village Institute & our third effort with a stall for the Sunday School. First year we made £9. Second year we made £12. This year we made £16.
A big boost to our stall this year was **sugar**, which has been in short supply lately, & we had a goodly store.

2nd December 1974 Monday

My interview with Mr. Sharp consisted chiefly in him telling me how to be a good E.O., how to be a good "manager" & leader of men. How to get the best out of people, how to get people to do what I want without upsetting them – diplomacy – tact – courtesy – charm & firmness.

4th December 1974 Wednesday

Mum has had the last of her teeth out this week. For many years she has had false teeth at the top & half false teeth at the bottom. The last 5 were removed in one fell swoop & a complete new set – top & bottom installed – cost £10. They look very good but are meant to be only temporary ones.

6th December 1974 Friday

Bought our very first ironing board - £6. We have always managed with a home made board, but a proper ironing board is much better for dresses & skirts.

Have also ordered a garden seat, 5 feet long (1.5 metres), called "The Wyvern Teak Seat" - £36-14p.

8th December 1974 Sunday

This afternoon at church I made my début in public – **playing guitar**. We had a Children's Service in which the little ones (Diane's class) sang "Away in a Manger", & the older ones (my class) sang a lively Calypso Carol, accompanied by guitar & also tambourines.

We had a lovely "manger" made by Mr. Land.

10th December 1974 Tuesday

As the price of petrol goes up & up, & the oil sheiks get richer & richer, **Mecca** the Holy City for the 475 million followers of Islam, is up for redevelopment. British architects have been chosen for the job. The big problem is – they are not allowed into **Mecca**. If the mountain will not come to Muhammed, Muhammed must go to the mountain.

12th December 1974 Thursday

King Faisal of Saudi Arabia now has a Mountain of Money. Money has been creamed off from the rich nations & the fate of the world lies very much in the hands of the oil producers. Faisal, aged 69, is a wise old king. He says "Petroleum is a gift from God & all humanity has the right to use it."

14th December 1974 Saturday

Slowly but surely the great new Licence Centre at Swansea is taking over the records from Motor Licence Offices all over the country. This week I received my first Driving Licence from Swansea. Records of new cars (starting 1st October 1974) are all at Swansea.

16th December 1974 Monday

Wrote a poem for the January Parish Magazine –

"God be with us every day, throughout the coming year,
Bless our village & our church & good folk living here.
Bless the old & bless the young & all who here belong,
Keep us ever close to thee, that we may shun the wrong.
Bless the miners in our midst & bless the miners' wives,
Remembering for good, O Lord, The men who give their lives. As we face another year, And tread the great

unknown, May we feel thy loving presence here in Ravenstone."

20th December 1974 Friday

Our lovely new garden seat has arrived. (All wrapped up for Christmas). We are keeping it indoors for the winter – in Mum's bedroom, where it is proving very useful.

All our other presents are now wrapped up, & Christmas cards dispatched. The lights are on the Christmas tree & the fairy on the top.

22nd December 1974 Sunday

Aunt Dos, Pat & I visited Auntie Cis at the Ava Private Nursing Home, 38 Ratcliffe Road, Leicester, & took her for an afternoon drive to Leicester's Town Hall Square to see the beautiful Christmas lights. Thousands of coloured lights hung like fruit on the bare trees & all was really lovely.

24th December 1974 Tuesday

Delightful weather – just like spring. Blue skies & sunshine have brought up all my little bulbs (planted in September). Tiny sturdy shoots are peeping out everywhere. We now have received the rose trees (ordered last August) & have already planted the **Magnolia**, chosen by Mum.

26th December 1974 Thursday

A day in the garden! Planted all my new roses.
Five standard roses – 2 yellow, 2 pink & one yellow & pink mixed; & 10 small bush roses –
1. Josephine Bruce. 2. Ernest H. Morse. 3. Mullard Jubilee. 4. Gay Gordons. 5. Vanda Beauty.
6. Prima Ballerina. 7. Pink Favourite. 8. Pascali. 9. Mischief. 10. Peace.

28th December 1974 Saturday

Tosca the beautiful, Tosca the beloved, is now so very crippled by arthritis in the 2 front legs that he moves only when absolutely necessary. He looks well & eats well, but it is so very sad to see him struggling along, a few painful steps at a time, and then resting like a kangaroo.

Note – Tosca has arthritis & rheumatism in both front legs, caused no doubt by jumping daily from the top of our closed entry gate.

30th December 1974 Monday

I have now taken over the role of "Money Receiver" from the sale of the Ravenstone Parish Magazine. Thirteen ladies – good & true – deliver each month 250 Parish Magazines @ 5p each. This means in a year I should collect £150, which I hand over at intervals to Sam Land, the Treasurer.

* * *

1975

2nd January 1975 Thursday
And so we come to the last quarter of the 20th Century. In the past year the price of petrol has gone up from 42p to 73p per gallon. This is the main reason we have such problems of inflation, with one firm after another going out of business – people made redundant, & uncertainty everywhere.

4th January 1975 Saturday
The flowers that bloom in the spring Tra-La, or indeed the flowers that bloom in the autumn, are now blooming in parks & gardens. With weather just like spring, & no signs of any night frosts, roses are still blooming, Michaelmas Daisies are flowering in our garden, & crocus are coming up.

6th January 1975 Monday
As a "life member" of the Friends of Leicester Cathedral, it occurred to me to give our rare old books "An Exposition of the Old & New Testament" by Matthew Henry, dated 1721, to the Provost, that the proceeds may be used towards the Cathedral Tower. (See 24th Dec. 1971)

8th January 1975 Wednesday
Wrote to the Provost – "Dear Provost, I would like to offer you 6 very old books which were given to my father in 1925 …….. If you can find the best home for them I would like the price offered to be given to the Cathedral Tower Appeal." I know the Provost likes very old books.

10th January 1975 Friday
Read in the Leicester Mercury – "The Provost Has an Operation" – "The Provost of Leicester, the Very Revd. John Hughes is in the Leicester Royal Infirmary after having a back operation. The operation was successful, & on leaving hospital shortly, he will have 2 months recuperation." Canon Gundry is standing in for him.

12th January 1975 Sunday
Because of the financial straits of our country, there is to be a set limit on how much heating we can have at work, & a considerable reduction in all flood-lighting.
But we have just had erected near our house, a lovely new street light, & we do appreciate its warm & friendly light.

14th January 1975 Tuesday
In 1973, there were 1,205,837 British cars sold in Britain, (including my KAY 7L). But our economic crisis brought the figures down in 1974 to 914,724. The top ten best sellers are –

1. Ford Cortina	6. Austin Allegro
2. Ford Escort	7. Chrysler Avenger
3. Mini	8. Ford Capri
4. Morris Marina	9. Austin Maxi
5. Vauxhall Viva	10. Hillman Hunter

It is estimated that figures for 1975 will be even lower. There is the threat of mass short-time working among the half-million people employed in car plants &

component factories. British Leyland in 1974 had 33% of the home market – Ford had 23%.

18th January 1975 Saturday
Received a letter from the Provost's secretary Miss M. R. Cumberland –
"Dear Miss Hewes, …… It is extremely kind of you to offer to the Provost six volumes of Matthew Henry's Exposition of the Old and New Testament. It may very well be that these would make a worthy addition to his own library; however, I note you wish the proceeds to go to the Cathedral Tower Appeal, & knowing how generously the Provost has personally contributed to this fund, he may have to forego them to sell to the highest bidder. I know how delighted the Provost will be to receive the books ….."

22nd January 1975 Wednesday
Our guitar lessons have now progressed from strumming with the chords to the more subtle "finger-picking". This is more sophisticated, & sounds gorgeous when done properly. I bought a book "Baxter's Finger-Picking Manual" - £1-75p, & am currently engrossed in learning "Jingle Bells".

24th January 1975 Friday
The Most Reverend Father in God, Donald Coggan, Archbishop of Canterbury was today enthroned at Canterbury Cathedral. Speaking of tribulation, violence & materialism, Dr Coggan said, "Did that secretary write more wisely than she knew when by an error of typing she referred to my enthornment?"

26th January 1975 Sunday
I have now delivered to the Provost's secretary the six books of Matthew Henry, & also I took "Splendour of the Heavens" which was given to me by Reg Hall in February 1971.
The Provost was at home in bed after his recent operation – the removal of a small bone pressing on a nerve in his back.

28th January 1975 Tuesday
The twins – Reevsie's sisters, now 23, both got married on Sunday 26th January. They were engaged October 9th 1971. Phyllis was engaged to Philip, & Sherry was engaged to Eric in our office. Phyllis & Philip parted company, & Phyllis married another – Ian. Sherry married Eric.

30th January 1975 Thursday
"Great Scott" is now one year old. He is a big bouncing baby.
Michael & Sheena who parted company last year (see 29th September 1974) are happily re-united: and Julian (my other nephew) is hoping to be married this year – May 31st.

1st February 1975 Saturday
Had a good old shopping spree in Leicester. Bought 16 prizes for my Sunday School class (to be presented February 16th) including crayons, felt tip pens, jigsaws & books. Bought a gorgeous black & orange glittery evening stole – to take to Rome, & had my photograph taken for a passport for April 6th.

3rd February 1975 Monday

Our guest preacher at church last night likened our life to a conducted tour on holiday, with Jesus as our courier. "Let us go on holiday with Jesus – to the promised land of Heaven."

He chose Proverbs 3. 6. as his text - "In **all** thy ways acknowledge him, and he shall direct thy paths."

5th February 1975 Wednesday

In view of the financial state of our country, the great Channel Tunnel Project linking Britain with France has been abandoned.

Oh dear! One machine which cost £546,000 was due to begin digging a 21 foot diameter access tunnel. There it was, assembled – **all ready to go** - & now it's all systems **stop**.

7th February 1975 Friday

Senior Engineer Ted Glover, a professional Tunnelling Engineer, has been associated with the Channel Tunnel Project for over 7 years. To any Tunnelling man the Channel project represented a once-in-a-lifetime challenge. Now it has all been abandoned. Everything now will be sealed off & made safe.

9th February 1975 Sunday

The great count-down begins. Only 8 weeks to **Rome**! To me this is the event of a **life-time**. All this & **Florence** too. I know how much **Robert Browning** loved Florence, & I am looking forward so much to seeing the architecture, & those gates described as "Worthy to be the Gates of Heaven".

11th February 1975 Tuesday

A pay rise for the Queen.

In December 1971, the Queen's allowance was raised from £475,000 per annum to £980,000 per annum. Such is the rate of inflation that this has now risen to £1,400,000. To meet this £420,000 increase the Queen has offered £150,000 of her own money.

13th February 1975 Thursday

Actually, £1,400,000 is more than enough to pay the royal bills. To pay all the servants & provide for the horses, to pay for the garden parties & provide gifts for visiting monarchs, premiers & politicians, & all the other expenses, last year amounted to £1,200,000, so there may be some change.

15th February 1975 Saturday

Today we met Shirley, who is to marry Julian on May 31st. The family clan assembled at Pat's house – Pat, Evelyn, Auntie Belle, Aunt Dos, Mum & me, Enid, Fanny & Thirza, Bill & Hilda, (relatives of Bunting's mother) Bunting & Mostyn, Julian & Shirley.

Pat leaves his house on 1st March.

17th February 1975 Monday

Yesterday was Sunday School Prize Giving. With the Rector at home ill & no visiting preacher I was officer in charge. We had a nice little half hour service with 3 hymns – prayers read by Lyndon and Karen – the lesson read by Diane, & the collection taken by Arthur & Jane. The children also sang to the guitar.

19th February 1975 Wednesday

And yet again Leicester City and Arsenal wrestle for the Cup. (See 17th January 1973)

In tonight's 5th round F.A. Cup Tie Replay, the score after extra time was 1 – 1. But what excitement! Leicester scored just in the nick of time & so we have a 2nd replay next Monday.

21st February 1975 Friday

Langham Kendrick, our friend and neighbour – just across the road – for many years, had a stroke today & is now in bed unable to speak & without the use of his right side. An ex-miner, he is 72 years old & has never needed a doctor in his life. A great character! Known to us all.

23rd February 1975 Sunday

Six weeks to Rome! And now I am the proud owner of British Passport P557189A, declaring me to be a British Subject: Citizen of the United Kingdom and Colonies. Occupation looks very much like "Gout Service" i.e. Government Service. This passport expires February 1985 & is worded thus: - "Her Britannic Majesty's Principal Secretary of State for Foreign and Commonwealth Affairs requests & requires in the name of Her Majesty all those whom it may concern to allow the bearer to pass freely without let or hindrance, & to afford the bearer such assistance & protection as may be necessary."

Note – I acquire my first passport, ready to visit Italy. I am hoping to join a coach trip organised by Betty Henn from Coalville's Christ Church.

27th February 1975 Thursday

Her Britannic Majesty – Queen Elizabeth II – is at this moment enjoying a State Visit to Mexico. My – what a welcome she received. Who but the Mexicans could dance such lively gay dances, or wear such exotic national costume? I thought of the great Montezuma himself (see 8th November 1974) & all Mexico's great past.

2nd March 1975 Sunday

London's worst Tube disaster took place on Friday 28th February 1975 when the 8-37 a.m. train arrived at Moorgate from Drayton Park full of passengers. Instead of the train stopping at the Moorgate terminus, it went full speed into a brick ended stretch of old tunnel, killing 29 & injuring 76.

4th March 1975 Tuesday

"Fiddler on the Roof" – Coalville Amateur Operatic's production begins tonight.

I have been asked to be assistant prompter. The prompter sits with the orchestra (right by the pianist) beneath the front of the stage. I am to relieve the regular prompter on Thursday evening & Saturday matinee.

6th March 1975 Thursday

Drew out all my money - £200 from S.A.Y.E. i.e. Save As You Earn, & spent £175.

Bought travellers cheques for Italy - £100. Bought £10 of Italian money. Bought a beautiful electric fire £25, electric kettle £10, purse £5, shoulder bag £7, sheet £5, pair of binoculars £13.

8th March 1975 Saturday

A wonderful write-up in the papers for "Fiddler on the Roof". This is a show which is full of pathos & full of humour at the same time, with superb musical numbers. I found as prompter that sometimes I could not see the words of the libretto because of tears in my eyes. What a great show.

10th March 1975 Monday

A letter from the Provost's secretary –

"Dear Miss Hewes, I had the books which you so very kindly donated to the Cathedral Tower Appeal valued by Mr Lance Harvey, Horsefair Street, Leicester. He said Matthew Henry's set of 6 were worth £4, & "The Splendour of the Heavens" £1-50p......."

12th March 1975 Wednesday

(letter continued) ….. The Provost himself has purchased these books on the valuation, & an amount of £5-50p has been paid into the Cathedral Tower Appeal …. Not only has this swelled the Tower Appeal, but also given pleasure to the Provost, & his son Simon, who is interested in astronomy."

14th March 1975 Friday

Kendrick, David Edward Langham, 54, Leicester Road, Ravenstone, dearly loved husband of Annie, loving father of Jean and Brian, dear grandfather of Susan, passed peacefully away on March 14th 1975. Funeral service at Swannington Methodist Church on Wednesday March 19th at 3 p.m. followed by cremation at Loughborough. Inquiries to Co-operative Funeral Service, Berrisford House, 101 Belvoir Road, Coalville. Telephone 36703.

16th March 1975 Sunday

Aristotle Socrates Onassis, possibly the richest man in the world, died yesterday. He married President Kennedy's widow Jackie in October 1968. Much of his £400 million fortune will go to his daughter Christina's son – yet to be born. His own son & heir, Alexander, was killed in a plane crash two years ago.

18th March 1975 Tuesday

"Scrap Car Tax Plan" – As more & more people are made redundant every day, the threat now comes to those employed in **Motor Taxation**. The newspapers announce that Chancellor Denis Healey is seriously considering plans to scrap the **Car Licence Tax** in next month's budget, & replace it with a **Petrol Tax**.

20th March 1975 Thursday

The great Vehicle & Driving Licence Centre at Swansea is proving to be an unprofitable proposition. Running costs have risen from an estimated £9 million a year to £23 million a year, & there are untold problems – "only as it progressed did the complexity of the task, & the demands it would make, become evident."

22nd March 1975 Saturday

Our Easter Garden at Sunday School this year is to have a "landscaped" touch – following my efforts at home in the garden last summer – see August 28th 1974.

So there is to be less soil & moss, & instead a green towel for a lawn, with impressive rocks to form the open tomb & background.

24th March 1975 Monday

Mum & I went to Staunton Harold Cheshire Home to hear the Coalville Amateur Operatic Society singing a selection from their latest show "Fiddler on the Roof". John Saunders, the producer, told the story in between the songs – Peter Jacques, musical director, conducted the singing, & Hilary was pianist.

26th March 1975 Wednesday

King Faisal of Saudi Arabia is dead. (see 6th December 1973 and 12th December 1974)

He was assassinated by his nephew yesterday morning – the anniversary of the birth of the Prophet Mohammed. Like Mohammed, whose religion was founded on the sword (see 7th February 1972) so was Faisal's kingdom founded. Faisal in Arabic is "sword".

28th March 1975 Good Friday

Our Easter Garden in church this year is very pretty. The metal tray is 2ft by 4ft. Inside we have a carpet base – then a green towel. In the centre at the back is the open tomb flanked by rocks which reach to the front. An angel sits on a rounded rock & flowers & foliage are all around.

30th March 1975 Easter Sunday

One week to Rome! Watched on television "Easter in Rome". Saw Pope Paul's Easter Mass celebrated in the open air at an altar in front of St. Peter's in a vast assembly of Holy Year pilgrims. Watched different people offering their gifts, including a little lamb.

1st April 1975 Tuesday

The fishermen of England have lined up their boats across harbour mouths all round our coast-line. An armada of 1,500 fishing boats has created a massive blockade of our ports. Why? The fishermen want the government to stop importing cheap foreign fish & to set up a 50 mile fishing limit for foreign boats.

3rd April 1975 Thursday

All Motor Vehicle Records are now on the move. Apart from brand new vehicles, which have been on the computer at Swansea since last October, all vehicles renewing their vehicle excise licence now – starting April 1st – are being sifted according to their age, with "L" "M" & "N" going to Swansea.

5th April 1975 Saturday

A day of exciting preparation for our Roman holiday which starts tomorrow.

We leave Coalville in our bus load at 8 a.m. & travel to Luton. Then by air from Luton to Rome. Then by coach across Italy from Rome to San Marino. One night in San Marino, one in Florence, & 2 nights in Rome.

7th April 1975 Monday

Have now seen one of the 7 wonders of the world. At 5-30p.m. in the evening sunlight we beheld the famous leaning Tower of Pisa. Also visited Assisi (see 27th September 1974), & arrived in Florence for the night. Tomorrow we explore Florence to see Michelangelo's "David" & the old Ponte Vecchio.

9th April 1975 Wednesday

The most memorable day of my life. Stood right in the middle of the mighty ancient Pantheon of Rome. Walked in the ruined Colosseum, visited the Vatican Museum & the Sistine Chapel, & most wonderful of all, entered St. Peter's. In the evening walked through the world famous Tivoli Gardens.

11th April 1975 Friday

Rome is a City of Fountains. One of the most beautiful fountains in Rome, & one of the best known in the world, is Trevi Fountain. It was here where we threw 3 coins in the fountain – this means we wish to return to Rome. We actually walked underneath a fountain in the Tivoli Gardens – like walking underneath Niagara.

13th April 1975 Sunday

And so we come back to earth, after the holiday of a lifetime. Like Hannibal we have crossed the Alps to reach Rome. But unlike Hannibal, who crossed under the most arduous conditions, we sailed high above the clouds. What a wondrous sight from above, those snow capped peaks, stretching far & wide beneath us.

15th April 1975 Tuesday

Budget Day! As predicted, Chancellor of the Exchequer Denis Healey brought about the strictest measures to bring another £1,000 million into the Treasury.
We were glad he did not "scrap car tax" (see 18th March 1975). He put car tax up from £25 to £40. Vehicle Excise Taxes will now rise from £500 million to £773 million.

17th April 1975 Thursday

With £60 left over from my Roman holiday, I bought a Calor Gas heater. So now we do not have a coal fire. The Calor Gas heater warms the room better than a coal fire, & has the added advantage of constant heat – is there at the press of a button - has no dirty ashes - & does not get smoky.

18th April 1975 Friday

On 18th April 1775 Paul Revere made his famous midnight ride from Charlestown to Lexington, accompanied by William Dawes, to warn the Massachusetts patriots of the arrival of British troops at the outbreak of the war of American Independence. (See Longfellow).

19th April 1975 Saturday

Brother Pat has a brand new fitted carpet for his new bungalow. So he has given Mum & me the carpet he had before. This is quite good, & we have been busy putting it down in our front bedroom. That means we have one unwanted old carpet from our bedroom – older than I am – to throw away.

21st April 1975 Monday

The great grass-cutting season is here.
Brian Land kindly offered to bring his super motor mower &, in 2 shakes of a cat's whisker, cut all the lawns in our garden. This job would have taken me hours & hours with our old machine. Mum & I decided then that we ought to buy a motor mower.

23rd April 1975 Wednesday

As an Executive Officer in the Civil Service, I have been asked to go on a 2 week's course at Swansea, on the art of "management". This will be the first 2 weeks in June. There will be 4 E.O.s from our office going on this type of course, but all at different times – Eric, Ralph, Steve and me.

25th April 1975 Friday

One thing I shall miss at the beginning of June is the great Common Market Referendum.
On June 5th the whole country is going to the polls to decide whether or not we wish to stay in the Common Market. Although we are in the Common Market now, it is up to the people to say whether we stay in.

27th April 1975 Sunday

Mum & I have now acquired a Qualcast Jetstream 15″ Rotary Lawn Mower – cost - £42.
This is a lawn mower run like a scooter on a mixture of ½ a pint of oil to 1 gallon of petrol. Like a scooter, it has a crankshaft, carburettor, flywheel, sparking plug etc. & needs the same sort of maintenance and servicing.

29th April 1975 Tuesday

Studied the Swansea holiday guide & register of accommodation for somewhere suitable to stay in June. Chose the page "Furnished Flats & Flatlets" & found that the Langland Court Hotel had one & two bedroom luxury flats with 1. Ample car park 2. Central heating 3. Radio in bedrooms 4. Telephone service for residents. So I rang them.

1st May 1975 Thursday

I have accepted the Langland Court Hotel's offer of "an apartment" for the first 2 weeks in June. "The luxury appointed apartments have a commanding view of the Bristol Channel, & consist of a large lounge with a sun balcony, one double bedded room, fully equipped kitchen, shower & toilet. Private steps lead to the beach."

3rd May 1975 Saturday

Tomorrow I shall be 16,000 days old.
Cup Final Day! West Ham beat Fulham 2-0. Needless to say poor old Leicester were knocked out in the 5th round. The Cup this year was presented by H.R.H. the Duke of Kent. Attendance was 100,000. Receipts: £303,000. This was an all-time record.

5th May 1975 Monday

Her Britannic Majesty – Queen Elizabeth II – is now enjoying a state visit to Japan. First of all she went to Jamaica for a few days, then on to Hawaii where she stayed last Thursday & Friday (on a private visit). On Saturday she made a brief stop in Guam, then on to Hong Kong from Sunday until next Wednesday, & then Japan.

7th May 1975 Wednesday

An indication of the problems facing the great Driver & Vehicle Licensing Centre (D.V.L.C.) at Swansea is the latest vacancy for a top salaried man to take charge of an "urgent & complicated exercise designed to move work involving some 600 – 700 posts (not yet filled) away from D.V.L.C. into the local office network".

9th May 1975 Friday

"Ballet for All". Again the dancers of the Royal Ballet were at Coalville, where Mum & I went to see them twice. First performance was "Sun King, Swan Queen" showing the development of ballet from the 17th century, Louis XIV as the Sun to Swan Lake; & secondly the creation of "La Fille Mal Gardée".

11th May 1975 Sunday

Our Sunday School Outing this year is to be on Mum's birthday – August 23rd – to Slimbridge Wildfowl Trust. It is hoped we may possibly be able to combine this with a visit to Gloucester Cathedral & also Berkeley Castle. This month, on May 24th, we have a Parish outing to Oxford & a guided tour of the Colleges.

13th May 1975 Tuesday

Another outing which has been arranged by our Rector – the Revd. Buckroyd – is to York on Saturday 21st June. A conducted tour of the Minster has been booked for 11 a.m. we are hoping also to have a boat trip on the river & maybe a tour of the ancient city walls. Our Rector certainly arranges some interesting outings for us.

15th May 1975 Thursday

Department of the Environment, Driver and Vehicle Licensing Directorate, sends regular memos to Local Licence Offices.

The latest memo says: "During the last few weeks many letters have been received from members of the public complaining about the way the new rates of duty have been applied to borderline cases. No doubt we shall continue for some time to receive complaints & to ask you in some cases to reverse your decisions. Please bear with us in this, & also apply these principles to any complaints made to you. We shall be looking again at our budget procedures in the light of our experience this year, & any comments you make will be considered."

19th May 1975 Monday

More news from D.V.L.C. Swansea – "It has been decided to set up 9 postal Local Vehicle Licence Offices (L.V.L.O.s) in various parts of the country during early 1976. All the present 81 L.V.L.O.s are to be grouped into ten areas, each of which will be under the control of an Area Manager responsible to D.V.L.C."

21st May 1975 Wednesday

Enid & I went to the pictures at Coalville. We saw the modern musical "Jesus Christ Super-Star". This was the story of Jesus Christ seen through the eyes of 20th Century beat groups. A clever combination of the original gospel story & the super-star hero of today. A moving picture about the last week in the life of Jesus.

23rd May 1975 Friday

This year – 1975 – is amongst other things "European Architectural Heritage Year".

The idea is to halt the steady loss of irreplaceable buildings & the erosion of character in historic European towns. We want to assure for ancient buildings a living role in society today. I have therefore become more observant of all styles of buildings.

25th May 1975 Trinity Sunday

How very interesting to visit Oxford yesterday in this year of architectural observance. Here the old & the new were very much interwoven. We had a 2 hour conducted tour, starting at Christ Church, where the great 6 ton bell **Great Tom** sounds 101 times every evening to commemorate the curfew imposed by the colleges long ago.

27th May 1975 Tuesday

Britain's worst ever road disaster occurred today – Spring Bank Holiday Tuesday – when a coach load of women on an outing crashed over Devil's Bridge in the Yorkshire Dales, killing 32 & injuring 14.

Apparently the brakes failed as the coach went down a one-in-six hill & it somersaulted 20 feet into the stream below.

29th May 1975 Thursday

Yesterday, Prince Charles was installed in Westminster Abbey as Great Master of The Order of the Bath. Like a knight in shining armour, he laid his sword on the altar, while the Dean said, "I exhort & admonish you to use your sword to the Glory of God, the Defence of the Gospel ...... & of all equity & justice to the utmost of your power."

31st May 1975 Saturday

Julian's Wedding Day. A beautiful wedding – a beautiful sunny day. The vicar stressed that they were "Called of God" to this Holy Estate of Marriage.

I motored 85 miles to the wedding in Malvern, & then motored another 110 miles to Swansea, where I am staying for the next two weeks.

2nd June 1975 Monday

My first day on "Management Appreciation Course". We have 18 members on this course, & we had a pleasant day together.

This evening I visited our old Rector – the Revd. Matthew Rice Lewis - & his wife, who live just outside Swansea. They invited me to have lunch with them on Sunday, after morning Church.

4th June 1975 Wednesday

The Management Appreciation Course gets harder each day. What with "Systems Analysis" & such like, I don't think I shall ever make a manager. Some of the course is interesting, but most of it is way beyond me. Fortunately I have my delightful flat, overlooking Langland Bay, to return to.

6th June 1975 Friday

"Yes to Europe". Yesterday the country voted on the Common Market Referendum, & for the first time in our history this was a case of "Direct Government by the People Themselves". We voted "Yes" by a majority of more than two to one. At a cost of £10 million it did not really cost too much.

8th June 1975 Sunday

Yesterday I took the train to dear old Tenby – a beautiful coast ride & a delightful sunny day. It cost me £2 return from Swansea, about 1 ½ hour journey.

Our Referendum Vote last Thursday ran very much with

the voting of M.P.s themselves, when they voted 28th October 1971.

10th June 1975 Tuesday

On Sunday morning I went to St. Mary's Parish Church, Swansea (where my dad's parents were married!). What a lovely service – Morning Prayer and Holy Communion combined; with the Sunday School children there at the beginning & again at the end. As we took Communion the choir sang like angels.

12th June 1975 Thursday

Today I entered the portals of the mighty D.V.L.C. – the Driver & Vehicle Licensing Centre at Swansea. What impressed me most of all was the amount of space each member of the staff has – so different from our tightly packed office.
Had lunch there with Charlie, another course member.

14th June 1975 Saturday

Home again from Swansea, after a week of glorious sunny weather.
Stopped at Hereford for elevenses, then on to Stratford-on-Avon for lunch. Spent the afternoon at Stratford – shopping – walking by the river - & lying on the grass by Shakespeare's delightful monument. **"I laid me down with a Will?"**

16th June 1975 Monday

Yesterday was our Sunday School Anniversary. With 11 children in my class aged 8 – 11, & 24 in Diane's class aged under 8, we had a lovely day. I played guitar for my class who sang & played tambourines. 1. The Lord of the Dance. 2. He's Got the Whole World in His Hands.
3. Stand Up, Clap Hands.

18th June 1975 Wednesday

Britain's first supply of North Sea Oil was proudly piped ashore today – the anniversary of Waterloo. Energy Secretary Tony Benn said, "This is far more significant & historic for Britain than a Moon shot. This is a day of national celebration. We will in time be one of the top ten oil producers in the world."

20th June 1975 Friday

Our proposed outing to York (see 13th May 1975) has been cancelled. We did not have enough people to make a bus load. Maybe we chose the wrong day. There are numerous fêtes & galas in the neighbourhood at this time of year – people are away on holiday & coming up shortly is the "Holiday Fortnight" for this area.

22nd June 1975 Sunday

Our new standard roses, planted last winter on 26th December, are just coming into bloom.
But what a surprise! The first one to flower was one of the pink ones – 2 beautiful pink roses right at the top, & **on the same tree** – one gorgeous **red** rose.

24th June 1975 Tuesday

Chancellor of the Exchequer, Denis Healey, today appealed on television for co-operation from everyone in the next few weeks to beat inflation. "Without it, we are all sunk" he warned. This means co-operation from the all powerful unions. Prime Minister Harold Wilson stressed "Consent & consensus."

26th June 1975 Thursday

Having drawn out all my money from S.A.Y.E. (6th March 1975), with virtually nothing in the bank – no premium bonds, & still owing Mum £400, I signed on the dotted line today to join the new index linked save as you earn scheme, operative from 1st July.
£20 per month. (The maximum allowed).

28th June 1975 Saturday

Remember my "Kings & Queens of England"? (See 10th August 1973). Well, I have now acquired these same Kings & Queens of England, from William I to Elizabeth II in picture form. The whole set in postage stamp form cost 50p – what a bargain!
So I have paid £5·75p to have them framed to match.

30th June 1975 Monday

After 4 weeks of continuous sunshine, the gardens are baked dry. The grass is wilting, but every-one looks beautifully sun-tanned. This week is the 2nd week of the great Wimbledon fortnight & we are all enjoying some great tennis on television.

2nd July 1975 Wednesday

Remember Alison Hewes, born 20th December 1967? Now a lively 7 year old, she is Enid's niece. Enid has offered to take Alison to London for the day during the long summer school holiday. She wants to show her Buckingham Palace, Trafalgar Square & Big Ben; & has invited me to accompany them.

4th July 1975 Friday

July 4th 1776 – American Independence.
So, next year America celebrates its bi-centenary. This week, one of only 21 recorded copies of the American Declaration of Independence was sold at Christie's for £40,000. It was "slit along folds and repaired at back with tape, some spots & stains".

6th July 1975 Sunday

Bunting, my half-sister, is **60** tomorrow! How the years fly.
Reevsie was 40 last month, and Mum will be 70 next month. It's funny how age progresses with you. When Bunting was 40 I remember thinking, "Oh dear – how old!" Now that I am over 40 I think, "How lovely to be 44 next week."

8th July 1975 Tuesday

Every year at work (November time) we have a Census. This is like an annual stock-taking, based on a one in ten study of the records. Today we receive a letter from Dept. of Environment saying 6 Local Taxation Offices (including ours) are to have a one in hundred extra sample census in August.

10th July 1975 Thursday

I have been chosen to "manage" our mini Census next month. The idea of this Census is to obtain information to measure the degree of error in the Annual Census. The 6 offices have been chosen on their Vehicle Population Totals.

Full instructions will be provided – so meet "**Manager Hewsie**".

12th July 1975 Saturday
Tosca the beautiful, Tosca the beloved, is now old & crotchety. Tosca's front paws are bent with rheumatism, so Tosca now has the antics of a kangaroo, developing powerful back legs, bounding along with front paws in mid-air, & sitting up like a dog. Or just waits to be carried – poor old "Hoppity".

14th July 1975 Monday
44 today = 2 x 2 x 11. This year I complete my 27 years of service in the Motor Licence Office, to qualify for 6 week's annual holiday.

Do you know what I would like best to do with my extra days' holiday? Answer – visit America during her bi-centenary next year, & see the giant redwoods of California.

16th July 1975 Wednesday
The first international space link-up is about to take place. Yesterday a Soyuz spacecraft was sent up from the Baikonur Launch Complex in Russia to go into Earth orbit. Shortly afterwards an Apollo spacecraft was launched from the Kennedy Space Centre in the U.S.A. Tomorrow they hope to dock together in space.

18th July 1975 Friday
Yesterday we followed on television the drama of the Apollo/Soyuz link-up. We saw Apollo Commander Thomas Stafford float weightless down the 10 foot metal tunnel linking Apollo with Soyuz & grasp the hand of Soyuz Pilot – Alexei Leonov. America & Russia joined hands across the universe.

20th July 1975 Sunday
The Apollo/Soyuz link-up reminded me so much of Michelangelo's masterpiece of painting in the Sistine Chapel in Rome, which I saw this year on April 9th.

Painted between 1508 & 1512, the frescoes which decorate the vault include "The Creation of Adam". Here God reaches to Man across the Universe.

22nd July 1975 Tuesday
Have been busy sorting out details of our Mini-Census, which is to take place August 4th.

I estimated a total of 240,000 vehicles on our files. We hope to work on blocks of 60 at a time. Ten teams of 2 people will monitor 4 blocks each.

24th July 1975 Thursday
"Matron" of Ashby Hospital, now aged 63 & retired, asked Mum & me to accompany her to the Cheshire Home, Staunton Harold, which she visits every week as a personal friend of so many of the patients there. It was a joy to see the happiness she radiated. They all absolutely adored her.

26th July 1975 Saturday
Mum & I went to Loughborough to see Mum's Cousin Cyril & his wife Elsie. Cyril is 74, & has not been at all well lately. He has difficulty getting up from a chair & walks very slowly, shuffling his feet along. He can no longer drive his car – his chief joy in life - & naturally feels very depressed.

28th July 1975 Monday
Three days holiday this week, so I ventured all alone in the car, 100 miles to Skegness. Managed to book bed & breakfast for a couple of nights at a little place in Life Boat Avenue. Visited Seacroft Drive, where Auntie Cis used to live, & called to see her neighbour Miss Ancient.

30th July 1975 Wednesday
Three days of scorching hot weather. Visited Sutton-on-Sea & Mablethorpe.
Came home today via Boston where I stayed from 11a.m. to 2p.m. Had a good look round Boston & lay on the grass in the shade of the mighty bell tower of the church. Then on to Grantham & spent an hour looking round Grantham.

1st August 1975 Friday
On August 11th this year a Viking spacecraft will blast off from Cape Canaveral U.S.A. to go on an 11 month 450 million mile journey to Mars.
The Viking will reach Mars on June 18th 1976, & go into orbit round the planet, photographing every detail before actually landing on Mars on 4th July.

3rd August 1975 Sunday
The scorching hot weather continues. By day the temperature is over 90°F (32°C) & throughout the night it is too hot for any bedclothes. The most ardent sun-seekers have to seek the shade. Tosca is out of doors day & night, either under the bushes, under the garden seat, or somewhere in the shade.

5th August 1975 Tuesday
You will be pleased to know our mini-Census went off very well & was finished in record time.
I thoroughly enjoyed being at the hub of events, with everyone – like the spokes of a wheel – working through me. I kept a record of all that was going on, with each team bringing me information.

7th August 1975 Thursday
Mary Moore, Mum's cousin from Colchester, arrived in a sizzling heat-wave to spend 10 days with Mum & me. We have all been invited to lunch on Sunday with Mary's friend Molly & her husband Eddie Donaldson at nearby Donington-le-Heath.

9th August 1975 Saturday
Enid & I have chosen Monday 11th August to take 7 year old Alison on her first visit to London. So we are all looking forward to this adventure. Alison has read a little picture book on London & has picked out the places she most wants to see. We are hoping to catch the 7-30a.m. train which arrives in London at 9a.m.

11th August 1975 Monday
A delightful day in London. Visited Madame Tussaud's – then to Trafalgar Square, which turned out to be Alison's favourite place in London – then Whitehall – Downing Street – St. James Park – Buckingham Palace – back down the Mall to see Trafalgar Square again, & finally a river trip to Tower Bridge.

13th August 1975 Wednesday
Visited Reg Hall's newly built luxury house in Main Street, Ravenstone. He had everything money could buy – gold taps in the bathroom – lighting in the lounge which could be dimmed or bright, beautiful pictures, & best quality wall paper.

15th August 1975 Friday
More news from D.V.L.C. Swansea (see 19th May 1975).
It has now been decided not to set up 9 postal Local Vehicle Licence Offices. All the present 81 L.V.L.O.s deal only with counter applications. Everything by post is passed to Swansea – Swansea cannot cope, so the 81 L.V.L.O.s may soon be dealing with post as well.

17th August 1975 Sunday
Last winter was the mildest winter since 1869. And this summer has been the hottest since 1869. Not even the oldest members of the family have ever known a British summer quite like this one. The reason we have had mild winters recently is that the **ice** appears to be retreating around Iceland.

19th August 1975 Tuesday
Auntie Doris of Mountsorrel is 80 today. Auntie Doris, formerly Doris Moore, related to Mary Moore, is related to Mum via Mum's father Tom Sketchley. We visited Auntie Doris last week & you would never have guessed she was 80. Full of vim & vigour, in a sleeveless white dress.

21st August 1975 Thursday
"**Work When You Like**" (see 20th March 1972). Leicestershire County Council has now decided to introduce "**Flexitime**" and "**Flexileave**". The scheme is to be launched in October, & we have been given full instructions. The scheme will be administered in each department by supervisors – so I may be a supervisor.

23rd August 1975 Saturday
Sunday School Outing to Gloucester Cathedral, Slimbridge Wildfowl trust & Berkeley Castle. We had conducted tours of both the Cathedral & the Castle which were most interesting. Saw where the 9 year old boy was crowned Edward II in Gloucester Cathedral, & where the same King Edward II, aged 43, was murdered in the Castle.

25th August 1975 Monday
Bank Holiday Monday. Spent the whole day re-arranging the landscaped garden. Moved turf back into the lawn where I had put 6 slabs, & set the slabs out in a different design where I had set the magnolia. Moved the magnolia to the lawn to allow it ample space to display its beauty.

27th August 1975 Wednesday
Meet Elizabeth Hewes, aged 44, member 080171 of S.C.S. Society of Civil Servants.
I resigned in disgust from C.P.S.A. on 27th February 1973. C.P.S.A. is the union which looks after Clerical Officers in the Civil Service. S.C.S. is a different union for Executive Officers & other higher grades.

29th August 1975 Friday
Auntie Cis is dying. After 2 heart attacks she is now very frail & has not been out of bed for a week now. Auntie Dos, Pat & I visited her in the Ava Nursing Home, Leicester, but she barely opened her eyes. For 80 years she enjoyed good health, but the last 3 years have been sad for her.

31st August 1975 Sunday
Hewes, Ethel May (Cis), late of Skegness, loving sister of Dos, passed peacefully away at the Ava House Nursing Home, Leicester, on August 31st, 1975, aged 83 years. Funeral service at Marlborough Square Methodist Church, on Thursday September 4th at 2-45p.m. followed by cremation at Loughborough. Cortege from 25b Leicester Road, Ravenstone.

2nd September 1975 Tuesday
Auntie Dos & I went to see Auntie Cis as she lay in her coffin in the Chapel of Rest at Coalville. She looked very beautiful in pink & white, & much younger than her years. As I looked at her, I could see myself in her features – the same shaped forehead & bone structure, more apparent than usual.

4th September 1975 Thursday
Today I went to 2 funeral services.
1.) 12-30p.m. at St. David's Broomleys, Coalville, for the funeral of Fred Burton, aged 62, Secretary of Coalville Amateurs for the past 17 years, &
2.) 2-45p.m. at Marlborough Square Chapel, Coalville, for the funeral of Auntie Cis, aged 83.

6th September 1975 Saturday
Again I came – I saw – I conked out. (see 2nd October 1970) There I was, at the A6 junction halfway between Ravenstone & Willoughby-on-the-Wolds, where I was going to pick Mum **up**. And again a Knight of the Road came to my rescue, staying with me for an hour, to make sure I was alright.

8th September 1975 Monday
In September 1970, 2 men from Swansea came to our office at County Hall, Glenfield, Leicester, & spent all day giving us a detailed account of the work covered by the Ministry of Transport. Now we have been invited to go to Swansea for a whole day conducted tour of the great Driver & Vehicle Licensing Centre.

10th September 1975 Wednesday
Driving Licences will cost £5 from January 1st next year, & last until the holder's 70th birthday, it was officially announced today.
At the moment Driving Licences are renewed every 3 years. In future, drivers over 70 will be able to renew their licence every 3 years. My present licence expires 31st December 1977.

12th September 1975 Friday
So great was the response from the staff of our Local Taxation Office to visit D.V.L.C. Swansea, that Swansea (yet again) cannot cope. So our names have gone into a hat & only the lucky few will be going. Six names were down for September 25th – including mine. Only one – Gladys – was chosen.

14th September 1975 Sunday

"And it came to pass, when King Hezekiah heard it ……" See II Kings, Chapter 19. Then see Isaiah, Chapter 37.

What have we here? Two chapters in the bible almost word for word alike. Well, I never knew that until today. This amazing fact was revealed to me by Mr Biggs our organist.

16th September 1975 Tuesday

Hail to the Champions! Leicestershire are County Cricket Champions – the amazing Grace Road Heroes are Champions of English County Cricket for the first time in 96 years. Best bowler was Captain Ray Illingworth; best batsman was Brian Davison.

18th September 1975 Thursday

The Leicester Cathedral Tower Appeal brought in £27,000. That means we need another £3,000. This last £3,000 is the hardest to get, so we are to have on 4th October a sponsored walk in Bradgate Park; & on 5th December an evening entertainment in Leicester.

20th September 1975 Saturday

The Revd. Gerald Vandeleur, Rector of Ravenstone 1890-1903, married a young couple in the village, & gave them a china tea service for a wedding present. The bride was Lizzie Hewes (sister of my grandpa George Harry) Cousin Audrey (her daughter) says she would like to give this now to me – "**To keep it in the family**".

22nd September 1975 Monday

Supervisors have now been chosen for our Flexitime. Jackie, John, Geoff, Frank, Eric, Ralph. (Not me) We start on 1st October. We may start work any time from 8-00a.m. – 9-30a.m. We may finish any time between 4-30p.m. and 6-00p.m., provided we total the necessary number of working hours.

24th September 1975 Wednesday

Gerald Ford, President of America since August 1974, is now campaigning for the 1976 Presidential Election.

Twice this month he would have been assassinated had it not been for split-second action by his magnificent bodyguards. But he insists, "I will not cower in the White House."

26th September 1975 Friday

The cost of computerising driving records at Swansea has more than doubled since the scheme was first planned, a Report of the Commons Public Accounts Committee announced today. When the scheme was costed in 1968, it was estimated it would take £145 million – now it will cost £350 million.

28th September 1975 Sunday

At 12 noon we assembled at little St. Mary's for the burial of Auntie Cis's ashes in her dad & mother's grave. At 3 p.m. we assembled again at little St. Mary's for the Harvest Festival. The new vicar of Snibston, the Revd. Peter R. Ince, took the service, & told us of his 5 years spent in Bengal.

30th September 1975 Tuesday

Yesterday the **Post Office** went **Metric**. The cost of the change over will be £1,500,000. Letters will be weighed at 60 grammes instead of the familiar 2 ounces. Later this will be reduced to 50 grammes. Next in line is milk – from pints to litres; meat is due for conversion in 1977; petrol in 1978, & then mileage.

2nd October 1975 Thursday

O.P.E.C. the 13 nation Organisation of Petroleum Exporting Countries have agreed to increase prices by 10%. The price will remain frozen for 9 months – until June 30th 1976. This means we shall be paying an extra 8p per gallon. The majority including Iran, Iraq, Gabon, Nigeria & Libya wanted 15% more.

4th October 1975 Saturday

Went with Sylvia (from the office) to Wanlip Church to see Charles & Renee married.

Charles & Renee are both in their sixties. Charles a widower, & Renee a widow, met at County Hall. Charles has a son Michael who is a parson & he conducted the service. A lovely service & a full church.

6th October 1975 Monday

More & more is our office feeling the effect of Swansea's take-over. In the office we have 2 distinct sections –

1. The L.T.O. which deals with vehicles not yet on computer record.
2. The L.V.L.O. which deals with Swansea.

We who are in L.T.O. are now enjoying comparative ease & leisure.

8th October 1975 Wednesday

Sylvia at work decided to invite her friend Pat to give a week by week course of crochet instruction at Sylvia's home to a few ladies interested in learning to crochet.

So, I joined the class & have had 2 lessons so far. I am hoping to complete a pretty sleeveless jacket in pink wool.

10th October 1975 Friday

Flexitime has a tremendous effect on County Hall, Glenfield, Leicestershire. No more dilly-dallying in the cloakroom first thing in the morning. Everybody comes to work on the dot. Many choose ½ hour lunch break instead of the usual 1 hour; & enjoy the benefit of leaving ½ hour early at night.

12th October 1975 Sunday

Harvest Festival at Ravenstone. At the Children's Gift Service this afternoon the children sang another "Song of Harvest" which I had written. I played guitar, & 5 little children sang with me – Arthur Needham, Elaine & Susan Gandy, Susan Land, and Jane Wright.

14th October 1975 Tuesday

Continuing my simplification of the garden, I have now ordered another 8 slabs to put in a diamond design inside the rose bed.

Also cleared one almighty overgrown rockery & have re-arranged the rocks into a pretty design; covered the rockery with a lot more soil, & set new plants.

16th October 1975 Thursday

Leicestershire Keep Fit Association presented a Festival

of Keep Fit at the De Montfort Hall, Leicester, & I had a seat on the front row of the balcony.

There were various items including skipping – balls & hoops – national dancing – scarves (produced by the **Cuz** – i.e. **Enid**) & gym display.

18th October 1975 Saturday

Stung again! I never knew anybody stung so often. 1969 – 1970 – 1973 & now today for the 4th time I have been stung by a wasp. There I was doing a bit of landscape gardening, picked up a great piece of rockery with my bare hands & …… you've guessed it …… there lurked a wasp!

20th October 1975 Monday

Prince Fahd, the Crown Prince of Saudi Arabia, arrived in England today for a four-day visit.

He was greeted with all the deference due to a mighty oil sheik. We are hoping to borrow millions of pounds from him to help us through our financial crisis; so out with the red carpet & magic carpet.

22nd October 1975 Wednesday

James Callaghan, Foreign Secretary, has arranged to fly to Saudi Arabia next month; and Harold Wilson, the Prime Minister, is to go also.

Prince Fahd told Mr Wilson his country wants Britain as a major partner in their great leap forward into the 21st Century. They will spend £80 million with us.

24th October 1975 Friday

Coalville's new Market Hall was in use today for the first time. A spanking new market to replace the old derelict tumble-down market with its rusty corrugated ramshackle roof & puddled ground. And what was the general verdict? – "Oh, we'd rather have the good old market."

26th October 1975 Sunday

Oh, the beauty of autumn. Mum & I went for an afternoon drive in the car to see autumn at its very best along the lanes of Charnwood Forest, where for mile after mile the trees meet across the road. "The most charming period of the year."

According to Ovid – the Autumn; according to Virgil – the Spring.

28th October 1975 Tuesday

"The £68,000-a-day monster that's driving us all mad". So heads an article in the Daily Express about D.V.L.C. Swansea. It says that D.V.L.C. admits to having had training problems – it has been hit by power crises – and a strike of civil servants. But D.V.L.C. says the worst is over.

30th October 1975 Thursday

Patrick Porter, chief information officer at D.V.L.C. who "confidently said the worst is over" answers critics of the Swansea set-up by saying, "On the Driving Licence side we just about break even. On the Vehicle side we are primarily a revenue gathering organisation netting £750 million a year in taxes."

1st November 1975 Saturday

And so we sadly say farewell to all our Vehicle Records which we have brought forth & cared for over the years. Every new vehicle goes direct to D.V.L.C. Swansea for computer record. Every registration ending L, M or N goes to D.V.L.C. on renewal of licence, & starting today "K" is also going to D.V.L.C.

3rd November 1975 Monday

The Irish, who have been blowing each other up for the past 6 years, are now concentrating their efforts in England – London in particular. They send letter bombs & parcels which blow up when opened; they plant bombs underneath parked cars & inside public buildings. They have now killed 60 people.

5th November 1975 Wednesday

Britain is now going deeper & deeper into debt. Chancellor Denis Healey is seeking a loan of £975 million from the International Monetary Fund. Already this year we have borrowed £1,000 million including £200 million from the Shah of Iran. Since 1973 we have borrowed altogether over £5,000 million.

7th November 1975 Friday

We are hoping to pay our colossal national debts with the help of our North Sea Oil. But before we benefit from this revenue we have to pay for actually getting the oil. As the government wants the maximum profit from North Sea Oil, it is to nationalise the lot - £900 million for The British National Oil Corporation.

9th November 1975 Sunday

Evening Prayer at 4 p.m. This is the latest idea at Ravenstone Church for the winter months. It is to preserve fuel, & is proving to be very satisfactory. It means we are home for tea, & can then settle by the fireside for the evening. Today we were joined by Coalville Male Voice Choir.

11th November 1975 Tuesday

Mr Sharp, Geoff, Steve, Miss Gazzard, Muriel & I went this morning to St Andrew's Church, Aylestone, for the funeral of our old colleague Mr Hollier, aged 72, who retired 7 years ago. The church was beautifully adorned with masses of poppies, being Remembrance Day, & the sun streamed through the windows.

13th November 1975 Thursday

The Department of the Environment was 5 years old yesterday. Sir Ian Bancroft is the new Permanent Secretary, & succeeds Sir James Jones, the Permanent Secretary since 1972. He in turn succeeded Sir David Serpell, DOE's Permanent Secretary from the start. Dr John Gilbert is Minister for Transport.

15th November 1975 Saturday

Went with a bus load from Coalville Amateur Operatic Society to Doncaster to see "Viva Mexico" which will be given by Coalville next March. A lively colourful show, which I thoroughly enjoyed. We had a very eventful journey, including one shattered windscreen, which exploded like a bomb.

17th November 1975 Monday

Remember Cousin **Hayden**? (See 26th May 1971) Well, now from the little town of Snowflake, Arizona, U.S.A.

comes the most astounding story of Travis Walton, aged 22, kidnapped on 5th November by a flying saucer, & released 5 days later – gaunt, 10lbs lighter in weight, & with a frightening tale to tell.

19th November 1975 Wednesday

Travis Walton, a tree trimmer in the Sitgreave-Apache National Forest, was pole-axed by a brilliant blue & white flash from a flying saucer hovering 15 feet above the trees. He was knocked unconscious, & when he woke up he was on his back on a table looking up at 3 weird creatures, about 5 feet tall.

21st November 1975 Friday

The three weird non-human creatures who kidnapped Travis Walton looked like well-developed foetus. They wore tan-brown robes, tight fitting. Their skin was white, like a mushroom, & they had no clear features. **They made no sound.** They had no hair, their foreheads domed, & their eyes were very large.

23rd November 1975 Sunday

God performs miracles with the help of Man. (See 27th October 1974)

The Rector of Ravenstone, the Revd. Buckroyd, spoke today about the miracle of feeding the 5,000. He talked of the starving millions & stressed the need for ordered discipline – "Make the men sit down .... in ranks by hundreds, & by fifties."

25th November 1975 Tuesday

Again the Queen has opened Parliament – the 24th Parliament of her reign, & again she closed with these words, "My Lords & members of the House of Commons, I pray that the blessing of Almighty God may rest upon your counsels."

As in 1605 we have gunpowder & plot.

27th November 1975 Thursday

The Queen said from the throne, "My Government will continue to strive for a constitutional solution to the problems of Northern Ireland ..... My Government will continue to give the highest priority to the attack on inflation & unemployment. The law of conspiracy in England & Wales will be reformed."

29th November 1975 Saturday

Our annual Christmas Fair in Ravenstone Village Institute & our 4th effort with a stall for the Sunday School. This year we made £18. The children brought lots of useful items for sale, & the children themselves served behind the stall. The photographer from the local press took their photograph.

1st December 1975 Monday

Had my 2nd interview with Mr Sharp, as last year (See 26th November 1974). Mr Sharp will be retiring next April, so the interview was more like a fond farewell. He talked of all the changes & improvements we have had over the years, & the changes we can expect in the near future, when we leave County Hall.

3rd December 1975 Wednesday

As we gradually go metric, the Metrication Board gives us little rhymes to help – example: -

A metre measures three foot three; it's longer than a yard you see. Two and a quarter pounds of jam weigh about a kilogram. A litre of water's a pint & three quarters.

But still I prefer division by 12.

5th December 1975 Friday

God does not measure in tens. God measures in twelves. (See Revelation Chap.21) See the Holy City, New Jerusalem. See the wall with 12 gates – on the east 3 gates, on the north 3 gates, on the south 3 gates & on the west 3 gates – the length & the breadth & the height are equal.

7th December 1975 Sunday

On February 16th this year we had our Sunday School Prize Giving (2 months late). So today we had our accepted time for the Prize Giving, just before Christmas. We had nearly 50 children, more than we have had for a long time, thanks mainly to the endeavours of Diane, who is so good with the infants.

9th December 1975 Tuesday

DOE World – the newspaper for the Department of the Environment, this month carries a 3 page article in fullest praise of DVLC Swansea. "The truth is a success story which has saved the whole system of maintaining driver & vehicle records from falling into total disarray." DVLC now employs 5,000 people.

11th December 1975 Thursday

DOE World says, "In 1950 there were 5 ½ million drivers in this country, compared with more than 20 million today. There were 4 ½ million vehicles, compared with 17 ½ million today.

By 1977 DVLC will be handling 500,000 items of mail every day – five tons of it – ⅔ of the town's mail.

12th December 1975 Friday

Dexter – John. In fond memory of John – from his many Friends and Colleagues in the County Motor Tax Office.

13th December 1975 Saturday

Harry Lorayne, America's top Memory Man, fascinated us on television with his amazing memory. He said he learned from Aristotle to memorise by association of ideas.

Example – transcribe a pack of cards into 4 different groups of people you know, 13 from work, 13 from the family, etc. & you will know who is missing.

15th December 1975 Monday

Harry Lorayne taught us how to give a speech lasting 6 hours without referring to notes.

Progress in thought from a certain place you know, & in the first place you talk about such & such, in the second place you go on to the next thought sequence, etc.

Hence the origin of the well known phrase – "in the first place".

17th December 1975 Wednesday

Auntie Cis has left me £500 in her Will, & I have received the cheque signed by brother Pat, "Executor of Miss E. M. Hewes, deceased."

So now I am able to pay off the remaining £250 which Mum gave me to buy my car in July 1973. I shall endeavour to save the other £250 for my next car.

19th December 1975 Friday

I have now purchased for our landscaped garden, a beautiful Witney Sundial in Doulting Stone from Fowkes Garden Centre, Syston, Leicestershire. This cost £30 – so you might say my Christmas present from Auntie Cis.

I thought immediately of the good King Hezekiah & his sundial. (Isaiah 38, 8.)

21st December 1975 Sunday

My beautiful electric type-writer which I bought for £100 in May 1969 has now been declared redundant & worth only £10 for spares. Like a motor car, it has depreciated rapidly.

So I have now exchanged it for a second-hand non-electric Olivetti 82, offered for sale at £80.

23rd December 1975 Tuesday

Meet **Nessiteras Rhombopteryx**, i.e. Nessie the Loch Ness Monster, now officially acknowledged after under-water cameras have finally managed to photograph this elusive monster.

The name means The Ness Monster with Diamond Fin, & has been put forward by British naturalist Peter Scott and Dr. Rines.

25th December 1975 Thursday

My beloved Provost this Christmas tells of a sermon preached before the King at Whitehall in 1606 by Bishop Lancelot Andrewes. He shows how Heaven & Earth meet in the Christ-Child. A manger for the child – a star for the Son of God; Shepherds see the child – a choir of angels see the Son of God.

27th December 1975 Saturday

"All through the life of Christ you see Heaven & Earth meeting together. Jesus hungered as a man, yet he fed 5,000 as the Son of God. He died as the son of Adam, at the same time disposing of Paradise as the Son of God."

So Bishop Andrewes, over the centuries gives us our Christmas message.

29th December 1975 Monday

Nessiteras Rhombopteryx has proved to be an anagram of "**Monster Hoax by Sir Peter S**." The name was put forward by Sir Peter Scott and Dr. Robert Rines – leader of the team from the Academy of Applied Science in Boston, Mass., who spent four weeks working at Loch Ness last summer.

31st December 1975 Wednesday

And so we come to the end of another year – a year of galloping inflation – of terrorists at home & abroad – of mass unemployment; the age of the computer, when we become a number rather than a member of Christ, or the child of God, but Christmas as ever brings love & hope to the world.

* * *

1976

1st January 1976 Thursday
1976 arrived with gale force ferocity & hurricane winds, the likes of which I have never before experienced. A trail of debris covered the whole of Britain & other countries of Western Europe. It smashed down our garden fence & completely severed a line post.

3rd January 1976 Saturday
Everyone today is gathering up the pieces after the dreadful gale. Keith Carter, our next door neighbour, helped me re-assemble our fence. Giant trees littered the roads, uprooted or snapped in two. People everywhere have been up ladders seeing to the roof & putting back the tiles.

5th January 1976 Monday
Today came news of the bloodiest murder yet in Northern Ireland. Every day we hear of one person or another shot dead, but today in South Armagh 10 Protestants, travelling home from work in a mini-bus, were ambushed & machine-gunned to death by Catholics known as the South Armagh Republican Action Force.

7th January 1976 Wednesday
A spokesman for the South Armagh Republican Action Force said, "We wish to claim full responsibility for the shooting of 10 Protestants. It was in retaliation for the killing on Sunday night of the Reavey brothers at Whitecross, & the O'Dowd family at Ballydougan. In future, every outrage against the Catholics will be met with accordingly."

9th January 1976 Friday
The Government of Italy collapsed in a sudden crisis this week. The Government was a coalition Government of Christian Democrats and Republicans who have agreed to differ. This leaves the way now wide open to the Communist Party who already control the municipal council of every major city in Italy except Rome.

11th January 1976 Sunday
America fears that Russia will turn Italy into a Russian beach-head in the Northern Mediterranean. Because of this, United States "Central Intelligence Agency" the C.I.A. has given £3 million of secret funds to Italy's Christian Democrats to boost their political strength. The C.I.A. is similarly supporting both Greece & Portugal.

12th January 1976 Monday
On this day the world's most successful detective story writer, Agatha Christie, died.

13th January 1976 Tuesday
As in the days of the rising Napoleon it was the Pope versus Napoleon, so today it is the Pope versus Communism. With Italy in almost total political & economic chaos, Pope Paul VI now aged 78, has begun to prepare for the battle ahead between Church & Communism. Today's Napoleon is Enrico Berlinguer.

15th January 1976 Thursday
The S.A.S. is the Special Air Service; their emblem is a winged dagger & their motto, "Who Dares Wins". They are Britain's toughest soldiers & they are now being sent to South Armagh in Northern Ireland to sort out the trouble there.

17th January 1976 Saturday
Now for the good news. The weather at the moment is just like spring, & the blackbirds sing to their hearts content. It is a joy to hear them.
Today I had a good old shopping bonanza in Coalville. I bought a new carpet for the kitchen £16, and a gorgeous new hearth-rug £21.

19th January 1976 Monday
All of a sudden we are overwhelmed with offers of help in Ravenstone Sunday School. Having plodded manfully on for many years, just managing to keep the Sunday School going, we now have an influx of dynamic teachers ready to revolutionise the whole system in 20th Century style.

21st January 1976 Wednesday
Concorde today made its historic maiden commercial supersonic flight.
Designed jointly by France & England, Britain's Concorde lifted off the runway at London's Heathrow Airport on its flight to Bahrain at precisely the same time that France's Concorde left Paris for Rio de Janeiro.

23rd January 1976 Friday
Passengers flying in Concorde are 11 miles high – over 55,000 feet – above troposphere (an elliptical layer of atmosphere) into the stratosphere. So at mid-day they see the sky above as midnight blue, separated from the usual sky-blue below by a band of indigo.
A journey indeed **out of this world**.

25th January 1976 Sunday
The Queen hopes to fly in Concorde next July to America for the U.S. bi-centennial celebrations, & then on to Canada to open the Montreal Olympic Games.
President Giscard d'Estaing of France also hopes to visit America in May this year, in their identical Air France Concorde.

27th January 1976 Tuesday
£3,000 per year. Such is the rate of inflation that my salary has trebled in 7 years. (See 30th April 1969) This of course has been helped considerably by my promotion to E.O.
Compare then June 1st 1974. Petrol is now 75p per gallon. I reckon £15 per week to live on, & save £20 per month S.A.Y.E.

29th January 1976 Thursday
Inflation and unemployment go hand in hand. This includes the Civil Service.
Right now Ministers are discussing means to reduce Civil Service manpower requirements over the next 2 years. They have already decided that expenditure on salaries & administrative costs in civil departments in 1978-79 should be less.

31st January 1976 Saturday

"**Viva Mexico**" – Coalville Amateurs' forthcoming production is taking shape very well.

I have been asked to be prompter & this week I joined them at rehearsals. The show will be the first week in March & I have arranged to have a week's holiday for then – lovely having 6 weeks holiday.

2nd February 1976 Monday

Leicester Cathedral's Jubilee Year is to start this year & culminate next February.

On June 13th there is to be open air Eucharist on Leicester City Football Ground, at which Dr. Coggan the Archbishop of Canterbury will preside & preach. In September there is to be "Jubilation in Flowers".

4th February 1976 Wednesday

Brian Lamming – my number one heart-throb – renewed his Driving Licence this week, & for the first time was asked to give his date of birth.

He was born on the 7th day of the first month of the year 1928. He belongs therefore to the Chalcedon sign of Capricorn – my perfect partner.

6th February 1976 Friday

Prince Charles came to Coalville this evening for the 6th annual dinner of the North West Leicestershire branch of the National Farmers' Union at the North Leicestershire Miners' Welfare Centre. He came by air to Castle Donington Airport and then by car down Wash Lane & past our house to Coalville.

8th February 1976 Sunday

Ethel May Hewes, - late of 3 Seacroft Drive, Skegness, who died on August 31 last, left £18,800 gross, £18,560 net. She left £500 each to Hinckley and District Society for Mentally Handicapped Children and the Salvation Army, for the use of the Skegness branch.

Auntie Cis provided for Auntie Dos in her Will by letting her have all the interest on her capital. I have been appointed trustee.

10th February 1976 Tuesday

The latest memo from D.V.L.C. says, "There has been some evidence recently that a small number of local office staff have made implied criticisms to the public about the performance of the D.V.L.C. Whilst not seeking to deny that we are having our troubles at the Centre, it must be emphasised that we are all L.T.O.s, L.V.L.O.s, & D.V.L.C., part of the same team. You can make a valuable contribution to good relations by continuing to deal with the public with sympathy & tolerance, & above all by emphasising that your colleagues at Swansea are making very real efforts to overcome the current difficulties or delays."

Signed R.J.Wood.

"**Delays**" are the major complaint.

14th February 1976 Saturday

We are hoping to produce some sort of historical pageant in Ravenstone Church in June, instead of the usual Sunday School Anniversary, so I am fully engrossed at the moment devising make-believe interviews with the children of the 14th Century, the

Rector of the 15th Century etc.

16th February 1976 Monday

Television tonight spotlighted D.V.L.C. Swansea – "**A Scandalous Affair**" How many more projects will grow into **Ugly Swanseas**?

There was no realistic original estimate of cost, & once a project of this kind gets under way, it is very difficult to stop. The foundation stone was laid in 1969.

18th February 1976 Wednesday

Whose fault is Swansea? Successive Ministers of Transport, starting in 1965 with Tom Frazer who took the initial decision to computerise. What has he now to say? "I honestly cannot remember about the decision. It didn't seem an important matter at the time."

Swansea started in 1973 with a hope & prayer.

20th February 1976 Friday

The Right Rev. Dom Basil Hume, Benedictine Monk & Abbot of Ampleforth, Yorkshire, aged 52, is to be the new Roman Catholic Archbishop of Westminster. There are 4 million Roman Catholics in England & Wales, & he succeeds the late Cardinal Heenan.

Nobody expected a monk to be appointed – least of all he himself.

22nd February 1976 Sunday

The Revd. Buckroyd, Rector of Ravenstone, preached today on the 2 gardens –

The Garden of Eden, where man turned away from God. The Garden of Gethsemane, where man again turned away from God. In the first garden man was punished; in the second – forgiven.

24th February 1976 Tuesday

Ravenstone Parish Magazine is now home made. The Rector provides all the material; a volunteer typist does the master copy. Another volunteer runs off 300 copies on our own machine & then more volunteers (including me) meet in church with stapling machines & staple the pages together.

26th February 1976 Thursday

Rumours are abroad of the break-up of the marriage of the Queen's sister, Princess Margaret & Lord Snowdon. Princess Margaret, aged 45, could not marry the man of her dreams because he was divorced. How tragic then that her so-called respectable marriage is now heading for divorce.

28th February 1976 Saturday

Princess Anne, this week rode through the streets of London in an open carriage to the Guildhall, to be given the Freedom of the City of London. The Princess was presented with a choker-style necklace of pearls, diamonds & sapphires as a gift from the corporation – then lunch at Mansion House.

1st March 1976 Monday

Viva Mexico! This is Coalville Amateurs' show being given this week.

I have taken a week's holiday from work to fulfil my role as prompter, & how I love it. At the moment we are enjoying blue skies & sunshine all day long, & the evenings are filled with fiesta music, dancing & colour.

3rd March 1976 Ash Wednesday
As I walk to my position as prompter with the members of the orchestra, I have now acquired a long black evening skirt, and a very smart black jacket trimmed with white.

The show is a great success & has a good write-up in the Leicester Mercury – our greatest asset the talented principles.

5th March 1976 Friday
What a joy it is to be prompter to such a talented cast as Coalville's "Viva Mexico". Tonight's performance was received with such acclaim. The audience burst into spontaneous applause **before** one of the more spectacular chorus numbers, immediately the curtains opened – at the sheer beauty of the arrangement.

7th March 1976 Sunday
Mum & I went to Willoughby-on-the-Wolds to see Mum's cousin Madge. Poor Madge was very distressed because her sister Bertha was so very ill. Bertha, aged 66, is now in hospital dying of cancer. Their eldest brother Rex, who lives in Sheffield, was with Madge & so was brother Johnty from Markfield.

9th March 1976 Tuesday
County Hall, Glenfield, Leicestershire (including a computer suite & workshops) was built for £1,866,511. Following local government reorganisation, County Hall now has an extension making it almost twice its original size. The cost of the extension is £2,200,000.

11th March 1976 Thursday
Bertha, Mum's cousin from Willoughby, has died. She died on Tuesday, and she will be buried tomorrow in Willoughby churchyard. This leaves Madge to live alone in the big family home which has a large garden – out buildings – stables, etc.

13th March 1976 Saturday
I have now prepared the full outline of our proposed Church Pageant. All I have to do now is persuade our 4 other Sunday School teachers to carry it out. We have a meeting tomorrow morning to discuss same. I have shown the birth of the Church of England – the birth of the Sunday School & the birth of our Diocese.

15th March 1976 Monday
Beware the Ides of March. At 4-34 p.m. a bomb exploded on the underground train leaving West Ham for Central London. The bomb went off earlier than planned, & the terrorist was caught in the act. In a panic, he then shot the train driver dead & finally shot himself. This is all part of the Irish troubles.

17th March 1976 Wednesday
The latest bombshell to hit this country is the resignation of Prime Minister Harold Wilson. With the Budget only 3 weeks ahead, he decided this was the best time to go, so that his successor can start & follow through all the discussions & the debates which will of necessity result from the Budget.

19th March 1976 Friday
"Scrap Road Tax Plan" – As this year's budget draws near again, the warning bells once more are sounded. The idea of scrapping road tax & getting the money from petrol is very much favoured. The main advantage would be the potential saving of millions of pounds at D.V.L.C. Swansea.

"**H.R.H. the Princess Margaret, Countess of Snowdon, and the Earl of Snowdon, have mutually agreed to live apart. The Princess will carry out her public duties & functions unaccompanied by Lord Snowdon. There are no plans for divorce proceedings.**"
This was officially announced today.

23rd March 1976 Tuesday
A letter from D.V.L.C. Swansea to Dear Miss Hewes – Assignment of L.V.L.O. posts.
"I am writing to inform you that on present indications it is unlikely that you will be offered an L.V.L.O. post in your locality when your present post in the L.T.O. comes to an end …." Signed P. L. Glover. PMA 2.

25th March 1976 Thursday
When I was promoted to E.O. in 1974 I had a letter which said, "….. You will, of course, be liable to transfer to any office of the Department in London or the Provinces employing officers of your grade if it is in the interest of the Department."
I therefore accepted the promotion on those terms.

27th March 1976 Saturday
How uplifting & inspiring to watch on television this week the ordaining of the new Roman Catholic Archbishop of Westminster. As when we heard the Abbot of Mount St. Bernard Abbey (22nd April 1974) again we heard a truly humble man of God. Called from Abbot to Archbishop – "Not to dominate, but to animate."

29th March 1976 Monday
Mum & I went to Staunton Harold Cheshire Home to hear the Coalville Amateurs' singing a selection from their latest show "Viva Mexico". Such a lively, colourful show on stage, it seemed to lose much of its magic without the exotic costumes & the action – the counter marching – the brass band - & all the comedy.

31st March 1976 Wednesday
A new "Chief Executive" for Leicestershire County Council.
The present Chief Executive, Mr Robert Thornton, will be retiring in July & over a hundred people applied for the vacancy. The man they have chosen is 36 year old Samuel Jones, at present head of the administrative & legal department at Sheffield.

2nd April 1976 Friday
"Oh, to be in England, now that April's here."
Our garden looks so beautiful with all the lawns mown for the first time this year. I certainly do appreciate the motor mower we acquired last year. And the rockery, cleared of all its overgrowth, looks so much better. My landscaped garden is really quite a picture.

4th April 1976 Sunday

Tonight at church we thanked God in our prayers for Buddha. Throughout Lent we have had a sermon each week on the world's great religions. This week the subject was Buddhism, the one which impressed me most. Like Christ, he fasted, was tempted by the Devil, but by self-discipline he overcame the world.

6th April 1976 Tuesday

Budget Day – and much to our relief another reprieve for Motor Taxation.

Following the recent resignation of Prime Minister Harold Wilson, a new leader was chosen yesterday – James Callaghan, the first Prime Minister to come into office without a General Election **first**. He was formerly Foreign Secretary.

8th April 1976 Thursday

Mary Moore, aged 64, is spending a week with Mum & me, so it is **All Systems Go**.

We have been to tea at Donaldson's, in their delightful new house at Donington-le-Heath.

We have visited Auntie Doris at Mountsorrel; & Mary has visited all her old friends – Joyce – Mary – Florrie – Ivy – Olive, etc.

10th April 1976 Saturday

A new Prime Minister & all change in the Cabinet. Anthony Crosland, (our boss) goes from Environment Minister to Foreign Secretary. Our new boss is Peter Shore. It is expected that next year Mr Crosland & Chancellor Denis Healey will swap jobs. Peter Shore, who was Trade Secretary, is replaced by Edmund Dell.

12th April 1976 Monday

The Leicester Mercury is full of suggestions "Where to go during the Easter Holiday".

The place which most appeals to me is Empingham Reservoir, where the first boat will be taking to the water there on Good Friday. Work began on this new reservoir 5 years ago, & it is slowly filling with water.

14th April 1976 Wednesday

Empingham Reservoir will eventually be the largest man-made lake in the country, holding 27,000 million gallons of water. This water is now being pumped from the River Welland & River Nene. It is hoped that by next Easter (1977) the reservoir will be used also for fishing, & even now is being stocked with trout.

16th April 1976 Good Friday

Yesterday I ventured in the car on a hundred mile round trip to Uppingham – where I bought a picture of "Rutlandshire" for £6-55p, then on to Stamford in Lincolnshire where I bought a clock showing the date & the day; back through Empingham, Oakham, Corby, Market Harborough, Leicester – home.

18th April 1976 Easter Sunday

Again our Easter Garden in church looks very pretty beside the font. We have also decorated the font itself. Here we have three crosses; with dainty little flowers all round the base of each cross individually, & backed by the larger flower arrangements. These look down on the garden.

20th April 1976 Tuesday

A day in Coventry. Perfect holiday weather with blue skies & sunshine, so I ventured forth alone in the car to explore Coventry. Walked for the first time in the ruins of the old cathedral which was destroyed by bombs on 14th November 1940, & visited the new cathedral, whose foundation stone was laid 23rd March 1956.

22nd April 1976 Thursday

Yesterday Her Majesty the Queen was 50, & on her birthday Princess Anne her daughter had a nasty fall from a horse. Princess Anne was knocked unconscious & taken by ambulance to hospital in Poole in Dorset. She spent the night there before being transferred to hospital in London, but was not hurt seriously.

24th April 1976 Saturday

Charles & Renee, who were married last October, invited Mum & me to their new home in Cosby about 18 miles from Ravenstone. They each sold their previous house & started married life together in a new environment. Charles has been organist at Cosby for 5 years, so they feel quite at home there.

26th April 1976 Monday

The Diocese of Leicester is now setting off on a great procession of celebration as we go forward into our Jubilee Year. The Bishop of Leicester – Ronald Ralph Williams – says, "The first sermon I heard preached in Leicester Cathedral was 'Speak unto the children of Israel that they go forward'". This is our motto.

28th April 1976 Wednesday

Mr Sharp, our office boss for the past 13 years, is 60 years old today & is now retiring. A record collection of £27 was made for him from the staff, & will be presented to him in the form of a cheque on Friday at 4 p.m.

The new boss will be Les Timson, who has worked there since school.

30th April 1976 Friday

What a strange thing it is when your boss ceases to be your boss. Mr Sharp came to work today almost like a visitor. Remember President Kennedy, when speaking of "passing the buck" said, "The buck stops here"? Well, the buck will pass no more to Mr Sharp. He can now view from afar.

2nd May 1976 Sunday

Yesterday was Cup Final Day.

Little Southampton – a second division team – beat the mighty champions Manchester United 1 – 0. The Cup was presented by Her Majesty the Queen. Attendance was 100,000, but ever rising inflation brought the receipts to an all time record of £420,000.

4th May 1976 Tuesday

Mum & I went to the Haymarket Theatre, Leicester, to see "**Mame**" presented by the Leicester Amateur Operatic Society – an excellent production which we thoroughly enjoyed. On Friday I hope to be going with Frances (from the office) to see Leicester Operatic Players latest production –"**The Mikado**".

6th May 1976 Thursday
It is not known exactly when my present post in L.T.O. will come to an end, but it is intended that complete L.T.O. closure will be effected by the end of March 1978.
At present there are about 6,000 people employed in L.T.O.s up & down the country. Of these 1,000 are Civil Servants & 5,000 Local Government.

8th May 1976 Saturday
On Thursday this week we all went to the polls for the local district councils. We had to choose between my good friend Alf & Ray Hextall.
The result was A.W.Hall (Ind.) 410, R.Hextall (Lab.) 277. So Alf now joins the North West Leicestershire District Council. There are 43 on the council; 19 Labour, 13 Conservative, 10 Independent, & 1 other.

10th May 1976 Monday
Aunt Dos & I went to St. Mary's Church at Cole Orton to see "Our Heritage" – a Festival of Flowers for the Leicester Diocesan Jubilee. Here we saw the most beautiful chair – used by the Archbishop of Canterbury at the coronation of William IV in 1831, & given to the Beaumont family of Cole Orton.

12th May 1976 Wednesday
I am one of about 70 E.O.s working in L.T.O. who will not be wanted in the new L.V.L.O.
A special message to us from our union says, "It is vital that members offered posts either elsewhere in D.O.E. or in other government departments give very careful consideration to the offers. Over the next couple of years posts in the L.V.L.O.s, D.V.L.C. and throughout the D.O.E. and other departments are going to be at a premium. Staff refusing to leave the L.T.O.s or who turn down offers of transfers in the hope that something better will turn up in 1977/78 are likely to be disappointed. The situation can only get worse ...."

16th May 1976 Sunday
Our Sunday School pageant is now showing every sign of promise.
June, our pianist, is full of bright ideas for her century – the 17th. Mrs Small has done a thorough research into the 16th century – Diane is 18th century, & Mrs Barras, who is doing the 19th century, is also making all the banners.

18th May 1976 Tuesday
This is "Christian Aid Week". It is the 20th campaign since 1956 when the churches made their first united appeal to the general public on behalf of the world's neediest people. I have been distributing & collecting envelopes in Wash Lane & Leicester Road, Ravenstone, helped by Susan Land.

20th May 1976 Thursday
Last year £2,474,837 was collected throughout the country for Christian Aid Week.
This seems to me such a little to provide for all the millions of starving people in the world.
What will £2 million provide? An extension to County Hall (9th March 1976).
Last year alone Britain borrowed £2,000 million.

22nd May 1976 Saturday
Spent all day painting & decorating our poor old pantry. Brushed down the white-washed walls till I was surrounded by a thick cloud of dust, & then proceeded to paint them anew with a good solid white undercoat of Woolworth's paint. Covered the shelves with pretty blue washable paper – a big improvement.

24th May 1976 Monday
Our forthcoming pageant has prompted the Rector – the Revd. Leslie Buckroyd – to lend me some very interesting books.
1. A History of the Church of England. 2. Official Year Book of the Church of England.
3. Part of "Nichols History of Leicestershire" hand written by Leonard Fosbrooke for us.

26th May 1976 Wednesday
Basil Hume, newly appointed Archbishop of Westminster, was in Rome this week to be made a Cardinal by the Pope. Nineteen others were also created cardinals, including the Archbishop of Manila, Jaime Sin. Archbishop Sin said, "Now I will be known as the **Eighth Cardinal Sin**." There are altogether 138 cardinals.

28th May 1976 Friday
Miss Gazzard, who has worked in our office for the past 40 years, will be retiring at the end of next month. I have been chosen to take her place as Cashier No.1 on the public counter.
I was on the counter as Cashier No.2 from 1967 to 1970. (When I met my best beloved)

30th May 1976 Sunday
Three weeks to go to our Sunday School Pageant. The children are singing the songs very well. And the teachers have done so much historical research that we have really more material than we can fit into the programme. The thing is – we've all got carried away with it. I've written 2 songs & a 21 verse epic poem.

1st June 1976 Tuesday
Spent the Bank Holiday gardening. Did a bit more re-arranging. Put the slabs in a different design & created another little lawn to give the garden seat a more suitable vantage place. We certainly do appreciate having such a good garden seat. We all enjoy it – Tosca, Mum & me.

3rd June 1976 Thursday
For our summer holiday this year Enid & I are hoping to go to London (just for one day).
We would like to go by river from Westminster Pier to Hampton Court Palace to see the Palace, the King's Privy Garden, the Great Fountain Gardens, the Tudor & Elizabethan Knot Gardens, the Maze, etc.

5th June 1976 Saturday
Ravenstone's Annual Summer Garden Fete, held in the beautiful garden of Mrs Brearley & opened by Cicely Williams, wife of the Bishop of Leicester. A glorious hot sunny day.
Mum & I later took 20 red carnations for the church, for Whit Sunday – our turn to do the flowers.

7th June 1976 Monday
I have now joined the many who have seen strange sights in the sky.
U.F.O. is the name given to Unidentified Flying Objects, & last night at 10-30 p.m. I saw a beautiful U.F.O. Like a giant star it crossed the heavens to disintegrate like a spectacular fire-work in a trail of glory.

9th June 1976 Wednesday
My U.F.O. was not seen by the great radio astronomy centre Jodrell Bank. From the way it was described to them, they suggested it was one of the thousands of man-made satellites which are orbiting the earth, burning up in the atmosphere. When I saw it, the sky was quite light, being midsummer, with no stars out.

11th June 1976 Friday
The biggest overdraft in Britain's history was announced by the Government this week. It gives Chancellor Denis Healey international credit totalling more than £3,000 million. The loan comes from the United States, France, West Germany, Japan & other "Group of Ten" countries, in a bid to save our falling £.

13th June 1976 Sunday
The great service of Thanksgiving for the Golden Jubilee of the Diocese of Leicester, held at Leicester City Football Ground, 10-30 a.m.

15th June 1976 Tuesday
Mum & I have asked John Bloomfield, our local painter & decorator, to decorate our old shabby kitchen. He has given us his estimate £84-50p, plus 8% Value Added Tax. This includes ceiling & woodwork undercoat & gloss; walls papered at £1-50p per roll; plus a shelf & incidental other extras.

17th June 1976 Thursday
Called to see my good friend Reg Hall, to ask him if he would take some photographs of the Sunday School children in our forthcoming pageant. He agreed to call in at our rehearsal in church on Saturday morning. Like me, Reg is particularly interested in the past present & future all being brought together.

19th June 1976 Saturday
Dress rehearsal for our Sunday School Pageant. Our banners are really magnificent, (7) for each century from 14th century to 20th Century, and one bearing the Leicester Diocesan Coat of Arms. "Speak unto the children of Israel that they go forward". This is beautifully illustrated in our procession.

21st June 1976 Monday
Our Sunday School Anniversary yesterday was a momentous occasion. We all enjoyed being part of the great procession of celebration for the Leicester Diocesan Golden Jubilee.
All over the county, churches are doing something similar, & there should be no doubt anywhere that this is our Jubilee Year.

23rd June 1976 Wednesday
A new home for Princess Anne! The Queen has bought Gatcombe Park for around £500,000 for Princess Anne & Captain Mark Phillips. As well as the 10 bedroom Georgian house, there are 730 acres of farmland & woodland in lovely Gloucestershire, situated deep in the Cotswolds.

25th June 1976 Friday
"**The Lady Jane Returns**". This was Newtown Linford's great Pageant, presented in the open air inside the ruins at Bradgate Park. Mum & I went to the opening night (last night) & saw again England's Nine Day Queen brought to life. This was the Queen who succeeded Edward VI.

27th June 1976 Sunday
We have just had one of the hottest weeks on record. It has been over 90°F **in the shade**, & only the bravest have dared to lie in the sun, at over 100°F.
Yesterday we took the Sunday School children out for a picnic, & were jolly thankful for the shade of the trees in Friar's field.

29th June 1976 Tuesday
Fifteen thousand people went to Bradgate Park to see the Pageant. About 200 people went to the church in Newtown Linford on Sunday evening, where the Bishop of Leicester was preaching. The Bishop said Mother Nature without Mother Church is not enough, for Nature can be so cruel.

1st July 1976 Thursday
Swansea is now nearly halfway there in taking on vehicle records. Eight million vehicles are now on computer record. The latest registration suffix is **P**. And the computer now has every **P** registration going back as far as **K**. As from today all vehicles with the suffix **H** & **J** will be recorded on renewal of licence.

3rd July 1976 Saturday
The sun has now been beating down relentlessly from a cloudless sky for 2 weeks, & we are all wilting away. I come home from work utterly exhausted, & have to strip off completely to wash not only myself, but my underclothes.
Bravely, the little antirrhinums are all coming into flower.

5th July 1976 Monday
July 4th 1976, 214 million Americans celebrated their Bicentennial. This side of the Atlantic, with the help of television, we shared all the excitement with them. From East to West the church bells rang, there were parades through every town, & beneath the Statue of Liberty an armada of ships.

7th July 1976 Wednesday
Seeing America enjoying "**The Biggest Birthday in the World**" made me want all the more to visit America.
We saw sunrise over the Grand Canyon – Niagara Falls – the Pacific Fleet off San Francisco – the old wagon trains – the Indians in full ceremonial attire, & fireworks at sea.

9th July 1976 Friday
The Queen is now on a state visit to America. She first visited Philadelphia, birthplace of American

Independence, then on to Washington for the biggest ever reception & banquet at the White House with President Ford; then on to New York, Charlottesville & Boston, before moving on to Canada.

11th July 1976 Sunday

"**Rain in Summer**" by H. W. Longfellow.
"How beautiful is the rain! After the dust & heat, in the broad & fiery street, in the narrow lane, how beautiful is the rain. Across the window pane it pours and pours; and swift & wide, with a muddy tide, like a river down the gutter roars the rain, the welcome rain!"

13th July 1976 Tuesday

Tosca the beautiful, Tosca the beloved is still with us, though now very, very lame. As a result Tosca likes plenty of fuss, & does not mind being carried upside down like a baby, or nursed for hours, never leaves the confines of the garden & spends hours & hours doing nothing at all but sleep.

15th July 1976 Thursday

Now I am 45, i.e. 3 x 3 x 5.
This week I acquired a super map of America showing the "Old West" – the pioneer trails & battles, Indian's territories, stagecoach lines, military forts & historical data of the frontier period circa 1840.

17th July 1976 Saturday

The 1976 Olympic Games in Montreal were opened today by Her Majesty the Queen. Once again, the rebellious African countries have refused to take part – Zambia, Uganda, Nigeria, Tanzania, Kenya, Somali & Ethiopia. They are protesting because New Zealand rugby players are touring Rhodesia.

19th July 1976 Monday

The Viking spacecraft which left America last August, for a landing on Mars this month, was not able to land on July 4th as planned. The proposed landing site was found to be dangerously strewn with rocks, so another site has been chosen, & it is hoped to land tomorrow.

21st July 1976 Wednesday

Now we have seen Mars in close-up. Perfectly clear pictures of the landscape were shown on television when America's Viking spacecraft landed there yesterday. The direct distance between Mars & Earth is 200 million miles & the pictures travelling at the speed of light took 20 minutes.

23rd July 1976 Friday

Montreal is 5 hours behind our time. Consequently, watching the Olympic Games means that we in England have to stay up till well past the midnight hour. As I like to be in bed by 10 p.m., I have missed quite a lot.
All our royal family are there to watch Princess Anne competing.

25th July 1976 Sunday

Princess Anne, aged 26, was part of our equestrian team at the Olympic Games. There was also Lucinda Prior-Palmer, Hugh Thomas and Richard Meade, but we didn't manage to win any medals in this event. The United States won the Gold Medal, West Germany the Silver, & Australia the Bronze.

27th July 1976 Tuesday

Mum's cousin Cyril can no longer move himself about. Two nurses come every evening to put him to bed, & then again mid-morning to get him up. He sits in a chair all day long, & is very, very unhappy. What a sad thing it is, not to be able to move your own body. I feel so sorry for him.

29th July 1976 Thursday

The 1976 Olympic Games have cost the Province of Quebec £800 million. The people of Montreal will be paying off taxes to cover this for the rest of their lives.
The 1980 Olympic Games are to be in Moscow, & in 1984 they are booked provisionally for Teheran – rich with oil.

31st July 1976 Saturday

Watched on television Cierpinski of East Germany win the marathon in a record time of 2 hours 9 ½ minutes.
The marathon means running for 26 miles along the public roads, & commemorates the run of Pheidippides, a Greek courier, who in 490 B.C. ran 22 miles from Marathon to Athens & then died.

2nd August 1976 Monday

It seems only yesterday that we watched the closing ceremony from the 1972 Olympic Stadium in Munich. And now once again we watched the closing ceremony from Montreal. What a magnificent spectacle. The mighty parade of athletes was headed by Red Indians in full ceremonial dress.

4th August 1976 Wednesday

And still the rumours persist that Motor Taxation is to be scrapped. Although we are never told directly, we hear that it will be announced in the Budget next April, & then brought into effect in 1978. As total Local Taxation Office closure is scheduled for the end of March 1978, this makes sense.

6th August 1976 Friday

A sickle with flint blades & a wooden handle, dating back 5,000 years & believed to be the first farm implement of its kind in Western Europe, has been unearthed at Peterborough. This was not only **Before Christ**; it was before **Moses**, before **Israel**, almost back to **Methuselah**.

8th August 1976 Sunday

What can we do with Ireland? We send out our soldiers to restore law & order & they are killed without mercy. Nineteen-year-old J. Borucki today became the 256th soldier to die. We send out our Ambassador, & he too is blown to pieces. Everywhere there is destruction, violence and mob hatred.

10th August 1976 Tuesday

The women in Ireland can be as belligerent as the men. Not only is there the I.R.A. to contend with, there is also the women's I.R.A. called the Cumann na Ban. The women shout & declare their intentions to march to victory, threatening to destroy not only Belfast, but English towns as well.

12ᵗʰ August 1976 Thursday
I am now weighing up the possibility of buying a new car. But oh, the rising costs! It is now almost double what it was 3 years ago, when I bought **KAY 7L**.
I think perhaps I might get £800 now for **KAY 7L**, Mum would kindly lend me £500, & I would provide £500.

14ᵗʰ August 1976 Saturday
Today I filled in all the necessary forms to apply for a new car through Godfrey Davis (Wembley) Ltd., who give discount to Civil Servants. They offer £158 discount, & even so the total price (with wireless) is nearly £1,800.

16ᵗʰ August 1976 Monday
Yesterday I fetched Auntie Doris (a sprightly 80 year-old) for tea. She had with her, Hilda, her younger sister. After tea, we went to Leicester Cathedral, where Canon Gundry read the 2 lessons. Canon Gundry is the best lesson reader I know. The Provost preached on the 2ⁿᵈ lesson, John 16. 33.

18ᵗʰ August 1976 Wednesday
The Provost told us that Jesus "came out **from** God" in Greek **para** …. from being at the side of God. But much more than that Jesus "came forth **from** the Father" in Greek **ek** …. that is "out of God". But what did the disciples say? "We believe that thou camest forth **from** God" in Greek **apo** …. just from God.

20ᵗʰ August 1976 Friday
Visited Hampton Court. An enchanting day. Enid & I thoroughly enjoyed the 3 ½ hour boat trip from Westminster, arriving at Hampton Court at 1-30 p.m. Saw more of Verrio's beautiful work, which I first saw at Burghley House in August 1971. Loved the grounds & gardens, & got lost in the Maze.

22ⁿᵈ August 1976 Sunday
Yesterday we all enjoyed our Sunday School outing to the West Midland Safari Park, Bewdley, in Worcestershire. I had the pleasure of the company of 6 year old Clare Allsoppe & her 9 year old sister Sally Ann. We had a 2 hour stop at Bridgnorth in Shropshire, & went by steam train from there to Bewdley.

24ᵗʰ August 1976 Tuesday
Mum's birthday yesterday, & we went out for the day. We motored to Peakirk Waterfowl Gardens, near Peterborough, about 60 miles from Ravenstone. We stopped at Uppingham, & bought Mum a pair of shoes – one of the few towns where you can park the car right in front of the shop window.

26ᵗʰ August 1976 Thursday
Spent a couple of days with Bunting at her home in Malvern. Motored there via Birmingham, over the fabulous "Spaghetti Junction". Visited Julian & his wife Shirley, whom I last saw on their wedding day 31ˢᵗ May 1975. Bunting is very vivacious & talks most of the time, making things larger than life.

28ᵗʰ August 1976 Saturday
"**Let the Flowers Die**". These are the sad headlines as Britain faces its worst drought for 250 years. Week after week of endless sunshine has resulted in a land parched so dry that firemen are working day & night to fight uncontrollable fires. Water is to be rationed, & priority given to industry, farming, health & essential use.

30ᵗʰ August 1976 Bank Holiday Monday
Around A.D. 1200 to A.D. 1400 England & much of Europe basked in a Mediterranean climate. This gave way around the 1600s to a "Little Ice Age".
Like some huge spaceship, Earth is buffeted by forces on the interplanetary ocean. Huge whirlpools in the outer layers of the Sun, known as sunspots, affect us greatly.

1ˢᵗ September 1976 Wednesday
Sunspots are closely connected with the so-called "solar wind", a one million miles per hour stream of charged atoms that escape from the Sun & tangle with our own atmosphere 100 miles up. This gives us those great westerly Atlantic gales, which have not been stirred up recently. The Sun's next rash of spots is due about 1980.

3ʳᵈ September 1976 Friday
Europe's present drought is a direct result of the weak westerly winds. When blowing at full force in the same direction as the Earth rotates, they keep everything in balance.
Now we have a wobble which can jar the drifting 50 mile thick plates of rock into which the seemingly solid land masses are divided on Earth.

5ᵗʰ September 1976 Sunday
Motor Taxation will not be scrapped.
Denis Healey, Chancellor of the Exchequer, has written to Sir Clive Bossom, chairman of the R.A.C., stating, "To abolish this duty would mean a 15p a gallon rise in petrol prices. Such a large increase would further expose this country to imports of small foreign cars and to loss of jobs in our own industry. On these grounds I decided against abolishing the duty. Whatever the merits of abolition on other grounds, I take the view that our industrial policies must have first priority."
So Mr Healey will not scrap the £40 a year car tax while we face such competition from imported cars.

9ᵗʰ September 1976 Thursday
Mary Moore, who spent a week with Mum & me in April this year, has arranged to spend the week with us again – next week. So, I have taken a few days holiday to get the house & garden ship-shape. I do appreciate having 30 day's holiday now. That means 6 weeks (5 day week) – i.e. one week every two months.

11ᵗʰ Sept 1976 Saturday
A cabinet reshuffle this week because Home Secretary Roy Jenkins has gone to be head of the European Commission in Brussels. The new Home Secretary is Merlyn Rees, who vacates the hot seat as Ulster Secretary. The new Ulster Secretary is Roy Mason, to wrestle with the unruly Irish.

13ᵗʰ September 1976 Monday
Jubilation in Flowers! Auntie Doris (aged 81) and I went to Leicester Cathedral yesterday for the Flower Festival to celebrate the Golden Jubilee of the Diocese. The preacher was my beloved Provost who said that the

flowers were really preaching to us – "Let the flowers die" indeed. (28th August 1976)

15th September 1976 Wednesday
Visited the Donaldsons at Donington-le-Heath who had recently spent a fortnight in America. I was fascinated with all their books & pictures of New York & Boston, & enjoyed hearing all they had to say about their luxury holiday.
You know how much I would love to see America – especially in her bi-centenary year. (See 14th July 1975).

17th September 1976 Friday
Now that Chancellor of the Exchequer Denis Healey has given the go-ahead to Motor Taxation, the staff in our office are all being sifted & sorted out for the forthcoming L.V.L.O. office in Leicester. Only Civil Servants will be accepted, & only four Executive Officers will be required. Following Geoff's promotion to H.E.O., I am now hoping to be included.

19th September 1976 Sunday
Mary Moore & I spent a most interesting afternoon at the "Battlefield of Bosworth" about 10 miles from Ravenstone. This historic site, recently opened to the public, is where Henry VII defeated Richard III in 1485. It ended the Plantagenet dynasty & founded the Tudor. We saw a half hour film on Richard III.

21st September 1976 Tuesday
We have in our office at the moment 6 E.O.s – Frank Pawsey, Ralph Richardson, Steve Sharpe, Eric Grewcock, Steve Browne & me. The first three have been E.O.s ever since we joined the Civil Service. Now we are all to have a "career development" interview, booked for next month.

23rd September 1976 Thursday
450 million tons of coal. The biggest untapped coalfield in Western Europe has just been discovered. Guess where! The beautiful Vale of Belvoir, Leicestershire. The coal board are hoping to sink three pits, but local residents, including the Duke of Rutland, are up in arms.

25th September 1976 Saturday
Sir Derek Ezra, chairman of the Coal Board, this week visited the £7 billion coalfield lately discovered in the Vale of Belvoir.
He said, "We cannot live for today & forget about the future. This coalfield will be essential when our offshore oil & gas pass their production peak in the 1990s."

27th September 1976 Monday
Yesterday the Provost came to Ravenstone Church. The Revd. Buckroyd, Rector of Ravenstone, & he, were both at Durham University together, & this week was the 25th anniversary of their ordination to the priesthood.
A major distraction during the service was a swarm of bees.

29th September 1976 Wednesday
Down & down & down goes the value of the £. So once more we have asked the International Monetary Fund for a further loan. £2.3 billion (that is £2,300 million).
But this time the world bankers are sending their auditors to Whitehall, to see why we cannot manage our finances better.

1st October 1976 Friday
Rhodesia (named after Cecil Rhodes) broke away from British rule 11 years ago, & has been a rebel state ever since. Rebel leader Ian Smith, as leader of 270,000 white people, said that the 6 million black people were not yet sufficiently educated to rule themselves. Now they are to do so.

3rd October 1976 Sunday
The 6 million black people of Rhodesia did not appreciate being ruled by the ¼ million whites. The Zimbabwe African Peoples Union (ZAPU) & the Zimbabwe African National Union (ZANU) were formed & resulted in guerrilla warfare. Now it is hoped to produce a peaceful independent Zimbabwe.

5th October 1976 Tuesday
Last week we had the pleasure of the Provost's company at Ravenstone Church, & this week we had the Bishop of Leicester, Dr. Williams.
Not only was it our Patronal Festival – St. Michael & All Angels, but also the dedication of a new Altar Cloth, which has taken many months to embroider.

7th October 1976 Thursday
The Bishop spoke to us of Angels. He mentioned the Angel with a flaming sword in the Garden of Eden. He mentioned the "Angels" who saved Elisha from the King of Syria, when Elisha said to his servant, "Fear not" & prayed, "Lord, I pray thee, open his eyes that he may see." II Kings 6. 17.

9th October 1976 Saturday
The Bishop mentioned the Angel in that other garden – the Garden of Gethsemane - & finally he mentioned the Angels on the Resurrection morning. The Bishop made us feel the strengthening power of the Angels – if Jesus himself could be given strength by an Angel, surely we could be similarly strengthened.

11th October 1976 Monday
Yesterday was our Harvest Festival at church. We met Miss Margaret Bettis, our "link" missionary from Nakuru, Kenya. We sang to her a song I had written especially for her, & we sang another song I wrote for the harvest. We all enjoyed meeting Miss Bettis, who showed us her slides.

13th October 1976 Wednesday
It is now dark each evening by 7 o'clock, so I just have time for about one hour each day in the garden. I have cleared our second rockery, rearranged the eight slabs into a border round yet another lawn, given the sundial a bigger base of 16 coloured slabs, & now have only the minimum of garden left to dig.

15th October 1976 Friday
Career Development Interview Number One.
Having been at work in the same office for 28 years, I was today given my first career development interview by a very kind & gentle understanding man from Swansea. He dwelt on my good points & assured me that

there was great opportunity for me in D.O.E.

17th October 1976 Sunday
At church tonight we sang Psalm 75. "For promotion cometh neither from the east, nor from the west; nor yet from the south ……"
At my interview on Friday, I was strongly urged to consider moving from Leicester. I was offered Birmingham, Nottingham or Bristol – if not immediately maybe in two years time.

19th October 1976 Tuesday
In our Civil Service journal "**Opinion**", I have this month won First Prize in a competition set by "Friar Tuck" – an extract from the report of a visitor from outer space arising from a brief sojourn in a civil service place of work. We could write ten lines of verse – and the prize is £1-50p.

> "And even though it made them choke,
> They sent their signals up in smoke,
> Engulfing them in such a haze
> I felt they went into a daze;
> And very shortly after three
> They needed topping up with tea,
> Which seemed to give them extra drive
> And kept them going until five,
> When in a flash, they all took fright
> And disappeared into the night."

23rd October 1976 Saturday
For the past 4 years, Mum has struggled manfully on with sclerosis. Walking any distance has been a real effort for her, but she has managed wonderfully well.
This week however, her legs seem to have taken a turn for the worse, & she has been really miserable, & able to get upstairs only with great determination.

25th October 1976 Monday
Following the great summer drought, we have had the great autumn rainfall, which means a less beautiful autumn than usual, but how thankful we are for the rain to fill the empty reservoirs.
This week we have put the clocks back one hour, so now it is dark shortly after 5 o'clock.

27th October 1976 Wednesday
Ronald Ralph, Bishop of Leicester, came to Ravenstone Church in February 1971. He chose for his text Genesis 9. 14. "And it shall come to pass, when I bring a cloud over the Earth, that the bow shall be seen **in the cloud**." Not after, but "**in the cloud**".
This week I saw a rainbow, & thought on this.

29th October 1976 Friday
This is a historic day in the Driving Licence saga.
Since 1904, driving licences have been issued by good old Leicestershire County Council.
For 14 years – from the time I left school, I worked in the Driving Licence section.
Now all the records are at D.V.L.C. Swansea, & today we issued our last.

31st October 1976 Sunday
This week is the American Presidential election.

150 million Americans have to choose between James Carter & Jerry Ford. Jimmy Carter, aged 52, is the Democratic candidate. Jerry Ford, aged 63, is the present Republican President thrust into the White House on 9th August 1974 following the Watergate scandal.

2nd November 1976 Tuesday
Jimmy Carter has won the American Presidential election. Pointing to the dawn he said, "The sun is rising on a beautiful new day, a beautiful new spirit in this country, & a beautiful new commitment to the future." So the Democrats have won the day & the new President will move into the White House in January.

4th November 1976 Thursday
Mum has had a very trying week, hardly able to do much at all. It is a real struggle to move from one room to the next, & she has great difficulty moving & carrying anything.
So I've been up with the lark, putting everything ready for her to eat on the table, doing all the housework, & keeping the home fires burning.

6th November 1976 Saturday
Today we took a party of 23 children & Sunday School teachers – Mrs Small, Mrs Bird, Diane, Louise & me – to Leicester Cathedral where 1,400 children from the whole Diocese met together as part of the Diocesan Golden Jubilee celebrations. The Bishop was there, the Provost, & various dignitaries.

8th November 1976 Monday
Enid & I went to the Little Theatre in Dover Street, Leicester to see Ursula Hall in "Hello Dolly". Ursula belongs to Coalville Amateurs as well as Leicester's I.D.O.L.S.
Coalville have just cast their latest show "**Showboat**" which they will be presenting next March, when I hope to be prompter again.

10th November 1976 Wednesday
Another death-blow today for our office. Gladys arrived home from work to find her husband Tom, aged 61, had collapsed & died.
Last year, John Dexter, a member of our staff, collapsed & died in a similar way.
Two years ago, Ruby died; Barbara's husband died aged only 50; & always it seems just before Christmas.

12th November 1976 Friday
The Department of the Environment is 6 years old today. Consisting of three former Ministries – 1. Transport 2. Public Buildings & Works 3. Housing & Local Government, it was created in order to co-ordinate all these various aspects of the environment. However, we now have within D.O.E. a new Department of Transport.

14th November 1976 Sunday
This year I have been asked to report on 2 members of our staff (see 22nd November 1974). They are both C.O.s but quite different characters. One is Peter, aged 30, slow & super cautious, but a likeable enough lad, except when under pressure. The other is Philip, aged 50, very industrious & always on the go.

16ᵗʰ November 1976 Tuesday
In August this year, I filled in all the necessary forms to apply for a new car through the Civil Service, but I decided in the end not to do so. Since then the price of a new Mini Clubman has gone up by £90. However, my good friend Alf has managed to obtain one for me at the old price from Loughborough.

18ᵗʰ November 1976 Thursday
In March 1963, Mr Rose retired from our office, where he was head of the Driving Licence Section. He & his wife then immigrated to Australia to be near their only daughter Margaret. Margaret is married with 4 sons, & Mr & Mrs Rose this year celebrated their golden wedding. He keeps in touch.

20ᵗʰ November 1976 Saturday
A letter this week from Mr Rose in Australia describes the most recent excitement – the eclipse of the Sun ….. "It was very fascinating; the whole eclipse was shown on TV as it happened. It was 350 years since the last total eclipse in this area; it was eerie, fantastic & wonderful; the light gradually faded until there was total darkness and the Sun was completely obliterated. All lights on the roads were turned on – motorists switched on their lights. There was total darkness for three minutes. The Moon was dark with the brilliance of the Sun around the edge, like a ring of gold."

21ˢᵗ November 1976 Sunday
Buckroyd, Madge Edith, The Rectory, Ravenstone, dearly loved wife of Leslie, mother of Martin and Paul, died peacefully in hospital on November 21ˢᵗ.
Funeral service at St. Michael's and All Angels Church, Ravenstone on Thursday November 25ᵗʰ at 1-30p.m. followed by cremation at the Sutton Coldfield.
Family flowers only, donations to the Leukaemia Research Fund (Leicester Branch) Care of Mrs D. Hornsby, 27 Winchester Road, Countesthorpe.

24ᵗʰ November 1976 Wednesday
Ravenstone Church was filled to overflowing for the funeral of our Rector's wife, Mrs Buckroyd, aged 55. The address was given by the Revd. Canon D. R. Michell, who married the happy couple, & recalled their marriage vows which they made so many years ago – a model Christian marriage.

26ᵗʰ November 1976 Friday
Again the Queen has opened Parliament beginning with, "My Lords & Members of the House of Commons, my husband & I look forward to the events being prepared to mark the 25ᵗʰ anniversary of my accession to the throne" …… & ending "I pray that the blessing of Almighty God may rest upon your counsels."

28ᵗʰ November 1976 Sunday
Memorial Service for Mrs Buckroyd at Ravenstone Church this evening, where the preacher was my beloved Provost.
He spoke on the 23ʳᵈ Psalm, & said how hard it is to relinquish to God your own greatest treasure. But God gave you this treasure in the first place – what treasure to have been given.

30ᵗʰ November 1976 Tuesday
Our Annual Christmas Fair in Ravenstone Village Institute last Saturday was our 5ᵗʰ effort for the Sunday School. We made £22. The Fair was opened by Dr Bladon, & our stall was manned by the Sunday School teachers – Mrs Bird, Diane, Louise & me. We sold lots of things left from last year.

2ⁿᵈ December 1976 Thursday
My 3ʳᵈ interview with my own boss. Having been promoted to E.O. in 1974, I have now had the stipulated 3 interviews in 3 consecutive years. This year of course, my boss changed from Mr Sharp to Les Timson, & this year's interview was very friendly & informal, discussing the final run-down of the L.T.O.

4ᵗʰ December 1976 Saturday
This week I took delivery of my new car. It is another Mini Clubman – colour antique gold, registration mark & number **PNR 867R**.
Alf took my other car **KAY 7L** in part exchange, with mileage 35,000. Dear old **KAY 7L** had been with me from the East to the West – from Skegness to Swansea.

6ᵗʰ December 1976 Monday
Poor old Mum is gradually grinding to a halt. She has struggled & struggled each night to climb the stairs to bed, until she can struggle no more. So, reluctantly, she now has her bed downstairs again. She gets so frustrated & miserable, & feels so hopeless & helpless. She wonders how much longer she can cope.

8ᵗʰ December 1976 Wednesday
Last Sunday we had our Sunday School Prize Giving. The service was taken by the Revd. Cole, Archdeacon of Leicester.
Our Rector, the Revd. Buckroyd, stayed at home to rest after his recent bereavement. All the clergy have been wonderfully kind to our Rector, offering to take services for him.

10ᵗʰ December 1976 Friday
One year later! The truth is **not** a success story at D.V.L.C. Swansea. *(See 9ᵗʰ December 1975)* Headlines in the newspaper this week "Computer Crazy" – Now car tax bungle boys throw away the forms you send. Hundreds of drivers notify change of ownership, but it is too complicated for the computer to be fed this information.

12ᵗʰ December 1976 Sunday
Police are angry because they want to know who really owns each car. So now police & officials from D.O.E. are holding talks to unravel the tangle at the much criticised D.V.L.C. The Centre, which has been under fire since the day it opened, now gets up to 1,700 complaints or queries every single day.

14ᵗʰ December 1976 Tuesday
As Britain gets deeper & deeper into debt, we have this week had a Mini-Budget. Chancellor of the Exchequer, Denis Healey, has announced £1,000 million cuts in public spending next year, and £1,500 million the following year. Included will be the Civil Service with cuts of £30 million & £10 million.

16th December 1976 Thursday

Our Sunday School Christmas Party in Ravenstone School, with a dedicated band of young mothers providing all the cakes & jellies etc. Entertainment by 4 young people with guitars, & lively songs for all the children to sing. Then the arrival of Father Christmas & all the sorrows of the world forgotten.

18th December 1976 Saturday

Words of comfort come today from my old friend Longfellow, on a beautiful Christmas card from Aunt Dos (bought originally by Auntie Cis).
"And the night shall be filled with music, and the cares that infest the day, shall fold their tents like the Arabs, and as silently steal away."

20th December 1976 Monday

Our landscaped garden is now just about complete. Recently we had the sides of the path re-concreted – bought some new coloured slabs to give the sundial a magnificent base – cleared the second rockery & bought £6 worth of rockery plants, & set pretty climbing roses to cover the wall.

22nd December 1976 Wednesday

Inflation continues. In January this year (see 27th January 1976) I needed £15 per week for everyday expenses. Now I need £20. This covers petrol – newspapers – laundry – hairdressers, & biggest item of all – **food**. A packet of tea used to be 10p. Now it is 20p. Coffee too has doubled, & almost everything.

24th December 1976 Friday

Christmas Day this year falls on a Saturday which means that Boxing Day is being accepted as Monday, & all the shops are shut for 4 days. This makes it rather tricky stocking up with food supplies. Fortunately Mum & I (and Aunt Dos) have been invited by Pat & Evelyn to have Christmas dinner & tea with them.

26th December 1976 Sunday

Christmas Day this year was bright with sunshine. As the sun streamed through the windows of Leicester Cathedral at morning service, the Bishop, Ronald Ralph Williams, spoke of the Light of Men – "The Light shines on in the dark & the darkness has never mastered it." St. John. Chap. 1.Verse 5.

28th December 1976 Tuesday

A Christmas card to gladden our hearts came from the Revd. Gustav Aronsohn, former Rector of Ravenstone. "With kindest thoughts & so many happy memories. May God indeed bless you both richly this coming new year, as ever The Revd. & Mrs Gustav Aronsohn." A painting by G. B. Benvenuti.

30th December 1976 Thursday

And so we say farewell to 1976 – a year of violence in Ireland – a year where Scotland & Wales want to break away from English rule – a year of ever rising prices, & the country borrowing more & more money. As always we look to a brighter New Year – a year of Jubilation for England.

* * *

In 1824 a few men of vision sat down in a London pub & talked – as a result the Royal National Lifeboat Institution was founded. Its purpose was, and still is, to preserve life from shipwreck at sea, regardless of nationality & in peace & war. Lifeboats are boats par excellence & their crews are experts with a wealth of knowledge about the sea.

When the good ship "Centralisation" was being built, "Lifeboatmen" were invited to comment on its construction, but the advice was declined because the "Builders" insisted that the sea in which it would sail was a permanent dead calm, & a crew was easy to come by.

The ship was duly launched & eventually sailed into the Sea of Vehicle & Driver Licensing, & instead of the dead calm expected, its crew found sandbanks, storms & shoal water, & its course gave rise to grave concern.

Messages were sent asking if assistance was required, but the reply was always the same – "We can manage."

The "Lifeboatmen" decided to keep a constant watch from their stations, for they knew the weather would worsen & the inadequate drain valves & pumps would not cope. They are still watching as steerage way is lost & the ship gradually turns beam to sea. The question the "Lifeboatmen" ask is "Why don't they ask for help? There is still time for us to launch & tow them to calmer water. Surely they know the service is voluntary, & it is not undignified to seek the help of a lifeboat."

Signed George Brown
Portsmouth LTO/LVLO
February 1976.

* * *

Y

Betty's Diaries / 1977

1977

2nd January 1977 Sunday

The Rector of Ravenstone, whose wife died so recently, spoke in his New Year sermon of his favourite Psalm, Psalm 27, which begins, "The Lord is my light & my salvation, whom then shall I fear; the Lord is the strength of my life, of whom then shall I be afraid? ..... Be strong, and he shall comfort thine heart."

4th January 1977 Tuesday

L. T. O. rundown is now really beginning to be felt, as the latest vehicles to be taken over by the computer are those with the suffix **E, F & G**. This means that only those which are over 10 years old are still with us.

Today we took £3,000 in cash over the counter – one of our last busy days.

6th January 1977 Thursday

Tomorrow is the 7th day of the year 77 when my best beloved will be 7 x 7. He does not come to our office at all these days. I saw him last in July 1976, & before that I had not seen him for 2 years. It is 10 years since I fell for him, & have never met anyone else to compare with him.

8th January 1977 Saturday

Mum, who was in the depths of despair a month ago, is now much more cheerful. Although she is virtually house-bound, the doctor has ordered a series of injections, which seem to have mastered her depression. Whereas she formerly spurned all help offered by others, she is now happy to accept their help.

10th January 1977 Monday

The Department of Health & Social Security is now helping Mum. Today we had a second handrail fixed upstairs (all pro gratis), & Mum has an appointment with the D. H. S. S. at Nottingham next week, at Sherwood Hospital. They say, "Our aim is to help you – that is what we are here for."

12th January 1977 Wednesday

Watched on television a week of scientific lectures for children by Professor Porter.

How very interesting & edifying. We learned how life developed on Earth from the beginning, before the grass was green. In the form of a clock we saw at what hour various changes had taken place.

14th January 1977 Friday

Professor Porter brought us right up to the present age of oil, & showed in a graph that we live at the height of the oil age, which rose so quickly & will die equally so. He said, "You are the scientists of tomorrow. You must discover new sources of energy." The new untapped sources include the sun, the sea, & the fearful radio-active uranium.

16th January 1977 Sunday

Dear, oh dear, now we have a leaking roof. Recent falls of snow have found all the weak spots, & my bedroom ceiling has a nasty smelly wet patch.

We have contacted "Coalville Roofing" who have given us an estimate for sealing the roof with Evo-seal, using fibre-glass - £239-60p.

18th January 1977 Tuesday

Went with Mum, by ambulance, to Sherwood Hospital, Nottingham, where she chose a light-weight wheel-chair, which will be provided free of charge. We travelled with 2 jolly disabled passengers, & were most impressed by everyone's kindness – the ambulance men – the doctor, & all the staff.

Note – Once Mum receives a wheel-chair, she never, ever, wishes to be seen in it. She hates other people looking down to her. She either stays indoors or goes out in the car.

20th January 1977 Thursday

America's 39th President, Jimmy Carter, today was officially sworn into The White House. He took the oath, "I do solemnly swear that I will faithfully execute the Office of President of the United States, & will to the best of my ability preserve, protect & defend the Constitution of the United States."

22nd January 1977 Saturday

"Constitutionally" Jimmy Carter is now Commander in Chief of the armed forces. He will never move far without the company of a man who carries a black attaché case. In that case are codes which the Commander in Chief has to use to unleash America's nuclear might in a doomsday war.

24th January 1977 Monday

Saw this advert & answered it.

"Recovery Assistant" £3,309 - £3,567 per annum. "Applications are invited from mature persons for this post, to deal with the collection & recovery of water charges. Applicants should be able to deal with members of the public at all levels. Experience of clerical and court procedures would be an advantage. The post holder may be required to travel throughout the County, & therefore a clean current driving licence is essential," Applied to Severn Trent Water Authority, Soar Division, Leicester Water Centre, Gorse Hill, Anstey.

28th January 1977 Friday

£8,000 million worth of coal! This is the latest estimate of coal in the Vale of Belvoir. It is now thought there are 500 million tons of coal there, 50 million tons more than the previous estimate. Instead of 3 pits, it is now proposed to have 4, possibly at Langar in Notts; & Hose, Asfordby & Saltby in Leicestershire.

30th January 1977 Sunday

"**Show Boat**" is Coalville's production for this year. I have just joined them in my role of prompter. The show opens with a chorus of blackies singing, "Niggers all work on de Mississippi, Niggers all work while de white folks play." The show includes that great song, "Ol' Man River" who jes' keeps rolling along.

1st February 1977 Tuesday

America is now suffering the worst winter of the century, the worst hit areas being Pennsylvania, Ohio, Indiana, Illinois and New York State.

In Buffalo, New York, six motorists froze to death in their cars. Temperatures were minus 25° Fahrenheit. (i.e. minus 32° centigrade).

3rd February 1977 Thursday
"Domine Dirige Nos" – "God – Direct us." This is the motto of the City of London, & one I often think of, especially in these uncertain times, when, as a spinster, I wonder what the future may bring. This week I have been visiting Mum's Cousin Cyril in the geriatric ward of hospital – oh, how sad to be old & helpless.

5th February 1977 Saturday
On February 6th 1952, King George VI died, & his daughter Elizabeth was proclaimed Queen Elizabeth II. Now, 25 years later, we celebrate her Silver Jubilee. There will be a special public holiday on 7th June, & great bonfires will be lit all across the country.

7th February 1977 Monday
The Queen & the Duke of Edinburgh will be setting off this week for the first of their Commonwealth Silver Jubilee tours. They will visit Australia, New Zealand, & British territories in the Pacific. This tour will last until the end of March.

9th February 1977 Wednesday
Bailey, Cyril, 29 Moor Lane, Loughborough. Beloved husband of Elsie. Passed peacefully away in hospital on February 9th, aged 76 years. Funeral service and cremation at Loughborough Crematorium on Monday at 1-30 p.m. Flowers to Loughborough and District Funeral Service. Tel. 215331.

Mum's Cousin Cyril died 1977.

Bailey, Mary (Elsie) of Hunters Lodge, Old Dalby, (formerly of Moor Lane, Loughborough) passed peacefully away April 10th 1992, aged 91 years. Funeral service and cremation at Loughborough Crematorium on Wednesday April 15th at 11 a.m.

Cyril's widow Elsie died 1992.

11th February 1977 Friday
As Napoleon was beaten by God's army of little snowflakes, so now, the new President of America Jimmy Carter is finding that his greatest problem is not the Russians but the grip of winter, which has almost totally paralysed the U.S.A.
Even the mighty Niagara Falls have frozen.

13th February 1977 Sunday
Went to Leicester Cathedral this evening, where we sang Whittier's most beautiful hymn, "Dear Lord and Father of mankind, forgive our foolish ways." This was Auntie Cis's favourite hymn, & we sang it at her funeral. Tonight, it was sung to perfection with the Cathedral choir & organ.

15th February 1977 Tuesday
Following last summer's great drought, we now have water in abundance. A new reservoir on the Leicestershire – Derbyshire border will ensure good supplies of water for Leicestershire until the year 2000. This is the Foremark Reservoir, supplied by water from the River Dove, & will hold 3,000 million gallons.

17th February 1977 Thursday
Water started to flow into the new Foremark Reservoir yesterday. This new lake will reach its top level in about 18 months. It will be twice as big as Staunton Harold Reservoir, which holds nearly 1,500 million gallons. Cropston holds 556 million, Blackbrook 506 million, and Thornton 324 million.

19th February 1977 Saturday
Foreign Secretary Anthony Crosland, aged 58, died today following a stroke last Sunday.
This poses a problem for Prime Minister James Callaghan who was hoping that Chancellor Denis Healey would swap jobs with Anthony Crosland (see 10th April 1976).
With the budget due on March 29th what now is best to do?

21st February 1977 Monday
Leicester Cathedral's 50th birthday.
Today I rejoiced to be in Leicester Cathedral at the re-hallowing "Jubilee Eucharist", where the preacher was the Bishop of Peterborough. We were able to use a special post box inside the Cathedral for first day covers "Leicester Diocesan Jubilee".

23rd February 1977 Ash Wednesday
Dr. David Owen is our new Foreign Secretary. He was Mr Crosland's young deputy & has now taken his place. This has caused the minimum of changes in the Cabinet, & means Denis Healey is still Chancellor.
No doubt there will be a major re-shuffle later on.

25th February 1977 Friday
February-fill-dyke has not only filled the rivers to overflowing, it has flooded fields & houses & been more like a monsoon. In fact it has rained & rained in torrents, & when at last a day dawned with blue sky, birdsong & sunshine, we all felt like Noah must have done when the flood abated.

27th February 1977 Sunday
Fifty years ago, when Leicester Cathedral came into being, this was the text of the 1st Sermon.
I Kings. Chapter 9, verse 3. "And the Lord said ….. I have hallowed this house, which thou hast built, to put my name there for ever; & mine eyes & mine heart shall be there perpetually." – God's covenant with man.

2nd March 1977 Wednesday
The lesson for the 1st Sunday in Lent (last Sunday) was most appropriately Genesis, Chapters 8 & 9 – the story of Noah coming out of the ark after the flood, & God's first covenant with man, "I do set my bow in the cloud, and it shall be for a token of a covenant between me and the earth."

4th March 1977 Friday
I guess the Severn Trent Water Authority did not require my services as "Recovery Assistant"
They acknowledged my application, & that was all.
As predicted last year (May 14th) it is becoming

increasingly difficult to get another job. Everywhere more & more people are being made redundant.

6th March 1977 Sunday
All aboard the show-boat "Cotton Blossom" for a week of music & togetherness, as a vital link in Coalville Amateurs' latest show.

Again I have a week's holiday & am looking forward to this lovely, lively musical, with Jerome Kern's great music. Only one more rehearsal, & then it is opening night on Tuesday.

8th March 1977 Tuesday
Opening night of "Showboat" was rather amateurish. With 8 scenes in the first Act, & 7 scenes in the second Act, this called for precision curtain opening & closing, but this was not always so. The orchestra played too loudly during dialogue, & much of the principal's noble work was spoiled by others' inadequacy.

10th March 1977 Thursday
"Showboat Sails into Coalville with Blaze of Colour."
After a shaky start, the show is now gathering momentum & received a very good write-up in the paper, as the above heading indicates. It's lovely being prompter – right at the very heart of it all, surrounded by the orchestra – just there – like an anchor.

12th March 1977 Saturday
League Cup Final Day. Aston Villa 0, Everton 0. Replay in Sheffield on Wednesday.

This has been a gorgeous week's holiday for me, catching up on the cleaning, shopping etc.

I have pruned the roses, started on the spring cleaning, had the stair carpet up, washed the bathroom curtains, & stocked up with provisions.

14th March 1977 Monday
A phone call at work today from Swansea asking for me. Had I worked on "**Enforcement**"? (That is work connected with enforcing the law) I said that I had – motorists who failed to pay up, etc. What does this imply? We thought perhaps we might be offered enforcement work.

16th March 1977 Wednesday
12 million vehicles (out of 18 million) are now on computer record at D.V.L.C. Swansea.

All Driving Licence records are now at Swansea (22 million). The number of vehicles on the road has trebled in the last 25 years. In 1952 there were 6 million.

League Cup replay: - Aston Villa 1, Everton 1.

18th March 1977 Friday
Ordered a **Refrigerator** from Coalville, £67.

Nearly everybody these days owns a "**Fridge**". Mum & I have never had one before, so we are looking forward to owning one – to keep the milk fresh, etc. Last summer, being one of the hottest on record, & plagued with flies, we decided we would like a fridge.

20th March 1977 Sunday
Mothering Sunday & a sad day for our Rector, the Revd. Leslie Buckroyd & his grown-up sons Martin & Paul, now motherless. We had a very nice service for

"Mothers' Day" with all the children given flowers for their mothers.

Susan Hewes is 21 tomorrow. As you know, I am her **Godmother**.

22nd March 1977 Tuesday
Spring is here, & although the weather is still very cold, the buds are appearing in the garden (including **one** bud on our magnolia). The birdsong is delightful, & one blackbird sings his heart out every evening, right at the top of the Hollies pear tree.

Last Saturday we put the clocks forward 1 hour, making longer evenings.

24th March 1977 Thursday
Into Leicester Market Place today came the 16th Century High Cross, 20 feet high & weighing 1½ tons. Consisting of plinth, pedestal & cross, it was lowered into place by crane. Market traders jeered at its arrival, but I love it. For the past 25 years the Cross has stood in Newarke House Museum gardens.

26th March 1977 Saturday
"Coin and Stamp Collectors Fair" at the Abbey Motor Hotel, Abbey Street, Leicester. Thousands of coins & stamps on display, all are for sale. Pre-1947 silver coins wanted, at least three times face value paid. All are welcome to buy, sell & exchange – so off I went with my little hoard of old coins & sold them for £8.

28th March 1977 Monday
Went to Staunton Harold Cheshire Home to hear the Coalville Amateurs singing a selection from their latest show "Showboat". Everyone loved the singing & joined in the well known chorus numbers. One of the most moving numbers was "Auld Lang Syne", when we all linked up as one, the strong & healthy & the helpless.

30th March 1977 Wednesday
Budget Day yesterday brought yet another increase in Vehicle Taxation. Up went the price of car tax from £40 to £50. Also, up went the price of petrol to 90p per gallon.

R.A.C. Chairman, Sir Clive Bossom, declared, "This is the biggest case of highway robbery since Dick Turpin."

1st April 1977 Friday
The world's worst air disaster. (See 3rd March 1974) Last Sunday at Santa Cruz Airport in the Canary Islands, 562 people were killed when a Dutch K.L.M. jet just taking off the runway collided with a Pan-American plane, also due for take-off, when they hit head-on.

3rd April 1977 Palm Sunday
All Motor Vehicle records are now closing in to the great D.V.L.C. Swansea.

With L.T.O. closure scheduled for 31st March 1978, this means that all **annual** licences issued, from 1st April this year onwards, go into the Swansea pipe-line. Suffix CD (4monthly will go on July 1st)

5th April 1977 Tuesday
Enid & I went to Ibstock School to watch the Danish Junior Gymnasts from Vojens, a little town of 7,000 inhabitants in the southern part of Jutland.

As I watched these flaxen haired children, I thought of Pope Gregory I, who saw such similar children for sale in Rome long ago.

7th April 1977 Thursday
When England was a pagan land, a long, long time ago, Pope Gregory the First in Rome said, "Tell me – I must know – what have we in the market place? Are children being sold?

They must have come from lands afar. Why was I never told?" - So began my 21 verse epic poem, written last year for our pageant.

9th April 1977 Saturday
"Oh Sire, they come from Angle-land where pagan Angles dwell; because the children are so fair, we find them good to sell."

"I will not have them sold as slaves. They are God's children dear, I see them not as Angles but as **Angels** standing here …" And so I thought of Gregory I.

11th April 1977 Easter Monday
"Tolstoy My Father" by Ilya Tolstoy.
This superb book from the library has given Mum & me hours of pleasure. Leo Tolstoy, the great Russian writer, and author of "War & Peace" (see December 1972) was born in 1828 (100 years before my beloved).
Born on August 28th, of the 28th year, his life was governed by number 7.

13th April 1977 Wednesday
What a great film could be made of Lev Nikolayevich Tolstoy, & his life at the Tolstoy country estate Yasnaya Polyana. "Leo Tolstoy – This is your Life" would indeed be an epic in its own right. Spanning the years from 1828 to 1910, you would see Socrates, the Buddha, & Christ himself personified.

15th April 1977 Friday
Count Leo Tolstoy married when he was 35 (5 x 7) & had 13 children. His thoughts were profound. He knew the depths of despair & the pinnacle of fame. He wrote an imaginary futuristic article for the April issue of "Russian Antiquity" in the year 2085 – like me, he wrote to people not yet born.

17th April 1977 Sunday
"Unto God's gracious mercy & protection we commit you. The Lord bless you and keep you. The Lord make his face to shine upon you, and be gracious unto you. The Lord lift up his countenance upon you & give you peace, both now & for evermore." These are the beautiful words we hear at church every Sunday evening. (See Numbers 6. Verses 24-26)

19th April 1977 Tuesday
The Department of Environment have written to the Department of Health & Social Security, Leicester, asking them if they could employ the 3 E.O.s from Leicester L.T.O. who cannot be accommodated in the Leicester L.V.L.O.
The 3 E.O.s are Eric Grewcock, Steve Browne, and **ME**.

21st April 1977 Thursday
League Cup Final Second Replay has at last decided the

winners (in extra time), & the final goal was scored **two minutes** from the end of extra time. Aston Villa 3 Everton 2.
This has been the biggest financial coup since the Great Train Robbery, over half a million pounds paid out for the three matches.

23rd April 1977 Saturday
Train Robber Ronald Arthur Biggs, who escaped from prison in 1965, was arrested in Rio de Janeiro in February 1974. Because his girl friend was pregnant by him at the time, he remained a free man (under Brazilian law). His 2 ½ year old son, Mike Fernand de Castro, is an absolute little darling.

25th April 1977 Monday
Mr Gardiner from D.H.S.S. interviewed Eric, Steve & me at County Hall. He said we could all be considered for work as E.O.s in his department following a period of training which would include 4 weeks away from home. As this was not so easy for me, I could wait & see how things progressed.

27th April 1977 Wednesday
I told Mr Gardiner I could not leave Mum to look after herself for 4 weeks, & he was very sympathetic. He said if later on I still wish to work for D.H.S.S. they would consider me, but of course I would be expected to undergo the necessary training. So, for the time being, I am hoping to stay at dear old County Hall.

29th April 1977 Friday
Mum & I have booked a holiday! We answered an advert in the paper "Self Catering Holiday Cottage – Downing House Cottage, Studley Roger, Ripon, North Yorkshire." We have booked for one week commencing June 18th & hope to travel by car, all the way from Derby along the A61 via Sheffield and Leeds.

1st May 1977 Sunday
Downing House Cottage is a fully furnished 3 bed roomed holiday cottage, attached to the farmhouse of a 268 acre mixed farm, situated in "glorious countryside" on the edge of Studley Royal Deer Park, 2 miles west of Ripon. We chose this place because it is near to Knaresborough, which I hope to visit.

3rd May 1977 Tuesday
"Except ye Lord keep ye citie ye Wakeman waketh in vain". This is Ripon's motto, & in the olden days one of the duties of the principal Burgess was the arranging for the watch each night. Even now, at 9 o'clock every evening, the horn is still blown in the market place. We hope we shall see this.

5th May 1977 Thursday
County Council Election Day.
Leicestershire County Council has 93 members. There are now 75 Conservatives, 17 Labour, & one Independent. It was an overwhelming victory for the Conservatives, as it was all over the country. The present Labour Government is struggling to command respect.

7th May 1977 Saturday
Had my ears pierced – **again**. I originally had my ears

pierced in April 1964, & have been able to wear ear-rings with only the thinnest of wires. Ear piercing now is much improved – none of the previous barbaric methods, and now I am hoping to be able to wear thicker wired ear-rings.

9th May 1977 Monday
Leicester's new Cheapside pedestrian precinct was officially opened today by the Lord Mayor, Mr Bernard Toft. Leicester Rotary Club paid for the landscaping - £10,000, to mark the Rotary Club's 60th Anniversary. The centrepiece of this delightful precinct is Leicester's historic High Cross.

11th May 1977 Wednesday
Our Sunday School Outing this year is to be on August 20th, to Whipsnade Zoo.
The Sunday School at the moment is doing quite well, thanks to the quality of the teachers. Mrs Bird is pianist & sorts out lots of interesting songs & activities. Mrs Barras, Diane, Louise & Anthea assist.

13th May 1977 Friday
Steve & Eric are now ready to leave the world of Motor Taxation to go & work with D.H.S.S. Steve will go on July 1st and Eric will go on October 1st – (I have a reprieve for the time being). This will mean "all change" & I shall be taking over Ralph's job in his office.

15th May 1977 Sunday
Ralph has a private office of his own within the big main office. He deals with all cheques and Postal Orders received by post each day in the Local Taxation Office. He does the work of Les Timson (The Boss) when Les is not there, but all this work is running down.

17th May 1977 Tuesday
This time next year there will be no Local Taxation Office at all. Les will then be head of the ever-expanding Local Vehicle Licence Office, which is ruled directly by D.V.L.C. Swansea. Although originally planned for 4 E.O.s, they now say 3 will suffice.

19th May 1977 Thursday, Ascension Day
A phone call from Swansea to say perhaps – only **perhaps** – there may be a vacancy for one E.O. (that means me) in Leicester's L.V.L.O. in connection with enforcement work.
Talks are now taking place at top level to determine the future of enforcement, which is being re-organised.

21st May 1977 Saturday
Jubilee Cup Final Day! Manchester United beat Liverpool 2 – 1. The cup was presented by the lovely Duchess of Kent. As last year, attendance was 100,000 & the receipts were £420,000. The Queen is now touring Scotland for eleven days as part of her several Jubilee tours. The whole country is now in Jubilee mood.

23rd May 1977 Monday
Correspondence Course in Written Communication.
This is the latest thing we are doing in our office with D.V.L.C. Training Branch at Swansea. It consists of 5 separate exercises, 2 on minute writing & 3 on letter writing. This is more in my line than "Management

Appreciation" two years ago.

25th May 1977 Wednesday
Have moved into my "Private Office". This is a lovely room with windows the whole length of one wall, where the morning sun shines in. I have an "executive" arm chair, lots of space, & working surface of 3 big desks, phone & big safe. Not too much work to do, so it is lovely.
Note – This is the life – suits me down to the ground – but I know it will soon be a new life altogether.

27th May 1977 Friday
Two years ago we had a staff of 50 in our L.T.O. As the work gradually transferred to the L.V.L.O. so our staff diminished. Last year we had a staff of 40, & now we have 20. Soon we expect to be down to 12. These 12 will be allowed to stay to the end – March 1978.

29th May 1977 Whit Sunday
How uplifting to hear the words of the Gospel for Whit Sunday – my favourite Chapter in the Bible – John 14. "...... peace I leave with you. My peace I give unto you ......" and then in the evening to hear Canon Gundry reading that mighty Chapter 8 from the Epistle to the Romans – my dad's favourite.

31st May 1977 Tuesday
Everyone today is cashing in on the Queen's Silver Jubilee. There are souvenir mugs, plates, glasses, tea cloths, books, trays, jumpers, socks, rugs, etc. etc.
East Midlands Electricity Board advertises, "If your wiring is reaching its Jubilee, don't rejoice – re-wire." So we have now had an estimate for re-wiring - £211.

Note – Mum & I decide we should have the house re-wired. All our plugs and sockets are different from the standard fittings of today.

2nd June 1977 Thursday
Next Tuesday is officially Jubilee Day. It has been made a national holiday (next Monday is the ordinary Spring Bank Holiday & I have booked a coach trip to London that day). Churches all over the country will be holding special services of Thanksgiving on Sunday, & I am hoping to go to the Cathedral.

4th June 1977 Saturday
Our Three in One God, who stamps everything with his three in one Trade Mark, can be seen yet again in the Jew, the Moslem, and the Christian, with their common Father-in-God Abraham. The Dome of the Rock, where once stood the Temple of Solomon in Jerusalem is the corner stone.

6th June 1977 Monday
The Dome of the Rock in Jerusalem was completed in 691. This is the very spot where Abraham nearly sacrificed Isaac his son. From this rock Mohammed ascended to heaven, and according to Moslems, this is where the Angel Israfil will sound the trumpet on Judgment Day.

8th June 1977 Wednesday
What a glorious day in London. I saw the City in Jubilee

mood on the day before the Queen was to ride to St. Paul's, & from there walk to the Guildhall for lunch with the Lord Mayor.

I walked along the processional route from Trafalgar Square via St. Paul's & St. Mary-le-Bow & on to Guildhall.

10th June 1977 Friday

"Domine Dirige Nos" – I saw this motto of the City of London high above the entrance of the Guildhall, & also on the crest of the Lord Mayor's car parked in front of St. Paul's. Also, I saw the thrilling sight of Tower Bridge being raised to admit the Royal Yacht Britannia.

12th June 1977 Sunday

The great service of Thanksgiving for the Silver Jubilee of the Accession of Queen

Elizabeth II was held in Leicester Cathedral last Sunday. The preacher was Ronald Ralph Williams, Bishop of Leicester, who chose for his text Psalm 144, "Happy is that people whose God is the Lord."

14th June 1977 Tuesday

Of all the messages sent to Her Majesty the Queen on her Silver Jubilee, this is my favourite: -

"Dear Queen Elizabeth,

Thank you very much for sitting on the throne for 25 years.

Lots of Love from Nicola. Aged 8."

Nicola wrote from Talavera School, Zoest, West Germany, where her father is a soldier with the Army of the Rhine.

16th June 1977 Thursday

"Charles to Marry Astrid" These are the newspaper headlines this week. Prince Charles is 28 and Princess Marie-Astrid of Luxembourg is 23. Her full names are Marie Astrid Liliane Charlotte Leopoldine Wilhelmine Ingeborg Antonia Elisabeth Anna. She will become Princess of Wales.

18th June 1977 Saturday

Yorkshire here we come! Mum & I started our week's holiday at Studley Roger, near Ripon, North Yorkshire. We had a good journey, calling en route at Harewood House, 7 miles south of Harrogate – a veritable treasure trove of Chippendale furniture, & Adam's work.

20th June 1977 Monday

Ripon is a dear little place (population 12,000) with a mighty Cathedral & a mighty history. Went to the Cathedral yesterday for evensong, & how beautifully the choir sang – 18 choir boys & 6 choir men. The most moving part of the service was listening to the choir sing Psalm 18, with stereo effect in 2 sections.

22nd June 1977 Wednesday

"Except ye Lord keep ye citie, ye wakeman waketh in vain." High above the Town Hall in Ripon this is written big & bold & clear. And now we have seen the hornblower, blowing his horn at 9p.m. in the Town Hall square. This custom is more than a thousand years old, dating back to King Alfred in 886 A.D.

24th June 1977 Friday

What a treasure trove of history we have found in North Yorkshire. Knaresborough is one of the most delightful places you could ever see. Richmond is also a quaint old place; & everywhere there are great country houses & estates with acres & acres of grounds with waterfalls, lakes, and lovely walks.

26th June 1977 Sunday

Ravenstone Sunday School Anniversary. Most of the credit was due to Mrs. June Bird, our pianist & teacher. The children sang some lively songs including "I Love the Sun", "The Flowers that Grow in the Garden", "We Must Learn to Play Together", "When I Needed a Neighbour", and "Let my Little Light Shine". (24 children)

28th June 1977 Tuesday

In one fell swoop our L.T.O. staff was sliced from 20 to 12 as the L.V.L.O. took over more staff. Plans are now ahead to re-design the whole lay-out of the office, with a completely new counter, & everything in accordance with government standards, rather than county council.

30th June 1977 Thursday

Steve Browne today finished work in our L.T.O. & starts tomorrow with D.H.S.S.

There are still 43 E.O.s in the country working in L.T.O.s who are surplus to requirements. This includes me. The enforcement vacancy in L.V.L.O. is by no means definite, but I am ever hopeful.

2nd July 1977 Saturday

Our second picnic for the Sunday School. Mrs Bird organised everything, & it was a great success. We had the use of Ravenstone Scout Hall, where we played games, & then had tea out of doors, behind the Scout Hall, by the cornfield. A lovely sunny day for us.

4th July 1977 Monday

With our little band of L.T.O. staff now reduced to 12, I am now "Executive Officer" in charge of the section. As most of the staff are not Civil Servants, it is a job that should not involve a dozen Staff Reports. I thoroughly enjoy running the section & would like it to last longer.

6th July 1977 Wednesday

Mum & I visited her cousin Elsie at Bosworth Hall, where she was convalescing after a recent hernia operation. The Hall at Market Bosworth was once the home of the Dixie family – a magnificent residence, standing in splendid grounds. We learned of Willoughby Dixie.

8th July 1977 Friday

"I, Willoughby Dixie, of Bosworth Park, without the aid of scribe or clerk,

Or pettifogger of the law, ready to make or find the flaw,

To my sister Eleanor of Bourne lest she her brother long should mourn,

The welcome news she must hear, that I give her eight hundred pounds a year.

And also on her I do fix to be my sole executrix.

To sister Rosamund whose bower of happiness ne'er knew one hour,

I twelve pence give, far more than's due to such a sad vexatious shrew …….."

So began the Will of Sir Willoughby Dixie, Bart. of Bosworth Park, Leicestershire, dated
1st June 1815. Proved in Doctors Commons 17th August 1815. Sworn under £300,000.

12th July 1977 Tuesday
Tosca the beautiful, Tosca the beloved is dead. At the end of the summer last year, Mum & I took Tosca to be put to sleep. Tosca lay on my lap in the waiting room at the vets, & completely ignored the other restless cats & dogs. Tosca gave me one last long look with those beautiful blue eyes, and goodbye.

14th July 1977 Thursday
46 today. Pat, Evelyn & 9 year old Steven (Mary Blue's son) came for the evening.
Evelyn retired from work this month after many years as a school teacher.
Steven lives with his grandparents at Ashby-de-la-Zouch (Mr & Mrs Jarman) (See July 11th 1971) but we see him occasionally.

16th July 1977 Saturday
Let me introduce you to Anthony Powell, a comparative new-comer to Ravenstone, who works at County Hall, Glenfield. He is a young man in his early twenties & sometimes has a lift to work with me. His unique job is caring for a battle-field, i.e. Bosworth Field; and he has to think up bright ideas to make it appeal to the public.

18th July 1977 Monday
You've no idea what a worry a battlefield can be. Having organised a **Joust** to take place on the battlefield on Sunday 7th August, Anthony cannot sleep at night worrying about all the incidental arrangements – tents to be hired & erected, litter bins, toilet facilities, etc. etc., all in the middle of nowhere.

20th July 1977 Wednesday
Guess who is coming to County Hall for lunch on Friday this week? His Royal Highness, the Duke of Edinburgh – the Queen's husband! He will arrive by helicopter in full view of our office windows. Such excitement! We had a rehearsal the other day, with a helicopter landing & taking off again.

22nd July 1977 Friday
The Duke of Edinburgh dined at County Hall. We had an excellent view of him going into lunch & also coming out. All the dignitaries of the county were there – Colonel Andrew Martin, Lord Lieutenant of the County, the Lord Mayor, the Bishop, the Duke of Rutland, etc.

24th July 1977 Sunday
A newcomer to my Sunday School class this morning was 9 year old Timothy Williams. I was showing the class how to find their way through the Bible – the Old Testament (stories **before** the birth of Jesus) – the New Testament (stories about Jesus), & the Epistles. He was thrilled to see an Epistle to Timothy.

26th July 1977 Tuesday
Having a few days holiday this week, Mum & I went out for the day to see the new Empingham Reservoir – now called Rutland Water. Dear little Rutland, now no longer a county, refuses to lose its identity. Signs at every boundary point proclaim Rutland, & a church in the water does too.

28th July 1977 Thursday
Went with a bus load from Ravenstone to Gladstone Pottery, Longton, Staffs. Expected to see pretty china in elegant surroundings. Instead we saw an old dirty building, with disused kilns, where we were taken on a conducted tour to see what used to be.

30th July 1977 Saturday
£500 at last. This is the total of my life's savings, which has been slowly but surely accumulating over the past 2 years in the index linked Save As You Earn scheme. (See 26th June 1975) If only I can manage to keep it going for another 3 years, this should be a worth-while lump sum on which to build.

1st August 1977 Monday
Apart from my £500 in S.A.Y.E. I have about £500 in the bank which I am about to spend. What with re-wiring the house - £211, a leaking roof, & other incidentals, Mum & I are hoping to have a modern sink unit in the kitchen & then an automatic up-to-date washing machine.

3rd August 1977 Wednesday
As the Local Taxation Office prepares for extinction – 8 months to go – various items, preserved over many years, are being given the chop. I managed to rescue one beautifully bound book – **"Register of Mechanically Propelled Road Vehicles" LAY 1 – LUT 999**.

5th August 1977 Friday
No rumours at the moment to scrap Motor Taxation. It provides such tremendous revenue for the government.
The latest proposal in Leicestershire is for the Department of Transport (Civil Service) to take over our office (part of County Hall, belonging to the County Council) & pay the County Council for its use.

7th August 1977 Sunday
Yesterday I paid £50 deposit on a new washing machine. I chose an automatic Hotpoint 1509 top loader from Coalville Co-op, on sale at £194. This will take up to 10lbs of washing, plus choice of 2 smaller loads – no tangle – any washing powder – I am hoping to pay £72 on September 3rd & £72 on October 1st.

9th August 1977 Tuesday
This Silver Jubilee Year the Queen has visited almost every corner of her kingdom. From Scotland to Wales – the Midlands – Devon & Cornwall & finally this week to Northern Ireland, where violence & shooting never stops. Thousands of soldiers & police are on full alert for the Queen's visit.

11th August 1977 Thursday
Despite threats by the I.R.A. to blow her up, the Queen made a 2 day visit to Northern Ireland. Yesterday she went by helicopter to Hillsborough Castle, near Belfast, & today she visited the University of Ulster in Coleraine.

Protected by 32,000 soldiers & policemen, she defied the I.R.A. threats.

13th August 1977 Saturday
Reg Hall now has yet another luxury residence in Main Street, Ravenstone. His latest house is 3 former derelict cottages made into one. Again the interior is expensively decorated, carpeted and furnished. He uses it mainly as a sleeping place, as he has his meals at his brother Alf's, across the road.

15th August 1977 Monday
David Page, a neighbour who works in the coalmine - Snibston Pit, has offered to take me on a conducted tour of the mine. We have fixed the date for Sunday 28th August. All my life I have lived in a mining area in a community of coal miners, & am most interested to see what it is like where they all work.

Note – I asked if I might go, having lived all my life on top of the coal-mine.

16th August 1977 Tuesday
Elvis Presley, *the King of Rock'n'Roll, died in Memphis, Tennessee, aged 42 years.*

17th August 1977 Wednesday
Presley, Elvis Aron, passed away August 16th in Memphis, Tennessee, U.S.A.
"Your passing caused more pain than words can ever say. God keep you safe in His arms until the Judgement Day. We'll remember forever."
This was in the "Deaths" in the Leicester Mercury, as grief stricken fans mourned the 42 year old greatest pop singer.

19th August 1977 Friday
Elvis Presley, idol of millions, & known as Elvis the Pelvis, has rocked the world for the past 21 years with gyrating music. President Carter says, "Elvis Presley's death deprives our country of a part of itself. His music & his personality, fusing the style of white country & black rhythm and blues, permanently changed the face of American popular culture. His following was immense & he was a symbol to the people the world over, of the vitality, rebelliousness & good humour of this country. He burst upon the scene more than 20 years ago with an impact that was unprecedented & will probably never be equalled."

23 August 1977 Tuesday
Sunday School Outing to Whipsnade Zoo last Saturday did not get a lot of support. We managed to fill only one 45 seater bus. We had 28 adults & 19 children (not all of the 19 children were Sunday School children). I spent a couple of hours in Dunstable, about 5 miles from the Zoo, looking around.

25th August 1977 Thursday
This week we have had our new sink unit in the kitchen, and our new washing machine plumbed in. The sink unit cost £66. The taps cost £15. George, the joiner, assembled the whole unit & made us a work top extension for £11. Eric, the plumber, fixed us up with a new bathroom rail at the same time - £60.

27th August 1977 Saturday
£50,000 was offered to the first man to become airborne without the aid of an engine. This week Bryan Allen achieved this by pedal power. He had to remain airborne for more than a mile, & this he did. He "flew" in a plane designed by Dr Paul McCready, costing £14,000.

29th August 1977 Monday
Dr Paul McCready, former international gliding champion, designed a plane with a wingspan longer than a jet liner & yet gossamer light. He called the plane "Gossamer Condor" & it was pedalled into history in California. And so, 4,000 years after Icarus took to the air, man does it again.

31st August 1977 Wednesday
This week has been August Bank Holiday. Mum & I ventured forth 60 miles to Ravenstone in Buckinghamshire, just to see our village namesake. We found a dear little village, & had our picnic lunch near to the church.
On the way home we called to see the Saxon church at Brixworth, Northamptonshire.

2nd September 1977 Friday
My proposed visit to the local coal mine was cancelled, because a party of 30 policemen decided to go, & they were given priority. So, we are hoping to go some other time, possibly September 25th. David Page, who has offered to take me, lives next door but one. He has a dear little girl named Joanne, aged 3.

4th September 1977 Sunday
Sunday School started again today, after our holiday for the month of August. I have several newcomers in my class, who have moved up from the younger class.
Today we had a look at our huge old family bible, dated 1811, & also a look at the "Red Letter" bible & its pictures.

6th September 1977 Tuesday
This week we are having the house re-wired, so I am having a week's holiday.
This week also, Aunt Dos is having a new tar-mac drive, so it is a hive of industry with workmen busy everywhere.
Our house is a proper shambles at the moment, but the garden is a picture, in fullest bloom.

8th September 1977 Thursday
John Bailey (Johnty), Mum's cousin, has joined the hive of activity around our house this week.
He came, complete with ladders & all the necessary paraphernalia, to climb up the roof & make it water-tight. He did a Herculean job, all alone, & would accept no more than £2.
(See 16th January 1977 for other estimate)

10th September 1977 Saturday
Next week we are expecting Mum's cousin, Mary Moore, to be staying with us. She will be coming by train from London to Leicester, & then by bus to Ravenstone, arriving Monday afternoon. She had originally thought of coming a week earlier, but changed her mind when she heard we were being re-wired.

12th September 1977 Monday
"Provost to be Country Vicar"
Today my beloved Provost, the Very Revd. John Hughes, celebrates the 15th anniversary of his arrival at the Cathedral, & the stunning news in the Leicester Mercury is that he is now leaving to become vicar of Bringhurst with Great Easton and Drayton.

14th September 1977 Wednesday
The house is now ship-shape again after a week of re-wiring. We had floor boards up in every room upstairs & on the landing. We had holes drilled through the walls, through the ceiling & through the floor. There was debris all over the place – but **now!** We are well pleased with the result & have all new fittings.

16th September 1977 Friday
Auntie Doris now a sprightly 82 year old, came for tea & spent the evening with Mary Moore, Mum & me. She thinks nothing of cycling 3 miles to visit her daughter; she also goes for long walks, & often sits up until after midnight, playing cards with her friends – one of whom is aged 91.

18th September 1977 Sunday
Victor, a 1 ton, 18 foot giraffe, 15 years old, did the splits with his back legs a couple of days ago & now cannot get up. He is one of the giraffes at Marwell Zoological Park, near Winchester, and his plight has caused nationwide concern. The cause of his downfall was Arabesque, one of his 3 wives, on heat.

20th September 1977 Tuesday
Victor, the giraffe, is dead. He died apparently from shock, minutes after being hoisted upright, 6 days after he collapsed.
The lifting tackle used today was supplied by the Royal Navy and is normally used for raising heavy naval guns. Scaffolders built a tower around him, & hoisted a sling round his midriff.

22nd September 1977 Thursday
"Seven Hundred Feet Down" Next Sunday I am hoping to go down Snibston mine, & remarkably there is an article this week in the Leicester Mercury by Joan Stephens, who went with a small press party to this very mine, & she describes in detail what it was like ….. "To my disappointment we did not go down in the miners' cage but were escorted down the drift."

24th September 1977 Saturday
"The drift was a long sloping tunnel, having a one in four slope, over ½ a mile long. Walking down the drift was quite difficult. The surface was uneven, & we squelched through sticky mud ……." So read the report by Joan Stephens, but my neighbour says he won't take me anywhere like that.

26th September 1977 Monday
One hundred fathoms deep & more I descended with my neighbour Dave to the pit bottom – like going down into some mediaeval dungeon; then out into what appeared like a never ending pitch black railway tunnel. We were equipped with helmets, lamps and emergency air supply.

28th September 1977 Wednesday
After a mile walk through the tunnel at the bottom of the pit, sometimes stooping low & often clonking my pit helmet on the roof, we met the foreman doing his safety rounds. He escorted us the rest of the way, & even provided me with coffee from a flask. Then a joyful return to sunlight.

30th September 1977 Friday
How very pleased I am with our new washing machine. It does all that I expected and more. The washing has never looked so good. First it gives the clothes a good old soak, then a thorough wash, then a double rinse, & finally a spin dry.
This week I bought a very useful fold-up clothes airer for £10.

2nd October 1977 Sunday
In this month's Cathedral News-Letter, my beloved Provost, the Very Revd. John C. Hughes, says that he will be instituted at Great Easton on the Feast of the Epiphany, January 6th 1978 at 7-30 p.m. He says, "I shall remain in the diocese, tucked away in the most beautiful Leicestershire countryside, in my view the finest in the world.
Handing on the torch is an exciting moment – as a rule the one who runs the next leg is a better runner – the anchor man is always the fastest – and in this case the anchor man is our Lord Jesus. So we're bound to win. As you hand over the torch & see your successor going away with great success you cheer with all the puff left in you."

6th October 1977 Thursday
Enid – The Cuz – is **50** today, & still she has boundless energy. She still plays hockey, running down the left wing & scoring goals. She still takes her keep fit class & goes for a weekly swim at the swimming baths.
Yesterday we were shocked to hear of the death of a neighbour, Jean Marlow, aged only 49.

8th October 1977 Saturday
At last there are signs of improvement in the financial state of the country.
Prime Minister James Callaghan is likened to Moses, leading Britain to the Promised Land flowing with **oil** and **money**. He tells us, "There are no short cuts, but there is a road ahead – **either back us or sack us**."

10th October 1977 Monday
Yesterday was our Harvest Festival at Ravenstone Church. We had a lovely service in the afternoon for the children when the preacher was the Revd. Ince, vicar of Snibston.
Mum's cousin "Johnty" came to our house for tea, & he went with me to church in the evening for Festal Evening Prayer.

12th October 1977 Wednesday
October 12th 1958 was my first day as Sunday School teacher. It was Harvest Festival at Ravenstone Church. What I would like to do, is complete 25 years, and "retire" when it is Harvest Festival 1983. But who knows what the next years may bring. Time alone will tell us.

14th October 1977 Friday
Bing Crosby, 73 year old crooner, admired by two generations for his easy-going style & relaxed way of singing, died today of a heart attack while playing golf in Spain, ten miles north of Madrid. He made the best-selling disc of all time, "White Christmas". Everybody knows "I'm Dreaming of a White Christmas."

16th October 1977 Sunday
The Queen is now on the last tour of her Silver Jubilee Year. On Friday she landed at Ottawa International Airport at the start of a 3 weeks tour of Canada & the Caribbean.
The French Canadians are at the moment threatening to break away from English rule, particularly in Quebec.

18th October 1977 Tuesday
It is now 7 years since my heart sank to "unfathomable depths". I thought of this when I went down into the depths of the coalmine.
You can imagine what a tremendous impression it had on me when we came up from the mine so swiftly – out of the darkness to the joyful mid-day sun.

20th October 1977 Thursday
Staff Reports. This year I have already done one staff report for Frank Lee when he transferred from the old L.T.O. to the new L.V.L.O. Still with the old L.T.O. are 4 C.O.s, so I have 4 more reports to do – David Love, aged 35, Philip Stevenson 51, Muriel Morris 58, and Colin Thomas 25.

Note – I have to perform the unwelcome chore of writing staff reports on 4 Clerical Officers at work. The Unions are fighting for "open reporting", & staff who so wish, may now read their reports. I find no pleasure whatsoever in writing staff reports. As the years go by it gets worse and worse, knowing whatever to say different from before. Equally, I find no pleasure whatsoever in being reported upon, knowing you are constantly under observation & being judged.

22nd October 1977 Saturday
A beautiful warm sunny day. Tonight we put the clocks back, so it will be dark after tea.
Have made the most of the hours of daylight this past week, getting the garden cleared up for the winter. Spiked all the grass, raked it, mowed it & fed it, & put all the plants in ready for spring.

24th October 1977 Monday
This week at work we are having one almighty clear-out of all the old L.T.O. stock. We are throwing out all the old account books, etc. & filling crate after crate of dusty papers galore. We really are on the last lap now. Only a very small proportion of vehicles still have the old style log books.

26th October 1977 Wednesday
Confirmation Service this evening at Ravenstone Church, conducted by the Right Revd. T. Garrett, Assistant Bishop of Leicester. Three girls from my Sunday School class were confirmed – Elaine Gandy, Susan Land & Heather Dickinson. I read one of the three readings from the Bible.

28th October 1977 Friday
Have spent many hours this week doing Staff Reports. It is like doing a character study, & I have to consider such things as "foresight" – penetration judgement – ability to produce constructive ideas – oral expression – expression on paper – relations with others – any particular strengths – any particular weaknesses.

30th October 1977 Sunday
"Blessed is the man whose strength is in thee; in whose heart are thy ways". This appropriately was the text chosen this evening by our Rector, the Revd. Leslie Buckroyd, from the beautiful Psalm – Psalm 84, after I had spent such a lot of time considering "What is his or her particular strength?"

1st November 1977 Tuesday
We now have a new County Treasurer. Mr Blackburn retired yesterday. He was not only County Treasurer, but also Local Taxation Officer, & as such his signature appeared on all the letters from our office – though he never signed one himself.
Ray Hale is now County Treasurer.

3rd November 1977 Thursday
Only a few hours after returning from her Jubilee tour of Canada and the Caribbean, the Queen opened Parliament today wearing her new half moon spectacles to read the speech from the throne. The Imperial State Crown worn with half moon specs looks stupid.

5th November 1977 Saturday
Civil Service Staff Reports have always been confidential. But the Unions are now fighting for "open reporting", & although this has not been agreed with top management, the Unions insist that staff who so wish, may now read their reports. Muriel & David chose so to do.

7th November 1977 Monday
The Civil Service in their negotiations with Leicestershire County Council regarding accommodation for the L.V.L.O. have come across an "insurmountable problem", viz – Bank Holidays.
While the County Council have Monday & Tuesday holiday, the Civil Service have Monday only. The County Council refuse to provide heat & light on days when the County Council are on holiday.

9th November 1977 Wednesday
Once upon a time there lived in Leicestershire a man of great local importance named Sir Robert Martin. He was for many years Chairman of the Leicestershire County Council. As a local benefactor, he proposed that staff of Leicestershire County Council should have 2 days Bank Holiday.

11th November 1977 Friday
What Sir Robert did not know, was that Motor Taxation was to grow beyond the confines of County control.
It grew & grew until the government themselves tried to harness it, but even the government found it was something they could never completely master.

13th November 1977 Sunday

Mum & I ventured forth into the Peak District of Derbyshire on a 100 mile round trip & found the treasures of the snow. We went through Ashbourne to Tissington, where we had our lunch, (we packed our own) & on as far as Newhaven, which was covered in snow.

15th November 1977 Tuesday

To Princess Anne a son, her firstborn, Peter Mark Andrew, a Jubilee grandson for the Queen. The baby weighing 7lbs 9ozs was born this morning at about 11 a.m. at St. Mary's Hospital, Paddington. It was on November 15th 1859 that two babies were born, who grew up, married and became my Grandpa & Grandma Hewes.

17th November 1977 Thursday

16 years ago – in November 1961, I bought a beautiful new winter coat, with a lovely warm fox collar. This coat has given 16 years wonderful service, & is now thread-bare. This week I have bought another gorgeous coat which cost £63. I wonder how long this will last.

19th November 1977 Saturday

Took a party of 18 Sunday School children & 6 teachers to Leicester Cathedral for the annual Sunday School "Get Together". From all over the County children brought Teddy Bears to be given to needy children. About 600 Teddy Bears sat in front of the High Altar.

21st November 1977 Monday

My beloved Provost, the Very Revd. John Hughes, was at the Cathedral to welcome the Teddy Bears. It was a most moving sight to see children by the hundred walking up the aisle past the Bishop of Leicester, while the organ played "The Teddy Bear's Picnic".

23rd November 1977 Wednesday

Saw this advert, & answered it: -

"Administrative Officer – Salary Grade AP3/4 £3,395 - £4,214 inclusive – N.W.Leics. District Council, Treasurer and Chief Executive's Department, at Ashby-de-la-Zouch. Duties will include control & distribution of mail, the make up & payment of wages, petty cash expenditure & staff control in the secretarial, machine room & cashiers sections. Responsible for the efficient running of the admin. function in a busy dept. of 47 staff."

27th November 1977 Advent Sunday

Only 4 weeks to Christmas Day. Brother Pat has invited Aunt Dos, Mum & me for dinner & tea. We are expecting 2 babies in the family any day now. Bunting's 2 sons are both waiting for their first-born, & Bunting (my half-sister), now 62, will be a granny twice over.

29th November 1977 Tuesday

Our Annual Christmas Fair in Ravenstone Institute last Saturday, & our 6th effort with a stall for the Sunday School.

We made £14 (not so good). Our stall was manned by Mrs Bird & me, with the help of 2 children, Heather Dickinson & Simon Brown.

1st December 1977 Thursday

"Announcing the arrival of
Lucy Victoria,
born to Sheena & Michael Stevenson,
on Sunday 27th November 1977. 8lb 1oz.
Mother and daughter well."

Received a card from Michael for the birth of their first baby.

3rd December 1977 Saturday

Tomorrow is our Sunday School Prize Giving, so we have been buying all the books for 45 children. I have 11 children now in my class – Susan Land, Heather Dickinson, Susan Roe, Debra Hickin, Sally Anne Allsop, Ruth Howkins, Tim Williams, Simon Brown, David Roe, Dale Fairbrother & Arthur Needham.

5th December 1977 Monday

Spent an hour or so at Ravenstone Rectory sorting out with the Rector, the Revd. Leslie Buckroyd, the rota of "Altar Flowers & Brasses" for next year. It is a work of art trying to suit everybody. Obviously it is much better to be on during the summer than in the winter.

7th December 1977 Wednesday

Our rota for "Altar Flowers & Brasses" is made up of ladies who work in twos, & have two consecutive weeks, because flowers sometimes last for two Sundays. We have enough ladies to span the whole year, so we have to make sure that they are not always given the worst time of the year.

9th December 1977 Friday

This week I have bought a pair of new winter boots. My good old green winter boots lasted for 14 years; these were replaced in 1969 by brown boots 9″ high.

Now I have the latest fashion of today – black leather Cossack style high heeled – knee high with a 15″ zip (40cm) £33.

11th December 1977 Sunday

Hewes, Helen (Nellie), widow of the late Frank Hedley Hewes and loving mother of Hilda and Walter, peacefully on December 11th 1977, aged 91 years, service Bramcote Methodist Church, Nottingham, Thursday December 15th at 10 a.m. prior to cremation Wilford Hill. Inquiries to R. Clower and Son, 105 Derby Road, Nottingham, Telephone 44035.

This is Auntie Nellie, wife of Uncle Hedley.

13th December 1977 Tuesday

Sir Winston Churchill, the greatest man of our times, died in January 1965. In 1908 he married Clementine Hozier, & afterwards he wrote, "I married, & lived happily ever after." Today his "Darling Clementine" died aged 92.

15th December 1977 Thursday

Our Sunday School Christmas Party in Ravenstone School was a joyous occasion with conjuror Eric Rose keeping the children well entertained. Outside it was cold & wet & windy, but inside, the children, dressed in their prettiest party clothes, were radiantly happy .....
"Except ye become as little children ...."

17th December 1977 Saturday

"Dinner in Honour of Retiring Provost" quote from the Leicester Mercury, "The retiring Provost of Leicester, the Rt. Revd. John Hughes, received one of his highest tributes last night, when the Lord Mayor, Mr Bert Baker, described him as one of the most remarkable friends a Mayor could wish for."

19th December 1977 Monday

"The Brandon Spire at Leicester Cathedral will be a lasting memorial to the Provost, the Rt. Revd. John Hughes, who is leaving after 15 years" writes the Bishop of Leicester in his letter to the diocese this month. Dr R. R. Williams praises the Provost's efforts to raise £30,000 for the spire.

21st December 1977 Wednesday

A Christmas card from Shirley, Julian & Baby Katherine, heralds the arrival of the second baby expected in our family. Born on December 16th, Katherine Louise is 3 weeks younger than her cousin Lucy Victoria. Both babies are born under Sagittarius, the Archer.

23rd December 1977 Friday

Received a letter from North West Leics. District Council. Dear Sir/Madam, Appointment of Administrative Officer. Thank you for your application for the above position. I have to inform you that the post has now been filled. Yours Faithfully, M. R. Davis, Deputy Treasurer

25th December 1977 Sunday

Christmas Day, & how lovely to have this Holy Day on a Sunday. Went to 11 a.m. service at Leicester Cathedral, where my beloved Provost was taking his last Christmas in his old recognised spot in the Cathedral.
To me, the Provost is John Hughes. I cannot imagine anyone else.

27th December 1977 Tuesday

Heaven & Earth met together in Leicester Cathedral this Christmas when we sang Psalm 85, "Mercy & Truth are met together; righteousness & peace have kissed each other. Truth shall flourish out of the earth & righteousness hath looked down from heaven."

29th December 1977 Thursday

The "insurmountable problem" mentioned on 7th November, seems to have melted away. It now seems almost certain that the Motor Licence Office will remain at good old County Hall. Plans have now been drawn up for re-designing the whole interior of the office, with the counter re-positioned.

31st December 1977 Saturday

From Auntie Belle this Christmas we had a card to remind us of St. Paul's message, II Corinthians Chapter 13, verse 11.
"Finally, brethren, farewell. Be perfect, be of good comfort, be of one mind, live in peace; & the God of Love and Peace shall be with you."

* * *

1978

1st January 1978 Sunday

This is year 78.

$1 + 2 + 3 + 4 + 5 + 6 + 7 + 8 + 9 + 10 + 11 + 12$

$7 + 8 = 15 = 1 + 2 + 3 + 4 + 5$ ___ $1 + 5 = 6 = 1 + 2 + 3$

3rd January 1978 Tuesday

Auntie Dos has very generously given me £50. When I launched out on a new sink unit and a washing machine last August, Aunt Dos said she would like to give me £50 towards the cost, & I said, "Leave it until Christmas." So with my bank balance now very low, I am hoping to build it up again.

5th January 1978 Thursday

L.T.O. rundown is now on its very last lap. As the last of the vehicles with current licences are swallowed up by the computer, it is total destruction of 50,000 records in our office of the vehicles which have not been licensed during the past year. We hate to destroy such valuable records.

7th January 1978 Saturday

Bringhurst, one of the tiniest villages in Leicestershire, which has embraced my best beloved for so long, yesterday acquired a new vicar. My beloved Provost became "the vicar". So the two men who have had the greatest effect on me may soon meet one another.

9th January 1978 Monday

What do you do when a motorist applies for a duplicate registration document for a car that has not been licensed lately & the records are destroyed? I rang Swansea to ask what to put for the "Date of Original Registration". This is so very important.

I was told, "Make up an imaginary date."

11th January 1978 Wednesday

A Wedding Invitation.

"Mr & Mrs Donald A. Hewes request the company of Miss E. Hewes at the Marriage of their daughter Susan Ann to Mr Michael Norman Richard Underwood at St. Michael & All Angels' Church Ravenstone on Saturday 25th March 1978 at 12 noon, & afterwards at the Grey Lady."

13th January 1978 Friday

The Royal Institution Annual Christmas Lectures to Young People was given this year by Professor Carl Sagan.

Entitled "Planets", it was of particular interest to me. Starting with the Planet Earth, we approached as if from outer space to find this tiny planet which is our world. From the Planet Earth we said, "Hello Universe." Like an echo we heard "Hello Universe" as the sound reached first the Moon (travelling at the speed of light), & then some time later Venus, & then Mars & Mercury. But most of the Universe was much too far away to hear.

Professor Carl Sagan is perhaps the world's greatest optimist for the existence of intelligent life elsewhere in the Universe. He does not expect that we shall make contact in our lifetime, but he told his young audience, "You are the scientists of tomorrow. It will be up to you

to continue this quest."

15th January 1978 Sunday

The Christmas Juvenile Lectures, as they were called by their founder Michael Faraday, began in 1826 and were intended to educate and entertain young people – Faraday's own great scientific career was inspired by attending just such a lecture.

17th January 1978 Tuesday

Miss M. Cumberland, Provost's secretary since November 1968, has left to take up an appointment with the Area Health Authority. So it is just as well I was not accepted when I applied for that job. I never thought at the time that within 10 years the Provost would be a country vicar.

19th January 1978 Thursday

Mum has now had her wheel-chair for a year, but she would never be seen in it. She prefers to stay in her old armchair, & on the rare occasions when she ventures out, she goes by car. She goes to the hairdressers by car – about once a month, but throughout the winter she virtually hibernates.

21st January 1978 Saturday

A covering of snow this week inspires me to tell the children at Sunday school of Napoleon & his mighty army being beaten by God's army of little snowflakes.

"Thank you God for snowflakes, so delicate and small; but when called into action, they are mightier than all." How I marvel at little snowflakes.

23rd January 1978 Monday

Transport Minister, William Rodgers, now admits that D.V.L.C. Swansea was a mistake. He says, "When the decision was taken to create it, some of the problems were under-estimated. It was the age in which we believed that **biggest** was best. Since then we have realised that the biggest is not necessarily the best."

25th January 1978 Wednesday

It costs £50 million a year to run D.V.L.C. Swansea, & a big campaign is being launched to scrap the centre & its mixed-up computer nicknamed "**The Nincomputer**". M.P.s, driven round the bend by complaints from constituents, plan to fire a new barrage of Commons questions at William Rodgers.

27th January 1978 Friday

Tomorrow I shall be 17,000 days old. 46 years old, grey haired (coloured brown), 2 teeth missing, weighing 9 ½ stone – an old maid. Trudging round town with the shopping I look & feel like an also-ran. Dressed in my elegant Sunday best however, I look and feel as good as any of the best of them.

29th January 1978 Sunday

Poor old Leicester City! Leicester's football manager Frank McLintock has done his utmost to bring us success, but week after week we fail to score & are heading fast for relegation from Division I to Division II. Yesterday we were knocked out of the Cup by 3rd Division Walsall.

31st January 1978 Tuesday

"La Vie Parisienne" is Coalville Amateurs' production for this year, & I am very pleased to be joining them once more in my role of prompter. Set in Paris in the 1860's, it is a lively musical by Offenbach with lots of singing for the chorus. There is more music than libretto, so not a lot of prompting.

2nd February 1978 Thursday

God's army of little snowflakes has this week been doing battle in the North of Scotland. Never in my whole life have I seen such terrifying snow scenes as on the television. Rescue teams using long poles have probed drifts 20 feet deep to find motorists completely buried underneath.

4th February 1978 Saturday

And now we come to the count down for L.T.O.closure – only 8 weeks left, & I have not been given a place in the L.V.L.O. My name has been given to the Department of Energy at Wigston, who have one E.O. vacancy coming up shortly. I am to go & see them on Feb. 21st.

6th February 1978 Monday

The most amazing rescue story from Scotland's blizzard was that of Billy Sutherland, 60 year old salesman, buried for 4 days in his Mini Clubman beneath 18 feet of snow. While others died in their cars, he survived by constantly poking an air-hole, by violent arm exercises & by eating snow.

8th February 1978 Ash Wednesday

"Thank God you found me!" These were the words of Billy Sutherland when rescuers freed him from the terrors of a snow tomb. They knew he was somewhere under the snow on the A9 near Wick. For 4 days a team of men with avalanche probes checked every step until they struck metal.

10th February 1978 Friday

Before I go to see them on February 21st at the Dept. of Energy, I have an appointment with Colin Payne, our present personnel officer. He has arranged to see me next Wednesday, at Birmingham L.V.L.O., where he is on his official rounds. I am hoping to go to Birmingham tomorrow to look around.

12th February 1978 Sunday

Went to Birmingham yesterday by bus to find the Motor Licence Office, where I have an appointment next Wednesday. I was looking for Oozells Street, off Broad Street, & it took me nearly 2 hours to find it – under busy roads, & over busy roads, but now I know exactly where to go.

14th February 1978 Tuesday

"Department of Energy" "Development of the Oil & Gas Resources of the U.K." & "Britain 1977" – including energy and natural resources.
Three books from the library at D.V.L.C. have been sent to me on loan via personnel to help me in my forthcoming interview at Wigston.

16th February 1978 Thursday

Had my interview with Colin Payne at Birmingham Motor Licence Office. He urged me to make every effort to get the job being offered to me at the Dept. of Energy, Wigston. He said I may not have another such offer in Leicestershire, & it was up to me to make the most of this opportunity.

18th February 1978 Saturday

After my interview in Birmingham, I had an opportunity to look round the shops. What a concrete jungle there is in the city centre. It's all up steps, down steps, subterranean walks & a shopping centre completely under cover, but not my choice of a city. Give me London or Paris or Rome.

20th February 1978 Monday

How very interesting I have found my books on "**Energy**". Having already marvelled at God's army of little snowflakes, now I can marvel at tiny atoms & molecules, at air pressures in tyres, at solids changing to liquid, changing to GAS. Molecules by the million make raindrops or oceans, snowflakes or icebergs.

22nd February 1978 Wednesday

I have now been offered the E.O. vacancy at the Dept. of Energy, Wigston, which I have accepted. But, oh, the turmoil of thoughts in my mind! I wept at the thought of leaving good old County Hall & all its associated memories. How I shall miss the world of Motor Taxation – my world for 30 years.

24th February 1978 Friday

"Gas Standards Branch", Dept. of Energy, Wigston, is a body of "Competent & Impartial Persons" (mainly scientists) who carry out tests of the gas supplied by B.G.C. (British Gas Corporation) for the purpose of ascertaining whether it is of the declared Calorific Value & conforms to prescribed standards.

26th February 1978 Sunday

I experienced the most heart-warming glow from the Lord's Prayer, after my initial fears at joining the Dept. of Energy (known at one time as the Ministry of Power). I was moved so deeply by those oft repeated words, "For thine is the Kingdom – **the Power** & the Glory."

28th February 1978 Tuesday

The declared calorific value of gas in our country means: – the number of British thermal units produced by the combustion of one cubic foot of gas, measured at sixty degrees Fahrenheit under a pressure of thirty inches of mercury, & containing a certain amount of water vapour.

1st March 1978 Wednesday

"Gas Standards Branch" Dept. of Energy, Wigston, is a body of "Competent and Impartial Persons" who also examine meters to ensure that they conform to prescribed standards – "No meter shall be used unless it is stamped by a meter examiner." Meters must be periodically overhauled & re-examined.

3rd March 1978 Friday

4 weeks to L.T.O. closure, & because I have accepted the E.O. vacancy at Wigston, I am leaving L.T.O. a little earlier than I expected. Officially, I shall leave next Friday, but actually I left today, because I had already

arranged to have a holiday next week for "La Vie Parisienne".

5th March 1978 Mothering Sunday
On this Mothering Sunday 1978, I am reminded of a poem I heard read at five minutes to midnight on the last day of the year 1967 ….. "Nothing left of a time that was but things remembered. We stand on a bridge between two shores, while under our feet eternity pours all the time dismembered."

7th March 1978 Tuesday
"We stand on a bridge between two shores." La Vie Parisienne is my bridge linking my old world of Motor Taxation to the new untrodden world of Gas Standards. It is a beautiful bridge, where girls in colourful costume dance & sing, & where I am swept along with them.

Note – The cross-roads of my working life. After 30 years in the good old Motor Licence Office, I am now thrust fully into the Civil Service, where there is a strict pecking order, & all the work moves up & down & round & round, with everybody writing their own special comments on the way.
Unlike the Motor Licence, where we endeavoured to clear the work daily, here, correspondence can take weeks or even months to clear, as it gets held up on its merry-go-round. Nevertheless, I am interested in the work of this unique place, & find there is plenty of time to explore the records in the Registry & the scientific journals in the library, for which I am now responsible. I must now "supervise" several staff & prepare their Staff Reports.

9th March 1978 Thursday
A letter from the Department of Energy, Thames House, South Millbank, London, S W 1.
"Dear Miss Hewes, I am pleased to inform you that arrangements have been made for you to transfer to the Dept. of Energy …. I would like to take this opportunity of welcoming you to the Dept. of Energy."

11th March 1978 Saturday
Last night of La Vie Parisienne. This week has sped by so quickly. A glorious week of blue skies, sunshine & birdsong, with every evening filled with the delightful music of Offenbach. Once again I have thoroughly enjoyed my role as prompter, sitting with the orchestra.

13th March 1978 Monday
Mum & I went to Staunton Harold Cheshire Home to hear the Coalville Amateurs singing a selection from their latest show "La Vie Parisienne". As the emphasis of this show is very much on the singing, the story could almost be told in song which sounded so good in their lovely big room.

15th March 1978 Wednesday
I am now acquainted with the 12 gas regions of our country, reminding me of the 12 tribes of Israel in the land of Canaan.
I have also been introduced to a whole new vocabulary, such as:- Hygrometric Surveys, Recording Calorimeters & Non-recording Calorimeters.

17th March 1978 Friday
His Excellency Shaikh Abdul Aziz Bin Abdullah Ale Shaikh, who is like the Pope of the Muslim world, came to Leicester this week. He is titled Imam of Haram Sharif & is the religious leader of the world's 900 million Muslims. We have 10,000 Muslims in Leicester, & this was the visit of a life-time.

19th March 1978 Palm Sunday
The Rector of Ravenstone, the Revd. Buckroyd, spoke today of the humility of Christ as described by St. Paul in his Epistle to the Philippians, Chapter 2. He spoke of the Peace of God which passeth all understanding – proclaimed by the Angels at the birth of Christ, "On Earth Peace" & finally "My Peace I give unto you".

21st March 1978 Tuesday
As I now stand on the shores of my new life in the world of Gas Standards, I am reminded that a little unborn baby is the reason for such an E.O. vacancy being offered to me. Christine the E.O. whose place I am taking is leaving because she is expecting a baby in June.

23rd March 1978 Thursday
Christine, the E.O. whose place I am taking, has now left. She has been with me every day since I started, teaching me the work, & has been a wonderful help. At night, she & her unborn baby have been out in the fields of her farmer husband "**lambing**", so I gave her a lamb.

25th March 1978 Saturday
Susan Hewes, aged 22, my goddaughter, was married today at Ravenstone Church. And again the Rector spoke of "the Peace of God which passeth all understanding" from Chapter 4 of St. Paul's Epistle to the Philippians. We sang two beautiful hymns, "O Perfect Love" and "O Father All Creating".
Note – Reception at the Grey Lady, Newtown Linford.

27th March 1978 Easter Monday
Easter once more proclaims to us "The Exceeding Greatness of the Power of God" as described by St. Paul in his Epistle to the Ephesians.
Having now joined the Department of Energy, which deals with the so-called power of man, it is nice to know that the greatest Power is in Mercy & Pity.

29th March 1978 Wednesday
It was in March 1972 that Britain struck oil in the North Sea. Where there is oil there is natural gas, & our country is now enjoying an abundance of both oil & gas. But by the end of this century we are expecting our oil wells to run dry & then we predict a major crisis energy gap.

31st March 1978 Friday
Local Taxation Closure. The former Leicestershire County Motor Licence Office is now the Local Vehicle Licensing Office, including Leicester City and Rutland. Staff from Leicester City L.T.O. held a party to mark the closure of their office after 55 years.

2nd April 1978 Sunday
The lesson at church this evening was taken from I

Kings, Chapter 17. Unlike our oil wells, which are of such limited duration, here was the story of Elijah & the promise of God, "The barrel of meal shall not waste, neither shall the cruse of oil fail."

4th April 1978 Tuesday

A day's holiday, so I called to see all my old work-mates at good old County Hall. They were absolutely over-whelmed with work. L.T.O. closure had reduced their ranks, & they had a mountain of post brought about by the forthcoming Budget, by the Easter holiday, & also staff on holiday.

6th April 1978 Thursday

Mr Ellis, Chief Gas Examiner of the whole country, who works in our office, spent a couple of hours today explaining to me the history & development of Gas in this land. He virtually controls the whole Gas flow throughout England, Scotland & Wales, & was very informative.

Note – Much of the clerical work is generated by the Chief Gas Examiner & his 12 Area Gas Examiners, located far & wide throughout England, Scotland & Wales, plus numerous "fee-paid" gas examiners located likewise, & continually testing gas for correct pressure & calorific value.
Mr Ellis appreciates my attention to detail & meticulous keeping of records. He says of my previous employers, "Their loss is our gain".

8th April 1978 Saturday

Mr Ellis, Chief Gas Examiner, told me how gas was first made from distilled coal. He explained that distilled water is the pure steam from boiling water, not allowed to escape, but kept in a closed vessel & cooled back to liquid. So coal was heated to make gas.

10th April 1978 Monday

North Sea Oil & Natural Gas are now bringing to this country "seven years of great plenty". (See Genesis 41. 29) But as in ancient Egypt, "there shall arise after them seven years of famine, & all the plenty shall be forgotten", we too must store against the years of famine.

12th April 1978 Wednesday

Budget Day this week, and at last (thanks to our North Sea Oil) the Chancellor, Denis Healey, can give us all some money back in the form of reduced Income Tax, and also pay off some of our colossal debts. (See 5th November 1975) Without North Sea Oil we would by now have sunk.

14th April 1978 Friday

I have now completed **one month** in my new world of Gas Standards. I am responsible for the work in our G.S.B. library, in our registry, & for the correspondence of the chief gas examiner & the chief gas meter examiner. I have much yet to learn, but I hope in time to succeed.

16th April 1978 Sunday

"**May Every Success be Yours**" This was the message signed by the 40 staff from Motor Tax, when I left last

month. I chose as my leaving present a beautiful gilt-edged oval mirror to "**reflect**" on thirty years in the world of Motor Tax from 1948 – 1978.

18th April 1978 Tuesday

My world of Motor Tax reached to the 4 corners of the county, but now my world of Gas Standards reaches to the 4 corners of the whole country, from Scotland in the north to Cornwall in the south west. I have now been introduced to the Quarterly Statements involving a detailed breakdown of the regions.

20th April 1978 Thursday

"**Watchdogs who can Sniff out Danger**" So heads an article in the Leicester Mercury all about Gas Standards Branch, South Wigston. Opened in 1969 as part of the devolution of Civil Service work to the provinces, it is Leicester's only Government department headquarters, and employs 50 technical experts.

22nd April 1978 Saturday

Cathedral News-Letter No. 156. What a surprise!
My beloved Provost, the Very Revd. John Hughes, stopped sending his news letter when he left the Cathedral four months ago, but now Canon Gundry has decided to keep in touch with us, & has compiled a letter from various folk.

24th April 1978 Monday

The new Provost of Leicester Cathedral will be the Revd. Alan C. Warren, aged 46. His installation has been fixed for 23rd June.
He is a keen sportsman, & has played cricket for the Leicestershire 2nd Eleven. He has also played in the Leicestershire Symphony Orchestra & conducted.

26th April 1978 Wednesday

Think Metric! This is what we are advised to do, but easier said than done. This week our load of coke was delivered for the first time in 50kg bags instead of 1cwt bags.
When I buy a jumper it says on the label, "To fit bust 38″ (inches) Tour de poitrine 97 cm."

28th April 1978 Friday

We still buy milk by the pint, & petrol by the gallon, & we still travel by the mile. (See 30th September 1975) Packets of seeds for the garden are to be sown so many centimetres apart, & this mystifies the gardeners. To change all the sign-posts & all the maps from miles into kilometres will take years & cost millions of pounds.

30th April 1978 Sunday

Mum & I have again booked a holiday in Yorkshire.
We have chosen Baldersby Park, Topcliffe, Thirsk, North Yorkshire. This is an elegant Georgian mansion set in 40 acres of parkland, by the River Swale. It has been converted into holiday flats & we have booked for June.

2nd May 1978 Tuesday

Our library in Gas Standards Branch is supplied & controlled by the Department of Energy's head library in Thames House South, London. This week Graham Hurford, from T.H.S. library, came to see us at Wigston;

& later on, Karen, C.O., Linda, C.A., & I hope to visit T.H.S. library in London.

4th May 1978 Thursday, Ascension Day

I am one of two E.O.s at Gas Standards. The other E.O. is Arthur, who has 5 girls working under him. I too have 5 girls working under me: - 1. Rose, C.O. married and a friend to all.
2. Karen, C.O. engaged & very bright. 3. Jan, divorced & difficult, C.O. 4. Ron (Irona) C.A. engaged & brazen. 5. Linda, C.A., new girl.

Note – Above the 2 E.O.s is a Higher Executive Officer, Reg Biggins. Over & above us all are the top scientists, plus the Department of Energy's head office in Thames House South, not far from the Houses of Parliament, in London.

6th May 1978 Saturday

Cup Final Day. Ipswich 1 – Arsenal 0. Well done little Ipswich! It was the first time they had reached the final, & they deserved their victory over the mighty Gunners. With an attendance of 100,000 the receipts were an all time record £500,000. The Cup was presented this year by Princess Alexandra.

8th May 1978 Monday

Had a most interesting conducted tour of the scientific laboratories at work. I learned of basic organic chemistry & was introduced to hydro-carbons – **methane** with its one carbon atom to four of hydrogen, **ethane** with two carbon atoms, **propane** with three, **butane** with four etc., & saw the gas being analysed.

10th May 1978 Wednesday

Hydro-carbons are made from carbon & hydrogen only. Methane = CH_4 Ethane = C_2H_6 Propane = C_3H_8 Butane = C_4H_{10} They are lighter than water & insoluble in it. Carbohydrates are something quite different. They are a compound of carbon, hydrogen & oxygen. (Water = H_2O)

12th May 1978 Friday

I have now completed 2 months in my new world of Gas Standards. I am being broken in gently & am more or less free to sort things out myself. Reg Biggins, the H.E.O. over Arthur & me, is retiring at the end of this month & up to now there is no one chosen to replace him.

14th May 1978 Whit Sunday

"At length had fully come, on mystic circle borne, of seven times seven revolving days, the Pentecostal morn; when as the Apostles knelt at the third hour in prayer; a sudden rushing sound proclaimed, that God Himself was there." – Hymn 152. This is the wonder of Whitsuntide, the Power & the Glory.

16th May 1978 Tuesday

Our registry in Gas Standards Branch, like our library, is controlled by the Department of Energy's head registry in Thames House South, London. We have about 7,000 files, including many which should have been extracted long ago. I have been endeavouring to sort & sift them this week.

18th May 1978 Thursday

Leicester Fiesta! "Oyez, oyez, oyez." Beneath the old High Cross in Cheapside, Leicester, a contest was held for a Town Crier. The winner was Mr Norman Roberts, who tomorrow, with the new Lord Mayor, Mr Albert Watson, will launch the Leicester Fiesta, a week of fun & jovial festivity.

20th May 1978 Saturday

Not since 1836 has Leicester had a Town Crier. The post was then disbanded, along with that of the city Mole Catcher. But from now until next Saturday, Leicester is in Fiesta mood, with dancing in the streets, bands, guitar groups, and Morris Men, all culminating in a grand public talent contest.

22nd May 1978 Monday

The most amazing aspect of the Trinity has been revealed to me in a sermon I heard at church on John 21. 11. "Simon Peter drew the net to land, full of great fishes, a hundred & fifty & three". i.e. $1 + 2 + 3 + 4 + 5 + 6 + 7 + 8 + 9 + 10 + 11 + 12 + 13 + 14 + 15 + 16 + 17$. Draw this on a graph & you have a perfect triangle.

24th May 1978 Wednesday

So then – how about this – $1 + 2 + 3 + 4 + 5 + 6 + 7 + 8 + 9 + 10 + 11 + 12 + 13 + 14 + 15 + 16 + 17 + 18 + 19 + 20 + 21 + 22 + 23 + 24 + 25 + 26 + 27 + 28 + 29 + 30 + 31 + 32 + 33 + 34 + 35 + 36$.
See Revelation Chapter 13. verse 18.
"Here is wisdom. Let him that hath understanding count the number of the beast, for it is the number of a man, & his number is 666."

26th May 1978 Friday

A day in London, & my first introduction to Thames House South. I met the 12 library staff & also Mr Bell, Mr Sewell & Mr Brown in Registry. High above the entrance to Thames House, linking Thames House South to Thames House North, I saw the City Coat of Arms, & its motto, "Domine Dirige Nos."

28th May 1978 Sunday

"Holy, Holy, Holy! Lord God Almighty" Tonight at church we sang this old familiar hymn which suddenly had more meaning than ever before. The impact of the Trinity. "So the all great were the all loving too" – "Merciful & Mighty", & of particular interest in my new job, "Perfect in power, in love & purity."

30th May 1978 Tuesday

A sizzling Bank Holiday with sunshine all day & everyday. We all got sun-tanned & I spent many hours in the garden, not only enjoying the garden seat, but clearing out all the tulips & wallflowers, digging afresh, & planting 300 new little plants – salvia, antirrhinum, pansies & petunias.

1st June 1978 Thursday

ERNIE, the Electronic Random Number Indicator Equipment, celebrates his 21st birthday today. In his 21 years he has given away £652 million. He has selected 15,600,000 prizes, ranging from £25 to £100,000. There are 21 million holders of premium bonds, which is 40% of the population.

3rd June 1978 Saturday

Mum & I arrived at Baldersby Park holiday centre & residential country house, Topcliffe, Thirsk, N. Yorks. We have a luxury flat on the ground floor, with lovely big rooms, in this elegant mansion built around 1710 A.D. You can imagine horse drawn carriages coming into the cobbled courtyard.

5th June 1978 Monday

Mum stayed in the luxury flat all day while I ventured alone to Harrogate and Knaresborough on a shopping spree.

Yesterday we watched all the veteran cars setting off from Ripon – just like the London to Brighton run, & also watched the new Lord Mayor's procession to the Cathedral.

Note – This is Mum's last holiday; soon she will be unable to walk at all.

7th June 1978 Wednesday

Had tea yesterday with Mr & Mrs Baxter, an elderly couple in Ripon, whom we first met last year when we stayed in the farm cottage. Today I motored to Northallerton & bought a pretty plum-coloured suit, while Mum enjoyed the luxury of the flat, and it poured with rain non-stop all day.

9th June 1978 Friday

Mum & I motored yesterday as far as Pickering, through beautiful Helmsley & through Kilburn where you see the White Horse on the hills. Today we finished our holiday with a trip to York & into the mighty Minster. The Minster had a wheelchair which we were able to borrow for Mum to see inside.

10th June 1978 Saturday

Bromell, *Christine (nee Naselli) and Roger are thrilled at the safe arrival of a delightful daughter, born June 10th. 7lb. 5oz. Many, many thanks to the staff of Ward 6. L.R.I.M.H.*

11th June 1978 Sunday

Ravenstone Sunday School Anniversary, and again most of the credit was due to Mrs Bird, who chose some lovely songs not only for the children but also for the congregation. We sang, "Immortal, Invisible, God only Wise", "Lord of all Hopefulness, Lord of all Joy", "Jerusalem" and "Glory, Glory, Alleluia".

13th June 1978 Tuesday

The Vicar of Snibston, the Revd. P. Ince, looks on little St. Mary's church as a "treasure". For many years it has been sadly neglected, and almost lost in a wilderness of long grass.

But now it looks better than it has looked for a long time, & next Saturday, the Bishop himself is coming.

15th June 1978 Thursday

You never saw such a hive of activity at little St. Mary's as it prepares for its open day & for a visit from the Bishop, Ronald Ralph Williams, who is retiring later this year. The little church has been painted & decorated inside and out, all the grass has been cut, & a spanking new notice board.

17th June 1978 Saturday

A Summer Fayre was held today on Snibston School playing field, for the benefit of St. Mary's church, Snibston. The fayre was opened by the Bishop of Leicester, who said he was pleased to see the little church so well cared for. The sun shone all afternoon & hundreds of people came.

19th June 1978 Monday

A letter from Department of Energy -

"Dear Miss Hewes, Pay documents received from Department of Transport, following your transfer to Department of Energy, indicated that you were still on the Entry Scale. We therefore asked why they had not transferred you to the Main Scale on 1st July 1977 on your completion of three years service as an Executive Officer. It appears to have been an oversight & Department of Transport will therefore be sending the arrears to us for onward transmission to you.

Yours Sincerely…………"

23rd June 1978 Friday

£4,579 per annum!

All of a sudden my salary has jumped by leaps & bounds to the top of the scale. This is the maximum of the Executive Officer main scale, following a new pay rise for the whole Civil Service with effect from 1st April this year. I do not expect to go any higher in rank than E.O.

25th June 1978 Sunday

"Peace I leave with you, my peace I give unto you". Tonight at church, I read my favourite chapter of the Bible, St. John, Chapter 14. This was the Second Lesson, including, "Let not your heart be troubled, neither let it be afraid." I once heard a sermon by the Revd. Aronsohn on "My peace I give unto you."

27th June 1978 Tuesday

"My peace I give unto you". This was one of the last things that Jesus said. Spoken on the night before He died on the Cross, it is in effect His last Will and Testament ….. "Not as the world giveth, give I unto you." He had no material gifts to leave behind. He had the greatest gift of all, "My Peace".

29th June 1978 Thursday

Had a most interesting conducted tour by Arthur, the other E.O. at work, of all the locked up parts of the building at Gas Standards. We went into the boiler room, the air-conditioning room, the room containing full gas canisters & empty gas canisters – saw the huge gas bags & went on the roof.

1st July 1978 Saturday

Civil Service pay settlement 1978 has brought the top of Clerical Officer scale to £3,280.

Executive Officer = £4,579. Higher Executive Officer = £5,718. Senior Executive Officer = £7,032. Then comes Principal, Senior Principal & Assistant Secretary.

3rd July 1978 Monday

Went to Leicester Cathedral yesterday to hear the new Provost, Alan Warren, preach his first sermon as Provost.

I was much impressed. He referred to Ezekial's Valley

of Dry Bones (Chapter 37) & likened us to this army which needed breath to live. He hoped to provide this breath.

5th July 1978 Wednesday

"Let the music breathe". This, said the new Provost, was something he once heard someone say. Meaning – allow pauses of silence for it to sink in. And this is what he aimed for in Leicester Cathedral. So we had some beautiful moments of absolute silence. Never was **silence** any more eloquent.

7th July 1978 Friday

"I can do all things through Christ which strengtheneth me" (Philippians 4. 13.)

The new Provost mentioned these words in his first sermon with us, as well as, "By this shall all men know that ye are my disciples, if ye have love one to another." (John 13. 35.) – not by your beautiful church alone.

9th July 1978 Sunday
A city with no traffic!

For one week now, Leicester has been a city centre for pedestrians only. Apart from the city buses, no traffic is allowed past the clock tower. The roar of Leicester's traffic has stopped to allow shoppers freedom to cross the road.

11th July 1978 Tuesday

Christine, whose place I have taken at work, brought her beautiful baby, Julie, into the office today. As, on 17th April 1967, I sat & held Reevsie's sleeping baby for about 10 minutes, so I held this special baby who has directed the course of my life into the world of Gas Standards.

13th July 1978 Thursday

I have now completed 4 months in my new world of Gas Standards. We now have our new H.E.O. Roy Ellison, a former E.O. in Atomic Energy Division, newly promoted. The great jigsaw of this new work is gradually taking shape. Each day a new piece goes into place.

15th July 1978 Saturday

47 yesterday. To mark the occasion I opened an account with the Leicester Building Society. Starting with £500, I would like to build it up at the rate of £1,000 per year. That means £100 every month & 2 bonanzas a year.

17th July 1978 Monday

My first Staff Report for G.S.B. I have reported on "Ronnie", my brazen C.A. "Her strength lies in her good nature. Her weakness lies in her limited talents, but she is never daunted. Her cheerfulness ensures harmony in the section."

19th July 1978 Wednesday

The boss at Gas Standards Branch is Mr Boreham – the Controller. He rules quietly but effectively, & has been very kind to me. He knows his staff individually, from the greatest to the least, & has shared with me the job of Ronnie's Staff Report, as our new H.E.O. hardly knows her.

21st July 1978 Friday

The planet Mars, which we saw in close-up for the very first time 2 years ago, was described in detail by Professor Sagan in his lectures earlier this year. Half the size of Earth, it has colossal dust storms, & the red dust makes the sky look Sky Blue Pink.

23rd July 1978 Sunday

Although the planet Mars is only half the size of Earth, it has a 24 hour day. The Earth has earth-quakes & Mars has mars-quakes. Venus is the nearest thing we know to Hell, being so near to the Sun, but the Rings of Saturn are masses of snowballs.

25th July 1978 Tuesday

Pieces of Eight are old Spanish coins worth eight reals = 2 pesetas = one eighth of a dollar.

In 1743, the Hollandia, a Dutch ship, sank off the Scilly Isles. She was carrying a cargo of recently minted coins, destined for the East Indies. This cargo has now been recovered, & coins are for sale.

27th July 1978 Thursday

Paid £78 for a piece of treasure which was lost and is found again. My lost treasure is a piece of eight bearing the Imperial Crown of Spain & the two Pillars of Hercules. It bears the inscription, "Philip V of Spain & the Indies by the Grace of God 1741".

29th July 1978 Saturday

Philip V of Spain reigned from the year 1700 – 1746. By the Treaty of Utrecht, imposed on the Spaniards by his grandfather, Louis XIV in the summer of 1713, Philip was recognised as King of Spain and the Indies, hence my piece of eight:- Philip V. D.G. Hispan et Ind Rex.

31st July 1978 Monday

Mary Moore is spending the week with Mum & me in Ravenstone. She arrived in Coalville on a long distance bus – from Clacton-on-Sea to Liverpool. She has my lovely big comfortable bed, and I am sleeping next door in Aunt Dos's bungalow.

2nd August 1978 Wednesday

One of my jobs at work is taking the minutes at various meetings. Once a year there is the Area Gas Examiners' Annual General Meeting, & there are meetings with Gas Engineers & such like. So far, I have attended only one small meeting, but this made best use of my shorthand, which I know slightly.

4th August 1978 Friday

In 1965 I did a correspondence course in shorthand, & now I am busy brushing up ready for my meetings. As I enjoy writing & reading, shorthand is naturally a subject I can also enjoy. You may therefore get a lesson or two.

6th August 1978 Sunday

Today is the 11th Sunday after Trinity, & the collect for today begins, "O God, who declarest thy almighty power most chiefly in showing mercy and pity." (See 26th August 1974)

And Psalm 62 says, "God spake once, & twice I have also heard the same that power belongeth unto God; & that thou Lord art merciful."

8th August 1978 Tuesday

Pope Paul VI died at 8-40 p.m. on Sunday, the eleventh Sunday after Trinity. He was aged 80, and had been Pope since June 1963. He was formerly Cardinal Giovanni Montini, Archbishop of Milan. He too, declared his almighty power most chiefly in showing mercy & pity to the 700 million Catholics he led.

10th August 1978 Thursday

Not only did Pope Paul VI die on the Eleventh Sunday after Trinity, which has that great collect, but perhaps more significantly it was also the day when the Church remembers "The Transfiguration". "With shining face and bright array, Christ deigns to manifest this day, what glory shall to faith be given."

12th August 1978 Saturday

"What glory shall to faith be given, when we enjoy our God in heaven."

These words are from Hymn No.760 in our hymn book.

Today we watched on television the open air funeral mass in St. Peter's Square, Rome, of Pope Paul VI. Never before had I seen all the Cardinals gathered together.

14th August 1978 Monday

Our Sunday School outing this year has been cancelled through lack of support. We had arranged the outing for next Saturday, but managed to get barely half a bus load. We were going to Derbyshire, visiting Chatsworth House and the Peak Cavern at Castleton, which has electric light.

16th August 1978 Wednesday

Presley, Elvis Aaron. Passed away August 16th 1977.

"Ours is but a simple prayer, give him Lord your tender care. We love him now still as ever, and we shall forget him never. A year has gone since he passed away, but to us it's only yesterday. In our hearts he'll always be, King throughout all history."

18th August 1978 Friday

Elvis Presley fans have filled the "In Memoriam" columns of the Leicester Mercury on the first anniversary of his death. The one reproduced here was signed, "Members of the Society of Elvis Friends." Others were signed, "House of Elvis", "Loughborough Rock 'n' Roll Society", "Devoted Fans", "Ever Loving Fans", "Faithful Fans" etc.

20th August 1978 Sunday

The Power of God was proclaimed to us this evening at church first by Isaiah in the first lesson (2 Kings 19) and secondly by St. Paul in the second lesson (1 Corinthians 1.) The same message spanned the centuries & reached us here in the 20th Century – not only the Power but also the Wisdom of God.

22nd August 1978 Tuesday

Mum's birthday tomorrow. She will be 73. She looks well, eats well & sleeps well. Just seeing her sitting in a chair, you would not know there was anything wrong with her. But as soon as she tries to stand up, it takes her a long time to get on her feet, & then she walks with great difficulty, & only a few steps.

24th August 1978 Thursday

"Be present, O merciful God, & protect us through the silent hours of this night, so that we who are wearied by the changes & chances of this fleeting world may repose upon thy eternal changelessness; through Jesus Christ our Lord." This is the prayer we have regularly at church – the "eternal changelessness" of God.

26th August 1978 Saturday

In 1969 Leicester City Football team was knocked out of Division I into Division II. But after "two hard years of slogging" we were back in the First Division.

We now start a new season back in the Second Division. We have a new manager, Jock Wallace, who hopes to get us "upstairs".

28th August 1978 Bank Holiday Monday

Pope John Paul I, the 263rd Pope, was chosen at the weekend after one of the shortest conclaves ever. Contrary to all expectation he was elected on the very first day of voting in the Vatican's Sistine Chapel – where I stood on that most memorable day 9th April 1975 when I went to Rome.

30th August 1978 Wednesday

The new Pope was born just north of Venice on 17th October 1912, & before becoming Pope he was Cardinal Albino Luciani, Patriarch of Venice. He said recently, "I am a little man accustomed to little things and to silence." Like many other great men he was much influenced by his devout mother.

1st September 1978 Friday

Sunspots are probably caused by the combined gravitational pull of the planets. When the planets are in a straight line & all pulling in the same direction, the Sun will experience unusually high tides resulting in intensive magnetic storms & many sunspots. A complete alignment of all the planets is very rare.

3rd September 1978 Sunday

A complete alignment in the same direction of all the planets (less Pluto) happens only once in 179 years! But such an alignment is almost on us. The outer planets are already taking up their positions and in 1982 they will all be in the same straight line. This may cause the most violent earthquakes on record.

5th September 1978 Tuesday

Now that I work with men of science, I can tell you that "**fusion**" creates the Sun.

Fusion power is the power from fusing light atoms. Man has not yet been able to create fusion power, but we are hoping to do so by the turn of the century. All we have to do first is create a temperature of 100 million degrees centigrade.

7th September 1978 Thursday

100 million degrees centigrade will fuse together the simple atoms deuterium and tritium. Up to now we can only achieve 60 million degrees centigrade. But, if we can create fusion power, we shall have no problems concerning waste materials, because the fuel would consume itself – unlike our problems with **fission power**.

9th September 1978 Saturday
Fission power is power from splitting heavy atoms. This is something we can do, but we have terrible problems with radio-active waste materials. Our nuclear power plants split the atoms of uranium and plutonium, but both have limited resources. Fusion power is boundless as the sea.

11th September 1978 Monday
Fusion power is boundless as the sea because fusion power is the fusing together of deuterium and tritium. These occur naturally in sea water. The nuclei of hydrogen isotopes fuse into a heavier helium atom & in the process **energy** is liberated.
But beware of a big bang.

13th September 1978 Wednesday
I have now completed 6 months at G.S.B. in spring time & summer time.
More often than not the amount of work we have in a day can easily be done in half a day, so we are by no means overworked. We have a pleasant airy office on the ground floor & look out to a sports field with trees & squirrels.

15th September 1978 Friday
Just as the man of my dreams, Brian Lamming, would stand right in front of me & all but break my heart – so now, the house of my dreams stands right in front of me at Wigston, within reach but not within grasp. Newly up for sale this week – offers around £23,000.

17th September 1978 Sunday
"As it is written, eye hath not seen nor ear heard, neither have entered into the heart of man, the things which God hath prepared for them that love him" – I Corinthians, chap 2 verse 9.
In one of his most moving sermons, the Rector of Ravenstone, the Revd. Buckroyd, brought these words to life.

19th September 1978 Tuesday
"Ah, but a man's reach should exceed his grasp, or what's heaven for?" Robert Browning.
Liking nothing but the best, I look at our poor old house with its damp patches here & there, cracked with subsidence through being on top of a coal mine, & sadly in need of decoration. Value about £7,000.

21st September 1978 Thursday
So, the next item on the agenda is house decoration. Practically the whole house needs decorating, so we are making a start with the front room and the hall.
We have chosen Barker and Weston of Ashby to do the work. They came with their new metric measure & estimated £200.

23rd September 1978 Saturday
The Severn Trent Water Authority, which came into being on 1st April 1974, is divided into 8, including the Soar division which covers most of Leicestershire. Most of the water for our division comes from the reservoir at Staunton Harold. The water is pumped from the River Dove, & this month they have had an open day.

25th September 1978 Monday
"**Open Day**" at Staunton Harold reservoir was most interesting. We saw the different processes the water goes through from river water to drinking water. We were able to look through microscopes at weird hairy monsters (magnified a hundred times) & ended up appreciating all that the Water Authority does.

27th September 1978 Wednesday
"Ghost Down a Coal Mine"
Earlier this year a young miner working at Cinder-Hill colliery at Sutton-in-Ashfield, Nottinghamshire was terrified by a ghost miner. He was working alone 3 miles from the mine-shaft, when the ghost miner joined him & then disappeared. The young miner ran for his life.

29th September 1978 Friday
Pope John Paul 1st, elected last month, is **dead**. What a shock for the world!
He seemed perfectly all right yesterday – he went to bed and died of a heart attack at 11 p.m. Early this morning he was found by his private secretary Cardinal Confalonieri. He was found with his light on, as if reading.

1st October 1978 Sunday
Pope John Paul, Pope for one month, had a lovely friendly smile. At his inaugural mass he said he had agreed to accept his election with surprised & understandable trepidation, but also with immense trust in God – in the powerful grace of God. His smile radiated joy and serenity.

3rd October 1978 Tuesday
Had a few days holiday this week & cleared the garden of all the summer flowers. Now that the garden is mostly lawn, with only borders for flowers, the biggest digging area is a piece 12 feet by 8 feet. I decided to make a half moon rockery in this to break it down further.

5th October 1978 Thursday
Had a gorgeous day shopping in Leicester. Bought another pair of winter boots – brown leather, flat heeled, sheepskin lined £33. These are intended for walking & driving in snow, ice & slush. The high fashion boots I bought last winter look super but are not very practical.

7th October 1978 Saturday
Apart from the winter boots I bought this week, I also bought two very pretty nightdresses for Mum, some books for Sunday School prizes, an up-to-date World Atlas showing the latest names in the Continent of Africa & the new counties of the British Isles.
I gave Enid a photograph album for her birthday.

9th October 1978 Monday
Harvest Festival yesterday at Ravenstone Church meant that I had completed 20 years there as Sunday School teacher. At the moment there is quite a good Sunday School, thanks very much to the dedication of Mrs June Bird, who does a lot of backstage preparation & is a great help.

11th October 1978 Wednesday
Cathedral News-Letter No.157. After a break of 6

months, a news-letter from the new Provost saying "Many people have urged me to continue the tradition of sending a Cathedral News-Letter, & indeed, I am delighted to do so." He mentions his wife Sylvia & daughters Sue, Katie & Helen.

13th October 1978 Friday
In the Cathedral News-Letter the Provost "warmly commends to all Cathedral members and friends the Lord Mayor's Appeal Fund for a head & body scanner to be installed at the Leicester Royal Infirmary." The Lord Mayor will need £500,000 – one of the largest appeals made in Leicester.

15th October 1978 Sunday
My second Staff Report for G.S.B. I have now reported on Linda, C.A., who joined the Branch in April this year. "She is a most attractive 17 year-old with a pleasing personality to match her good looks. Because of her beautiful eyes she is eloquent in silence" - (the eyes have it).

17th October 1978 Tuesday
Pope John Paul II, the 264th Pope, was chosen yesterday. He is Cardinal Karol Wojtyla, aged 58, Archbishop of Krakow, Poland, & the first non-Italian Pope for more than 400 years. He described himself as "this man called from a distant country".

19th October 1978 Thursday
For three consecutive weeks we are having an hour's talk for all the staff at G.S.B. from our top men of science on the various aspects of their work. These are very interesting & show how we inter-relate with Europe & how we share our oilfields with Norway.

21st October 1978 Saturday
"The Cycles of Heaven" by Playfair & Scott is my latest book of revelation. Newly published this year, it describes how man relates to the great electro-magnetic forces of the whole universe, and in particular to our own solar system, where the planets are attuned like music into harmonic movements.

23rd October 1978 Monday
These are the notes of music of the planets: - For every 11 notes for Earth there are 18 for Venus, 46 for Mercury and 6 for Mars. (i.e. how many orbits round the Sun over an 11 year period) Once in every 11 years these planets are lined up to play a **chord**.

25th October 1978 Wednesday
Meanwhile, every 179 years, Saturn completes 6 orbits & Jupiter completes 15 orbits to form a fuller chord with the other planets. At the same time there are all sorts of planetary conjunctions, to form a continual harmony of geometric symmetry & perpetual motion.

27th October 1978 Friday
The Area Gas Examiners Annual General Meeting. There I was, the only woman with about 20 men of science, listening to their accounts of gas examining & all the associated work carried out by our staff at G.S.B. I was there to take the minutes with the help of a tape recorder.

29th October 1978 Sunday
Spent many hours this weekend on the minutes of the Area Gas Examiners' meeting. They discussed their problems of testing the pressure of gas in difficult places – kiosks that let the rain in – vandals who smash up the kiosks & all sorts of conflicting instructions which add to the confusion.

Note – The minutes are a marathon job. Everything I write is scrutinised in detail, amended, adjusted time & time again, first by one, then by another of the 20 men who were at the meeting, until the final product, typed & re-typed countless times by the typists, bears only the slightest resemblance to what was actually said.

31st October 1978 Tuesday
Ronald Ralph Williams, Bishop of Leicester for the past 25 years, will retire at the end of this year. The new Bishop was named today – the Revd. Richard Rutt aged 53.
His wife Joan said, "We are pleased that Leicester has a large Asian population. Asia is one of our dear loves."

2nd November 1978 Thursday
Gas Standards Branch deals with the metering & computing systems for gas passing through North Sea treatment & compression platforms. Each of the two Frigg Field platforms carries a gas metering system capable of measuring the treated gas to a maximum flow of 1000 million cubic feet a day.

4th November 1978 Saturday
Like Her Majesty the Queen, I now have a pair of specs for reading. Mine cost £50 & have the minimum of frames – just a thin band of gold across the top.
I went to Curry and Paxton Ltd., of Coalville – "The Visionaries" who have shops all over the country, & have been going since 1876.

6th November 1978 Monday
House for Sale: – Priced to sell at £9,950 is this eye-catching, end of four, modern, gas centrally heated house, situated at 156, Aylestone Lane, Wigston. A truly pleasing property, spacious & not cramped, yet easily managed. Splendid décor & appointments. Small private garden & garage.

8th November 1978 Wednesday
My good friend Alf went with me to see the house for sale at £9,950. Not only was this house within reach, but within grasp. It was the best you would ever find at the price, & I was delighted with it. Alf advised me to get our house in Ravenstone valued, & put it up for sale.

10th November 1978 Friday
House for Sale in the popular residential village of Ravenstone, price £8,500.
Two reception rooms, kitchen, solid fuel central heating, two bedrooms, bathroom, nicely laid out rear garden.
(I like that bit – all my own work & many years toil, sweat and tears). Rates - £70.

Note – Mum & I put our house up for sale & seriously consider moving nearer to where I work. The office is 18 miles from home & the journey in winter is likely to be difficult. However, we do not have enough money to buy the sort of house we would really like, & eventually abandon the idea.

12th November 1978 Sunday

Now here I am, ready & willing, but not yet able to buy the house I have chosen. The agents selling the house want £9,950 - **now**.

Meanwhile our agent Geoffrey Snushall sends Mum & me a letter, spelling out a whole list of commitments which we have now let ourselves in for.

14th November 1978 Tuesday

Geoffrey Snushall writes, "I would confirm that my firm's charges in this matter will be 1¾% of the selling price, **plus** value added tax, **plus** advertising. The charges will be payable when a prospective purchaser has been found who is ready able & willing to sign a contract."

16th November 1978 Thursday

"**Ready – Able – and Willing.**" The house I was ready & willing to buy is now **sold**. No use being ready & willing if you are not able. We have had one or two tentative enquiries about our poor old house at Ravenstone, but nobody yet is ready able & willing to sign a contract.

18th November 1978 Saturday

My latest book of absorbing interest is called simply, "The Book of the Hand" by Fred Gettings. Just as everyone has an individual face, so everyone has individual hands, & what a lot is revealed, not only in the lines of the hand, but in fingerprints & the length & shape of the fingers.

Note –It is amazing what is written in a hand, if only you knew how to read it. I make a full imprint of my hands to preserve in my diary.

20th November 1978 Monday

So, what can you see in my hands? In the left hand you see the Head & Heart lines are two. In the right hand you see they are one. When these two are one there is inner conflict & you are either a criminal or you are religious or you are creative – a devil or a saint.

22nd November 1978 Wednesday

What else do you see in my hands? Can you see a triangle formed by the line of Fate which goes straight up the middle of the hand to join the Head line & is swept into a triangle by the Life line? So here again, as in the whole Universe, is geometry.

24th November 1978 Friday

Reading a hand is like reading a book. Every line is written by your own inner self – your own nervous energy directed by the undercurrents of temperament & behaviour.

So your innermost self is there for all to see & read all the time, but few there be who learn how to read.

26th November 1978 Advent Sunday

Again the Queen has opened Parliament. This time she wore prettier specs than last year, but it seems to me that any specs look stupid with the Imperial State Crown.

She said, "My government's economic policies will continue to be directed to overcome the evils of inflation & unemployment."

28th November 1978 Tuesday

The Queen mentioned **gas** in her speech. She said, "Bills will be introduced to improve safety & discipline at sea, to help control marine pollution & to amend other aspects of Merchant Shipping legislation & also to strengthen the enforcement powers for the safety of offshore oil & gas installations."

30th November 1978 Thursday

Motor Taxation will be Scrapped. (See 5th September 1976) After years of rumour & speculation it has finally been agreed to scrap Motor Tax. It will be replaced by a petrol surcharge, & will be done gradually over the next five years. 1 in 10 at present dodges Car Tax - £70 million per year loss.

2nd December 1978 Saturday

We have now had 6 lots of assorted house hunters to inspect out poor old house at Ravenstone. The one showing any sort of genuine interest at the moment is Dr. Graham, a local doctor, who is considering it for his daughter. She has a dog, & is attracted to the "nicely laid out garden".

4th December 1978 Monday

Yesterday was our Sunday School Prize Giving at Ravenstone Church.

Since Mrs Barras left I have more children now in my class – Susan Roe, Debra Hickin, Yvonne Tivey, Jenny Gould, Joanne Freestone, Caroline Ottewell, Tim and Nick Williamson, James & John, Simon & Andrew.

6th December 1978 Wednesday

Venus is in the news this week.

Two spacecraft from the United States & two from Russia have been sent to study the atmosphere & weather on a global scale. The first of these spacecraft, American Pioneer Venus I, which set off last May from Earth, arrived safely this week – 24 million miles.

8th December 1978 Friday

Venus is hell.

For clouds, Venus has transparent clouds of sulphuric acid, & it is as hot as an oven at ground level - 470°C. It is too hot for oceans – even too hot for steam – so it can only rain sulphuric acid in a gaseous form. So if you are thinking of going to Venus, be sure to take an acid proof space suit.

10th December 1978 Sunday

On Venus, the axis of rotation is perpendicular to its orbital plane. This means that there are no seasons – spring, summer, autumn, winter.

And Venus rotates the opposite way to the Earth. It takes 243 Earth days to rotate one day, but 225 days to orbit the Sun. One day is longer than a year.

12th December 1978 Tuesday

House Sold! (Subject to contract). Just as we were beginning to despair of selling the house, along came a

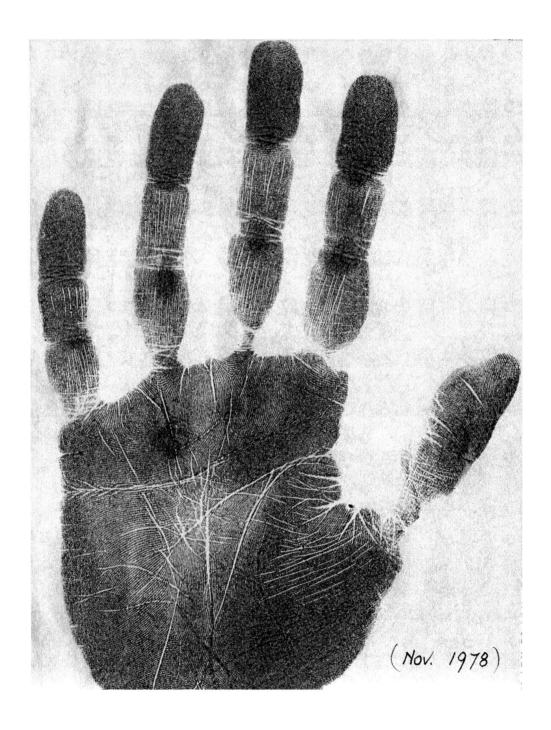

(Nov. 1978)

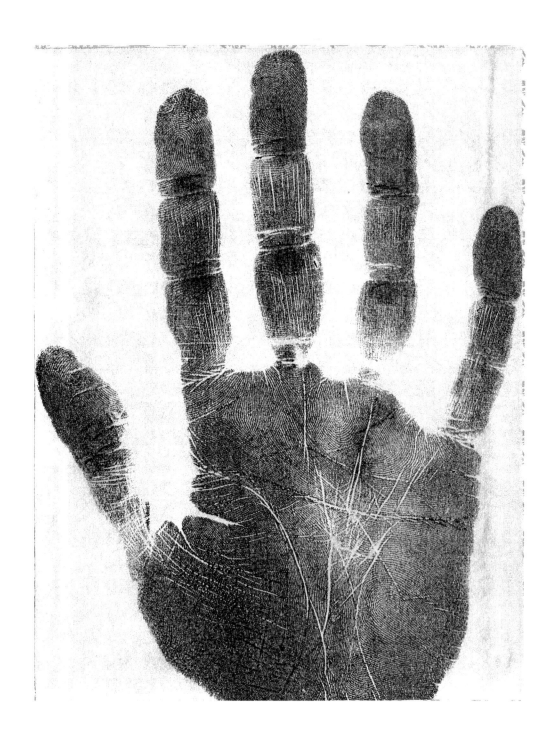

dynamic young fellow named Tom Barson with his fiancée of 2 weeks – Jenny – both raring to get married & both impressed with the potential of our house. He offered £8,250 and we accepted.

14th December 1978 Thursday

Tom Barson & Jenny with stars in their eyes chose our house as their love nest. He is an engineer & also an expert guitar player. As soon as he saw my guitar he just had to play it. He is a man who can make instant decisions & while Dr. Graham dithered on the brink, he snaffled up our house.

16th December 1978 Saturday

Lord Snowdon, who married Princess Margaret (the Queen's only sister) on 6th May 1960, was married yesterday to divorcee Mrs Lucy Lindsay-Hogg. The children of Lord Snowdon's 18 year marriage to Princess Margaret are Viscount Linley, 17, & Lady Sarah Armstrong Jones, 14. The marriage ended in divorce.

18th December 1978 Monday

Country Cottage – just superbly modernised & gas central heating installed. Attractive lounge with bay, splendid dining room & well fitted kitchen. Two good sized bedrooms – super bathroom, new avocado suite, lovely large garden.

38, Leicester Road, Fleckney. Rare find at £11,000.

20th December 1978 Wednesday

Mum & I went to Fleckney, complete with the key of the door, to see the "rare find".

We both loved the house which was completely empty but freshly painted & decorated throughout. From the front windows we looked across beautiful undulating open fields where sheep were grazing peacefully.

22nd December 1978 Friday

Ready – able & willing. For the second time we choose a house and again we are told we cannot buy. Tom Barson & Jenny, who have offered to buy our house at Ravenstone, are planning to get married on March 3rd 1979 & we are very limited financially where we can go. We are hoping **third time lucky**.

24th December 1978 Sunday

As we expect this to be our last Christmas in this house at Ravenstone, I am hoping to continue with the Sunday School here until the end of July when we have a month's break & then the children change classes. I would like to present to the Sunday School, when I leave, a Nativity set costing £100.

26th December 1978 Tuesday

"Of His Kingdom there shall be no end"

Ronald Ralph – Bishop of Leicester for the past 25 years, chose this as his text for his last sermon before he retires. In this fleeting world where nothing endures for long, he spoke of the promise made before Christ was born in Isaiah 9 & Luke 1.

28th December 1978 Thursday

"For unto us a child is born, unto us a son is given: and the government shall be upon his shoulder: and his name shall be called Wonderful, Counsellor, the mighty God, the everlasting Father, the Prince of Peace. Of the increase of his government & peace **there shall be no end** …….. from henceforth even for ever." Isaiah 9.

30th December 1978 Saturday

"So – let it be written: so – let it be done."

This was the command of ancient Egypt. In Israel the Ten Commandments survived because they were **written**. That which is written remains. And to Mohammed it was revealed, "Thy Lord is the most bountiful, who teaches by the pen, teaches man what he did not know."

* * *

1979

2nd January 1979 Tuesday
"Thy word is a lamp unto my feet, and a light unto my path" – Psalm 119, verse 105.
The Rector of Ravenstone, the Revd. Leslie Buckroyd, used these words to launch us into a new year. He also referred to Psalm 18, verse 28 – "For thou wilt light my candle: the Lord my God will enlighten my darkness."

4th January 1979 Thursday
Selling a house is fraught with pitfalls and hidden dangers. The secret of success is being **ready – willing & able** both to buy & to sell at one & the same time.
Our prospective buyer has now backed out of the deal, so Mum & I have now taken the house off the market for the time being.

6th January 1979 Saturday
Britain is now on the threshold of a new technological revolution, which could be the most rapid industrial change in history. We are giving £3,000 million to the National Enterprise Board to support the development of the **micro-chip** industry – that means **micro-electronics** to bring wide-spread automation.

8th January 1979 Monday
Geo-thermal power is the subterranean heat of the Earth itself. Sometimes, where there is a geological freak, hot water will spring from the ground of its own accord, as in Iceland, Italy, Japan & Russia. The city of Rotorua, New Zealand, has underwater hot springs which provide heat for the city.

10th January 1979 Wednesday
So when the oil wells run dry, there is all the energy in the world as well as in the sun to draw on. Most of the Earth's 260 billion cubic miles of rock, beneath the top layer, is at melting point. And the melting point of rock is a lot higher than the melting point of water – $2,200°F$ or $1,200°C$.

12th January 1979 Friday
The season of goodwill has now ended, and it is time for the January strikes.
Men demanding more & more money are all on strike & grinding the country once more to a halt. Tanker drivers are not delivering petrol; other drivers are not delivering food, & pigs & poultry are dying.

14th January 1979 Sunday
Tonight at church we had once more our Rector's favourite Psalm – Psalm 27. How lovely in the gloom of winter, battling against the elements & with fog all around, to hear again, "The Lord is my **light** & my salvation; whom then shall I fear? – Put thou thy trust in the Lord."

16th January 1979 Tuesday
The National Debt is now £79,180 million. Compare this with 4th August 1966 when it was £31,327 million. It would then have cost £577 each to wipe out the debt. Now it would cost £1,417 each. As far as I can understand the situation, we owe this money to our own country, so it is all very strange.

Note – The National Debt came into being in 1694 when William III had to raise £1.2 million to finance war with France. The financiers who raised the money were given a charter to form a bank. It became the Bank of England. (See 17th January 1989)
The Bank of England, also popularly known as the Old Lady of Threadneedle Street, was set up in 1694 and is one of the world's oldest central banks. It started life as a commercial bank but was nationalised in 1946.

18th January 1979 Thursday
"At Inverness the castle stands, where I shall be a king, and read the Leicester Mercury – or from the great west wing I'll watch the splendid sunsets & have daylight till eleven; and maybe then my merry men will see the power of heaven."
Wrote this for a competition organised by the Mercury.

20th January 1979 Saturday
The competition organised by the Leicester Mercury showed pictures of eight different castles which you had to name – you were given some help – for each castle you had 3 names to choose from; & then you had to say which castle you would choose to live in & why.

22nd January 1979 Monday
"**Hello Dolly**" is the show chosen this year for Coalville Amateur's production in March.
I am pleased to say that I have again been asked to be prompter, & went along to rehearsal this evening to order £20 worth of tickets.
Coalville Amateurs and I have been together now for **thirty years**.

24th January 1979 Wednesday
Apart from all the people on strike – lorry drivers – train drivers – hospital laundry workers & other low paid public employees, the weather also is doing its best to grind everybody to a halt. We have to battle against snow, ice and freezing fog, & God's mighty army of little snow flakes.

26th January 1979 Friday
"In the winter we will build a snowman". Having struggled to & from work from Monday to Thursday in treacherous conditions, I chose to have a day's holiday today & enjoy the snow. The world is a veritable wonderland with hoar frost on all the trees, & I made a very impressive snowman.

28th January 1979 Sunday
"God is working His purpose out as year succeeds to year …….. What can we do to hasten the time, the time that shall surely be; when the earth shall be filled with the glory of God as the waters cover the sea?" This is part of the stirring hymn No. 735 to inspire us in these strike-bound days.

30th January 1979 Tuesday
How nice to know that God's almighty power is so different from the seemingly almighty power of the Unions who at the moment are disrupting so many public services – hospitals are turning the sick away –

the dead are not being buried, & there is general chaos, & many firms are going out of business.

1st February 1979 Thursday

After the snow, the rain. After the rain the floods & February Fill Dyke was off to a good start with so many roads in the county impassable that driving conditions were almost impossible. All the traffic seemed to converge on one road, & it took me two hours to get to work.

3rd February 1979 Saturday

Bought a Grundig Elite Boy 700 from Coalville - £35. This is a very nice slim-line wireless to replace our old Grundig wireless which is of no further use. All the wavelengths have changed recently (23rd November 1978). Now for the first time we can listen to Radio Leicester on the U/FM band. (V.H.F.)

5th February 1979 Monday

It has now been decided by American scientists that the magnetic field of the Earth, which makes compasses point north, is caused by heat from the gravitational collapse of heavy matter deep inside the Earth's core. Millions of years ago huge quantities of iron & nickel poured into Earth's core.

7th February 1979 Wednesday

When the iron & nickel cooled down from its great heat inside the Earth, it created electrical energy, & this slowly seeped out to become a magnetic field. The infall of heavy matter would be accelerated by the Earth's rotation. Venus therefore, rotating so slowly, has no magnetic field.

9th February 1979 Friday

"At Inverness the castle stands ..." My castle remains a castle in the air, as the winner of the Leicester Mercury's recent competition is announced today – Mr John Pither, 4a Elmdale Road, Earl Shilton. He & his wife Josie and children are keen caravan tourers, & have visited lots of castles.

11th February 1979 Sunday

Septuagesima Sunday – and the Gospel for today tells this strike ridden country of ours the Parable of the labourers in the vineyard – Matthew, Chapter 20. This is how God deals with his men, rewarding them in accordance with their opportunities rather than achievements.

13th February 1979 Tuesday

Ronald Ralph Williams – Bishop of Leicester for the past 25 years, who retired at the end of last year, died suddenly today.

Both he and his wife Cecily always loved the snow, & his body will be brought across snowbound Britain from London to Leicester Cathedral next Monday.

14th February 1979 Wednesday

On this day in 1779 Captain James Cook, British explorer, was murdered by natives in Hawaii.

15th February 1979 Thursday

Man versus Snowflake – today the little snowflakes joined forces & showed man who was the greatest. Arctic winds whipped the snow into huge drifts which overhung in curves.

I battled home from work and was thankful to arrive safe & sound. Many were stranded completely, all night.

17th February 1979 Saturday

While we shiver in the Arctic weather, the Queen is presently enjoying the sunshine of the Middle East. This week she flew to Kuwait for a 3 week tour of the Gulf States. Not only is she the first reigning British monarch to set foot on Arab soil, she is the first woman to be accorded equal rights.

19th February 1979 Monday

Today in Leicester Cathedral was the funeral service of the Bishop of Leicester.

The Bishop had chosen much of the music himself, including his favourite Psalm, Psalm 121. "I will lift up mine eyes unto the hills from whence cometh my help." The anthem was Nunc Dimittis, "Lord now lettest Thou Thy servant depart in peace."

21st February 1979 Wednesday

The Bishop chose the two hymns which were sung at his funeral – No. 517 "When all Thy mercies O my God, my rising soul surveys, Transported with the view, I'm lost in wonder love & praise." No. 235 "Oh what the joy & the glory must be, those endless Sabbaths the blessed ones see ......which to the Angels & us shall belong."

23rd February 1979 Friday

The Civil Servants are on strike today. I am pleased to say that no-one at Gas Standards Branch answered the call to strike. The main targets for picketing have been the Cabinet Office, Ministry of Defence, Department of Trade, the Home Office, D.V.L.C. Swansea, Customs Officers at ports & airports and D.H.S.S.

25th February 1979 Sunday

The Queen's visit to the land of rich Arab oil sheiks has been likened to the Queen of Sheba's visit to the court of King Solomon. (See I Kings, Chapter 10.)

She has been to the Garden of Eden, enjoyed fabulous Arabian nights, & the oil sheiks, like Solomon, have given her of their bounty.

27th February 1979 Tuesday

"Stars & Planets" – my latest book from the library has taught me how to recognise not only the Plough (alias the Great Bear or the Big Dipper or the Ursa Major), but from that to locate Leo the lion & watch his nightly prowl across the heavens, & even tell time by the stars.

1st March 1979 Thursday

Dr. Richard Rutt, aged 54, formerly Bishop of Taejon, Korea, and latterly Bishop of St. German's Cornwall, was confirmed this week in his appointment to the see of Leicester. The ceremony took place in St. Margaret's, Westminster. In law he is now our Bishop, & can sign Richard Leicester.

3rd March 1979 Saturday

The new Bishop of Leicester will do homage to the Queen next Wednesday when he is presented to her at

Buckingham Palace.
He plans to move into the Bishop's Lodge, Springfield Road, Leicester, in early April, but he will come to the city on March 24th to be installed in the Cathedral.

5th March 1979 Monday
"Hello Dolly" – After the gloomy winter of snowstorms, icy roads, and people forever on strike, what a joy it is to have a week's holiday where the birds sing all day long & the evenings are packed with music & drama. How I love being prompter, & how I am stirred every time the orchestra starts up.

7th March 1979 Wednesday
Having a gorgeous week's holiday & have managed to do quite a bit of spring cleaning. Washed the curtains in my bedroom & Mum's bedroom, & moved Mum's bed downstairs. Mum's knees gave way & we had to dial 999 for 2 ambulance men to lift her up again, so we decided to have her bed downstairs again.

9th March 1979 Friday
A good write-up in the Leicester Mercury for "Hello Dolly" ….. "Ursula Hall, in gorgeous gowns & wide brimmed hats, handles the part of Dolly with consummate ease …. Hughie Adcock, one of the funniest men in county amateur operatics, is irrepressible as Ambrose Kemper. (And no-one needs prompting).

11th March 1979 Sunday
Poor old Mum has had such a trying day today. She just could not stand on her legs at all. The Doctor came to see her & summoned help from two nurses to attend to her. She is in continual pain & I feel so helpless & hopeless. It is more than I can do to hoist her up; & toilet presents quite a problem.

13th March 1979 Tuesday
Oh, how it grieves me to see my poor old Mum so helpless. I feel like Peter, who, beginning to sink, cried, saying, "Lord, save me." St. Matthew, Chapter 14.
"And immediately Jesus stretched forth his hand & caught him & said, "O thou of little faith, wherefore didst thou doubt?"

14th March 1979 Wednesday
"Through the night of doubt & sorrow …" Mum & I saw the sleepless hours pass slowly by, while we wept with despair. While all around the world lay sleeping, Mum cried out with pain, & I tried in vain to haul her into a more comfortable position. We both ended up exhausted – weary, worn & sad.

16th March 1979 Friday
In the middle of an Arctic blizzard Mum was fetched by ambulance & transported to Market Bosworth Hospital. Aunt Dos & I visited her later in the day & found her tucked up snug & warm in this beautiful mansion – formerly the home of landed gentry; & being given every possible loving care.

18th March 1979 Sunday
Cousin Johnty (aged 74) and I visited Mum in Market Bosworth Hospital.
She is by no means a model patient. As in January 1973

she finds the place too hot & she falls out with the nurses. She demands to be sent home, & then she calms down & decides, "If you can't beat 'em – join 'em."

20th March 1979 Tuesday
"Dum Spiro Spero" – While I breathe I hope. I learned today that this is my family motto. Paid £23 for the **Hewes Coat of Arms** & it arrived by post today.
Now that Mum & I are feeling so sad, we certainly **hope** for better days. Mum is really miserable in the geriatric ward, where all hope seems lost.

22nd March 1979 Thursday
Mum is being well fed – has even been given a bath, & has had her hair washed & set, but oh how she longs to be back home again. She sits all day long in a big room with 14 other very old & feeble ladies & she gets so depressed. But she cannot stand up by herself & cannot be independent.

24th March 1979 Saturday
"Hiawatha! Hiawatha!" And the desolate Hiawatha, far away amid the forest; miles away among the mountains; heard that sudden cry of anguish; heard the voice of Minnehaha; calling to him in the darkness, "Hiawatha! Hiawatha!"
So it was I twice heard the anguished cry of Mum in the night, "Bet! Bet!"

26th March 1979 Monday
Yesterday was Mothering Sunday and Auntie Doris & I went to Leicester Cathedral in the morning to a "Service of welcome to the new Bishop of Leicester – the Rt. Revd. Richard Rutt." I had lunch with Auntie Doris & we visited my poor old Mum in the afternoon – such a sad day for her.

28th March 1979 Wednesday
I stood at the magnificent entrance to the hospital where so many inside were so sad, & where I had left my poor old Mum in tears. The scene before me was breathtakingly beautiful. It was just getting dusk & the birds were singing in all the trees. I heard the lambs, saw the new moon, & the clock in the lovely church struck 8.

30th March 1979 Friday
Murder at the House of Commons! The bloody Irish planted a bomb underneath the car of Mr. Airey Neave, 63 year old M.P. for Abingdon & Shadow Minister for Ulster. As he drove his car up the ramp from the House of Commons underground car park he was blown to smithereens at 3 p.m.

1st April 1979 Sunday
The present Labour Government and Prime Minister James Callaghan are about to collapse. Following a recent vote of "no confidence" from Opposition leader Mrs. Margaret Thatcher, a General Election has been called for 3rd May; but the murder of M.P. Airey Neave has humbled them all.

3rd April 1979 Tuesday
Mary Moore arrived today for a week in Ravenstone, so that she can go & visit my poor old Mum. I met her at Leicester Station, & I have arranged a few days holiday

while she is here. But Mum, like Jacob, refused to be comforted. (See Genesis 37. 35.)

5th April 1979 Thursday
John Bloomfield, our local painter & decorator, spent the day wall papering our bathroom. We chose a pattern of ducks and swans & water lilies on the water, with the occasional flamingo. I then bought a new mirror for the bathroom wall, & it now looks very smart.

7th April 1979 Saturday
Today I bought two new saucepans – Prestige stainless steel with copper base.
2 pints, base diameter 4½ inches, which being interpreted is 1.2 litres, 115mm, reduced from £12·95p to £11·50p.
3 pints, base diameter 5⅜ inches = 1.7 litres, 135mm, reduced from £14·25 to £12·80.

9th April 1979 Monday
Through visiting my poor old Mum in the geriatric ward at Bosworth Park Infirmary, I have become acquainted with a dear old lady, aged 95, who tells me such lovely tales of her early life, & the handsome rich young man who loved her so dearly, & bought her such expensive presents.

11th April 1979 Wednesday
The dear old lady, aged 95, has the most unique engagement ring, engraved "**Dearest**". For every initial of this word, there is a precious stone – a **d**iamond – an **e**merald – an **a**methyst – a **r**uby – another **e**merald – a **s**apphire - & a **t**opaz.

13th April 1979 Good Friday
Saw the full suffering of the Crucifixion in the "Holy Shroud" on television. The Turin Shroud is thought to be the burial cloth of Jesus, & apart from showing every whiplash, every wound, & a whole bunch of thorns on the head, to mark the shroud so, it shows the very features of his face.

15th April 1979 Easter Sunday
The Turin Shroud has been carefully saved by faithful Christians for 2,000 years, but it has taken 20th Century technology & men of science to analyse it in microscopic detail & find what must surely belong to our three in one God. Whipped by a 3 lash whip & a 3 so clearly in his wounds.

Shroud is a Fake
Tests have shown that the Shroud of Turin, revered by many Christians as Christ's burial cloth, is a medieval fake. Tests carried out by laboratories in England, United States and Switzerland, showed with 95% certainty that the cloth dated from between 1260 and 1390. (Proved in 1988)

17th April 1979 Tuesday
Psalm 118, which we sang in church on Easter Sunday, reminded me that, "The Lord is on my side; I will not fear…….. it is better to trust in the Lord than to put confidence in man.
It is better to trust in the Lord than to put confidence in princes…….the Lord is my strength and song."

19th April 1979 Thursday
This week we are having the front room papered & decorated – and the hall. It was in a very scruffy state, & Mr Weston from Ashby is making a very good job of it – slow but thorough. It will cost £200 for the front room and the hall, and another £200 for them to be carpeted.

21st April 1979 Saturday
Mum has now been in hospital 5 weeks. They have done all they possibly could to help her stand again on her own feet. First she was encouraged to stand between 2 parallel bars, and then walk between the bars.
Although she is still depressed, she can now walk with a walking aid.

23rd April 1979 Monday
On St. George's Day at St. George's Parish Church, Ticknall, my dad's cousin Cecil Hewes was buried today. I went to the funeral with Pat & Auntie Dos. A horseman all his life, he had from his wife Dorothy, the most beautiful wreath, made into a perfect horseshoe.

25th April 1979 Wednesday
£5,000 per year. The latest Civil Service pay award takes the maximum E.O. salary to £5,043 with effect from 1st April 1979. This will be increased to £5,272 on 1st August 1979, with yet a further increase to £5,700 on 1st January 1980.

27th April 1979 Friday
With the General Election next week we are being bombarded with election literature first from one party & then another.
We are in the Loughborough constituency & have five people to choose from – Conservative – Labour – Liberal – National Front – and my choice an Ecologist.

29th April 1979 Sunday
Working at Gas Standards Branch has shown me, perhaps more than most people, the problems of providing North Sea oil & gas without upsetting the balance & rhythm of Nature. Hence my choice of an Ecologist – one who studies plants, animals & people in relation to environment.

1st May 1979 Tuesday
Mum has been told that she can come home on Thursday – Election Day – after 7 weeks in hospital. Although she has been longing to come home, she is not altogether sure that she will be safe in the house on her own. Her legs only just support her & she is afraid of falling.

3rd May 1979 Thursday
Election Day – and a win for the Conservatives. Margaret Thatcher, aged 53 (same age as the Queen) makes history by becoming the first ever woman Prime Minister. Conservatives 339 seats, Labour 268, Liberal 11, others 17. This gives the Conservatives an overall majority.

5th May 1979 Saturday
"Where there is discord, may we bring harmony; where there is error, may we bring truth; where there is doubt, may we bring faith; where there is despair, may we bring hope."

On the steps of 10, Downing Street, Margaret Thatcher, newly elected Prime Minister, quoted the prayer of St. Francis of Assisi.

7th May 1979 Monday
All change in the Government -
Prime Minister = Margaret Thatcher, aged 53. Home Secretary = William Whitelaw, aged 60. Foreign Secretary = Lord Carrington, aged 59. Chancellor of the Exchequer = Sir Geoffrey Howe, aged 52. Energy Secretary (my boss) = David Howell, aged 43.

9th May 1979 Wednesday
The bravest man in the new Government is the newly appointed Northern Ireland Secretary Mr Humphrey Atkins – number one target for the I.R.A. Asked how he felt on being offered a job which has been likened to a poisoned chalice, he said, "Very, very honoured. I look forward to it immensely."

11th May 1979 Friday
Our poor old coalhouse has lately become like the leaning tower of Pisa.
Fearing that it might come crashing down at any minute we finally gave it the final push. Keith (next door) and Brother Pat, with the help of a plank, knocked it flying, & with one almighty crash it was down.

13th May 1979 Sunday
Cup Final Day yesterday. Arsenal 3 – Manchester United 2. This 51st Wembley Cup Final was an "unforgettable epic". The score at half time was Arsenal 2 – Man. United 0. Then Manchester drew level & at the last minute lost. Prince Charles presented the Cup. Receipts were £500,000.

15th May 1979 Tuesday
Two nights in London! Accepted an invitation from Library H.Q. at 1, Victoria Street for a two day course connected with work in the great governmental libraries in London. A most interesting couple of days, including a conducted tour of the huge library at 1, Victoria Street, dealing direct with M.P.s.

Note – Absolutely fascinating to see how facts & figures are found for Members of Parliament, & the system for cross referencing, etc. Just the sort of work I love – more in my line than "managing" staff.

17th May 1979 Thursday
Pat & Evelyn kindly took Mum under their wing while I went to London. Mum is still very shaky & she was glad to be somewhere where she was watched over & cared for day and night. At home she is left alone when I go to work & she is scared of falling while in the house on her own.

19th May 1979 Saturday
Having made the front room so beautiful with its new wallpaper & new fitted carpet, I have now ordered a smart new Parker Knoll chair – colour Windsor Rose – and a new piano stool to match. The chair is £50 & the piano stool is £40. Also, we have a new electric fire & pink Venetian blinds.

21st May 1979 Monday
Having seen the great library at 1, Victoria Street, London & been given a clearer insight into Government publications, I have become much more interested in "Hansard" which comes every day to our library at Gas Standards Branch & tells you what everybody said in Parliament the day before.

23rd May 1979 Wednesday
How interesting to be in such close touch with all that is said in Parliament when we have just had a General Election.
I found of particular interest the first number of the first "session" of the 48th Parliament of the U.K. & Northern Ireland in the 28th year of the reign of Her Majesty Queen Elizabeth II.

25th May 1979 Friday
Hansard No. 1 (Volume 967) showed the history of Parliament from William the Conqueror to the present day. It also listed every Member of Parliament returned at this month's General Election & gave details of Principal Officers now in the Government. Finally it recorded the Election of the Speaker – G. Thomas.

27th May 1979 Sunday
Quote from Hansard, "The duties of Mr Speaker include ensuring compliance with the First Epistle of St. Paul to the Corinthians, Chapter 14, verse 40. 'Let all things be done decently & in order'. Mr Speaker replied, "….. I shall quote St. Paul's advice to the Thessalonians, 'Stand fast & hold the traditions ye have been taught.'"

29th May 1979 Tuesday
The Parish Church of Saint Mary and All Saints, Willoughby-on-the-Wolds, is celebrating its 800th Anniversary 1179 – 1979. To mark this auspicious occasion there was a special evensong on Sunday where the Bishop of Southwell preached. I went with Johnty, his brother Eric, & Eric's wife, May.

31st May 1979 Thursday
The world's first international general election is being held on June 7th. Voters will elect 410 M.P.s to the Euro-Parliament in Strasbourg. These Euro-M.P.s will speak on behalf of 260 million people in the 9 E.E.C. countries – Ireland, U.K., France, Italy, Denmark, Holland, Belgium, Luxembourg & West Germany.

2nd June 1979 Saturday
In the European Parliament, Britain has 81 seats, France 81, Italy 81, West Germany 81, Holland 25, Belgium 24, Ireland 15, Denmark 16 & Luxembourg 6.
These are The Nine – but beware – Greece will become the 10th member 1st January 1981.
(See 24th January 1972) and see Revelation, Chapter 17.

4th June 1979 Monday
Yesterday was Whit Sunday and it was my privilege & pleasure to read both lessons in Ravenstone Church at Evensong – Isaiah, Chapter 11 & Romans Chapter 8, including those powerful words of St. Paul, "We know that all things work together for good to them that love God ….. if God be for us, who can be against us?"

6th June 1979 Wednesday

What a marathon task it has been clearing a ton of bricks & rubble after knocking down the coalhouse. Once again this has meant re-landscaping the garden. The coalhouse floor was laid on curved bricks which I have now set out in a perfect circle round the sundial.

8th June 1979 Friday

Our Sunday School Anniversary this year has for its theme, "The International Year of the Child". The songs include, "I belong to a family, the biggest on Earth", "The ink is black, the page is white", "We are one in the Spirit, we are one in the Lord", "All night, all day, angels watching over me".

10th June 1979 Trinity Sunday

And yet another thought for our three in one God who stamps everything with his three-in-one Trade Mark. St. John 13. 38. Jesus said to Peter, "The cock shall not crow till thou hast denied me thrice". Then later (St. John 21) Peter was asked three times "Lovest thou me?" & was able to acknowledge Jesus thrice.

12th June 1979 Tuesday

£100,000 was offered to the first man to "fly" across the English Channel without the aid of an engine. Today Bryan Allen achieved this by pedal power. (See 27th August 1977) He went from Folkestone to Calais in just under three hours in "Gossamer Albatross" by pedal power.

14th June 1979 Thursday

Dr. Paul McCready, former international gliding champion, designed "Gossamer Albatross", weighing 55lbs & a wing span of 96 feet. The £100,000 prize, held by the Royal Aeronautical Society, was put up by English industrialist Henry Kremer. The machine flew at 10 feet.

16th June 1979 Saturday

Budget Day this week & new Chancellor Sir Geoffrey Howe brought Income Tax down & put prices of everything up with 15% V.A.T. (i.e. Value Added Tax) To make more money, the Government might yet sell British Gas, so who knows what will happen to "Gas Standards"?

18th June 1979 Monday

Stuart David Page was born today. A baby son for our neighbours David & Sue, a brother for 5 year old Joanne. He was born in the Leicester Royal Infirmary & weighed in at 5lbs 3ozs. David Page, you remember, is a miner who took me down the mine in September 1977.

Note – A brother for 5 year old Joanne, who now seeks undivided attention by becoming a regular visitor to our house – she lives next door but one.

20th June 1979 Wednesday

Yesterday I went with David Page to visit Sue & one day old baby Stuart. The baby was so beautiful & so tiny, but wide-eyed & alert.
As David held him in his arms I thought of Henry VIII & all that he did to get a baby son, & I thought of old age & all its sorrow.

22nd June 1979 Friday

Went with Auntie Dos to visit Cousin Audrey in Leicester Royal Infirmary. She had a nasty fall & has ended up with her leg in plaster.
She has no children of her own & no nieces or nephews. Like me, she is very much alone in this world, & I felt so sorry for her – old, frail & helpless.

24th June 1979 Sunday

"Blessed is the man whose strength is in thee, in whose heart are thy ways.
Who going through the vale of misery use it for a well; & the pools are filled with water."
We sang this tonight at church (Psalm 84) after Mum & I have spent the day shedding many tears – Mum so helpless, not able to stand on her feet.

26th June 1979 Tuesday

Holiday on the Costa Ravo. With Mum once again bed-ridden, I have taken a week's holiday to attend to her. She suffers absolute torments & cries out in pain. Like Hiawatha she calls to heaven for help, "….. but there came no other answer than the echo of his crying."

27th June 1979 Wednesday

Mum landed helpless on the floor & was picked up by 2 ambulance men who then took her to Leicester Royal Infirmary as a "casualty". However, no bones broken, no fracture, so she was sent home for us to continue the struggle of bed-pans – wet beds - & continual washing.

28th June 1979 Thursday

"And what is so rare as a day in June? Then, if ever, come perfect days"
And again, "O perfect day, wherein shall no man work, but play."
As Mum & I struggle each day, heart-broken & in despair, how we both long for better days.

30th June 1979 Saturday

While Mum & I have our sorrow & tears, the problems of the world at large loom around us. The energy crisis is of major concern at the moment. The Western world is so utterly dependant on Middle East oil, but recently the Shah of Iran has been deposed & Iran no longer is producing oil for the West.

2nd July 1979 Monday

The Psalms & Hymns at church continue to cheer us on our way. Tonight we are reminded, "Let not sorrow dim your eye, soon shall every tear be dry; let not fears your course impede, great your strength if great your need (Hymn 291) …. The clouds ye so much dread, are big with mercy & shall break - in blessings on your head. (Hymn 373)

4th July 1979 Wednesday

On a beautiful sunny day Mum was yet again fetched by ambulance & transported this time to the new hospital at Glenfield. Visited her in the evening & oh, how pathetic she looked in bed. "God in heaven – why must I suffer so – but then He never has liked me. I wish I were dead, but He doesn't want me." So my poor old Mum lost all hope.

Note – Mum is taken by ambulance to Glenfield Hospital, never again to return home. Once Mum became completely bed-ridden a few weeks ago, we hardly knew how to cope, & I took a week's holiday "on the Costa Ravo". Poor Mum was in such pain, & we both shed many tears; Mum was in the very depths of despair, & would never walk again. She was to spend the next 3 years suffering the indignities of life in the geriatric ward, first at Glenfield & then at Market Bosworth Hospital.

6th July 1979 Friday
Seeing my Mum in such a sorry state, I thought of Elijah sitting under a juniper tree, "And he requested for himself that he might die." I Kings, Chapter 19. "And as he lay & slept under a juniper tree, behold, then an angel touched him & said unto him, arise and eat."

8th July 1979 Sunday
"And behold, the Lord passed by, and a great & strong wind rent the mountains, & brake in pieces the rocks before the Lord; but the Lord was not in the wind; & after the wind an earthquake; but the Lord was not in the earthquake; & after the earthquake a fire; but the Lord was not in the fire; & after the fire a still small voice."

10th July 1979 Tuesday
Leicester's Scanner Appeal was launched by the Lord Mayor of Leicester, Mr Albert Watson, last September. Although Albert Watson finished his term as Lord Mayor earlier this year, he is still in charge of the appeal. The target £500,000 is now in sight & the body scanner is being ordered for the Infirmary.

12th July 1979 Thursday
How sad to see your own lovely mother looking like an old woman of the workhouse. Unable to stand, she has to endure the anguish & discomfort of a geriatric chair all day long, & is dressed in drab geriatric clothing. She feels like a prisoner & suffers absolute torment & torture.

14th July 1979 Saturday
48 today – 2 x 2 x 2 x 2 x 3. As I wept at the bedside of my poor old Mum, I thought – what a birthday!
Mum was in a turmoil of agonising pain & anguish. As she thrashed about the bed with her face screwed up in her torture, I wondered how much more she must suffer.

16th July 1979 Monday
Having worked in Motor Taxation with the constant threat – "Scrap Motor Tax", I am now in Gas Standards Branch where the latest rumour is "Reduce G.S.B. by 50%". We are only an incidental extra in the Department of Energy – just keeping a check on British Gas.

18th July 1979 Wednesday
Seven years ago thousands of British Asians were expelled from Uganda & many found refuge in Leicester. The latest problem is even more refugees fleeing from Vietnam. They are called "the boat people" as they cram themselves into boats to flee from Vietnam.

19th July 1979 Thursday
On this day in history – in 1553 – Lady Jane Grey was sent to the Tower of London and Mary Tudor proclaimed Queen of England.
And in 1588 – "There's plenty of time to finish this game of bowls and thrash the Spaniards too" said Sir Francis Drake on Plymouth Hoe as he played bowls.

20th July 1979 Friday
Rudolph, Leicester's fund raising reindeer, is to be put out to grass & is to be replaced by a younger model called "Son of Rudolph". Rudolph was found in 1949 when he was a dilapidated stage cow & was transformed into a reindeer. "Son of Rudolph" will cost £900.

22nd July 1979 Sunday
"God Bless Ireland". These were the words of the Pope today as he prepares for a visit to Ireland from 29th September to 1st October. It will be the first visit by a Pope to Ireland since St. Patrick himself in the 5th Century. From Ireland the Pope will go to America & the U.N.
(U.N. = United Nations)

24th July 1979 Tuesday
On Budget Day last month, the new Chancellor Sir Geoffrey Howe said, "In order to reduce the borrowing requirement & the burden of direct taxation we must make savings in public spending & roll back the boundaries of the public sector." £4,000 million cuts are planned.

26th July 1979 Thursday
"Roll back the boundaries of the public sector" – that means the Civil Service – that means Gas Standards Branch of the Dept. of Energy – **but!** - Our expenses are re-claimable from British Gas, and British Gas has just announced a profit over the year of £360 million.

28th July 1979 Saturday
"We all agreed that nuclear energy was the answer." These sad prophetic words were spoken by our new Prime Minister, Mrs Margaret Thatcher, after a meeting of world leaders to discuss the energy crisis. I thought of the seven last plagues described in Revelation.

30th July 1979 Monday
Britain plans to build five more nuclear power stations, adding to the 15 we have already. It seems to be "Hobson's Choice" in the face of the alternative power sources – wind, sun, wave and tide. These are all economically unviable. And so like lemmings we rush headlong towards destruction.

1st August 1979 Wednesday
Metric measurements are slowly sneaking up on us. Coffee this week changed from 8oz. (227g.) to a slightly smaller 200g. Margarine changed from 8oz. (oz. = ounces) to a slightly larger 250g. & the weatherman talks of temperatures around 21C, instead of 70F which we have been used to.

3rd August 1979 Friday
The Vietnamese boat people are chiefly of Chinese origin – an ethnic minority being expelled from Vietnam. Estimates are that as many as 1,500,000 may be forced out of Vietnam & there is a fear that other

countries might decide to get rid of their minorities.

5th August 1979 Sunday
Britain is to take in 10,000 Vietnamese refugees, with the only stipulation that they must come from Hong Kong. Some 4,000 refugees from Vietnam, including those picked up on British ships, have already arrived in Britain. The extra 10,000 will gradually be brought in over a period of time.

7th August 1979 Tuesday
On the 7th day of September 1964, I bought a Grundig portable tape recorder, which cost
65 guineas = £65 plus £3-5/-. This has now given up the ghost – ruined by battery corrosion. Today I saw an advert in the Leicester Mercury for a second-hand Grundig tape recorder & bought it for £40.

9th August 1979 Thursday
Telephone bills usually come every 3 months – February, May, August and November. However, a strike by Post Office computer staff numbering no more than 123 has meant no bills since last February, & this strike is costing the Post Office £10 million every day in lost revenue.

11th August 1979 Saturday
Conducted my very first solo interview yesterday after watching Arthur my companion E.O.
interviewing various applicants for "trainee typist" at Gas Standards Branch. We asked their name, address & educational record, told them about G.S.B., the salary & holidays etc. & gave them a 10 minute typing test.

13th August 1979 Monday
To be a "trainee typist" in the Civil Service, you complete a form which asks your age, height, weight – eyesight – hearing – speech - any defect or disability - serious accident - radiotherapy – fits, fainting, heart trouble, asthma, bronchitis, gastric, bowel, kidney, bladder, arthritis, blood, skin, etc. etc.

15th August 1979 Wednesday
To be a "trainee typist" in the Civil Service you complete another form which asks your nationality & also your nationality at birth if different – your parents & husband or wife – their date & place of birth & occupation & nationality – have you been charged before any court or placed on probation or bound over?

17th August 1979 Friday
Our Sunday School outing last year to Chatsworth House & the Peak Cavern at Castleton was cancelled through lack of support. Our Sunday School outing this year to Warwick Castle & possibly Charlecote Park or Stratford has also been cancelled through lack of support.

19th August 1979 Sunday
The planets prepare for their great line-up of the eighties & already Earth is feeling the effect. The biggest disaster in the history of ocean racing overtook the 333 yachts in the Fastnet International Yacht Race this week when a sudden storm force 10 gale struck.

21st August 1979 Tuesday
The Fastnet International Yacht Race is from Cowes to Fastnet Rock (Off the southern coast of Ireland) & back to Plymouth.
The Fastnet Rock lighthouse keeper said he had never seen such bad weather in the area in August. Many luxury yachts from 20 nations were lost completely.

22nd August 1979 Wednesday
Roll of Honour
Plantagenet, Richard, King of England, killed at Battle of Bosworth, August 22nd 1485. Wreath laying by the Provost, West Bridge, 11 a.m. Wednesday.

23rd August Thursday
Mum's birthday. 74 today. Confined to a geriatric chair in the Glenfield Community Centre, it was hardly a "Happy Birthday". Mum wished she could be at home & wished she could stand & walk.
Cousin Johnty (aged 75 – who renewed contact with Mum in 1967)) & I both took her flowers & stayed with her till bedtime.

25th August 1979 Saturday
An invitation – "You are cordially invited to an informal Re-union Party at the Ravenstone Institute on Saturday 22nd September. The gathering is to give friends of Esme Hill (née Wallis), who will be on a visit from Canada, an opportunity of meeting her again."
(A neighbour)

27th August 1979 Monday
Ten years ago, in August 1969, the British Army's emergency peacekeeping force was sent to Northern Ireland "To help out the police for a few weeks". The army is still there, & although no war officially exists, 300 regular soldiers & 2,000 ordinary people have been killed.

29th August 1979 Wednesday
Lord Louis Mountbatten, aged 79, the Queen's favourite uncle, is the latest victim of the bloody Irish. He was on holiday at Mullaghmore, County Sligo, where he spent the month of August every year for many years. He & his family were in his 29ft boat, Shadow V, when it blew up.

31st August 1979 Friday
Lord Louis Mountbatten was a hero of the last war 1939 – 45. The handsomest man of his day, he became First Sea Lord, & survived the perils of the deep. His ship was torpedoed & sunk, but he was destined to die at sea in a quiet Irish harbour – murdered by the I.R.A.

2nd September 1979 Sunday
The I.R.A. have issued the following statement, "The I.R.A. claim responsibility for the execution of Lord Louis Mountbatten.
This operation is one of the discriminating ways we can bring to the attention of the English people the continuing occupation of our country. The British Army acknowledges that over ten years of war they cannot defeat us, yet the British Government continues to oppress our people & torture our comrades in the "H" blocks. For this we will tear out its imperialistic

sentimental heart, etc.etc." Statement issued in Belfast.

Brooks, Pauline, 7 Jacqueline Road, Markfield.
Passed peacefully away at home Sunday September 2ⁿᵈ,
after a long illness. Beloved wife of Alf, mother of
Malcolm and Kevin, mother-in-law of Kathleen. Much
loved grandmother of Richard and David. Funeral
arrangements later.

6ᵗʰ September 1979 Thursday
Today was the funeral of Pauline Brooks who, like Ruby, worked at my side on the counter in the Motor Licence Office, & who, like Ruby, suffered the slow agonising death of cancer. Ruby died in November 1974 in her early fifties, & Pauline too died in her early fifties.

8ᵗʰ September 1979 Saturday
King Edward VII College, Coalville, offers among other things for night school this autumn, "Travel Club Course".
So I have enrolled for this course which will begin next Thursday. I was told that it will be concerned chiefly with travel abroad & it was noted that I have been to Rome.

10ᵗʰ September 1979 Monday
I went with three other members of staff from Gas Standards Branch on a conducted tour of Meadow Hall Gas Holder Station at Sheffield. We heard the gas roaring through huge pipes, went into the Calorific Value Test Room, & did a mock test on the calorific value of the gas.

12ᵗʰ September 1979 Wednesday
The garden at the moment is a vision of delight. All the toil of past months & past years has resulted in a landscape of lawns & paved edges, flowers just as a border decoration, with the minimum of digging now – sun dial & bird bath.

14ᵗʰ September 1979 Friday
Went to my first evening "Travel Club Course" & was told that only four people had enrolled. The class was therefore cancelled & my money was refunded.
That then was the end of my night school for this season. I wasn't particularly sorry. It's nice not to turn out on wintry nights.

16ᵗʰ September 1979 Sunday
Since the birth of baby Stuart, our 5 year old neighbour Joanne Page, has spent many hours with me. With her vivid imagination & ceaseless chatter, she keeps me well entertained.
She is in turn the Bank Cashier, the Shopkeeper, Customer, District Nurse, Teacher, Telephone Operator, etc. etc.

18ᵗʰ September 1979 Tuesday
My darling Mum suffers all the indignity of being helpless & at the mercy of others.
The nurses are uncouth & maintain that she is a malingerer. They say her tears are "crocodile tears" & that she could stand & walk if she tried.
And her daughter – "She never speaks to anyone".

20ᵗʰ September 1979 Thursday
"Why are you so lucky?" asked five-year-old Joanne. "In what way?" I replied. "You've got such a lot of nice things."
I thought of all my blessings – of my father who was so well-loved & who provided much of my home – of my mother who provided much of the rest & gave me all she possessed.

22ⁿᵈ September 1979 Saturday
While I enjoy all the blessings of my home, my poor old Mum is confined to a geriatric chair in hospital – unable to move her own body. She is so unhappy & looks like a pauper in a horrible geriatric dress & hair unkempt. It grieves me to see her so.

24ᵗʰ September 1979 Monday
Last night at church, I read the first lesson – Job, Chapter 1.
The introduction read thus, "The Book of Job is a dramatic poem which attempts to solve the age-old mystery of undeserved suffering. Job has been upright all his days, yet he is terribly afflicted. Why should God allow this?"

26ᵗʰ September 1979 Wednesday
Having followed all the suffering of Job through the 42 chapters of the story, how good to know that "The Lord turned the captivity of Job, when he prayed for his friends; also the Lord gave Job twice as much as he had before. So the Lord blessed the latter end of Job more than his beginning."

28ᵗʰ September 1979 Friday
Gracie Fields, aged 81, known to millions as "Our Gracie", died yesterday in her luxury home on the Isle of Capri. Born over a fish & chip shop in Rochdale she became the world's Queen of Song. She had the gift of moving audiences from laughter to tears in minutes.

30ᵗʰ September 1979 Sunday
Pope John Paul II is spending 3 days in Ireland & his message is "Love your enemies, do good to those who hate you." Well, he is called the Pontiff – the Bridge Maker, as he captivates the hearts of all. The youth of Ireland flock to him & pour out their hearts to him in dance & song.

2ⁿᵈ October 1979 Tuesday
Pope John Paul II is perhaps the most powerful man to have hit Ireland since Saint Patrick. Who else could have emptied a city and the entire human population out of the hills & valleys? Dublin on Saturday was devoid of all life. Everyone was in Phoenix Park waiting.

4ᵗʰ October 1979 Thursday
The Pope not only went to Phoenix Park, he went to the west coast where he conducted an open air mass at Galway on a racecourse, & then on to the shrine at Knock in County Mayo.
He drove through the ranks of people in a specially designed vehicle called a "Popemobile".

6th October 1979 Saturday
Like St. Paul, the Pope is now on his apostolic mission thousands of miles from home. The Philadelphia of the ancient world has become the Philadelphia of the U.S.A., but the meaning is the same – brotherly love. The Pope is, however, firm – the Church must not bow to modern fads.

8th October 1979 Monday
"Pensions at 50 Plan to Cut Civil Service". The Sunday Express yesterday announced, "Seventy-five thousand Civil Servants are to be encouraged to take pensions at 50, plus cash pay-offs up to £20,000 plus, under plans being considered by the Government to cut the Civil Service by 10%.

10th October 1979 Wednesday
The Government would like to reduce the number of Civil Servants from the present 750,000 to around 675,000. Early retirement, on index-linked pensions, is regarded by Ministers as less likely to disrupt the work of departments than a prolonged ban on recruitment. This might include me!

12th October 1979 Friday
I told you we look out from our office window to a sports field with trees & squirrels. (September 1978) Well, we now have a squirrel who is so tame; she comes regularly to see us & sits up & begs like a little dog, while we delight in throwing monkey-nuts to her. Some she eats & some she buries.

14th October 1979 Sunday
Harvest Festival today at Ravenstone Church marks my 21st Anniversary as a Sunday School teacher. To mark this auspicious occasion I wore my very smart new suit which I bought yesterday - £80. Tonight at church we had the Stanton Brass Band to play for the hymns.

16th October 1979 Tuesday
Our friend the squirrel brought two of her babies with her to visit us this morning. While she came right up to the window for nuts, the babies ran up & down the trees or chased each other across the grass. They wash their faces like a cat & then use their bushy tails as a towel.

18th October 1979 Thursday
The Post Office strike affecting the sending out of telephone bills is now over. But the outcome of it all is that the Post Office has no idea who now has a telephone & who has not. So letters of explanation are being sent to every address in Britain - 21,500,000 – including 5 million homes without a telephone.

20th October 1979 Saturday
Now that petrol costs more than £1 per gallon, there are thousands of petrol pumps which cannot calculate the price. When the pumps were made they did not anticipate needing 3 figures, so it has been decided to switch to the metric system as quickly as possible & buy by the litre instead of the gallon.

22nd October 1979 Monday
What a joy it is to be greeted on my arrival home from work by my little 5 year-old neighbour Joanne. She

helps me unload my shopping & then makes herself quite at home for an hour or so, playing the piano, or crayoning, or typing, or cleaning the brasses, or cooking, etc.

24th October 1979 Wednesday
Mum was transferred yesterday from the hospital at Glenfield to St. David's ward in the Bosworth Park Infirmary. This is an annexe in the grounds of the mansion where she was taken on March 16th. I am pleased to say that now, she is not so depressed, & has settled in quite well.

26th October 1979 Friday
Went with Aunt Dos (aged 77) to dear old County Hall where the Lord Lieutenant of Leicestershire, Colonel Andrew Martin, presented 47 people with awards for their public service. There were Police, Firemen & W.R.V.S. – including Aunt Dos, who received recognition for 39 years service.

28th October 1979 Sunday
Samuel Charles Stevenson born 19th October 1979 is the latest member of the family. Bunting's first grandson, born to Michael & Sheena, & a brother for little Lucy, he weighed 8lbs 9ozs at birth.
Bunting arrived on a brief visit today & went with me to visit Mum in hospital.

30th October 1979 Tuesday
The "Battle of Belvoir" began today. (See September 23rd 1976) To dig for coal or not to dig for coal? That is the question. The coalfield is the biggest find of coal in Europe's recent history & the Coal Board would like to have 3 mines at 1.Asfordby, 2.Saltby & 3.Hose.

1st November 1979 Thursday
The mammoth public inquiry into the future of the beautiful Vale of Belvoir is expected to go on for 6 months. It is the Coal Board versus "The Vale of Belvoir Protection Group". We have to decide whether it is vital to have this coal **now**, or whether to save it for the future.

3rd November 1979 Saturday
The Coal Board, in their argument for mining in the Vale of Belvoir, have leaked the information that all six Leicestershire mines at present in production will close by 1990. Bagworth - 154 years old. Desford – 79 years old. Ellistown – 105 years old.
Snibstone – 145 years old. South Leicester – 104 years old. Whitwick – 152 years old.

5th November 1979 Monday
Meet Elizabeth Hewes – shareholder.
The following offer appeared in the paper today – "The Governor & Company of the Bank of England on behalf of the Lords Commissioners of Her Majesty's Treasury offer for sale 80 million shares of the British Petroleum Co. Ltd. at £3-63 per share."

7th November 1979 Wednesday
The Government & the Bank of England at present hold 51% of the B.P. ordinary capital.
By offering 80 million shares to the public they will then

hold 46%. Applications must be for at least 100 shares & I have bought 100 = £363. My interest in the B.P. group is its connection with gas.

9th November 1979 Friday
Who owns B.P.? The Government owns 31% = 477 million shares. The Bank of England 20% = 311 million shares. (The Government hopes to acquire the Bank of England's holding eventually) 160,000 members holding 757 million shares, & now I have jumped on the bandwagon with 100 shares.

11th November 1979 Sunday
Went yesterday to Leicester Cathedral for the Annual Children's Festival. The money this year was collected to help the blind children in Nigeria. We were given the Braille alphabet & a text printed in Braille which we brought home with us & then tried to transcribe.

13th November 1979 Tuesday
This was the text in Braille – "The God who said out of darkness the light shall shine is the same God who made His light shine in our hearts."

17th November 1979 Saturday
The new Bishop – Richard – spoke to the children of darkness & its fears & said how the light makes us feel safe, & how plants all need light to grow.

19th November 1979 Monday
"The Times" daily newspaper is now back in circulation after a strike which lasted almost a year. It recalls the great items of news which swept the world in its absence. These include the overthrowing of the Shah of Persia & all its terrible repercussions being felt now.

21st November 1979 Wednesday
The Shah of Persia is one & the same thing as the Shah of Iran. (See 30th June 1979)
In 1971 the Shah indulged in "the biggest beano since Babylon" (See 11th October 1971)
And in 1975 he loaned £200 million to Britain (See 5th November 1975) but now he is in exile & very ill in America.

23rd November 1979 Friday
Ayatollah Ruhollah Khomeini is the present spiritual & temporal leader in Iran. He has stirred up all the people to follow the old ways & have nothing to do with the ways of the western world. The American Embassy in Iran has been attacked and 49 Americans are held hostage.

25th November 1979 Sunday
With the western world so utterly dependant on the Arabs for oil, the present troubles in the Middle East are causing great concern. The latest drama is the seizure of the Grand Mosque at Mecca, holiest of all Islam's shrines, & likely to have far reaching repercussions.

27th November 1979 Tuesday
America versus Iran. The world waits with bated breath to see what fate will befall the 49 American hostages held in the American Embassy in Teheran for the past 24 days by 400 Muslim students who have the full support of the Ayatollah Khomeini & his 35 million followers.

29th November 1979 Thursday
In the year 1054 there was a great split in the Christian Church. Pope John Paul II is again showing himself as a true bridge-maker (i.e. Pontiff) by visiting Istanbul. He was met at the airport by Eastern Orthodox, Armenian Orthodox, Armenian Catholic, Roman Catholic, Greek Catholic & Anglican representatives.

1st December 1979 Saturday
Our Annual Christmas Fair in Ravenstone Village Institute & our 8th effort with a stall for the Sunday School. This year we made £18. Father Christmas (namely Jimmy Williamson) came to our house to robe and disrobe & it was a tricky business keeping Joanne away.

3rd December 1979 Monday
Yesterday was our Sunday School Prize Giving. About 40 children received a book each including 12 in my class – Samantha & Lorna Toon, Sally Anne & Clare Allsop, Debra Hickin, Joanne Freestone, Vernis Brooks, Susan & David Roe, James Ritchie, Andrew Vernon & John Nicholls.

5th December 1979 Wednesday
Went with Pat & Evelyn to the Haymarket Theatre, Leicester, to see "Oklahoma". This was a super production which is starting in Leicester for 2 months & then touring the country. It was of particular interest to us because both Pat & I had taken part in Coalville's production.

7th December 1979 Friday
The axe has fallen. The Government have announced cuts in the Civil Service which will reduce the numbers by 40,000. Gas Standards Branch is to be pruned, but the full details have not yet been spelled out. Motor Tax has been given another reprieve.

9th December 1979 Sunday
What is religion? Our Rector, the Revd. Buckroyd, explained that the word "religion" meant "binding" "by covenant" (religare = to bind) & as such there were therefore only **three** religions in the world – those where God made a covenant with man – Jews, Christians & Moslems.

11th December 1979 Tuesday
"Faith in God" as professed in common by the descendants of Abraham – Christians, Jews and Moslems ….. "is a secure foundation for dignity, brotherhood & the freedom of men". This was the message taken by the Pope to Istanbul. The spiritual links which unite them should be developed.

13th December 1979 Thursday
"Blessed Lord, who hast caused all Holy Scriptures to be written for our learning, grant that we may in such wise hear them, read, mark, learn & inwardly digest them, that by patience and comfort of thy holy word, we may embrace & ever hold fast the blessed hope of everlasting life."

15th December 1979 Saturday

The collect for the 2nd Sunday in Advent gives it the name of Bible Sunday.

Our Rector, the Revd. Buckroyd chose for his text I Kings 17. 14. "Neither shall the cruse of oil fail" & likened the word of God impregnated into our hearts as the cruse of oil which would never fail us.

17th December 1979 Monday

Mum went to see Dr. Kaye, psychologist, at the hospital where she herself worked for many years – Ashby-de-la-Zouch. He asked her in detail her full life story in an effort to find out what her illness really is. They have decided it is in the mind & not sclerosis.

19th December 1979 Wednesday

My lovely Mum is more contented with life at the moment than she was earlier in the year. Although she cannot walk or even stand up, she is not in the depths of despair, & is able to enjoy all the pre-Christmas comings & goings in hospital, including a personal visit from Santa himself.

21st December 1979 Friday

"Liking nothing but the best, we have to wait" - So, I wrote in my diary on 30th September 1970. You will be pleased to know that we now have a spanking new fitted carpet in the middle room. It is over fourteen years since the room was papered & decorated, but now it has been freshly done.

23rd December 1979 Sunday

"And the angel said unto her, "Fear not, Mary." I thought of my Mum, as I read these words during our 9 lesson Carol Service at Ravenstone Church this evening. Earlier in the year, during the Easter period, I thought of my Mum when Jesus said to Mary Magdalen – "Mary".

25th December 1979 Tuesday

Pat & Evelyn took under their wing the widow and the orphan for Christmas day. They invited Doris Roberts (widow), Mod Fletcher (widow), Aunt Dos & me.

I visited Mum during the afternoon in Bosworth Park Infirmary and wondered if she would ever be able to come home again.

27th December 1979 Thursday

Gale force winds and torrential rain have given everybody a bashing today. I drove through the worst flood water I have yet encountered and was thankful to arrive home safely. Wales was hardest hit and people were drowned in their own homes as well as out of doors.

29th December 1979 Saturday

1979 has been a vintage year as far as studies of the planets are concerned. Voyager space craft have sent us incredible pictures from Jupiter & are now on their way to Saturn. The first is due to arrive in November 1980 & we are hoping to see Titan, the largest moon in the solar system.

31st December 1979 Monday

Voyager II should reach Saturn in August 1981, & will then continue to the outer planets, arriving in January 1986 at Uranus and hopefully in the autumn of 1989 at Neptune. There are also plans to orbit Venus & if possible fly a probe past Halley's Comet when it approaches.

* * *

Homes, Gardens, Pets & Parents

Looking north, up Wash Lane from the Ibstock road, where Leicester Road crosses; this is now a busy main road with traffic lights. On the right, The Hollies circa 1900. At the time this was taken, 27 Leicester Road (Betty's home) was the next house after The Hollies out of the picture to the right. Other houses have since been built on what were once The Hollies' lawns.

George Harry Hewes, Betty's Grandfather, bought the land in 1897 and had the Hollies built.

The front of 27 Leicester Road Ravenstone in the winter of 1947. The tree and wall were removed in 1987

Betty's grandparents, George Harry and Mary Susannah Hewes, who had six sons and two daughters

With Grandad Tom Sketchley at Yew Tree Farm in the late 1930s.
The Sketchleys moved here from Willoughby on the Wolds in 1912 when Betty's mother was seven years old. The farm stood on the right hand side of Mary's Lane just along from the church going towards Jenny's Lane.

15th November 1964 Sunday: "I went for a walk in the afternoon sun-shine & met Don & Susan at the old farmhouse where Mum used to live. It was empty & derelict with no windows, no doors & the ceilings caving in. We wandered all through, & went upstairs; reminiscing back to the days when I used to visit Grandad, when I was only six."

Above, mum Mary & dad Reg at the garden gate of
Yew Tree Farm, Snibston, before Betty was born…

…and below, at Yew Tree Farm afterwards

Grandpa George Harry Hewes in the rear garden of Oak
Tree Cottage, 52 Leicester Road, Ravenstone, circa 1944,
when he lived there with his younger daughter, Betty's
Aunt Dos

Brother Robin with Dorothy Yates, who was *"at
one time our maid."* Probably around 1937 in the
garden of 27 Leicester Road

6th August 1984 Monday

"From a small photograph of my dad, taken about 75 years ago when he was a young soldier in the Coldstream Guards, I have now acquired a large colour photograph. Mr Stanyard, photographer at Whitwick, went to great pains to do this for me & I am delighted with the result. How smart my dad looks in his guard's uniform.

As Leslie Hale reminded me when he wrote to me in 1982, "I met your father 60 years ago & I can see him now as he stood always upright..."

My dad looks you straight in the eye & his brightly polished buttons (in pairs) show which Regiment of Guards he belonged to.

The Grenadier Guards – buttons regularly spaced
The Coldstream Guards – buttons in pairs
The Scots Guards – buttons in threes
The Irish Guards – buttons in fours
The Welsh Guards – buttons in fives
Each Regiment also has a distinctive bearskin."

Reg Hewes outside the office of G. H. Hewes & Sons,
Marlborough Square, Coalville in the 1930s

Summer 1947: in the garden of Oak Tree Cottage with
Bill, Aunt Dos's collie dog.

1956: in the garden of 27 Leicester Road,
Ravenstone, with mum

Betty, in her late teens, with Judy.

A walk with Vicky, Mary Blue's fox terrier

387

Left: garden of 27 Leicester Road 1976 and
above in 1999, showing 'The Croft' under
construction at the far end...
...and left: in 1976

Betty, the gardener

Tosca, the cat, in 1970

27, LEICESTER ROAD, RAVENSTONE
LEICESTERSHIRE. LE67 2AR

PRICE : £59,500

27 Leicester Road, up for sale in 2001

1980

1st January 1980 Tuesday
This is the decade when the planets line up together. Jupiter & Saturn will be within two degrees of conjunction from November 1980 to March 1981. The astrological action will go on until 1988/89 with a rare triple conjunction of Uranus, Neptune & Saturn.
It is predicted that there will be world shaking political upheavals of great might.

3rd January 1980 Thursday
American Presidents who died in office form a 20 year cycle – Lincoln elected 1860, Garfield elected 1880, McKinley elected 1900 – all were assassinated. Harding elected 1920, died in office; Roosevelt elected 1940, died in office; Kennedy elected 1960, was assassinated.

5th January 1980 Saturday
It is predicted that the President elected in 1980 will break the 7 year cycle & survive. Conjunctions of Jupiter & Saturn, the two largest planets, repeat at intervals of just under 20 years. It is an awe-inspiring sight when seen from Earth. Was this then the Star of Bethlehem?

7th January 1980 Monday
And so we go into the uncertain Eighties. My finances are at rock bottom after spending all my money on home improvements. The world in general dithers on the brink as Russian troops invade their neighbour Afghanistan, only one step away from the great oil producing countries – life-line of the Western world.

9th January 1980 Wednesday
Geo-thermal power is gathering momentum. Scientists now want to bore a shaft 12 miles down into the Earth where the temperature is 600°F. The deepest wells up to now are 6 miles down. The distance from Earth's surface to its interior is 4,000 miles, where the temperature is 10,000°F.

11th January 1980 Friday
"Gipsy Love" by Franz Lehar is the show chosen this year for Coalville Amateurs' production in March. I joined them this evening in my now accepted role as prompter & it was lovely to share with them again the drama – the pathos – the fun & the sheer joy of belonging to the stage.

13th January 1980 Sunday
"May you live to see a thousand reasons to rejoice." Hearing these words in a televised showing of the film "Fiddler on the Roof" I began compiling my own list of reasons to rejoice. I read again diaries written long ago when I was at school & re-lived situations and events long since forgotten.

15th January 1980 Tuesday
The Leicester Mercury told the story of Kirby Muxloe Castle.
It was begun in 1480 for William, Baron Hastings, Sheriff of Leicestershire & Warwickshire, who supported England's first Yorkist King, Edward IV, and who, charged with treason, was executed in 1483.

17th January 1980 Thursday
William, Baron Hastings, appears in Shakespeare's "King Richard III". In Act 3, Scene 5, Lord Lovel says (standing by the Tower of London), "Here is the head of that ignoble traitor, the dangerous & unsuspected Hastings."
1483 was a bloody year when England had 3 Kings.

19th January 1980 Saturday
King Edward IV died in 1483, and his son and heir Edward V was one of the princes who were murdered in the Tower. Another Leicestershire connection is the marriage of King Edward IV with Elizabeth, the widow of Sir John Grey of Bradgate. Lady Jane Grey was Queen for 9 days in 1553.

21st January 1980 Monday
Even the finances of the Vatican are shaky. Pope John Paul II, Bishop of Rome, Vicar of Jesus Christ, Successor of the Prince of the Apostles, and Sovereign of the Vatican State, says, "We are short of money." Although the Vatican Bank buys & sells land & shares, it is making an annual loss of £9 million.

23rd January 1980 Wednesday
A week of prayer for Christian Unity. For the first time this week we had the Roman Catholic Parish Priest of St. Wilfrid's, Coalville, Father Brian Dazeley and his flock in our Church of England Church at Ravenstone to share our service with us. A most moving experience.

25th January 1980 Friday
Father Brian Dazeley preached a mighty powerful sermon at Ravenstone. He said that the idea of Christian Unity had started in 1909 but had never got off the ground because the Roman Catholics had always expected others to do what they did. Now they were not quite so dogmatic.

Note – Every January since 1909 we have had a week of prayer for Christian Unity. The Roman Catholics & Protestants are prepared to enter each others place of worship & say a few prayers together, but otherwise they are as divided in what they actually believe as ever they were. The Protestants have simply "protested" about the worshipping of saints; the many corrupt practices which were taking place in the 16th century; & latterly in 1870, the doctrine of the Pope's infallibility.

27th January 1980 Sunday
"O Lord of the Church, make us the Church of the Lord." This was the prayer for the week of Christian Unity, when for the first time in my life I went to a service in St. Wilfrid's Roman Catholic Church at Coalville.
The Salvation Army band played for the hymns & the church was full.

29th January 1980 Tuesday
The crossed keys of St. Peter were on the front wall of Coalville's Roman Catholic Church & inside I saw picture postcards of Michelangelo's Pieta, that most famous of his works which I had gazed on in St. Peter's Basilica, Rome. The Vicar of Christ Church, Coalville was guest preacher.

31st January 1980 Thursday

The Revd. Roger Hinton, M.A., Vicar of Coalville, likened the gathering of all denominations in the Roman Catholic Church to the miraculous draught of fishes in St. Luke, Chapter 5, when Jesus said to Simon Peter, "Launch out into the deep" ……. "& they beckoned to their partners to come & help."

2nd February 1980 Saturday

Saw Roy Johnson in his role as Dame at the Concordia Theatre, Hinckley. The Pantomime was "Babes in the Wood", & it was one of the most enjoyable shows I have ever seen. The scenery, the sets & the lighting were wonderful. Real rabbits could be seen in the woodland scenes – truly a wonderland.

4th February 1980 Monday

Roy Johnson is the best Pantomime Dame you could wish to see. Many years ago he left a lasting impression on me when he undressed as a Dame, taking off his corsets & then rubbed his released body with such relief. I think of him doing this when I get undressed myself.

6th February 1980 Wednesday

So when Roy Johnson again undressed himself as a Dame, I've no doubt I appreciated it more than most.
It is over ten years since I have seen him in Pantomime, & during that time his wife Brenda, who played Principal Boy so many times with him, has been stricken with cancer & is dying.

8th February 1980 Friday

Funny how one incident can be remembered for ever while others pass away.
Gilbert Harding spoke once of the little boy sitting on a fence & waving to the passing train. That little boy is still there, & every time I see such a boy, I think of Gilbert Harding.
Gilbert Harding died in 1960. The boy never dies.

10th February 1980 Sunday

Similarly I think of Douglas (who married my Dad's cousin Dorothy) every time I see people flat out, sunning themselves face upward on the beach.
He told a tale of God making a batch of people & laying them out to be "cooked". To test whether or not they were done, he had to poke each one in the tummy.

12th February 1980 Tuesday

Terry Thomas once did a sketch in which he explained that he was the one who did all the wrong "noises off" that you hear on the television, such as a great clatter in the middle of the desert where there should be no noise.
Whenever I hear a wrong noise I think its Terry Thomas.

14th February 1980 Thursday

The Bishop of Leicester, Richard Rutt, visited All Saint's Church of England School, Wigston. The Bishop, who was a missionary in Korea for 20 years, explained the different ways the Koreans have for saying "Thank you". The more important a person was the longer the "Thank you" then became.

16th February 1980 Saturday

"Who do you think is the most important person you have to say "Thank you" to?" the Bishop of Leicester asked the children at All Saint's Church of England Junior School.
"Mother" – "Father" – "The Queen" answered the children. Then, after a short silence, one boy put his hand up & said, "Please Sir, is it the Pope?"

18th February 1980 Monday

The Queen is coming to Leicester on March 14th & will dine at County Hall.
My little 5 year old neighbour, Joanne, spends a couple of hours with me most evenings, & loves dressing up as the Queen with my stage jewellery, evening stole, etc. while I bow & curtsey & call her "Your Majesty".

20th February 1980 Wednesday

What a joy it is to be entertained by a 5 year old whose imagination is endless & whose energy is boundless. As the Queen, she puts on her specs to sign the visitors' book at the Town Hall, she chats to the patients in hospital & compliments all who have worked so hard to create the floral displays, etc.

22nd February 1980 Friday

While I play every imaginable role from Lord Lieutenant of the County, to the shy child who reluctantly gives a bouquet of flowers to the Queen, Joanne in turn changes from Queen to prima ballerina, to music hall artiste & to every conceivable act in the Circus – lions, elephants & ponies.

24th February 1980 Sunday

Joanne is never still for long. If I sit in the armchair having a drink, she skips & jumps round & round & round the chair until I feel that I am in a magic fairy circle.
She loves to clear a space big enough to dance or do acrobatics, & we play the music on my tape recorder over & over & over again.

26th February 1980 Tuesday

Joanne performs not only on the carpet but also on the table. She tells me to put my hands together & say after her, "Our Father, which art in heaven – Harold be thy name."
Or else, "For what we are about to receive, may the Lord make us truly fat and full."
How the Lord must love her.

28th February 1980 Thursday

A night in London. Stayed at No.11, Cardinal Mansions, Carlisle Place – opposite Victoria Palace. This was the home of Mrs Fuge, an elegant widow who offered Bed & Breakfast to help pay the ever increasing rates. I was given every possible home comfort – including a hot water bottle.

1st March 1980 Saturday

Went to London for a one day course on "Finance & Accounts" in the Department of Energy. We learned how financial estimates are prepared & then go to the Cabinet for final approval & then translated into the "vote". We learned about "Internal Audit" & "Exchequer & Audit".

3rd March 1980 Monday

A day of sunshine. It was warm enough for Mum to be taken outside into the grounds of the hospital. She has a wheelchair, complete with tray, which she sits in every day – better than a geriatric non-moving chair. She is looked after very well, but misses the freedom & fresh air of home life.

5th March 1980 Wednesday

"Gipsy Love" & Coalville Amateur Operatic's production this week transports me to another world of music & dance & to the freedom of Romany life. How I love being at the very heart of it all as prompter at the front of the stage.

If however, anyone needs prompting, I get a hot flush.

7th March 1980 Friday

Sir Peregrine Plomley, played by Brian Wardle, says, "I shall purposefully pursue that poppet & pop the question." - "You find me devilish, devastating & disturbingly dangerous."

"This roaming Romany Romeo." - "A fallacious phantasmagorical figment."

"Ravishingly rustic." - "I have proposalled to the Lady, and we are to be espousalled."

9th March 1980 Sunday

The Rector of Ravenstone, Leslie Buckroyd, spoke of the story of the Good Samaritan, Luke 10, & said this was not only an example of "love thy neighbour" but also a lesson in "humility" for the victim, who normally would despise the Samaritan.

"For the Jews had no dealings with the Samaritans." John 4.

11th March 1980 Tuesday

"White marble bust of a Pope" sold by Christies for £85 along with the rest of the contents of Swithland Hall in October 1978, has now been identified by experts at the Victoria & Albert Museum as being of Pope Gregory XV & is the work of Bernini in 1621.

It is therefore worth half a million pounds.

13th March 1980 Thursday

Pat & Evelyn this week are celebrating their Ruby Wedding Anniversary.

They invited Evelyn's brother Vin, his wife Olive; Angela, their daughter & family; the Stacey's (Pat's mother's family); Doris Roberts, Bunting, Mostyn, Aunt Dos & me, & Mary Blue & family to a re-union party – a rare old mixture.

15th March 1980 Saturday

Her Majesty the Queen yesterday came to Leicester. The weather was terrible. It rained most of the time & was freezing cold, but what a great & glorious day to remember. I joined the merry throng in front of the Town Hall Square & also joined the merry throng at County Hall. A right royal subject.

17th March 1980 Monday

It was lovely to stand in front of the Town Hall & listen to the band as we waited for the Queen. And when the Queen arrived, the band played the National Anthem, & it was great to sing this, so lustily, to the Queen herself.

The Queen did walk-about in Leicester & at County Hall & we all loved her.

19th March 1980 Wednesday

Mum was taken to Hinckley to look round the shops. Four patients, all in wheelchairs, were taken in a special bus with its own hydraulic lift & were taken into several different shops & were treated to morning coffee. This service was provided by Rehab – friends of the hospital.

21st March 1980 Friday

"Thought for Today" on Radio Leicester this week has had the rare distinction of coming from Mount St. Bernard's Abbey. Who could be more of a man of God than a monk? Rather than fleeing from the realities of life, they explained that we who indulge in holidays, entertainment & theatre are the escapists.

23rd March 1980 Sunday

Mothering Sunday this year was much happier for my lovely mother than it was last year. She is now reasonably settled in hospital at Market Bosworth & has the mobility of a wheelchair. She has company & care & no major worries. She is more interested now in others & more like her old delightful self.

25th March 1980 Tuesday

The most Reverend & Right Honourable Robert Alexander Kennedy Runcie yesterday became the 102nd Archbishop of Canterbury. After his enthronement he took the text for his sermon from St. Luke, Chapter 1. "….. and the Lord God shall give him the throne of his Father David."

27th March 1980 Thursday

Budget Day yesterday increased Vehicle Excise Licence from £50 to £60. It also replaced the present 4 monthly licence by a 6 monthly licence. Petrol is also up by 10p a gallon to £1-33p. There will also be further cuts in the number of Civil Servants.

28th March 1980 Friday

Johnson, Brenda Patricia (nee Clitheroe), 29, Broome Leys Avenue, Coalville, a devoted wife and mother, passed peacefully away March 28th at the Royal Marsden Hospital, London, after a long illness.
Funeral service at Christ Church, Coalville, on Thursday, April 3rd at 10 a.m. followed by cremation at Loughborough Crematorium.

Brenda (Aladdin) See 9th January 1969.

29th March 1980 Saturday

The Queen's allowance is now £2,716,300. The Queen Mother's allowance is now £244,000. The Duke of Edinburgh's allowance is £135,000. Princess Anne's allowance is now £85,000. Prince Andrew's allowance is now £20,000. Princess Margaret's allowance is now £82,000.

31st March 1980 Monday

The worst tragedy in the history of the North Sea Oil industry happened last Thursday at 6-30p.m. when a floating oil rig lost one of its 5 giant legs & turned completely upside down in a matter of minutes, entombing about 100 men. It happened in the Norwegian Ekofisk field.

2nd April 1980 Wednesday

April Fool Hewsie wept yesterday to be told by Mr Boreham, boss at work, that her latest staff report (written by Roy Ellison) showed that she was not as good as she should be as an E.O. at Gas Standards Branch. She did not exercise enough control, command or authority.

Note – This certainly was a humiliating experience. I stood firm & told him that I had done my best & could not do any better; but afterwards I was in tears, feeling that I was not appreciated & ready to look for another job. Throughout the coming year I applied for 3 different jobs, but all to no avail.

4th April 1980 Good Friday

Feeling hard done to & not appreciated for my true value at work, I am reminded today of all that Christ suffered at the hands of his fellow men.

If ever any-one was hard done to & not appreciated for his true worth it was the Lord himself who asked only that we love one another.

6th April 1980 Easter Sunday

Easter Sunday gave us again Psalm 118 which tells us that "…… I called upon the Lord in trouble; & the Lord heard me at large. The Lord is on my side ….. It is better to trust in the Lord than to put any confidence in man …… This is the day which the Lord hath made; we will rejoice and be glad in it."

8th April 1980 Tuesday

Scientists, testifying before the U.S. Senate energy & natural resources committee, have warned that the world could be facing an ecological disaster unless we control the amount of carbon dioxide pumped into the atmosphere.

Clearing the world's forests, & burning coal, oil & natural gas are the causes.

10th April 1980 Thursday

Unless a global strategy is developed to control the amount of carbon dioxide pumped into the atmosphere, within 40 or 50 years the Earth could be like a greenhouse. The polar ice caps would melt; the level of the oceans would rise & coastal towns would be flooded.

We must have trees.

12th April 1980 Saturday

North West Leicestershire District Council – Technical & Planning Services Department – Depot Clerk wanted at the Highfield Street Depot, Coalville. Grade Misc. 5. £3,375 - £3,585. I applied for this vacancy, and I have a salary right now of £5,700.

The District motto is "Ex Terra Opes."

14th April 1980 Monday

N. W. Leicestershire District was born on April Fool's Day 1974.

It is made up of 6 former authorities – Coalville Urban District Council (U.D.C.), Ashby-de-la-Zouch U.D.C., Ashby Woulds U.D.C., the Rural Districts of Ashby-de-la-Zouch & Castle Donington and the Parish of Ibstock. Total population = 76,400.

16th April 1980 Wednesday

What a beautiful spring this year. The whole of the Easter holiday was warm & sunny & everyone set to work with a will on the garden. Suddenly the world was re-awakened and burst into new life more dramatically than usual. Our magnolia, now 6 years old, also burst into bloom.

18th April 1980 Friday

Rhodesia, Britain's last African colony, rebellious & war-weary, finally attained recognised & legal independence at midnight last night & is now known by its African name of Zimbabwe. It becomes the 43rd member of the Commonwealth. The Revd. Canoon Banana is president.

20th April 1980 Sunday

"I bless God, I do find that I am worth more than ever I yet was, which is £6,200, for which the Holy name of God be praised." So wrote Samuel Pepys in his diary on 31st October 1666. The latest Civil Service pay rise takes the maximum E.O. salary to £6,745.

22nd April 1980 Tuesday

The Rotary Club of Wigston, No. 1248, District 107, invited 4 members of staff from Gas Standards Branch to their meeting at the Officers' Mess, Glen Parva. We had a most enjoyable social evening.

24th April 1980 Thursday

"Service above Self" – This is the motto of the Rotarians. The Wigston Rotary Club called their evening "Meet the Public Servants" & extended their fellowship to the Army, Prison Officers, Ministry of Agriculture & Fisheries, & D.H.S.S. as well as Gas Standards Branch.

26th April 1980 Saturday

America versus Iran. (See November 27th 1979)

The world waits with much more bated breath to see what fate will befall us all following an abortive attempt by the Americans to rescue the hostages still being held in Iran. Poor President Carter accepted sole responsibility for the decision to strike.

28th April 1980 Monday

In April 1975, Mum & I acquired our first petrol driven lawn mower - £42. After 5 years loyal service it is now much worse for wear, & so I decided to replace it with another identical model. The new mower cost £103. Such is the rate of inflation.

30th April 1980 Wednesday

Mum has an ulcerated leg which has become much worse lately & is now suffering considerable pain. She has drastic doses of pain killing tablets & looks very poorly at the moment. The palms of her hands, bearing many sharply defined crosses, tell the story of her suffering.

2nd May 1980 Friday

"Rejoice in the Lord alway; and again I say, rejoice." These joyful words from the Epistle of St. Paul to the

Philippians were given to us on Radio Leicester this morning as our "Thought for Today". How nice also to have "the peace of God, which passeth all understanding".

4th May 1980 Sunday
As the sister in hospital knelt at the feet of my mother to bathe & dress her ulcerated foot, I thought of Jesus, who after the last supper took a towel & girded himself. After that he poureth water into a basin & began to wash the disciples' feet & said, "Ye also ought to wash one another's feet." John, Chapter 13.

6th May 1980 Tuesday
America versus Iran = the Western World versus Islam = Luke-warm Christianity versus the devoted Moslem.
The lesson reading at church this week included the letters written to the 7 churches in Asia, including the letter to the "Luke-warm" church of the Laodiceans. (Revelation III)

8th May 1980 Thursday
Special Air Service troops (the S.A.S. – see 15th January 1976) this week were in action in the Iranian Embassy in London. A six-day siege ended when they were ordered into action to rescue 20 hostages who were about to be killed by terrorists. We watched live on television the whole action.

10th May 1980 Saturday
Cup Final Day. Second Division West Ham beat the mighty Arsenal 1 – 0. It was Arsenal's third successive appearance in the F.A. Cup Final. With an attendance of 100,000 the receipts hit the jackpot £700,000. The Cup was presented by the Duchess of Kent.

12th May 1980 Monday
"Jesus said – Whatever ye shall ask the Father in my name, he will give it you." John. 16. Yesterday was Rogation Sunday – asking Sunday. Our preacher at Ravenstone Church was the Venerable R. B. Cole, Archdeacon of Leicester, who is soon retiring. He gave a fine sermon on how to ask.

14th May 1980 Wednesday
The Venerable R. B. Cole stressed the difference between "Whatsoever ye shall ask the Father" and "Whatsoever ye shall ask the Father **in my name.**" The secret lies in being in tune with heaven & thinking of others. I thought of Job …. "And the Lord turned the captivity of Job, when he prayed for his friends."

16th May 1980 Friday
In 1964 we gave a children's concert in Ravenstone Institute. Eleven year old Diane Woodward was dancer & "choreographer". This week I went to the Town Hall, Ashby-de-la-Zouch, where **Diane King Academy of Dancing** put on a show with 85 children – produced & choreographed by **Diane.**

18th May 1980 Sunday
I thought of man – hopeless on this earth without God. And I thought of God – hopeless on this earth without man. Example – a garden looked after by God & man together.

"The heaven, even the heavens, are the Lord's; but the earth hath he given to the children of men." Psalm 115.

20th May 1980 Tuesday
The new Lord Mayor of Leicester is Mr Herbert Sowden. He hopes to plant an avenue of young oaks, named to commemorate the Queen Mother's 80th birthday – August 4th this year. "I take this opportunity to invite gifts of young oak trees – I thought eighty in number."

22nd May 1980 Thursday
A mighty oak is growing in our garden. Planted with loving care it now has a trunk 4 " high. Three splendid branches reach out & measure 5", 6" and 7". Already this fine tree is in leaf &
I look forward to the day when the birds of the air come & lodge in the branches.(Matt.13. 31)

24th May 1980 Saturday
Shareholder Hewsie received her first cheque from the British Petroleum Co. Ltd., £12 for the year ending 31st December 1979. I am one of 159,525 B P shareholders. The British Petroleum Co. Ltd. is the parent company of the B P group which has 1,300 subsidiary companies in 67 countries.

26th May 1980 Monday
"God, who as at this time didst teach the hearts of thy faithful people, by the sending to them the light of the Holy Spirit, grant us by the same Spirit to have a right judgement in all things, & evermore to rejoice in his Holy comfort." The joyful collect for yesterday - Whitsunday.

28th May 1980 Wednesday
Leicester City football team have ended the season in some degree of triumph. Having fallen in disgrace from the First Division they have now emerged triumphant as holders of the Second Division Cup.
The Lord Mayor said, "Make sure you bring another cup back next year."

30th May 1980 Friday
Peter Martin Hewes, son of Cousin Donald, was married in October 1966 to Miss Christine Hill. They now have three daughters – Sarah, Kirsty & Emma.
But sadly the marriage is now on the rocks & their lovely home in the grounds of the Hollies is now for sale. Asking price - £50,000.

1st June 1980 Trinity Sunday
I saw the Trinity yet again in a world map. Jerusalem was at the centre of a shamrock-like design – the great continent of Asia was one leaf, the great continent of Europe was another & the great continent of Africa was the third.

3rd June 1980 Tuesday
"Our forefathers Abraham – Isaac & Jacob." Notice again the Trinity. Abraham is the man of great faith – not a perfect man, but chosen by God for his faith. Isaac is the middle of the road man – just ordinary – the vast majority of mankind – and Jacob the go-getter – he represents those with ambition.

5th June 1980 Thursday

The planets begin to line up and - Whoosh! Mount St. Helens on the western coast of America blows her top. The volcano erupted 60,000 feet into the air & the huge cloud of smoke & ash floated halfway round the world. In the immediate neighbourhood ash fell by the ton.

7th June 1980 Saturday

Dear Madam,

<u>Depot Clerk</u>

With reference to your application for the above post, I have to inform you that the vacancy has now been filled & thank you for your interest – Signed, P. Brown.

9th June 1980 Monday

My 6 year-old little friend Joanne continues to visit me daily & is a constant source of joy & delight. She loves to play the piano or listen to a story or perform cartwheels or roll head over heels or play snakes & ladders or eat gingerbread men or draw a picture or be some-one else.

11th June 1980 Wednesday

As more & more people become out of work with firms cutting back or closing down, the chances of getting a job anywhere is getting harder.

We have a vacancy at the moment at Gas Standards for a Clerical Assistant & have been flooded with applications, mostly from sixteen year-old school leavers.

13th June 1980 Friday

N.W. Leics. District Council – Chief Executive & Clerk's Department – Clerical Assistant. Clerical 1 / 2 up to £4,356. Applications are invited for the above post within the Chief Executive & Clerk's Department. This is a new post created to deal with vehicle licensing matters, etc. I applied.

15th June 1980 Sunday

Yesterday was the Annual Garden Fete held in the beautiful grounds of Bosworth Park Infirmary. The weather was terrible but the rain stopped for a fine display of marching & playing from Leicester's pipe & drum band resplendent in their kilts. One piper played a tune just to my Mum.

17th June 1980 Tuesday

At Market Bosworth garden fete, I saw for the first time real horse shoes for sale. They were painted in a variety of colours & I bought two. One was silver & one was black. They were 50p each & the black one now has pride of place on the wall above "Rutlandshire".

19th June 1980 Thursday

Mary Moore is coming on Sunday to spend a week with me in Ravenstone.

I have taken a few days holiday to clean the house, room by room, from top to bottom – upstairs, downstairs & in my lady's chamber. All the brasses are gleaming bright, furniture polished, curtains washed & windows sparkling.

21st June 1980 Saturday

The Olympic Games this year are to be held in Moscow.

However, Russia's invasion of Afghanistan (only one step away from the vital oil supplies in the Middle East) has caused such unrest in the Western world, that many athletes have decided not to compete, & there is considerable tension all round.

23rd June 1980 Monday

Yesterday was our Sunday School Anniversary at Ravenstone. This year marks the 200th Anniversary of the founding of Sunday Schools by Robert Raikes in Gloucester in 1780.

We sang six songs including "God make my life a little light" & "One more step along the world I go."

25th June 1980 Wednesday

Another holiday on the Costa Ravo. Mary Moore (now aged 69) is spending a week in Ravenstone & visiting her many friends and relations.

Auntie Doris, still very mobile in her eighties, came for tea & then we all went to Molly Donaldson's to spend the evening in her gorgeous home.

27th June 1980 Friday

Wimbledon fortnight has come in the monsoon season this year. It not only thunders & lightens & pours heaven's hardest, it hails great hailstones. The best place to be on holiday at the moment is at home. The sun makes brief appearances, & the grass is so beautifully green.

29th June 1980 Sunday

Auntie Doris & I went to Ulverscroft Priory for an open air service where the Bishop of Leicester, the Rt. Revd. Cecil Richard Rutt was to preach. But the incessant rain meant the service had to be held indoors at St. Peter's Church Copt Oak. The Bishop spoke of monks & monasticism – from "monos" meaning alone.

1st July 1980 Tuesday

The Bishop spoke of the last prayer of Jesus when he asked God that "they all may be one; as thou Father art in me, & I in thee, that they also may be one in us." John 17. 21.

The Bishop said, "Let us pray that ……" but before he finished his sentence, the congregation disappeared, thinking he said, "Let us pray."

3rd July 1980 Thursday

My dear old Mum has now been away from home, in hospital, for a whole year. I visit her two or three times every week and sometimes I find her in tears – sometimes bright & cheerful. Her ulcerated foot, which was so bad a little while ago, is at last responding to treatment & beginning to heal.

5th July 1980 Saturday

Wimbledon fortnight ended today in the most exciting cliff-hanger battle I have ever seen on the centre court. Bjorn Borg, aged 24 from Sweden, won for the 5th consecutive year. He beat America's John McEnroe, aged 21, in a ding-dong battle which lasted 3 hours 53 minutes.

7th July 1980 Monday

Joanne has performed on the carpet once too often.

While no-one was looking she wet on the front room carpet & made a nasty smelly patch. I told her mother who said, "I'll give her a good hiding." So ends a beautiful relationship. "Give me a child until he is seven & I will give you the man."

9th July 1980 Wednesday
A Wedding Anniversary to beat all records. On July 9th 1900 John Orton, aged 24, married Harriet Harris, aged 22. What a remarkable couple. They are both devout Methodists & every day Mr Orton reads to his wife from the Bible they had as a wedding gift.

11th July 1980 Friday
Mr & Mrs John Orton were married at the parish church in Little Casterton, Rutland. They now live at Great Gidding in Cambridgeshire. We saw them on T V – a lovely couple, holding hands, & when asked about their ambition – "Love each other to the end."

13th July 1980 Sunday
Tomorrow I shall be 49 (7 x 7).
Number 7 is my special number, & I am reminded of the Whitsuntide hymn, "At length had fully come, on mystic circle borne, of seven times seven revolving days, the Pentecostal morn."
When I was 7 years old, my dad died. He was 49 (7 x 7).

15th July 1980 Tuesday
Mum was in tears on my birthday. She wept with pain & utter despair. As she sat in her wheelchair with other silent sufferers, she was in such discomfort & longed to be able to stand & walk. She longed for home & independence, for fresh air and freedom & joy instead of sorrow.

17th July 1980 Thursday
"Isabella's – 14, Friar Lane, Leicester. Dine & Dance the night away in the best appointed Night Club in England for £6-50p. Telephone 50649."
(See 17th November 1967)
This is our Motor Licence Office, which has been empty all these years since we left in the moonlight.

19th July 1980 Saturday
"Dine & Dance the night away at 14 Friar Lane, Leicester." I recall the times we worked long hours into the night every January in the days when all vehicle licences were due for renewal during the first 14 days of January. It was sometimes midnight before the cashiers managed to balance.

21st July 1980 Monday
Once again I have joined the ranks of Premium Bond holders. In one fell swoop I bought £100 worth.
"A bond is not eligible for inclusion in the prize draws held in respect of the first three calendar months following the month in which it is purchased." The National Debt Act 1972.

23rd July 1980 Wednesday
King Richard III who lost his crown & his kingdom in Leicestershire is now to be honoured in Leicester's Castle Gardens. A new £20,000 larger than life bronze statue will be unveiled on July 31st by the present Duke of Gloucester – the first Richard, Duke of Gloucester since King Richard III.

25th July 1980 Friday
Dear Miss Hewes,
Appointment of Clerical Assistant.
With reference to your application for the above position, an appointment has now been made & I am sorry that on this occasion you were not successful.
Signed, P. Briggs – Personnel Officer.

27th July 1980 Sunday
Saved again by the hand of Providence.
Hymn 657 reminds me again, "Praise to the Lord, who o'er all things so wondrously reigneth – shieldeth thee gently from harm, or when fainting sustaineth. Hast thou not seen how thy heart's wishes have been granted in what he ordaineth?" "Ponder anew what God can do."

29th July 1980 Tuesday
What encouragement I find in the hymns and Psalms we sing at church.
Psalm 37 says, "Trust in the Lord & do good; so shalt thou dwell in the land, and verily thou shalt be fed. Delight thyself also in the Lord, and he shall give thee the desires of thine heart. Commit thy way unto the Lord; trust also in him."

31st July 1980 Thursday
The Shah of Persia, Mohammad Reza Pahlavi, aged 60, King of Kings, Centre of the Universe, Shadow of the Almighty, Regent of God, & Light of the Aryans, died this week in exile in Egypt. Toppled from his peacock throne he was a broken man & his people rejoiced at his death.

2nd August 1980 Saturday
"The bloodsucker of the century is dead." Thus the people of Iran were officially informed of the death of the Shah. He tried to raise his people in one generation to the level of western civilisation, but he learned to his cost that culture & tradition win through in the end.
(He crowned himself.)

4th August 1980 Monday
President Sadat of Egypt treated the exiled Shah with every respect & gave him a state funeral. Huge wreaths were carried in procession shaped like peacocks in full display – in honour of the Shah's peacock throne. In London, his faithful followers held his portrait & decked it with flowers.

6th August 1980 Wednesday
£1,735-08p in favour of Elizabeth Hewes.
This is my Save as you Earn, now complete after 5 years saving £20 per month. Such is the rate of inflation that my "index-linked" savings have turned payments of £1,200 into £1,735-08p. So I am now ready to buy a new car with a new **W** suffix.

8th August 1980 Friday
D.V.L.C. Swansea have invited suggestions for the future format of Vehicle Registration Marks & Numbers. I wrote & said, "The answer I declare, would never raise a hair, if we all just reverse, and go straight on from

there." As an example I chose the number **A123 ABC**.

10th August 1980 Sunday
Mum & I went to St. Peter's Church, Market Bosworth, to morning service. How lovely to go with Mum to church again. The church is next door to Bosworth Park Infirmary. The first hymn we sang was No. 657 …. "Hast thou not seen how thy heart's wishes have been granted in what he ordaineth?"

12th August 1980 Tuesday
Received a reply from D.V.L.C. Swansea.

Dear Miss Hewes,

Mr. Bayly has asked me to thank you for your letter about the future format of vehicle registration marks. Your comments have been noted & will be taken into account before a final decision is made.

Yours Sincerely, C.E.Roberts –

Policy Branch.

14th August 1980 Thursday
As the third anniversary of the death of Elvis Presley approaches, his fans still idolise him & fill the "In Memoriam" column of the Leicester Mercury with their tributes –

*"**Presley**, Elvis Aaron, 1935 – 1977,*
Always and forever, we shall love thee eternally –
Love Joyce."

16th August 1980 Saturday
*"**Presley**, Elvis Aaron, died August 16th 1977.*
The years pass by but memories stay.
Quietly I remember you Elvis, every day –
Love Steph."

"Long after this & the summer is gone,
I'll remember you.
I'll be lonely, oh so lonely,
Living only to remember you." –
Mick, Val & Lisa Haywood. "House of Elvis"

18th August 1980 Monday
Our Sunday School outing this year is to be Alton Towers, near Uttoxeter.

After 2 years of cancelled outings, we have now managed to get a bus load sufficiently interested to go. We have 22 Sunday School children, 22 adults, 6 choir members & a few non-Sunday School children.

20th August 1980 Wednesday
A statue of Ethelfloeda, daughter of Kind Alfred, who expelled the Danes from Leicester in 968, went on display again today. The Lord Mayor of Leicester, Mr. Herbert Sowden, unveiled the Ethelfloeda Fountain in the new Dolphin Square.

A former statue in Victoria Park was stolen 2 years ago.

22nd August 1980 Friday
Roll of Honour
***Plantagenet**, Battle of Bosworth, August 22nd 1485. There died fighting bravely, Richard III, king, statesman, soldier, gentleman. "Loyalty binds me". Annual wreath laying, noon, August 22nd at new statue in Castle Gardens, all welcome. – Dorothy Cooke.*

Went on a guided walk from Leicester Cathedral to Castle Gardens to see the newly erected statue of Richard III. He looked very handsome – so unlike the pictures usually shown of him. It was a perfect summer evening walk & I saw so much in Leicester that I had never seen before.

24th August 1980 Sunday
Mum was 75 yesterday. The weather was kind & we were able to sit out of doors in the beautiful grounds of the hospital. Mum was subdued & rather sad & did not feel very well.

Today however she was much brighter & we had a lovely afternoon together in the sunshine.

26th August 1980 Tuesday
On Sunday morning I went with Pat, Evelyn & Sharon (Mary Blue's step-daughter) to St. James Church, Snibston.

Canon Oscroft talked of our Lord – a broken man, with head hanging down – not the proud champion leading us to heaven. I thought of my suffering broken Mum.

28th August 1980 Thursday
"You must come up to Scotland & let me take you on my boat on Loch Lomond" said the Scottish Area Gas Examiner to me on the telephone today.

"You must come to Hong Kong" said Mr Basu, a visitor from Hong Kong, whom I had the pleasure to take in my car to the station.

30th August 1980 Saturday
Two million people in Britain are now out of work. This is the highest total since the depression of the 1930s. And with the recession tightening its grip & increasing numbers of firms laying off workers, the outlook is grim. Where are we heading? Nuclear Energy, costing £40,000,000,000.

1st September 1980 Monday
Ethelfloeda has gone again.

There she was – a £350 bronze statue fitted with a special anti-vandal device which should have made her burglar proof – but she lasted only 10 days after being unveiled with due ceremony by the Lord Mayor.

I'm glad I managed to see her.

3rd September 1980 Wednesday
September 2nd is the date when Hindus remember the birth of Lord Krishna, who was born in a jail 5,000 years ago & smuggled out in a basket by his uncle.

The celebration known as Janmastami is at midnight – Indian time, so in Leicester the celebration starts 4 hours early at 8 p.m.

5th September 1980 Friday
Tomorrow is our Sunday School outing to Alton Towers.

We have booked a 53 seater bus & interest has gathered momentum until we now have more people than we have seats on the bus.

Mrs Bird's mother died this week, so she would like to take her father with her. I offered not to go.

7th September 1980 Sunday

Moore, Harold Arthur, The Red Lion, Horninglow, Burton-on-Trent, late of 52, Ibstock Road, Ravenstone, dearly loved son of Harold and the late Ellen Edith, loving brother of Betty, Margaret and brother-in-law of Derrick, passed away suddenly on September 7th after a short illness, in Perth Royal Infirmary, aged 52 years. Funeral service at St. John's Church, Horninglow, Burton-on-Trent, on Monday September 15th at 2 p.m. followed by cremation at Bretby Crematorium. Cortege will leave from 52, Ibstock Road, Ravenstone. In heavenly love abiding.

This is Harold – stalwart worker for Ravenstone Church for many years until he moved with his friend Dennis Collier to the Red Lion. He was Sunday School Superintendent until he left in 1971.

9th September 1980 Tuesday

Ethelfloeda was lost and is found. An anonymous telephone call led to her discovery.

With the statue was a message –

"It was the lager on Friday night that possessed us to move such a beautiful sight,

It wasn't for lust, and it wasn't for money, it was just at the time we thought it was funny."

11th September 1980 Thursday

"N. W. Leics. District Council Relief Cashier/Clerk – salary on scale rising to £3,990.

Applications are invited for the full time post of relief cashier/clerk in the Treasurer's Dept. Ashby-de-la-Zouch. Applicants should have experience in handling cash. The post will be based initially in Ashby but will be transferred to Coalville upon completion of new office extensions in approximately 12 months time. Applicants should hold a current driving licence. Closing date 23rd September 1980."

I applied.

15th September 1980 Monday

Harold's funeral today at Horninglow.

Ravenstone was represented by Mr Burne, Stan Taylor, Alan Roulston, Moyra Jones & me. The church was full & Harold's poor old dad wept as he followed the coffin. I wept to see him & thought of Jacob as his daughters walked with him, but could not comfort him.

17th September 1980 Wednesday

Sir Thomas White, one time Lord Mayor of London, today stands guard on one of the four corners of Leicester's clock tower.

When he died in 1566 he left £1,400 to form a charity fund which time & careful investment have converted into a current income of £40,000 a year. He wanted to encourage business,

19th September 1980 Friday

Sir Thomas White, 400 years after his death, is still helping others to launch themselves into a business career. His money is for young men in Leicester of "fair name and fame" to expand their business. Up to £2,000 is available – interest free for 9 years. Applicants must live in Leicester. Age 18 – 35.

21st September 1980 Sunday

"What shall I do?" The Rector of Ravenstone, the Revd. Leslie Buckroyd, gave a fine sermon based on the 4 occasions where this question is raised in the New Testament.

First, the rich young man, Matt. 19. Then another rich man, Luke 12. Saul of Tarsus, Acts 9, & the jailor, Acts 16. The answer is, "Believe on the Lord Jesus Christ."

23rd September 1980 Tuesday

Ashby Statutes, the great fair that takes over the whole of the street every September, is here again. I took 6 year old Joanne to gaze in wonder at all the flashing lights & share in the fun of the fair. She came home with a hydrogen filled balloon & brandy snap.

25th September 1980 Thursday

"Oyez, oyez, oyez." In May 1978, a contest was held in Leicester for a Town Crier.

Mr Norman Roberts, who was the winner, has gone from strength to strength & has now become World Champion. Mr Roberts of 26, Gorse Lane, Oadby, won the title in Halifax, Nova Scotia, Canada.

27th September 1980 Saturday

As the price of everything goes up & up – rates – electricity – fuel – food – clothing, I hesitate to spend all my hard earned savings in one fell swoop on a new car.

So I am marking time for a while & have decided to launch out into a deeper store of Premium Bonds, hoping for a catch.

29th September 1980 Monday

Mum & I went to the Harvest Festival Service yesterday at 10 a.m. in Market Bosworth Church.

Johnty & I went to the Harvest Festival Service yesterday at 3 p.m. at little St. Mary's, which holds only 35 congregation, & was just filled.

1st October 1980 Wednesday

Gas is going metric! Good old British Thermal Units per cubic foot will be Megajoules per cubic metre. 1 BTU/ft^3 = 0.03796 MJ/m^3.

With effect from 1st December 1980, Calorific Values must be expressed in MJ/m^3, but the Therm will continue in use and be defined as 105.5 megajoules.

3rd October 1980 Friday

"How are the mighty fallen." As was said so long ago of King Saul, so is now said in the boxing world of Muhammad Ali, formerly Cassius Clay. Possibly the most glittering career in boxing ended when he was beaten this week by Larry Holmes. Bruised & battered, "The Greatest" lost.

5th October 1980 Sunday

Marjorie Hayes, my next door neighbour for many years, now lives in style & comfort as the wife of George Merrill, who owns a thriving millinery in Coalville. They have a lovely home in Ravenstone & are very kind to me. They often ask me to have Sunday lunch with them. Marjorie's son Ian is now 13.

7th October 1980 Tuesday

Enid's birthday yesterday. She is now 53 & although

still as energetic as a teenager, she has reluctantly hung up her hockey boots this season because she feels out of place playing in a team where everyone else is so much younger. She wishes more people in her age group would continue to play.

9th October 1980 Thursday
Navrati, one of the main celebrations of the year for Hindus begins this week.
It is a 9 day festival of singing & dancing & is being celebrated in Leicester at 4 places -
1. The De Montfort Hall. 2. The Granby Halls. 3. A huge marquee near the cattle market. 4. Gipsy Lane.
Mahishasur was an evil demon. The 3 "super-powers" – Brahma, Vishnu & Shiva, created a goddess named Ambaji who fought the evil demon for 8 days & on the 9th day killed him. All the gods rejoiced & on earth people joined in the celebrations with singing & dancing. That is Navrati.

13th October 1980 Monday
Harvest Festival yesterday at Ravenstone Church marked my 22nd anniversary as a Sunday School teacher. A lovely sunny day when my 6 year old friend Joanne gladdened my heart with her spontaneous joie de vivre & song. She herself is a ray of sunshine & visits me daily.

15th October 1980 Wednesday
Dear Miss Hewes,
<u>Appointment of Relief Cashier/Clerk</u>
I thank you for your application for the above appointment and have to advise you that the post has now been filled.
Yours Sincerely, A. G. Meekings,
Deputy Treasurer.

17th October 1980 Friday
The Queen is now in Rome on a week long State Visit to Italy. They will see the Vatican & Genoa, Naples & Palermo. The Queen referred to Julius Cæsar & Shakespeare, whose plays were often set in Italy – from Rome to Messina, Venice & Verona, and Verdi's Macbeth.

19th October 1980 Sunday
"Luke, the beloved physician" (See the Epistle to the Colossians 4. 14.)
"Luke my fellow labourer" (Epistle to Philemon 1. 24.)
"Only Luke is with me" (2nd Epistle to Timothy). The Rector of Ravenstone, the Revd. L. Buckroyd, gave a fine sermon on St. Luke, physician & evangelist.

20th October 1980 Monday
Barnett. On October 20th 1980, suddenly at her home, The White House, Cossington, Lady Isobel Morag Barnett, wife of the late Geoffrey and dear mother of Alistair. Funeral service at St. Mary's Church, Knighton, Leicester, on Friday, October 24th at 12 noon, followed by private cremation. Family flowers only, please, but donations in lieu may be sent for her various charities c/o Mr G. Culshaw, 14 New Street, Leicester.

21st October 1980 Tuesday
St. Luke wrote the Gospel according to St. Luke and also the Acts of the Apostles. Thanks to him – a gentile – we know so much & yet only 12 words in the Bible tell us all we know of him – Luke, the beloved physician. Luke, my fellow labourer. Only Luke is with me.

23rd October 1980 Thursday
Tomorrow I shall be 18,000 days old. For my 18,000th birthday I have arranged a day's holiday from work.
With massive public spending cuts on the way, our work is being axed left, right & centre. Gas examiners are being given the chop all over the country.

25th October 1980 Saturday
"One, two, **thlree**" says Joanne, aged six. As she endeavours to distinguish between fingers and fumbs, Fursday and Thriday, she is a fountain of joy to me.
She has now learned the art of losing a game without being all upset, & if I beat her at "Draughts" says, "Well done!"

27th October 1980 Monday
Spent all day at work reading the Annual Reports issued by the British Gas Corporation, and before that the Gas Council, & then wrote an interesting précis of the development of the gas industry. I started in 1868, from gasworks to Natural Gas & measurement now in megajoules.

29th October 1980 Wednesday
From Italy, the Queen travelled to North Africa & is presently in Morocco where King Hassan, aged 51, is giving her what has been described as an Arabian nightmare.
She is kept waiting for meals & not treated at all with the respect she is used to. He certainly is a mad Arab.

31st October 1980 Friday
Twins in the family!
Latest Census Report says, "You may have heard the rumour – and here's the confirmation – Some-one (amended to Some-two) new have just arrived to change the population.
Andrew Thomas 6lbs 3ozs and Helen Clare 6lbs 10ozs to Shirley & Julian."

2nd November 1980 Sunday
Joanne (aged 6) and I have now become star-gazers. We find the seven stars of the Plough   part of the constellation of Ursa Major – the Great Bear, & with the help of our star-gazing book find other animals who roam the heavens. At the moment Pegasus is riding high.

4th November 1980 Tuesday
A new President for America! Ronald Wilson Reagan, born 6th February 1911, was today elected as the 40th President of the United States. Formerly a film star, he will officially take over as President next January.
As he will then be nearly 70, he may well die in office. (See 3rd January 1980)

6th November 1980 Thursday
As the British Government presses for more & more cuts in the number of Civil Servants, Gas Standards Branch are now considering the possibility of chopping themselves off from the Department of Energy &

"branching out" as an independent body under the auspices of British Gas.

8th November 1980 Saturday

Leicester's 40,000 Hindus, Sikhs & Jains yesterday celebrated Diwali, the colourful festival of lights. Today is their new year 2037, in a lunar calendar. The legend behind the celebration is slightly different for Hindus & Sikhs but each recognises the triumph of good over evil.

10th November 1980 Monday

Yesterday was Remembrance Sunday & the Rector of Ravenstone, the Revd. L. Buckroyd, spoke of war & peace. He spoke of the coming of Christ when all the Angels sang, "Glory to God in the Highest, & on Earth Peace." The risen Lord Jesus said to his disciples, "Peace be unto you."

12th November 1980 Wednesday

"Rejoice in the Lord always and again I say rejoice …. And the peace of God which passeth all understanding shall keep your hearts & minds through Christ Jesus." St. Paul wrote these words to the Philippians (Chapter 4) to sum up perfectly the "Peace" of the God of Peace.

14th November 1980 Friday

Spacecraft Voyager I has reached Saturn to send mortals on Earth photographs they have never seen before.
The rings of Saturn defy all scientific knowledge & one seems like a coil of rope. There are hundreds of rings & ringlets, some spoked, some jagged, some smooth.

16th November 1980 Sunday

Took Joanne yesterday to Leicester Cathedral for the annual Children's Festival. There was a procession of banners depicting the saints of the different parishes. We sang "Rejoice in God's Saints …." & then Joanne rejoiced to see the city lights & moving escalators.

18th November 1980 Tuesday

What a wealth of wisdom lies in the Book of Ecclesiasticus (in the Apocrypha).
How I loved reading for the lesson this week Chapter 11, "There is one that laboureth, and taketh pains, & maketh haste, & is so much the more behind etc……..wisdom knowledge & love are from God."

20th November 1980 Thursday

Two nights in London! Stayed again at 11, Cardinal Mansions, Carlisle Place, where I had every comfort including electric blanket.
Went primarily for a "Registry Seminar" at Thames House South, where I enjoyed meeting staff again from both Thames House South Registry and Library.

22nd November 1980 Saturday

While I went to Thames House South, the Queen, on her 33rd wedding anniversary, went to the State Opening of Parliament. There I was, practically next door, & didn't have a chance to see her.
She said, "My Government look forward to the accession of Greece to the E.E.C."

24th November 1980 Monday

Greece will join the European Community on 1st January 1981. This will bring the number of member countries to 10.
I thought of the beast with 7 heads & 10 horns …. "and power was given unto him to continue 42 months." This beast would bring an overall dictator – 666.

26th November 1980 Wednesday

Charles Panati, a leading American scientific journalist, predicts in 6 years time sleep patterns will determine the exact time of a person's death.
In 7 years time vitamin E will be used to prevent lung cancer. By the year 2020, women could give birth at 60 & everyone live to be 110.

28th November 1980 Friday

Southern Italy this week has suffered a major earthquake. Every day brings news of more people being brought out alive from underneath a mountain of debris. Thousands have died & many of the dead cannot be identified. The homeless are cold & desolate.

30th November 1980 Sunday

What a sad world we live in. It is so very, very sad to see the survivors of the dreadful earthquake in Southern Italy as they embrace their dead loved ones. Huddled together, they are battered by the elements, homeless & without proper food supplies, helpless & hopeless.

2nd December 1980 Tuesday

Our Annual Christmas Fair in Ravenstone Village Institute & our 9th effort with a stall for the Sunday School. Not a very good effort this year. Diane Roberts (teacher) and I held the fort & made only £8-65p. Mr Brooks took over the role of Father Christmas.

4th December 1980 Thursday

Reynolds, George Herbert, 5a Leicester Road, Ravenstone, passed away suddenly on December 4th, the beloved husband of Joyce, dearest father of Stuart and Angela, Keith and Fiona, much lived granddad of Neil. Funeral service at Ravenstone Parish Church on Wednesday December 10th at 1-30 p.m. followed by interment in the churchyard.

This is George, aged 62,
Who used to work for Mr Prew,
A farmer here in Ravenstone,
Where Cocky worked – my very own
Beloved Cocky, mine for sure;
But I loved Brian Lamming more.

6th December 1980 Saturday

Auntie Belle's brother George, aged 83, is now in Bosworth Park Infirmary. Auntie Belle, aged 85, a very elegant & charming old lady, and I went on a joint visit to visit George & Mum. We all sat together in the therapy room where Mum had just made a pretty Christmas flower arrangement.

8th December 1980 Monday

Office Notice 173/80.
Thames Tidal Flooding: There is a continuing possibility that in exceptional weather conditions the level of the Thames might rise above the present flood defences, putting at risk 45 square miles in Greater London. This

includes Thames House South.

The tidal barrier at present under construction at Woolwich will eventually contain the threat of flooding, but completion of the barrier is not expected before late 1982. Emergency accommodation facilities have been earmarked in Turnstile House, High Holburn.

12th December 1980 Friday

"Son of Rudolph", Leicestershire's new Christmas fund raiser, comes to town tomorrow.

A city legend, the Rudolph story started in 1949 when a fireman found a model cow at a local sports ground. It was transformed into a reindeer & with a motorised sleigh captivated Leicester.

14th December 1980 Sunday

Took Joanne, aged 6, to Leicester yesterday to see Rudolph. We saw him arrive at the clock tower at 10 a.m. & oh how we loved him! Joanne stroked him for about ½ hour. He is perfect. He can move his neck, his face, his ears; open & shut his eyes; & lets the children kiss him.

Santa Knew Her Dad!

Mr Hurt of Enderby recalls Leicester Fire Station Officer Tommy Kershaw, one of the main driving forces behind the original Rudolph project and also Father Christmas on the reindeer's sleigh, was a wizard with electrics and animated displays. "The display firm where I worked used Tommy's ingenuity," he says.

Mr Hurt remembers going to Tommy Kershaw's house where he kept a large stuffed polar bear (understood to have once been used to promote Fox's Glacier Mints) in the bedroom. "The bear moved its head and growled when the heat of your hand passed near it," he explains. One year, Mr Hurt made some acrylic stars for the sides of Rudolph's sleigh. He took his small daughter to see Rudolph in the Town Hall Square and when Santa saw him in the crowd he stood up and gave him the thumbs up sign. He shouted, "The stars are just the job, Tony!" says Mr Hurt. "My daughter was flabbergasted that Santa knew her dad!"

16th December 1980 Tuesday

The front bedroom is being decorated this week. From Scandecor Ltd., 3, Armadale Road, Feltham, Middlesex, I have chosen a Palm Beach scene mural which covers the whole of one wall. The room was last decorated in February 1964 by Philip Bancroft. This time it is Barker and Weston.

18th December 1980 Thursday

Mr Ellis, the Chief Gas Examiner, & his wife Elaine, entertained Linda, Rose & me to a slap up Christmas luncheon at the Old Barn Inn, Glooston, near Market Harborough.

Situated in the beautiful Welland Valley this 16th Century inn had a huge fireplace & log fire.

20th December 1980 Saturday

Went to Snibston School to see my little 6 year old friend Joanne in the Christmas concert.

I saw the school as it was 45 years ago when I was there in the Infants' Class.

Then, at night, I dreamed of the future & saw Reevsie

mourning the loss of Phyllis, her younger sister, who is a twin.

22nd December 1980 Monday

Liking nothing but the best, we have waited to have a spanking new fitted carpet in the front bedroom.

But poor old Mum cannot enjoy the comforts of her own home, being confined to a wheelchair in hospital. How she would love to "run & not be weary" to "walk & not faint". Isaiah 40. 31.

24th December 1980 Wednesday

"Please convey to the Worshipful Master, Officers & Brethren of the Grace Dieu Lodge, my warmest thanks for their Christmas gift, which was such a lovely surprise & very much appreciated." I wrote this for Mum to send to Coalville Freemasons. My dad was a Freemason & sowed the seed for us to reap.

26th December 1980 Friday

Pat & Evelyn took under their wing the widow (Doris Roberts) & three old maids for Christmas Day – Aunt Dos aged 78, Katherine aged 76, and me aged 49.

How lovely to meet Katherine, a lady who had travelled the world & had such interesting tales to tell. She was grand.

28th December 1980 Sunday

Mary Blue & Murdo entertained us for tea & the evening on Boxing Day. There was Doris Roberts (Evelyn's sister-in-law), Pat & Evelyn, the 3 children Murdo, Sharon & Scott & me. We laughed & laughed as we played "Give us a Clue" – a miming game.

P.S. I forgot to mention Aunt Dos also.

30th December 1980 Tuesday

It was a joy to share in the Holy Communion Service at 9 a.m. on Christmas Day in dear little St. Mary's Church, Snibston, where we remembered "The birth, death, passion & resurrection" of Christ all in one & the same service.

Here my Mum & Dad were married & here I was Christened.

* * *

Wedding Anniversaries

First Cotton, Second Paper, Third Leather, Fourth Flowers, Fifth Wood, Sixth Candy, Seventh Copper, Eighth Bronze, Ninth Pottery, Tenth Tin, Eleventh Steel, Twelfth Linen, Thirteenth Lace, Fourteenth Ivory, Fifteenth Crystal, Twentieth China, Twenty-Fifth Silver, Thirtieth Pearl, Thirty-Fifth Coral, Fortieth Ruby, Forty-Fifth Sapphire, Fiftieth Gold, Sixtieth Diamond, Seventieth Platinum.

* * *

Ravenstone = Hrafn's Settlement

* * *

1981

2ⁿᵈ January 1981 Friday

Here I am – Elizabeth Hewes – aged 49, now an old maid, weighing in the New Year at eleven stone. Since April last year, when I was April Fool Hewsie, I have acquired the Middle Age Spread. Then for the last time I was like slim-line Rachel. (See Genesis 31. 35.)

4ᵗʰ January 1981 Sunday

1981 has in its favour the fact that it is divisible by 7. My best beloved Brian Lamming was born on 7ᵗʰ January. My beloved brother Rob was born on 21ˢᵗ January & Cocky, my first true love, was born on 28ᵗʰ January. My perfectly balanced partner would be born on 14ᵗʰ January.

6ᵗʰ January 1981 Tuesday

Joanne, who will be 7 years old on 7ᵗʰ March, has now learned how to do simple cryptic clue crosswords which I design.

She can find "Something very cold in Le**ice**ster", "Where a baby sleeps in S**cot**land", "Boy seen in ap**ron**", "Upside down pets", "Ten backwards" etc.

8ᵗʰ January 1981 Thursday

To enhance the beauty of our newly decorated front bedroom I have now bought a beautiful gilt edged mirror 4 feet x 3 feet. It was in the January sales reduced by 10% from £135 to £122, plus £3 to be delivered and put up on the wall. A real bargain at £125.

10ᵗʰ January 1981 Saturday

Today I saw another bargain in the January sales – carpet remnant 11 feet by 9 feet in pretty pink, reduced from £80 to £40. I snapped this up for the bathroom to replace the tatty old piece of carpet which Pat & I put down in January 1973 & was never very good.

12ᵗʰ January 1981 Monday

Like Little Red Riding Hood, my little friend Joanne comes in the dark & in the snow to knock on my door, She has such enthusiasm for all that she does & we go out into the darkness to gaze in wonder at the night sky. Now is the time to see Orion the hunter with his belt of 3 stars.

14ᵗʰ January 1981 Wednesday

Went to the Haymarket Theatre, Leicester, & saw from the front row a superb production of Gigi. I quote, "The Haymarket Theatre has acquired through successes like Oliver, My Fair Lady, Camelot, Oklahoma & Joseph, a national reputation for producing possibly the finest large musicals in the country."

15ᵗʰ January 1981 Thursday

I now have a cassette player to give me the music of my choice.

How I love listening to the music of Tchaikovsky – to the beautiful music of Swan Lake & the Nutcracker which includes the delightful "Dance of the Sugar Plum Fairy" which Joanne dances to without any prompting.

16ᵗʰ January 1981 Friday

Mohammed the prophet was born in Mecca, according to tradition, in 570 A.D. Leicester's Muslim community will be celebrating Mohammed's birthday this weekend with two days of festivities. The Archangel Gabriel appeared to him & said, "Thy Lord is the Most Bountiful who teaches by the pen."

18ᵗʰ January 1981 Sunday

"I will greatly rejoice in the Lord, my soul shall be joyful in my God; for he hath clothed me with garments of salvation, he hath covered me with the robe of righteousness ..... as the garden causeth the things that are sown in it to spring forth, so the Lord God will cause righteousness to spring forth." (Isaiah. Chapter 61.)

20ᵗʰ January 1981 Tuesday

"Finally, my brethren, rejoice in the Lord." (Philippians, Chapter 3.)

The 2 lessons I have read this month at church have emphasised – "Rejoice in the Lord."

St. Paul defines "righteousness" as that which is through the faith of Christ, which is of God.

22ⁿᵈ January 1981 Thursday

"Waltzes from Vienna", the story of Johann Strauss, is the show chosen this year for Coalville Amateur's production in March. Like the Queen, I now need my specs to read the script in my role as prompter. This show culminates in the Finale Act 3 with "The Blue Danube".

24ᵗʰ January 1981 Saturday

America rejoiced this week at the freeing of 52 American hostages held in captivity in Iran since November 1979. They were released as the new Republican President Ronald Reagan was being sworn in. Aged 69, he is the 40ᵗʰ & the oldest to take office.

26ᵗʰ January 1981 Monday

Took Joanne to the Concordia Theatre, Hinckley, to introduce her to the magic of the stage. We saw Roy Johnson playing Widow Twanky in the pantomime "Aladdin".

She was fascinated by the lighting effects & mystified by the changing scenery, but had problems with her self-raising seat.

28ᵗʰ January 1981 Wednesday

What a sad world it is when business starts to boom in Nuclear Bomb shelters. Even the government is advising people how to prepare for survival in case of Nuclear War.

The shelters are grotesque & remind me of "Aida" where two lovers are buried alive together in a sealed tomb.

30ᵗʰ January 1981 Friday

Polly Alexandra, born on 24ᵗʰ January is the latest member of the family.

Weighing in at 5lbs 1oz she was 6 weeks premature. Born to Michael & Sheena, she is sister to Sam and Lucy; & Bunting's 6ᵗʰ grandchild.

My dad has now produced 9 great-grandchildren, but none named Hewes.

1st February 1981 Sunday
Grandpa Hewes had 6 sons & 2 daughters. His sons all married & produced 8 boys and 9 girls. While the girls reproduced boys, the boys reproduced girls, & the name of Hewes, which at one time was so abundant, in two or three generations almost disappeared.

3rd February 1981 Tuesday
Leicester City football team came home triumphant in May last year as holders of the Second Division Cup & were promptly back in the First Division.
This year they have gone from bad to worse & have lost practically every game. Third Division Exeter knocked them out of the cup.

5th February 1981 Thursday
"What is innus?" asked the child after a service in church. Was it used by God when he did his cleaning?
He had distinctly heard the priest say, "O God, make clean our hearts within us." Such are the problems when the ears alone try to do the job.

7th February 1981 Saturday
My darling Mum is meeting people in hospital who knew the world when she was young.
She has met people who knew Reg (my dad, who this year would be 92!). She has met someone who knew her as Mary Sketchley & she has met someone who knew my brother, Rob.

9th February 1981 Monday
Joanne went with me yesterday to visit Mum at Bosworth Park Infirmary. The Sister made Joanne a real nurse's cap which she brought home & then became a little nurse. I made her a nurse's apron & she looked lovely. – "Of such is the Kingdom of Heaven."

11th February 1981 Wednesday
Prince Charles made an official visit to Leicester & was given a very warm welcome. The sun shone all day long & young girls kissed him.
Having recently made a tour of India he was able to communicate with the Indian community of Leicester, & even joined in the Indian stick dancing.

13th February 1981 Friday
I am now building up a lovely selection of music to listen to on my cassette player. My choice so far includes a collection of the best Military Music, "The World of Charlie Kunz – Piano", Music of Johann Straus & Tchaikovsky. I much prefer this sort of music to the popular music of the present day.

15th February 1981 Sunday
My darling Mum, who has given me her all, has now suggested that our house & home is transferred from her name to mine.
"We brought nothing into this world, & it is certain we can carry nothing out." I Timothy 6. 7. My Mum is so honest & generous & must surely have treasure in heaven.

17th February 1981 Tuesday
Such is my mother's genuine love and generosity to me that she hopes the house will be a blessing & not a burden to me. Such was her honesty when I was a child that she did not want me to believe in Father Christmas. "Seek ye the truth and the truth shall make you free."

19th February 1981 Thursday
Gas did not go metric in December 1980 as originally forecast. But all is now set for metrication to take effect from 1st April this year. An announcement in the Leicester Mercury says that the calorific value of gas supplied by the B.G.C. on or after 1st April 1981 in the East Midlands shall be 38.3 mj/metre^3.

21st February 1981 Saturday
Gas supplied by the British Gas Corporation from the North Sea is good dry gas with a calorific value at present of about 1035 British Thermal Units per cubic foot. This being interpreted into metric units is 38.6 megajoules per cubic metre. Some gas is wet & some partial dry. (As in East Midlands).

Note – Working at Gas Standards Branch, I am well acquainted with the great 19th Century scientist J. P. Joule (1818 – 1889) who gave his name to the new standard unit of heat.

23rd February 1981 Monday
"Charles Will Marry Diana – Official"
"It is with the greatest pleasure that the Queen and the Duke of Edinburgh announce the betrothal of their beloved son, the Prince of Wales, to the Lady Diana Spencer, daughter of the Earl Spencer & the Honourable Mrs Shand Kydd."

25th February 1981 Wednesday
Lady Diana Spencer was born on 1st July 1961. She is now 19 years old & is to marry the 32 year old heir to the throne.
So Lady Diana, after the wedding, will become Her Royal Highness the Princess of Wales & this title will not be for Princess Marie-Astrid. (See 16th June 1977)

27th February 1981 Friday
While everyone is delighted with Prince Charles' choice of a wife, Mum & I do not think she is the best choice in the world. Mum is an excellent judge of character – she does not trust those who are too sweet & sugary, & both she & I suspect that Lady Diana loves "for richer" & her own glory.

2nd March 1981 Monday
Final rehearsal this evening for Coalville Amateurs' "Waltzes from Vienna".
As prompter, sitting with the orchestra, centre stage, I enjoy every word & detail. There are no Prima Donna tantrums, just one big happy family who give their all, & move me to tears.

4th March 1981 Ash Wednesday
"Waltzes from Vienna" – in a world of violence & unrest, how lovely to be transported to another world where music & love & peace reign supreme.
Every year I rejoice with Coalville Amateurs during the week of the show. It is such a wonderful concentration of team-work.

6th March 1981 Friday

Where is my Parker 51 pen? I have searched the house and it is nowhere. Is it possible that it has been stolen? Is it possible that my little friend Joanne has taken it? My little friend is 7 years old tomorrow & I shower her with gifts. She has the complete run of the house.

Note – The pen which Cocky gave me for my 21st birthday is lost, never to be seen again.

8th March 1981 Sunday

The Rector, the Revd. Leslie Buckroyd, spoke this evening of "The good man of the house." St. Mark, Chapter 14, verse 14. He suggested that this may have been the house where St. Mark lived. Was the house where Jesus had his last supper the same house where the Apostles received the Holy Ghost?

10th March 1981 Tuesday

Budget Day! Petrol went up from £1-34p to £1-54p – the biggest tax increase on record. Car Tax went up from £60 to £70. Cigarettes – beer, also up. The country certainly is in a sorry state with more & more unemployment & the cost of living ever rising.

12th March 1981 Thursday

"Deed of Gift"

Mrs M. Hewes to Miss E. Hewes of messuage or tenement situate & being No. 27 Leicester Road Ravenstone in the County of Leicester. The Grantor is seised of the property hereinafter described for an estate in fee simple free from incumbrances .....

So is worded Mum's transfer of the house to my name.

14th March 1981 Saturday

"In consideration of her nature love and affection for the Donee the Grantor hereby conveys unto the Donee all that messuage or tenement with the yard garden outbuildings and appurtenances thereto belonging known as No. 27 Leicester Road Ravenstone."

My Mum gave me her all.

16th March 1981 Monday

The Civil Service on Strike. 400,000 out – Union Members at certain key Government sites are now on permanent strike, including naval supplies and dockyards, D.H.S.S., Driving Test Centres, ports and air-ports, Inland Revenue, Customs & Excise, Ministry of Defence.

18th March 1981 Wednesday

A nurse at Bosworth Park Infirmary said to me today, "Your mother is so lovely. She is no trouble at all."

No longer the rebel she was 2 years ago, Mum is now a model patient. She has now given up all hope of ever living at home again, & is able to calm others who are in great distress.

20th March 1981 Friday

From the window of St. David's Ward at Bosworth Park Infirmary, I watched a farmer rounding up his sheep & his lambs into a barn where they were shut in for the night. The naughty little lambs skipped & ran away & one had to be retrieved from the farthest corner of the field & carried home rejoicing.

22nd March 1981 Sunday

The Revd. Buckroyd, Rector of Ravenstone, spoke tonight of the Good Shepherd looking for his lost sheep. He said that man has been trying to hide from God ever since Adam hid in the Garden of Eden. He mentioned Zaechaeus hiding in the tree, & referred to Psalm 139, "Wither shall I go from thy spirit?"

24th March 1981 Tuesday

"Wither shall I go from thy spirit?" or wither shall I flee from thy presence? If I ascend into heaven, thou art there; if I make my bed in hell, behold thou art there. If I take the wings of the morning & dwell in the uttermost parts of the sea, even there shall thy hand lead me & thy right hand shall hold me."

26th March 1981 Thursday

Yesterday we had a Holy Communion service at 7 p.m. at little St. Mary's, Snibston. March 25th is "The Annunciation of the Blessed Virgin Mary", the day when the Angel Gabriel said, "Hail Mary". It was the first time I had ever been to little St. Mary's in the dark.

28th March 1981 Saturday

Watched the little lambs again at Market Bosworth. Saw one standing on the back of its mother who was lying down resting. When it was time for them all to go into the barn at

4-30 p.m. they were quickly rounded up and only one needed to be carried. He was limping.

30th March 1981 Monday

The Social Democratic Party was launched officially on March 26th 1981.

This is a new political party formed chiefly from members of parliament who disagree with the way their former party is heading. The Labour Party is going too far to the left & the SDP is more liberal.

1st April 1981 Wednesday

The London Marathon at the weekend was from Greenwich to Buckingham Palace.

7,000 people took part in this race which was 26 miles 385 yards. A million people cheered them all the way through 66 closed roads, cheering & ringing bells & spurring them on.

3rd April 1981 Friday

£1,000 in Premium Bonds. This is how far I have launched out at the rate of £100 per month over the past 10 months & this is as deep as I expect to go. With this amount I am hoping to win something. It is a gamble where you may win nothing at all or £100,000.

5th April 1981 Sunday

Census Day. This is the day which comes once every ten years. Mum & I have both been included for our home address at 27, Leicester Road, Ravenstone. The form says, "Include any person in hospital" & then asks where did you spend this night – at home or elsewhere.

7th April 1981 Tuesday

The 1981 Census has cost £50 million & at least one life. The unruly rebels of Northern Ireland have refused to complete their census forms & have made a public exhibition of burning them, together with an effigy of British Prime Minister Margaret Thatcher. They murdered a census enumerator.

9th April 1981 Thursday

Census enumerators have had some hair-raising experiences including being raped, being chased across the field by a bull, butted by a goat, hissed at by geese. One had to climb a mountain, one had to go by boat to the middle of a loch & one even encountered a cave-man up in Scotland.

11th April 1981 Saturday

House for sale! Our neighbours, Keith Carter, his wife Margaret & teen-age son Simon, who moved in on June 3rd 1974, are now ready for off. They are hoping to buy a house with a garage & somewhere to park their caravan. They have been good neighbours for the past 7 years.

13th April 1981 Monday

Voyager I has shown us Titan, the largest moon in the solar system, which is the outermost moon out of 15 moons which go round Saturn. Titan is waiting, as it were, in the wings to warm up to life in 41,000 years time, when Earth is swallowed up.

15th April 1981 Wednesday

When Earth is swallowed up by the Sun in 41,000 years time, the Sun will be bigger & hot enough to support life on Titan before it then gets smaller & smaller & disappears altogether. The oceans on Titan are liquid gas and it rains methane.

17th April 1981 Good Friday

The Rector of Ravenstone, the Revd. Leslie Buckroyd, spoke today of Judas Iscariot.
Judas was "treasurer" (he had the bag – John 13) He was like a member of the National Front – out with the Romans – and Satan was able to enter into him because he allowed himself to be tempted.

19th April 1981 Easter Sunday

Neither God nor Satan can tell us what to do if we will not listen.
Abraham Lincoln said, "No man is good enough to govern another man without that other's consent." And Joshua said, "Choose you this day whom ye will serve .... As for me & my house, we will serve the Lord." (Joshua 24)

21st April 1981 Tuesday

We are free to make our own decisions – free to choose. Jesus said to his disciples, "Ye have not chosen me, but I have chosen you." (John 15. 16) and Psalm 25 says, "What man is he that feareth the Lord? - him shall He teach in the way that he shall chose."

23rd April 1981 Thursday

The world's first space liner made a successful maiden voyage this month. John Young aged 50, and Bob Crippen aged 43, were the first Americans in space for 6 years. A short 2 day trip into orbit at 16,000 m.p.h. then landing like an aeroplane at 220 m.p.h. on a 7 mile runway.

25th April 1981 Saturday

Chipperfield's Circus came to Oadby Racecourse this week.
I took Joanne, aged 7, to introduce her to the world of trapeze stars & to see the many animals including polar bears, elephants, tigers, camels, horses, even two huge pigs, beautiful parrots & a baby llama, 6 days old.

27th April 1981 Monday

Two and a half million people in Britain are now out of work – i.e. more than 10% of the working population. In April last year 1 ½ million were out of work & in August last year 2 million were out of work. And yet the Civil Servants, who are lucky to have a job, are continually going on strike.

29th April 1981 Wednesday

"Oh, to be in England, now that April's there" said Robert Browning. (1812 – 1889)
Last weekend an unexpected Arctic blizzard struck & absolutely wrecked the electric power grid in Leicestershire. With poles at jaunty angles & cables down everywhere, it meant a prolonged black-out.

1st May 1981 Friday

Britain's longest lasting marriage, which began at Little Casterton village church Rutland, in 1900, ended this week with the death of 103 year old Mrs Orton (See 11th July 1980).
Mr & Mrs Orton celebrated their record breaking 80th wedding anniversary in their own home last July.

3rd May 1981 Sunday

"God hath chosen the foolish things of the world to confound the wise; and God hath chosen the weak things of the world to confound the things which are mighty; and base things of the world & things which are despised hath God chosen, yea and things which are not, to bring to nought things that are." I Corinthians 1. 27.

5th May 1981 Tuesday

County Council elections this week (which come once every 4 years) showed a dramatic swing away from Conservatism after two years of Margaret Thatcher (The Iron Lady) as Prime Minister. She rules with a rod of iron, and relentlessly pursues her course, convinced she is right.

7th May 1981 Thursday

Cup Final Day this year ended in a 1-1 draw. Manchester City were playing Tottenham (Spurs). Tommy Hutchison created a piece of Cup Final history by scoring both goals.
The Queen Mother (aged 80) was there to present the cup & receipts totalled £703,250.

9th May 1981 Saturday

My dad died when he was aged 49 years, 9 months and 25 days.
That is how old I am today.
The Reverend Wallace wrote of my dad, "He served his England, served his fellowmen, because he loved & served his God & Christ. So he was loved & honoured by his friends. Then he passed. Now he is standing at the Tryst and answering true & unafraid, "Lord, I am here."

Captain Bamber of the Salvation Army wrote of my dad:
"Many the hearts that chill at his absence;
from many skies the sun will have gone;
Still there is left us memory's sweet incense
pointing the way to heaven's 'Well done'."

13th May 1981 Wednesday
Leslie Hale wrote of my dad, "I never remember an unkind word. To his advice & guidance & help I owe much. It was Reg who helped to found my practice, Reg who introduced me to my wife, Reg who helped me to build my first house & to provide me with an office.
I am not a man who makes friends readily & Reg was one of the few that I had – and certainly the closest & the finest & the best. Reg has left behind him the most that any man can hope to leave – the affection of his friends, the respect of all who knew him & the gratitude of hundreds."

17th May 1981 Sunday
Mary Blue's two children from her first marriage, Steven (13) and Karen (10) had a rare get together this week. They were both at Pat & Evelyn's today, where I joined them for Sunday lunch.
Steven is a Leicestershire lad & Karen is a Bedfordshire lassie with a delightful Bedfordshire accent.

19th May 1981 Tuesday
We live in a world of violence and disquiet. Every day someone is blown up in Northern Ireland. There has been an attempt to assassinate President Reagan, & also an attempt to assassinate the Pope. Our royal family & all top people need to be on their guard day & night.

21st May 1981 Thursday
Climbed with Joanne (aged 7) 138 steps to the top of Loughborough Carillon. It was a bit scary as we went round & round, up a spiral staircase which seemed to close in on you, but we made it to see the massive bells at the top. We also saw a peacock in spectacular display.

23rd May 1981 Saturday
"The Yorkshire Ripper", the man who murdered 13 women & attempted to murder seven others, was yesterday sentenced to life imprisonment.
Peter William Sutcliffe, aged 34, was obsessed by prostitutes. They held some fatal fascination for him & roused him to murder them.

25th May 1981 Monday
Shareholder Hewsie has sold her shares. Disillusioned with the amount of interest they made I have found a stock-broker in Leicester – Hill Osborne & Co., & managed to sell them for slightly more than the price I paid for them. I bought them for £363 & sold them for £388.

27th May 1981 Wednesday
Pat & Evelyn now belong to St. James Church, Coalville, which is twinned with Mary de Castro in Leicester.
This week I have been introduced to a service in Mary de Castro which is very "High Church" where for the first time in my life I have learned how to genuflect properly.

29th May 1981 Friday
Ascension Day yesterday and High Mass at St. Mary de Castro, Leicester, where the Bishop of Leicester gave a fine sermon in which he explained how the Ascension was neither the end nor the beginning, but the very centre of all that Christ came to earth for.

31st May 1981 Sunday
Jesus said, "It is expedient for you that I go away; for if I go not away, the Comforter will not come unto you." John 16. 7. The Bishop emphasised the word "go". Not only must Jesus go, but his last instruction also was to "go & teach all nations". Matthew 28. 19.

2nd June 1981 Tuesday
No longer like children dependant on another, the Ascension prepares us to stand on our own two feet & speak up for ourselves. Christ did not say "Cheerio – I'll see you later." He said, "I am with you always, even unto the end of the world." Matthew, Chapter 28, verse 20.

4th June 1981 Thursday
Last Sunday I took Joanne to the Family Service (with Holy Communion) which is held once a month at Ravenstone Church.
This was the first time she had ever been to a church service & we had a rehearsal in advance so that she knew what she was to expect.

6th June 1981 Saturday
Joanne's summing up of her first church service was, "I liked it." She followed the words in the prayer book, did her best to sing the hymns, knew how to say "The Lord's Prayer" & reverently knelt to pray. She joined the others at the communion rail where she received a blessing.

8th June 1981 Monday
"Career Development Interview Number One at Gas Standards Branch" (See 15th Oct. 1976)
A kind young girl from London told me that my last 2 staff reports had shown that my work was not up to the standard required. I did not understand the work, lacked judgment & had no authority.

Note – Again it was more in my line to enter the latest competition.

10th June 1981 Wednesday
In our Civil Service journal "**Opinion**", I won Second Prize in a competition set by "Friar Tuck" (See 19th October 1976) – ten lines of verse rhyming with "pay". I began, "So many bills there are to pay, no wonder I am turning grey, and sometimes want to run away …." Three pounds to "Liz Hewes".

12th June 1981 Friday
Took Joanne, aged 7, to the East Midlands Airport at Castle Donington (10 miles away from Ravenstone) where she was so thrilled & excited to see a huge plane coming straight towards us to land just as we arrived.
There was then lots more activity to watch & we had the "**binoclears**".

14th June 1981 Trinity Sunday

Look at your hand & you will see the sign of the Trinity in every finger. Do you see the 3 phalanges of each finger? Total 12 phalanges.

What a mighty passage of scripture is appointed for Trinity Sunday – Isaiah, Chapter 40. There are now thought to have been 3 people who wrote "Isaiah".

16th June 1981 Tuesday

The world wept at the plight of 6 year old Alfredo Rampi who slipped fathoms deep into a foot wide shaft leading down & down & down into a well near the town of Frinscati outside Rome. Day & night they did their utmost to get him out, but were beaten by a great stratum of solid rock & so he died.

18th June 1981 Thursday

Swithland Woods in Summertime. On a beautiful sunlit evening without a cloud in the sky I went on my first "Guided Walk in the County of Leicester". We met at 7 p.m. & walked for

3 ½ miles through Swithland Woods & village. It was absolutely lovely, with birdsong & jovial company.

20th June 1981 Saturday

Mary Moore (now 70) is spending a week with me again. So it has been all systems go to get the house & garden looking spick & span.

Johnty (now 76) is very fond of gardening, so he gladly trimmed all the edges of the lawns & cleared the weeds in the paths, & the result is very pleasing.

22nd June 1981 Monday

Yesterday was our Sunday School Anniversary at Ravenstone.

In this, the year when we are thinking particularly of the disabled, we sang "Jesus' hands were kind hands, doing good to all", "Hands to work & feet to run" & "Lord Jesus Christ, You have come to us".

We also learned about the cripple Mephibosheth. (2. Samuel. 9.)

24th June 1981 Wednesday

Almost a repeat performance of this time last year. Auntie Doris, still as mobile & smart as ever, went with Mary Moore & me to visit my poor old immobile Mum in Bosworth Park Infirmary. Then we all went to Donaldson's for the evening, where Eddie (aged 68) had to be held at bay.

26th June 1981 Friday

Mary Moore had a nasty fall earlier this year, which has left her with a weakness in her back & she is now walking with the aid of a stick.

She & I motored to Derby to visit one of her old friends – Edith Whittaker, who together with her husband, Bill, entertained us to tea & made us very welcome.

28th June 1981 Sunday

Took Joanne to Bradgate Park. We parked the car at the Cropston end & walked the whole length of the park into Newtown Linford & back again.

Deer were grazing by the edge of the path & we bravely marched through, hoping they would not charge at us with their huge antlers.

30th June 1981 Tuesday

Took Joanne to Leicester to see the dismantling of the Great Central Railway Bridge near Sanvey Gate.

We then motored to Doncaster Road to see Indian ladies in their colourful saris.

We then visited Castle Gardens & walked to Leicester Cathedral where we were beckoned by the lovely bells.

2nd July 1981 Thursday

"Please pray for John Hewes to be ordained Deacon by Robert, Archbishop of Canterbury in the Cathedral Church of Christ, Canterbury, and for the Rector and people of the Parish of St. Andrews, Buckland, Dover, where he is to serve." This is Cousin John.

Note – Cousin John, son of Uncle Charlie, is ordained deacon in Canterbury Cathedral.

4th July 1981 Saturday

Wimbledon fortnight ended today in an action re-play of last year's final. Bjorn Borg, aged 25, hoping to win for the 6th consecutive year, was finally beaten on the 4th July, by an American, John McEnroe, aged 22.

Bjorn Borg was dignified in defeat, losing 4 – 6, 7 – 6, 7 – 6, 6 – 4.

6th July 1981 Monday

The Royal Wedding – (Prince Charles and Lady Diana) – is to be on 29th July 1981. This day will be a general holiday for all & at the moment the shops are choc-a-bloc with Royal Wedding souvenirs. Just as with the Queen's Silver Jubilee (See 31st May 1977), there are souvenir mugs, plates, glasses, tea cloths, etc.

8th July 1981 Wednesday

"**Read the Riot Act**" are the newspaper headlines as violence erupts in London, Liverpool & Manchester. Hundreds of youths gather together & begin an all out attack at a chosen place. They hurl fire-bombs, bricks & stones, smash shop windows, steal what they want, injure the police, & set the place on fire.

10th July 1981 Friday

The Riot Act, introduced in 1714, aimed to give authorities power to disperse an unruly mob. Magistrates or police had to read a clause of the Act to the rioters ordering them to break up & leave the streets. Anyone who failed to do so within one hour was guilty of a felony. It was abolished in 1967.

12th July 1981 Sunday

My darling Mum is still enduring the discomfort of having to sit all day & every day in the same chair, but at least she has the mobility of a wheelchair, which is much better than a geriatric chair. She also wears her own clothes & has her hair washed & set nicely, & looks very well with a good sun-tan.

14th July 1981 Tuesday

My Golden Birthday. Never do I want to turn back the clock & be any younger than I am. Like St. Paul, "Forgetting those things which are behind & reaching forth unto those things which are before, I press toward the mark for the prize of the high calling of God in Christ Jesus." (Philippians 3. 14.)

16th July 1981 Thursday

Joanne (7), Alison (13), Enid (53) & I all went to Coalville baths for a most enjoyable swim. It was the first time I had taken Joanne, who cannot swim, but who is quite happy in the water having been taken from school. I had not been to the Baths for years & it was lovely to be swimming again.

18th July 1981 Saturday

The £91 million Humber Suspension Bridge was officially opened yesterday by H. M. The Queen. This is the largest super-structure in the world and completes a hat-trick for the Queen who had the privilege of opening both the Severn Bridge & the Forth Bridge. Traffic has been using the bridge for 3 weeks.

20th July 1981 Monday

Riots continue to erupt in our major cities, particularly in the trouble-torn Toxteth area of Liverpool. Leicester had a mini-riot, but nothing too serious. The situation now is that gangs of black youths congregate ominously around the city centre while police in police vans keep constant watch.

22nd July 1981 Wednesday

From all over the world people are coming to London for the Royal Wedding.

The King & Queen of Spain are not coming because we have managed to upset them.

The President of the United States is not coming but sent his wife, & saddest of all, Princess Marie Astrid is not coming. (She had hoped to be bride.)

24th July 1981 Friday

Mr C. V. Whittaker, Area Gas Examiner based at Reading, retired today.

Mr Ellis, the Chief Gas Examiner took Rose & me in his car to Reading for the farewell party.

Seventeen people, 13 men – (Gas Examiners) and 4 ladies, sat down to luncheon at the beautiful Swan Hotel, Pangbourne.

26th July 1981 Sunday

Yesterday I took Joanne to the Monastery where she bought £2-50p worth of religious items from the Monastery shop. From there we went to Leicester to the Haymarket Theatre, where we had seats on the front row to see "Godspell", & from there home via a little ride along the M 1.

28th July 1981 Tuesday

Royal Wedding fever has now gripped the country. Houses everywhere are decked with flags & large photos of Prince Charles & Lady Diana.

Swannington Road, Ravenstone, has hundreds of flags spanning the width of the road in a triumphal arch & my small effort is a gold shield supporting 3 flags.

30th July 1981 Thursday

The sun shone for the Royal Wedding held yesterday in St. Paul's Cathedral. I went to Willoughby & watched the whole ceremony with Madge (aged 82) on her colour television. I was not impressed by the bride's over fussy wedding gown. I much preferred Princess Margaret's wedding in May 1960.

1st August 1981 Saturday

Civil Servants have been in dispute over their pay settlement for the past 21 weeks. It has been the longest national pay dispute since the miners in 1926. Selective strikes have disrupted airports, denied the Government £8,000 million in revenue & generally created chaos. It also cost the Unions £9 million.

3rd August 1981 Monday

Civil Servants have at last reached a pay settlement with the Government.

In the first place, the Government offered a 6 ½ % increase. The Civil Servants demanded more. They said they needed 15%. But the Government stuck to their guns & have only conceded now to a 7 ½ % increase.

5th August 1981 Wednesday

A day in London! Caught the 7-15a.m. train from Leicester for a lovely Royal Wedding flavour day in London.

Walked from Buckingham Palace to St. Paul's along roads bedecked with flags. Inside St. Paul's the last remaining garlands of flowers hung beside huge "Prince of Wales" emblems.

7th August 1981 Friday

"**Domine Dirige Nos**" I was greeted again by London's motto high above the bridge as I walked back from St. Paul's to the Old Curiosity Shop off Kingsway.

I then visited the Science Museum Library in South Kensington for an interesting browse among their books.

9th August 1981 Sunday

"In the year that King Uzziah died I saw the Lord ….." Isaiah, Chapter 6, verse 1.

A mighty powerful sermon tonight from a visiting parson who told us, "In the year of our Lord 1981, on the 9th August in Ravenstone Church, I saw the Lord." "High & lifted up" on Calvary's cross in heaven.

11th August 1981 Tuesday

£7,000 per year. The latest rise in Civil Service pay after a 21 week campaign for yet more has brought the top of the Executive Officer grade to £7,247. This will be back-dated to 1st April 1981. The H. E. O. salary is now £9,000 & the S. E. O. £11,000.

13th August 1981 Thursday

The Prince & Princess of Wales are now on a Mediterranean cruise in the Royal Yacht Britannia for their honeymoon.

They have been swimming & sunbathing in a secluded cove of golden sands in the legendry island of Ithaca, where Penelope waited for Odysseus to return from Troy.

15th August 1981 Saturday

A new neighbour! Mrs Yelland, an elderly widow, moved in this week to be between our house & Joanne's house. That means we now have three ladies all in a row living alone – Aunt Dos – me – Mrs Yelland. I am very glad it's not a noisy houseful of folks.

Note – Mrs Yelland is a Londoner – she moved to be nearer her son.

17th August 1981 Monday

My little 7 year old friend, Joanne, greeted me today with a "gat-toothed" smile, because today her 2 front teeth came out. She is so pretty with long hair & big beautiful blue eyes, rosy cheeks & a lively sense of humour, but she hates having no front teeth.

19th August 1981 Wednesday

Everything we now buy is wrapped up with a sort of electronic code number – a barcode. This is one step nearer to the prophecy in the Book of Revelation (Chapter 13).

Every person will also have a number. European economists are already allocating a number for everyone on earth. Whenever anyone starts a new job, receives a pay-slip, or pays income tax, it is recorded in a 3-storey computer in Brussels. The computer is known as "The Beast". A European trade stamp in use in Italy is No. 666.

23rd August 1981 Sunday

Mum's birthday. 76 today and quite a happy birthday. The hospital provided a lovely big birthday cake. Mum asked me to take two bottles of sherry, so everyone had cake & sherry & then it was sunny enough to sit out of doors. Bosworth Park Infirmary is now almost "home" to Mum.

25th August 1981 Tuesday

"Raksha Bandhan" is a celebration in Indian communities, on 25th August each year, to honour the special relationship of brother & sister. The girl gives her brother a special bracelet for his right wrist, fringed with silver paper & bearing a replica of one of the Hindu gods to look after him.

"Raksha Bandhan" is the time for an Indian boy to give to his sister a token of love, usually money around £20, or a gift. At the same time, he renews his promise that, no matter what happens, he will look after his sister and safeguard her. (We learn a lot from the Indians.)

29th August 1981 Saturday

American spacecraft Voyager II has now reached Saturn 1,000 million miles away, and has sent us more exciting pictures of this mighty planet with its necklace of whirling ice chunks. But America now will concentrate more on its defence programme in lesser orbits to counter Russian achievement of a permanent military base in orbit.

31st August 1981 Monday

Yesterday was the Eleventh Sunday after Trinity whose collect for the day tells us that God shows his almighty power most chiefly in showing mercy.

The lesson from Proverbs, Chapter 8, also told us of the quality of wisdom – "All the things that may be desired are not to be compared to wisdom."

2nd September 1981 Wednesday

Read the "Proverbs" of Solomon after the Book of Psalms in the Bible and you will find wisdom personified. "Her ways are ways of pleasantness & all her paths are peace." "Blessed is the man that heareth wisdom. For whoso findeth her findeth life, and shall obtain favour of the Lord."

4th September 1981 Friday

Read the Book of Ecclesiastes after the Book of Proverbs in the Bible, and you will find yet more wisdom. You will no doubt have a good laugh at the conclusions reached, but remember we all share the same lifestyle – here today and gone tomorrow. Just trust in the Lord.

6th September 1981 Sunday

Our Sunday School outing yesterday was to Drayton Manor Park (once the home & magnificent grounds of former Prime Minister & founder of our police system – Sir Robert Peel). I had the pleasure of the company of Joanne, aged 7, & we had a lovely day.

8th September 1981 Tuesday

At Drayton Manor Park Zoo we saw tigers, lions, a huge alligator & other wild animals, as well as reconstructed monsters now extinct.

Joanne loved best of all riding on the Carousel astride a horse. We went on the Ghost Train, on a chair lift, & the sun shone the whole of the day.

10th September 1981 Thursday

Linda (C.A., new girl in May 1978) is now leaving to have a baby. Promoted to C.O. early in 1980, she has been a joy to work with. She is radiantly beautiful with huge dark eyes & is loved by everyone. She is never any trouble & I have never known her be unkind to anyone.

12th September 1981 Saturday

Petrol is now preparing to go metric. In the County of Leicestershire there are 1,569 petrol pumps which have to be adapted to sell petrol in litres instead of gallons. It will take about 3 months to complete this changeover.

My car holds about 5 gallons. There are 4.5 litres to one gallon.

14th September 1981 Monday

Took Joanne (aged 7) to the East Midlands Airport, Castle Donington, her favourite place, to see the runway lit up on a dark & rainy evening. She was absolutely enchanted with all the lights & activity, including someone carried from a plane into an ambulance.

16th September 1981 Wednesday

A Cabinet re-shuffle & it's all change again in the Government.

The Secretary of State for Energy (my boss) is now Nigel Lawson. He is described as the hardest of all the hard-line monetarists in Mrs Thatcher's team. The new Secretary of State for trouble-torn Northern Ireland is Jim Prior – "an immense challenge."

18th September 1981 Friday

From a large group photograph including my Mum & Dad, which was taken many years ago, I have now acquired a picture of my Mum & Dad together. Fisher and Potter Ltd. have provided me with a picture I can treasure of my well beloved dad and mother.

20th September 1981 Sunday

"I bear in my body the marks of the Lord Jesus" – Galatians, Chapter 6, verse 17.

The Rector of Ravenstone, the Revd. L. Buckroyd,

spoke of love & human suffering & how people suffer when those they love are suffering.

I thought of the sharply defined crosses in the palms of Mum's hands. (See 30th April 1980)

22nd September 1981 Tuesday

Ashby Statutes! Joanne (7), Alison (13), Enid (53) & I shared once again in the hurdy-gurdy of the great fair which seems to have more advanced scientific equipment every year. Death-defying apparatus spins screaming eager teenagers high into the air – up & down & round & round.

24th September 1981 Thursday

A fifty pound note! Such is the rate of inflation that we now have £50 notes.

I cashed £100 from the Building Society & was asked if I would like it in £50 notes. I chose to have one £50 note – the first I had ever seen – with Sir Christopher Wren & St. Paul's shown on the back.

26th September 1981 Saturday

Tomorrow we have the honour of the Bishop of Leicester, Richard Rutt, at our 10 a.m. Family Service & Holy Communion at Ravenstone.

He is a Bishop who likes to extend his visit to the highways & byways of the Parish, & meet the old & infirm, where possible, in their own homes.

28th September 1981 Monday

Morning coffee with my Lord Bishop of Leicester.

Yesterday morning, Joanne & I paid our regular Sunday morning visit to Miss Emily Walker, who is an old friend of Mum's and now house-bound, & had the pleasure of a pastoral visit from the Bishop of Leicester, accompanied by the Rector.

30th September 1981 Wednesday

Carsington Reservoir, in Derbyshire, is now being built and is due to be completed by 1985 – 1986. Costing £37 million, it will hold 7,700 million gallons of water & be able to supply 52 million gallons a day.

It will back up the reservoirs in North Derbyshire, Yorkshire & North Leicestershire.

2nd October 1981 Friday

Mum is sometimes bright & cheerful, & sometimes in utter despair. She is well fed & kept beautifully clean, but surrounded by old & helpless people, with no hope of ever being free again, her only thought of escape is to die. If only she could be cared for & be really happy again.

4th October 1981 Sunday

"Were there not ten cleansed? But where are the nine?" St. Luke 17. 17.

The Rector of Ravenstone, the Revd. Leslie Buckroyd likened the story of the cleansing of the ten lepers to the world in general, where only one in ten gives thanks to God & nine out of ten never give glory to God.

6th October 1981 Tuesday

President Sadat of Egypt (aged 63) who befriended the exiled Shah of Persia in his darkest hour (see 4th August 1980) was himself assassinated today. He stood

resplendent in uniform taking the salute of his troops, when from a grand parade of artillery, he was gunned down.

8th October 1981 Thursday

As the wild winds of autumn howl around the house & dark clouds loom ominously above, how I appreciate the warmth & comfort of home. Home is a haven & I love being in my own home more than seeking such pursuits as night school, women's' meetings, night clubs, coffee evenings, etc.

10th October 1981 Saturday

The bloody Irish have struck again. Their target today was an army bus carrying Irish Guardsmen back to their barracks in Chelsea after ceremonial duty at the Bloody Tower.

A booby trap nail-bomb killed a woman who was passing by & injured 39 others, some seriously.

12th October 1981 Monday

Harvest Festival yesterday at Ravenstone, & we were reminded again of those reassuring words of St. Paul, "The harvest of the spirit is love, joy, peace, patience, kindness, goodness, fidelity, gentleness & self-control." Galatians 5, 22. This is the fruit we must produce when we are harvested.

14th October 1981 Wednesday

"Star Maps", a book written by W. R. Fix, is my latest book of fascinating information which explains how all mankind came from the outer galaxies in spirit form & will return again. Heaven is in many different orbits, and only those with the highest credentials reach the highest spheres.

16th October 1981 Friday

Joanne has now changed from an ugly duckling (with no front teeth) to a beautiful young lady. It has taken only 2 months for her new teeth to grow & with a completely new hairstyle, short & nicely tapered, she looks a little smasher.

How she has grown up in so comparatively short a time.

18th October 1981 Sunday

"I knew a man in Christ above fourteen years ago, (whether in the body, I cannot tell; or whether out of the body, I cannot tell; God knoweth) such an one caught up to the third heaven ...... and I knew such a man caught up into paradise." The 2nd Epistle to the Corinthians.

19th October 1981 Monday

On this day in **1781** the American War of Independence ended when British commander Lord Cornwallis surrendered to George Washington at Yorktown, Virginia.

20th October 1981 Tuesday

In praise of St. Luke – the Rector of Ravenstone, the Revd. Leslie Buckroyd, gave a fine sermon on Sunday, being the very day itself when we remember St. Luke.

He mentioned all the things which St. Luke alone spoke of in his Gospel – things not recalled by anyone else at all.

21st October 1981 Wednesday

Hudson, Albert Henry, 185 Ashburton Road, Hugglescote, former head of Snibston School, died on Wednesday, October 21st aged 80 years, loved husband of Ivy Josephine and devoted father of Hazel. Funeral service at St. James Church, Highfield Street, Coalville. My teacher 40 years ago.

22nd October 1981 Thursday

Nigel Lawson, our new Secretary of State for Energy, has announced "The biggest programme of privatisation ever to come before Parliament." He is one of the staunchest supporters of Prime Minister Margaret Thatcher's hard line & is one of the toughest fighters at Westminster.

24th October 1981 Saturday

Nigel Lawson proposes to – 1. Transfer to the private sector the entire oil-producing business of the British National Oil Corporation. 2. Privatise the British Gas Corporation's off-shore oil business. 3. Abolish the Gas Corporation's monopoly power to buy and sell gas.

26th October 1981 Monday

Albert Henry Hudson taught me many things. He was one of the corner-stones of my life.
He taught me, "If a man lets you down once, shame on him; if he lets you down twice, shame on you." He taught me how to multiply by 11.
E.g. 43 x 11 (Add 4 & 3 & put between)

28th October 1981 Wednesday

Aunt Dos (aged 79) and I went to Leicester City General Hospital to visit her cousin Audrey (aged 79). Poor old Audrey was in a sorry state, talking in a mixed up state of past & present. She was a pathetic frail old lady while Aunt Dos in contrast seemed so much younger.

30th October 1981 Friday

 This is **Rubik's Cube**, invented by Erno Rubik, a Hungarian professor of architecture & interior design.
It has 6 sides, 6 colours & 27 sub-cubes. Rows of the cube rotate vertically or horizontally to make over 3 billion colour combinations.

1st November 1981 Sunday

Rubik's Cube is the latest craze to hit the shops. Nearly everybody now has one to try & puzzle out. It looks innocent enough, but a few simple turns will mix the colours up and it is well nigh impossible to return all 6 sides to their original solid colours. It just gets worse.

3rd November 1981 Tuesday

A123 ABC - This was my suggestion for car numbers which I offered in August 1980. In Parliament this week, a question was asked about the new format of Vehicle Registration numbers & the answer was, "We hope to complete consideration of the many responses received & announce our decisions later."

5th November 1981 Thursday

Please to remember the Fifth of November!
Took Joanne, aged 7, on an evening drive to see the local bonfires & fireworks. We went to Whitwick & up to the Monastery, to look down over the whole of Coalville, & then to Ibstock where there was a huge bonfire behind the "Hastings".

7th November 1981 Saturday

"Charles to Marry Astrid" These were the newspaper headlines in June 1977 when Prince Charles was supposed to be marrying Princess Marie-Astrid of Luxembourg. These are again newspaper headlines as Princess Marie-Astrid is now to marry Charles Christian de Hapsburg Lorraine, son of Archduke Charles Louis of Austria.

9th November 1981 Monday

Joanne (aged 7) and I went to see Sir Robert Fossett's circus at Oadby race-course. To a mere handful of people in the audience, some of the greatest acts you could see in any circus were performed. A troupe of 8 elephants, 12 beautiful ponies, 4 tigers, & marvellous trapeze.

11th November 1981 Wednesday
"Congratulations, you're a Cubist!"

This is the message at the end of instructions on how to solve the Rubik Cube. Even with the book of instructions it has taken me hours and hours – burning the midnight oil - to solve the cube. But what a sense of achievement! Absolutely great!

13th November 1981 Friday

The Rubik Cube reminds me of life. Everyday you move this way or that in over three billion possible colour combinations. Every now & then some semblance of pattern emerges, but in order to reach the next stage, the whole thing gets mixed up again, till finally – whoopee – you're there!

15th November 1981 Sunday

"Morning Glory" by Harold Clayton. This is a beautiful picture of roses and other flowers in a vase which I have chosen as my 50th birthday present with money given to me earlier this year by Mary Moore. I saw the picture for sale in Coalville & liked it immediately.
Note – It was a case of "Coup de Foudre" – love at first sight.

17th November 1981 Tuesday

Jim Prior, the new Secretary of State for Northern Ireland, went to a funeral service at Dundonald, near Belfast, for the Revd. Robert Bradford, M.P. for South Belfast, who was shot dead by the I.R.A. Jim Prior was jostled, jeered & booed & fled for his life.

19th November 1981 Thursday

The Protestants of Northern Ireland are constantly under attack from the I.R.A., & yet they accuse the British Government of being responsible because they are not tough enough to quell the I.R.A. That is why Jim Prior was mobbed & why he was called "murderer".

21st November 1981 Saturday

Cousin Audrey (my dad's cousin) is 80 years old tomorrow. She is now in such a sorry state mentally that she has been taken to Carlton Hayes Hospital,

Narborough. I visited her there in Beatty Ward & oh, how sad to see so many people in such a hopeless state of confusion.

23ʳᵈ November 1981 Monday
Taylor, Stanley, 36 Leicester Road, Ravenstone, passed away in hospital November 23ʳᵈ, beloved husband of Dorothy, father of Patricia and Clive, grandfather of Helen and Ruth. Funeral service at Ravenstone Parish Church on Thursday November 26ᵗʰ, at 10 a.m., followed by cremation at Loughborough Crematorium. Family flowers only, please. Donations in lieu to Ravenstone Church, c/o Rev. L. Buckroyd, Ravenstone Rectory, Ravenstone.

This is Stan, Deputy Church Warden at Ravenstone, and a regular lesson reader. He married my 2ⁿᵈ cousin Dorothy Hewes & was brother Pat's close friend.
He died suddenly of a heart attack

25ᵗʰ November 1981 Wednesday
Joanne, aged 7, keeps me well entertained as she struggles with the complexities of the English language. Apart from difficult words like "binoclears", she gets mightily confused with the microscope – or is it a horoscope? The word she is looking for is telescope.

27ᵗʰ November 1981 Friday
The National Debt goes up & up & up. On 4ᵗʰ August 1966 it was £31 thousand million.
On 16ᵗʰ January 1979 it was £79 thousand million. And the latest figure is £112,780 million. Inflation means that everything is costing more all the time and wages also go up & up to keep pace.

29ᵗʰ November 1981 Sunday
Our Annual Christmas Fair in Ravenstone Village Institute and our 10ᵗʰ effort with a stall for the Sunday School. Following our poor effort last year we were given all sorts of things to sell by other stall holders and the result was a record £25 towards the £600 total.

1ˢᵗ December 1981 Tuesday
"Cashless Society". Britain's big banks are preparing to take another major step towards the cashless society. They plan to introduce a new payments system based on the use of computer terminals at High Street shops. Shoppers will have a card which automatically debits their bill to their bank. (See Revelation, Chapter 13.)

3ʳᵈ December 1981 Thursday
Visited Cousin Audrey again in Carlton Hayes Hospital. She wept to see me & said I was an answer to her prayers. Feeling utterly deserted & not knowing how to get in touch with anyone she knew, she prayed that someone would contact her. She was completely lost in a hostile world.

5ᵗʰ December 1981 Saturday
The Atherstone Hunt met this morning at The Globe, Snarestone. Took Joanne to see the meet & what a magnificent spectacle. There were approximately 100 people on horseback & they all rode past up the hill towards Measham.

7ᵗʰ December 1981 Monday
Ravenstone Sunday School Christmas party. Thanks entirely to the efforts of two young mothers – Wenda Hickin & Rita Freestone, about 40 children had a sit-down tea with jellies and ice-cream, cakes etc., followed by entertainment from a local conjurer & finally the entrance of Santa Claus.

8ᵗʰ December 1981 Tuesday
Rose. To Linda (nee Edwards) and David, a daughter, Carly Jane, 7lb 15ozs.
Thanks to all concerned at R. M. H.

9ᵗʰ December 1981 Wednesday
"Thought for Today" this week on Radio Leicester has been most uplifting. A Roman Catholic priest has spoken about people he has known who have helped him to see Christ in what they have said or done; especially in those unexpected heart-warming fleeting moments which are so precious.

11ᵗʰ December 1981 Friday
Winter came with a vengeance today. It took me 2 hours to get to work as traffic ground to a halt in arctic conditions.
We were allowed to leave work at 3-15 p.m. & I travelled home through a veritable winter wonderland. The scene was so breathtakingly beautiful, I was moved to tears.

13ᵗʰ December 1981 Sunday
Ravenstone Sunday School Prize-giving Day.
Like good King Wenceslas I battled through a blizzard to Ravenstone Church & back.
As I walked through snow, deep & crisp & even, I sang, "Mark my footsteps good, my page – tread thou in them boldly." Nearly all the children came.

15ᵗʰ December 1981 Tuesday
The Queen also, like good King Wenceslas, went out into the snow. She went in her Range-rover vehicle to visit her daughter Princess Anne in Gloucestershire.
On her return to Windsor Castle her car was stuck in the snow & she took refuge in the Cross Hands Hotel, Old Sodbury.

17ᵗʰ December 1981 Thursday
Went to Ibstock High School to see the children perform "Zoe Diakos", a Christmas Circus.
It was in fact the Zodiac performed in a circle like a circus, with the Age of Aquarius ready to take over from the 2,160 years of Pisces, the age of the Christian era.

19ᵗʰ December 1981 Saturday
Went to Snibston School again to see Joanne, aged 7, in the Christmas Concert.
As I looked around the audience, I saw parents whom I had known as babies themselves.
I thought of my Mum, who had been there when she was aged 7; & saw the children of today 70 years hence.

21ˢᵗ December 1981 Monday
The Penlee lifeboat Solomon Browne, from Mousehole in Cornwall, yesterday answered the call to the stricken 1,400 ton freighter Union Star.

Mountainous seas claimed the lives of all eight of the heroic lifeboat crew and all eight of the people they fought in vain to save. Waves were 60 feet high.

23rd December 1981 Wednesday

A wonderful tribute to the lifeboat men in the Daily Express says, "Whether we go to sea or not, we are all in the debt of the lifeboat men. The death of the 16 was tragic & saddens the heart. But in its way it gladdens the mind, which is uplifted by the brave story."

25th December 1981 Friday

A White Christmas! For the past 2 weeks we have been in an Arctic grip of snow & ice. This year I lit a candle for Poland. For the past 2 weeks Poland has been under martial law with mass arrests, killings & the setting up of concentration camps to stamp out trade unions.

27th December 1981 Sunday

"It is predicted that there will be world shaking political upheavals of great might." (See January 1st 1980) Already there are indications of this as the East & West threaten to come to blows over Poland. America has warned Russia that Moscow will be made to pay dearly for its "crime", alleging that Russia had directed operations in Poland.

29th December 1981 Tuesday

"Peace I leave with you." "My peace I give unto you." "Not as the world giveth, give I unto you." "Let not your heart be troubled, neither let it be afraid." (John 14. 27.)
Am I thankful to have a God of Peace, "Who is above all". (Ephesians 4. 6.)

31st December 1981 Thursday

And so another year ends. After 50 years at 27, Leicester Road, Ravenstone, sleeping in the very bed where I was born, this is "home".
So many people I know, live in houses, but do not live "at home". They say, "When I was at home" meaning where they lived with their parents.

* * *

1982

1ˢᵗ January 1982 Friday
1982 is to be launched by a total eclipse of the Moon (January 9ᵗʰ).
It should be seen from anywhere in the world. The Moon does not disappear completely, but takes on a whole range of colours dependent on the weather. Maybe red, maybe even blue – hence "once in a blue moon".

3ʳᵈ January 1982 Sunday
Marjorie Merrill, my friend since I was a small child, invited Joanne (aged 7) & me to join their New Year party. What a lovely time we all had (13 altogether). We played games with paper & pencil, searched for tiny objects in the room, played "Pass the Parcel" and had a good old sing-song.

5ᵗʰ January 1982 Tuesday
Staff Reporting is one job that I certainly **do not like**. Every year I have to report on 6 members of staff & spend hours & hours wondering what to put. I am pleased to say that the report form has now been revised to "Reflect current needs" & it is not now quite so bad.

7ᵗʰ January 1982 Thursday
Ravenstone is featured in this week's Leicester Advertiser - "A Delightful Village."
"In the 'olde' part of the village are the famous Ravenstone Almshouses, the biggest complex of its kind in England. St. Michael & All Angels Church is one of the most picturesque village churches in the county."

9ᵗʰ January 1982 Saturday
The eclipse of the Moon this evening was a wonderful sight. On a clear frosty night we watched the Moon slowly change colour. Not exactly a blue Moon, rather a dusky pink. Spent the whole day clearing snow after another blizzard struck yesterday & sub-zero temperatures.

11ᵗʰ January 1982 Monday
"Brigadoon" is the show chosen this year for Coalville Amateurs' production. Set in the Scottish Highlands, it requires someone to be able to play the bag-pipes. Took Joanne to rehearsal where she was completely engrossed watching the chorus learning the Sword Dance & Reel – Finale Act 1.

13ᵗʰ January 1982 Wednesday
"Colder than Iceland". Temperatures in Leicestershire during the night have plunged to minus 19 degrees Centigrade. A prolonged spell of sub-zero temperatures, snow, ice & freezing fog has brought people out in the most daring outfits – igloo boots, striped woollen socks & chunky warm hats.

15ᵗʰ January 1982 Friday
During the past 12 months I have collected a lovely selection of music to listen to on my cassette player. I now have 24 cassettes including the music of Beethoven, Offenbach, Elgar, Johann Strauss & Tchaikovsky, as well as songs by Elvis Presley, music from the "Shows" and Brass Bands.

17ᵗʰ January 1982 Sunday
Every day we are entertained in one way or another by people who are now dead, but who, through the wonders of 20ᵗʰ Century technology, remain very much alive on film & on records. I am serenaded by Elvis Presley, played to on the piano by Charlie Kunz & moved deeply by old films on television.

19ᵗʰ January 1982 Tuesday
"**Moon Blues**" Such excitement, for Joanne aged 7 & for me, when the letter she had written to the Leicester Mercury appeared not only in print but in pride of place in the centre of the page, accompanied by a lovely caricature of a little girl watching through binoculars the eclipse of the Moon.
This was Joanne's letter, prompted by me but drafted almost entirely by her, "On Saturday night I saw the eclipse of the Moon. I saw it change colour. I was told that it was supposed to look blue. It looked pinky-brown to me. Is it true that it is supposed to look blue? When I looked through the binoculars it looked like an egg being hatched."

23ʳᵈ January 1982 Saturday
Cousin Johnty (my Mum's cousin) aged 77, married for over 40 years, with 2 grown-up sons & grandchildren, has just recently become divorced. He & his wife lived a cat & dog existence & he has alienated himself not only from his wife but also from his sons & grandchildren. He now lives like a hermit.

25ᵗʰ January 1982 Monday
Three million people in Britain are now out of work. (See April 27ᵗʰ 1981, when the figure had reached 2 ½ million) This represents one in eight of the working population & is the worst since the depression of the nineteen thirties. And still the government dares to say that things are now looking up.

27ᵗʰ January 1982 Wednesday
Took Joanne (aged 7) to the Concordia Theatre, Hinckley, to see her second pantomime – Humpty Dumpty. We were lucky enough to have seats on the front row & we enjoyed all the wonder & joy of seeing the nursery rhyme characters brought to life. As always, the scenery & costumes were great.

29ᵗʰ January 1982 Friday
After nearly 3 years in hospital, my darling Mum has been asked if she would like to have a fortnight's holiday.
Apparently it is possible for severely disabled people to have a holiday through "Wing Fellowship Trust" & she has been offered a holiday at Nottingham later this year.

31ˢᵗ January 1982 Sunday
"O ye ice and snow, bless ye the Lord." Alan Warren, the Provost of Leicester Cathedral, in the Cathedral Newsletter No. 177 covering Feb/March 1982, quotes from the Benedicite, that great Canticle found in the Prayer Book where in turn all ye works of the Lord give praise.

2ⁿᵈ February 1982 Tuesday
Kim Tracey, aged 42, is a clairvoyant & this is what she

predicts, "Prince Charles & Princess Diana will have 3 children: - 1. A boy. He will be extremely good at drawing & painting & will become known as the Artist King. He will marry when he is about 22 or 23. The other 2 children will be girls, totally different from each other.

4th February 1982 Thursday

The painters & decorators are now at Gas Standards Branch, painting all the rooms one by one. Today they are in Room 007, the room where Rose (aged 49), Lisa (aged 18) & I work. Also at the same time we are having a large extension built on to our present laboratories.

6th February 1982 Saturday

Visited Cousin Audrey (aged 80) at Tillson House, Coalville. Sadly, she is no longer capable of administering her own affairs & is totally confused.

Her little home in Ravenstone Almshouses is being cleared out ready for someone else to move in & all her life-long treasures sold or given away.

8th February 1982 Monday

A123 ABC. This was my suggestion for car numbers which I offered in August 1980.

At last a decision has been reached. Apparently there were thousands of suggestions, but this was the most popular one, submitted by most people, & has been chosen as the one to be adopted next year.

David Howell, who is now Secretary of State for Transport, has now given his formal approval of the new format for car numbers. He says, "Some ingenious ideas were put forward, but the majority of the motoring public & the motor trade overwhelmingly wanted a simple system which would minimise the cost."

12th February 1982 Friday

£1 notes are to be replaced by £1 coins. Such is the rate of inflation that it has been decided to have £1 coins instead of £1 notes & they will be introduced next year.

The Royal Mint asked for ideas on the shape of the new coin & the winning design was offered by Eric Sewell, a retired engraver.

14th February 1982 Sunday

Winged Fellowship Trust, 2nd Floor, 64/68, Oxford Street, London, is the organisation which offers holidays for physically disabled people. It has 3 holiday centres – 1. Chigwell in Essex. 2. Redhill, Surrey. 3. Holme Pierrepont, Near Nottingham. Volunteers help the small residential staff on these holidays.

16th February 1982 Tuesday

Conducted 7 interviews on my own for a C. A. vacancy in the Registry. Cheryl, aged 18, who was appointed last year, is leaving to take up nursing.

Each applicant first of all filled in a lengthy questionnaire, which is a great help, & I actually enjoyed interviewing – much better than when being watched.

18th February 1982 Thursday

Ramases II had a sister, Princess Tia. British archaeologists excavating at Saqqara, near Cairo, have now discovered a Royal tomb about 3,300 years old, of an Egyptian princess. It was the burial place of Princess Tia, who was born sometime before 1304 B.C. & who could possibly be the Princess who found baby Moses.

20th February 1982 Saturday

Took Joanne (aged 7) to Nottingham. What a lovely day we had. The sun shone all day long & we were able to sit in the Square feeding the pigeons. We climbed up to the castle & walked all round the castle walls to look at the caves. I bought a ship mural 7 feet high.

22nd February 1982 Monday

Tomorrow is Shrove Tuesday. The French call it Mardi Gras.

We call it Pancake Day, because on Shrove Tuesday butter & eggs were used up by making pancakes before the shriving bell called everyone to Church, where the priest "Shrove" or absolved them after confession, before Lent began.

24th February 1982 Wednesday

"And God shall wipe away all tears from their eyes; & there shall be no more death, neither sorrow, nor crying, neither shall there be any more pain; for the former things are passed away."

(Revelation, Chapter 21, verse 4.)

As my darling Mum wept with pain & utter despair, I shared her sorrow.

"These are they which came out of great tribulation ….. the Lamb which is in the midst of the throne shall feed them, & shall lead them unto living fountains of waters; & God shall wipe away all tears from their eyes."

Rev. 7. 17.

My darling Mum has had more than her share of sorrow & tribulation.

28th February 1982 Sunday

When my Mum was aged 10, her twin sister died of diphtheria. When she was aged 15, her mother died. She was married at 23 and was a widow at 33. Her only son died when he was 17. She has had a lifetime of seeing those she loved suffer & die, & now she has nothing to look forward to, being confined to a wheelchair & in great pain.

1st March 1982 Monday

Final rehearsal this evening for Coalville Amateurs' "Brigadoon".

We were there until 11-30 p.m. Yesterday we had a 6 hour rehearsal from 2 p.m. – 8 p.m.

This is a lovely show if done to perfection, but we are somewhat amateurish this year, with our best talent lined up in the chorus.

3rd March 1982 Wednesday

"Young Talent Shone Through Scotch Mist"

"Coalville Operatic Society coped reasonably well when Brigadoon popped out of the Highland mists. The singing was nothing to rave about (i.e. the principals) but the musical arrangements & chorus singing were a credit to Peter Jacques." – Leicester Mercury.

5th March 1982 Friday

Although Brigadoon has its weak spots it also has moments of glory.

I consider myself well blessed to have the best seat in

the middle of the orchestra where, as prompter, I see & hear more than anyone else. I live through every moment with them all & thrill to the magic of the music.

7th March 1982 Sunday

Joanne's birthday! 8 years old today. As a 5 year old, 6 year old and 7 year old, she has been to me a friend & companion & has brought me untold joy. Like Minnehaha she runs to greet me the minute I arrive home & we spend many happy hours together.

"Give me a child until he is 7, and I will give you the man."

9th March 1982 Tuesday

Tomorrow is the day when the planets come closest to being in alignment. They are not strictly in a straight line, but they are in the same 90° quadrant.

The next time they will be in the same quadrant will be in the 24th century.

11th March 1982 Thursday

Budget Day! Car Tax went up yet again from £70 to £80.

The Chancellor, Sir Geoffrey Howe, was anxious to encourage innovation in industry.

He said, "There is no more important area to which this applies than micro-electronics & information technology." New schemes will be announced. (See January 6th 1979)

13th March 1982 Saturday

Aunt Dos's 80th birthday. Pat & Evelyn gave her a party at their house & invited her old pal Dol Dean (now 88) and me (aged 50).

After tea we had a film show by local naturalist Peter Williams. We saw the most beautiful pictures of wild birds feeding their young – especially the baby woodpeckers.

15th March 1982 Monday

23VK 636291 – Premium Bond winner!

"Dear Sir/Madam, I am glad to tell you that the bond number on the enclosed crossed warrant has been drawn for a prize." Such excitement to receive an official envelope bearing the postmark Blackpool. "Pay Miss E. Hewes the sum of £50."

17th March 1982 Wednesday

St. Patrick's Day & my dad's birthday.

What a strange thing it is to think if my dad's wife Julia had not died so tragically at so early an age, he would never have re-married to my darling Mum & I would never have been born as I am, but as somebody else, entirely different.

19th March 1982 Friday

From model patient (this time last year) Mum has gone into the depths of despair again. She is in such pain & discomfort sitting every day in a wheelchair & has for company old & helpless people who make her feel even worse. She is so sad & utterly forlorn that nothing seems to cheer her up.

21st March 1982 Sunday

Mothering Sunday. The children at Sunday School were a real joy to me today.

Angela (a little Angel indeed) was celebrating her 6th birthday & was so happy when we all sang "Happy Birthday" to her. The children all gave flowers to their mothers & we had a lovely "Mothering Sunday Service".

23rd March 1982 Tuesday

Pope John Paul II, elected 16th October 1978, will be the first Pope ever to visit our shores.

He is to make a pastoral visit (not an official State visit) to the Roman Catholic community of England, Wales & Scotland, at Pentecost, 29th May – 2nd June 1982.

He almost died last year following an assassination attempt.

25th March 1982 Thursday

"Sweeney Todd – the Barber of Fleet Street."

Pat, Evelyn & I saw this most popular of the Victorian melodramas performed as a musical in a style of acting & production of yesteryear. The audience hissed & booed & applauded the actors & we thoroughly enjoyed the drama & over-acting. Sweeney Todd the Barber put his clients in a specially designed chair which tipped them up & over into the basement. He cut the throats of so many victims & robbed them, but they came back to haunt him & drive him out of his mind. A host of eccentric characters came into & out of his life.

29th March 1982 Monday

The Quorn Hunt, the Belvoir, the Fernie, the Cottesmore, the Atherstone & the Pytchley, together with the Oakley Foot Beagles, North Warks. Beagles & Westerby Basset Hounds, all joined forces to converge on County Hall at Glenfield with an 8,000 signature petition not to ban foxhunting on County Council land.

The League Against Cruel Sports, 83 Union Street, London, has recently enjoyed considerable success in gaining co-operation from Councils in different parts of the country to ban blood sports on council owned land. Labour councillors have now tabled a motion to ban foxhunting on 10,000 acres of council land in Leicestershire.

1st April 1982 Thursday

Chick, Dr. Frederick Henry, M.R.C.S., L.R.C.P., of Mountfield, Upper Packington Road, Ashby-de-la-Zouch, passed peacefully away in hospital on April 1st 1982, aged 87 years.

2nd April 1982 Friday

The Battle of Belvoir (See 30th October 1979) has been fought to save the beautiful Vale of Belvoir from being turned into 3 coalmines. A verdict has at last been reached & a compromise solution offered with the chance to mine at Saltby & Asfordby, provided waste is dumped elsewhere. The village of Hose has had a reprieve.

3rd April 1982 Saturday

Stacey, Frances E., 172 Thornborough Road, Coalville, passed peacefully away in hospital, April 3rd, loving sister of Thirza and William (and the late Julia and Simeon, 1918)and sister-in-law Hilda, auntie of Bunting, Pat, Janet and Sheila.

4th April 1982 Sunday

Peter Mould, now aged 38, is a spastic confined to a wheelchair. On New Year's Eve he became engaged to Bernice, a widow aged 62, who is also severely handicapped following a stroke which left her unable to speak. They are to be married on July 3rd when he will be 39, at Breedon-on-the-Hill.

6th April 1982 Tuesday

Fox hunting is to continue. Leicestershire County Council voted in favour of fox hunting on public land. Labour's motion to ban fox hunting on 10,000 acres of council land was defeated by 46 votes to 42. Julian de Lisle said that hunting & Leicestershire were synonymous. The Co-op have banned hunting on their land.

8th April 1982 Thursday

Mr Howe, Gas Meter Examiner for more than 40 years, retired last week from work at Gas Standards Branch. We were all invited to a farewell buffet & drinks at Blaby Bowling Club from 12 noon – 2 p.m. It was a very pleasant informal occasion in a most delightful setting.

Howe, Walter James, of Glen Parva, husband of Pearl, father of Wendy and Linda, father-in-law of Ian and Grandpa of Stephen, died on July 14th 1992, at L.R.I.

10th April 1982 Saturday

When Trojan Paris stole the lovely Helen, the Greeks launched a thousand ships to rescue her. This week our Royal Navy put to sea in wartime order to sail 8,000 miles to rescue the people of the Falkland Islands from the clutches of General Leopoldo Galtieri of Argentina.

12th April 1982 Easter Monday

"The Lord is Risen!" "He is risen indeed."

What a lovely Easter for me this year as Joanne, aged 8, accompanied me on Good Friday to the Devotional Service at Christ Church, Coalville; to the Monastery on Saturday; & to Leicester Cathedral on Easter Sunday. This was her first "Christian" Easter & she said she "understanded" most of it.

14th April 1982 Wednesday

"The Doctor's Walking Book" written by Dr. Fred Stutman, has prompted me to take a good walk every day. "Walking builds the capacity for energy output & physical endurance by increasing the supply of oxygen to skin and muscles. It stimulates the lungs & heart" etc. etc.

"Walking opens up narrowed areas in the coronary blood vessels, lessening chances of a heart attack. Walking may also increase the elasticity of the blood vessels, decreasing the likelihood that they will rupture under pressure – one cause of strokes." Etc. etc.

Note – Amongst several "Readers Digest" little books which Mum had been given to read, I came across an extract from "The Doctor's Walking Book" written by Dr. Fred Stutman. He so extolled the virtues of taking a good walk every day, to keep the blood circulating freely, & at the same time keep a check on Middle Age Spread, that I set about going for a daily half-hour walk before setting off to work in the car.

18th April 1982 Sunday

"The same day at evening, being the first day of the week, when the doors were shut, where the disciples were assembled for fear of the Jews, came Jesus & stood in the midst, and saith unto them, Peace be unto you." John 20. 19.

The Rector of Ravenstone chose this text this evening.

20th April 1982 Tuesday

The Rector, the Revd. Leslie Buckroyd, said that the risen Lord did not come & stand in the midst, but was there all the time unseen. He allowed himself to be seen here & there for a short while to help us understand – "Where two or three are gathered together …… Christ is in the midst."

22nd April 1982 Thursday

The calorific value of walking is 3,500 calories to lose one pound in weight.

Similarly 3,500 intake of calories will put on one pound. A one hour walk, at a moderate pace will burn up 300 calories. I am hoping therefore to reduce my 11 stone weight by walking off 300 calories each day.

24th April 1982 Saturday
"On the Brink of War".

These are the sad headlines in the Leicester Mercury this evening as Britain prepares to do battle with Argentina over ownership of the Falkland Islands. These islands situated off the coast of South America lie in hostile seas where Antarctic storms rage in all their fury.

26th April 1982 Monday

Britain took possession of the Falkland Islands about 150 years ago. A community of some 1,800 people, all British, now lives there.

However, long before that, the islands belonged to Argentina, & the Argentine military leaders have decided it is high time they re-claimed what is theirs.

28th April 1982 Wednesday

"Deadline at Dawn on Friday" – Britain has given the Argentines a deadline of dawn on Friday to get off the Falkland Islands – or else there will be war. If the Argentines fail to leave voluntarily by noon in London (8 a.m. in the Falklands) the fleet's commander Sandy Woodward will launch an attack.

30th April 1982 Friday

"Princess Ida" or "Castle Adamant", one of Gilbert & Sullivan's lesser known works, is being given this week by Leicester Operatic Players. I went this evening with Reevsie & Nancy (who works in the Motor Licence Office) and got up to date on all the happenings at work.

2nd May 1982 Sunday

The congregation at Ravenstone Church this evening numbered 15. At one time it used to average about 50. This is typical of the trend throughout the whole country as a new generation has grown up which shows no interest in the church. Soon we shall be sharing one parson with Packington & Normanton-le-Heath.

4th May 1982 Tuesday

May Day Holiday Monday yesterday. Went for a 3 ½

mile walk to Hoo Ash – Altons – home.

Then took Joanne (aged 8) to Castle Donington Airport where we stayed from 10-30 a.m. until 2 p.m. We took a packed lunch with us & then went into Castle Donington to see the Mediaeval Market & from there to Kings Mills.

6th May 1982 Thursday

Leicester Royal Infirmary's Scanner has now been unveiled.

In 1978 the Lord Mayor of Leicester, Albert Watson, launched his appeal which raised almost £900,000 to provide Leicester with a Whole Body C. T. Scanner which is a highly sophisticated X-ray machine used with a computer.

Albert Watson, former Lord Mayor of Leicester, unveiled the plaque for the room in which the Scanner will do its work – the Albert Watson Suite. He was moved to tears as he saw his dream fulfilled & was presented with a gleaming metal model of the Scanner which gives "sliced bread" pictures.

10th May 1982 Monday

The London Marathon last year attracted 7,000 runners. This year there were 16,350. The race started at Greenwich & finished on Westminster Bridge. Again there were a million people to cheer them on their way & the majority completed the course. The winner was Hugh Jones.

To run 26 miles 385 yards is certainly a "Marathon" effort. The winner this week romped home in 2 hours 9 minutes 24 seconds. Way ahead of all the others, he turned the last miles into a one-man state procession through the City of London, down the Mall & to his lonely glory on Westminster Bridge.

Note – This is London's 2nd "London Marathon".

14th May 1982 Friday

My darling Mum, who was told she could have a fortnight's holiday this year, has now been informed that she cannot be accommodated this year. She has been promised a holiday – next year. However, you will be pleased to know that Mum doesn't mind at all. In fact she has brightened up & is happier now.

16th May 1982 Sunday

We are now learning the songs at Sunday School for the Sunday School Anniversary which will be on 20th June. Mrs Bird, our pianist & teacher has chosen the theme "God's Creation" & we are hoping to have posters & various displays showing the wonders of all that God has created.

18th May 1982 Tuesday

Apart from the wonders of sun, moon & stars, trees, fish, animals, etc., we are hoping to illustrate all the by-products from wood & mineral wealth. Doll's house furniture will show "wood". A toy farm-yard set for the animals & we will extol the virtues of coal (our local commodity) of oil & of **gas**!

20th May 1982 Thursday

Open-cast coal mining now stretches from Heather to Ibstock & is slowly advancing down Heather Lane &

down Ibstock Lane towards Ravenstone. Joanne (aged 8) & I went for a walk down Heather Lane to see this extraordinary landscape which reminded me very much of Arizona & the Grand Canyon.

22nd May 1982 Saturday

The mighty oak in our garden now measures 4″ high. Three splendid branches reach out & measure 5″ 6″ and 7″.

"Ah" you may say. You've heard that before. But these splendid branches have now sent out more branches which are longer than themselves & are in full leaf.

23rd May 1982 Sunday

Wainwright, Megan Doreen, 4 Wash Lane, Ravenstone, passed away suddenly at home on May 23rd, beloved wife of Michael, dearly loved mum of Carole, dear daughter of Mrs Fern. Ours is just a simple prayer, God bless and keep you in His care.

24th May 1982 Monday

Cup Final Day this year ended in a 1 - 1 draw (after extra time). First Division Tottenham were playing Second Division Queens Park Rangers.

Princess Anne was there to present the Cup & again there was an attendance of 100,000 but receipts hit an even higher jackpot of £918,000.

26th May 1982 Wednesday

E. R. N. I. E. – the Electronic Random Number Indicator Equipment has now been selecting Premium Bond winners for 25 years. During that time ERNIE has selected more than 20 million winners & paid out over £1,000 billion. With more than 1,400 million bonds in the draw the chances of winning are 14,000 – 1. There are 100,000 prizes every month.

28th May 1982 Friday

"**John Paul Two, We Love You**". This was the cry today when, for the first time ever, a Bishop of Rome set foot on English soil. Pope John Paul II began a 6 day visit to this country with the words of Christ, "Peace be with you" as Britain is fighting with Argentina right now.

30th May 1982 Sunday

Yesterday, on the Eve of Pentecost, Pope John Paul II went to Canterbury Cathedral. He was moved to tears as the packed congregation burst into spontaneous applause loud & long. Pope Gregory had sent Augustine to evangelise the English. Here was Pope John Paul II himself.

1st June 1982 Tuesday

From England to Scotland Pope John Paul II continued his triumphal tour. "Will ye no come back again" they sang. He spoke to them of St. Andrew (Peter's brother) & they hailed him as their own brother. He spoke of the wonderful power of the Holy Spirit – the Spirit of Truth; the Spirit of Counsel & Might.

3rd June 1982 Thursday

From Scotland to Wales, the Pope took his blessing, before returning to Rome from Cardiff airport. He brought 6 days of sunshine & hope. For him it was a marathon effort – 26 speeches & a non-stop programme – and on the 7th day he rested.

"May God bless you all" he said, as he bid us fond farewell.

5th June 1982 Saturday

What a wonderful Whitsuntide this year to have literally seen the power of the Holy Spirit in Pope John Paul II. A brilliant man, able to speak 7 languages, we heard him speak in our own tongue the wonderful works of God. (See Acts, Chapter 2.)

I sent him a "Thank You" picture postcard of Rome.

6th June 1982 Trinity Sunday

In the Garden of Gethsemane, Jesus prayed 3 times, "Abba, Father, all things are possible unto thee; take away this cup from me; nevertheless not what I will, but what thou wilt."

Peter then three times denied Christ & finally the risen Lord asked Peter three times, "Lovest thou me?"

7th June 1982 Monday

Coalville Amateur Operatic Society Annual General Meeting this evening brought about several changes in the Appointment of Officers for 1982 – 1983.

John Lewin replaced John Saunders as Producer & a new Treasurer was appointed following the resignation of Pam Moore. Guess who is the new Treasurer – ME!

9th June 1982 Wednesday

I was delighted to be offered the job of Treasurer. This means I now relinquish my role as Prompter which I have thoroughly enjoyed.

My dad went from Prompter to President & I now go from Prompter to Treasurer. I take over at a time when the Society has £3,000 in hand.

Note – Treasurer is a post I continue to hold until I retire from work when I reach the age of 60 in 1991.

11th June 1982 Friday

Spent the evening with Pam Moore, who handed over to me all the accounts etc. for my new role as Treasurer.

"Brigadoon", performed earlier this year, was the Society's 58th show & our accounts date from the post-war period when production resumed after the war years 1939 – 1945.

13th June 1982 Sunday

"Tea at Trinity". Joanne (aged 8) & I went on a guided walk in Leicester. We started from the Town Hall & went to the ancient Guildhall. From there we went to St. Mary de Castro (St. Mary of the Castle), through the Castle Gardens & into the Trinity Hospital in the Newarke, founded in 1331 A.D.

15th June 1982 Tuesday

The Battle for the Falkland Islands has been won by Britain.

We lost 4 ships – 1. H.M.S. Sheffield. 2. H.M.S. Ardent. 3. H.M.S. Antelope. 4. H.M.S. Coventry. We lost 237 men & now we have the major problem of garrisoning the islands. This will cost around £1,000 million a year. Is it worth it?

17th June 1982 Thursday

We plant a community of settlers on the Falkland Islands 8,000 miles away from home & insist that we have a right to sovereignty for all time.

The Argentinians, however, firmly believe that these islands, which they call the Malvinas, are theirs. They will fight another day.

Hewes, Mary, 27 Leicester Road, Ravenstone, loving wife of the late Reginald Arthur, dearly loved mother of Betty, passed peacefully away June 17th 1982 at Bosworth Park Infirmary. Funeral service at St. Mary's Church, Snibston on Wednesday June 23rd at 10-15 a.m., followed by cremation at Loughborough Crematorium. No flowers by request, donations if so desired to the Friends of Market Bosworth Hospital, c/o Mr Wood, 151 The Park, Market Bosworth, Nuneaton. Tel. 290074.

My Darling Mum.

19th June 1982 Saturday

After 3 years of pain & anguish, Mum is now at peace. She became desperately ill last Thursday & I was called from work to her bedside. I arrived at 2 p.m. & she knew I was there. She said, "Lift me up" & within half an hour she had died. I am so pleased to know she can suffer no more.

21st June 1982 Monday

A Prince is born. At 9.03p.m. the Princess of Wales gave birth to a baby boy – 7lbs. 1 ½ oz. This is the first child born to a Prince & Princess of Wales since 1905 (the year my Mum was born). The baby was born at St. Mary's Hospital, Paddington, London.

23rd June 1982 Wednesday

My darling Mum's funeral. We went to dear little St. Mary's Church, Snibston, where a little gathering of friends & relations gathered to bid her farewell. The Vicar, the Revd. David Jennings, conducted the service beautifully, & Pat & Bunting were either side of me as pillars of support.

The hymns I chose for Mum's funeral were – 1. God that Madest Earth & Heaven. 2. Forever with the Lord. I also requested Isaiah, Chapter 40, verses 28 – 31. So my Mum was carried up to heaven on eagle's wings to stand before God. (See 11th May 1981.)

Mum's funeral procession went from home via Snibston School to St. Mary's Church, just as my dad's had done in 1939. After the service, it then continued down the little lane past where her old farm-house once stood. Outside the farm gate the procession halted for Mum to say goodbye, before cremation at Loughborough.

29th June 1982 Tuesday

William Philip Arthur Louis.

The new baby Prince will be called His Royal Highness Prince William of Wales.

He is second in line to the throne after his father, Charles. The 1st King William was of course William the Conqueror. The new baby will be King William **V**.

1st July 1982 Thursday

Mum's ashes were laid to rest this morning inside my dad's grave. There were 7 of us standing by the grave as the Vicar held a very brief service including Cardinal Newman's prayer, "May he support us all the day long …….. Then in his mercy may he give us a safe lodging, a holy rest, and peace at the last."

3ʳᵈ July 1982 Saturday
"Peace I leave with you. My peace I give unto you." This was the last Will & Testament of the Lord Jesus Christ. Today I made my Will. £1,000 to each of my 3 churches – St. Martin's, St. Michael's & St. Mary's. £1,000 each to Mary Blue, Michael & Julian.
All the rest to you, dear child.

5ᵗʰ July 1982 Monday
The solicitor thought it very strange that I should think such a lot of you. But I know how much I share with my dad's mother, who died in the year that I was born. She was a child of the 19ᵗʰ Century. I was a child of the 20ᵗʰ Century, & you are a child of the 21ˢᵗ Century.

7ᵗʰ July 1982 Wednesday
£7,700 per year. The latest rise in Civil Service pay has brought the top of the Executive Officer grade to £7,700. As fast as wages go up, so up & up go the cost of petrol, telephone bills, fuel bills, food, etc. My next big expense will be buying a new car.

9ᵗʰ July 1982 Friday
My darling Mum's Death Certificate says that she died of – A. Septicaemia. B. Pyelonephritis. C. Chronic Pyelonephritis.
This means that her kidneys failed completely & her blood became septic. There was nothing to indicate why she was unable to stand up and walk.

11ᵗʰ July 1982 Sunday
The one & only wreath for my Mum (by request) was from me. I chose one in the shape of an anchor to symbolise "anchored safe in the harbour of Heaven". When my dad died in the prime of his life he had 99 wreaths. The 99 and the one are now complete.

13ᵗʰ July 1982 Tuesday
Leslie Hale, my dad's best friend, is 80 years old today. He wrote such a lovely letter to my Mum in 1939 when my dad died, & he wrote such a lovely letter to me when my Mum died. He said, "I could see you at the House of Lords, where I am entitled to go. The afternoon tea is very good."

15ᵗʰ July 1982 Thursday
51 yesterday – 3 x 17. My first birthday as an orphan. Reevsie (viz Mrs Patricia Walsom) my old friend from the Motor Licence Office, invited me for tea & the evening. She & Tony will be celebrating their Silver Wedding next year. Their daughter Joanne is now a lovely lively teenager.

17ᵗʰ July 1982 Saturday
Susan Hewes (my god-daughter) who married Richard Underwood in March 1978, has now left her husband for a fellow school teacher. There are so many broken marriages today, I am thankful to belong to my Mum & Dad whose love was profound & of whose memory I can always be very proud.

19ᵗʰ July 1982 Monday
Leslie Hale, in his recent letter to me, said, "You had parents to be proud of. I met your father 60 years ago, & I can see him now as he stood always upright ……"
I was pleased to be able to write to Leslie Hale & thank him for all that he did for us (when my dad died) & say, "I am equally proud of you."

21ˢᵗ July 1982 Wednesday
The latest victims of an I.R.A. bomb in London are members of the Household Cavalry, both men & horses. They were just coming from Hyde Park when the remote-controlled bomb exploded.
Shortly afterwards a second bomb, planted under the bandstand in Regent's Park, killed six of the bandsmen.

23ʳᵈ July 1982 Friday
"Salad Days" – a light-hearted musical, is now showing for the summer season at the Haymarket Theatre in Leicester. I took Joanne (aged 8) and her cousin Tina (aged 9) to the matinee on Wednesday & went again this evening with Pat & Evelyn. Sitting on the front row I loved seeing it all over again.

25ᵗʰ July 1982 Sunday
St. James Day. Pat & Evelyn invited Katherine (aged 78) & me to the Patronal Festival Service at St. James, Snibston, where the preacher was The Venerable Harold Lockley, Archdeacon of Loughborough. It was a memorable service where we learned all about James, who followed Christ "immediately".

27ᵗʰ July 1982 Tuesday
"They immediately left their ship & their father & followed Jesus." – Matthew 4. 22.
Jesus chose those who were impulsive. They were decisive & active. They did not always make the right decision, but that did not matter. Far better to be bold & brave than to dither about & achieve nothing.

29ᵗʰ July 1982 Thursday
James & John were brothers whom Jesus surnamed Boanerges – "The Sons of Thunder" Mark 3. 17. They were inseparable brothers & teach us the importance of brotherly love.
The Archdeacon told us the story of a boy carrying his brother on his back up a big hill.
"He is no burden" said the boy, "He is my brother."

31ˢᵗ July 1982 Saturday
Baby Prince William will be christened next week on August 4ᵗʰ – the Queen Mother's 82ⁿᵈ birthday. Baby Prince William is the son of Charles, & is the eldest child of the Queen – Elizabeth; & Elizabeth the Queen Mother is the baby's great grandmother. The baby is 2ⁿᵈ in line to the throne.

2ⁿᵈ August 1982 Monday
Prince William will be the 21ˢᵗ Century King. He will be the 42ⁿᵈ monarch since the Norman Conquest, & will be the 14ᵗʰ in direct descent from James I of England & VI of Scotland.
(See Matthew Chapter 1 verse 17) "From Abram to David – from David to captivity in Babylon – from Babylon to Christ."

4th August 1982 Wednesday
Luncheon with my Lord Hale. What a rare joy & a privilege it was for me today to visit the Hale family at their home in Dulwich, South London. Meeting Leslie Hale was for me like meeting the great Winston Churchill. With the roar of a lion he can devour or befriend you. (See 30th November 1964)

Note – Lord Hale lives with his daughter Lesley & son Bill, both unmarried, & just a little older than me.

Spent the night in London at St. James Hotel, Buckingham Gate, after visiting Leslie Hale. Never have I enjoyed such sumptuous luxury in a single bedroom. I had my own private toilet & bath – coloured television in the bedroom, phone, radio, writing paper & envelopes, & no noisy traffic. According to the brochure, St. James Hotel was built in the 19th Century to accommodate the overflow of guests from Buckingham Palace. It is the closest hotel to Buckingham Palace & yet the traffic could hardly be heard from the bedroom which I had. How I loved this momentous trip to London.

10th August 1982 Tuesday
St. Augustine, being asked, "What is the first thing in religion?" replied, "Humility".
"And what is the second?" "Humility". "And what is the third?" "Humility".
Leslie Hale talked to me of his days as a lawyer. He told me about a proud man who learned humility & how he wept like a child.

12th August 1982 Thursday
Sitting at the feet of Leslie Hale was like sitting at the feet of Socrates & learning from him great wisdom. All his life he has been such a learned & busy man that he has been almost inaccessible. Can you imagine then, how much it meant to me to have his undivided attention last week?

14th August 1982 Saturday
Following Prime Minister Margaret Thatcher's glorying over victory in the Falkland Islands conflict, where so many lives were lost & much suffering resulted, a Franciscan monk has written to the Leicester Mercury to say she clearly knows nothing about the life or the aims of St. Francis – Signed Robert Widdowson, Franciscan Tertiary. (See 5th May 1979)

16th August 1982 Monday
Gas Standards Branch is at the moment being landscaped. Having recently had an extension to the building to house bigger laboratories, the whole of the forecourt is now being transformed into a picturesque frontage. There are mountains of rubble, sand & soil, kerb stones, slabs etc. & a hive of activity.

18th August 1982 Wednesday
The future of Gas Standards Branch, which at present is part of the government's Department of Energy, is being discussed at ministerial level. After considering a variety of options it is now thought likely that the Branch might be split between the "Department of Trade" & the "Health and Safety Executive".

20th August 1982 Friday
"**Divine Providence**" – In the current Cathedral Newsletter, No. 180, the present Provost, the Revd. Alan Warren, aged 50, says, "A recent letter to me was addressed to the Very Revd. The **Providence** of Leicester." Earlier in his life, when he was Canon Missioner, he was called **Commissionaire**.

22nd August 1982 Sunday
Roll of Honour
Plantagenet. *August 22nd 1485 at Bosworth Field.*
There died fighting bravely, Richard III, King of England, soldier, statesman, gentleman.
Remember him O God for good, and bring him unto glory through the suffering and death of the captain of our salvation. Service in the cathedral, August 22nd at 2-30 p.m. All welcome. – Dorothy Cooke.

Went to Leicester Cathedral to the "Battle of Bosworth Memorial Service & Dedication of the Richard III Memorial Stone." – A magnificent slab set in the floor of the chancel.

24th August 1982 Tuesday
Yesterday would have been my darling Mum's 77th birthday. After all her suffering, her pain, her tears, & her utter despair, there is nothing better she would have wished for than to be celebrating her birthday at rest with my dad, reaping in joy what was sown in tears. Psalm 126

26th August 1982 Thursday
To celebrate my Mum's 77th birthday, the World Cycling Championships began their track events in Leicester – one of the finest and fastest cycle tracks in Europe.
It is 12 years since the World Cycling Championships were held in Leicester, when Mum & I were so thrilled to see them.

28th August 1982 Saturday
World Cycling Championships in Leicester!
Joanne (aged 8) & I spent the afternoon at Saffron Lane Sports Centre, where we cheered & yelled with all the rest as the champions of the world whizzed round & round the 333.3 metres track with its 37° angle of inclination. Really super!

30th August 1982 Monday
In August last year, my little friend Joanne greeted me with a "gat-toothed" smile because her 2 front teeth came out. Now, 12 months later, she has 2 beautiful front teeth, with a gap either side, as another 2 teeth have come out. Soon she will be a grown young lady.

1st September 1982 Wednesday
The latest model in the Mini range of cars is the Mini Metro. I cannot afford a brand new car at £4,700, but have chosen an ex-demonstration model which is on offer at £3,850.
I have £1,000 from my darling Mum; £1,850 in the Building Society; & all my Premium Savings Bonds £1,000.

3rd September 1982 Friday

Coalville Amateurs Publicity Committee.

Viz. The new producer, John Lewin; the Secretary, Olive Meakin; the Treasurer – me (with the help of the retiring Treasurer, Pam Moore); House Manager, Brian Moore; & Wardrobe Mistress, Betty Henn, met to discuss the cost of our next show – Calamity Jane.

5th September 1982 Sunday

We estimated that it would cost about £4,000 to stage Calamity Jane.

Costumes £400; scenery £800; hire of hall £600 (that includes rehearsals every week from September to March); printing - posters, programmes & tickets £450; royalties £600; insurance, orchestra, lighting, etc.

7th September 1982 Tuesday

Our Sunday School outing this year was to Wicksteed Park on the outskirts of Kettering.

We had one bus-load. I sat on the front seat with the Rector, the Revd. Leslie Buckroyd, with Joanne & her dad immediately behind. It was a lovely sunny day & I enjoyed the company of Joanne & Dave.

9th September 1982 Thursday

Joanne (aged 8) was able to go on more adventurous equipment with her dad at Wicksteed, while I was quite content to watch them. They went time & time again on the Dodgem Cars; they went up & down & round on the Big Wheel; & the outcome of it all was that poor Joanne felt sick.

11th September 1982 Saturday

B.B.C. Television's "Antiques Roadshow" came to Leicester this week.

We all took our treasured antiques for valuation & comments from the experts who could tell in an instant the date, the country of origin & every detail of the items shown to them. I took Mum's white jug – 1845.

13th September 1982 Monday

I sold for £100, a brass lamp, a brass jam kettle, a brass saucepan, a brass candlestick & a mahogany bed-table which belonged to Mum, & which have lain tucked away for a long time. I did not sell Mum's white jug which is a "Minton" & valued by the experts at £20.

15th September 1982 Wednesday

Princess Grace of Monaco, aged 52, died yesterday from injuries suffered in a car crash on Monday. She truly was a fairy-tale Princess, having started her career as a beautiful Hollywood film star. While in Monaco she fell in love & married the eligible Prince Rainier & now leaves 2 daughters and one son.

17th September 1982 Friday

Sir Thomas White (see 17th September 1980) is believed never to have set foot in Leicester. A new book has just been written about him by A. Daly Briscoe called "A Marian Lord Mayor". He was a devout Catholic who became Lord Mayor of London in 1553. In turn each year, Coventry, Northampton, Leicester, Nottingham & Warwick benefit from his will in a repayable loan.

Sir Thomas White originally gave £1,400 to Coventry Corporation to rescue the city from its ruin & decay. On his death a loan system was established whereby £40 would go to one recipient from Coventry every fifth year & that in each of the intervening years that sum was to be lent in turn to young men from Northampton, Leicester, Nottingham & Warwick.

£40 to Leicester every 5th year has grown over a 400 year period of investment to an income of £40,000. So, when the time comes to think about making a Will, you could take as your example Sir Thomas White, who at the age of 12 was apprenticed to a London merchant tailor, & who made good.

23rd September 1982 Thursday

Mini Clubman, with radio, R registration, 68,000 miles, lady owner, £950. Telephone Coalville 36583.

PNR 867R - Only one person came to inspect my car – Mr. Edwin English, 44 Piers Road, Glenfield.

He said he would give me £750 & so I sold it to him for the price he offered & he paid me – **cash**.

25th September 1982 Saturday

This week we have had the front of our house painted & decorated by Barker & Weston of Ashby-de-la-Zouch, so instead of being the scruffiest in the row, it now looks better than the others. The front door & the nearby supporting post are green & all the rest is cream. The next job will be the stairs.

27th September 1982 Monday

I have now been at Gas Standards Branch for 4 ½ years. The great extension is now complete & so it is all change as regards office accommodation.

I have moved from Room 007, which I shared with Rose (aged 50) and Lisa (aged 18), to the Registry which is a bustling busy noisy thoroughfare.

29th September 1982 Wednesday

Mary Moore (now 71) is spending a week with me again, so I have taken a few days holiday.

Yesterday we motored to Derby to visit Edith Whittaker; & she is also visiting her other old friends – Molly, Joyce, Ivy, Florrie, Olive, etc. Next Saturday she is joining the merry throng for a re-union of old scholars at Coalville Grammar School.

Note – Mary Moore went to school at Coalville Grammar School & lived here until she married her cousin Mick Dunn & moved to Essex.

1st October 1982 Friday

UBC 783X is the beautiful Mini Metro which I have now acquired. It is ex-demonstration & is one year old. Tyre pressures have now gone metric – 28 lbf/m^2 is 2.0 bar (front wheels) and 26 lbf/inch^2 is 1.8 bar (back wheels). This is a hatch-back car which allows lots of room for carrying things.

3rd October 1982 Sunday

Harvest Festival at little St. Mary's this year was very special to me. As we sang "…. All good gifts around us are sent from Heaven above", I thought of the good gift of my Mum & Dad, now together just outside the walls of the church. We also sang, "...... who from our

Mother's arms hath blessed us on our way ...." Here I was brought as a baby to be christened.

5th October 1982 Tuesday

Coalville Grammar School re-union which was held last Saturday drew old scholars from as far back as 1909, when the school first opened. Auntie Doris from Mountsorrel, now aged 87, was guest of honour, being the very first pupil. She looked very smart and sprightly.

7th October 1982 Thursday

What an amazing experience it was to meet again after 35 years people I had last seen at school. I met Elaine Cooper, Jean Merchant, Margaret White, Jean Roddis, Audrey Cooper, Margaret Pegg, Teresa Lardner, Marie Adcock, Mina Hart, Nancy Lee etc., all looking remarkably good & so friendly.

9th October 1982 Saturday

Joanne, aged 8, has spent so much time with me that I can now see myself reflected in her. She reacts with the self-same words & makes observations which I would make. She has picked up my expressions & is happy to share my interests, even though at times she is the only child in a gathering of grown ups.

11th October 1982 Monday

Word Processors are the latest form of type-writers, which display all the wonders of modern technology. We have been given several demonstrations at work & have marvelled at the way they can literally think for themselves, correcting errors, erasing, balancing accounts, and even spelling.

13th October 1982 Wednesday

The Tudor warship "Mary Rose" sank in 1545 off the coast of the Isle of Wight as she went into battle against the French. King Henry VIII watched the pride of his fleet sink.

This week 437 years on, Prince Charles watched this same ship hoisted from the depths at a cost of £4 million.

15th October 1982 Friday

A letter from the Vatican! "His Holiness Pope John Paul II has directed the Secretariat of State to express his gratitude for the kind message sent to him with regard to his pastoral visit to Britain. His Holiness appreciates the kind sentiments which prompted this gesture and prays that God will fill all hearts with his gifts of peace and joy." Signed Monsignor G.B. RE.

17th October 1982 Sunday

The letter which I received from the Vatican came from Nottingham in a "Diocese of Nottingham" franked envelope. It contained a small picture of the Pope, signed "Joannes Paulus II in apostolic itinere ad Philippinarum 16 - 27th February 1981"

"Jesus Christ the same yesterday & today & forever" Hebrews 13. 8.

19th October 1982 Tuesday
Snibston School Diary 1907 – 1941.

This fascinating book was loaned to me & I spent many hours reading in detail its 500 pages. The Hewes family was in the book from beginning to end. It spanned the 2

Great Wars, the poverty of the 1920s, the Royal Weddings, Jubilees, Coronations & Eclipses.

The old School Diary showed my Mum & Dad's lives leading them together. It mentioned my Mum's twin sister, Cissie Sketchley aged 10, in 1915 when she died of diphtheria.

It mentioned my dad's funeral in 1939.

"Alderman R. Blower called to ask that playtime might not coincide with the funeral of Mr. R. Hewes. 16th January 1939."

Albert Henry Hudson, who became Headmaster at Snibston School in 1937, wrote with such sincerity in the School Diary, "November 10th 1937 – I have heard today with great regret that Mr. Sketchley passed away last evening." (This was Mum's dad)

The School Reports said of him that he was a vigorous & stimulating teacher.

Snibston School Diary 1941 – 1975.

This diary is another fascinating record of school life interwoven with the joys & sorrows of the village and the nation.

February 11th 1944 reads, "Rita Hewes was present in the afternoon despite having received news that her father had died of wounds received in action."

Norman Hewes, my cousin, son of my dad's brother Aubrey, died during the 1939–45 war in Italy.

June 11th 1951 in the School Diary reads, "Received sad news of death of Robert Hewes, one of our old boys." This was my brother, who died at the age of 17, now at rest in little St. Mary's Churchyard with other scholars & teachers.

In the Churchyard at little St. Mary's is my dad. Embraced within his grave is my Mum. At his feet lie the ashes of his brother Hedley and Hedley's wife Nellie. Immediately opposite is his dad, his mother & sister Cis. Immediately behind are Mum's dad, Mum's mother & also step-mother. Together for ever.

31st October 1982 Sunday

Yesterday I bought my second pair of specs. They are bi-focal, with the bottom part magnifying & the top part ordinary vision. They cost £73 & I am very pleased with them. This month also I have launched out on a new camera £80 and a gorgeous sheepskin lined suede ¾ length coat £160.

2nd November 1982 Tuesday

A day in Coventry. Took Joanne to Coventry to show her the old Cathedral & the new. Showed her Lady Godiva's statue & then we wandered through the shopping precinct where we bought one or two Christmas presents. The sun shone for our visit & the ruined Cathedral had a backcloth of blue sky.

4th November 1982 Thursday
"A Girl for all Seasons"

I like Spring because all the pretty flowers start to grow. Spring is lovely because people can get out and about. Summer is even better because people do gardening and go on holiday and sunbathe, of course.

Autumn is very attractive because all the trees and flowers go a beautiful colour. The flowers look gold and rich. Winter has great gale force winds. All the trees

swish and sway. And all the people get blown away.
Joanne Page, 31 Leicester Road, Ravenstone.

Once again my little friend has a letter she has written to the Leicester Mercury in pride of place with a framed edge. (See 19th January 1982) There is now a "Junior Page 4" in the Leicester Mercury and they encourage children to send them interesting letters.

6th November 1982 Saturday
"Do not have to say something. Have something to say." I am reminded of these words of wisdom when there is little of consequence to write in my diary.

I was delighted to see Sharon (Mary Blue's step-daughter) writing in a make-shift home-made diary a detailed account of her daily activities, so I have bought her a diary for 1983.

8th November 1982 Monday
London is now safe from floods. Modern technology has triumphed where King Canute failed. Yesterday afternoon in London the tide was stopped when the vast gates of the River Thames flood barrier were raised in a successful test. It is the world's largest moveable flood barrier, 570 yards long & should last for 100 years.

The River Thames flood barrier has taken 8 years to construct & has cost £450 million. It has 10 steel gates which span the width of the river and when fully raised are 50 feet above the river. Tide levels have risen 2 feet at London Bridge over the past 100 years because London is sinking on its clay bed.

12th November 1982 Friday
London sinking on its feet of clay reminds me of the dream which Nebuchadnezzar, King of Babylon, had. (See the Book of Daniel, Chapter 2.)

He dreamed of a great image whose head was of fine gold, his breast & his arms were of silver, his belly & his thighs were of brass, his legs of iron, and his feet were part iron & part clay.

14th November 1982 Sunday
Leonid Brezhnev, Soviet leader for the past 18 years, died last Wednesday, aged 75.

His predecessor was Nikita Khrushchev & he will be succeeded by Yuri Andropov, former KGB Chief, aged 68, who ran the Soviet KGB secret police for 15 years before retiring this spring. The Bolshevik Revolution took place in 1917.

16th November 1982 Tuesday
Maurice Williams, Senior Gas Engineer at Gas Standards Branch retired this month & we had a lovely farewell party in the Conference Room at work. He provided an excellent buffet for about 75 people including people he had worked with previously from North Thames Gas, other retired members of staff, wives & husbands.

18th November 1982 Thursday
"The Donkey Sanctuary" – This was my darling Mum's charity which she supported. Today she received a newsletter inviting her to spend a week next year from 3rd – 10th May in Sidmouth, Devon, where 4 hotels have agreed to keep the majority of their rooms free for supporters of the Donkey Sanctuary. Arrangements will be made to visit the donkeys.

20th November 1982 Saturday
Having spent 1979, 1980 & 1981 holidaying on the Costa Ravo, I have accepted the invitation from Mrs Svendsen, administrator of the Donkey Sanctuary, to holiday at the Hotel Riviera, Sidmouth, next year. The Donkey Sanctuary looks after hundreds of donkeys which have suffered from neglect or cruelty & helps them to live happily ever after.

22nd November 1982 Monday
"Privatisation" is the Government's bright idea to get themselves more money, but their bid to give the public a stake in North Sea oil has been labelled a fiasco after ¾ of the £550 million issue were not sold. Energy Secretary Mr Nigel Lawson (M.P. for Blaby) has been accused of converting a successful national corporation into a stock exchange flop.

24th November 1982 Wednesday
The Cashless Society is coming. "As part of the general movement throughout the economy to systems of cashless pay, the Government is committed to accelerating the move to cashless monthly pay among non-industrial civil servants." Staff are being offered £100 "incentive payment" if they agree to transfer to monthly pay by Credit Transfer.

26th November 1982 Friday
Joanne, aged 8, now puts me right as her knowledge increases. "How do you spell symmetry?" she asked me. I did not know, but she did.

She has a very interesting life at school, & learns about a wide range of topics. She goes out & about & visits museums, castles, churches, a blacksmith at work & other such things.

28th November 1982 Sunday
"Know ye not that ye are the temple of God & that the Spirit of God dwelleth in you? If any man defile the temple of God, him shall God destroy; for the temple of God is holy, which temple ye are." I Corinthians. 3. 16. The Rector of Ravenstone, the Revd. Leslie Buckroyd, reminded us that each one of us is a holy living temple.

30th November 1982 Tuesday
Our Annual Christmas Fair in Ravenstone Village Institute & our 11th effort with a stall for the Sunday School. We made only £10-80p towards the £500 total. I have mentioned to the Rector, the Revd. Leslie Buckroyd, & to the other teachers Mrs Bird & Diane Robert, that I hope to "retire" next summer.

2nd December 1982 Thursday
Next Sunday is our Sunday School Prize Giving & my little friend Joanne has been chosen to read the lesson – I Corinthians, Chapter 12, verses 4 – 12. This is the first time she has ever read the lesson & it gladdens my heart to hear her, as she reads it over and over again to me, until she almost knows it off by heart.

4th December 1982 Saturday
Visited poor old cousin Audrey, who was in such a sorry

state that it was impossible to hold any coherent conversation with her at all. Being bent almost double with curvature of the spine, she wandered from one person to another, not knowing who she was talking to, & they not knowing what she was saying.

6th December 1982 Monday

"Bloodbath at Ballykelly" "At 11 o'clock on Monday night, an active service unit of the South Derry brigade of the Irish National Liberation Army placed a bomb in the Droppin Well pub, Ballykelly, known to be frequented by the British Army." Sixteen people died, including 9 soldiers, and 60 were injured – "Massacre without Mercy".

8th December 1982 Wednesday

Ravenstone Sunday School Christmas Party. Thanks again to Wenda Hickin & Rita Freestone the children had a lovely party. "Uncle Harry" another local conjurer came & kept the children well entertained after they had eaten; & finally Father Christmas arrived & gave each child a present. The younger children were really angelic.

10th December 1982 Friday

What is Joy? In the Ravenstone Parish Magazine this month, the Rector quotes part of a poem written by Robert Bridges 1844 – 1930.

"Ah heavenly joy! But who hath ever heard, who hath seen joy, or who shall ever find Joy's language? There is neither speech nor word; nought but itself to teach it to mankind."

12th December 1982 Sunday

Susan Hewes, my god-daughter, who married Richard Underwood on March 25th 1978, yesterday married John Stuart. (I was not invited to the wedding.)

Peter Hewes, her brother, also remarried recently following the break-up of his marriage.

Lesley, their sister, remains happily married to her first cousin, John Sear.

14th December 1982 Tuesday

Went to Packington Church to see 3 of my girls from Sunday School confirmed – Clare Allsop, Joanne Freestone & Catherine Groocock.

The Bishop of Leicester, Dr. Richard Rutt, spoke about the great season of Advent – the coming of Christ & how we should all be prepared – "The Kingdom of God is nigh."

16th December 1982 Thursday

The Bishop of Leicester at Packington Church said that by regular worship & regular listening to the Word of God, we would find the Kingdom of Heaven within our hearts here on Earth. It was not just a question of "Be good & you will eventually go to heaven". Trust God & let the Holy Spirit work in you.

18th December 1982 Saturday

Jubilate! I have just finished writing this year's Staff Reports – Angela & Eileen, the 2 typists, Karen aged 18, C.A., Lisa, Rose & Jan, C.O.s. How thankful I am that the form has been revised to "reflect current needs" & does not require so many comments.

20th December 1982 Monday

Went to Snibston School again to see Joanne, aged 8, in the Christmas concert. It was the infants who stole the show in their Nativity Play. The little angels were little angels indeed & I thought how quickly they change from infants to juniors to seniors & then parents to grandparents.

22nd December 1982 Wednesday

I seem to notice the changing pattern of life in the village more particularly because I have not followed the normal course of life.

I have not married & raised a family of my own, but seem to be more like an onlooker, a listener & a recorder, & do not notice how much I change myself.

24th December 1982 Friday

"At this time I remember with you your dear mother now cared for by those Guardian Angels we are all privileged to possess, in one of the mansions of God's House. So parting is only temporarily & I am sure that you will find great strength in this teaching of our Church at this festive season. So be of good cheer.

Your old Rector & friend, Gustav Aronsohn."

26th December 1982 Sunday

It was Christmas 1965 when we said fond farewell to our Rector, the Reverend Gustav Aronsohn, but every year since then he has sent a Christmas card to Mum & me. As I told you in December 1965, he can stir me to the very depths of my soul, & I have a tremendous affinity with him. Like Leslie Hale, he is a wise and learned old man.

28th December 1982 Tuesday

Holy Communion at little St. Mary's on Christmas morning was very special to me this year, with my Mum & Dad & brother all there in spirit. Being very much alone in this world, I feel more in tune with heaven than with earth; & in the Communion Service we pray that we may be fulfilled with, "Thy Grace and Heavenly Benediction."

30th December 1982 Thursday

King Charles II, having been restored to his throne, was determined never to go on his travels again. The great thing about England, he said, was that it was the only country in the world where you could go for a walk every day of the year. This I have endeavoured to do since I began in April.

* * *

1983

2nd January 1983 Sunday

"Jesus saith unto her, Mary." John 20. 16.
This is the text I have chosen to be put in the Book of Remembrance at Snibston Church. The book was acquired only last year in memory of my old teacher – Albert Henry Hudson. On the page for June 17th is my Mum's name & this simple meaningful text.

Note – On June 17th last year my Mum, Mary, died. Now her name is entered in the Book of Remembrance held at St. James Church, Snibston.

4th January 1983 Tuesday

The painters & decorators – Barker & Weston – started work today on the staircase and landing. I have chosen "Manders" wallpaper at £3-78p per roll, & we need 10 rolls. I have also chosen another mural from "Scandecor" – the good ship Esmeralda. I am hoping to have new fitted carpets also in due course.

6th January 1983 Thursday

How I love being "Treasurer" to Coalville Amateurs. Every day in the post I receive applications for tickets from our 100 patrons or from one of the local Darby & Joan clubs.
I have bought a very smart executive case to hold the books of tickets & a very nice "Treasurer's bag" for every day use.

8th January 1983 Saturday

Joanne & I went to the Haymarket Theatre, Leicester, to see the musical, "South Pacific". We had seats on the front row & enjoyed the show very much. Joanne, now nearly 9 years old, was able to follow the story & was aware that Lt. Cable had been reported killed in action. Why, then, did he appear in the finale?

10th January 1983 Monday

Prime Minister, Margaret Thatcher, has gone to the Falkland Islands for a surprise visit to boost the morale of the islanders. "Hello – how are you?" she says to them all, one by one, without waiting to hear their answer. She has been given the Freedom of the Falkland Islands, as like Napoleon, she almost crowns herself.

12th January 1983 Wednesday

Auntie Dos's best friend Dol Dean, officially Mrs Dorothy Uridge, whose husband when he was a little boy spoke to Queen Victoria, died today aged 89. Auntie Dos has been feeling very low & listless for the past month or two & the news of Dol's death was a great blow to her. They had been pals for 60 years.

14th January 1983 Friday

Today I had new fitted carpet on the stairs and landing to enhance the newly decorated walls. I chose Axminster "Acropolis" which blended reasonably well the carpet in the front bedroom & which cost just under £10 per square yard. The total cost with underlay etc. was £183. The cost for papering and decorating was £200.

16th January 1983 Sunday

Epiphany II. "Almighty & everlasting God, who dost govern all things in heaven and earth, mercifully hear the supplications of thy people, and grant us thy peace all the days of our life; through Jesus Christ our Lord."
This is the lovely collect set for today, helping us to evaporate into heaven.

18th January 1983 Tuesday

Brother Pat & I went to Hugglescote Church for Dol Dean's funeral. We met her brother Fred, aged 91 – a wonderful old man who could hardly walk & was almost blind, but was so pleased to meet us. He had a marvellous memory & it was a joy to talk to him. He had journeyed from Birmingham.

20th January 1983 Thursday

Mount St. Bernard Abbey opened its doors yesterday for an Ecumenical Service* where monks sat intermingled with all who wished to attend. I was delighted to take with me Joanne, brother Pat and Katherine. We arrived early & went into the monastery shop where I bought "Jesus, the Good Shepherd."

(*A week of prayer for Christian Unity. I went with 8 year old Joanne, 64 year old brother Pat & 78 year old Katherine Sullivan, who is a devout Roman Catholic.)

I Corinthians 12. verses 4-12. Imagine how Joanne & I felt when we heard this familiar passage read to us at the Monastery, (See 2nd December 1982).
After the service we walked under the starlight on the crunchy frosty ground to the Refectory where we had cream cakes & trifle; & all the monks circulated freely.

24th January 1983 Monday

The Bishop of Leicester, Dr. Richard Rutt, has asked for all Sunday Schools in the Diocese to give him a report on their particular activities & curriculum. This is the first time in my 25 years as a Sunday School teacher that I have been asked to do this, but I have enjoyed writing the report with the help of June & Diane.

26th January 1983 Wednesday

Allocation for tickets for "Calamity Jane". Spent the evening at the home of Peter Jacques (Chairman & Musical Director of Coalville Amateurs) where we spent from 7p.m. until midnight issuing tickets for over a hundred applications. There were 8 of us on the job including Olive (Secretary) & me (Treasurer).

28th January 1983 Friday

Took Joanne, aged 8, to the Concordia Theatre, Hinckley, to see her third Pantomime – "Cinderella". Again we were fortunate enough to have seats on the front row & what a magnificent Pantomime it was. I laughed until I cried at the antics of the Ugly Sisters, & we adored the Shetland ponies.

30th January 1983 Sunday

The wearing of seat belts in motor cars comes into force at midnight tonight.
After 10 years of attempts in the House of Commons & Lords, Lord Nugent, aged 75, has finally won through. He was formerly President of "The Royal Society for the

Prevention of Accidents" = R.O.S.P.A. The new law is called "Nugent's Law".

1st February 1983 Tuesday

What a busy time I am having as "Treasurer". I had a day's holiday to sort out all the tickets we had allocated. I went through them all one by one & made a small replica chart of each day, keeping a record of exactly which tickets were for which particular member or patron.

We can accommodate approximately 500 people in one sitting at our show, & we give 6 performances during the week. This means we have about 3,000 tickets to sell. On our advance booking night we allocated over 2,000 including children.

Children & pensioners pay £1 & others pay £1-60p. The opening night (i.e. Tuesday) & Saturday matinee are for pensioners. There are no reduced prices on Friday or Saturday evening. We also have a small balcony of 3 rows only, where tickets are £1-20p.

7th February 1983 Monday

My darling Mum is hopefully now in a better world "now cared for by those guardian angels we all are privileged to possess, in one of the mansions of God's House" as my old friend & Rector, Gustav Aronsohn, put it so beautifully. How good it is to know that the Lord Himself has prepared a place for us. (See John 14.)

9th February 1983 Wednesday

St. John, Chapter 14, is my favourite Chapter in the whole Bible. It starts with those wonderful words of Christ, "Let not your heart be troubled .... I am the way, the truth and the life ..... Peace I leave with you, my peace I give unto you. Let not your heart be troubled, neither let it be afraid."

11th February 1983 Friday

"The Church & the Bomb". For 5 hours the Bishops of the Church of England wrestled with the problem of nuclear warfare. Do we or do we not build up our stock of nuclear weapons? The vote was 338 to 100 in favour of maintaining our nuclear weapons, hoping that this would serve to deter any aggressors.

13th February 1983 Sunday

Joanne has a younger friend Simone, aged 7, who comes with us to Sunday School. Joanne and Simone amuse themselves for a while on the piano in our front room. Simone is quite impressed by Joanne's piano playing & asked me today if I would give her lessons.

15th February 1983 Tuesday

Real life drama at work this week as young Lisa comes between young Karen and her fiancé David. The wedding fixed for May this year is now cancelled & it has been decided to move Lisa to another office where she & Karen will not be obliged to work side by side.

17th February 1983 Thursday

The house & home my mother has given to me is a blessing indeed. How I appreciate my haven & my home.

The kitchen & rear quarters, however, are in need of drastic alteration. The fire in the kitchen is smokey & needs at least £1,000 to change the boiler. A complete new kitchen would cost £10,000.

19th February 1983 Saturday

Visited poor Cousin Audrey at Tillson House, Coalville. She was in bed & appeared to be heavily drugged. She was asleep most of the time & only occasionally said a few words to herself. How very sad to be old & helpless. I just sat there in silence & thought of us all growing old and dying.

21st February 1983 Monday

"Everyone will be met either at Exeter St. David's Station or Exeter Coach Station & taken to their hotel & there will be shuttle services twice a day up to the Donkey Sanctuary. We shall also arrange day visits to our other farms." I am hoping to travel by coach from Leicester to Exeter on 3rd May.

23rd February 1983 Wednesday

It is 3 years since my little friend used to skip & jump round & round & round my chair making me feel that I was in a magic fairy circle. She still brings magic into my life as she visits me daily & we can now follow more & more new pursuits, going further afield & broadening our horizons.

25th February 1983 Friday

Mahatma Gandhi, who was assassinated while I was still at school, is the inspiration behind the latest epic film "**Gandhi**" which I saw this week. This man of God, like Socrates & like Christ, spoke of love in a world of wickedness. The world was not worthy of him, yet he died for it.

27th February 1983 Sunday

Dress rehearsal for "**Calamity Jane**". As treasurer, I am so busy trying to balance the books. I have overall control of the tickets until they are on sale to the public & then we have a rota of people on duty at the Booking Office. It is not always clear what exactly they have sold.

28th February 1983 Monday

Leicester University scientist Professor Alec Jeffreys is the man who invented & developed genetic fingerprinting. The secret of DNA was actually discovered 30 years ago by James Watson & F. Crick.

2nd March 1983 Wednesday

"A bit genteel, but no calamity." Not a very good write-up for our show this week in the Leicester Mercury. "John Lewin's production – his first for Coalville Amateur Operatic Society – was a bit too genteel, but it was an impressive initiation. Lighting was good & costumes were excellent."

4th March 1983 Friday

Have enjoyed my role as treasurer this week, being in the Box Office each evening at the theatre & seeing the other side of the story.

As treasurer I get to know all the members much better & can enjoy my individuality, while at the same time being very much part of a fine society.

6th March 1983 Sunday

Where is my Parker 51 pen? I do not know. I have now purchased a new Parker pen, but the Parker 51 is no longer available. I have chosen therefore a "Golden Falcon". I told the salesman what excellent service my Parker 51 had given me – over 25 years – and he said he hoped this would too. It cost £30.

8th March 1983 Tuesday

Lammiman. On March 8th 1983, in hospital, Herbert Askey Lammiman, aged 80 years, of Kenneth Gamble Court, Wigston. The loving husband of Marjorie, father of David, and stepfather of Michael and Mary and a loving grandfather. Funeral service at St. Mary's Church, Knighton on Monday, March 14th at 1-15p.m. Cremation following at Gilroes Crematorium. Family flowers only. Further inquiries to Ginns and Gutteridge Ltd., Funeral Directors of Leicester. Tel. 56117.
(See 7.4.67.)

10th March 1983 Thursday

"Where the handshake is a little stronger, and the smile is a little longer, that is where the West begins." The Queen quoted these words this week as she visited the West Coast of America. She toured 5 countries – Jamaica, the Cayman Islands, Mexico, the United States & Canada during her month's trip.

12th March 1983 Saturday

Tomorrow is Mothering Sunday. This is my first Mothering Sunday without a mother. It is also my last Mothering Sunday as Sunday School Teacher where I say, "Dear Lord Jesus, bless us all and keep us in your care; especially our mothers and our loved ones everywhere."

14th March 1983 Monday

St. James Church, Snibston, has recently formed its "**100 Club**". This consists of 100 people who pay £1 per month. Every month there is a Prize Draw where one person wins £40.
£10 is set aside to snowball into a £120 win once per year. £50 per month goes to the Church.

16th March 1983 Wednesday

Budget Day yesterday increased car tax to £85. Petrol & cigarettes are also up in price.
With my car tax due at the end of this month I was very pleased to learn that I had won the £40 prize this month in the newly formed "St. James Church Hall Fund 100 Club".

18th March 1983 Friday

Ex-King Umberto of Italy died this week in exile. He left Italy voluntarily in 1946 after reigning for only a month when a referendum rejected the monarchy by a majority of 2 million votes. His father, Victor Emmanuel III, died in Egypt where he is buried. So ends the Royal House of Savoy, although he has a son.

20th March 1983 Sunday

Emily Walker, aged 77, is confined to a wheelchair in her home in Ravenstone where she lives alone. Every Sunday morning after Sunday School, Joanne & I visit her & have morning coffee with her. Oh dear, what a sad life she has as she struggles every day, with all the odds against her.

22nd March 1983 Tuesday

Inside Emily Walker's house is Cardinal Newman's prayer, "May He support us all the day long of this troublous life .... Then in His mercy may He give us a safe lodging, a holy rest and peace at the last." After all her suffering in this life, may she indeed find a holy rest & peace at the last.

24th March 1983 Thursday

Public Notices – St. Mary's Churchyard, Snibston. "Notice is hereby given that it is the intention of the Secretary of State for the Environment, acting on an application by the Priest-in-charge and churchwardens, to apply to the Privy Council for an order requiring the discontinuance of burials in St. Mary's Churchyard."

26th March 1983 Saturday

Let me fill you in with a few details about myself. I am right-handed. I like to get up early in the morning & like to go to bed early at night. I am not very good at remembering faces & only recognise those who are special in some way. I am taller than average, about 5ft. 8inches & now weigh 10 stone.

28th March 1983 Monday

"The Blues" 167, Uplands Road, Oadby, is the name of a pub which depicts The Blues of the Household Cavalry. Mr Taylor, Chief Gas Meter Examiner, who retired this week, held his retirement party at "The Blues", & we all went there from 12 noon to 2 p.m. A most enjoyable party.

30th March 1983 Wednesday

Molly Donaldson invited me to spend the evening with her & Eddie. After a delicious dinner we talked about the 150th Anniversary of Coalville, which is to be celebrated at the beginning of June. I was pleased to be able to take her a copy of a poem written in 1898 by Auntie Belle's father.

1st April 1983 Good Friday

Auntie Belle's father, Arthur Clarke, was a much loved man in his day. He died in his prime at the age of 53 & the streets of Coalville were lined with people for his funeral. He was very musical & wrote hymns for the Sunday School as well as his moving poem to the Whitwick miners.

3rd April 1983 Easter Sunday

The Rector of Ravenstone, the Revd. Leslie Buckroyd, spoke of St. Luke & pointed out that in his account of the crucifixion, he saw Jesus, as it were, beyond the suffering of the cross.
It is Luke who tells us that Jesus said to the dying thief on the cross, "Today shalt thou be with me in paradise." He observed the detail of all the people who were there, & did not look upon Jesus as forsaken.

5th April 1983 Tuesday

In the Ravenstone Parish Magazine this month the Rector says, "Miss Betty Hewes, who has been a Sunday School Teacher for many years & Superintendent since I came here 13 years ago, has intimated that she wishes to resign from office at the end of July.

We shall be sorry to lose her, but we are most grateful for her work etc. ….."

7th April 1983 Thursday
The Diocesan Board of Education is sponsoring a Hymn Competition in connection with the Diocesan Pilgrimage to St. Albans on 28th May 1983. Entries are invited for the writing of a hymn on the pilgrimage theme "All for Jesus" to be sung in St. Albans Abbey (to a well known tune). I entered.

9th April 1983 Saturday
Brother Pat tells me that with effect from 1st April 1984 the Council will take over the care of the Churchyard at little St. Mary's, Snibston.
Ever since my dad died in 1939, first Mum & then I have kept the grass cut around my dad's grave, but much of the churchyard is a wilderness.

11th April 1983 Monday
"May you live to see a thousand reasons to rejoice" (see 13th January 1980). These words are from the musical "Fiddler on the Roof" which was first seen in London in 1967 (the year I fell hook, line & sinker for Brian Lamming). Well, the great Topol, who plays the lead, is to return in his starring role at Coventry, 27th May to 4th June.

13th April 1983 Wednesday
"The Doctor's Walking Book" written by Dr. Fred Stutman has certainly done me a world of good. For the past 12 months I have made a determined effort to walk round the village (1 ½ miles) every day. This has helped get my weight down from 11 to 10 stone & the extra 500 miles has made me more alive & alert.

15th April 1983 Friday
"I would like to present to the Sunday School when I leave, a Nativity set costing £100."
This is what I wrote in my diary in December 1978, when Mum & I were thinking of leaving Ravenstone.
There is a Nativity set for sale at the Monastery (£120) which I would like to buy.

17th April 1983 Sunday
Judas was "Treasurer" (he had the bag). I think of this now that I am treasurer & hope I will always be worthy of the trust given to me. I remember when I was a child reading something which said, "God knows what He wants you to be in life. Let yourself go His way, rather than say – I shall do this or that."

19th April 1983 Tuesday
Confirmation Service this evening at St. James, Snibston. The Bishop of Leicester, as is his custom, spent the whole day in the parish. He visited little St. Mary's & he said he could understand why we were all so proud of the little church & loved it so. He visited Snibston School & Coalville Council offices.

21st April 1983 Thursday
"Decus et Tutamen" – an ornament & safeguard. This is the motto milled around the edge of our new £1 coin which is out today. It is a return to the wording on our coinage in the 17th Century. The new coins are made of cupro nickel and zinc & 250 million have been delivered to the banks.

Note – the £1 coin replaces the £1 note.

23rd April 1983 Saturday
"The Card" is Coalville Amateurs' choice of show for next year. We went in a bus load to Lichfield to see the show & I was not much impressed. Set in the north of England in the early 1900s, it tells the story of a self-made man who is a bit of a "card". I much prefer a show with more dignity & pathos.

25th April 1983 Monday
£8,000 per year. The latest Civil Service pay award takes the maximum E.O. salary to £8,078 with effect from 1st April 1983. The maximum H.E.O. salary (i.e. Higher Executive Officer) is now £10,000. It costs me about £50 per week for everyday housekeeping – food, petrol, hairdressers, etc.

27th April 1983 Wednesday
Voluntary Early Retirement.
With so much unemployment in the country, the Civil Service now offers a new Voluntary Early Retirement scheme. Applications are invited from staff aged 55 & over. They will receive a pension & lump sum immediately. This is 5 years before the recognised retirement age of 60.

29th April 1983 Friday
"Mum has chosen a magnolia." This is what I wrote in my diary in August 1974.
It took 6 years for the magnolia to bloom & by that time Mum was in hospital & never saw it.
This year, the magnolia is making excellent progress & speaks to me of my mother's love & life renewed.

1st May 1983 Sunday
I am now all set for my week's holiday at Sidmouth, Devon, May 3rd – May 10th. It has been so cold & wet this week that I have packed all my winter woollies & decided to go in my winter boots. My little friend Joanne has agreed to write to me to keep me up to date on all the news at home.

3rd May 1983 Tuesday
"Sidmouth! Silvery pink & creamy Sidmouth", so says our poet John Betjeman,
What a joy it was to come to the Hotel Riviera in Sidmouth in blossom time. I was privileged to have as my table companion, Mrs Blanche Alexander, a widow from Stratford-on-Avon, who was most interesting & entertaining.

5th May 1983 Thursday
"National Donkey Week". From all over the country we came (150 in all) to see about 500 donkeys which lived at various farms. We visited Slade House Farm, Salcombe Regis, Paccombe Farm, Harcombe & Brookfield Farm, Honiton, where we were made so welcome by staff & donkeys.

7th May 1983 Saturday
Although the weather was poor we loved visiting the Donkey Sanctuary & were especially pleased to come at Rogationtide. Tomorrow being Rogation Sunday, we are having a short service in the yard with the donkeys, as well as in church. "O all ye beasts and cattle, bless ye the Lord."

9th May 1983 Monday
The London Marathon is now so popular it is definitely here to stay. This is the race where people give their very all, not to win, but just to complete the course at all. Friendships are forged as strangers jog along together & the marvellous crowds lining the route shout & encourage those who begin to wilt.

11th May 1983 Wednesday
It was due entirely to my mother's love of the poor humble donkey that she supported the Donkey Sanctuary. I therefore represented her on my holiday & know how much she would have loved to have gone herself. I thought of her especially at church where the dear departed were all remembered.

13th May 1983 Friday
My darling Mum, who was promised a holiday this year, had her dream fulfilled to escape from her wretched wheelchair, to escape from her pain, to escape from her life sentence in hospital, to escape from this world of woe & be transported to realms on high & be free as a bird to enjoy heaven & live happily ever after.

15th May 1983 Sunday
Mrs Blanche Alexander, 3 Sanctus Court, Stratford-on-Avon, whom I met on holiday, was an authority on the stage & theatre. She travelled the world to lecture & yet was full of fun & mischief. She lectured on ships on world cruises, or Mediterranean cruises & had visited everywhere of interest in the world.

17th May 1983 Tuesday
I asked Mrs Alexander which was the most beautiful country in the world she had ever visited. She said, "Great Britain"! Nowhere else was there such infinite variety, such green grass & such history.
 I asked her why she was so fond of donkeys and, like St. Augustine, she said, "Humility" "Humility" "Humility".

19th May 1983 Thursday
The donkey has a cross on its back. This humble, lovable, creature speaks to us of Christ.
It was lovely to be in the midst of so many donkeys & to hear them all braying in chorus at our Rogation Sunday Service in the yard. And then followed absolute silence, as the vicar gave his blessing.

21st May 1983 Saturday
There will be a General Election next month on 9th June. Again I will choose the Ecology Party, although they never win. When it burst on to the national political scene in 1979 it had 50 candidates, but this time it has 100. It seems to me the only party which is not hell bent on destruction. It cares for all creation.

23rd May 1983 Monday
Margaret Thatcher, Conservative Prime Minister for the past 4 years, has tremendous drive & stamina. She is greatly admired by her own party but not by her opponents. She is hard as iron and always wants to be top dog. Members of the 2 major parties, Labour & Conservative, never have a kind word for each other.

25th May 1983 Wednesday
Diocesan Pilgrimage Hymn Competition.
"Thank you very much for your hymn for the above competition; in all there were 41 entries. After careful consideration we decided to divide the prize & use the hymns written by Mrs V. Costerton of Thornton and Mrs J. Cooper of Hugglescote." Signed Richard Leicester.

27th May 1983 Friday
"North West Leicestershire" is a new constituency for the forthcoming General Election, formed out of chunks from Loughborough & Bosworth. It has an electorate of 69,398.
We have 4 names to choose from: 1. David Ashby, Conservative; 2. Mrs Read, Labour;
3. Geoffrey Cort, Alliance; 4. Dinah Freer, Ecologist.

29th May 1983 Trinity Sunday
For our three in one God see Revelation, Chapter 16, verse 19.
"And the great city was divided into 3 parts, & the cities of the nations fell; & great Babylon came in remembrance before God, to give unto her the cup of the wine of the fierceness of his wrath."

31st May 1983 Tuesday
Roy Ellison, Higher Executive Officer at Gas Standards Branch for the past 5 years, made an abrupt departure this week. It has been rumoured for a long time that his job would become redundant, but it seemed that almost without any warning, there he was, **gone**. We were all quite amazed.

2nd June 1983 Thursday
Milk Race 1983. Joanne (aged 9) & I watched the champion cyclists of the world as they sped along the A447 from Desford to Ibstock with their vast entourage of lorries, vans, ambulance, 45 cars & 15 motor cycles. They started in Bournemouth & will finish in Blackpool. The Milk Race began 26 years ago.

4th June 1983 Saturday
"Fiddler on the Roof", one of my favourite musicals, has been showing this week at Coventry. Joanne & I went this afternoon to see the great Topol in his starring role. What drama! What pathos! What a wonderful moving lively show. Afterwards Topol signed Joanne's autograph book, "Shalom - Topol."

6th June 1983 Monday
Cup Final Day this year was a re-play after a draw on the actual day. The final outcome was a resounding victory for the favourites Manchester United against Brighton. Brighton 0 -Manchester United 4. At the end of the season Leicester City go up again to Division I.

8th June 1983 Wednesday
£80,000 needed for Leicester Cathedral.
The mighty organ is now being extensively renovated -
£50,000. A further £30,000 is required for "the fabric" -
i.e. masonry repairs, belfry repairs, window restoration,
lighting, etc.

10th June 1983 Friday
Election Day yesterday and a landslide victory for
Margaret Thatcher, Conservative Prime Minister for the
past 4 years. Conservatives = 397, Labour = 209,
Liberals and Social Democratic Party = 23, others = 21.
Boundary changes mean we now have 650 M.P.s

12th June 1983 Sunday
Pioneer 10, carrying a message from Planet Earth, has
become the first spacecraft to leave the solar system,
travelling possibly for ever among the stars. The
American spacecraft was launched on 2nd March 1972 &
has now passed the outer planets Neptune and Pluto.

14th June 1983 Tuesday
Pluto is usually the outermost planet but, because of its
egg-shaped orbit, it will be inside the orbit of Neptune
for the next 17 years. Neptune therefore, at the moment,
is the outermost planet. Pioneer 10 should meet its first
star in 10,507 years time, by which time its message will
be out of date.

16th June 1983 Thursday
All change again in the government: - Foreign Secretary
= Sir Geoffrey Howe. Home Secretary = Leon Brittan.
Chancellor of the Exchequer = Nigel Lawson.
(See 22nd October 1981) Secretary of State for Energy =
Peter Walker. Minister of State for Energy = Alick
Buchanan-Smith.

20th June 1983 Monday
Sunday School Anniversary yesterday marked the
official date of my retirement as a Sunday School
Teacher at Ravenstone 1958 – 1983.
A beautiful sunny day & thanks to the endeavours of
Mrs Bird & Diane I was presented with a gorgeous
arrangement of flowers, & from the parishioners a £20
cheque.

22nd June 1983 Wednesday
I was delighted to be able to give to the Sunday School a
"Nativity Set" which I bought from the Monastery,
costing £78. It consisted of 13 pieces, Baby Jesus, Mary,
Joseph, 3 shepherds, 3 Kings, a cow, a donkey & 2
lambs. Made in Italy, the pieces are breakable, but I
hope they will be well looked after.

24th June 1983 Friday
"Dear Miss Hewes, I am writing this letter to say how
sorry I am to hear that you are leaving, but how glad I
am that you taught me and many others. Theresa &
myself thank you very much for what you have done for
us & we have learnt a lot. Again, thank you very much.
              Debra & Theresa Hickin XXX"

26th June 1983 Sunday
Cousin Minna (Uncle Aubrey's daughter) died
yesterday. Apart from her brother Norman, who was

killed in action during the war, she is the first one of my
generation to die in the family. Not forgetting, of course,
my own brother Robert who died at the age of 17.
I hardly know some of my cousins.

28th June 1983 Tuesday
Cousin Enid (Uncle Cyril's daughter) is the one I know
best. She is 4 years older than I am, but lives across the
road from me, & we see other cousins less often – Don
& Isobel (Fred's children); Basil, Norman, Minna
(Aubrey's); Hilda & Walter (Hedley's); Mary, Jean &
John (Charlie's); Margaret, Enid, David (Cyril's).

30th June 1983 Thursday
Sunday School Teacher Mrs Frances Brown has doubled
my record. She has retired after more than 50 years as a
Sunday School Teacher at Castle Donington.
Another Sunday School Teacher at St. Barnabas,
Leicester, completed 40 years. I am very pleased,
however, to have completed 25 years.

2nd July 1983 Saturday
King Olav of Norway today celebrates his 80th birthday.
When he was a little boy he used to visit Buckingham
Palace. How the guardsmen on duty loved him when he
discovered that every time he ran up to look at them on
sentry duty they saluted him.
One of those guardsmen was my dad.

4th July 1983 Monday
Mr Boreham, Controller at Gas Standards Branch for the
past 10 years, has announced that he will be retiring in
October this year.
Today a new Chief Gas Meter Examiner joined the
Branch. He is Mr Fulton, who comes to us from the
Department of Transport. He replaces Mr Taylor who
retired earlier this year.

6th July 1983 Wednesday
Staunton Harold Hall, the Cheshire Homes local base for
28 years, was sold this week for £209,000. The buyer
comes from within the Cheshire organisation and will
use the hall as a training centre for volunteers working
among the terminally ill & disabled. Cheshire Homes
will be moving its local base to a new £1.5 million unit
in 1985.

8th July 1983 Friday
"Dear, oh dear," I wrote in my diary 12 years ago, when
Mary Blue ran away from her husband Terry.
"Dear, oh dear, oh dear," as poor Mary Blue has run
away from her drunken husband Murdo & has now
landed in the "home for battered wives".
Murdo's downfall has been his love of whisky.

10th July 1983 Sunday
Mary Blue's second marriage to Murdo appeared on the
surface to be so successful. But her mother Evelyn tells
me that all has not been well for the last 2 years. When
he has had too much to drink he repeatedly beats her up
and loses all control of himself.
They have one son, Scott.

12th July 1983 Tuesday
90°f (32°c) these are the temperatures in Great Britain at

the moment, as we all swelter in a heat wave which has been with us now for a fortnight, and which shows no signs of abatement. It is hotter here than Rome or the Costa Brava, and while some revel in it, there are those who cannot stand it.

14th July 1983 Thursday
52 today. "O gift of God, O perfect day, whereon shall no man work, but play; whereon it is enough for me, not to be doing, but to be ….. And over me unrolls on high, the splendid scenery of the sky, where through a sapphire sea the sun, sails like a golden galleon."
Had a lovely birthday, on holiday.

16th July 1983 Saturday
Had a couple of days off work to celebrate my birthday. Spent one day with Joanne, aged 9, in Stratford-on-Avon. It was scorching hot, but we had a most enjoyable day sitting in the shade by the river, taking a boat trip and visiting Anne Hathaway's Cottage & took photographs.

18th July 1983 Monday
Another farewell function. Doreen Holland, C.O. at Nottingham for many years, was given a farewell luncheon at Toton Grange Farm Restaurant. I went with Mr Ellis, Chief Gas Examiner, & his wife. There were 12 altogether including Area Gas Examiners Mr Preston, Mr Lewis & their wives, Mr Cox, Mr Rogers & wives.

20th July 1983 Wednesday
19,000 days old tomorrow. One day and night of Brahma = 8,640,000,000 years.
864 is the important number, whether it be seconds, minutes, hours, days, months, years, or millions of years. Whether it be inches, feet, yards or miles.
Hence the diameter of the Sun = 864,000 miles = 12 x 12 x 6,000.

22nd July 1983 Friday
Like the Universe, a human being consists of body & spirit. The circle squared is a symbol of the union of two incommensurable elements. A true image of the cosmos is created when a square & circle of equal perimeters are combined. Stonehenge, built circa 2160 B.C. is a perfect example.

26th July 1983 Tuesday
£663 million profit – this is British Gas 1982/83 profit, more than twice the level for 1981/82. The British Gas Corporation is the goose that lays the golden egg for Britain at the moment. At the same time the Coal Board have losses amounting to £111 million. We spend £100,000 million in a year.

28th July 1983 Thursday
What an idyllic month this has been. The sunniest July this century, with everyone suntanned and wearing only the minimum of clothes. The great heat wave at the beginning of the month gave way to more pleasant sunny days (not quite so hot), lovely - especially early mornings and evenings.

30th July 1983 Saturday
Joanne & I visited cousin Johnty (aged 79) in his new "town house" at Markfield. We had tea with him there & sat in his garden. Afterwards he took us in his car to Bradgate Park where, on a lovely warm summer's evening, we enjoyed a stroll through the park, eating ice cream & seeing the deer.

1st August 1983 Monday
"A" very special day today as the format of vehicle registration changes from a suffix letter to a prefix letter. First of all we had **AAY 1** etc. When we reached **YAY 999** we went into reverse, **1 AAY**. Then we went to **AAY 1A**, and having reached **YAY 999Y** we now have **A1 AAY**.

3rd August 1983 Wednesday
A marble temple for Indian Jains is to be made out of a chapel in Oxford Street, Leicester. The foundation stone will be laid this week & 250 tons of Rajastan stone is being hand carved for this transformation. It will be the European headquarters of Jainism - £800,000.

5th August 1983 Friday
Leicester's Jain temple will bring a look of the mystic East into our midst. The temple will be part of a complex which will include a permanent Jain exhibition, library, auditorium, conference rooms & dining hall. Many of the rooms in the building will be used by non-Jains. It will be ready by 1985.

7th August 1983 Sunday
"But thou art the same Lord, whose property is **always to have mercy**."
These words, which I have heard so many times in the service of Holy Communion, seemed to register most particularly when I heard them today.

9th August 1983 Tuesday
"The quality of **mercy** is not strained; it droppeth, as the gentle rain from heaven, upon the place beneath: it is twice blessed; it blesseth him that gives & him that takes: 'tis mightiest in the mightiest ….. it is an attribute to God himself." - Shakespeare's Merchant of Venice.

11th August 1983 Thursday
"Holy, holy, holy! Lord God almighty! Early in the morning our song shall rise to thee.
Holy, holy, holy! Merciful & mighty! …. Perfect in power, in love and purity."
And the great collect for Trinity XI reminds us that God declares his almighty power most chiefly in showing mercy.

13th August 1983 Saturday
What a glorious summer we are having this year. Joanne (aged 9) & I are enjoying the summer evenings watching the ducks on Groby Pool, or visiting Abbey Park, where the trees are literally alive with thousands of migratory birds, sounding just like an aviary. We also enjoy visiting Beacon Hill.

15th August 1983 Monday
On April 28th 1980 I paid £103 for a new petrol driven lawn mower. Although it does a good job, it is very noisy & in the present hot spell it has almost choked me with its excessive exhaust. I have therefore launched out

on yet another – this time an electric, reduced from £180 to £130.

17th August 1983 Wednesday

A day in Birmingham. Thanks to my old friend the poet Longfellow who wrote "Hiawatha" there is to be a "spectacular children's show – Longfellow's classic poem Hiawatha" adapted and directed by Michael Bogdanov for 6 – 12 year olds.

I went to explore Birmingham to find the Hippodrome Theatre.

19th August 1983 Friday

Booked seats for Joanne & me for "Hiawatha" at Birmingham Hippodrome on 17th September. The concrete jungle which I last penetrated in February 1978 led me this time to an Aladdin's Cave of quality shops in the city centre, beyond the garish arcades & junk shops which you see first.

21st August 1983 Sunday

Auntie Doris celebrated her 88th birthday on Friday 19th August.

Looking remarkably good for her age, she still manages to live in her little old cottage at Mountsorrel.

Today she is having a party for her immediate family, sister Hilda, daughter Maureen & great-grandchildren.

23rd August 1983 Tuesday

Today my darling Mum would be 78. (3 x 26). I am now 52 (2 x 26).

What a lot can happen in 26 years. When my Mum was 26 years old I was born.

When I was 26 I was not as strong & healthy as my Mum was at 52. I suffered then from claustrophobia, while Mum was very fit.

25th August 1983 Thursday

Department of Energy. "Gas & Oil Measurement Branch" Office Notice 94/83 –

"It has been decided that Gas Standards Branch, Leicester will in future be known as the Gas & Oil Measurement Branch. The change reflects the growing importance of petroleum measurement."

27th August 1983 Saturday

"Once in a Blue Moon". It is exactly 100 years ago that there was an almighty volcanic eruption on the island of Krakatoa in the Dutch East Indies. 36,000 lives were lost as waves 120 feet high & fiery lava took their toll. On the island of Ceylon, the Moon was blue.

29th August 1983 Monday

Water means life. The Diocese of Leicester has launched an appeal to individual church members to support numerous projects concerned with the U.N. Water Decade in the Third World.

31st August 1983 Wednesday

The Diocese of Leicester Appeal needs a "Parish Representative" to help in launching the appeal. I volunteered. I felt that I was in a better position than anybody else since I can distribute literature via the Parish Magazine. I am happy to co-ordinate if others will co-operate.

2nd September 1983 Friday

Annual meeting at work with B.G.C.

While all the learned men discuss what is taking place now, & what is expected to happen over the next 10 years, I sit in their midst & take the minutes. Fortunately, I have the assistance of the Chief Gas Examiner, Mr Ellis, to finalise the minutes.

4th September 1983 Sunday

The 27th Veteran Cycle Rally was held today in Leicestershire (for the first time). Joanne & I watched the start at Rothley as 200 riders set off on the most amazing array of cycles, dating back to the 1860s. Suitably dressed in period costume they looked terrific.

6th September 1983 Tuesday

Our Sunday School outing this year was again to Drayton Manor Park.

I had the pleasure of the company of Joanne, now aged 9. Her favourite ride this time was the "Dodgem Cars". She also went with other children on the "Waltzers", the Ghost Train & the exciting high water chute.

8th September 1983 Thursday

Maurice Williams, Senior Gas Engineer, who retired from our office last November, has received the tragic news that his only son has been killed on holiday while mountain climbing in Switzerland. The funeral service will take place on Saturday 10th September at his home in Newton Harcourt.

10th September 1983 Saturday

How about a glass of champagne! To help brother Pat celebrate his 65th birthday on 29th August, I bought him a lovely bottle of champagne - £10.

To help George Merrill & my old friend Marje celebrate their 10th Wedding Anniversary next Tuesday I also bought them one.

12th September 1983 Monday

Not only are George & Marje celebrating their 10th Wedding Anniversary, but sister Sybil is celebrating 40 years of service with the Ashby Standard Soap Co.

Also Marjorie's son Ian, by her first marriage, is celebrating 7 "O" levels in his recent school examinations. So its drinks all round.

14th September 1983 Wednesday

B.P.'s Magnus Oilfield, North East of Shetland, the deepest & most northerly in Europe, was officially inaugurated by the Prime Minister, Mrs Margaret Thatcher, today.

The 75,000 ton Magnus platform, 100 miles north of the Shetlands, cost £1.3 billion & is the biggest in the world.

16th September 1983 Friday

B.P.'s Magnus Oilfield, like other B.P. discoveries, is named after a Scottish saint. The Magnus platform is a masterpiece of engineering. Giant steel legs anchor the platform 600 feet below sea-level. It must withstand 100ft. waves & 100 m.p.h. winds. It is 4 storeys high.

18th September 1983 Sunday

"Hiawatha" was brought to life wonderfully at Birmingham Hippodrome yesterday by the National

Theatre. I learned from the programme that Hiawatha was a real Indian who lived about 500 years ago.

Joanne loved the theatre which was the biggest & best she had ever been inside.

20th September 1983 Tuesday

Mary Moore, now 72, is spending a week with me again, so I am on holiday for a week. Yesterday we entertained Edith Whittaker from Derby for tea. Her husband Bill died only a month ago, on Mum's birthday August 23rd, so she was naturally feeling very sad & lonely. They were a gentle loving couple.

22nd September 1983 Thursday

£170 Haul

Thieves who broke into 28 Leicester Road, Ravenstone, between 10 a.m. and 12.15 p.m. yesterday stole £170.

Visited Mary's cousins, all looking remarkably good for their years. Auntie Doris at Mountsorrel, now 88; her sister Hilda at Wigston, now 86. Also cousin Florrie Moore, aged 89, she is a really colourful character.

24th September 1983 Saturday

Again I read the lesson at church for Trinity XV – Job, Chapter 1. I thought of my dear Mum & all that she suffered.

In the congregation this year was Sunday School Teacher Diane Robert, whose father has died this month. I felt for her & her Mum as I read the lesson.

26th September 1983 Monday

"The days of our age are three-score years and ten; & though men may be so strong that they come to four-score years, yet is their strength then but labour & sorrow. So teach us to number our days; that we may apply our hearts unto wisdom. O satisfy us with thy mercy, so shall we rejoice ………." Psalm 90.

28th September 1983 Wednesday

"People who know everything & do nothing."

This was the description of our government given by Sir John Hoskyns, former head of the Prime Minister's Downing Street Policy Unit, when he spoke to the Institute of Directors this evening.

Delivering the annual lecture, he said four main changes were needed -

1. The Prime Minister should not be restricted to the small pool of career politicians in Westminster in forming a government.
2. Whitehall should be organised for strategy & innovation.
3. Adequate numbers of "high quality outsiders" should be brought into the Civil Service.
4. Workload on ministers must be reduced.

2nd October 1983 Sunday

"Yet is their strength then but labour and sorrow" (Psalm 90). Oh, how very sad it is to be old & helpless. I visited poor old cousin Audrey, aged 82. She was asleep in bed & when she woke up she did not know I was there. I visited poor Miss Walker; she sat huddled up in her wheelchair & hardly spoke a word.

4th October 1983 Tuesday

Area Gas Examiners Meeting.

I took the minutes which included the latest problem - "privatisation". The British Gas Corporation up till now has had monopoly supply of gas, but private suppliers now pose the problem of not odorising their gas satisfactorily. What must we do?

If there should ever be a major gas explosion because the gas was not recognisable by its smell, we must be able to produce our own experts trained in the art of distinguishing a "distinctive smell". If we go to court to prosecute, we must have some expertise – some experienced sniffers.

8th October 1983 Saturday

"What a strange thing it is when your boss ceases to be your boss". This is what I wrote in my diary in April 1976 when my boss Mr Sharp retired. The same thing now applies that Mr Boreham, Controller of Gas Standards Branch for the past ten years, has retired.

10th October 1983 Monday

"There is no such thing as Perpetual Motion". Mr Ellis, chief gas examiner, explains to me, in simple language, the many wonders of science. He does all the talking while I listen spell-bound. But, much to my amazement, he was stopped in his tracks when I asked, "Is there then, no such thing as Eternity?" He was silent.

12th October 1983 Wednesday

Went to the Mothers' Union meeting at St. James, Snibston, at Evelyn's invitation, to hear a most interesting talk on the ritual of the church & the meaning of everything worn by a priest. Everything showed the suffering of Christ, from the Y cross of a man being crucified, to the whip cord.

14th October 1983 Friday

"To every action there is always opposed an equal reaction".

This is another gem of wisdom I have learned through working with men of science. It is one of Sir Isaac Newton's three laws of motion. He established a relationship between the forces on Earth & those throughout the whole Universe.

16th October 1983 Sunday

It was Galileo (1564 – 1642) who first pointed man in a new direction towards science. Like a rocket requiring lift-off, it was Galileo who provided the first lift-off in the world of science.

And then it was Newton (1642 – 1727), born in the year that Galileo died, who put the world into orbit. Both Galileo & Newton became more & more firm in their belief in God with each revelation of the wonder of nature. For Newton, the mechanistic universe – the giant clock that kept time precisely & ran without ending – was an argument against atheism. His belief in God was absolute. God was eternal.

20th October 1983 Thursday

Mr G. R. Boreham, Controller of Gas Standards Branch for the past 10 years, has now been replaced by Mr J. Plant, Director of Gas and Oil Measurement Branch.

22nd October 1983 Saturday

Roy Johnson's Music Hall, sponsored by the Rotary Club of Coalville for their Jubilee Year, has been delighting audiences all week at the Technical College Theatre, Coalville.

I went with Pat & Evelyn & Enid, & we were fortunate to have front seats where we sat & laughed all night.

23rd October 1983 Sunday

Walker, Emily Elizabeth, of Ravenstone, a dearly loved sister, aunt and great-aunt, passed peacefully away at 40 The Green, Thrussington, on October 23rd 1983. Funeral service at Ravenstone Parish Church, Wednesday October 26th at 2.30 p.m. followed by interment. Family flowers only please.

24th October 1983 Monday

"A holy rest & peace at the last."

Emily Walker, life long friend of my Mum, and in her prime the best needlewoman in the county, who made dresses for Mum in her younger days, died yesterday after many years being crippled with arthritis & rheumatism; at the home of her niece.

26th October 1983 Wednesday

Diwali, the Hindu Festival of Lights, is here again. Five thousand lights went on in Belgrave Road, Leicester, making it the first city in Europe to stage major civic decorations for this festival. They will be used again at Christmas for the Christian Festival.

This week is "One World Week".

28th October 1983 Friday

"Put off thy shoes from off thy feet, for the place whereon thou standest is holy ground". Exodus 3. 5.

For the first time in my life I entered a Hindu Temple – Shree Sanatan Mandir in Catherine Street, Leicester, formerly a Baptist Chapel. I also went inside the Raja Yoga Centre. Through "Leicester Inter - Faith" in conjunction with "One World Week", I went on a conducted tour which started at Leicester Cathedral and then by bus to the Shree Sanatan Mandir and the Raja Yoga Centre. It is only because we have so many Indians here that we have such opportunity.

1st November 1983 Tuesday
"Privy Council Office" Burial Act 1853.

Notice is hereby given that representations have been made to Her Majesty in Council by the Secretary of State for the Environment, that burials should be discontinued in St. Mary's Churchyard, Snibston, Leicestershire.

3rd November 1983 Thursday

A nine foot high bronze statue of Lord Louis Mountbatten, murdered by the I.R.A. in August 1979, was unveiled by the Queen this week. The public & Lord Louis's many friends around the world raised the £100,000 needed to pay for the statue, plinth and other expenses.

5th November 1983 Saturday

Took Joanne, aged 9, to see her first ballet. We went to the Hippodrome, Birmingham, to see the London Festival Ballet performing "Cinderella". The music was by Prokofiev. Lovely as it was, we did not particularly like the music, & altogether we preferred the Pantomime we saw in January.

7th November 1983 Monday

American Cruise Missiles are now arriving in Britain. The deadly shipment has triggered a storm of protest throughout the country. The first dozen missiles, armed with nuclear warheads, have been flown into the Greenham Common base in Berkshire. There will be 160.

9th November 1983 Wednesday

Russia versus the Western powers is the reason why America is sending all these deadly weapons to Britain. Each warhead has an explosive power equal to 200,000 tons of T.N.T. The missiles have a range of 1,500 miles & will be based also at Molesworth, Cambridgeshire

11th November 1983 Friday

A day in Birmingham, Christmas shopping. Thanks entirely to my old friend Longfellow I now know & love Birmingham. I bought £50 worth of presents & also bought myself a new mac for the winter with warm lining & a big hood to keep out the wind & snow.

13th November 1983 Sunday

A futuristic laser system will flash multi-coloured greetings across the Leicester night sky this Christmas in a spectacular display never before seen in the Midlands. Leicester & County Chamber of Commerce & Industry have leased a sky-writing machine from Laser Systems, South Wales – for £3,000.

15th November 1983 Tuesday

Leicester's Christmas laser system is to be installed on a city centre roof-top & switched on by the Lord Mayor on 7th December. If the weather is favourable, the highlight will be the projection of a Happy Christmas message on the clouds which will be seen eight miles away.

17th November 1983 Thursday
"Horse & Cart Funeral for Dealer"

Jack Toon, a well known local character in the horse & scrap metal business, has died, aged 78. His last wish was granted when his coffin was carried from his home to Whitwick Church on an open cart covered with flowers & pulled by his six year old horse, Flicka.

19th November 1983 Saturday

"For the sin ye do by two and two ye must pay for one by one". Mr Ellis came out with this quotation when I said I would like to check some columns of figures with him – one by one. I was so amused that he loaned me a book written by Rudyard Kipling, containing these words in a poem.

21st November 1983 Monday

"Tomlinson" by Rudyard Kipling, is the funniest poem I have ever read. It is the story of Tomlinson who gave up the ghost in his house in Berkeley Square, "And a Spirit came to his bedside & gripped him by the hair."

It carried him far away. He was taken up & then down & finally sent home.

"Stand up, stand up now, Tomlinson, & answer loud &

high – the good that ye did for the sake of men or ever ye came to die." Thus spoke St. Peter.

"Sit down, sit down upon the slag, & answer loud & high – the harm that ye did to the Sons of Men or ever you came to die." Thus challenged the Devil.

Tomlinson had no passport to heaven nor hell.

"The good souls flocked like homing doves & bade him clear the path, and Peter twirled the jangling keys in weariness & wrath."

While down below, "The Devil he blew on a brandered soul & set it aside to cool – do you think I would waste my good pit coal on the hide of a brain-sick fool?"

27th November 1983 Sunday

"Heaven has its own Civil Servants who man an inquiry office where you can find out which of your loved ones is next destined to die. Houses and surroundings are produced by thought, so everything is exactly as you want it to be."

These are the words of the Revd. Robert Hugh Benson. The Revd. Robert Hugh Benson had been dead for more than 50 years, when in 1975 through a medium, he spoke to Anthony Borgia who had once been his pupil at the Westminster Cathedral Choir School. Sometimes contact was by voice and at other times by "automatic writing".

"Highlands of Heaven" by Reverend G. Vale Owen, is a book of "automatic writing" whereby someone in heaven named Zabdiel describes, as best he can to mortals on earth. what his life in heaven is like. He spoke through the writer from 3rd November to 3rd January 1914. Zabdiel said, "People differ in brightness according to the degree of holiness in each.

i.e. according to the degree in which each individual in himself is able to reflect the divine light of spirit. Some appear very dim & these will go to regions dim or less dim according to their own dimness."

Along the road to heaven, the light ever increases & spiritual bodies grow in brightness & beauty the further they go. Above & beyond the plane of earth lie the spheres. Zabdiel, at the time he spoke, was a member of the tenth sphere. He could see on earth who were shining. Those who love beauty will find in heaven a never-failing supply. As light and holiness go hand in hand, so, as they progress in the one, will they in the larger enjoyment of the other. This is the Beauty of Holiness. "Look up & be fearless for all is fair ahead & all is well."

9th December 1983 Friday

What is faith? Our guest preacher, Arthur Crane of Ashby, referred us to Hebrews 11. 1.

"Faith gives substance to our hopes and makes us certain of realities we do not see."

As a magistrate & lawyer, he compared faith with the magistrate's court where a witness must see a thing to prove a point.

Arthur Crane told us the true story of an old man who drove his car & knocked down a bollard. He was really too old to be a safe driver. A policeman, sheltering in a doorway at the time, heard the crash. Did he see the crash? Answer, "No". Therefore the case was dismissed.

13th December 1983 Tuesday

Eighteen Christmas presents all wrapped up & ready for Christmas – how lovely they look.

1. Pat, 2. Evelyn, 3. Mary Blue, 4. Scott, 5. Bunting, 6. Aunt Dos, 7. Enid, 8. Auntie Gladys, 9. Madge, 10. Auntie Belle, 11. Elsie, 12. Johnty, 13. Matron, 14. Joanne, 15. Stuart, 16. Rose, 17. Jan, 18. Karen.

15th December 1983 Thursday

Pamela Cassell, now Mrs Chessell, 15 Croftside, Vigo Village, Meopham, Kent, was an evacuee at our house during the War 1939 – 1945. She arrived with her twin sister Ann & her mother & spent several years with us. After the war we lost touch with them, but today she re-appeared.

17th December 1983 Saturday

Snibston Colliery, which was opened in 1832, closed officially yesterday. It is the first of the 6 Leicestershire pits which will end their lives during the next few years. It was in September 1977 that Joanne's dad took me fathoms deep to see what it was like down pit. I'm glad I had the opportunity.

19th December 1983 Monday

"A Licence to Relax – After 44 Years."

"The manager of the Leicester Vehicle Licensing Centre, Mr Les Timson, has retired after 44 years service with the centre. Mr Timson of 43 Palmerston Boulevard, Knighton, joined the centre as an office boy."

I worked with him for 30 years.

21st December 1983 Wednesday

From my dad's best friend, Leslie Hale – "Dear Betty, How very nice of you to send me a card all to myself & I reciprocate with the mixed but warm greetings below – (pre-printed) Seasons Greetings, Meilleurs Voeux, Felices Fiestas, Frohe Festtage." Leslie.

23rd December 1983 Friday

"To dear Betty with all good wishes for Christmas & the New Year & every God's Blessing on you for much good health & happiness in the years to come, with my wife's & my own thoughts of our love for all you have done in His name. Bless you for it."

Pauline & Gustav Aronsohn.

25th December 1983 Sunday

Christmas morning Holy Communion at 9.00 a.m. at little St. Mary's. I then went with cousin Johnty, now aged 79, to morning service at the Methodist Chapel at Markfield. The chapel was filled to capacity & we sang heartily all the old favourite Christmas carols. A lovely bright sunny day.

27th December 1983 Tuesday

Mary Blue, whose 2nd marriage ended recently in disaster, spent Christmas with her mother & dad (Evelyn & Pat).

There was also Scott, aged 9, Doris Roberts, Katherine, Aunt Dos & me. Mary Blue looked pale & tired and Katherine, alert & lively at 79, said, "Take vitamin E."

29th December 1983 Thursday

Thanks to the influence & example of Katherine, I take vitamin E every morning. Thanks to the good advice of Dr. Fred Stutman, I walk a mile every day. Thanks to my good friend Reevsie, I gave up smoking long ago. What would we do without a helping hand from others?

31st December 1983 Saturday

"Sleeping in the very bed where I was born"

(See 31st December 1981).

Have just read an article about beds. Every night you lose 1 ¼ pints of body moisture during ordinary sleep.

(57 gallons per year) Much of it is absorbed into the mattress.

The skin constantly sheds minute scales of stale worn out tissue. Much of it goes into the bed as bed dust.

"Never buy a second hand bed."

* * *

1984

1st January 1984 Sunday

"Remember where you stand" (Hebrews 12. 18.) You stand before the city of the living God, heavenly Jerusalem, before myriads of angels ...... and God the judge of all.

For thus saith the Lord of hosts, "Yet once, it is a little while, & I will shake the heavens & earth. I will shake all nations." (Haggai 2. 7.)

3rd January 1984 Tuesday

"A staff inspection will be taking place shortly in the area where you work. The purpose of the staff inspection is to ensure that work which is done in Government Departments needs to be done, that the organisational structure and the numbers of staff employed on it are right."

Note – Normally our scientific staff, including two Doctors of Science, can "baffle with science" any so-called inspectors and justify the vast amount of money we spend on our laboratories at work; & the equally vast amounts of money spent visiting oil rigs, gas terminals, & meetings with Europeans in Paris & Brussels to agree European "Standards".

5th January 1984 Thursday

Old Moore's Almanack, which prophesies the forthcoming year, and has been doing so since 1697, says for December 1984, "Moves to restructure the British Civil Service and lessen the expenditure of Local Government is likely to be met with some stiff resistance."

7th January 1984 Saturday

The Government has already committed itself to reducing the number of Civil Servants. It has set a target for April 1984 of 630,000. The Department of Energy, one of the smallest Departments, is to be reduced to 1,100. Is your job really necessary?

9th January 1984 Monday

"The great jigsaw is gradually taking shape. Each day a new piece goes into place."

This is what I wrote in my diary in July 1978 when I began working on the great jigsaw of my new job in the world of gas testing.

Today, as I finished my updated "E.O. Desk Notes", it was complete.

11th January 1984 Wednesday

My E.O. Desk Notes fill a book. They tell the whole story of gas testing from its beginnings in 1868 to the present day.

They also show the progress of the work through various Departments of Government & show, not only the part I play in it all, but tell you how & why.

13th January 1984 Friday

"County Put Tight Rein on Staffing"

Not only Central Government (The Civil Service) but also Local Government, are cutting down on staff. The Leicestershire County Council Policy Committee agreed this week both to monitor future vacancies and also carry out a review to ensure value for money.

15th January 1984 Sunday

"Midland Fox – your new bus service arrives January 15th. Midland Fox is Leicestershire's exciting new bus service. From January 15th we'll be introducing more of the bright red and yellow buses you may already have seen in some areas, to run throughout Leicestershire. Join the Midland Fox Hunt."

17th January 1984 Tuesday

"I am the bright and morning star" Revelation 22. 16. This was the text of a sermon given long ago by my old friend & Rector, the Revd. Gustav Aronsohn. At this time of year, when the stars are at their brightest, I journey to work each day with Venus as my guide.

19th January 1984 Thursday

How I love the stars. This is the month when Orion dominates the sky. On a clear night you can see his sword hanging from his belt & close by you can see Sirius which really does twinkle. (This is because its light comes at such an angle through our atmosphere.)

21st January 1984 Saturday

Took Joanne, aged 9, to the Concordia Theatre, Hinckley, to see the pantomime "Jack and the Beanstalk". Now a sophisticated young lady, she seems to have outgrown the fairy tales. Already at school she is learning about the Prime Minister, the Cabinet, & Chancellor of the Exchequer.

23rd January 1984 Monday

The lesson at church yesterday for the Third Sunday after the Epiphany was from the book of Amos (Chapter 5). Appropriately it spoke of the stars and in particular – Orion! "Seek him that maketh the seven stars and Orion." "Can you loosen the belt of Orion?" (See Job. 38.)

"Can you bring out the signs of the zodiac in their season?" (Job. 38. 32.) "Did you proclaim the rules that govern the heavens, or determine the laws of nature on earth?" (Job. 38. 33.)

"Did you give the horse his strength?" These were the questions given to Job by God.

27th January 1984 Friday

Coal mining in the Vale of Belvoir has now been given final approval by the Government. Energy Secretary, Mr Peter Walker, earlier this month unveiled the £400 million development of the new coal mine project at Asfordby. It will take about 7 years to be in production & will provide partial replacement for the declining North West Leicestershire field. Six pits in Leicestershire will be closed down by the 1990s. It will take another 2 years to reach the first seams of coal in the Vale of Belvoir.

31st January 1984 Tuesday

Staff inspection in our office has now been completed. Two Staff Inspectors spent 3 weeks with us. Every member of staff was interviewed individually & each interview lasted about 2 hours. They asked in detail about each job & how long it took to do.

2nd February 1984 Thursday

Sirius is the brightest star in the sky only when it is viewed from Earth. If all stars could be observed from the same distance the night sky would look very different. So, to show how bright a star really is, astronomers have selected a "Standard Distance" of 32 light years.

32 light years is the distance that a ray of light will travel in 32 years. Imagine therefore, that you can position yourself exactly 32 light years away from any star you choose. Then you would see Rigel, at the bottom right in the constellation Orion, 16 times brighter than Venus.

6th February 1984 Monday

"Gas Safety Section" in our office has now transferred to the Health & Safety Executive, under the Department of Employment.

Four members of staff – Tim Gye, Keith Walker, Peter Castle & Shaun Welsh, together with hundreds of registered files, have all been transferred to London.

8th February 1984 Wednesday

Guess where I have chosen for my summer holidays? – Pencombe Hall.

"Never heard of it" do I hear you say?

Neither had I, until I sent for holiday literature round & about Malvern, in order to visit Bunting & family. Pencombe Hall in Herefordshire offers self-catering.

10th February 1984 Friday

Coalville A.O.S. have chosen Tony Hatch and Jackie Trent's potteries musical "The Card" for their 1984 production. Tickets are not on sale from society members or Betty Hewes on Coalville 36583, dates are March 5th to 10th. (Newspaper cutting)

"Tickets are not on sale" should read, "Tickets are **now** on sale". All the difference in the world.

12th February 1984 Sunday

Yuri Andropov, Soviet leader for the past 15 months, died last Thursday, aged 69. He had been dogged by ill-health throughout the 15 months in office & had not been seen in public since last August. His death has come at a moment of extreme danger in the Middle East. (Russia's backyard).

14th February 1984 Tuesday

War in the Middle East affects the whole world. At the moment the position is very volatile. If Iran & Iraq engage in warfare it would in turn bring Russia & America into conflict. These two super-powers would fight for possession of the **oil** fields. Already Russia has invaded Afghanistan.

16th February 1984 Thursday

"Such was my mother's genuine love and generosity to me that she hoped the house would be a blessing & not a burden to me". (See February 17th 1981)

How thankful I am to have a home of my own, but this winter has found all the weak spots, with snow & gale force winds.

First of all came the snow which found its way through the roof into the false floor. Then came gale force winds which completely wrecked the fence, & finally the incessant beating rain penetrated the middle bedroom window.

I can cope well enough with the summer, but not with the winter.

20th February 1984 Monday

What an interesting week Joanne & I have just had as we tackled her "home-work".

We have searched the encyclopaedias & reference books in the library, read Hansard, & cut pictures from the newspapers in an attempt to answer a long questionnaire all about Parliament & all therein.

We have learned about the Lord Chancellor, the Woolsack, the Peerage – Duke, Marquis, Earl, Viscount & Baron.

We have learned about Lords Spiritual, Lords Temporal – "What is a referendum?" "Find out all you can about your M.P."

Even my diaries were consulted. (See 14th November 1966 and 6th June 1975).

24th February 1984 Friday

I have dreamed a dream & in my dream I saw the whole orchestra walk out on strike in the middle of a performance of Coalville Amateurs' forthcoming production, "The Card".

Brian Moore of the Amateurs' also dreamed that the musical director, Peter Jacques, did likewise. What does this mean?

26th February 1984 Sunday

As fast as Joanne & I finish one load of homework the teacher comes up with more & more. We have now had to find out all about "Black Rod", "Suffragettes", "The Civil War in the days of Charles I" and "What are Civil Servants?" I had no problems with the last question.

Fortunately, Joanne possesses a volume of "Children's Encyclopaedias" which have been handed down to her from her mother. They are most useful to us as we search their pages for facts & figures. We read what it says in the book & then I "translate" & dictate in simple language.

1st March 1984 Thursday

Our Member of Parliament, David Ashby, has now made a personal visit to Snibston School to talk to the children about Parliament.

Joanne & I have now arranged to join a bus load going to London for a conducted tour of the Houses of Parliament – scheduled to take place on 9th May.

3rd March 1984 Saturday

My little friend grows in wisdom and stature every day. She will be 10 years old next week and she now has the confidence to ask for things herself when we go to the library or shopping. She is becoming quite a writer & although she has no concept of punctuation her spelling is very good.

5th March 1984 Monday

What a lowering of standards there has been at Coalville Amateurs'. Final Dress Rehearsal of "The Card" this evening saw new producer, John Lewin, at his worst. As he swore at the cast and the stage hands, I was ashamed of him. The show itself is by no means perfect.

6th March 1984 Tuesday
On this day in 1836 Western heroes Davy Crockett and Jim Bowie died when the siege of the Alamo ended.

7th March 1984 Wednesday
Joanne's birthday! Ten years old today.
I bought her a "Project Book" in which you can both write & stick pictures or draw; writing paper; a roller damper; Tippex correction fluid; Pritt stick adhesive; fluorescent text liner; Books 1 & 2 "Kings & Queens of England" and a jigsaw of horses.

9th March 1984 Friday
Coalville Amateurs' production of "The Card" has been quite successful, but by no means a sell-out.
At least it survived without anyone going on strike, although earlier in the year we lost 3 of our stalwarts, Ursula Hall, Mick Rooney and Shirley Bettison, following a division of loyalties.
When Roy Johnson produced his highly successful Music Hall last October, he asked Ursula, Mick & Shirley to take part. They wrote explaining the situation to Coalville Amateurs' & said they would join rehearsals for "The Card" later. However, they were told it would be too late.

13th March 1984 Tuesday
Six years ago today I "stood on a bridge between two shores" as I left my old world of Motor Taxation for the new untrodden world of Gas Standards – now Gas & Oil Measurement.
After a shaky start, when I tried 3 times to escape, I am glad to be at the heart of British Government.

15th March 1984 Thursday
What a lot I learn from helping Joanne with her homework & what a lot she learns from me. Like Monna Giovanna & her friend in Longfellow's poem "The Falcon of Ser Federigo" we are "each by the other's presence lovelier made".
We certainly bring out the best in each other.

17th March 1984 Saturday
My dad's birthday. Young Steven, Mary Blue's firstborn, now a 16 year old about to leave school, looks so much like my dad looked when he was a teenager. As my dad's son & heir, I have therefore taken him under my wing, & have done all I can to help him apply for a whole variety of jobs. With so many people unemployed it is very hard to get a job at all these days. Steven, therefore, has chosen to be –
 1. A Butcher; 2. Miner; 3. Railwayman; 4. Policeman; 5. Fireman; 6. See the world as a Marine Radio Officer; 7. Porter at a hotel; 8. Ambulance Driver; 9. Electrician; 10. Mechanic.

21st March 1984 Wednesday
Visited Madge at Willoughby. Madge, now aged 85, lives alone in the old family home while all around the outbuildings are falling into decay. Once a hive of activity, relics of yesteryear now lie idle – the old hay forks, the horse's bridle, a sturdy wheel-barrow, feeding troughs, ladders & old farm machinery.

How soon we change from one generation to another. It seems but yesterday that Madge was in the prime of life, preparing meals for a large family gathering with Mum & Rob & me there as guests. She prepared an extra dinner for Aunt Agnes down the road. Now she is like Aunt Agnes.

25th March 1984 Sunday
Madge would rather die than move from her old home where she has lived all her life. She has been offered a place in an old peoples' home but much prefers to be in her own home.
As my old friend Longfellow says, "Happy he whom neither wealth, nor fashion, nor the march of the encroaching city, drives an exile from his ancestral homestead."

27th March 1984 Tuesday
"The stranger at my fireside cannot see the forms I see, nor hear the sounds I hear; he but perceives what is; while unto me all that has been, is visible and clear."
"And the boy that walked beside me, he could not understand, why closer in mine, ah! closer, I pressed his warm, soft hand!" Longfellow.

29th March 1984 Thursday
Joanne's latest homework has sent us to Coalville Library in search of Boadicea, the Great Fire of London, the Great Plague & London Bridge. It is amazing how one thing leads to another and how everything inter-relates. There stands Boadicea, right next to the Houses of Parliament, where we started.

31st March 1984 Saturday
Steven has chosen to be - 1. A Butcher.
For some unknown reason, this really is his first choice.
I offered to buy him a smart outfit if he should be asked to go for an interview.
He chose black trousers, black jacket, red tie, red belt & a striking striped shirt – like a butcher's apron.

2nd April 1984 Monday
Poor Cousin Audrey died last Thursday aged 82. What a sad life she has had for the past 2 years since she was forced to give up her own home through being old & senile. How right the Psalmist was when he wrote, "Yet is their strength then but labour & sorrow."

***Revell**, Audrey May, passed peacefully away on March 29th 1984. Funeral service at Ravenstone Church on Tuesday April 3rd at 2 p.m. followed by cremation at Loughborough Crematorium. No flowers by request, but donations if so desired for the Ravenstone Church Fund.*

4th April 1984 Wednesday
"April 4th 1984", so wrote a fictional character by the name of 6079 Smith Winston, when he dared to open a diary. If detected it was reasonably certain that it would be punished by death. For whom, he wondered, was he writing this diary? **For the future, for the unborn.**
George Orwell's book, entitled "Nineteen Eighty Four" was written about 35 years ago. It is the story of young Winston Smith who is the victim of a supposedly post revolutionary period when the world is made up of 3 super powers. It is a time when "Big Brother" rules.

"Down with Big Brother" – over & over again, wrote 6079 Smith Winston in his diary. But the all powerful Big Brother knew everything that Winston did or even thought. Winston was therefore taken away to be interrogated, humiliated & tortured. Independent thought had to be extinguished.

10th April 1984 Tuesday

"Cardinal Wolsey" – This is Joanne's homework today. We learned how he rose to great power – dined in state and lived like a king. Then came his great fall from power and the final charge of high treason. He died a broken man at Leicester Abbey in the year 1530 A.D.

Roman Baths, Roman Amphitheatres and Roman Temples.

Another interesting subject for homework as we delved into the story of Rome. We studied that greatest of all temples – the Pantheon, meaning "All Gods", and that greatest of all amphitheatres (seats all round) the Coliseum.

14th April 1984 Saturday

A thousand miles I have walked, thanks entirely to Dr. Fred Stutman.

It is now 2 years since I read "The Doctor's Walking Book" and have maintained my effort to walk round the village every day. If I had not been guided by Dr. Stutman I am quite sure I would now be a middle-aged matron.

16th April 1984 Monday

Following the death of Cousin Audrey, her life-long pal and one time play-mate, Aunt Dos, has been ill in bed.

What a demanding patient she is! Pat & I have tried in vain to satisfy her every whim but nothing is ever right. You wouldn't think it possible to be so hard to please. The bed was not made right; the curtains were not opened properly; the tea was not in the right cup; the butter was too salty; the egg was the wrong egg, so she could not drink the whisked egg in milk; the cupboard doors were not shut properly; the taps were turned too tight, etc.

20th April 1984 Good Friday

Went to St. James, Snibston, for Evensong, where I sat with brother Pat. I thought my dad would be pleased if he could see us there together. The vicar, the Revd. David Jennings, gave a fine sermon & told of the "Cross" in the church at Hinckley, where you literally go through the Cross into the church.

22nd April 1984 Easter Sunday

Glorious weather for the whole of the Easter holiday. How lovely to be reminded again at church of those uplifting words of Psalm 118. "I called upon the Lord in trouble & the Lord heard me at large. The Lord is on my side. This is the day which the Lord hath made; we will rejoice & be glad in it."

24th April 1984 Tuesday

"Well, I've never had a dinner like that! I never do liver like that. I've never had cabbage with liver. I wish I'd let Evelyn send me some dinner. She was going to send me some lamb."

Guess who? The one and only Aunt Dos. What a holiday

I've had. The porridge was too thick, but oh, the weather was perfect.

26th April 1984 Thursday

Another farewell at work as Alan Hart left to take up a new job in Aberdeen connected with North Sea Oil. It was drinks all round at "The Fairfield" Wigston. Highlight of the occasion was a "kissogram" when a scantily clad girl arrived with a message of fond farewell & kisses.

28th April 1984 Saturday

Homework in the sunshine on the garden seat & newly acquired garden table. The character studies this week were the Duke of Wellington, who managed to defeat Napoleon at the Battle of Waterloo, and the notorious King Henry VIII who had 6 wives.

30th April 1984 Monday

Like a seven branched candlestick the magnolia blooms in all its glory. Planted ten years ago, it now boasts 30 flowers, but it has grown into its own chosen shape of perfect symmetry. It is 4 feet wide and 4 feet high. The mighty oak, growing nearby, is also 4 feet high.

2nd May 1984 Wednesday

At 10 a.m. on 17th April (2 weeks ago) a demonstration was taking place in London, outside the Libyan People's Bureau. This was the name given to the Libyan Embassy in 1979.

Shots were fired from a window of the bureau injuring 12 people, including a police woman who died.

The murder of police woman Yvonne Fletcher was an unprecedented breach of British law, international law and the Vienna convention on diplomatic relations. We have therefore now broken off diplomatic relations with Libya. Libya's leader is named Colonel Gaddafi.

6th May 1984 Sunday

"Did not our heart burn within us?" The Rector of Ravenstone, the Revd. L. Buckroyd, spoke this evening about the Walk to Emmaus, when the risen Lord Jesus was recognised at last by Cleopas & his friend. Like them, we who have recognised the presence of Christ, must tell you "this hour". "When did you recognise Christ?" challenged the Rector in his sermon. When I was a child, we always sang "The Story of the Cross" during Lent. This most moving of anthems reached the very depths of one's soul & now my heart "burns within me" in the silence of "The Blessing".

10th May 1984 Thursday

A day in London yesterday. Took Joanne, aged 10, on her first ever trip to London.

This was the North West Leicestershire Conservative Women's organised trip to the Houses of Parliament. I had never seen inside the Palace of Westminster before & was spell-bound.

What a wonderful day we had, we had an excellent guide inside the Palace of Westminster & also enjoyed the company of our M.P. David Ashby. We were taken through the House of Lords, the House of Commons, into the great Hall of Westminster & down into the Crypt.

Joanne & I had an afternoon stroll to Trafalgar Square,

where we fed the pigeons, then down the Mall to see Buckingham Palace, back through St. James Park, in time for tea with our M.P. inside the Palace of Westminster – a truly memorable day.

16th May 1984 Wednesday
"Fifty Miners on Riot Charge" - These are the headlines in "The Daily Mail" today as miners get out of control in their efforts to force others to go on strike. Threatened pit closures have caused many miners to go on strike. When they got really out of hand the Riot Act was read to them. Miners in Nottinghamshire & Leicestershire have chosen not to go on strike, but for the last ten weeks pickets from other mining areas have been doing their utmost to stop them getting to work. Police have been brought to Coalville from London & work day & night guarding the entrance to the mines.

Note – The coal miners of Britain, desperate to defend their livelihoods, are causing mayhem by going on strike themselves & forcing those who prefer to work to join the strike.
The Nottinghamshire & Leicestershire miners do not wish to go on strike, but miners from elsewhere descend on the area & we have police stationed day & night at the pits, just to protect our miners.

20th May 1984 Sunday
F. A. Cup Final yesterday. Watford 0 – Everton 2. The attendance was 100,000 and the receipts totalled £915,000. The Cup was presented by the Duchess of Kent. The referee, J. Hunting, was from Leicestershire. Pop millionaire Elton John is the Watford Chairman.

22nd May 1984 Tuesday
Thomas, Colin Neal, 8 Repton Road, Wigston. Loving son of Ted and Evelyn, passed away tragically May 14th, 1984, aged 32 years. Funeral service Bethel Evangelical Free Church, Burleigh Avenue, Wigston, Tuesday May 22nd at 11.30 a.m. followed by interment at Oadby Cemetery. Further inquiries and flowers please to R. C. Weston and Son Ltd., Funeral Directors, Saffron Road, South Wigston. Tel. 783381.

This is the tragic story of Colin, who worked with me in the Motor Licence Office. About 10 years ago he became a victim of multiple sclerosis. He committed suicide when he could bear it no longer.
Motor Licence staff turned out in force for Colin's funeral. We had known him as a young promising lad & watched him change into a broken man. He was battered in body, mind and spirit. He had nothing to live for, nothing to hope for and died in despair, wondering where was God.
I met Colin occasionally in Wigston during the dinner hour. He would come into the café where I had lunch. He had to walk with the help of a walking frame & his illness had made him almost blind. A tall, good-looking young man, with beautiful teeth, and very smartly dressed. Colin talked to me about his illness & about the so-called advice he was given by others. More than once he tried to commit suicide & was warned that he would not go to heaven. I wondered, if the tables were turned and he was the strong healthy one, how the others would fare.

30th May 1984 Wednesday
Guided Walks in and Around Leicester –
"About the City Coat of Arms – Tracing the Origins of Leicester's Coat of Arms."
Joined this most interesting walk & learned how the cinquefoil was first used by Robert de Bellomonte, first Earl of Leicester.
In 1239 Simon de Montfort was Earl. Simon de Montfort was killed at Evesham on 4th August 1265 A.D. fighting against King Henry III. The Earldom of Leicester passed to the King's 2nd son, Prince Edmund, whose son Thomas is remembered in Leicester. These were the Dukes of Lancaster, giving us ducal coronets in the Coat of Arms. (Earls, prior to 1351 A.D.)

3rd June 1984 Sunday
Here I am at Pencombe Hall in the beautiful County of Hereford. Went to Evensong at this Ascensiontide in Hereford Cathedral. What a wonderful Cathedral. The mighty Norman pillars & arches filled me with awe. I was thrilled to be carried up to heaven by those great Norman conquerors.

Note – I spend a week all on my own, on a self-catering holiday at Pencombe Hall, Herefordshire, to be within reach of Bunting & family whom I would like to visit.

5th June 1984 Tuesday
Went on a guided walk around Hereford. Stood inside "The Old House" & from the 2nd storey looked out from the windows of the 17th Century to the 20th Century scene below.
Saw the world famous chained library & the World Map of 1290 A.D. – a flat circular world.

7th June 1984 Thursday
Yesterday I visited Bunting & Mostyn at Malvern.
I also climbed the Malvern Beacon, 1395 feet. Saw Julian's 3 children for the first time.
Today I went to Ledbury and had an interesting guided "walkabout" with the help of a leaflet. Ledbury is a fascinating old town, steeped in history.

9th June 1984 Saturday
"O gift of God – O perfect day" A cloudless sky all day long. I was up at 4 a.m. for an early morning start from Pencombe Hall – home. What an enchanting ride. I left at 5 a.m. & saw rabbits, squirrels & sheep on the road. Missing all the traffic, I was home by 7.30 a.m.
An 85 mile ride.

11th June 1984 Monday
European Parliament – Election No. 2 takes place this week. "Vote for Robert Moreland, Conservative." Robert Moreland was elected to the European Parliament in 1979 as member for the Staffordshire East constituency.
Now there's a funny thing. How have we got into Staffordshire East?
When we had our first European Election, 5 years ago, we were part of Midlands East, but recent boundary changes have created a new local North West Leicestershire Constituency. This has now joined Burton, Mid & S.E. Staffordshire, South Derbyshire & Stoke-on-Trent in "Staffordshire East".

15th June 1984 Friday

"Heraldry" - This is my latest interest following the Leicester Guided Walk "About the City Coat of Arms". I am now intrigued to learn the hidden meaning of other Coats of Arms. I find it particularly interesting to see how the Royal Coat of Arms has developed & changed over the years.

From Richard I to Edward III the Royal Arms were 3 lions only. Then Edward III quartered the arms of France in token of his claim to the French throne – Fleurs-de-lis came in. With the accession of the Stuarts the arms of Scotland & Ireland were introduced – but not Wales.

At a banquet given by King Edward III in 1348 A.D. the blue silk garter of one of the noble ladies fell off. To spare her embarrassment, the King himself gallantly picked up the garter and fastened it round his own leg with the words, "Honi soit qui mal y pense".

(Shame to him who thinks it evil.) The Most Noble Order of the Garter is now the premier Order of Chivalry. Since the reign of Edward III, the Garter, charged with the motto "Honi soit qui mal y pense" has encircled the shield of the Royal Coat of Arms. Knights of the Garter may encircle their shields similarly. The Order of the Garter consists of 25 Knights Companions, the Sovereign, members of the royal family & some foreign monarchs. The late Sir Winston Churchill was created a Knight of the Garter, the highest honour in this country. St. George's Chapel, Windsor, shows their arms.

25th June 1984 Monday

The HVT Honeywell Recording Calorimeter is the latest scientific invention I have been writing about at work – "It consists of a gas/air proportioning device which maintains the amount of air for combustion at an amount extremely close to the **stoichiometric** quantity."

How about that for a good word?

This clever new Recording Calorimeter has a zirconium oxide sensor, i.e. $Zr\ O_2$ sensor, which can detect the presence or absence of oxygen in the products of combustion and the resulting signal is sent to a microprocessor which in turn adjusts a valve to maintain the stoichiometric air/gas ratio. However, if you are thinking of using the HVT Honeywell Recording Calorimeter, remember –

> The gas must not contain free hydrogen. (H_2)
> The gas must not contain air prior to testing.
> The specific gravity of the gas must be right.
> The gas mixture must be either alkanes or alkenes.

26th June 1984 Tuesday

*The **Pied Piper** lured 130 children of **Hamelin** away on this day in 1284. They were never seen again.*

1st July 1984 Sunday

"Each member country of the EEC likes to retain its own nationality". This is what I wrote in my diary on 28th January 1972.

Well this week it was decided to appoint a special "Task Force" to look into ways of crossing national borders within the Common Market & eliminating barriers to trade.

The Common Market has no official insignia at present. The tune from Beethoven's Ninth Symphony the "Ode to Joy" is however repeated in Strasbourg & Brussels as a kind of quasi-anthem. Moves to establish a common EEC passport have failed because of language problems.

5th July 1984 Thursday

"Europe", launched circa 1957 with the Treaty of Rome, ploughed tranquil seas until Britain joined the Community in 1973 bringing with it an Atlantic climate that led to the vessel being docked on grounds of cost, seaworthiness & hitherto unrevealed problems concerned with navigation.

"Europe" is rather adrift at present. In the recent election very few people took the trouble to vote. The European Parliament means nothing to the majority of people & no-one really knows where the EEC is going, including its leaders. Nevertheless, a United Europe is essential for survival.

9th July 1984 Monday

Meet Elizabeth Hewes, B.L.O. i.e. Branch Liaison Officer.

Following the Staff Inspection earlier this year, there have been several changes at work.

I have now moved from Registry, where I have been for the past 2 years, back to Room 007 which I now share with Alan & Lisa.

As Branch Liaison Officer, I no longer deal with the work of the Branch, but with the people who do the work. I sort out sick leave, holidays, personal details, updating staff changes & sorting out accommodation, etc. I keep our head office in London up to date with all that we are doing.

13th July 1984 Friday

My birthday tomorrow – age 53.

"Only 7 years from today, only 7 years from today"

Seven years to being an **Old Age Pensioner!** I have now completed 35 years of "Superannuation" at work, i.e. ⅞ of the 40 years required for full pension & an invitation to the Garden Party at Buckingham Palace.

It is thanks entirely to the guiding hand of Providence that I have completed 35 years towards my superannuation. When I started paying at the age of 18, I expected to get married & leave. Several times I have applied for jobs outside the Service but now am thankful for my job.

17th July 1984 Tuesday

Visited Jodrell Bank in Cheshire to see the mighty radio telescope & the Nuffield Radio Astronomy Laboratories of the University of Manchester. I went on a coach tour organised by Leicester City Transport & had a wonderful day, stopping at Ashbourne and also at beautiful Lyme Park.

The mighty radio telescope at Jodrell Bank is used for studying radio emission from radio galaxies, quasars & pulsars. It is also used as part of a network of interconnected telescopes. Sir Bernard Lovell was the inspiration behind the building of the great telescope in 1957. Lord Nuffield helped pay.

What an exciting moment in my life when I first beheld the leaning Tower of Pisa (April 1975). It was a similar experience when I first saw the Jodrell Bank radio telescope. Like the Queen of Sheba, who had heard of the fame of Solomon; when she actually saw it all for herself, was so moved.

The Queen of Sheba visited King Solomon at Jerusalem & marvelled at the mighty temple he had built. "And when the Queen of Sheba had seen all Solomon's wisdom & the house that he had built …… and the attendance of his ministers & their apparel, there was no more spirit in her." I Kings. Chapter 10.

The Queen of Sheba said to King Solomon, "It was a true report that I heard of thy acts & of thy wisdom. Howbeit, I believed not the words until I came & mine eyes had seen it; & behold the half was not told me; thy wisdom & prosperity exceedeth the fame which I heard."

I Kings Chapter 10. Verse 7.

27th July 1984 Friday

An exciting adventure for the new Branch Liaison Officer this week, thanks to the Post Office in Leicester being on strike. Our "Data-post" from London was stranded at Peterborough, so I had the pleasure of a 45 mile drive to Peterborough to go & fetch it.

29th July 1984 Sunday

The XXIII Olympic Games was opened this morning (according to British time) by the President of America, President Ronald Reagan, at Los Angeles.

I sat up till 3.30a.m. to watch the opening ceremony live from Los Angeles (afternoon there). What a spectacular occasion – really great.

31st July 1984 Tuesday

Viking Coaches, Burton-on-Trent, have organised a visit to the International Garden Festival – Liverpool, 1984. Joanne & I have booked for this – "Don't miss Britain's first ever International Garden Festival ………"

It is advertised as the largest & most spectacular event of its kind ever held in Britain. Reclaimed dockland has been transformed into 125 acres of flowers, fun & entertainment in a breathtaking garden paradise on the banks of the River Mersey.

4th August 1984 Saturday

Joanne & I had a lovely day visiting the International Garden Festival at Liverpool. The weather was warm & sunny & we were able to sit on the grass for our sandwich lunch & tea. We travelled on the M6 and were able to see the Jodrell Bank radio telescope.

6th August 1984 Monday

From a small photograph of my dad, taken about 75 years ago when he was a young soldier in the Coldstream Guards, I have now acquired a large colour photograph. Mr Stanyard, photographer at Whitwick, went to great pains to do this for me & I am delighted with the result. How smart my dad looks in his guard's uniform.

As Leslie Hale reminded me when he wrote to me in 1982, "I met your father 60 years ago & I can see him now as he stood always upright ……"

My dad looks you straight in the eye & his brightly polished buttons (in pairs) show which Regiment of Guards he belonged to.

The Grenadier Guards – buttons regularly spaced.
The Coldstream Guards – buttons in pairs.
The Scots Guards – buttons in threes.
The Irish Guards – buttons in fours.

The Welsh Guards – buttons in fives.
Each Regiment also has a distinctive bearskin.

11th August 1984 Saturday
Keyword

Keyword entrants must have stayed up late every night of the week to get the full effect to this week's puzzle. The topical clue at one across was Olympic Games, and sporting attempts by Mr O. Prosser, 20 Brendon Close, Shepshed and Elizabeth Hewes, 27 Leicester Road, Ravenstone, took them through the tape first to get the gold - £5 worth.

12th August 1984 Sunday

The Glorious Twelfth! As the Olympic Games draw to their glorious finale, we are reminded this evening at church of the words of St. Peter: - "More precious than perishable gold is faith which has stood the test. Trials come so that your faith may prove itself worthy of all praise…." I Peter. 1. 7.

14th August 1984 Tuesday
"Car Salesman was Unfairly Dismissed"

"An Evington car salesman, who was sacked for not reaching sales targets, won his appeal against a dismissal at a Leicester industrial tribunal last week.

Mr Brian Lamming, aged 56, was sacked after ten years with Erringtons of Evington. Mr Lamming, who lives in Bringhurst, near Market Harborough, was dismissed on February 10th and given two weeks' notice. Erringtons claimed his sales performance had dropped dramatically, his timekeeping was poor and he regularly came back from lunch late and appeared to be drunk. Mr Andrew Browne, industrial tribunal chairman, said there was little evidence to show Mr Lamming's sales performance was poor enough to warrant his sacking. The fact that he was often seen to be unsteady on his feet, slurring his speech & drowsy after lunch was possibly the result of his diabetes. Mr Lamming admitted to drinking two or three pints of lager most lunchtimes.

Mr Browne said Erringtons had shown a woeful lack of understanding of industrial relations and the laws relating to the protection of employees, but he said Mr Lamming was not free from criticism."

My heart missed a beat when I read about Brian Lamming in the Leicester Mercury. He settled for £6,000 compensation. But what is that compared to a good salary & pension? I thought of the time he all but broke my heart by doing absolutely nothing. He simply ignored me.

"You would really wonder why I care for him at all, but I do. (And I know that on 2nd November 1965 he was fined £40 or 3 months imprisonment for driving under the influence of drink …..)" This is what I wrote in my diary in April 1967. "He must surely be the most impossible man to love." 22nd November 1969.

26th August 1984 Sunday

Richard Burton, one of our finest Shakespearean actors, with a wonderful speaking voice, & in his younger days a most beautiful face, died on 5th August this year, aged 58. Like my beloved Brian Lamming, he changed from a Prince Charming into a "lost lamb" by drinking too much.

28th August 1984 Tuesday
"Thanksgiving Service for the Life of Mr Richard Burton, C.B.E. at St. Martin-in-the-Fields, Trafalgar Square, London W.C.2. Thursday 30th August 1984 at 12 noon."

I applied for this ticket to Marjorie Lee, The Dorchester, W.1 & was delighted to receive it.

30th August 1984 Thursday
What a moving, majestic, memorial service to Richard Burton. Elizabeth Taylor, the great Cleopatra of his life, was there, together with many stars of screen & stage. The incomparable voice of Burton himself was heard & the singing was led by the Rhos Cwm Tawe male voice choir, plus trumpeter. The hymns chosen were – "Guide me, O thou great Jehovah!" "Jerusalem" and "Mine eyes have seen the glory of the coming of the Lord."
As we sang "He is sifting out the hearts of men" I thought of Tomlinson.
(See 21st November 1983)

1st September 1984 Saturday
Mr Cyril Moseley, Area Gas Examiner based at Shrewsbury, aged 58, died suddenly and unexpectedly from a heart attack. This was my first "death" to deal with as Branch Liaison Officer. I was mightily impressed at the great response from all quarters – Welfare, Union & Establishment, for his widow.

5th September 1984 Wednesday
"Quiet retiring type, somewhat slightly aloof."
Reading through my own file, I found this description of myself when I transferred from Motor Taxation to the Department of Energy. It is most enlightening being Branch Liaison Officer. There's no doubt about it, the Civil Service does its homework thoroughly.

7th September 1984 Friday
"Isabella has Danced her Last"
In July 1980 our Motor Licence Office, which had been standing empty for years, was brought to life as "Isabella's – the best appointed night club in England". Now, after only 4 years, "Isabella's" has turned into Harpers Discotheque, Harpers at 14 Friar Lane, Leicester.

9th September 1984 Sunday
The Government is planning to sell shares in British Telecom to the public. The "Crown" is to be a promoter for the flotation of B.T. shares. But what is the "Crown"? It is a concept rooted in antiquity, whose significance has changed over time & which rests on a combination of prerogative & statutory powers & interpretation by the Courts. The Courts regard the Crown as representing the "sum total of Government powers", including: - a) The Royal Household,
b) Ministerial Offices, c) The Armed Forces, d) Government Departments operating under the direction of Ministers. For more details see Section 17 of the Crown Proceedings Act 1947.

13th September 1984 Thursday
Severn Trent Water Authority – Soar Division.
"Dear Sir/Madam, In order to alleviate the problem of discoloured water in your area, the Authority are intending to "air-scour" the water mains which supply your property. This involves inducing turbulence in the mains by introducing air from a compressor."
After a glorious summer with hardly any rain the reservoirs are now very low. There is a lot of loose material in the water mains, causing the water to be discoloured. The "air scour" will carry the loose material to selected hydrants which will then be flushed until the water runs clear. It will take two days.

17th September 1984 Monday
Prince Henry Charles Albert David (Prince Harry) was born at 4.20 p.m. on Saturday. The 2nd child of the Prince and Princess of Wales, he is 3rd in line to the throne.
1. Prince of Wales. 2. Prince William. 3. Prince Henry. 4. Prince Andrew. 5. Prince Edward. 6. Princess Anne.

19th September 1984 Wednesday
Mary Moore is spending the week with me. We have visited Florrie Moore, aged 90, daughter of Will. We have visited Auntie Doris & Hilda, daughters of David Sketchley Moore, & we have also met Peter Reynolds & family from Australia, grandson of James Sketchley Moore. James Sketchley Moore, referred to as Uncle Jim, was the eldest of the 12 children of Godfrey Moore & Harriet Anne Sketchley. He was the black sheep of the family – a bigamist. He went to Australia & under the name of James Sketchley raised a second family, now thriving well.

23rd September 1984 Sunday
Mary returned home to Wivenhoe, near Colchester. Joanne (aged 10) & I took her to Leicester in the car where she caught the coach to Colchester. Mary, now aged 73, is a mine of information. She has the most amazing memory & can hold long intelligent conversations on almost any subject.

25th September 1984 Tuesday
"What is light?" Young Alan at work asked Dr. Joe Jeannon at work, and I listened in wonder to the answer which lasted for well over an hour. This prompted me to get from the library my latest book, "Einstein's Universe" & learn yet more about the wonderful world of science.

Note – Young Alan, who shares the same office with me, is only partially sighted; he suffers from Retinitis Pigmentosa & year by year sees the light less clearly. He has never seen the stars.

27th September 1984 Thursday
"Wonder is the beginning of philosophy." So said Aristotle. Dr. Jeannon at work is a Doctor of Philosophy – Ph.D. Einstein wondered with an intense, child-like curiosity about the working of nature. He was introverted, being happier with his own thoughts than with company – just like me.

29th September 1984 Saturday
The miners' strike has lasted now for more than 6 months. Never in my life have I seen such fighting between miners and police who carry riot shields &

charge on horse-back like knights in armour riding into battle. So far this strike has cost the country £1,500 million.

1st October 1984 Monday

"Review of Accommodation" – Having been staff inspected at the beginning of the year, we are now about to be inspected again to see why the Department of Energy with a staff of 1,100 needs to spend about £7 million each year on all its bills for furnishings & upkeep.

Guess who has the overall responsibility at work for "Accommodation"? – The B.L.O.

So, with the minimum of warning, I must jump to & give an account of my stewardship. I must know why we need to spend so much money on rent, rates, maintenance, running costs, capital costs, etc.

5th October 1984 Friday

As a result of our "Accommodation Review" I now know a lot more about the duties of our "Accommodation" aspect of the work than I did before. We were all questioned in great depth about the job & I was thankful I had done my homework. The first question was, "What exactly does "Accommodation" cover?"

Our "Accommodation Section" at work is responsible for the upkeep of our whole building, together with rented accommodation in various parts of the country. We see to all the bills for fuel & utilities, telephone bills, cleaning bills, night watchman, etc. We buy new furniture, have repairs done & grass cut, etc.

9th October 1984 Tuesday

"How I appreciate the warmth & comfort of home". This is what I wrote in my diary three years ago. It seems that this is the time of year when I really appreciate my home most of all. Every time I go by Leicester Prison I think of those behind those great austere walls, & all who have no home at all.

12th October 1984 Friday

An assassination plot, second only in severity to the Guy Fawkes plot, took place this morning at the Grand Hotel, Brighton, where the Prime Minister, Margaret Thatcher, and members of the Cabinet were assembled for the Annual Tory Conference. A bomb went off at 3 a.m. killing 4 people & injuring 32.

13th October 1984 Saturday

Prime Minister Margaret Thatcher today celebrates her 59th birthday, having missed assassination by the I.R.A. who claimed responsibility for the detonation of 100lbs of gelignite in Brighton against the British Cabinet & what they referred to as "Tory Warmongers".

The I.R.A. said, "Mrs Thatcher will now realise that Britain cannot occupy our country (Ireland) & torture our prisoners and shoot our people on our own streets & get away with it. Today (3a.m. 12th October) we were unlucky. But remember, we have only to be lucky once."

17th October 1984 Wednesday

Young Steven, Mary Blue's first-born, left school this year with no qualifications for a job & at a time of record unemployment. I did my best to help him get a job & was delighted when he was accepted by the Leicestershire Co-operative Society as a trainee butcher. Sadly, he did not like it & has left.

It was because Steven reminded me so much of my dad that I was so eager to help him. But was I helping him to find his own true identity or was I leading him up the wrong path?

I only know that my dad joined the army as a young man & more than once ran away before proving his wonderful worth.

21st October 1984 Sunday

Madge from Willoughby, now old & frail, has had a fall & landed in hospital at Nottingham. Oh, how sad it is to be old & helpless & alone. I visited her in the geriatric ward where she was one of many in such a sorry state. She wished she could die & was so unhappy, but was pleased to see me.

23rd October 1984 Tuesday

The world wept this week to see the plight of Ethiopia, where millions could die of starvation. Film shown on television has brought the tragic situation home to people all over the world, who in one almighty combined effort have pulled out all the stops to try & help.

25th October 1984 Thursday

Ted Ludlow, one of our gas meter examiners at work, is an ardent Roman Catholic. I listen enthralled to the many amazing stories he relates. He has loaned me some fascinating books related to the Faith, telling the life stories & experiences of visionaries and saints.

"Thou wilt not suffer thine Holy One to see corruption" Acts 2. 27. I am now reading a book called, "The Incorruptibles". It tells of many holy people who were dead & buried but whose bodies did not rot away. Such is St. Bernadette Soubirous of Lourdes who died in 1879.

History indicates that the first saint whose body experienced the phenomenon of incorruption is St. Cecilia (seen in one of the windows in Ravenstone Church). She belonged to a wealthy Roman family & was put to death in 177 A.D. for being a Christain. She lived in Rome. Inside the Basilica of St. Cecilia in Rome, which is believed to have been built on the site of St. Cecilia's family mansion, is one of the most celebrated & best known Italian works of art by Stefano Maderno. It is a statue of St. Cecilia, lying exactly as she died.

2nd November 1984 Friday

"Let every Indian eat a little less rather than let one Indian die of hunger." So said Premier Mrs Indira Ghandi in November 1966. This week, on 31st October 1984, Mrs Indira Ghandi was assassinated. Two members of her own bodyguard, ardent Sikhs, fired at her with a pistol & a sten gun.

4th November 1984 Sunday

"We sat with Mr Tindall" (See 2nd October 1966).

This year is the Centenary of Leicester City Football Club. I went to Leicester Cathedral to a thanksgiving service for this Centenary & sat with my old friend Mr Tindall, who has given years of devoted & loyal service to the Cathedral, but oh, how sad & subdued he seemed, like a lost lamb.

6th November 1984 Tuesday

President Reagan of America, now aged 73, was today re-elected for a further 4 years in office. He had an amazing victory, winning 49 of the 50 states. His rival, Walter Mondale, a Democrat, won only his own state of Minnesota.

"You ain't seen nothing yet" is Reagan's catch phrase.

8th November 1984 Thursday

"For goodness sake and no mistake, choose "Cold Shield" for your windows."

The middle bedroom window, which gets the full impact of the cold north wind & wintry weather, is so much worse for wear now that I have launched out on a £500 replacement de luxe double-glazed up to date window.

10th November 1984 Saturday

Visited poor old Madge in hospital at Nottingham. It seems she will never be able to live in her own home again.

On the same day I visited Johnty (Madge's brother) in hospital at Leicester. He too has had a fall, but is hoping to return home as soon as he is up on his feet again.

12th November 1984 Monday

"Celtic Britain" – This is Joanne's interesting homework this week. So we have gone back to the beginning, from the Stone Age, when man used little more than stones, through the Bronze Age, circa 1800 B.C. to 500 B.C., to the Iron Age, up to the Roman Conquerors, when "Ancient Britain" ended.

14th November 1984 Wednesday

"Millions could die of starvation". Feeding the 5,000 has become the problem now of feeding almost the whole of Africa, where famine "looks with haggard eyes & hollow", as it did at the lovely Minnehaha. The problem is so vast, that it seems completely out of control as drought spreads everywhere.

16th November 1984 Friday

Oakham & Uppingham Schools, those two venerable seats of learning, are celebrating their Quatercentenary (400 years). For this auspicious occasion Her Majesty the Queen & her consort, Prince Philip, today visited both towns & once more put Rutland on the map – this dear County which refuses to die.

18th November 1984 Sunday

"Your Sun Signs" by Russell Grant is a hilariously funny book which I am currently enjoying.

It describes me perfectly – "Crabs prefer to hide at home rather than go out into the big wide world and face whatever it may have to offer them. Their energies are all directed towards the family & fireside. Crabs will scuttle home at the first opportunity. They may go out for the evening, but before they've started on the soup they'll slope off home. Their home is a fortress against the world, a little cocoon they can crawl into at the end of the day and pull up the drawbridge. Their claws can clutch & crush."

22nd November 1984 Thursday

Today is the feast of St. Cecilia, the patroness of musicians, who died for her faith. First she was confined to the vapour bath of her home to die of suffocation, but she remained unharmed, & then an executioner made 3 attempts to behead her, only half succeeding.

24th November 1984 Saturday

Having a de luxe double glazed window in the middle bedroom, I am now hoping to have the room papered & decorated. Barker & Weston have given me an estimate £137. Then I would like a new carpet.

When I can afford it I would like a new window in the bathroom & also in the kitchen.

26th November 1984 Monday

Conducted 4 interviews with John Norburn, Higher Scientific Officer at work, for a "handy-man, sweeper-up, unload the lorries etc." vacancy. We were both amazed at the way the applicants so readily and willingly poured out their hearts to us. There was just no stopping them & we would gladly have given any of them the job.

28th November 1984 Wednesday

Maximum & Minimum Thermometer! Joanne came home from school almost in tears because she had some homework in connection with maximum & minimum, but she was not what, other than a thermometer with a press button. How pleased we were to find it defined in the dictionary - "A maximum & minimum thermometer is one which shows the highest and lowest temperatures which have occurred since the last adjustment." The children at school are to have such a thermometer to keep, during the winter, to see how low the temperature falls & to record it.

2nd December 1984 Sunday

Advent Sunday. Went to Evensong at Leicester Cathedral. Because there were so few in the congregation (only about a dozen) we sat in the choir stalls. It was my pleasure & privilege to sit between Mr Tindall & the Church Warden in his tailcoat. I enjoyed singing with this pair of good singers. The First Epistle to the Thessalonians, Chapter 5, was the powerful lesson for Advent, bidding us all to watch & not be caught napping. "They that sleep, sleep in the night, but let us, who are of the day, be sober, putting on the breastplate of faith & love ..... follow that which is good ..... Rejoice evermore."

6th December 1984 Thursday

Dr. Jeannon at work, a man of science, explained to me in detail his views on Christianity. Everything must be questioned & looked at from every angle. From his detailed analysis, he reasoned that Jesus Christ was born of a Virgin, but was not conceived by the Holy Ghost. He did not believe in the Holy Trinity.

8th December 1984 Saturday

St. Martin's new shopping centre was officially opened yesterday. A commemorative plaque on the inside of the archway leading to the shops was unveiled by Leicester City Council planning committee chairman, Mr Derek Fryett. This development cost £3 million – a combination of many different styles of architecture.

10th December 1984 Monday

"At the third stroke ..." it will be the voice of Mr Brian Cobby, aged 55, British Telecom's new Speaking Clock. The previous voice was that of Miss Pat Simmons, who has been the voice telling the time on the telephone since 1963. Mr Cobby was chosen from 5,000 entrants & will be heard in the New Year – precisely.

12th December 1984 Wednesday

All wrapped up for Christmas – how lovely the presents look, & more than ever this year.
1. Pat, 2. Evelyn, 3. Mary Blue, 4. Scott, 5. Sharon, 6. Bunting, 7. Aunt Dos, 8. Enid,
9. Auntie Gladys, 10. Madge, 11. Auntie Belle, 12. Elsie, 13. Johnty, 14. Matron, 15. Joanne, 16. Stuart, & this year I have 9 staff at the office.

14th December 1984 Friday

Fined £10! "Motor Vehicle No. **UBC 783X** was seen in Station Street, South Wigston, from 12.40 to 12.50 on 14th December 1984 in circumstances giving me reasonable cause to believe that the offence shown at 01 was being or had been committed."
Signed by Traffic Warden No. 0052, E. Wilkinson. (On double yellow lines.)

16th December 1984 Sunday

"Time" – This is the subject we have for homework for the Christmas holidays. What a stupendous subject for a 10 year old. Within our limits we have written about time on Earth – clocks & watches, the calendar, the days & the years. We have mentioned Venus (see 10th December 1978) where a day is longer than a year.

18th December 1984 Tuesday

Snibston School Christmas Concert. This is Joanne's last Christmas at Snibston School & she was the Angel Gabriel. It seems but 5 minutes that she was a 5 year old little angel & now she is the tallest girl in the school. This year she won the school shield for "Best Endeavour" – all the homework we do.

20th December 1984 Thursday

Ellis. On December 20th 1984, peacefully in hospital, after a long illness courageously borne, L. Elaine Ellis, aged 57 years, of Eglwys Cottage, Clipston, Market Harborough. Loving wife of Martyn and beloved mother of Hywel and Nicola. Funeral service All Saints' Church, Clipston on Friday December 28th at 2.30 p.m. Followed by cremation at Kettering Crematorium (Albert Munn Chapel) 3.30 p.m. No flowers by request, donations for Talbot Butler Ward Fund, c/o Northampton General Hospital.

Mrs Ellis, wife of Mr Ellis, Chief Gas Examiner.

Note – This leaves Mr Ellis, Chief Gas Examiner at work, a widower ...

"Keep Your Hands Off" – The Leicester Mercury leaps to the defence of the County boundary as the neighbouring county, Warwickshire, applies to the Boundary Commission for some 10,000 acres of our land, which would include Twycross Zoo. Everyone is up in arms, including the chimps at the zoo, holding high their banners.

22nd December 1984 Saturday

"Only a decade ago, all England was rocked by a so-called improvement in local government. Whole counties disappeared (including Rutland), people were shifted willy-nilly from one administrative area to another, generations of loyalty were pushed aside; & the tinkering persists even today. The Boundaries Commission has asked for ideas, with the result that the empire building North Warwickshire Borough Council has cheerfully claimed a chunk of West Leicestershire. Were the wishes of the local people consulted? Not at all. Were the wider social implications discussed? No ...... we will fight for you."

25th December 1984 Tuesday

Christmas Day at Pat's, where there was Pat, Evelyn, Aunt Dos, Catherine, Doris Roberts & her son David.
By far the liveliest and most interesting character was Catherine, now aged 80, who recounted her experiences in India. Only once in 20 years did the summit of Everest show itself.

28th December 1984 Friday

"The Hong Kong Treaty" was signed this month in Peking by Prime Minister Margaret Thatcher and China's leader Teng Hsiao-Ping. This will become operative on 1st July 1997, when Britain hands Hong Kong back to China after 99 years of British occupation. The Queen has been invited to visit China in late 1986.

30th December 1984 Sunday

And so we come to the end of 1984, prophesied as the year of doom through George Orwell's book, "Nineteen Eighty Four".
Thankfully, the year was a happy year for many, although it was tragically sad for the millions who are at this very moment victims of drought, and man's inhumanity to man.

* * *

1985

1st January 1985 Tuesday

The world's population is 4.8 billion at the start of 1985 and, by the year 2000, will reach 6.1 billion, a United Nations report says. By the turn of the century 80 percent of people will be living in developing countries.

2nd January 1985 Wednesday

Started the New Year in Wonderland. Went to the Phoenix Theatre, Leicester, to see a delightful production of "Alice in Wonderland". Saw all the characters, which we tried in Ravenstone without success, in 1965, to create, brought to life. The costumes were excellent & the cast quite crazy.

4th January 1985 Friday

I have bought myself an office desk. "Genuine Government Surplus Sales – Leicester Road, Loughborough." So, I now have a desk at home exactly like the ones we have at work. I bought the desk for £25 – a real bargain, with 2 good drawers where I can file all my various papers & letters.

6th January 1985 Sunday

What a delicate situation has arisen. Mr Ellis, Chief Gas Examiner, whose wife died so very recently, rang me at home, invited me out to the theatre, & suggested I stay overnight at his house, in the spare bedroom! His grown up son & daughter live with him. I refused to stay overnight.

8th January 1985 Tuesday

Cousin Audrey, who died last year, left me £100 in her will. I have now received this money, which will help me to pay for the middle bedroom to be decorated.

One of the sad things about receiving money from anyone who has died is that you are not able to say, "Thank you".

Now then, the same thing will happen (or has happened) to you. So I will accept your thanks now in anticipation. Just remember that you & I are kindred spirits. I have loved you even before you were born; so that gives us a very special relationship. But of course we are both special.

I remember with gratitude all my good friends who died long before I was born. Those whose music has enriched my life – those whose writings have stirred my soul, and the countless labourers who have built for me roads & bridges; built me a home; & built the mighty wonders of the world.

"Let us now praise famous men, and our fathers that begat us …… such as did bear rule in their kingdoms, men renowned for their power, giving counsel by their understanding …… such as found out musical tunes & recited verses," etc. etc.

Ecclesiasticus. Chapter 44. (In the Apocrypha).

16th January 1985 Wednesday

"Julius Cæsar" is the subject for Joanne's homework this week. Fortunately we found some very good books in Coalville library and learned such a lot about this mighty conqueror. Born in 100 B.C., he went from strength to strength until, at the age of 56, he was murdered.

18th January 1985 Friday

"Behold, I stand at the door & knock; if any man hear my voice & open the door, I will come in to him & I will sup with him & he with me." Revelation 3. 20.

Went to the monastery & bought this beautiful picture of Christ for £7. One of the monks took my arm & walked me through the snow.

20th January 1985 Sunday

Sunday lunch at Clipston, Northamptonshire, with Mr Ellis, Hywel & Nicola.

We also went to Clipston Parish Church for morning service and Holy Communion at 11 a.m. How picturesque the church looked in the snow.

Mr Ellis gave me some of his wife's clothing from her large wardrobe.

Note – Sunday lunch was in lieu of the theatre & an overnight stay.

22nd January 1985 Tuesday

This week, for the very first time, the House of Lords was televised live. It is a 6 months' experiment to see whether or not it succeeds. The House of Commons is not being televised. It was interesting to see all the noble Lords; & the Lord Chancellor on the woolsack.

24th January 1985 Thursday

Mount St. Bernard Abbey again held an "Ecumenical Service" for this week of Christian Unity. I went with Katherine, a sprightly 80 year old. It was wonderful to be in the midst of these holy men – monks on either side of us, the Abbot immediately in front of us & monks all around us.

We sang only one hymn – "The King of love my shepherd is." We chanted "Antiphons" with the monks, but the most moving part of the service for me was the absolute silence we had after the sermon. This indeed was the Peace of God.

28th January 1985 Monday

"£1 billion Water City Planned for Royal Docks." A scheme to create a new city only 5 miles from the heart of London has been unveiled. The "Royals" form one of the largest remaining urban re-development sites in Europe. The new city is being planned for the 21st Century.

The £1 billion new city, north of the River Thames near Woolwich, which is the old Victoria Dock, Royal Albert Dock & George V Dock, will be an innovative & visionary water city for business & commerce, & a dramatic waterfront for surfing, powerboat racing, exhibitions and a large marina.

1st February 1985 Friday

John Lewin, Producer of Coalville Amateur Operatic Society for "Calamity Jane" 1983, "The Card" 1984, and for this year's "Oklahoma" (next month), has announced that he will be resigning after he has completed "Oklahoma". We have therefore to find a new producer for next year's "Music Man".

3rd February 1985 Sunday

Again it is all systems go, as booking gets under way for Coalville Amateurs' "Oklahoma". This is the busiest time of the year for the Hon. Treasurer, who, of course, loves being in charge of everything & everybody. I really do enjoy having complete control of all the tickets and their custody.

5th February 1985 Tuesday
Joanne's homework today is "A Limerick" on water safety -
"There once was a man in a boat, who thought he was going to float, when up came a whale, which flicked up its tail, and there he was - gone down its throat."

7th February 1985 Thursday
£3 million sports complex and industrial museum planned for the Snibston Colliery site.
Now that Snibston Colliery has exhausted itself as a coal mine, it is hoped to transform it into a unique sporting centre with artificial ski slope 170 metres in length, cycle circuit, cricket, football, etc.

9th February 1985 Saturday
Snow, snow, thick, thick snow. After a spell of spring-like weather, we had a day of snow yesterday, which stopped us all in our tracks. I have been visiting Madge in hospital every Saturday since last October, but I did not manage to get there today. Spent much of the day clearing snow.

11th February 1985 Monday
Sub-zero temperatures, day & night, have turned last Friday's day of snow into a veritable winter wonderland. Snow drifts six feet high sparkle like diamonds in the sunshine.
All the windows in the house (except the new de luxe double glazed) are beautifully painted by Jack Frost.

13th February 1985 Wednesday
"Old Mother Shipton". This is Joanne's homework today. Thanks to the holidays in Yorkshire which Mum & I enjoyed in 1977 and 1978, I knew all about Old Mother Shipton from Knaresborough. I had a little book all about her, telling of her amazing prophecies.

15th February 1985 Friday
"How thankful I am to have a home of my own." Again I reiterate these words. How thankful I am to have my new de-luxe double glazed window in the middle bedroom. I could never afford to buy a house. It takes all my money just to keep going & pay all the bills.

17th February 1985 Sunday
After a week of arctic weather, I have abandoned my daily walk round the village, until it is safe to walk on the footpath again. Snow drifts, 6 feet high, completely cover some of the footpath in Wash Lane & much of the rest is so icy it is quite treacherous underfoot.

19th February 1985 Tuesday
Madge's birthday today. What a sad birthday for her. She is now almost completely blind from glaucoma and just sits all day & every day in the geriatric ward at Nottingham General Hospital. She is so miserable and wishes she could die. Oh, the sorrows of old age & infirmity. I feel so sorry for her.

21st February 1985 Thursday
Mr Ellis, Chief Gas Examiner aged 60, again invited me to go with him to the theatre in London. I told him that I thought it would be better for us not to go at all. It would not work. After all, I am not in love with him. We have very little in common & what if we met Brian Lamming!

23rd February 1985 Saturday
Having loved Brian Lamming so much & having been completely spurned & rejected, I have now evolved as a self-sufficient odd-bod. But even my best beloved turned out to have "feet of clay". I am sure I could not have endured his excessive drinking. He might well have broken my heart completely.

25th February 1985 Monday
Like a judge, I sat and listened at work to two sides of a reported incident. Maurice, the messenger, had upset Stuart, the craftsman in the workshop. First I heard the story from Stuart, where Maurice was the villain. Then I heard the story from Maurice, where Stuart was the villain.
Maurice, the messenger at work, reports to me as his E.O. (Executive Officer). I must therefore reprimand him for any misdemeanours. I thought of the time when I had stood before Mr Boreham (April Fool Hewsie) in 1980. And so I said I would see how things improved & see them again.

Boost for church fund
The fund for the renewal of the electric wiring at St. Mary's Church, Snibston, received a welcome boost when £260 was raised by Mr and Mrs George Merrill of Ashby Road, Ravenstone, through a coffee evening.
St. Mary's Church is one of the smallest churches in the country. It is nearly one and a half miles from St. James, the parish church of Snibston.

2nd March 1985 Saturday
The I.R.A. have struck again. They launched a mortar attack at the police station in Newry, County Down, killing 9 Royal Ulster Constabulary officers. The I.R.A. in East Tyrone claimed responsibility. The casualties were the worst suffered by the R.U.C. since the present troubles began in 1969.

4th March 1985 Monday
"He marched them up to the top of the hill, and he marched them down again." After being on strike for 12 months, the miners have at last agreed to go back to work. Only the most militant formed a picket line. This happened at Barrow, near Barnsley, where access was denied.

6th March 1985 Wednesday
Joanne's birthday tomorrow, 11 years old.
No longer the little girl who chatted to me non-stop. As the problems of life mingle with the joys of childhood she is now more pensive. Sometimes I wonder what is on her mind as she sits wrapt in thought, unable to communicate freely.

8th March 1985 Friday
"Oklahoma", Coalville Amateurs' production for this year, is going well. It has virtually been sell-out, and the

Treasurer is delighted. But you would be surprised how many problems arise from the sale of tickets. People book for the wrong night; & changing tickets is quite a job.

10th March 1985 Sunday

God's army of little snowflakes came in full force on February 8th. How proud and majestic the snowdrifts stood in their glittering shining armour.

But see them now. Shrivelled and dirty. They hide in the ditches. They shrink away & they flee in fear, beaten by "gentle spring".

12th March 1985 Tuesday

Konstantin Ustinovich Chernenko, who replaced Yuri Andropov as Soviet leader early last year, has died at the age of 73. Like his predecessor, he had been dogged by ill-health throughout his brief spell in office. He died last Sunday from pulmonary emphysema.

14th March 1985 Thursday

Mikhail Gorbachev, aged 54, is the new Soviet leader. Within hours of Chernenko's death he was proclaimed the new leader. Young & vigorous, he is expected to hold office for many years. Margaret Thatcher, Britain's Prime Minister, attended Chernenko's funeral yesterday in Moscow.

16th March 1985 Saturday

Mothering Sunday this year falls on St. Patrick's Day, March 17th, so, on one & the same day, I remember my mum & dad. What a wonderful thing it is to have a good mother & a good father. According to figures just published, one in four marriages today is ending on the rocks.

18th March 1985 Monday

"Thank you God for a home." How I love my home. It is a haven of peace where I can do exactly as I please.

At our "Mothering Sunday Service" at Ravenstone Church yesterday, the Rector, the Revd. Leslie Buckroyd, spoke of our heavenly home, more wonderful than any here, waiting for us.

20th March 1985 Wednesday

Barker & Weston, decorators, have begun work on our middle bedroom. I have chosen a pale yellow paper with white flowers @ £4.38p per roll. Gradually the whole house is getting ship-shape, but there is a lot to be desired in the kitchen & back quarters. That just has to wait.

22nd March 1985 Friday

"Gentle Spring! In sunshine clad, well dost thou thy power display! For winter maketh the light heart sad, & thou, thou makest the sad heart gay" – Longfellow.

Never have I welcomed the spring more than this year, after an arctic winter, struggling to keep the house warm. You would never believe how cold I have been this winter. I have worn a snug woolly hat, underneath a fur bonnet, underneath a shawl, when I have gone to bed.

I have covered the pillow with another shawl. Fuel has cost me over £300 & now I am thankful it is spring.

26th March 1985 Tuesday

Car tax is now £100 per year! Chancellor Nigel Lawson is now known as the "ton up" Chancellor, following this month's budget, when car tax went up from £90 to £100. Also, petrol went up from £1.99p to £2.03p per gallon. I was able to beat the budget by one day for a £90 car tax.

28th March 1985 Thursday

Long service medals and bars were presented at Coalville Amateur Operatic Society Annual Dinner & Dance, as follows – Joan Dillow, Peter Jacques and Vera Jacques were presented with their bars for 40 years service. John Saunders and I received our bars for 35 years service. Gillian Carpenter, Noreen Measures and Brian Wardle received their 25 year medal. This year the President, Roy Hunt, the Chairman, Peter Jacques, & Vice Chairman, Frank Goddard, were all too ill to attend the Amateurs' Dinner, a most amazing combination of circumstances, never known before.

1st April 1985 Monday

Visited poor old Elsie, aged 84, in the Old People's Home, Shelthorpe House, Loughborough. What a struggle it was for her to walk into the dining room. She shuffled, oh so slowly & painfully, with a walking aid. Her ulcerated leg caused her great distress, but she put on a brave face.

The world of the old & infirm is such a very sad world. At Shelthorpe House, those of a bossy nature enforced their will on others who were totally confused & helpless. It seems that all through life there are some who take it upon themselves to dominate & humiliate their companions.

5th April 1985 Good Friday

15 million people in the world today are refugees. Christian Aid Week, this year from May 13th – 18th, will concentrate on helping the homeless. The campaign theme is "Charity begins with the homeless". It was the British churches compassion for the plight of the homeless which first started "Christian Aid".

7th April 1985 Easter Sunday

"Down with Big Brother." I am reminded of this when I visit poor old Madge in the geriatric ward at Nottingham General Hospital. Those who are old and helpless, sit all day long under the ever-watchful eye of the nurse in charge, who immediately challenges anyone daring to stand up.

9th April 1985 Tuesday
A proposal of marriage!

Old Maid Hewsie was very moved when Mr Ellis, Chief Gas Examiner, opened his heart and assured her that his intentions were honourable. Would she perhaps like longer to think about it? But there was no doubt in her mind. It simply would not work.

Old Maid Hewsie, like Hiawatha, guarded the secrets of her own heart – "Not a word he said of arrows, not a word of Laughing Water."

I think perhaps if I had been born when my old friend Longfellow was around, I could well have chosen him as my perfect partner.

13th April 1985 Saturday
1,500 miles I have now walked, thanks to Dr. Fred Stutman. The Royal Family all endeavour to keep themselves fit with exercise and balanced diet. Prince Charles has become the chief disciple of "Holistic Practitioners", who believe in the whole man – body, mind & spirit, & in natural medication.

15th April 1985 Monday
Poor Madge has now transferred from Nottingham General Hospital to a Nursing Home at West Bridgford. "Byron Nursing Home" is situated in ½ acre of well kept garden, with a very pleasant sun-lounge overlooking the garden, but Madge, being almost blind, cannot enjoy this.

17th April 1985 Wednesday
"May you both be favoured with the future of your choice .... May you live to see a thousand reasons to rejoice." These words from the great musical, "Fiddler on the Roof", were brought to life again by Leicester Operatic Players this week. Enid & I thoroughly enjoyed their production.

19th April 1985 Friday
Young Steven, Mary Blue's first-born, now aged 17, gets more handsome as he changes from schoolboy to manhood. In the full bloom of young love, he has a girl friend named Ruth. As they look lovingly into each others eyes, I think of Ruth the Moabitess, & wonder if this love will endure.

21st April 1985 Sunday
Went to the Church of St. James the Greater, Leicester, for a Centenary Service of Thanksgiving for the Soldiers' Sailors' & Airmen's Families Association. The address was given by the former Chaplain General to the Forces, the Venerable Peter Mallett, Hon. Chaplain to H.M. the Queen. The Venerable Peter Mallett, being small of stature, said that he appreciated the high pulpit in St. James the Greater. Sometimes, he said, he was reminded of St. Paul's journey to Damascus, when "the men which journeyed with him stood speechless, hearing a voice, but seeing no man." Acts 9.

Note – The Ven. Peter Mallett, CB, Chaplain-General to the Forces, 1974-80, died on June 5th 1996, aged 70. He was born on September 1st 1925.

25th April 1985 Thursday
"Diaphanous" – This is the description of Princess Diana, in the Italian newspapers, as she and Prince Charles begin a grand tour of Italy. Highlight of the tour will be a meeting with the Pope next Monday.
Later in the year, on 27th June, the Prince & Princess will be visiting Leicestershire.

27th April 1985 Saturday
Katherine Sullivan, friend of Pat & Evelyn, yesterday celebrated her 81st birthday. She invited Pat & Evelyn & me to her home, where we celebrated her birthday with sparkling champagne and sparkling rhetoric, from this widely travelled, and widely read, fascinating lady.
Katherine is as nimble and alert as anyone half her age. She can read without the aid of spectacles; she can run;

and she can recount in detail her life story, from life in India, Paris or Spain, to the many interesting people she has met along the way.
Katherine is a fine example of how to be glamorous in old age. She eats all the right food – plenty of fresh fruit and vegetables, wheat germ, etc.; does her daily exercise after her bath (when the muscles are relaxed), and with hair swept back in a pleat, looks a smasher.

3rd May 1985 Friday
County Council elections this week (which come every 4 years) showed mounting support for the up & coming "Alliance" party as people become more & more disillusioned with both Conservative's & Labour's endeavours.
Being a floating voter, I gave my support to the "Alliance".

5th May 1985 Sunday
"East Midlands International Airport".
This is Joanne's homework for the weekend, so off we went to the airport's newly opened "Visitor Centre" where there is a splendid display telling the story of the airport & flying in general. We watched an interesting film in the 50 seat lecture room.

7th May 1985 Tuesday
Elizabeth Hewes – "Stationery Co-ordinator". How about that for a high-faluting title?
All it means is that I am responsible for checking all orders for stationery, submitted by "Gas and Oil Measurement Branch", to our Head Office in London. The Civil Service generally must economise.

8th May 1985 Wednesday
May 8th 1945 = V.E. Day. Victory in Europe after 5 years and 8 months of war.
Today, 40 years on, we remember V.E. Day.
140,000 British soldiers were killed in the war. 69,000 R.A.F. men, 50,000 Royal Navy men, 60,500 civilians died, and 30,000 merchant seamen.

9th May 1985 Thursday
Hale – on May 9th, Leslie Hale former Member of Parliament for Oldham West and Life Peer. Peacefully at home. Cremation at Honor Oak Crematorium at 2 p.m. on Friday 17th May. Family flowers only.

Leslie Hale, friend of my dad, has died.

> "So, when a great man dies,
> For years beyond our ken,
> The light he leaves behind him lies
> Upon the paths of men."
>
> Longfellow.

11th May 1985 Saturday
The new-look St. Margaret's bus station, rebuilt at a cost of £1.4 million was officially opened this month (May 3rd). The station became operational last Sunday morning, in time to cater for the Bank Holiday (first Monday in May). The official opening was by Derek Fryett, Chairman of the City Council's Transport Committee.

13th May 1985 Monday

Mount Pleasant Airport, in the Falkland Islands, was officially opened yesterday. Following the war with Argentine in June 1982, Britain has spent £395 million building a large runway & airport in order to fly big aircraft direct to the Falkland Islands.

15th May 1985 Wednesday

"British Gas Corporation for Sale". The Government has announced that it plans to privatize the whole of the British Gas Corporation "as speedily as possible". BGC is the goose that lays the golden egg for Britain. Profits last year were in excess of £1,000 million.

The decision to bring the British Gas Corporation into the private sector and sell it on the Stock Market was announced in the House of Commons by Mr Peter Walker, Secretary of State for Energy. The Gas Act 1948 first nationalised the industry when it was all coal gas.

17th May 1985 Friday

I went to Honor Oak Crematorium London, S.E.23 for the funeral of Leslie Hale.

Champion of the helpless, and all in need, the lesson was appropriately taken from St. Matthew's Gospel, Chapter 25 …. "Inasmuch as ye have done it unto one of the least of these my brethren, ye have done it unto me."

The newly elected Mayor of Oldham, members of the House of Lords, & members of the House of Commons attended the funeral of Leslie Hale. They spoke of his compassion, & recalled how his persuasive oratory saved men who were threatened by imminent execution.

19th May 1985 Sunday

F.A. Cup Final Day yesterday, Everton 0 – Manchester United 1. Attendance was 100,000 and receipts totalled a record £1,100,000. Kevin Moran, one of the Manchester United players, went down in soccer history as the first player ever to be sent off in an F.A. Cup Final

27th May 1985 Monday

The soccer season this year ended in tragedy when fire destroyed the 77 year old stand at Bradford during their game with Lincoln on Saturday 11th May.

52 people were burned to death, trapped behind the padlocked turnstiles, and hundreds suffered from burns. The fire spread so quickly because there was a lot of old paper and rubbish underneath the wooden seating. And as soon as the roof caught fire, the entire stand was ablaze, with burning asphalt falling on to the people. Some of the bodies had to be freed from each other.

29th May 1985 Wednesday

"A mighty oak is growing in our garden". This mighty oak is now taller than I am. Standing about 8 feet high, this sapling is being trained to reach upwards rather than outwards. Every year I remove the lower branches so that it can devote all its energy to reaching higher.

2nd June 1985 Trinity Sunday

How I love Trinity Sunday. What power and wisdom there is in the scripture readings for today.

Isaiah, Chapter 40, shows the soccer hooligans of today where true strength lies. Read this chapter, and you will share with me in its wonder.

This is the lesson I read today at church.

4th June 1985 Tuesday

The Reverend John King Hancock will be officially licensed by the Bishop of Leicester on Thursday 6th June as the new Priest in Charge of Snibston Parish. A former horticulturist, he was born in Boston, Lincolnshire, & trained at St. Steven's House, Oxford. A 37 year old bachelor, he replaces David Jennings.

6th June 1985 Thursday

Went to St. James, Snibston, to welcome the new Priest in Charge, John King Hancock. Richard, Bishop of Leicester, officiated wearing a mitre which he had knitted himself – it looked very good. He spoke of the importance of the Bible & its teaching.

Today also is "Corpus Christi".

8th June 1985 Saturday

British soccer hooligans at the European Cup Final, held at the Heysel Stadium in Brussels on May 29th this year, caused such violence before the start of play that the game was 1 ½ hours late starting. 40 people died when a wall collapsed and riot police were called in.

Juventus (Italy) v. Liverpool.

10th June 1985 Monday

As a result of the dreadful behaviour of English football hooligans at the European Cup Final this year, the Union of European Football Associations (U.E.F.A.) has banned all English football clubs from competing in Europe for an indefinite period. (Not Scotland, Wales or Northern Ireland.)

12th June 1985 Wednesday

As a result of the dreadful behaviour of English football hooligans at the European Cup Final this year, the Federation of International Football Associations (F.I.F.A.) has banned all English professional football clubs from playing anywhere in the world outside England.

14th June 1985 Friday

The new Netherseal Cheshire Home, built at a cost of £1.5 million, to replace the existing Staunton Harold Home, has now been officially handed over to be occupied by residents. The Cheshire Home at Staunton Harold will close at the end of this month. The Netherseal Home is for 34.

16th June 1985 Sunday

The world wept at the plight of 6 year old Alfredo Rampi, in June 1981, when he slipped fathoms deep into a well. This month at Ventnor, in the Isle of Wight, Romanus Giranus, aged 22, was working down a 50 foot well when it collapsed on him. The well was on a one in eight hill. Romanus Giranus had gone down into the well with a wandering lead light to examine the bottom. He had a rope tied around his waist and secured at the top of the shaft. Then there was a loud thudding & shaking of the ground & the well filled with earth & stone within seconds.

It took rescue workers 4 days & nights to reach Romanus Giranus, entombed at the bottom of the 50 foot well. They believed he could have been alive in an air pocket, if the well flared out at the bottom like an upturned funnel. But, after a gallant effort, they found Romanus dead.

22nd June 1985 Saturday
Open Day at the opencast coalfield on the outskirts of Ravenstone. "Coalfield North" site was granted authorisation for opencast coal working in October 1980. The contract was for 9 years to recover 7 million tons of coal. It was great to visit the site & see the colossal machines.

The opencast coal mine is like the Grand Canyon. A vast hole in the ground marches forward, continually opening up ahead as it closes behind. I have never seen such huge excavators, weighing over 1,600 tons, like a house inside, & vehicles whose wheels were 8 feet high.

24th June 1985 Monday
Midsummer Day! But, according to Jeffrey Graham, amateur weatherman from Manchester, we can expect winter to be "the worst winter on record".

Apparently, we are in the middle of a sunspot cycle – the second most active cycle on record – and records began in the year 1701 A.D. Sunspots (explosions on the surface of the sun) spell bad weather for planet Earth. Sunspot activity takes about 10 years to complete a cycle and the most severe winters occur during the last 4 years of sunspot cycles. The very worst winters occur when the moon is full in late November – see 27th November.

30th June 1985 Sunday
"Concorde", the most wonderful aircraft of today, paid a rare visit to the airport at Castle Donington. Aunt Dos (aged 83) and I went to experience the thrill of seeing this magnificent machine take off. It glided majestically down the runway before roaring away for its supersonic flight.

2nd July 1985 Tuesday
"The Bayeux Tapestry". Joanne's final homework as a pupil at Snibston Junior School is the fascinating story of the Bayeux Tapestry. From Coalville library we acquired a superb book which showed the whole tapestry and told its story.

4th July 1985 Thursday
The Bayeux Tapestry was commissioned by Bishop Odo, half brother to William the Conqueror, to be hung in Odo's Cathedral at Bayeux, a little town in Normandy, 10 miles

from the sea. It is one of the world's greatest art masterpieces, 230 feet long, & tells the story of the Battle of Hastings.

6th July 1985 Saturday
Halley's Comet, last seen in 1910 A.D., will soon complete its 76 yearly elliptical orbit and be with us again.

A spacecraft set out from Earth this week on an 8 month journey of 93 million miles to intercept Halley's Comet on March 13th – 14th next year. It hopes to take close-up colour pictures of the comet.

8th July 1985 Monday
What a lovely year I have had at work as Branch Liaison Officer. It has been a pleasure to work with young Alan Norris (Accommodation Officer), who is so helpful. He & I now have a big room to ourselves, where we can spread our wings & enjoy our freedom.

10th July 1985 Wednesday
"The Microcomputer Handbook" is my latest book from the library. I am interested to know how to program a computer & am fascinated by the 3-fold memory of the computer.

I marvel at the human brain with its similar 3-fold memory, a computer indeed of the very highest order.

12th July 1985 Friday
The world-wide ban on English soccer clubs playing abroad was lifted by F.I.F.A. yesterday. F.I.F.A., the international football federation, banned all English clubs from playing abroad on 6th June, eight days after the Heysel Stadium tragedy in which Italian & Belgian spectators were crushed to death.

14th July 1985 Sunday
My birthday! 54 today (2 x 3 x 3 x 3).

The Collect for today, the 6th Sunday after Trinity, is, "O God, who hast prepared for them that love thee, such good things as pass man's understanding, pour into our hearts such love toward thee, that we, loving thee above all things, may obtain thy promises, which exceed all that we can desire; through Jesus Christ our Lord," Amen.

16th July 1985 Tuesday
Bob Geldof is a young man with his own rock music group, known as the Boom-Town Rats. He is Irish and he is a rebel, but when he saw the plight of famine-stricken refugees in Ethiopia on T.V., he was stirred into action.

Rock star Bob Geldof wrote a hit song last Christmas called, "Do they know it's Christmas?" He raised £8 million for famine relief. He has now master-minded the biggest rock concert the world has ever seen. The concert took place last Saturday in London's Wembley Stadium and Philadelphia's John F. Kennedy Stadium.

This magnificent music marathon to give hope to Ethiopia's starving millions featured all the top pop groups of the day. It began at 12 noon in London & finished there at 10 p.m. to be continued in America until 4 a.m. It was televised virtually to the whole world, inviting viewers to send money for aid.

22nd July 1985 Monday
"The National Trust welcomes you to Calke Abbey and Park Open Weekend, 20th July and 21st July 1985." Aunt Dos & I joined thousands of others at Calke Abbey's open weekend. We drove down the noble avenue of limes to this magnificent stately home, where time has stood still for a century.

Calke Abbey, set in a thousand acres of glorious parkland on the Derbyshire/Leicestershire border, was built in 1701 – 1703 for Sir John Harpur. Although Calke remained one of the greatest landed estates in the Midlands, Sir Henry Harpur began a tradition of eccentric seclusion, & nobody saw the place.

Visiting Calke Abbey was like visiting the Sleeping Beauty who was to wake up after a hundred years.

Everything was as it was a hundred years ago. Even the nursery contained dolls' houses & toys of that era. Calke Abbey is now closed until 1989 for restoration.

The National Trust has recently acquired Calke Abbey from Mr Henry Harpur-Crewe & is now faced with the great challenge of putting it back to its former glory. It will take more than 10 years to repair the roof, secure crumbling stone & perished wood, & preserve all the contents.

30th July 1985 Tuesday
Willoughby on the Wolds
Brentwood House
To be sold by auction in the early autumn

Large family house in need of improvement. Gardens of one-third acre. Good range of outbuildings including stables. Lovely village location in heart of good hunting country.

> Edward Bailey & Son,
> 20 Market Street, Bingham.
> Telephone Bingham 38341. Ref: 3167.

With poor old Madge now confined to a nursing home, the old family home is to be sold.

1st August 1985 Thursday
This month marks the 500th Anniversary of the fighting of the Battle of Bosworth here in Leicestershire. This battle marked the effective end of the Wars of the Roses, the demise of the Plantagenet dynasty & the rise of the Tudors. This quincentenary is being celebrated in quite a big way.

3rd August 1985 Saturday
The children & staff at St. Peter's Primary School, Market Bosworth, dressed for a whole week in medieval costume. We were able to visit the school & see the children at their lessons. They also performed "Dick Whittington" – Lord Mayor of London in 1397, 1406 & 1419. They sang and danced.

5th August 1985 Monday
Mary Moore is arranging to spend a week with me this year to coincide with the climax of the Bosworth Quincentenary. An excellent newspaper has been produced, dated August 23rd 1485 telling the supposed news of 500 years ago. The headlines read, "King Richard Dead." The quincentenary newspaper tells not only the full story of the Battle of Bosworth, but gives other world news – "China's Ming Government – The Austrian Emperor, Frederick III, flees Vienna – Captain Christopher Columbus believes that the world is round; he may seek backing of King of Spain."

9th August 1985 Friday
The Prince & Princess of Wales came to Bosworth Battlefield, where they unveiled a plaque commemorating the quincentenary of King Richard III's defeat.
Later, Prince Charles unveiled a plaque to Dr. Richard St. Barbe Baker, the founder of the "Men of Trees" at Nanpantan.

11th August 1985 Sunday
The Pakistan Ambassador, Mr Ali Arshad, & the Lord Mayor of Leicester, Mrs J. Setchfield, were among the many guests from all parts of the country at the opening of Europe's first purpose-built Muslim burial centre (Janazgah) at Saffron Hill Cemetery, Leicester - £76,000.

13th August 1985 Tuesday
Joanne & I went with Viking Coaches on a most delightful tour of the Yorkshire Dales. We had lunch at "The Woolpack" and afternoon tea in Harrogate.
Joanne, aged 11, is now like Rachel (See Genesis 31. 35.) In two weeks time she will be starting at her new school in Ibstock. She has already been to see the school & has been given a very good little booklet telling her exactly what to expect & what to provide,

17th August 1985 Saturday
The Battle of Bosworth is being re-enacted this year in as much detail as possible. Henry Tudor Earl of Richmond, alias Geoffrey Davies, with his army has marched over 200 miles from Wales to Bosworth, while Richard III, alias Robert Streeter, has been received in Leicester & promised support.

19th August 1985 Monday
In Leicester's ancient Guildhall, Mary Moore & I met the soldiers who were preparing to fight for Richard III. A huge fire was burning in the great hearth, while soldiers were polishing their armour & letting us try on their heavy helmets and gauntlets & answering all our questions.

21st August 1985 Wednesday
Mary Moore, aged 74, on holiday with me this week, Joanne, aged 11, & I went to Leicester to see the Lord Mayor present Richard III with the Leicester Militia and a cannon. The King & his men then left for Bosworth. We had a picnic lunch in Castle Gardens beside King Richard III's statue.

23rd August 1985 Friday
What a wonderful sight on Bosworth Field yesterday when Henry Tudor & his men approached from one direction & King Richard & his men from the other. On huge horses, chosen specially to bear the weight of armour, these 2 men greeted each other & clasped hands. "You've no idea what a worry a battlefield can be!" So I wrote in my diary 18th July 1977, but as Geoffrey Davies, alias Henry Tudor, says, "History provides the finest marketing platform that anyone could devise." The Bosworth Battlefield Quincentenary has attracted thousands upon thousands.

27th August 1985 Tuesday
"Oyez, oyez, oyez!" From 1836 to 1978 we had no Town Crier in Leicester, but with so much medieval revelry just lately, we have now appointed a Deputy Town Crier, Mr Anthony Green of Judgemeadow School, to assist Mr Norman Roberts, the Town Crier,

29th August 1985 Thursday
A.I.D.S. = Acquired Immune Deficiency Syndrome.
This is a new virus in humans which is now giving cause for alarm. First reported in 1981, it produces persistent blood disease for life & causes slow, progressive

degeneration of the brain. The aids virus is transmitted in blood.

31st August 1985 Saturday

Mrs June Bird, Sunday School teacher since the beginning of 1976, when we had a sudden influx of dynamic teachers at Ravenstone, has now relinquished this role, leaving Diane the faithful to hold the fort alone. We hope some of the other members of the Sunday School will help.

2nd September 1985 Monday

Monks from Mount St. Bernard Abbey recently celebrated its 150th anniversary by returning to the medieval headquarters of their order, Fountains Abbey, Yorkshire, for a special mass. Founded by Ambrose de Lisle with just 6 monks, it is now the biggest Cistercian Abbey in the United Kingdom, with 45 monks.

4th September 1985 Wednesday

At a time set by astrologers, three marble images have now arrived at Leicester's new Jain Temple, the European headquarters of Jainism one of India's oldest religions. The images are of 3 of the 24 Jain Tirthankaras or prophets. Shantinath is the image in the middle.

The Jain Tirthankaras, or prophets, were human beings who achieved total knowledge and broke free of the cycle of birth and rebirth and achieved eternal bliss. Shantinath was the 16th of the 24 Tirthankaras, who consolidated the faith of the Jains & is especially auspicious for Leicester.

8th September 1985 Sunday

Lord Avon, aged 54, died on 17th August this year from A.I.D.S. He ended his days a gaunt, nearly blind, shell of a man, in a wheelchair. Cause of death was brain inflammation. And yet, in the prime of manhood, he was a handsome soldier and also Parliamentary under Secretary of State. He was the son of Anthony Eden, Tory Prime Minister 1955 – 1957. Lord Avon, Nick to his friends, was Parliamentary under Secretary of State, Dept. of Energy 1983-1984.

Williams, Cicely (Bim) on September 8th 1985 at Leicester General Hospital, loved and loving wife of the late Bishop Ronald Ralph Williams, Bishop of Leicester 1953 – 1978. Funeral service at Leicester Cathedral on Monday September 16th at 12 noon, followed by private cremation.

12th September 1985 Thursday

The Titanic, the "unsinkable" super luxury liner, which hit an iceberg & sank on 14th April 1912, was found this month in an ocean canyon where the water was two and a half miles deep, 500 miles south-east of Newfoundland.

1,513 people died when the Titanic sank. It is still in almost mint condition.

14th September 1985 Saturday

The "Hoolivan" is the latest vehicle used by the police to combat hooliganism at football matches. The "Hoolivan" is an ordinary van with cameras working through a submarine-like periscope perched on top.

Costing £60,000 the Hoolivan's cameras can turn 360° and get close-ups.

16th September 1985 Monday

Today in Leicester Cathedral was the funeral service of Cicely Williams, six and a half years after the death of her husband. She too, chose Psalm 121 and the Anthem "Nunc Dimittis" (19th February 1979).

Cicely was "late for her own funeral". The Cathedral clock struck 12 noon, the choir walked in solemn procession to form a welcoming line-up with all the clergy & civic dignitaries, the vast congregation all stood & waited & waited. But soon the coffin arrived for a most impressive service. The lesson from Holy Scripture was read by Canon Gundry. There is no finer lesson reader than Canon Gundry. From I Corinthians, Chapter 15, the words resounded "O death, where is thy sting? O grave, where is thy victory?" And so, victorious, Cicely left her Cathedral.

22nd September 1985 Sunday

"The Shaftesbury Society" founded by the 7th Earl of Shaftesbury in 1844 as the "Ragged School Union" is my number one charity which I have supported since 1960. Today the society maintains residential schools for multiple-handicapped children. It also has 29 Christian mission centres.

On 14th July 1970, a letter was sent to me from the Shaftesbury Society –

"I see from our records that you have been supporting our work for a long number of years & should like to say how much this continued interest & support is appreciated."

Signed A.T.Wright, Accountant.

The reason that "The Shaftesbury Society" is my number one charity is because it brings Christianity into its work. Christian caring is the basis for all its work and it seeks to provide a very high standard of personal care, love and attention.

The Earl of Shaftesbury lived from 1801 to 1885.

1885 – 1985, one hundred years since the death of the seventh Earl of Shaftesbury, founder of "The Shaftesbury Society". There will be television & radio documentaries, a new biography, an art exhibition & many other events, including a special Memorial Service in Westminster Abbey on 1st October.

Eros at Piccadilly Circus, generally taken to be Cupid, is really Anteros, the spirit of charity. The work of Sir Alfred Gilbert (1854 – 1934), it was unveiled in 1893 to commemorate the Seventh Earl of Shaftesbury. This is the motif of the Society – "Love – Serve".

2nd October 1985 Wednesday

From Harvest Festival last Sunday at dear little St. Mary's Snibston, to Westminster Abbey yesterday for the Service of Thanksgiving on the Centenary of the death of the 7th Earl of Shaftesbury.

One hundred years ago the streets of London were lined by the halt, the blind & ragged urchins. One hundred years ago Cecil Ashley, son of the 7th Earl of Shaftesbury, wrote - "When I saw the crowd which lined the streets, as my father's body was borne to the Abbey, the halt, the blind, the maimed, the poor & the naked, I thought it the most heart stirring sight my eyes had ever looked on." Again they came to honour the 7th

Earl of Shaftesbury. Children in wheelchairs tragically deformed and stunted in growth, who are cared for today by the Shaftesbury Society, were brought into Westminster Abbey to see wreaths laid at the 7th Earl's Memorial inside the Abbey.

8th October 1985 Tuesday

A new quartz electronic watch - £50 and a new pair of specs - £111.85p. My old watch conked out & my specs snapped in half both together. So I chose a beautiful watch which I saw in Samuel's at Coalville & replaced my specs which have given 3 years good service.

10th October 1985 Thursday

"Off the Shelf" An introduction to the library – layout – classification; fiction, non-fiction, general reference.
Joanne's homework at her new school has taught us how to understand the code numbering on the library books using the Dewey System (after the American, Melvyn Dewey).
Melvyn Dewey divided all knowledge into ten parts;
000 General Reference Books, etc. 100 Philosophy,
200 Religion, 300 Social Sciences, 400 Languages,
500 Science, 600 Technology, 700 Fine Arts (music, drama, sport), 800 Literature, 900 Geography,
920 Biography and History.

14th October 1985 Monday

"It's Tally Ho, and Quick, Quick, Go."
This little ditty has won for me a day's outing on Coalville's recently launched Minibus Service. The Minibus is called a "Fox Cub" and my prize is – "A Fox Cub & driver for a Sunday to take you and your friends anywhere you choose (up to 10 hours)."
I have invited all my neighbours to share my "Fox Cub" outing with me, and they have all accepted.
1. Next door, Mrs Yelland. 2. Joanne (next door to Mrs Yelland) with her little brother Stuart, aged 6, and her mum and dad. 3. Next door to Joanne, Peter & Angela & 2 little boys.

18th October 1985 Friday

Mary Blue, now aged 41, is at present in Leicester City General Hospital, following a hysterectomy. She had a large cyst on one of her ovaries which caused her some considerable pain earlier in the year and it was decided to remove the whole womb. She was remarkably bright and cheerful.

20th October 1985 Sunday

Remember George, aged 62, who used to work for Mr Prew? (See 4th December 1980)
Joyce, his widow, and Sally Springthorpe, her friend, also a widow, will be joining us on our "Fox Cub" outing.
It is sad to recall that George died from a heart attack after running across a field to see the local hunt.

22nd October 1985 Tuesday

Today at work I made my longest distance phone call yet when I phoned Oslo, capital of Norway. (See 11th August 1966). In my interesting role as Branch Liaison Officer, I arrange for members of staff to go on different courses, including this particular one which is to be held in Oslo.

Note – Our scientists inter-relate with Norway in connection with gas & oil-fields in the North Sea.

24th October 1985 Thursday

"The Wonder of Guadalupe."
This is the latest book loaned to me by Ted Ludlow, following Mexico's latest devastating earthquake.
It tells the wonderful story of Juan Diego, who on 12th December 1531, not only saw the Virgin Mary, but her image was miraculously imprinted on his cloak.
The Virgin Mary told Juan Diego that she desired a temple to be built on the hilltop where she appeared to him. Today, the Basilica of Our Lady of Guadalupe in Mexico is the greatest Marian shrine in the world. Here you can see Juan Diego's cloak, bearing her reflection.

28th October 1985 Monday

B407 NJF was the little "Fox Cub" bus which yesterday took our party of 12 out for the day. Complete with driver Mark Pickering, a young man tall dark & handsome, we set off at 9 a.m. via Charnwood Forest to Coventry for half an hour break & on to Warwick Castle, our chosen destination.
"A Royal Weekend Party, 1898" by Madame Tussaud's really brought Warwick Castle to life as we went from room to room & actually saw life-like people. The principle guest was the Prince of Wales, who later became Edward VII. He stood chatting to Lord Curzon in one of the bedrooms. We saw (in wax-work figures) the Duke of York & the Duke of Marlborough playing cards. In another room we saw the infant Marquess of Blandford in the arms of his nurse. In another room the Countess of Warwick was taking tea with Millicent, Duchess of Sutherland – 1898.
In stark contrast to "A Royal Weekend Party, 1898" in the splendour of the State Rooms, we went to the dreadful dungeon where French prisoners of war, captured at the Battle of Poitiers were held in 1356. The dungeon has an oubliette, even worse – a dungeon within a dungeon. The weather was fine for our outing to Warwick Castle, but not sunny. We enjoyed riding along in our own little bus, especially when we met people who had never seen such a little bus before. They stood in obvious amazement and were intrigued at this novel form of transport.

7th November 1985 Thursday

An invitation to a Christening! - "We look forward to seeing you at the Christening of Hannah Louise Stuart on Sunday 8th December, 3.00p.m. at Ravenstone Parish Church & afterwards at "Littlecroft" Ravenstone."
Hannah is the daughter of Susan, my god-daughter, who was christened on 7th October 1956.

9th November 1985 Saturday

Steven, Mary Blue's firstborn, who will be 18 years old next month, has now passed his driving test.
Alison (daughter of Cousin David) who will also be 18 years old next month, has also passed her driving test.
Ian Merrill, son of my friend Marjorie, 18 last March, has passed the test also.

11th November 1985 Monday

"Ishi, the last of his tribe". Saw this film on television. The true story of Ishi, the last wild Indian to survive in

North America. As a young boy, Ishi watched as his tribe was brutally murdered. With a few members of his family he fled, until he alone was left. He died in 1916. (See Hosea 2. 16.)

13th November 1985 Wednesday

"The Emerald Forest" – the adventure movie of the year. Went to the Odeon Cinema in Leicester to see this great film about a little boy who was captured in the great forest by the Amazon, by a tribe of wild Indians who, unlike the Indians of North America, still live their own natural life-style. They were known as the invisible people because they could move so stealthily through the forest & blend in with the foliage so well, that no-one ever found their hiding place. They crushed emeralds to powder for their war-paint, & never left the forest.

17th November 1985 Sunday

The planets line up and – Whoosh! In June 1980, it was Mount St. Helens on the western coast of America which blew her top. The volcano erupted 60,000 feet into the air.

This week it was the Colombian volcano Nevado Del Ruiz, in South America, which erupted, killing thousands of people.

Not since the Krakatoa disaster, over a hundred years ago, (see 27th August 1983) has a volcanic eruption caused so much loss of life as Nevado Del Ruiz. The town of Armero, 30 miles away from the volcano, took the full impact of the eruption & was completely buried.

21st November 1985 Thursday

The "Grand Planetary Alignment" which began building up in 1976, will not abate until 1993. It has been predicted that, "When the Moon is in the Seventh House, and Jupiter aligns with Mars, and with the other seven planets of the solar system, Los Angeles will be destroyed." Apart from the line-up of the planets, we have the arrival of Halley's Comet, another traditional portent of evil. Its last appearance in 1910 saw the build-up to the Great War 1914 – 1918. Halley's Comet was seen in the 1520s by Nostradamus who made many amazing predictions, & mentioned comets.

25th November 1985 Monday

Scientists believe that there is a link between earthquakes, volcanic eruptions, and sun-spots. There is also a link between sunspots and planetary positions. Planetary alignments cause sun-spots, which in turn cause unusual & extreme weather patterns. Electromagnetic tides trigger movements at fault lines on the Earth's crust.

27th November 1985 Wednesday

Full Moon! The most severe winters occur during the last four years of sunspot cycles, & the very worst winters occur when the Moon is full in late November, due to sea level & tidal effects on air pressure. This coming winter is the 7th year of the present sunspot cycle, & is expected to be really bad.

29th November 1985 Friday

"Worlds in Collision" was the title of a book published in 1950. Dr. Immanuel Velikovsky said that in about 1500 B.C. a fireball erupted from the planet Jupiter to become a comet. This comet had a near collision with planet Earth, before settling into its own orbit & becoming the planet Venus.

According to Dr. Velikovsky, the story of the plagues of Ancient Egypt in the days of Moses, were what happened when the comet Venus had its near collision with Earth. The comet's tail of fine red dust turned rivers blood coloured, it caused hail stones, and an unprecedented tide rolled back the Red Sea.

The comet Venus was to the children of Israel a pillar of cloud by day and a pillar of fire by night. (See Exodus, Chapter 13) This was the comet's blazing tail seen through a pall of smoke. But Earth was never the same after that. Changes in weather patterns finished off the might of Troy.

Changes in weather patterns nearly finish me off sometimes (see 24th March this year). Apparently, the warm weather of the past 50 years is coming to an end. Now it's back to normal. From 1430 to 1850 weather in the Northern Hemisphere was severely cold & was known as the "Little Ice Age".

2nd December 1985 Monday

Reeves, *William Arthur. Much loved father of Ken, Pat, Phyllis and Sherry, dear granddad of Joanne, Kelly and Paul, passed away December 2nd after much suffering. Your place in our hearts can never be filled.*

My friend Reevsie's dad.

7th December 1985 Saturday

Dr. Jeannon, my good friend and doctor of science, died today aged 49. Yesterday he was at work although he was not at all well. He had suffered 2 heart attacks and had been away from work for several months, but it seemed that he came back to work for a word with us all before he died.

9th December 1985 Monday

What a sad day as news reached everyone at work that Dr. Jeannon had died. There was a subdued hush about the place all day. Eyes brimmed with tears as each recalled some special memory. Josué Marc Jeannon was from the Island of Mauritius & known to us all as "Joe".

I remember with gratitude the many things I learned from Dr. Jeannon. He it was who showed me how to draw a perfect circle using only a pencil, paper & your own hand in a fixed position. Only one day before he died he brought me a book to read, entitled, "An Introduction to Logic & Scientific Method."

13th December 1985 Friday

Today I went all alone to see Dr. Jeannon as he lay in his coffin in the Chapel of Rest, not far away from our office. I informed the man on duty that I had come to see some-"body". Could I please see Dr. Jeannon?

I had to wait a little while & I had to smile as I recalled what Dr. Jeannon would have said to me. Whenever I went to his office I said, "Could I see the Doctor please?" & he would suggest I take off all my clothes & lie on the couch.

Now he lay at peace. Although we could no longer communicate with words, we said, as it were, "Au revoir".

17th December 1985 Tuesday

Dr. Jeannon, like Cicely Williams 3 months ago, was late for his own funeral. But unlike the impressive service for Cicely in Leicester Cathedral, poor Joe had an impersonal service in the chapel at Gilroes Cemetery. There was no music & we had to sing unaccompanied the one hymn, "The Lord's my Shepherd."

19th December 1985 Thursday

Steven, Mary Blue's firstborn, and his 15 year-old girl friend Ruth are hoping to become engaged on Christmas Day. Ruth is still at school & will be leaving school next Easter.

Steven now has a job as a window-cleaner. He works in a three-some team with Ruth's father & Ruth's brother.

21st December 1985 Saturday

"With kindest thoughts and many happy memories. I have not been well at all these last 8 months, but seem to improve. Hope you are well and I wish you a very happy Christmas.

God bless you." A Christmas card greeting from my very dear old friend, the Revd. Gustav Aronsohn.

Recalling the beautiful blessing used so often by the Reverend Gustav Aronsohn, I wrote on my Christmas card to him, "May the love, the power and the joy of the Lord Jesus be with you. May the love of the Lord Jesus draw us to himself; may the power of the Lord Jesus strengthen us in his service; may the joy of the Lord Jesus fill our souls."

25th December 1985 Wednesday

Christmas Day at Pat's, where Evelyn once again rounded up all the odd bods.

There was Pat, Evelyn, Doris Roberts, Katherine Sullivan, Aunt Dos & me, and for good measure the new young vicar, the Revd. John Hancock.

In the morning I called to see Johnty, aged 81, also alone.

26th December 1985 Thursday

Mary Blue, now feeling much better after her recent hysterectomy, invited us all to her house for Boxing Day. There was Pat & Evelyn, Doris Roberts, Aunt Dos & me. There was her firstborn Steven & his girl friend Ruth, young Murdo & Sharon (with boyfriend Darren) & 11 year-old Scott.

29th December 1985 Sunday

Remember Comet Kohoutek? Hailed as the biggest & brightest comet ever recorded & expected to be seen around Christmas 1973? Well, it came & went without being seen at all. Now the great Halley's Comet is just the same. For this visit the Earth & the comet are in the wrong places for viewing.

31st December 1985 Tuesday

Halley's Comet is now moving through Pisces into Aquarius, but we cannot see it. It sets earlier each night and is lost on the horizon. Soon it will be so far south that it will not rise at all over the British Isles. The only hope of seeing it will be from the southern hemisphere.

* * *

1986

1st January 1986 Wednesday
North-South, East-West. The Pope has chosen peace, the bonds between East & West, and North & South relations as keynotes of his World Day of Peace message. Only the just solution to the existing inequalities between North & South can ease the tensions between East & West.

3rd January 1986 Friday
Spain & Portugal have now joined the Common Market. So now we are 12. When Greece joined on 1st January 1981 I thought of the beast with the 7 heads and 10 horns. (See Revelation, Chapter 13) I am pleased that we are now 12 rather than 10. The beast with 10 horns sounds a fearsome creature.

5th January 1986 Sunday
I have bought another bargain from "Genuine Government Surplus Sales – Loughborough."
I just happened to see the very thing I have wanted for a long time and snapped it up immediately. A folding card table 36″ by 36″ which doubles into a wooden table 18″ by 36″. Reduced from £89 to £69.

7th January 1986 Tuesday
"And when they were come into the house, they saw the young child with Mary his mother and fell down and worshipped him." Matthew, Chapter 2, verse 11.
The Rector of Ravenstone, the Revd. Leslie Buckroyd, said that Julius Cæsar came & saw & conquered. The wise men, however, came and saw and worshipped.

9th January 1986 Thursday
Cicely Williams (the Bishop of Leicester's widow) who died last September has left estate valued at £101,893. Having no children, she has left her money to many organisations, including Leicester Cathedral, with a request that it be used to enhance the musical tradition of the Cathedral.

11th January 1986 Saturday
Poor Madge has now been in the Byron Nursing Home at West Bridgford for 9 months. I visit her every Saturday afternoon & have watched all the spirit taken out of her. She is now reduced to a state where she sits all the time with head bowed low, eyes closed, and has nothing to say to anyone.
I know it would have upset my Mum to see Madge in such a sorry state. They were such close friends. When they were very young they had such fun together. One day they lost all sense of time when they spent many happy hours throwing ducks into the ponds. The ducks came back for more.

15th January 1986 Wednesday
"Midland Fox" now has a minibus service as well as the normal bus service. The minibus is called the Fox Cub. These minibuses are only the second such scheme in the country and were introduced in Coalville last year on 27th July. They mean a more frequent service.

17th January 1986 Friday
The United States census for 1890 asked for the colour of the respondee – whether he or she was Black, Mulatto, Quadroon or Octoroon.
Mulatto = offspring of a Black and a White. Quadroon = offspring of a Mulatto and a White. Octoroon = offspring of a Quadroon and a White, i.e. ⅛ Negro blood.
I have learned the meaning of Mulatto, Quadroon & Octoroon from the book entitled, "An Introduction to Logic & Scientific Method" which Dr. Jeannon brought me to read. So although Dr. Jeannon is now dead, I am still in effect learning from him & able to benefit from his knowledge.

21st January 1986 Tuesday
Michael Ray Dibdin Heseltine, Defence Secretary, resigned in sensational fashion on 9th January when he walked out of a Cabinet Meeting at 10, Downing Street. He is the 16th Government figure to retire or to be dismissed since Margaret Thatcher became Prime Minister in 1979. She is too dominating.

23rd January 1986 Thursday
Remember Voyager II the NASA space-craft, scheduled to reach out as far as Uranus by January 1986? (See 31st December 1979) Well, after 8 years, it is just about there. It is the furthest reaching odyssey of exploration launched from Earth, going on to Neptune by 1989.

25th January 1986 Saturday
Remember the Channel Tunnel Project which we had to abandon in February 1975 because we ran out of money? Well, we have now decided to try again. Britain & France are to be linked by a 31 mile twin-bore rail tunnel which will cost £2.3 billion. It is expected to be ready in 1993.

27th January 1986 Monday
And yet another Cabinet Minister hits the dust. Leon Britton, Secretary of State for Trade & Industry, took measures which were not politically acceptable to his colleagues. He sprang leaks deliberately, to further his own cause, & even though Prime Minister Margaret Thatcher approved, he resigned.

29th January 1986 Wednesday
America had its worst space disaster yesterday when the space shuttle Challenger, with 5 men & 2 women on board, exploded at 1,977 miles per hour just 72 seconds after launching.
The 90 ton shuttle blew up like a bomb, at an altitude of 10 miles, becoming a scorpion shaped inferno. (See 29th January 1988).

31st January 1986 Friday
Auntie Gladys, Enid's mum, widow of my dad's brother Cyril, celebrates her 90th birthday tomorrow. She is now in a hopeless state mentally, but Enid attends to her every need & although there are times when she drives Enid to screaming point, Enid looks after her & also goes to work full time.

2nd February 1986 Sunday
"This beginning of miracles did Jesus in Cana of Galilee,

& manifested forth his glory." The Rector of Ravenstone, the Revd. Leslie Buckroyd, spoke of the "manifestation" of Christ, in his first miracle, when he turned water into wine. He said that in his last miracle he explained that his blood is our wine.

4th February 1986 Tuesday

The last miracle of Jesus was his death & resurrection. We have been given a continual remembrance of his death in the service of Holy Communion. Christ himself, at the Last Supper, said, "This cup is the new testament in my blood; this do ye, as oft as ye drink it, in remembrance of me."

(I Corinthians, Chapter II, verse 25.)

6th February 1986 Thursday

The Revd. Norman Hulme, Rector of Elmesthorpe and Vicar of Earl Shilton, near Hinckley, Leicestershire, has been driven out of his home and job by vandals. Stained glass windows have been broken, church doors daubed with obscenities, and stones have been thrown at him in his own doorway.

8th February 1986 Saturday

Tomorrow is the start of the Chinese Year of the Tiger. For the first time in Leicester, the Chinese New Year will be celebrated in traditional style, with a carnival procession through the streets followed by a concert at the De Montfort Hall.

10th February 1986 Monday

Perihelion = the point of the orbit of a planet or a comet at which it is nearest to the Sun. Perihelion for Halley's Comet was yesterday, but the comet was behind the Sun, and therefore not visible at all from Earth. Like the cuckoo, it will come northward again in April & fly away in July.

Although the return of Halley's Comet is the worst for 2,000 years, as far as seeing it from Earth, it is nevertheless possible for the first time to send space-probes right up to it. Five different vehicles are on their way now and hope to rendezvous next month; two Russian, two Japanese and one European.

The European space-probe "Giotto" (named in honour of the Florentine painter who included the comet in his great paintings) has a date with Halley's Comet on March 13th – 14th. It will penetrate right into the head of the comet & if all goes well send back close range pictures, although it may be destroyed in the effort.

16th February 1986 Sunday

"God save the Queen and God help the Consort" – thus read the banners of welcome 25 years ago when the Queen last visited the Kingdom of Nepal, between North India & China.

Today she began another State Visit, arriving at the capital Katmandu before going to Australia.

18th February 1986 Tuesday

"It seemed good to me to write unto thee, in order ….." (St. Luke, Chapter I, verse 3.)

Like St. Luke, I like to record things in order. As Hon. Treasurer for Coalville Amateurs', I am once again in my element, as we get into full swing selling tickets for our next production "Music Man".

20th February 1986 Thursday

On the recommendation of Peter Jacques, we chose a professional producer - £300 – for our forthcoming production "Music Man". But we have not been at all satisfied with the services of the lady in question – Thea Craine of Leicester. The show seems to be in a shambles & morale is low.

22nd February 1986 Saturday

The oldest man in the world died yesterday, aged 120. Shigechiyo Izumi of Asan, on Tokunoshima, an island 820 miles south west of Tokyo, Japan, was born on 29th June 1865. His recipe for a long life was, "Do not worry. Leave things to God, the Sun, and Buddha."

24th February 1986 Monday

From 23rd February to 6th March 1836, the Alamo, at San Antonio in Texas, was the scene of bloody battle. The Alamo, once a mission, became a fortress where 180 brave men fought in vain against an army of 4,000 Mexicans. These men (including Davy Crockett) were willing to die for Texas.

Texas today is celebrating the 150th anniversary of its independence from Mexico. Although the glorious story of the Alamo may have looked like a defeat for our heroes, very shortly afterwards the Mexicans were well & truly beaten at San Jacinto, as the Texans shouted, "Remember the Alamo!"

28th February 1986 Friday

What a bitterly cold month it has been this February. A biting easterly wind has been blowing straight from Siberia. It is the coldest February since 1947, but fortunately it has not brought much snow. I'm thankful it is not 1947 when conditions really were austere.

During the last 3 months of freezing wintry weather I have been well pleased with my central heating. The old Cavendish boiler has kept going day & night with anthracite.

3rd March 1986 Monday

Final Dress Rehearsal for "Music Man". Although not one of Coalville Amateurs' greatest productions, the dress rehearsal went very well.

Brother Pat is House Manager this year because House Manager Frank Goddard is ill. For a number of years Pat has been the Assistant House Manager.

5th March 1986 Wednesday

All the officials of Coalville Amateur Operatic Society receive a little gift in recognition of their services.

Last year I chose "The Complete Works of William Shakespeare" and this year I have chosen an up-to-date World Atlas which contains lots of useful snippets of information.

6th March 1986 Thursday

Remember The Alamo – March 6th 1836. On this day Western heroes Davy Crockett and Jim Bowie died when the siege of the Alamo ended.

7th March 1986 Friday

Joanne's birthday! Twelve years old today.

She still pops round to see me, but her visits are now less frequent. As she develops more of her own personality she shares less of my interests. She has no interest in Coalville Amateur Operatic Society and shows very little interest in the theatre in general.

9th March 1986 Sunday

After the big freeze of February we have had a week of beautiful weather for our show. The sun has shone & all the birds have started to sing again. What a joy it is to see signs of spring after the long & dreary winter.

This afternoon I went with Pat & Evelyn to visit Doris Roberts in hospital. Doris Roberts, aged 84, was taken to hospital last week following a slight heart attack. She is a compulsive talker and can talk non-stop all day long. As we sat round her bedside she did all the talking, although she was connected up to a cardiograph, which gave a continuous record of her heartbeat.

13th March 1986 Thursday

Hayes, Sidney George, 11 Newstead Avenue, Wigston, dearly loved husband of Betty, loving father of Simon, Andrew, Philip and Doral, passed away suddenly but peacefully on March 13th aged 53 years. Funeral service at St. Thomas's Church, South Wigston, on Tuesday March 18th followed by interment at Wigston Cemetery.

Remember Mrs Hayes, my next door neighbour who used to say, "Gee awe, Sid."?
(See 26th August 1969)

15th March 1986 Saturday

What a shock it was to hear that Sidney Hayes had died. Like his mother, he died quite unexpectedly. I remember him so well as a child & even recorded in my diary the day he "went into long trousers" – 29th July 1945.
His mother's "Ghee awe, Sid" meant "Stop it! Sid"
(i.e. Gi' o'er – give over.)
Sidney Hayes married Betty Brown and set up home at Wigston. He was a good bass singer and was in the choir at St. Thomas's Church. He worked in Lloyds Bank. He was at work up to last Wednesday and then on Thursday morning, while sitting at the breakfast table, he died of heart failure.

19th March 1986 Wednesday

The funeral of Sidney Hayes was very impressive. There was a large choir of 28 men and boys and a church full of people. The singing was loud and clear (so different from the funeral of poor Joe – Dr. Jeannon). The theme was "peace" & we ended with an Easter hymn, "Jesus Lives" Number 140.

21st March 1986 Friday

A Royal Engagement!
"It is with the greatest pleasure that the Queen and the Duke of Edinburgh announce the betrothal of their beloved son, the Prince Andrew, to Miss Sarah Ferguson, daughter of Major Ronald Ferguson and Mrs Hector Barrantes."

23rd March 1986 Sunday

Following the announcement of the Royal engagement, it is expected that Prince Andrew will soon be created "Duke of York".
This title, traditionally associated with the 2nd son of the sovereign, was created in 1385 by Richard II & conferred upon his uncle Edmund of Langley.

25th March 1986 Tuesday

"The noble Duke of York, he had 10,000 men, he marched them up to the top of the hill, and he marched them down again."
This particular Duke of York was Prince Frederick, the 2nd son of George III. He was commander-in-chief of the English army, but had to resign from the post.

27th March 1986 Thursday

The new "Gas Bill" had its third reading this week. Peter Walker, Secretary of State for Energy, said, "I am delighted that the House has seen the Bill through its Second Reading & through Committee stage. I rejoice that the Bill went through Report & now it is before the House for its Third Reading."

29th March 1986 Saturday

"And it was night" (St. John, Chapter 13, verse 30)
At our Good Friday Service yesterday, the Rector, the Revd. Leslie Buckroyd, spoke of the tremendous meaning of these words. On the night of the Last Supper, it was indeed as though the Light of the World was being extinguished, the moment Judas left.

31st March 1986 Monday

"Jesus saith unto her, Mary." I thought of my mum as I read these words in the lesson at church on Easter Sunday.
The congregation at Ravenstone Church gets lower & lower in numbers. Row upon row of empty seats and on Easter Sunday at Evensong a congregation of 7.

2nd April 1986 Wednesday

Half a million homes in this country (including mine) need repairs costing more than £7,000 each. A state fund to help householders who cannot afford repair bills has been proposed by the National Economic Development Office. Tax concessions make no provision for maintenance.

4th April 1986 Friday

"Everyone should have the right to freedom to have or adopt a religion or belief of his choice, & freedom either individually or in community with others and in public or private, to manifest his religion or belief in worship, observance, practice & teaching."
Article 18, U.N. Convention on Human Rights.
An Anglo-American human rights team recently visited Nepal to examine allegations of torture & brutality against the small Christian minority there. In 1985, over 80 people were charged with "Preaching Christianity" & causing a "Disturbance to Hinduism". Nepal does not like Western influences.

8th April 1986 Tuesday

The Greater London Council together with 6 other Metropolitan County Councils, have now been scrapped, because they were considered to be an unnecessary layer of Local Government and wasted too much money; Tyne & Wear, Merseyside, West Midlands, South Yorkshire, West Yorkshire and Greater Manchester.
Abolishing the Greater London Council cannot be done overnight. Apart from the magnificent building of

County Hall, across the River Thames from the Houses of Parliament, there are another 10,000 pieces of Greater London Council property to be disposed of. The work will be absorbed in Borough Councils.

It will take about 5 years to wind up the estate of the Greater London Council. Most loose ends will be tied by the newly appointed "London Residuary Body", with a staff of 4,331 headed by Sir Godfrey Taylor, aged 60.

The Greater London Council computer alone will take 9 months to move.

Roberts, Doris, of St. Mary's Court, Hugglescote. In hospital on April 8th 1986, aged 83 years. Beloved wife of the late George Cecil, and much loved mother of David and family. May she rest in peace, and rise in glory. Funeral arrangements later.

14th April 1986 Monday

2,000 miles I have now walked, thanks to Dr. Fred Stutman. Round and round the village I go, usually about 7 a.m., & meet the occasional jogger or the paper boy. Again this year I had a break in the severe winter weather, when the wind was so bitingly cold & conditions underfoot were bad.

16th April 1986 Wednesday

Today I am 20,000 days old. Full many a glorious morning have I seen. (Shakespeare)

This afternoon we all attended the funeral of Doris Roberts, Evelyn's sister-in-law. We assembled at the Co-operative Funeral parlour in a pleasant waiting room, with Doris Roberts next door in her open coffin. As we wandered freely in & out of the room where Doris Roberts lay in her coffin, it seemed that she was very much with us. Always so loquacious, for the first time now I saw her perfectly silent. She had lived a full & active life, and many people came to pay their last respects.

20th April 1986 Sunday

"Remember the Sabbath Day to keep it holy. Six days shalt thou labour, and do all thy work, but the seventh is the Sabbath of the Lord thy God, in it thou shalt not do any work."

(Exodus Chapter 20.)

The Government were defeated this week on a Bill to allow shops to open on a Sunday.

"The Shops Bill" was defeated at the 2nd Reading, thanks to such stalwarts as Sir Peter Miles who said "I make no apology for taking the Christian view. This may be a minority view, but it is important. A nation which ignores God and his commandments is bound to fail, & fail miserably. I must give that warning."

If we fail to allow this land of ours to enjoy her Sabbaths, then God himself will make our cities waste & bring our sanctuaries into desolation. "Then shall the land enjoy her Sabbaths, as long as it lieth desolate ..... As long as it lieth desolate it shall rest; because it did not rest in your Sabbaths when ye dwelt upon it." (Leviticus 26)

26th April 1986 Saturday

The Duchess of Windsor, aged 89, died this week on 24th April. A Buckingham Palace statement said, "It is announced with deep regret that the Duchess of Windsor died at 10 a.m. at her residence near Paris." Her residence was on the edge of the Bois de Boulogne – the mansion Bagatelle.

The Duchess of Windsor lived in exile in Paris with her husband (who died in May 1972). He was Britain's uncrowned King Edward VIII who gave up his throne to marry the woman he loved. Being twice divorced, she was not accepted as Queen. However, her body will be brought to Windsor for burial.

Instrument of Abdication

I, Edward the Eighth, of Great Britain, Ireland, and the British Dominions beyond the Seas, King, Emperor of India, do hereby declare My irrevocable determination to renounce the Throne for Myself and for My descendants, and My desire that effect should be given to this instrument of Abdication immediately.

In token whereof I have hereunto set My hand this tenth day of December, nineteen hundred and thirty six, in the presence of the witnesses whose signatures are subscribed.

Edward R

Signed at Fort Belvedere in the presence of

| Albert | Henry | George |

30th April 1986 Wednesday

King Juan Carlos of Spain & his wife Queen Sofia have recently made a historic 3 day State Visit to Britain.

Not since 1905, when King Alfonso XIII came in search of a bride, has a Spanish monarch paid a State Visit to Britain. Much of this century Spain was ruled by Dictator Franco.

2nd May 1986 Friday

Katherine Sullivan, now aged 82, who has met so many interesting people in her life, lived for a while in Paris. One day, while walking her dog, it was attracted by another dog which was with his master. "Come here," she said, in English, & that led to a long chat with the dog's owner – King Edward VIII.

4th May 1986 Sunday

The London Marathon has now become the greatest one day sporting event in Britain.

Over 18,000 runners set off in the pouring rain from Greenwich to run the 26 miles 365 yards to Westminster Bridge. We shared in the ecstasy and in the agony of the race. The winner was Toshiako Seko.

6th May 1986 Tuesday

A radioactive cloud now covers most of Europe following an explosion at a Soviet nuclear power station. The accident happened at the Chernobyl nuclear plant, near the town of Pripyat, 80 miles north of Kiev in the Ukraine. Deadly particles of radioactive Caesium & Iodine were released.

8th May 1986 Thursday

Ascension Day!

As at Christmas, God through Christ came down to earth from heaven, so at Ascension tide, man through Christ can aspire to heaven. "He ascended into heaven, and sitteth on the right hand of God the Father Almighty." We are called to be God's right hand men.

10th May 1986 Saturday
Tomorrow is Cousin Donald's 46th Wedding Anniversary. He built his home in Ravenstone during the war & has lived there ever since. The house is now up for sale, as he feels now that he would like somewhere smaller.
His daughter Lesley, who married in 1966, has now parted from John.

12th May 1986 Monday
A day in London! I attended the Civil Service College at 11 Belgrave Road, S.W.1 for an interesting & enjoyable one day "workshop" called "Employment Law for Line Managers". We learned about the latest laws concerning race & sex discrimination & the laws relating to the protection of employees.

14th May 1986 Wednesday
"Employment Law" which we learned about this week dwelt very much on the rights of employees.
I thought of my best beloved Brian Lamming, who won his appeal against unfair dismissal at a Leicester Industrial Tribunal in August 1984. His employers were criticised by the tribunal chairman for incorrect procedure.

16th May 1986 Friday
"The Meaning of the Glorious Qur'an" by Abdullah Yusuf Ali.
While in London this week, I bought this book, a translation of The Koran, the Mohammedan Scriptures. It is now the month of Ramadhan, the month in which was sent down the Qur'an, as a guide to mankind, so very like the Bible.

18th May 1986 Whit Sunday
Whit Sunday is "The great roll-call of the world". Parthians and Medes and Elamites, & the dwellers in Mesopotamia & in Judea and Cappadocia, in Pontus & Asia, Phrygia and Pamphylia in Egypt, & in the parts of Libya about Cyrene, & strangers of Rome, Jews & proselytes, Cretes & Arabians. (Acts 2.)

20th May 1986 Tuesday
F. A. Cup Final this year resulted in a win for Liverpool, who beat Everton 3 – 1. This was the first ever all Merseyside Cup Final. Liverpool have also won the League Championship (the 3rd team this century to claim the League & Cup double). Receipts again totalled £1,100,000.

22nd May 1986 Thursday
Sonja Folarin, E. O. from Thames House South (our head office), came to G. O. M. B. (Gas & Oil Measurement Branch) today, where she and I interviewed 5 girls who had applied for our typist vacancy. We had invited 7 for interview but one telephoned to say she had another job & one simply did not turn up.

24th May 1986 Saturday
"Praise & Celebration for Everyone – Ravenstone Parish Church."
This week we held an ecumenical service where Roman Catholics, chapel members & church members all joined in unison for a moving mid-week get-together. This was organised by Mary Danaher, a Roman Catholic.

26th May 1986 Monday
Rock star Bob Geldof has done it again! (See 16th July 1985) He has now master-minded the biggest mass participatory sports event the world has ever seen. At 4 p.m. on Sunday the whole world staged a fun-run. Sport Aid was a knock-out success raising more money for the starving people of Africa. The worldwide series of races began when Sudanese athlete Omar Khalifa lit a symbolic flame outside the U. N. building in New York. Every runner paid £5 & ran 10 kilometres to help Band Aid & Unicef.

30th May 1986 Friday
The Prince & Princess of Wales came to Leicester today. They arrived by helicopter at County Hall at 11.20a.m. Then at 11.30a.m. they arrived at Leicester's Hospice close by, where they stayed for a buffet lunch. Then on to London Road Station, Leicester, to open the new booking hall.

1st June 1986 Sunday
What a revelation it is to read the Glorious Qur'an. "And thus have we, by our command, sent inspiration to thee; thou knowest not (before) what was revelation and what was faith; but we have made the Qur'an a light ….." (See Sura XLII Ayat 52) The Qur'an, like every religious book, has to be read not only with the tongue & voice & eyes, but with the best light that our intellect can supply, & even more, with the truest & purest light which our heart & conscience can give us. As Sura XV says, "These are the Ayats of Revelation."

5th June 1986 Thursday
"So hold thou fast to the Revelation sent down to thee; verily thou art on Straight Way. The Qur'an is indeed the message for thee." (Sura XLIII)
"Those who listen to the Word, & follow the best (meaning) in it, those are the ones whom Allah has guided, & those are the ones endued with understanding." (Sura XXXIX)

7th June 1986 Saturday
The new Moon tonight signals the end of the Muslims' month-long daylight fast of Ramadhan. During this month I have read the whole of the "Glorious Qur'an".
"We have indeed revealed this message in the Night of Power. The Night of Power is better than a thousand months."

9th June 1986 Monday
Man found dead by brook.
Twelve year old Scott, son of Mary Blue & Murdo MacLeod, was coming home from school across the fields when he found the body of a man in the brook at the back of Ethel Road. It was the body of an elderly man. When Scott found the dead man in the brook, he thought at first he was a stuffed dummy. Then he saw the man's hand & wrist, complete with wrist watch. Scott ran across the field to tell someone. The first person he met was the Vicar who did not believe him & told him not to tell such tales. The next man he encountered was also dubious, but Scott managed to

persuade him to go back with him to the brook. The police were then called & the body was eventually taken away. Scott was not frightened by this incident. He simply said to Pat, "Guess what I found?"

15th June 1986 Sunday

Auntie Belle, widow of my dad's eldest brother Fred, is now 90 years old. She is a wonderful 90 year old, living in her own home & to celebrate her birthday she had a "party" this evening, where 14 of us gathered to a sit down spread with chicken, ham, salad, trifle, etc. and champagne. Auntie Belle has nieces – June & Averil & a nephew George, who with their respective partners & children, now grown up, all think the world of her & joined forces to prepare food for a good old get-together. Auntie Doris at Mountsorrel, now also aged 90, has her own grandchildren who do likewise.

19th June 1986 Thursday

Apartheid (the segregation of black & white communities) has now brought a state of National Emergency in South Africa. Apartheid, conceived by the Nationalists in 1948 was intended to make South Africa a "white" country. 5 million whites live in luxury while 24 million blacks live in squalor.

The 24 million blacks in South Africa have been banished from the elegant quarters of the wealthy whites. They were told that they were not South African at all; they belonged to one or another of the "Homelands" according to their tribal origins. Foreigners in their own land, they now rebel.

South Africa today is poised on the brink of catastrophe. The Government in Pretoria says that there has been an attempt to get away from classic apartheid for 10 years, but it will not tolerate the A.N.C. (African National Congress) whose leader Nelson Mandela is kept in prison.

25th June 1986 Wednesday

The Reverend Gustav Aronsohn, Rector of Ravenstone from December 1959 to December 1965, has died. An announcement in today's Daily Telegraph says – *"Aronsohn. On June 19th 1986 peacefully at Eastbourne, Sussex, Rev. Gustav, much loved by his family & many friends. Funeral private. No flowers."*

What a lasting impression the Reverend Gustav Aronsohn made on me. Remember the beautiful words he wrote to me at Christmas 1982, following the death of my Mum? Now he, too, is cared for by Guardian Angels. May the love, the power & the joy of the Lord Jesus be with him.

Note – Remember what the Churchwardens wrote when he left Ravenstone in December 1965 "No Parish could have enjoyed the services of a more Godly man – a learned & well read scholar."

29th June 1986 Sunday

"And I saw the dead, small & great, stand before God; and the books were opened; & another book was opened, which is the book of life; & the dead were judged out of those things which were written in the books, according to their works." Revelation 20.

This description of the Day of Judgment signalled Domesday.

1st July 1986 Tuesday

A message to each household from British Gas announces, "Great News! Gas could be coming to Ravenstone soon! To ensure it does, we need a minimum of 123 houses to take a supply."

3rd July 1986 Thursday

Visited the "Domesday Exhibition" at the Public Record Office, Chancery Lane, W.C.2.

1086 – 1986. Saw this great treasure of English history & was held spellbound by Living Image creations of the monk of Peterborough who wrote about the Conqueror in 1086 and now "spoke" to us.

Living Image Ltd. create life-like models which are made to speak. Their eyes blink & look realistically from side to side. They "swallow" & their mouths move to perfection with the words. I was absolutely fascinated by the monk of Peterborough, who voiced his displeasure at William.

After experiencing the presence and power of the monk of Peterborough, I next encountered the great Conqueror himself. Living Images Ltd. say, "We are proud that our craft & artistry breathes stunning life into the Domesday Exhibition." I was indeed captivated.

The Domesday Exhibition in London spans from William the Conqueror to our 4 year old Prince William who one day should become King William V. He will be the 42nd monarch since the Norman Conquest (See 2nd August 1982).

At this exhibition I bought "Diary of a Lifetime" (My hundred year diary.)

11th July 1986 Friday

Polaris (The Pole Star) was the name given to Britain's first fleet of submarines equipped with nuclear warheads. Polaris is now to be replaced by Trident (the 3 pronged spear of the sea-god Poseidon or Neptune). Trident's first submarine, H. M. S. Vanguard, is now being built.

"Trident remains the key to our defence policy & we regard it as a cost-effective deterrent."

So say the Conservative Government, at present in power. With over 500 warheads & a nautical range of 4,000 miles it will cost £10 billion. The Labour Party say they will cancel Trident if they get into power.

15th July 1986 Tuesday

I have now reached the age of 55 (5 x 11).

As I read in Hansard, our learned Members' of Parliament debate on the Defence of this realm, the facts & figures they produce are frightening. In Russia, there are 300,000 tonnes of chemical weapons stockpiled ready for use.

The major threat to the West is from the Warsaw pact, dominated by the Soviet Union. Russia spends 15% of its gross domestic product an weapons, compared with 5.2% in Britain & 6.9% in the United States. It is protected by buffer states, countries all round it, which it dominates & works through.

In 1920 the Soviet leader Lenin said, "As long as capitalism & socialism exist we cannot live in peace. One or the other will triumph in the end."

Russia & America today are the 2 superpowers. Russia is a military superpower, but only at the expense of its people's quality of living.

21ˢᵗ July 1986 Monday
Prince Andrew, the second son of Her Majesty Queen Elizabeth II, will marry Miss Sarah Ferguson on Wednesday this week at Westminster Abbey. On his wedding day he will become Duke of York, Earl of Inverness and Baron Killyleagh. (A town in Northern Ireland)

23ʳᵈ July 1986 Wednesday
The wedding of the newly created Duke & Duchess of York. The bride wore the most beautiful wedding dress (£8,000) & had 4 little bridesmaids & 4 little pages, including Prince William.

25ᵗʰ July 1986 Friday
The 13ᵗʰ Commonwealth Games have just begun in Edinburgh. There were supposed to be 58 nations competing, but 32 nations have refused to take part. They have decided to boycott the event because Britain will not impose economic sanctions on South Africa.

27ᵗʰ July 1986 Sunday
In praise of "The Civic Amenities Tip".
It is amazing how much rubbish we all need to dispose of. The "tip" at Coalville does a roaring trade. There are half a dozen huge skips which you throw things in from above. They take all the garden & household rubbish. No need for bonfires.

29ᵗʰ July 1986 Tuesday
"How to Build a Human Being".
American biologists would like to map & read the whole of the human "genome".
The genome is a set of complete instructions for building a human being, written in DNA on 23 chromosomes & divided into about 50,000 genes.
The human genome is written in the DNA alphabet of 4 letters known as bases. It is 3.5 **billion** bases long. So far 6.7 million bases have been read, i.e. 2%.
To complete this project in 10 years would take 3,000 people. All that is needed now is £1 billion a year to pay for it.
The map showing how to build a human being is hidden inside everyone. We all carry 2 copies of it in every cell in our body, one from each parent. If one person donates a few cells the scientists can "clone" his genome.
Human genomes differ as much from each other as do humans.

4ᵗʰ August 1986 Monday
"Civil Protection". Following the Chernobyl nuclear disaster earlier this year (see May 6ᵗʰ 1986), the Home Office is stepping up its plans for tightening up the civil defence regulations of 1983. Local authorities must be prepared for emergencies, not just for the nuclear option, but for the range of disasters that could occur any time.
These are some of the plans for improving our "Civil Protection". Local authorities have been given a targeting programme. By 1ˢᵗ April 1987 their objectives must be quite clear; by 1ˢᵗ April 1988 they must have the resources, plans for accommodation & plans for the prevention of disease; by 1ˢᵗ April 1989 further plans.
Mr Giles Shaw, Minister of State, Home Office, said in Parliament, "It is clear that, post-Chernobyl, authorities should take seriously the need to protect their citizens.

The Government are determined not only to put civil protection firmly on the map, but to ensure that regulations are implemented according to a time scale."
"Chernobyl" is the Ukrainian word for wormwood. In the Book of Revelation, chapter 8, it says, "And the third angel sounded, & there fell a great star from heaven, burning as it were a lamp, & it fell upon the third part of the rivers - & the name of the star is called Wormwood."

12ᵗʰ August 1986 Tuesday
"To Schlumberger, Branche Comptage Domestique Gaz, 47, Rue Gosset, BP 327-51061, Reims Cedex" – For the first time in my life I drafted a Telex at work **in French** when 5 gas meters arrived at Birmingham Airport from France on their way to our laboratories for testing.
"Compteurs de gaz pour approbation de modele gasmeters gallus 2000 – Cinq compteurs sont a l'aeroport, Birmingham, ou ils attendant payement de passer la douane. Voulez-vous avoir la bonte de prendre les dispositions necessaires pour ce payement, et tenez moi au courant de ce qui ce passe."

16ᵗʰ August 1986 Saturday
Ravenstone Gas Exhibition, Monday 11ᵗʰ – Saturday 16ᵗʰ August, Primary School, Church Lane.
Great news! Gas could be coming soon! See our proposals for laying gas mains through your village.
One step nearer to having gas at Ravenstone, which we hope to have later this year.

18ᵗʰ August 1986 Monday
Peter Gregson – Permanent Under-Secretary of State, Department of Energy, visited our Branch (Gas & Oil Measurement Branch = G.O.M.B.) & subsequently wrote to Mr Plant, our boss, "I was greatly impressed with the skill & commitment of the staff at all levels,
Yours ever, Peter."

20ᵗʰ August 1986 Wednesday
Leicester Markets Festival, Monday 18ᵗʰ – Saturday 23ʳᵈ August 1986.
More medieval merry-making in Leicester this week. I signed the Festival's Book of Records (in the "H" department for Hewes). The Book is to be buried in the foundation of a new city building. I've signed the Book! – have you?
The theme of this year's celebrations is the investiture of Simon de Montfort as the sixth Earl of Leicester. The Book of Records has been signed by our acting King Henry III & our Simon de Montfort.
Simon de Montfort was born in France in 1208 A.D. He moved to England & quickly won favour in the court of King Henry III. He became Earl of Leicester in 1218 A.D. & married the King's sister in 1238 A.D. However, the King turned against him & he eventually was killed in 1265 A.D.

26ᵗʰ August 1986 Tuesday
The Gas Act 1986 came into force this month. This replaces the Gas Act 1972. It means that British Gas is now privatised.
For my week-end August Bank Holiday reading I have read the whole of the new Gas Act & found it very interesting, informative & clearly set out.

28th August 1986 Thursday

Auntie Gladys, aged 90, has been very poorly this week. Enid has taken a week's holiday from work to be with her & give her undivided attention.

Enid is now 58 and is finding it difficult to work full time & also care for her mum. She has even considered giving up her job.

30th August 1986 Saturday

The long school summer holidays are now ending and the new term sees the introduction of the new exam system which means all change for pupils & teachers alike. The General Certificate of Secondary Education (G.C.S.E.) is a completely revolutionary system of education. The G.C.S.E. is designed to test not only memory & presentation of facts, but also understanding, practical skills & ability to apply knowledge to real life contexts. Emphasis will be on problem solving, rather than mechanical knowledge & is of particular relevance to this age of the computer.

3rd September 1986 Wednesday

Mary Moore, now aged 75, will be arriving tomorrow, to spend a week with me. I have been busy cleaning the house, tidying up the garden & getting up to date with all the jobs which need to be done. We are hoping, during her stay, to visit all the old friends & relations hereabouts.

5th September 1986 Friday

"Visit a Power Station – come & see how electricity is made – Ratcliffe-on-Soar Power Station - open Saturday & Sunday 6th & 7th September." The first power station in Britain to generate more than 13,000 million units of electricity over a single year & now produces more power than any other station.

7th September 1986 Sunday

"For thine is the Kingdom, the <u>Power</u> and the glory ….."
I thought of God's almighty power as I marvelled at the colossal machinery, the Dante's inferno, at the heart of Ratcliffe-on-Soar Power Station where 20,000 tonnes of coal a day provide the heat to make the steam to drive the huge turbines.

I stood beneath the high chimney at Ratcliffe-on-Soar Power Station & marvelled at its very construction. It is 200 metres high (656 feet), taller than the 600 foot National Westminster Tower in London, Britain's tallest building. Against the background of a blue sky with moving clouds, it seemed to move.

The Times Friday May 21st 1999

Shanghai: An optical illusion that a skyscraper in Shenzhen, northern China, was falling sent thousands of people running for their lives on two occasions this week, the official *Wenhui Daily* reported. Experts said that unusually fast-moving clouds created the illusion.

11th September 1986 Thursday

The first visible signs that Ravenstone is to have gas are the 40 foot long yellow pipes, stacked in blocks of 24, at various vantage points on the wide grass verges of the village. I watched 3 men with a large "spider map", walking all round the village. We see lots of "spider maps" at work, showing the network of pipes.

13th September 1986 Saturday

Mary Moore has returned home after a hectic week visiting all her old friends.

We entertained Auntie Doris for tea on Monday, Katherine on Tuesday & Edith on Thursday.

Pat & Evelyn took Aunt Dos (aged 84) for a week's holiday in Cromer, where they stayed in a chalet.

15th September 1986 Monday

Christ was born on September 15th 1993 years ago! Doctor Seymour, a fellow of the Royal Astronomical Society and principal lecturer in astronomy at Plymouth Polytechnic, used a computer to work out the date when Christ was born.

This really should be the year now, 1993 A.D.

17th September 1986 Wednesday

"Caution – Caution – Caution – Gas Main Below." As the gas pipes are laid to rest approximately 30 inches below ground, a continuous strip of caution is buried immediately above them. The gas main, 180mm in width, is now making its way down Wash Lane. Smaller piping 90mm, 60mm & 30mm lies waiting for use in huge coils.

19th September 1986 Friday

Coalville Amateurs' are now rehearsing for their next show – "Oliver!" We have performed this show once before, in 1969, when Frank Goddard excelled in the role of Fagin. How very sad to see Frank Goddard now, stricken with gastric cancer, hardly recognisable, being so very frail and weak.

21st September 1986 Sunday

"Come!" …. "Go!" The Rector of Ravenstone, the Reverend Leslie Buckroyd, spoke of Christ who first called his disciples with the words, "Come ye …" and whose last words to his apostles were, "Go ye therefore, & teach all nations …."

"Come unto me, all ye that labour & are heavy laden, & I will give you rest." Matthew 11. 28.

23rd September 1986 Tuesday

Hewes, Gladys M. E., 50 Leicester Road, Ravenstone (wife of the late Cyril) and dearly loved mother of Enid, David and Margaret. Passed peacefully away September 23rd 1986, aged 90 years. Mother-in-law of Irene and Dai, grandmother of Alison, David and Steven. Funeral Service at Saint Michael and All Angels Church, Ravenstone, on Monday September 29th at 10.15 a.m., prior to Cremation at Loughborough Crematorium. Family flowers only please, but donations in lieu, if so desired, to Ravenstone Church.

This is Auntie Gladys. Cousin Enid was able to care for her virtually single-handed to the end, and she died in her own home.

25th September 1986 Thursday

Cousin Enid, like me, has lived all her life in the house where she was born. We both have now outlived our parents and are left as orphans alone in the family home. While our contemporaries have roamed the world & become grandparents themselves, we are still here, almost old age pensioners!

27th September 1986 Saturday
"Meadowcroft" 17, Fosbrooke Close, Ravenstone – Called this morning to see Cousin Donald, now settled in his spanking new beautiful bungalow at the other end of the village. He enjoys long panoramic views across the valley & can see the glory of the sunset.
Leonard Fosbrooke, long ago, was "Squire" of Ravenstone.

29th September 1986 Monday
On St. Michael's Day, at St. Michael's Church Ravenstone, we assembled for Auntie Gladys' funeral – Enid, David, Irene, Alison, Margaret & Dai, Bunting, Pat & Evelyn & me, Cousin Walter & his 2nd wife Jeannie, Cousin Don & Phyl.
Auntie Dos, now aged 84, and having recently had a nasty fall, was not able to join us.
Like a well trained choir we sang at Auntie Gladys' funeral. Cousin Walter has a fine deep voice & Bunting is a rich deep contralto. David, Irene & Alison are all in the choir at Packington.
We sang hymn 166 – "All people that on earth do dwell, sing to the Lord with cheerful voice" & 197 – "The King of Love."

3rd October 1986 Friday
Canon Hughie Jones, Rector of The Langtons & Stanton Wyville, is the new Archdeacon of Loughborough.
He replaces the Ven. Dr. Harold Lockley, who has been Archdeacon for 23 years.

5th October 1986 Sunday
"Man doth not live by bread only, but by every word that proceedeth out of the mouth of the Lord doth man live …. Remember the Lord thy God; for it is he that giveth thee power to get wealth." Deuteronomy Chapter 8.
This was the message given to us this year at little St. Mary's Harvest Festival.

7th October 1986 Tuesday
From British Gas East Midlands to Miss Hewes –
"Your changeover boiler quotation – one Baxi 501 floor standing boiler; supply and install a gas supply from meter position in front room to the boiler; change D.H.W. cylinder & install new F/E tank, programmer, cylinder thermostat & room thermostat; supply & install a new radiator in ground floor back room; change pump; move towel rail on to back wall.
Price £918 plus Value Added Tax (V.A.T.) 15% = £1,055.70p"
This will replace the 20 year-old solid fuel Cavendish boiler & hopefully be cleaner & easier to operate.

11th October 1986 Saturday
Patrick Magee - this is the man who planted the bomb two years ago in the Grand Hotel, Brighton. He was finally caught and given life imprisonment. Now aged 35, he will not be released until he is 70.

13th October 1986 Monday
Diane the faithful (Diane Robert) who became a Sunday School teacher at Ravenstone exactly 12 years ago, has indicated that she wishes to relinquish this duty at the end of this year.
In the Parish Magazine the Rector says, "... we owe her a great debt of gratitude for her tenacity & forbearance."

15th October 1986 Wednesday
Her Majesty the Queen is enjoying a fabulous week in China. This is the very first time a reigning British monarch has visited China, and television brings us close up pictures from the initial welcome in Peking, a walk on the Great Wall, to Shanghai.

17th October 1986 Friday
From Shanghai, Her Majesty the Queen flew to the ancient city of Xian (which incidentally is twinned with Edinburgh). Here, in the 3rd century B.C., the first emperor to unify China, Qin Shi Huang, built himself a colossal tomb, guarded by an army of terracotta warriors, only re-discovered 12 years ago.
The 6,000 terracotta warriors who guard the tomb of the Emperor Qin have lain buried for centuries. Today they are one of the greatest archaeological discoveries of this century. The Queen descended the 30 foot pit & inspected this ghostly guard, absolutely life-like, each with a different face.

21st October 1986 Tuesday
Ravenstone – Best Kept Village! Four villages which have been judged to be the best kept in Leicestershire have been given their appropriate awards. Market Bosworth (large) Ravenstone (intermediate) Barrowden (small) & Sibson (hamlet). The "Trophy" is an outdoor shield.

23rd October 1986 Thursday
"Hello America!" How exciting to be asked at work to ring the American Gas Association 1515 Wilson Boulevard, Arlington, Virginia. This is the first time I have ever spoken on the telephone to America. I was booking a place for Gilbert Paul-Clark on the International Symposium there.

25th October 1986 Saturday
The Archbishop of Canterbury, Dr. Robert Runcie, yesterday came to Leicester and today he came to Coalville! He spoke to us at the Miners' Centre, where he arrived in gale force winds with his entourage, including the Bishop of Leicester, the Rt. Revd. Dr. Richard Rutt and the newly appointed Archdeacon of Loughborough.
Canon Hughie Jones introduced himself to the assembled audience as, "Your friendly Archdeacon". He was a merry soul & said to me outside, when the wind blew his red shoulder cape over his head, "This Father Christmas outfit was not made for this weather."
(I looked like a monk in my hooded coat.)
The Archbishop of Canterbury, Dr. Robert Runcie, was late arriving at the Miners' Centre. Everyone wanted to keep him talking. As he walked down the centre aisle at the end of his visit, he chatted to various clergy. The Bishop, like the rabbit in "Alice in Wonderland", said to me, "We're late! We're late!"

31st October 1986 Friday
Hallowe'en! Leicestershire's most famous landmark, the ale tankard-shaped Old John Tower in Bradgate Park, has been specially opened to the public for a 200th anniversary.

Exactly 200 years ago, on Hallowe'en, an estate retainer named Old John was killed when the central pole of a huge bonfire burnt through & fell among revellers celebrating the 6th Earl of Stamford's coming of age. The earl decided to name the crenellated tower in memory of Old John. Knowing the old man's liking of ale, he ordered a "handle" buttress to be added to the tower, giving it a tankard shape.

1st November 1986 Saturday

Choyce, *Dorothy Esther, passed peacefully away on Saturday, November 1st aged 85, a loving mother to June and George, mother-in-law to Terry and Shirley, grandmother to Beverley, Richard, Darren, Lynne and Andrew, great-grandmother to Amanda and Rebecca and a loving sister to Isabelle. Funeral service and cremation at Loughborough Crematorium on Thursday November 6th at 2 p.m. With thanks to all at Berrystead Nursing Home.*
Auntie Belle's sister "Dot".

4th November 1986 Tuesday

Nezar Hindawi – this handsome young man came to England from Jordan. He is an Arab terrorist who planted a bomb in the luggage of his pregnant girlfriend, Ann Murphy, hoping to blow up the plane taking her to Tel Aviv.
It was on 17th April this year that the El Al Jumbo flight 016, with 375 people on board, left Heathrow for Israel carrying many Jews for the Feast of the Passover. Nezar Hindawi, aged 32, gave his girlfriend a bag containing 3lb 2oz of explosives, which she unwittingly carried to the check-in. Thanks to the vigilance & thoroughness of El Al security at Heathrow Airport, the bomb planted in his girlfriend's luggage by Hindawi was found. This was cold-blooded emotional manipulation & ultimate betrayal – the Judas kiss. Hindawi is now in a British jail – sentenced to 45 years imprisonment.
The bomb, with which Hindawi hoped to destroy an Israeli jumbo jet, was actually made inside the Syrian Embassy in Belgravia, London. The explosive contained in it was brought into this country in a Syrian diplomatic bag. Britain has therefore severed diplomatic relations with Syria.

12th November 1986 Wednesday

"British Gas will deliver central heating materials on Friday 14th November and start work installing on Wednesday 19th November a.m."
Message through the letter box from Mr I. Gubb, Service Officer, British Gas, East Midlands. This includes new radiator, boiler, cylinder, pump, copper piping, etc.

14th November 1986 Friday

Joanne, now aged 12 ½, is busy learning French. As French was one of my best subjects at school, I love helping her with her French homework. She has a very interesting book, full of pictures and helpful examples, which take you step by step through lots of everyday situations – shopping – conversation – travel, etc.

16th November 1986 Sunday

"Trust in the Lord and abide in thy labour; for it is an easy thing in the sight of the Lord on the sudden to make a poor man rich."

These words of encouragement are from the Book of Ecclesiasticus, Chapter II. This Book, from the Apocrypha, which is so full of wisdom, forms the reading for Trinity XXIV.

18th November 1986 Tuesday

The Civil Service Benevolent Fund is celebrating its Centenary this year. I represent our office on the C.S.B.F. Leicestershire Area Committee and this year I have had the pleasure of co-ordinating the Christmas Raffle – 5,000 tickets to allocate to all the Government Departments throughout Leicestershire.

20th November 1986 Thursday

Gas is now being installed at 27, Leicester Road, Ravenstone. Work began yesterday morning and the job will be completed in 2 ½ days. The whole plumbing system is being updated, with a separate new water tank in the roof, ready for a completely new system of central heating, operative from tomorrow.

21st November 1986 Friday

Goddard, *Frank, late of 6 Beechway, Ibstock, passed peacefully away at home after a long illness November 21st 1986, aged 59 years, dearly loved father of Paul and Carol, and grandfather of Christopher and Kathryn, also beloved of Marlene. Funeral service St. Denys Church, Ibstock, 11a.m. Thursday, November 27th prior to interment at Hugglescote Cemetery.*
All inquiries Gillivers Funeral Directors. Telephone Market Bosworth 290356.

22nd November 1986 Saturday

Wonderfuel Gas! So reads the British Gas advertisement. I find my new gas central heating absolutely wonder-fuel. For the first time in my life I have heat that I can control at the touch of a button. On the sudden I feel like a poor man made rich. How I appreciate the luxury of a warm home.

24th November 1986 Monday

How encouraging to receive by post at work the money & counterfoils of sold raffle tickets from so many different sources – the D.H.S.S. (Department of Health and Social Security), the Inland Revenue, the M.O.D. (Ministry of Defence), the M.A.F.F. (Ministry of Agriculture, Fisheries & Food), the Crown Court, etc etc

26th November 1986 Wednesday

Colour Television! Most people these days have a colour television & have now joined the ranks. I bought a "Philips" 14″ portable, reduced from £180 to £150, to replace the old black & white Mum & I had in 1970. So now its £78 instead of £18 for a TV licence.

28th November 1986 Friday

"Consider yourself one of the family ......"
At Frank Goddard's funeral yesterday, attended by a large contingent from Coalville Amateur Operatic Society, the Rector of Ibstock, the Revd. Buxton, referred to Frank's role as Fagin, when we last did "Oliver!" in 1969. He said that Coalville Amateurs considered him as "one of the family".

30th November 1986 Sunday

5,000 raffle tickets @ 10p per ticket equals £500. However, of those we sent out, there were 500 tickets which did not return sold. We therefore reaped a harvest of £450.

All the prizes (23 altogether) had been donated by one or another of the larger local offices, including our own.

2nd December 1986 Tuesday

A.I.D.S. Acquired Immune Deficiency Syndrome (first mentioned in this diary in August last year) is gradually taking hold more & more, not only in this country, but world-wide. It is causing such alarm that the warning bells are sounding loud & clear, as for the plague.

"Leicester City to get A.I.D.S. Officer." An A.I.D.S. Liaison Officer has been included in plans for the new health education unit of the City Council in response to an "urgent need" to co-ordinate local action against the killer disease. The officer will work with voluntary groups & all connected with health services.

The killer disease A.I.D.S. is the result of our promiscuous society. The Roman Catholic Church is the lone voice crying in the wilderness – repent. The Pope does not approve of contraception. But 20th Century man is supposedly too smart to listen to the Pope. Wine, women & song is the order of the day.

Since October 1985, the national blood transfusion service has screened all blood donations for antibodies to the Aids virus. No cases of Aids virus transmission have been reported in patients given blood since that date. Before screening, some patients did receive blood infected with the Aids virus.

The Aids virus is about one sixteen thousandth the size of a pin head, but like the snowflake, can marshal its armies to bring about the complete downfall of man. The virus is called HIV – Human Immune deficiency Virus. It first attacks & about 5 years later becomes effective. It is a pirate of the body's cells.

12th December 1986 Friday

"Handled Stolen Goods.

Two local unemployed teenagers were given conditional discharges after they admitted handling stolen property. Steven Terence Jarman, 19, of Paulyn Way, Ashby, pleaded guilty to taking a stolen bar towel from Ashby Bowling Club."

This is Mary Blue's son, Steven. What a worry Steven is to the family at the moment. Like so many of his generation he is unemployed & bored.

It is precisely this state of affairs that leads to the taking of drugs to add a little spice to life. The Aids virus thrives among our injecting drug misuser population, who are now carriers.

"Don't Aid Aids" This is the message emblazoned loud & clear in every newspaper, in teenagers' magazines, & soon to be delivered in leaflet form to every household in the country.

18th December 1986 Thursday

Aunt Dos, aged 84, has been very poorly for the last few weeks. Sandra, who used to be her next door neighbour & now lives about 7 miles away at Field Farm, Osbaston, has been like a daughter to her, visiting her every day, and giving her the strength & encouragement to pull through.

20th December 1986 Saturday

"Burmese", the lovely horse which Her Majesty the Queen has ridden side-saddle each year for the ceremony of Trooping the Colour for the past 18 years, is now to retire. In future, the Queen will ride in a carriage.

22nd December 1986 Monday

The Revd. Gustav Aronsohn, who died in June this year, is very much in my thoughts at this time of year, when all the Christmas cards arrive. I keep and treasure the cards he sent me in other years. He was able to reach so very deep into my heart, I still expect him to remember me.

24th December 1986 Wednesday

Remember Colin who used to work with me at the Motor Licence Office? He was struck down by the dreadful illness of multiple sclerosis & was eventually driven to suicide. I now work with Alan Norris who sadly suffers from retinitis pigmentosa, another dreadful illness, which is slowly sending him blind.

26th December 1986 Friday

Christmas Day & Boxing Day at Pat's where Evelyn again gathered up the waifs and strays. Auntie Dos this year was the "granny" in the corner, who was either too hot or too cold, who thought the television was too loud or not loud enough, & had everybody pandering to her every whim. Auntie Dos is becoming more & more dependant on others, as the problem of old age & frailty begins to tell. Unlike Auntie Belle & Auntie Doris, both aged 90, who are still going strong, she is now very forgetful, & spends most of the time in her armchair, expecting constant attention.

30th December 1986 Tuesday

Margaret Thatcher, Conservative Prime Minister since 1979, has pressed forward with a massive programme of Privatisation. There has been the sale of council houses, the privatisation of British Telecom, the Trustee Savings Bank, British Gas & more to come – British Airways, the Water Authorities, etc.

* * *

1987

1ˢᵗ January 1987 Thursday
And one makes five billion ….. Somewhere on earth, a child born will become the 5 billionth person living on the planet, according to estimates by the population institute.

2ⁿᵈ January 1987 Friday
Privatisation forms an important part of the present Conservative Government's overall strategy for long term economic growth. Since coming to power in 1979, twelve major companies have been privatised, with plans for a further twelve to be transferred to the private sector. (Former state-owned companies.)

4ᵗʰ January 1987 Sunday
Brother Pat & I started the New Year with an almighty clean up & clear out of Aunt Dos's home, which is chock-a-block with so much rubbish, she can never find anything she wants & is forever accusing folk of stealing her things. She refuses to have a "home help" since the last one supposedly "stole" all manner of things.
"I wish you would leave my things alone," announced Aunt Dos (as expected), following the marathon effort made by Pat & me to remove a mountain of filth & litter from her home. Now that the dust has settled, nothing is where it should be, & she has so much more to complain about & declare "missing".

8ᵗʰ January 1987 Thursday
Her Majesty in Council agreed on 5ᵗʰ November 1986 to the proposals set out in the Order in Council confirming the formation of the establishing of The United Benefice of Hugglescote with Donington, Ellistown & Snibston. The result being the legislation of the United Benefice from 1ˢᵗ December 1986.

10ᵗʰ January 1987 Saturday
Inauguration Service – tomorrow at 3.30 p.m., Hugglescote Parish Church, a special service to mark the uniting of 3 parishes – 1. Hugglescote with Donington, 2. Ellistown, 3. Snibston, to form the new united Benefice. Special preacher – The Ven. T. H. Jones, Archdeacon of Loughborough.

12ᵗʰ January 1987 Monday
"The North Wind doth blow, and we shall have snow."
Actually, it is a North Easterly wind blowing straight from Siberia & the East coast of Britain is taking the worst of the weather at the moment. As night time temperatures fall well below zero, am I thankful for my gas heating!

14ᵗʰ January 1987 Wednesday
"Snow had fallen. Snow on snow. In the bleak midwinter. Long, long ago." Well, that was today. All night long, the snow fell, until this morning we were buried under 18 inches of snow. The whole country has been affected by some of the worst conditions we have seen for a very long time. I managed to dig my car out of the snow, where it was buried as it stood in Aunt Dos's drive, & get to work on time. I started clearing the snow at 6 a.m. & was out on to the road by 7.15 a.m. The

roads had been cleared by the good old snow ploughs & I reached our office by 8.30 a.m., but the whole car park was buried. Several members of staff never made it to work. Only the main roads were open.

18ᵗʰ January 1987 Sunday
Just 24 hours of continuous snow brought complete havoc. Fortunately the westerly winds reached us in time, & no sooner had we been buried under the snow than the thaw set in, & the worst of the snow beat a hasty retreat. This morning, I was able to resume my daily walk.

20ᵗʰ January 1987 Tuesday
Tonight we were up until after midnight dealing with the annual allocation of tickets for Coalville Amateurs. We assembled once more at Peter Jacques' house, where Peter Jacques & his daughter, Lisa, Betty Henn, Brian Gadsby, Olive Meakin, George Taylor & I spent a very enjoyable evening together.

22ⁿᵈ January 1987 Thursday
6ᵗʰ Development / Petroleum Measurement Inspectorate Meeting today at work where I took the minutes. This was an all day meeting where our 6 top men, involved with metering the gas & oil from the North Sea, did all the talking & I listened & wrote – with the help of a tape recorder.

24ᵗʰ January 1987 Saturday
What a busy week I have had.
Spent all day Wednesday getting the tickets ready for posting to the Patrons & for giving to the members. I like to keep a "visual aid" chart for each performance, which shows exactly who has which tickets. I like to know who is sitting where on the different nights.

26ᵗʰ January 1987 Monday
Mr Tindall, my very good friend at Leicester Cathedral, died today, aged 66. It was he who made my Mum & me so welcome at the Cathedral when we first joined the "Friends of Leicester Cathedral", 20 years ago.
Mr Tindall was Chairman of Leicester Cathedral Fellowship. He was President of the Leicester Battalion of the Boys Brigade. He was Chairman of the governing body of Lancaster Boys School, Knighton, & Vice Chairman of the governing body of Sir Jonathan North School, Knighton, etc.
Mr Tindall was, until his retirement, Head of the School of Building at Leicester Polytechnic. At his funeral, held at Leicester Cathedral, Canon Gundry referred to him, during the prayers, as a wise masterbuilder. (See I Corinthians, 3. 10.) I was privileged to sit on the front row, nearest to him.

1ˢᵗ February 1987 Sunday
To a congregation of only four, the Rector of Ravenstone, the Revd. Leslie Buckroyd, spoke of those who are "called by God". He spoke of the years of study & the training of those who are called to be priests – of their responsibilities to all in their parish.
Parishioners too, are "called" to help the priest.

3ʳᵈ February 1987 Tuesday
How interesting it has been for me to write the minutes

of our Petroleum Measurement Inspectorate Meeting. Measuring the mighty flow of North Sea Oil & Gas is indeed a fascinating subject. I have learned about the viscosity of oil & gas (i.e. the thickness) and how the viscosity changes as temperature rises.

5th February 1987 Thursday
Department of Energy – Gas and Oil Measurement Branch. That is where I work. That is why I marvel at those who can measure the flow of fluids contained in pipes, where, like a motorway, there are fast lanes & slow lanes, even swirling lanes. There is the thermal expansion coefficient & compressibility.

The thermal expansion coefficient of a fluid is the fractional increase in specific volume (or the fractional decrease in density) caused by a temperature increase of 1°. The compressibility of a fluid is the fractional decrease in specific volume (or the fractional increase in density) caused by unit increase of pressure.

It is because temperature makes all the difference to precise measurement of gas and oil that our laboratories at work need to be air-conditioned. Having overall responsibility at work for "accommodation", I am now better able to appreciate the need for the unique design of the building.

The Department of Energy collects royalties on oil and gas produced in British territory.

A recent question asked in Parliament was, "What is the total amount of revenue raised through North Sea Oil since 1978 - 79?" Answer - £56 billion.

This has helped to pay off some of our huge overseas debt.

13th February 1987 Friday
"If music be the food of love, play on." I have now acquired a second-hand radiogram, which has suddenly brought to life my collection of records, which have lain sadly silent for many years. What a joy it is to hear the wonderful music of Strauss, Tchaikovsky, Berlioz, Mendelssohn & all the masters.

15th February 1987 Sunday
Terry Waite, the Archbishop of Canterbury's special envoy, makes trips to the Middle East for the sole purpose of negotiating deals with terrorist groups who take innocent people hostage in order to exchange them for their own friends held in jail. Terry Waite has secured the release of several such hostages.

Terry Waite went to Beirut a month ago in an attempt to free more innocent people who had been taken hostage; and was taken hostage himself. He has not been seen or heard of since. There is no reliable news – just lots of conflicting reports, and everyone now is very concerned about his safety.

19th February 1987 Thursday
Jack Lee is producer for our forthcoming show "Oliver!" & a very good producer he has shown himself to be. He has taken part in several of our productions & has also produced shows elsewhere. "Oliver!" is a great improvement on last year's show, and we are all hoping it will be a huge success.

21st February 1987 Saturday
"And Jesus departed into the coasts of Tyre & Sidon."

Hearing the news at the moment is almost like reading the Bible, as Syrian forces gather strength. The present Islamic revolution had its roots in the villages east of Tyre.

Iran's leader, Ayatollah Khomeini, now aged 86, is dying. It was Ayatollah Khomeini who overthrew the Shah of Iran in 1979.

Today there are Iranian backed gunmen in lots of different little groups, at work in several countries, but most especially in Lebanon, & in particular in West Beirut, where Terry Waite has been held captive since 20th January.

25th February 1987 Wednesday
"The World Held Hostage" – This is the title of my latest book from the library. In an attempt to understand the background of the problems of the Middle East, I have learned quite a lot. There are some 2 million terrorists specially trained to try & bring down freedom & democracy.

The terrorists receive a lot of help from Syria, which encourages the establishment of Palestinian terrorist organisations who operate from different bases south of Tarsus and also north & south of Damascus. Colonel Gadhafi of Libya gives the Palestinian terrorists £1 million per month.

The Palestine Liberation Organisation (the P.L.O.) is the major destabilising factor in the Middle East. It is the central perpetrator of international terrorism & its aim is to embrace global terrorism. Countries who support the terrorists are not attacked by them – hence all the secret subtle support.

4th March 1987 Wednesday
"Oliver!" – Coalville Amateurs' production for this year is now in full swing.

I never tire of watching them on stage, having seen them for the past 6 months learn every movement & action. But what a difference it makes with full make-up, costumes, scenery, and a fine orchestra.

6th March 1987 Friday
This evening we sold every single seat for "Oliver!" both in the main hall (483 seats) and in the balcony (63 seats). We usually have a few empty seats at the back of the balcony. Brother Pat is busy as House Manager and I am in my element as Treasurer, receiving all the money.

8th March 1987 Sunday
On this First Sunday in Lent, the Rector of Ravenstone, the Revd. Leslie Buckroyd, spoke of the parable of the lost sheep. First he spoke of St. Luke's version, (Luke, Chapter 15) where Jesus was speaking to the Scribes & the Pharisees, & then St. Matthew's version, as told to the disciples.

According to St. Luke, Jesus told the parable of the lost sheep to the Scribes and Pharisees. According to St. Matthew, this parable was told to the disciples. The Rector suggested that we are all entitled to bear witness according to what we notice ourselves. We all see things from different angles.

12th March 1987 Thursday
I have now completed 9 years at work in the Department of Energy's Gas & Oil Measurement Branch.

Secretary of State for Energy, Mr Peter Walker, is not one of Prime Minister Margaret Thatcher's favourites. With a general election due this year, there could well be changes ahead. Rumour has it that Secretary of State for Energy, Peter Walker, is due for the chop. Rumour has it also that the Department of Energy is due for the chop! With a staff of only 1,000 but more money than all the rest put together, it is considered to be "too big for its boots" & must be merged.

16th March 1987 Monday
We have a vacancy at work at the moment for a junior clerk (officially entitled Administrative Officer). Interviews are conducted by the two E.O.s - i.e. Catherine Wells & me.
We advertised the vacancy at Wigston Job Centre and received about a dozen applications for the job.

18 March 1987 Wednesday
With 3 million people in the country unemployed, we find that those who apply to our office for a job apply at the same time to every other possible vacancy going. They go from one interview to another, knowing that it is all the luck of the draw if they will ever be accepted.

20th March 1987 Friday
I continue to visit poor old Madge in the Byron Nursing Home, but there is virtually no communication between us. Now aged 88, she is reduced to such a sorry state, & lives in a world of her own. Huddled up in her chair, with head bowed & eyes closed, she utters sounds but does not speak.
I see Madge as she is today & think of her as she was 40 years ago. You would not believe that she is one & the same person. She is in a room with others who, like her, are in the same sad state. Their visitors, too, recall the days of yesteryear, when they were lively & loving relations.
"Madge would rather die than move from her old home where she has lived all her life." This is what I wrote 3 years ago. But she did not die. She was condemned to a living death & the light has gone completely from her. It seems that this world casts its bright beams only on the young.

26th March 1987 Thursday
Coalville Amateurs' Dinner Dance this year coincided with the Silver Wedding of our Secretary, Olive Meakin. We danced therefore to "The Anniversary Waltz" amongst other tunes. This year also marked 50 years membership by Vincent Hardy, our first member ever to receive the 50 year gold bar.

28th March 1987 Saturday
"We all liked Sheena & thought she and Michael were well matched." So I wrote in my diary on 28th March 1970, when Michael proudly introduced his pretty fiancée to his Ravenstone relations. Sadly, their marriage has now ended in divorce & the heartache has been felt particularly by Bunting, now aged 72.

30th March 1987 Monday
Mothering Sunday yesterday & how good to see Ravenstone Sunday School doing so well under the leadership of Joanne Freestone and Clare Allsopp, who were once in my Sunday School class and are now most attractive young ladies. At the Mothering Sunday Service the 20 children sang beautifully.

1st April 1987 Wednesday
Notice to quit! April Fool Hewsie was asked by her Aunt Dos to find somewhere else to park her car. For the past 20 years Aunt Dos has very kindly allowed me to park in her drive, as my own home has no parking space. But this happy arrangement has now come to an end.
With nowhere to park my car & with the rain coming down in torrents, I felt rather like King Lear, abandoned to the elements. However, I went out in search of somewhere to settle; & felt then more like the dove which Noah sent out from the ark. As the waters abated, I found a parking space.
Keith Woodings, whom I remember so well as a little baby in 1945 & who now farms at Grange Farm, Snibston (right next to little St. Mary's Church) has agreed to me parking in his spacious grounds. I am very grateful for this – any port in a storm - & so my car is safe each night – right near to my mum & dad.

7th April 1987 Tuesday
Joanne has been asked at school to prepare a ten minute speech on any subject of her choice. This should be ready by the end of the summer term – July. She asked my advice, and we eventually settled on "The Six Wives of Henry VIII", allowing about 1 ½ minutes per wife.
How much better acquainted we now are with –
1. The virtuous Spanish Princess Catherine of Aragon,
2. Anne Boleyn, 3. Sweet Jane Seymour (the one and only true love), 4. Princess Anne of Cleves (described by Henry VIII as the Flanders Mare), 5. The wanton Catherine Howard, 6. Catherine Parr.

11th April 1987 Saturday
Bailey – *Marguerite (Miss) aged 88 years, of Willoughby on the Wolds. Passed away peacefully at the Byron Nursing Home on 11th April. Sadly missed by all her family. Service Willoughby on the Wolds Church, Wednesday 15th April at 3.30 p.m. followed by interment. Flowers may be sent to Radcliffe and District Funeral Service or Willoughby Church.*
"Madge" Mum's cousin and life-long friend.

Madge will now return to the fold, to be buried by the side of her sister Bertha in the churchyard at Willoughby-on-the-Wolds. She will be re-united with Bertha on Bertha's 77th birthday. And so, another cycle of life has been completed; together with each other & their parents.

15th April 1987 Wednesday
In this Holy Week, the Bishop of Leicester, in "The Bishop's Easter Meditation" tells us that Christ hung naked on the cross. Shame forbids us to paint a picture of him thus. The brutality of the time included the humiliation of stripping his clothes from the condemned man. The nakedness of the crucified reflects the truth of the event at the deepest level.

17th April 1987 Good Friday
On 17th April 1984, the shooting of police woman Yvonne Fletcher outside the Libyan Embassy in London

led to Britain breaking off diplomatic relations with Libya.

Exactly 2 years later, on 17th April 1986, the planting of a time bomb led to Britain breaking off diplomatic relations with Syria.

19th April 1987 Easter Sunday

Derek Buxton, former Precentor of Leicester Cathedral, who became Rector of Ibstock in September 1969, leaves Ibstock this Easter to become Vicar at Woodhouse Eaves.

How well I remember his Induction Service at Ibstock when the Bishop likened their relationship to St. Paul & Timothy.

21st April 1987 Tuesday

In this Easter Week, the Bishop of Leicester tells us that nakedness in the Bible means not only a sign of want & of vulnerability, but also means perfection. God made Adam & Eve naked before shame & cruelty entered. Naked we come into the world. Christ left his grave clothes in the tomb.

23rd April 1987 Thursday

A mighty pre-historic monster was dug from a brick-pit in Great Casterton on 19th June 1968. Known as the Rutland Dinosaur – Cetiosaurus, this huge skeleton has pride of place at Leicester Museum. I gazed in wonder at the size of this monster, which roamed this land 175 million years ago.

25th April 1987 Saturday

The Duchess of Windsor, who died 12 months ago, had fabulous jewels valued at £5 million. This month they were sold by auction at the Beau Rivage Hotel, Geneva. The millionaires of Europe, Asia & America made this auction one where altogether £31,380,197 was bid.

The astonishing assault of High Society money on the Duchess of Windsor's jewels reached such frenzy in Sotheby's Geneva, that some bids reached up to 885 times estimate. That is why the auction made a total of £31,380,197 instead of the projected £5 million. The Duchess of Windsor's wedding ring, platinum, inscribed "Wallis 18.10.35. Your David 3 VI 37" sold for £74,074 (estimate £300 to £500). Her emerald engagement ring, inscribed "We are ours now 27 X 36" sold for £1,312,000. There were 306 items for sale.

1st May 1987 Friday

Contacted Mr. Jarram of Jarrams Landscapes, Loughborough, for a quotation to convert my front garden into a space for car-standing. It involves the removal of a tree & a wall.

3rd May 1987 Sunday

"Mum has chosen a magnolia" (30th August 1974). With the magnolia in full bloom & looking better & bigger every year, I learn that in Europe they were named after Pierre Magnol, a French botanist of the 17th Century. They were introduced first to the King of Spain, having been brought from Mexico.

5th May 1987 Tuesday

"Staff Reporting is one job that I certainly **do not** like." These were my sentiments 5 years ago & now we have a new system which, once more, I certainly **do not** like.

You never saw such an array of questions to be answered, plus the listing by everyone of "Specific Objectives".

Staff Report – Comment on the following –

Results achieved: - planning, quality & output of work.

Management: - Use of staff and other resources.

Communication: - Oral / written, relations with others.

Acceptance of responsibility; judgement; ability to produce constructive ideas; drive & determination; etc. etc.

9th May 1987 Saturday

Hoorah, hooray! At last! Today! Finished the new staff reporting session.

I have 2 Admin Officers (known previously as Clerical Officers), 1 Admin Assistant (known previously as Admin – Clerical Assistant), 2 Typists & 2 Messengers.

Alan Norris, Jan, Varsha, Angie, Val, Maurice, Alan Gamble.

11th May 1987 Monday

Remember Ethelfloeda, daughter of King Alfred, whose statue was erected in Leicester in 1980? Well, I have now made the acquaintance of this great "Lady of the Mercians" once more, as I explored the delights of Tamworth, which was the capital of the Kingdom of Mercia. King Offa (757 – 796) built his palace at Tamworth.

In more recent times, Thomas Guy paid for the building of the Town Hall in 1701. He was the local M.P. who is famous for founding the London hospital which bears his name.

In front of the Town Hall is a statue of Sir Robert Peel. M.P.

The treasures of Tamworth unfolded to me as I spread my wings in a new orbit. As I browsed among the shops, I bought a new musical record, one of a collection of 8, called "100 Greatest Classics"; the music moved me to tears in "Easter Hymn from Cavalleria Rusticana".

17th May 1987 Sunday

"100 Greatest Classics" – "This unique collection brings you the top 100 pieces of classical music of all time. Here is a golden opportunity to own a priceless collection, which will never date, of these great pieces of classical music performed by the finest artists in the world."

Here's to the next!

19th May 1987 Tuesday

Guess what! My car is back in Aunt Dos's drive. During the short time I was banished from her kingdom, the weather was particularly good, after the initial deluge, and like the dove I have returned briefly to the ark. I have arranged to have the front garden converted to car parking space in June.

21st May 1987 Thursday

F. A. Cup Final this year – Coventry 3 – Spurs 2. Attendance was 98,000 and receipts totalled £1,286,737 – 50p. It was the first time that Coventry had ever reached the final & there was great jubilation when they beat seven times winners Spurs, by 3 – 2.

23rd May 1987 Saturday

Leicester's new Lord Mayor is Indian born Mr. Gordhan Parmar.

He was born in Gujarat State, India, on 22nd July 1937. His parents moved to Tanzania in 1949 & he was educated in Dar-es-Salaam, moving to England in 1966. He is Leicester's first Lord Mayor of Asian origin.

25th May 1987 Monday

Milk Race 1987. How exciting to see the champion cyclists racing round Leicester's city centre after their long 111 mile lap from Gloucester. Leicester's new Indian Lord Mayor was there to present the trophy.

27th May 1987 Wednesday

Leslie Hale, my dad's best friend, who died 2 years ago, lived with his unmarried daughter Lesley and his unmarried son Bill. They have now sold their house in London and are moving back to Leicestershire. They have bought "The Grove", Swannington, where long ago their granny lived.

29th May 1987 Friday

By The Queen – A Proclamation – For Dissolving the Present Parliament & Declaring the Calling of Another. "….. and We being desirous & resolved, as soon as may be, to meet Our People & to have their advice in Parliament, do hereby make known to all our loving subjects, Our Royal Pleasure to call a new Parliament."

31st May 1987 Sunday

The London Marathon this year was won by another Japanese runner – H. Taniguchi.

Again it was a magnificent effort by all concerned, both runners (28,000 accepted, out of the many applicants) whose ages ranged from 18 to 81; organisers, throngs who lined the streets, and an army of valiant helpers.

The St. John Ambulance Brigade give tremendous help at the London Marathon, to those who literally buckle at the knees. The runners in turn help many charities - £5 million this year.

4th June 1987 Thursday

"100 Greatest Classics" – Added to my priceless collection of classical music by buying 2 more records from the collection of eight.

How my soul is stirred by this great music & what a moving experience to hear for the first time such treasures as Verdi's "Chorus of Hebrew Slaves".

6th June 1987 Saturday

Mr. Ellis, Chief Gas Examiner, aged 62, today married Veronica Branson, aged 56, a divorcee. They were married at Clipston Baptist Chapel & are going to Austria for their honeymoon.

8th June 1987 Monday

"Bridges" – This is Joanne's latest subject at school. As we have learned more and more about the world's great bridges & the men who built them, we have marvelled at them all. We learn that Leonardo da Vinci was a bridge engineer; & know all about Thomas Telford.

Thomas Telford (1757 – 1834) was Britain's greatest civil engineer since the Romans. He built roads, bridges, tunnels, canals, harbours & aqueducts. He was called "Pontifex Maximus".

12th June 1987 Friday

The General Election yesterday gave the Conservatives a further term in office and meant a hat-trick for Prime Minister Margaret Thatcher. They gained their victory with their Defence Policy. They intend to increase spending on nuclear weapons, whereas the Labour Party would scrap them.

14th June 1987 Trinity Sunday

On Trinity Sunday, with its 3-fold trade-mark of God, we are reminded of the tremendous 3-fold promise made at our Baptism, rehearsed again in the Catechism of the Prayer Book, and confirmed in the Confirmation service, whereby we are preserved through God's "most mighty protection".

16th June 1987 Tuesday

Prime Minister Margaret Thatcher wasted no time in removing Peter Walker, Secretary of State for Energy, from office. He has been replaced by her well favoured Cecil Parkinson, aged 55. He will be concentrating his efforts on preparing Privatisation for the electricity industry.

18th June 1987 Thursday

Our telephone at 27, Leicester Road, Ravenstone, was installed in June 1971.

Now, after 16 years, I have ordered a new up-to-date model, with push button numbers instead of dialled numbers, together with an extension in the middle bedroom, where I have my lovely office desk.

20th June 1987 Saturday

Trooping the Colour this year did not seem right, with the Queen being the only one not on horse-back. She looked more like the elderly Queen Victoria, as she rode in an old perambulator-like carriage-for-one, with a rug over her knees, wearing a matronly flimsy outfit.

22nd June 1987 Monday

In the Queen's "official" birthday honours, Princess Anne (born 15th August 1950), has been given the title "Princess Royal". She is the 7th Princess in history to hold the title. The last Princess Royal was H.R.H. Princess Louise Victoria Alexandra, who gained the title in 1905.

24th June 1987 Wednesday

The State Opening of Parliament this year takes place in June, rather than the usual time of November, because of the recent general election.

In her speech to Parliament, the Queen (like a puppet) had to rehearse all the things which the government now proposes to do -

"My government will stand fully by their obligations to the N.A.T.O. Alliance. They will sustain Britain's contribution to Western defence by modernising the independent nuclear deterrent through the introduction of the Trident submarine programme." (See 13th July 1986).

"My government will continue to pursue policies of sound financial management designed further to reduce inflation & to promote enterprise & increased employment.

Legislation will be introduced to enable the water & sewerage functions of the water authorities in England and Wales to be privatised."

30th June 1987 Tuesday

"O God, who art the author of peace and lover of concord, in knowledge of whom standeth our eternal life, whose service is perfect freedom, defend us …….. that we, surely trusting in thy defence, may not fear the power of any adversaries." (God is a lover of concord.)

2nd July 1987 Thursday

King Olav V of Norway today celebrates his 84th birthday. I sent him a birthday card depicting the guardsmen, resplendent in their red tunics & busbies, & sent a covering note which began, "Your Majesty, Long, long ago, a little Prince from Norway visited England & discovered to his great delight that when he approached the guardsmen on sentry duty at Buckingham Palace, they came to life & saluted him ……… One of those guardsmen was my late father …….. Today, I salute you, etc. (See 2nd July 1983)

6th July 1987 Monday

"And Mary arose in those days, & went into the hill country with haste, into a city of Judah; & entered into the house of Zacharias, & saluted Elisabeth." (Luke 1. 39.)

The preacher at Ravenstone yesterday told us that July 2nd is the day when we remember "The Visitation of the Virgin Mary." He spoke of the debt we owe to Mary & Elisabeth. He spoke of the importance of good holy women, without whom mankind would be lost. He stressed the importance of this visit by Mary to Elisabeth, which prompted that most wonderful song, "Song of the Blessed Virgin Mary."

10th July 1987 Friday

"Educational Holidays at Home and Abroad."

Saw this interesting brochure in the library at Coalville & sent for details of a holiday in Florence ….. "What better way to study the art & architecture of Florence than in the company of an expert art historian – February 1988."

Other fascinating holidays offered include - Jordan and Lower Egypt £800; Madrid £330; Wildlife Safari to Zambia £1,000; Art & Music in Vienna £450; Art & Architecture in Mexico; The Bicentenary of Australia; Armada Anniversary.

14th July 1987 Tuesday

My Birthday! 56 today (2 x 2 x 2 x 7).

The collect this year is for the 4th Sunday after Trinity, "O God, the protector of all that trust in thee, without whom nothing is strong, nothing is holy, increase & multiply upon us thy mercy, that thou being our ruler & guide, we may pass through things temporal, that we finally lose not the things eternal."

16th July 1987 Thursday

The front garden has now been converted to a tarmac car parking space, at a cost of £300.

"Dig out for drive to level and lay down base for tarmac, then lay tarmac to recommended thickness of approx 2

½ inches. Total price £300."

At the moment it certainly looks very good.

18th July 1987 Saturday

Took Katherine, aged 83, to the Monastery. As we walked in the monastery garden, Katherine showed me in detail the exquisite beauty of the roses.

"This one" she said, "is named 'Peace'. The seed was taken from France to America in wartime & reached perfection as the war ended."

Katherine, a devout Roman Catholic, knelt in prayer before the altar rail at the monastery. Beside her, in a shopping bag, her pampered Dachshund, Alison, knelt reverently with bowed head. This was a moving sight, in the otherwise empty church, with only the beautiful Madonna keeping watch.

From the monastery, Katherine & I motored to Mountsorrel, to see Auntie Doris, aged 92 next month. What a lot they had to tell each other, of shared experiences travelling through the Holy Land & Egypt, where they had each experienced "seeing" baby Moses in the bulrushes.

Auntie Doris served as a nurse in Egypt during the 1914 – 18 war. She talked of the day she met Lawrence of Arabia. Katherine, who could talk for ever, told of the day she got into a "spate" – crossing a dry river bed which suddenly, without warning, became a raging flood.

26th July 1987 Sunday

From British Gas, East Midlands, to Miss Hewes, 27 Leicester Road, Ravenstone –

"We have pleasure in submitting the following quotation – Appliance price (inc. fixing) £176 including V.A.T. Pipework to provide point £13-62p."

I now have a lovely new gas fire.

28th July 1987 Tuesday

Mary Moore, now aged 76, arrived for a week's holiday in Ravenstone, so the house has been given its annual "spring clean".

Tomorrow she is having lunch with Betty Stiles of Coalville, another day with Molly, another day with Joyce & another day with Edith Whittaker.

30th July 1987 Thursday

Steven, now aged 19, has a new girl-friend named Kim. He also has a new job which he really enjoys. He drives a van for a local firm, delivering small items throughout the county.

He is therefore a transformed character, with all the charm of a handsome happy young man in love.

1st August 1987 Saturday

I invited Katherine (aged 83) and Aunt Dos (aged 85) to join Mary & me for tea & the evening. Katherine, in a league of her own, took centre stage, while we were her audience. Mary & I took her home & admired her exquisitely decorated home & treasures.

3rd August 1987 Monday

Yesterday evening, while spending the evening at Molly Donaldson's, Mary Moore suffered a slight stroke.

For a little while her speech was blurred & her right hand & right foot were limp. She managed to walk with difficulty to the car & we were able to get her safely to bed.

5th August 1987 Wednesday

The doctor came to see Mary, following her mild stroke & said she should be alright to travel home on Thursday (tomorrow) by bus. He advised her to rest & said she should soon be back to normal. Her speech is alright again & the use has returned to her right hand & foot.

7th August 1987 Friday

Yesterday I went with Mary by bus from Coalville to London & saw her safely on her next bus from London to Colchester. She looked tired & weary & I wondered whether she would be coming to see me ever again.

Then like Hiawatha, I returned home into the portals of the sunset.

9th August 1987 Sunday

Auntie Belle, now aged 91, is beginning to feel her great age. Living alone, she finds it increasingly difficult to look after herself.

"I have lived too long," she said to me the other day, when her niece Avril asked me to be one of the signatories to Auntie Belle's latest Will.

11th August 1987 Tuesday

The Driver & Vehicle Licensing Centre (D.V.L.C.) at Swansea has a new £35 million computer system and, with an inquiry team of 107 women & 25 men, can cope with all telephone queries in a matter of seconds. They receive about 2,400 queries every day.

No longer the "Nincomputer" (as recorded in my diary 25th January 1978). No longer the major complaint about D.V.L.C. being "delays" (as recorded 12 February 1976), but now a super-efficient "help team" with a high speed licensing computer which is "driver friendly".

Help line: 0792 – 72151.

Over 1,000 people "lose" their driving licences every week & telephone D.V.L.C. "help line" to enquire about a replacement. If they need their "Driver Number" the help team give it to them over the 'phone. Only pink Euro licences are now being issued as duplicates.

17th August 1987 Monday

Sahara sand falls over Britain. Sand from the Sahara blows 900 miles to Britain! What an amazing thing to see everyone's car covered in sand-bearing rain spots. Small deposits of sand lurk in the corners of the car windows. After a moderately light rainfall all the cars in southern Britain needed a good clean.

19th August 1987 Wednesday

Rudolf Hess, Hitler's former deputy & the last known survivor from the Nazi leadership died on Monday this week, aged 93. He spent the last 40 years of his life in Spandau Prison in Berlin, after being sentenced to life imprisonment at Nuremburg for war crimes.

21st August 1987 Friday

Afternoon tea at "The Grove" Swannington.

Aunt Dos & I were invited by Lesley & Bill Hale to visit their newly acquired home at Swannington. "The Grove" is a listed building, built by the landed gentry 2 centuries ago. It has stables & coach houses & a truly beautiful garden with huge trees.

23 August 1987 Sunday
And 30 years rolled by.

And the telephone rang.

"I am speaking from Lancaster Prison – do you know John Marsden? Do you know him as Cocky? It's just that we didn't believe him. He works with us & we are just checking. He is here now. Would you like a word with him?"

"How did you know my telephone number?" I asked Cocky.

"I've known it for years" he said. And in a few minutes on the phone we bridged the last 30 years as if in a story book, & each gleaned from the other the salient points, & Old Maid Hewsie wept tears of sorrow & tears of joy.

Note – My long-lost love Cocky, now a prison officer at Lancaster Prison, telephones me; we then continue to keep in touch by telephone.

27th August 1987 Thursday

For the past 5 years I have been saving £50 per month in "Save as you earn". This has now reached fruition & I have received a cheque for £3,548 – 56p.

Out of this I have bought a new wheelbarrow £40, new curtains £40, matching chair covers £40, new Electrolux cleaner £80 & a car.

29th August 1987 Saturday

E479 EAY is the beautiful new car which I acquired today. This is my 5th car –

1. **FBT 638D** (2nd hand – 1967) 2. **KAY 7L** (new – 1973) 3. **PNR 867R** (new – 1976)

4. **UBC 783 X** (ex-demonstration 1982) 5. **E479 EAY** (new silver Metro, as was the previous make & colour, £6,300 from Fowkes Bros., Ibstock).

I paid 60% of the price of my car & have 12 months to pay the rest – 0% interest!

I paid £2,400 – was allowed £1,350 on my old car, making a total of £3,750.

This leaves £2,550 to pay, which has finally been adjusted to £2,499-96p = 12 monthly payments of £208-33p.

2nd September 1987 Wednesday

£10,000 per year. The latest Civil Service pay award (effective from 1st September 1987) takes the maximum E.O. salary to £10,100. This modest achievement provides me with a life of comfort, if not of luxury.

Cocky tells me that his daughter Yvonne has a salary of £40,000 p.a.

4th September 1987 Friday

Double retirement party at work as Mr. Ellis, Chief Gas Examiner, and Derek Moody, Higher Scientific Officer, both retired. I had a long interesting chat with Veronica, the newly wed Mrs. Ellis, & liked her very much. She is kind & gentle & likes the simple things in life.

6th September 1987 Sunday

"John of Gaunt" is the subject for this year's medieval merry making in Leicester.

He was the 4th son of King Edward III. He married Blanche, only child of Henry, the first Duke of Lancaster

& 10th Earl of Leicester, and by right of his wife acquired his father-in-law's Earldoms. John Plantagenet – of "Gaunt" or Ghent – was born at Ghent, Flanders, in 1340A.D. He married Blanche in 1359A.D. & became the 2nd Duke of Lancaster in 1362A.D. He and Blanche had a son, Henry Bolingbroke, who became the usurper King Henry IV, founder of the Lancastrian Kings.

Because Henry Bolingbroke, the 3rd Duke of Lancaster, decided he ought to be King that was, in effect, the last time anyone held the title "Duke of Lancaster" because it was united with the crown. Henry, however, preserved its identity & the Duchy of Lancaster still exists.

12 September 1987 Saturday

Survivors of the Titanic, which sank in 1912, would like the ship to be left alone as a memorial to the dead. The U.S. expedition which found the ship 2 years ago, have kept its exact location a secret. However, French salvagers have now found the ship & are retrieving the ship's safe. The treasure hunters who have found one of the Titanic's safes are planning to open the safe in a live broadcast on television in Monte Carlo next month. Tales of a fortune in diamonds & jewels from the millionaire passengers on board have circulated ever since the liner went down.

16th September 1987 Wednesday

Pope John Paul II, presently touring the United States, addressed all 320 American Bishops in Los Angeles & stressed the importance of the teachings of the Church on sexual and conjugal morality, divorce & re-marriage. He also said, "Women are not called the priesthood. The teaching of the Church on this point is quite clear."

18th September 1987 Friday
Olav Feast
King Olav of Norway (84), Europe's oldest reigning monarch, celebrated three decades of rule with a banquet for 1,500 people.

20th September 1987 Sunday

14th Sunday after Trinity and the Epistle for today tells us again that the harvest of the spirit is love, joy, peace, patience, kindness, goodness, fidelity, gentleness & self-control.

(Galatians 5. 22 – N.E.B.) This was the text chosen by the Provost in 1966 at the Harvest Festival.

22nd September 1987 Tuesday

Dawn Henn (now aged 37), choreographer for Coalville Amateurs, became engaged last Saturday to David Cox, after a courtship which lasted for many years.

Also at the weekend (on Sunday) Joan Dillow, another member of Coalville Amateurs, celebrated her Ruby Wedding.

24th September 1987 Thursday

On the office desk at work, of Senior Scientific Officer Vijay Weerasinghe, sits a large figure of the Buddha ("The Enlightened One"). Vijay talked to me about the Buddha & said that if you concentrate on looking at the Buddha, you are filled with peace.

Buddhism is based on the teachings of Siddhartha Gautama, who lived in the 6th Century B.C. He made up his mind to solve the riddle of life. He sat down quietly under a tree – the sacred Bodhi tree, with legs crossed and with right hand pointing down. After 49 days of meditation, he achieved the enlightenment he was seeking.

The symbol of Buddhism is the wheel whose spokes represent the Eightfold Path. Right Knowledge, Right Intention, Right Speech, Right Conduct, Right Means of Livelihood, Right Effort, Right Mindfulness, Right Concentration.

30th September 1987 Wednesday

Canon Gundry, Chancellor of Leicester Cathedral since 1963, is retiring after 48 years service in the ministry. How I love to hear Canon Gundry read the lesson at church; but he is also a great writer & is retiring to devote more time to his writing.

He was ordained at Southwark in 1939.

2nd October 1987 Friday

Coalville Amateur Operatic Society (founded 1919) Grand Re-Union.

What a wonderful evening when a lifetime of shows was contracted into one night to remember. Stars of yesteryear were moved to tears as we all sang again the songs of love which they knew so well.

The Hewes family was well represented at the Coalville Amateurs Grand Re-Union.

Aunt Dos was able to represent the "Nineteen Twenties". Bunting was there from the "Thirties". Pat Enid & I were there from the "Forties" & Mary Blue was there from the "Fifties". There were 200 people there.

6th October 1987 Tuesday

Enid is 60 years old today, and is retiring from work. However, she neither looks nor acts at all like an old age pensioner. She regularly attends her "Keep Fit" class and has a very trim figure. Her bubbling personality makes her very popular with colleagues, both male & female.

8th October 1987 Thursday

Memorandum from Officer Marsden, H. M. Prison, Lancaster – Tel: 68871 Ext. 261.

"Dear Betty, Enclosed is a photograph of me. I often wonder what you are doing & if you still thought of me.......... Still Love You."

Note -I receive a photograph of Cocky in uniform.

If Cocky were not a married man, I would right now be running to him, falling on his neck and kissing him. But I know that if I were his wife of 30 years, it would break my heart if I knew that he was sending his photo to another woman and writing to her to say that he still loved her.

On 12th October 1949, my diary records "**Primaus**" – one of the happiest days of my life, when Cocky first kissed me. However, our love was not able to withstand the strong opposition from most of my family & we said goodbye – at least we tried to say goodbye, time & time again "**diximus vale**".

14th October 1987 Wednesday

Cocky & I had a long heart to heart chat on the telephone and he poured out the troubles of his heart to me.

For the past 6 years his wife Joan has been suffering

from deep depression, subsequent to the death of her parents. She is so unhappy that, like my mum (3rd April 1979) she refuses to be comforted.

Cocky & Joan have 2 children. Yvonne, aged 26, is a chartered accountant & works in London as Area Controller for the great Guinness brewery. She is Cocky's pride & joy and is planning to marry shortly.

Jonathan, aged 14, is still at school & he is a pupil at Lancaster Royal Grammar School.

20th October 1987 Tuesday

"And the people of Sevenoaks, Kent, discovered that they were only the people of One Oak."

Britain's worst weather disaster for nearly 300 years brought death & destruction to the whole of southern Britain last Thursday night, when 100 m.p.h. winds brought everything to a halt.

Not only Sevenoaks, Kent, lost 6 of 7 oak trees, which symbolise its name, in last weeks devastating storm, but Kew Gardens was equally devastated. Damage was so great it will take at least 25 years to recapture the beauty of the world's most famous botanical gardens, in London.

24th October 1987 Saturday

"Medjugorje" (pronounced Med-jew-gory-ay). This is the latest book loaned to me by Ted Ludlow. It tells the story of the continued appearance of the Blessed Virgin Mary, since 24th June 1981 to 5 young people who live at Medjugorje in Yugoslavia. Her messages include: - "Pray, pray, pray!" & "Peace, peace, peace".

Medju Gore = between the mountains. This is where the Blessed Virgin Mary continues to speak to her chosen children. Pray, pray, pray, is her constant request.

"I do not know what else to tell you, because I love you & wish that in prayer you come to know my love & the love of God."

"Pray, pray, pray" and "Peace, peace, peace" The Virgin Mary explains that prayer is the only way to peace. "Without prayer there is no peace. Turn your hearts to prayer & ask the Holy Spirit to be poured on you. I wish to fill you with the peace, joy & love of God. Pray, pray, pray! In prayer you will come to know the greatest joy & the way out of every situation that has no way out. Pray with conscious attention & in prayer you will know the majesty of God. Open yourselves to God & God will work through you & give you everything you need."

1st November 1987 Sunday

My beloved Provost, the Revd. John Hughes, now aged 63, has retired altogether from the ministry. He has taken his last service at St. Nicholas Church in Bringhurst, & will live at Hallaton.

3rd November 1987 Tuesday

In May 1979 Mum & I acquired a "new" garden shed. Actually, it was a second hand site-hut, 10 feet x 8 feet, & was erected on the site of the old tumble down coalhouse. I have now sold this shed to Joanne's dad for £100 & have turned the site into a paved patio.

5th November 1987 Thursday

Bunting & Mostyn, who were married in January 1946, reached their Ruby Wedding Anniversary in January 1986, but with all the upset of Michael's divorce from

Sheena, they did not feel like celebrating at the time. Now we are to have a belated get-together on 14th November 1987.

Bunting & Mostyn have recently bought a new house jointly with Michael at Kidderminster. Michael's 3 children visit them every weekend.

Michael will be bringing Bunting & Mostyn to join Pat, Evelyn & me for a six-some dinner party next Saturday at the de-luxe Gatsby at Osgathorpe.

9th November 1987 Monday

"Poppy Day Massacre"

These are the grim headlines in today's newspapers, telling the world what happened at Enniskillen, County Fermanagh, in Northern Ireland yesterday morning, as people gathered round the Statue of Remembrance for the annual wreath-laying ceremony to honour their dead.

11th November 1987 Wednesday

A 30lb bomb of home-made explosives had been planted by the I.R.A. behind the gable wall of an old community centre, only yards from the Cenotaph in Enniskillen last Sunday morning. In one of the worst terrorist outrages in Ulster, 11 people were killed & 63 injured, 5 very seriously.

13th November 1987 Friday

DNA = Deoxyribo-Nucleic Acid of the Human Mitochondria. (See 29th July 1986)

Today, for the first time, the DNA fingerprinting test, which was pioneered at Leicester University, has been used to help secure a conviction. Labourer Robert Melias was jailed for rape. This wonderful test identifies the unique human cell structure.

Genetic fingerprinting was invented in 1983 by Dr. Alec Jeffries at Leicester University. (Ordinary fingerprinting was first discovered in 1901).

Genetic fingerprinting enables scientists to match DNA from any minute sample of blood, hair, tissue or semen with the DNA from any individual. We are all unique.

14th November 1987 Saturday

Dinner party for 6 people at the Gatsby. What a splendid dinner we had to celebrate (nearly 2 years late) Bunting & Mostyn's Ruby Wedding. We were treated like royalty as we were fussed over at the best round table, complete with 5 candle centrepiece, & served from silver & gold dishes.

15th November 1987 Sunday

Following Saturday's dinner party for 6 people, we had Sunday lunch for 9, kindly provided by Evelyn. There was Pat, Evelyn & their daughter Mary Blue, with her 13 year old son Scott. There was Bunting, Mostyn & their son Michael, Aunt Dos & me.

Michael fell for his cousin Mary Blue. Michael & Mary Blue last saw each other 20 years ago. He said to her, "I could write a book about what I have gone through since we last met, & I guess you could too." - "Yes," she said, and her heart melted.

(Note by Mary Blue—This is Betty being fanciful!)

19th November 1987 Thursday

Kings Cross underground station became a blazing

inferno last night, when fire engulfed the top of one of the wooden slatted escalators, while people frantically tried to escape.

30 people died, including one fireman – Station Officer Colin Townsley, the one who had to go in first & assess how bad the situation was.

25th November 1987 Wednesday
"No need to ask them questions, their faces tell it all. They came back riding four; there were five before the call."

Was there ever a more moving sight than the fire engine festooned with floral tributes bearing the coffin of Colin Townsley through the streets of London, lined with thousands of firemen?

27th November 1987 Friday
Hewes, Rene, of Leicester Road, Ravenstone, passed peacefully away in hospital, November 23rd 1987, aged 82 years. Beloved wife of the late Norman, dearly loved mother of Norma and Eric, Rita and John, devoted grandma of Ian, Nigel, Philip, Jane and Paul.

Funeral service at Ravenstone Parish Church on Friday November 27th at 2 p.m., to be followed by cremation at Loughborough. Family flowers only by request, but donations if so desired for Ravenstone Parish Church. Donations and further inquiries to Coalville and District Funeral Service, Gutteridge Street, Coalville. Tel. 38600.

This is "Auntie Rene", widowed for 43 years when my cousin Norman, her beloved "Norm", was killed in the 1939 – 1945 war. At her funeral today the Rector said that her name means peace.

Auntie Rene was the same age as my Mum. They were young girls together & the young Norman Hewes might well have married either of them. He might then have been my father instead of my cousin. My Mum however preferred Reg Hewes, & both she & Auntie Rene became widows for 43 years. How very sad to lose your partner so early in life. Those who stay together for 40 years are showered with gifts, while those who weep alone have nothing to celebrate. Every Sunday morning you could see Auntie Rene lovingly placing fresh flowers at the War Memorial in Ravenstone.

3rd December 1987 Thursday
"O for yesterdays to come" – These poetic words were quoted by Canon Gundry as he started his retirement, (not too retiring, he hoped) after having served for 24 years as Chancellor of Leicester Cathedral. Question – What do you name a large cat? Answer – Magnificat.

5th December 1987 Saturday
"When Christ was born, midnight gloom lightened into midday brightness."
"When Christ died, midday brightness darkened into midnight gloom."
These words are quoted in the Parish Magazine "The Grapevine" for this month, December.

7th December 1987 Monday
Ravenstone Sunday School Gift and Prize Giving Service yesterday showed that the Sunday School is still doing well, under the leadership now of the parents,

since the teenage girls have now moved on to College. I was delighted to see my nativity set on display; & dear angelic Angela, now 11. (See 21st March 1982).

9th December 1987 Wednesday
As a prelude to a "Census" of some 3,000 registered files at our office, the 2 E.O.s (Catherine Wells & I) did a thorough search of the whole building, looking into everyone's cupboards & drawers, & recording every file we found anywhere. What a lot of other interesting things we found as well.

11th December 1987 Friday
All wrapped up again for Christmas – 1. Pat, 2. Evelyn, 3. Mary Blue, 4. Scott, 5. Sharon, 6. Bunting, 7. Aunt Dos, 8. Enid, 9. Auntie Belle, 10. Johnty, 11. Matron, 12. Katherine, 13. Joanne, 14. Stuart, plus 2 hairdressers, plus 9 at the office. How lovely the presents look all together, plus 53 cards.

13th December 1987 Sunday
And the people of Sevenoaks, Kent, are once more the people of 7 oaks, following a ceremony attended by several thousand people at which 7 saplings were planted at the Vine Cricket Ground, to replace the 7 mighty oaks destroyed with thousands of others during October.

15th December 1987 Tuesday
Brother Pat, married to Evelyn for 47 years, came face to face this week with his first love Rachel Clark, whom he had completely lost all trace of. As they held each other in fond embrace in the middle of the Co-op shop, Coalville, he learned that she is now a widow, living in Bristol.

17th December 1987 Thursday
Snibston School Christmas Concert. Every year, since Joanne was a little angel in the Infants Class, I have accompanied her mother to the Christmas Concert. We go now to see her little brother, Stuart; & every year I am filled with nostalgia, remembering when I was there myself as a child.

18th December 1987 Friday
Hall, Alf, of Main Street, Ravenstone. Beloved husband of Amy and dearest brother of Reg, passed peacefully away on December 18th 1987. Funeral service at Loughborough Crematorium on Wednesday December 23rd 1987 at 11a.m.
Time will not dim the face we love, the voice we heard each day. The many things you did for us, in your own special way. All our lives we'll miss you, as the years come and go; But in our hearts we'll keep you, because we loved you so.

My very good friend Alf.

21st December 1987 Monday
"Thinking of you at Christmas" – "This comes to wish you happiness when Christmas is here, and remind you of how very much you're thought of through the year."
"Best wishes and love to the woman of my dreams."

For the first time at Christmas my true love sent to me, a card chosen specially for me.

23rd December 1987 Wednesday

"To a Special Friend at Christmas" – "Thinking of you at Christmas and sending this cheery 'Hello', to greet you very warmly and then to let you know, you're wished a pleasant season, the kind that will impart, the happiness that will remain forever in your heart."
From Joanne, (aged 13).

25th December 1987 Friday

A beautiful warm sunny Christmas Day. Pat & Evelyn gave us another warm welcome – Aunt Dos & me, Katherine & the Vicar, the Reverend John Hancock.
The warm glow in my heart told me that Cocky was "Thinking of me at Christmas" and I felt less like an odd bod or a waif & stray.

27th December 1987 Sunday

On the third day of Christmas, my true love sent to me, five gold rings. The telephone gave 5 rings & Cocky was talking to me from Lancaster Prison.
He had spent Christmas with Joan, Jonathan, Yvonne & her boy-friend David. Joan feels more secure when Cocky is with her.

29th December 1987 Tuesday

How hard a thing it is to love a married man. Knowing that we all are God's children, we are given the clearest of instructions how to play the game of life. When Cocky married Joan he was no longer mine ......
"Forsaking all other, keep thee only unto her, so long as ye both shall live – I will."

31st December 1987 Thursday

Only Cocky was able to search the depths & bring my heart to the surface again. Like my "piece of eight" my heart has known what it was like to sink to unfathomable depths (18th October 1970) and then to re-surface. Until Cocky found me again I seemed to be immune to all romantic overtures.

* * *

1988

1st January 1988 Friday
Pope John Paul II, a devotee of the Blessed Virgin Mary, has decreed that we have a Marian Year, spanning from Whit Sunday 1987 to the Assumption of the Blessed Virgin, 15th August 1988. That is the day when Roman Catholics celebrate their belief that the Virgin was taken, body & soul, into heaven.

3rd January 1988 Sunday
"In 1988 a terrible comet will appear in the heavens & by a cruel blow on earth will raise water from the seas & drown whole lands."
Thus predicted a Polish monk in the 18th Century. He also predicted a universal earthquake in 1996 which will destroy Italy, Sicily, Spain & Portugal.

Buckroyd. On Sunday January 3rd 1988, Rector of St. Michael's and All Angels' Church, Ravenstone, Leslie, beloved husband of the late Madge, loving father of Martin and Paul, passed suddenly but peacefully away aged 71 years. Funeral service at St. Michael's and All Angels' Church, Ravenstone, on Wednesday January 13th at 11 a.m., followed by cremation at Sutton Coldfield Crematorium, 1 p.m. Family flowers only please, donations in lieu for British Heart Foundation, c/o Leicestershire Co-operative Funeral Services, 128 London Road, Coalville. Tel. 36703.

The Reverend Leslie Buckroyd
Rector of Ravenstone
1970 - 1988

Note – The Reverend Leslie Buckroyd, Rector of Ravenstone since 1970, died in church at the Sunday morning service. He had suffered with a bad heart for many years.

5th January 1988 Tuesday
"Mutiny on the Bounty" – Watched on television this true life story which began in reality exactly 200 years ago. What a story – charged with such emotions. On 23rd December 1787 Captain William Bligh & his crew set sail for Tahiti. They experienced every possible emotion a man could endure.

9th January 1988 Saturday
The great jigsaw of my job embraces gas testing and gas meter testing. Over the years I have gleaned enough facts & figures to be able to produce a chart which shows the history of gas testing & gas meter testing. This chart is now framed & on display in the foyer.
My B.L.O. Desk Notes now fill a book. As Branch Liaison Officer, it is my pleasure and privilege to know everything first at work & then communicate to those concerned. I love being asked by Mr Plant, the Director, to find out what is happening here, there & everywhere, & then report back.

13th January 1988 Wednesday
My mum had beautiful blue eyes. One of her admirers once said that she had eyes to bring a duck off water.

Little did he know that my mum had indeed brought more than one duck off water – time & time again, when she & Madge were young, a long time ago.
(See 13th January 1986).

"What are these which are arrayed in white robes? And whence came they?" Revelation 7. 13.
I thought of this at the funeral procession for our Rector, the Revd. Leslie Buckroyd, when a seemingly never ending procession of clergy followed his coffin into Ravenstone Church. I was moved to tears.

17th January 1988 Sunday
"Thy word is a lamp unto my feet, and a light unto my path." Psalm 119, verse 105.
"The Lord is my light & my salvation." Psalm 27.
These were the words from Holy Scripture which meant so much to our Rector, the Reverend Leslie Buckroyd, who died in church 2 weeks ago.
"That was the true light, which lighteth every man that cometh into the world." John 1. 9.
Mr Godfrey Pill, resident "reader" at church, spoke of the light which lighteth every man in the world. There is not one single person who does not possess some spark of divine light.

21st January 1988 Thursday
Letter from East Midlands Electricity –
"Dear Madam, The electricity meter in your premises has now reached the age where it must be removed for testing. The Board is obliged to do this under the terms of the Electricity Supply (Meters) Act 1936." Meters are tested every 20 years.

23rd January 1988 Saturday
7th Development / Petroleum Measurement Inspectorate Meeting this week at work where I took the minutes.
The great oil fields of the North Sea begin life as oil wells. Before any oil well can come into production it must be tested. It must, as you may **well** imagine, be **well** tested.
Gas & Oil Measurement is a mighty tricky operation. British Gas experts have now come up with a different method of measurement for the Morecambe & Rough fields, containing a "deviation of the isentropic exponent".
Well, well, well. Our experts are not sure they can agree to that.

27th January 1988 Wednesday
"Sound of Music", Coalville Amateurs' production this year, is proving to be a firm favourite. The initial allocation of tickets was almost an all time record. Once more we assembled at Peter Jacques' house & were there until the early hours. (7 of us working for 7 hours).

29th January 1988 Friday
Those who died in the inferno of the space shuttle Challenger, 2 years ago, were –
1 The Commander of the flight, Francis Scobee, 46,

2. The Pilot, Michael Smith, 40, 3. Ronald McNair, 35,
4. Lieutenant Colonel Ellison Onizuka, 39,
5. Gregory Jarvis, 41, 6. Judy Resnik;
7. Mrs Christa McAuliffe, a teacher, 37.

481

31ˢᵗ January 1988 Sunday

Die Zauberflöte = The Magic Flute. Watched on television this fairy tale opera by Mozart & found it truly enchanting. The hero, an Eastern prince named Tamino, with the help of his magic flute, wins the hand of his true love, Pamina, after undergoing trials of initiation into higher life.

2ⁿᵈ February 1988 Tuesday

To a congregation of only four, the Rector of Ravenstone, the Revd. Leslie Buckroyd, spoke a year ago of those who are "called by God". At his funeral service last month, to a church overflowing with people, he was described as "God's officer & gentleman – a very parfit gentleman."

4ᵗʰ February 1988 Thursday

Chlorofluorocarbons (CFCs) were invented 60 years ago. They are used as propellants in aerosols, in refrigerators and air-conditioning systems, in the dry-cleaning industry, fire-fighting, etc.

The CFCs, after use, escape into the stratosphere, where they are decomposed by sunlight to free chlorine, which is now destroying the ozone.

750,000 tonnes per year of chlorofluorocarbons are now destroying the protective ozone layer around the earth. There is now the so-called Antarctic hole which appears for about 2 months during the Antarctic spring & is getting bigger every year. The threat to the ozone layer is a global problem for the whole world.

8ᵗʰ February 1988 Monday

Septuagesima Sunday once more reminds of the sacredness of marriage. From the 2ⁿᵈ Chapter of Genesis, the words ring out loud & clear – "In the beginning God created ……"

From the 10ᵗʰ Chapter of St. Mark, the words of Christ himself, "What God hath joined together, let not man put asunder."

10ᵗʰ February 1988 Wednesday

"Read the Apocrypha – the short Book of Tobit has some beautiful prayers, shows how God gives healing, & also stresses the holiness of marriage." – This month's Parish Magazine prompts us to read again the beautiful story of Tobias & the Angel Raphael, one of the seven holy angels.

12ᵗʰ February 1988 Friday

£157 billion pounds!

That is how much the government is expecting to spend during the next financial year. By far the greatest chunk goes to the Department of Health & Social Security with £50 billion for Social Security & £22 billion for Health. £22 billion for Education & £20 billion for Defence.

14ᵗʰ February 1988 Sunday

Valentine's Day.

Coalville Amateurs' were well represented yesterday at the marriage of Dawn Henn & David Cox at Christ Church, Coalville. What a lovely wedding. The church was filled to capacity, with people standing at the back. Dawn was a truly radiant smiling bride.

15ᵗʰ February 1988 Monday

Hewes, Donald Arthur, of Ravenstone. Beloved husband of Phyl, devoted father of Peter, Lesley and Susan, loving grandfather of Sarah, Kirsty, Emma, Ruth, Clare, Karen, Hannah and James, passed suddenly but peacefully away February 15ᵗʰ 1988, aged 73 years. Funeral service at Ravenstone Church on Monday February 22ⁿᵈ at 11.30a.m. followed by cremation at Bretby Crematorium.

Cousin Don, who died today.

16ᵗʰ February 1988 Tuesday

The Angel Raphael is like the Branch Liaison Officer of Heaven. He says to Tobias, whose wife has been "made whole" again, "I am Raphael which present the prayers of the saints, & which go in & out before the glory of the Holy One. Fear not … but write all things which are done in a book."

20ᵗʰ February 1988 Saturday

Called to see Phyl, following the sudden death of her husband. (Cousin Don). She was bearing up well, but the poor old dog, Tina, a golden Labrador, was utterly bewildered & lost. She wandered in vain from room to room, went eagerly to the door, only to return completely dejected.

22ⁿᵈ February 1988 Monday

Ravenstone Church was filled to overflowing for the funeral of cousin Don, Churchwarden & Freemason. His many cousins were well represented, plus the next generation & the next. Aunt Dos was the sole representative of his father's generation. Now, almost 86, she is now a very frail old lady.

How interesting to meet Don's grandchildren, now beautiful young ladies. Peter's eldest daughter, Sarah, an attractive 21 year old. His second daughter, Kirsty, a reincarnation of Don's sister Isobel. Lesley's eldest daughter Ruth is truly beautiful. Don was blessed with 7 grand-daughters & one grandson.

26ᵗʰ February 1988 Friday

In praise of the Postal Service! Went on a 2 hour guided tour of Leicester's sorting office which handles 1 million letters every day. Leicester is one of 80 mechanised letter offices, capable of sorting mail at a rate of 16,000 items per hour. It was absolutely fascinating.

Note – A tour which I organised from work for a small group of interested folk. Our post at work is special delivery each day & collected by van each afternoon. We saw the different stages a letter goes through, including mail being mechanically sorted.

28ᵗʰ February 1988 Sunday

"Sound of Music" – Coalville Amateurs' production this week and a sight never seen before, as the books of tickets are all reduced to stubs. A complete sell out! What a turn-up for the books! What a delight for yours truly, the Hon. Treasurer, who loves receiving all the money.

1st March 1988 Tuesday

"Forward, Master March!"

"Master March looked like Fasting itself, but carried his nose very high, for he was related to the "Forty Knights" and was a weather prophet. But that's not a profitable office & that's why he praised fasting." – So wrote Hans Christian Andersen.

3rd March 1988 Thursday

What a joy it is to bask in the glory of the success of Coalville Amateurs' "Sound of Music". There has never been a more popular show. Its magnetic appeal stems from the film which captivated everyone. People never tired of seeing it again & again.

Mary Blue saw the film 16 times.

5th March 1988 Saturday

And so we come to the end of Coalville Amateurs' most successful show "Sound of Music". How I love the world of music & drama.

What a moving experience to see the procession of nuns singing so superbly, from the back of the hall, up to the stage, & hear the mighty organ resounding.

7th March 1988 Monday

Joanne's birthday! 14 years old today. She now knows exactly where she wants to go in life. She has decided she would like to train to be a hairdresser, and is plotting her school career accordingly.

Later this year she will transfer from Ibstock School to Ashby, & will be able to attend Coalville Technical College.

9th March 1988 Wednesday

"Gastroenteritis in Coalville" – A letter from Dr. G. M. Morgan, Specialist in Community Medicine (Environmental Health) Leicestershire Health Authority, Princess House, Leicester. "Dear Miss Hewes, As you may be aware, a number of people have developed gastroenteritis following performances of the Sound of Music. I am attempting to identify the cause of the episode & would be very grateful for your help. Could you please complete the enclosed questionnaire ….."

About 100 people were ill after eating food at the Amateurs' buffet. I did not attend the late night buffet on Friday 4th March, which seemed to be the cause of the Coalville Amateurs' outbreak of gastroenteritis. I was at the Saturday afternoon tea, provided by the same caterers & the questionnaire covers both.

"Please answer (detailed questions) whether or not you were ill."

15th March 1988 Tuesday

Aunt Dos, who celebrated her 86th birthday on Sunday, has not ventured outside again since she attended cousin Don's funeral 3 weeks ago.

She is distressed because she has lost so many of her belongings (usually hidden by herself) and is for ever telephoning the police.

17th March 1988 Thursday

My dad's birthday! He would now be 99. I think of the day he was born and consider all that has happened since then. It reminds me of the time when God spoke to Job. (Job, Chapter 38)

"Where wast thou when I laid the foundations of the earth? … declare if thou knowest it all."

19th March 1988 Saturday

Man's inhumanity to man was seen on the television news screen today as two British soldiers serving in Northern Ireland were attacked & killed. Like a pack of angry wolves, a mob of about 100 young men cornered them in their car, dragged them out, stripped them & beat them to death.

Never have I seen such scenes reported on the television news as the "Murder Most Foul" of the two British soldiers serving in Northern Ireland. They were Corporal Derek Wood, aged 24, and Corporal David Howes, aged 23, of the Royal Corps of Signals. We saw them battered to death.

I thought of Christ at the mercy of an incensed mob, as I watched Corporal Derek Wood, a fine young man in the prime of life, dressed in his casual civilian clothing, torn to pieces by his attackers & left naked except for his underpants – left lying prostrate with arms outstretched, as one crucified.

25th March 1988 Friday

Cocky telephoned from Lancaster Prison at 7.30 p.m. He was on duty until 9 p.m. & we had a long heart to heart chat. He is the only one I can communicate with "heart to heart".

He told me that Yvonne has fixed her wedding for 21st May, & will be honeymooning in the Seychelles.

27th March 1988 Palm Sunday

The lesson at church this evening was from Isaiah, Chapter 53. Written 6 centuries before Christ, it tells of His dreadful sufferings & death. "……a man of sorrows and acquainted with grief. He was cut off out of the land of the living. He hath poured out his soul unto death."

29th March 1988 Tuesday

What a lovely day for G.O.M.B.'s Branch Liaison Officer today, organising for the whole Branch a photographic session. First we all assembled on the front steps of the building for a big group photograph & then a pre-arranged progress from laboratory to laboratory showing the scientists & gas meter testing staff at work.

The Government's Central Office of Information in London contacted a local Wigston photographer to take photographs of our staff at work, to accompany an article to be printed in the Department of Energy's latest journal, "Power-Points". We all felt highly honoured to belong.

2nd April 1988 Saturday

On 2nd April 1805, Hans Christian Andersen was born. I have been reading the story of his life (written by himself) and find in him a kindred spirit. He and I have so very much in common, you would think we had been cast in the same mould, to share so many identical experiences.

3rd April 1988 Easter Sunday

The Collect for Easter Sunday – Almighty God, who through thine only-begotten son Jesus Christ hast overcome death & opened unto us the gate of everlasting life; we humbly beseech thee, that as by thy special grace preventing us thou dost put into our minds good desires, so by thy continual help, we may bring the same to good effect."

The preacher on Easter Sunday stressed the "good desires" which are put into our minds by God's special grace "pre-venting" us – i.e. going before us. He spoke of the "continual help" which God gives to us all to enable us to bring the same to good effect.

8th April 1988 Friday

Cousin Johnty, now aged 84, is enjoying the benefits of his £50,000 inherited from his sister Madge. (Her £100,000 estate was divided equally between her 2 surviving brothers Eric & John.) Johnty has bought himself a new bungalow & I have acquired the settee, which he did not wish to take with him.

10th April 1988 Sunday

"Cavalleria Rusticana" – Watched on television a superb film of this hot-blooded opera which includes the "Easter Hymn". It was this piece of music which moved me to tears when I first heard it. (15th May 1987). How uplifting to see the grand procession to church, while this music was playing.

12th April 1988 Tuesday

Mr Mordechai Vanunu, aged 34, worked for 10 years as a nuclear technician. He then resigned for ideological reasons. He broke the Israel Official Secrets Act to tell the world that his country has stockpiled the world's 6th largest armoury of nuclear warheads. The Israeli Government firmly denies this.

Peace activists in Israel have taken Mr Mordechai Vanunu's revelations as proof that Israel does have the Atom Bomb & have nominated him the Nobel Peace Prize. However, like Christ, he has been subjected to a supposed "trial" in Jerusalem, accused of treason & jailed for 18 years.

16th April 1988 Saturday

Cocky telephoned from Lancaster Prison at 12 noon. He was on duty until 4 p.m. and we had a short chat. He told me that he will retire from work on his 60th birthday – January 1990.

It is the most amazing thing to share life with someone into your twenties & then renew contact 30 years later.

18th April 1988 Monday

"Brian Lamming, whose name is engraved on my heart, is constantly in my thoughts, although I never see him at all these days." – This is what I wrote in my diary 20 years ago.

"Cocky now lives in Lancashire, so I never see him & rarely give him a thought." – This is what I wrote in July 1973.

20th April 1988 Wednesday

Russian troops invaded Afghanistan in January 1980 & there has been fighting there ever since.

Russia & America have now signed a peace deal, promising to refrain from any form of interference or intervention in this war-torn land, after 15th February next year. There are five million Afghan refugees.

22nd April 1988 Friday

The world's longest hi-jack came to a peaceful end this week in Algiers. The 16 day ordeal began when a Jumbo jet from Bangkok to Kuwait was threatened by gun-men aboard – diverted to Cyprus, 2 passengers killed & others threatened with death unless demands were met. Demands were not met.

24th April 1988 Sunday

"La Traviata" – (meaning the lost woman, i.e. the one who has gone astray) Verdi's opera founded on Alexandre Dumas' novel "La Dame aux Camelias" based on incidents in his life, was shown on television.

Violetta Valery, a Parisian lady of easy virtue, meets Alfredo Germont, who loves her truly.

26th April 1988 Tuesday

Katherine Sullivan is 84 today.

Having lived for 20 years in India in the days of the Maharajahs, & as one who talks of "the Princess" as the most natural thing, she loaned me her latest book "The Maharajahs of India" which I find most enlightening. Once there were 565 ruling Princes.

How magnificent were the great Princes of India, before Prime Minister Mrs Ghandi removed their titles in 1972. They were rich beyond belief, with diamonds & pearls, rubies & emeralds. One of the Princes, the Maharajah Dhuleep Singh, owned the Koh-i-noor diamond. The British seized it in 1849.

30th April 1988 Saturday

"I felt like a King!" – This is what Cocky told me today when he spoke to me on the telephone from Lancaster Prison. He had been to try on his top hat & tails ready for Yvonne's wedding in 3 weeks time.

Jonathan, however, aged 14, was rather too embarrassed to feel like a Prince.

2nd May 1988 Monday

"Soon we shall be sharing one parson with Packington & Normanton-le-Heath." This is what I wrote in my diary exactly 6 years ago. However, this has now changed. Legal aspects are now going ahead in preparation for the creation of a different merger – Ravenstone and Swannington.

4th May 1988 Wednesday

The London Marathon this year was won by Henryk Jorgensen from Denmark.

I thought of Hans Andersen who once wrote, "And those whose names end with "sen", said she, they cannot be anything at all. One must put ones arms akimbo & keep them at a great distance, these "sen".

6th May 1988 Friday

What a jolly gathering we had for the Silver Wedding Anniversary of David & Irene. Cousin David (Enid's brother) lives in a lovely bungalow right in the country at Normanton-le-Heath. All the happy Hewesies were making each other laugh & we were all recalling fond memories of childhood.

8th May 1988 Rogation Sunday

Rogation Sunday teaches us God's great commandment (Deut. Chap. 6) – Thou shalt love the Lord thy God with all thine heart, and with all thy soul, and with all thy might. When Christ quoted these words, he added – Thou shalt love the Lord thy God with all thy mind. (Mark. Chapter 12)

10th May 1988 Tuesday

Tina, the Golden Labrador who never recovered from the sudden death of her master (Cousin Don), died today. I called to see Phyl, Don's widow, as she nursed the sick dog, no longer able to stand or walk unaided. How sad & lonely Phyl was feeling without Don, & now without Tina.

12 May 1988 Thursday

A day in London! I attended the Civil Service Benevolent Fund Annual General Meeting at the Institute of Education, University of London, 20 Bedford Way, London W.C.1. Within easy walking distance from St. Pancras, I had a most enjoyable day, returning at 4.30 p.m. on the "Master Cutler".

14th May 1988 Saturday

"We will be playing Happy Families" – so said Lesley, Cousin Don's daughter, now separated from her husband John Sear. John, however, will be returning briefly this week to celebrate the 21st birthday of their eldest daughter, Ruth. Mother, father & 3 daughters will be dining out together.

16th May 1988 Monday

The prison population in England & Wales increases every year. It has now reached 50,000. The prison system is designed to hold 44,000. Leicester prison was built to hold 200 prisoners but now has a record 435. The overcrowding in prisons is now a major problem.

Most of our prisons were built in the last century & are in urgent need of improved access to sanitation. The government therefore is planning the biggest prison building programme this century. There will be 26 new prisons and also major improvements to many of the existing ones.

20th May 1988 Friday

F. A. Cup Final this year brought the mighty Liverpool team back to Wembley, confident of clinching another double – League Championship plus the Cup. However, underdogs Wimbledon beat the Merseyside giants 1 – 0. Wimbledon's hero goalkeeper & captain Dave Beasant received the trophy.

21st May 1988 Saturday Cocky & Joan's daughter

Yvonne, aged 26, marries David Bond.

22nd May 1988 Whit Sunday

"God, who as at this time didst teach the hearts of thy faithful people, by the sending to them the light of thy Holy Spirit; grant us by the same spirit to have a right judgement in all things, and evermore to rejoice in his holy comfort ...." Again we are reminded of the joyful collect for Whit Sunday.

"And we know that all things work together for good to them that love God." (Romans 8. 28.)

This is the great & glorious lesson appointed to be read every Whitsunday. The preacher at Ravenstone Church chose this as his text at our 6 o'clock service today.

26th May 1988 Thursday

Cocky telephoned from Lancaster Prison at 7.15 a.m.

"Are you all right?" I asked, and he proceeded to tell me that neither he nor Joan had been able to attend Yvonne's wedding last Saturday. At the last minute Joan knew that she simply dare not face it & Cocky stayed to comfort her.

What turmoil of emotions for everyone concerned on Yvonne's wedding day. And yet the depth of anguish turned Cocky from a King to a Saint.

As my beloved Provost once said, "Where there is suffering there is love; and where there is love there is suffering." (See August 28th 1966)

29th May 1988 Trinity Sunday

"And it came to pass after three days they found him in the temple, sitting in the midst of the doctors, both hearing them and asking them questions" – St. Luke 2. 46.

And yet another example of the "three-in-one" trademark of God. This was when the child Jesus was twelve years old.

30th May 1988 Monday

"Glasnost & Peristroika" – These are 2 Russian words we hear a lot about these days as their leader Mr. Gorbachev tries to encourage his people to behave more like individuals than mass produced puppets. Journalists are now free to express more of their own thoughts.

Little has changed in Russia during the past 40 years. Prices set then are still the same today, but they bear no relation to the true value of things. Metro & bus fares are a standard fixed amount & everyone receives the same wages. But Peristroika means reconstruction, renewal & regeneration.

Peristroika in Russia is developing very slowly. Old habits die hard.

As one Russian said, "It may take another 40 years to reach the Promised Land. Moses himself could have reached the Promised Land in 5 years, but it took 40 years because it was something to be remembered for all time."

5th June 1988 Sunday

The Civil Service Benevolent Fund, Leicestershire Area Committee's Annual Bazaar was held yesterday. This is, in effect, a glorified rummage sale. You never saw anything like it when they open the doors. Like a horde of locusts they charge in to grab the best.

7th June 1988 Tuesday

Two members of our staff who work in Scotland – one Admin Officer from the Area Gas Examiner's Office in Glasgow and one Admin Officer from the Petroleum Measurement Inspector's Office in Aberdeen will be coming to our office at Wigston next week to see what work is done there.

9th June 1988 Thursday

Our A.O.s from Scotland will arrive at Birmingham Airport where they will meet each other for the first time. I therefore made a special trip to Birmingham Airport to find out exactly what it is like inside to determine where to advise them to meet.

I decided "underneath the digital clock".

11th June 1988 Saturday

Spent the whole day listening to the taped record of the recent meeting held at work by the Area Gas Examiners, and wrote in detail what they said, in order to compile the minutes of the meeting. I find all these meetings most enlightening & learn such a lot from these men of science, who are so clever.

13th June 1988 Monday

How I have enjoyed making all the arrangements for our two A.O.s in Scotland to visit G.O.M.B. Wigston. I arranged travel by air; taxi to & from the airport; hotel accommodation; & the full programme of talks by the Area Gas Examiners, the Gas Meter Examiners & 3 different Senior Scientific Officers.

15th June 1988 Wednesday

And a good time was had by all. It was most rewarding to hear everyone say how much they had enjoyed the in-house training given at G.O.M.B. Those who gave the talks enjoyed the experience as much as those who listened.

In the evening we had a social get-together & the weather was perfect.

17th June 1988 Friday

"We heard it on the grape-vine" – What the Scottish Area Gas Examiner said about the Chief Gas Examiner reached the ears of the retired Scottish Gas Examiner, now living in Western Australia, who passed it on to another retired Gas Examiner on the other side of Australia & the message got back to G.O.M.B.

19th June 1988 Sunday

Archimedes' principle states that when a body is wholly or partially immersed in a fluid, the upthrust is equal to the weight of the fluid displaced. Good old Archimedes, who lived circa 287 – 212 B.C. is often referred to in the work of gas & oil measurement. This made quite an impression on our A.O.s from Scotland.

21st June 1988 Tuesday

"Make his paths straight" – Matthew 3. 3.

I thought of John the Baptist, as I struggled single-handed to remove all the old blue paving bricks from our entry & replace them with 48 small slabs, which ended up anything but straight. I called on the expert assistance of Mr. Jarram.

23rd June 1988 Thursday

Microwave Oven!

Most people these days have a microwave oven, & as in November 1986 with a colour television, I can say again that I have joined the ranks. I bought a Sharp's Carousel II, one cubic foot capacity, i.e. 345mm wide, 217mm high & 364mm deep, reduced from £200 to £180.

25th June 1988 Saturday

Mary Blue's daughter Karen, who lives in Bedford and hardly knows me, celebrates her 18th birthday tomorrow. I sent her a birthday card which said, "Wouldn't you be surprised to open this card and find a £50 note inside?" As you may guess, I placed inside the card a £50 note.

27th June 1988 Monday

A change in world climate of a sort not rivalled in the history of civilisation was predicted today at an international conference held in Toronto. "The Changing Atmosphere Conference" was attended by 350 experts from 40 different countries. Leading climatologists warned that the greenhouse effect is here. (See 10th April 1980).

Global air pollution is causing the greenhouse effect on earth. Gases, such as carbon dioxide produced by fossil fuels & chlorofluorocarbons (which also damage the ozone layer) accumulate in the atmosphere, trapping infra-red radiation & heating the earth, causing shifts in rainfall patterns & a rise in sea levels.

Britain may cool, as a result of the "greenhouse effect" which will bring increased warming at the poles. This in turn will reduce the thermal gradient between the equator & the high latitude regions. It will change the global pattern of winds, ocean currents – such as the warming Gulf Stream - & rainfall.

3rd July 1988 Sunday

The Lambeth Conference takes place once every 10 years. While University of Kent students are on holiday their place will be taken by 600 Anglican Bishops and Archbishops from all over the world. They will be meeting in Canterbury for 3 weeks from 16th July to 7th August.

5th July 1988 Tuesday

American warships sent to the Persian Gulf to keep the peace in the volatile Middle East, shot down in error an Iranian passenger jet, killing 298 passengers & crew, including 66 children. The Ayatollah Khomeini rose from his sick bed to call for revenge on America & her allies.

7th July 1988 Thursday

The world's worst ever oil rig disaster took place last night in the North Sea when a gas explosion wrecked the Alpha platform in the Piper Field, 120 miles north-east of Aberdeen.

There were 228 men on the platform & only 64 survived, many of those badly burned in the inferno. (See 31st March 1980).

Not only were there 164 oil workers burned to death on the 34,000 ton, £600 million oil rig Piper Alpha, but 2 rescuers died when their fragile dinghy was engulfed by a fireball.

The scream of escaping gas which was heard before the dreadful explosion was likened to the wail of a banshee from hell.

11th July 1988 Monday

Alan Norris, who shares the same room with me at work, suffers from Retinitis Pigmentosa and finds it easier to work with a computer than with pen & paper. He has therefore been given a new £2,000 computer & word processor, which I have been delighted to have a go with & try to learn.

13th July 1988 Wednesday

Tomorrow is my birthday – aged 57.

Another "Golden Number" – Three times nineteen. I have now completed 3 Metonic Cycles of 19 years.

Remember Meton, the Greek astronomer who discovered that the great planets move in a set pattern lasting 19 years? (See 13th July 1969)

15th July 1988 Friday

Cocky telephoned from Lancaster Prison early in the morning yesterday to say "Happy Birthday". He sent me, via Interflora, a bouquet of flowers to say "Happy Birthday, all my love J", and he sent me a birthday card to say "Happy Birthday, I will always love you for ever. xxxxx." You would hardly believe that Cocky & I have not seen each other for years & years. We seem to be closer to each other than many who are married. We speak the same language, share the same thoughts & can communicate involuntarily, by telepathy, as if our hearts are linked in some way by a "heart telephone".

19th July 1988 Tuesday

As a direct result of the jolly gathering of all the Hewes' cousins at David & Irene's Silver Wedding in May this year, Evelyn organised another get-together this evening for 16 of us. In spite of all the tears shed over the past 12 months by some of those assembled, we had another jolly evening together.

Cousin Don's beautiful grand-daughter, Ruth aged 21, had a boyfriend who was killed on a racing motorcycle. In due course she had a new boyfriend & he too has been killed on a racing motorcycle. All the tears shed by the cousins have been associated with the problems of "man-woman relationship".

Cousin Don's widow Phyl was devastated by his sudden death, but manages to smile through her tears. Lesley, his daughter, was shattered when her husband John Sear left her for another woman, but can still make us all laugh. Mary Blue, stunned by two divorces, can also contribute to a jovial gathering.

25th July 1988 Monday

"I hope the house will be a blessing and not a burden to you," said my Mum in 1981, when she signed the property over to me. As I mentioned before (17th February 1983) the rear quarters are in a sorry state, but help is at hand. The government are offering considerable financial aid for "home improvement".

27th July 1988 Wednesday

Received from N. W. Leicestershire District Council the necessary forms to apply for House Repairs Grant. I did not like the idea of signing, "I hereby certify that I intend that, on or before the first anniversary of the certified date & for the following 4 years, the dwelling will be my only residence – occupied exclusively by me."

"Housing Act 1974 – Section 60" – Certificate of future occupation – to accompany application for house renovation grant … "Your application for grant approval should be made within 6 months from the date of this letter."

To sign or not to sign? That is the question.

31st July 1988 Sunday

"Finally, be ye all of one mind, having compassion one of another." I Peter, 3. 8. The preacher spoke of the need for us all to show compassion. We are all God's children and we are all on a journey through life, as it were from Jerusalem to Jericho, where we may be like the priest, the Levite, or the Good Samaritan.

2nd August 1988 Tuesday

"They looked like twins" – this is how Cocky described Yvonne & Jonathan when he was telling me about the wedding photos he has now obtained from Yvonne's wedding in May.

Cocky is a twin. He has a twin sister. My Mum was a twin. Long, long ago I wondered if I might have twins.

4th August 1988 Thursday

Mary Moore, now aged 77, has not been 100% fit since the slight stroke she had last year. Nevertheless she hoped to be able to make her annual pilgrimage to Ravenstone & meet once again her many friends; but when the time, came she decided after all, not to attempt the journey.

6th August 1988 Saturday

August 6th is the day the church remembers "the transfiguration of our Lord". (See Luke, Chapter 9.) Peter said to Jesus, "Master, it is good for us to be here." Our preacher at church chose this text for us to remember, not only today, but every time we attend a place of worship.

8th August 1988 Monday

On the eighth day of the eighth month of the 88th year, Katherine aged 84, and I enjoyed a sunlit afternoon in the peace and beauty of a Monastery Garden. Brother Gabriel gave us permission to wander through the private grounds & into the walled graveyard.

10th August 1988 Wednesday

"Improving Management in Government" – The latest recommendation is that the Executive functions of Government, as distinct from Policy Advice, should be carried out by units known as "Agencies". Each agency will be accountable to a Minister, who will in turn be accountable to Parliament.

Ministers have been asked to identify functions & administrative services that are right for an agency. The Driver & Vehicle Licensing Centre (D.V.L.C.) at Swansea plus all Motor Licence Offices will be one of the first agencies. D.V.L.C. has been chosen because it is an autonomous unit.

14th August 1988 Sunday

How lovely it was to hear the bells of Lancaster Priory, coming to me through the telephone, when Cocky rang me from the prison. I hear such a variety of background sounds. Sometimes I hear the clank of keys, sometimes all the alarm bells ringing, & other noises off.

16th August 1988 Tuesday

Joanne, aged 14, has now virtually severed all links with me. She is fully engrossed with the thrills & excitement of teenage romance. How beautiful she looks in full make-up and carefully tended hair as she sets off to charm and capture the heart of many local young men.

18th August 1988 Thursday

"The Winthrop Woman" – Katherine loaned me this excellent book which tells the true life story of Elizabeth, born 1610, and whose own history, like mine, is commingled with national affairs. From Suffolk she sailed to a new life in the New World and experienced every possible human emotion.

20th August 1988 Saturday

"The Lord Mayor & councillors of the City of Leicester do hereby proclaim a special week of celebration to mark the 400th anniversary of Charter of Incorporation by Her Majesty Queen Elizabeth I and invite the people of Leicester & those who visit the city to attend and enjoy these festivities." Oyez!

What a "Year of Wonders" as long foretold, the year 1588 proved to be. It was then that one of the greatest victories in English history took place, when the Spanish Armada was defeated. And it was then that Queen Elizabeth I granted Leicester its charter, making it a Borough, & her motto became Leicester's.

24th August 1988 Wednesday

"Providence had meditated better things for me than I could possibly imagine myself." These are the words of Nathaniel Hawthorne (1804 – 1864) who became imbued with poetic sentiment at Longfellow's hearthstone & to whom I have just had the great pleasure of being introduced.

26th August 1988 Friday

And Old Maid Hewsie wept again when she received in the post from Cocky a photograph of Yvonne in her bridal outfit, looking lovingly into the eyes of her father. Cocky is the only one whose eyes I have ever looked into close enough to see myself reflected there.

28th August 1988 Sunday

"Some authors," wrote Nathaniel Hawthorne, "indulge themselves in such confidential depths of revelation as could fittingly be addressed, only and exclusively, to the one heart & mind of perfect sympathy, as if the printed book were certain to find out the divided segment & complete his circle of existence."

"But," continued Nathaniel Hawthorne, "as thoughts are frozen & utterance benumbed unless the speaker stand in some true relation with his audience, it may be pardonable to imagine that a friend is listening; & then we may prate of the circumstances that lie around us, but still keep the inmost **me** hidden."

As with Hans Christian Andersen, so with Nathaniel Hawthorne, I find myself in the company of a kindred spirit. Like me, he worked as an Executive Officer, but never considered it other than a transitory life. There was always a prophetic instinct, a low whisper in his ear, that one day a change would come.

3rd September 1988 Saturday

Cocky, who now belongs so very much to Lancashire, spoke to me of "home".

He was referring to Ravenstone, where he was born & bred. He was one of a large family – Nellie, Wilfred, Norman, Kathleen, Midge, Mavis & twins John & Betty. Midge is the only one still living in Ravenstone.

5th September 1988 Monday

Mary Moore, who thought about visiting me last month & then decided against it, is now hoping to try again this week.

A new train service is now in operation from Colchester to Leicester without having to change stations at London. All being well, she will be staying with me from 8th to 20th September.

7th September 1988 Wednesday

"Important Announcement – North West Leicestershire District Council – Refuse Collection. Dear Householder, In an effort to provide a cleaner healthier district, and a more efficient refuse collection service, N.W.L.D.C. has decided to extend the wheeled bin system, following successful trials in Coalville & Ashby.

"The Wheeled Bin System" – who benefits?

1. The Householder – no extra containers / boxes are needed. Larger capacity – 2 ½ times the capacity of your normal bin. 2. The environment – less rubbish dumped. 3. The operatives – no lifting. 4. The Local Authority.

11th September 1988 Sunday

Mary Moore arrived safely at Leicester Station on Thursday and is following her normal programme, on a reduced scale. No longer able to dash about, she spends a leisurely morning with a "lie-in" until lunchtime, and then visits friends & relations in the afternoon or early evening.

13th September 1988 Tuesday

Mary Moore & I visited Auntie Doris, now a sprightly 93 year-old, in her olde worlde cottage at Mountsorrel. Auntie Doris & Mary talked of the old days & of their numerous cousins & other relations, many of whom are only a name to me, but included my mum & her family.

15th September 1988 Thursday

As in August 1972, Auntie Cis was taken by ambulance, very much against her will, to the psychiatric hospital at Narborough, so in exactly the same circumstances her sister, Aunt Dos now aged 86, was whisked away today, protesting strongly that she was perfectly alright & not in need of help.

17th September 1988 Saturday

The XXIV Olympic Games are being held this year in South Korea. Watched on television the spectacular opening ceremony, which drew on 7,000 years of history, and included the long march of 160 nations, like a global fashion show. Saw the Olympic torch lit & the flag paraded & hoisted.

18th September 1988 Sunday

A beautiful Ming vase was sold at Sotheby's, Hong Kong, for an all time record of £1,159,864.

It was made during the reign of the Hongwu Emperor, the first of the Ming Dynasty. (Circa 1370 A.D.)

The Ming Dynasty in China spanned from 1368 A.D. to 1644 A.D. What a wonderful history China has.

While Britain was illiterate, China's first Dynasty, the Ch'in Dynasty, 200 years Before Christ, had created a uniform and standardised written language – also built the Great Wall.

19th September 1988 Monday

Brother Pat, aged 70, Mary Blue, aged 44, & I, aged 57, visited Aunt Dos, aged 86, in the psychiatric hospital and were agreeably surprised to find her in a more contented frame of mind.

We walked with her in the grounds and sat out of doors in a pleasant sheltered little alcove.

23rd September 1988 Friday

Another major fire aboard a North Sea oil rig yesterday resulted in the death of one man, radio operator Timothy Williams, aged 25, of Kent. He remained at his post sending out urgent messages while the other 66 men took to the lifeboats to escape from the stricken oil rig, Ocean Odessy.

When I heard on the television news about the fire on the oil rig, Ocean Odessy, the name Timothy Williams brought to mind immediately the 9 year-old Timothy Williams in my Sunday School class. (See 24th July 1977) How pleased he was to see his name in the Bible.

My little 9 year-old Timothy Williams would now be aged 20. The radio operator Timothy Williams was aged 25. I thought at first they were possibly one & the same person. And so, although totally unknown to me, I was very much aware of the death of this young man.

29th September 1988 Thursday

The two wells in our backyard at 27 Leicester Road, Ravenstone, are to be filled in. I could never leave this house without ensuring their safety.

The estimate states, "To totally fill up both wells with 20 tons of mill waste & rubble; to then clear any rubbish left – total price £188-20p.

1st October 1988 Saturday

"I long for a kindred spirit to communicate with freely and find at the end of a perfect day, the soul of a friend." These were my longings exactly 20 years ago, when Cocky seemed gone for ever and Brian Lamming simply did not wish to know me.

Where, I wonder, will we all be 20 years hence?

3rd October 1988 Monday

The Venerable T. H. Jones, Archdeacon of Loughborough, was the preacher at our Patronal Festival held at St. Michael & All Angels, Ravenstone.

Every hymn, every prayer, the Psalm, the lessons and the sermon spoke of God's Angels, until we felt one with the whole company of heaven.

"And behold a ladder set up on the earth & the top of it reached to heaven; & behold the Angels of God ascending & descending on it."

The Archdeacon said that the Angels go up & down. They do not come down & up. They are with us down below & go up for help from heaven to mortals below.

7th October 1988 Friday

Received in the post from Cocky twelve postcard size colour photos taken of Yvonne's Wedding Day. Although Cocky & Joan did not actually go to the church, they were able to be photographed with Yvonne in her own home; & so I now know what they all look like, including Joan & Jonathan.

Yvonne and Jonathan certainly do look like twins. Both have thick dark straight hair & identical features.

Their mother Joan, aged 53, looks bright-eyed, bonny & well preserved, while poor old Cocky, aged 58, with dark rings under his eyes, looks as though he has taken a bashing.

11th October 1988 Tuesday

I have just completed the most unusual job – knocked down an indoor wall, all by myself with the help of a sledge-hammer, & made a clearway from the old back pantry, through the old outside toilet to the backyard. This entailed six consecutive visits to the council tip – toilet and all.

13th October 1988 Thursday

Now that I have removed the outside toilet, I can bring under cover for the winter my new giant-size "wheeled bin" & also my wheelbarrow. The door to the old toilet is so rotten that it must be replaced, as the wind blows straight through now into the house. That is the next priority.

15th October 1988 Saturday

The Reverend John Hewes, Uncle Charlie's son, who was ordained at Canterbury Cathedral in July 1981, and whom we have not seen for years, came knocking on my door today to say, "Hello." Just like Cousin Johnty (February 1967) and just like Cocky (August 1987) he was the 3rd John to return to me.

17th October 1988 Monday

When house-holder Hewsie saw grass growing out of the guttering above her bedroom window she took immediate action & responded to the following advertisement –

"If you'd like your guttering cleaned out ready for winter, telephone Loughborough 213139."

A bucketful of silt was removed.

19th October 1988 Wednesday

How very poorly we found Aunt Dos this evening when we visited her in hospital. She sat in an armchair beside her bed & looked too ill to be out of bed. She hardly spoke. Her only words were, "Lift me up" – "Don't leave me" – and "Pray for me." She has slowly grown worse since being in hospital.

21st October 1988 Friday

And again the people of Sevenoaks, Kent, have discovered that they are only the people of One Oak. The replacement saplings planted last December have been destroyed by vandals. But plans are ahead to replace the saplings with more mature trees, hopefully able to survive.

23rd October 1988 Sunday

Aunt Dos is now looking & feeling much better after being given a life-support drip feed. She was found to be dehydrated after virtually refusing all food & drink. Severe constipation had made her very ill & she had been quite sick as well, but now she is full of praise for all the nurses.

25th October 1988 Tuesday

"Garabandal" – This is another book loaned to me by Ted Ludlow. It tells the story of the appearance of the Blessed Virgin Mary to four children in San Sebastian de Garabandal, Spain, during the years 1961 – 1965. The children's names were Conchita, Loli, Jacinta and Marie Cruz.

The Virgin Mary told Conchita that there would be only

three more Popes after Pope John XXIII. That means that everything must happen within the reign of the present Pope, John Paul II. First there will be "the warning" – an event unique in the history of mankind, & then there will be "the miracle".

29th October 1988 Saturday
Long, long ago, Cocky was my sweetheart. Now, 40 years on, he has a wife & family of his own & I am more like "the other woman". He phones me two or three times a week and I still think of him as my sweetheart, but we never make any plans to meet each other; & love each other from afar.

31st October 1988 Monday
Cashless shopping is slowly creeping up on us all. I have now acquired from Lloyds Bank the latest "payment card". It can be used to draw cash from Lloyds 2,000 Cashpoints, plus the cash dispensers of other banks; but can also be "swiped" through an electronic terminal when shopping without cash.

2nd November 1988 Wednesday
In November 1961 I bought a beautiful new winter coat with a lovely warm fox collar. It gave 16 years wonderful service. Imagine my surprise today when I saw in a second hand shop in Leicester a replica of this very coat, as good as new, which I bought for £8.

4th November 1988 Friday
To complement my new (second-hand) coat, I have now bought a lovely Cossack-style black astrakhan hat - £14. Not only did the hat cost more than the coat, so did the gloves at £11. My most expensive item of clothing to date is my sheep-skin coat at £160 in 1982.

6th November 1988 Sunday
"You ain't seen nothing yet!" – the catchphrase of Ronald Reagan, America's President from 1980 – 1988, has been taken up by Margaret Thatcher, British Prime Minister for the last 9 years and still going strong. "Ten more years!" is the boast of her ardent supporters, who regard her as some sort of super-woman.

8th November 1988 Tuesday
64 year-old George Bush was today elected as America's 41st President. Mr Bush, now officially president-elect, is a Republican with a quarter-century in politics and eight years apprenticeship as Vice-President during President Reagan's term of office. His inauguration will be in January 1989.

10th November 1988 Thursday
The streets of Ravenstone are all being paved with beautiful new kerbing stones & the work has reached our house. I asked the workmen if I might have a lower kerb in order to drive up to the front window & they have obliged. So, after all, it was as well that I had to quit next door for car parking in April last year.

Although I was prompted to have the front garden converted into car-parking space, I have continued to park in Aunt Dos's drive since I was allowed to return there in May 1987. However, I may have to vacate the drive at any time, if Aunt Dos is not well enough to live there again.

14th November 1988 Monday
Like a judge, I sat and listened again at work to two sides of a reported incident. (See 25th February 1985). This time, Maurice the volatile messenger had upset Senior Scientific Officer Vijay – the one imbued with the peace of the Buddha. You could not imagine two more opposite types.

16th November 1988 Wednesday
"European Single Market" – This is aimed for 1992, and all business men are asked to start preparing now. Some 200 measures have already been agreed, including the mutual recognition of professional qualifications. Future measures include public procurement, financial services and standards.

18th November 1988 Friday
Having worked at "Gas Standards" I know all about British Standards. Now we have to prepare more & more for European Standards.

As China became great through a uniform & standardised system for everything, so Europe hopes to have everything interchangeable by 1992.

20th November 1988 Sunday
"Tranquillisers" prescribed by doctors for the past 20 years have brought more sorrow & depression than ever they have cured. Valium was one such "anti-depression" tablet prescribed to my poor old Mum. The powerful "Ativan" prescribed to Cocky's wife Joan has had a devastating effect on her for years.

There are believed to be one million people in Britain on tranquillisers. One man whose life was wrecked for 17 years by tranquillisers has now formed a group in Leicester to help people get away from tranquillisers. He is Cyril Capenerhurst, founder member of Tranx-Leics. Tranx-Leics support group meet at 32 De Montfort St., Leicester (Tel – 555600). One of the members who got hooked on the powerful Ativan is Mrs Meg Machin. She says, "I was on Ativan for 18 months & getting off it is worse than coming off heroin – it was horrific."

The effect of these so-called "tranquillisers" is as follows – Your life is in ruins. Your powers of concentration evaporate. You develop phobias about going into shops; sometimes you cannot walk straight & think you are going mad. You are dizzy, disoriented & have dreadful aching limbs.

Cocky's wife Joan imagines such frightening things sometimes that Cocky has to stay & comfort her instead of going to work. Sometimes he is called home from work. Sometimes Joan has dreadful nightmares. Cocky does all the housework, the cooking, the washing, the shopping & the ironing.

30th November 1988 Wednesday
Aristotle Socrates Onassis, possibly the richest man in the world when he died 15th March 1975, left the bulk of his fortune to his daughter's son, **not then born or even conceived**.

His daughter Christina died this month, aged 37, leaving no son but a 3 year-old daughter, Athina, to inherit the fortune.

2nd December 1988 Friday
Christina Onassis died from "pulmonary edema" or fluid

in the lungs. But actually she died of a broken heart. Four times married, her only true love was her 4th husband Thierry Roussel. She loved him truly, but he did not truly love her. Married in 1984, divorced in 1987, she never stopped loving him.

4th December 1988 Sunday

"Gather up the fragments that remain that nothing be lost." John 6. 12.

The preacher emphasised this aspect of the story of the feeding of the 5,000. The fragments refer also to mankind. No-one is lost to God. All who have been broken in heart or mind are equally precious in the sight of God.

6th December 1988 Tuesday

Sometimes I feel very much like one of the "fragments that remain". In this world of happy families and partnerships, I do not belong anywhere. Cocky is the only person in the world who loves me, but he is not mine, and I wander alone like a lost sheep, seemingly lost but ever hopeful of being truly found.

8th December 1988 Thursday

After 12 weeks in hospital – first in Carlton Hayes, then in Leicester City General, and finally in Coalville's new hospital, Aunt Dos returned home yesterday (on Jonathan's fifteenth birthday). But oh, how frail & helpless she is. With failing eyesight she feels afraid to be left on her own.

10th December 1988 Saturday

How sad to see Aunt Dos, now a helpless old woman. In complete contrast I see Joanne, on the threshold of young womanhood, so exquisitely beautiful, and I think – this once was Aunt Dos. I wonder what God thinks of all his children as he watches their progress year by year & century by century?

12th December 1988 Monday

"Shall the thing formed say to him that formed it, why hast thou made me thus?" Romans 9.

God is a Spirit and "The Spirit itself beareth witness with our spirit that we are the children of God." Romans 8. 16. God sees all his children not as we are in human form, but as heavenly children.

14th December 1988 Wednesday

After only one week struggling against all the odds, alone in her own home, Aunt Dos has now returned to the care of the hospital. Three months ago she protested strongly that she did not require hospital care. This time she insisted that she ought never to have been sent home.

16th December 1988 Friday

Snibston School Christmas Concert - another nostalgic return to Snibston School with Joanne's mum, to see 9 year-old Stuart on stage. As the little children, in single file, passed by me down the centre aisle, looking more like cherubs & angels, I thought how sad to have to grow old & decrepit.

18th December 1988 Sunday

How good to see Ravenstone Church filled to overflowing for the candle-lit Carol Service. The Christmas Carol which touched me most deeply this year was, "It Came upon the Midnight Clear." Never before have the words been brought to life so vividly, as I literally saw myriads of angels coming to earth.

"For lo! The days are hastening on, by prophet bards foretold, when with the ever circling years, comes round the age of gold; when peace shall over all the earth its ancient splendours fling, and the whole world send back the song which now the angels sing!"

But man hears not the song of the angels.

22nd December 1988 Thursday

"Best wishes & love to the woman of my dreams" – So wrote Cocky to me last Christmas. And now Cocky has dreamed a dream, more real than any dream he has ever dreamed; so real that when he woke up he could hardly believe that it had not happened & that he & I were miles apart.

24th December 1988 Saturday

"With very special love at Christmas" – a Christmas card from Cocky to say "Merry Christmas darling. All my love. I wish I could be with you." And via Inter Flora, a bouquet of flowers to say "All my love J."

I wonder if Cocky & I actually met again, our love would be as wonderful as it appears in our dreams?

25th December 1988 Sunday

Christmas Day this year at Mary Blue's, where Mary Blue kindly entertained & provided for seven. There was Mary Blue & 14 year-old Scott. There was Murdo Junior in his early twenties, Pat & Evelyn, Aunt Dos, whom we collected from the hospital at mid-day & returned in the evening, and me.

28th December 1988 Wednesday
Steven's 21st Birthday!

Terry, his father, hosted a dinner party at The Mews, Ashby-de-la-Zouch for 18 of us.

What a banquet! And how lovely to see Steven looking so handsome, & to see Terry again after 17 years, now a prosperous middle-aged man with a lovely new 27 year-old wife.

30th December 1988 Friday

On the fifth day of Christmas, my true love sent to me a tiny heart-shaped silver locket & chain. Forty years ago he gave me a photograph of himself which I have kept & treasured all these years & which now fits perfectly (head & shoulders) into the locket.

And this is the man I chose not to marry.

* * *

Prayer for the Marian Year 1987 – 1988

Mother of Hope, Star of the Sea, sure consolation of the pilgrim people, guide our steps in our journey through life, so that we may walk along paths of peace and harmony, of progress, justice and freedom. Reconcile brothers and sisters; may hatred and rancour disappear, may divisions and barriers be overcome, may rifts be closed and wounds healed. May Christ be our Peace, may His pardon renew our hearts during this Marian Year.

Pope John Paul II

1989

1st January 1989 Sunday
"Why", you may ask, "do we now have a gardener's diary?" The answer is simply that Collins have changed the format & style of their five-year diaries, and & have tried in vain to find one like my others. As you can see, this was printed in 1973, and was the best I could find, anything like the others.

3rd January 1989 Tuesday
Treasurer Hewsie is in her element again receiving all the applications for tickets for Coalville Amateurs' forthcoming production "Charlie Girl". The recent closure of the Miners' Centre means that we now have a new venue, "King Edward VII Community College" where we can seat only 200 per night instead of 500. We have usually given 6 performances at our Annual Coalville Amateurs production. This has allowed for an audience capacity of 6 x 500 = 3,000. This year however, we are giving ten performances & will have 10 x 200 seating capacity = 2,000. Allocation of tickets will therefore require the wisdom of Solomon.

7th January 1989 Saturday
"Time, like an ever rolling stream, bears all its sons away. They fly forgotten as a dream dies at the opening day." Today I think of Brian Lamming – 61 today!
And in three weeks time Cocky will be 59. So we all progress towards the three score years & ten, allotted to man on earth.

9th January 1989 Monday
Tomorrow I shall be 21,000 days old. My 21st one in a thousand. This may indeed be 3,000 weeks, but remember the Glorious Qur-ăn, which tells us that the Night of Power is better than a thousand months, and also the teachings of Brahma (Hindu god), where one day & night of Brahma is 8,640 million years! And we learn from St. Peter in his Second Epistle that "one day is with the Lord as a thousand years, & a thousand years as one day." Psalm 90 also.

10th January 1989 Tuesday
A major air disaster last Sunday evening resulted in 44 people dead & 82 injured when a Boeing 737 from London to Belfast crashed on the M 1 at Kegworth in Leicestershire, just 500 yards short of the runway at East Midlands Airport. The pilot tried in vain to make an emergency landing at the airport.
The co-ordination of all the rescue teams – police, ambulance, fire service, motorists on the M 1, villagers from Kegworth, the Salvation Army, local priests & even a lifeboat crew from Withernsea on their way home, helped to save so many lives in the recent air disaster. They formed a human chain to pass the injured to the line of ambulances.
Catholic Moves – US Roman Catholic bishops modifying Scripture readings to be more considerate to women. Ballot at three-day meeting of 250 bishops at University of Notre Dame in Indiana expected to approve changes. Phrases such as "He who believes" will be changed to "Those who believe" and "Brethren" will become "Brothers and sisters."

11th January 1989 Wednesday

"Public Hall – Coalville – Grand Concert.
January 9th, 10th, 11th, and 12th.
Piano – Miss Hewes; American Organ – Mr G. H. Hewes; Conductor – Mr J. E. Hewes;
Programme printed by J. Hewes, Bookseller, Stationer, Printer, etc. Post Office, Coalville (for the last 30 years)"

All this was 100 years ago – 1889.

17th January 1989 Tuesday
The National Debt is now £171.3 billion. Ten years ago it was £79.2 billion. Twenty years ago it was £31.3 billion. It would appear that we go from bad to worse, but it does not seem to affect anybody. Each one has his own financial orbit.

19th January 1989 Thursday
To sign or not to sign? That was the question posed last July. I was given 6 months to decide & I have now signed on the dotted line. Mr Adams has given me an estimate to do the work (with the cheapest windows etc.) £4,500. So let it be written ... so let it be done.
Grant Works Estimate – Chimney stack £286. To level kitchen floor & asphalt £196. Three new windows (*middle room, kitchen & bathroom*) £680. New back door £235. Repoint gable & replace bricks £724. Re-render wall £300. Re-tile roof £1,694. Renew guttering & down pipe £146. Re-build outside out-house £239. Total - £4,500.

23rd January 1989 Monday
Freedom Day – Revolutionary leader Ayatollah Ruhollah Khomeini has pardoned 4,500 convicts on occasion of impending 10th anniversary of establishment of Islamic regime in Iran, official Islamic Republic News Agency reported.
Iran's leader, Ayatollah Khomeini, was reported to be dying 2 years ago. Last July he supposedly rose from his deathbed to call for revenge on America & her allies, but still he holds tremendous power in the world.

25th January 1989 Wednesday
America now has a new President.
Republican George Bush, aged 64, has been sworn in as 41st President. After President Reagan who had tremendous charm and charisma, George Bush in contrast seems rather "lack lustre".

27th January 1989 Friday
"I have to refer to your application for repairs grant in respect of 27 Leicester Road, Ravenstone, & enclose the formal approval of my Council to the making of a grant. The Council have determined £4,227 – 60p as being the amount of expenses eligible & the grant will be 60% = £2,536."

28th January 1989 Saturday
On this day in history – 814 – Emperor Charlemagne, King of the Franks and Holy Roman Emperor, died.
His embalmed body, 8 feet tall, was dressed in royal robes with crown and sceptre and he sat on a marble throne for 400 years until Frederick II had him buried in

a gold and silver casket in Aix la Chapelle.

29th January 1989 Sunday

As in June 1973, Auntie Cis tumbled out of bed at Carlton Hayes Hospital and was transferred to Leicester Royal Infirmary, so now Aunt Dos is in exactly the same predicament.

I think of Grandpa & Grandma Hewes & their lovely family life with eight children, but oh the suffering those children were to endure.

31st January 1989 Tuesday

Ravenstone's new Rector, The Revd. Kerry Emmett, his wife Tricia & 2 daughters, Elisabeth, aged 8, and Nesta, aged 6, have now taken up residence in the new Rectory, 9 Orchard Close, The Limes, Ravenstone.

For the first time ever, we are to have "The Joint Benefice of St. Michael & All Angels, Ravenstone with St. George, Swannington."

2nd February 1989 Thursday

Ravenstone Parish Magazine this month contains an introductory letter from the new Rector whose official licensing service takes place on Saturday, 4th February at Swannington.

He says, "..... We shall be very happy for you to call us Kerry and Tricia – rather than Rector & Mrs Emmett."

4th February 1989 Saturday

The "licensing" of the Revd. Kerry Emmett as Priest in Charge of the parishes of Ravenstone & Swannington took place during a power cut and was conducted therefore in the semi-darkness. I was reminded of Dr. Coggan (3rd October 1974) who under similar circumstances said, "The trouble with us – our light has gone out."

6th February 1989 Monday

"O God of unchangeable power and eternal light, look favourably on your whole church, that wonderful and sacred mystery; and by the tranquil operation of your perpetual providence carry out the work of man's salvation ...." – So began this moving prayer which formed part of Saturday's service.

8th February 1989 Wednesday

Auntie Dos, who has dominated brother Pat and me for the whole of our lives, watched our every move, and cross-examined us at every turn, now lies helpless in the Leicester Royal Infirmary, hardly aware that we visit her, but gradually acquiring an inner peace, as all her aggression dies.

10th February 1989 Friday

"Mark the perfect man, and behold the upright; for the end of that man is peace." Psalm 37.

I thought of these words, as Pat and I sat by the bedside of Aunt Dos. All her life she has upheld strong Christian principles and been a staunch "Methodist", & for her the end is peace.

12th February 1989 Sunday

I am delighted to say that allocation of tickets for "Charlie Girl" has been achieved with the maximum success.

Every-one was allowed a first, second & third choice of which evening they wished to attend, and by switching from one to another, we managed to accommodate all concerned.

14th February 1989 Tuesday

 "A heart for a heart; yours for mine; love for always to my Valentine" In the thirty-seventh year of the reign of Her Majesty Queen Elizabeth II, I received from my true love, for the very first time, a Valentine Card.

16th February 1989 Thursday

Cocky & I had a long heart to heart chat on the telephone. "Will you marry me?" he asked, knowing that he will never break his marriage vows to Joan & will never forsake her.

I thought of the words of St. Paul, "We then that are strong ought to bear the infirmities of the weak & not to please ourselves."

It was in April 1954 that Cocky & I vowed to each other that we would always love one another, but I would not leave my family to marry him. Now, one by one, my family have gone & I am left alone.

Cocky, who was not considered good enough for me, is the only one now who cares for me.

20th February 1989 Monday

"We've been together now for forty years!" – That is, Coalville Amateurs' & I. This year's production of Charlie Girl is my fortieth show. Brother Pat, currently House Manager, has been a member even longer. Now that he is aged 70 he has decided to "retire" this year.

22nd February 1989 Wednesday

Colonel Sir Andrew Martin has been the Lord Lieutenant of Leicestershire since 1965. Now aged 75, he is retiring from office and the new Lord Lieutenant will be Mr. Timothy Brooks, aged 59 of Wistow Hall with effect from 23rd April. The appointment lasts until the age of 75.

23rd February 1989 Thursday

Thought for the day – For ye shall go out with joy, and be led forth with peace; the mountains and the hills shall break forth before you into singing, and all the trees of the field shall clap their hands.
Isaiah 55, v 12, King James Bible

24th February 1989 Friday

A questionnaire to each house in the Parish of Ravenstone: - Address, Surname, Number in household, Number of children, Ages; Do you attend the Parish Church? Do you attend another church? If yes, which one? To help plan parish activities, would any of your family like to .....?

Clergy from all over the deanery assembled recently at Ravenstone Church. Then, two by two, they went to every household in the parish & delivered the questionnaire in preparation for the arrival of the new Rector. The last question on the questionnaire being, "Would you like a visit from the new Rector?"

25th February 1989 Saturday

Moore, Florence Annie, of 41 Station Road, Ratby, formerly of Coalville, passed peacefully away in hospital on February 25th aged 94 years. Funeral service and cremation at Gilroes Crematorium on Monday March 6th at 3.45 p.m. All flowers and inquiries to Ginns and Gutteridge Ltd., Funeral Directors of Leicester.

"Florrie Moore"

28th February 1989 Tuesday

Aunt Dos has now been transferred from the Leicester Royal Infirmary to Carlton Hayes Hospital, where she hovers between life and death. One day she is expected to die any minute and the next day she is well enough to be sitting with all the others in the sitting room.

1st March 1989 Wednesday

Evelyn is now in hospital. She was taken to Leicester City General with a perforated stomach ulcer. Brother Pat has not known which way to turn – worried about Evelyn, concerned about Aunt Dos, and anxious about his duties as House Manager for Coalville Amateurs' – opening night on Friday.

3rd March 1989 Friday

All the troubles of the world disappeared for a while as we revelled in the opening night of Coalville Amateurs' "Charlie Girl". The sheer magic of the stage lifted all our spirits. The mere smell of the empty stage before the audience arrives; the music, the laughter & the camaraderie all thrill me.

5th March 1989 Sunday

Mothering Sunday and our first united service at church with Swannington & Ravenstone. The Mothers Union banners of both churches were taken in procession up the aisle & the children from Swannington sang their "Hosanna" song. All the mothers received flowers from their children & one old maid wept alone.

7th March 1989 Tuesday

Joanne's birthday – 15 years old and a glamorous young lady – though still at school. I see very little of her now. Her world & mine are not the same any more and we each go our separate ways. It is a remarkable coincidence that Cocky's children have their birthdays 7th December and 7th June.

9th March 1989 Thursday

What a lovely week for my 40th show. How I enjoy being part of the front of "House" team. The theatre foyer itself this year allows us to line up in spectacular formation like a guard of honour, the men resplendent in evening dress & the ladies in black & white, with blue sashes.

11th March 1989 Saturday

And so we come to the end of our 1989 production "Charlie Girl". All the ladies on stage were sent bouquets & baskets of flowers. I saw them all arrayed in the reception area & thought of a great funeral; but one bouquet, a bouquet of red roses, came to me at home – "All my love, John."

13th March 1989 Monday

Aunt Dos is 87 today. Oh how frail & pathetic she looked propped up in the hospital reclining chair with her feet on the foot-stool. She was so pale & wan & could hardly keep her eyes open, but she was pleased to welcome her birthday visitors & with trembling hand, accepted chocolates offered to her.

15th March 1989 Wednesday

Cousin Johnty, aged 84, has bought a super de luxe relaxing therapy armchair. It cost well over £2,000 and is the most amazing chair I have ever sat in. In-built electrically controlled rollers literally massage up & down your whole body and send delightful shudders up & down your spine.

17th March 1989 Friday

In the year of our Lord 1889, exactly 100 years ago today, Reginald Arthur Hewes, my dad, was born. And in the year of our Lord 1939, fifty years ago, he died. I hardly knew him and yet I feel very much a part of him and sometimes, he appears so clearly to me in my dreams.

19th March 1989 Sunday

Evelyn is now making good progress at home after her brief spell in hospital with a perforated ulcer. She arrived home to masses of flowers from well-wishers & received lots of "Get Well" cards. Today is Mary Blue's birthday & this month is also Evelyn's birthday & Wedding Anniversary.

20th March 1989 Monday

On this day in history – 43BC – Ovid, Roman poet who wrote Medea, born in Sulmona.

21st March 1989 Tuesday

The first day of spring, but the weather is anything but gentle. It seems that March has decided to go out like a lion rather than like a lamb. Part of my fence has been bashed down; but overall, the winter has been one of the mildest on record, with no snow falls.

23rd March 1989 Thursday

Licence Move

The Vehicle Registration Office based at County Hall, Glenfield, is moving to new premises on Good Friday.
The new offices at the Rutland Centre, Halford Street, Leicester, will be open from Tuesday, March 28th.

And so at last our good old Motor Licence Office severs its last link with the County Council and the insurmountable problem of Bank Holidays (see 7th November 1977) is a problem solved.

25th March 1989 Saturday

How beautiful the garden looks after my first full grass cutting session this year. I now can look up to the mighty oak planted with loving care when it was only 4 inches high. I guess it is now about 12 feet high. With the wells now filled in & the house due for improvements "we are getting there".

27th March 1989 Monday

Easter Sunday introduced Ravenstone Church to a new

format of Holy Communion which reduced me to tears. Gone was all the solemnity, & instead of being lifted up to the very gates of heaven, we stayed well & truly down to earth, with the clank of tea-cups & the sound of a kettle boiling in the background.

29th March 1989 Wednesday

I am pleased to read in the latest Cathedral News-letter, that the Provost, the Very Revd. Alan Warren shares my views concerning the form of church worship. He writes, "What has been gained lately in many churches in terms of warmth & fellowship has sometimes been lost in terms of worship & adoration."

31st March 1989 Friday

Fusion Power! "Man has not yet been able to create fusion power" – so I wrote in my diary in September 1978. Now, two scientists claim to have achieved nuclear fusion in a simple test-tube experiment at room temperature, rather than at a temperature of 100 million degrees Centigrade, previously considered necessary.

Professor Martin Fleischmann of Southampton University, a former examiner at Leicester Polytechnic, was the man who achieved nuclear fusion in an experiment he did with Professor Stan Pons of the University of Utah in Salt Lake City. However, continued work is needed to further understand the science & to determine its value.

Nuclear fusion releases energy by joining the nuclei of atoms such as deuterium & tritium. The trick is to overcome the mutual repulsion of the positively charged nuclei & make them fuse. This has now been achieved by using electrochemical techniques and squeezing the nuclei into fusion under an electric current.

7th April 1989 Friday
On this day in history

1739 – The notorious highwayman Dick Turpin was hanged in York for the murder of an innkeeper from Epping – he was buried in York as John Palmer.

8th April 1989 Saturday
"You are invited to a Wedding"

Mr & Mrs Walter Asbury would like you to join them to celebrate the marriage of their daughter Carolyn and Mr. Michael Stevenson at Berkswich Methodist Church, Walton on the Hill, Stafford, on Monday 29th May 1989 at 3 p.m. (Bunting's son is re-marrying).

"We all liked Sheena ......" – so I described Michael's first wife in 1970. What a lovely wedding they had in July 1971, but sadly it ended in divorce. They have 3 children who are absolutely beautiful, Lucy, Sam & Polly, whom I have never met, but maybe we shall see them when Michael marries Carolyn next month.

10th April 1989 Monday

"Calculation of Isentropic Exponent" (see 25th January 1988). British Gas metering group forwarded a massive dossier to our scientific experts at work showing page after page of calculations of how they meter the gas from the Morecambe & Rough fields, giving an example with methane, ethane, propane & nitrogen.

Take 0.92 Methane, 0.05 Ethane, 0.01 Propane and 0.02 Nitrogen. Total volume = 1.00

Use a temperature of 15°c. Have a mixture pressure of

14.504 p.s.i.

Take account of the mixture molecular weight, mixture critical pressure & temperature etc. & find the ratio of specific heat capacities; & the isentropic exponent = 1.29376.

I told you that gas & oil measurement is a mighty tricky operation. The word isentropic means "of equal entropy". And the word entropy means a measure of unavailable energy – energy still existing but lost for the purpose of doing work – a measure of heat content, from the Greek, signifying "transformation-content".

16th April 1989 Sunday

Britain's worst sporting disaster happened yesterday during the Liverpool – Nottingham Forest F A Cup semi-final at Sheffield. Barriers which had been erected to keep the fans off the pitch became a cage to them as the pressure of fans behind them surged forward. Over a hundred were crushed to death.

18th April 1989 Tuesday
"Here comes my John of Lancaster"

Reading through my "Complete Works of William Shakespeare", I came across my John of Lancaster, son of King Henry IV – the Prince, Lord John and Duke of Lancaster. So, just as Brian Lamming was once my prince, now I imagine Cocky as my Prince.

20th April 1989 Thursday

Attended the funeral of Jack Thomas, aged 63, one of our retired gas examiners. As the funeral was at Stafford Crematorium, brother Pat made the 40 mile journey with me and we combined the outing with a visit to Bunting who just happens to live at Stafford now.

22nd April 1989 Saturday

Seven hundred & fifty six red tiles now are stacked at the front of 27 Leicester Road Ravenstone, in readiness for a new roof. The tiles are strongly bound in 21 "bundles" of 36. Also today British Telecom arrived on the scene to renew the overhead wires which connect to our phones.

24th April 1989 Monday

"Cry – God for Harry! England! And Saint George!" So exhorted King Henry V when he went – "once more unto the breach, dear friends."

Yesterday, being St. George's Day, & Ravenstone Church now being united with St. George's Church, Swannington, we found ourselves sharing in Swannington's Patronal Festival.

26th April 1989 Wednesday

Katherine Sullivan, whose life was centred for 20 years from 1939 – 1959 in India, is 85 today. Today she loaned me another of her fascinating books – the story of a Westerner who went to India in search of the great Holy Men – the wise men of the East & through them was "born again". (See John, Chapter 3.)

28th April 1989 Friday

From Maharajahs to Maharishees. Just as India's Maharajahs were "great kings" rich in this world's jewels, so the Maharishees were "great wise men" whose spiritual riches were the true pearls of great price;

who knew deep and lasting happiness because they had known spiritual rebirth.

30th April 1989 Rogation Sunday

On this Rogation Sunday I learn from India's Maharishee, what we all should be really asking, "Who am I?" Solve this problem and all other problems will be solved. All human beings are ever searching for happiness, but happiness is inborn in the true self which will live on beyond this mortal life.

"When a man knows his true self for the first time, something else arises from the depths of his being & takes possession of him – something infinite, divine, and eternal. Some people call it the Kingdom of Heaven, others call it the soul, still others name it Nirvana, or Liberation. Only when this happens has a man found himself."

"Every man is divine & strong in his real nature" says the Maharishee. "The greatest error of a man is to think that he is weak or evil by nature. What are weak & evil are his habits, his desires & thoughts, but not himself. The divine nature reveals itself anew in every single human life."

6th May 1989 Saturday

Cousin Johnty, now aged 84, who divorced his wife after 40 years of marriage and severed relationships with his 2 sons, Philip & Neville, has now landed in Coalville Hospital for a brief spell, where they contacted his next of kin. The happy outcome of all this is a fond reunion with the long lost 2 sons.

8th May 1989 Monday

"O God of unchangeable power and eternal light, look favourably on your whole Church, that wonderful and sacred mystery; And by the tranquil operation of your perpetual providence carry out the work of man's salvation, and let the whole world feel and see that things which were cast down are being raised up, and things which had grown old are being made new, and all things are returning to perfection through him from whom they took their origin, even Jesus Christ our Lord. Amen."

The induction of the Reverend Kerry Emmett as Rector yesterday in Ravenstone Church, three months after his initial "licensing", again included the beautiful prayer which he first read during a power cut at Swannington. The Archdeacon of Loughborough officiated.

10th May 1989 Wednesday

The Venerable Hughie Jones, Archdeacon of Loughborough, at this season of Ascentiontide, said that Christ is in us; we are in Christ; Christ is risen; we are risen. Not "we will rise" but "we are risen". As the Mararishee also knows, it is possible for man to seek & find those things which are above, even while living here on earth. (See Colossians, Chapter 3.)

11th May 1989 Thursday

On this day in history – 1811 – Chang and Eng Bunker, twins who gave the name "Siamese" to joined babies, born in Maklong, Siam. Joined for life, they worked as travelling showmen, became American citizens and married two sisters. Between them they had 21 children and have more than a thousand descendants in America.

12th May 1989 Friday

Cocky, who was planning to retire from the Prison Service on his 60th birthday (next January) is now hoping to get a little part-time job as a Security Guard at "Granby Garments" in Morecambe – 2 hours in the morning, when the staff arrive, & 2 hours in the late afternoon, when they leave.

14th May 1989 Whit Sunday

The glorious message of Whitsunday came to us again in Holy Scripture, in Hymns & prayers. The words of Hymn 156 especially reached me, "Come, thou Holy Spirit, come …. On the faithful, who adore & confess thee, evermore in thy sevenfold gifts descend; give them virtues sure reward ….. give them joys that never end."

The sevenfold gifts of the Spirit are – Wisdom, Understanding, Counsel, Fortitude, Knowledge, Righteousness and Godly Fear.

The seven sins are – Pride, Wrath, Envy, Lust, Gluttony, Avarice and Sloth.

I think Whitsunday holds for me the greatest of all the Church teachings.

18th May 1989 Thursday

Cocky has now been offered the job of Security Guard at Granby Garments and is due to start working there on Monday 3rd July.

He has therefore handed in his notice at the Prison where he has worked for over 20 years. He will be hosting a farewell buffet for all his mates on 30th June.

20th May 1989 Saturday

Flags were at half-mast on Wembley's famous twin towers for this years F A Cup Final, following the disaster at the semi-final on 15th April. The unruly crowd drowned the National Anthem with their own rowdy chants but observed the one minute's silence for their dead comrades. Liverpool 3 – Everton 2.

22nd May 1989 Monday

"European Single Market". As the count-down to 1992 gathers momentum, insular Britain finds it progressively harder to accept all the conditions. We want to keep our own British money & not have a single European currency & a central European Bank. We want our own sovereignty.

There are other issues on which Britain & Europe cannot agree. We are not prepared to lower our high standards for such things as health checks on imported animals & plants. The threat to quarantine rules is of particular concern as the Channel Tunnel is expected to be ready by the early 1990s.

26th May 1989 Friday

At the 11th hour Michael (Bunting's son) has told Carolyn that he cannot go through with the wedding. Having known her only for 5 months, he feels that she has taken over his life more than he likes. She bought the engagement ring. She arranged the wedding & the honeymoon; but now it is all off.

28th May 1989 First after Trinity Sunday

Another thought for God's 3 in 1 trademark. Emotion, knowledge, and conation are the 3 groups of the phenomena of the mind. Emotion is a moving of the feelings – agitation of the mind. Knowledge is enlightenment and understanding. Conation is the active aspect of mind, including desire ……. "I will".

30th May 1989 Tuesday

Cousin Johnty, in all his long life, has never been to London. I therefore gladly offered to go with him on a Viking Coach trip which included a guided tour through London plus time to yourself. We booked the tour & then Johnty was taken ill; & so it was that brother Pat went with me.

What a great day brother Pat & I had in London. We spent all our free time in Whitehall. After savouring the delights of Trafalgar Square, we went inside the magnificent Banqueting Hall in Whitehall & also visited the Cabinet War Rooms below ground. The sun shone for us & we took lots of photographs.

3rd June 1989 Saturday

As a newly appointed member of King Edward VII Community College "Arts Committee", I was asked if I could arrange for an evening's entertainment of "Songs from the Shows".

What a joy it was for me when this all came to fruition as a result of Coalville Amateurs & our brilliant pianist, Anthony Wilson, giving their all.

5th June 1989 Monday

His Holiness Grand Ayatollah Haj Sayyed Ruhollah Mussavia Khomeini, who was born 24th September 1902 & who was reported to be dying in early 1987, died on Saturday in Tehran. Having overthrown the Shah of Persia, he formed the Islamic Republican Party (I.R.P.) & led his country – Iran – back into the past.

6th June 1989 Tuesday

On Monday morning, June 5th 1989, the Coalville Miners Welfare was burnt to the ground. The inferno destroyed what was the town's most important venue and mirrored the decimation of the North West Leicestershire coalfield. Building of the new welfare started in 1955 and the centre – which cost £125,000 to build – was officially opened on Sept.18, 1965.

7th June 1989 Wednesday

"To – Miss E. Hewes,
You are invited to my retirement party.
Place – Boot & Shoe,
Date – 30th June 1989,
Time – 22.00 hours
From – John."

Miss E. Hewes, of course, will not be attending.

9th June 1989 Friday

Meet Diamond Word Processor Hewsie. For the first time at work, I was allowed to use the Diamond Word Processor in our typing pool. At the moment we have only one typist & she will shortly be on leave, so I was delighted to have a go myself as "back-up" to the temp who will be covering for us.

11th June 1989 Sunday

Bailey – *George Eric (Bill) of West Bridgford. Passed away peacefully in hospital on Wednesday 7th June, aged 86 years. Loving husband of May and devoted father of*

David and Paul, in-laws June and Gill, grandchildren Helen, Sarah, Catherine and Richard. Service and cremation at Wilford Hill on Tuesday 13th June at 10 a.m. Family flowers only please. Enquiries to Radcliffe and District Funeral Service.

This is Mum's cousin Eric, brother of Rex (now dead), Madge & Bertha (now dead) & Johnty. Their father Tom Bailey and Mum's mother, Ann Eliza Bailey were brother and sister.

13th June 1989 Tuesday

Johnty & I motored together to his brother Eric's funeral at West Bridgford. After his recent illness, Johnty is still frail & shaky & not able to walk any distance. Eric's widow May was remarkably bright and chirpy & was given wonderful support by her 2 sons & their lovely wives who were the hostesses.

15th June 1989 Thursday

European Parliament – Election No. 3. These elections are held once every 5 years for the European Parliament in Strasbourg. Britain has 43 million voters to pick 78 Euro – M.P.s. There are 3 more Euro – M.P.s in Ulster, giving a total of 81 seats for the U.K. There are now 12 countries in the community.

The European Parliament is made up as follows – France (81 seats), Germany (81 seats), Italy (81 seats), United Kingdom (81 seats), Spain (60 seats), Netherlands (25 seats), Belgium (24 seats), Greece (24 seats), Portugal (24 seats), Denmark (16 seats), Ireland (15 seats) & Luxembourg (6 seats), Total = 518 Euro – M.P.s.

19th June 1989 Monday

Fusion Power! Just when we thought we had cracked it, scientists at Harwell Laboratory in Oxfordshire have announced that cold fusion is nothing more than a "mad idea". They have spent £320,000 trying to make this "mad idea" work & have now given up after conducting 125 experiments.

20th June 1989 Tuesday

On this day in history –
451 – Battle of Chalons in which Attila the Hun was defeated by the Romans.
1389 – John of Lancaster born.
1756 – Night of the "Black Hole of Calcutta". One hundred and forty six English prisoners were put into a cell 18feet x 14 feet on a hot June night when Surajah Dowlah, Nawah of Bengal, captured Fort William. Twenty three survived the night.

21st June 1989 Wednesday

In January 1985 the House of Lords was first televised. It has now been decided to televise the House of Commons, starting with the State Opening of Parliament in November this year. Strict rules have been laid down to make sure the end result is what the M.P.s want & not what the film crew want.

23rd June 1989 Thursday

To make sure that the Palace of Westminster is not made to look like the Palace of Varieties, the television cameramen must film only the head & shoulders of the

M.P. actually speaking & they must not wander all round the Chamber showing shots of other M.P.s, or of the Gallery. The idea is to **inform** – not to **entertain**.

25th June 1989 Sunday
In the year of our Lord 1929, exactly 60 years ago today, Reginald Arthur Hewes, my dad, aged 40, married Mary Sketchley, my mum, aged 23 at little St. Mary's Church, Snibston. This marriage was solemnized (attended with an appeal to God, as an oath) by the Revd. Duncan Wallace.

27th June 1989 Tuesday
A get-together of my dad's 3 children as Pat, Evelyn & I spent the day with Bunting and Mostyn in their luxury home at Stafford.
Michael, still reeling from his recent near-miss wedding, appeared briefly at tea-time, only to announce that he was going out. Nobody asked where was he going.

29th June 1989 Thursday
Joanne, aged 15 ¼, now has her own boyfriend Tyrone, who happens to live in the house behind Aunt Dos's bungalow – built in the grounds of the old family home "The Hollies". He is several years older than Joanne – drives a car - & takes her all over the place. This weekend they will be off to Blackpool.

30th June 1989 Friday
The Prison Officers' Magazine
Lancaster
June saw the retirement from the service of John "Jack" Marsden. Jack joined the service in 1967 here at Lancaster and after his training period at Wakefield O.T.S. he was posted to Preston. He obtained a transfer back to Lancaster in 1968 and since that time he has been one of the main pillars of the staff here at the Castle, always keen to help out when the need arose. He has been the Officer's Mess Treasurer for a number of years, threatening to resign from that particular post on numerous occasions, but still kept on doing the job until his retirement. We must thank you for a job well done in that respect, Jack. An officer of great experience and ability his professionalism will be sorely missed. When the service loses an officer, through retirement, of Jack's calibre, then it requires two from the training school to replace him, to make up for his efficiency and commitment to the job.
Jack, at the end of the day you get nothing from the job, only the memories and heartaches that it gives you. May we wish your good wife Joan and yourself a long and a happy retirement and hope that you will still remember your friends and colleagues, as we will remember you.

1st July 1989 Saturday
Received in the post from Cocky his badge of Office which he has worn as a Prison Officer; together with two table mats – Lancaster Prison, to keep among my souvenirs.
It was "Wine, Women & Song" at Cocky's farewell "do" from the Prison Service. He paid out about £350 for food & drink for some eighty people. A scantily clad "Kissagram" girl sat on his knee & read a poem telling his life story. They all sang to him, "For he's a jolly good fellow". (& I stayed at home).

5th July 1989 Wednesday
Hewes, Alison, Congratulations on gaining a
BA Honours Degree in History (Class 2 : 1)
at Warwick University.
Well done – Love Mum and Dad.

This is Alison, who on the day she was born, sent me a Christmas card – via her parents David & Irene (See December 1967).

7th July 1989 Friday
Last week we received the stunning news that cousin Eric's widow May had died of a heart attack. One minute we were at Eric's funeral & now today, it is May's funeral.
So, in one & the same month, after 55 years of marriage, they died almost together and almost in the same way.

9th July 1989 Sunday
As I approach the completion of my 40 years contribution to Superannuation, I feel rather like the Children of Israel approaching the Promised Land after 40 years in the wilderness.
My so called "career" in the Civil Service has been more of a slow meandering journey than a true vocation.

11th July 1989 Tuesday
The Quatorze Juillet this year is of special significance because it marks the 200th Anniversary of the storming of the Bastille. Revellers in Paris dance through the night in the street; & where the Bastille prison once stood, they have now erected a magnificent opera house, the Opera Bastille.

13th July 1989 Thursday
"What a delicate situation has arisen" – so I wrote in my diary in January 1985, when Mr. Ellis, whom I did not love, tried to woo me.
What a delicate situation has now arisen when Cocky, whom I love with all my heart, sends me a cheque for my birthday for £25, in the joint names of J & J Marsden.
As I refused to stay overnight with Mr Ellis, I refused to cash the cheque from Cocky; but I spent £25 on a heart-shaped brooch, whose value lies not so much in its monetary worth as in the price paid in tears, not only when we were young, but even now when we are almost pensioners.

17th July 1989 Monday
Vic Adams, the builder, arrived with Glyn, his right hand man, to erect the scaffolding at 27 Leicester Road Ravenstone, in preparation for the new roof. When the scaffolding was almost erected, the ladder slipped, Glyn fell to the ground & was whisked off to hospital by ambulance, very badly shaken.

19th July 1989 Wednesday
Rising Damp!
This is the latest problem to be tackled. It may even be the result of having the wells filled in, but the Council have agreed to help towards the estimated cost of £1,000 which will involve a complete & almighty upheaval of every room downstairs, with dust & debris.

21st July 1989 Friday

Auntie Dos, who was at death's door at the beginning of the year, has now been discharged from Carlton Hayes Hospital, to take up permanent residence at Markfield Court Nursing Home. Although she is still very confused & unable to stand or walk, she is always pleased to see us & hear the latest news.

23rd July 1989 Sunday

Johnty, my John number two, is 85 years old today. He is the only one now left who can recall the old days at Willoughby – whose childhood memories are those of my mum – of "Aunt Green" & "Aunt Skinner" & all the other colourful characters they both knew & who made a lasting impression on them.

25th July 1989 Tuesday

As in November 1967, the County Council moved lock, stock & barrel into County Hall at Glenfield, so now the Department of Energy in London is moving from Thames House South (neat to the Houses of Parliament) to Number 1, Palace Street (near to Buckingham Palace). Again they move with military precision.

The Department's move to 1, Palace Street will cost more than £12.5 million. That includes complete refurbishment and air-conditioning. Now the question arises, "Do we need the Department of Energy?" Created in 1974, after the oil crisis & problems with the oil sheiks, it could soon be abolished.

29th July 1989 Saturday

"I find" said 'e, "things very much as 'ow I've always found; for mostly they goes up & down or else goes round & round." These words, written in 1912 by P. R. Chalmers are amazingly true.

I thought of them when I visited Aunt Dos in the nursing home at Markfield Court where she & Thirza Stacey sat together.

It was on 17th March 1915, that my dad, aged 26, married Julia Tabitha Stacey, aged 23. They each had a younger sister – one my Aunt Dos & the other Thirza Stacey. Neither Aunt Dos nor Thirza ever married & now in their late eighties, both being frail & in need of care, they find themselves together.

2nd August 1989 Wednesday

"From the Gas Act 1948 to the Gas Act 1986, from the Nationalisation of the Gas Industry to the Privatisation of the Gas Industry." I had the pleasure of providing this "modern history" at work in answer to a questionnaire sent to the Department of Energy by a modern historian, interested in how we compile our records.

4th August 1989 Friday

Iran's new leader Ali Akbar Rafsanjani is making a brave attempt to woo the West and ease some of the tension in the Middle East. And even Colonel Gaddafi of Libya, arch enemy of the West, is able to joke that Arabs not only taught Europeans astronomy, algebra, etc. but obviously gave us Sheikh-speare.

6th August 1989 Sunday

"The Transfiguration of Our Lord" and a very fine sermon from our new young Rector, the Reverend Kerry Emmett. To all who seek God, to all who want to see Him, and all who want to hear His voice …. This is it."

Read the story in Luke, Chapter 9, & retold by St. Peter in II Peter, Chapter 1.

"And, behold, there talked with him two men, which were Moses & Elijah, who appeared in glory, & spake of his decease which he should accomplish at Jerusalem."

The transfiguration of our Lord was the time when Jesus "steadfastly set his face to go to Jerusalem" knowing only too well what manner of death lay ahead of him.

"All things whatsoever ye would that men should do to you, do ye even so to them; for this is the law and the prophets" Matthew 7, 12.

"Think not that I am come to destroy the law, or the prophets; I am not come to destroy, but to fulfil" Matthew 5, 17. Moses = the Law. Elijah = the Prophet.

12th August 1989 Saturday

When Enid first went to work at Coalville Police Station in November 1964, my dear friend & Rector, the Revd. Gustav Aronsohn said, "The law and the profits."

But it was through him that I learned the deepest meanings of Holy Scripture, & I value his influence on my life.

14th August 1989 Monday

"Don't let me stay here, Betty. Please take me home" pleaded Aunt Dos, when Pat & I visited her in the Nursing Home at Markfield Court. She wept & sobbed at the very thought of being put in "a home".

"Please take me home" echoed Thirza, who felt similar abandonment. Nothing we said or did was any comfort.

16th August 1989 Wednesday

Twenty years ago this month, British troops moved into Northern Ireland as a "short-term measure" to help the police control the warring factions – Catholics versus Protestants. The troops are still there & the situation is just as bad as ever. In the past 20 years, nearly 3,000 people have died & there seems no end to the problem.

18th August 1989 Friday

Auntie Doris at Mountsorrel is 94 tomorrow, and still going strong. She lives in her own home – goes to Loughborough shopping – has long telephone conversations with all her friends & relations – always has someone or another calling to see her, & is celebrating her
birthday in style.

20th August 1989 Sunday

From Bombay to Delhi to Kashmir to Calcutta, the preacher had journeyed when serving in the army during the 1939 – 1945 war. How he marvelled at those who had built the roads to the top of those mountainous regions, zigzagging from side to side, even downwards sometimes. Such, he said, is life.

22nd August 1989 Tuesday

Seven hundred & fifty six red tiles which have been stacked in front of the house for the past 4 months are now beautifully in place on the roof. What a transformation! Again the house looks as good as the others in the row, and it is reassuring to have a good roof overhead.

24ᵗʰ August 1989 Thursday

Office Notice 103/89 – Members of staff will be interested to know that a letter this month from the Prime Minister to Sir Eldon Griffiths, M.P. said, "The Department of Energy should be retained as a separate department at least until the end of this Parliament."

26ᵗʰ August 1989 Saturday

Neptune – a remote planet of the solar system discovered in 1846. How exciting to see the very first close-up pictures of Neptune sent to Earth this week by Voyager 2, a space-craft which was launched from Cape Canaveral, Florida, in August 1977. The 3 billion mile journey has taken 12 years.

Neptune is 300 times larger than Earth! To reach Neptune, Voyager 2 (thanks to the line-up of the planets) was able to fly past Jupiter, Saturn & Uranus. But it will not stop there. Next it will leave our solar system & continue into interstellar space, taking greetings from Earth.

30ᵗʰ August 1989 Wednesday

The more I consider the size of the Earth, the size of our solar system, the size of our galaxy & the size of the universe, the more I marvel that God came down to Earth from heaven. We who think we are the centre of the universe could disappear & never even be missed.

1ˢᵗ September 1989 Friday

F I N M I S = Financial Management Information System. This is the latest computerised system used by the great Department of Trade & Industry & soon to be adopted by the Department of Energy, whereby every item of expenditure is pre-coded, & strict budgetary control continually maintained.

3ʳᵈ September 1989 Sunday

"……. for mostly things goes up & down or else goes round & round." Earth goes round & round & even our galaxy rotates on its axis. It takes the Sun about 250 million years to go round this great axis. The Milky Way with its millions of stars belongs to our galaxy. But there are millions of other galaxies.

5ᵗʰ September 1989 Tuesday

"H.R.H. the Princess Royal and Captain Mark Phillips have decided to separate on terms agreed between them. There are no plans for divorce proceedings."

Another sad announcement from Buckingham Palace, as it was in the case of Princess Margaret in March 1976. First the Queen's sister – now the Queen's daughter.

H.R.H. the Princess Royal had "a real fairy tale wedding" in November 1973. She has two children, Peter, now aged 11, and his sister Zara, now aged 8. According to "rumour", the Princess now has a Timothy in her life – former Royal Equerry & bachelor Commander Timothy Laurence, aged 35.

9ᵗʰ September 1989 Saturday

3,000 witches & pagans have gathered in Leicester this weekend for a Pagan Federation Conference because Leicester, like Stonehenge, is part of the "magic circle".

11ᵗʰ September 1989 Monday

"Dear Sir/Madam – Housing Act 1985. Re – 27

Leicester Road, Ravenstone.

A cheque is enclosed for £1,600 being an instalment on the repairs grant approved on 26ᵗʰ January 1989. The remainder of the grant will be paid on satisfactory completion of the whole improvement works."

13ᵗʰ September 1989 Wednesday

What started as a £4,500 job has now turned into a £6,000 job, for the simple reason that I like nothing but the best. Instead of choosing the cheapest windows & doors, I have chosen de luxe double glazed windows to match my existing one, & 2 doors which cost £700 each.

15ᵗʰ September 1989 Friday

Diamond Word Processor Hewsie has had a hectic week at work, not only trying to deal with correspondence at work using the Word Processor, but sending messages by Telex to various oil companies, to the Petroleum Measurement Inspectorate at Aberdeen & the Norwegian Petroleum Division, who share the North Sea with us.

17ᵗʰ September 1989 Sunday

And the preacher talked of scarecrows. He likened the prophets to scarecrows whose purpose in life was to scare away all the wrong-doers.

He saw the scarecrow pointing straight in both directions; & then he saw Christ crucified, looking like a scarecrow – a scarecrow to save us all.

19ᵗʰ September 1989 Tuesday

Rising Damp! Thanks to cousin David (Enid's brother) I have discovered the cause of my rising damp. The down-pipe from the guttering was still sending all the water from the house roof to a non-existent well. This has now been diverted to take the water down the drain & a £1,000 bill has been averted.

21ˢᵗ September 1989 Thursday

And another wheel turns full cycle as Alison Hewes has a spell of teacher practice at Snibston School, in preparation for her teaching career. It was in September 1907, that Pupil Teacher Cissy Hewes, my Auntie Cis, did exactly the same thing & showed every promise of making a good teacher.

23ʳᵈ September 1989 Saturday

This week has been more of an "up and down" than a "round & round". Window replacement in the back bedroom (now a bathroom) has been the ideal opportunity to take out 2 large wardrobes – Pat was pleased to have one of them & Vic Adams the builder the other, & I have a lovely new fitted wardrobe.

25ᵗʰ September 1989 Monday

Mary Moore, now aged 78, is now on her annual pilgrimage to Ravenstone. Being a compulsive talker & extrovert, she interests herself in anyone & everyone, dead or alive. We visited Bardon Churchyard & Snarestone Churchyard where she knew practically everyone buried beneath the old graves.

27ᵗʰ September 1989 Wednesday

Mary Moore can associate herself in one way or another with almost anyone she meets. She has a fantastic memory and can join in any conversation. But when she eventually flakes out in the armchair & nods off, then she reminds me of Falstaff, in outline so very similar.

29th September 1989 Friday

St. Michael & All Angels Day. Again at church we felt the undoubted presence of Angels as we were reminded of Christ's words, "Take heed that ye despise not one of these little ones; for I say unto you that in heaven their angels do always behold the face of my Father which is in heaven." Matthew 18.

1st October 1989 Sunday

Twice a year – April & October, I pay "the rates" based on the value of the house. The total for the year at present is £266 – 75p. With effect from 1st April next year, domestic rates are to be abolished & replaced by the Community Charge (Poll Tax) whereby people rather than property will be taxed.

The Community Charge is a "charge" for local government services, such as education & personal social services. In the 19th Century local government services were largely property services, hence "the rates" which were paid only by property owners. Like any other major change, it generates fierce opposition.

5th October 1989 Thursday

A new "accompanied" motor cycle riding test became operative throughout Great Britain with effect from Monday 2nd October this year. The examiner, instead of conducting the test on foot, will accompany the candidate on another motor cycle with radio link.

(I got lost during my test in 1963.)

7th October 1989 Saturday

"To level kitchen floor & asphalt - £196."

I had no idea what this meant until the workmen arrived. A rough looking crew with a purpose-made vehicle containing hot steaming gas tar quickly spread the molten substance over the red quarry tiles & it soon set into a black shiny surface.

9th October 1989 Monday

Slowly but surely the poor old kitchen at 27 Leicester Road, Ravenstone, is beginning to look more like a 20th Century kitchen as the newly blackened floor now boasts a wall to wall fitted vinyl carpet to complement the newly fitted window. The new door has not yet been put in.

11th October 1989 Wednesday

Do you remember Hayden Hewes of Oklahoma, who in May 1971 supposedly saw aliens from outer space?

Today's news is that aliens 12 feet high with tiny heads landed in a large shining ball in the Soviet city of Voronezh, 300 miles south east of Moscow, & strolled around.

12th October 1989 Thursday

The kaleidoscope of life, in which we see an ever-changing variety of beautiful colours & forms, on this 40th Anniversary of my first never-to-be-forgotten kiss by Cocky, shows Cocky & Joan looking forward to the birth of their first grandchild, as Yvonne confirms that she is now pregnant.

13th October 1989 Friday

Friday the 13th & it was my pleasure at work to speak on the telephone to Brussels to book bed & breakfast for Gilbert Paul-Clark for one night next Tuesday. The Europa was fully booked. The Central - the Metropole – fully booked. And in the end, the whole of Brussels was fully booked.

15th October 1989 Sunday

The Archbishop of Canterbury defended his doctrine that people with conflicting views can all be right. We all see God through our own eyes as did Matthew, Mark, Luke & John. Matthew's gospel reflects his own particular viewpoint, as do the others. One sees one thing & one sees quite another.

17th October 1989 Tuesday

Commons TV

Proceedings in the House of Commons will be televised for the first time today when M.P.s return after the summer recess. Closed-circuit preparations will take place before experimental public coverage begins at the end of next month.

The Conservative government are having rather a rough ride at the moment. Their drastic changes – self governing agencies; & doctors to be paid according to out-put, are not going down very well.

19th October 1989 Thursday

"Ravenstone Church Bell Fund"

Ravenstone Church has 3 bells, but the tower was built to accommodate 6 & we have now decided to buy 3 more bells. The Bell Fund is being launched to restore & re-hang the old bells & buy 3 new ones, approximately £3,000 each.

21st October 1989 Saturday

"Ravenstone Parish Church St. Michael & All Angels – Grand Open Day

Saturday 21 October 1989. 3p.m. – 7p.m. – Your opportunity to see how the church bells operate & a chance to "have a go" yourself."

A most interesting & enlightening experience with experts on hand to advise.

"They went & told the sexton, and the sexton tolled the bell" – Thomas Hood.

I thought of these words as I sat in the belfry at Ravenstone Church, watching the bell-ringers demonstrating the art of bell-ringing. For the first time in my life I heard the bells & understood them.

My Grand-dad Sketchley (mum's dad) was a bell-ringer. He could listen to the bells of Hugglescote from his farm at Snibston & know exactly where & when they went wrong. Maybe then it is the Sketchley blood in me which makes me thrill to the sound of a full glorious peal of bells.

27th October 1989 Friday

"Loveable Loughborough Archdeacon, far out of his depth, seeks knowledgeable computer buff to help set up data on Amstrad 1640HD20."

So reads an advert placed by Canon Hughie Jones in the "Diocese of Leicester – News & Views." This is the same man who introduced himself as "Your friendly Archdeacon" in 1986.

29th October 1989 Sunday
Churches Count Up
Will you be seen in church on Sunday 29th October?
No, it's not expected to be Judgment Day (if that could ever be anticipated), but the day of the English Church Census when it is hoped, on an "average Sunday", to count every churchgoer in the country.
Each church or fellowship, of every denomination, has been asked to fill in a questionnaire. The results will be analysed by Marc Europe and published to help churches plan and understand patterns of church attendance in the various parts of England.

31st October 1989 Tuesday
Cocky, who so often provided a shoulder for me to cry on in our teens & twenties, is today comforting Yvonne, who has sadly lost the baby she was expecting. Yvonne is Cocky's baby. She is Joan's baby; & her loss is equally their loss. United in their sadness, they are all able to comfort one another.

2nd November 1989 Thursday
Discovered the delights of Derby on a pre-Christmas shopping spree.
Every Thursday there is a bus through Ravenstone to Derby allowing 3 hours to browse around the shops. And what an unexpected pleasure to find so many shops of quality, which at this time of year are fully stocked.

4th November 1989 Saturday
Joanne poured out the troubles of her heart to me today when she informed me that her boyfriend Tyrone has found himself another girlfriend.
Like me, she has wept many tears, but she is still at school, and has plenty of young suitors waiting in the wings; all only too willing to woo & win her.

6th November 1989 Monday
Aunt Dos poured out the troubles of her heart to me as she suffered the indignities of old age & infirmity in the confines of a Nursing Home. How she longed to be in her own home, but unlike Joanne, whose tears could soon be dried, for Aunt Dos there seems no hope left in this weary world & vale of tears.

8th November 1989 Wednesday
One new de luxe double glazed back door, & one to match as a replacement for the old tumble-down outside toilet, & we are nearly there. How lovely to have more light in the kitchen & more light where the toilet wall once blocked out all the light. This brings my finances to rock bottom again.

10th November 1989 Friday
Glasnost & Perestroika (see 30th May 1988). In 1946, the great Winston Churchill said, "From Stettin in the Baltic to Trieste in the Adriatic, an iron curtain has descended across the continent." In 1961 a hundred mile wall was built in Berlin to keep East & West apart. Today people freely crossed this barrier.

12th November 1989 Sunday
"Hymns Old & New" and "The Shorter Prayer Book"
Ravenstone's new Rector, the Revd. Kerry Emmett has introduced new hymn books and prayer books, which are now in use. I opened my new hymn book to see written inside the front cover, "In Loving Memory of Irene and Norman Hewes".

14th November 1989 Tuesday
In the year of our Lord 1859, exactly 130 years ago tomorrow, on the 15th November, my grandfather George Harry Hewes was born at Swannington, the son of Thomas Hewes and his wife Anne (née Martin).
On exactly the same day, his wife to be, (my grandma) Mary Jones was born.
And because George Harry Hewes fell in love & married Mary Jones, here I am, now 700 months old.
We in this world see things only from our present day viewpoint, but visiting the old & so-called senile, we find that they live in the distant past & in the present at one & the same time.

18th November 1989 Saturday
Yelland, Ethel. Of Leicester Road, Ravenstone. Much loved mum, nan and great-grandma. Died peacefully in her sleep Saturday, November 18th aged 86 years. All enquiries to the Co-operative Funeral Service, 128 London Road, Coalville. Tel. 36703.

My next door neighbour from 1981 to 1989.

Mrs Yelland my next door neighbour for the last eight years was a Londoner through and through who had more go in her than most folk. She was out & about as usual on Friday & died during the night. What a shock to see her carried out of the house as a corpse on Saturday morning.

22nd November 1989 Wednesday
"WELCOME" says my new doormat to all who step into my newly furbished kitchen. But the old house, sad & lonely between two now empty houses, has only me for company & thinks of the time when it knew love & laughter, when its walls echoed with lively chatter & children at play.

24th November 1989 Friday
Good King Wenceslas looks out today from Wenceslas Square in Prague, the capital of Czechoslovakia, where the winds of change sweeping through Eastern Europe are bringing out the masses in their hundreds of thousands to express their jubilation at their new found freedom.
Good King Wenceslas was a Prince of Bohemia, as Czecho-Slovakia was known, a thousand years ago. He was a saintly & holy man who was assassinated in the year 929 A.D. by his own brother. By his martyr's death he was beatified by the Catholic Church & became Saint Protector of Bohemia.

28th November 1989 Tuesday
As the "Iron Curtain" dividing Eastern & Western Europe is "rent in twain from the top to the bottom", I think of Christ. At the moment of his death, after 9 long agonising hours of torture the veil of the temple was rent in twain from the top to the bottom. (Mark 15, 38.) The barrier was broken.

30th November 1989 Thursday
Old romantic Hewsie today opened an account with a new Building Society, the Heart of England.
Ruled more by my heart than by my head, I chose it purely for its "heart", & the fact that my finances being at rock bottom, I am ready to start again.

2nd December 1989 Saturday
"Elizabeth Hewes, 27 Leicester Road, Ravenstone, Leicester. No. 110130270012.
Notification of entry in the Community Charges (Poll Tax) Register.
Type of charge = personal,
Registration start date = 1st December 1989.
Your liability to pay the Community Charge will commence 1st April 1990."

4th December 1989 Monday
Since the first North Sea oil well was drilled in December 1964, more than 1.2 billion tonnes of oil have been brought ashore & more than £64 billion invested in developing 44 oilfields, 25 gas fields & 2 gas condensate (i.e. oil & gas) fields. We are hoping to keep going for another 25 years.

6th December 1989 Wednesday
A new pair of specs to update the ones I bought 8th October 1985. There is now a charge for eye testing - £10. The total bill, including this £10, was £142 for "bi-focal spectacles". They are very similar to my other specs, with a hint of pale blue in an otherwise transparent frame.

8th December 1989 Friday
Wonderfuel Gas! In praise of Gas Central Heating. As we wake each morning to a fog enshrouded world, how wonderful to have central heating at the touch of a button. How thankful I am to have the benefits of 20th Century technology; & the old house is equally thankful to be so warm & cosy.

10th December 1989 Sunday
What a masterpiece of a sermon from Mr. Pill, our one time lay reader, now newly ordained deacon. He brought to life the whole story of the Book of Job as if it was a 3-Act play, with inset scenes which spanned every emotion. We saw how Job reacted to all that befell him, & triumphed in the end.

12th December 1989 Tuesday
As I write the Christmas cards this year, I realise how many on my list are now dead. Most recently of course, Mrs. Yelland; earlier in the year both Eric & May, & during the past few years, cousin Don, Auntie Rene, Auntie Gladys, & my old friend The Revd. Gustav Aronsohn, who holds a special place in my heart at Christmas.

14th December 1989 Thursday
To my love, Happy Christmas, All my love X X X X
From my love, by post, a gold necklace for Christmas.

16th December 1989 Saturday
Open Day at the Town Hall, Leicester. For the first time ever we were allowed to see the Inner Sanctum of the Town Hall. We were given a guided tour of the Council chambers, the Lord Mayor's office & the courts. David Taylor, the present Lord Mayor, is eager to share his delight in office with us all.
The Magistrates Courts which are housed at the moment in the Town Hall will move in the next 2 or 3 years to new premises. We were invited to write down our ideas for future uses of the vacated areas. Inspired by the "Living Images" which I saw at the Domesday Exhibition in July 1986, I recommended them.

20th December 1989 Wednesday
In praise of Thomas Cranmer & Shakespeare. Prince Charles today made a powerful speech in defence of the King James' version of the Bible & the wonderful language of Cranmer in the Book of Common Prayer. He voiced my sentiments entirely, having been fed on the Word of God in this format all my life.
Ravenstone Church is losing much of its solemnity now that the old is giving way to the new.
As Prince Charles says, "The fear of being considered old fashioned seems to be so all powerful that the more eternal values & principles which run like a thread through the whole tapestry of human existence are being abandoned".

24th December 1989 Sunday
"No Evensong" – This blunt message in the Parish Magazine informs us that there is no service at Ravenstone Church this evening. There will be Midnight Communion & that's it. No service at all on Christmas Day. I will just have to recall the wonderful words of yesteryears, embedded in my heart.

26th December 1989 Tuesday
A lovely Christmas Day yesterday. First a phone call from my beloved. Holy Communion at dear little St. Mary's where I felt my "soul washed", & an invitation to dinner & tea at Mary Blue's. I told Pat & Bunting that I would like a gathering of all my dad's offspring when I celebrate my Diamond Birthday in 1991.

28th December 1989 Thursday
"To all Staff – 1989 has been another busy & exciting year for the Department of Energy, & one which has seen us move to our splendid new Headquarters Building ....."
Greetings to us all & thanks for our hard work & dedication, from the Secretary of State for Energy – John Wakeham.

29th December 1989 Friday
December 29th is St. Thomas of Canterbury's Day when wassailing moves into full swing. Wassail is an old Anglo Saxon toast, waes heil, which means good health. Something to say regularly over the festive season!

30th December 1989 Saturday
A sad sign of the times is the fact that no-one today is allowed to walk freely along Downing Street in London. New security gates at the Whitehall entrance now stand 10 feet high and are accompanied by an automatic steel trap in the road, which will spring up, if an attacker should get in.

31ˢᵗ December 1989 Sunday

"Watchman, what of the night? Watchman, what of the night? The watchman said, "the morning cometh, & also the night; if ye will enquire, inquire ye; return, come." Isaiah 21.

Another brilliant sermon by Mr. Pill as we see the dawn of a new year and the dawn of a new decade.

* * *

The Story of Ozone (O_3)

Ozone in the upper atmosphere protects us from the sun. Ozone at ground level is toxic. Ozone at ground level is caused by the polluting emissions from motor vehicles, factory emissions, paint solvent, manure, etc.

Oxygen does not like to be alone; it forms a union with whatever comes along.

Nitrogen & Oxygen form Nitrogen-Oxide. Oxygen & Oxygen form Dioxygen.

Then they decide to make a 3-some $N + O + O =$ Nitrogen-Dioxide, $O + O + O =$ Ozone. Ozone is formed when ultraviolet light breaks down $N + O + O$ into $N + O$ and atomic oxygen – both very re-active. When the bachelor oxygen has been separated from the $N + O$, where it enjoyed life as a 3-some, it then seeks solace with $O + O$, and forms a new 3-some, $O + O + O =$ Ozone.

Hydro-carbons – the polluting emissions from motor vehicles, etc. interfere with all the happy relationships forged by Nitrogen & Oxygen. They too have eligible virile oxygen bachelors who form a 3-some with $N + O$, making a new colony of $N + O + O$, at ground level. They upset the balanced relationships of the original partners by dispensing with the chemical path that breaks down the ozone; until we are clogged up & choked up with ground level Ozone, & a hole up above.

* * *

C.A.O.S

(No, not misspelt mayhem - Coalville Amateur Operatic Society)
Betty was a stalwart member for more than 50 years

The Lilac Domino - 1952
Left to right: Betty, Marianne Shilliam, Betty's brother Pat and Peter Jacques

'Goodnight Vienna' 1954
Clockwise from the left: Betty,
Jack Barrs, Betty's brother
Pat, Vincent Hardy and
Christine Gough

Right - Lilian Dunkley as the
romantically inclined Mabel in
'Pirates of Penzance' 1937 -
she was Betty's singing
teacher from April 1954 to
November 1956

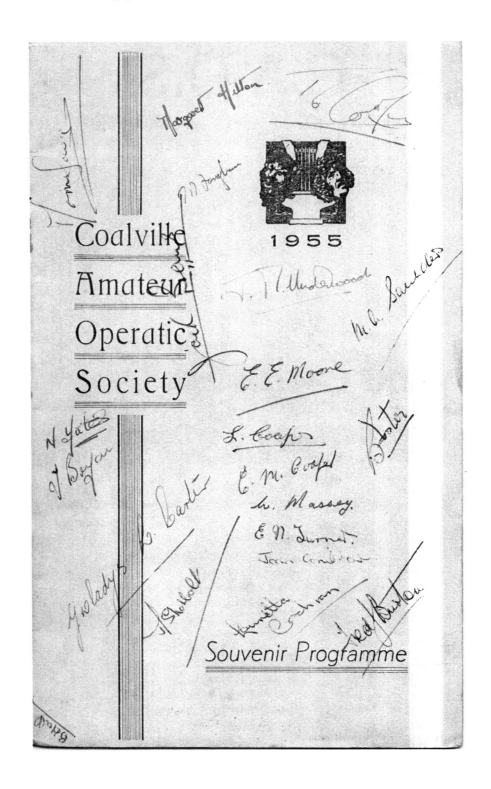

Coalville
Amateur Operatic Society

(Affiliated to the National Operatic and Dramatic Association)

PRESIDENT :

G. S. TAYLOR, Esq.

FOR THEIR 36th ANNUAL PRODUCTION

PRESENTS

THE SUCCESSFUL MUSICAL COMEDY

"MARITZA"

(By arrangement with Samuel French Ltd.)
English Book by Robert Layer-Parker and Eddie Garr.
Lyrics by Arthur Stanley.   Music by Emmerich Kalman.

THE REGAL THEATRE, COALVILLE

THURSDAY, FRIDAY, SATURDAY,
MARCH 24th, 25th, 26th, 1955
AT 7.20 P.M.

Matinee : Saturday, March 26th, at 2.15 p.m.

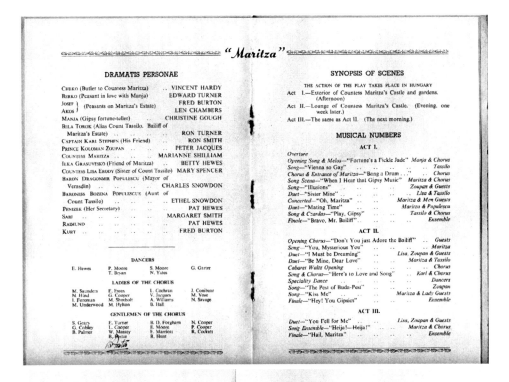

"Maritza"

DRAMATIS PERSONAE

CHEKO (Butler to Countess Maritza)	VINCENT HARDY
BERKO (Peasant in love with Manja)	EDWARD TURNER
JOSEF ⎫ (Peasants on Maritza's Estate)	FRED BURTON
AKOS ⎭	LEN CHAMBERS
MANJA (Gipsy fortune-teller)	CHRISTINE GOUGH
BELA TOROK (Alias Count Tassilo, Bailiff of Maritza's Estate)	RON TURNER
CAPTAIN KARL STEPHEN (His Friend)	RON SMITH
PRINCE KOLOMAN ZOUPAN	PETER JACQUES
COUNTESS MARITZA	MARIANNE SHILLIAM
ILKA GRASUVESKO (Friend of Maritza)	BETTY HEWES
COUNTESS LISA ERODY (Sister of Count Tassilo)	MARY SPENCER
BARON DRAGONMIR POPULESCU (Mayor of Verasdin)	CHARLES SNOWDON
BARONESS BOZENA POPULESCUE (Aunt of Count Tassilo)	ETHEL SNOWDON
PENIZEK (Her Secretary)	PAT HEWES
SARI	MARGARET SMITH
RADMUND	PAT HEWES
KURT	FRED BURTON

DANCERS

E. Hewes	P. Moore	S. Moore	G. Garter
	T. Bryan	N. Yates	

LADIES OF THE CHORUS

M. Saunders	E. Essex	L. Cochran	J. Conibear
N. Hind	G. Cooper	V. Jacques	M. Vose
I. Foreman	M. Shotbolt	A. Williams	N. Savage
M. Underwood	M. Hylton	B. Hall	

GENTLEMEN OF THE CHORUS

S. Geary	E. Turner	B. D. Forgham	N. Cooper
G. Cobley	L. Cooper	E. Moore	P. Cooper
B. Palmer	W. Massey	E. Marriott	R. Cockett
	B. Foster	R. Hunt	

SYNOPSIS OF SCENES

THE ACTION OF THE PLAY TAKES PLACE IN HUNGARY

Act I.—Exterior of Countess Maritza's Castle and gardens. (Afternoon)

Act II.—Lounge of Countess Maritza's Castle. (Evening, one week later.)

Act III.—The same as Act II. (The next morning.)

MUSICAL NUMBERS

ACT I.

Overture	
Opening Song & Melos—"Fortune's a Fickle Jade"	Manja & Chorus
Song—"Vienna so Gay"	Tassilo
Chorus & Entrance of Maritza—"Bang a Drum . . ."	Chorus
Song Scena—"When I Hear that Gipsy Music"	Zoupan & Guests
Song—"Illusions"	Lisa & Tassilo
Duet—"Sister Mine"	Lisa & Tassilo
Concerted—"Oh, Maritza"	Maritza & Men Guests
Duet—"Mating Time"	Maritza & Populescu
Song & Czardas—"Play, Gipsy"	Tassilo & Chorus
Finale—"Bravo, Mr. Bailiff"	Ensemble

ACT II.

Opening Chorus—"Don't You just Adore the Bailiff"	Guests
Song—"You, Mysterious You"	Maritza
Duet—"I Must be Dreaming"	Lisa, Zoupan & Guests
Duet—"Be Mine, Dear Love"	Maritza & Tassilo
Cabaret Waltz Opening	Chorus
Song & Chorus—"Here's to Love and Song"	Karl & Chorus
Speciality Dance	Dancers
Song—"The Pest of Buda-Pest"	Zoupan
Song—"Kiss Me"	Maritza & Lady Guests
Finale—"Hey! You Gipsies"	Ensemble

ACT III.

Duet—"You Fell for Me"	Lisa, Zoupan & Guests
Song Ensemble—"Heija!—Heija!"	Maritza & Chorus
Finale—"Hail, Maritza"	Ensemble

MINUTE HON. SECRETARY :

"Cheko"
VINCENT HARDY

"Ilka Grasuvesko"
BETTY HEWES

Ladies of the Chorus in 'Rose Marie' 1958. Betty is standing far right and Mary Blue kneeling second from right.

Below left: 'Kiss Me Kate' 1970

Below right: 'My Fair Lady' 1973

When their acting days were done Pat and Betty played various other roles behind the scenes. Pat was secretary at one time while Betty was treasurer and prompter.

The photo on the right was taken in 1990, when Pat was House Manager with Betty as Assistant House Manager

Below - the Front of House team

11th March 1993 Thursday: "All the forces at work behind scenes of 'Guys & Dolls' were again in evidence to Assistant House Manager Hewsie as she saw the tea-ladies preparing for the interval mad rush; watched the electricians at work in their control room; & culminated in the delivery of red roses from my true love –
All my love, John".

C.A.O.S. Re-union October 1997

Among the ladies are: Betty - 5th from left on the back row and her cousin Enid - 1st on the left, third row back. Betty's half-sister Bunting is 6th from right, third row back, and Aunt Dos 5th from the right, third row back. Mary Blue - second row back, 4th from left and Mary Blue's mother Evelyn is second row back, 5th from the left.

2nd October 1987 Friday: The Hewes family was well represented at the Coalville Amateurs Grand Re-Union. Aunt Dos was able to represent the "Nineteen Twenties". Bunting was there from the "Thirties". Pat, Enid & I were there from the "Forties" & Mary Blue was there from the "Fifties". There were 200 people there.

C.A.O.S. Re-union October 1997

Among the gentlemen is Betty's brother Pat, second row back, 4th from the left.
Peter Jacques is in the centre on the front row.

2ⁿᵈ October 1987 Friday: Coalville Amateur Operatic Society (founded 1919) Grand Re-Union. What a wonderful evening when a lifetime of shows was contracted into one night to remember. Stars of yesteryear were moved to tears as we all sang again the songs of love which they knew so well.

1990

2nd January 1990 Tuesday

"Almighty God, unto whom all hearts be open, all desires known, and from whom no secrets are hid; cleanse the thoughts of our hearts by the inspiration of thy Holy Spirit ...."

As we begin the last decade of our 20th Century, this opening Collect for Holy Communion comes to mind.

4th January 1990 Thursday

"Hello Universe" we said in January 1978, when the Royal Institution Christmas Lecture was entitled "Planets".

"Hello" again, as this year we explore the science of music and with the help of an oscilloscope "see" the different wave lengths of sound produced by different music & different voices.

6th January 1990 Saturday

Treasurer Hewsie is once more busy receiving applications for tickets for Coalville Amateurs' forthcoming production "My Fair Lady".

Things are "going round" again as we repeat our production of "My Fair Lady" last performed by our Society in 1973, when I was in my last production on stage.

8th January 1990 Monday

All written instructions in the Civil Service must now be "non-sexist". No such thing as an officer receiving his salary. It must be his/her salary.

I wonder how long it will be before the Word of God has to be "updated" to this so-called improved format? Jesus said, "Everyone that asketh receiveth, & he that seeketh, findeth."

10th January 1990 Wednesday

Jesus said, "I am the bread of life; he that cometh to me shall never hunger; & he that believeth on me shall never thirst. Verily, I say unto you, he that believeth on me hath everlasting life. I am the resurrection & the life; he that believeth in me, though he were dead, yet shall he live."

12th January 1990 Friday

The computer was asked to delete any reference to the word "man", and it created more problems than ever it solved. So we kept our manhole and mankind, our man-made and our man-of-war. We kept Manchester & Mansfield, but when we wanted a handyman, we had to ask for a handy-person.

14th January 1990 Sunday

18 months to retirement & the countdown now begins. Already I have distributed calendars at work for the last time. (The calendars cover two years – one either side).

The one job I shall not be sorry to relinquish is that of "staff reporting". This is the annual chore which nobody at work likes.

16th January 1990 Tuesday

Just when we all thought that 1990 had brought us into "the nineties", we are reminded in the Leicester Mercury Postbag, by Mike Scott of Oadby, that the nineties will not begin until 1st January 1991. The first recorded year was 1 A.D. A decade begins No. 1 and ends at 0.

18th January 1990 Thursday

Now, how about this for an interesting extra job I have been given at work – Approval of Gas Meters for use in E.E.C. countries. All our learned scientists check every minute detail of every manufactured meter; & any alteration whatsoever in pattern or construction has to meet with our approval.

20th January 1990 Saturday

Where is Terry Waite? Three years ago today, Terry Waite, the Archbishop of Canterbury's special envoy, was seized in the Lebanon while on a mission to rescue others who were held hostage. Not a word of his whereabouts has been heard since.

22nd January 1990 Monday

A Service of Confirmation was held at Ravenstone for one candidate only. Michael Anker was confirmed by the Assistant Bishop of Leicester, the Right Reverend Godfrey Ashby. I was asked to read the Old Testament Reading and Mr. Pill read the New Testament Reading.

I walked up the aisle at Ravenstone Church to read the lesson. The Bishop sat there in front of me and my knees turned to jelly. I felt like a drunken man (or woman) as I walked unsteadily to & from the lectern, but thankfully my voice held steady as a rock.

26th January 1990 Friday

Gale force winds brought death and destruction to much of Southern Britain yesterday. Falling masonry & fallen trees killed 45 people including one of our staff from the Department of Energy in London. Mr Norman Marguerie from Petroleum Engineering Division was struck by a falling wall.

28th January 1990 Sunday

"Happy Birthday to my ain wee Darling"

This is what I wrote in my diary in 1957, when Cocky & Joan were shortly to be married. Now, in the twinkling of an eye, as if overnight, Cocky has changed from a 27 year old to a 60 year old.

The day Cocky married Joan I thought the world would surely end. But the world carried on regardless, and it was only my own little world which ground to a halt. When Cocky renewed contact with me in 1987, my heart resurfaced, and I was back in orbit once more.

1st February 1990 Thursday

The world itself seems in turmoil at present. Apart from storm & tempest, the people are also unsettled.

Every day we see on the news masses in their thousands up in arms about one thing or another – blacks against whites in South Africa; Islam versus Christianity; hooliganism & vandalism.

3rd February 1990 Saturday

But still amidst all the unrest in the world, the cycle of life continues.

The birds each morning delight us with their dawn chorus, assuring us that spring is not far away; and Cocky tells me that Yvonne is pregnant again, after suffering the trauma of a miscarriage not so long ago.

5th February 1990 Monday
"Dear Betty, Please join us to celebrate our Golden Wedding on Sunday 18th March 1990 at 1.00 p.m. at St. James Church Hall, Highfields Street, Coalville."
From Pat & Evelyn.
This year marks the Golden Wedding of brother Pat & also cousin Donald, who sadly died 2 years ago.

7th February 1990 Wednesday
With one tumble-down fence, and one rotten gate at the end of the entry, I asked "Ashby Fencing Specialists" (A. J. Hicklin) for an estimate.
I accepted their quotation of £70 for a gate & £547 for a fence 5 feet high – 13 panels, with concrete posts & gravel boards – for early March.

9th February 1990 Friday
Department of Energy – Fire Drill. "To all occupants of 1, Palace Street (London) – A fire drill has been arranged for the week of 12 – 16 February 1990. The exercise will involve the full evacuation of staff from the building to the external assembly point in St. James Park."

11th February 1990 Sunday
Glasnost & Peristroika in Russia have now brought to an end 72 years of Communist rule & opened up the road to Democracy. Russian leader Mr. Gorbachev has managed to persuade his people that without democracy they are isolated from the mainstream of world civilisation.

13th February 1990 Tuesday
 "Valentine, my heart is yours, & always will be too; because you're very special, and I think the world of you."
Happy Valentine's Day, All my love
XXXXXXXXXXXXXXXX
From my darling John Marsden.

15th February 1990 Thursday
In the year 1528 A.D. King Henry VIII wrote to Anne Boleyn, his then mistress, "Mine own sweetheart, these shall be to advertise you of the great aloneness that I find here since your departing, for I ensure you, methinketh the time longer since you departing now last than I was wont to do a whole fortnight."

17th February 1990 Saturday
Nelson Mandela, champion of the blacks in South Africa, has this week been granted his freedom after spending 27 years in prison. As he walked hand in hand with his wife in public again after a quarter of a century apart, I was so deeply moved, I wept much.

19th February 1990 Monday
Nelson Mandela is now aged 71. He is a black man of noble birth. He received a first class education and, like Moses, he is ready to release his people from the bondage of "Apartheid". For this he was sentenced to life imprisonment, and now he is free to save his people.

21st February 1990 Wednesday
Salman Rushdie wrote a book called "Satanic Verses"

which was published at the beginning of last year. "Blasphemy!!" said the great Ayatollah Khomeini. "He must be put to death."
$3 million reward was offered to any Iranian who could find him & kill him, but no-one has yet found him.

23rd February 1990 Friday
Ten years ago I had a little friend – Joanne, who skipped & jumped round and round and round the chair, until I was inside a magic fairy circle.
Now she is almost "sweet sixteen" and casts her magic spell elsewhere. The sweet innocence of childhood has long since gone.

25th February 1990 Sunday
"My Fair Lady", Coalville Amateur's choice for this year, brings back memories of our 1973 production, when Margaret Lillyman excelled as Eliza Doolittle & I played the elegant Mrs Higgins. I now watch Margaret playing the elegant Mrs Higgins while she in turn watches young Karen Adams playing Eliza.

27th February 1990 Tuesday
Alison, the pampered Dachshund, who knelt at the alter rail at the Monastery in July 1987, died last week; & Katherine, now aged 86, like Hiawatha when his beloved Minnehaha died, "Uttered such a cry of anguish, that the very stars in heaven shook and trembled with his anguish. Then he sat down still and speechless, on the bed of Minnehaha, at the feet of laughing water ...... with both hands his face he covered. Seven long days & nights he sat there, as if in a swoon he sat there, speechless, motionless, unconscious of the daylight or the darkness."
This too was Katherine.

2nd March 1990 Friday
Like Hans Andersen I watch people on stage and think of them as they were in other years. As I lose myself again in the magic of the stage, I see Gladys Watret, now a Cockney wench high kicking, doing the knees up, & think to myself, here is the Mother Abbess of 1988.

4th March 1990 Sunday
"My Fair Lady" this year is our longest running production – 12 performances in all from Wednesday 28th February to Saturday 10th March, with two matinees. This is simply because the Harley Theatre in King Edward VII Community College has only a 163 seating capacity, making an overall total of less than 2,000.

6th March 1990 Tuesday
Chettleburgh, Kenneth George, of Romans Crescent, Coalville, the dearly loved husband of Margaret, loving father of Mark and Emma, passed peacefully away in hospital on March 6th 1990. Funeral service at Christchurch, Coalville, on Friday March 9th at 12.15 p.m. to be followed by cremation at Gilroes Crematorium, flowers and or donations as desired. Donations for The Midland Asthma and Allergy Research Association. Flowers, donations and inquiries to Coalville and District Funeral Service, Belvoir Road, Coalville. Tel. 38600.
My boyfriend in 1949, but I preferred Cocky.
Chettleburgh & I enjoyed riding a bicycle made for two.

8th March 1990 Thursday

How beautiful the garden now looks with a magnificent new fence, built to resist the gale force winds which we have experienced lately.

Also there is now a much improved "patio" where the shed once stood, with slabs laid perfectly, and for which I readily paid an additional £225.

10th March 1990 Saturday

And so we come to the end of another memorable, moving, magical week of music & drama. Brother Pat, House Manager, who was talking of retiring from this role, now wanting to continue until he is 80; & for old romantic Hewsie a bouquet of red roses – "All my love forever, John."

12th March 1990 Monday

"A daughter of the gods, divinely tall, & most divinely fair."

This may well describe Marlene who heads our front of house team at Coalville Amateurs. In the line-up of tall girls – Marlene, her sister Margaret, Ann Bradford, Olive Meakin, etc. I feel very much at home with them & the male stewards.

14th March 1990 Wednesday

Aunt Dos, who was at death's door a year ago, celebrated her 88th birthday yesterday in much better spirits. Although her waking thoughts seem more like dream thoughts, where those long since dead intermingle freely with those still living, she enjoys the company of her visitors.

16th March 1990 Friday

"Pat & Evelyn – Congratulations on your Golden Wedding 16th March 1940 – 1990"

I had these words hand-painted in gold on a china plate & even written on the back – **"Love from Betty"** from a stall in Loughborough Market.

18th March 1990 Sunday

Hewes, Pat and Evelyn. Congratulations on your golden wedding anniversary. Lots of love – From Mary, Scott, Sharon, Darren, Murdo, Lian, Karen and Graham

What a glorious golden day of summer sunshine for Pat and Evelyn's Golden Wedding Day celebrations, which began with a Church Service where they walked arm in arm to the Altar for a blessing.

The Golden Wedding celebration began with the 9.30 a.m. Church Service, continued with a sit down meal for about 50 guests, and continued then into the night, when half the guests gathered at the house for a jolly old get-together. Pat & Evelyn declared it was better than their Wedding Day.

22nd March 1990 Thursday

Found Aunt Dos in a sad & sorry state. Like poor Emily Walker, when her life was drawing to its close in October 1983, Aunt Dos sat huddled up in her wheelchair and hardly spoke a word. In complete contrast, earlier in the day, I met Sophie, aged 4 weeks, baby daughter of Veronica at work.

24th March 1990 Saturday

Johnty, my John Number 2, now aged 85, is in Leicester City General Hospital at the moment with fluid on the lung. Nev Bailey, his son, telephoned to tell me & I visited him in No 7 Ward, where he looked very frail & tired. He hardly touched his evening meal & seemed heavily drugged.

***Gundry**. On March 24th 1990, the Revd. Canon Dudley William Gundry, lately chancellor of Leicester Cathedral, aged 73 years. Funeral service at Leicester Cathedral on Monday April 2nd at 12 noon followed by private cremation; if desired donations in lieu of flowers to Leicester Cathedral or Leicester Grammar School.*

26th March 1990 Monday

"Bailey Beats the Big Guns"

This is Johnty's son, Nev Bailey, aged 44, whose photo appears in the paper this week.

"Nailstone sharpshooter, Neville Bailey, is celebrating following his British Open Double Rise Clay Pigeon Shooting championship win."

In July he will captain the English team.

30th March 1990 Friday

***Bailey**, John Skinner. Dearly loved father passed away peacefully March 30th.*
Just as you were you will always be,
Someone very special in our memory.
Dad you will be sadly missed.
Love always – Neville. Marie, Tracey and Dale.

This is Johnty – the last of Mum's cousins from Willoughby. After a long turbulent relationship with his 2 sons, all was forgiven before he died; & he died on Cocky's 33rd Wedding Anniversary.

1st April 1990 Sunday

The Community Charge – known as the Poll Tax, comes into force today. But, you never saw or heard such opposition as there is to this new legislation. The main reason for the outcry is the exorbitant amount demanded. Thousands cannot afford to pay.

3rd April 1990 Tuesday

Leicester Cathedral yesterday provided a funeral service befitting so eloquent a man as Canon Gundry. Heaven & Earth were indeed united when we sang, "Ye holy angels bright, who wait at God's right hand, or through the realms of light fly at your Lord's command, assist our song." And they did.

5th April 1990 Thursday

Johnty would have been proud of his 2 sons who today led the mourners at his funeral. Two fine young men in the prime of life – men of the outdoors; & Nev, wearing his blazer & tie with the "England" badge of marksmanship. "You must keep in touch" they each said to me.

7th April 1990 Saturday

Queen Ethelfloeda is back on her pedestal!

Remember Ethelfloeda who featured in my diary in 1980, & whose beautiful statue seemed irresistible to the lads about town when displayed out of doors? Well, she is now safely under cover in the foyer of the City Rooms, after being renovated.

9th April 1990 Monday

"Toffee"- the new pampered Dachshund acquired by Katherine met me today & greeted me like a long lost friend. This is a 6 year old dog, owned formerly by a rich family in the south of England, who likes constant love & affection & who was reluctant to share such a life with their new baby.

11th April 1990 Wednesday

"Astronaut Wanted – no experience necessary" - Glavcosmos, the Soviet Space Administration, has offered a place to a British astronaut on the Juno Mission space flight of 8 days, scheduled for April 1991, the 30th Anniversary of the first flight.

13th April 1990 Good Friday

Cocky & Joan were in Ravenstone visiting Midge – just up the road from me. My heart missed a beat when I saw their car parked outside Midge's house – **REC 732Y**.

15th April 1990 Easter Sunday

While I still yearn for Cocky, the Commandments of God remind me that "Thou shalt not covet thy neighbour's house – wife – etc."
And the Epistle for Easter Sunday, Coloss. 3. v. 5 & 6, admonishes me further still – "Covetousness is idolatry for which the wrath of God cometh."
No wonder I cry so.

17th April 1990 Tuesday

Elizabeth Hewes – No. 11 013 027 0 012 has received her first Community Charge Bill – the controversial Poll Tax, which has had the population in uproar. I now pay £358 – 67p per annum, as opposed to £266 – 75p last year. I am only thankful that I have enough money to absorb this increase.

19th April 1990 Thursday

The new Poll Tax is a standard charge for everyone aged 18 upwards, according to their address, but not according to their ability to pay. £358 from a salary in excess of £10,000 per year is a totally different concept from expecting £358 from those who can hardly make ends meet.

21st April 1990 Saturday

At 49, Leicester Road, Ravenstone, lives Elaine Barkby, all alone in the world, in her mid -40s. Having never enjoyed the best of health, her continuing ailments have now been confirmed as Multiple Sclerosis. I called to see Elaine, to cheer her up & found she was a bundle of fun & good humour.

23rd April 1990 Monday

O'Mara, Francis Martin, of Ashburton Road, Hugglescote, passed suddenly away at home April 17th 1990 aged 58 years, dearly loved husband of Gillian, loving father of Ruth and Rachel.
Funeral service and requiem mass at Holy Cross R.C. Church on Monday April 23rd at 1 p.m. to be followed by cremation at Loughborough. No flowers by request, but donations if so desired for The British Heart Foundation, donations and further inquiries to Coalville and District Funeral Service, Belvoir Road, Coalville. Tel. 38600.

This is Martin O'Mara, who was at Coalville Grammar School with me, in the same classroom, sharing the same education, and who did not live to see so much as three score years.

25th April 1990 Wednesday

To celebrate Katherine's 86th birthday, I took her to the recently opened "Marks & Spencer" de luxe store at Fosse Park, where she bought all manner of provisions & potted plants. We then went to the Monastery where she captivated Brother Ambrose, who in turn captivated us with his tales of Medjugore.
Brother Ambrose visited Medjugore earlier this year & spoke to us of the continuing presence & appearances of the Blessed Virgin Mary. He took with him 4 rosaries, and one of them turned into gold. He said that Pope John Paul II was destined to become greater than St. Peter himself.

29th April 1990 Sunday

In these weeks between Easter & Pentecost, we feel most strongly the presence of the risen Lord Jesus. The preacher spoke of the appearance of the Lord at break of day by the sea-shore. (St. John, Chap. 21).
Just when we think we have failed in all our endeavours, we find that all turns out well.

1st May 1990 Tuesday

"Hello Universe", as the very latest telescope, about the size of a bus, weighing 12 ½ ton, and 43 foot long, is now in orbit 380 miles above the Earth. It is called the Hubble Space Telescope and will be able to observe distant planets, stars & galaxies with up to 10 times the clarity of instruments on Earth.

3rd May 1990 Thursday

"Frogmore Gardens – Windsor" – a once a year opportunity to visit the Queen's private gardens – the Royal Mausoleum will also be open. Katherine & I accepted this unique offer by Viking Coaches & on a scorching hot day travelled from Coalville to Windsor to see the gardens.
The Royal Mausoleum at Frogmore, Windsor, is the magnificent "tomb-house" of Queen Victoria & her beloved Albert. The recumbent marble effigies of Victoria & Albert were both made at the same time, and show them therefore both young & beautiful, kissed by the sun and at peace together.
Inside the Royal Mausoleum at Frogmore, Windsor, is a beautiful marble angel taking a well earned rest. You never saw such workmanship – to portray out of a solid block of marble, a tired angel, sitting with eyes closed, leaning almost asleep, but serenely content.

9th May 1990 Wednesday

"Mr & Mrs T. W. Jarman request the pleasure of the company of Miss B. Hewes at the Marriage of his daughter Karen Mary to Graham David Oliver at St. Paul's Church, Kirby Road, Leicester, on Saturday 7th July 1990 at 2.00 p.m. and afterwards at The Gables Hotel, 368 London Road, Leicester."

11th May 1990 Friday

Don & Phyl's Golden Wedding Day. At least, it would have been if Don had lived to see today. Instead, Phyl wept alone in their lovely home. I visited her with a beautiful basket of flowers and she recounted the details of the day Don died. She wept & smiled alternate.

13th May 1990 Sunday
"Where there is no vision, the people perish" – Proverbs 29. 18.
The preacher was a good man – the Reverend Derek Goodman, who had inspired many by his powerful preaching, & he spoke to us of God's great goodness & purpose for us all, if only we have the vision to see & understand.

15th May 1990 Tuesday
Diane King Dancing Academy this year celebrates its 21st birthday. Now with over a hundred children – Beginners; Friday Juniors; Saturday Juniors; Lower & Senior Class; they go from strength to strength.
As I watched their latest polished performance, I recalled our poor effort of December 1964.

17th May 1990 Thursday
I dreamed a dream so vivid & so real. Mikhail Gorbachev, Soviet leader, held me in fond & loving embrace & I thought of the words of the Blessed Virgin Mary at Fatima in July 1917, "I ask for the consecration of Russia to my Immaculate Heart. If my request is heard Russia will be converted."
"If my request is heard" said the Blessed Virgin Mary, "there will be peace. If not, the errors of Russia will spread throughout the world promoting wars & persecution of the Church. The good will be martyred & the Holy Father will have much to suffer. In the end however Russia will be converted & consecrated to me."

21st May 1990 Monday
Sandringham (including admission to house and grounds) and a visit to Caithness Crystal – glassware factory & shop. Enid & I went on this Viking Coaches outing & enjoyed strolling through the Queen's beautiful garden, through the splendid rooms of the house, the museum, & Sandringham Church.
Our visit to the crystal glassware factory reminded me of my visit in 1986 to Ratcliffe-on-Soar Power Station with its Dante's inferno. Glass is made from the finest sand, almost like powder, brought to a molten state in the open furnace and handled with great rods & tongs by slave-like workmen.

25th May 1990 Friday
F.A. Cup Final this year was a re-play; Manchester United beat Crystal Palace 1 – 0.
Gone are the days of 100,000 attendance at Wembley. As a direct result of recent disasters at football games, all terraces where people used to stand and watch have been converted into seating areas – total capacity now 80,000.

27th May 1990 Sunday
Ascension Day last Thursday and Ravenstone Church held an evening service, the likes of which it had never experienced before. It was attended by a lively contingent from the Coalville Council of Churches, who freely held their arms aloft, & led the prayers as if at a Music Hall.

29th May 1990 Tuesday
Elaine Barkby, suffering from Multiple Sclerosis, chatted to me non-stop for 4 hours when I called to see her. She looks so very frail and can walk only very slowly with a walking aid, but she has some very good friends, including retired Doctor Sheila Lee, who is taking her to Scotland for a holiday.

31st May 1990 Thursday
Gas Meters Variation of Fees Regulations 1990 – Statutory Instrument 1990 No. 686.
Our Gas Meter examiners are the only people in Britain who are authorised to "approve" the pattern and construction of gas meters, and the only people authorised to test the accuracy of used meters. Modest fees are charged for checking the accuracy of household gas meters, but much larger fees are charged for "approving" the pattern & construction: -
Diaphragm Meters = £562 - 50p. Rotary Positive Displacement Meters = £1,312 – 50p. Turbine Meters = £1,487 – 50p. Any others = £2,343 – 75p.

4th June 1990 Monday
Whitsuntide never ceases to inspire us and assure us again that, "All things work together for good to them that love God." Romans 8. 28.

6th June 1990 Wednesday
Coalville Amateur Operatic Society Annual General Meeting when Treasurer Hewsie presented her accounts & was re-elected for another year.
As so much of the work relies on back-up facilities at the office – photo-copier in particular – I expect this to be my last term of office.

8th June 1990 Friday
The full contents of Aunt Dos's bungalow were sold by auction. In a couple of hours the accumulated hoard of almost a century was virtually scattered to the four winds as one lot after another went at knock-down prices. It was rather sad to see all her family treasures no longer treasured.

10th June 1990 Trinity Sunday
"I besought the Lord thrice ……. that the thorn in the flesh might depart from me."
II Corinthians, Chapter 12. Another thought for God's 3 in 1 trademark, when St. Paul, like Christ, prays earnestly, only to be told by God himself, "My grace is sufficient for thee; for my strength is made perfect in weakness."

12th June 1990 Tuesday
The Social Democratic Party – a new political party launched on 26th March 1981 – has now "wound up". It died on 4th June 1990. Originally its founder members, known as the Gang of Four, belonged to the Labour Party, which is thriving at the moment by opposing the unpopular Poll Tax.

14th June 1990 Thursday
First time advertised – Ravenstone – 25B Leicester Road. *Valuable detached bungalow in village location. Entrance hall, lounge, breakfast kitchen, 2 bedrooms, bathroom. Garage, private gardens, immediate*

possession.
Further details from Arnold & Son, Coalville 32140.
Aunt Dos's bungalow for sale brings to an end the Hewes' domination of Hewes' Corner, Ravenstone. Built on the lawn of the old home, all is now gone.

16th June 1990 Saturday

Leicester Amateur Operatic Society 1890 – 1990, celebrated its centenary in style with a lavish production of "Merry Widow".
This romantic story, which Coalville Amateurs portrayed in 1968, reminded me of my own life story in reverse – one, not good enough for the other, proves to be better.

18th June 1990 Monday

Leicester's new Lord Mayor, Councillor Peter Kimberlin, aged 59, is the son of Alderman Kimberlin who was Leicester's Lord Mayor in 1964. The Lord Mayor's Appeal this year is to raise £250,000 to buy a surgical laser – designed to unblock hardened arteries – for Leicester Royal Infirmary.

20th June 1990 Wednesday

Ravenstone Darby & Joan, founded in November 1948 by Auntie Belle, and once a thriving concern, has now been forced to close through lack of members. As the old stalwarts have gone, one by one, a new generation of pensioners has come along who simply are not interested.

22nd June 1990 Friday

"Somewhat slightly aloof" Hewsie was brought down to earth with a jolt this week when she was told what had been written about her on her Annual Staff Report – Grade 4 marking – not up to the standard required of an Executive Officer – not able to motivate staff.
Ten years ago, in 1980, I had a similar adverse staff report (written by Roy Ellison).
The reporting officer this year is Dr. Courtenay Sayer. After a lifetime at work, you might not think I have achieved much, but apart from being hopeless in some respects, I am not completely without merit.

26th June 1990 Tuesday

"What a sad world we live in" – these were my sentiments in November 1980, following the dreadful earthquake in Southern Italy. And now we are witnessing similar scenes following the latest earthquake in Iran where 50,000 people have been killed.
When I told Aunt Dos, she said, "They will be busy in heaven."

28th June 1990 Thursday

"Golly, what are we going to do?" This was the immediate reaction of everyone who attended a meeting hosted by Prime Minister Margaret Thatcher for members of the Cabinet and department heads to address the problem of Global Warming. Our very lifestyle creates the problem.

2nd July 1990 Monday

Salmon Rushdie, whose book "Satanic Verses" so offended the great Ayatollah Komeini and all devout Muslims, dare not venture from his secret hideout for fear of being assassinated by the Iranians. However, the recent terrible earthquake in Iran has prompted him to give £5,000 to help the victims.

4th July 1990 Wednesday

"Othello" was shown again on television and I enjoyed it just as much as when I first saw it in January 1974. This time I followed it word for word with my "Complete Works of William Shakespeare" and marvelled at the skill of the actors to give such life to the written word.

6th July 1990 Friday

Bunting's birthday tomorrow – 75! And Karen's Wedding Day tomorrow – just 20. Karen is Mary Blue's daughter, brought up by her father Terry when Mary Blue ran away to Scotland, but happily now equally at home with either of her parents; secure in the love of her Graham.

8th July 1990 Sunday

No expense was spared by Terry, father of the bride yesterday, when his only daughter Karen married her beloved Graham. A white Rolls Royce – a lovely church wedding – a splendid reception at "The Gables", where even the serviettes proclaimed Graham & Karen 7th July 1990. Mary Blue, mother of the bride, was not able to enjoy this role to the full, as Terry's wife No. 3 took centre stage in this part, with wife No. 2 and wife No. 1 acting more like understudies. The Hewes' representation was minimal; with old maid Hewsie in her role as maiden aunt.

12th July 1990 Thursday

18/8 Stainless steel 44 piece canteen of cutlery – i.e. 18% Chromium, 8% Nickel.
After a lifetime using the old mixed medley of cutlery belonging to my mum, I have at last acquired, like a new bride, an exquisite set of knives, forks & spoons, reduced in the summer sales to £250.

14th July 1990 Saturday

Cocky has bought me a new Parker pen for my 59th birthday. Cocky bought me my first Parker pen for my 21st birthday shortly after we had said goodbye; but such is our love for each other, that I am still aged 21 in the eyes of Cocky, & he is still the young man I think of as mine.

16th July 1990 Monday

"You are invited to my retirement family get-together on Sunday 14th July 1991, afternoon and evening" – location not yet decided. I sent out my initial tentative invitations to all my dad's progeny, with an assortment of brochures to peruse, for them all to consider where they would like to go.

18th July 1990 Wednesday

"The moving finger writes; and having writ, moves on."

"Here with a loaf of bread beneath the bough; a flask of wine, a book of verse – and thou beside me singing in the wilderness – and wilderness is paradise enow."

Enid gave me a 70 year-old little treasure of a book, "The Rubáiyát of Omar Khayyám".

> "'Tis all a Chequer-board of Nights and Days,
> where Destiny with Men for Pieces plays;
> hither and thither moves, and mates, and slays,
> and one by one back in the Closet lays."

Thus observes Omar Khayyám, Persian poet of the 12th century, who like Salman Rushdie of today, offended his fellow countrymen.

22nd July 1990 Sunday

St. James Church, Highfield Street, Coalville 1915 – 1990.

The 75th anniversary was celebrated in style with a Solemn Mass where the Archdeacon of Loughborough was the preacher and where 5 priests – concelebrating priests – all in unison blessed & consecrated the Bread & the Wine. The Archdeacon likened the building of St. James Church in 1915, when so many young men were being killed in the battle-fields of the First Great War, to the building of the Church at Staunton Harold in 1653; taking for his text the inscription seen above the entrance to that church -

"In the yeare 1653, when all thinges sacred were throughout y nation either demolished or profaned, S[r] Robert Shirley Barronet founded this church whose singular praise it is to have done the best thinges in y worst times and hoped them in the most callamitous."

All the old records, both of little St. Mary's & St. James Church, Snibston, were on display at the 75th anniversary, including Parish Magazines all beautifully bound, year by year, for preservation.

I was most interested to read of my own baptism in the September magazine of 1931.

30th July 1990 Monday

Another get-together of my dad's three children as Pat, Evelyn & I again spent the day with Bunting & Mostyn in their luxury home at Stafford.

Michael, fully recovered from his brief fling with Carolyn, & now openly discussing his happy relationship with Josie, joined us for afternoon tea.

1st August 1990 Wednesday

As in March 1979, a terrorist bomb was planted underneath the car of Mr. Airey Neave, 63 year-old M.P. for Abingdon, killing him as soon as he drove away, so now top Tory M.P. Mr. Ian Gow, 53 year-old M.P. for Eastbourne, has been killed in a car bomb blast in the drive of his home.

3rd August 1990 Friday

99° Phew! It is so hot this week, that I am now sitting absolutely stark naked in my boudoir writing today's entry in my diary.

I feel for Yvonne, who is now 8 months pregnant.

Readers might, perhaps, be interested to know that at precisely 56 seconds past 12.34 (a.m. or p.m.) next Tuesday, August 7th 1990, the time date sequence will be

12.34.56 7/8/90

5th August 1990 Sunday

Yvonne is expecting her baby on 28th September and she already knows that it is a boy. So Cocky & Joan look forward to the birth of their first grandchild. As Psalm 128 says, "Thus shall the man be blessed that feareth the Lord. Yea, thou shalt see thy children's children."

7th August 1990 Tuesday

On 7th August 1679 Nicholas Postgate, a Roman Catholic priest, was martyred at York in the reign of Charles II, subsequent to the Oates Plot. His crime? Being a Roman Catholic priest on English soil. "The Priest of the Moors" is the latest book I have been loaned by my work colleague, Ted Ludlow.

The more I read about the bloody conflict between Protestants & Roman Catholics, the more I wonder whatever the good Lord in heaven above thinks of us all. Every day brings us news of continued bloodshed in Northern Ireland over this very issue – the latest victim, an innocent man.

11th August 1990 Saturday

Another book loaned to me by Ted Ludlow, a devout Roman Catholic himself, is the story of Ronald Walls, a Presbyterian minister in the Highlands of Scotland, who after much soul searching gave up his job & his religion with its limited horizons in favour of the University of the Roman Catholic Church.

13th August 1990 Monday

"How lovely it was to hear the bells of Lancaster Priory coming to me through the telephone when Cocky rang me from the prison." That is what I wrote in my diary in August 1988. Imagine, then, how pleased I was to find in a second-hand shop in Leicester a picture of the Castle Prison & Priory.

15th August 1990 Wednesday

Meet "Cordon Bleu Cook Hewsie" – the Blue Ribbon of cooks. Having never owned a decent cooker, & never having baked anything in an oven, I have now purchased a table top size cooker called a "Cordon Bleu Mini Kitchen" - £100, & for the first time ever made an oven cooked meal.

17th August 1990 Friday

President Saddam Hussein of Iraq, known as the Butcher of Baghdad, after numerous threats & much sabre-rattling, has now brought the simmering cauldron of the Middle East to boiling point by overthrowing the Emirate of Kuwait, and threatening next to usurp the oil rich Kingdom of Saudi Arabia.

19th August 1990 Sunday

On this 11th Sunday after Trinity when we are reminded that God declares his almighty power most chiefly in shewing mercy & pity, all the military might of the world is gathered in the Middle East where Saddam Hussein has called for a jihad – a Holy War; & both sides pray for victory.

21st August 1990 Tuesday

As the Western world rushes to defend Saudi Arabia, simply because the oil fields there are so vital to the West, the bitter conflict is becoming more of a conflict between East & West; between Arabs & Westerners; between Islam & Christianity; with those of the same faith joining forces together.

23rd August 1990 Thursday

The Iraq of today was probably where Adam & Eve walked in the Garden of Eden. Here are those two great rivers – the River Euphrates & the River Tigris. Here were the Hanging Gardens of Babylon, which have now been rebuilt by order of Saddam Hussein, with bricks cast in his own name.

Ancient Babylon had two periods of greatness. Its first empire from about 1900 B.C. to 1600 B.C. and its second empire 1,000 years later when Nebuchadnezzar II carried away to Babylon, the Children of Israel & destroyed their temple in Jerusalem. "By the rivers of Babylon we sat down and wept, when we remembered thee, O Zion.........." Psalm 137.

27th August 1990 Monday

It seems that the history of the world has now gone full cycle as the Garden of Eden prepares for battle. When Baghdad was sacked by invading Mongols in 1258 it was said that mankind was unlikely to see the like of such a calamity until "the world comes to an end & perishes".

29th August 1990 Wednesday

The more I consider the age of the Earth, the more I marvel at the provision of oil and gas for this generation alone. 65 million years gave us the Frigg & Forties fields. 150 million years gave us the Morecambe field, while the Buchan field goes back to the Carboniferous age – up to 395 million years.

31st August 1990 Friday

Mary Moore, aged 79, is on her annual pilgrimage to Ravenstone, where again we met up with her Australian cousins, descendants of black sheep & bigamist "Uncle Jim". We last saw them in September 1984 at Mountsorrel at the home of Auntie Doris, & met up with them there again.

2nd September 1990 Sunday

"... who went about doing good." Acts of the Apostles, Chapter 10.

The preacher said that these five words spoken by St. Peter to describe our Lord said it all – in a nutshell. He was talking of Naaman who was cured of his leprosy when he accepted small duties rather than great.

4th September 1990 Tuesday

Joanne, aged 16, has now left school & started work in a hairdresser's shop. She has one day each week at Coalville Technical College learning the mechanics of the job, & every Thursday has a day off; working Monday to Saturday. She loves the job, as it is what she has always wanted to do.

6th September 1990 Thursday

Katherine Sullivan, aged 86, & I enjoyed a full day together in Nottingham. We shopped at Debenhams, had lunch across the road from the Castle, went into the Roman Catholic Cathedral Church of St. Barnabas, & booked seats at the Theatre Royal for 2 forthcoming productions.

8th September 1990 Saturday

September 8th is the Birthday of the Blessed Virgin Mary – so the Roman Catholic priest told me. Speaking on the radio, he said that when Christ was on the Cross, he said (not only to his disciple John, but to everyone), "Behold thy mother."

The Roman Catholics have an indirect influence on me.

10th September 1990 Monday

The Roman Catholics had a direct influence on my mum.

In the First World War 1914 – 1918, refugee nuns from Belgium came to the convent at Coalville & taught my mum in her early teens.

When diphtheria killed my mum's twin sister in 1915, only the nuns came anywhere near.

12th September 1990 Wednesday

What is a Priest?

In the year 1614, a Benedictine priest, Blessed Maurus Scott, asked Dr. John King, Protestant Bishop of London, "Are you a priest?"

"No", said the Bishop, "I am not a massing priest."

"Sacrifice", replied the Benedictine priest "is essential to priesthood. Massing is the same as sacrificing. If you are no massing priest, you are no sacrificing priest; if no sacrificing priest, no priest at all, & therefore no bishop." For saying this to the Protestant Bishop of London, he was put to death.

To understand the priesthood of Christ, know Melchizedek. Christ is more than a priest. Christ is "A high priest after the order of Melchisedek".

(Hebrews 5, 6.)

Melchizedek, King of Salem, King of righteousness, King of peace, without father, without mother, without genealogy, having neither beginning of days nor end of life, first appears in the Book of Genesis, Chapter 14.

"The Lord hath sworn, & will not repent; thou art a priest for ever, after the order of Melchizedek". (Psalm 110). Christ was born of the tribe of Judah, unlike Moses & Aaron who were born of the tribe of Levi – the priesthood tribe. It is because Christ is priest for ever, that his priesthood is special. (See Hebrews, Chapter 7.)

20th September 1990 Thursday

"I was most impressed by Lord Caradon, a man of infinite wisdom & compassion". Thus I wrote in my diary in February 1972.

Lord Caradon, PC, GCMG, KCVO, OBE, who as Sir Hugh Foot was governor of Cyprus from 1957 to 1960, died earlier this month, aged 82. He was born on 8th October 1907.

Lord Caradon's wisdom & compassion made him a "peace-maker". His wisdom was to teach the warring Greeks & Turks of Cyprus to think for themselves & sort out their own problems. As a direct result of my adverse staff report, I too am more inclined to think for myself than ask, "Shall I?"

24th September 1990 Monday

"Gorbachev Glasnost & The Gospel" – This was the title of this year's Annual Ashe Lecture, given at St. Helens, Ashby-de-la-Zouch by Michael Bordeaux, recognised as the most authoritative commentator on Christians in the Soviet Union. I was able to buy his book of the same title.

Mikhail Sergeyevich Gorbachev, like me, was born in

1931. Gorbachev's mother, like mine, was a practising Christian & he was baptised. But at an early age his education included lessons on Marxism – Leninism & scientific atheism. Last year on 1st December 1989 however, he met the Pope at the Vatican.

28th September 1990 Friday
The Bishop of Leicester, the Rt. Revd. Dr. Richard Rutt is to retire on 1st October 1990.
It was 9 years ago, in September 1981 that he came to Ravenstone & had morning coffee with us at the home of Emily Walker.
It was he too who knitted his own Bishop's mitre. (See 6th June 1985).

30th September 1990 Sunday
Godfrey Pill, aged 65, was today ordained as "Priest" in Leicester Cathedral. Katherine & I attended this impressive service followed by a social gathering & sit-down meal at Hugglescote Church Hall, attended by many Ravenstone parishioners. Mr Pill will now be priest at Hugglescote.

2nd October 1990 Tuesday
In 1945 at the end of the Second World War, the victors split Germany into four zones –
1. U. S., 2. British, 3. French, 4. Soviet. Zones 1, 2 and 3 became the Federal Republic while Zone 4 became the German Democratic Republic. At midnight tonight Germany will be made whole again.

4th October 1990 Thursday
October 4th is the Feast of Saint Francis. Last Sunday "well behaved pets" were invited to a Service of Thanksgiving for creatures great & small at St. Andrew's Church, Jarrom Street, Leicester, where the retiring Bishop of Leicester gave the address. Katherine, Toffee & I were delighted to attend.

6th October 1990 Saturday
Matthew Lawrence John Bond, who was expected to make his entrance into this world at the end of September, delayed his entrance until the early hours of tomorrow, to carry on the family tradition of a birthday on the 7th. He is Cocky and Joan's first grandchild, born on the Sabbath Day.

8th October 1990 Monday
"What a strange thing it is when your boss ceases to be your boss" – This is what I wrote in my diary in October 1983, and before that in April 1976. But how much more strange a thing it is to contemplate your own retirement and prepare to step out of one orbit into another.

10th October 1990 Wednesday
Having moved in the sphere of full time employment for 42 years, I feel rather like Zabdiel (see 5th December 1983) about to be launched into a higher sphere, which can only be done at the precise moment of contact of the 2 spheres.
I feel also like Elijah, about to cast off my mantle.

12th October 1990 Friday
Enthronement Date – Dr. George Carey will be enthroned as 103rd Archbishop of Canterbury in Canterbury Cathedral on Friday April 19th next year, dean and chapter of cathedral have announced.

14th October 1990 Sunday
9 months to retirement and I now feel like Zabdiel – Elijah - Christian in Pilgrim's Progress at the end of his journey - a chrysalis about to change into a butterfly - & altogether a new and different me.
Already I have attended a Pre-Retirement Training Course & am preparing for lift-off.
"Preparing for lift-off" means getting rid of excess baggage. The amount of clutter I have accumulated at work over the years is slowly being sorted & sifted, until only the essential paper work, etc. is left.
Likewise at home, I am glad to have discarded all bulky & cumbersome furniture.

18th October 1990 Thursday
My "Pre-Retirement" course was held at Vaughan College in Leicester. Situated right in the centre of what used to be the Roman city of Ratae Corieltauvorum, I explored the remains of the Roman public baths, built about 150 A.D. & the Jewry Wall, meaning Jurat's Wall – a medieval town councillor.

20th October 1990 Saturday
Mikhail Sergeyevich Gorbachev, Soviet leader, who appeared so vividly to me in a dream earlier this year, has been nominated 1990 winner of the Nobel Peace Prize. He has been given this honour for the historic changes he has instigated - for the greater openness in Soviet society, promoting international trust.

22nd October 1990 Monday
And 1,000 years rolled by. And thanks to Mikhail Gorbachev, the Christians of Russia, persecuted from the days of the Revolution 1918, until 1988, were allowed to celebrate their Orthodox Millennium 988 – 1988 to commemorate the baptism of Prince Vladimir & the end of paganism.

24th October 1990 Wednesday
"Tomorrow is Saint Crispian"
So said King Henry V on the eve of his greatest victory, at the Battle of Agincourt, when his 6,000 archers gained a great victory over more than 30,000 French knights, leaving 10,000 French & a mere handful of English slain. I saw this on the cinema screen.

26th October 1990 Friday
"We've won the forest" proclaims the Leicester Mercury as Leicestershire is chosen as the site for the first major forest planting since the days of William the Conqueror. There were 5 contenders -
1. Leicestershire's Charnwood & Needwood,
2. Shakespeare's Forest of Arden,
3. Rockingham Forest,
4. Wyre Forest,
5. Sherwood Forest.
The planting of our new forest will take 30 years. It will be a "broad-leaved" forest of oak, birch, ash and elm and will cost £90 million. It will cover 150 square miles of North West Leicestershire & parts of Staffordshire, Derbyshire and Warwickshire. The forest will not reach maturity until circa 2100 A.D.

30th October 1990 Tuesday

Lee, Francis (Frank), the devoted and dearly loved husband of Beatrice, passed suddenly but peacefully away at his home at Anstey, on October 29th 1989, aged 67 years.

Without goodbye you fell asleep, memories of you I will always keep. Goodnight sweetheart, till we meet again. I will love you always and thank you for 41 wonderful years – your devoted wife Beatrice.

Funeral service Anstey United Reformed Church, Tuesday, November 7th followed by interment in Anstey Cemetery. Family flowers only please, donations in lieu to the British Heart Foundation Fund, if so desired, may be sent to the Co-operative Funeral Service, 131 Humberstone Road, Tel. 516906.

This is Frank Lee, whose staff report I wrote in 1977. (See 20th October 1977)

I wrote then, "In the final analysis he will be counted as a winner." What more can a man wish for than a devoted wife to love & call him sweetheart?

1st November 1990 Thursday

The Channel Tunnel is expected to be finished & operative by June 1993. There are 2 parallel train tunnels with a smaller diameter service tunnel between. The first contact between British & French excavators with a long metal probe in the service tunnel is imminent, with men meeting later.

3rd November 1990 Saturday

"Put my tears into a bottle" – Psalm 56.

Having wept so much over the years, I wonder how large a bottle my tears would fill. No doubt our tears, like choicest perfume, come in varying degrees of worth, according to what lies behind them. But all is revealed in God's diary. "Are not these things noted in thy book?"

5th November 1990 Monday

"Diorissimo" - choicest perfume by Christian Dior of Paris has the fragrance of lilies of the valley. This is the perfume which Katherine chooses, and this is the perfume which I have now acquired. Katherine not only opens my eyes to things I have never seen before, but awakens other senses too.

7th November 1990 Wednesday

The latest book to be loaned to me by Katherine is "The Rothschilds – a Family of Fortune". Spanning more than 200 years, it tells the remarkable story of this Jewish family, who amassed colossal wealth and had palaces fit for a king all over Europe. One such palace is Ferrières, where Katherine once worked.

Katherine taught English to the young David René James Rothschild who was born in 1942. She taught him in his own home, Ferrières, in the Brie district near Paris.

Joseph Paxton, the designer of Crystal Palace, was the architect of Mentmore Towers in Buckinghamshire (another Rothschild home) & also of Ferrières.

11th November 1990 Sunday

Imagine my delight on my "Pre-Retirement" Course when a member of the National Trust showed coloured slides of places of interest now in the care of the National Trust which included Waddesdon Manor in Buckinghamshire, former home of Ferdinand Rothschild, and also Ascott House.

13th November 1990 Tuesday

The Reverend Royston Grandfield Davis has now been "licensed" as Team Vicar in the United Benefice of Hugglescote with Donington, Ellistown & Snibston, replacing John King Hancock whose 5 year tenancy finished earlier this year. Again we heard that beautiful prayer, "O God of unchangeable power ...."

Being Bishopless at the moment, the licensing of Snibston's new Vicar was conducted by our loveable Archdeacon, the Venerable Hughie Jones. The service was held at St. Christopher's, Ellistown, where I chose to sit on the back row, & was then absolutely amazed to be asked to lead the way to Communion in the porch.

16th November 1990 Friday

"Spy" Shuttle – Space shuttle Atlantis thundered into space on a secret mission that civilian experts say will launch a spy satellite to monitor Iraqi troops in the Gulf.

17th November 1990 Saturday

£200 thousand million pounds! That is how much the government is proposing to spend in the 1991 – 1992 financial year commencing 1st April. Again the biggest slice of the spending cake goes to Social Security (62.8 billion). Health = £25 billion, Defence – £22.8 billion, Local Government = £23 billion.

19th November 1990 Monday

Saint Elizabeth's Day. (So I am informed by Katherine) Saint Elizabeth (1207 – 1231) of Hungary was the daughter of King Andrew II. Married at 14, she was widowed at the age of 20, and died so young because of her excessive asceticism & charitable works. She is honoured at Marburg in Germany.

Elizabeth of Hungary was born into a royal family in 1207. She married Ludwig of Thuringia and became his queen. But she didn't forget the poor people who lived nearby.

21st November 1990 Wednesday

As in 44 B.C. Julius Cæsar was stabbed in the back by members of the Senate, so today Britain's first woman Prime Minister, Mrs Margaret Thatcher, after 11 years in office, is being hounded out by members of her own cabinet and other supposedly loyal Tory M.P.s, all now against her.

23rd November 1990 Friday

Prime Minister Margaret Thatcher, much against her own will, yesterday tendered her resignation. For 11 years she has enjoyed the power and the prestige of being Number One, pressing purposefully forward as the "Iron Lady", loved by many but hated by many more, especially the poor & under privileged.

25th November 1990 Sunday

"Blessed are the peacemakers; for they shall be called the children of God" (Matthew 5, 9.)

With the world on the brink of war, Ravenstone's new young Rector, the Reverend Kerry Emmett, spoke of the blessedness of the peacemakers – not the peace keepers, but the peacemakers, in every sphere of life.

27th November 1990 Tuesday
John Major has been "elected", by the 372 Conservative M.P.s at present in Parliament, to replace Margaret Thatcher as Prime Minister. He was Mrs Thatcher's Chancellor of the Exchequer, and now takes her place with her blessing, having supported her throughout, when others resigned or were given the chop.

29th November 1990 Thursday
Snibston's Industrial Heritage Museum on the site of the old Snibston Colliery is due to be fully operative by 1992. However, as a foretaste of things to come, we had a most interesting lecture this week in the "New Gallery" called simply "Flames" & presented by British Gas. Admission **Free**. "Flames" the very first lecture to be given in the New Gallery at Snibston's Industrial Museum, covered everything under the sun including the Sun itself. From pre-historic man to the blacksmith at his anvil – the glass maker – jet aeroplanes & launching rockets into outer space.

3rd December 1990 Monday
And 8,000 years rolled by & Britain became linked again to the continent, for the first time since the Ice Age, when the Channel was frozen.
At 11.00a.m. last Saturday, 1st December, French tunnellers made contact with British tunnellers 160 feet beneath the Channel. The tunnel has cost £7 ½ billion.

5th December 1990 Wednesday
"Britain has therefore severed diplomatic relations with Syria" – thus I wrote in November 1986 when explosives brought in by a Syrian diplomatic bag blew up the El Al Jumbo Flight 016. However, diplomatic relations with Syria have now been restored as Syria joins the West in readiness for war with Iraq.

7th December 1990 Friday
Jonathon, Cocky's son, is 17 years old today & celebrating with a family get-together – Cocky, Joan, Yvonne, David, and 2 month old baby Matthew.
It was when Cocky himself was 17 and I was 16 that we first fell in love, but I never expected to spend all these years as an old maid.

9th December 1990 Sunday
As the world stands on the brink of war, I wonder how God surveys the scene, beyond the confines of space and time. Does he see all that ever was and all that ever will be? Does he see the antics of this world like a video, which he can move backwards or forwards at will, at high speed or switch off?

11th December 1990 Tuesday
Car numbers for sale! Now that the government has overall control of the allocation of car numbers, they have stopped releasing numbers 1 to 20, saving them for auction at exorbitant cost. Latest offers include;
G 1 LES, **H 1 LDA**, **SUS 1 E**, and even **1 MAY** & **1 SAY**, which were never genuinely issued.

13th December 1990 Thursday
From my love, by post, a tiny golden heart-shaped locket brooch beneath a golden bar, shaped into a pretty beribboned bow, and a Christmas card which said, "Special wishes at Christmas to the one I love" – "Have a nice Christmas darling. All my love for ever, John xxxxx XXX
I arrive at work early – Department of Energy, Gas and Oil Measurement Branch, 3 Tigers Road, South Wigston, Leicester LE8 2US Telephone 0533 785354.
Dr. Sayer, my reporting officer, receives written communication from Personnel Section, London, concerning my retirement. (7 months in advance) He confirms in writing that I expect to retire on my 60th birthday July 14th 1991.

14th December 1990 Friday
As Treasurer of Coalville Amateur Operatic Society, I prepare at work a covering letter to send out to 25 different "groups" in the area, and forward applications to attend C.A.O.S. forthcoming production "Hello Dolly".
Dr. Sayer sends a written minute to Registry staff: – File Handling Procedures – The P.U.S. has recently taken an interest in the handling of registered files within the Department & as a result we are required to ensure that a file is closed & new part opened when a part is 5 years old or more than 1 ½ ″ thick.

15th December 1990 Saturday
"Coppélia" – That most exquisite of ballets with equally enchanting music composed by Léo Delibes, was performed this week at Nottingham's Royal Centre. Thanks to Katherine's love of Delibes' music we found ourselves on the front row, transported to realms above by the heavenly performance which moved me to tears.

Flashes of sheet lightning actually between the sheets each time I turned over in bed, wearing brushed nylon pyjamas, convinced me I was a highly activated electro-magnet.
Regular dreams of flying over the roof-tops also made me think I was by no means earth-bound.
Belonging to no-one, but still in the nest where I was hatched, I feel out of place.

16th December 1990 Sunday
Advent III - "Today I am coming to your house" – This is the thought given to us today as we are reminded of Christ's words to Zacchaeus. (Luke, Chapter 19)

17th December 1990 Monday
A lovely all-go day. Up with the lark and a phone call from Cocky at 6.20 a.m.
Off to Nottingham for a good old pre-Christmas shopping spree, savouring the delights of the city in festive mood.
Called in at the "Amateurs" rehearsal of "Hello Dolly" and collected one or two members' subscriptions - £3-50p each.
Home by 9 p.m. and a phone call from Roy Hunt, President of Coalville Amateur Operatic Society, to finalise details of "The President's Letter" which I, as Treasurer, send out to the Patrons.
10 p.m. I telephoned Auntie Doris (aged 95) at Mountsorrel and arranged to visit her tomorrow morning.

"History is Planted" – so proclaims the Leicester Mercury as the first sapling, a tiny oak, was planted in Leicestershire's forest of the future. The first of 30 million trees for our "New Forest" was one of several hundred planted near to Ashby-de-la-Zouch, some given by the "old" New Forest in Hampshire.

18th December 1990 Tuesday

Up with the lark again & after breakfast a brisk 3 mile circular walk. Ravenstone – Coalville – Ravenstone.

Katherine Sullivan, aged 86, Toffee her pampered dachshund & I motored to Mountsorrel & had morning coffee with 95 year old Auntie Doris.

I bought a pretty outfit for £35 at the shop across the road from Auntie Doris' house, by the Butter Cross.

In the afternoon I took Katherine to the newly opened Morrison's supermarket at Coalville, where she was delighted to buy lots of provisions from so vast a choice of quality foods.

19th December 1990 Wednesday

Back to work after my last 2 days annual leave for this year.

Our office party this afternoon. A telephone call in the middle of the party from our head office in London to confirm from me that I am expecting to retire from work next July; in which case they will forward letter spelling out the details.

I despatched all the letters from Coalville Amateur Operatic Society to the patrons, enclosing applications for tickets. Price of tickets ranges from £2 to £4.

We arrange at work to throw out all the old typewriters, now overtaken by word processors and computers.

A pre-Christmas blizzard brought havoc to Leicestershire with power blackouts which lasted for more than a week in the worst hit areas. As the snow hit electricity & telephone wires it was frozen by winds causing a phenomenon known as **ice accretion** – a very rare occurrence.

Ice accretion = the growing together of parts externally – continuous coherence. It will only form with wet snow falling, and a moderate to strong wind, and temperatures at exactly the right level to freeze the wet snow into cylindrical formations of ice, making all the wires up to 9″ thick.

20th December 1990 Thursday

Twice a week I visit Aunt Dos, now aged 88 and confined to Markfield Court Nursing Home.

This evening I found her in bed, protesting loudly at having been put to bed against her will & demanding that I take her home with me.

A dozen times or more she asked me, Where was she? Why was she there? When was she supposed to be going home?

Gradually, however, her aggression died down as she snuggled into the bedclothes, with her sister-in-law Thirza Stacey, in the twin bed beside her.

These two are, for brother Pat, his father's sister & his mother's sister.

21st December 1990 Friday

As I approach my three score years, I recall Aunt Dos at that age, when she owned her own car and took me for rides with her, while I still rode a scooter as a "learner".

Gosh, what a decade or two can do to us! I remember once on holiday with Enid we saw inside a church some recumbent effigies and a plaque which read, "As you are, so were we. As we are, so you'll be."

And so often I hear those who are now old and infirm say, "I never thought I would ever come to this."

22nd December 1990 Saturday

Twice a week Cocky telephones me from Lancashire. He & I were teenage sweethearts.

In 1957 he married Joan & after 30 years of marriage he rang to say he still loved me. He has no idea what I look like after all these years, but we talk to each other on the phone as though time has stood still for us. We never meet, but love each other from afar.

23rd December 1990 Sunday

All wrapped up for Christmas – and we are reminded that when Christ was born he too was all wrapped up by Joseph & Mary. But, more than that, when he died, he again was all wrapped up by Joseph of Arimathaea.

In my reluctant role of Maiden Aunt, I was grateful to be invited for Christmas Day to the home of Mary Blue & family; and for Boxing Day to the home of Pat & Evelyn.

Snibston's new vicar, the Reverend Davis, has stipulated that no-one in his parish must be alone for Christmas. He has gathered them up, like "the fragments that remain, that nothing be lost".

24th December 1990 Monday

Our 3 day Christmas break at work this year is Monday, Tuesday, Wednesday.

Katherine Sullivan and I booked seats for "Cinderella" this afternoon at the De Montfort Hall, Leicester. We chose front central gangway seats on the balcony. Imagine our surprise when we arrived to be told that those seats ought not to have been sold to us. They were intended for the Lord Mayor & Lady Mayoress. Would we be so very kind & accept alternative seats further along the row? Katherine, at her most charming, graciously accepted & we were provided with interval ice-cream, compliments of the Lord Mayor.

25th December 1990 Tuesday

Cocky, whom I have not seen for decades, was in closer contact with me than anyone else today as he whispered words of love to me on the telephone.

What a sad thing it is that we cannot all find our life's partner and live together in harmony without such things as love triangles, jealousies and broken hearts.

Christmas Day at the home of Mary Blue, where Pat & Evelyn & I joined Mary Blue, Scott and Murdo Junior for a lovely day together.

Sharon & Darren called in briefly during the evening & we saw their beautiful wedding stationery, specially printed in readiness for their wedding next year on 22nd June.

Mary Blue, now aged 46, after 2 marriages, 2 divorces, and with 3 grown up children of her own, plus Sharon & Murdo who know her as "Mum", looks younger than ever & is enjoying life to the full, with lots of friends & plenty of parties and outings. In her household, love rules without a sword; love binds without a cord.

26th December 1990 Wednesday

Boxing Day at the home of Pat and Evelyn.

Pat, Evelyn, Mary Blue & I had lunch together and were joined later by the local hospital chaplain Colin Patey, his wife & 2 young sons, plus the new Vicar of Snibston, the Revd. Royston Davis, his wife, and two Chinese students they had under their wings for a few days. We all sang with gusto, as first one then another played the electronic organ. One of the Chinese students was a Christian & the other was a Confucian. (We were told he was a Confusion)

27th December 1990 Thursday

Received the letter I was expecting from our head office in London concerning my retirement next July, together with "Declaration of Entitlement and Application for Payment" and explanatory notes...... "Because of the need to keep down costs, the Paymaster General's Office will not be able to send you details of your pension each time a payment is made. Any enquiries about the payment of your pension should be made to the Paymaster General's Office, quoting your personal pension reference number which will be notified to you when your pension begins."

"To All Staff – 1990 has been a very active year for the Department; electricity privatisation, the international oil market, the Piper Alpha inquiry, the financial restructuring of the coal industry, and environmental issues are just a few of the subjects which have caught the headlines........ the Department has achieved a great deal. This has been made possible through the dedicated efforts of staff at all levels .... I have been most impressed by the enthusiasm & commitment shown by staff in this very busy year & the hard work which has made it such a success" – John Wakeham.

28th December 1990 Friday

Completed the form G59/CS – application for payment of pension, which was countersigned by my work colleague Alan Norris, who certified that "this declaration was signed in my presence by the declarant whom I believe to be the person named above."

"Please notify the Paymaster General's Office, Sutherland House, Russell Way, Crawley, West Sussex RH10 1UH of any permanent change of your private address or bank account details as far in advance as possible. With well over a million pensioners being paid, it is most important that you quote your personal pension reference number in full, to make sure that your enquiry is dealt with promptly."

29th December 1990 Saturday

Having been introduced through the library at work to Whitaker's Almanack – "An amazing variety of subjects in one renowned annual volume, all the facts at your fingertips at home or at work" – I have chosen the 1991 edition as my "gift to the Treasurer" to be presented by Coalville Amateur Operatic Society next March. Today I bought the book in Leicester, as I happened to see it while I was in a book shop. (£20)

30th December 1990 Sunday

Never has the world been so close to its "Armageddon". The vials of the wrath of God seem almost ready to be poured out. (Revelation, Chapter 16)

31st December 1990 Monday

And so the year ends with the world poised for battle. President Saddam Hussein of Iraq, having invaded and conquered Kuwait, declares that Kuwait is, and always has been, part of his rightful territory. To defend this claim he is prepared to launch chemical & biological weapons against any would-be attacker. Chemical weapons contain poison gas. Biological weapons deliver deadly germs to produce such things as typhoid, cholera and anthrax.

President Bush of America is equally determined to save the oil supplies of both Kuwait & Saudi Arabia & has threatened nuclear warfare if Saddam is not out by 15th January.

* * *

"And as the evening twilight fades away
The sky is filled with stars, invisible by day"
Longfellow

* * *

1991

1991 - The year I reached retirement age.

1991 - The first palindromic year since **1881**.

"The world then to an end will come, in nineteen hundred and ninety one"

Old Mother Shipton (1488 – 1561)

1st January 1991 Tuesday

Cocky, who has smoked ever since he was a teenager, has decided to give up smoking for his New Year Resolution. When I told him that I would not like to kiss him with his breath fouled by tobacco smoke, he said, "I will give up smoking for you." Not that we are planning to meet & kiss, but we live in a make-believe world.

Cocky means more to me than anyone else in the world. We share confidences and are almost as one, and yet we keep our distance – a hundred and fifty and three miles apart. I will never arrange a clandestine meeting with him. That is my constant resolution.

2nd January 1991 Wednesday

Saddam Hussein's New Year message to the West is this – "Kuwait is Iraq's 19th Province & there is no reverse to this reality & there is no negotiation on the basis of withdrawal from Kuwait." He has invoked God's curse on President Bush, and branded Saudi Arabia's King Fahd "the traitor of the two holy mosques" for allowing foreign troops into his kingdom.

"In the same way as did the renegades and hypocrites betray the principles of Islam in the life of the Prophet Mohammed, so has the so-called Custodian of the Two Holy Mosques betrayed the trust given to him, the principles of Islam."

3rd January 1991 Thursday

A New Year and new neighbours either side of 27 Leicester Road, Ravenstone.

Into Aunt Dos's bungalow Mr & Mrs Taylor – Douglas & Eileen with their 26 year old son Peter. They invited Mrs Kath Nichols & me to see the New Year in with them & kept us well entertained with all their reminiscences.

1991 is Census Year and as Branch Liaison Officer at work, I have received all the necessary paperwork for anyone interested in applying to be a Census Enumerator. As it sounded just the job for me, I have filled in the form to be an enumerator myself.

"Please give reasons why you believe you are suitable for the post of Enumerator."

Answer – "Suitably qualified. Mature, responsible and conscientious. Capable of carrying out the work. Looking forward to this opportunity."

It all depends what area you are given, whether it is a pleasure or not.

4th January 1991 Friday

"The Government has decided that a Census of Population should be taken on 21st April 1991." The Census will be the 19th in a series carried out every 10 years in Great Britain since 1801, except in 1941. (The War)

105,350 Enumerators will be needed for the delivery & collection of the Census forms, & they will be recruited, trained & managed by 2,255 local managers (Census Officers), helped by 6,765 Enumeration Supervisors (Assistant Census Officers). Above the Census Officers will be 115 Census Area Managers, reporting to Census H.Q., The Office of Population Censuses & Surveys (O.P.C.S. Recruitment) Titchfield, Fareham, Hants. PO15 5RR

Telephone 0329 84 44 44

5th January 1991 Saturday

Having artificially coloured my hair brown ever since my first few grey hairs appeared, half a lifetime ago, I have decided to go into retirement as a blonde. The gradual transition has now begun, and after the first session I am one degree lighter. What colour I really am underneath I have no idea. The roots appear to be pure white, so maybe I am indeed white headed.

Epiphany Sunday tomorrow sees the launching of "The Decade of Evangelism" a joint venture by all Britain's leading Christian denominations in a bid to swell the dwindling congregations, now less than 7 million. The "new" Christians will be offered more colour & flair in their worship.

6th January 1991 Sunday

The Epiphany – "As with gladness men of old, did the guiding star behold, As with joy they hailed its light, leading onward, beaming bright; So, most gracious Lord may we – evermore be led to Thee."

7th January 1991 Monday

What a dreadful thing it is to make provision for bloody warfare. While soldiers in the desert practise gunfire, ready to inflict untold damage on one another, here in rural England preparations are being made to receive the war wounded. The Trent Regional Health Authority is preparing 2,500 hospital beds; & schools & halls are also ready for use as makeshift transfusion centres, with voluntary services, including St. John Ambulance & the Red Cross ready to assist. Leicester Royal Infirmary in an emergency can deal with burns & plastic surgery.

Joanne, almost 17 years old, is finding as I have found, that the course of true love never did run smooth. As I think of Brian Lamming on this, his birthday, Joanne, fighting to hold back her tears, confides in me that the boy of her dreams chooses to ignore her & deliberately walks away from her.

8th January 1991 Tuesday

How even more dreadful a thing it is to see healthy young men, in the prime of life, being despatched in their thousands to do battle in the Middle East.

While half the world suffers from malnutrition & starvation, astronomical amounts of money are being poured into weaponry & protective clothing against chemical and biological weaponry. And what of the anguish of wives, sweethearts & mothers left in tears as their men-folk leave by the ship-load?

I think of Longfellow who wrote – "And in despair I bowed my head; 'There is no peace on earth', I said."

9th January 1991 Wednesday

"Christmas Bells" by Longfellow.

I heard the bells on Christmas Day
their old familiar carols play,
And wild and sweet the words repeat
of Peace on Earth, Goodwill to men!
Then from each black accursed mouth
the cannon thundered in the south,
And with the sound the carols drowned
of Peace on Earth, Goodwill to men!
It was as if an earthquake rent
the hearthstones of a continent,
And made forlorn the households born
of Peace on Earth, Goodwill to men!
And in despair I bowed my head;
"There is no peace on earth" I said,
For hate is strong & mocks the song
of Peace on Earth, Goodwill to men!
Then pealed the bells more loud & deep,
"God is not dead; nor doth he sleep!
The wrong shall fail; the right prevail,
with Peace on Earth, Goodwill to men!"

*****

While Joanne suffers all the heartbreak of feeling spurned & rejected, her close relative Tina, who is a few years older than Joanne, is happily engaged to Wayne Tyers, is planning to get married this year & will live next door to me, between my house & Joanne's. Wayne is already living in the house vacated by Mrs Yelland.

10th January 1991 Thursday

Bunting and Mostyn's Sapphire Wedding Anniversary (married 45 years). It was in January 1946 that they were married at Ravenstone Church and I was one of the bridesmaids.
Like Cocky, Mostyn lived in Ravenstone. As I fell in love with Cocky at Ravenstone Institute, so Bunting fell in love with Mostyn at Ravenstone Institute. As Cocky & I have loved each other since first we met, so Bunting & Mostyn's love has continued to this day – they are united in Holy Matrimony, while Cocky and I tried & failed to say goodbye.
Cocky and Joan are united in Holy Matrimony. I am just a spare part.
As St. Paul stresses in Chapter 7 of his First Epistle to the Corinthians, "Let every man have his own wife, and let every woman have her own husband."
And as the Lord himself says, "What God hath joined together, let not man put asunder." (Matthew 19)
Only in heaven can we all be together as one, "For in the resurrection they neither marry, nor are given in marriage, but are as the angels."

11th January 1991 Friday

Living today under the threat of total annihilation, with all the military might of the world poised for battle on top of oil supplies which, if set on fire, would darken the sun, is like living, as Christ said, in the dark days of Noah when people carried on regardless, right up to the end. – Matthew, Chapter 24.

12th January 1991 Saturday

How grotesque our soldiers look in their N.B.C. suits (nuclear biological & chemical) as they anticipate the most horrendous attack of weaponry devised by man. Every square inch of flesh must be covered. As knights in shining armour long ago had to protect themselves in battle, the soldier today needs protection from the very air he breathes; from mustard gas & nerve gases, which are nightmare means of warfare.

13th January 1991 Sunday

"The End is Nigh" – For as long as I can remember, there have been those who were convinced that the end of the world was imminent. Now, however, the bookmakers are receiving bets from people that Jesus Christ will return to earth during this year 1991. They have been given 1000 – 1 odds.
Epiphany I, Psalm 67 – "God be merciful unto us & bless us ….. God shall bless us; and all the ends of the earth shall fear him."

14th January 1991 Monday

And still in my dreams, I fly at treetop level – mile after mile, looking down at the scene below. While cars grind to a halt when floodwater covers the road, I carry on, unhindered in my progress. Last night, however, I found myself veering to the left when I was trying to go to the right. And then I managed to get into someone's house, flying around the huge drawing room, but unable to get out. The good man of the house showed me the way out & when I apologised for intruding he said it had been a pleasure to have such a visitor.

Newspaper cutting – Flying – this represents ambition. If you fly on a steady path, you will achieve your goals. If you have difficulties or crash, you are grasping for more than you can reach. The experience of soaring is equated with aspiration and the desire to be upwardly mobile.

15th January 1991 Tuesday

While I fly merrily along in my dreams, in grim reality our leaders prepare for war. Encased in a nuclear-proof bunker at R.A.F. Strike Command, High Wycombe, Buckinghamshire, which goes down four storeys to a depth of 80 feet, 500 personnel control the communications systems which link up with the Gulf & defence establishments around the world. This is home to the Joint Headquarters for "Operation Granby" as Britain's Gulf deployment is known. The computer system, known as Air Staff Management Aid (A.S.M.A.) is linked up with air, land & naval bases; & there is direct communication with the Ministry of Defence in Whitehall.
6 months to retirement and the countdown is changing from months to weeks. As Staff Reporting looks set to become an ever more arduous chore, I shall be thankful to get away from "Work Objectives", "Management Objectives" & "Personal Development Objectives", but will miss the more delightful elements of the job.

16th January 1991 Wednesday

But it is President Bush of America who bears the burden of responsibility of giving the final go-ahead for war. Never has anyone had so dreadful a decision to make.

Saddam Hussein of Iraq is pinning the colours of Islam to his war banners. He has ordered that the Iraqi flag be embroidered with the words, "**Allah Akbar**" (God is Greatest), the Muslim battle cry. And God looks down on us all. Are we not all God's children? And surely, as a father, he loves us all.

17th January 1991 Thursday

"**Lord, keep us safe this night**" As we prayed the prayer we have known since childhood, it seemed to me like the night of the "Passover"....... "And Moses said, thus saith the Lord, About midnight will I go out into the midst of Egypt, and all the firstborn in the land of Egypt shall die ......"

And it was about midnight that war exploded in the Gulf. Military targets in Iraq and Kuwait were pounded with 18,000 tonnes of bombs, as "Operation Desert Storm" was launched. The raids were said to be the biggest air raids in history.

The National Debt is "The Liabilities of the National Loans Fund". It is not the most useful or comprehensive measure of public sector indebtedness because it does not cover the whole of central government. It is the Net Public Sector Debt which covers everything – local authorities and the lot. (See 16th January 1980)

18th January 1991 Friday

As the Western world with all its superior weaponry relentlessly attacks Saddam Hussein of Iraq, it nevertheless is aware of the strong influence & power of Islam. One false move or inadvertent attack on a holy place and the whole Moslem population, 300 million strong, would retaliate. Mecca, the birthplace of Mohammed and most revered place of all, is in Saudi Arabia & it is in Saudi Arabia that all the military might of the West is assembled.

In any war, land has to be fought over and taken. Following the bombardment by air, a million soldiers will be there for a campaign on the ground – a far more deadly prospect.

19th January 1991 Saturday

Abraham is the father of all who now fight each other in the Gulf War. Jews & Christians are sons of Abraham through his son Isaac. Arabs are sons of Abraham through his son Ishmael. But, without a doubt, the sons of Ishmael show greater respect for their faith. The word "Islam" means submission (to the will of God). A "Moslem" is "One who submits".

Olav Mourning

The Queen has ordered eight days of court mourning for her cousin, King Olav of Norway, who died on Thursday night. Members of the Royal Household will wear black on official engagements.

His Majesty King Olav V of Norway has died at the age of 87. He is the little Prince who loved to run up to my dad on guard duty at Buckingham Palace, for the sheer thrill of receiving a salute.

King Olav of Norway was half Danish & half English by birth. He was born Prince Alexander Edward Christian Frederick of Denmark. But he was born on the Royal Sandringham Estate, in 1903. When he was aged 2,

Norway severed its union with Sweden. His father was elected King & he became Olav.

"Sometimes being a King is a lonely life" – these were the sentiments once expressed by King Olav. His wife, Princess Martha, died in 1954, and his father, King Haakon died in 1957, making Olav a King without a Queen. However, he had 3 children & his son Prince Harald succeeds him as King.

20th January 1991 Sunday

Epiphany II – "Almighty and everlasting God, who dost govern all things in heaven and earth .... Grant us Thy peace all the days of our life." (Collect for today).

21st January 1991 Monday

Katherine Sullivan teaches me how to understand & appreciate great music and art. Sibelius is her favourite composer.

In a recent letter to me she wrote, "I remember the first concert in India that Peter Gwyn took me to. He had a job I can tell you, trying to make me like Sibelius' music – then, after making me like it, I fell so deeply in love with this music that now it is my favourite. It's really wonderful music when you really know it, but it is not everyone's cup of tea."

When Katherine saw that the Halle Orchestra were to be performing Sibelius this week at Leicester's De Montfort Hall, we obtained tickets for Wednesday evening.

22nd January 1991 Tuesday

Other cultural influences in my life at the moment are Rachel Goddard and Pamela Horsepool whom I encountered recently on my "Pre-retirement Course". We three, being all old maids together, formed an alliance, as we seemed to share the same interests. We have therefore booked to see "The Winter's Tale" by Shakespeare, on Saturday 9th February.

How I love Shakespeare. "The Winter's Tale" has all the makings of a real fairy story, but filled with rich word-power, and covering every emotion from the very depths to the highest elevation of joy, when loved ones, long since lost, are joyfully re-united.

23rd January 1991 Wednesday

Symphony No. 5 in E flat. Op 82 was my introduction to Sibelius. This work was commissioned by the Finnish government in honour of the composer's 50th birthday.

It was impossible not to be deeply moved by this music, being in the company of Katherine who loved it so much.

Sibelius lived from 1865 – 1957, so this particular work was written during the First World War. I enjoyed particularly the "fantastic whispering" by the strings, and the dramatic finale, when Katherine turned to me with such a look, I guessed she was thinking of Peter Gwyn.

24th January 1991 Thursday

War weapons in use at the present time in the Gulf war - the Iraqi Scud Missile is launched against Saudi Arabia and against Israel, while America's Patriot anti-missile rocket meets it in mid-air. At the precise moment the Patriot explodes, the Scud explodes & disaster is averted.

25ᵗʰ January 1991 Friday

"Lack lustre" President Bush, now exactly half way through his term of office, was destined to be in command at a time in history when events in the Middle East came to a head.

With enough potential armoury to blow up the whole world, he had the unenviable task of declaring war.

The "Allied Forces" now massed against Saddam Hussein of Iraq are overwhelmingly American. 650,000 troops (350,000 = United States), 150 ships (50 = United States), 1,500 aircraft (1,000 United States), 3,500 tanks (2,000 = United States).

We have the "United Nations", an association founded in 1945 to secure peace & justice in the world, but they tried in vain to prevent this latest war. General Perez de Cuellar, Secretary-General of the United Nations, went personally to Baghdad as a messenger of peace, but came home in despair, having achieved nothing.

26ᵗʰ January 1991 Saturday

Such is the enmity between East & West, Saddam Hussein is the arch-villain of all time, while according to the followers of Saddam Hussein, the "Imperialistic West" are the villains of the piece. In this 9ᵗʰ day of warfare, like a nine days' wonder, each side assures its supporters that **it** is right, and is fighting to defend that right.

27ᵗʰ January 1991 Sunday Septuagesima

Septuagesima Sunday reminds us each year of the sacredness of marriage. From Genesis to the teaching of Christ, it is the same message, "Marriage is sacred." (Mark, Chapter 10).

War in the Middle East is now into its second week. Supposedly the "Allied Forces" freeing innocent Kuwait from the clutches of President Saddam Hussein of Iraq. In effect it is mainly America acting as the Giant, with Britain giving full support & nobody else wanting to be involved.

28ᵗʰ January 1991 Monday

"A nation at war must surround itself with a bodyguard of lies" – This was said by Winston Churchill during the First World War. This seems to be true today, as we hear so much one-sided news of the Gulf War.

The truth is – "There is no justification for this war" – These are the sentiments of the Pope, and the sentiments of thousands of others the world over.

It was after the 1914 – 1918 war that the remains of the Ottoman Empire were carved up, and countries like Iraq, Jordan and Lebanon came into being. Then in 1948 Israel came into being for the Jews; & there has been trouble ever since.

29ᵗʰ January 1991 Tuesday

The State of Israel was created by partitioning Palestine and providing 55% for the Jews and 45% for the Arabs. But since then the Jews have taken over more & more territory.

Today Israel occupies the West Bank of the River Jordan & the Gaza Strip, both being seized in 1967 in defiance of United Nations resolutions.

Did "The Allies" then go to war to defend the rights of the Palestinians? – No. Quite the contrary. It suited the West to support Israel for its own ultimate gain. Israel

guards Western interests in the Middle East – namely "OIL".

"If Kuwait grew carrots, we wouldn't give a damn" – L. Korb.

The Gulf War absolutely dominates the news at the moment. Practically all day long there is news on the radio & on the television; and the newspapers too are filled with news of the war. I am reminded of the stories of "Brer Rabbit" and "Brer Fox" as first one, then the other, scores in the battle of wits.

30ᵗʰ January 1991 Wednesday

Saddam Hussein has attacked Israel in this present Gulf War knowing how much all Arabs hate the Jews. His idea is to exploit this hatred of Israel to undermine those who are backing the United States.

In 1982 Israel invaded Lebanon and bombarded the capital – Beirut – with cluster and phosphorous bombs, causing untold suffering.

Since the "Intifada" uprising (Arab uprising against Israeli occupation) began in December 1987, Israeli troops have murdered thousands of Palestinians.

And America blocked attempts to condemn Israel at the United Nations after 21 Arabs were slaughtered on Jerusalem's Temple Mount.

31ˢᵗ January 1991 Thursday

Saddam Hussein of Iraq is Brer Fox. The Allied Forces attack him with all their military might and "Brer Fox – he lay low". Then, when they wonder what he is up to, he foxes them by sending all his air force & planes to Iran – why? Is he running away, or is this a deviously cunning plan?

As in the days of Moses the waters that were in the river were turned to blood, and the fish died, and the Egyptians could not drink the water, so now Saddam Hussein has contaminated the waters of the Gulf which supply water to the multinational coalition fighting Iraq. He achieved this simply by turning on pumps which can move 100,000 barrels of oil a day, at the Sea Island terminal 10 miles offshore from Kuwait's main petroleum refinery at Al Ahmadi.

All the oil is now flowing in the waters of the Gulf and represents the worst oil pollution ever encountered in the world.

1ˢᵗ February 1991 Friday

To understand the problems of the Middle East, you must know something of its history.

Once upon a time there was a land known as Mesopotamia meaning "between the rivers". The rivers were the Tigris & the Euphrates, now being Iraq.

Kuwait (meaning the Little Fort) was recognised in 1914 as an independent principality under British protection. In 1961 Iraq pressed its claim to Kuwait so strongly that British troops were sent, at the ruler's request, to Kuwait's defence.

(Kuwait was given its freedom from Britain after the Suez War in 1956).

2ⁿᵈ February 1991 Saturday

Candlemas – This is the Feast of the Purification of St. Mary the Virgin. This is the day when Mary & Joseph brought their baby Jesus to Jerusalem to present him to the Lord. (Every male that openeth the womb shall be

called holy to the Lord. - St. Luke, Chapter 2)
Candles in church depict the light of Christ. One candle can give light to another, without ceasing to burn itself.

"Brer Fox" = Brother Fox.
Saddam Hussein of Iraq spoke to Muslim leaders at the beginning of the Gulf War & said, "The showdown, dear brothers of today, is not a showdown for land or territory, it is a showdown between infidels & believers, not for temporary objectives."

3rd February 1991 Sunday
Sexagesima - Just as two, joined together in Holy Matrimony are no more two, but "one flesh", so he that is joined to the Lord is "one spirit". (1 Corinthians, Chapter 6).

4th February 1991 Monday
A day in London. Visited the Department of Energy's new H.Q. at 1, Palace Street, and was given a conducted tour of the building by Maureen who works there.
Visited the "London Map Centre" in Caxton Street & bought an up-to-date map of the world. Identifying with "Christian" I bought Bunyan's "Pilgrim's Progress".
I volunteered to go to London with our typist – Christine Bolsover – who was taking part in a 2 days' training course on Word Processing. Being of a timid nature, she lacked the courage to venture alone to Palace Street, and I was only too pleased to see her safely there, & then do as I pleased.
Note – At work we throw out all the old typewriters. It is now the age of word processors & computers.

Iraq is divided by race & religion as follows –
1 Arabs (majority) 2. Kurds 3. A few Persians, etc.
The vast majority of Arabs, Kurds and Persians are Mohammedan, but they are split into 2 main sects –
1. The Shi'as 2. The Sunnis.
Shi'as outnumber Sunnis by 3 – 1, although in the Arab world as a whole the Sunnis outnumber the Shi'as. The difference stems from the question of Mohammed's successor. The Sunnis believe it to be the first caliph elected after the Prophet's death. The Shi'as, on the other hand, revere the Prophet's grandson Hussein.

Newspaper cutting - Shia Muslims – Shias make up the 10% minority of the world's Muslims, compared to the 90% Sunni majority. The split between the two communities came with the death of the prophet Muhammad in 632, & centred on the question of authority and succession. The Shia believe that Ali, Muhammad's son-in-law, inherited the prophet's spiritual abilities, & still look to the prophet's closest family members, the Ahlul Bait.
Shia Islam began with the martyrdom of Ali and his son Hussein, and today places a strong emphasis on the inner spiritual life, the meaning of suffering and rejection. In Sunni Islam, fundamentalism can be conservative, such as in the interpretation of the Koran and the law. In Shia Islam, fundamentalist extremes have been seen in the revolutionary Hezbollah, and the fatwa against Salman Rushdie, the author.

5th February 1991 Tuesday
Holy War is defined thus in the Koran – "Warfare is

ordained for you, though it is hateful unto you; but it may happen that you hate a thing which is good for you, and it may happen that you love a thing which is bad for you. Allah knoweth, ye know not. Fight in the way of Allah against those who fight against you, but do not begin hostilities. If they attack you, then slay them. Such is the reward of disbelievers."
Saddam Hussein insisted all along he would not begin hostilities with the West, but would respond in accordance with how he was attacked.

6th February 1991 Wednesday
Exactly 6 months ago, it was too hot to wear any clothes, and I wrote my diary absolutely starkers. Now it is so cold I have the central heating on – plus 4 bars of the gas fire. Outside the snow has fallen and the easterly winds are blowing straight from Siberia. Temperatures are expected to stay below zero both night & day.
How thankful I am to have a gas fire & gas central heating & enough money to pay the gas bill. At times like this it certainly is, "Wonderfuel Gas".

7th February 1991 Thursday
As the Western Allies continue to blast Iraq, blowing up the beautiful bridges which span the River Euphrates, injuring & killing innocent civilians in the process, I look at the victims on the television screen & in their beautiful dark lustrous eyes I see those Companions of the Hereafter as described in the Holy Koran – "And there will be Companions with beautiful, big and lustrous eyes, like unto pearls, well guarded. A reward for the Deeds of their past life. No frivolity will they hear therein nor any taint of ill – only the saying, "Peace! Peace!" Sura LVI

8th February 1991 Friday
The I.R.A. yesterday launched an attack into the back garden of No. 10 Downing Street from a vehicle parked outside the Banqueting Hall, opposite the entrance to Horse Guards Parade Ground, in Whitehall. There was a loud explosion and No. 10 was shaken quite badly, but there were no casualties.

The closure of Bagworth Colliery today brings the end of a great era in Leicestershire. Bagworth Colliery is the last remaining pit in the North Leicestershire coalfield. First sunk in 1825 it started as a small privately owned mine on the estate of Viscount Maynard. The Viscount died in 1865, leaving the pit to his grand-daughter, the Countess of Warwick, who, five years later, sold the lease to the Bagworth Coal Company. In 1947, Bagworth Colliery was taken over by the National Coal Board.
Having been born & bred in a mining community, & living on top of a coalmine (and having actually been down the mine), I feel a strong affinity with the miners.

9th February 1991 Saturday
Now I am superficially a blonde.
The initial transformation took effect a fortnight ago and caused quite a stir for the first few days. Most people genuinely liked the change; some pretended they had not noticed any difference, and some diplomatically said, "Well, do you like it?"
Cocky, who has not seen me for half a lifetime, loves me

whether I am blonde, brunette or grey-headed.

10th February 1991 Sunday
Quinquagesima – (fifty days before Easter Sunday) – "O God, thou hast taught me from my youth; and hitherto have I declared thy wondrous works. Now also when I am old and grey headed, O God, forsake me not." (Psalm 71)

Last Thursday's I.R.A. bomb attack on No. 10 Downing Street was the first missile bomb attack used by them on mainland Britain. Three bombs were "launched" like rockets from a van which cleverly concealed them. The main missile landed in the garden of No. 10 but was deflected when it hit a cherry tree.

11th February 1991 Monday
On a winter's day (9th February 1991) saw "The Winter's Tale" by Shakespeare, at Leicester's Haymarket Studio. We sat on the front row, which was in effect part of the stage. A cast of eight people, plus one boy, managed to portray the whole cast, which could have been portrayed by 50 people or more. But the magic and majesty of Shakespeare was brought to life in grandiose eloquence.
"Did you see the meeting of the two Kings?" We saw this indeed as clearly in our mind's eye, as the day I actually saw the meeting of the two Kings on horseback, when we commemorated the Battle of Bosworth in 1985.
The two Kings in Shakespeare's "The Winter's Tale" are Leontes, King of Sicilia & Polixenes, King of Bohemia.
Before they ever appear on stage, we are introduced to them thus – "Sicilia cannot show himself over kind to Bohemia. They were trained together in their childhoods; and there rooted betwixt them then such an affection which cannot choose but branch now since their more mature dignities & royal necessities made separation of their society, their encounters, though not personal, have been royally attorneyed with interchange of gifts, letters, loving embassies, that they have seemed to be together, though absent; shook hands, as over a vast, & embraced as it were, from the ends of opposed winds."

12th February 1991 Tuesday
From British Telecom – **important** – your telephone number will change. British Telecom is pleased to advise you that in about 12 months time a new digital telephone exchange will replace the existing exchange which serves Coalville 3xxxx numbers. Your present number Coalville 36583 will become 836583.

13th February 1991 Wednesday
On this first day of Lent, we are directed to the Epistle to the Hebrews.
"Today, if ye will hear His voice, harden not your hearts, as in the provocation. For some when they had heard, did provoke. With whom was He grieved forty years? ..... them that believed not. They could not enter in because of unbelief. They could not enter "into his rest". God did rest the seventh day from all his works. There remaineth therefore a rest to the people of God. Let us labour therefore to enter into that rest."

14th February 1991 Thursday
"For my Darling Valentine"
Roses are red; violets are blue; oh, how I wish I could marry you.
I will always love you till the end of time, so please be my Valentine. Xxxxxxxx

While sweethearts everywhere know only one language – the language of love, on this 29th day of the Gulf War, the confusion of battle, where men do not speak the same language, reminds us of the building of the Tower of Babel.
Built long ago in the land of Shinar (now Iraq), the great city & tower was something like the splendid building erected by Saddam Hussein & inscribed with his name; but without love, there was a breakdown in communication.

15th February 1991 Friday
"And the whole earth was of one language and of one speech. And it came to pass, as they journeyed from the east, that they found a plain in the land of Shinar; and they dwelt there. And they said, "Go to, let us build us a city and a tower, whose top may reach unto heaven; & let us make us a name, lest we be scattered abroad upon the face of the whole earth."
And the Lord said. "Behold, the people is one, & they have all one language; & now nothing will be restrained from them, which they have imagined to do. Let us go down, and there confound their language, that they may not understand one another's speech." Genesis, Ch. 11

16th February 1991 Saturday
Treasurer Hewsie has been busy this week allocating tickets for Coalville Amateur Operatic Society's forthcoming production, "Hello Dolly". With demand outstripping supply for the most popular nights, it has entailed quite a lot of juggling & switching of tickets to achieve best results all round.

Being a blonde, Katherine has advised me to condition my hair with olive oil. Every time I wash my hair, I therefore "anoint my head with oil". Not just any old olive oil, but the best "extra virgin olive oil" pre-heated, liberally rubbed into the scalp, covered for an hour or so with a plastic bag, and then thoroughly washed. The result is the softest shining hair I've ever had.

17th February 1991 Sunday
The First Sunday in Lent
"O lord, open thou my lips; and my mouth shall show forth thy praise." (Psalm 51)
Stacey, Thirza, late of Thornborough Road, Coalville. Sister of William, sister-in-law of Hilda, aunt of Bunting, Pat, Janet and Sheila, passed away peacefully at Markfield Court, Markfield on February 17th 1991, aged 87 years. Funeral service at Marlborough Square Methodist Church on Monday February 25th at 11.15 a.m., followed by cremation at Loughborough Crematorium.
This is Thirza, my dad's sister-in-law, who for the past year or two has shared a bedroom with Aunt Dos at the Nursing Home at Markfield Court; but being so frail & confused, hardly aware of each other.

18th February 1991 Monday, Presidents' Day
(Holiday U.S.A.)

Today is a holiday in America, but it is no holiday for the people of Iraq, who on this 33rd day of war continue to be bombarded day and night by the relentless onslaught of the American air attack. "One day," they say, "President Bush will be assassinated for what he is doing today – just as surely as President Kennedy was assassinated, following the war in Vietnam."

We see on the TV, innocent families blasted to death, with maybe one solitary survivor utterly grief-stricken and left to face life all alone – too heart-broken for words, and completely shattered.

19th February 1991 Tuesday

Just as Iraq today plants Iraqis in Kuwait and calls it Iraq's 19th Province, so Britain in days gone by planted Protestants in Northern Ireland and claimed it as theirs. The result has been trouble and strife ever since. The I.R.A. is for ever seeking revenge. British troops are sent to Northern Ireland in an effort to keep the peace, but the I.R.A. is ready to fight the British Army, the British Government, the British Police and indeed the British general public.

Yesterday morning the I.R.A. planted a bomb at Victoria Station in London which killed one traveller and injured many others, some seriously. Another bomb exploded at Paddington.

20th February 1991 Wednesday

While mankind engages in warfare and wilful destruction the world over, God's lesser creatures do their best to survive in a hostile environment.

At this time of the year, my early morning walk – 6 a.m. to 6.30 a.m. – coincides with the Dawn Chorus. What a joy it is to hear the birds singing their hearts out. The thrush high up in the tree seems to rise above all earth-bound troubles.

The cock crowing each morning reminds me of the Lord's words to St. Peter – "Before the cock crows twice, thou shalt deny me thrice." And my heart goes out to St. Peter.

"What is light?" was the question we asked in September 1984. A letter I was given to answer at work this week prompted me to ask further from our learned scientists, "What is energy?"

I was amazed to learn that energy can be neither destroyed nor created. It is there in one form or another.

Question – Has the explosive force of the Big Bang ever been calculated?

Answer – The energy in the Big Bang equals the total amount of energy in the universe; energy in the form of radiation and mass added together. So far the sums don't add up because there doesn't seem to be enough mass. This is one of the most fundamental questions in cosmology today so, no, it hasn't been done yet.

21st February 1991 Thursday

The recent heavy fall of snow transformed much of our country for a few days into a Winter Wonderland. The loveliest sight I saw was a piebald horse alone in a field of white. This horse galloped from one end of the field to the other for the sheer joy of it. Then it galloped all the way back again. Children too, delighted in the snow, and some artistic adults created the most beautiful "snow sculptures" – clever arches & geometric shapes which looked like permanent edifices. But others, who were less fortunate, suffered dreadfully in the extreme cold & bitter easterly winds.

22nd February 1991 Friday

Extract from a letter written 22nd February 1971 to my mum –

Ashby-de-la-Zouch and District Hospital

Dear Mrs Hewes,

At our last House Committee meeting I was requested to convey to you the Committee's most sincere appreciation for the valuable service rendered to this hospital during a period of over 20 years. The Committee realise that throughout this long term of employment you have carried out your duties in a most satisfactory manner, working efficiently and conscientiously. With thanks and every good wish for your future from the Committee and the entire staff of the hospital.

Hospital Secretary.

F. W. Woolworth opened his first "nothing over 5 cents" store in New York on this date, 22nd February, in the year 1897 – and nearly went broke.

*However, when he moved to **Lancaster**, in Pennsylvania, he changed it to "nothing over 10 cents" and the result was that he became a multi-millionaire.*

23rd February 1991 Saturday

High noon today (12 noon in Washington) (5 p.m. in London) (8 p.m. in Baghdad)

Saddam Hussein was told by President Bush of America to get out of Kuwait by today or "face annihilation". This heralds the beginning of an all-out land offensive, after 5 weeks of non-stop bombardment of Iraq by air. However, Saddam Hussein will not be dictated to by the West. He is setting fire to Kuwait's oil wells.

24th February 1991 Sunday

Lent II - "For ye have need of patience, that, after ye have done the will of God, ye might receive the promise. For yet a little while, & he that shall come will come, & will not tarry."

(Hebrews 10, 36.)

"The Pilgrim's Progress" by John Bunyan is a book which literally poured out of him. It is a book which has no division of chapters, but just goes on & on to the end. It appeals to me because it speaks the language of the Bible which I know so well – I can identify so well with Christian.

25th February 1991 Monday

Gulf War – Day 40. As half the oil wells of Kuwait blaze out of control, we are told that it is part of Saddam Hussein's "scorched earth" policy. Air-men returning to base after flying over the blazing oil-wells said it was like flying over hell. Apart from the fire, there is so much black smoke that day is turned into night. The ground is so hot that the sand, as in a furnace, is likely to turn into glass – "A sea of glass mingled with fire" (Revelation 15)

26ᵗʰ February 1991 Tuesday

The City of Kuwait has been liberated by the Allied Forces. Saddam Hussein's army was not able to withstand the overwhelming onslaught by the Allies, by air, by sea & on land. Thousands upon thousands of Iraqi soldiers, weary & worn, frightened & hungry, gladly gave themselves up to the Allied soldiers.

One Iraqi soldier, who had been hiding for days in a dugout in the sand, had ventured into the open in search of food, only to be killed. I saw him (on TV) being buried in the sand, & I thought of Moses who "slew the Egyptian & hid him in the sand". I also thought of his mother & all who loved and cared for him.

"What shall I do?" – Remember this fine sermon given by the Rector of Ravenstone, the Revd. Leslie Buckroyd, in September 1980? The answer always being "Believe on the Lord Jesus Christ". Well, the opening paragraph of Pilgrim's Progress is poor old Christian in despair saying, "What shall I do?"

27ᵗʰ February 1991 Wednesday

Saddam Hussein had an army of half a million regular troops, half a million reserves and over half a million "militia".

As the U.S. troops advanced towards the City of Kuwait, they were amazed to see one Iraqi "soldier" dressed in a t-shirt & Bermuda shorts. He told them, "I came home from Chicago to visit my grandmother & they enlisted me in the army."

You never saw such a mixed medley of soldiers, ill equipped and with any old sort of footwear – more like a medieval army of rogues & vagabonds, who would not have been out of place in one of Shakespeare's plays.

28ᵗʰ February 1991 Thursday

"Gulf War has Ended" – "Kuwait is liberated. Iraq's army is defeated ….. Tonight the Kuwaiti flag once again flies above the capital of a free and sovereign nation. Seven months ago, America & the world drew a line in the sand. We declared that the aggression against Kuwait would not stand, & tonight America & the world have kept their word." – Thus began the speech given by President Bush of America this morning.

N.B. "America and the world" (America is not on another planet.)

"While everyone is delighted with Prince Charles' choice of a wife, Mum & I do not think she is the best choice in the world ……."

These were my observations ten years ago. However, Princess Diana has in the past 10 years blossomed into the most beautiful elegant lady, performing royal duties superbly.

Princess Diana is stunningly beautiful. She loves modern music & dancing. She swims every day & keeps herself in trim. Rumour has it that she & Prince Charles have very few shared interests & live almost separate lives – he being the misfit.

1ˢᵗ March 1991 Friday

Mr Ken Weaver, Census Officer appointed for our locality, visited me at home in response to my application to be a Census Enumerator. He explained briefly what the job would entail, including three sessions of instruction commencing in March.

There would later be at least 3 visits to each household –
1. To deliver a leaflet to say the Census Form would be due shortly.
2. To deliver the Census Form in person to the householder.
3. To collect the completed Census Form.

Census Day is 21ˢᵗ April 1991. The peak day of action for the Census Enumerator is the following day – best to have the whole day free.

2ⁿᵈ March 1991 Saturday

"Gulf War has Ended" (As reported on Baghdad Radio)

"Iraq has fought, stood fast, & triumphed. Iraq fought on your behalf the entire group of atheism led by War Criminal Bush.

Iraq has triumphed. Iraq is victorious because it fought against atheism with faith & fought the evil & aggression in defence of land, dignity & holy places."

3ʳᵈ March 1991 Sunday

Lent III – "Again the High Priest asked Jesus – Art thou the Christ, the Son of the Blessed? And Jesus said, I am; & ye shall see the Son of Man sitting on the right hand of power, & coming in the clouds of heaven."
(Mark, 14)

Poor old Christian is a man clothed with rags, with a book in his hand (the Bible) and a great burden on his back. The book promises him such wonderful things, if only he can get rid of his burden.

"How comest thou by thy burden at first?" he is asked by Mr Worldly-Wiseman.

"By reading this book in my hand."

4ᵗʰ March 1991 Monday

The High Priest asked Jesus – Art thou the Christ, the Son of the Blessed?

And Jesus said – "**I am**". Herein lies the secret of Christ's divine nature. When Moses first heard the call of God, he asked, "When I come unto the children of Israel & shall say unto them, the God of your fathers hath sent me unto you; & they shall say to me, what is his name? What shall I say unto them?" And God said unto Moses, "**I am that I am**" & he said, "Thus shalt thou say unto the children of Israel, **I am** hath sent me unto you."

5ᵗʰ March 1991 Tuesday

Cocky's twin sister Betty, aged 61, died suddenly & unexpectedly at the weekend. She lived at Normanton-on-Soar, near Loughborough. A heavy smoker all her life, she appeared on the surface to be in good health – unlike poor Midge, their elder sister, who has had cancer for several years.

"Hello Dolly" is Coalville Amateur Operatic's choice for this year. Producer is Brian Gadsby. Musical Director is Peter Jacques. Choreographer is Dawn Cox. Secretary is Olive Meakin. Treasurer is me. (Treasurer from 1982 – 1991) House Manager is Brother Pat. (Aged 72)

The venue is The Harley Theatre, within the King Edward VII Community College, with a seating capacity of 163. We have 12 performances.

6th March 1991 Wednesday

Opening night of Hello Dolly. Thoroughly enjoyed being part of the impressive "Front of House" team, resplendent in long black skirt, white blouse, blue sash emblazoned with "Coalville Amateurs", & long service medal with 3 bars, denoting 40 years with the Society.

Joan Dillow, my trusty helpmate, in charge of the sales of programmes, kept meticulous record of numbers of programmes sold & monies taken. She has an ongoing record year by year. I told her that I will be relinquishing the role of Treasurer at the A.G.M. in June. We have worked as a team over the years.

I recall the words of my beloved Provost, the Very Revd. John Hughes, in the Cathedral Newsletter of October 1977.

"Handing on the torch is an exciting moment ...... as you hand over the torch & see your successor going away with great success, you cheer with all the puff left in you."

7th March 1991 Thursday

"Hello Dolly", Coalville Amateurs' show for this year, is now in full swing. As this is my last show as Treasurer, I am enjoying this fleeting moment of glory, before fading into the background. I have been Treasurer since 1982 & have really loved the job, but am ready now to hand over the torch to my successor.

Received from Mr Weaver, Census Officer, the relevant papers for me to be appointed as a Census Enumerator.

"Detailed instructions about your duties will be issued to you in due course, during your training, & as may become necessary, during the conduct of the Census itself. Enumerators will be asked to sign a declaration that they are not known to a substantial number of people in an area to which they are appointed.

Please come to Ibstock Community College on Thursday 14th March 1991 at 6.30 p.m. when you will be appointed, issued with your supplies & briefed on your work."

8th March 1991 Friday

1991 Census – Extract of undertaking, Census Act 1920, Section 8 –

"If any person employed in taking a Census, without lawful authority publishes or communicates to any person otherwise than in the ordinary course of such employment any information acquired by **him** in the course of **his** employment; or having possession of any information which to **his** knowledge has been disclosed in contravention of this Act, publishes or communicates that information to any other person; **he** shall be guilty of a misdemeanour and shall on conviction be liable to imprisonment for a term not exceeding 2 years, or to a fine, or to both imprisonment and fine – currently £400."

"You will be required to give an undertaking to carry out your duties & obligations faithfully."

9th March 1991 Saturday

"And it came to pass in those days, that there went out a decree from Cæsar Augustus, that all the world should be taxed. (And this taxing was first made when Cyrenius was governor of Syria). And all went to be taxed every one into his own city. And Joseph also went up from Galilee, out of the city of Nazareth, unto Judea, unto the city of David, which is called Bethlehem; (because he was of the house & lineage of David) to be taxed with Mary, his espoused wife, being great with child." (Luke 2).

10th March 1991 Sunday

4th Sunday in Lent – "Jesus Christ the same yesterday and today and for ever."
Pope John Paul II's chosen text. (Hebrews 13)

11th March 1991 Monday

"Hello Dolly" has given enormous pleasure to those on stage, to the supporting cast behind scenes & to the audiences this week at Coalville.

As usual, there were masses of flowers & bouquets to round off the production; & for one old maid a bouquet of red roses, "All my love forever, John."

The Poll Tax, which came into being on 1st April last year, has caused nothing but disquiet & rebellion ever since. Thousands of people have simply refused to pay. The Conservative government, responsible for its introduction, are pondering what to do to win back the electorate for the next General Election.

A recent by-election in the Conservative stronghold of Ribble Valley indicated the feeling of the general public. It was one of the most humiliating defeats for the government since it came to power in 1979. Victorious Liberal Democrat Mike Carr overturned a 19,000 Tory majority & won by 4,000.

12th March 1991 Tuesday

"When the Poll Tax is finally put to rest in the grave, its epitaph will read –
'Here lies the Poll Tax, killed in the Ribble Valley'." – Thus said newly elected M.P. Liberal Democrat Michael Carr.

With the dreaded Poll Tax due for payment again on 1st April, the government, in desperation, is pouring £1.7 billion into the funds to help cushion the blow.

The Leicester Mercury sums up the position thus – The high fever of the Poll Tax has been masked with a bracing dose of quack medicine – but unless the patient is given the hi-tech treatment of a fairer tax, the disease will return.

13th March 1991 Wednesday

What a very sad birthday for Aunt Dos. She has now completely lost the will to eat & the will to live. It is hard to imagine that she was once the happy-go-lucky person who always looked on the bright side & enjoyed being the life & soul of the party. Now, huddled in her shell, she has nothing to live for.

Katherine Sullivan & I went to the Theatre Royal at Nottingham to see the ballet Cinderella. The music was by Rossini, and it was the most exquisite production you could wish to see. The last time I saw Cinderella, as a ballet, the music was by Prokofiev & I certainly preferred Rossini. Katherine and I both love the theatre & both have the same extravagant tastes – choosing the best seats available. While at the theatre we booked for two forthcoming events – 1. Merchant of Venice, 2. Iolanthe. We already have tickets for "Giselle".

14th March 1991 Thursday
1991 Census. Attended my first meeting at Ibstock Community College, "Appointment & Briefing". Was given Ordnance Survey Map of my Enumeration District which consists mainly of Donington-le-Heath. Was given also "Enumeration Record" for listing all addresses, "Field Manual" giving detailed examples of all eventualities, "Guide to Delivery" telling you what to do, in what order, plus a complete set of "Census Forms" (my estimated area is 170 households, although it may be more – it may be less) plus 1991 Census Enumerator Authority Card.

15th March 1991 Friday
An early morning walk along the little lanes of Donington-le-Heath to note down the sort of residences I will be contacting on my Census rounds. I noted each house, bungalow, shop, farm, indicating which looked vacant, which were newly built & "For Sale", which said "Beware of the Dog", and which were houses, but not houses – example – "The Manor House" Ancient Monument, 13th Century House. People pay to enter and look round, but nobody actually lives there. Donington also has a unique "Iron Age" encampment for tourists, with wigwam-like dwellings of yesteryear.

£250,000 appeal by Leicester's Lord Mayor, Peter Kimberlin, for a surgical laser to unblock hardened arteries, has just reached the £200,000 mark. It is hoped that the remaining £50,000 can be raised before the Lord Mayor hands over his chains of office in ten weeks time.

16th March 1991 Saturday
1991 Census. The addresses at Donington-le-Heath indicate what a delightful place it is.
"The Manor House" Manor Road.
"Green Acres" Berry Hill Lane.
Then there are – Tweentown, Blackberry Lane, Farm Lane, Townsend Lane and The Green. A truly rural spot.

17th March 1991 Sunday – St. Patrick's Day
Christ within me, Christ before me, Christ beside me, Christ beneath me, Christ above me, Christ in hearts of all that love me … (St. Patrick's Prayer).
Matthew Laurence John Bond, Cocky & Joan's first grandchild, born last October, was christened today, on my dad's birthday.
I thought of the lifespan of us all – cherished & loved at birth, and then cast on to the Ocean of Life, to sink or swim, & maybe, like Aunt Dos, have nothing left to live for.

18th March 1991 Monday
Coalville Amateur Operatic Society "Hello Dolly" – Treasurer Hewsie's marathon count-up of monies received.
The majority of the members leave it until the show is over to hand over their money in payment for tickets. The total receipt for tickets this year is £6,575. I then take the money to the bank, much of it in coins which are really heavy – mostly £1 coins.
Then come the big bills for payment – scenery – costumes – stage furniture, etc. & the whole thing is wound up ready for the A.G.M. in June.

19th March 1991 Tuesday
The new Bishop of Leicester will be the Rt. Revd. Dr. Thomas Butler. He is due to take over as Bishop of Leicester in the autumn. Aged 51, he was born in Birmingham & educated at Leeds University. It is the most amazing thing to find myself older than the Bishop, the supposedly venerable elder of the church.
Today I visited the Council Offices at Coalville & asked whether I was allowed to see the list of "Register of Electors" for Donington-le-Heath. I was allowed to study the list & even copy the names and addresses, but was not allowed a photo-copy of their records. Nevertheless, my own hand-written copy was a great help to me in sorting out my "Census" territory. Being such a rural community, it is not always apparent which road is the address for which house – some seem to be in the middle of nowhere, & those on a corner could be either one or the other – so now I have sorted them all out.

20th March 1991 Wednesday
The Budget this week has caused complete chaos. New Chancellor Norman Lamont announced a £140 per person cut in the Community Charge (i.e. the Poll Tax). What a time to announce such a cut. All over the country councils had already prepared their bills & many had actually been dispatched. Re-billing will cost more than £100 million. What a way to run a country!
The people who have had the best deal are the people of Wandsworth. With the lowest Poll Tax in the whole country – agreed at £136 – they will now have to pay nothing at all.

21st March 1991 Thursday
So where is all this money coming from to deduct £140 from everyone's Poll Tax?
Answer – V.A.T. = Value Added Tax. This is the amount added to virtually everything you buy, except food. V.A.T. has been 15% for some years now, but will go up to 17 ½% on 1st April. In a last ditch bid to do away with the Poll Tax, we are to have the "People & Property Tax", but this will take a year or more to sort out. The idea is to tax every household according to the value of the property, plus the number of adults living there.

On this first day of spring when a young man's fancy lightly turns to thoughts of love, Karen is overjoyed to announce – "I'm pregnant!"
Not only is she over the moon, but Mary Blue is thrilled at becoming a grandma & Pat & Evelyn are delighted at the prospect of becoming great-grandparents.

22nd March 1991 Friday
"Virgin Births" are the latest scientific so-called masterpiece. There are now some 160 clinics which provide fertility treatment, including test-tube baby conception and surrogacy arrangements.
Single women are allowed to obtain such fertility treatment. The newly created Human Fertilisation & Embryology Authority will operate with effect from August this year & will be responsible for licensing & supervising standards in the 160 clinics which provide fertility treatment – test-tube baby conception, sperm & egg donation, etc. A ceiling of 10 is being placed on the

number of children which may be fathered by any one sperm donor.

23rd March 1991 Saturday

Just as my mum hoped the house would be a blessing & not a burden to me, so now John Bunyan from 17th Century England, referring to his "Pilgrim's Progress" which I recently acquired, says, "Now may this little book a blessing be, to those that love this little book & me – not money thrown away."

Never has the world seen such a fire as the oil wells of Kuwait all ablaze. They have now been burning for a month & could burn for a hundred years if not tackled. Was there ever such a fire-fighting operation? You would think it was impossible to attempt such a thing – but attempt it we shall. At the moment we are still sizing up the problem and deciding where to start. I will keep you informed of developments.

24th March 1991 Palm Sunday

"Ride on! Ride on in majesty! In lowly pomp ride on to die; Bow Thy meek head to mortal pain, then take, O God, Thy power, and reign."

25th March 1991 Monday

Lady Day – the day when the angel told the Blessed Virgin Mary that she was to be the mother of Christ.
What a contrast to the so-called virgin births of today. The Government are not getting involved with this difficult issue. Although it raises exceptionally difficult ethical issues for the doctors concerned, the Government have decided that the situation does not lend itself to political intervention. They were willing to give the go-ahead for doctors to pursue their embryonic work & let them deal with the consequences themselves. The Church, however, is opposed to the idea.

The Treaty of Rome, signed 25th March 1957 was the beginning of the European Community. Being somewhat slightly aloof, Britain did not join until assured by Prime Minister Edward Heath that there was no question of eroding our national sovereignty. We were prepared to join a common market, not a United States of Europe.

26th March 1991 Tuesday

The 10 Commandments really do cover every eventuality in life. And even so, Christ managed to condense them into two, namely – "Thou shalt love the Lord thy God with all thy heart with all thy mind with all thy soul & with all thy strength." This is the first and great Commandment. And the second is like, namely this – "Thou shalt love thy neighbour as thyself."
On these two Commandments hang all the law & the prophets. When questioned by the Pharisees or the Sadducees, who tried to "entangle him" Christ said, "Ye do err, not knowing the scriptures."

27th March 1991 Wednesday

When I was a child, I was introduced to "the scriptures" by the Rector of Ravenstone, the Revd. Dowling, a revered old man who, a generation earlier, had likewise introduced my mother, as a child, to the scriptures.
"To read the Bible", he said, "do not start at the beginning, as in other books. Start by reading one of the

gospels. Read the Gospel According to St. John. Then maybe read the Gospel According to St. Luke – then Mark – then Matthew. Note how they tell the same story from different angles. Then try the Acts of the Apostles, & just carry on from there."

Note – Make time to read John's gospel in the Bible. It's the best book ever written.
It starts, "In the beginning was the Word".
Why the "Word"? Because Jesus is God's chief way of speaking to us.

The European Parliament, for which we have our own local M.E.P., is a "Talking Shop" - something akin to shareholders scrutinising a company's affairs. The European Parliament is not the body from which the European government is drawn, because there is no European government – yet. We await further developments.

28th March 1991 Maundy Thursday

"Now before the feast of the Passover, when Jesus knew that his hour was come that he should depart out of this world unto the Father, having loved his own which were in the world, he loved them unto the end. And supper being ended, he laid aside his garments; & took a towel & girded himself. After that he poureth water into a basin & began to wash the disciple's feet & to wipe them with the towel wherewith he was girded. ...... and he said, "Whither I go ye cannot come; so now I say unto you .... a new Commandment I give unto you, that ye love one another." (Commandment in Latin = Mandatum = Maundy Thursday)

29th March 1991 Good Friday

"And it was the preparation of the Passover & about the sixth hour & Pilate saith unto the Jews, "Behold your King!" But they cried out, "Away with him, away with him, crucify him!"
And Pilate wrote a title & put it on the cross. And the writing was, "Jesus of Nazareth, the King of the Jews". This title then read many of the Jews; for the place where Jesus was crucified was nigh to the city; & it was written in Hebrew & Greek & Latin.
Then said the chief priests of the Jews to Pilate, "Write not the King of the Jews; but that he said, I am King of the Jews." Pilate answered, "What I have written, I have written."

"Fellowship" is again referred to by the Provost of Leicester in his Newsletter -
"Fellowship all too often becomes associated with what I would term the Holy Huddle. I believe that what matters at the end of our pilgrimage is not our cosy human fellowship, but the fellowship of the Holy Spirit."

30th March 1991 Saturday

The blazing oil wells of Kuwait pose a major problem, but those which were exploded & then failed to blaze are an even greater problem. They are now gushing forth acrid smoke & lethal quantities of hydrogen sulphide - H_2S. To stem this flow of H_2S, they must first be set alight. Only then can work begin on stemming the flow of hell-fire & brimstone. The air in the vicinity is not safe to breathe.

31st March 1991 Easter Sunday

"I, John, was in the isle that is called Patmos & heard behind me a great voice, as of a trumpet, saying, "**I am** Alpha & Omega, the first & the last; & what thou seest, write in a book".

John Bunyan, who had a blind daughter, would be very pleased to know that 3 centuries after he wrote his "little book" The Pilgrim's Progress, it would be available as a "talking book" for the blind.

My good friend & workmate Alan Norris, who is registered as blind, has acquired this talking book from the library.

1st April 1991 Monday

"If negative energy forces get too strong, the earth will be finished by 1997" – so predicts David Icke, one time sports presenter & member of the "Green Party".

He now claims to be a channel for the Spirit of the Son of God, & says he is on a mission to save the world from destruction. He expects a huge earthquake to devastate the Isle of Arran. He also claims that the Channel Tunnel is doomed. A sequence of disasters is likely to start with a major eruption on Mount Rainier in the U.S.A.

2nd April 1991 Tuesday

Social Security – About your retirement pension –

"Our records show that you are nearly 60. When you are, you may be entitled to a weekly State Retirement Pension of £53 – 36p. This amount is based on our records of your National Insurance contributions.

The different parts of your retirement pension are – Basic Pension £52 (based on National Insurance Contributions, not on your earnings), Graduated Pension £1 – 36p (based on Graduated Contributions between 1961 & 1975).

Please complete the enclosed form for Retirement Pension".

Alan Norris & I have shared our room at work for 7 years. Although he is registered as blind, he can just manage to see enough to work at a desk. He is a computer whiz-kid & a great thinker. Having no religious inclination, he nevertheless liked what I told him about Pilgrim's Progress, enough to get the book.

"Now may this little book a blessing be, to those that love this little book & me ......

Yea may this second pilgrim yield that fruit, as may with each good pilgrim's fancy suit,

And may it persuade some that go astray, to turn their foot & heart to the right way" – is the Hearty Prayer of the Author John Bunyan.

3rd April 1991 Wednesday

Joanne Page, my young neighbour who adopted me as her friend & confidante when she was a little 5 year old, is now a stunning 17 year old. At the moment she is out of work & very much in love with Jeff Walker who seems reluctant to return such love.

She popped round this evening to bring me up to date on her affairs or, rather, non-affairs. How she longs for love & romance. How she longs for a satisfying & rewarding job. How she longs for enough money to learn to drive a car – to own a car. And how I feel for her in her longings.

4th April 1991 Thursday

1991 Census

On your marks – get set – get ready – Go!

I have been ready for off for the past 3 weeks, but we must all act in unison over the whole country.

Advance Round Leaflets must be delivered not earlier than Friday 5th April & not later than Monday 8th April. So I have a day's leave tomorrow to deliver my leaflets.

The Leicester Mercury this evening paves the way – "Over the next couple of days leaflets about the once-a decade Census will be delivered to households all over the country".

5th April 1991 Friday

1991 Census – Delivered my Advance Round Leaflets to all my households except one. The exception was "Berry Hill Nurseries", Berry Hill Lane. The gate at the entrance to the long drive was bolted and barred & the whole of the grounds were hidden behind high hedges on every side. However, I contacted them by phone & arranged to visit them next week-end with the Census Form.

In Holts Lane I found 3 cottages now equalled one house, & was surprised to find so many houses completely empty; & houses owned by people who lived somewhere else altogether.

6th April 1991 Saturday

Jubilate! Liberate!

You've no idea what a pleasure & what a relief it was to throw away all my accumulation of papers & instructions concerning Staff Reporting. Freed from the shackles of this annual chore, I was reminded of Bishop of Hippo's prayer –

"O Thou who art the light of the minds that know Thee; the life of the souls that love Thee; & the strength of the wills that serve Thee; help us so to know Thee that we may truly love Thee, so to love Thee that we may fully serve Thee, whom to serve is perfect freedom."

I have a 1991 Census Enumerator Authority Card – 3 ½ " x 5".

I determined that I had 175 Residential Premises in my E.D. (Enumeration District). Each individual address had to be listed in my "Enumeration Record" Part 1 – Advance Round.

Then I had to telephone the Assistant Census Officer, Steve Marsden to report progress so far.

7th April 1991 Sunday

1st Sunday after Easter. But the mercy of the Lord is from everlasting to everlasting upon them that fear him & his righteousness unto children's children; to such as keep his covenant & to those that remember his Commandments. (Psalm 103)

8th April 1991 Monday

Gulf War has ended but ....

There is now Civil War in Iraq as Saddam Hussein orders mass killing of the Kurds in his land. Saddam Hussein's Republican Guard who fled recently from the might of the West, are able to terrify the unarmed Kurdish population who are now fleeing in their hundreds of thousands to the mountains of the north, hoping to escape to Turkey or Iran.

Turkey & Iran simply cannot accommodate so many refugees & they are stranded in the mountains – cold and hungry and dying. And the world weeps.

9th April 1991 Tuesday

I think of the Lord Jesus as he was led away to be crucified. "And there followed him a great company of people, and of women, which also bewailed & lamented him. But Jesus, turning unto them, said, 'Daughters of Jerusalem, weep not for me, but weep for yourselves & for your children. For, behold, the days are coming, in the which they shall say, blessed are the barren & the wombs that never bear, & the paps which never gave suck. Then shall they begin to say to the mountains, fall on us; cover us. For if they do these things in a green tree, what shall be done in the dry?' "

10th April 1991 Wednesday

The Exodus of Kurds from Iraq is reminiscent of the great Exodus of the Children of Israel from bondage in Egypt. The lesson appointed for last Sunday at Church was the Song of Moses – Exodus, Chapter 15. What a mighty powerful reading – "The Lord is my strength and song & he is become my salvation. Thy right hand, O Lord, is become glorious in power. Thou shalt bring them in & plant them in the mountain of thine inheritance, in the place, O Lord, which thou hast made for thee to dwell in. The Lord shall reign for ever & ever."

How lovely to have fitted carpets in every room in the house. For the first time in my 60 years at 27 Leicester Road, Ravenstone, I have now achieved this with my latest purchase – a new fitted carpet for the middle bedroom £182. Liking nothing but the best, we certainly do have to wait.

11th April 1991 Thursday

1991 Census – Attended my 2nd meeting – "Delivery Training Course".

Having delivered the Advance Round Leaflets to every household, the next "Delivery" is the Census Form itself. We saw a half hour film which showed a Census Enumerator going from door to door & learning from him exactly what to do & say in a variety of circumstances. Many of the householders he met were paragons of virtue who all gave precise and accurate answers to all his questions. One, however, shut the door in his face.

12th April 1991 Friday

1991 Census – 12th April to 18th April, Friday to Thursday deliver Forms.

Phew! Another day's leave to make a start on delivering Census Forms in person to the house-holder. I started at 9 a.m. Finished at 7 p.m. & after all that had delivered only 37 of my 175 forms. Half the houses I visited had no-one at home. One man refused point blank to have anything to do with the form. Another man standing chatting to a neighbour said, "They're a funny lot at Donington. They'll deliberately dodge you, whenever they see you coming".

13,000 applications were received in answer to the advertisement for an **Astronaut**.

The winner is **Helen Sharman**, aged 27, a chocolate technologist who comes from **Mars**,

i.e. Mars, at Slough, Buckinghamshire, the chocolate firm. She is Britain's first astronaut & ready for blast off.

13th April 1991 Saturday

1991 Census – A most exhilarating & interesting day as Mary Blue & I, working in perfect harmony, delivered another 70 Census Forms. We were invited into many of the homes & met such an interesting cross section of the community. We even managed to deliver a form to the house where the man yesterday refused to accept the form. It was a real pleasure today being a Census Enumerator.

"Madge will now return to the fold, to be buried by the side of her sister Bertha in the churchyard at Willoughby-on-the-Wolds" – So I wrote in my diary in 1987.

Exactly 3 years later, Johnty's ashes were taken to Willoughby, to return likewise to the fold & complete yet another cycle of life.

14th April 1991 Sunday

2nd Sunday after Easter – Know therefore this day, & consider it in thine heart, that the Lord he is God in heaven above & upon the earth beneath; there is none else. Thou shalt keep therefore his statutes & his Commandments. (Deut. 4)

Three months to retirement!

15th April 1991 Monday

1991 Census – The 175 Residential Premises in Enumeration District No. FJ 06 of Census District No. MP 03 have now been brought to life for me.

I have met 2 weeks old baby Boot. I have learned that both occupants of No. 22 Manor Road are recently deceased. I have been guilty of opening a garden gate & letting escape a little dog who ran up the lane & out of sight. I have discovered 15 completely empty houses and have met such a lot of helpful "neighbours" who volunteered advice & readily gave advance warning of what to expect next door.

16th April 1991 Tuesday

1991 Census – Received my own Census Form – Census District MP 02 Enumeration District FS 05.

Total No. of Rooms = 5, Own the property – yes, Use of bath – yes, Indoor flush toilet – yes, Central heating – yes, No. of cars – one, Anyone else here on the night 21st – 22nd April – No.

Elizabeth Hewes. Born 14th July 1931. Single (never married). Same address a year ago.

Born in England. "White". No health problem.

In full time employment. "Executive Officer" Civil Service. Drive car to work.

No qualifications after the age of 18. Census 1991 - "It counts because you count"

Twelve years ago, in March 1979, I stood at the magnificent entrance to the hospital at Market Bosworth. The scene inside was the sorrow & desolation of old age, while the scene outside was the joy & promise of spring.

Again this dual scene was experienced, visiting Aunt Dos at Markfield.

17th April 1991 Wednesday
Saddam Hussein's Slaughter of the Kurds.
Never in my life have I seen so many people fleeing to the mountains, only to find a worse state than they left behind. The anguish of the Kurds of Iraq is shown nightly on television & the West must accept some blame. Encouraged by the West to rise up against Saddam Hussein, they have now been crushed, & pursued to the hills where there is neither food nor shelter.
There are 12 million Kurds; 2 ½ million live in Iraq; 2 ½ million live in Iran; 5 ½ million in Turkey; ½ million in Syria & the rest are scattered around.

18th April 1991 Thursday
<u>Alton Towers</u> - Mary Blue & I went on a day trip to Alton Towers to confirm its suitability for a family get-together on July 14th. We decided we would choose this venue for my 60th birthday get-together.
Hailed as Europe's Premier Leisure Park, it was once the home of the Earls of Shrewsbury & one of the grandest private homes in Europe. The grounds are magnificent – 500 acres of parkland, beautiful walks – a sky-ride at tree-top level in alpine-style gondolas, plenty of entertainment for all ages & a gorgeous setting for lots of photographs.

The London Marathon goes from strength to strength. When it was first run in 1981, there were 7,000 taking part in the run. Every year since then the numbers have increased & this year (April 21st) there will be 34,000 crossing the start line, including fun runners, eccentrics, exhibitionists & world champion runners.

19th April 1991 Friday
<u>1991 Census</u> – Attended my third meeting – "Collection Training Course".
Next Monday we start to collect the Census Forms which should be completed by the householder. We have to check the answers, especially "Where the person was on the night of 21st – 22nd April 1991", "Does the person have any long-term illness?", "Did the person have a paid job last week?"
We had a practice on a mock Census Form filled in by an imaginary family, & had to indicate where it was wrong. We also learned how to complete the final return & overall balance.

20th April 1991 Saturday
"Woe to us if we fail to hand on to future generations the unsearchable riches of Christ which are the very heartbeat of the Church and its mission" – so said Dr. George Carey, the new Archbishop of Canterbury, in his enthronement sermon yesterday. He intends to reach out to the young.
"And God saw everything that he had made, & behold it was very good." (Genesis 1, 31.)
The more I see of the suffering masses, suffering untold hardship & deprivation, struggling to keep alive in the midst of death & disease, with neither food nor shelter; the more I wonder how God can bear to see his children in such a desperate plight, without rescuing them.

21st April 1991 Sunday
3rd Sunday after Easter – And there are also many other things which Jesus did, the which, if they should be written every one, I suppose that even the world itself could not contain the books that should be written. (John 21.)

22nd April 1991 Monday
St. George's Swannington, Patronal Festival yesterday attended by Ravenstone & Swannington combined congregations showed us not only the "Dragon" of disease & hunger which we have to fight against, but showed us the love of God, over & above all earthly love.
We saw the risen Lord Jesus at the dawn of a new day, welcoming the despondent disciples to a seashore breakfast. He, the Bread of Life, who had accepted death on the Cross to provide us with the true bread from heaven, life everlasting, entrusted the feeding of his lambs on this earth to mankind .... "Feed my lambs" (St. John, Chapter 21.)

Yesterday was Census Day & was also the day of the London Marathon. Hence this lovely cartoon – Picture of lady handing census form to enumerator at the door and saying, "I had to leave Eric off the form – he's still running in the London Marathon."

23rd April 1991 Tuesday
<u>1991 Census</u> – "Behold, I stand at the door & knock" (Rev. 3, 20.)
I have never knocked at so many doors in my life before. Standing outside the fortress of a closed door, not knowing whether there is anyone there or not, is quite an experience. Sometimes I stand for quite a while & then, much to my amazement, somebody stirs from within. I have encountered every possible type of door, from the baronial solid oak to the fragile frame with broken glass panes. Some doors have push-button bells which you never know for sure are working.

24th April 1991 Wednesday
<u>1991 Census</u> – The Census is, as it were, a snapshot of the nation at one moment in time. I feel very privileged to have been part of this marathon exercise. The organisation is absolutely first class & the precision timing of every action is excellent. Nothing is left to chance. We report to our A.C.O. (Assistant Census Officer) at every stage of events. This week, we are allowed from Monday to Thursday to collect all the completed forms, reporting progress all the time.

"Buy a Brick! Go down in history" – Because this is the Year of the Maze, there is going to be a "maze" in Horsefair Street, Leicester. Engraved bricks will be laid in the maze and nearby. So we are invited to make a name for ourselves by buying a brick with our name on, for £20.

25th April 1991 Thursday
<u>1991 Census</u> – "All is safely gathered in". This evening I collected my last elusive Census Form & was delighted to report 100% success. Some Enumerators have had a much harder time than I have had. I am thankful to have been given Donington. It is so convenient, being so near

to home, to pop in for light refreshments & zoom off again to round up the odd stragglers. It reminds me of God in heaven delivering all his children to earth & then collecting them all back again, all marked by his own hand.

26th April 1991 Friday

1991 Census – Now comes the homework. We have an "Enumeration Record".

At the "Advance Round" stage we listed, in order, the addresses within our Enumeration District. At the "Delivery" stage we listed them all again & wrote down the number of persons in each house. We ticked off every house which received a Census Form.

At the "Collection" stage we ticked off every house where we collected the form.

Now we check the forms in detail & list how many people were actually there & how many were "elsewhere".

"It is with regret that Steven cannot accept your kind invitation to your retirement celebrations on 14th July 1991 as he will be away on holiday."

However, a more encouraging response from Bunting & family who have all agreed to come; & please may they bring an extra one – Josie's daughter.

27th April 1991 Saturday

1991 Census – Mission complete! The forms have been checked & double checked. They have all been numbered in accordance with their record in the "Enumeration Record". Lists have been made (10 households per page) of everyone in each house who was present on Census Night, plus those who were not present, separately. All packed in E. D. box & returned to the Census Officer.

28th April 1991 Sunday

4th Sunday after Easter – Therefore thou shalt love the Lord thy God, and keep his charge, and his statutes, and his judgments, and his commandments always. (Deut. 11)

"A rose by any other name ....." North West Leicestershire Tory M.P. David Ashby has dared to suggest that Coalville should be re-named. With coal mining now nothing more than a memory, he contends that Coalville needs a new name & a positive image, if it is to win the high-tec jobs of the future.

29th April 1991 Monday

Ted Ludlow, my work colleague, who is a staunch Roman Catholic, explained to me the interpretation of the beast with seven heads & ten horns. (Revelation 13). The horns are not growing out of the head of the beast. They are rather the horn of the horn-blower making a sound proclamation. And what is the message of the beast with these ten horns?

Answer – The 10 commandments turned from "Thou shalt not......." Into "Thou shalt ......"

It is the voice of the Permissive Society, giving licence to steal, to commit adultery & disregard God's laws.

30th April 1991 Tuesday

"Here is wisdom. Let him that hath understanding count the number of the beast; for it is the number of a man; & his number is - six hundred, threescore and six. (Revelation 13, 18.)

Because **666** is the number of the Devil, there is a belief that it has satanic connections.

Car registrations **666** have been involved in so many accidents that it has now been scrapped as a vehicle registration number. People complained that funny things happened when they came up against a vehicle with the number. You would be surprised how much some numbers mean to us.

"**Outrageous**" was the initial reaction to David Ashby's proposal to change the name of Coalville. However, a telephone poll held by the Leicester Mercury showed that the majority of voters favoured the idea. It has been suggested therefore that we have a local referendum to see what we all think.

1st May 1991 Wednesday

The Empire State Building in New York, like me, is celebrating 60 glorious years. Standing 102 stories high, it was the tallest building in the world until it was surpassed in 1971 by the World Trade Centre's twin 110-storey towers, & further still by the Sears Tower in Chicago.

60th birthday celebrations start today & will continue throughout the month of May. They are aptly described as birthday high-jinks! The Empire State Building dominates mid-town Manhattan & is visited each year by more than 2 ½ million tourists.

2nd May 1991 Thursday

1991 Census – When you consider how many hours & hours of work were involved for me to count up 411 people, you can imagine what was involved nationwide. The 1991 Census for Great Britain has cost £135 million. About 130,000 Enumerators were involved, including Census Officers & A.C.O.s. New questions this time included – central heating, hours worked, long term illness, term time address of students, ethnic group. The Census has covered England & Wales & Scotland. I think we've given up on Northern Ireland.

Trouble with Hubble. No sooner had the multi-billion dollar telescope been launched in April last year, when it was apparent that its two mirrors did not focus properly together in outer space. So what was intended as a glimpse into 14 billion years back into the history of the universe, resulted in "seeing through a glass darkly."

3rd May 1991 Friday

No sooner do we pour all our resources into saving the Kurdish refugees, struggling to survive on the mountains of Iraq, than we learn that famine in Africa is likely to be worse than ever before.

And now we hear of the worst cyclone in living memory, in Bangladesh, which has made 10 million people homeless and has killed more than 100,000. The cyclone, with winds up to 145 m.p.h., pounded Bangladesh's densely populated coast & a dozen offshore islands this week, flattening buildings, flooding farmland and sinking boats. Bangladesh Prime Minister Begum Khaleda Zia has appealed for aid.

4th May 1991 Saturday

"Mum has chosen a magnolia ……." – thus I wrote in August 1974. This same magnolia is now in full bloom & looks absolutely beautiful. The old cherry tree in the Hollies orchard is also in full bloom, showering me with confetti as I mow the lawn, making me feel like a bride without a bridegroom.

The Driver & Vehicle Licensing Agency (D.V.L.A.) is the modern day equivalent of the old Local Taxation Office where I worked for 30 years. We allocated new car numbers in strict order, never deviating from the correct sequence.
But now! Anything goes. Owners of new cars are invited to create their own numbers, and pay astronomical amounts to acquire a special number, so long as it is not already allocated.

5th May 1991 Sunday

5th Sunday after Easter – Jesus said, "Ask, and it shall be given you; seek, & ye shall find; knock, & it shall be opened unto you". (Luke 11, 9.)

Hewes, Hilda May, aged 92, beloved wife of the late Charles and a dearly loved mother, grandmother and great-grandmother, passed away peacefully on May 5th in Chelmsford.

6th May 1991 Monday

"What is so sweet & dear as a prosperous morn in May, the confident prime of the year, when nothing that asks for bliss, asking aright is denied, and half the world a bridegroom is and half the world a bride" – W. Watson.

David Icke, who now claims to be a channel for the Spirit of the Son of God, is aged 38. He wears turquoise because this colour shares the same frequency as the energies of love and wisdom. Interviewed on television he was asked if he could supply any proof of his extraordinary status. "Yes", he said, "Saddam Hussein is dead, although he is still being shown very much alive on TV."
Might David Icke indeed be the Messiah? Was not ICHTHYS, the acronym for Jesus Christ, Son of God, & the Greek for fish, the secret sign of the early Christians?

7th May 1991 Tuesday

At this "Rogationtide" we are reminded of Christ's teaching – (St. Luke, Chapter 11.)
First we are taught "The Lord's Prayer" & then we are taught, "Ask & it shall be given you; seek & ye shall find; knock & it shall be opened unto you". ….. "If ye then, being evil, know how to give good gifts unto your children; how much more shall your heavenly Father give the Holy Spirit to them that ask him?"
Why then should not David Icke be a channel for the Holy Spirit? Why then should not we all be a channel for the Holy Spirit? We are all one in the Spirit.

8th May 1991 Wednesday

On the night before Christ died, he said, "And now I am no more in the world, but these are in the world & I come to thee. Holy Father, keep through thine own name those whom thou hast given me, that they may be one, as we are. Neither pray I for these alone, but for them also which shall believe on me through their word; that they all may be one; as thou, Father, art in me, & I in thee, that they also may be one in us …. I in them, & thou in me, that they may be made perfect in one". (St. John, Chapter 17).

Elizabeth Hewes – No. 11 013 027 0 012 has received her second Community Charge Bill – the still controversial Poll Tax - £260 – 73p.
This amount is after knocking off £140, paid this year for everyone by the government in an attempt to appease the populace and prevent rebellion.

9th May 1991 Thursday Ascension Day

"Lift up your heads, O ye gates; & be ye lift up, ye everlasting doors; & the King of Glory shall come in. Who is this King of Glory? The Lord strong & mighty, the Lord mighty in battle. Lift up your heads, O ye gates, even lift them up, ye everlasting doors; & the King of Glory shall come in. Who is this King of Glory? The Lord of Hosts, he is the King of Glory. (Psalm 24).

10th May 1991 Friday

"Mr & Mrs Murdo MacLeod request the pleasure of the company of Miss E. Hewes at the marriage of their daughter Sharon Helen with Darren Pickering at St. Mary's Parish Church, Sileby, on Saturday 15th June 1991 at 2 o'clock, and afterwards at Six Hills Country House Restaurant A46."

11th May 1991 Saturday

The Tigers – The "Tigers" was the name given to the Royal Leicestershire Regiment after its magnificent service in India during the 19th century. Founded in 1688 the unit was disbanded 22 years ago. But the famous name is to be used again by the county's T.A. infantry battalion. The 7th (volunteer) Battalion the Royal Anglian Regiment will make military history when it officially adopts the Tigers nickname on 12th May.
Glen Parva Barracks, South Wigston was the home of the Tigers. Here, too, is the home of the new "Tigers".
The original Parade Ground at Glen Parva Barracks has long since gone. It is now the site of the Department of Energy. Hence my address at work – 3, Tigers Road, South Wigston, Leicester.

12th May 1991 Sunday after Ascension Day

Jesus himself stood in the midst of them & said, "Peace be unto you". (Luke 24)

Yesterday, on Don & Phyl's Wedding Anniversary, their beautiful grand-daughter, Ruth Lesley Sear, was married at Ravenstone Church to Neville Martin Balls.
Next month is the Silver Wedding Anniversary of the bride's parents – Lesley & John, but sadly that marriage has ended in divorce.

13th May 1991 Monday

Leicester Cathedral Festival, May 10th – May 13th
Brother Pat & I attended the Provost's Reception at the Cathedral & heard the most interesting 45 minute talk by the Provost – "What is the Cathedral Foundation?" or in other words, "Who's Who" in the running of the Cathedral & what are the rules laid down in the

"Cathedral Statutes"?
All the Canons were there & all other officials involved in the running of the Cathedral. One by one they all stood up to be identified; & a brief résumé of their duties was given. It was a most enlightening address.

14ᵗʰ May 1991 Tuesday
14ᵗʰ May 1643 – Louis XIV ascended the throne of France, aged four years 231 days, on the death of his father Louis XIII – and reigned for more than 72 years.

Louis XIV of France reigned for more than 72 years!! Here in England we had – Charles I – then no King for 11 years – Charles II – James II – William & Mary.

In an antique shop in Coalville I saw a dear little table for sale - £35. This little table & I seemed to be meant for each other, so I snapped it up quickly, brought it home, polished it & set it underneath the old copper pan where it felt completely at home immediately.
Looking at this dear little table, I wonder what is its life story. Who fashioned it with such loving care? How many years has it stood firmly on its four good strong legs? Unlike me, it will live on from century to century, no doubt recalling its former days as a great living tree.

15ᵗʰ May 1991 Wednesday
The great living trees in Swithland Woods were all around us as Katherine Sullivan & I enjoyed the annual "Bluebell Service" last Sunday afternoon. On a perfect spring day with blue skies, sunshine & birdsong, we sat on a grassy bank and sang the old familiar hymns accompanied by the Loughborough Salvation Army Band. I thought of my good friend Longfellow, whose poem, "My Cathedral" spoke of such an outdoor "Cathedral" whose towers were the trees ….. "Listen! The choir is singing; all the birds, in leafy galleries …"

16ᵗʰ May 1991 Thursday
Kowalski, Joseph Anthony, watchmaker and jeweller of 1, Ashby Road, Coalville, loving husband of Nina, father of Christopher and Richard, passed peacefully away following a long illness, on May 12ᵗʰ 1991 at Coalville Community Hospital. Funeral service to be held at St. Wilfred's Catholic Church, London Road, Coalville at 12 noon on Friday May 17ᵗʰ 1991.

Elaine Barkby, now suffering with multiple sclerosis, was for many years Mr. Kowalski's assistant.
She loved him much as I love Cocky, & he loved her as much as Cocky loves me; but, like Pulcinella, she now weeps alone.
Who is Pulcinella? He is one & the same Punchinello who evolved into Punch (Punch & Judy). Hans Andersen knew him in his story "What the Moon Saw" – "I know a Pulcinella" the Moon told me. He was the sad hunchback who loved Columbine & grieved more than Harlequin when she died.

Fatima – In the middle of Portugal, in the year 1917, The Virgin Mary appeared to three little shepherd children.
1. Lucia de Jesus Santos
2. Francisco de Jesus Marto
3. Jacinta de Jesus Marto

The Virgin Mary appeared 6 times – 13ᵗʰ May 1917, 13 June 1917, 13ᵗʰ July 1917, 13ᵗʰ August 1917, 13ᵗʰ September 1917, 13 October 1917.
"I will return here yet a seventh time" said the Virgin Mary. On 13ᵗʰ May 1917 at the same hour of that memorable day, the future Pope Pius XII was consecrated Bishop. He eventually consecrated the world to the Immaculate Heart of Mary.

17ᵗʰ May 1991 Friday
Lucia de Jesus Santos, now a Carmelite nun, is the only surviving witness of the vision of the Virgin Mary. Now aged 84, she was entrusted with the "Third Secret of Fatima".
The First Secret of Fatima was a brief glimpse of Hell.
The Second Secret of Fatima was being told that "The Holy Father will consecrate Russia to me & it will be converted. In the end, my Immaculate Heart will triumph".
The Third Secret was kept by Lucia until 1960 when she wrote it down for safe-keeping by the Bishop of Leiria.
On 13ᵗʰ October 1917 at Fatima, the sun spun & danced in the sky.
And now Pope John Paul II is to meet the nun, Lucia.

18ᵗʰ May 1991 Saturday
Leicester City 1 – Oxford United 0.
On their last match of the season, Leicester City had to win to avoid relegation to the Third Division. Always the 2 teams right at the bottom when the season ends are relegated. Leicester City, by the skin of their teeth, lived to play again in the 2ⁿᵈ Division.

19ᵗʰ May 1991 Whit Sunday
"And we know that all things work together for good to them that love God, to them who are the called according to his purpose". (Romans 8, 28.)

20ᵗʰ May 1991 Monday
F. A. Cup Final this year was between Tottenham Hotspurs & Nottingham Forest.
This was the 110ᵗʰ F. A. Cup Final & although Nottingham scored the first goal, the final result, after extra time, was a 2 – 1 win for Spurs.
I was in Nottingham when the match started – a deserted city.

Ted Ludlow has now interpreted for me the meaning of the number **666**.
It is the number of Satan himself who declares that if God, the great Trinity of Trinities, can be **333**, then Satan can double that.
Thus, in the year **666**, Islam came to denounce the teaching of the Holy Trinity.
Twice **666** = **1332** & in that year man began to expand himself until he felt almost too clever to need God any more.
Three times **666** = **1998**. That will be the year of Anti-Christ, when Satan has his last great fling of power.

21ˢᵗ May 1991 Tuesday
"The adjudication officer has decided that you are entitled to a weekly rate of Retirement Pension of £56 – 26p from Monday 15ᵗʰ July.
Basic Pension = £52. Graduated Pension = £1 – 36p.

Additional Pension of £37 – 05p is based on earnings from 1978 Contracted-out (COD) deductions of £34 – 15p are taken away leaving £2 – 90p. The Contracted-out deductions (£34 – 15p) will be paid by a different pension scheme".

Elizabeth Hewes, ZA 19 21 72 D is entitled to a N. I. Retirement Pension.

22nd May 1991 Wednesday

£250,000 needed to buy the laser for cardiovascular surgery at Leicester Royal Infirmary has now been raised by Leicester's Lord Mayor, Councillor Peter Kimberlin, just in time before he hands over his chains of office. Professor Peter Bell, expert in vascular surgery, will choose which laser to buy.

"I just don't know what the world is coming to" – so said President Bush of America on hearing the news that Rajiv Gandhi of India had been assassinated during an election campaign.

Rajiv Gandhi became Prime Minister in 1948 when his mother Indira Gandhi was assassinated. Rajiv Gandhi was assassinated in Sriperumpuour, 25 miles from Madras.

He was accepting garlands of welcome when a hidden bomb killed at least 14 people.

There was an enormous blast and Rajiv Gandhi was decapitated.

Aged 46, he leaves a widow & 2 teenage children.

23rd May 1991 Thursday

The bomb which decapitated Rajiv Ganghi on Tuesday this week raised new fears that the world's largest so-called democracy could also be blown to pieces.

India is a tinderbox mixture of races & religions & 16 different languages. Since its independence 44 years ago it has only just managed to hold itself together. India was born in violence as Moslem Pakistan was hived off in 1947. Rajiv Gandhi's grandfather Nehru became the first Prime Minister of India following "Independence" in 1947. Then his mother Indira Gandhi became Prime Minister.

24th May 1991 Friday

A Day in Stafford – Brother Pat, Evelyn & I spent the day with Bunting & Mostyn at their new home in Stafford.

Now almost 76, Bunting was having doubts about living so far out of town. They live in a lovely spot known as "Wildwood" – home of those delightful creatures of "Wind in the Willows". But, having no car of their own, it is becoming increasingly difficult to carry the weekly provisions home. Michael, however, living nearby with his new lady-love, Josie, is on top of the world – in the prime of life & looks as happy as a sand-boy.

Bunting, who has always been the life & soul of the party, making everything larger than life, & devoting all her energies to the well-being of her family, is now feeling rather depressed. She feels almost surplus to requirements, as though her life is meaning less, & wishes she could be doing something really worthwhile – something more challenging, with a real sense of purpose; to give her a sense of achievement.

St. Bartholomew's Hospital has pioneered laser surgery on arterial blockages in Britain. The laser can tackle rock-hard blockages up to a foot long without the need for open heart surgery. The laser fires a rapid succession of 100 kilowatt pulses through an insert fibre and breaks up the blockage.

26th May 1991 Trinity Sunday

The grace of our Lord Jesus Christ & the love of God & the fellowship of the Holy Ghost, be with us all evermore. (The Holy Trinity) (2 Corinthians)

And another thought for our 3 in 1 God. Jesus chose 12 disciples, but 3 were more privileged than the others to witness certain events. The 3 were Peter, James & John. They witnessed the raising to life of the daughter of Jairus, and they witnessed the glorious Transfiguration of Christ.

27th May 1991 Monday

Trinitas – And still I prayed, "Lord let me see, how three are one and one is three, read the dark riddle unto me!"

Then something whispered, "Dost thou pray for what thou hast this very day, the holy three have crossed thy way. Revealed in love and sacrifice, the holiest passed before thine eyes, one & the same in three-fold guise. The equal Father in rain & sun, his Christ in the good to evil done. His voice in thy soul, and the three are one." J.G.Whittier.

28th May 1991 Tuesday

Ascension Day this year (9th May) was more way out than ever.

This time the Coalville Council of Churches assembled at Swannington & the "service" was led by a guitar playing, tambourine slapping, hand clapping group, with plenty of reaction from the congregation, who seemed carried away by it all.

Fides, Spes. i.e. Faith, hope. These two, Fides, spes, are personified in the stained glass windows of Ravenstone Church. Hope holds the Anchor.

The Rector of Ravenstone, the Revd. Kerry Emmett, spoke to us on Trinity Sunday of the "sure & certain hope of the resurrection to eternal life". Not the uncertain hope that we have of so many things in life, but sure and certain hope of the resurrection to eternal life.

As St. Paul also reminds us, "….to lay hold upon the hope set before us; which hope we have as an anchor of the soul, both sure & steadfast". (Hebrews 6, 18.)

29th May 1991 Wednesday

With only a few more weeks before I retire from work, it is all systems GO all day long. Instead of a gradual slowing down, it is more a case of doing half a dozen jobs at once.

Mr Plant, the Director, has no secretary, so I am opening his mail & being allowed to read all sorts of interesting confidential letters which I would never normally see.

I am arranging recruitment for a new Confidential Personal Secretary & also for a new Office Junior in the Registry. And I am bringing some of my work home, to ensure that the fragments that remain are gathered up & nothing is lost.

30th May 1991 Thursday

Remember little Rowlie Jarvis, aged 11, who accompanied me to the Easter Sunday service in Leicester Cathedral in 1969? ……. "It was a pleasure to have such a model child with me."

Well, another wheel turns full circle as he & his wife now take on the role of Sunday School teachers at Ravenstone Church.

Milk Race – The 1991 Milk Race has hit the road. The cream of the world's cyclists are racing, stage by stage, from Humberside to Merseyside, including the 62 mile seventh stage from Kettering to Leicester, with 8 laps round the city centre. It is called the Milk Race because it is sponsored by the National Dairy Council; & this year the race includes Bridlington, Hull, Cleethorpes, Lincoln, Skegness, Norwich, Great Yarmouth, Bury St. Edmunds, Ipswich, Milton Keynes, Kettering, Leicester, Birmingham, Gloucester, Cardiff, Sheffield, Leeds & Liverpool.

31st May 1991 Friday

Milk Race – It is always so exciting to see the champion cyclists hurtling at top speed, all massed together, as they go round & round the city streets. The race started on 26th May & will finish on 8th June. Leicester this year has the pleasure of a weekend finish to a Race Stage, which means we have the cyclists with us for longer than usual. I love seeing all that goes on behind scenes – the entourage parked in adjoining streets - & a huge van with one side that lets down to open up into a 6 tier seating arena for 153.

1st June 1991 Saturday

And still the oil-wells of Kuwait are ablaze day & night. In fact night never falls in parts of Kuwait where the desert skies glow with the flames of more than 500 burning oil-wells. Kuwait City is surrounded by a circle of fire belching out plumes of putrid black smoke into the atmosphere. Twelve weeks after Kuwait was liberated, more than 100 fires have been put out, but it will take many months to complete the task.

Karen expects her baby in November, but she wishes it were November **NOW!** She is so looking forward to having a baby that it seems much too long to have to wait until November.

"What does he want for Christmas?" asks brother Pat, while Evelyn knits baby clothes for the new baby.

2nd June 1991 Sunday

Trinity I – Be strong & of a good courage; be not afraid, neither be thou dismayed; for the Lord thy God is with thee whithersoever thou goest. (Joshua 1, 9.)

3rd June 1991 Monday

And the preacher spoke of God's call to Abram – a single command – Genesis 12, 1.

"Get thee out of thy country, & from thy kindred, and from thy father's house, unto a land that I will show thee." Then God made 7 promises to Abram, even though his reward was intangible & not to be in his lifetime.

"And I will make of thee a great nation, & I will bless thee, & make thy name great; & thou shalt be a blessing; and I will bless them that bless thee, & curse him that curseth thee; & in thee shall all families of the earth be blessed."

And Abram obeyed God's call. Is God calling you?

"New Scientist" – a scientific journal I am privileged to read at work, this week reviews a new book, "The Conscious Universe". It explains quantum physics. A property of the quantum world is "non-locality". Subatomic particles, such as phatons which have interacted at one time, continue to "know" about each other, even if there is no possibility of a signal passing between them. It is because all particles in existence interacted once – during the fireball of the big bang – that they all are still, in some sense, in communication instantaneously. Therefore we all are one.

4th June 1991 Tuesday

Silver Wedding Day of cousin Lesley & John Sear. But sadly, the marriage ended in divorce.

Today then, Enid & I spent the evening with Lesley, where we saw on video the recent wedding of Lesley's eldest daughter Ruth.

Lesley's other daughters, Clare and Karen, are now grown up and at work, still living with their mum.

Lesley has recently been promoted to "Sister" at Coalville Hospital & is enjoying this newly acquired status, which gives her a sense of fulfilment & a feeling of being somebody worthwhile in her own right.

5th June 1991 Wednesday

The Merchant of Venice – Katherine Sullivan & I enjoyed a superb production by the English Shakespeare Company at Nottingham's Theatre Royal. Apart from the great dialogue of the main characters …. "The quality of mercy is not strained" … etc., I was enchanted by the young lovers Lorenzo and Jessica …. "The moon shines bright! In such a night as this, when the sweet wind did gently kiss the trees & they did make no noise, in such a night, Troilus, methinks, mounted the Trojan walls … In such a night …." etc. etc.

6th June 1991 Thursday

The Leicestershire Hospice has advertised for a part-time clerk. To provide clerical support to admin. & nursing staff. The position requires a mature person with good communication skills and flexible approach. Hours 1 p.m. – 4.30 p.m. Mon – Friday. £2-67p per hour.

I thought this sounded just the job for me, so I have applied.

"To keep notes – "Trolley and Sister" – in proper order. To answer the telephone according to Hospice policy. To liaise with general office – collect and distribute post to patients."

7th June 1991 Friday

Phew! The end of another hectic week at work.

Kim, (who will be taking my place when I leave) and I, have now interviewed the prospective candidates for the "Junior" in the Registry. We chose a young 15 year old boy who will be 16 years old next month. His name is Daniel, and I thought of old Shylock ready to claim his pound of flesh, referring to the learned doctor of the law as a Daniel come to judgment!

Yea, a Daniel. And then when the same learned doctor

made it impossible to be done, the others repeating, "A Daniel".

Coalville Amateur Operatic Society Annual General Meeting when Treasurer Hewsie presented her accounts & gracefully retired from office, leaving £8,000 to launch next year's show. From Prompter to Treasurer to Assistant House Manager. This is my latest role, assisting brother Pat.

Having formally tendered my resignation from the role of Treasurer to Coalville Amateur Operatic Society, I have thereby created a void. No-one volunteered to take over the job & it was finally decided to look outside the Society for a replacement.

8th June 1991 Saturday
"I think the nightingale, if she should sing by day when every goose is cackling, would be thought no better a musician than the wren".
"He is well paid that is well satisfied".
"Her sunny locks hang on her temples like a golden fleece, and many Jasons come in quest of her" – just a few of the many gems strewn into Shakespeare's "Merchant of Venice".

9th June 1991 Sunday
Trinity 2 – The Lord bless thee & keep thee; the Lord make his face shine upon thee & be gracious unto thee; the Lord lift up his countenance upon thee & give thee peace.
(Numbers 6, 24.)

10th June 1991 Monday
Happy Birthday to Auntie Belle **95** today!
Auntie Belle, widow of Fred, my dad's eldest brother, celebrated her 95th birthday in her own home with a party organised by her niece Averil.
Also celebrating his birthday today is Prince Philip, Duke of Edinburgh, consort to her Majesty the Queen. Prince Philip is 70 today & is unhappy about ageing. He has refused permission for an official portrait to commemorate his birthday; so it will be an official photograph taken 2 years ago which we will see.

11th June 1991 Tuesday
"Virgin Births" Axed - Family planners have decided to drop the "Virgin Birth" service which caused such controversy earlier in the year. The British Pregnancy Advisory Service says it will close all artificial insemination clinics next month, & will concentrate on its prime function, which is to provide an abortion and advice service.
The first baby in the world to be born as a result of fertilisation in vitro (conception outside the body) was Louise Joy Brown, delivered by caesarean section in Oldham General Hospital on 25th July 1978.
"Snibston Museum Sneak Preview" – A behind-the-scenes sneak preview of what is going on at the Snibston Museum & Country Park project will be given tomorrow evening. It is hoped to open the 130 acre park site in October 1992. Tim Shadla-Hall, Director of Leicestershire Museums, is in command.

12th June 1991 Wednesday
Music! Hark! "It is your music, madam, of the house".

Having so recently enjoyed Shakespeare's Merchant of Venice, where music crowns the final Act, I have now launched out on the latest "Integrated Compact Disc Hi-Fi System".
This is a 3 in 1 unit, which will play music on tape, on compact disc & also on the radio.
My very first compact disc is "New Year's Concert in Vienna", 17 items consisting chiefly of Strauss, but also including Mozart & Schubert.
Every New Year's Day we enjoy this superb concert from Vienna, shown on television.

13th June 1991 Thursday
What an interesting sneak preview we had of Snibston Museum. Apart from all the mining interests, there were some wonderful old vehicles on display, including a splendid old horse drawn hearse; & there were such fascinating scientific exhibits, such as a model tornado in action, & the miracle of D.N.A.

Joanne, aged 17, having tried her hand briefly at office work, hair dressing, curtain making, etc, has now applied for a job as a PCB Assembler (i.e. a personal computer base). I took her to Market Bosworth for an interview with Flowtronics Systems Ltd & she was told that she could start work next Monday.
But oh, what hard task-masters they are. Start work at 7-30 a.m. Finish at 5 p.m. Monday to Thursday. Then on Friday 7-30a.m.to 11-30a.m. Half an hour lunch. It will mean leaving home at 6-30 a.m. It is factory-like work, sitting at a conveyor belt.
Flowtronics Systems Ltd. (Electronic & Telecoms Equipment Manufacturers) make all those complicated workings that are usually hidden inside the electronic equipment of today. They are concerned with Weighing Technology, Telecommunications, Scientific Instruments, and Control Equipment & Telemetry. PCB – Hand soldering & Flow soldering, wiring – cabinets, chassis, and racks. Cable forming – laced or tied gunwrapping chassis, backplanes, PCBs.
Poor Joanne – not altogether her choice of a job. But it is all she has on offer at the moment. £80 per week.

15th June 1991 Saturday
Sharon & Darren were married today at St Mary's Parish Church, Sileby. The reception was held at Six Hills Country House Restaurant. The wedding was originally planned for next Saturday 22nd June, but had to be changed because of problems with catering arrangements. Sharon wore the most beautiful wedding dress you could imagine, but the weather was awful. It rained & it rained & it rained all day long.
In torrential rain we all went to Sharon & Darren's wedding. But "many waters cannot quench love; neither can the floods drown it". Darren & Sharon met at school & each has been for the other, the one & only true love. Darren concluded his speech by saying to Sharon, "I will always love you".

16th June 1991 Sunday
Trinity 3. The God of all grace, who hath called us into his eternal glory by Christ Jesus, after that ye have suffered a while, make you perfect, strengthen & settle you. (1 Peter, 5.)

17th June 1991 Monday
"You are invited to my retirement "Oldies" get-together at County Hall Restaurant on 16th July at 12 noon"

Sent out half a dozen invitations to the original Old Brigade of the Motor Tax Office, some of them who were there when I first started work in 1948 at good old 14 Friar Lane, Leicester.

Principal Volcanic Eruptions
Santorini, Greece, 1550BC: Island destroyed
Vesuvius, Italy, 79AD: Destroyed Pompeii
Etna, Italy, 1669AD: 20,000 killed
Kelud, Java, 1586AD: 10,000 killed
Tambora, Indonesia, 1815: Largest eruption: 90,000 killed
Krakatoa, Indonesia, 1883: Biggest explosion 36,380 dead
Mont Pelée, Martinique, 1902: 26,000 killed
Mount St Helens, USA, 1980: 66 killed
Lamington, Papua New Guinea, 1951: 3,000 killed
Nevada del Ruiz, Colombia, 1984: 24,000 killed
Mount Unzen, Japan, 1991: 38 killed

The latest volcanic eruption of **Mount Pinatubo**, 60 miles north of Manila in the Philippines, brings into focus the whole question of volcanic activity.
Vulcan was the god of devouring flame. The ancient Romans used to sacrifice to Vulcan regularly on 23rd August (my mum's birthday). How tragic then that in A.D. 79 on the day following the sacrifice to Vulcan, on 24th August, Vesuvius erupted & destroyed Pompeii. Filipinos fled in their thousands from the volcanic eruptions of Mount Pinatubo. A whole series of thundering explosions shot a giant plume of ash more than 15 miles high and rained down a deadly cascade of molten rock. Nearby Angeles City (City of the Angels) is now buried beneath the ash. As if a volcano erupting were not enough, there has also been a typhoon & earthquakes.

19th June 1991 Wednesday
"You are invited to my retirement party in the Conference Room on 12th July 1991, 12 noon – 2 p.m."

Sent out about 40 invitations to all my work-mates at the Department of Energy.
So I prepare to go out with a bang – 3 parties in one week to celebrate my 60 glorious years.

Auntie Doris, also aged 95, is still as alert as ever, & looking forward to a Centenary birthday celebration underneath the ancient Butter Cross at Mountsorrel, just across the road from her little old cottage in Watling Street. She rang me up for a long & lively chat, to bring me up to date on all her latest activities. Still busy knitting for African babies; & every Monday entertaining her younger sister Hilda (aged 93) at her home for the day.
"One of these days" she said, "I will have to consider what arrangements to make for when I am old!!"

20th June 1991 Thursday
Poor old Aunt Dos, aged 89, is really old & frail &

helpless. How sad to see her in such discomfort as she sits day in & day out in a world of her own. Her eyes are always closed & are often her major cause of distress. The eyelids swell grotesquely making her look like a frog; & she sits with her head constantly drooped, so that it is difficult for her to eat or drink. Brother Pat & I are now her sole visitors. We sit with her for an hour or so, but she hardly says a word to us until we say we are going, and then she says, "No – don't go. Please stay with me".

21st June 1991 Friday
Civil Service Benevolent Fund
Methodist Church Rooms, Clarendon Park Road, Leicester,
Saturday 22nd June Adm.10p Doors open 1-30 p.m.

Preparing as I am for "Lift Off", the C.S.B.F. Annual Rummage Sale provided a good opportunity for me to discard a whole load of clutter from the house.

The longest day, but a very pleasant hectic day at work following another hectic week trying to do 2 jobs at once. I love acting as Mr Plant's secretary, being entrusted with all his confidential work – opening his mail each day and receiving all his phone calls. He is off to Berlin next month on official business & will not be at work on the day I retire.
Today we had a VIP visitor at work – Permanent Under Secretary Geoffrey Chipperfield, so we all got dressed up in our best attire & had drinks with him in Mr Plant's office.

22nd June 1991 Saturday
Having drinks at work with the Permanent Under Secretary of State means that I am again bringing work home, in order to keep up with myself. Some of the letters I have to prepare are so full of technical jargon that it is a work of art sorting out what they are all about. There are first drafts, second drafts, third drafts and more, before they are finally signed.

23rd June 1991 Sunday
Trinity 4. O God, the protector of all that trust in thee, without whom nothing is strong, nothing is holy, increase & multiply upon us thy mercy, that thou being our ruler & guide, we may so pass through things temporal, that we finally lose not the things eternal. (Collect).

Being so close to retirement, I am pleased to say that I have managed to escape the annual P.P.I. (Progress & Performance Interview) following each staff report. So I shall never know what was written about me this year. How we all love the praises of men, even though one & the same thing can be either praised or denounced.
Cartoon in paper – Dad to schoolboy – "Same old notes on your report!" – "Could do better!"
Schoolboy to Dad – "See – there's hope for me yet!"

24th June 1991 Monday
Never have I known such exquisite music as I now enjoy on my new compact-disc player. The sound quality is a vast improvement on my old second-hand radiogram. My choice of compact discs so far is –

1. New Year's Concert in Vienna 1991.
2. New Year's Concert in Vienna 1990.
3..Classic Experience II – 36 of the most popular classics.
"What would you like for your birthday?" asked Bunting, & I knew immediately, "A compact disc!"
How privileged are we who live in this age of high technology to enjoy such benefits.

25th June 1991 Tuesday
"**Dieu et Mon Emu**" An indication of Britain's reluctance to be swallowed up in European monetary union, with loss of our own sovereignty, is a caricature in today's paper of the royal coat of arms supported by a suspicious lion & strutting EMU.

The most eligible bachelor in the county, 32 year-old David Charles Robert Manners, Marquis of Granby, son & heir of the Duke of Rutland of Belvoir Castle, with its 18,000 acres of grounds, has announced his engagement. His fiancée is Emma Watkins, aged 27, daughter of a Welsh farmer, who runs her own business Eardisley Park Interiors, in Herefordshire. The couple plan to marry in the chapel at Belvoir Castle next spring. Lord Granby is an antique & modern sporting weapons dealer. The Duke of Rutland is now aged 72.

26th June 1991 Wednesday
"Sure-shot Bailey" hits the headlines again. Nev Bailey, cousin Johnty's son, is pictured in the Leicester Mercury under the heading "Sure-shot Bailey hits full house for national crown"
"Leicestershire's Nev Bailey notched up a perfect score of 300 points as he fulfilled a long-held ambition to win the Clay Pigeon Shooting Association's English down-the-line title. Bailey, from Nailstone, who has been trying to win the title for 11 years & has been runner-up twice, hit all 100 clays on first barrels amid competition from 366 other guns at Bywell Shooting Ground, Northumberland."

27th June 1991 Thursday
Hewes, Isobel, passed away peacefully in hospital, June 27th 1991, aged 95 years, a dearly loved and devoted aunt. She will be sadly missed by all who knew her. Funeral service and cremation at Loughborough Crematorium on Thursday July 4th at 1 p.m. All flowers and inquiries to Co-operative Funeral Services, Stuart House, 128 London Road, Coalville. Tel. Coalville 36703
This is Auntie Belle, who died today, aged 95. Born in June, she also died in June. She was Uncle Fred's second wife. His first wife Lucy (Cousin Don's mother) died early in the war, in 1942.
Auntie Belle died in Glenfield Community Hospital. Shortly after her birthday on 10th June, she was taken to hospital in great pain. The pain was cancer, which unbeknown to anyone, had taken hold & affected her chest & ribs, & even inside her head.
I have visited her every Sunday morning for some years now. I last saw her on 23rd June, when she was in considerable discomfort, but was able to hold a long conversation with me, telling me all that had been happening in the hospital ward. She was a charming old lady, loved by everyone.

28th June 1991 Friday
Happy Birthday to Henry the Eighth!
Henry Tudor, 2nd son of Henry VII, was born on 28th June 1491 in Greenwich. The 500th anniversary of his birth is being celebrated throughout this year, but especially today; there are pageants, plays, Tudor music recitals, banquets & such-like, here , there & everywhere.
Greenwich, more than anywhere else, lays claim to Henry VIII. He was born there in the Palace of Placentia, whose foundations lie below the Royal Naval College. He was christened there; he was married there to Catherine of Aragon & Anne of Cleves; & his two daughters, Mary and Elizabeth were both born there.

29th June 1991 Saturday
When I finished work at the Motor Licence Office in 1978, I chose as my leaving present a beautiful gilt edged oval mirror to "reflect" on 30 years in the world of Motor Taxation. Now, as I finish work at the Department of Energy's Gas & Oil Measurement Branch, I have chosen a de-luxe camera, for a more lasting picture.

Red Adair, aged 76, the world's most experienced oil trouble-shooter, is in charge of capping the burning oil wells of Kuwait. Dressed in his red boiler suit & sweating from the 300°F heat around the wells he said, "This is going to take 5 years". He cited red tape, problems of water, shortages of equipment, mines, lack of roads & fatigue, as some of the major reasons for the long time-scale of the operation.

30th June 1991 Sunday
Trinity 5. What is man, that thou art mindful of him? And the son of man, that thou visitest him? For thou hast made him a little lower than the angels, & hast crowned him with glory & honour. (Psalm 8.)

1st July 1991 Monday
"Quiet retiring type, somewhat slightly aloof Hewsie" is now retiring, but not so quietly. This is the July holiday fortnight & a time for high jinks & frivolity. As Shakespeare says in "King Richard II" Act 3 – "Awhile to work, & after the holiday". So, after 42 years at work, it is now time for the holiday.

"Part-Time Ward Clerk"
"Dear Miss E. Hewes, Thank you for your application form for the above post. Unfortunately you have not been successful on this occasion, but may I take this opportunity of wishing you well in your future career. Yours Sincerely, Bernadette Fenn (Mrs) Administrative Assistant."
At the grand old age of 60, one is not so much "mature" as "over-ripe" for launching out on a new career. Having meandered through life thus far, I will let the stream of life take me with it along its course.

2nd July 1991 Tuesday
The Princess of Wales celebrated her 30th birthday yesterday, going about her daily "business as usual" & declining the offer of a birthday party. This has added fuel to the rumours that she & her husband now live separate lives & prefer to go their own separate ways.

She is however much more in demand than he is, being by far the most glamorous member of the family, dressed in the finest outfits money can buy & completely at ease with old & young alike.

Poor Prince Charles, heir to the throne, cannot compete with her. Old before his time, he has to cancel some of his engagements because of his bad back; & looks very sad.

3rd July 1991 Wednesday

I think of the last Prince of Wales. He too suffered untold agonies for the love of a beautiful woman. Not only did he give up his throne for her, but he finished in the end a broken man.

Katherine Sullivan, who met him one day walking his dog near his home in Paris, spoke to him in English. Oh, how he longed to be able to visit England as freely as anyone else. Just to meet someone by chance who belonged to England stirred him to the depths of his soul; but only as a corpse could he return to England.

Cocky's retirement party cost about £350. My triple bonanza is costing twice as much as that, if not more. But, as the good book says, "Give and it shall be given unto you; good measure, pressed down, & shaken together, & running over, shall men give into your bosom" (Luke 6)

4th July 1991 Thursday

An idyllic day; a day of blue skies & sunshine for Auntie Belle's funeral. On the coffin was placed the most beautiful basket of flowers from her niece June, together with the more conventional "wreath" from her niece Averil. Auntie Belle, who had in her lifetime created many gorgeous flower arrangements, would have been well pleased with the flowers at her funeral. Loughborough crematorium is in a delightful setting & through the picture windows we could see masses of roses forming a complete hedge of roses beneath the lovely old trees. Afterwards we gathered at Auntie Belle's.

5th July 1991 Friday

On 5th July 1841 Thomas Cook, of Adam & Eve Street, Market Harborough, organised his very first excursion from Leicester to Loughborough by train. Leicester therefore is proud to call itself "the birthplace of tourism" and is celebrating the Thomas Cook 150th Anniversary in a big way. From the tiny acorn of this first trip in 1841, the mighty oak of the tourism industry of today has grown. 1841 – 1991, the Thomas Cook Festival starts on 5th July & culminates with a Thanksgiving Service on 14th July.

Othello which was shown on television a year ago (MCMXC) was repeated for our entertainment again this year. I loved following it all over again with my "Complete Works of William Shakespeare" & was again held spellbound at the skills of the actors in bringing the words to life.

6th July 1991 Saturday

Motored to Stafford to deliver to Bunting by hand tickets of admission for Alton Towers. For the first time ever, I met Michael's three beautiful children.

I was delighted to make the acquaintance of Michael's 3 children – Lucy, Sam & Polly. What a joy it was to walk along the edge of the wood which reaches the bottom of Michael's garden, hand in hand with 10 year old Polly. She had never seen me before, but gladly offered the hand of friendship.

7th July 1991 Sunday

Trinity 6. O God, who hast prepared for them that love thee, such good things as pass man's understanding, pour into our hearts such love toward thee, that we, loving thee above all things, may obtain thy promises which exceed all that we can desire. (Collect for today)

8th July 1991 Monday

My last week at work. Kim has now taken up permanent residence at my desk and I have virtually moved out – lock, stock and barrel. I feel completely liberated, like a little bird ready to fly for the first time. The whole world is there for me to explore, but I have no desire to fly too far afield. The only place which beckons me at the moment is Copenhagen because of my strong affinity with Hans Christian Andersen. But I am quite content with dear old England, whose many treasures lie waiting for me to discover.

9th July 1991 Tuesday

As I approach the completion of 42 years at work, I feel as though I have conquered Everest. No wonder I am planning such an extravagant birthday celebration. There has never been anything in my life to celebrate before. Even my 21st coming of age was very low key, having said goodbye to Cocky, but still loving him.

"The universe is full of magical things patiently waiting for our wits to grow sharper"

Eden Philpotts

All the wonderful technology of today is magic to me; the telephone – the television – the radio – and of course my delightful compact disc player. The whole of creation is magic to me – birth & re-birth – the seasons & the instincts of animals & birds. And what is more magical than a perfumed flower? The house is well blessed at this very moment with masses of flowers for my retirement, & choicest music.

10th July 1991 Wednesday

An hour long telephone call from my former workmate Reevsie. She brought me up to date on all her family news. Her sister Sherry has been completely shattered & on the verge of suicide following her desertion by her husband. Her American pen-friend Sherry, whom she has known for 40 years or more but never actually met, eventually made it to England & spent a memorable week with Reevsie – one of the happiest weeks Reevsie has ever known.

Reevsie's Mum now has cancer, but is bearing up very well. Her mother-in-law died suddenly, just sitting in her chair. Her sister-in-law Eileen has some dreadful illness which is gradually paralysing her. Her other sister-in-law Shirley has been widowed at a relatively early age, and Reevsie & Tony take her out & about with them; but Shirley misses her Geoff, particularly as they both enjoyed ballroom dancing so very much. Reevsie's one

& only daughter Joanne is still at home, but has a steady boyfriend, although she is in no hurry to get married. Reevsie's brother Ken, married for 18 years to Maureen, has fallen hopelessly in love with another woman. In all this family turmoil of mixed joy & sorrow, Reevsie seems to be the central linchpin holding them all together – their confidante & advisor.

11th July 1991 Thursday

Dr Sayer was asked to prepare a "Valedictory Letter" for my retirement, but knowing absolutely nothing about my 30 years work in the Motor Licence Office & not being over-impressed with my managerial capabilities, he asked me what had been the highlights in my life. "No highlights," I said, "only low lights."

12th July 1991 Friday
Exit Stage Left - Betty Retires.

My last day at work and a wonderful "send off" from the office. We had a lovely buffet lunch together in the staff tea-room & everyone rallied round to help. I was made to feel like a queen for the day – showered with gifts & good wishes from as far afield as our head office at 1, Palace Street, London, to our other office at Aberdeen.

A beautiful large card with 3 red roses pictured on the front was signed by them all, including one which said, "Betty exits stage left for a long and happy retirement!" Then a basket of red roses at home from Cocky.

13th July 1991 Saturday

Surrounded as I am at home today with more flowers than I have ever been given in my life before, the perfume of so many roses fills the air completely.

Flowers have been given to me from the office, from the Committee of the Civil Service Benevolent Fund, "Phyl & Lesley", "Sharon & Darren", Joanne, Enid, Reevsie, Caroline the Caterer (for the office buffet) & from Cocky – "Love forever John".

All set for my great birthday celebration tomorrow and I am delighted to say that every single one of my dad's progeny have now agreed to come. Steven has parted company with his latest girl friend, cancelled his holiday, & will come to Alton Towers with us. Only Mostyn will be missing. He is not well at the moment.

14th July 1991 Sunday

Trinity 7 – "This is the day which the Lord hath made; we will rejoice and be glad in it."

(Psalm 118)

15th July 1991 Monday

My first day of retirement; thought for the day – Hymn 276…

"O Lord, how happy should we be if we could cast our care on Thee; if we from self could rest, & feel at heart that One above, in perfect wisdom, perfect love, is working for the best.

How far from this our daily life, how oft disturbed by anxious strife, by sudden wild alarms; Oh, could we but relinquish all our earthly props, & simply fall on Thy Almighty arms.

Could we but kneel & cast our load, e'en while we pray upon our God, then rise with lightened cheer; sure that the Father who is nigh to still the famished raven's cry, will hear in that we fear. We cannot trust Him as we should; so chafes weak nature's restless mood to cast its peace away; but birds & flowerets round us preach, all, all the present evil teach sufficient for the day. Lord, make these faithless hearts of ours such lessons learn from birds & flowers; make them from self to cease; leave all things to a Father's will, & taste, before Him lying still, e'en in affliction, peace.

What a glorious day we all had yesterday at Alton Towers. The weather was absolutely perfect & it was lovely to have the whole of my dad's family together for the very first time. We all met at 12 noon & then dispersed until 5 p.m. when we had a birthday tea together, & a birthday cake presented by Henry Hound.

17th July 1991 Wednesday

O.A.P. Hewsie has now applied for…

1. Senior Railcard No. 10287, £16, valid for one year. This entitles the holder to cheaper rail travel.

2. Concessionary Travel for Elderly People. i.e. Half fare pass to travel by bus on all local bus services as far as Derby, Nottingham, Grantham, Stamford, Peterborough, Northampton, Rugby, Coventry & Burton-on-Trent.

O.A.P.s (Old Age Pensioners) are also entitled to cheaper tickets at the theatre & other places of entertainment. My first outing as an O.A.P. was to Alton Towers on my birthday.

Luncheon in the restaurant at County Hall, Glenfield, where I was delighted to meet up again with my old Motor Tax colleagues – Charles, Pam & Les, & Reevsie. How we laughed at all the hilarious episodes we could all remember – all the old eccentric characters we knew & the experiences we shared.

Charles is now aged 80; remember his wedding in October 1975 to Renee? He & Renee in the autumn of their lives have found happiness together & they have now invited me to spend the day with them next Wednesday, for old time's sake.

Miss Gazzard & Muriel, two other "oldies" from the Motor Licence Office who were invited to my get-together, were not able to attend but sent their apologies & said we can meet later on, at Muriel's home in Leicester. Miss Gazzard now lives in Yorkshire, but maintains close contact with Muriel.

18th July 1991 Thursday

Joanne, aged 17, who was offered a job 5 weeks ago at Market Bosworth, packed the job in before she even started. The very thought of it convinced her that it was not the job for her.

Today I took her for another interview – this time to Shepshed to work in the factory of Mansfield Knitwear as a machinist, making jumpers etc. Part of the vast Coats Viyella group, it seemed a much better place for Joanne. Hours 8 a.m. – 5 p.m. with an hour lunch; near to the shops – on a bus route - & a friendly workforce.

19th July 1991 Friday

Inland Revenue – no sooner do you retire than you get Form P161 to complete.

Ref – 946/500/HEW ZA 19 21 72 D

How much is your pension a week? £56 – 26.
Other pensions – What is the name & address of the payer? Paymaster General, authorised by the Treasury, via Department of Energy.
How much is the pension? £6,258 – 71 p.a.
Details of interest from bank & building society.
£15-16 from bank, £50-54 from building society.

20ᵗʰ July 1991 Saturday

Lump Sum – 42 years at work culminated in a lump sum of £19,000. This has now been dispersed as follows – £10,000 Heart of England Building Society (extra high interest), £5,000 National Savings, £2,000 Premium Bonds, £2,000 to spend.

21ˢᵗ July 1991 Sunday

Trinity 8 – Verily for the righteous there will be a fulfilment of the heart's desires.
                    The Koran (Qur'an) (Sura LXXVIII)

22ⁿᵈ July 1991 Monday

Les Misérables – This masterpiece by Victor Hugo has been translated and transposed into one of the greatest musicals of all time. It has been playing to packed houses in London since 1985 and Mary Blue has seen it. So impressed & inspired was she that she has offered to take me on 31ˢᵗ August to see it with her. Full of pathos, full of truth, full of high eloquence, it has always been & will always be a best seller.
When it was first published Hugo sent a telegram to his publisher. It said **"?"** The answer came back **"!"**

23ʳᵈ July 1991 Tuesday

Retirement suits me very nicely because it enables me to make haste slowly. As one of life's dreamers I like to "stand & stare", to wander at leisure & browse all day in little back street arcades, book shops, libraries & museums. When choosing a birthday card or a Christmas card I usually look at every card in the shop first. And how lovely it is to have time to do the shopping, the house-work & the garden just whenever it suits; or on an impulse spread my wings & fly further afield. But best of all is freedom from "Staff Reports" & official rules.

"Clean Water & Adequate Sanitation for all by 1990" This was the goal set by the United Nations when they declared 1981 – 90 the International Drinking Water Supply & Sanitation Decade. I volunteered to be "Parish Representative" in August 1983, but sadly the response was minimal.

24ᵗʰ July 1991 Wednesday

116,000 Soldiers – The British Army is to be reduced to 116,000 soldiers (cut by a quarter) following the collapse of the Warsaw Pact military allowance & the withdrawal of thousands of Soviet troops from Eastern & Central Europe. This supposedly has ended the "cold war" between East & West. The Ministry of Defence however will be retaining 120,000 civil servants; more than the entire strength of the Army. Famous Regiments will now have to amalgamate with others.

25ᵗʰ July 1991 Thursday

Sherwood Forest – Enid & I enjoyed a coach trip to Sherwood Forest.
First port of call was Rufford Abbey & Country Park where we wandered at will from 12-15p.m. to 2-15p.m. Then on to the coach, well beyond the Sherwood Forest Visitors Centre, in order to drive back through the magnificent double avenue of lime trees stretching over 2 miles & known as the "Duke's Drive" in Clumber Park.
And so to Sherwood Forest from 3-15p.m. to 5-15p.m. where we walked a mile to see the famous Major Oak and savoured the atmosphere of Robin Hood.

Mostyn's sickness has now been confirmed as cancer. For several weeks he has been very poorly, unable to keep any food down & intermittently having projectile sickness which Bunting describes as emitting in a great arc like a rainbow. He has been in & out of hospital not knowing what was really wrong.

26ᵗʰ July 1991 Friday

Citizen's Charter – Not quite as memorable or momentous as Magna Carta, but this latest Citizen's Charter has been launched this week by Prime Minister John Major. It includes more than 70 measures whereby Mr & Mrs Joe Public (shown inside logo) are guaranteed value for money. e.g. Postal Services, Train Services, Local Government, Central Government, Gas, Electricity, etc. Public servants who come into contact with the public will be expected to wear name badges. Everything & everybody will have to be accounted for.

27ᵗʰ July 1991 Saturday

Thomas Cook 1808 - 1892 – Katherine Sullivan & I enjoyed an afternoon at the Haymarket Theatre Leicester, watching a theatrical extravaganza about Thomas Cook. "Follow the Man from Cooks" was a Victorian Music Hall type of show spanning the years 1808 – 1892. It was a superb portrayal of the times, the world & the Leicester which Thomas Cook lived in.

An idyllic summer's day culminating in an idyllic summer's night, complete with full moon. Katherine Sullivan & I, after an afternoon at Leicester's Haymarket Theatre, took "Toffee" her dachshund for an evening romp through the bracken at the top of the Beacon, our local high spot.

28ᵗʰ July 1991 Sunday

Trinity 9 – Verily over you are appointed angels to protect you – kind and honourable – writing down your deeds. The Koran (Sura LXXXII)

29ᵗʰ July 1991 Monday

The jungle which was Aunt Dos's garden at the back of her bungalow, next door to my house at Ravenstone, has now been completely transformed, & this week a newly seeded lawn has sprung to life. So another wheel turns full cycle as the old Hollies lawn is seen again from my bedroom window.

Castle Park Festival Week 24ᵗʰ – 31ˢᵗ August.
Castle Park is the historic core of Leicester.
"Take a leisurely walk around Castle Park in the company of famous historical figures who will explain the history as you go along. Each day a different

historical character will be your guide, including Mr Thomas Cook the well known temperance reformer & travel entrepreneur."

Today I went to the Information Centre, St. Martin's Walk, Leicester, and booked 2 tickets for a guided walk with Thomas Cook on Tuesday 27th August.

30th July 1991 Tuesday

Mostyn comes home from hospital. Mostyn is dying from cancer, but today he was discharged from hospital to be cared for at home by Bunting. I motored to Stafford this morning to comfort Bunting, but found her to be a tower of strength – never doubting for one moment that **all things work together for good**, and truly casting all her care on God; feeling at heart that "One above, in perfect wisdom, perfect love, is working for the best."

Michael & his lady love Josie, having sold their large 5 bedroom house, have now bought a smaller house nearby complete with "Granny Annex" attachment.

31st July 1991 Wednesday

Leicester City football stadium at Filbert Street is to be converted into a de-luxe all-seater stadium by the end of 1993. It will cost £7 ½ million and will hold 21,000 seated spectators. The main stand will be the new North Stand along Filbert Street. It will have 3 levels & will contain health & leisure club, sports shop, dressing rooms, ticket office, conference & banqueting facilities, restaurant, club offices, V.I.P. facilities & 30 executive boxes. (28 being 10 seaters & 2 being 20 seaters) Puzzle – where to find £7 ½ million? Apart from grants, it is hoped that business investment will help bridge the gap.

A new "Chief Executive" for Leics. County Council. The present Chief Executive, Sam Jones, appointed in 1976, is going on to higher things – Town Clerk to the City of London. His successor is 43 year-old David Prince. He faces an uncertain future, maybe the abolition of County Councils.

1st August 1991 Thursday

A day of discovery. Explored Victoria Park, Leicester – found "Peace Walk" leading from the War Memorial & so to Welford Road Cemetery where I then found the grave of Thomas Cook, which looked as good as new. Then down the lovely "New Walk" to the Museum where I bought a little book "The Tigers" – a short history of the Royal Leicestershire Regiment. In 1944 the Regiment was granted the honour of the Freedom of the City of Leicester. The vellum scroll recording this is now held in the ancient Magazine, which today is the Museum of the Royal Leicestershire Regiment – so I will endeavour to visit that in due course.

2nd August 1991 Friday

The marriage of Tina Marie & Wayne Lee Tyers takes place tomorrow at St. George's, Swannington. Joanne is one of the bridesmaids. She will be wearing a dark green off-the-shoulder dress with a garland of flowers on her long blonde hair. Seeing her dressed thus, she reminded me of a Grecian nymph.

"Leicester – Streets Ahead" This is Leicester's latest slogan having been chosen to be Britain's first Environment City. Leicester has been given its Environment City title for four years from the start of 1991 until the end of 1994. The award was made by the Civic Trust, which is part of the Department of Environment & the Royal Society for Nature Conservation. So, we are all set now for a massive programme of improvement with a cartoon caterpillar as our mascot. Our caterpillar will turn into a butterfly on 21st September 1991 when the Environment City campaign really takes off. It is envisaged that on 21st September 1991 the world's biggest caterpillar will be created in a huge conga of thousands of local people and celebrities. The conga will shuffle into Leicester's town hall and be transformed into a butterfly, portrayed in an expensive laser display. The top priority in all this is to give local residents pride in where they live; & give Leicester a national identity.

4th August 1991 Sunday

Trinity 10 – God is not the God of the dead, but the God of the living. To Moses he said, "I am the God of Abraham & the God of Isaac & the God of Jacob." (Mark, Chapter 12)

Abbey Park 8.00a.m. This morning I went on another voyage of discovery and found Abbey Park in its fullest beauty, before most people had stirred from their beds. I watched squirrels foraging in the litter bins, and virtually had the Park to myself. The flower beds – the lawns – the lake – the trees were a sheer delight. I chose a seat on an elevated glade overlooking the lake and drank in the beauty of the scene. The bells of nearby St. Margaret's pealed across the meadows & I was transported out of this world. I also discovered some useful parking places.

Lunch at Pat & Evelyn's home where we were joined by Mary Blue & Karen (6 months pregnant). Karen is hoping in due course to have the baby Christened, but has doubts about all that it might entail, being a non-churchgoer. Could she in all honesty make her responses, not really believing in the Holy Spirit?

The lesson appointed for today was Acts 15. This dealt with the vexed question of the early church concerning what to do to become a Christian. The Rector, the Reverend Kerry Emmett, brought this up to date by likening it to the non-churchgoers of today needing help & support to christen their babies.

5th August 1991 Monday

The Magazine Gateway in Leicester was originally the main gateway to the Newarke, built in the 14th century. During the Civil War it was used for the storage of arms; hence its name. It now houses the Museum of the Royal Leicestershire Regiment. What an interesting time I had visiting this oasis of peace at the very heart of the bustling city. I was the only visitor & spent an hour or more looking at all the treasured souvenirs of centuries of warfare; & then sat outside in the afternoon sun answering a lengthy questionnaire about Museum services.

"For Valour" Seeing the Victoria Crosses which were won by those fighting "Tigers" of the Leicestershire Regiment, & seeing the horrendous scenes of battle which they endured beforehand, made me think what a good thing it is that we no longer require their services. I thought of those words of the prophet Micah, "They shall beat their swords into plowshares & their spears into pruninghooks; nation shall not lift up a sword against nation, neither shall they learn war any more." But although our fighting services are being reduced at the moment, there still remains plenty of bloodshed in the world.

National Army Museum – Inside the Museum of the Royal Leicestershire Regiment I found a little booklet, "National Army Museum" – Five Centuries of History – Free!!

The National Army Museum in London tells the history of the Armies of Britain, from the raising of the Yeomen of the Guard in 1485 to the soldiers of today. So, guess where I will be heading for one of these fine days? It seems that one museum helps lead you to another.

And all because I happened to work at 3, "Tigers" Road.

8th August 1991 Thursday

Hostage John McCarthy Free – On 17th April 1986, John McCarthy, now aged 34, journalist for Worldwide Television News from Barnet, North London, was kidnapped while working in the Lebanon. Today he was released by Islamic Jihad.

Hostage John McCarthy has been released by his captors with a letter which he is to deliver to General Perez de Cuellar, Secretary-General of the United Nations. They are seeking his help & influence to release many of their own fellow countrymen held captive in other lands. They in turn will then release other hostages.

9th August 1991 Friday

Birmingham – Motored to Birmingham & got hopelessly lost both going in and coming out. Once inside, I went in search of its treasures & found the City Museum & Art Gallery where I was fascinated by the collection of coins, going back before Christ.

"Show me the tribute money" Christ said to the Pharisees. "And they brought unto him a penny." There it was in Birmingham "Tiberius Caesar".

From the City Museum to the monstrous Central Library – one of the largest libraries in Europe. I have never seen so many books. (9 floors)

Lunch in Victoria Square & on to Birmingham Cathedral – St. Philip's.

"If you have time to stand & stare……" So said the little guide book entitled "Exploring Birmingham" which I sat & read inside the mighty library, surrounded by over a million books. At one end of New Street is the railway station but at the other end is Paradise Street & it is here where you find Chamberlain Square, named after the Mayor Joseph Chamberlain, who in 1874 laid the foundation of all you see today – he parked – paved & watered.

11th August 1991 Sunday

Trinity XI "O God, who declarest thy almighty power most chiefly in showing mercy & pity …….. grant that we may be made partakers of thy heavenly treasure. (Collect for today).

12th August 1991 Monday

Neville Chamberlain – In 1916, the Lord Mayor of Birmingham was Neville Chamberlain, son of Joseph, who had been Mayor before Birmingham was granted "City" status in 1889.

When I was a child Neville Chamberlain was Prime Minister. I attended Snibston School where the caretaker was one by the name of Chamberlain. Not knowing the difference between a Prime Minister & school caretaker, I was taught that "Prime Minister Mr Chamberlain has been to see Hitler in an attempt to prevent warfare" & I knew that Mr Chamberlain had failed.

"Just Married" - Tina & Wayne (my next door neighbours) arrived home from honeymoon to find the front of their house festooned with banners & balloons announcing to the world that they were newly-weds. And so Tina now takes up permanent residence in her new home. She wept at leaving her family home.

13th August 1991 Tuesday

Spike Milligan – Time to stand and stare and time to read more library books. How interesting to read the life story of Spike Milligan (Terence Alan Milligan) born in India on 16th April 1918.

His father was named Leo Alphonso Milligan (named after the Pope in 1888) & Spike was taught by nuns in a Roman Catholic School for girls in India.

On 10th March 1922 when he was almost 4 years old he saw Mahatma Gandhi go by. He was being taken to prison. "'He's not as black as he's painted' said my kind grandmother. But I found out he was not painted. It was his real colour."

14th August 1991 Wednesday

Who Am I? To those who know me well – "Bet". To Enid – "Cuz". To those who are not on such familiar terms – "Betty". To those who know me by my signature – "Elizabeth". To Katherine, who knows everyone as "Darling". To those who hardly know me "Miss Hewes". To the shopkeepers "Madam" (which makes me feel really old). And to Cocky who thinks I am forever young – "My Darling".

Who Was I? To my dad I was "Snip" or "Snippy". My dad died when I was aged 7. My mum continued to call me "Snip" for a while. Uncle Aubrey called me "Snip" until he died during the war. Nobody now knows "Snip". To my younger brother Robin I was "Liz" or "The Lizard" & he was "Bin-Bon". Nobody now knows "The Lizard". Bin-Bon died aged 17, so he really is forever young.

Who Will I Be? Ah! That I do not know. You now know that, better than I. The remarkable thing about keeping a life-long diary is that you can skim through the years which have gone & see whole decades as it were in a matter of moments, but the years ahead do not reveal their secrets. We are so attuned to what is happening "today" that it takes precedence over all other times; & the Lord himself has taught us to take no thought for the morrow; for the morrow shall take thought for the things of itself.

(Sermon on the Mount, Matthew, Chaps. 5, 6, 7.)

All the brasses in the house are gleaming bright, the old copper warming pans are looking their best, every room has been cleaned & tidied, & old house-wife Hewsie is now flopped out in the chair after her annual "spring clean" in preparation for the arrival of Mary Moore tomorrow. I certainly have no time left for going to work.

16th August 1991 Friday

Cordon Bleu Cook Hewsie has now bought a new Electrolux freezer to supplement my "fridge" which has its own built-in freezer, but which is not always as good as it should be. So many pre-packed frozen dishes are available today which require nothing more than popping into the oven, cooking is no trouble at all.

17th August 1991 Saturday

"Every Hand is a Winner" (Cards) all you have to know is what to keep and what to throw away". Heard these words sung on the radio in a Country & Western song & thought how applicable to life in general. We spend our whole life acquiring & discarding. "We brought nothing into this world & it is certain we can carry nothing out." (I Timothy, Chap. 6)

18th August 1991 Sunday

Trinity 12 – I said, not so, Lord; for nothing common or unclean hath at any time entered into my mouth. But the voice answered me again from heaven, "What God hath cleansed, that call not thou common." And this was done three times. (Acts II)

Mary Moore, now aged 80, is finding it increasingly difficult to fulfil her programme of activities as she would like to – the spirit is willing but the flesh is weak. She still retains her wonderful memory, knowing virtually everybody she meets & knowing all their family relationships.

19th August 1991 Monday
Gorbachev Overthrown –
Troops on the Streets of Moscow.

These are the headlines today in the Leicester Mercury following the shock news that Soviet leader Mr Mikhail Gorbachev has been toppled from power by hard-line Communists. President Gennady Yanayev has taken over as head of an eight-man State Emergency Committee which includes the chiefs of the armed forces & the K.G.B. According to some "The gates of hell are going to open on Soviet Union." Civil war & chaos is expected as a 6 month state of emergency is declared in some areas.

Mikhail Gorbachev became Soviet leader in March 1985. He brought about great reforms including "Glasnost" (openness) & "Perestroika" (re-structuring). Last year he was named Nobel Peace Prize winner for his many & decisive contributions, including his drive for greater openness & promotion of international trust. Only last month, U.S. President George Bush & Mikhail Gorbachev signed landmark nuclear arms limitation treaty, an agreement to reduce levels of ballistic missiles & long range bombers. Hence the decision on our part to cut by a quarter the size of our army. But the old hard-line Communists have toppled him.

20th August 1991 Tuesday

Warwick Castle – Mary Blue & I went on a Leicester City Coach trip to Warwick Castle & Stratford-on-Avon, and on a glorious summer's day we saw them at their best. While Mary Blue (aged 47) walked high on the "cat-walks" from tower to tower, & then ascended to the top of the highest tower (Guy's Tower), old maid Hewsie stayed on terra firma, enjoying the scene from ground level. What a splendid castle is Warwick Castle, unlike so many of our castles which now lie in ruins. There is so much to see you could stay all week. Again I saw the dreadful dungeon & oubliette which I last saw in October 1985. It is hard to believe that man is capable of such brutality when you see what punishments were inflicted on prisoners in days of old.

Stratford-on-Avon – While in Stratford, Mary Blue & I visited the house where Shakespeare was born & also went inside the church to see his grave & monument.
> **"Stay passenger, why goest thou by so fast?**
> **Read if thou canst whom envious death hath placed**
> **within this monument – Shakespeare."**

Like Warwick Castle, Stratford is a place to stay & not go by so fast. But with only 3 hours at each place we saw only a fraction of all there was to see. Nevertheless, we had a wonderful glimpse of them & bought literature to peruse further.

Mary Moore is compiling a "Family Tree" scrapbook, complete with photographs of as many as she can find. Her father, Philip Moore, was one of 12 children. His father, Godfrey Moore, married Harriet Anne Sketchley whose brother John was my great-grandfather. The family now spans the whole globe.

23 August 1991 Friday

Arrested – Vice-President Yanayev. Three days in office & the eight men headed by Yanayev have themselves been overthrown & are now on trial as traitors. Events have moved so fast in Russia this week that you never know what will happen next. The statue of Felix Dzherzhinsky (founder of the secret police) in the square outside the KGB headquarters has been removed. The dreaded KGB boss, Kryuchkov, one of the 8 "Junta" men who plotted against President Gorbechev, is now inside his own jail. The "hammer & sickle" flag has been replaced by the white, blue & red, as a new USSR emerges.

24 August 1991 Saturday

In July 1917, the Virgin Mary appeared at Fatima in Portugal & said, "I ask for the consecration of Russia to my immaculate heart. If my request is heard Russia will be converted & there will be peace. If not ...... the good will be martyred & the Holy Father will have much to suffer & various nations will be annihilated. In the end however my immaculate heart will triumph. The holy father will consecrate Russia to me."

Mary Moore returned home by train from Leicester via Peterborough where she had to change. I travelled with her from Leicester as far as Peterborough – saw her safely on the next train & then had an interesting browse around the shops in the splendid Queensgate shopping centre.

25th August 1991 Sunday

Trinity XIII – The Lord is my shepherd therefore can I lack nothing. He shall feed me in a green pasture & lead me forth beside the waters of comfort. (Psalm 23)

26th August 1991 Monday

"Be ye therefore perfect, even as your father which is in heaven is perfect" (Matt. Ch.5)

The Rector of Ravenstone, Kerry Emmett, told us yesterday that this should be our "objective". Although it may be impossible to achieve, it is where we should aim. And here I was, thinking I had escaped from objectives.

Leicester Castle Park Festival, 24 – 31 August.
"The past is brought to life again at the Jewry Wall Museum. Travel back in time to the English Civil War & see how Leicester fared in the fight for supremacy between Roundheads & Cavaliers. Take a leisurely walk around Castle Park in the company of famous historical figures who will explain the history as you go along. Tour the Jain Centre; Leicester Castle; etc. & discover Leicester's rich and colourful past. Re-live the Seige of Leicester……. Enjoy the past & the present at the Castle Park Festival."

27th August 1991 Tuesday

The Jain Centre – Jainism is one of the oldest religions of India. Like Buddhism, it was a revolt in the 6th Century B.C. against Hinduism. Looking rather like Buddha, their great prophet Bhagwan Shree Shantinathji sits in full lotus position, in the centre of great arches which you can see at the far end of the temple immediately you step through the door at the top of a grandiose staircase. He was the 16th of the 24 prophets (Tirthankaras) who consolidated the faith of the Jains. Like Buddha, he proclaims peace to all.

"Take off thy shoes, for this is holy ground." As I walked in my stockinged feet in the Jain Temple, I was left alone to take in the whole impressive scene before me. I gazed at the 3 central images, Shantinath in the middle, with Parswanath and Mahavir on either side. I learned about the 24 prophets (Tirthankars also known as Jinas) especially the last prophet Mahavira, who was 30 years older than Buddha. His life story was in stained glass windows.

28th August 1991 Wednesday

"Enthronement of The Right Reverend Thomas Butler, B.Sc. M.Sc. Ph.D. on Saturday 7th September 1991 at 3 p.m."

Thanks to the influence of our new Rector the Revd. Kerry Emmett, I have an invitation to attend the Enthronement of the new Bishop of Leicester at Leicester Cathedral on 7th Sept.

29th August 1991 Thursday

Leicester Castle – How wonderful to see inside the great hall of Leicester Castle, now divided into law courts, but once the favourite residence of the dukes & earls of Lancaster.

It is reputed to be the oldest & only pure example in England today of the great hall of a Norman baron. Here, Henry, Earl of Leicester & good Duke of Lancaster lived, & died of the plague in 1361 A.D. Here in 1300 A.D. Edward I was entertained – then Edward II & Edward III. Here John of Gaunt lived & entertained Richard II, who later was brought again as a prisoner.

30th August 1991 Friday

"What is man, that thou art mindful of him? And the son of man, that thou visitest him? For thou hast made him a little lower than the angels & hast crowned him with glory & honour. Thou madest him to have dominion over the works of thy hands; thou hast put all things under his feet." Psalm 8.

Old Times Coach Trip with Authentic Coach and Four Horses.

To celebrate Pat's 73rd birthday yesterday, we went on the most delightful "Old Times Coach Trip".

Pat, Evelyn, Mary Blue & I rode in style on the top of this splendid coach for 7 miles from the White Hart at Billesdon (9 miles south of Leicester) along lovely country lanes in truly rural countryside, including gated roads, up hill & down dale via Illston & Gaulby, returning to the White Hart for roast beef lunch.

Halfway round we stopped for the horses to take a well earned rest, while we were handed a glass of wine, as we sat aloft.

Benedicite Omnia Opera – I thought of this great canticle of the Prayer Book where everything in turn rejoices in being part of God's creation, as we made our magnificent progression with coach and horses. Cows in the fields ran alongside us – horses responded – people in their gardens waved spontaneously – motorists smiled & waved & we were made to feel like royalty.

1st September 1991 Sunday

Trinity XIV – Who can find a virtuous woman? For her price is far above rubies…… Strength & honour are her clothing; & she shall rejoice in time to come. Proverbs, Chapter 31.

The preacher spoke of the Ten Commandments & stressed the word "Command" ments. In this wishy-washy age of ours where anything goes, he said they would probably have been considered rather as the Ten Suggestions offered by God to see us through life. But we must know that they are commands.

2nd September 1991 Monday

U.S.S.R. – Union of Soviet Socialist Republics. Following the recent failed coup, the so called Union of U.S.S.R. is rapidly disintegrating. The foundations of more than 70 years of Soviet power are now shattered. The Soviet republics are "spinning quickly out of the Kremlin orbit". The 3 Baltic republics – Estonia, Latvia & Lithuania, have re-claimed the independence they lost in 1940; and one by one others are following suit. Proudly they unfurl their old national flags.

U.S.S.R.
1. Armenian Soviet Socialist Republic
2. Azerbaijan Soviet Socialist Republic
3. Estonian Soviet Socialist Republic
4. Georgian Soviet Socialist Republic
5. Byelorussian Soviet Socialist Republic
6. Kazakh Soviet Socialist Republic
7. Kirghiz Soviet Socialist Republic
8. Latvian Soviet Socialist Republic
9. Lithuanian Soviet Socialist Republic
10. Moldavian Soviet Socialist Republic
11. Russian Soviet Federal Socialist Republic

12. Tadzhik Soviet Socialist Republic
13. Turkmen Soviet Socialist Republic
14. Ukranian Soviet Socialist Republic
15. Uzbek Soviet Socialist Republic

The flag of the U.S.S.R. since the Revolution has been plain red with the golden hammer & sickle in the top left hand corner beneath a 5 pointed star, symbolising the unity of the peoples of 5 continents. The hammer and sickle represent the workers & the peasants. The white – blue- red tricolour which we are now seeing in U.S.S.R. is the old flag of Tsarist Russia.

S.S.S.R. is Russian for U.S.S.R. = Soyuz Sovetskikh Sotsialisticheskikh Republik.

There is also another alphabet called the Cyrillic Alphabet (attributed to Saint Cyril) in which S.S.S.R. = C.C.C.P. This is the alphabet which has some letters like ours & others completely different, such as – И П Ф Ц Ш Э Ю Я Ж Б Г Д

3rd September 1991 Tuesday
"What manner of man is this, that even the winds & the sea obey him?" (Matthew 8, 27.)
Sailing calmly through life, we may not feel the need to say, "Lord, save us." But when the great tempest blows up & there we are, crying for help, while God seems to be fast asleep, then we appreciate his power to command.

5th September 1991 Thursday
The mighty Norman pillars & arches of Hereford Cathedral filled me with awe 7 years ago. Now I have discovered within 10 miles of Ravenstone one of the greatest Norman parish churches in the whole of England – the Church of Saint Michael with Saint Mary, Melbourne, which I never knew was there.

Stolen Car – At Abbey Park, Leicester, I recently discovered "some useful parking places".
Here you could park all day free of charge. Here, therefore, Mary Blue & I each parked our cars last Saturday, when we went to London for the day to see Les Miserables at the Palace Theatre in Shaftesbury Avenue. When we arrived back in Leicester at 10-30 p.m. my car was nowhere to be seen. It had been stolen by a local young joy-rider, who had ripped out the ignition & buckled the wheels in a reckless adventure.

A Day in London – What a lovely day Mary Blue & I had in London last Saturday. The sun shone the whole of the day & I was introduced to parts of London I had never seen before. We took the London underground from Golders Green to Leicester Square and from there we sampled the delights of nearby Gerrard Street with its strong Chinese flavour (China Town). We entered the tinselly garish world of Soho & visited Covent Garden. We had lunch in the exclusive restaurant of the National Gallery looking out on to Trafalgar Square and then off to the theatre for the matinee performance.

Les Misérables – Never have I sat in such expensive theatre seats. Mary Blue paid £27-50p each for us to sit in the best seats of the Stalls – this was her present to me for my 60th birthday; she also paid for the coach tickets. How we loved "Les Misérables" & how everyone else

loved it too. For the first time ever I experienced standing in the midst of an elated audience to give a standing ovation at the end of the show.

7th September 1991 Saturday
The Enthronement of The Right Reverend Father in God – Thomas Frederick Butler as Lord Bishop of Leicester. What a service! I was reminded of Pilgrim's entry into the Holy City.
"All the bells were ringing welcome. The King's trumpeters made heaven echo with their sound, as if heaven itself was come to meet them."
It took half an hour for the "Processions" to enter the Cathedral for the Bishop's enthronement. There was the Civic Procession of all the local Mayors & M.P.s. There was the Diocesan Procession of retired clergy, serving priests, etc. Visiting dignitaries from all over the world – choir – Canons of the Cathedral, etc.

8th September 1991 Sunday
Trinity XV – All flesh is as grass & all the glory of man as the flower of grass. The grass withereth & the flower thereof falleth away; but the word of the Lord endureth for ever.
(I Peter, Chapter 1.)

9th September 1991 Monday
Glenholm – Following the death of Auntie Belle, the widow of Uncle Fred, their house & home is handed down to Uncle Fred's daughter Isobel, now aged 75. Isobel arrived with her elder son Miles & his wife Sarah to sort & sift through all the treasured possessions of Uncle Fred, going back to the beginning of the century.
Miles was delighted to find he had a family inheritance where he, more than anyone else in the world, was the rightful son & heir to this special family home. Built by Uncle Fred & owned exclusively by him, Miles was ready to buy.

10th September 1991 Tuesday
Joy Riders – The joy riders who steal cars today are known as "hotters". They can break into a locked car in a few seconds – rip out the ignition & they are away, driving as fast as the car will go, and then delighting in doing handbrake turns. This is what happened to my car, resulting in the following list of damage :-
2 wheels, 2 tyres, 2 wheel-trims, steering lock assembly, wiper switch , indicator switch assembly, steering column assembly, front bumper.
These joy riders are turning many city areas into race tracks & no-go zones & are a major problem to the police.

11th September 1991 Wednesday
Bible Radio – A star cast including Sir John Gielgud and David Kossoff will read the Bible from beginning to end on Radio 4 starting on September 16th and finishing next August.

Elaine Barkby – Elaine, who lives alone at 49 Leicester Road, Ravenstone, suffers from that most dread disease Multiple Sclerosis. She has no-one in the world who truly belongs to her & is totally dependant on good neighbours & the so-called "Home Help" service, which she describes as the "Home Helpless". She is so painfully thin & frail & can only just manage to walk on matchstick legs which have no feeling. She can stick needles into her leg & not feel a thing. She smokes incessantly, having no desire to prolong her life. She has no-one & nothing to live for.

12th September 1991 Thursday

Darren Preston – Darren Preston is the young man who was caught driving my car after it had been stolen. P.C. Marshall, who is dealing with the case, visited me at home this evening & gave me a few details. Darren celebrated his 17th birthday on 29th August this year – the same day as brother Pat's birthday, & 2 days before my car was stolen. He did not steal the car. Others in his gang showed him the car after it had been stolen & asked him if he would like a go driving it. It was his misfortune to be spotted by the police, who gave chase.

It was when the police gave chase that Darren drove the car as fast as he could, round a corner, up the kerb, screeching to a halt, & then running away across the fields. But, it so happened that the police had radioed their H.Q. nearby, where a Police Dog was at the ready for action. Darren was caught with the help of the Police Dog. Since the age of 14 he has been in & out of the police courts for one thing after another. He will be taken to court for this latest offence on 1st October at Leicester's Town Hall.

13th September 1991 Friday

Cousin Don's widow Phyl has now suffered a stroke, which has paralysed her left side. I visited her in Coalville Hospital, where she is being given daily physiotherapy.

"Feel the weight of my left hand" she said to me. And I was amazed how heavy the useless hand was. As poor Phyl sat in her wheelchair, a prisoner in her own body, with no use in her left side, it was so sad to see the expensive diamond ring & wedding ring adorning a useless hand. She who had lived in the lap of luxury was now utterly dejected & completely at the mercy of others.

14th September 1991 Saturday

Glenholm – The mantle of Uncle Fred has definitely fallen on the shoulders of Miles, his grandson.

Uncle Fred, my dad's eldest brother, prospered in life & was known locally as "The Baron". Now, along comes Miles, like the youthful Hiawatha, "a youth with flaunting feathers", with all the confidence of an up-and-coming new "Baron", ready to take the helm and carry on exactly where Uncle Fred left off.

15th September 1991 Sunday

Trinity XVII – The Lord is my light & my salvation; whom then shall I fear? The Lord is the

strength of my life; of whom then shall I be afraid? (Psalm 27)

16th September 1991 Monday

"Did you see the meeting of the 2 Kings?"

Having seen the meeting of the 2 Kings at the re-enacted Battle of Bosworth, & again through the pen of Shakespeare in "The Winter's Tale", I have now seen yet another meeting of the 2 Kings in my latest library book about Cardinal Wolsey. In 1520 AD the most elaborate meeting was organised by the over-inflated Cardinal for King Henry VIII to meet his counterpart, François I of France.

The Field of Cloth-of-Gold was between Guisnes & Ardres in France, where 2,800 tents were erected and a temporary "palace" richly decorated with cloth-of-gold. Cardinal Wolsey led the way to inform François that Henry VIII had arrived.

"In rich velvet robes & wearing a red hat with large hanging tassels, he rode in state on his mule (to signify humility). The mule was gorgeously decked in gold & crimson velvet. With hundreds of archers in front and behind, plus gentlemen ushers carrying great gold maces, and the bearer of the double cross of gold which always preceded him on state occasions, he set the scene for the Kings to meet."

Henry VIII had a retinue of 4,000 people & 2,000 horses, as he, & the French King likewise, met and embraced on horseback.

17th September 1991 Tuesday

"Pazzo è chi non sa da che parte vien il vento" (He is a fool who does not know which way the wind blows). I think of this proverb as I now look out from my kitchen window to the roof top of my neighbour's house, built in the grounds of The Hollies, where a weather-vane aeroplane has been erected. The weather-vane aeroplane is one of the best weather-vanes I have encountered. It flies above the roof-top where Tyrone (former boy friend of Joanne) lives. Whichever way the wind blows it flies accordingly. Tyrone & family cannot see it themselves – I have the best grandstand view.

18th September 1991 Wednesday

Deanery Festival – The Diocese of Leicester is divided into 13 deaneries, including Akeley East, Akeley West and Akeley South. Ravenstone is within Akeley South, but immediately borders on Akeley West which covers Normanton, Packington, Snarestone, Appleby Magna with Swepstone, Blackfordby, Donisthorpe with Moira, Ashby St. Helens with Coleorton. Ashby Holy Trinity, Worthington with Newbold & Griffydam, Breedon-on-the-Hill with Isley Walton. (and Staunton Harold) Akeley West is holding a Deanery Festival starting this evening with the Dedication Service & culminating on Sunday 29th September. The Festival includes an Open Air Service next Sunday at Normanton-le-Heath. Next Wednesday the new Bishop of Leicester the Right Reverend Thomas Butler will preside at the Mothers' Union Festival Service at Donisthorpe. On Saturday 28th September there will be a grand parade & praise march through Ashby, followed by an evening social event & praise service at Breedon-on-the-Hill. The Festival began as "a seed sown at Blackfordby, it has been nurtured by prayer & nourished by grace." (Reverend Michael Penny – Rural Dean)

19th September 1991 Thursday

The weathervane aeroplane is one of the best weathervanes I have encountered. It flies above the rooftop where Tyrone (former boyfriend of Joanne) lives. Whichever way the wind blows it flies accordingly. Tyrone & family cannot see it themselves – I have the best grandstand view.

20th September 1991 Friday
Custom Marks are what once were known as "cherished" vehicle registration numbers. The Government have now turned the whole business into a money making bonanza. Having held back all the low numbers for the past 8 years, they are now up for sale. The scheme was launched 19th August 1991 and so far more than 10,000 Custom Marks have been sold by the D.V.L.A. (Driver and Vehicle Licensing Agency). This has brought in £2 million. This is in addition to the "select registrations" where you invent your own number, and the "classic collection" schemes, totalling £42 million in the last two years.
The Motor Car Act, effective from 1st January 1904, first provided for the registration and numbering of cars in this country. Prior to that, would you believe, the R.A.C. (at that time the Automobile Club) insisted that compulsory numbering would damage the motor industry. They said that the stigma implied by the numbering of a motor carriage would not be tolerated in this country. The English gentleman did not want public identification.

21st September 1991 Saturday
Sponsored Bicycle Ride/Walk. The Leicestershire Historic Churches Trust joined by 24 other counties is holding its 2nd Sponsored Bicycle Ride/Walk.
I have volunteered to "man" Ravenstone Church for 2 hours to record those who come and go.

22nd September 1991 Sunday
Trinity XVII – The days of our age are threescore years and ten; & though men be so strong that they come to fourscore years, yet is their strength then but labour and sorrow. (Psalm 90)

23rd September 1991 Monday
With one garden wall looking as though it may fall down any minute, I have accepted the following quotation from Steven Brooks, 7 Elder Lane, Griffydam: - Set foundations for pillar, construct 18″ square pillar, to taper off using facing brickwork to match the existing - £230 plus V.A.T.

Car Theft – In Leicester, cars are now being stolen at the rate of almost 1,000 per week. Car crime has more than doubled since last year. It is not quite so bad in the county – about 1,000 per month. Car insurance covers fire and theft but the upward spiral of car theft, mostly by so-called joy riders who cause such costly damage, is making the insurance companies reconsider their terms. Teenage car-thieves compete with each other to see how many thefts they can notch up in one session. It is their latest pastime and gives them excitement.

24th September 1991 Tuesday
Charles V, 1500 – 1558 Holy Roman Emperor. From the confines of British history, I have now spread my wings to Europe. We, who know only the shenanigans of King Henry VIII, are totally unaware of far greater drama being enacted elsewhere. How interesting to meet Charles V – King of Castile & Aragon, Lord of the fabulous treasures of the Indies & great Holy Roman Emperor. Before he was 12 months old, his father made him a member of "The Order of the Golden Fleece".

Named after his great-grandfather Charles the Bold, he was destined to become the most powerful monarch of his age. Charles V in his lifetime had more to concern him than did insular Britain. He had to keep the great Ottoman leader Suleman the Magnificent at bay, otherwise Christendom would have sunk without trace. He had to deal with the great schism in the Christian Church introduced by Martin Luther – he who was disillusioned with the established Church of Rome & was obliged to protest – hence the beginnings of Protestantism. He had to release the pope after his over-zealous soldiers had been responsible for the Sack of Rome. And he kept a diary.

25th September 1991 Wednesday
Brother Pat, married to Evelyn for 51 years, has done it again! Come face to face with one of his old flames. There we were – Pat, Evelyn, Mary Blue & I at the Adult School, Coalville, to see their latest stage production "One for the Pot" when Pearl Haywood, after more than half a century, re-appeared.

26th September 1991 Thursday
In praise of those who write. The Chroniclers of old, the foreign ambassadors and other such writers are our only means of knowing intimate details of our forebears. We know such a lot about Queen Victoria because she kept a journal. We know about Jesus Christ because there was some-one to write about him. When there is no-one to write about you, you either sink into oblivion or become a distorted legend. Even Adam & Eve had some-one to write about them. How about you then?

27th September 1991 Friday
Leicester's new £125 million Shires Shopping Centre sprang into life today, after 10 years of marathon re-development. With 74 shop units all under cover, in 500,000 square feet of space, centred on a spectacular glazed atrium & parking for 2,000 cars, it has transformed Leicester's tumble-down High Street.

Charlemagne (768- 814 A.D.) Never before in my life have I had such an opportunity to meet so many wonderful characters from history as I now have the pleasure of meeting. Charlemagne = Charles the Great. He lived in splendour at Aix-la-Chapelle where the most treasured relic in the possession of his family was the cloak of St. Martin (Capella sancti Martini). Our word chapel is derived from "capella" i.e. St. Martin's cloak. It was Charlemagne who helped to mould the civilisation of Western Europe, which began to take shape in his powerful reign.

28th September 1991 Saturday
Glenholm – Uncle Fred's grandson Miles celebrates his birthday today, assured of his "noblesse oblige" i.e. the obligations imposed by his rank. I gave him an outline of our "Family Tree" starting with John Hewes born in 1801, and he was absolutely delighted to be such an integral part of it. The more he learned about his grandfather the more he wanted to follow in his footsteps.

29th September 1991 Sunday
St. Michael's Day – Lord, give thy Angels every day,

command to guide us on our way, & bid them every evening keep their watch around us while we sleep. (Hymn 335)

Harvest & Patronal Festival combined this year at Ravenstone. The result was that St. Michael & all the angels were totally ignored. Only rarely does St. Michael's Day actually fall on a Sunday & for the day to pass without so much as a mention of the great archangel seemed to me very remiss.

30th September 1991 Monday
Constantine the Great, Roman Emperor, reigned 306 – 337 A.D.

Christendom has to thank Constantine the Great for his tremendous contribution to all that it is today. He was the Emperor who first accepted Christianity and he founded the impregnable city of Constantinople where the Byzantine Church – i.e. the Eastern or Greek Orthodox Church – stood firm as a rock for 1,000 years. All through the "Dark Ages" when Britain & much of the west sank into oblivion, Eastern Europe, thanks to Constantinople, went from strength to strength. Written records were maintained, thus preserving the historiographical traditions of ancient Greece, giving us our "Creed".

1st October 1991 Tuesday

Constantinople – When the Turks finally breached the citadel of eastern Christianity in 1453 A.D., that was the end of the Christian Church in Constantinople.

Muhammed II was the Ottoman Sultan who entered the Christian sanctuary where he personally destroyed the altar. So ended a thousand years of history. The desecration of the Holy City was unbelievable. There was treasure untold & "books beyond all counting & number"- Aristotle – Plato, etc. Some were destroyed but thankfully some were sold & preserved so that we today should not be totally ignorant of our heritage.

"Dear Betty – Just to let you know that my retirement "do" will take place on Thursday 10th October between 12 noon and 2p.m. Do hope you can come. I look forward to seeing you & hearing how your first months of retirement have been".

Invitation from Rosemary Todd, Scientific Officer at G.O.M.B. Wigston.

2nd October 1991 Wednesday

The Monks. It is thanks to the monastic communities which all through the Dark Ages sheltered not only the life of prayer and meditation, but also writing, learning and the arts. One of the earliest monks of renown was St. Benedict born circa 480 A.D. His code of guidance & discipline – the Rule - was taken in the 8th century to Germany, by the greatest of English missionaries, St. Boniface. The self-governing autonomous community designed by Benedict enabled each monastery to stay afloat like an ark, in the deluge of barbarism which swept across Europe in those Dark Ages.

3rd October 1991 Thursday

Rugby World Cup – Watched on television the opening ceremony of Rugby Union's second World Cup at Twickenham. There are 16 teams from all over the world, including the famous New Zealand "All Blacks",

meaning they wear all black. Their captain is Gary Whetton whose twin brother Alan is also in the team. The final is 2nd November.

4th October 1991 Friday

The Friars. The Friars did not appear on the scene until much later. Originally they were revolutionary off-shoots in the 12th century, when all manner of sects were setting themselves up, only to be dealt with as heretics. Faced with this outbreak of heresy, the Church of Rome managed to win some of the radicals to its side. These were the friars who in the end enabled the papacy to triumph over heresy. The 2 first orders of friars were the Dominicans, founded by St. Dominic, & the Franciscans, founded by Saint Francis of Assisi. (1182 – 1226A.D.)

The friars were members of the mendicant monastic orders in the Roman Catholic Church. That means they went around like beggars. The Franciscans were Grey Friars. The Dominicans were Black Friars. The Carmelites were White Friars. The Friars of the 12th century were known for their poverty and for their preaching, but by the 14th & 15th centuries they had become quite wealthy. They became such a lot of rouges, offering indulgencies & suchlike, until in the end there was rebellion & people broke away from the church.

5th October 1991 Saturday

Cousin John – Attended the Dixie Grammar School, Market Bosworth, Founder's Day Service at St. Peter's Church, where the "address" was given by the Reverend John Hewes, son of my dad's brother, Charlie.

Cousin John, a few years older than me, tells me that he was born in the same house as me, 27 Leicester Road, Ravenstone. Now with a white beard, he looks like a real elder of the church.

"Divine Providence" – Remember the Provost of Leicester receiving a letter addressed thus? (See 20th August 1982) He now tells us that this has been capped by the Right Revd. David Leake, an assistant Bishop, who was once listed as "The Ass Bishop – correction The Right Bishop"

6th October 1991 Sunday, Trinity XIX

"Where shall wisdom be found? And where is the place of understanding?

.........and unto man he said, Behold, the fear of the Lord, that is wisdom; and to depart from evil is understanding". Job: 28.

"Service of Thanksgiving for all Creatures Great & Small"

Again Katherine, Toffee & I attended this service in Leicester where the preacher stressed the fact that all God's creatures, including man, are flesh & blood. He reminded us that "The Word was made Flesh" (St. John 1: 14) All flesh is one.

7th October 1991 Monday
Thomas Hewes 1834 – 1912

From cousin John, now living in Kent, I received the most interesting copy of "Articles of agreement indented made concluded and agreed upon the twenty sixth day of May, one thousand eight hundred and forty nine" whereby Thomas Hewes, my great-grandfather, aged 15 years or thereabouts promised & agreed as follows:-

That he will diligently & faithfully serve Sampson Sherwood of Hungerton as servant for the term of five years to commence from 26 May 1849, to be employed in the trade or business of Carpenter & Wheelwright and shall and will work & labour from 5 o'clock in the morning to 8 o'clock in the evening in Summer & from 7 o'clock in the morning to 8 o'clock in the evening in Winter in every working day during the said term if required so to do by his said Master. And in all things obey the lawful commands of his said Master & not waste or purloin his goods or absent himself from his Master's service day or night unlawfully, but in all things behave as a good & faithful servant during the said term.

No wonder Thomas came to Ravenstone in 1889 & took up farming.

8th October 1991 Tuesday

Dimitrios I – His All Holiness Dimitrios I, 269th Oecumenical Patriarch of Constantinople, died earlier this month, aged 77. So, all is not lost at Constantinople. The conquest of the city by the Turks in 1453 A.D. did not diminish its ecclesiastical dominance. The Patriarch of Constantinople, if not quite the Pope of Orthodoxy (because the eastern churches reject the notion of absolute authority concentrated in one figure-head) is recognised as "Primus inter Pares" of the 4 ancient patriarchies of Constantinople, Antioch, Alexandria and Jerusalem.

9th October 1991 Wednesday

Film star Elizabeth Taylor, aged 59, this week married Larry Fortensky, aged 39. This is her 8th marriage. She married Richard Burton twice, so this is the 7th man she has married. She wore a £17,000 dress & invited 223 guests. It was a million dollar wedding ceremony.

10th October 1991 Thursday

Orthodox Christians – Such is the rivalry between Turkey and Greece that it is not easy being the Patriarch of Constantinople. By the treaty of Lausanne in 1923 Turkey subjected the Patriarch's continued presence in Constantinople to stringent conditions - from that time, both he & those who worked for him had to be Turkish citizens & his appointment required government approval. Today there are only 5,000 Greeks in Istanbul (the present day name for Constantinople). For years Dimitrios lived in seclusion in Istanbul to avoid offending the Muslims. However, he burst out of his cocoon in 1987.

Modern Orthodoxy is made up of various national churches (Russian, Greek, Romanian & others). There are 250 million Orthodox Christians. St. Andrew is regarded as the founder of Orthodoxy, while his brother St. Peter was the first Bishop of Rome. A theological stumbling block with Rome is the doctrine that the Holy Ghost proceeds from the Father – "Son and the". Orthodoxy rejects this. There are also the difficulties with papal infallibility.

However, with the recent collapse of Communist regimes in Europe & Russia, there is renewed hope for Orthodoxy.

11th October 1991 Friday

Canon Gundry Memorial – A memorial stone to Canon Gundry (the best lesson reader I have ever known) will be dedicated in the sanctuary of St. Dunstan's Chapel in Leicester Cathedral on Sunday 3rd November. Thus it is written! (So says Cathedral Newsletter 235).

12th October 1991 Saturday

Mostyn is dying. Mostyn, now in hospital, is dying from cancer. Bunting keeps long bedside vigils with him & has wonderful support from their 2 sons, Michael & Julian. So much so that Bunting, even now, has asked that we do not attend the funeral. She wants to be alone with her own immediate family at the cremation, with the larger family gathering at the interment.

13th October 1991 Sunday, Trinity XIX

Whatsoever things are true, whatsoever things are honest, whatsoever things are just, whatsoever things are pure, whatsoever things are lovely, whatsoever things are of good report… think on these things. (Phil: 4)

Sahara sands drift to our doorsteps. As in August 1987, sand from the Sahara Desert has blown 900 miles to Britain. Again my silver Metro car has known sand lurking in all the crevices after sand-bearing rain has deposited its residue on cars, dustbin & everywhere.

14th October 1991 Monday
ECUs & EMUs.

Next year, in 1992, Britain's entry to the common market will be complete. But one subject still remains unsettled – a common European currency. At the moment each country has its own currency:-

Luxembourg: Franc
British: Sterling
German: Deutschmark
Portuguese: Escudo
Danish: Kroner
Belgian: Franc
French: Franc
Greek: Drachma
Irish : Punt
Dutch: Guilder
Italian: Lira
Spanish : Peseta
The European Currency Unit = E.C.U.
Economic and Monetary Union = E.M.U.

15th October 1991 Tuesday

"Whenever opposite views are held with warmth by religious-minded men, we may take it for granted there is some higher truth which embraces both. All high truth is the union of two contradictions" Revd. Frederick Wm. Robertson (1816-1853)

The Three Creeds – We have 3 creeds at church: -
1. The Nicene Creed,
2. The Apostles Creed,
3. The Athanasian Creed.

The early church was so unsure about the precise relationship of God the Father, God the Son and God the Holy Ghost that the learned elders had to have at least 3 goes at making it clear. So at Holy Communion we say the Nicene Creed as agreed at the Council of Constantinople in 381 A.D. At Evensong we say the Apostles Creed, the end product after centuries of development. Finally, in the prayer book "Quicunque Vult" the Athanasian Creed fully expounds its meaning.

16th October 1991 Wednesday

Quicunque Vult – Whosoever will be saved.......

So begins the Athanasian Creed & goes on to say:-

The Catholick Faith is this: - That we worship one God in Trinity & Trinity in Unity.

.... So the Father is God, the Son is God & the Holy Ghost is God. And yet they are not three Gods but one God.

.... The Father is made of none: neither created nor begotten. The Son is of the Father alone: not made, nor created, but begotten. The Holy Ghost is of the Son: neither made, nor created, nor begotten, but proceeding.

17th October 1991 Thursday
"Work Objectives – Management Objectives – Personal Development Objectives"

All these objectives from which I am so thankful to have escaped, are about to be introduced by the new Bishop of Leicester for his clergy. He says "The Church learns from other professions how best to train".

So from next Easter the poor old clergy will come under a new "Assessment" scheme. Every one will meet the Bishop regularly to review their ministry & their plans for the future. They will be interviewed for about 2 hours & asked what they have achieved so far & what are their future plans.

18th October 1991 Friday
Mary – Queen of Scots – Having heard of Mary, Queen of Scots, but never knowing for sure exactly who she was or where she fitted into all the web of intrigue lurking in British history, my latest library book has helped me to know her better.

Henry VII, as I knew, was the father of Henry VIII. What I did not know was that he was also the father of Margaret Tudor. She was the elder sister of Henry VIII & heiress to the English crown if Henry VIII did not produce an heir. She married James IV of Scotland who was killed at Flodden in 1513. Their son James V was father to Mary.

Mary, Queen of Scots was born 8th December 1542. Her father died 6 days later. Although she was by then a Queen, she needed first to grow up. Her mother belonged to the French aristocracy and Mary, when she was aged 6, went to live in France & at the age of 15 married the sickly & feeble French Dauphin who shortly became King. Mary was then Queen of France & also Queen of Scots. She dreamed of next being Queen of England. But on 5th December 1560 her boy husband died. She returned to Scotland & married Lord Darnley who was her cousin & they had a son James who became England's James I.

In 1567 there was gunpowder, treason & plot & Lord Darnley was blown up, leaving the way clear for Mary to marry the Earl of Bothwell. But her subjects were then up in arms & she fled for her life to England.

Queen Elizabeth saw her as a possible rival & kept her in her place, a prisoner who was ever plotting to escape. In the end public opinion clamoured for her execution &

she was beheaded 8th February 1587.

20th October 1991 Sunday, Trinity XXI
"O Lord my God, I hope in thee; my dear Lord Jesus, set me free; in chains, in pains, I long for thee. On bended knee I adore thee, implore thee to set me free" (Mary, Queen of Scots)

"Be not afraid" - The lesson at church from the Gospel according to St. Matthew, Chap. 14 told the story of Jesus feeding the five thousand & later, "in the 4th watch of the night" walking on the sea to his disciples who were in their boat in very rough weather. The disciples cried out for fear "But straightway Jesus said - Be of good cheer, it is I, be not afraid. And Peter answered him & said - Lord, if it be thou, bid me come unto thee on the water. And Jesus said☐ "Come"☐. The wonderful story of Jesus walking on the sea tells us how the Lord is there to rescue us immediately we begin to sink. "And when Peter was come down out of the ship, he walked on the water to go to Jesus. But when he saw the wind boisterous, he was afraid and beginning to sink he cried saying - Lord, save me. And immediately Jesus stretched forth his hand & caught him & said unto him - O thou of little faith, wherefore didst thou doubt? And when they were come into the ship the wind ceased.

21st October 1991 Monday
Mostyn died yesterday, on the 21st Sunday after Trinity.
So now, for Mostyn, the storm of life is over.

The Nobel Prizes are awarded each year from the income of a trust fund established by the Swedish scientist Alfred Nobel who died 10 December 1896. There are 6 prizes: - a) Physics b) Chemistry c) Physiology or Medicine d) Literature e) Peace f) Economic Sciences. They are awarded every 10th December.

22nd October 1991 Tuesday
Peter Hewes – While Miles, aged 45 in the prime of life, takes on the mantle of Uncle Fred, his cousin Peter, aged 50 (Don's son) fears that he may now be dying from cancer of the liver.

Peter complained of stomach pains & was taken to hospital where tests revealed that he had cancer. This was a double blow to his family, coming so soon after his mother Phyl had her stroke, leaving her paralysed down the left side.

To me it seems but yesterday that Peter & Lesley were young children – so often I stayed with them as their child-minder when Don & Phyl went out.

24th October 1991 Thursday
In loving memory of Mostyn Stevenson.

Stevenson – On October 20th 1991 in Stafford District General Hospital, Rupert Mostyn, dearly loved husband of Bunting, father of Michael and Julian, grandfather of Lucy, Sam and Polly, Katherine, Helen and Andrew. He will be laid to rest in the family grave at Ravenstone, in accordance with his wishes. Donations, if desired, to Stafford Hospice Appeal, c/o Co-operative F/S, 94 Queensville, Stafford ST17 4NX Inquiries to 0785 59847.

Mostyn died last Sunday & another wheel turns full cycle as he, like Madge in April 1987, returns to the fold to be buried where his parents lie.

Brother Pat & I joined Bunting & her immediate family for Mostyn's funeral service at Stafford Crematorium.

We were seven. Bunting, Michael & Josie, Julian & Shirley, Pat & me.

On either side of Bunting, like the Pillars of Hercules, stood her two sons. Both over 6 feet tall & well-built, they towered above the diminutive figure of Bunting.

Bunting, strong in spirit, sang with us all the two chosen hymns – "Abide with me" and "He who would valiant be 'gainst all disaster".

25th October 1991 Friday

To be a Pilgrim –Mostyn's ashes were laid to rest in the family grave at Ravenstone, where again we sang the same two chosen hymns at a Service of Committal taken by the Rector of Ravenstone, the Revd Kerry Emmett.

Mostyn's illustrious family descended on the scene rather like a gathering of the Rothschilds. They quite overwhelmed & outshone all lesser mortals assembled there. But we held our heads high & I thought of Christian in Pilgrim's Progress as we all made the same commitment to labour night & day to be a pilgrim & fear not what men say.

25th October 1991 Friday

Today is Saint Crispin & Saint Crispian (brother shoemakers who were martyred) remembered for all time, thanks to Shakespeare's Henry V who inspired his men to fight & win at Agincourt, saying "And Crispin Crispian shall ne'er go by, from this day to the ending of the world, but we in it shall be remembered".

26th October 1991 Saturday

"Save the Tigers" No sooner does the T.A. 7th (Volunteer) Battalion adopt the proud name of "The Tigers" which belonged to the Royal Leicestershire Regiment, than it learns that it could be axed as part of the government's drastic cuts in the armed forces.

27th October 1991 Sunday, Trinity XXII

God created man to be immortal, and made him to be an image of his own eternity.

The Wisdom of Solomon (The Apocrypha)

Last night we put the clocks back an hour ready for the winter. This usually means a change of time for Evensong at Ravenstone Church from 6 p.m. to 4 p.m. However, this year a vote was taken & the majority favoured 6 p.m. So 6 p.m. it remains. I was one of the minority who preferred 4 p.m.

28th October 1991 Monday

Rugby World Cup – This month we have seen the cream of the world's Rugby players battling for supremacy. How interesting to be introduced to this great game by such great players.

The climax will be next Saturday when the 2 finalists emerge & meet in combat. I now know all the 15 positions of the players & marvel how they spend so much time locked in mortal combat & emerge unscathed. The 8 forwards seem for ever head down in a scrum appearing headless as the "hooker" with his 2 props either side, 2 locks & 2 flankers behind, & No.8

central rear, all shove with all their might & then emerge with heads intact.

29th October 1991 Tuesday

European Economic Area: – E.C. + E.F.T.A. = E.E.A.
Nineteen European nations have agreed on the formation of the E.E.A.

334 million people of the 12 nation European Community will join 32 million people of the European Free Trade Association (E.F.T.A.) i.e. Switzerland, Austria, Finland, Norway, Sweden, Liechtenstein and Iceland to create a vast free trade area stretching from Greece to the Arctic. They will share in the "four freedoms" of the E.C.'s internal market – the free movement of goods, people, capital and services with effect from the end of next year.

The Council Tax (property & people tax) is the latest bright idea proposed by the government to replace the disastrous Poll Tax. It is planned to come into force in England, Wales & Scotland on 1st April 1993. Property will be put into different bands according to its value – bands A, B, C, D, E, F, G, and H. The Council Tax will enable people living in cheaper houses to pay less than those living in expensive houses.

Band A is for properties worth less than £40,000 and is charged at two-thirds band D.

Band B (£40,000 to £52,000) is charged at seven-ninths band D.

Band C (£52,000 to £68,000) is charged at eight-ninths.

Band D (£68,000 to £88,000) is the benchmark.

Band E (£88,000 to £120,000) is charged at eleven-ninths.

Band F (£120,000 to £160,000) is charged at thirteen-ninths.

Band G (£160,000 to £320,000) is charged at fifteen-ninths.

Band H (more than £320,000) is charged at double.

30th October 1991 Wednesday

A-spiring Bishop – Just 3 months into his role as Bishop of Leicester, the Rt. Revd. Thomas Butler is planning to raise money for the Church Urban Fund by climbing to the top of 50 church spires round the county. He has challenged congregations across the county to sponsor him for this intrepid task. He will climb the spires from the steps inside.

No ordinary Bishop this. Only last month he joined in the charity cycle ride for the Historic Churches Preservation Trust. Now he hopes to be further "inspiring".

31st October 1991 Thursday

A Day in Birmingham – Courtesy of "Viking Coaches Day Trips" had a lovely day in Birmingham.

Visited the Museum & Art Gallery again & penetrated further into its labyrinthine depths to discover Tyrannosaurus (Rex) the biggest creature that ever roamed this earth – 20 feet high & 50 feet in length. It lived in the cretaceous period over seventy million years ago. Also saw the great copper statue of the Buddha from Sultanganj on the Ganges, unearthed in 1862. Bought one or two Christmas presents and a de-luxe house number 27.

1st November 1991 Friday

Quorn Hunt – Leicestershire's famous Quorn Hunt, 200 years old, is in disgrace.

Lord Crawshaw, confined to a wheelchair as a result of a riding accident early in life, has been chairman of the hunt committee for the past 20 years. Now he has offered his resignation. Senior Master Mr Joss Hanbury and Master of Foxhounds Mr Barry Hercock have both been suspended. The League Against Cruel Sports filmed two incidents in separate September cub hunting meets showing cubs being pulled & dug out of their holes, only to be devoured by the pack of angry hounds.

2nd November 1991 Saturday

Meet calligraphist Hewsie. Today I bought a calligraphy set £22 complete with 8 different sized nibs.

The Rugby World Cup Final at Twickenham was between Australia and England. Heralded as the modern day equivalent of a gladiatorial tournament, I was one of the millions who screamed with anguish & expectation as the game progressed.

The Queen, there to present the trophy, was just about the only one who maintained her equilibrium. In the end the "Wizards of Oz" beat England 12 – 6.

3rd November 1991 Sunday, Trinity XXIII

I am created to do something or to be something for which no-one else is created. I have a place in God's counsels & in God's world which no-one else has. I am a link in a chain.

(Cardinal Newman.)

4th November 1991 Monday

"That very law which moulds a tear, and bids it trickle from its source; that law preserves the earth a sphere and guides the planets in their course"   Samuel Rogers 1763 – 1855

("That very law" = the law of gravitation)

Darren Preston sentenced – Darren has been sent to a young offenders' institution for 4 months after taking 3 cars and driving them while disqualified.

Unemployed Darren Robert Preston (17) of 3 Salcombe Drive, Glenfield, had previously been given a 6 months driving ban, but he was caught in April, May and August driving stolen cars. 1 – Vauxhall Nova, 2 – Vauxhall Cavalier, 3 – Austin Metro (mine).

He was sentenced to one month's detention for the April offence, a further one month for the May offence and two months for the August offence.

5th November 1991 Tuesday

Pope not welcome in Russia – For a thousand years and more Christianity has been split between the Eastern Orthodox Church & the Western Catholic Church. Each vied with the other for supremacy until 1453 A.D. when the Orthodox Church was virtually overthrown by the Turkish conquest of Constantinople. Now, however, there is re-birth of the Orthodox Church as Russia is freed from 70 years of Communism. Patriarch Aleksiy of Moscow came to London this week & in a bitter attack on the Roman Catholic Church said that the Pope is not wanted in Russia. Patriarch Aleksiy accused the

Vatican of breaking an agreement not to recruit new members in the Soviet Union. He is deeply offended by the Pope's decision to appoint a Catholic Archbishop of Moscow. Also the Ukraine is now a major target of Catholic expansionism & many other parts of Russia. This is in clear breach of an agreement between the two churches not to proselytise each others members.

(Like true love, the course of true religion ne'er did run smooth.)

6th November 1991 Wednesday

Katherine Sullivan & I went to Leicester Cathedral on Sunday for the Dedication of the Memorial Stone to Canon Gundry. He was Canon Chancellor from 1963 – 1987. The Address was given by Bishop John Mort, now retired, who spoke so lovingly of his friend – Dudley.

"O God our Father, who hast called us into the fellowship of thy Holy Church, we praise thee for those who have been lights of the world in their generation & in whose lives others have seen the likeness of thy mercy & love." So began one of the prayers at the dedication. "Accept, we beseech thee, this memorial of thy servant Dudley who by thy grace rendered unto thee in many ways & in many places such true and laudable service; & grant that it may inspire those who come after him to honour thee in like manner".

Canon Gundry certainly inspired me, lifting me up to heaven.

7th November 1991 Thursday

Madrid Peace Conference – The sons of Isaac & the sons of Ishmael are still fighting over their homeland. America has now taken the initiative & invited them all to get together in neutral Madrid, to see if they can possibly talk "peace". President Bush of America has appealed to Israelis & Arabs to forgive & forget. But at the conference table of the royal palace in Madrid, beneath beautiful frescoes of Greek gods & nymphs, Jews & Arabs seem more like combatants in a Rugby scrum. Their grievances go back 4,000 years.

Jews v. Arabs – Throughout the whole of the "Holy Land" Jews & Arabs are at variance with one another. The key disputed areas of territory are – the Gaza Strip, the Golan Heights, the West Bank and Jerusalem.

Every day the Jews settle themselves in more & more "settlements" while the displaced Arabs live as refugees. The Jews maintain that much of the land is rightfully theirs. About 100,000 Jews have "settled" in the West Bank & Gaza Strip in 143 settlements. 140,000 have moved into the ring of buildings tightening around East Jerusalem & 12,000 on the Golan Heights.

9th November 1991 Saturday

Blazing oil wells all extinguished – The Emir of Kuwait threw a party this week in the desert to celebrate the extinguishing of all his country's oil well fires. After 8 months of darkening the skies & blackening the land, the 727 fires set by Iraq's vandalising army were out.

27 teams from ten different nations accomplished this feat.

10th November 1991 Sunday, Trinity XXIV

Jesus said unto him, if thou canst believe, all things are possible to him that believeth. And straightway the

father of the child cried out & said with tears – Lord, I believe; help thou mine unbelief
(Mark: 9)

11th November 1991 Monday
Burgan 118 – Burgan 118 is the name of the last oil well in Kuwait to be capped. Burgan was one of the largest producing oil fields in the world.

Over 400 of the blazing oil wells set ablaze by the Iraqis were in the Burgan field. Over 10,000 fire-fighters tackled this worst oil disaster on record.

Mr Red Roberts of Dickinson, North Dakota, one of the supervisors, said the biggest hazard was the heat coming from all directions – sand, fires & sun – like walking through a fiery furnace.

12th November 1991 Tuesday
Fusion Power! (See 31st March 1989) Scientists at the Joint European Torus experimental fusion reactor in Oxfordshire have now succeeded in putting "real" fusion reactor fuel into their machine. As the temperature inside the reactor rose 20 times hotter than the sun, the tritium & deuterium particles fused.

Fusion Power! I sometimes wonder if Cocky & I have been fused together by fusion power. We never meet & communicate only by telephone; & yet our hearts seem to be as one. The fact that we are not aware of each other's weaknesses & blemishes elevates us in our mind's eye to a much higher plane.

Vivat St. Petersburg – In November 1917 the Bolsheviks stormed the Winter Palace in St. Petersburg, Russia's second city. The anniversary of the 1917 revolution has always been marked by military parades & Communist processions, but not this year. With the fall of Communism it is now "Vivat St. Petersburg" to celebrate the restoration of the city's original name & its effective rebirth. The city's name was changed to Leningrad but this week the mayor promised to "open the door into Europe wide" in the tradition of the city's founder – Peter the Great.

13th November 1991 Wednesday
Opera Spectacular – Enid & I made our first acquaintance with Birmingham's vast N.E.C. arena, with a seating capacity of 12,681, where we enjoyed the most splendid "Opera Spectacular".

On stage were the Royal Philharmonic Opera Orchestra and the Chorus of the Royal Opera House, Covent Garden, plus Fanfare Trumpeters from the Band of the Irish Guards.

What great music we heard – Verdi, Wagner, Puccini etc.

My favourite items were Mascagni's Cavelleria Rusticana, Verdi's Chorus of the Hebrew Slaves & his Grand March from Aida.

14th November 1991 Thursday
Hamlet – Saw the film "Hamlet" at the cinema in Leicester & was held spellbound by the magic of Shakespeare. The film, unlike a stage production, was able to show the sea & the sky in all their beauty.

"But, look, the morn, in russet mantle clad, walks o'er the dew of yon high eastern hill"

The ghost of Hamlet's father was able to appear & disappear just like a real ghost.

And the great soliloquies were all there, spoken to perfection: - "To be, or not to be – that is the question". How Shakespeare would have loved to see the film version of his play. Set in Denmark it held a special attraction for me, as I thought of Hans Christian Anderson. It was such a sad, sad story, with the two young lovers, broken hearted & both dying, that we in the cinema sat long in stunned silence when the film ended.

Was there ever anyone like Shakespeare who could see into every man's soul, from monarch to serving wench – old men, young men, rich & poor, wise & foolish? Everyone to him was totally transparent.

"O, that this too, too solid flesh would melt, thaw & resolve itself into a dew"

"Murder most foul ......"

"There are more things in heaven & earth, Horatio, than are dreamt of in your philosophy"

"What a piece of work is man! How noble in reason! How infinite in faculties! In form and moving, how express & admirable! In action, how like an angel"

Just a few of the many gems strewn into Shakespeare's "Hamlet".

16th November 1991 Saturday
"And a partridge in a pear tree"

We now have our very own partridge – as tame as a pigeon – which shares its affections with me & my neighbours. We all provide it with food & all love it dearly. It just arrived out of the blue a few weeks ago & decided to make itself at home here.

17th November 1991 Sunday, Trinity XXV
In the beginning God created the heaven & the earth. And the earth was without form and void; & darkness was upon the face of the deep. And the Spirit of God moved upon the face of the waters. And God said, Let there be light: & there was light. (Gen: 1: 1 – 3)

18th November 1991 Monday
Hostage Terry Waite Freed!
(After 1763 days in captivity)
Was there ever a home-coming quite like that of Terry Waite, envoy of Dr Runcie, Archbishop of Canterbury? On 20th January 1987 he was taken hostage in Beirut by Islamic Jihad. Islamic Jihad is controlled by the Mugniyahs & the Hamadeis, two of Lebanon's most powerful clans. They held Terry Waite in chains in a darkened room. For 4 years he was in solitary confinement, but for the last year he had the pleasure of the company of other western hostages. All men of great intellect & character, they were able to sustain one another. Latterly they were given a radio & all paid tribute to the World Service of the BBC which operated 24 hours a day.

"Dr Runcie I presume" said Terry Waite, as the Archbishop met him again after 5 long years. And then Terry Waite spoke to the world, "I'll tell you a story" he said "I was kept in total & complete isolation for four years. I saw no-one & spoke to no-one apart from a cursory word with my guards when they brought me food. And one day out of the blue a guard came with a postcard. It was a postcard showing a stained glass

window from Bedford showing John Bunyan in jail & a message from someone whom I didn't know simply saying "We remember. We shall not forget."
Once again a blessing from Bunyan.

Bradgate Park – How wonderful to be retired from work & be able to enjoy a brisk morning walk through Bradgate Park. On a glorious late autumn November morning, beneath a clear blue sky, I walked the whole length of Bradgate Park & back (3½ miles) stopping to drink in the scene from an elevated seat overlooking the water at the far Cropston end.
It was mostly young mothers with infants in pushchairs, or retired people with dogs, who had the opportunity to walk in the park mid-week. I met Mike Paterson, like me, recently retired from G.O.M.B.

19ᵗʰ November 1991 Tuesday
Much Ado about Nothing – Another of Shakespeare's 37 plays has now been added to my repertoire, with more treasured quotations:-
"And look, the gentle day, before the wheels of Phoebus, round about dapples the drowsy east with spots of gray"
"Good morrow, Benedick. Why, what's the matter, that you have such a February face, so full of frost, of storm, and cloudiness?"
And Benedick's thoughts on Claudio might well describe Shakespeare himself: - "And now is he turned orthographer; his words are a very fantastical banquet, just so many strange dishes".

20ᵗʰ November 1991 Wednesday
And so the stork prepares to deliver baby Suzannah tomorrow. Mary Blue's daughter Karen has been wishing it were November "NOW" for such a long time – spring, summer and autumn. Now we are almost there.

Lady Jane Grey – Watched on TV the film telling the tragic story of Lady Jane Grey, England's queen for nine days.
On the death of Henry VIII the throne passed to his ailing young son Edward VI. What intrigue & scheming there was, to proclaim Lady Jane from Bradgate Park Leicestershire, England's new queen, to uphold the protestant faith. No sooner was the young boy king dead, than Jane was queen. However, Catholic Mary, daughter of Henry VIII and rightful heir, soon claimed her rights.
Nine Days' Wonder – The most astonishing event is reckoned to hit the headlines for no more than nine days. A nine days' wonder is something that astonishes everybody just for nine days.
How poignant therefore that Lady Jane Grey should reign for nine days. Because she happened to be born when she was, & who she was, she was one of many who faced the block of the executioner in the turbulent days of the Reformation. The oaks in Bradgate Park were beheaded in tribute to her.

21ˢᵗ November 1991 Thursday
Oliver, to Karen (nee Jarman) and Graham,
Congratulations on the birth of your daughter,
Suzannah Mary, on November 21ˢᵗ weighing 7lb. 5½oz. -
Love and best wishes from Mum, Murdo, Scott, Sharon and Darren.

Baby Suzannah was born on a Thursday.
"Thursday's child has far to go".
Born at the time of the full moon, she belongs to Scorpio, suggesting that she may therefore be determined, passionate, resourceful, aggressive, independent, intuitive, intense, secretive & mesmerisingly magnetic.

22ⁿᵈ November 1991 Friday
The Ashe Lecture – Endowed by Francis Ashe in 1654, this annual lecture in St. Helen's Church, Ashby-de-la-Zouch, was given this year by Leicester's new Bishop the Rt. Revd. Thomas Butler.
In the week which saw the release of hostage Terry Waite, it co-incided with the ringing of church bells throughout the land in celebration of his safe return.
The Bishop paid tribute to Terry Waite, who had thrown himself at a "wall of injustice & oppression" in the Lebanon. Although the wall collapsed on top of him, he had made it possible for others to make their way to freedom.

23ʳᵈ November 1991 Saturday
£2,000 to spend – I have arranged to have the kitchen at 27, Leicester Road, Ravenstone, decorated & re-furbished with up-to-date fitted units in "New England – Medium Oak".
A leaflet came through the door advertising Bob Parker, a superb service for all aspects of property maintenance. The service to "turn your home into a house".
No doubt it meant "turn your house into a home".

24ᵗʰ November 1991 Sunday, Sunday before Advent
Fear God & keep his commandments; for this is the whole duty of man. For God shall bring every work into judgment, with every secret thing, whether it be good, or whether it be evil. (Ecclesiastes 12 – 14)

Baby Suzannah's home-coming was shared by her mother Karen, dad Graham, grandmother Mary Blue, great grand-dad Pat and yours truly, great-great half-aunt Betty. We drank champagne & each in turn held this precious bundle of joy. Like Auntie Cis, a century ago, she was "perfect" & as good as gold.

Note by Mary Blue – Auntie Cis was Ethel May Hewes the 1ˢᵗ girl born to Mary Suzannah and George Harry in 1892 after four boys (hence the nickname "Cis" which she was known by all her life & indeed signed herself as such). The fourth boy had been Uncle Hedley who was born with a cleft palate & harelip, therefore when Cis was born the telegram sent to inform relatives of her safe arrival read, "Baby perfect".

25ᵗʰ November 1991 Monday
United Nations –General Perez de Cuellar, Secretary General of the United Nations, has been instrumental in securing the release of Western hostages from the Middle East. Now, aged 70, his term of office will finish at the end of this year.
His successor will be Mr Boutros Boutros Ghali, who is Egypt's Deputy Premier for Foreign Affairs. He is the first Arab to be elected to the U. N.'s top post. But he is no ordinary Arab. He is a Christian Arab, being a member of the minority Coptic Christian community.

Furthermore his wife Leia is Jewish. As much of his work will be concerned with Middle Eastern affairs he should be able to see things from 3 angles.

26th November 1991 Tuesday

Vivat St. Petersburg – How lovely to be introduced to the great treasures of St. Petersburg. Prior to the 1917 Revolution, it was Russia's capital city. Set on 100 islands with more than 300 bridges connecting them, it was designed by Italian & French architects who built the most magnificent buildings you can imagine.

Peter the Great's Winter Palace, known latterly as the Hermitage is the most fantastic place of all. Consisting of five buildings it contains so many works of art that if you stopped & viewed each one for 30 seconds it would take you 7 years.

Bible Radio! – The reading of the whole Bible which began in September this year has now reached the story of Samson in the Book of Judges. "Then went Samson to Gaza ....."

As I listened to this sad story of conflict between Israel & the Philistines over 3,000 years ago, I thought of today's Palestinian problem.

The Philistines of old were the first Palestinians. In the days of Samson "the Philistines had dominion over Israel". But today, Israel has dominion over the Palestinians. The 6 day war in June 1967 may have resulted in victory for Israel, but it has caused more problems than it has solved, with never-ending repercussions.

27th November 1991 Wednesday

UNIKOM – The United Nations Iraq-Kuwait Observer and Monitoring Force (UNICOM) is a unique experiment in international peace-keeping. For the first time in U.N. history, all 5 permanent members of the Security Council – Britain, France, China, the United States and the U.S.S.R. – are represented. They contribute 30 officers each & another 28 nations supply 7 officers each. They patrol a de-militarised zone 15 kilometres wide (5 into Kuwait and 10 into Iraq) and keep the warring factions ay bay.

Similar peace-keeping forces are to be used in other troubled areas.

28th November 1991 Thursday

Peter the Great (1672 – 1725) – Gosh! Having met Constantine the Great & Charles the Great (Charlemagne) I have now met the one & only **Peter** the Great, founder of St. Petersburg.

"He was your Samson, O Russia" cried Prokopovich in the funeral sermon which he preached in 1725. "He was your Moses, O Russia". He was your Solomon, O Russia". He was your David & your Constantine". He was "a brilliant comet in European history", but he was a very hard taskmaster.

Peter the Great was 6 feet 7 inches tall. When he took over the reins as Tsar, Russia wondered what had hit it. He was so dynamic & had such boundless energy that few could possibly keep up with him. "How many died that Caesar might be great" could also be said of Peter the Great. Out of nothing in the dreary marshes of the Gulf of Finland he built a new city, St. Petersburg.

Alexis, his son, was a great disappointment to him. All he wanted was a quiet life. He literally fled from his father, only to be severely punished & put to death.

In less than three decades Peter the Great introduced more innovations to Russia than it had seen in centuries. He brought it into line with Western Europe – changed the calendar in 1700 from the Russian year 7208 (the alleged creation of the world) – built up a navy from scratch – had the landscape mapped – had a Census & even introduced the Poll Tax.

30th November 1991 Saturday

The committee of Coalville Amateur Operatic Society, prompted by Chairman Peter Jacques, recently agreed to acknowledge my services over the years by a gift, of my choosing, to the value of £75.

What would I like? I chose a lovely wall clock with pendulum & chimes in a 24 inch high case, to be presented to me next Monday.

1st December 1991 Sunday, Advent I

And I heard a voice saying unto me, Write, Blessed are the dead which die in the Lord from henceforth: Yea, saith the Spirit, that they may rest from their labours & their works do follow them. (Revelation 14)

2nd December 1991 Monday

This evening, with the full company assembled for rehearsal of Coalville Amateurs' forthcoming production "Half a Sixpence", I was graciously presented with my lovely clock. It was the pinnacle of my long association with the society & I was pleased to give the society in return my de-luxe "Treasurer's Case" for their use.

A Visit to St. Petersburg – My latest library book has taken me on a guided tour of St. Petersburg. First, we went by bus on a tour of the city, to get the feel of the spread of this Venice of the North, with its islands & bridges and interconnecting waterways. We visited the Hermitage, saw the Petropavloskaya (= Peter & Paul) Fortress, where Peter the Great's son Alexis was the first prisoner to be held there & was tortured to death. Saw where Tchaikovsky lived & died in 1893. Saw St. Isaac's Cathedral, looking like London's St. Paul's on the skyline. And Alexander's Column, like Nelson's Column in the vast Palace Square.

By Boat to Peterhof – 21 miles from St. Petersburg is Peterof (known also as Petrodvorets). Founded by Peter the Great it was his intention to make it the Russian equivalent of Versailles.

It reminded me of Tivoli, on the outskirts of Rome, where the world famous Villa D'Este fountains cascade in waterfalls down & down & down.

At Peterhof the Grand Palace stands on a terrace 39 feet high. The façade of the palace, facing the sea, towers over the Grand Cascade, a great system of fountains which descends in broad steps to the 300 acre park below. There are 129 fountains, including the Samson Fountain which rises 66 feet into the air.

4th December 1991 Wednesday

Kitchen & Middle Room Decoration.

What an almighty mess! You never saw anything like the state of the house at 27 Leicester Road, Ravenstone. Bob Parker is tackling the job, but calls in additional experts for injecting a damp course, fixing new electric wiring etc. The house is a buzz of activity – drilling, hammering & lively banter.

Vivat Tchaikovsky – Katherine and I saw the ballet "Nutcracker" at the De Montfort Hall, Leicester. Was there ever such exquisite music as Tchaikovsky's Nutcracker? The Nutcracker is in fact a Nutcracker Doll, a Christmas present for Clara. That night Clara goes to bed & in her dreams all the toys, including the Nutcracker Doll, come to life. The Nutcracker then turns into a handsome Prince & we are transported to the Palace of the Sugar Plum Kingdom, where Clara & the Prince are greeted by the Sugar Plum Fairy, who in turn introduces all the enchanting inhabitants of the Sugar Plum Kingdom.

5th December 1991 Thursday
The Ukraine – A referendum held this week showed that 90% of Ukrainians supported secession from the Kremlin. As the Ukraine breaks away from Soviet domination the prospect of a new "Union of Sovereign States" becomes less likely. Following the Russian Revolution in 1917, Lenin said, "Losing the Ukraine would be like losing our heads." The republic of the Ukraine, whose capital is the lovely city of Kiev, has a population of 53 million. It is now ready to shake off 3 centuries of rule from Russia.

6th December 1991 Friday
Birmingham again - Courtesy of "Viking Coaches Day Trips" I discovered more of Birmingham's hidden depths. As one who searches out the oases of calm in the heart of a bustling city, I visited the Church of St. Martin in The Bullring – had lunch with "Nelson" sitting out of doors in the bright winter sunshine – had afternoon tea in the roof restaurant of Rackhams & then gazed in wonder at the Aladdin's cave of merchandise in this elegant store – and finally browsed in the great book shop "Waterstones" with eight floors of books & bought for £5 a book which took my fancy "Who's Who in Shakespeare".

Bible Radio! Not since Canon Gundry have I enjoyed such eloquent bible reading. And never have I heard so many great bible stories brought to life. The bible readings at church cover the same limited ground year after year, & it is wonderful to explore new territory, following the whole story from beginning to end.

7th December 1991 Saturday
Long Case Regulator Quartz Wall Clock – The Westminster chimes of my new wall clock are saying – "Lord through this hour, be thou my guide, that through thy power, no foot shall slide". This clock was a gift presented to me this week by Coalville Amateur Operatic Society. Also this week I bought a de-luxe mirror, costing £135.

8th December 1991 Sunday, Advent II
Delight thyself also in the Lord; & he shall give thee the desires of thine heart. Commit thy way unto the Lord; trust also in him; and he shall bring it to pass. (Psalm 37) Like Michelangelo, young Bob Parker, aged 36, decorated the ceiling in the Middle Room. It was artexed – a smooth runny paste slapped on to the ceiling & then

transformed into swirling patterns with swift dextrous movements before it set hard. He even managed to incorporate my initials as a monogram.

9th December 1991 Monday
Granada Television Studios Tour – Mary Blue & I went on a Viking Coach Trip to Manchester to sample the workings of a television studio. We were shown behind the scenes to see the tricks of the trade. A boat-load of us with wind blowing on us were shown on screen out at sea. We walked down the street in two popular television programmes –
1) Baker Street of Sherlock Holmes fame. 2) Coronation Street, still shown regularly on television after 30 consecutive years. We walked also along Downing Street, and enjoyed a lively light-hearted debate in a perfectly reconstructed House of Commons.

10th December 1991 Tuesday
Turn your house into a home – Working like a Trojan, Bob Parker is slowly but surely transforming the poor old Kitchen at 27 Leicester Road, Ravenstone into a thing of beauty. All last week he worked from 8 a.m. to 8 p.m. tackling the Middle Room & Kitchen together. First the house was full of steam as he steam stripped the old paper from the walls. Then the house was full of dust as he knocked off great chunks of crumbling plaster & ripped out rotten skirting boards. Then the walls were drilled & injected with damp proofing. Then the walls were re-plastered – kitchen units assembled, & all set now for papering.

11th December Wednesday
Worldlife Centre - £35 million wildlife plan for Leicester. Space-age centre a world first.
An ambitious £35 million plan to put Leicester at the forefront of wildlife conservation was unveiled today. The Worldlife Centre planned for Western Park will be the first in a new generation of zoos. Instead of animals in cages, Worldlife will use satellites & computers to show visitors more about the natural world. Worldlife is due to open in June 1995 & Leicester has been chosen because of its excellent road & rail links & because it is the first Environment City.
The Worldlife Centre will take up around 50 acres of the 170 acres of Western Park. In Worldlife you will be able to go live to the Serengeti in Africa & to the Amazon. A Worldlive News Station will link people to what is happening with the environment in the world today. There will be exhibits called Worldlife Review & the amazing technology will include Virtual Reality, where you wear a computer-linked head set & have your own private 3 dimensional view of life in the wild. You can even become a lizard or a lion.

12th December 1991 Thursday
Elizabeth Hewes
27 Leicester Road
Ravenstone
Leicester
LE6 2AR
0530 836583
British Telecom have committed themselves to a multi-billion pound modernisation programme which is transforming the U.K. telephone network. This has now

reached my telephone at Ravenstone, as the local telephone exchange is being converted to digital technology – hence the new telephone number.

13th December 1991 Friday

Friday the Thirteenth – This is the day when **Triskaidekaphobics** keep a low profile.

A Christmas Carol – In sub-zero temperatures Katherine & I motored to Nottingham through a winter wonderland of hoar frost to see "A Christmas Carol" by Charles Dickens. We parked on the 14th floor of the 16 storey car park & then saw on the pavement below, someone lying on the pavement being attended by ambulance men. Later, as we sat in the theatre foyer having Christmas lunch prior to the matinee performance, we learned that the person lying on the pavement had committed suicide by jumping from the top of the car park. This added to the pathos of the day – a moving story which stirred all the emotions.

I was able to identify myself with Scrooge as he found himself standing on the outside, looking on the inside, & seeing those he loved long ago now happily ensconced in the bosom of their families, while he was excluded. Christmas is certainly no time for the also rans. There is no pleasure being a tagger-on – an incidental extra – a maiden aunt – or an old cross-patch uncle. I know exactly how Scrooge felt.

14th December 1991 Saturday

From my love, by post, a framed picture of Lancaster Castle in the snow & a Christmas card "For the One I Love" – "to wish you special happiness & then to tell you, too, on Christmas day & every day, my heart belongs to you"

Have a nice Christmas darling.

Love for ever. John X X X X X

15th December 1991 Sunday, Advent III

All scripture is given by inspiration of God & is profitable for doctrine, for reproof, for correction, for instruction in righteousness that the man of God may be perfect. (Timothy II)

16th December 1991 Monday

"British Telecom has modernised your telephone exchange. And now we can offer you a choice of two types of bill... .free. You can have a simple summary of calls. Or if you prefer, your bill can give you a free itemised breakdown listing the numbers called, date, time, length of call and how much it cost." I chose the latter.

Meals on Wheels! Thirty years ago Aunt Dos, the driver, helped deliver meals on wheels to the elderly housebound. Enid & I have now joined the ranks of those delivering meals on wheels. Enid is the driver & I am her assistant. How sad to see those whom we knew in the prime of life, now so lonely & housebound.

17th December 1991 Tuesday

Louis XIV (1638 – 1715) – My latest library book has introduced me to the great Louis Quatorze. What a king! He had so many children but only one authentic son & heir – Louis the Grand Dauphin. He in turn had 3 sons, the eldest Louis, duc de Bourgogne, also having 2 sons.

No problem then for a suitable heir – one heir – 5 spare. Imagine the grief then, when one by one they died. First the Grand Dauphin, aged 53, died of small-pox. Then his son, the duc de Bourgogne died of measles, leaving 2 little boys – the elder boy also died of measles. When Charles II of Spain died in 1700, aged 35, he left no immediate heir but chose Philippe d'Anjou, the second son of the Grand Dauphin, as his successor. The Grand Dauphin therefore had the unique distinction of being able to say, "The king, my father & the king, my son."

"The king, my son" was then Philip V of Spain – one & the same Philip V on my piece of eight which lay for 200 years at the bottom of the sea!

The 3rd son of the Grand Dauphin died in the prime of life, following a hunting accident.

When the great king Louis XIV was on his deathbed, he sent for his great-grandson, the five year old sole surviving Dauphin. He came with his governess, Mme de Ventadour. She lifted him on to the bed & the two men who between them reigned in France for 131 years, looked gravely at each other for the last time.

"Mignon" (my little darling), said Louis XVI, "you are going to be a great king". He kissed the child, saying, "My dear child, I give you my blessing with all my heart".

18th December 1991 Wednesday

Louis XV – Little darling Louis XV grew up to be the darling of all the ladies. All his lady loves knew him as the Bien Aimé. His long-suffering queen, who had ten children within twelve years, had to put up with one mistress after another, most notably Jeanne Antoinette le Normant d'Etoiles (née Poisson) = Fish. She was housed in splendour, in her own apartment inside the Palace of Versailles and was made a marquise – Marquise de Pompadour.

i.e. Madame de Pompadour.

Like his great-grandfather before him, Louis Quinze died at Versailles. He died from small-pox on 10th May 1774.

19th December 1991 Thursday

Louis XVI (1754 – 1793) – Louis XVI, when he was the Dauphin, aged 16, married Marie - Antoinette – Josèphe – Jeanne of Austria, aged 15.

Four years later he became king, with his queen, Marie–Antoinette. How she loved being queen. She revelled in luxury, wore the most beautiful dresses & had the most elaborate hair styles. She was so very extravagant that eventually the Bishop of Nancy made a public attack on court luxury and the prodigality of its members.

Finally, on the 14th July 1789, the Bastille was stormed by the people of France who said enough was enough.

"So" said the king, "There is a rebellion."

"No, Sire. It is a Revolution."

From the pinnacle of luxury, Louis XVI and his family found themselves at the mercy of the people of France. In desperation, they tried to flee the country in disguise, but were caught in the act & brought back again.

On 21st January 1793 Louis XVI was sent to the guillotine. His body & head were thrown into a pit 15 feet deep, where they were consumed by quicklime.

20th December 1991 Friday

King James Version of the Bible. Bible Radio, which I

am enjoying so very much, is taking its daily reading from the King James Version, whose rich language is engraved in my heart, after hearing it for over half a century. At Ravenstone Church we have modern terminology which means very little to me.

The question is: "Why the Authorised Version of the Bible?"

The answer, one suspects, is that actors prefer Elizabethan language

as a vehicle for their histrionic skills; it sounds better and comes out more meatily.   (Newspaper cutting)

22nd December 1991 Sunday, Advent IV

"For with God nothing shall be impossible." (St. Luke, Chap. 1 Verse 37)

"Carols by Candlelight" – Ravenstone Church was full this evening for the Carols by Candlelight. As everyone assembled in their respective family groups, Old Maid Hewsie was so pleased to be joined by Cousin Miles and Sarah, together with their mothers, and also Cousin Lesley.

Cousin Isobel (mother of Miles) who was born in Church Lane, Ravenstone, where Cocky also was born, is spending this Christmas once more in Ravenstone after half a century elsewhere. She is hoping to move house & buy a cottage somewhere near to Miles.

There is actually one for sale in Church Lane.

23rd December 1991 Monday

Alma Ata – Alma Ata is the capital of Kazakhstan where leaders of eleven former republics of the Union of Soviet Socialist Republics – U.S.S.R. – have now met to establish a new Commonwealth of Independent States. The 4 states who have rejected formal links with the others are the Western oriented Lithuania, Latvia, Estonia & the fiercely independent Georgia. The heartland of the new Commonwealth are the Slav Republics of Russia, Ukraine & Byeloruss, joined by Christian Armenia & Muslim Azerbaijan, both south of the Caucasus mountains, 5 central Asian states & Moldova, akin to Romania.

24th December 1991 Tuesday

Snow White – Katherine Sullivan & I booked seats for "Snow White" this afternoon at the De Montfort Hall, Leicester. Unlike last year when we were given the Lord Mayor's seats by mistake, we chose to sit near the front in the stalls. The theatre was less than half full & we were able to sit more-or-less where we liked. The show itself was mediocre compared with "Snow White on Ice" which enthralled me many years ago. The entrance of the seven dwarfs from the vast backcloth of the diamond mine on to the ice was a sight never to be forgotten.

25th December 1991 Wednesday

Christmas Day again at the home of Mary Blue.

Pat, Evelyn & I joined Mary Blue, Scott & Murdo Junior for another lovely day together.

Grandma Hewes, who died in 1931, played an integral part in the day's activities as we read again the letter she wrote over a hundred years ago to her sister Emma...

Kingsthorpe House
Coalville
Feb. 17th 1886

My Darling Emma,

I am going to be a good girl this time and write to you early, many thanks for your letter, my Harry & I were very pleased to receive it. Harry thanks you for all your good wishes for the "New Year" & as I have not written a letter to you since we entered it I heartily wish you every blessing this world can afford, and may you have a very happy bright New Year.

It is true as you say we cannot have all we wish, I'm afraid if we could we should be poor selfish creatures, & not nearly as happy as we are now, God knows what is best for each of His children, although we cannot see it always, but as you say I'm sure each little sorrow & care draws us nearer to Him, for who have we in trouble like unto Him, look upon me in the hour of trouble and I will comfort thee, Oh Emma what a blessing Christianity is – what should we do without it? My darling Harry does try daily to walk in the right path, and I can say from my heart, that we are happier each day of our lives, Emma it is such a comfort to have a dear Christian husband. We often enjoy a little talk to help each other onward.

You say what a beauty my little darling must be, I assure you he is, I love him more every day, but as you laugh at what I tell you about him I must not tell you so much, but there, I couldn't help it if I tried. About a week since, he was very ill, in fact I thought I should have lost him, I shall always think he had a touch of croup, for he was so hoarse and almost barked when he coughed, I had a fire in the bedroom for nearly a week and kept him in the sitting room by day. For two nights I had no sleep scarcely, I was so anxious about him, but I'm thankful to say he is better now, except a cold. He was such a good little soul all the time, you should have seen the style of my room with all his toys, but I gave him all I could think of to amuse him. When he wanted me he would go to the sitting room door and call Ba – Ba, he cannot say Ma yet. He was 16 months old yesterday and we have been married 2 yrs & 7 months today. How quickly the time flies Emma, I often look back to my wedding day with very great pleasure, I must say ours has been a very happy union so far, God has so wonderfully blessed us but we do not expect it all sunshine.

I'm now busy making my little pet a new set of pinafores as he has grown out of his first ones. You know when I begin I've such a lot to make, only having my wash once every three weeks. I've a very pretty pattern, one of Mrs Morgan's little boys. Bessie sent it, with 10 or 12 shillings worth of embroidery from Evan's remnants. Some of it is lovely, his best ones I am making very pretty, 4 yards of wide embroidery beside 2 pieces of insertion up the front on one pinafore, but I can get on very nicely with my little machine, and besides I've lots of time now. Now laugh at this if you don't feel interested, I want to get most of my sewing done before the summer comes, as when I'm in my new house I shall want to take my little pet for nice walks as you know how pleasant it is up there. We shall have a very nice home, shall build close up to Mr Bertenshaw's, and such a lovely garden. The land has cost just £100. The plans and specifications are out for tenders and all being well we hope to begin to build in March. They say it will take 10 or 12 weeks to complete it. You can fancy how full Harry is of it. He said dinner time how much he should like you to come and see us in our new house and that you are to make haste. We often wish you were here. As regards the name Dany-Graig – Harry's Uncle Gibbs said he should have something that people would understand, so I altered it to Lansdowne Villa, will that do dear? Tell me.

I don't expect Harry will go home this summer, so I'm thinking of going when Uncle John Stark comes over. It would be so nice to meet all together! I hope dear Cousin Lo ….. keeps better, and little Frankie as well, I should like to see him.

Yes dear Emma I just was happy at Christmas to have my dear ones with me, I think dear Ma stood the journey wonderfully, and you know how Da enjoys himself when he goes anywhere, he does look so well. He played ball with Freddy in fact they were great friends. Ma and Bessie were just fit to eat him. He is always having something sent him.

When the news about Harry came we all felt very much upset, in fact I just pitied dear Ma, it made her ill. I'm so thankful he has a situation, and hope sincerely that he will be a good boy, give my fond love to him.

Mrs Hall, my neighbour that was, has a little son about 6 weeks old. She is going to name him Freddy. She is very proud of it.

Now I must thank you for your very pretty Xmas card, I think it was sweet. Please give my fond love to Aunt Emma and Frank and thank them both for the very pretty cards. I hope she is better ere this.

Yes Emma dear I do hope my little pet will grow up to be a comfort to me, I shall not fail if he lives to tell him of his dear Uncle who died so soon after his birth. Oh if he is only such a noble Christian, what a blessing it will be.

Ta, Auntie for nice kiss come and see me I'm a good little boy, I've got a gee gee. Tatta Auntie

What do you think of your nephew's first letter? He is very fond of writing, often sends a line to Gam-Ma.

We have had a very severe winter, such a quantity of snow, more than we have had for years. I too should have liked to have seen your Canadian snow, I enjoyed the remarks you made on it.

It was rather strange but the same day that I received your letter I read this beautiful little piece in the Christian Herald and I said, Well, I must send this to Emma. Did you receive Spencer's Almanack dear? Excuse me for not sending it before.

I'm sorry Aunt Harry fell, how unfortunate she has been that way, give her my fond love and tell her I should just love to see her. Harry often says I should like Aunt Harry to come and see us.

I heard from Bessie this week, she said dear Ma kept about the same, and she should be very glad when the warm weather comes. I think she has stood the winter well, and was surprised to see her look as well as she did at Christmas. Now my dear I think I have told you all my stock of news, and as my darling has just come I must get the teas.

Accept our united fond love

From your Affectionate Sister

Mary –

To all my dear Uncles Aunts and Cousins God bless you dear, Goodbye XX

P.S. I did not tell you that dear Bessie sent me a half dozen yards of such pretty crotchet that she's made. It is nearly 2 inches deep and so lacey. So I have plenty of trimming for my pinafores. I have cut one out since tea and made it, trimming as well except the neck. I should not like to be without my little machine.

Good night duckie

Just struck 10

26th December 1991 Thursday

Boxing Day! Pat & Evelyn invited Evelyn's brother Vin, Mary Blue & me for lunch & we were joined later in the day by the Revd. Royston Davis & his wife & also the Revd. Colin Patey & his family. We played several of the good old Christmas party games.

27th December 1991 Friday

Gorbachev Resigns –Mikhail Gorbachev, Soviet leader for the past 6 years, whose vision of a new free country brought an end to 70 years of stifled Communist rule, resigned on Christmas day as Soviet President.

Things have not turned out as he hoped. He is not happy that his great country should fragment into separate states. The nationalism, which has now been unleashed, is proving to be a formidable force beyond his control. In his farewell speech he said, "The most dangerous situation facing us now is the disintegration of the country. All that we have achieved so far could be lost."

28th December 1991 Saturday

C.I.S. – Leaders of the new Commonwealth of Independent States are meeting next week to sort out the problem of their vast nuclear arsenal.

Four of the "States" have nuclear weapons – Russia – Ukraine – Byelorussia – Kazakhstan.

Only one man has his finger on the nuclear button – Mr Yeltsin, the Russian leader. Mr Kravchuk, the Ukrainian leade4, does not approve of this.

"To all Staff……."

How wonderful to be retired from work & not have to bother with such things as the international oil market or the financial restructuring of the coal industry.

How lovely not to be confined to the office day after day, but absolutely free to come & go as I please.

29th December 1991 Sunday after Christmas

"For I the Lord thy God will hold thy right hand, saying unto thee, Fear not; I will help thee."

(Isaiah 41 : 13)

30th December 1991 Monday

Cousin Miles – Pat & Evelyn invited Cousin Miles, with his wife Sarah, his mother Isobel & me for an evening get-together.

Cousin Miles held centre stage as he recounted some of the bizarre experiences of his life, including the prankish escapades of the "Cock Robin" choir to which he belonged in his younger days.

A true extrovert, his life seems to have been one adventure after another. Not for him the mundane humdrum life of a stick-in-the-mud, but the swash-buckling excitement of the go-getter.

He has a brother, Murray, equally successful, living in America.

31st December 1991 Tuesday

New Year's Eve – Mr & Mrs Taylor, my next-door neighbours, invited Mrs Nicholls (widow), Cousin Enid & me to see the New Year in with them. We had a jolly time together & heard more of the tales they had to tell of life with the landed gentry, which they have experienced through Mr Taylor's interest in shooting.

He regularly visits Catton Hall in Staffordshire (near Alrewas) where he acts as a beater, etc. at the pheasant shoots. There he comes across anyone from Jackie Kennedy (widow of President Kennedy of the U.S.A.) to members of the British Royal Family.

* * *

60 years in the same house. And so another year ends with the old mirror on the wall reflecting a beautiful newly decorated room, leading to a delightful newly fitted kitchen: & the lady of the house, having reached three score years, now an ash blonde.

* * *

1992

1st January 1992 Wednesday
Every New Year's Day I love to listen to the "New Year's Day Concert from Vienna." The Vienna Philharmonic Orchestra plays all the great Strauss waltzes, polkas & gallops & we are transported to realms above.

Cocky & I shared a few magic moments listening to the music together, as he happened to telephone from Lancaster in the middle of the concert.

Remember his New Year Resolution last year, to give up smoking? It didn't last very long.

2nd January 1992 Thursday
"Happy New Year" said the old man to me. He was a total stranger who stepped aside for me to walk by in the narrow jitty.

"Happy New Year" said the girl in the Building Society, as she updated my account.

"Come in, to be wished Happy New Year" said Cousin Miles, as I walked by his house. There I was kissed by Miles & his mother Isobel.

It seemed as if the whole world was ready for a Happy New Year, unlike last year, when the whole world was poised for bloody battle.

"My view is that the most important thing in life is never to have too much of anything"

Terence - circa 190 – 159 B.C.

Or if you prefer – "Moderation in all things, and some things to excess"

4th January 1992 Saturday
The Royal Institution Christmas Lecture is given this year by Dr Richard Dawkins who explains & defends Darwin's Theory of Evolution.

Gone completely is God the Creator, as in the vastness of geological time we see ourselves gradually emerge from a blob of protoplasm.

"We all see upside-down" – so said Dr Richard Dawkins as he explained the evolution of the eye. Then we were shown a magnificent real live eagle, whose eyesight is reckoned to be the very best: - "He watches from his mountain walls, and like a thunderbolt he falls."

(Alfred Lord Tennyson)

I thought of Pooh Bah, in The Mikado, who could trace his ancestry back to a protoplasmal primordial atomic globule.

And then I thought of Christ who said, "Father, the hour is come ...... glorify thou me with thine own self with the glory which I had with thee before the world was." (John 17)

Snibston Discovery Park – Visitors will flock to North West Leicestershire with the opening in Coalville next June of Britain's largest ever science museum.

A huge display of technology & engineering will be just part of the new Snibston Discovery Park which is being built on the site of the former Snibston colliery.

The park should be open to the public on 27th June 1992. An official opening ceremony is to take place later in the year.

The museum will be just one of numerous attractions at the park – a nature trail & a special arena to host rallies & fairs.

A prize from E.R.N.I.E.   Bond Number 14HN 331400
Dear Bondholder, Congratulations, one of your Premium Bonds has won a prize and a warrant for the money is enclosed.

"Pay Miss E. Hewes Fifty Pounds Only"   Good luck in future draws – Alan McGill.

5th January, 2nd Sunday after Christmas
Surely goodness and mercy shall follow me all the days of my life; and I will dwell in the house of the Lord for ever   (Psalm 23)

10th January 1992 Friday
"They all absolutely adored her." This was "Matron" of Ashby Hospital, aged 63 in July 1975. Now, poor Matron, old & frail, is no longer able to walk following a heart attack 6 months ago. Her sisters in Yorkshire have taken her affairs in hand & are arranging nursing home accommodation.

12th January 1992 Sunday
Jonathon, Cocky's 18 year old son, has now passed his driving test. He passed last Thursday at the first attempt. He has left school, but is still without a job. He is one of many at the moment out of work. There are millions unemployed & for every vacancy there are scores of applicants.

14th January Tuesday
6 months of retirement & the most wonderful time of life. No longer forced to do what others would have you do. Free to do what you choose to do yourself, & a steady income to pay the bills. In summer time and in winter time it is absolutely lovely to be free as a bird.

16th January 1992 Thursday
"Six days shalt thou labour & do all thy work; but the seventh day is the Sabbath of the Lord thy God; in it thou shalt not do any work."

"Six years thou shalt sow thy field ..... but in the seventh year shall be a Sabbath of rest."

Six decades .... & in the seventh decade, we retire.

18th January 1992 Saturday
"So let it be written – so let it be done"

"Let it be written among the laws of the Persians and the Medes" Bible Radio has now reached the Book of Esther. What a story! To hear it read to perfection is a joy indeed. What a glorious Kingdom for Queen Esther (a Jewess) stretching from India even to Ethiopia.

Carried away from Jerusalem to Babylon with the captivity, Esther the little orphan was destined by her beauty to become Queen of the great Ahasuerus & live in sumptuous splendour. "The King loved Esther above all women & made a great feast unto all his princes & his servants, even Esther's Feast, & granted all her requests."

"And it was written ..." Thanks to Esther the Queen, the Jews in captivity were given preferential treatment. The King's scribes were called & it was written unto the

Jews & to the lieutenants & the deputies & the rulers of the provinces (127 provinces) from India to Ethiopia, to every people according to their language.

24th January 1992 Friday
Mount St Bernard Abbey again held an "Ecumenical Service" for this week of Christian Unity. And again I went with Katherine, now a sprightly 87 year old.
As on 24th January 1985 it was indeed wonderful to be intermingled with the monks, plus the added joy of having Leicester Cathedral Choir.

26th January 1992 Sunday
The Provost of Leicester Cathedral, the Very Revd. Alan Warren was the preacher at the Ecumenical Service held at the Monastery. Referring to Chap. 4 of St. Paul's Epistle to the Ephesians, he said we must endeavour to "**keep** the unity of the Spirit in the bond of peace". That unity is there already for us to keep.

28th January 1992 Tuesday
Happy Birthday to my ain wee darling – now 62.
Remember George, aged 62, who used to work for Mr Prew? A farmer here in Ravenstone, where Cocky worked – my very own Beloved Cocky.
But now a great gulf divides us & he is no longer mine.

30th January 1992 Thursday
"**Victory is of God**" – This was the watchword of Judas Maccabeus that great man of God whose many noble deeds are recorded in the Apocrypha – "As for the other things & noble acts which he did, and his greatness, they are not written; for they were very many".
The First Book of the Maccabees and the Second Book of the Maccabees help to bridge the gap between the Old & New Testament.
How about this excellent descriptive writing? – "Now when the sun shone upon the shields of gold & brass, the mountains glistered therewith & shined like lamps of fire".

3rd February 1992 Monday
Bible Radio! Every morning at 10-15a.m. for a quarter of an hour the Bible literally breaks forth into life. Can you imagine the story of Shadrach, Meshack & Abednego in the fiery furnace? (Daniel: Chapter 3) Never have I heard this story read so brilliantly and with such humour.
How thankful I am to be retired from work & able to enjoy Bible Radio each morning. The star cast of readers are really superb. Unlike those who read the Bible so solemnly in Church, they are free to act the role of all the eccentric characters, whispering in the King's ear, or giving vent to their emotions.

7th February 1992 Friday
"**Buy a Brick**" – More than 200 people chose to buy a brick engraved with their name.
The maze in Horsefair Street, Leicester, has now been completed & we who have become part of Leicester's history by being "immortalised in stone" are invited to the official opening on 14th February.

9th February 1992 Sunday
"To me the Provost is John Hughes. I cannot imagine anyone else".
So I wrote on Christmas Day 1977, & since then I have had to accept the Very Reverend Alan Warren as Provost of Leicester Cathedral. Now we are told – Provost is to retire. He will retire at Easter & will move to Hunstanton, Norfolk.
Not only is the Provost of Leicester Cathedral to retire – now we are told further that the Archdeacon of Loughborough is also to retire. Canon Hughie Jones endeared himself to us when he first introduced himself in October 1986 as "Your friendly Archdeacon". He will retire at the end of September.

14th February 1992 Friday
"A loving Valentine's Day wish to the one I love"
I dream of you every night and wish I could hold you tight. Therefore be my Valentine today & every day. Love for ever.

15th February 1992 Saturday
Former Treasurer Hewsie has been busy this week preparing all the necessary facts and figures for the new Treasurer to proceed with the business of receiving money for Coalville Amateurs' forthcoming production "Half a Sixpence". Hayley Smith, a new member, is the new Treasurer.

17th February 1992 Monday
Saunders, *Eric*, *of Greenhill Road, Coalville, passed peacefully away in hospital on February 8th 1992, aged 86 years, beloved husband of the late Madge, loving father of Ann and John, proud grandfather and great-grandfather. Funeral service at Hugglescote Parish Church on Monday February 17th at 11a.m. followed by cremation at Loughborough Crematorium. Family flowers only by request, donations if so desired may be sent direct to Age Concern, St. Martins, Leicester. Further inquiries to Coalville and District Funeral Service, 89 Belvoir Road, Coalville. Tel. 838600.*

This is Mr. Saunders, also a former Treasurer to Coalville Amateurs' & Hon. Life Member of the Society. He reigned supreme for many years; & a goodly contingent of older members attended his funeral.

19th February 1992 Wednesday
Spellbound by Taj Mahal! The Princess of Wales asked to be left entirely alone for a while to absorb the perfect peace & beauty of the Taj Mahal.
"Fascinating" she said, "A very healing experience". This most exquisite mausoleum at Agra was built by the Emperor Shah Jehan for his wife Mumtaz, who died in 1629.

21st February 1992 Friday
Oh, how I love the freedom of retirement. To breathe the pure fresh air of Charnwood Forest & walk the broad footpaths through bracken & woodland, to & from Beacon Hill, meandering here & there, enjoying distant views, & drinking in the whole delightful scene around me.

23rd February 1992 Sunday
"For ye shall go out with joy & be led forth with peace; the mountains & the hills shall break forth before you

into singing, & all the trees of the field shall clap their hands".

Now is not that the sort of applause to stir you to the very depths?

All this & more is in Isaiah, Chap. 55.

25th February 1992 Tuesday

In the Diocese of Leicester we have 13 deaneries: - Akeley West (Ashby), Akeley East (Loughborough), Akeley South (Coalville), Framland, Gartree I & II, Goscote, Guthlaxton I & II, Sparkenhoe West (Hinckley & Bosworth), Sparkenhoe East, Christianity North (Leicester North), Christianity South (Leicester South).

27th February 1992 Thursday

Twenty five years ago today I took a particular fancy to a certain garage man, but he remained quite aloof. Gosh, how I loved that man. He all but broke my heart, but now, a quarter of a century later, I can say again, as I said of Cocky in July 1973, "I never see him, & rarely give him a thought."

29th February 1992 Saturday

A day in Birmingham.

"Not my choice of a city" I said in February 1978, when it took me 2 hours to find Oozells Street. Now I know exactly where I am & really love the place. A major programme of pedestrianisation has transformed the city centre & given it new life.

While in Birmingham I searched out St. Chad's Roman Catholic Cathedral & had my sandwich lunch in the Kennedy Gardens, another oasis of peace in the heart of the bustling city.

I bought a little book, "Consecration to the Immaculate Heart of Mary" by St. Louis de Montfort.

4th March 1992 Wednesday

The whole world was consecrated to the Immaculate Heart of Mary on 31st October 1942 by Pope Pius XII. He thereby set in motion, as it were, the express train to the Heart of God. But we must board it of our own free will. He set up the ladder to heaven, which again, we ourselves must climb.

6th March 1992 Friday

"Half a Sixpence", Coalville Amateurs' show for this year, sees Brother Pat as House Manager, with me as Assistant House Manager. This is a pleasant little role, ensuring that all the 163 seats in the theatre are numbered correctly, & erecting various signs, then graciously receiving all the patrons.

8th March 1992 Sunday

"Graciously receiving all the patrons" is a joy indeed. "Half-a-sixpence" is a great success. We are blessed with a fresh new intake of talent & we "Elders" of the Society bask in their reflected glory. Resplendent in our matching attire, complete with long service medals, we line up like a guard of honour.

10th March 1992 Tuesday

As Assistant House Manager, I have yet another perspective of the theatre. I seem to be more aware of all the forces at work from far & near, all converging into one beautiful whole.

From as far away as Israel came red roses for my John of Lancaster to send to me. "Love forever, John"

12th March 1992 Thursday

Aunt Dos reaches the landmark of four score years & ten tomorrow. Having been at death's door three years ago, she has battled on to become a nonagenarian. But what a sad life it is. She spends all day & every day slumped in her chair & exists in a world of her own, almost forgotten by this world.

14th March 1992 Saturday

"For I am prudent" says the Lord. (Isaiah 10: 13)

The British Government love this word "prudent". It was well aired this week in Chancellor Norman Lamont's budget speech, even though he proposed a Public Sector Borrowing Requirement (P.S.B.R.) of £28 billion to see us through.

The fact is – Britain is struggling at the moment in a deep recession. The Conservatives have been in power for 13 years & are anxious about the outcome of the next General Election in a few weeks time. Borrowing £28 billion is not prudent, according to the Opposition, but a panic-stricken election bribe.

18th March 1992 Wednesday

"Beware the Bribes of March" – So warn the newspaper headlines on the Budget. Not that there is much to improve my somewhat limited financial affairs. Motor taxation has gone up from £100 to £110, & petrol has also gone up. Much of the high financial changes are way above me.

20th March 1992 Friday

Department of Social Security, Benefits Agency, Central Pensions Branch, Newcastle-upon-Tyne. Dear Sir or Madam, I am writing to say that from 6th April 1992, the rate of your pension will be increased from £56 – 26p to £59 – 82p per week. (A welcome £15 extra per month)

22nd March 1992 Sunday

"I shall light a candle of understanding in thine heart" II Esdras 14. Was ever there a more godly man than Esdras, the scribe who studied the law & commandments of God & taught all the people? And yet he dared to challenge God, & ask why the world was in such a state.

"Surely it would have been better not to have given the earth to Adam; or else, when it was given to him, to have restrained him from sinning?"

"Why could not God have made those that have been made, those that are here now & those who are yet to come, at once, & thus have Judgement day sooner?"

These were but 2 of the questions posed by Esdras, who also said, "I know that the Lord is merciful & patient. I know that he is bountiful & that he pardoneth, otherwise that would be the end of most of us." It was the Archangel Uriel who came to enlighten him.

28th March 1992 Saturday

"Two Gentlemen of Verona" – what a lovely light-hearted tale of love & heartache, told as only Shakespeare could tell.

Even Launce, the servant of one of these gentlemen, is smitten by love of a milkmaid, & recites a "cat-log" of her virtues & vices, including one vice – "she has no teeth".

30th March 1992 Monday
35 YEARS WED

Cocky married 1957

Cocky & Joan today celebrate their Coral Wedding Anniversary

1st April 1992 Wednesday
How much has the Poll Tax wasted? £14 billion! 30% in extra staff, buildings, computers, plus sky-high collection costs & sundry sweeteners. This amounts to £350 per adult & still there are many who refuse to pay. My Poll Tax for this year is £268.

3rd April 1992 Friday
The new Provost of Leicester Cathedral will be Canon Derek Hole, at present Vicar of St. James the Greater, Leicester. Aged 58, and a bachelor, he has been priest in charge at St. James the Greater since 1973.
I'm sure Shakespeare would find words to take us from A. Warren to De'Hole.

5th April 1992 Sunday
"Love's Labour Lost" – I was prompted to read this delightful Shakespearean play following a quote by Conservative leader John Major in one of his verbal attacks on Labour leader Neil Kinnock – "He draweth out the thread of his verbosity finer than the staple of his argument."   (Act V, Scene I)

7th April 1992 Tuesday
"Love's Labour Lost" – And yet another win for the Conservatives.
For the first time in the 20th century, one party has won four successive General Elections. With mass unemployment & the country in deep recession, it was almost more than they dared hope.

9th April 1992 Thursday
Euro Disney, located on a 5,000 acre site, 20 miles east of Paris, will open on Sunday 12th April 1992. Construction will continue at the Euro Disneyland Theme Park until the year 2017.

11th April 1992 Saturday
Astronaut Helen Sharman said of her amazing experience, "While I was up there I really felt as though I had seen infinity. The stars seemed to go on forever."
Orbiting the earth she witnessed 16 days & 16 nights every 24 hours. From outer space the scenes were a beautiful blue, unlike the blue we see.

14th April 1992 Tuesday
Appeal Fails
The Israeli Supreme Court rejected an appeal yesterday by Mordechai Vanunu, the scientist jailed for 18 years in 1988 for revealing atomic secrets.   (newspaper cutting)
This is Mr Mordechai Vanunu, who appeared in my diary exactly four years ago.
How very sad that he – **a man of peace** – must suffer so much as a prisoner of conscience in Jeru-salem (=peace)

"Vanunu was hijacked in Rome ITL 30/9/86, 2100. Came to Rome by BA FLY 504"
These sad words were written by Mordechai Vanunu on the palm of his hand in December 1986 while he was in a car being taken to court in Jerusalem. He was secretly smuggled back to Israel from Italy in September 1986 after breaking the Israel Official Secrets Act to tell the world that his country (Israel) had stockpiled the world's 6th largest armoury of nuclear warheads.
As the vehicle bringing him from his top security prison slowed to go down the lane behind the East Jerusalem Court, where he was to appear, he flattened the palm of his hand against the window. Before his guards could pull his hand away the message had been photographed.
It seems that Mordechai Vanunu was lured from Britain to Italy by a blonde girl called Cindy who had befriended him in London.

Extract from Alfred Nobel's Will
"... The whole of my remaining realizable estate shall be dealt with in the following way:
the capital, invested in safe securities by my executors, shall constitute a fund, the interest on which shall be annually distributed in the form of prizes to those who, during the preceding year, shall have conferred the greatest benefit on mankind.
The said interest shall be divided into five equal parts, which shall be apportioned as follows:
One part to the person who shall have made the most important discovery or invention within the field of physics; one part to the person who shall have made the most important chemical discovery or improvement; one part to the person who shall have made the most important discovery within the domain of physiology or medicine; one part to the person who shall have produced in the field of literature the most outstanding work of an idealistic tendency; and one part to the person who shall have done the most or the best work for fraternity between nations, for the abolition or reduction of standing armies and for the holding & promotion of peace progress."
Paris, 27th November, 1895
Alfred Bernhard Nobel

15th April 1992 Wednesday
Five thousand miles and more – I have walked, thanks entirely to Dr Stutman who wrote "The Walking Book". When I was at work I walked round the village every day (1½ miles). Having now retired from work I have the great pleasure of walking further afield.

17th April 1992 Friday
From the narrow confines of life behind an office desk, it is so lovely to be able to do a hundred & one other things in the daytime, & to be more aware of current affairs.
There are excellent daily programmes on television "Today in Parliament". There is time to read – time to explore – time to do whatever you like.

19th April 1992 Easter Sunday
Bunting, now a widow aged 76, has booked a short holiday in Harrogate with me as her companion. We are booked in at the "Alexa House Hotel" 26 Ripon Road, Harrogate, for 4 nights commencing 21st April.

"Britain's largest & most beautiful early spring flower show" is there this week.

21ˢᵗ April Tuesday
Bunting & I set off on our little holiday in Harrogate, in my 5 year old silver metro car E479 EAY. We are staying at the Alexa House Hotel, a Victorian house built for the Baron-de-Ferrier. We have a single bedroom each, complete with en-suite facilities, TV, radio, etc.

23ʳᵈ April Thursday
What a lovely holiday we are having. An afternoon in Knaresborough, which is one of the most beautiful places you could wish to visit. A whole day at Harrogate's 65ᵗʰ Spring Flower Show. And tomorrow we hope to visit dear old Ripon with its mighty cathedral; & a guided tour of Fountains Abbey.

Princess Anne, Queen Elizabeth's only daughter, is granted a divorce from Captain Mark Phillips.

25ᵗʰ April 1992 Saturday
And so ends our little holiday in Harrogate which was certainly spiritually uplifting. Never have I seen such exquisite flower arrangements. They had been judged by experts whose comments were most enlightening. Then our guide at Fountains Abbey inspired us further, by bringing the ruins to life again.

27ᵗʰ April 1992 Monday
"Heaven on Earth" – The Natural Law Party is a new political party whose goal is for everyone to enjoy Heaven on Earth through the implementation of Maharishi Mahesh's programme of Transcendental Meditation. Their splendid H.Q. is Mentmore, Bucks, built by Rothschilds.

29ᵗʰ April 1992 Wednesday
"Classical Spectacular" – Having enjoyed the "Opera Spectacular" last year at Birmingham's vast N.E.C. Arena, with its seating capacity of 12,681, we ventured to the equally vast National Indoor Arena at Birmingham for another superb "Spectacular" – Enid driving & me navigating. Needless to say, we got hopelessly lost.

1ˢᵗ May 1992 Friday
In the year 1750, Lancelot Brown, better known as Capability Brown, for his habit of saying a place had "capabilities", designed a garden, a natural landscape, for the 2ⁿᵈ Earl of Egremont at Petworth Park, West Sussex, but it got no further than the drawing board. Now, from the original drawings, the dream comes true

3ʳᵈ May 1992 Sunday
"Go you through the town to Frogmore" – Katherine & I have again booked with Viking Coaches for the once a year opportunity to visit the Queen's private gardens.
This has given added meaning to my reading of Shakespeare's "Merry Wives of Windsor", written for Queen Elizabeth I, for her express delight & amusement.

5ᵗʰ May 1992 Tuesday
By taxi from Coalville to Colchester Crematorium for the funeral of Mary Moore who died in Colchester General Hospital on 27ᵗʰ April, following a perforated ulcer & subsequent cardiac arrest. Molly & Joyce, her

friends since school days, went with me by taxi.
So ends another link with the past.

7ᵗʰ May 1992 Thursday
County Hall, London, the former Greater London County Council headquarters in prime position on the south bank of the River Thames, has now been sold for £200 million (Ecu 280 million) to the Japanese Shirayama Corporation for a hotel, residential & conference complex.

9ᵗʰ May 1992 Saturday
A day in London! Went on a coach trip, where we were dropped in Park Lane. This gave me the opportunity to circumnavigate Mayfair & Soho, walking the length of Park Lane, Piccadilly and Haymarket, to Trafalgar Square, Charing Cross Road & Oxford Street.
I bought a book, "Myths of Greece & Rome" - £10.

11ᵗʰ May 1992 Monday
Gosh! Was there ever a family tree like that of great Jupiter, whose illustrious progeny came from his union with so many varied and different partners? From his union with Eurynome came the Three Graces – Euphrosyne, Aglaia & Thalia, seen on the latest Five Ecu coins.

Antonio Canova's famous sculpture of the Three Graces is valued today at £7.6 million. It was commissioned in 1817 by the Duke of Bedford for the Temple of Graces in the grounds of Woburn Abbey. It is now jointly owned by the National Galleries of Scotland and V & A.

13ᵗʰ May 1992 Wednesday
The Muses, not to be confused with the Graces, were the daughters of Jupiter & Mnemosyne. There were nine – Calliope - the muse of epic poetry, Clio - of history, Euterpe - of lyric poetry, Melpone - of tragedy, Terpsichore - of choral dance & song, Erato - of love poetry, Polyhymnia - of sacred poetry, Urania - of astronomy & Thalia - of comedy.

15ᵗʰ May 1992 Friday
Venus, also known as Aphrodite, was the daughter of Jupiter & Dione.
Mercury was the son of Jupiter & Maia.
Cupid was the son of Venus & Mercury.
Jupiter, through other liaisons, was the father of Mars, Apollo, Diana, Bacchus & mighty Hercules, renowned for all his heroic deeds.

17ᵗʰ May 1992 Sunday
"Do I not fill heaven & earth? saith the Lord. I have heard what the prophets said, that prophecy lies in my name, saying I have dreamed, I have dreamed. The prophet that hath a dream, let him tell a dream; & he that hath my word, let him speak my word faithfully." Jeremiah 23 : 24.

19ᵗʰ May 1992 Tuesday
F. A. Cup Final – Liverpool, who won the F.A. Cup in 1965, 1974, 1986 & 1989, have now gained their fifth victory by beating Second Division Sunderland 2 – 0.
The game was shown on TV to 60 nations, including U.S.A.

21st May 1992 Thursday

Another day in London. Caught the 6 a.m. train & enjoyed my morning walk from St. Pancras to the Science Museum, South Kensington (4 miles). Discovered new delights all along the way, especially "The Fountains" at the end of the Serpentine & the squirrels in Kensington Gardens.

23rd May 1992 Saturday

My interest in DNA (Deoxyribonucleic Acid) led me to the Science Museum where there was a special DNA exhibition. I bought a little book, "The Double Helix" – an account of the discovery of the structure of DNA.
Also at the SPCK shop I bought "The Rule of Saint Benedict" & N.I.V. Bible.

25th May 1992 Monday

It was our guide at Fountains Abbey who prompted me to buy "The Rule of St. Benedict". So imbued with the scriptures was St. Benedict that their teaching & very words are all interwoven into his Rule. Only a "Rule" founded on love could have stood the test of 15 centuries, as this Rule has done.

27th May 1992 Wednesday

"Seven times a day do I praise thee" (Psalm 119 : 164)
Thus St. Benedict says in his Rule: - This sacred number of seven will be performed by us if we carry out the duties of our service at Lauds, Prime, Terce, Sext, None, Vespers and Compline; & at night get up to praise Him.

29th May 1992 Friday

In the course of one week, the monks who follow the Rule of St. Benedict, including our monks at Mount St. Bernard's Abbey, sing every Psalm, following the same daily pattern. Three psalms are sung at each service except Vespers when four psalms are sung. Long psalms are subdivided.

31st May 1992 Sunday

"You shall go out with joy" (Isaiah 55) "and all the trees of the field shall clap their hands."
This exhilarating new hand-clapping hymn was sung at Charnborough Road Baptist Church, Coalville, where we assembled to see 11 year old Elisabeth Joy Emmett totally immersed in Holy Baptism & Confirmation.

2nd June 1992 Tuesday

Leicester's new £8 million magistrates court building, on the corner of Pocklington's Walk & Newark Street, became operational yesterday. This replaces the old courts at the Town Hall and at Leicester Castle. Features include underground parking for magistrates & high security cells for prisoners.

4th June 1992 Thursday

Leicester's ancient Castle County Magistrates Court, which has now closed down, was a seat of judgement from as far back as 1274.
The County Magistrates & City Magistrates are now one single administrative unit known as the Leicester Division. The new courthouse has 10 courts for Leicester's Division.

6th June 1992 Saturday
35th Milk Race Tour of Britain

The great exciting Milk Race this year by-passed Leicester completely.

8th June 1992 Monday

Meet Internal Auditor Hewsie. At the Annual General Meeting of Coalville Amateur Operatic Society, brother Pat relinquished his long held role of Internal Auditor. So I now hold two minor offices – Assistant House Manager & joint Internal Auditor with Basil Newbold.

10th June 1992 Wednesday

A day of discovery. Caught the 6 a.m. train to London – a 3 mile morning walk from St. Pancras, through the very heart of the city to Liverpool Street Station & on to Colchester where I spent 6 hours browsing here, there & everywhere, including a delightful guided walk.

12th June 1992 Friday

"What is life?" My little book "The Double Helix" explains in simple language how some 40 years ago scientists first solved the structure of DNA. They had then found the secret of life. Deoxyribonucleic acid (DNA) is a molecule found in the cells of living things.
Professor Alec Jeffreys in 1984 = DNA fingerprints (see 13th November 1987)

14th June 1992 Trinity Sunday
Rosary – Reparation – Consecration.

These three were the vital ingredients referred to by the Virgin Mary at Fatima (Portugal) in 1917. Praying without distraction – aligning your will to that of God – and renewing the vows & promises which were made at Holy Baptism & again at Confirmation.

16th June 1992 Tuesday

"There's a quart d'ecu for you".
Having acquired the United Kingdom ECU set of coins, including one quarter ecu, & being told that ECU is an abbreviation of the term European Currency Unit, I find that the ecu was around even in Shakespeare's time, as quoted in "All's Well that Ends Well".

18th June 1992 Thursday

Shakespeare for 4 year olds! A revolutionary scheme aimed at teaching Shakespeare to school children as young as 4 years old is to be launched in Leicestershire. The county's education authority has joined forces with the Royal Society of Arts for a pilot scheme due to start in September.

19th June 1992 Friday

Hewes, Peter Martin, of Main Street, Netherseal, a much loved husband of Jacqueline, devoted father of Sarah, Kirsty and Emma, beloved son of Phyllis and the late Donald, brother of Lesley and Susan, passed peacefully away after a very brave fight, on June 12th 1992, at home, aged 50 years. The funeral service will be held at St. Peter's Church, Netherseal, on Friday June 19th at 11 a.m., followed by cremation. Family flowers only please, donations in lieu, if so desired, for the Patient's Amenities Fund, Meacham Medical Unit, and all inquiries may be sent to J.P. Springthorpe and Co., Castle Lodge, South Street, Ashby-de-la-Zouch.

On the day that Auntie Cis would have been 100 years old (19th June) we attended the funeral of Peter. His poor mother Phyl, in her wheelchair, wept as the preacher said that God knew what "seeing your son die" meant.

20th June 1992 Saturday
"O, had I but followed the arts!" exclaims Sir Andrew Ague-Cheek in Shakespeare's Twelfth Night. Now, thanks to Mr Maurice Gilmour the drama advisor to Leicestershire County Council, young children are to be given the opportunity to know & love Shakespeare, starting with simplified plays.

22nd June 1992 Monday
Father, to small boy, reading school report, "Same old notes on your report! Could do better!!"
Small boy, "See…… there's hope for me yet!"

24th June 1992 Wednesday
Needless to say, I did not receive an invitation to the Garden Party at Buckingham Palace, as originally expected (July 1984). My 40 years service was not considered worthy of any such recognition.
I am reminded of the letter I received in July 1971, "…….. you have not been recommended."

26th June 1992 Friday
How wonderful to know the Rule of Saint Benedict. If we could all behave as monks learn to behave, what a different world it would be. What amazing discipline; what true humility; what obedience. Possessing absolutely nothing & yet possessing heaven itself – quietly & serenely climbing the ladder heavenwards.

2nd July 1992 Thursday
An impromptu private guided tour of Nottingham's magnificent Council House where the city fathers conduct their business. Councillor C. A. Clarke, former Lord Mayor, showed me the great ballroom, the civic silver & the council chamber, where I sat in the Lord Mayor's seat.
I learned also that Nottingham still maintains its famous Sheriff of Nottingham, elected annually, & I was invited to sit in his seat in the council chamber. How I loved looking through the windows on to the scene in the square below, as on 5th June 1984.
This year Nottingham City & County are commemorating the 350th anniversary of the English Civil War. It was in August 1642 that King Charles I raised his personal standard at Nottingham Castle & the Civil War began. So it is a summer of pageantry, entertainment & drama.

8th July 1992 Wednesday
"For me the Commons has never been just a career. It's my life" – so said 62 year old Miss Betty Boothroyd, recently elected the 155th Speaker of the House of Commons. For the past five years she has been Deputy Speaker, but this is the first time ever that we have had a woman Speaker.

10th July 1992 Friday
Joanne, now 18 years of age, has a boy friend named Glen. She poured out her troubles to me when she discovered that she had an unwanted pregnancy. She could not wait to arrange for an abortion & went through torments of body & mind in an eventual miscarriage-cum-abortion.

12th July 1992 Sunday
Collision at the Cross Roads!
Driving home from visiting Aunt Dos at Markfield Court Nursing Home, with brother Pat as passenger, we arrived at Hugglescote Cross Roads to find the traffic lights out of action & crossing the junction we were hit from the left & knocked into a 3rd car.

14th July 1992 Tuesday
A subdued 61st birthday after last year's bonanza.
Fortunately no-one was injured in our 3 vehicle collision the other day, but all 3 cars took a bashing. My 5 year old silver Metro E479 EAY is now at Parkin & Jones garage waiting for the report from the insurance company re. the damage.

16th July 1992 Thursday
"Dear Sir,
Re - Vehicle E479 EAY
We have received the engineer's report which indicates that the vehicle is damaged beyond economic repair. The pre-accident market value is assessed at £2,725 which we are prepared to offer ……"
Yours faithfully, Zurich Insurance.

18th July 1992 Saturday
"In a Monastery Garden" – Katherine & I enjoyed an afternoon at Mount St. Bernard Abbey where people from far and near assembled on the lawns in the summer sunshine for a "pilgrimage" organised by local Anglican Churches. Brother Gabriel provided tea for us.

20th July 1992 Monday
Buried Treasure! – The largest haul of Roman coins ever found in Leicestershire has been unearthed about a mile away from my house.
2,784 coins, some bearing the head of Probus, Roman Emperor from 276 – 282A.D, were discovered in a broken pot buried on a building site near Hoo Ash.

22nd July 1992 Wednesday
Marriage Split – The noble Duke of York & his wife Sarah who were married exactly 6 years ago, have now parted company.
The poor old royal family is struggling to hold its own. Prince Charles, heir to the throne, & Princess Diana live separate lives.

24th July 1992 Friday
"The Merry Wife of Windsor" – Lady Helen Windsor, aged 28, daughter of the Duke & Duchess of Kent, has married her 29 year old sweetheart Tim Taylor, an art dealer. The wedding took place last Saturday at St. George's Chapel, Windsor, & was conducted by the Dean of Windsor, the Very Revd. P. Mitchell.

26th July 1992 Sunday
In the Diocese of Leicester we have 13 deaneries. Members of the Leicester Diocesan Synod have now agreed to appoint a part time youth officer in each of the 13 deaneries in an attempt to woo the younger

generation into the church. Young people find church boring & want more active Christianity.

Life is one long balancing act. The role of the church's new part time youth officers is to find out what are the type of questions young people are asking & see if they can work towards a balance of keeping the tradition of the church with the values of today's technologically-orientated society.

30th July 1992 Thursday

Invincible Spirit! - Loughborough pigeon expert, Mr Michael Massarella has just paid £110,800 for this 4 year old pigeon.

Invincible Spirit recently won the Barcelona International & will now be used for breeding purposes.

1st August 1992 Saturday

Today the new cars have the prefix "K". My new car is K49 PUT, a Peugeot 106 – XR.

The choice of a Peugeot was because my garage Parkin & Jones are Peugeot dealers.

Costing £7,413 plus £250 for an alarm system, I have paid half, with the remainder spread over the next 12 months.

(*Note by Mary Blue – Enid took one look at the new car and said, "It's KAPUT!"*)

3rd August 1992 Monday

"A drum, a drum! Macbeth doth come!"

Katherine & I have booked to see "Macbeth" this week at the Theatre Royal, Nottingham.

This is another of Shakespeare's plays with outrageous stage directions such as: - "Witches vanish" – "The Ghost of Banquo rises" – "Ghost disappears" – "Enter with Macbeth's head".

Shakespeare reminds us in "Macbeth" that "Life's but a walking shadow; a poor player that struts and frets his hour upon the stage & then is heard no more; it is a tale told by an idiot, full of sound & fury, signifying nothing." The scene is set at Macbeth's castle, Inverness.

7th August 1992 Friday

"Macbeth, probably the greatest & most famous murder story ever." What a play! How we sat spellbound in the theatre. It was Macduff who moved me to tears when he learned what had happened to his wife & children – "Did heaven look on, and would not take their part?" (Act 4.)

9th August 1992 Sunday

"Chad Varah – The Good Samaritan" – This evening on television we were introduced to the Anglican priest who founded the Samaritans. The Reverend Dr. Edward Chad Varah – O.B.E., born 12th November 1911, is currently Rector of the Lord Mayor's Parish Church of St. Stephen in the City of London.

11th August 1992 Tuesday

"Pill for the Pigeons" – The city of Milan has more pigeons than it can cope with. Droppings from an estimated 400,000 pigeons are eating away at historic monuments & churches, particularly the famous Gothic Cathedral. So now the pigeons face mass deportation & also contraceptive pills.

13th August 1992 Thursday

Meet Elizabeth Hewes – Friend of the Settle – Carlisle Line. Having recently enjoyed a wonderful 400 mile round trip by chartered train from Leicester to Carlisle & back by the famous Settle to Carlisle Line, I paid £4 to become one of the "Friends of the Settle – Carlisle Line".

14th August 1992 Friday

On this day in history in 1040, Macbeth slew King Duncan of Scotland and succeeded him.

15th August 1992 Saturday

Cordon Bleu Hewsie is now into the full swing of cooking. Having replaced the table top size cooker with a proper full size "circa-fan" cooker, plus four hot plates, and enjoying the freedom of retirement, it is wonderful to be able to produce exciting & interesting meals, with home made delicacies.

17th August 1992 Monday

Mary Moore, who had such a wonderful memory, is now in the home of the Blessed & will be visiting me no more. How I miss her annual pilgrimage to Ravenstone. It is hard to imagine that all that vast accumulation of knowledge she had amassed over the years can never be tapped again.

19th August 1992 Wednesday

Bible Radio! – And so we come to the last book in the Bible – The Revelation of St. John the Divine: - "Blessed is the one who reads the words of this prophecy, and blessed are those who hear it and take it to heart what is written in it, because the time is near." Revelation 1 : 3.

22nd August 1992 Saturday

1642 – August 22: *King Charles raises his Standard at Nottingham.*

King Charles I did not gain the support of the good people of Nottingham. Many a skirmish took place between the Roundheads of Nottingham & the Royalists, including "Willoughby Field".

"History provides the finest marketing platform that anyone could devise" – so said Geoffrey Davies, alias Henry VII, in August 1985. I thought of his words as I stood at the entrance of Nottingham Castle & watched the impressive procession of armed men & horses leading King Charles I up the hill.

24th August 1992 Monday

On this day in 1572 the St. Bartholomew's Day Massacre took place in Paris – the killing of thousands of French Huguenots, by order of the Catholic French Court.

25th August 1992 Tuesday

40,000 to wed – the South Korean-based Unification Church is to break the record it had set for mass weddings by marrying 20,000 couples from 81 nations in Seoul's Olympic Stadium today.

Bible Radio! – While 20,000 brides appear together in Seoul's Olympic Stadium, we end our year long Bible reading with a glimpse of heaven itself. "Come," says the Angel, "I will show you the bride of the Lamb."

27th august 1992 Thursday

Not to be outdone by King Charles I, the Royal Mail announce that they too are now "Raising the Standard". Apart from official business, they support numerous good causes including the planting of 10,000 trees in the "Royal Mail Wood" in our new forest.

29th August 1992 Saturday
Joseph Hewes (1730 – 1779)

The present I have chosen for brother Pat's 74th birthday – a brief history of the name Hewes – tells us that one of our illustrious forebears from North Carolina was one of the founding fathers who signed the American Declaration of Independence.

31st August 1992 Monday

Siamese twins Chang & Eng Bunker (1811 – 1874) eventually bought a farm in a remote area of Mount Airy, Wilkes County, North Carolina, where they met & married Adelaide & Sarah Yates, the daughters of a local farmer.

Chang & Adelaide had ten children. Eng & Sarah had eleven children. (See 11th May 1994)

2nd September4 1992 Wednesday

"The Tempest" – Who like Shakespeare, could describe a storm at sea?

The King of Naples & all his retinue returning from the wedding of his daughter in Tunis are shipwrecked. "This Tunis, sir, was Carthage."

Who like Shakespeare could give such stage directions as "Enter Ariel, invisible"?

4th September 1992 Friday

And another Norman Church!

Visiting Bunting so often in her home on the outskirts of Stafford, we have discovered the dear little Norman Church of St. Chad's, tucked away in the centre of the town, midst all the comings & goings of the shops. A perfect example of "Christ in the midst". (See 20th April 1982)

6th September 1992 Sunday

Radio Pilgrim's Progress! Following on immediately from Bible Radio which covered the whole Bible from Genesis to Revelation, we are now being treated to a superb rendering of Pilgrim's Progress, which itself is written almost as a play, with the most delightful & extravagant characters.

8th September 1992 Tuesday

"Merry Wives of Windsor" – To Stratford-on-Avon where we saw the Royal Shakespeare Company perform to perfection this hilarious comedy.

How Shakespeare would have appreciated the interpretation of his play, especially the jealous husband Mr. Ford, who went berserk with rage.

10th September 1992 Thursday

As in September 1973, I enjoyed "An Armchair Voyage Round the World" through someone else's travels, so now I am enjoying through television the latest voyage "Around the World with Thomas Cook". It is almost as good as being there in person, without all the hassle of getting there & having to pay £20,000.

12th September 1992 Saturday

Radio Pilgrim's Progress – How John Bunyan would have enjoyed hearing his great story brought to life each morning on the radio.

We have now come as far as Mr By-ends. You never heard such a brilliant character portrayal. "As very a knave in our company as dwelleth in all these parts"

14th September 1992 Monday

The heaviest object ever moved by man was the 1.5 million tonne Gullfaks C oil production platform, one of Norway's 50 platforms in the North Sea. The Troll platform, due on site in 1996, will be heavier still.

The big problem will come when these giants come to the end of their working life. What then?

North Sea ageing oil rigs will need to be demolished, but how? And at what astronomical cost? Norway's oil industry is already gearing up for a technological & financial headache. And it is estimated that eventually in Britain too, more civil servants will be employed planning rig disposals than planning new oilfields.

18th September 1992 Friday

Today I saw Stone Henge! Enjoying a few days holiday with cousin Enid, and staying at Bath, we experienced the magic of the great stones. Like a water diviner I held two metal rods which moved of their own accord in response to the magnetic forces of this sacred site.

Stonehenge and the surrounding 30 acres of land was sold at auction for £6,600 to Mr C. H. Chubb who later presented it to the nation in 1915.

20th September 1992 Sunday

17 years ago I was given a family heirloom by Cousin Audrey to be kept in the family – a china tea service which had been given to her mother as a wedding present by the Revd. Gerald Vandeleur. This has now been given to Mary Blue for safe keeping & for further handing down.

22 September 1992 Tuesday

With one garden wall that has withstood the elements for almost a century; I have accepted Bob Parker's quotation for £1,500 for complete renovation. At the same time he will tackle the derelict rear quarters of the house to include a new toilet, for a further £2,500.

24th September Thursday

"Little Nook"- Having obtained the Deeds of the House from the solicitor, to peruse at leisure, I have been fascinated by all that they reveal. Where I have lived all my life was once part of a field of land called "Little Nook" bought by my Grandpa in 1897.

26th September 1992 Saturday

"Little Nook" is the name I have given to 27 Leicester Road, Ravenstone. Bought in 1897 by George Harry Hewes and transferred over the years to his wife; to their son Reg; to his wife; and to me. The land is 18 feet wide & 198 feet long (6 yards x 66 yards).

This is my home, 396 square yards.

28th September 1992 Monday

Uncle Fred's grandson Miles celebrates his 46th birthday today, having worn the mantle of his grandfather for one year & having immersed himself so fully in his family heritage that his wife Sarah has upped & gone back to her mother.

"I know just how she feels," said Cocky.

30 September 1992 Wednesday

While I spend £4,000 transforming the dilapidated rear quarters of "Little Nook", Enid is likewise spending £4,000 on her home, No. 50 Leicester Road, Ravenstone. Every window in her home has now been replaced by de luxe double glazed windows, matching the others to perfection.

2nd October 1992 Friday

Mary Blue, aged 48, cousin Miles, aged 46, & I, spent much of the day at Leicestershire's Record Office delving into the old records & discovering all manner of interesting facts about our local history. It was so interesting to read the Census of 1891 where we found Uncle Fred, aged 6, & my dad, aged 2.

4th October 1992 Sunday

Harvest & Patronal Festival combined again this year at Ravenstone, so again the great Archangel Michael & all the angels were ignored.

But at least I had the pleasure of the company of cousin Miles – an elegant, well spoken, well mannered "young man" all on his own at the moment.

6th October 1992 Tuesday

"Service of Thanksgiving for all Creatures Great & Small" – Again Katherine, Toffee & I attended this service in Leicester, where the preacher was the Bishop of Leicester, Thomas Butler. Are there animals in heaven? "Oh yes" said the Bishop. See Revelation, Chap. 4.

"For God created man to be immortal, and made him to be an image of his own eternity"

(The Wisdom of Solomon, Chapter 2, verse 23. The Apocrypha.)

Do animals go to heaven?

The answer is no. All living things have souls – the soul being the animating and vital principle of life. In earth we have three degrees of life: plant life, animal life and human life. An animal has a soul but that soul is mortal, finite; it dies with the death of the animal. An animal, therefore, has no potential whatsoever for life after death. Only humans possess an immortal soul, made in the image of God. Only we have the potential or possibility, by God's grace, of entering into the everlasting happiness of heaven. Rev A Winn, Pontefract, W Yorks. (Newspaper cutting)

8th October 1992 Thursday

Film star Elizabeth Taylor, like me, celebrated her 60th birthday at an amusement park.

Her birthday in February was celebrated at Disneyland in Anaheim, California. She took over the whole park for 1,000 guests & paid £500,000 for her birthday bash, for adults only.

10th October 1992 Saturday

Nicholls, Kathleen. Wife of the late Frank, much loved mother and grandmother, passed away October 3rd after an illness bravely borne. Funeral at Ravenstone Parish Church on Friday October 9th 1992 at 12-30p.m., followed by cremation. Family flowers only please, donations if desired to the Sue Ryder Foundation, Staunton Harold Hall, via the family.

This is my near neighbour for many years.

She lived at the other end of our row of houses & saw the new year in with me both last year & the year before. Little did we think then that she would die.

12 October 1992 Monday

You may have noticed that I try to write my diary, using the 6 lines provided, making each entry fit as precisely as possible in the space allowed.

Very occasionally I hit the jackpot when I achieve this in one single sentence. You can see an example of this at the top of the page – 1989.

Note by Mary Blue – Betty's diaries were mainly written in 5 year diaries with the 5 years running concurrently – hence 12th October 1989 was at the top of this page.

She also kept a separate "Travel Journal" after she retired, which I have transcribed in a separate volume.

14th October 1992 Wednesday

"The Black Death" – This was the headline this morning as British Coal axed 31 coal mines in one fell swoop. It is the most sweeping closure programme since post-war nationalisation, & miners, who in 1984 caused havoc when they went on strike, are now devastated.

British Coal is no longer king. Power generating companies today are moving away from coal because gas-fired stations are cheaper to build & less vulnerable to industrial action. British coal also contains 1.5% of sulphur & when burnt in furnaces the sulphur turns to sulphur dioxide.

18th October 1992 Sunday

Installation of Canons!

What a pleasure it was for me to be escorted to Leicester Cathedral by cousin Miles for the installation of G. K. J. Moore as Lay Canon, together with 2 other Honorary Canons.

A truly majestic service which was interpreted in sign language for a party of deaf people.

20th October 1992 Tuesday

"My heart is framed in black" – I wept to read the sad life story of the great Swedish scientist Alfred Nobel (1833 – 1896). He was fabulously rich but desperately lonely; and he did not enjoy good health. All alone in the sleepless hours of the night, he longed for a kindred spirit.

"Everything in this mean world can be explained, except possibly the magnetism of hearts, to which that same world owes its continued existence. It would seem that I lack this magnetic quality, since there is no such person as Madame Alfred Nobel."

No wonder I wept.

24th October 1992 Saturday

King Henry V - Saw on television the 1945 film version

of this wonderful play, starring Sir Laurence Olivier. Following the script with my "Complete Works of William Shakespeare" I was able to savour every minute of it & marvel yet again at the skills of our greatest actors & the skills of our greatest writer.

26th October 1992 Monday

Having "won" the forest, we are now asked to donate £100,000 in order to plant 50,000 young trees (£2 per tree) on three sites in Leicestershire – Willesley Wood, Coleorton & Western Park in Leicester. £2 pays for planting, after care & initial preparation & fertilising the sites.

28th October 1992 Wednesday

"Wasteland to Wonderland" – Leicester Mercury reporter **John Marsden** gives us a detailed account of our New National Forest. There will be 30,000 trees at Willesley Wood, 10,000 at Coleorton & 10,000 at Western Park, Leicester. **"WE'LL STUMP UP FOR WOODY" by John Marsden**

30th October 1992 Friday

Senior Leicestershire County Council Forester, Mr Nick Fell, is the "architect" of the New Forest. He has devised a series of woodlands, glades and pathways whereby important lines of vision are maintained. So when you enjoy the delights of this New Forest, think of old Nick & all of us who gave it birth.

1st November 1992 Sunday

All Saints' Day – Cousin Miles & I went to Leicester Cathedral for the Collation & Installation of the Reverend Prebendary Ian Thomas Stanes as Archdeacon of Loughborough.

St. Michael and All Angels Church, Ravenstone, requires a minimum of £100,000 for a major restoration scheme. Work on the first phase of repairs to the roof will commence in the next few months. Supporters of the church have planned a series of fund-raising events.

3rd November 1992 Tuesday

John Montagu, 4th Earl of Sandwich, was born on this day, 3rd November in 1718 A.D.

The sandwich was named after him in 1762 A.D. when he spent 24 hours at a gaming table & could only snatch refreshment from a passing footman. He absentmindedly put a slice of cold beef between 2 slices of toast.

5th November 1992 Thursday

Talking Newspaper! – The Royal Leicestershire, Rutland & Wycliffe Society for the Blind advertised recently for new readers of the "Coalville Times" Talking Newspaper. So there are now 5 teams each with 5 readers & I am delighted to be in one of the teams.

7th November 1992 Saturday

Carthusian Monks! – The re-establishment of the Catholic hierarchy in England took place in 1850. The Carthusian Order, founded by St. Bruno in 1086, returned to England with the building of Saint Hugh's Charterhouse at Parkminster, in Surrey in 1883.

St. Hugh's Charterhouse (Carthusian Monastery) is the only one of this order in our country. Just north of Henfield, it was known to Cousin Miles when he lived at

Worthing & he has been able to describe it in detail to me. More austere than the Cistercians, each monk lives by himself.

Like the Trappist monk, the Carthusian monk lives an austere & silent life. At Parkminster, round the Great Cloister, there are 35 "cells" where each monk lives alone. Theirs is not the ministry of preaching the Gospel to every creature. Theirs is the ministry of Divine Union through prayer & penance.

13th November 1992 Friday

The Revd. Royston Davis, writing in the Snibston Church Parish Magazine, stresses the importance of incarnational spirituality – that is Christ/we. We all are one body – not Christ/me.

On this day in history -

1511 - King Henry VIII decides to join The Holy League and thus enter European politics.

1687 - Nell Gwynne died, aged 37. The mistress of King Charles II and best known orange seller of all time, she bore him two sons, and his last words as he lay dying are reputed to be, "Let not poor Nelly starve".

1914 – The brassiere was patented in the United States by heiress Mary Phelps Jacob. Previously women had worn a version of the child's liberty bodice to protect them when playing sport.

15th November 1992 Sunday

The partridge (Perdix) has a place in Greek mythology. Perdix, unlike his cousin Icarus, who flew on wings made by Daedalus, was maliciously hurled to his death by this same Daedalus. The goddess Minerva saved his life by changing him into a bird. The bird, to this day, avoids high places.

17th November 1992 Tuesday

Another prize from E.R.N.I.E. Bond number 14HN 330261

Dear Bondholder, Congratulations. One of your Premium Bonds has won a prize and a warrant for the money is enclosed. "Pay Miss E. Hewes fifty pounds only"

Good luck in future draws – Alan McGill, Controller.

19th November 1992 Thursday

The Swift Tuttle, a comet last seen by observers in 1862, has made a rare appearance in our skies this week. It is not due again until 2126 A.D. when, according to the experts, there is a one in ten thousand chance that the comet could crash into Earth with catastrophic effects.

21st November 1992 Saturday

"Welcome" says my new doormat to all who step into my newly furbished "Little Nook".

How wonderful at last to have the rear quarters of the house looking so good. The old house, no longer feeling sad & neglected, has taken on a new lease of life, ready to embrace one & all.

23rd November 1992 Monday

"Little Nook" & I have invited Bunting to spend Christmas with us.

Bunting, now feeling more like an odd-bod than the focal point of her family, does not wish to spend Christmas with Michael her elder son whose children live elsewhere, nor with Julian, as an incidental extra.

25th November 1992 Wednesday

Bromell, *Roger John, passed away at Leicester Royal Infirmary after a courageous fight, November 20th 1992, aged 50 years. Dearly loved husband of Chris, loving father to Julie and Steven. Funeral service to be held at Gilroes Crematorium on Thursday November 26th at 1-45p.m. No flowers by request, donations in lieu if so desired to Leicester Haematology Research Fund, c/o Leicester Royal Infirmary. Further inquiries to Leicestershire Co-operative Funeral Service, Windsor House, 131 Humberstone Road, Leicester.*

Remember the "special baby Julie" that I held in my arms on 11 July 1978 – who directed the course of my life into the world of Gas Standards – this is her father Roger, sadly dying at 50.

27th November 1992 Friday
Terry's Freedom

Former hostage Terry Waite and the Archbishop of Canterbury, Dr George Carey, will be awarded the Freedom of the City of Canterbury at a ceremony on November 27th.

On this day of special importance in Canterbury, I appreciate how well blessed we are to live in "this sceptred isle" with our own safe bounds, as opposed to many who are tossed from one regime to another.

29th November 1992 Sunday
900th Anniversary of the Archdeaconry of Leicester!
Cousin Miles & I went to Leicester Cathedral for a splendid service of Thanksgiving & Dedication to celebrate this momentous occasion.

From 1092 to 1992 A.D. From early Norman influence to new merging with Europe.

1st December 1992 Tuesday
To celebrate the 900th anniversary of the Archdeaconry of Leicester, the Bishop of Leicester, the Rt. Revd. Dr. Thomas Butler, on behalf of the Diocese, has handed over a cheque for £900 to pay for the planting of 450 trees in our new forest "to benefit the next 900 years of worshippers".

3rd December 1992 Thursday
And 350 years rolled by, and we have a special newspaper edition giving us the latest news as it might have been in the year 1642.

"After one of the most turbulent years in its history, the nation stands on the brink of all-out civil war." The Leader states, "We must have peace".

5th December 1992 Saturday
A new pair of specs to update the ones I bought 3 years ago. "Exclusive offer for people aged 60 and over – bifocals from £55. Please hurry – offer ends 24th December". The total bill, including £15 for eye testing, was £100. These have a hint of brown in the frame & look very good.

6th December 1992 Sunday
Today is the feast day of St. Nicholas, patron saint of youth, popularly known as Santa Claus.

Christopher Columbus discovered Hispaniola, now Haiti and the Dominican Republic, 1492.
The Irish Free State was proclaimed, 1921.

7th December 1992 Monday
Our Annual Christmas Fair in Ravenstone Village Institute saw "yours truly" in a most enjoyable new role, seated with Mr Jim Bailiss (Church Warden) at the Prize Draw table.

3,000 tickets were sold making £300 – the majority sold in advance – making this a very pleasant little job, much easier than our Sunday School.

8th December 1992 Tuesday
Spencer, *Caroline (Matron). Passed peacefully away at Ashby Court Nursing Home. Funeral service at St. Helen's Church on Monday December 14th at 12.30pm followed by cremation. Enquiries to A E Grice, 4 Derby Road, Ashby-de-la-Zouch. Tel (0530) 412229.*

Hall, *Leslie, of Agar Nook, Coalville. Beloved husband of Ursula, a loving father of Jonathon, passed suddenly away December 8th 1992 aged 62 years. Funeral service and cremation at Loughborough Crematorium on Monday December 14th at 3.30pm. Peace after pain.*

9th December 1992 Wednesday
"An Important Message from the Royal Mail" – To streamline the letter mail system & improve quality of service we need to change postal addresses in your area. It would help if you would start using your new form of address immediately. LE6 2AR will become LE67 2AR.

11th December 1992 Friday
"The Queen & Duke of Edinburgh are pleased to announce that the Princess Royal will marry Commander Timothy Laurence, MVO, RN, at Crathie Church, Balmoral, at 3pm on Saturday December 12th. The wedding will be a private family occasion".
The Princess is 42. Commander Laurence is 37.

13th December 1992 Sunday
From my love, by post a Christmas card "To the One I Love", containing two £10 notes.
"As the candles add their brightness when this festive time is here, your love can brighten every day for me throughout the year" Love you for ever. John x x x x X

15th December 1992 Tuesday
The Palace
It is announced from Buckingham Palace that, with regret, the Prince and Princess of Wales have decided to separate.

It is now official. The Prince & Princess of Wales:
"Have no plans to divorce"
"Their constitutional positions are unaffected"
"They will continue to carry out full & separate programmes of public engagements"

17th December 1992 Thursday
And a welcome Christmas Prize from E.R.N.I.E. Bond Number 14HN 330040.
Dear Bondholder, Congratulations.
One of your Premium Bonds has won a prize & a warrant for the money is enclosed.

"Pay Miss E Hewes one hundred pounds"
"Good luck in future draws" Alan Mc Gill, Controller.

19th December 1992 Saturday

Vivat Tchaikovsky! Katherine Sullivan, aged 88 & I, who enjoyed the ballet "Nutcracker" last December at Leicester, saw this same ballet again in Nottingham, performed by the English National Ballet. What a magical performance "a performance exploding with colour & imagination" Truly out of this world.

21st December 1992 Monday

"Civil Service Retirement Fellowship"
My first Christmas party with the Coalville group at the home of Charlie – Mr Tyrrell,
54, Blackwood. What a lovely party! We have about 20 members & we each took food & a wrapped present. Then we had a Christmas quiz & all had a gift from "Santa".

23rd December 1992 Wednesday

How lovely this year to spend Christmas at home in the role of hostess, with Bunting under my wing. With the old house looking so homely & cosy, Bunting declared, "This house is not a house – it is a home." And "Little Nook" has been well & truly appreciated.

25th December 1992 Friday

A happy Christmas Day for Steven & his girlfriend Jane who became engaged today.
A day tinged with sadness for Bunting, as we visited Mostyn's grave in Ravenstone churchyard. What a mixture of emotions as Bunting recalled what the church had seen – her wedding & Christenings.

27th December 1992 Sunday

"To All Staff" ......
As the Good Book says, The wisdom of a learned man cometh by opportunity of leisure & he that hath little business shall become wise. How can he get wisdom ... whose talk is of bullocks?
(Or maybe the international oil market?) Ecclesiasticus 38 – 24.

29th December 1992 Tuesday

"But he that giveth his mind to the law of the most high & is occupied in the meditation thereof, will seek out the wisdom of all the ancient….. He will seek out the secrets of grave sentences & be conversant in dark parables. When the great Lord will, he shall be filled with the spirit of understanding".

31st December 1992 Thursday

Shakespeare's vocabulary = 25,000 words.
He, more than anyone, sought out the secrets of grave sentences. How I love his pun on words – example –

"In thy tale"
"In thy tail?"
"What news with your mastership?"
"With my master's ship?"
"What is your will?"
"My will? I ne'er made my will yet".

* * *

Aids on Increase

Further 363 cases of Aids in UK reported in second quarter of year, Department of Health said.
 Total of Aids cases now stands at 6,140, of whom 3,839 (63%) have died, with HIV infection cases now amounting to 17,868.
Figures show Aids among women is increasing at a faster rate than men.

* * *

"Getting the Coal"

Impressions of a 20th century mining community.

This little book, printed in 1992, consists almost entirely of extracts from tape-recorded interviews carried out by Coalville's Mantle Oral History Project over a period of 6 years.
What a story! I know personally so many of the central characters. The extracts are in the very words of the contributors & so it is a tale told with some "me ducks" & some "oh ya buggers".
Good times & bad times are remembered; impressions from children of miners, wives of miners, & of course, the miners themselves.
The most telling extract is from Herbert Blake –
"The shortest shift I ever did was my last. I went & left home about ten minutes to ten at night & by a quarter to eleven I was back home. See, you never worked your last shift. You just went, took your tally out, handed it back in, then came home – said cheerio to everybody & came home. It went back to the days when Ball was the manager, before nationalisation, actually. When anybody retired, he used to say, "They don't work on their last day. I couldn't bear to have a man killed on his last day at work".

* * *

Management Consultants!

To Jesus, Son of Joseph, Nazareth,

From Jordan Management Consultants, Jerusalem.

It is our opinion that the 12 men you have picked to manage your new organisation lack the background, educational & vocational aptitude for the type of enterprise you are undertaking. They do not have the team concept.

Simon Peter is emotionally unstable & given to fits of temper.

Andrew has no qualities of leadership.

The two brothers James and John place personal interest above company loyalty.

Thomas demonstrates a questioning attitude that would tend to undermine morale.

We feel it our duty to tell you that Matthew has been blacklisted by the Greater Jerusalem Better Business Bureau.

James, the son of Alphaeus & Thaddeus have radical leanings & both registered high on the manic-depressive scale.

One of the candidates, however, shows great potential. He is a man of ability and resourcefulness, has a keen business mind & contacts in high places. He is highly motivated & ambitious.

We recommend Judas Iscariot as your controller and right-hand man.

(From a Church Magazine)

* * *

The 1992 Olympic Games were held in Barcelona. A Spanish archer shot a flaming arrow high into the bowl of the Olympic flame to herald the opening of this 25th modern Olympiad.

The opening ceremony was watched by King Juan Carlos & Queen Sofia of Spain & millions of television viewers throughout the world. A record number of 172 nations took part.

Britain managed to win only 5 gold, 3 silver and 12 bronze medals, unlike Germany who won 33 gold, 21 silver & 28 bronze.

The German canoeists alone won 7 gold, 2 silver & 2 bronze – "oar-inspiring".

The closing ceremony was the most spectacular event, culminating in a grandiose firework display.

In 1996 the Olympic Games will be held in the U.S.A.; in the southern state of Georgia, in the city of Atlanta.

* * *

1993

1ˢᵗ January 1993 Thursday
The Single European Market is operative from today, heralding the "FREE" movement of people, services, trade & commerce throughout Europe.
In Greek mythology Europa was a demi-goddess, daughter of Agenor, King of Phoenicia. Zeus, in the guise of a bull, carried her off to her new home, Europe.

3ʳᵈ January 1993 Saturday
Princess Diana, the Princess of Wales, now officially separated from her husband, Prince Charles, the Prince of Wales, continues to dazzle everyone, as she carries out public engagements.

5ᵗʰ January 1993 Monday
The Royal Institution Christmas Lecture has been given this year by Professor Charles Stirling, Head of the Department of Chemistry at Sheffield University. Of particular interest to me was a detailed explanation of the structure of D.N.A. whose 3-unit make up bore the trademark of a 3 in One God.

7ᵗʰ January 1993 Wednesday
"The Characteristics of Left & Right-handedness"
This was the theme of Professor Stirling's lecture. He produced a model of the double right-handed helix, like a spiral staircase, whose banisters were made of sugar, linked by phosphate & whose millions of steps were adenine-thymine (A...T) & guanine-cytosine (G...C).
D.N.A. = Deoxyribonucleic Acid. Deoxyribose = sugar.
D.N.A. is the molecule found in the cells of living things. But the most amazing thing (discovered in 1984 by Professor Alec Jeffreys at Leicester) is that the chemical bonds – the steps of A...T or T...A & G...C or C...G form unique codes.
"The very hairs of your head are all numbered"
(Luke 12 : 7)
Not until the numbering of the steps on the staircase of the molecules of the cells of all living things was unravelled did we appreciate that we all carry our own code number in every single hair, in every drop of blood & every minute detail.

13ᵗʰ January 1993 Tuesday
Durham Cathedral this year celebrates the 900ᵗʰ anniversary of its foundation. There will be major events throughout the year, including St. Cuthbert's Day on 20ᵗʰ March, when the Archbishop of Canterbury will attend a celebration service.

15ᵗʰ January 1993 Thursday
18 months of retirement & all those long years spent at work have passed into history. They seem a million miles away, as if they related to someone else in the realms of "once upon a time". Now, like someone re-born, it is wonderful to be myself, & be more at one with God & nature.

17ᵗʰ January 1993 Saturday
The National Debt can increase, despite the public sector debt repayment. This may happen if sterling is drawn from the National Loans Fund to finance a big rise in the gold & foreign exchange reserves. There are other factors not included in the National Debt, such as short term assets.

"The days when governments spent money freely and cheerfully ran up the national debt are long gone."
(Newspaper cutting)

19ᵗʰ January 1993 Monday
"So let it be written – so let it be done"
Was there ever anyone more than Christ himself who knew the dreadful impact of such words?
Time and time again he referred to the ancient writings of scripture concerning his own destiny: - "for it is written" – "have ye not read?" - "did ye never read in the scriptures?"
And when Jesus had accomplished all that was written of him, he walked as the risen Lord to Emmaus & spoke to Cleopas & his companion "beginning at Moses & all the prophets, he expounded unto them in all the scriptures the things concerning himself" (Luke 24 : 27)

The risen Lord Jesus then appeared to his disciples in Jerusalem: - "And he said unto them, These are the words which I spoke unto you, while I was yet with you, that all things must be fulfilled which were written in the law of Moses and in the prophets an in the psalms – thus it is written". (Luke 24 : 44 – 46)

"What I have written I have written" (St. John 19 : 22)
This was the answer given by Pontius Pilate to the chief priests after he had written a title & put it on the Cross of Christ : - "Jesus of Nazareth the King of the Jews"

27ᵗʰ January 1993 Tuesday
"Civil Service Retirement Fellowship" - My first "annual January lunch" with the Coalville Group at The Bulls Head, Thringstone. Mr & Mrs Jim Bailiss invited me to go with them & I was pleased to sit by Mr & Mrs Baxter from The Beeches, Ravenstone.
The Fellowship celebrates its Silver Jubilee this year.

29ᵗʰ January 1993 Thursday
Nottingham's pantomime this year was Robin Hood & the Babes in the Wood. Katherine & I enjoyed this most excellent of entertainments from the Dress Circle front central seats. How we laughed at the antics of the "Acroloons". They were almost as funny as the "Ugly Sisters" in 1983.

31ˢᵗ January 1993 Saturday
"Reprieve for the Coal Miners" – Following the devastating news that 31 coal mines were to close (see 14ᵗʰ October 1992) the Commons Trade & Industry Select Committee have now recommended a re-think. They have called for a £500 million subsidy to British Coal over 5 years to save the industry.

2ⁿᵈ February 1993 Monday
George Washington (1732 – 1799) – Having just read the interesting life story of America's first President, I discovered that in those days false teeth were made of wood. His unsmiling portrait shows a distorted mouth. Such was the unpleasant taste, he soaked his teeth overnight in wine.

4th February 1993 Wednesday

"Paradise Lost" – Having enjoyed "Bible Radio" followed by "Pilgrim's Progress" we have now been introduced to "Paradise Lost" by John Milton, born 1608. Not since "Tomlinson" which delighted me in November 1983 have I encountered such a poem, but this of epic proportion.

What a masterpiece of descriptive writing. You never heard anything like the journey undertaken by Satan, lately cast out from heaven into hell & setting out in quest of fledgling Earth. This was all that Tomlinson ever encountered & more, much much more.

8th February 1993 Sunday

Septuagesima Sunday & Evensong at Ravenstone Church with lay reader Mr B. Daws transported us to the very gates of heaven. The 2nd lesson was Revelation, Chapter 4, which itself paved the way, as St. John described for us his vision of Heaven, where the worship of God never ceases.

10th February 1993 Tuesday

"Guys & Dolls" is this year's choice for Coalville Amateurs.

I was very pleased to be asked to join those assembled at Peter Jacques' house for the annual allocation of tickets: - Peter & his wife Vera, Basil Newbold, Vincent Hardy, Olive Meakin, George Taylor, Betty Henn & Hayley (8 months pregnant).

12th February 1993 Thursday

"Operation Sickleforce" was the disastrous Invasion of Norway in April 1940 by some 5,000 young British soldiers, including brother Pat.

Veterans of this campaign have now arranged a grand reunion & this evening the Lord Mayor of Leicester is hosting a civic reception & supper at the Town Hall for up to 100 men.

14th February 1993 Saturday

"Happy Valentine's Day"
From guess who? Yes, your only true
Valentine
X xxx X

16th February 1993 Monday

"I thought about you on Valentine's Day" said John Dolman to me as we came away from Ravenstone Church on Sunday evening.

How lovely it was for Old Maid Hewsie to be thought about by her two rival boyfriends of 40 years ago, both of which have long since been married to another.

18th February 1993 Wednesday

James Bulger, aged 2, went shopping with his mum Denise, in the New Strand shopping centre in Bootle last week, when he was lured away by 2 young boys.

These 10 year old boys have now been charged with his abduction & murder. They are among the youngest this century accused of murder in a British court.

20th February 1993 Friday

As brother Pat & I sat by the bedside of Auntie Dos, so emaciated & weak, with sunken cheeks & no fight left in her, I thought of the dying Minnehaha & her uninvited guests: - "Looked with haggard eyes & hollow at the face of Laughing Water – the Beloved – the dying Minnehaha."

22nd February 12993 Sunday

Salman Rushdie, author of the book "Satanic Verses" which so offended the Muslim world, is still in hiding following the declaration of "The Fatwa" 4 years ago. He is guarded day & night & lives like a prisoner, never daring to venture out alone. Freedom of Speech has given him no freedom.

24th February 1993 Tuesday

A £4 million project is under way at Donington Park, Leicestershire, to upgrade the track & facilities for the European Grand Prix. On Easter Sunday, 11th April, the first-ever round of the F1 world championship will be held at Donington. A crowd of 100,000 is expected, with visitors from all over the world.

26th February 1993 Thursday

"What shall I do?" Shakespeare puts these words into the mouth of Falstaff in Act 4 of the Merry Wives of Windsor. Lured by Mrs Ford into her house while her husband is out a-birding, news of the husband's imminent return puts Falstaff in a dilemma.

"What shall I do? I'll creep up into the chimney."

28th February 1993 Saturday

"What shall I do?" Shakespeare also puts these words into the mouth of Hamlet's mother, Queen of Denmark, when Hamlet has a long heart-to-heart talk with her, exposing her new husband as a murderer & a villain – a King of shreds & patches - & she herself almost as bad.

1st March 1993 Monday

"Fred was alive & is dead –
there is no more to be said"
This was said of a former Prince of Wales (father of George III) who died in March 1751. At one time he too considered marrying another Lady Diana Spencer.

3rd March 1993 Wednesday

Opening night of Coalville Amateurs' "Guys & Dolls" – a rip-roaring hilarious show, when again it is such a pleasure to be an integral part of the front of house team, as Assistant House Manager to brother Pat, & one of the "magnificent seven" line-up of "girls" – Ann, Olive, Marlene, Margaret, Enid, Joan and me.

"Guys & Dolls" is a real family affair. Keith Crockett & his wife Anne play the comedy leads. Brian Gadsby & his son Duncan sing a duet. Peter Jacques conducts the orchestra while on stage his wife Vera is conducting the Salvation Army band. Mothers & daughters are there, plus brother Pat, cousin Enid and me.

7th March 1993 Sunday

Stacey, William of Whitwick, passed peacefully away in hospital, March 7th 1993, aged 85 years, beloved husband of the late Hilda, father of Janet and Tony, Sheila and Jack, granddad of Alison, Andrew, Sarah and Rachael, great-grandad of Christopher, Sarah and Emma. Funeral service at Marlborough Square Methodist Church, Coalville, Wednesday March 17th at 12.45p.m. followed by cremation at Loughborough

Crematorium. Family flowers only by request, donations in lieu for the Heart Association for Midland Hospitals may be sent to Mrs J. Wilson, 29 Hough Hill, Swannington.

Bill Stacey is uncle to Pat and Bunting.
He is the last of his line – the youngest brother of Julia, my dad's first wife. His sister Thirza died in February 1991 at Markfield Court.

9th March 1993 Tuesday

"Bishops in Lent" – How interesting to hear different bishops giving lunchtime talks during Lent at Leicester Cathedral. Bishop John Howe, a retired bishop, spoke to us of the world-wide Anglican Church. He said we know that we exist when we are known by people, dead or alive or yet to be.

11th March 1993 Thursday

All the forces at work behind scenes of "Guys & Dolls" were again in evidence to Assistant House Manager Hewsie as she saw the tea-ladies preparing for the interval mad rush; watched the electricians at work in their control room; & culminated in the delivery of red roses from my true love – "All my love, John".

13th March 1993 Saturday

Our last Spring Budget, & with a Public Sector Borrowing Requirement (P.S.B.R.) of £50 billion for the next twelve months, we are all to be heavily taxed – not immediately – but over the next 3 years. Car Tax goes up immediately from £110 to £125, but Value Added Tax on gas & electricity is to be phased in.

15th March 1993 Monday

"O prudent discipline" declares the bastard son of King Richard I, in Shakespeare's King John.
Brought up as Philip Falconbridge, then Knighted as Sir Richard Plantagenet, it is he also who says, "Zounds! I was never so bethump'd with words since I first called my brother's father dad." (Act 2)

17th March 1993 Wednesday

Shakespeare's "King John" is a blend of fact & fantasy. It is satirical, farcical & tragic. As always, Shakespeare himself has an overall Olympian view of everybody as they all scheme & plot to overthrow one another; but there is never a mention of Magna Carta, which John was forced to sign.

19th March 1993 Friday

The Bishop of Leicester, the Rt. Revd. Dr. Thomas Butler, is now in training for the London Marathon! He will be running alongside the Bishop of Ripon, the Rt. Revd. David Young, leading a team of 7 church runners & hoping to raise £50,000.

21st March 1993 Sunday

"When a young man's fancy lightly turns to thoughts of love". Have you ever heard of Leander? Every night he used to swim across the Hellespont to his beloved Hero, but one night in a tempest, he was drowned. The waves bore his body to the shore & Hero, broken hearted, drowned herself.

23rd March 1993 Tuesday

"Judge not, that ye be not judged. For with what

judgment ye judge, ye shall be judged; & with what measure ye mete, it shall be measured to you again" (Matthew 7: 1.)
This is precisely the meaning of "Measure for Measure", Shakespeare's play, where justice prevails in the end.

25th March 1993 Thursday

"Give me justice, justice, justice, justice" pleads Isabella, to the noble Duke of Vienna, in Shakespeare's "Measure for Measure".
Having already gleaned all the true facts, disguised as Lodowick, a hooded friar, the noble Duke not only shows justice & mercy to all concerned, but makes Isabella his wife.

27th March 1993 Saturday

"What, is there none of Pygmalion's images, newly made woman, to be had now ....?"
Not knowing who this Pygmalion was in Shakespeare's "Measure for Measure", I subsequently learned that he was a sculptor who carved an ivory image of Aphrodite, which came to life in a story written by Ovid.

29th March 1993 Monday

"The grace of our Lord Jesus Christ, and the love of God, and the fellowship of the Holy Ghost, be with us all evermore. Amen." (2 Corinthians: 13) *(See 29th March 1989 and also 1991)*

31st March 1993 Wednesday

"Justice, most gracious duke; oh, grant me justice", pleads Antipholus of Ephesus in another of Shakespeare's plays "The Comedy of Errors" where much confusion arises with two sets of identical twins. The story is very far fetched, but was adapted from an ancient tale by Plautus who also purloined it from 500 B.C.

2nd April 1993 Friday

Mr & Mrs William Mobberly request the pleasure of the company of Miss Betty Hewes at the marriage of Josie & Mike on Friday 30th April 1993 at Stafford Register Office at 11 a.m. & afterwards at the Moat House, Acton Trussell.
(Bunting's son is re-marrying – see 8th April 1989, 26th May 1989, 30th July 1990)

4th April 1993 Sunday

Yesterday's Grand National was a complete disaster. Thirty-nine riders lined up & after two false starts the jockeys did not know whether they were to race or not. Some held back, some raced on, but the race was declared void. £75 million which had been placed on bets all had to be returned.

6th April 1993 Tuesday

H. M. The Queen has today for the first time paid "Income Tax" on her personal income.
"Expenses which can be offset against tax" include £879,000, which used to be paid to her three younger children, her sister & her aunt through the Civil List Payments, but now to be paid by the Queen herself.

8th April 1993 Thursday

"And Herod with his men of war set him at nought &

mocked him" Luke 23 – 11. The preacher spoke of all those who cruelly mocked our Lord: - The men that held Jesus. Luke 22 – 63. And the soldiers also mocked him; and they that passed by; and the chief priests. Mark 15.

12th April 1993 Monday
"Grand Prix   □93" - With the European Grand Prix almost on our doorstep, we have suddenly become much more interested and knowledgeable in the sport. Donington Park is only one of 16 circuits throughout the world where the race is run, starting in March & finishing in November.

13th April 1993 Tuesday
Shared with 500 million television viewers across the world the thrill of Grand Prix racing at Castle Donington. With the help of TV cameras, we were at times actually in the car with Brazilian Ayrton Senna as he sped to victory.

16th April 1993 Friday
£50 worth of British Rail Travel Vouchers!
"It gives me great pleasure to inform you that you have won one of the runners-up prizes worth £50 …Your entry was one of those chosen from the thousands that we received."
This competition was open to "Senior Railcard holders". Five £10 vouchers, valid until April next year.

18th April 1993 Sunday
Elizabeth Hewes – No. 811 013 027 0 012 has received her first Council Tax Demand Notice, which has replaced the disastrous "Poll Tax". Every-one who lives alone is given 25% discount.
I now pay £250 – 72p. i.e. £334 – 29p less £83 – 57p.

20th April 1993 Tuesday
The London Marathon at the weekend, Sunday 18th April, was won by Eamonn Martin (Great Britain) in 2 hours 10 minutes.
The Bishop of Leicester, the Rt. Revd. Dr. Thomas Butler completed the run in 4 hours 36 minutes. We were all invited to sponsor him, in a bid to raise money for the Church Urban Fund.

24th April 1993 Saturday
Leicestershire County Council Elections, Thursday 6th May 1993. Coalville Division: Cousin Miles is putting up as Conservative candidate against Adeline Smith (Labour) who holds the seat at present.
Miles Robert Wilson, whose wife Sarah left him last year and who now has a new live-in girlfriend – Gwen.

26th April 1993 Monday
To celebrate Katherine's 89th birthday, we motored to Melton Mowbray where we had lunch with Mrs Richey at the House of Anne of Cleves and saw inside the magnificent Church of St. Mary's. Then on to Waltham Hall Private Nursing Home to see Auntie Doris aged 97, now resident there.

28th April 1993 Wednesday
"Heaven on Earth" – A theme park of enlightenment has now been proposed by the millionaire mystic Maharishi Mahesh. Veda Land (Veda meaning knowledge) is envisaged for those seeking the meaning of life, love, peace and understanding; with a levitating house & all things heavenly.

30th April 1993 Friday
"I felt like a king!" – So said Cocky, 5 years ago, as he prepared for Yvonne's wedding day. On his birthday this year he was moved to tears by a card from Yvonne which said she had been dealt by the cards a father who was not a Jack; he was not a King; he was The Ace.

2nd May 1993 Sunday
The wedding of Michael & Josie on Friday 30th April was a cosy family affair with only 25 guests & Julian again in the role of best man. (See 31st July 1971)
The weather was absolutely perfect all day long.

4th May 1993 Tuesday
"Go you through the town to Frogmore" – Katherine & I again enjoyed a Viking Coach trip for this once a year opportunity to visit the Queen's private gardens, plus this year a chance to see inside Frogmore House & inside Windsor Castle, so recently devastated by fire. I loved all the magnificent clocks in every room.

6th May 1993 Thursday
Coalville
(Electorate................................7,687)
*A Smith (Lab)...........................2,076
M Wilson (Con)........................... 667
Lab hold Majority 1,409
County Council Election & Cousin Miles was well & truly beaten by the Labour candidate.
 It was the same story nationwide as the Conservatives fell from favour.

8th May 1993 Saturday
Katherine & I again enjoyed the Annual Bluebell Service in Swithland Woods.
Katherine, who was born at the time of the year when all the bluebells were out, almost had the name "Bluebell" given to her. "Let's call her Bluebell" said her proud father on the day she was born, as he saw the bluebells from his window.

10th May 1993 Monday
Review of Local Government Structure! – A year long review begins today to determine the future of Local Government services in Leicestershire. The Local Government Commission made up of 14 members & chaired by Sir John Banham, formerly director-general of the Confederation of British Industry, will report.

12th May 1993 Wednesday
"The Conservatives fall from favour" – Why do we now have so many disaffected Conservative voters? The government, in a bid to squeeze more and more money out of everyone, is closing hospitals, closing coal mines, privatising British Rail, putting more taxation on fuel, which they promised not to do, & generally upsetting everybody.

14th May 1993 Friday
Cousin Miles, who jumps on the band-wagon of anything that is going, has now become a school

governor of Snibston School. The children are currently involved in a project covering local history & I was invited to visit the school with him at 3p.m.

It was in March 1907 that Geo. H. Hewes did just the same.

"Visited the school at 3 o'clock" – So wrote my grandfather George Harry Hewes on 27th March 1907. Snibston School was officially opened on 29th Jan. 1907 & in September that year Cissy Hewes (Auntie Cis) commenced as Pupil Teacher.

Cousin Miles is delighted to have this family connection.

18th May 1993 Tuesday
And again Karen is overjoyed to announce "I'm pregnant" as she looks forward to a baby early next year. Her first baby Suzannah is now 18 months old.

Also Yvonne, Cocky's daughter, is looking forward to her second baby later this year. Her first baby Matthew Lawrence John Bond is now 2½ years old.

20th May 1993 Thursday
F.A. Cup Final this year was again a replay. Arsenal beat Sheffield Wednesday 2-1 (after extra time). Described as a brawl, there was plenty of rough play. Andy Linighan who scored the winning goal, had his nose broken in play.

22nd May 1993 Saturday
Monaco Grand Prix! – Tomorrow is the celebrated Monte Carlo Grand Prix, the world's most famous race, always held at Ascension tide & attended by princes, film stars & the cream of society. Host of the Monaco Grand Prix is His Serene Highness Prince Rainier III, 70 this month.

The Monaco Grand Prix is No. 6 in the round of 16 circuits. Brazilian-born Ayrton Senna who won at Donington on Easter Sunday, won also at Monaco where he had won 5 times before, since he started in 1984 as a 24 year old.

26th May 1993 Wednesday
"The seas are quiet when the winds give o'er, so calm are we when passions are no more."

As brother Pat & I kept vigil by the bedside of Aunt Dos I thought how calm and peaceful she looked. "Gone was every trace of sorrow…….." as though she was gliding silently into heaven.

28th May 1993 Friday
Azalea Pontica! (belonging to Pontus)

How inspiring to have this new exquisitely perfumed plant in the garden for Whitsuntide: - "And how hear we every man in our own tongue, wherein we were born. Parthians & Medes & Elamites & the dwellers in Mesopotamia….in Pontus & Asia."(Acts 2: 8 – 11)

30th May 1993 Whit Sunday
Elaine Barkby, suffering from Multiple Sclerosis, can still talk to me non-stop, but oh how sad it is to see the slow but inexorable progress of this dreadful illness. Now incontinent, she has the "Home Help" service daily, to get her up and dressed each day; & wonderful help from her neighbour, Paul.

1st June 1993 Tuesday
"Sometimes he appears so clearly to me in my dreams."

So I said of my dad on 17th March 1989. But never more clearly than he appeared to me this night. As on 17th May 1990, Soviet leader Mikhail Gorbachev held me in fond & loving embrace, so my dad held me, & I thought, "This is no dream. This is real."

3rd June 1993 Thursday
Society for the Blind – presentation of certificates to long serving volunteers.

I went to the centre in Gedding Road, Leicester, where the Society's Blind Chairman, Brian Embry, presented about 30 certificates to long serving volunteers. This year's Lord Mayor's appeal is for the blind of Leicestershire.

5th June 1993 Saturday
Ravenstone Parish Church Summer Fair, held for the first time in the grounds of Ravenstone Hospital. A glorious sunny day & I revelled in my role at the Prize Draw table with Church Warden Mr Jim Bailiss. We have 20 assorted prizes & part of my job is writing down the names & numbers of the winners.

6th June 1993 Trinity Sunday
The 3 promises & vows of Baptism.

I should renounce the devil & all his works & all the sinful lusts of the flesh.

I should believe all the articles of the Christian faith.

I should keep God's Holy Will & Commandments and walk in the same all the days of my life.

7th June 1993 Monday
Coalville Amateur Operatic Society Annual General Meeting when Treasurer Hayley, complete with her beautiful bonny 3 month old baby Katy, presented her accounts & resigned as Treasurer. Wendy Miles volunteered to take over this role. Brother Pat was pleased to become Vice President.

9th June 1993 Wednesday
Lancaster is celebrating 800 years as a borough & on Monday this week Prince Charles was in Lancaster to be given the freedom of the city. Cocky & Joan saw him.

11th June 1993 Friday
Mary Blue buys new home!

Mary Blue, aged 49, has now moved from her home in Leicester to 23, Blackthorn Road, Glenfield, immediately opposite her close friend Pam.

Pat and Evelyn took me to see Mary in this pretty little semi with every mod con & all the latest electronic equipment.

13th June 1993 Sunday
"And the evening & the morning were the first day" Genesis 1 – 5.

Not the morning and the evening, but the evening & the morning. The preacher pointed out that the beginning of the first day was "the evening". I'd never even thought of that. "And the evening & the morning were the second day …." etc.

17th June 1993 Thursday
Hewes, Doris Annie (Dos), formerly of Ravenstone, passed peacefully away at Markfield Court Nursing

Home on Saturday June 12th 1993. Funeral service at Coalville Marlborough Square Methodist Church on Monday June 21st at 12 noon, followed by cremation at Loughborough Crematorium, no flowers by request, donation in lieu if desired for the Marlborough Square Methodist Church, c/o Revd. D. Allen, 71 Jackson Street, Coalville.

Aunt Dos, the last of her line, has died aged 91. Cousin Miles has offered to have the family get-together after the funeral at his home "Glenholm", where much of our family drama has been enacted.

19th June 1993 Saturday

According to the death certificate, Aunt Dos died of "cachexia". Brother Pat, Evelyn & I went to see her this morning in the Chapel of Rest at Coalville, where her poor emaciated body lay wrapped in pretty pink & white coverings & all you could see was her sunken face & almost skeletal hands.

21st June 1993 Monday

"I remember, I remember, the house where I was born; the little window where the sun came peeping in at morn."

At the high noon of summer I think of these words written by Thomas Hood, when the sun peeps so early into my bathroom window, as it has done since the day I was born.

"I remember, I remember" by Thomas Hood is actually a very sad poem. The joys of childhood have now gone & all that remains are the sorrows of age: - "My spirit flew in feathers then, that is so heavy now; and summer pools could hardly cool the fever on my brow." (He died, aged 46)

And so it was at the high noon of summer that we assembled for Aunt Dos' funeral.

The cortege left from my house & as the hearse moved past Aunt Dos' bungalow & past "The Hollies", it was led by the funeral director, complete with black top hat, who walked in solemn dignity to the crossroads. There were 24 family members who walked into chapel with Aunt Dos & a goodly representation of friends & neighbours already assembled. For one who had been out of circulation for so long, it was good to see so many gathered together to pay their last respects.

29th June 1993 Tuesday

Joanne, aged 19, has now set up home with her boyfriend Glen.

The roller-coaster of her emotions lifts her one day to the heights of bliss & another to the depths. One day Glen is all she can desire & another he is just the reverse; but right now they have their own little love nest – a flat in Coalville.

1st July 1993 Thursday

"Awhile to work, & after holiday"- While women in this country can receive their state pension at 60, men have to work until they are 65. Cocky has now decided to retire from his part time job as Security Guard, which he has had for 4 years, on his 64th birthday next January.

3rd July 1993 Saturday

Mr & Mrs D. A. Hewes request the pleasure of the company of Betty at the marriage of their daughter Alison to Mr Simon A. Chalkley at Holy Rood Church, Packington, on Sunday 29th August 1993 at 1-00p.m. & afterwards at The Priest House Hotel, Castle Donington.

5th July 1993 Monday

Internal Auditor Hewsie, with Basil Newbold, did their first audit for Coalville Amateurs. We went to Hayley's house at 79 Thorndale, Ibstock & spent about 2 hours checking the accounts which were in good order, apart from several missing invoices. New Treasurer Wendy Miles actually works in a bank.

7th July 1993 Wednesday

Ravenstone Church was filled for the funeral of Doris Land, farmer's wife & stalwart of the church for many years. The Rector stressed the appropriateness of the words of the funeral service to a farmer's wife – I Corinthians, Chap. 15. "Like a seed, we are sown at death to rise more glorious."

Land, Mrs Doris May, Ashby Road, Ravenstone, left estate valued at £128,437 gross, £126,996 net.
(newspaper cutting)

9th July 1993 Friday

Gilbert Paul-Clark, second in command at G.O.M.B. (Gas & Oil Measurement Branch) has retired from work & I was invited together with other retired members of staff to his farewell "Do". It was lovely to see them all again but sad to see Mr Ellis looking frail & suffering from arterial sclerosis.

11th July 1993 Sunday
Alfred Lord Tennyson (1809 – 1892)

Having just read the life story of this truly great poet, who knew such heart-ache & sorrow in his life, I thought of "no highlights – only low lights" when he was asked for a "biographical paragraph" in 1837. He said, "My life has been one of feelings, not of actions."

13th July 1993 Tuesday

"The Hollies", 25 Leicester Road, Ravenstone.
Entrance porch with mosaic tiled flooring. Reception hallway with mosaic tiled flooring.
Living room to the front with original fireplace. Dining room to the front with original fireplace.
Breakfast room. Rear hallway. Ground floor bathroom.
First floor: 4 double bedrooms. Study/box room. Bathroom and separate WC.
2nd floor: Attic room.
Externally: Gardens to 3 sides with lawns, trees and shrubs. Gravelled driveway to rear with car standing space and 2 separate concrete sectional garages.
Offers around £100,000.

Seeing the once splendid family home for sale, with virtually no trace of the family left in the vicinity, apart from a couple of lonely old maids – Enid & me, I thought of Tennyson's poem "Aylmer's Field". Now, nothing more than a field, this was once the family home of Sir Aylmer Aylmer.

14th July 1993 Wednesday

For my 62nd birthday, the biggest surprise was a cheque for £100 from Cousin Enid. Having been on a tight budget after spending such a lot of money on the house & on a new car, Enid offered to pay £100 for me to go on holiday with her, maybe in September. We hope to go to Windsor.

17th July 1993 Saturday
Financial Crisis in Church of England!
The incompetence of the Church Commissioners, who manage £2.2 billion of ecclesiastical assets, has contributed to a loss of £624 million between 1989 & 1991. Large sums were invested in commercial property & in "speculating", but then came the slump.
St. Michael's & All Angels Church, Ravenstone, requires at least £100,000 immediately for a new roof (see 1st November, 1992). We are but one of the many churches in the 43 different dioceses struggling against all the odds to survive at all. We could well do without this loss of £624 million.

21st July 1993 Wednesday
Scott, Doris E. M. Widow of J. H. (Bert) late of Hugglescote and Mountsorrel, died peacefully on July 15th in hospital, aged 97 years. Funeral arrangements later.
"......and one by one back in the closet lays" (Omar Khayyam) .The death of Auntie Doris, the only one left who shared with me my first day in this world, closes another chapter in my life.
With no-one left for me to call "Auntie" (or Uncle), and already a great-great half-aunt myself, I feel suddenly plummeted into the top strata of "the older generation".
But through all the changing scenes of life, Christ remains the same yesterday & today & for ever. (Hebrews 13 : 8)
Auntie Doris was actually quite a remote relation, daughter of David Sketchley Moore & grand-daughter of Godfrey Moore, who in 1855 had married Harriet Anne Sketchley.
While Auntie Doris & Mary Moore were direct cousins, my mum, Mary Sketchley, came down in line from Harriet's brother John.

27th July 1993 Tuesday
Scott, Doris Evelyn Mary. Passed away peacefully on July 15th 1993 at Grantham Hospital, aged 97 years. Funeral service to take place on Tuesday, July 27th at St. Peter's Church, Mountsorrel at 11 a.m. followed by cremation at Loughborough Crematorium. Flowers and inquiries to Stevens, Goodburn, Funeral Service, 33 Scalford Road, Melton Mowbray. Tel. 0664 63037.
Two British Legion Standard Bearers led the funeral procession of Auntie Doris into a well filled church at Mountsorrel. I was moved to tears when these British Legion standards slowly dipped at the end of the service.

Lawrence of Arabia's nurse Doris dies, 97
A county woman, who nursed Lawrence of Arabia when he was suffering from gunshot wounds in Egypt, has died at the age of 97 years.
Mrs Doris Scott, who was one of Mountsorrel's oldest residents, was trained in 1914 by St. John Ambulance before leaving England for Egypt and what was then Palestine, for service in the Voluntary Aid Detachment. She served for five years and returned in 1919, following a bout of malaria.

It was during that period that she nursed T E Lawrence who, when he recovered, thanked the medical team by entertaining them to a special dinner at the legendary Shepherd's Hotel in Cairo. Mrs Scott remembered in that in the centre piece of the dining table there was an arrangement of red roses with ribbons from it leading to each nurse. They found each ribbon pulled a rose from the arrangement – one for each of them.
The grandeur of Shepherd's Hotel was a sharp contrast to when Mrs Scott first arrived in Egypt in 1915. She worked in the fever block of the 17th General Hospital in Alexandria. The hospital coped with a maximum of 2,000 patients – many accommodated outside under canvas.
One enduring memory was of her first Christmas there and the staff giving all their spare time to making decorations and tying parcels for patients. "On Christmas Day it was very touching seeing the poor boys who were not able to sit up wearing their paper hats", she would recall.
Mrs Scott served in Egypt and Palestine often close to The Front and moving northwards into Lebanon and Syria.
"Only fairly recently did my grandmother disclose just how dangerous it all was, with shells and bullets hitting the front line hospitals", says Mr Graham Stocks of Quorn.
In 1918 Doris Scott contracted malaria very badly – a disease which recurred throughout her life.
After the First World War Mrs Scott trained as a midwife under the tutorship of the then Royal Physician at Queen Charlotte's Hospital in London.
Mrs Scott was the daughter of Mr & Mrs David Sketchley Moore, of Glebe Farm, Hugglescote, and her late husband, Mr Herbert Scott, was commandant of the Special Constabulary in the Coalville area for many years.
In 1963 she moved from Hugglescote to Mountsorrel, where she became involved in work for the Royal British Legion and the Mothers' Union and was a member of the congregation at St Peter's Church..

(Newspaper cutting)

(See 18th July 1987)

31st July 1993 Saturday
David Prince, Leicestershire County Council's Chief Executive, has now joined the elevated rank (29,000) of those listed in the 1993 edition of "Who's Who". This year's "Who's Who" marks the 145th annual edition.

2nd August 1993 Monday
Cathedral Newsletter No. 246, covering August/ September shows the new Provost Derek Hole making a determined effort to increase the number of "Friends of Leicester Cathedral". There are at present 290 members & he is hoping to double that number. Life membership is now £100.

4th August 1993 Wednesday
"Service of Thanksgiving & Blessing for the Birth of Suzannah Oliver"
This service held earlier this year was in lieu of Holy Baptism. No responsibility lay with anyone to do anything about a "Christian" upbringing. No mention of believing God's Holy Word or keeping his

commandments. And so little Suzannah cannot learn to recite "The Catechism".
Question - Who gave you your name?
Answer - My Godfathers & Godmothers in my Baptism; wherein I was made a Member of Christ, the Child of God & an inheritor of the Kingdom of Heaven.
I thought of the 2nd Epistle to Timothy, Chapter 1 Verse 5.

8th August 1993 Sunday
"Almost thou persuadest me to be a Christian" – So said King Agrippa to St Paul (Acts of the Apostles – Chapter 26). My latest book on the history of Ireland makes me feel like Agrippa, hearing the background to present day troubles & almost persuaded to support the I.R.A.
No wonder the Irish fight for freedom from British domination. Centuries of brutal repression have provoked the terrorism of today. Seeds of disquiet were first set in 1172AD when Henry II invaded Ireland. Things went from bad to worse, particularly during Cromwell's time, circa 1649AD.
It was Gladstone who more than anyone else devoted all his energies to the Irish cause. In 1868 he said, "My mission is to pacify Ireland". He did his utmost to provide "Home Rule" for Ireland, but defeat of his second Home Rule Bill by the House of Lords in 1893 finished the "Grand Old Man" of English politics.

14th August 1993 Saturday
A day in Windsor! Joined a Leicester City coach day-trip to Windsor for a reconnoitre of the town & its hotels with a view to staying there in September. I chose Fairlight Lodge Hotel, Frances Road, a small hotel with only 10 bedrooms – one time home of the Mayor of Windsor.

Children Tagged –A plan to postcode children, so they can be delivered home if lost will be launched by the Royal Mail and NSPCC next month. For less than the cost of an 18p stamp, parents can buy stickers with personal identification numbers for fitting into children's shoes.

Freedom of City – The pioneer of the genetic fingerprinting technique, Professor Alec Jeffreys, is to be given the freedom of the City of Leicester. He will be made an honorary freeman at a ceremony at Leicester's Town Hall next Friday.

Archdeacon off to Australia – The Archdeacon of Leicester, the Venerable David Silk, has accepted a job in Australia. The staunch traditionalist, who is 56 and hit the headlines with his fight against the priesting of women, is to become Bishop of Ballerat, Victoria. He has been archdeacon for 13 years.

18th August 1993 Wednesday
The tragic news today is that three miners have been killed by a rock fall 2,000 feet underground at Bilsthorpe Colliery near Mansfield, Notts.

Pit was Reprieved – Bilsthorpe was one of the 31 threatened with closure last October in the Government's controversial shake-up of the industry. The pit was reprieved and in March was designated a

"market tested" pit when the results of the White Paper review were announced. But this failed to guarantee a future for the mine – and has only served to fuel speculation about its possible fate amid a dwindling industry.

20th August 1993 Friday
"It's on with his head" – The statue of Cardinal Wolsey in Abbey Park was decapitated by vandals 18 months ago. Now he is back in one piece & restored to his former glory. The statue was carved in 1920 for Wolsey Ltd., a hosiery firm. In 1979 the 8 foot high statue moved to Abbey Park.

22nd August 1993 Sunday
"Dear Aunty Cuz,
Thank you very much for the dish which you bought us for our wedding. It was very kind of you & we are looking forward to using it. Simon & I are both looking forward also to seeing you on the 29th.
Love from Alison & Simon xx.
28 Rosslyn Way, Thornbury, Bristol BS12 1SG"

24th August 1993 Tuesday
St Bartholomew's Day – He is one and the same Nathaniel, of whom Christ was able to say in advance, "An Israelite indeed, in whom is no guile". (John 1 – 47) As Andrew first brought his brother Simon Peter to Jesus, so Philip brought the doubting Nathaniel to see for himself the Christ – "Come and see."

26th August 1993 Thursday
"With Visa's Delta Card, I'm an Ex-chequer" – As the cashless society continues its forward march, it becomes more & more a cheque-less society. I have a Lloyds Bank Visa Delta, which not only withdraws cash from a cash dispenser, but also from a bank account.

28th August 1993 Saturday
"**Had higher results**" – This briefest of detail recorded in my diary, exactly 45 years ago, marked the end of my academic career, when I gained only 2 "A" levels, instead of the 3 required for university. As this year's results are announced, I feel for those who have failed.

29th August 1993 Sunday
Today we celebrated brother Pat's 75th birthday & also Alison's wedding to Simon.
The wedding was at Packington Church at 1 p.m. followed by the reception at The Priest House, Kings Mills, Castle Donington.
What a lovely wedding & what a fairytale setting for the reception for some 100 guests.

30th August 1993 Monday
"Learning never in vain – whatever the A-level grade" – These encouraging words of wisdom in the Leicester Mercury are to all who are classed as failures. *"Their two years' work has not been in vain. What must never be forgotten is that the learning process can never be taken away – merely built upon"*

3rd September 1993 Friday
One cup - £10-25p, one saucer - £5-40p, two plates - £7-50p each. Last year, on Midsummer's day, I bought my

first exquisite cup & saucer "Royal Garden" made by Royal Worcester. Now my collection has grown to 2 cups, 2 saucers & 2 plates. I spied them in Lewis's, Leicester, closing down sale. Closing next February.

5th September 1993 Sunday
St Michael & All Angels Church Ravenstone "Restoration Club" Monthly Draw – in a bid to raise money for the church we now have a monthly draw whereby half the money goes to the church & half is for prize money. Some 200 people pay £1 each per month for 1st, 2nd, 3rd or 4th prize.

7th September 1993 Tuesday
From Greenwood Page & Ward, Solicitors, Colchester – "Mrs Phyllis Dunn's Estate" (Mary Moore)
"We are just finalising Mrs Dunn's estate, which has been quite complicated, & now have pleasure in enclosing a cheque in your favour for £500 to pay the legacy Mrs Dunn left you by her Will dated 6th February, 1992."

9th September 1993 Thursday
As when Cousin Audrey left me £100 I felt that I wanted to say "thank you" (8th January 1985), so now I feel that I must say "thank you" to Mary.
On the very day that I received £500 from Mary, cousin Miles dug up in his garden a cash box full of "hidden treasure", probably buried by his grandfather.

11th September 1993 Saturday
A legacy of Arabic Numerals – My latest book "The Guinness Book of Numbers" gives the history & development of numerational systems throughout the world. What a legacy for us all. Who must we thank for the now internationally common Arabic numerals? Not the Arabs! The Indians.

13th September 1993 Monday
"The Grand Climacteric" – From my latest "Book of Numbers" I learn that every seventh year in a person's life is critical, or climacteric, when some important change in health or fortune occurs. But most critical of all is 63 (7 x 9), called the Grand Climacteric. Cocky is now 63 & I am 62.

15th September 1993 Wednesday
"I sent £5 to the Lord Mayor of London for the Kennedy Memorial Appeal. The £1 million is to be divided between a memorial plinth & steps & scholarships in the U.S. for British students"
Thus I wrote in my diary in May 1964. Today I visited Runnymede & walked up these steps. .

17th September 1993 Friday
Enid & I are enjoying a few magical days in Windsor, where we have fallen in love with Windsor Castle & St George's Chapel with its quire stalls for the use of illustrious Knights of the Garter. Each knight has his sword, helmet, crest and banner above his stall, and here today we sat for Evensong.

19th September 1993 Sunday
From the great royal splendour of St George's Chapel Windsor to the lesser splendour of St George's

Swannington for Harvest Festival, where the preacher stressed the value of being led by God in the wilderness "to humble thee, & to prove thee & to know whether thou wouldst keep his commandments" (Deut. 8)

21st September 1993 Tuesday
Bromage, Lawrence Walter (Jim) of Saxons Rise, Ratby, passed suddenly away September 19th 1993, aged 62 years. Beloved husband of the late Kathleen, dearly loved father of Susan and Stephen, devoted and much loved granddad of Marie and Alan. Funeral service Ratby Parish Church Friday September 24th at 2-30p.m. followed by cremation Gilroes Crematorium. All flowers and inquiries to Coalville and District Funeral Service, 89 Belvoir Road, Coalville. Tel (0530) 838600.
Bromage, Jim, left us suddenly, Sunday, September 19th 1993. Beloved brother and uncle, a kind and gentle man. Rest a while. – John, Georgina and family.
Like Martin O'Mara, who died in April 1990, this is another of the lads who was in my class at school. Both passed suddenly away. How good to be called a kind & gentle man.

23rd September 1993 Thursday
We meet our teacher of 50 years ago. Enjoying an evening stroll by the lakeside at Melbourne, Enid & I encountered Miss Smith, now in her seventies, who taught us at Grammar School. What an amazing reversal of role-playing. It seemed that she, the teacher, now looked to us for reassurance.

25th September 1993 Saturday
"The green shoots….." - At the Conservative Party Conference 2 years ago, Chancellor of the Exchequer, Norman Lamont said, "It is clear that Britain is coming out of recession …. the green shoots of economic spring are appearing once again".
The green shoots however, soon took another dip.

27th September 1993 Monday
Cousin Miles & I spent the afternoon in Coalville library delving into the 1907AD edition of the Coalville Times, now stored on microfilm. We found details of Grandpa Hewes & his brother John who were declared bankrupt on 17th June in the paper dated 28th June – "Coalville Builders Failure".

29th September 1993 Wednesday
Harvest & Patronal Festival combined yet again this year at Ravenstone with no mention at all of Michael "The Great Prince" (Daniel, Chapter 12)
Guest preacher was the Revd Derek Goodman whom we last encountered in May 1990. He spoke this year about Jesus the vine – the true vine (St John, Chapter 15)

1st October 1993 Friday
Cocky also has spent £4,000 on his home, No 37 Yealand Drive, Lancaster. LA1 4EW.
Like Enid, he has had double-glazing throughout. (30th September 1992)
Yealand Drive is in the Scotforth district, south of the city centre & not far from Lancaster University.

3rd October 1993 Sunday
A real live horseshoe! In June 1980, at Market Bosworth

Garden Fete, I bought two horseshoes, one painted silver & one painted black. But today, on my morning walk, I found a horseshoe which had only just parted company with its owner, complete with loose nails & bits of hard hoof.

5th October 1993 Tuesday

Honi Soit Qui Mal Y Pense – "Dear Miss Hewes, I warmly welcome you as a Life Member of the Society of the Friends of St George's, Windsor"   T.C.M. O'Donovan, Honorary Secretary.

7th October 1993 Thursday

"Service of Thanksgiving for all creatures great & small" For the 4th time, Katherine, Toffee & I attended this service where we were reminded that "the stable cattle first adored the newborn Christ on Christmas morn; and on a donkey was the Lord triumphant to his passion borne". Preacher was Hughie Jones.

9th October 1993 Saturday

Was there ever a lovelier bride than Princess Margaret, the Queen's sister, when on 6th May 1960 she married Anthony Armstrong-Jones?
Yesterday their son, Viscount Linley aged 31, married Serena Stanhope, aged 23, in a bridal outfit copied from that of Princess Margaret, now sadly divorced & alone.

11th October 1993 Monday

Visa Delta 4921 8108 0090 7511 – This week I made my first ever purchase without cash & without a cheque. From Canyon Mountain Sports Shop, Leicester, I bought a maroon coloured, waterproof, windproof, quilt-lined "Berghaus" winter jacket reduced by 25% from £150 to £112-50p.

13th October 1993 Wednesday

Electronic Identity Tags – About 3,000 people who regularly use County Hall at Glenfield have now been issued with electronic identity tags. These admit holders to any of the dozen entrance doors to the building. People without tags have to go in via reception & be accounted for.

15th October 1993 Friday

"Hopes fade for threatened pits" – Despite prospects of a reprieve (see January 1993) 21 of the 31 coalmines threatened with closure have now closed & the remaining 10 are not likely to survive much longer. More than 20,000 miners have taken redundancy & left the industry in the last year.

17th October 1993 Sunday

Alexander, Cocky & Joan's second grandchild, was born on Friday 15th October weighing 6lbs 9ozs. He might well have been born a week earlier on his brother Matthew's 3rd birthday, but decided to break the family tradition of a birthday on the 7th. Jonathan has been asked to be godfather.

19th October 1993 Tuesday

Whirlwind romance for young Murdo! – 29 year old Murdo, step-son of Mary Blue, living all alone in the house vacated by Mary Blue earlier this year, has now found himself a 29 year old girl friend, become engaged almost immediately & is getting married on Friday 22nd October, in Scotland.

21st October 1993 Thursday

Dr Alfred Bernhard Nobel was so great a man that no-one had the "magnetism of heart" to match his. He was a genius who specialised in chemistry – in explosives – and yet he was a dreamer of dreams. He dreamed of a world where everyone might live in peace.
"I myself have never known any great joy – though I have indeed experienced deep sorrow". So wrote the great Alfred Nobel in September 1878. So it was that this chemical engineer was inspired to leave the bulk of his fortune to future generations – to great people yet to be born.
(See 20th October 1992)

25th October 1993 Monday

Unearthing the glorious past – China is to start excavating the final unopened vault at the tomb of Emperor Qin Shihuang, bringing to light the last regiments of the famed 2,000 year old Terracotta Warriors.

Record value – A rare £1 note fetched £52,000 at a London auction, a world record for a European banknote. The 1797 note, only the second-ever £1 printed, was bought by an Essex collector. It fetched nearly three times its estimated value.

Screen shop – TV addicts were today relishing Britain's first ever electronic home shopping channel. The new 24 hour satellite station means viewers can now buy goods ranging from sporting equipment and designer clothes to power tools and toys from the comfort of their living rooms.
QVC – The Shopping Channel will be beamed across the UK from today by BSkyB.

27th October 1993 Wednesday

Shakespeare's Forest of Arden is the setting for his play "As You Like It" where the banished Duke lives in exile & enjoys a "life more sweet than that of painted pomp". Here we learn that "All the world's a stage & all the men & women merely players" listing the seven ages of man.

29th October 1993 Friday
….. it's an Autumn Windfall

Dear Miss Hewes, Re – Doris Annie Hewes (Aunt Dos) Cheque enclosed £12,500. Aunt Dos has kindly made brother Pat & me the main beneficiaries in her will, resulting in £12,500 each.

2nd November 1993 Tuesday

Another prize from E.R.N.I.E. "Pay Miss E. Hewes £50 only"
With statistically average luck a person holding £2,000 worth of bonds, which is my holding, may expect to win two prizes a year. Altogether in one year ERNIE pays out £140 million, ranging from £50 to £250,000.

4th November 1993 Thursday

And again Joanne poured out the troubles of her heart to me, after she had seen her boyfriend Glen with another girl, complete with his baby. She has taken on another job at "Granby Garments" in Whitwick – an offshoot of the very same "Granby Garments" of Cocky in Morecombe.

5th November 1993 Friday
Henn, *Betty, passed away at the L.G.H. on November 1st 1993, aged 70 years, loving wife of the late Gordon, much loved mum and special friend of Dawn and David and nan to Jonathan and Matthew. Funeral service at Christchurch on Friday November 5th 1993.*

Coalville's parish church was packed to capacity for the funeral of a Coalville woman whose life was given to the service of others. Betty Henn, 70, died unexpectedly in hospital. A lifelong member of Christ Church, she was a member of the Parochial Church Council and Choir. She was also associated with the Mothers' Union, Flower Guild, Social Committee and Crèche and organised many UK and European holidays and outings. Betty Henn was treasurer for the local branch of the Spastics Society for 21 years. Many will remember her as Wardrobe Mistress for Coalville Amateur Operatic Society. A parish church spokesman said, "So many people who knew Betty had their lives enriched, and there's no doubt she will be greatly missed across a wide spectrum of Coalville life." Mrs Henn leaves a daughter Dawn, son-in-law David and two grandchildren

(newspaper cutting)

6th November 1993 Saturday
Visa Delta 4921 8108 0090 7511 – My second purchase without cash & without a cheque.
Having joined the ranks of the "ex-chequers", it was so much more convenient simply to hand over my payment card when buying a new pair of trainer shoes "Step Reebok" £49-99p from Stylo Instep, Nottingham.

8th November 1993 Monday
With baby Alexander less than three weeks old, his mother Yvonne is already warning her husband David that if he spends £5,000 joining an exclusive golf club he is likely to end up being divorced. After all, she is the major bread winner, contributing to their life of luxury.

10th November 1993 Wednesday
TART, *John, of Ravenstone, died suddenly in hospital on November 10th 1993. Dearly loved husband of Rita, very dear father of Nigel, Philip and Dawn. Funeral service at St. Michael and All Angels Parish Church, Ravenstone, Tuesday November 16th at 2 p.m. followed by interment in the churchyard. Family flowers only please. Donations if so desired for St. Michael and All Angels Parish Church, Ravenstone, c/o Coalville and District Funeral Service. All inquiries to Coalville and District Funeral Service, 89 Belvoir Road, Coalville. Tel. 838600.*
John Tart (1920 – 1993) was cousin Rita's husband. Like Jim Bromage who died recently, he was remembered as a kind & gentle man. He & Rita were a devoted couple with 2 adopted sons, Nigel & Philip.

12th November 1993 Friday
To Leicester Cathedral yesterday for the Patronal Festival – "God all powerful, who called Martin from the armies of this world to be a faithful soldier of Christ,

give us grace to follow him in his love & compassion for the needy & enable your church to claim for all people their inheritance as children of God."

14th November 1993 Sunday
The Revd. Royston Grandfield Davis did not last long at Snibston. So upset was he over the vote in favour of women priests that he packed his bags & went. His place has been taken by the Reverend Michael David Webb who was "licensed" as Assistant Priest at Hugglescote this summer.

16th November 1993 Tuesday
"We in this world see things only from our present day view-point" (16th November 1989)
But Esdras, the man who ventured to question God's seemingly unfair way of dealing with mankind, was encouraged to "consider that which is to come, rather than the present."

18th November 1993 Thursday
£250 thousand million! This is the present annual spending of our government. In order to achieve this, the government needs to borrow £50 billion & there is now therefore a searching long term review of public spending, lasting another 3 years, whereby each government department will have its budget studied in detail.

20th November 1993 Saturday
"The way of the Lord is not equal" (Ezekiel 18 – 29) So man sees the unequal way God seems to treat his children. But in Chapter 18, God spells out to Ezekiel exactly what are his ruling principles. "The soul that sinneth, it shall die, but if a man be just, he shall surely live."

22nd November 1993 Monday
"Venus & Adonis" by Shakespeare - Not since I first read "Tomlinson" by Rudyard Kipling, ten years ago, have I enjoyed a poem so much as "Venus & Adonis".
Venus, the goddess of love, could win the heart of any man – any man that is, except Adonis. Her frustrations when wooing him are quite hilarious.

24th November 1993 Wednesday
Charles "plans to wed Camilla"
Prince Charles has promised to divorce Princess Diana and marry his friend Camilla Parker-Bowles, royal watcher Nigel Dempster claimed today.
In June 1977, we read in the newspapers "Charles to marry Astrid". Now we read "Charles to wed Camilla".
He certainly loves her dearly, but she is already married.

26th November 1993 Friday
James Bulger, aged 2, who lived in Oak Towers, a small block of flats in Kirkby near Liverpool, went shopping with his mum on 12th February this tear in Bootle & was lured away by 2 young boys. Yesterday, at Preston Crown Court, Robert Thompson and Jon Venables, now aged 11, were charged with his murder.

28th November 1993 Sunday
"I believe in the Holy Ghost ... who spake by the prophets"

It was this aspect of the Nicene Creed which burst into life for me, having just been fully immersed in the writings of all those great prophets of the Old Testament - Isaiah, Jeremiah, Ezekkiel, etc.
(See Ezekiel, Chapter 8 as a prime example)

30th November 1993 Tuesday
Old romantic Hewsie opened an account with the Heart of England Building Society, purely for its **heart** & now it is no more. On October 2nd this year it merged with Cheltenham & Gloucester Building Society for us to benefit from a larger organisation.

2nd December 1993 Thursday
The Chancellor's old battered case may have been in use since the year 1860, but his new budget extends into the 21st century with plans to raise the age of pensions for women to 65 by 2020A.D.
Budget – From December 1993 the Budget will be amalgamated with the annual spending statement.

4th December 1993 Saturday
British Gas has won a major contract to develop the Dolphin Gas Field in Trinidad. The field is thought to consist of more than a trillion cubic metres of gas. What would Columbus have thought of this sort of treasure? He named the place Trinidad.

6th December 1993 Monday
The 1905 editions of the Coalville Times have provided cousin Miles & me with many hours of pleasure. Grandfather George Harry Hewes had such a time with the newly appointed Sanitary Inspector who delighted in taking him to court for failing to comply with the local council's bye-laws.
"Have you had a copy of the bye-laws?"
"I presume so" said George Harry.
"Well don't presume. You must answer".
Mr Ward suggested that if Mr Hewes had misled the Council he should be asked to appear before them again.
"We don't want him here again" said the Chairman, who actually supported George Harry.

10th December 1993 Friday
O.A.P. Hewsie is just one of a rapidly aging population. Today one person in 15 in Europe is aged 75 or over. By 2010 AD the ratio will be one in ten. By then one in four will be of retirement age.

12th December 1993 Sunday
A sad Princess of Wales has announced that she intends at the end of this year to reduce the extent of her public life. Beneath the brave dazzling exterior, the excessive intrusion of the media has reduced her to tears.

14th December 1993 Tuesday
From my weary & worn love, by post, a Christmas card, "Especially for the One I Love", containing two £10 notes – "The happiness we're sharing is a very special reason for you & I to celebrate a merry Christmas season" All my love, merry Christmas darling. John xxxx xxxx

16th December 1993 Thursday
"Remember the Sabbath Day to keep it holy" – In April

1986 the Government were defeated on a Bill to allow shops to open on a Sunday. Now M.P.s have voted 333 to 258 in favour of Sunday trading. From June next year the big stores can open for up to 6 hours on Sundays, providing the House of Lords agree.

18th December 1993 Saturday
Hundreds of elderly and disabled people in Leicestershire are celebrating the meals on wheels service's 50th anniversary, helped by members of the Women's Royal Voluntary Service. In the year up to March 1992, 1,530 customers enjoyed 156,160 meals supplied by 2,600 volunteers in the county. And the WRVS is now looking for new helpers.

20th December 1993 Monday
A nostalgic trip to Willoughby-on-the-Wolds where all whom I once knew so well now lie side by side in the churchyard, watched over by the great east window of the church – Madge & Bertha & Johnty & old Uncle Tom, their father.
50 years ago I knew most of the villagers. Now I am a complete stranger.

22nd December 1993 Wednesday
For the second time, I have the pleasure of playing hostess at Christmas to Bunting, now aged 78 & beginning to feel very lonely & lost in the world without Mostyn. She arrived today in a low & weepy state, having been brought by Michael; & dreading returning to the solitude of her home.

24th December 1993 Friday
"Do you remember?"
"I can remember when ….."
After a couple of days reminiscing with Pat & Evelyn over a lifetime of shared memories, Bunting blossomed into her old familiar self.
We visited Phyl at Ashby Court Nursing Home & Bunting was greeted & welcomed from all directions.

26th December 1993 Sunday
As in September 1989, Mary Moore & I visited Bardon Churchyard & Snarestone Churchyard to renew acquaintance with those long since dead, so Bunting & I visited Ravenstone Churchyard where Mostyn lies with his parents; Snibston Churchyard where so many of the family now lie & Coalville Cemetery where others lie.

28th December 1993 Tuesday
The Secretary of State for Energy no longer exists. Following the General Election in April last year, the whole Department was swallowed up once more in the Department of Trade & Industry. How thankful I am to have escaped just before another Staff Inspection & all the attendant consequences.

30th December 1993 Thursday
"Now I lay me down to sleep, I pray thee Lord my soul to keep. If I should die before I wake, I pray thee Lord my soul to take." Every night, my soul is offered to God's safe keeping.

Bolsover, *Christine, Healey Street, South Wigston, loving daughter of Dora and the late Bernard, dearest* *sister of Brian, passed away suddenly December 20th 1993, aged 50 years.*

Expert baffled by woman's death

A Home Office pathologist was baffled by the sudden death of a Leicestershire spinster, an inquest has heard. Typist Miss Christine Bolsover, 50, died after collapsing at her South Wigston home.

A post mortem examination and tests by Dr Clive Bouch failed to reveal a medical cause of death. The Home Office pathologist told an inquest, "There was no evidence to suggest that she died of anything other than natural causes".

The inquest heard that Miss Bolsover had been treated for depression for 14 years. But Dr Bouch said there were only normal levels of her usual anti-depressants in her system. A verdict of death by natural causes was recorded.

(newspaper cutting)

(See 4th February 1991)

Medical Mystery
The man who just died.

Richard Wai Hung Tang, a 35 year old bachelor was found dead in the bedroom of his home in Avon Street, Highfields, Leicester, on 4th May 1993. He worked as a special effects artist in London & was seen in good health by a friend five days before his death. His friend, Martin Wong, said, "He was perfectly normal. He didn't even complain of having a cough or anything".

Home Office pathologist & head of the Leicester Pathology Centre, Dr Clive Bouch, said he could find no evidence of disease or injury to cause death.

Foul play, suicide, asphyxiation, exposure to drugs, alcohol, poisons & carbon monoxide were all eliminated by forensic analysis.

Mr Michael Charman, Leicester's assistant deputy coroner, recorded a verdict of death by a cause unable to be determined by a post mortem examination but clearly of an unknown natural cause.

(newspaper cutting)

* * *

The Royal Institution Christmas Lectures 1993
Over the Rainbow

In 1826, Michael Faraday conceived the idea of the Royal Institution Christmas Lectures. These lectures introduce teenagers to the amazing world of scientific exploration & thanks to television we can all now share in the wonder of the latest scientific discoveries. So it is then that we have been taken on the most amazing journey back in time to the birth of the universe 15 thousand million years ago! Our guide has been Professor Frank Close, Head of Theoretical Physics at Rutherford Appelton Laboratory whose lecture is called "The Cosmic Onion", unpeeling for us the layers of matter from atoms, to get to the atom's nucleus & the very beginning of creation.

The more science advances, the more we can see "the invisible". Our normal vision is limited to only one form of electromagnetic radiation—our rainbow is but one octave on a piano. Light is a form of electromagnetic radiation & our eyes are able to detect it. We can see all the colours of the rainbow from red to deep purple. This is our "octave" of light, but either side of this octave lie many more types of electromagnetic radiation that our eyes cannot detect, such as x-rays, radio waves & microwaves. Modern science enables us to "see" the whole cosmic rainbow & thus the composition of the whole universe. $E = mc^2$ is Albert Einstein's famous equation. E represents energy, m represents mass & c is the speed of light. Because energy can turn into matter, scientists believe that the universe began with the Big Bang. But what was there before that? The first steps towards that answer may come from the Large Hadron Collider which is due to be built in the 21st century to simulate the very beginning; ready for another Christmas Lecture.

The best space telescope we have at the moment is the optical telescope "Hubble". This of course is limited to our "one little octave on the piano" & astronomers are now more excited by what they can observe in other parts of the electromagnetic spectrum, particularly by x-rays. Europe is set to lead the field in x-ray observations in the early part of the next century. Part of an ambitious research programme is the launch in 1999 by the European Space Agency (E.S.A.) of a major x-ray observation satellite, XMM (x-ray multi-mirror). Larger than an average house & carrying x-ray observation instruments about 100 times more powerful than any on previous satellite or rocket missions, it will help answer questions such as how galaxies are formed & die; & it will provide much more accurate information on very high energy sources, such as quasars & black holes, which emit most of their radiation in x-rays rather than visible light.

* * *

1994

1st January 1994 Saturday

"Welcome to Neighbourhood Watch" – Tina & Wayne, my next-door young neighbours, have organised a Neighbourhood Watch scheme for our immediate neighbourhood, so we are all now keeping watch for each other, hoping to deter any burglar.

3rd January 1994 Monday

"Skills & Capabilities" – This is what young people need today as well as "Knowledge" when they are launching out on their 40 years at work. The 6 skills needed are – Communication, Problem Solving, Team-working, Social & Interpersonal Skills, Information Technology and Numeracy.

The Capabilities are – Adaptability, Originality, Discretion, Leadership, Ability to Absorb Training and Exercising Judgment.

"Hybrid Capabilities" will be needed much more in the future in this rapidly changing world. Young people will need to acquire & develop a high level of core skills. They will also need to be flexible, adaptable & capable of coping with uncertainty. Not only must they have been taught at school, but they must also have acquired the habit of learning. I am thankful to have had such a good education.

7th January 1994 Friday

No longer obliged to learn or study what others demand, it is lovely to have the freedom to read or explore whatever is of interest to me. From the elevated viewpoint of retirement I can watch the world go by without being swept along with it. I can even think dispassionately about Brian Lamming on his 66th birthday – "so calm are we when passions are no more".

9th January 1994 Sunday

No sooner do we set up our Neighbourhood Watch scheme than the burglars arrive. The three houses they broke into were – Dorothy Taylor, No. 36 (jewellery), Sam Land, immediately opposite to me No.54, & Sally Springthorpe, No. 41 (cash).

Newspaper cutting – Three houses in Ravenstone were the target of burglars on Friday evening. The houses, all in Leicester Road, were entered between 5p.m. and 9p.m. From one house the burglars took jewellery, including bracelets and rings, valued at £900 and £30 in cash. A further £90 and £50 in cash was taken from the two other properties.

11th January 1994 Tuesday

Cardinal Basil Hume, the leader of the Roman Catholics in Britain is to receive the lovely 60 year old Duchess of Kent into the Catholic faith on 14th January at a service at his private chapel at Westminster Cathedral.

*Newspaper cutting - **Duchess of Kent turns to Rome** – The Duchess of Kent is to be received into the Roman Catholic Church on Friday in an unprecedented move by a member of the royal family.*

13th January 1994 Thursday

A new Type-writer! – Bought a smart new Smith Corona XL1850 (made in Singapore) Model 5A, Serial No. 2031840 for £70. In this age of the computer & word processor, the humble type-writer is almost a thing of the past, but I preferred a simple machine with the minimum of complications for the amount of typing I reckon to do.

15th January 1994 Saturday

"I will always love you" said Darren to Sharon on their wedding day 15th June 1991.

But now, new-age woman Sharon in her executive role at work, complete with company car & expecting to clinch deals worth £1 million & more, finds Darren too boring in her present elevated status. She has therefore turned him out of their home, which of course is more hers than his.

17th January 1994 Monday

"Anything Goes" is this year's choice for Coalville Amateurs & again I was very pleased to be asked to join those assembled at Peter Jacques' house for the annual allocation of tickets – Peter & his wife Vera, Basil Newbold, Vincent Hardy, Olive Meakin, George Taylor, Ann Day & new Treasurer Wendy Miles, complete with the de luxe "Treasurer's Case".

19th January 1994 Wednesday

Mount St. Bernard's Abbey Annual Ecumenical Service this week was led by "Broomleys Churches Together". A more unlikely combination of worshippers you never did see. The monks as usual sat interspersed with the congregation & allowed their most sacred Abbey to resound to guitar-playing, hand-clapping, arm-waving guests.

21st January 1994 Friday

Professor Alec Jeffreys, pioneer of the genetic finger-printing technique, who last year was given the freedom of the City of Leicester, has now been made a Knight in the New Year's Honours List. Aged 43, he is a "genetic scientist" at Leicester University.

23rd January 1994 Sunday

My latest library book "Kept – the Other Side of Tenko" is the result of a secret diary kept by Leslie Leonard Baynes in a Japanese prisoner of war camp from 1941 until 1945. What a story of courage & tenacity under the most atrocious conditions. Shunted in cattle trucks, or force marched from Singapore to Burma, these men built the railway.

25th January 1994 Tuesday

"Kept – the Other Side of Tenko" – This means saved by the hand of Providence, against all the odds, after years of deprivation & the daily roll-call, which in Japanese = "Tenko". Paraded night & morning for "Tenko", often barely able to stand; when at long last in August 1945, the author was liberated, he dumped everything but his diary.

27th January 1994 Thursday

"Civil Service Retirement Fellowship" – My second "Annual January Lunch" with the Coalville Group, the venue this year being Coalville Technical College where students prepare a good selection of dishes for up to 50 people. Again I was pleased to go with Mr & Mrs Jim Bailiss & enjoyed the company of 2 Loughborough ladies as we sat at one long table.

29th January 1994 Saturday

Lewis William, brother Pat's second grandchild's second child, delayed his arrival to be born yesterday, on Cocky's 64th birthday. Weighing in at almost 10lbs, he was a bumper bundle for his mum Karen, making Mary Blue a grandmother twice over at the age of 49. A brother for Suzannah (Sue & Loo), he is named after the Isle of Lewis, birthplace of MacLeods.

31st January 1994 Monday

An out-of-the-blue invitation to lunch with Mary Moore's life-long friend Molly Donaldson. Now in her eighties, Molly is the perfect hostess in the sumptuous surroundings of her home at Donington-le-Heath.

It was in June 1981 when Eddie, Molly's husband, then aged 68, had to be "held at bay". Today he was the perfect host as we all chatted together by the fireside.

2nd February 1994 Wednesday

Cousin Miles, described in his last venture as the "mercurial Miles Wilson" & also the "indefatigable Miles Wilson" is now in his element dealing with the publicity of a Hinckley based firm "Crane Electronics". He has access to all the very latest computer technology & is given freedom to develop & expand his own grandiose schemes to promote & sell the company at home & abroad.

4th February 1994 Friday

The Gingerbread Person takes a bow – Gingerbread Men, who have been around in some shape or form since the 17th century, have now been swept off the supermarket shelves to make way for Gingerbread Persons. Not even God himself is sacrosanct & beyond question in today's insistence on political correctness. Only by a whisker was "God" allowed to be mentioned in school assemblies & not "Divine Being or Power".

6th February 1994 Sunday

While "chatting by the fireside" at Molly's, she told me that she regularly visited an old retired miner & his wife who lived nearby in St. Mary's Avenue. Eddie told me that he now needed a new gardener. As Joanne's dad Dave has just lost his job as gardener to Mrs Moseley at Loughborough, I was able to act as catalyst & get them all together. The retired miner turned out to be Dave's dad!

8th February 1994 Tuesday

"We pay instant cash!" – "The Trent Antique Roadshow is in Burton at the Queens Hotel, Bridge St. Two days only offering highest possible cash settlements for all your items – broken or not ...."

So off to Burton I went with "the family silver", an oil painting, the prized chinaware, etc.

All I got was £20. Most of the items they didn't want at all. Just like Aunt Dos' sale in 1990.

10th February 1994 Thursday

New V.A.T. headquarters! (Value Added Tax) The Princess Royal officially opened Liverpool's magnificent new VAT headquarters on 1st February this year. Known as The Vatican, it cost £35 million & boasts a £400,000 hi-tech lighting system, crèche, £45,000 sculpture, £50,000 aeration plant, 260-seater restaurant, library & fitness centre for 1,800 office staff.

12th February 1994 Saturday

A sponsored walk through the Channel Tunnel, soon to be opened, raised £1.7million for charities. 118 walkers marched into history from Calais to Folkestone, the first time Man has been able to go on foot from France to England since the end of the last Ice Age, 15,000 years ago. It was a subterranean street party & cross-Channel carnival.

14th February 1994 Monday

"For my Valentine with love"
Although we are miles apart, you are always in my heart. You are my one & only Valentine. Love you for ever
xxxxxx

On this day in history: St Valentine's Day Circa 270: St. Valentine was martyred by Roman Emperor Claudius II Mystery surrounds why a day devoted to lovers should be named after the early Christian martyr St. Valentine. Bishop Valentine, who was executed on February 14th in the fourth century by being beaten with clubs and beheaded, is reputed to have hated women. But it seems the day of his death was close to an annual Roman festival in honour of the goddess Juno, who protected women and marriage. So as not to miss out on the celebrations, the early Christians linked them to one of their saints rather than a Roman god. By the Victorian era, St. Valentine's Day had become a frivolous affair. But in its early years it was customary on February 14th for young men to choose a wife by drawing her name from a box.

16th February 1994 Ash Wednesday

"From Land's End to John O'Groat's" – The speakers at this month's meeting of our local Civil Service Retirement Fellowship were the Revd. David Greenwood, Rector of Appleby Magna, Swepstone & Snarestone, and David Pilgrim who together cycled from Land's End to John O'Groat's in July 1992. A most interesting illustrated account of their adventure.

18th February 1994 Friday

New Archdeacon – The son of an East Midlands miner is to return to the region to take over as Archdeacon of Leicester, it was announced today.

The Reverend Mike Edson (53) steps into the shoes of The Venerable David Silk, who has accepted a post as a bishop in Australia, on September 1st.

At the moment, Mr Edson, who has a wife, daughter and three sons, is the warden of a religious community at the Lee Abbey Conference Centre in Devon. He was born in Nottinghamshire and graduated from Birmingham University with a degree in pure science and chemistry. Mr Edson worked for the Inland Revenue and in management consultancy before training for the ministry. He was ordained a deacon at Exeter in 1972 and as a priest a year later. He served as a curate and team vicar in Barnstaple until 1982 and then became a vicar in the London Diocese. Mr Edson, who is interested in walking, swimming and the theatre, moved to his present post in 1989. As Archdeacon of Leicester, he will be responsible for the deaneries covering Leicester, Melton Mowbray, Market Harborough, Wigston and Syston. Staunch traditionalist Mr Silk, who hit the headlines with a fight against the ordination of women as priests, is taking up the post of Bishop of Ballarat in Victoria.   (Newspaper cutting)

20th February 1994 Sunday
Flying Bishops! – Two traditionalist "flying bishops" have been appointed to minister to opponents of women priests.
John Richards, aged 60, becomes suffragan Bishop of Ebbsfleet & John Gaisford, 59, becomes suffragan Bishop of Beverley. They are officially called "Provincial Episcopal Visitors" & are there to administer to those who will not accept women priests.

22nd February 1994 Tuesday
The season of Lent is here again & we are reminded of the temptation of our Lord by the devil. The Rector of Ravenstone, the Revd. Kerry Emmett spoke of the three different temptations (Matthew, Chapter 4) & how Christ's own knowledge of the scriptures enabled him to come up with the right answer to Satan. Each temptation was dismissed with, "It is written ……."
Even the devil can quote scripture. "If you are the Son of God" he said to Christ, "throw yourself down. For it is written he will give his angels charge concerning thee & in their hands they shall bear thee up, lest at any time thou shalt dash thy foot against a stone". (Psalm 91)
Jesus replied, "It is written again, thou shall not tempt the Lord thy God."

26th February 1994 Saturday
John Richards – Suffragan Bishop of Ebbsfleet (named after a sand-bank off the Kent coast).
This pretty well sums up the sorry state of the Church of England at the moment – well & truly a house built on the sand (see Matthew 7 : 26)
The Rt. Revd. Dr. Richard Rutt, former Bishop of Leicester, is leaving the Church of England to become a Roman Catholic, as are many others.

28th February 1994 Monday
£250 thousand million is what the government spends in one year. Welfare handouts take up one third of this spending, eclipsing the defence budget. The biggest part of the benefits bill is £26 billion for 10 million state retirement pensions (including me). £7 billion goes to one million single parents. The Welfare State is cracking at the seams & some say it will have to be abolished.

1st March 1994 Tuesday
"Can we be sure of God?"
During Lent we have a series of talks at Leicester Cathedral. During this talk by Bishop Bill Ind of Grantham, he said that to find God we have to search in depth. As the aged King Lear said to Cordelia, "We'll take upon us the mystery of things, as if we were God's spies". We will be God's "secretary", i.e. one entrusted with his secrets.

I was reminded of the prophet Elisha who calmed the fears of his servant when they were surrounded by the horses & chariots of the enemy. (II Kings, Chapter 6). And Elisha prayed & said, Lord, I pray thee, open his eyes, that he may see. And the Lord opened the eyes of the young man & he saw & behold, the mountain was full of horses & chariots of fire round about Elisha.

4th March 1994 Friday
On this day in history in 1924 "Happy Birthday to You" was published by Clayton F Summy.

5th March 1994 Saturday
"Anything Goes" – We are now well into the swing of Coalville Amateurs' production which began last Wednesday & runs until next Saturday. A lively colourful show by Cole Porter & set in the 1920s, the action takes place on a luxury liner sailing from New York to Southampton. Again it is my pleasure to be "Assistant House Manager".

7th March 1994 Monday
Joanne celebrates her 20th birthday today, looking forward to becoming a mother later in the year. Now 4 months pregnant, she & her boyfriend Glenn are happily ensconced in their love-nest at Coalville & I see very little of her. Her mother Sue, pleased to be becoming a grandmother, is my near neighbour & keeps me up-to-date on all their news.

9th March 1994 Wednesday
"Can we be sure of God's will for the human race?"
This talk at Leicester Cathedral was by Bill Flagg, Assistant Bishop of Southwell, who quoted liberally from the scriptures to provide us with the answer.
Deut. 29 : 29, Psalm 8, Isaiah 11 : 6 – 9, Luke 15 : 3 – 32, Revelation & various other snippets, all summarised in the fact that "God so loved the world that he gave his only begotten Son".

11th March 1994 Friday
An innovation for this year's Coalville Amateurs' production has been a raffle during the interval which Joan, Enid & I have enjoyed running. All we did was stand there for 15 minutes while people flocked to us for tickets. Each night we presented 3 prizes – whisky, wine & chocolates - & over ten nights made an overall profit exceeding £300.

13th March 1994 Sunday
"We've been together now for 45 years!" That is Coalville Amateurs' & I.
This year it was lovely to welcome Ursula back into our midst as prompter after an absence of 10 years. The Society, founded in 1919, celebrates its 75th anniversary this year & we golden oldies shine with reflected glory. For one golden oldie a dozen red roses from her true love.

15th March 1994 Tuesday
Sharon has now relinquished her married name "Pickering" & reverted to her maiden name "MacLeod". Now in possession of a de luxe company car, complete with telephone & almost an in-built office, she offered to take Mary Blue & me to London & back for our theatre

trip in honour of Mary Blue's 50th birthday. She was on her weekly business trip to London as a "rep".

17th March 1994 Thursday
Civil Service Retirement Fellowship – Coalville Group Annual General Meeting, when to my surprise I learned that the Group had only been in action since 1988.
Our Social Account stood at £124 & I won the monthly raffle – a packet of Sainsbury's Red Label Tea & a packet of Sainsbury's biscuits.
One of our members – Muriel Harding – then gave an interesting talk on Calligraphy.

19th March 1994 Saturday
"Le bébé d'Evelyn était born" –Thus I wrote in my diary 50 years ago, when as a 12 year-old I had been given for Christmas by Mrs Cassell, our evacuee from war-torn London, my most treasured gift – a Desk Diary. So secret was my precious diary that it had to be written in school-girl French or Latin & other coded formats, now forgotten.

21st March 1994 Monday
How many Premium bond holders are aware that before the introduction of the £1 million monthly payout, the total monthly payout was cut by £3 million and the odds reduced from 11,000 to one to 15,000 to one, from March 1993?
It's now worth considering whether it's better investing money in the football pools than Premium Bonds.
C. Richards, Kittle, Swansea.

ERNIE's total monthly payout has been cut by £3 million & the odds of winning have been reduced. Now I know why last year I had only one win, rather than the expected two. Such information is not broadcast by the National Savings Office.

23rd March 1994 Wednesday
"Can I be sure of God's will for me?"
This talk at Leicester Cathedral was by Leicester's own Assistant Bishop Ashby. Again we were reminded of God's promises to Abram, which would take effect long after his limited time on earth (see 3rd June 1991), suggesting that God's will for each of us extends well beyond life on earth. God does not expect us all to be great achievers, but to trust him.
Bishop Ashby told us about Joseph II, born 13th March 1741, who died aged 48, convinced that he had failed in everything he ever attempted. Although he was Holy Roman Emperor, his conflict with the Roman Catholic Church caused him great problems. All his great ideas for reform – education, health, etc. met with resistance, but today are accepted.

27th March 1994 Palm Sunday
On 5th June 1984, I visited "The Old House" in Hereford & from the 2nd storey looked out from the windows of the 17th century to the 20th century scene below.
I have now had another similar experience visiting Steven & his fiancée Jane in their newly acquired rented upstairs flat, an 18th century property, in the old part of Ashby – No. 7, The Green.

29th March 1994 Tuesday
"Can we be sure of Jesus?"
Bishop Ashby said that Jesus was acknowledged not only by Christians but by many others as a great prophet & teacher. It is "through Jesus Christ our Lord" however, that Christians address their prayers to God. "Whom say ye that I am?" (Matthew 16 : 15) As Peter recognised Christ as the Son of the living God, so he founded the Christian Church, where God & not man reigns supreme.

31st March 1994 Thursday
"They covenanted with him for thirty pieces of silver" (Matthew 26 : 15)
This was the sum for which Judas Iscariot betrayed Christ with a kiss. Thirty pieces of silver (probably Greek tetradrachms) was the value of a slave if killed by a beast. In the Old Testament, Joseph was sold for 20 pieces of silver (Genesis 37 : 28), i.e. two thirds the price of an adult slave.
Cousin Peter Hewes, who married Christine Hill on 15th October 1966, died of cancer in June 1992, aged 50. Now Christine has died of cancer in March 1994, aged 51.

3rd April 1994 Easter Sunday
Bunting arrived in Ravenstone for another week's holiday at my home, 27, Leicester Road. Again she was brought by Michael & Josie, arriving at 4p.m. Bunting & I then went to Evensong at Ravenstone Church where there were only 8 altogether in the congregation – Easter Sunday - & the church almost empty. What a sad sign of the times, on Easter Day.

4th April 1994 Easter Monday
"Had a long talk with Cocky after church parmi multos lacrimos"
This was my entry in my diary, exactly 40 years ago. Having kept Cocky dangling on a string for such a long time, I had to decide once & for all whether to accept his proposal of marriage or not. As there would be no happy joint family get-together, midst many, many tears, I had to decide.

6th April 1994 Wednesday
"Rursus multos lacrimos" As you can see, it was a decision which was not taken lightly. Even John Dolman was involved. He wrote to me offering his advice. Finally I decided to let Cocky go & find himself a new girl-friend. I wrote to Mum telling her of our momentous decision.
Now, 40 years on, Cocky is a father & a grandfather, but we still love each other.

8th April 1994 Friday
"Don't let me stay here Betty. Please take me home" pleaded Aunt Dos in the Nursing Home, five years ago, on 14th August 1989.
"What shall I do Betty? Don't let Michael put me in a home" pleaded Bunting today, as she finds herself totally confused & unable to remember what she has done or where she has been recently & living completely in the past.
How sad to see Bunting in such a sorry state of confusion. Since Mostyn died, 2½ years ago, she has

gone completely to pieces. Living in Stafford, she feels like a fish out of water & certainly cannot recognise it as home. When Michael was transferred to Stafford with the bank, Bunting & Mostyn moved house with him & then Mostyn died.

12th April 1994 Tuesday
A new lawn-mower. Qualcast Quadtrak. This is to replace my old Qualcast Jetstream whose wobbly wheel finally broke off altogether. The new £80 mower is my first purchase since the 282 Single Market Directives came into being. It conforms to the specifications of directive 84/538/EEC relating to noise level, with guaranteed maximum sound level.

14th April 1994 Thursday
Thanks to Dr. Stutman, I have now walked 7,000 miles. Starting in 1982, at 500 miles each year, I now have the opportunity to walk 1,000 miles per year. The number of motor cars & lorries emitting poisonous gases from their exhaust pipes makes walking along the pavements most unpleasant, so whenever possible I prefer to walk across the fields.

16th April 1994 Saturday
Windsor Sideboard – Golden Dawn - £1,280-00p.
18 piece "Duchess" – Memories - 6 cups/saucers/plates £50. Thanks to the money left to me by Mary Moore, I paid £320 deposit on our first ever sideboard – on castors. This was in Fenwick's sale, reduced by 10% from £1,425 & payable over 12 months at £80 per month. Also, I just happened to see the lovely tea-service in a nearby shop.

18th April 1994 Monday
The Reverend John King Hancock, who was "priest in charge" at St. James, Snibston from 1985 until 1990, is another Church of England priest who is unable to accept women priests & is hoping to become a Roman Catholic priest. He says, "For some time now I have felt that the Church of England is drifting away from Gospel truth into a form of worldly liberalism".

20th April 1994 Wednesday
Another disillusioned member of the Church of England is Leicester Cathedral's Organist & Master of the Music, Peter White, aged 57, who for the past 25 years has given his all to Leicester Cathedral, only to be told in the 1993 Bishop's "Visitation Charge" that he must change with the times. He has therefore retired to make way for a younger man to meet the proposed changes.

22nd April 1994 Friday
The reverend Kerry Emmett, Rector of Ravenstone, is a young man happy to accept women priests & to go along with all the revolutionary changes in the Church today. "For as many of you as have been baptized into Christ have put on Christ. There is neither Jew nor Greek, there is neither bond nor free, there is neither male nor female; for ye are all one in Christ Jesus". (Galatians 3 : 27)

24th April 1994 Sunday
"Why is an eagle, a bird of prey, on the front of the lectern in churches?"
The eagle has become the traditional model for the lectern because it was considered the strongest & highest-flying bird, best able to carry the Word of God to the greatest number of places.
Some lecterns are modelled on the pelican because of the myth that the pelican fed its young with blood from its own breast.

26th April 1994 Tuesday
Having only just learned why an eagle is on the front of the lectern at church, I saw the very fine eagle in Ravenstone Church, almost ready for lift-off, as the Rector, the Revd. Kerry Emmett, addressed us this Easter-tide. On my recent visit to Norwich Cathedral, I saw for the first time a lectern in the form of a pelican feeding its young from its own breast.

28th April 1994 Thursday
….. it's an Autumn Windfall.
Dear Miss Hewes, Re – Doris Annie Hewes (Aunt Dos)
Cheque enclosed £1,094-55p in accordance with the attached Final Cash Statement.
So, my poor old Aunt Dos has now given her all to brother Pat & me – a total of £13,594-55p each, after expenses.

30th April 1994 Saturday
And another new lawn-mower. The recently acquired Qualcast Quadtrak, costing £80, was quite useless. I was so disappointed with its performance, I took it back to the shop "Higgott of Ibstock" & traded it in for a Mountfield Princess, costing £169. This too conforms to the specifications of Directive 84/538/EEC.

The county council's new chief executive, Mr John Sinnott, has admitted he is taking over the council at a difficult time. But he is determined to ensure the survival of the Glenfield-based local authority. Mr Sinnott was speaking shortly after beating three internal colleagues to land the £70,000 plus post. He replaces Mr David Prince who is leaving. (Newspaper cutting)

2nd May 1994 Monday
"Trouble with Hubble" (Ref: 2nd May 1991)
The multi-billion dollar telescope whose two mirrors did not focus properly together in outer space, making us see through a glass darkly, has now been put right & astronomers are delighted with the results. Hubble was designed to provide sharp images of objects in space as far as 15 billion light years away, including black holes.

15 billion light years away! How far is that you might ask? One light year is the distance light travels in a year, about 6,000,000,000,000 miles. Just multiply that then by 15 billion & you reach an "astronomical" figure. It makes the distance of the earth from the sun – a mere 92.9 million miles – fade into insignificance, but this is one astronomical unit.

Hubble, a lawyer-turned-astronomer, was the first person to posit the idea of an expanding universe. His reasoning was based on the observation that galaxies are moving apart. It seemed logical to deduce that all matter in the universe was once contained in a single spot.

Minnesota – Scientists say they have discovered the

largest prime number ever – a 258,716-digit monster that would take eight newspaper pages to print. Prime numbers are those divisible only by themselves or one and the latest is defined as two multiplied by itself 859,433 times, minus 1. (Newspaper cutting)

6ᵗʰ May 1994 Friday

Dr. Graham Leonard, aged 72, former Bishop of London, i.e. the third most senior Anglican bishop in England, is the most prominent Anglican to leave the Church of England & become a Roman Catholic priest. More than 240 Anglican priests have resigned or indicated they will resign since the vote to ordain women priests in November 1992.

8ᵗʰ May 1994 Sunday

"Evensong" at Ravenstone Church which I have enjoyed for 40 years & more, is slowly but surely being squeezed out for the more popular "Songs of Praise", consisting only of hymn singing. The Rector, the Revd. Kerry Emmett, has invited people not only to choose a hymn, but to give a testimony, saying what their religion, or the hymn, means to them. Not my scene.
Vicars are abandoning favourite hymns for meaningless evangelical choruses, traditionalists have claimed (newspaper cutting)

10ᵗʰ May 1994 Tuesday

"Perhaps the young man would like to say a few words?"
Mum's cousin, Cyril Bailey, who died in February 1977, aged 76, never forgot this experience he had as a youth in his chapel at Willoughby-on-the-Wolds, when it was the accepted thing to stand up & give a testimony.
The last thing he ever wanted to do was "say a few words" like his elders did.

11ᵗʰ May 1994 Wednesday

The original Siamese twins, Chang and Eng, were born of Chinese parents in Siam, on this day in 1811.
(See 31ˢᵗ August 1992)

12ᵗʰ May 1994 Thursday

A church service made up only of hymn singing is to me like a 5 course meal stripped of everything except the sweet course. Having been fed on the Word of God by so many great and learned men & having been transported to the very gates of heaven through inspired sermons, through prayers which move you to tears, I am now quite unmoved.

14ᵗʰ May 1994 Saturday

C & G = the Cheltenham & Gloucester Building Society & is the UK's 6ᵗʰ largest society. In the past 10 years it has swallowed up 16 other societies, including my "Heart of England", taking its assets to over £16 billion. Now the C& G has agreed to be taken over itself by Lloyds Bank, with effect from May 1995.
"Project Paul" was the code-name of talks leading to the marriage of Lloyds Bank to the Cheltenham & Gloucester Building Society. As St. Paul was "converted" on the road to Damascus, so the C & G expects to convert from building society to bank when the deal goes through. However, it promises to carry on still acting as a Building Society, just as before.

18ᵗʰ May 1994 Wednesday

65, Leicester Road, Ravenstone has recently been sold. Like my house, it was "link-detached" to an existing row of 4 houses. The new owners seemed to be stripping the roof – then the whole of the upstairs was dismantled, then the downstairs & foundations, leaving a post-box – No. 65.

On this day in history – 1804 – Napoleon Bonaparte was proclaimed Emperor of France.
1830 – Edwin Budding of Gloucestershire signed an agreement for the manufacture of his invention, the lawn mower. The first customer was Regent's Park Zoo.

20ᵗʰ May 1994 Friday

"The Hollies", the old family home, has been sold to Mr Alex Cook, a Scotsman who has a wife Eve & 3 children, Ian 9, Jasmine 7 and Alastair 4. They are currently in the process of restoring the house to its former glory, but with the benefit of up-to-date luxuries. Cousin Miles, Pat, Evelyn & I had a nostalgic guided tour of the house.

21ˢᵗ May 1994 Saturday

Houses raided – Detectives have launched an investigation after burglars struck three times in one morning in Ravenstone. Hundreds of pounds worth of gold jewellery was stolen in the raids.
Two houses in Leicester Road and another in Ibstock Road were broken into between 10a.m. and 1p.m. on Thursday. (Newspaper cutting)

For the 2ⁿᵈ time this year 3 houses in Ravenstone have been the target of burglars, including "Glenholm" No.46, Leicester Road, home of cousin Miles & his lady-love Gwen. They were in London for the day when burglars broke into their sun lounge.

22ⁿᵈ May 1994 Sunday

Manchester United 4 – Chelsea 0. This year's winner, the mighty Manchester United, have won both the League & the Cup – only the 4ᵗʰ such double win this century.
The money taken in tickets at the F.A. Cup Final was £3 million. The attendance was 79,634, headed by the Duchess of Kent.

24ᵗʰ May 1994 Tuesday

Scotland! Here we come again. Enid & I have booked a holiday in Edinburgh, starting out tomorrow & returning home the following Wednesday. We are travelling in Enid's car, staying overnight in the Lake District tomorrow & again on the return journey.
It is 25 years since Mum & I went to Edinburgh, when I wrote, "A city indeed to return to again".

28ᵗʰ May 1994 Saturday

"Ventrolla – The Sash Window Renovation Specialists. A national network of local companies"
Thanks to the money left to me by Aunt Dos, I have now spent £1,800 on my last remaining sash windows at the front of the house, 27 Leicester Road, Ravenstone.
The large bay window downstairs & the two bedroom windows are all now as good as new.#

30th May 1994 Monday

Alexander William David Bond, second grandchild of Cocky & Joan, was christened on 15th May this year, aged exactly 7 months. Although Jonathan was asked to be godfather, he preferred not to accept such a responsibility. Jonathan is 20 years old (he will be 21 in December) & his chief delight is in "Train Spotting", which takes him all over the British Isles.

1st June 1994 Wednesday

What a lovely holiday Enid & I have had at Edinburgh. No wonder my mum always saved the picture postcards sent from Edinburgh by my dad in 1934. It is interesting to compare the scene as it was then with the scene of today. My dad said, "Will tell you all when I'm home. It's far too much to write about. Everything is excellent in every way. All my love, Darling".

3rd June 1994 Friday

Leicester City's promotion to football's top flight, the Premier Division, has been the cause of great celebration this week. It has been 7 years since City were in "The Top Flight", when "First Division" meant the top. "First" now is lower.

5th June 1994 Sunday

Ravenstone Parish Church Summer Fair was held indoors yesterday inside Ravenstone Institute, due to inclement weather. Arthur Beesley, local Nurseryman, was the opener & brought along lots of colourful potted plants for sale. Again I sat at the Prize Draw Table with Church Warden Jim Bailiss & I actually won one of the 20 prizes – a hand knitted cuddly toy.

6th June 1994 Monday
D-DAY June 6th, 1994
50th Anniversary

D-Day = the opening day (6th June 1944) of the Allied invasion of Europe which led to the eventual liberation of Paris, Brussels, all of France & Belgium & ultimate victory over Nazi Europe. It was the day of the Normandy landings, planned long in advance when the exact day could not be known precisely. D-Day is any critical day of action.

7th June 1994 Tuesday

"Catechism looks all set to be a bestseller" - The long-awaited English version of the new "Catechism of the Catholic Church" is now on sale in the shops. Published first in French & approved by the Pope in 1992, it updates the previous "Roman Catechism", produced by the Council of Trent in 1566.

9th June 1994 Thursday

Pope John Paul II, now aged 74, says that he feels called to lead the Church into the year 2000. When he was elected Pope in 1978, his old friend Cardinal Stefan Wyszynski of Poland told him, "If the Lord has called you, you must lead the Church into the third millennium".

Like Moses, leading his people to the Promised Land, it is a long struggle.

11th June 1994 Saturday

Coalville Amateur Operatic Society A.G.M. this week saw brother Pat, aged 75, re-appointed as House Manager, with me as Assistant House Manager. The show chosen for next March is "Kiss Me Kate" which we last performed in 1970. Joan Dillow will be celebrating 50 years with the Society next March & was delighted therefore to be made a Vice President.

13th June 1994 Monday

H.M.S. Vanguard, Britain's first Trident ballistic missile submarine, launched in April 1992, has now fired its first test missile. There were 48 admirals, captains & contractors crowded into Vanguard more than 100 feet below the waves off Cape Canaveral in Florida for the occasion – "enough brass to sink it". The original plan for 128 warheads has now been reduced to 48.

15th June 1994 Wednesday
Magna Carta – 15th June 1215

John, by the Grace of God, King of England, Lord of Ireland, Duke of Normandy & Aquitaine & Count of Anjou …All counties, hundreds, wapentakes & tithings (except Our demesne manors) shall remain at the old rents, without any increase …… etc. etc. etc.

Given by Our hand in the meadow
which is called Runnymede.

17th June 1994 Friday

Lady Sarah to wed – *Buckingham Palace has announced the date of the wedding of Lady Sarah Armstrong-Jones and Daniel Chatto.*
The couple will wed at St. Stephen Church, Walbrook, in the City of London on July 14th. A Palace spokeswoman said just 200 people would attend the service at St. Stephen, a small church in the heart of the capital's financial district. The reception will be held at the Queen Mother's residence, Clarence House. Lady Sarah, 30, the daughter of Princess Margaret and Lord Snowdon, has known actor-turned-artist Mr Chatto, 37, for 12 years. *(Newspaper cutting)*

19th June 1994 Sunday

"Shafts of the Glory of God can touch us in any context, at any moment, allowing us to glimpse a deeper purpose & significance behind our everyday concerns".

Who but Cardinal Hume, the revered Archbishop of Westminster, could fashion such a sentence? Speaking in Westminster Abbey to councillors & the Lord Mayor, he said we must not see ourselves as the centre of the world.

21st June 1994 Tuesday

The tolling of the great bell at Windsor Castle at 4 a.m. on 21st June 1837 announced the death of King William IV. He had succeeded his brother George IV in 1830. His short reign is noted for measures of reform including the abolition of slavery & the Reform Bill itself.

And now today, our Prince William of Wales is 12 years old.

23rd June 1994 Thursday

"A historical memento of the most famous love story of the 20th century" – Thus Mohammed Al Fayed, owner of Harrods, describes the former home in Paris of the late Duke of Windsor, who was born 100 years ago tomorrow. Mr Al Fayed has devoted five years to

restoring the mansion at 4, Route du Champ d'Entrainement to its former condition, complete with all its belongings.

"The most famous love story of the 20th century" – when a King gave up his crown for the woman he loved, had the saddest of endings. He died of cancer of the throat after a lifetime of smoking. With the pivot of her life gone, the Duchess took to drink & after a serious haemorrhage spent 11 years unable to eat, speak or move, fed only through tubes.

27th June 1994 Monday
In 1909, the 16,000 ton liner Waratah left Australia for England & disappeared completely (see 28th June 1966). Scientists have now come up with their latest solution to disappearing ships – methane hydrate, i.e. frozen methane locked in the depths beneath the sea-bed, suddenly breaking apart & releasing a gas blow-out, making sea buoyancy impossible.
Bermuda Triangle – Latest figures say at least 50 ships and 20 aircraft have disappeared without trace in the Bermuda Triangle since it became known as an area where mysterious happenings occurred.
(Newspaper cutting)
Shanghai – China's imbalance of males over females could produce 70 million single men by 2000. Birth records show an average of 114 boys born for every 100 girls. (Reuter) *(Newspaper cutting)*

29th June 1994 Wednesday
Saint Peter's Day – *O Almighty God, who by thy Son Jesus Christ didst give to thy Apostle Saint Peter many excellent gifts and commandest him earnestly to feed thy flock, make we beseech thee, all Bishops & Pastors diligently to preach thy Holy Word & the people obediently to follow the same, that they may receive the crown of everlasting glory.* *(Collect for today).*

"To preach thy Holy Word" – The preacher spoke of the importance of the Word of God. He said that many today felt that preaching was irrelevant & out of date; that dialogue was more important than monologue. But God's unchanging Word was vital in a rapidly changing world, as Christ himself said, "Go into all the world & preach the Gospel to every creature". (Mark 16)

30th June 1994 Thursday
Court Circular, St. James's Palace - The Prince of Wales this morning visited Tower Bridge on the One Hundredth Anniversary of the opening of the bridge.

3rd July 1994 Sunday
Today I am 23,000 days old. Matthew, who was 1 year old when I was 22,000 days old, is now therefore 1,000 days old, plus 365 (he was born 7th October 1990).
It was on 3rd July 1982 that I made my will. Today it is almost impossible to say what anyone can expect to leave in a will as nothing remains constant & the future for many is so insecure.

5th July 1994 Tuesday
Another Charter! "Our Children's Education" – The Updated Parents Charter.
Twenty million copies have been sent to every home in the country, including lone souls like me. Secretary of State, John Patten explains, "What is happening in schools today is of vital interest to all members of the community". It is hoped by the year 2000 to see the true benefits.

National Targets for Education and Training
The Department for Education is committed to helping secure achievement of the National Targets for Education and Training. These set challenging goals for schools and colleges as well as employers and the Government, including:
By 1997, 80% of young people to obtain five A-C passes at GCSE, an Intermediate General National Vocational Qualification (GNVQ) or an NVQ at level 2;
Education and training to NVQ level 3 (or the equivalent of two or more GCE A levels or an Advanced GNVQ) to be available to all young people who can benefit;
By 2000, 50% of young people to obtain two or more GCE A levels, an Advanced GNVQ or an NVQ at level 3; and education and training provision to develop self-reliance, flexibility and breadth.

7th July 1994 Thursday
Bunting's birthday, 79 today.
Pat, Evelyn & I motored to Stafford, calling en route at Cannock to see "Bill" Wilson. What a contrast – Bill's home & garden maintained so beautifully. Bunting's home & garden looking totally neglected.
Michael & Josie joined Pat, Evelyn, Bunting & me for lunch in Stafford after which they had other interests they were anxious to pursue.

9th July 1994 Saturday
Seven Pips! How exciting to hear 7 pips instead of the usual 6, when the earth on its journey round the sun was one second behind time. BBC radio broadcast 7 pips to mark the occasion. Atomic clocks were first introduced at the London based National Physical Laboratory in the 1950s & since then 19 seconds have been added for perfect timing.
In a million years, the best atomic clocks lose or gain less than a single second. Yet clocks a hundred or a thousand times more accurate may soon be possible.
(Newspaper cutting)

11th July 1994 Monday
Internal Auditor Hewsie with Basil Newbold did their second audit for Coalville Amateurs. We went to Basil's house at 222, Forest Road, Coalville, where new Treasurer, Wendy Miles, presented her accounts in very good order for our last show "Anything Goes". The show was a financial success & we now have a healthy balance of £10,000 to launch our next show.

12th July 1994 Tuesday
The Queen is to visit Russia in October, Buckingham Palace announced yesterday. The four-day state visit will be the first by a British monarch since 1908. The visit, at the invitation of President Yeltsin, will take place between October 17th and 20th. The Queen and the Duke of Edinburgh will be accompanied by Douglas Hurd, the Foreign Secretary.
(Newspaper cutting)

13th July 1994 Wednesday

The Grand Climacteric!

Every 7th year in a person's life is climacteric. But when you reach the age of 63 (7 x 9), this is the Grand Climacteric, so here we go. 3 x 3 x 7, or 21 again – and again. Some people say "I wish I was 21 again" but I have no wish whatsoever to turn the clock back.

Our county motto is "For'ard, for'ard".

14th July 1994 Thursday
Bastille Day
Happy Birthday to Me!

To celebrate my birthday, Pat & Evelyn took me out to lunch to The Queen's Head, Belton – a most delightful country pub on the forest. After lunch we went to Shackerstone Station which has been "lovingly restored by members of the preservation society". We went into the Victorian Station Tea Room & saw the old steam train which runs at weekends along the Battlefield Line.

16th July 1994 Saturday

Ginger Rogers, dance partner of Fred Astaire, is 83 today.

17th July 1994 Sunday

__Williamson__, James Brewin, of Ravenstone, much loved husband of Doreen, father of Susan and Peter, Phillip and Carole, grandfather of Kelly and Penny. Passed peacefully away in hospital on July 11th 1994 aged 71 years. A man in a million, who fought right to the last.
In peace now after pain so bravely borne. Funeral service Ravenstone Parish Church, Monday July 18th at 1p.m. followed by private family cremation at Loughborough Crematorium. All flowers and inquiries to Coalville and District Funeral Service, 89 Belvoir Road, Coalville. Tel. (0530) 838600.

"Father Christmas (namely Jimmy Williamson) came to our house to robe & disrobe & it was a tricky business keeping Joanne away" *(1st December 1979)*
Now "Father Christmas" is dead, after a long battle with cancer. He married Doreen Carter of Wash Lane.

19th July 1994 Tuesday

"Chaplain decides on conversion"

And yet another Church of England clergyman is leaving to become a Roman Catholic. The Reverend Colin Patey, aged 44, who lives at the old Rectory, Ravenstone & is chaplain to 6 local hospitals, will relinquish this post on 30th September. "I now feel my spiritual home is in the Roman Catholic Church".

21st July 1994 Thursday

Poor old Bunting poured out her heart to me on the telephone.

"I was a land-girl once – a long time ago", she had remarked to Michael & Josie.

"Nobody is interested in that", said Josie, "all we hear about is what happened in the past".

"Yes", agreed Michael, "You are always going on & on about dad".

"Of course I am", said Bunting, "he would not want me to forget him, after all he meant to me".

23rd July 1994 Saturday

Giant wind turbine for Snibston Discovery Park – Three project partners, the County Council, Environ (a Leicester-based Green action group), & De Montfort University want to set up a huge wind turbine permanently at Snibston & they have called on the Government to provide money from its Non Fossil Fuel Obligation (N.F.F.O.).

The turbine, fitted with two 12 metre blades, is 50 metres high.

25th July 1994 Monday

The Reverend Michael David Webb, a bachelor, was 'licensed' 12 months ago as Assistant Priest in the United Benefice of Hugglescote, Ellistown & Snibston, living at St. James Vicarage, & in effect priest at St. James, Snibston. Now he has been 'licensed' as Team Vicar, having completed 4 years as a Curate (Deacon).

He has also fallen for the Lady Organist.

__Boy Baptised__ – Rome: The son of Rosanna Della Corte, 62, the oldest woman to give birth, has been baptised in the Roman Catholic Church despite Vatican anger that he was conceived artificially using donor eggs at Dr Severino Antinori's clinic. (Reuter)

(Newspaper cutting)

27th July 1994 Wednesday

"Civil Service Retirement Fellowship" – Our July meeting was held at the home of Roy & Brenda – namely Mr & Mrs J. R. Derbyshire, 16 Groby Road, Ratby. Not so much a meeting as a garden party as we sat in the shade on another glorious summer's day in their lovely garden. What a magnificent home they have; & afternoon tea on the lawn.

29th July 1994 Friday

On 29th July 1991 my diary recorded "The jungle which was Aunt Dos's garden at the back of her bungalow has been completely transformed & this week a newly seeded lawn has sprung to life". Now, exactly 3 years later, the jungle which was Aunt Dos's garden at the front of her bungalow has been similarly transformed; after months & months of preparation.

31st July 1994 Sunday

__Colver__, Paul John, beloved son of Terence and the late Susan, passed suddenly away July 29th, aged 19 years. Funeral service at Ravenstone Parish Church on Friday, August 5th at 3p.m. followed by interment in the churchyard. All flowers and inquiries to Co-operative Funeral Service, Stuart House, 128 London Road, Coalville, Tel. 0530 836703.

"Susan leaves today as she is shortly expecting her first baby" –Thus I wrote in June 1974.
Paul John, beloved son of Terence & the late Susan, now aged 19, is that very baby, who died in a road accident on Friday. His 125cc motor bike collided with a Ford Cortina at 7-40a.m.

2nd August 1994 Tuesday

£100 thousand million is spent each year in this country on state benefits. Social Security Secretary Peter Lilley has now been given an extra minister to cope with the most radical overhaul in years. The department will be expected to find ways to cut the amount spent on benefits for the unemployed, disabled, pensioners & the sick. Two new controversial Bills are expected.

4th August 1994 Thursday

Nuclear Power! The Department of Trade & Industry this year is undertaking a review of nuclear power. It was in 1955 that the Government decided to embark on a *civil* nuclear power programme. "Nuclear Electric" now has 6 Magnox & 5 advanced gas-cooled reactor (AGR) nuclear power stations in England & Wales which supply 25% of electricity used nationally.

"Scottish Nuclear" has two advanced gas-cooled reactor (AGR) nuclear power stations which supply nearly half of Scotland's electricity requirement.

A crucial outcome of the "nuclear review" will be a decision on the construction of new power stations & the major problem of decommissioning old power stations. New power stations will be based on a pressurised-water reactor (PWR).

Sizewell B nuclear power station on the Suffolk coast will be Britain's first pressurised water reactor (PWR) station. Sizewell B, which cost £2 billion, is expected to start feeding electricity into the national grid next February.

Our 6 Magnox power stations are now nearing the end of their lives. Decommissioning has begun on Berkeley in Gloucestershire & will take years & years.

How to decommission a Nuclear Power Station! Nuclear power stations cannot be handed over to a scrap dealer for demolition. High levels of radiation mean the dismantling procedures are complex & costly, & have to be spread in stages over 100 years. De-fuelling began at Berkeley in 1989 & parts dismantled. After 30 years of monitoring, a 9 metres high wall will be built.

12th August 1994 Friday

"*Royal family discovers Columbus*" – This Columbus is about to discover his new world. Columbus George Donald, son of Lady Helen and Timothy Taylor, was born on 6th August 1994.

He is 23rd in line to the throne, his mother being Lady Helen Windsor who was married at St. George's Chapel, in July 1992. *(See 27th December 1996)*

14th August 1994 Sunday

"The Battle of the Bogside" in Londonderry exactly 25 years ago – 1969 – was the beginning of the "Troubles" of the last quarter of a century in Northern Ireland when the army was sent in to keep order. Since then things have gone from bad to worse & the I.R.A. has gone from strength to strength, while the army is still there in what the I.R.A. calls The Long War.

Twenty-five years of violence in Northern Ireland have claimed the lives of more than 3,160 people.
Men, women, children, soldiers and police officers have died by bomb and bullet. While the police and Army have fought it out with terrorists from both sides, it has been civilians caught in the middle who have borne the brunt. A total of 2,219 have died, including several hundred terrorists. The Army, sent into Northern Ireland on August 14th 1969, has lost 445 men; the R.U.C. 195 and its Reserve 101. The U.D.R. lost 197 before being
amalgamated into the Royal Irish Regiment, which has lost five members. *(newspaper cutting)*

16th August 1994 Tuesday

Shed raided – *Goods worth £867 were stolen when burglars broke into a shed at the back of a house in Ravenstone. Among the items taken from the shed, in Leicester Road, were a lawnmower and fishing equipment.* *(newspaper cutting)*

Would you believe we could have so many break-ins at Ravenstone & all on Leicester Road? At the beginning of the year, they were all 'down the village'. This latest one is 'up the road' next door to Midge & Ron Ball. (Cocky's sister)

18th August 1994 Thursday

Proposed new Driving Licences! Dr. Brian Mawhinney, Secretary of State for Transport, has released details of the Government's proposed new plastic driving licence, which could be in place within 2 years. It will carry a photograph of the holder & will also be able to accommodate a microchip to transform it into a 'smart card' & will include security features.

One of the main aims of the proposed new driving licence is to prevent impersonation at driving tests. According to estimates, at least 1,000 a week become 'qualified' by paying someone else to take the test for them. When I think of the humble hand-written driving licence which we stuck into a folder year after year, how things have changed.

22nd August 1994 Monday

The Driver and Vehicle Licensing Agency is to cut 1,500 jobs and shut 51 regional offices in addition to the loss of 700 jobs at its headquarters in Swansea.
The efficiency drive, which will save an estimated £12 million, will continue until 1997 with DVLA closing its nationwide network, which registers about 2 million vehicles a year. It will allow car dealers to take over work normally done by its own regional counter staff. A pilot scheme enabling new cars to be registered from dealers' premises by use of computer links with the DVLA is expected to be in place by the end of next year. The work of 500 staff who deal in specialist number plates will be handled inside the Swansea headquarters.
(newspaper cutting)

And so we come towards total close-down of our dear old Motor Licence Office.

24th August 1994 Wednesday

A new Hoover – turbo power 1000 including 'edge cleaning' to replace the 7 year-old Electrolux purchased exactly 7 years ago 24th August 1987.

The poor old Electrolux never recovered properly after being used by workmen to 'hoover' debris including fragments of still wet concrete.

The new Hoover was on offer at £180, reduced from its original £220.

26th August 1994 Friday

Mother Teresa, born 27th August 1910 at Skopje in the former Yugoslav Republic of Macedonia, is a saint of our time. Known originally as Ganxhe Agnes Bojaxhiu, she belonged to a Catholic family & became a nun in

1931, choosing the name Sister Teresa. Her work among the sick & dying in Calcutta is legendry & Mother Teresa's homes now reach every corner of the world.

28th August 1994 Sunday

"The Sunday Trading Act" takes effect from today, which means that most of the larger shops, including supermarkets, D.I.Y. (Do It Yourself) outlets & out-of-town stores are allowed to open for a maximum of 6 hours. It was in April 1986 that 'The Shops Bill' to allow shops to open on a Sunday was defeated by those who upheld the Christian view saying, "A nation which ignores God & his commandments is bound to fail".

30th August 1994 Tuesday

Young, David, passed tragically away on August 21st 1994 aged 18 years. Much loved son to Peter and Margaret. Funeral service to take place at Ravenstone Church on Friday August 26th 1994, at 1-45p.m. followed by cremation at Bretby Crematorium at 3p.m. All flowers welcome or donations to Ravenstone Church c/o Mr S. Land, 54 Leicester Road, Ravenstone. All inquiries and flowers to Coalville Co-operative Funeral Service, Stuart House, 128 London Road, Coalville. Tel. 0530 836703.

Following the tragic death last month of Paul Colver, aged 19, whose mother & grandmother I knew so well, we now have the tragic death of David Young, aged 18, whose mother & grandmother I know even more closely, being Mabel Woodings & Margaret.

1st September 1994 Thursday

"Why is every room in our house as clean as a new pin?" (June 1974)

We had then purchased a beautiful new Electrolux cleaner to replace our old Hoover. Once again "I have swept clean every carpet in every room & have never seen the house quite so smart" as this time, in a reverse situation, a beautiful new Hoover has replaced the old Electrolux.

3rd September 1994 Saturday

Another prize from E.R.N.I.E.

Bond number 14 HN 330174.

Dear Bondholder, Congratulations, one of your Premium Bonds has won a prize & a warrant for the money is enclosed. 'Pay Miss E. Hewes Fifty Pounds only'. 'Good luck in future draws'.

Alan Mc Gill.

On this day in history –

1658, Oliver Cromwell, statesman, Puritan leader and Lord Protector of England from 1653, died in Whitehall of pneumonia, and was succeeded by his son Richard, as Lord Protector.

1752, What should have been September 3rd became September 14th with the introduction of the Gregorian calendar, and crowds flocked through the streets crying 'Give us back our 11 days'.

5th September 1994 Monday

St. Michael & All Angels Church, Ravenstone "Restoration Club" monthly draw, which was launched last September, is going from strength to strength.

A print-out from David Winterton tells us that we now have 350 members who have contributed £3,500 (half for prize money – half for the church).

Our recent "Open Gardens" resulted in a further £1,000 for the church.

7th September 1994 Wednesday

I.R.A. declares a ceasefire

"The I.R.A. have decided that as of midnight, August 31st, there will be a complete cessation of military operations. All our units have been instructed accordingly. At this historic crossroads the leadership of the I.R.A. salutes and commends our volunteers, other activists & supporters who have sustained the struggle against all odds for the past 25 years."

"A complete cessation of military operations".

"How long for?" people wonder.

It all depends on the next moves by everyone concerned. The I.R.A. say, "Partition of the 6-county state of Northern Ireland has failed. Freedom is going to embrace Unionist, Nationalist, Catholic, Protestant & dissenter in a free & united Irish Republic". "Oh, no!" say the Unionists.

11th September 1994 Sunday

Tea Party for six! How glad I was to have my lovely knives, forks & spoons (acquired July 1990) & my 18 piece 'Duchess' tea service (acquired April 1994) when I invited Pat, Evelyn, Bunting, Miles & Gwen for tea. Bunting was staying at Pat's house for a few days & we had a lovely get-together at 27 Leicester Road, Ravenstone. This was the first time my cutlery & china were put to full use.

13th September 1994 Tuesday

597A.D. is the year that St. Columba died.

597A.D. is also the year that St. Augustine landed in Kent, arriving at – guess where? – Ebbsfleet. (One of our so-called 'Flying Bishops' has been given the title 'Bishop of Ebbsfleet') He represents the Archbishop of Canterbury. In 1997, Canterbury will host the celebrations for the 14th centenary of the arrival of St. Augustine.

15th September 1994 Thursday

If men can go topless, so can women.....

(Newspaper cutting)

Women, for ever wanting to prove equal rights to men, have now been given authority to travel topless on the New York subway. The decision followed a campaign by women anxious to obtain equal treatment with male commuters who have long been permitted to travel without shirts.

17th September 1994 Saturday

Duck feather & down quilt 12 tog £34-99p. At last I have caught up with the fashion of the day with a 'Continental Quilt' made up as follows – 85% duck feather & 15% down – 'extra light for warmth without weight – ten year guarantee, 135 x 200cm (54 inches x 78 inches)' plus a pretty floral cover, purchased separately for a further £7.

19th September 1994 Monday

"Complete cessation of military operations" has brought to an end the dreadful practice of 'knee-capping' which the I.R.A. began in the 1970s. Victims are shot at the back of their knee & the knee-bone is shattered. But still those on the other side of the terrorist divide, the Ulster Freedom Fighters, continue this practice, while the I.R.A. now use batons.

21st September 1994 Wednesday
St. Matthew's Day! Christ called Matthew from being a tax gatherer to be an Apostle and Evangelist. I thought of St. Matthew when I read in the Leicester Mercury that £47 million is owed in arrears to Leicester City Council. This includes over £22 million still outstanding for the infamous poll tax, plus Council Tax, rates, rents etc.

Nearly £1.5 billion in poll tax is still owing two years after the tax was abolished. Figures issued today by the Audit Commission and Cipfa, the public finance institute, show that most of the money will have to be written off. Authorities found they could not keep information up to date on people's addresses, making it harder to keep accurate poll tax records. Added to this, the high numbers who simply refused to pay made it unfeasible to seek a committal in every case.

(Newspaper cutting)

23rd September 1994 Friday
Elaine Barkby, bravely battling on with Multiple Sclerosis, is finding it increasingly difficult to cope in her own home. Recently she had a spell in the new 'Rowans Nursing Home' in Owen Street, Coalville, which gave her a bed-sore & she ended up in hospital. When she returned home she could hardly walk at all & is now back again in 'The Rowans'.

25th September 1994 Sunday
"Songs of Praise" – Harvest & Patronal Festival this year at Ravenstone found us singing –
"If I were a fish in the sea, I'd wiggle my tail & I'd giggle with glee …..If I were a wiggly worm I'd thank you Lord that I could squirm & if I were a Billy Goat, I'd thank you Lord, for my strong throat & if I were a fuzzy wuzzy bear I'd thank you Lord, for my fuzzy wuzzy hair".

Czar's last resting place – The remains of Czar Nicholas II, his wife and three daughters will be buried in Peter and Paul Cathedral, St. Petersburg, next March. The family were executed by the Bolsheviks in 1918 and their bones were discovered in a pit in the Ural Mountains in 1991. They were identified by forensic scientists.
(Newspaper cutting)

27th September 1994 Tuesday
New Railway Station planned for Coalville. Once upon a time we had a railway station at Coalville, built in 1848 & closed down in September 1964. Now we are to have a new station costing £400,000. It is hoped that by 1996 the station will be built & the line open linking Coalville with Leicester, Loughborough, Derby & Nottingham.
(See 28th September 1995)

28th September 1994 Wednesday
A baby son for Joanne "Dale Andrew" (5lb 9oz)

29th September 1994 Thursday
St Michael & All Angels Day – Now that St. Michael &

All Angels are so sadly neglected at Ravenstone Church, here then is the collect for today – *'O everlasting God, who hast ordained & constituted the services of Angels & men in a wonderful order; mercifully grant that, as thy Holy Angels always do thee service in heaven, so they may succour & defend us on earth'.*

1st October 1994 Saturday
Donor Egg – Immediate Availability
Did you ever in your life see such an advertisement in the 'Times' newspaper?
Placed by The Genetics & IVF Institute, 3020 Javier Road, Fairfax, Virginia 22031 U.S.A.
"… has a large selection of donors available now for patients requiring donor oocytes. No waiting list. Suburban Washington D.C."

The institute is well known internationally, and to many in Britain, for its high quality and innovation in several areas of assisted reproduction, including non-surgical in vitro fertilisation (IVF), embryo cryopreservation, sperm injection into eggs for the treatment of male infertility, and pre-implantation genetic diagnosis. We are one of the first and largest IVF centers in the United States and have achieved more than 800 IVF pregnancies. Our donor egg-IVF pregnancy rate is highly satisfactory – approximately 40% per treatment – and we provide a choice of over 100 donors. Our screening policies for donors involve extensive medical, psychological, genetic and infectious-disease testing at standards equivalent to those required in Great Britain. In addition, our programme adheres to the guides of the American Fertility Society and the Society for Assisted Reproductive Technologies, which perform certain functions in the United States analogous to the Human Fertilisation and Embryology Authority of Great Britain. Health services are now provided internationally. A decade ago Americans came to England for IVF, which was brilliantly invented in your country. It will do no harm for a modest number of Britons to now come to the United States for a related type of medical care.
Yours Sincerely,
Joseph D. Schulman, Director, Genetics & IVF Institute, 3020 Javier Road, Fairfax, Virginia 22031, USA
(Newspaper cutting)

Eggs in short supply
An article in last week's Mail said Leicestershire women are being urged to donate eggs to childless couples, in the wake of a desperate shortage across the UK. The article stated that women over the age of 35 are needed. In fact it is women under 35, with a proven fertility. Anyone who is interested in donating eggs or sperm should ring Leicester Royal Infirmary's Assisted Conception Unit on 0116 2585922.

A shortage of Asian women donating their eggs for fertility treatment has led to desperate minority couples using white donors, it has been revealed.

An Australian judge has rules that a frozen embryo is legally entitled to inherit its father's estate, even if implanted in the mother's womb after the father dies. The ruling is in stark contrast to the law in Britain, where frozen embryos have no legal status which would enable them to inherit under the Human Fertilisation and Embryology Act, 1990. But medico-legal experts said they could not see any reason to object to the ruling in principle.

Cloning of human beings is no longer a mad scientist's dream, although it may be a sane scientist's nightmare.
(4 more newspaper cuttings)

3rd October 1994 Monday

Wardle – Reginald Arthur (Reg) passed away suddenly, but peacefully, at home on September 30th 1994, aged 78 years. Most loving husband of Elsie, devoted dad of Brian and Christine, Mary and Mick, granddad of Stephen, Iain, Tricia and Nick. Earth has one gentle soul less and Heaven one angel more. God's work well done, at peace with his Lord. Funeral service to be held at Worthington Church on Thursday October 6th at 11-30a.m. followed by interment at Worthington Cemetery. Donations in lieu of flowers to Mr M. J. Hunt, 2 Belmont Drive, Coalville, LE67 3LQ to establish a memorial to Reg at Worthington Church.
Coalville Amateur Operatic Society has lost 'one gentle soul' from the front of house team in the death of Reg Wardle. He & I spent much time together during the week of the show, keeping watch in the foyer & ushering in late-comers.
Note: Elsie Wardle died on Friday March 10th 2000, aged 84 years.

5th October 1994 Wednesday

"Seek him that maketh the seven stars & Orion, & turneth the shadow of death into the morning" (Amos 5 : 8) I thought of these words when I watched on television the most amazing programme about Egypt's great pyramid whose inner chambers are in perfect alignment with the constellation Orion; the 3 great pyramids themselves forming the belt of Orion.

7th October 1994 Friday

"Service of Thanksgiving for All Creatures Great & Small" – Katherine, Toffee & I attended this service again in Leicester, where the preacher was The Venerable Michael Edson, newly appointed Archdeacon of Leicester. Apart from the usual gathering of cats, dogs, hamsters, etc. we had a 'well-behaved' duck, which stole the show.

9th October 1994 Sunday

Dog-collar Union - A clergy section of the MSF union for skilled & professional people has been launched in response to fears over the future of the 'Clergy Freehold', which in the past guaranteed work until retirement. Now the clergy no longer feel secure.

11th October 1994 Tuesday

Pat, Evelyn & I, plus Honey, their dog, spent the day with Bunting at Stafford. We all went out for lunch together at The Moat House, Acton Trussell, where we last assembled 18 months ago, for the wedding reception of Michael & Josie.
Michael & Josie are now in Barbados, enjoying a 3 weeks holiday, while Bunting feels utterly bereft on her own.

13th October 1994 Thursday

"I thought of Henry VIII & all that he did to get a baby son, & I thought of old age & all its sorrow" – Thus I wrote in June 1979 when I met Joanne's newborn baby brother, Stuart. I have now met Joanne's newborn baby son, Dale, a perfect little darling – how Henry VIII would love to have fathered such a son. Joanne & her boyfriend Glenn absolutely adore him.

14th October 1994 Friday

On this day – in 1066 the Battle of Hastings was fought at Senlac Hill, near Pevensey.

15th October 1994 Saturday

The huge £35 million Nestlé distribution centre at Bardon was officially opened this week. It is the central 'finished goods store' for all Nestlé grocery, food & food service products; & services eastern England, London & the Home Counties. It will hold 58,000 pallets, process 200 vehicles in & out **per day!** & process 156 million cases of produce per year.

16th October 1994 Sunday

Bet goes – Actress Julie Goodyear today told how leaving Coronation Street after 25 years had broken her heart. The actress will bid farewell to Britain's best-loved soap tonight when her character Bet Gilroy leaves the Rovers Return for the last time.
(Newspaper cutting)

Vanunu birthday – Mordechai Vanunu, the nuclear technician kidnapped by the Israeli secret service in 1986 and jailed for 18 years after revealing details of Israel's nuclear programme to The Sunday Times, passed his 40th birthday in solitary confinement yesterday. *(Newspaper cutting)*
(See 14th April 1992)

17th October 1994 Monday
Road Closure Alert

A Coalville road is to be closed for four weeks for sewer and road works to take place. Standard Hill will be closed to through traffic from its junction with Highfield Street, Coalville, to its junction with Wash Lane, Ravenstone. Work starts at 9-30a.m. on September 26th and will continue until midnight on October 23rd with the road re-opening on October 24th. The alternative route for traffic will be via Central Road, Belvoir Road, Ashby Road, Swannington Road and Wash Lane.
(Newspaper cutting)

Not since I was a child, playing whip & top all the way to Snibston School, along the middle of the traffic-free road, have I enjoyed the pleasure of our road being so quiet & peaceful. It is a joy to take my morning walk up Standard Hill with not a car in sight, during these few weeks of 'Road Closure'. The traffic, however, is causing havoc elsewhere.

19th October 1994 Wednesday

"Stewart House" – a modern purpose-built residential home for long term mentally ill patients has opened in the grounds of Carlton Hayes Hospital, the old Victorian mental hospital which will close next year, in Narborough, Leicestershire.

On this day in history 439 – Carthage, the Phoenician city, was devastated by the Vandals, an East German tribe who captured and used it as their capital until it was re-taken by Belisarius in 533. The word 'vandal' for someone who attacks and destroys, dates from this era.

21st October 1994 Friday

'Formosissimus Annus' – the most charming period of the year. (According to Ovid, the autumn; according to Virgil, the spring).

A good summer this year followed by a mild dry spell has given us an exceptionally beautiful autumn. In a wet year the leaves do not colour so much. Maple leaves are responsible for many of the glories of autumn in New England, because they turn such a rich red.

The spectacular display of autumn glory at the maple glade in Westonbirt Arboretum near Tetbury, Gloucestershire, is the nearest we can emulate the glories of 'fall' in New England. Other recommended areas are – Grizedale Forest Park, Cumbria, Wye Valley in southeast Wales, Bedgebury Pinetum near Goodhurst Kent, & the Queen View Visitor Centre near Pitlochry, Tayside, Scotland.

25th October 1994 Tuesday

Loyalist ceasefire starts - First the I.R.A. called for a complete cessation of military operations. Now those on the other side of the terrorist divide have announced a ceasefire.

A statement by the Combined Loyalist Military Command, i.e. the Ulster Volunteer Force, the Ulster Defence Association, & the Red Hand Commando said that the 'Command' would universally cease all operational hostilities as from midnight 13th October.

The Loyalists

The Ulster Volunteer Force was revived in 1966 to oppose what its leaders saw as mounting republican violence. The UVF was originally founded in 1912 to oppose Irish Home Rule.

The Ulster Defence Association, which was founded in 1971, carries out its attacks under the name of the Ulster Freedom Fighters. It has been more militant and less predictable than the UVF.

The Red Hand Commando, which was founded in 1972, is the smallest loyalist paramilitary group. It is believed to have links with the UVF.

28th October 1994 Friday

On this day in 1886 – The Statue of Liberty was dedicated by President Cleveland, as a present from France to commemorate friendship between the two nations.

29th October 1994 Saturday

Tyrell, Annette. I think of you in silence, and always speak your name, but all I have is memories and your picture in a frame. Happy birthday Annette – Love always and forever Mitchell xxx

Annette Tyrell died on 23rd February 1993, aged 30. I did not know her at all, but so impressed was I when I read the 241 notices of her death in the Leicester Mercury from hundreds of people who loved her so very dearly, that I went to her funeral – Requiem Mass at Holy Cross Priory, Leicester. Her beautiful grave is in Saffron Hill Cemetery.

31st October 1994 Monday

Tomorrow is the Feast of All Saints, which originated in the 4th century & has been associated with the first of November since the 8th century. The Commemoration of All Souls (2nd November) began with a letter of St. Odilo of Cluny in 998 A.D. encouraging the monasteries of his order to add to the celebration of the saints of God the solemn remembrance of all the faithful departed.

1st November 1994 Tuesday – All Saints Day

"We will remember them". The solemn remembrance of all the faithful departed means simply that we re-member them – that is, we acknowledge them as members of God's family, as alive to God as all those still here on earth. In our Christian Creed we say, 'I believe in ...... the Communion of Saints; the forgiveness of sins; the resurrection of the body & the life everlasting. Amen'.

2nd November 1994 Wednesday – All Souls Day

Bikes Stolen – Two motorbikes worth a total of £5,000 were stolen from Leicester Road, Ravenstone, yesterday. The orange, red and white Honda XR600 Enduro bikes were taken at 12-30p.m. One is registered E799 SEL and the other is E814 SEL.   *(newspaper cutting)*

No doubt about it – our 'Neighbourhood Watch' Scheme is no use whatsoever. It is obviously impossible to watch everything, everywhere, all the time.

4th November 1994 Friday

"The Prince of Wales" by Jonathan Dimbleby, is the latest book on the market, telling in graphic detail the sad story of Charles, Prince of Wales, born to be King & more-or-less forced into marriage to Diana against his innermost wishes. He very much wanted to do the right thing for his country & for his family, but this loveless marriage "had all the ingredients of a Greek tragedy".

It makes clear he was never in love with Diana and felt he had to propose after he came under pressure from his father.

Princess Diana, Princess of Wales, once described herself as "Prisoner of Wales". The latest photograph of her waving through a car window, taken in America, reminded me of the last photograph we have of Mordechai Vanunu. On the palm of his hand were the sad words -'Vanunu was hijacked in Rome 30/9/86'. What do you suppose is written on Diana's hand, with the fingers in disarray?

(photograph cut from newspaper)

8th November 1994 Tuesday

Duke in Israel – On the slopes of the Mount of Olives, in the Russian Orthodox Church of St. Mary Magdalene, is the grave of Princess Alice of Greece, mother of Philip, Duke of Edinburgh, consort or our Queen, Elizabeth II.

This week, the Duke of Edinburgh paid his first visit to his mother's grave; being in such a politically sensitive part of the world 'he tiptoed through the Arab/Jewish conflict'.

The Spastics Society announced yesterday that in future it will be known as Scope. The change, which has cost the charity £175,000, has been introduced because of the way in which its name has been used as a term of abuse.

(Newspaper cutting)

10th November 1994 Thursday

"World History" – What a fascinating book I have acquired. From the narrow confines of British history, how wonderful to see the whole world, as it were, from Mount Olympus, in one overall view, as the centuries skim swiftly by.

Author Rodney Castleden says, "I hope that what emerges is a vivid & kaleidoscopic picture, like an endlessly complicated symphony, where we today are but a passing note".

Court Circular

St James's Palace, November 10 – The Prince of Wales arrived at Heathrow Airport, London, this morning from Hong Kong. Mr Stephen Lamport, Major Patrick Tabor and Mr Allan Percival were in attendance.

Kensington Palace, November 10 – The Princess of Wales, Colonel-in-Chief, The Light Dragoons, this evening attended the Officers' Annual Dinner at the Cavalry and Guards Club, Piccadilly, London W1. Viscountess Campden was in attendance.

(The separated Prince & Princess of Wales)

12th November 1994 Saturday

"What the Moon Saw" – Hans Andersen & I again shared our thoughts as my 'World History' showed me all the wonderful & dreadful events that this world has ever experienced.

The moon glided over the waters of the Flood & smiled on Noah's ark – 'Ah! What tales the Moon can tell. Human life is like a story to him'

'I will give you a picture of Pompeii' said the Moon. It was 79 A.D.

Science probes secrets of Vesuvius – Research dentists in Sydney, Australia, are examining the teeth of a woman who died in Pompeii in 79 A.D. after the eruption of Mount Vesuvius. Nearly 2,000 years later, her teeth will give scientists clues about the health of the citizens of the Roman Empire. *(Newspaper cutting)*

14th November 1994 Monday

Tickets for Britain's National Lottery go on sale for the first time today.

What a marathon job it has been to set the system up. The telecommunications network is phenomenal. Racal Network Services (R.N.S.) is the network which will link 27,000 terminals in newsagents, supermarkets, etc.

15th November 1994 Tuesday

Next year the British Red Cross Society celebrates its 125th anniversary. Continuing the energetic support Britain's royal family has given to the Red Cross, the Princess of Wales yesterday announced that she has agreed to be patron of the anniversary appeal.
(Newspaper cutting)

16th November 1994 Wednesday

A photograph in the paper shows the Imperial State Crown being driven in splendour to Westminster for the State Opening of Parliament.

We watched this age-old ceremony on television today & saw the Queen on the throne wearing her crown & her coronation robe. According to custom the Queen sent Black Rod to the House of Commons to summon the M.P.s. According to custom the door was slammed in his face, reminding us of the incident in January 1642 when King Charles I came with soldiers to the House of Commons to arrest five M.P.s whom he regarded as troublesome (one of whom was Leicestershire M.P. Sir Arthur Haslerigg).

Very shortly afterwards Charles I had to flee London for his own safety. He did not return until after his defeat in the Civil War & to suffer his trial & execution seven years later.

From that historic day in 1642 to this, no monarch has ever set foot in the House of Commons. The ceremony of slamming the door reminds us how our liberties were won through bloodshed. Even the ambling procession of M.P.s from the House of Commons to the Lords, chattering to each other while Her Majesty waits on her throne, is symbolic. It shows that the elected House is not the servant of the Sovereign alone. It comes when summoned, but at its own pace & after keeping her waiting. It has to be known that the Monarch reigns, but the government, answerable to parliament & the electorate, rules.

"Camelot" is the consortium which is running the 'National Lottery'. R.N.S. began working with Camelot last November. The company hired 80 people solely to work on the lottery system. They chose the international communications standard X25, which can send data at the rate of about 2,400 pieces of information a second. It can also ensure that all data is correctly transmitted & received.

It has cost £100 million just to get the National Lottery started – building the terminals & setting up the network. Satellite communications will also be involved, linking 5,000 of the terminals to the central computers (20% of the network traffic). Terminals will link to satellites such as Eutelsat, Orion or Intelsat. So now we are all ready for lift-off.

One quarter of the money spent playing the National Lottery will go to 'worthy causes' divided between – the four Sports Councils, the four Arts Councils, the National Heritage Memorial Fund, the National Lottery Charities Board and the Millennium Commission.

The first national lottery was in 1596 to repair the Cinque Ports.
Britain's last national lottery was banned in 1826 after treasury officials absconded with the money.

Choose 6 different numbers between one & 49. My choice – the birthdays of my dad, mum, Rob & me, plus Cocky & Brian Lamming – 7 - 14 – 17 – 21 – 23 – 28. There are about 14 million different combinations of the numbers 1 – 49. Match 5 numbers is a chance in 2 million (with the extra bonus drawn number).

There will obviously be a lot more losers than winners.

Crowie, *Jean Elizabeth, loving mother to Angela, Andrew and Ian.*

Put your arms around her Lord; treasure her with care, make up for all she suffered and all that seemed unfair.

Funeral service to take place at St. James's Church, Highfields Street, Coalville on Friday November 18th 1994 at 2p.m., all welcome, followed by private interment at Markfield Cemetery. All flowers welcome. Further inquiries and flowers to Coalville Co-operative Funeral Service, Stuart House, 128 London Road, Coalville. Tel. (0530) 836703.

No common-or-garden death. This was murder.

As reported earlier in the Leicester Mercury –

"A body found buried in a Coalville garden was that of missing mother-of-four Mrs Jean Elizabeth Crowie. North Leicestershire coroner Mr Philip Tomlinson adjourned the inquest & issued a disposal order for the body to be interred. Home Office pathologist Dr Clive Bouch identified a gold wedding ring which had been dug up along with human remains from the garden of 229 Highfield Street, Coalville, in August. He said that given all factors, including DNA testing results, he had to conclude beyond all reasonable doubt that the remains were those of Mrs Crowie. But he said he was unable to give a cause of death".

William Joseph Henry Crowie, aged 56, was charged with the murder of Mrs Crowie, his former wife, between 24th June 1978 & 23 August 1994.
(See October 14th 1995)

24th November 1994 Thursday
"Kiss Me Kate" is now into the full swing of rehearsals (2nd time around). Last time we did "Kiss Me Kate", 25 years ago when I was one of the casting committee, Ursula was chosen to play the lead, with Frank Goddard the leading man 'Petruchio'. The story evolves around Shakespeare's 'Taming of the Shrew'. Joan Dillow is delighted that her daughter Ann is our new 'Kate'.

26th November 1994 Saturday
Important notice! Water supply interruption. A letter from Severn Trent Water Ltd.
"Over the next 10 years we will be investing millions of pounds to improve the water quality throughout the Severn Trent region. As part of this programme we will be renovating the water mains in your street & the surrounding area".
This means renewal of the water main – new polyethylene main.

Cathedral to be jazzed up – The vaults of Leicester Cathedral will pulse to improvised melodies and syncopated rhythms next month. For the first time in its history the cathedral is hosting a jazz concert. The acclaimed Modern Jazz Trio will present a two-hour concert on December 1st at 8p.m. The programme will feature a variety of light jazz music as well as modern pieces and numbers by Oscar Peterson and Dave Brubeck. The cathedral precentor, the Rev John Craig, said, "I think it's great. Perhaps the church is lumbered with the image of a certain type of music and its makes a nice change to have some jazz". Tickets for the ground-breaking concert are available from the Tourist Information Centre in Leicester's Town Hall Square.
(Newspaper cutting)

28th November 1994 Monday
This month has seen 'the biggest shake-up in the dairy industry in more than 60 years'. The good old Milk Marketing Board, which for many years has sponsored the exciting 'Milk Race' – cycling tour of Britain, has been scrapped & replaced by Milk Marque which some 70% of the 28,000 dairy farmers in England & Wales have agreed to join. The idea is to make the industry more efficient.

UK dairies fear for future – The future of many British dairy firms is in doubt following the deregulation which ended the Milk Marketing Board's 61-year monopoly. Farmers can now sell milk to the highest bidder, free of the MBB monopoly, although Milk Marque, a huge farmers' co-operative, is expected to dominate the market. The Dairy Trade Federation, the industry body representing dairy farmers, said the co-operative had driven prices up by forcing dairy companies to bid against each other for milk supplies, which are always in shortage because of EU production quotes.
(Newspaper cutting)

30th November 1994 Wednesday
Civil Service Retirement Fellowship, usually held each month in Coalville Library, had to seek alternative accommodation this month as the library is closed for refurbishment. We met therefore in the home of Jack & Muriel Harding, 103 Castle Rock Drive, Coalville.
We had a very interesting talk given by Mrs Betty Wood, on her 25 years of experience in the community as a magistrate.

2nd December 1994 Friday
Budget – Chancellor Kenneth Clarke has managed to reap a harvest of £278.9 billion. Last year we were borrowing £50 billion, & in order to reduce this amount of Public Sector Borrowing Requirement (P.S.B.R.), taxes have increased & the big spending government departments have had to tighten their belts, especially 'Social Security', now reduced to £69 billion.

4th December 1994 Sunday
"Blessed Lord, who hast caused all holy scriptures to be written for our learning, grant that we may in such wise hear them, read, mark, learn, & inwardly digest them, that by patience & comfort of thy holy word, we may embrace & ever hold fast the blessed hope of everlasting life, which thou hast given us in our Saviour Jesus Christ".

6th December 1994 Tuesday
The 2nd Sunday in Advent always reminds us in its 'Collect for the day' of the importance of God's holy word & is known as Bible Sunday.
Each Sunday also we hear this prayer, 'O Lord, grant that in the written word & through the spoken word, we may behold the Living Word'.
'Thy word is a lantern unto my feet' - Psalm 119 verse 105.

8th December 1994 Thursday

Bardon Hill restoration plan!

Bardon Quarry has been eating away at Bardon Hill, Leicestershire's highest point at 912 feet, for many years. Now, at a cost of £5 million, the area around the summit, known as the Rookery, is about to be planted with 100,000 trees in the final phase of a 3 year restoration scheme. It is hoped by next April to be able to walk from Greenhill to the summit.

9th December 1994 Friday

A wetland which should attract a wide variety of birds and wildlife is being created in Leicestershire. The Kellam Bridge Farm site, near Coalville, will be home to ducks, owls and wading birds. It is being developed by local conservationists in conjunction with Severn Trent Water, which owns the land. Work begins tomorrow on the scheme which will take three years to complete.

"Seeing nature at such close quarters is sure to whet locals' appetites" said English Nature spokesman Ian Butterfield.

(Newspaper cutting)

10th December 1994 Saturday

D1ANA

The Princess of Wales may have had her eye on it for her sporty Audi convertible. But she was beaten to **D1ANA** *at an auction yesterday as a housewife paid £17,600 for the number plate – and then revealed that she did not even own a car. Diana Hudson, 41, who travelled from Wiltshire to Christie's in London by train, said afterwards, 'I never believed* **D1ANA** *would come up. I suppose now I'm going to have to get a car.'*

The highest price paid at the DVLA auction was £93,500 for the plate **1RR**. *The mystery London dealer, who last year set a world record by snapping up* **K1NGS** *for £235,000, also bought* **1J** *for £66,000,* **1PB** *for £31,100,* **1H** *for £27,500 and* **M15 SPY** *for £4,950.*

M1TCH *went to an anonymous London buyer for £28,600 as a gift for a relative and* **M1LAN** *was bought for £23,100 by an Asian businessman for his son.*

Tom Mason, 44, broke down in tears after getting **1TM** *for £23,100. 'I have been waiting 44 years for this moment' he said. The 80 plates sold boosted Treasury coffers by £1,565,355.* *(Newspaper cutting)*

"Martin Chuzzlewit" by Charles Dickens - Written in 1844, this masterpiece has now been brought to life by television's finest actors & actresses. How Charles Dickens would love to see all his larger than life characters brought to life so brilliantly. He was not interested in those who 'were strangely devoid of individual traits of character, insomuch that they might have changed minds with each other & nobody know'.

12th December 1994 Monday

'Civil Service Retirement Fellowship' – My 3rd Christmas party with the Coalville Group – this year at the home of our Chairman, Terry Watson and his wife Audrey, at 16 Coverdale, Whitwick.

No longer the 'new girl', it is lovely to know & be known by everybody & feel at home with them all. Since I joined we now have 4 more retirees, 2 singles & a couple.

14th December 1994 Wednesday

Canadian pine luxury Christmas tree!

Our dear little Christmas tree, 18 inches high, purchased by my dad for 7/6d, & still going strong, is sharing the honours this year with the most beautiful new tree, 4 feet high & bedecked & be-jewelled to perfection. Never have I seen such decorated trees as on display at Stapleton's Garden Centre & I have endeavoured to copy them.

Leicester Cathedral will get a new £25,000 visitors' entrance next year as part of a major refurbishment programme.

16th December 1994 Friday

Duck feather & down quilt 13.5 tog £39.99p. - After 3 months luxuriating each night under my lovely warm 12.0 tog 'Continental Quilt', I have now launched out on an extra warm 13.5 tog quilt, so that Bunting (whom I have invited for Christmas) & I can both enjoy the pleasure of such luxury & comfort. We have been invited to spend Christmas Day with cousin Miles.

Clerical moves – Leaving the area is the Rev Royston Davis, who goes from being priest in charge of Gilmorton to be rector of Ogwell and Denbury in Exeter in February. (Former Vicar of Snibston.)

18th December 1994 Sunday

'Holme Lodge', Cheshire Home, West Bridgford, is now home for Peter Mould, aged 50, whom we have known since he was a young boy. Enid & I spent the afternoon with him & were brought up to date on his news.

He is now a Roman Catholic & has 2 very good friends who are monks. Dermot & Tim had both written to him & I wrote a reply to each of them, dictated & signed by Peter.

20th December 1994 Tuesday

From my love, by post, a Christmas card "For the One I Love", containing two £10 notes.

"I may not put my love in words too often through the year, and maybe I don't say enough to make my feeling clear, but even so I'm sure you know that each day all year through, my greatest happiness in life depends on loving you"

Merry Christmas darling.

All my love for ever. John xxxxxx

The Facts on De Montfort

January 1994 – The £4 million refurbishment work began.

July 25th – City Council announced De Montfort Hall would re-open September 23rd.

July 30th – The opening date was delayed and five events cancelled when sub-contractors Eurotrak collapsed.

September 2nd – The Festival of Remembrance was cancelled.

October 31st – The cost of refurbishing the hall rose from £3.9 million to £4.25 million.

November 3rd – Constructors Costain announced the hall was not ready for Frank Skinner the next day. Two other events are cancelled.

November 15th – A revised opening date of December 3rd was announced and fifteen events thrown into doubt.

22nd December 1994 Thursday

MacLeod – Debbie and Murdo are proud to announce the birth of their son Murdo Alexander, born December 22nd 1994. Many thanks to the Foxton Team. L.G.H.M.U.

Remember young Murdo's whirlwind romance last year? (Married 22nd October 1993)
Now, exactly 14 months later, Debbie & Murdo have another Murdo – Murd the Third.
The new baby, like his father & grandfather, is a true Scot, dressed up for Christmas in the tartan & carrying on the full family name.

24th December 1994 Saturday

"U.S. Postal Service takes the Christ out of Christmas" – American Postmaster General, Marvin Runyan, bowing to the demands of politically correct censors, has decreed that the commemorative Christmas stamps will no longer include the Madonna & child.
Post Offices will be banned from mounting displays or hanging posters that refer to Christmas. Displays will relate only to Post Office services.

25th December 1994 Sunday

Bunting & I enjoyed Christmas Day at the home of cousin Miles, his lady-love Gwen & also his mother Isobel sharing the festive board with us.
His home 'Glenholm' is ideal for a get-together, with a grandiose dining table capable of seating 8 & a separate spacious lounge where the log fire ablaze in the hearth added just the right touch for Christmas Day.

28th December 1994 Wednesday

Another get-together at 'Glenholm', where there were 8 of us for tea & the evening – Miles, Gwen, Isobel, Pat, Evelyn, Enid, Bunting & me. I volunteered to provide the food for teatime & later we played the old favourite family games – Chinese writing, etc. etc.

30th December 1994 Friday

Intelligence Quotient (I.Q.) is measured on a scale on which the average of the population is 100, most people are somewhere between 70 & 130.
Only the mentally retarded fall in the I.Q. range 0 – 70.
Only the intellectual elite fall in the range 130 – 200.
Whereas in the past there was unskilled work for those in the range 70 – 100, these now form the bulk of the long-term unemployed.

* * *

Worth hunting Orion

The constellation of the month has to be Orion.
In Greek mythology he was a mighty hunter, unafraid of any foe. Annoyed by his audacity, the Earth goddess sent a lowly scorpion which gave Orion a fatal sting. The gods put Orion & the scorpion in the sky as constellations – as far apart as possible. Orion rules the winter skies, while Scorpius appears only in the summer.
Orion is one of the easiest constellations to recognise. Seven stars make up a distinctly humanoid shape; four stars for his shoulders & knees, & three for his belt. In the sky tableau Orion is facing his old foe Taurus, the bull.
Nearby are the beautiful Pleiades, a cluster of 'young' stars, only one million years old. The Pleiades are also called the Seven Sisters. (Seven daughters of Atlas).

* * *

1995

2nd January 1995 Monday

And so we face this New Year with many social problems, including chronic unemployment, single motherhood, welfare dependency & crime. Low I.Q. is thought to be a significant component of all these. The average I.Q. of the mothers of illegitimate children is 88; of recidivist criminals, 80; and of the long term unemployed, 77. Things only go from bad to worse as the cycle of deprivation is enlarged.

Marriage freedom – Nationwide: Couples will be able to get married in a register office anywhere in the country, and not just in the area they live, from Tuesday, January 3rd 1995. (Newspaper cutting)

4th January 1995 Wednesday

'The rich get rich & the poor get poorer …….'
Latest figures show that the number of people in Britain who earned more than £1 million doubled last year. Sir Andrew Lloyd Webber, who has composed several hit musicals, is top of the list with a salary of £11 million, topped up by £14 million in dividends from his 'Really Useful Company' which stages his musicals.

6th January 1995 Friday

'**Twelfth Night – or What You Will**' - Just call this masterpiece of Shakespeare's comedies anything you like. It is a play of light-hearted revelry; and Twelfth Night is such a night to round off the Christmas festivities. Set in a world of make-believe, it is a masquerade, where ambiguity reigns, & begins thus – "If music be the food of love, play on".
Shakespeare chose the make-believe land of Illyria for his setting of Twelfth Night. Here amidst the foolish comings & goings of the aristocracy, Feste, the clown, with his ready wit & intellectual agility, proves wiser than them all. Feste, the jester, was indeed a role created especially for the great theatrical jester of Shakespeare's day – Robert Armin.
Robert Armin, as well as playing the original Feste, the jester in Twelfth Night, was also the original Touchstone (As You Like It), Grave-digger (Hamlet), Lavache (All's Well That Ends Well), and Fool (King Lear). He was a professional 'fool' & had his own one man show. He also wrote a rhyming jest book, full of quips upon questions; & he in fact inspired Shakespeare.

12th January 1995 Thursday

Divorce leads to royal marriage speculation – An announcement that Brigadier Andrew Parker Bowles and his wife Camilla, who has had a long-standing affair with the Prince of Wales, are to divorce increased speculation that the Prince's own marriage could end shortly.   *(Newspaper cutting)*

Camilla Parker Bowles (née Shand) aged 48, is known to be the love-of-the-life of Prince Charles.
He & Princess Diana are expected to divorce; but for the heir to the throne to re-marry & live happily ever after, is well-nigh impossible. A royal marriage involves public opinion.

13th January 1995 Friday

Land, Florence, beloved wife of Sam, loving mother of Brian, mother-in-law of Jean, grandmother of Susan and John, great-grandmother of Jade and Lauren, passed peacefully away January 13th 1995. Funeral service at Ravenstone Parish Church on Thursday January 19th at 1p.m. followed by interment in the churchyard.

14th January 1995 Saturday

Visited poor Elaine in Coalville Hospital where she has gone for a fortnight's physiotherapy. Found her in bed in Ward 3 'Ellistown Ward' & oh, how poorly she looked. It seemed as though all her strength had been drained from her.

On this day – 1776 – The first cocktail was shaken by an American barmaid named Betsy Flanagan in New York. A drunk demanded that a handful of bantam tail-feathers decorating the bar be added to his drink. The barmaid mixed up as many coloured liqueurs as she could find and added the feathers – presenting the man with a 'cocktail'.

16th January 1995 Monday

A 25-acre site next to Moira Bath-Yard is to become part of our new National Forest which will be designed specially for the benefit of the disabled. The first phase of work to create a car park, pathways & early tree planting will begin this year. Phase 2, starting next year, will create picnic areas & a building for visitors. Bikes, motor vehicles & horses will be banned inside this area.

17th January 1995 Tuesday

'Civil Service Retirement Fellowship' – My third "Annual January Lunch" with the Coalville Group, the venue this year being 'The Robin Hood' at Swannington. Again I was pleased to go with Mr & Mrs Jim Bailiss & enjoyed the company of 'Charlie' at our table for 4. Tables were set out in 4s to seat 24. A very good meal where I chose 'chicken' & roly poly pudding.

20th January 1995 Friday

"Kiss Me Kate" is this year's choice for Coalville Amateurs & again I was pleased to be asked to join those assembled at Peter Jacques' house for the annual allocation of tickets. We were the same team as last year. This is a very special year for Peter & his wife Vera, as this marks their 50th year with the society. I was sorry to learn that Marlene will not join us in March.

22nd January 1995 Sunday

1902 Teddy Bear – Brooklyn candy store owner Morris Michtom made the first teddy bear of brown plush and named it for that great huntsman, Theodore Roosevelt.
Ready, Teddy, Go! – First produced in Germany in 1903, the teddy bear was named after American President Teddy Roosevelt.

(Newspaper cuttings)

Meet 'Honey Bear' – an irresistible 10-inch high teddy bear dressed in nothing but a navy blue jumper, emblazoned with the Royal Coat of Arms & the wording 'Theatre Royal, Drury Lane, London'.
Mary Blue & I went on a guided tour of this great theatre the other day & there, on sale, was this darling little

bear. Like President Roosevelt, I just had to take care of this little bear.

24th January 1995 Tuesday
The Royal Commission for the Exhibition of 1851 are still going strong. What are they doing?

You might well ask. Thanks to Queen Victoria's consort, Prince Albert, the mighty exhibition of 1851 was such a financial success that even today there is a £12 million nest-egg. Every year 18 fellowships, each worth up to £14,000 are handed out to post graduate science researchers & such-like.

The Royal Commission for the Exhibition of 1851 was set up in 1846 to stage the Great Exhibition & then to increase the means of industrial education. It therefore acquired 87 acres of South Kensington & built 'Albertopolis' including the Victoria & Albert Natural History, Science & Geological Museums, Imperial College, & the Royal Albert Hall. Rents from this area = £340,000 per year.

1.2bn Chinese – China's population will exceed 1.2 billion by the middle of next month, five years earlier than planned, the China Daily says. Last year the population grew by 58,000 a day.

28th January 1995 Saturday
Happy Birthday
♥ To My Ain Wee Darling – now 65 ♥
In the twinkling of an eye, Cocky changed from a 27 year-old to a 60 year-old. Now, in another twinkling of the eye, Cocky is a fully fledged O.A.P. old age pensioner, like me, eligible for the state pension. Meanwhile, baby Lewis, on the threshold of life, is one today.

30th January 1995 Monday
Sizewell B nuclear power station on the Suffolk coast, Britain's first pressurised water reactor station (P.W.R.) will be switched on tomorrow. With a dome bigger than that of St. Paul's Cathedral, the station has a life span of 40 years. More than 750,000 gallons of sea water will flow through the station every minute.

1st February 1995 Wednesday
The Victoria Cross, a bronze Maltese cross, awarded only to the bravest of the brave, is a rare honour indeed. Founded by Queen Victoria (1856) it is a decoration for 'conspicuous bravery on the field'. Only 3 men have ever won two Victoria Crosses, i.e. V.C. & Bar. Arthur Martin-Leake, Noel Godfrey Chavasse & Charles Upham who died recently.

3rd February 1995 Friday
'Renewal of the Water Main' – What a marathon task this is! For the past few weeks the whole of Leicester Road, Ravenstone, has had workmen here from 8a.m. until 8p.m., working in the dark after 5p.m., digging out great holes by hand, making huge mounds of earth, removing the earth by nightfall & covering the holes with steel boards.

M. Holleran Ltd., Civil Engineering & Pipeline Specialists, together with Underground Systems Ltd. of Sandy, Bedfordshire, supply the expertise and wherewithal for removing the old water main & literally threading through the underground the beautiful new polyethylene pipes for Severn Trent Water to proclaim:-'Working to improve our service to you'.

6th February 1995 Monday
On this day 6th February 1695 King Charles II died.

7th February 1995 Tuesday
Visited Durham! Enid & I are considering a holiday in Durham this year, so I went to 'inspect' the place. How I loved the great Cathedral where I would like to have lingered much longer.

At least I managed to walk all round the cloisters & also stand & gaze at the splendid lectern – a pelican feeding its young from its own breast – surpassing the one at Norwich.

9th February 1995 Thursday
Mary Blue, who will be 51 next month & has worked at 'Walkers Crisps' for the past 20 years, has now been made redundant. The potato crisp industry is facing a cut-throat price war where Walkers boasts the greatest market share in a £900 million per year market. Owned by the American group PepsiCo, Walkers will stop at nothing to out-manoeuvre all rivals.

One in five bank workers will lose their jobs in the next few years as the industry undergoes wholesale rationalisation similar to that suffered by British manufacturing, the head of one of Britain's leading banks predicts. Sir Brian Pitman, chief executive at Lloyds, estimated that 75,000 jobs would go, on top of the 90,000 lost since 1989. At its peak in 1989 the banking industry employed 460,000 people, since when some 3,000 bank and building society branches have closed. Computer technology, telephone banking and increased automation of some tasks formerly performed by clerks have all seen banks lose thousands of staff.
(Newspaper cutting)

11th February 1995 Saturday
F.A. Carling Premiership – Leicester City's promotion to football's top flight, the Premier Division, was the cause of great celebration last year (see 3rd June 1994).

Now, firmly established as 'the premiership's bottom club', there is little left to celebrate. They managed to scrape through to the F.A. Cup 5th round where they were knocked out by Wolves.

It is not too early to start wondering how on earth we will write the date when we reach the year 2000. Today's date can be written as 12.2.95, but in five years it will be 12.2,00 – and that will mean the year doesn't exist.   *Mrs B. Desborough.*
(Newspaper cutting)

13th February Monday
In this year of war-related anniversaries, we remember today the bombing of Dresden on 13th February 1945. This was 'the greatest single night's slaughter in the history of Europe'. Beautiful Dresden, magnificent baroque capital of Saxony was reduced to a smouldering ruin. Like Coventry Cathedral the baroque Frauenkirche (Church of Our Lady) was destroyed. Coventry & Dresden are now friends.

14th February 1995 Tuesday

"With love to my Valentine – you mean much more
than words could ever say……."

"Valentine, you mean much more than words could ever
say. That's why I'm sending all my love & warmest
thoughts today"

Roses are red, violets are blue.

Oh! & I love you always.

All my love for ever.

xxxxx

xx

The most romantic place in England on Valentine's Day
is 'Lover' which is situated mid-way between Salisbury
& Southampton. Taking advantage of its name, it now
does big business at its little Post Office where lovers
come from far & near to post their Valentine Cards &
receive a special post mark. When many other little Post
Offices were closed, Lover was reprieved.

*Defending City's motto – A county woman feels that
people asking for Leicester's motto to be changed should
look to its real meaning.*

*Author Sue Townsend started the debate when she stated
that Leicester is a progressive city and should change its
motto, 'Semper Eadem', which has been popularly
translated as 'Always the Same'.*

*Elizabeth Hewes of Ravenstone, near Coalville, was
reminded of something she read 28 years ago. She said,
"In 1967, under the heading What Our Motto Really
Means, the Leicester Mercury printed an excellent
explanation of why Leicester's motto should never be
changed." Semper Eadem was the personal motto of
Queen Elizabeth I. It was deemed appropriate for
Leicester after she incorporated the Borough of
Leicester at the end of the 16th century.*

*Mercury reader Mr J S Donaldson of Castle Street,
Whitwick, suggested that the motto may be interpreted
as – 'Be Always One'.*

*He wrote, "Elizabeth the Great never forsook a real
friend or servant and even the lowest of menials
dismissed from her service was either pensioned off or
found another place." He continued, "She was 'always
one' to England and her people. They understood her
motto and knew she stood by it."*

(Newspaper cutting)

*"The 'eadem' is not a neuter plural meaning 'the same
things'. It is a feminine adjective agreeing with the noun
mente which is understood" wrote Mr Bowden,
headmaster of Leicester's St John the Baptist Junior
School some decades ago. He added, "The adverbial use
of an adjective with mente was common in late Latin.
This is the origin of the French adverb in 'ment' and
eventually the feminine adjective in the ablative case
was adverbially without a substantive. Semper Eadem
then means Always in the Same Spirit – and is a fine
motto for a fine city if its citizens are not unmindful of
the heritage they enjoy".*

(From part of a further newspaper cutting)

19th February 1995 Sexagesima Sunday

"Man dies after freak fall in air pressure" – Don Tollett,
aged 60, of Hebburn, Tyne & Wear, was walking along,
not hurting anybody, when all of a sudden underground
carbon dioxide from old mine workings surfaced &
killed him. He died from suffocation after weather
conditions caused a drop in air pressure & the carbon
dioxide pushed out breathable air.

21st February 1995 Tuesday

Jeanne Calment, believed to be the world's oldest
person, is celebrating her 120th birthday today at Arles in
Provence, where she was born. The last person who
lived to be 120 was Shigechiyo Izumi of Japan who died
on 21st February 1986, aged 120 years and 237 days.

22nd February 1995 Wednesday

The Duchess of Kent celebrates her 62nd birthday today.

23rd February 1995 Thursday

Bunting's son, Michael, is involved with 'The Prince's
Trust' & so it was that yesterday, when the Prince of
Wales visited Lichfield, Michael was one of the
favoured few to shake hands with the Prince. Bunting
went along too & loved being so close to 'Charlie'.

*The Prince of Wales toured Lichfield Cathedral and
viewed recent restoration work. His Royal Highness,
President,*
*The Prince's Trust, later attended a meeting with
business and voluntary organisations at Lichfield
Cathedral Visitors'*
*Study Centre to discuss the trust's project in support of
the homeless. The Prince of Wales afterwards attended
E v e n s o n g   i n   L i c h f i e l d   C a t h e d r a l.*
(Newspaper cutting)

24th February 1995 Friday

*Marriage rates have fallen to their lowest level since
records began 150 years ago, while divorce rates have
risen to a new peak, a report shows. According to
figures from the Joseph Rowntree Foundation, the
number of people marrying each year has declined
steadily for the past 20 years, from 17 per 1,000
population to 11. The previous lowest rate – during the
two world wars – was 14 per 1,000. Forecasts of the
death of the traditional family are exaggerated though.
Despite the six-fold increase in divorce since 1961,
seven out of ten families are still headed by both birth-
parents. The report, based on evidence presented at a
series of seminars organised by the foundation, says that
the rise of cohabitation has postponed rather than
replaced marriage. Sixty per cent of couples live
together before their wedding day, compared with 6 per
cent in the 1960s. Most cohabiting couples marry or
b r e a k   u p   b e f o r e   h a v i n g   c h i l d r e n.
(Newspaper cutting)*

25th February 1995 Saturday

"It's a celebration – Occasion – Emerald Wedding –
55 years.
Date – Saturday 25th March 1995. Time – 7-30p.m.
Place – The Station Inn, Swannington.
Given by – Pat & Evelyn – Hope you can come!"

Invitation to dinner for fourteen in recognition of Pat &
Evelyn's Wedding Anniversary which is actually 16th
March.

27th February 1995 Monday
Wanted – Sheriff of Nottingham – The post of Sheriff of Nottingham is to go unfilled for the first time in more than 800 years because no one eligible for the office will accept it. Four members of the Labour majority on Nottingham City Council, which makes the annual choice, refused to be nominated and no volunteers could be found among the remaining 37 Labour councillors. (Newspaper cutting)

In July 1992, I had a wonderful impromptu private guided tour of Nottingham's magnificent Council House when I sat in the Sheriff's seat. The present Sheriff, Ron McIntosh, will retire in May & no other Labour councillor is prepared to fill this post.

2nd March 1995 Thursday
'The Church' – During Lent we again have a series of talks at Leicester Cathedral given by different Bishops. Starting on 9th March & finishing on 6th April, the subjects are – 'The People of God', 'The Church of England as by Law Established', 'The Holy Spirit at Work', 'The Body of Christ' and 'Society at Prayer'. They are from 1p.m. – 1-35p.m.

*Titanic memorial – A memorial garden for the 1,490 people lost in the sinking of the **Titanic** will be opened next month at the National Maritime Museum at Greenwich, southeast London.   (Newspaper cutting)*

4th March 1995 Saturday
Poor Elaine is now in Leicester Royal Infirmary where she was taken with a broken hip – broken by simply lying in bed. However, that seems to be mending itself, just as it managed to break itself. Her bed sores have broken out again, so she is in a private room; & because of the infection each time I visit her I have to wear a throw-away apron & rubber gloves.

6th March 1995 Monday
"Kiss Me Kate" – We are now well into the swing of Coalville Amateurs' production which began last Wednesday & runs until next Saturday. Another Cole Porter show, this time based on Shakespeare's 'The Taming of the Shrew'. I never cease to be thrilled by the magic of the stage & love being an integral part of the front of house team – Assistant House Manager to brother Pat.

Sheriff to rescue – Nottingham has got a new sheriff after fears that the post would be unfilled when four councillors turned it down. He is Roy Greensmith, 65, a Labour councillor for three years. (Newspaper cutting)

8th March 1995 Wednesday
Joanne yesterday celebrated her 21st birthday by becoming engaged to her boyfriend Glenn. Already the proud mother of baby Dale, born last September, she is now on top of the world.
"When will you be getting married?" I asked her.
"Oh, not yet. Not until Dale is old enough to be page boy!"

10th March 1995 Friday
'The People of God' – Bishop Godfrey Ashby (Bishops

in Lent) spoke of God first assembling his people at Sinai when Moses received the Ten Commandments. The Lord Jesus later assembled his disciples & the worldwide Christian Church.
The Bishop referred to all those through the ages who have been pillars of the church & said that Lord Melbourne called himself a buttress, supporting from the outside.

Christian women unite in prayer –Throughout the world the first Friday in March each year is Women's World Day of Prayer. It is a time when Christian women get together for a service of prayer and worship. Each year the service is prepared by women from a different country. This year it was prepared by the women of Ghana whose country, when the service went to print, was peaceful and hospitable. Since independent and in spite of its socioeconomic difficulties, Ghana had put aside the evils of ethnicity and tribalism and the people had been able to live as one nation. Today Ghana is a place of conflict and prayers are being asked for a solution to the problems and for people to help. Prayers are also asked for forgiveness and grace to be able to build a new Ghana of love, peace and forgiveness. With this in mind women of Ravenstone and Swannington, Anglicans, Roman Catholics and Methodists, joined together in Ravenstone Parish Church for this year's service. The service was led by Miss Betty Hewes, the soloist was Mrs Christine Koop and the organ was played by the Rector. Mrs Jan Shepherd spoke on the theme of the service, 'The earth is a house for all people'.

11th March 1995 Saturday
Wheelwright, Charles, of Cosby, beloved husband of Irene, father of Michael, brother of Freda and grandfather of Rachel, passed peacefully away in hospital on Saturday March 11th.
Funeral service on Friday March 17th at the Parish Church of St. Michael and All Angels, Cosby at 11a.m. followed by cremation at Gilroes Crematorium.
(See 17th July 1991)

12th March 1995 Sunday
"Kiss Me Kate" Coalville Amateur Operatic Society 75 years 1919 – 1994. Listed in the programme this year are all the Presidents, Chairmen, Secretaries, Treasurers, Musical Directors, Choreographers, Producers & Pianists we have had during those 75 years. How lovely to see my dad & mum's name in the list of Presidents. Evelyn's brother, Cecil Roberts, recorded all these names.

Hewes, John Neville, died Sunday March 12th 1995, aged 67 years. Beloved father of Stephen, Peter, Virginia and Martin, grandfather of James, Kathrine, Victoria, Matthew and Natalie. He will be greatly missed. His funeral service is to be held at 12 noon on Saturday March 18th at Loughborough Crematorium Chapel.

14th March 1995 Tuesday
And so we come to the end of our lovely 1995 production of "Kiss Me Kate". Our 'magnificent seven' line up of 'girls' this year included Barbara Webster in

place of Marlene. She is another of the golden oldies, but not like Marlene – 'daughter of the gods, divinely tall & most divinely fair'.

As once again we shine only with reflected glory, my darling sends me red roses.

16th March 1995 Thursday

Sharon, who works as a 'rep' for British Shoe United, now has a new man in her life. He too works for B.U. (British United Shoe Machinery Ltd.) as Area Manager. He is Jim Reason & has 2 children, Carly & Sam. Sharon & Jim, together with Carly & Sam, now all live together in sumptuous luxury in a de luxe new house, complete with double garage, in Melton Mowbray.

17th March 1995 Friday

In October 1975, Wanlip Church was full when Charles (my work-mate) married Renée.

Now, nearly 20 years on, Cosby Church was full to overflowing for Charles' funeral (on my dad's birthday). Charles was steeped in the music of the Church, having been organist in his locality for many years. For his last hymn he chose a 'Holy Communion hymn' which ended – 'And grant us never more to part with thee'.

18th March 1995 Saturday

'The Church of England as by law established' (Bishops in Lent). The dynamic Bishop Colin Buchanan, Assistant Bishop of Rochester, kept us well entertained as he spoke at a rattling speed of the 20th century Church of England trying to perform the impossible task of functioning in a multi-cultural society under laws laid down in a different age when all the parishioners attended church.

20th March 1995 Monday

Letter from America!

"Dear Betty, In 1948 you & I exchanged a few pen-pal letters & then ceased.

Today I was going through some papers I had accumulated over the years & found two of your letters. It has been more than 45 years & everything has changed of course. I can only hope to find you & to hear from you ……..."   Jean Brister, Arkansas.

22nd March 1995 Wednesday

Sales of Premium Bonds have increased four-fold since the jackpot went up from £250,000 to £1 million last year. The Government takes in an average £150 million a month in bond sales. Each month £19 million is distributed in prize money, i.e. 295,000 prizes per month.

Increasing the top prize has however made the other wins smaller. So, once again, the rich get rich & the poor get poorer.

24th March 1995 Friday

Westminster Cathedral, the Roman Catholic largest & most important church in England, is 100 years old this year. It was in 1895 that Cardinal Vaughan laid the foundation stone & the centenary year will begin tomorrow, 25th March and continue until 13th October.

In May there will be an international festival of flowers & other celebrations.

26th March 1995 Sunday

Pat & Evelyn's Emerald Wedding Feast took place yesterday evening in the Upper Room of the Station Inn, Swannington.

Of the original 14 who were to attend, Bunting declined, Karen & Graham could not make it from Bedford & Mary's friend Pam came to balance the party.

Pat said to me at the table, "We are in the Upper Room" and we thought immediately of the Last Supper.

     Jane   Steven   Scott   Sharon   Jim
Pat [///] Evelyn
     Betty Pam Mary Blue Debbie Murdo

28th March 1995 Tuesday

"A former investing member of the Heart of England Building Society will qualify as a 2-year Investing Member of Cheltenham & Gloucester Building Society ……..."

So, along with more than a million other members of the C & G, I have now voted for the C & G to join the Lloyds Bank Group – a £1.8 billion takeover. Cash incentives have been offered to eligible members.

30th March 1995 Thursday

'The Body of Christ' – Bishop Bill Ind of Grantham spoke first of the Holy Communion Service where we all acknowledge being 'one body'. How many people did God have to create to make you? he challenged. 'This is my body' said Christ at the Last Supper. 'Do this in remembrance of me'. And what is re-membrance? Being alive again, as to God. The whole Church of Christ is his body.

Thought for the day – Then Judas, which had betrayed him, when he saw that he was condemned, repented himself, and brought again the thirty pieces of silver to the chief priests and elders.   Matthew 27, v 3, King James Bible.

1st April 1995 Saturday

A new pair of specs to update the ones I bought in December 1992. As you might be sure, I chose just about the most expensive frames in the shop – gold rimmed, with the slenderest of black edge across the top, making them virtually colourless. The total bill, including £16-50p for eye testing, was £233-50p. You would wonder how specs could be so expensive.

Britain has lost 50,000 jobs in the first three months of this year, maintaining a strong sense of job insecurity and a 'feel-bad' factor at work, a new survey suggests. (Newspaper cutting)

5th April 1995 Wednesday

Elaine has now taken up residence in The Meadows Nursing Home, 94 Loughborough Road, Thringstone – for the Chronic Sick, the Physically Disabled & those in need of Terminal Care.

It has 42 beds & is part of a larger group of Nursing Homes called Craegmoor Healthcare.

Now confined to a wheelchair, she looks so tragically pale & so very frail, she is not expected to go back to her own home again.

6ᵗʰ April 1995 Thursday
Local folk are being invited to deposit their hard-earned cash with North West Leicestershire District Council in a new savings scheme. The Safe and Secure Deposit Account comes into force today and is open to all residents living in the district.
(Newspaper cutting)

7ᵗʰ April 1995 Friday
'Society at Prayer' – Bishop Godfrey Ashby, who will soon be retiring, referred again to God first assembling his people at Sinai, where through God's Commandments, the people were all under his command. The Christian Church, on the other hand, seemed to have the most unlikely beginnings, but on the Day of Pentecost, it was 'inspired'. He told us about Dante's Divine Comedy, which I then purchased.

9ᵗʰ April 1995 Palm Sunday
"Oriana", one of the names given to Elizabeth I by poets who wrote in her praise, is the name given to P. & O.'s latest super liner, which set sail today on her maiden voyage. What a magnificent sight – a block of luxury flats afloat, complete with all the services residents in such places expect. With 14 decks, a 500 seat theatre with rotating stage, giant waterfall & absolute sumptuous luxury.

10ᵗʰ April 1995 Monday
New Era – The world's first computerised DNA database started work today in Birmingham. The Forensic Science Service laboratory will keep genetic fingerprint information on hundreds of thousands of people and help police link criminals to crime.
(Newspaper cutting)

11ᵗʰ April 1995 Tuesday
The Church of England – the Anglican Church – has 2 Archbishops in England – Canterbury & York; but throughout the world it has 36 Archbishops, also referred to as Primates. They represent some 70 million Anglicans worldwide. The chief Primate, 'primus inter pares' = first among equals, is the Archbishop of Canterbury. Recently they all gathered together in London.

Wilkinson. Suddenly on April 3ʳᵈ 1995 at home Charles Fredrick, age 70 years. Dearly loved husband of Andrea Marianne formally of Coalville. The service was at St Pauls Church, Bishopton Road, Stockton-on-Tees, Friday 12.30p.m. prior to interment at Durham Road Cemetery. Thank you to all friends for letters, cards and flowers. Please accept this as recognition.

On November 8ᵗʰ 1961, Marianne married her beloved Charles. Formerly Miss Shilliam, she was a leading lady & also dancing mistress for Coalville Amateur Operatic Society.

13ᵗʰ April 1995 Maundy Thursday
'The Divine Comedy' – Thanks to Bishop Godfrey Ashby, I have been introduced to 'The Greatest Poem of the Middle Ages' Dante's 3 in 1 Trilogy in which Dante the pilgrim journeys through the Afterlife, first through Hell (Dante's Inferno) then through Purgatory & finally to Paradise. Only when there is justice & order do we find paradise.

15ᵗʰ April 1995 Saturday
According to statistics, the average person takes 18,000 steps a day & walks 70,000 miles in a lifetime. So one would suppose then that 'the average person' walks 1,000 miles per year. (See 14ᵗʰ April 1994)

16ᵗʰ April 1995 Easter Sunday
Phone code – As from April 16ᵗʰ 1995, the new national code for Leicester will change from 0533 to 0116 and all local codes will be prefixed by the figure 2. (See 22ⁿᵈ April 2000)

17ᵗʰ April 1995 Monday
All change in the telephone codes nationwide. This has been a major operation announced a year in advance to allow businesses time to re-programme switchboards, print new telephone & fax codes on stationery & ensure signs & advertising carry the new number. The change has been necessary to make sure we do not run out of telephone codes & numbers in years to come.
The new phone codes are planned to give enough numbers for several more generations to come. All UK area codes already started with an 0. All that was needed was to add a 1 after the 0. Five cities were exceptions to the rule & were given totally revised numbers because of local needs. They were Bristol, Leeds, Leicester, Nottingham & Sheffield.

21ˢᵗ April 1995 Friday
'Terrible news filled paper about Concentration Camps' – Thus I wrote in my diary in April 1945.
Commemorations of the 50ᵗʰ anniversary of the liberation of Auschwitz earlier this year brought us face to face with Lt. General Vasily Petrenko, now 83, who as a 33 year-old colonel in the Soviet army, liberated this hell on earth.
"Nothing" he said, "had prepared us for what we saw".
While the Russian army liberated the hell on earth of Auschwitz where an estimated 1,300,000 died in the gas ovens, the British army liberated another hell on earth, Belsen, a small village in a thick wood 60 miles south of Hamburg, where an estimated 37,000 died. There were no gas ovens at Belsen; its inmates were simply left to die from starvation & disease.

25ᵗʰ April 1995 Tuesday
Cousin Miles invited me to see his wonderful new & very latest 'all singing & all dancing' computer – cum fax – cum everything else you could imagine. He has now converted one of his bedrooms into an office, complete with super de luxe mahogany desk, swivel chair, & shelves stacked high with everything required by latest technology. He still works for 'Crane Electronics', but from home.

If you think cousin Miles is a dynamic whiz-kid you should meet his brother, Murray, who is 'President' of T.P.S. Inc., Technical Production Services, i.e. technical consultants to the Broadcast & Television Production Industry, 231 Stephenson Avenue, Savannah, Georgia, 31405.

Tel: – 912-353-7609. Fax: – 912-353-7775. Email: –
cserve70404, 3530.
Murray is master of 'Digital Video Technology'.

When Murray visits his mother Isobel in Colchester, it is
a fleeting visit in a strictly timed schedule.
Day 1: - Depart Savannah 3-15p.m. Day 2: - Arrive
Gatwick 6-15a.m. Rent vehicle & drive to Colchester.
Overnight at Dedham Hall. Day 3: - Depart early from
Dedham for France via Portsmouth for 14-30 sailing.
Arrive at Caen 19-30 etc. etc. Day 9: - Depart Gatwick
11 a.m.

*Church assets halved – The Church of England's assets
of £2.4 billion are to be halved to pay the burgeoning
clergy pensions bill, church sources disclosed last night.*
(Newspaper cutting)

29th April 1995 Saturday
A new seven-storey building, dubbed the new palace of
Westminster, is to be built in time for the year 2000, on a
site opposite Big Ben, overlooking the Thames. It will
provide new palatial offices for M.P.s, complete with
restaurant, courtyard, balconies, shop & hairdressers. It
is to be built above a new Westminster underground
station & work will start when the station is completed
in 1997.

*Following a review of local authorities throughout
England, it was decided to allow Rutland to once again
become an independent county. Elections for the new
unitary authority will take place in May 1996 with the
reorganisation coming into effect from April 1st 1997.*
(Newspaper cutting)

3rd May 1995 Wednesday
Edwin Powell Hubble, the American astronomer, was
born in 1889. He discovered that all the observed
galaxies were rushing away, or receding, from Earth.
The Universe seemed to be expanding & the further
away the galaxies were receding, the faster they were
moving. This relationship indicated a general rate of
expansion which is measured by what is called the
'Hubble Constant'.

*Hubble, a lawyer-turned-astronomer, was the first
person to posit the idea of an expanding universe. His
reasoning was based on the observation that galaxies
are moving apart.*
*It seemed logical to deduce that all the matter in the
universe was once contained in a single point..*
(Newspaper cutting)

The Hubble Constant sets the scale of the Universe. It
sets the sizes of everything; it sets the age of the
Universe.
Hubble's Law = 'v(elocity) = H x d(istance)'.
The constant H is called the Hubble Constant.
The trouble with the Hubble Constant is that nobody
knows exactly what 'H' is.
How many kilometres per second per megaparsec?
A megaparsec is 3.26 million light years, the distance
light travels in that time.

The Milky Way is a galaxy measuring 60,000 light years

in diameter. Earth belongs to this galaxy.
Andromeda is our nearest galaxy neighbour & is 2
million light years' distant from us.
In our galaxy there are 100 billion stars, all like our sun.
Within the horizon of the observable Universe, it is
estimated that there are 100 billion galaxies. This defies
calculation.

Have I got news for you!
Michael Pierce says that, without doubt, the Hubble
Constant is 85.
But, hold on a minute. Gustav Tamman says it is 50.
Meanwhile, George Jacoby says 80.
Brian Schmidt, 70. Michael Rowan Robinson 50, &
John Tonry 80. So there you have it.
As far as we know at present, the Universe is about 15
billion years old, but we are not really sure.

*The Big Bang theory has been vindicated by a new study
which shows that the universe is about 15 billion years
old*
(Newspaper cutting)

8th May 1995 Monday
"A nostalgic evening to commemorate the 50th
Anniversary of V.E. Day" – On Monday 8th May, Enid
& I joined the merry throng at Ravenstone Institute
looking back to Victory in Europe in 1945. All decked
out in our red, white & blue, & with flags I had acquired
earlier in the day in London, we had a lovely evening,
with everyone happy to be there.

*Oh, Mr Porter! – A train driver on the Shrewsbury to
Aberystwyth line had to radio ahead for spare trousers
after he took his off to cool down and they flew out of the
window. British Rail said train cabs often became too
hot on sunny days.*
(Newspaper cutting)

13th May 1995 Saturday
'Christ Church Coalville, 4th Annual Gala Concert' –
After an afternoon walk through Normanton Woods,
carpeted by bluebells, Enid & I continued the day's
delights at Coalville's Christ Church where we enjoyed
the most wonderful concert. We heard Sheila Harrod, the
champion whistler, & we heard great singing & music,
including 'The Lost Chord' played on the organ.

15th May 1995 Monday
Duck feather & down quilt 4.5 togs £24 - 75p.
Having launched out on a 12 tog continental quilt last
September (£35) & a 13.5 tog quilt last December (£40),
I have now bought a summer weight one, making a total
of £100 spent on continental quilts. At least I have never
in my life had to buy a bed, thanks to my dad buying the
very best & still as good as new.

*Not surprisingly, Silentnight, the UK's largest maker of
beds, backs the Sleep Council's verdict that the British
don't change their beds as often as is hygienic.*
*Our health-conscious sleeping partners in the US
change their beds once every ten years on average,
compared with every 16 years in the UK..*
(Newspaper cutting)

17th May 1995 Wednesday

Meet Elizabeth Hewes 'a member of the Women's Royal Voluntary Service entitled to wear the WRVS badge'. "The members of the W.R.V.S., in partnership with the public & private sectors, are committed to being the premier providers of voluntary assistance to those in need of care within their local community". Enid & I qualify by delivering "Meals on Wheels".

The now famous WRVS is the largest active voluntary service in the United Kingdom, with more than 140,000 members. It was formed as the Women's Voluntary Service in 1938, to help local authorities prepare for civilian care in the event of war.

(Newspaper cutting)

19th May 1995 Friday

65, Leicester Road, Ravenstone, which used to be link-detached, was sold & completely dismantled, leaving nothing more than a post-box, has now, like a phoenix, risen from the ashes to become a delightful brand new detached house; while nearby, poor old Elaine's elegant house (No. 49) languishes empty, now that Elaine is no longer strong enough to live in her own home.

21st May 1995 Sunday

"And there was light!" Of all the fruit trees in the Hollies Orchard, none has been more trouble to me over the years than the one planted by 'Auntie Emma', Grandma Hewes' sister, who lived there for many years & helped raise the family. She planted this tree so close to the wall that it has almost pushed the wall over & has cast a great shadow over our garden. Now it has been cut down.

23rd May 1995 Tuesday

Everton 1 – Manchester United 0.
This year saw the 114th F. A. Cup Final. Although Manchester United had hoped to repeat their double win of League & the Cup, they managed to reach the final in both, but were beaten in both.
The Cup was presented by Charles, Prince of Wales, accompanied by his 2 sons, Prince William aged 12 & Prince Harry aged 10..

25th May 1995 Thursday Ascension Day

Letter from America – No 2.
"Dear Betty, You cannot imagine how thrilled I was to get your letter ……… I would love for you to come visit for a week or two. You could fly to Dallas, Texas, & I could meet you there (350 miles) or you can fly from Dallas to Little Rock. Arkansas' lakes & mountains are beautiful. Let me know the things you like to do."

27th May 1995 Saturday

Tony Blair, Labour's new young dynamic leader, born 6th May 1953, is busy formulating "The New Labour Party". Out goes the 1917 declaration (clause 4) which committed the party to wide-scale nationalisation by promising to 'secure for the workers by hand or by brain the full fruits of their industry'. In comes a pledge to create a community where 'wealth & opportunity are in the hands of the many & not the few'.

29th May 1995 Monday

Question – Why is May 29th known as Oak Apple Day?

Answer - In September 1651, my ancestors, the five Penderel brothers, hid King Charles II from Cromwell's troops in the Royal Oak at Boscobel, Shropshire, after the battle of Worcester. The romantic idea of a king hiding in the most English of trees caught the public's imagination and when Charles II was restored to the throne on his 30th birthday, on May 29th 1660, the day became known as Oak Apple Day and was celebrated as a public holiday until the middle of the 19th century. It is still commemorated at the Royal Hospital, Chelsea, founded by Charles II, and at Groveley, near Salisbury, by the wearing and carrying of oak leaves. We should still celebrate Oak Apple Day because, but for my ancestors' courage, we might be without our constitutional monarchy.
Geoffrey Whittington, Crossmichael, Castle Douglas.

(Newspaper cutting)

31st May 1995 Wednesday
49 Leicester Road, Ravenstone

A spacious Victorian style semi-detached residence having GCH, UPVC d/g to the front, comprising – Reception Hall – Lounge – Separate dining room/day room – Breakfast room – Kitchen & pantry – ground floor shower room – 3 bedrooms – bathroom – gravelled foregarden area, driveway and large mainly lawned rear garden - £56,950
This is Elaine's elegant house, now sadly for sale after belonging to her family all its life. Built by her grandfather & handed on to Elaine's mother, Ena Lakin, it has always been home to Elaine, who planted those bushes at the front.

2nd June 1995 Friday

Enid & I are now on holiday in County Durham, staying at Helme Park Hall Country House Hotel, near Fir Tree, Bishop Auckland. We arrived here yesterday & have booked 5 nights bed & breakfast. Never have we enjoyed such a magnificent view as enjoyed by our hotel. We are in the heart of the countryside & love seeing & hearing the abundant wild life.

4th June 1995 Sunday

Enid & I celebrated Whit Sunday today in Durham Cathedral, where in the power of the Holy Spirit, we joined the Venerable Bede & Saint Cuthbert & a host of other saints & holy men, whose lives of devoted service to God literally permeate those massive Norman pillars, & who, being alive to God for all time, shared in the service.
Thought for the day – I am the God of Abraham, and the God of Isaac, and the God of Jacob. God is not the God of the dead, but of the living. Matthew 22, v 32,
King James Bible.

8th June 1995 Thursday

Mr & Mrs Robert Thomson,
13 Hornbeam Road, Newbold Verdon, Leics.
request the pleasure of the company of
Miss B. Hewes
at an Evening Reception to be held at Appleby Inn Hotel,
Appleby Parva on Saturday 5th August 1995 at
8 o'clock to celebrate the marriage of their daughter
Dawn with Mr Philip Andrew Tart.
(Philip is the adopted son of cousin Rita).

10th June 1995 Saturday

"This Sceptr'd Isle" – This is Radio 4's latest year-long daily 15 minute readings to give us the history of Britain from the arrival of Julius Caesar up to the present day. In 200 episodes, covering 50 hours of broadcasting, we will hear extracts from Churchill's "History of the English Speaking Peoples" plus extracts from other historians & contemporary chronicles.

12th June 1995 Monday

Coalville Amateur Operatic Society AGM this year saw brother Pat, aged 76, re-appointed as House Manager, with me as Assistant House Manager. The show chosen for next March is "Countess Maritza", an updated version of the original "Maritza" which we have given twice before – 1955 and 1974. Pat is hoping to complete 50 years of service with the society.

14th June 1995 Wednesday

"Dear Motorist, The registration number on your vehicle may be more valuable than you think. One of our agents has assessed it as being worthy of a free valuation. Please post this reply paid card to us …"
Elite Registrations, P.O.Box 100, Devizes, Wiltshire, SN10 4BR attached the above message to my Peugeot K49 PUT while I was shopping at Coalville Co-op.

Number plate sell-off. Unissued number plates such as M1 DGE and L1 DYA will be auctioned today and tomorrow by the Driver and Vehicle Licensing Agency at Basingstoke, Hampshire.
M1 DGE is expected to fetch about £5,000, L1 DYA £4,200 and 2 BEN £3,000. To date, over 10,000 registrations have been sold, raising £45 million for the exchequer.   (Newspaper cutting)

16th June 1995 Friday

Stocks, Maureen (nee Scott), fell asleep on June 12th aged 72 years. Loving wife of Ken, dear mother of Graham and Roger. Funeral service and cremation at Loughborough Crematorium on Friday June 16th at 10a.m. Family flowers only, donations for Oncology, made payable to Leicester Royal Infirmary, may be sent to Stevens, Goodburn Funeral Service, 33 Scalford Road, Melton Mowbray. Tel. 01664 630337.

Today was the funeral of Maureen, only child of 'Auntie Doris' who died, aged 97, two years ago.
How sad that we all gathered today at 'The Cedars' Loughborough, for Maureen's funeral, when next Friday, 23rd June, she & Ken would have celebrated their Golden Wedding.

"What relationship are we to each other?" Maureen's elder son Graham said that he & his mother had always meant to sort out a family tree, but had never got round to it. Now it was too late. However, thanks to Mary Moore's great interest in her family tree & details she had given to me, I was able to provide a worthwhile printout for Graham spanning 200 years.

19th June 1995 Monday

Group Captain Peter Townsend, CVO, DSO, DFC and Bar, Battle of Britain pilot and former equerry to King George VI, 1944-52, and Queen Elizabeth II, 1952-53, died on June 19th aged 80.
He was born on November 22nd 1914.

Group Captain Peter Townsend & Princess Margaret fell in love over 40 years ago in 1952 when King George VI died. He was 16 years older than the Princess; he was married with 2 sons & was about to divorce his wife – he being the 'innocent party'.
But poor Princess Margaret could not follow the dictates of her own heart. She had to consider the Church of England's teaching on divorce; the Queen, her sister, being Supreme Governor of the Church, & the fact that being then aged only 22, Princess Margaret could not, under the law setting out the rules for royal marriages, become engaged without her sister's formal consent. Even then, at the age of 25, she would need parliamentary approval, not just in the United Kingdom, but throughout the Commonwealth. They tried a 'separation' following the Coronation in 1953, until her 25th birthday. They could, if all else failed, be married by civil ceremony, with the Princess giving up all her royal privileges & financial rights. But with so much opposition from all quarters, they chose in the end not to marry. In time they each married someone else, but their love for each other never ceased. It was in 1959 that Group Captain Peter Wooldridge Townsend married for his second wife a Belgian, Marie Luce Jamagne. They made their home in France, where he is now buried.

20th June 1995 Tuesday

"Civil Service Retirement Fellowship" – Our June meeting was held at the home of Roy & Brenda (see 27th July 1994) where again we were blessed with a glorious summer's day in the garden. Mr & Mrs Baxter took me in their car & I found myself next to our Chairman Terry Watson who told me all about his life-long work as a forensic scientist.

22nd June 1995 Thursday

27, Leicester Road, Ravenstone, is now looking very smart after being painted & decorated on the outside. Pat's friend & neighbour, 63 year-old Mr Moore has done the job - £258. The new colour scheme at the front is black & white, replacing the former green front door with green & cream lower eaves. All that was green & cream is now black & white.

24th June 1995 Saturday, Midsummer Day

"A Midsummer Night's Dream" – This hilarious Shakespearean play was written originally as a masque for a private celebration – so popular with the Elizabethans. The motley crew of patches, tinker, tailor, etc. who perform their little play - 'a tedious brief scene of young Pyramus & his love Thisbe' - manage to turn a tragedy into a merry comedy.
Pyramus & Thisbe – the play within the play "A Midsummer Night's Dream" was the saddest story of true love taken from ancient times. Pyramus was the most handsome young man & Thisbe the most beautiful maiden in all Babylonia. Their parents did not approve of their love for each other, & like Romeo & Juliet, they died for their love of each other, when one thought the other dead.

28th June 1995 Wednesday
Barkby, Elaine, of Snibston, died June 23rd 1995, after a long illness bravely borne. Funeral Loughborough Crematorium, Wednesday June 28th at 3.30p.m. No flowers please. Donations to Multiple Sclerosis Society.

Poor Elaine certainly had a long illness, bravely borne. Being all alone in this world, she had no relations at all at her funeral. But her good neighbours rallied round to give her a good funeral & then each dispersed, with no formal get-together.

29th June 1995 Thursday
On St. Peter's Day, 29th June 1895 – one hundred years ago – the foundation stone of Westminster Cathedral was laid. The architect, John Francis Bentley, had been to Italy for 12 months to study the Byzantine style & prepare his plans. Although he would have preferred to design the cathedral in the Gothic style, he was asked to design a Byzantine Church, glistening with gold.

1st July 1995 Saturday
Hong Dong – China is to build a 99 tonne bronze bell, the world's largest, in Hong Kong to ring in the takeover of the British territory. The bell, known as Huaxia Dazhong, will be completed by the end of 1996 and will be tolled on July 1st 1997 when Peking regains sovereignty.   *(Newspaper cutting)*

2nd July 1995 Sunday
"What shall we do?" (Acts of the Apostles 2 : 37) Following the first great inspired sermon delivered by St. Peter on the Day of Pentecost, the people were so wonderfully impressed that they asked Peter & the other apostles what they should do. As these words were read in church this evening, I was reminded yet again of the sermon I heard in September 1980 – "What shall I do?"
"What shall we do?" Peter's answer to this question was, "Repent, & be baptised every one of you in the name of Jesus Christ for the remission of sins & ye shall receive the gift of the Holy Ghost. For the promise is unto you & to your children & to all that are afar off, even as many as the Lord our God shall call"
(Acts of the Apostles 2 : 38 – 39)

On 2nd July 1995, the Sikh community celebrated the 400th anniversary of the birth of Guru Hargobind, 6th Guru of the Sikhs. Guru Hargobind lived at a particularly difficult time in the history of India. The Mogul Emperor Jahangir was on the Peacock Throne in Delhi & he embarked on a ruthless persecution, forcing conversion of those of different religious beliefs. In Punjab, Hargobind's own father, the saintly and scholarly Guru Arjan Dev, had started the construction of the famous Golden Temple with its 4 doors signifying a welcome to people from all directions, both geographic & religious. He also collected the writings of his predecessors to produce a compendium of Sikh scriptures, called the holy Granth & included the writings of Hindu & Muslim saints.
Emperor Jahangir would not tolerate such actions as this. Guru Arjan Dev was duly arrested & tortured to death. His crime was advocating tolerance & respect for other faiths. Hargobind was only a boy at the time of his father's martyrdom. He recalled Guru Nanak's teaching that tolerance should not be extended to mute acceptance of evil. Bigoted behaviour which threatened the lives of others should be opposed by all means available & by force as a last resort. He encouraged Sikhs to look to physical fitness, learn martial arts & become expert horsemen to protect the rights of themselves & others. Sikhs were to be 'sant sipai', saint soldiers.
In later years, when Guru Gobind Singh was the Sikhs' 10th Guru, the Sikhs were again being attacked by the Mogul armies. One of the Sikh water carriers, named Ghanyia, took water to the enemy wounded when he felt so sorry for them. He was duly summoned to the tent of Guru Gobind Singh who wanted to know why he had done this.
"Is it not the duty of Sikhs to show care & compassion to all God's beings?" he pleaded. Whereupon the Guru embraced Ghanyia, calling him Bhai, or brother. Furthermore the Guru gave Bhai Ghanyia ointments & bandages to further his work of alleviating suffering.

6th July 1995 Thursday
Elaine's birthday. Today she would have been 52, but she died just 2 weeks short of her birthday. What more could she have wished for her birthday than to be freed from the dreadful burden of Multiple Sclerosis, which relentlessly bore her down & drained her of all her strength. A few weeks ago I asked her what she would like for her birthday. "Nothing" she said.

8th July 1995 Saturday
Bunting's 80th birthday party took place yesterday evening at the Moat House, Acton Trussell, where eleven of us assembled for a late evening meal. It was a hot summer's evening & we stayed in this idyllic setting until almost midnight. Bunting was treated like a queen & although feeling lonely & lost without Mostyn, had the love & support of her family.

Mary Blue	Pat	Julian	Bunting	Michael	Shirley
Josie's Dad	Josie's Mum	Josie	Betty	Evelyn	

10th July 1995 Monday
The latest government department to be abolished is the Department of Employment.
The unemployment department is itself now unemployed. Founded in 1893 as the Labour Department, a branch of the Board of Trade, it has now split into four – 'Training' to the latest Department for Education & Employment, 'Labour Statistics' 'Health & Safety' and the rest to D.T.I.

The information age has already produced a global shift in opportunity, as did the first Industrial Revolution. A relatively small group of people have the brains and education to take full advantage of the new age; they are becoming steadily richer. Opportunities for the unskilled are declining.   *(Newspaper cutting)*

12th July 1995 Wednesday
Four years of retirement & oh how thankful I am to be retired when I read of all the work-related stress there is today, brought about by redundancies & cost-cutting.

Redundancies mean employees are doing the work of up to four people. People at work have too much to do, while those unable to find work are bored. It is even worse in Japan where death from overwork is commonplace.

The Confederation of British Industry estimates that time off work because of stress and anxiety account for one-third of all sick leave.

(*Newspaper cutting*)

14th July 1995 Friday

My birthday! 64 today (2 x 2 x 2 x 2 x 2 x 2).

Cocky telephoned from Lancaster early in the morning to say "Happy Birthday".

He sent me a birthday card to say 'Happy Birthday darling. Wish I could be with you. Love you for ever. John xxxx XXXXX. And he enclosed two £10 notes.

It was 45 years ago, in 1950, that Cocky gave me £3 to buy some shoes.

16th July 1995 Sunday

To celebrate my birthday, Pat & Evelyn, plus Mary Blue, took me out to lunch to The Bull's Head, Thringstone.

Mary Blue, having been made redundant from work earlier this year, is enjoying the luxury of liberation from 'the daily grind'; & after lunch we went to Staunton Harold Hall for a stroll around the grounds & an afternoon 'cuppa' in the Tea Room.

18th July 1995 Tuesday

America is suffering its worst heatwave for many years. Temperatures over 38°c (100°f) have killed people, cattle & poultry. The majority of deaths have occurred in Chicago, where victims were mainly poor people living in flats where temperatures reached 49°c, In Central Park, New York, it was 39°c, just short of their hottest day in 1936.

Killer heatwave – A heatwave with temperatures of over 100 degrees Fahrenheit has hit the United States, causing at least 91 deaths.

(*Newspaper cutting*)

20th July 1995 Thursday

Queen Elizabeth, the Queen Mother, widow of King George VI, who died in 1952, has undergone an operation to remove a cataract from her left eye. The operation was performed at King Edward VII's Hospital for Officers, central London. Also this week, Katherine Sullivan, my 91 year-old friend, has had exactly the same operation at Leicester Royal Infirmary.

Cataract operation – Queen Elizabeth the Queen Mother has had a successful operation to remove a cataract from her left eye just weeks before her 95th birthday.

(*Newspaper cutting*)

22nd July 1995 Saturday

"They do blaspheme who say, 'Allah is Christ the son of Mary'. They do blaspheme who say, 'Allah is one of three in a Trinity; for there is no god except One Allah'.

In the heart of the city of Leicester, I watched two devout Muslims hanging up a huge banner, proclaiming these words from the Koran – Sura 5.

I thought of the death threat to Salman Rushdie. (See 21st February 1990).

24th July 1995 Monday

"Erected 1868" – The words engraved on Leicester's clock tower, which I had never noticed before, jumped out at me after I had spent much of the morning at Coalville police station being questioned in detail about the sexual antics of my 'flashing' near neighbour.

I was reminded also of Mistress Quickly's observations, "They mistook their erection".

(Merry Wives of Windsor, Act 3, Scene 5)

The flasher is often a weak man who is, or has been, dominated by his mother. If he is married, the wife is often dominant and a mother substitute.

(*Newspaper cutting*)

26th July 1995 Wednesday

The Reverend Michael David Webb, aged 35, Vicar of Snibston, has now married the organist, Elaine Conway, a widow aged 46. It was a parish celebration, with all the parishioners invited to the wedding ceremony & a get-together in the evening. He now has a ready made family including 15 year-old Mark who had his leg amputated last year due to cancer.

28th July 1995 Friday

"The Gypsy's Warning" – Coalville police have now severely reprimanded my erstwhile good neighbour, but of late too fond of disporting himself naked to the ladies nearby in their gardens. Fearing he might become a rapist, they have taken not only full particulars, but recorded his DNA.

The 1994 Criminal Justice and Public Order Act gives police the power to take DNA samples from anyone arrested in connection with a recordable offence (crimes that carry a prison sentence).

All forces are now taking samples from suspects held for sexual crimes, burglary or crimes of violence.

DNA backlog – Britain's DNA criminal database has been overwhelmed by samples sent by police and faces a backlog of more than 27,000 records waiting to be put on computer. The Birmingham collection, the first of its kind, was opened in April.

(*Newspaper cuttings*)

31st July 1995 Monday

Hewes, Phyllis Mary, formerly of Ravenstone, the beloved wife of the late Donald, loving mother of Lesley, Susan and the late Peter, dear grandmother of Ruth, Clare, Karen, Hannah, James, Sarah, Kirsty and Emma, great grandma of Charlotte and Daniel, passed peacefully away on July 25th 1995 at The District Hospital, Ashby-de-la-Zouch aged 77 years. The funeral service will be held at St. Michael and All Angels Parish Church, Ravenstone on Monday July 31st at 10.30a.m. followed by cremation at Bretby, family flowers only please. Donations in lieu of flowers if so desired for Ravenstone Parish Church and any inquiries may be sent to J.P.Springthorpe and Co. Funeral Directors, Castle Lodge, South Street, Ashby-de-la-Zouch.

Poor Phyl, widow of cousin Don, has died, after suffering for the past 4 years confined to a wheelchair, following a stroke which took the use of her left side. She & Don were so very good to me in the early post-war period.

Scorching July – Temperatures over the past month will secure July 1995 a place in the record books, probably as the third hottest July this century.

Tonight's weather: Phew!   *(Newspaper cuttings)*

1st August 1995 Tuesday
Lammas Day (Loaf Mass) – Feast of first fruits – the original time for Harvest Festival.
Ever since Moses led the children of Israel to the Promised Land, three thousand years ago, the 'first fruits of the land' have been given to God as a thanksgiving & acknowledgement that all that we have comes from God (See Deuteronomy 26)

3rd August 1995 Thursday
Reform of our Welfare System is now imminent. In 1949, when it began, it cost less than one thousand million pounds, or 4.7% of Gross Domestic Product. Now it swallows so much we are being devoured by it. The number of pensioners has doubled to 10 million & state pensions cost £28 billion. Within two more generations there will be 16 million pensioners & fewer at work to provide for them.

4th August 1995 Friday
1900: Queen Elizabeth, the Queen Mother (Elizabeth Angela Marguerite Bowes-Lyon) was born.

5th August 1995 Saturday
The wedding of Dawn & Philip. (See 8th June 1995).
Although Enid & I were invited only to the evening reception at Appleby Inn Hotel, Appleby Parva, we walked to Ravenstone Church to see the church service at 3p.m. They chose to be married at Ravenstone in order to share the occasion with John Tart who died in November 1993 & now lies buried in Ravenstone churchyard.

6th August 1995 Sunday
On this day 1945:
American bomber Enola Gay dropped the first atomic bomb, on the Japanese city of Hiroshima.
American bomber Enola Gay was a Boeing B29 Superfortress aeroplane which carried the uranium bomb to Hiroshima. The bomb floated down by parachute & exploded 1,900 feet above the ground. Three days later, on August 9th 1945, a further bomb, using plutonium fusion, obliterated Nagasaki. And so finally ended World War II, V.J. Day. Victory in Japan.

8th August 1995 Tuesday
Since the 1994 Marriage Act took effect in April, 465 hotels, stately homes and other buildings have been approved as venues for weddings. The list includes Woburn Abbey, Ripley Castle, Cheltenham and Epsom race courses, several football grounds and Terminal Four at Heathrow Airport.   *(Newspaper cutting)*

9th August 1995 Wednesday
Buckingham Palace! Tour of the State Rooms.
Yesterday, Enid & I saw inside Buckingham Palace. Having so recently (17th June) visited the splendid residence of the Duke of Wellington, Apsley House, No. 1 London, & seen Antonio Canova's marble sculpture of the fig-leaf clad Napoleon, now we saw Canova's 'Mars & Venus', similarly attired & commissioned by George IV. As in Apsley House, Mary Blue & I saw priceless treasures which had at one time belonged briefly to Napoleon, so in Buckingham Palace Enid & I discovered something similar.
In the Blue Drawing Room is the 'Table of the Grand Commanders' showing Alexander the Great & 12 other commanders from antiquity. Commissioned by Napoleon in 1806, it came to George IV.

13th August 1995 Sunday
'A nostalgic evening to commemorate the 50th anniversary of V.J. Day – Victory in Japan'
Yesterday Enid & I again joined the Golden Oldies of the village to celebrate the final liberation of our prisoners of war from the cruel clutches of the Japanese. I sat beside one such man – Horace Hardy, now aged 75, who was 'kept the other side of Tenko' & was one of the few who survived.

> **"When you go home, tell them of us & say,**
> **for your tomorrow we gave our today"**

The Burma Star Association reminds us of the solemn nature of Victory in Japan.
The notorious Burma Thailand Railway was one of the war's great acts of slave labour. (See cut out from 'The Times' below, dated 15:8:95)
See also 'Kept – The other Side of Tenko' the book referred to 23rd & 25th January 1994.

To the soldiers of the Imperial Japanese Army, being taken prisoner was the ultimate disgrace. They could barely understand why the thousands of Allied prisoners they took at the fall of Singapore did not commit suicide in shame, and they had no compunction in putting them to work as slaves with minimal regard for their lives. Building the 258 miles of the Burma-Thailand railway was one of the war's great acts of slave labour. A total of 61,806 British, Australian, Dutch and American prisoners were sent to hack the line through dense jungle from Kanchanaburi in Thailand to Thanbyuzayat in Burma. By the end of the war at least 12,400 had died. To supplement the PoWs, the Japanese rounded up 300,000 natives from their occupied lands of South-East Asia. They fared even worse than the prisoners, and some estimates suggest that 100,000 of them died. The British bore the brunt of PoW casualties, with 6,904 dead. In a single six-month period, under a monsoon sky and with the ever-meagre food rations, 7,000 men died. Few who survived did not bear some hideous permanent scar in body or mind.
Captain Alan Butterworth, a British officer in the Indian Army and a survivor of the 'Death Railway', recalls, "I do not know what force kept us alive .... It would have been so easy just to have given in."
From February 1942, the Japanese controlled South Asia from Singapore almost to the Indian border. Their far-flung occupation troops in Burma were sent by sea

to Rangoon, but after naval defeats at American hands in the Pacific battles of Midway and the Coral Sea, Japan feared that its seaborne supply route from Singapore was no longer safe from Allied attack. An overland route became an urgent necessity. Burma, Thailand and Malaya all had their internal railway networks, but there was a gap in the middle. British imperial engineers with similar dreams had surveyed the gap long before the war, but dismissed the scheme as impossible. To the Japanese, the rails had to be laid at any cost. The first prisoners were sent from Singapore to work on the railway in June 1942. In October 1943 the rails being laid from either end were finally joined at kilometre 253. The labourers had no mechanical power and only the most primitive of hand tools, yet they built 688 bridges, mostly of wood hewn from the jungle. The most famous of those – over the River Khwae – was of concrete and steel and not of wood as in the film. At the start of construction, a prisoner's typical task was to shift 1.2 cubic metres of earth a day, a reasonable workload for a healthy, well-fed man in a cool climate. They were, however, fed insufficient amounts of third grade rice, supplemented by whatever they could forage: wild bananas, bamboo shoots, even snakes and lizards. As the Japanese, increasingly desperate to see the line completed, demanded ever more "speedo speedo", the work became harder, the rations fewer, the men weaker from malnutrition and recurring bouts of dysentery, and the casualties higher from exhaustion and disease. Sweating, dirty bodies covered in bites and cuts rapidly turned septic and gangrenous; many a life-saving amputation was carried out by heroic PoW doctors on even more heroic victims without any anaesthetic. The guards, both Japanese and Korean, were brutal. Beatings sufficient to break a man's bones were a daily occurrence. Yet when the railway was completed the Japanese allowed their slaves a short holiday, before shipping them in overloaded vessels to camps in Japan, often to be torpedoed by Allied warships on the way. Today, only 80 miles of the metre-gauge line are still in use, but the impeccably-tended Commonwealth war cemeteries along its route remain as permanent memorials to a terrible inhumanity.   (The Times)

***Leicestershire Regiment.** In memory of the 1ˢᵗ Bn., the first British regiment in action against the Japanese at Jitra in the Malayian Campaign, 1941-42 who fought at Gurun, Alor Star, Kampar and Singapore. To the 179 officers and men killed in action and the 173 who died as Prisoners of War on the Burma Thailand Railway. When you go home, tell them of us and say, 'For their tomorrow we gave our today'.   (The Coalville Times)*

19ᵗʰ August 1995 Saturday

This year of war related anniversaries draws to a close this weekend as Services of Remembrance & Commitment, all following the same set format, take place inside churches & also out of doors, throughout the length & breadth of Britain. Television coverage & involvement of young & old has meant that we all now share together 'A Collective Memory'.

Each Service of Remembrance & Commitment, from the forecourt of Buckingham Palace to our own Parish Church, included these words, "Will you always acknowledge how precious are the gifts which God has

entrusted to us & exercise the freedoms & opportunities you have with gratitude & humility?"
To which we replied, "By the help of God, we will".

23ʳᵈ August 1995 Wednesday

And now, another delicate situation. Remember how Mr Ellis, Chief Gas Examiner, rang me at home & wanted to take me out in January 1985, almost immediately following the death of his wife Elaine?
Well, today I had a telephone call from Ken Stocks, whose wife Maureen died in June this year, wanting to take me out to lunch. And we hardly know each other.

25ᵗʰ August 1995 Friday

Driest summer since 1659 (newspaper cutting).
This summer has been a real scorcher; day after day of sunshine from sunrise to sunset. It has been declared the third warmest since records began in 1659. You never saw such a sight as overweight middle-aged & elderly folk attired in their shorts. How thankful I am to be retired & able to keep in the shade.

Britain has had one of the hottest, driest and sunniest summers for years. As it draws to a close, it will go into the record books as one of the three hottest ever registered. The last scorcher was 1976 and the previous record-breaker was 1826.

27ᵗʰ August 1995 Sunday, Trinity XI

"O God, who declarest thy almighty power most chiefly in showing mercy and pity …."
                                    Collect for today.

***Carl Giles**, OBE, Daily and Sunday Express cartoonist, died on August 27ᵗʰ aged 78. He was born on September 29th 1916.*

29ᵗʰ August 1995 Tuesday

Brother Pat's birthday! 77 today.
Both he & his sister Bunting were born during the First World War 1914 – 1918. We all step into this world at a certain moment in history at a certain spot on the globe, & then take all our bearings from there. Pat's bearings are slightly different from Bunting's, being brought up in separate households.

31ˢᵗ August 1995 Thursday

Notification of road closure! – Works to replace the sewer system in Ashby Road, Coalville, are programmed to start on 4ᵗʰ September & be completed by early November. The 'foul and surface water systems' are being updated. This marathon job is the culmination of years of work analysing the existing sewers network & getting it computerised.

1ˢᵗ September 1995 Friday

It took from the dawn of humanity to around 1800 before there were a billion of us. A child starting secondary school this September has seen a billion added in its brief lifetime.   (Newspaper cutting)

Rugby turns professional – Rugby union is to go professional following a historic decision yesterday by its world governing body. The revolutionary move by the International Rugby Football Board to abandon 125 years of amateurism and allow players to be paid was announced after three days of tortuous discussions behind closed doors in Paris.

(Newspaper cutting)

From Amateurs to Professionals. An amateur performs purely for love. (Latin *amator-oris*= a lover).
A professional performs for the love of money.

4th September 1995 Monday
Prize from E.R.N.I.E. Bond No. 14HN331205.
Pay Miss E. Hewes fifty pounds only,
Yours Sincerely Alan Mc Gill.

Premium bond sales rise 300% to £1.8bn.
Sales of premium bonds leapt 300 per cent in the past financial year, in spite of competition from the National Lottery. National Savings' annual report says that 1994-95 was its best year for premium bond business, with sales quadrupling to £1.8 billion – producing a net contribution to Government coffers of £1.49 billion.

(Newspaper cutting)

6th September 1995 Wednesday
"Old Maid Hewsie, like Hiawatha, guarded the secrets of her own heart" (See 11th April 1985).
Almost a repeat performance of 10 years ago, as this time I was wined & dined by Ken Stocks, whose wife Maureen died in June this year, after 50 years of marriage. He told me that their supposed happy marriage was really fraught with tension & life had been one darned thing after another.

7th September 1995 Thursday
Prince William today began his first full day at Eton – and became the only future king to attend the prestigious public school.

(Newspaper cutting)

8th September 1995 Friday
Holders of the Victoria Cross now number 33. Holders of the George Cross (awarded for civilian gallantry) now number 48. Many of these medal holders are in their eighties. In recognition of their great bravery & self-sacrifice they receive £100 per year. What an insult! Following the commemorations marking the 50th anniversary of the end of World War II, this will be increased.

10th September 1995 Sunday
43 Winchester Way, Ashby - £57,500
An extended detached family home with gas central heating and offering the following accommodation: Entrance porch, lounge, dining area, enlarged dining kitchen with appliances, inner hallway and to the first floor 3 bedrooms and the bathroom/wc. Outside a single garage and lawned gardens front and rear. Contact agent for viewing.
(newspaper cutting)

This is Steven's new house. He & Jane became engaged on Christmas Day 1992 & then 18 months ago set up home together in a rented upstairs flat, No. 7, The Green, Ashby. Now they have a lovely new home.

12th September 1995 Tuesday
Heritage Open Days – this is a European-wide programme, when magnificent buildings, normally closed to the public, open briefly for one weekend during the year. In London, next weekend, the star exhibit is the newly restored Mansion House (but you must book in advance: 0171-332 3075).
So I phoned this Residence of the Lord Mayor. "Sorry, we are fully booked".

Heritage Open Days in this country is organised by the Civic Trust, with funding from the Department of National Heritage. Now established as an annual event, there will be more than 1,000 buildings open throughout the country this weekend, including 300 across London. Mary Blue & I are hoping to be in London on Saturday & savour some of these delights.

16th September 1995 Saturday
Mary Blue & I had a lovely day in London enjoying its 'Open House □95'.
The problem was which 'Open House' to choose out of so many on offer. We would love to have seen inside 'Guildhall'. 'Shakespeare's New Globe Theatre', 'Lancaster House', 'Royal Courts of Justice' etc. etc. but nevertheless were delighted to see Brompton Cemetery Catacombs & Somerset House.

18th September 1995 Monday
The 14th Sunday after Trinity yesterday reminded us once more of the Harvest of the Spirit: - Love, Joy, Peace, Patience, Kindness, Goodness, Fidelity, Gentleness & Self-control. (Galatians 5 : 22)
The Rector of Ravenstone, Kerry Emmett, spoke of the man who asked the Angel if he could supply him with such fruits. "No", said the Angel, "We only supply seeds".

20th September 1995 Wednesday
"Complete cessation of military operations" – The IRA made this declaration 12 months ago & much to everyone's surprise & delight they have kept their word, but have nevertheless doggedly 'stuck to their guns'. They refuse point blank to hand over their guns & the dialogue between the two opposing sides is, as always, anything but friendly.

22nd September 1995 Friday
Holiday of a lifetime for Mary Blue!
Mary Blue has won a holiday for two in America & next Wednesday she & her friend Pam will be flying to Los Angeles (California) for a few days; then off to Las Vegas (Nevada) and a visit to the Grand Canyon. Finally, on to San Francisco (again California), returning to London on Thursday 12th October.

24th September 1995 Sunday
Harvest Festival & Patronal Festival - "Patronal Festival" at St. Michael & All Angels, Ravenstone is absolutely non-existent. All we had this evening was a 'Songs of Praise', which consisted only of a string of harvest songs, with the odd reading here & there. There was no mention at all of St. Michael – no mention of angels nor Archangels.

26th September 1995 Tuesday

"Ravenstone House" – Cousin Miles has had one almighty redecoration & refurbishment of his old family home **"Glenholm"**, both inside & out. No longer the white house on the corner, it is now a vibrant terra-cotta colour, with every room totally transformed inside. The dining room has changed places with the drawing room & it is given a posh new name.

28th September 1995 Thursday

"Once upon a time we had a railway station at Coalville" (1848 – 1964). Last year we were all led to believe that Coalville could expect to have a new railway station. Now it is the old, old, story – "Increased costs leave County Council with a shortfall of £4 million which signals the end of Coalville's hopes to join the Ivanhoe Line". The rail dream is now on hold.

30th September 1995 Saturday

How thankful I am to have 'sat at the feet' of such knowledgeable men of the Church as the former Bishop of Leicester – Ronald R. Williams & the former Rector of Ravenstone – Gustav Aronsohn, whose inspired sermons of long ago help to spur us on in this unfamiliar new age, where 'political correctness' takes precedence & angels are not mentioned.

Falling Angels – The Roman Catholic Church is diluting its belief in angels… (Newspaper cutting)

2nd October 1995 Monday

"Love notices detail" - A most uplifting 'thought for the day' on the radio, where in a few minutes we heard a wonderful mini-sermon, in which we were taught to see into & through & beyond what appears on the surface. We saw angels, and were reminded once more of Elisha: - "And Elisha prayed & said, Lord, open his eyes that he may see". (II Kings 6 : 17)

4th October 1995 Wednesday

Metrication – from pints to litres & from pounds & ounces to kilogrammes.
With effect from 1st October this year we have moved into the next phase of metric measurement.
"A quarter of ham" I said automatically, meaning a quarter of a pound in weight, & was duly presented with 0.125kg. The new price was 66p per 100g & I was charged 83p.

6th October 1995 Friday

"Can you bind the sweet influences of Pleiades or loose the bands of Orion?" Thus God challenged Job (Job 38 : 31). Pleiades = the seven stars in Taurus. "Seek him therefore that maketh the seven stars & Orion" (Amos 5 : 8) Taurus & Orion face each other in the night sky.

8th October 1995 Sunday

7th annual service of thanksgiving for all creatures great & small - Katherine (aged 91), Toffee the dog & I attended this service again at St. Andrews, Jarrom Street, Leicester, where the preacher was the retiring Assistant Bishop of Leicester, Dr. Godfrey Ashby. He spoke about Baalam & his ass which could see the Angel, 'Then the Lord opened the eyes of Balaam & he saw the angel' (Numbers 22 : 31)

10th October 1995 Tuesday

The MSF union which the clergy are joining = the Manufacturing, Science & Finance Union. Hardly the right union for clergy, you might think. But in September last year it was this union (aptly dubbed the 'white-collar' union) which opened a clerical section, & more & more vicars are joining. Clergy today are given fixed-term contracts, which can be ended at a bishop's whim.

Episcopal fake – The Bishop of Bath and Wells took his diocesan ring to the 'Antiques Roadshow', and was told that it was a fake. The ring, made in 1945, contains real gold sovereigns but its 'sapphire' is made of coloured glass.

(Newspaper cutting)

12th October 1995 Thursday

New metric shopping has caused plenty of confusion. Most of us have no conception of kilograms, metres or litres. We buy petrol by the litre but usually opt for £10 worth.

Metric madness has struck the county, leaving shoppers and traders confused by the changeover to the new measurement system. As we say farewell to pounds, yards and gallons, in come the kilograms, metres and litres, leaving us with the biggest change in shopping habits since decimalisation 25 years ago. The changeover applies to pre-packed produce. Loose goods such as fruit can be sold using the old measurement until the year 2000. Sizes in clothing will also remain the same, as will miles for road distances, descriptive measurements such as 12inch pizza and 'quarter pounder' burgers.

(Newspaper cutting)

14th October 1995 Saturday

Postcard from America – from Mary Blue.
"Dear Betty, This is the life! There are so many wonderful things to see & do. We've been to Beverly Hills, Sunset Boulevard, Hollywood Boulevard, Mann's Chinese Theatre, Universal Studios, etc etc. Everywhere is so clean & everything is so big. Everyone is so friendly & helpful & tells us to 'have a nice day' every 5 minutes."

16th October 1995 Monday

"Coronation Street", the television 'soap' which has been going strong since 1960, centres on the corner pub, the Rovers Return, where landlady Bet has reigned supreme for many years. Now she has chosen to 'retire' from this role & in the script she therefore packed her bags & left.

Bet goes – Actress Julie Goodyear today told how leaving Coronation Street after 25 years had broken her heart. The actress will bid farewell to Britain's best-loved soap tonight when her character Bet Gilroy leaves the Rovers Return for the last time.

(Newspaper cutting)

18th October 1995 Wednesday

Civil Service Retirement Fellowship meeting - Remember Muriel Harding who gave an interesting talk on Calligraphy? (17th March 1994). Today she gave another interesting talk on Poetry. She brought along about a dozen different poetry books & read to us a selection of her favourite poems. We all then looked through any book we chose & picked our own favourite to read or listen to.

20th October 1995 Friday

Front room refurbishment & total transformation – Last decorated in April 1979, & used of late more like a junk room, it has now been beautifully papered in predominantly rose-pink paper with a pretty floral chimney breast & matching border. A gorgeous new fitted carpet described as 'Persian Jewel Cottage Garden' & altogether an elegant sitting room with new curtains & cintique chairs.

22nd October 1995 Sunday

"And when you pray, do not be like the hypocrites, for they love to pray standing in the synagogues & on the street corners to be seen by men". (Part of the Sermon the Mount – Matthew 6 : 5).
The Rector of Ravenstone, the Revd. Kerry Emmett, told us that the word 'hypocrite' meant 'actor'. That was the Greek meaning in the original text.

Prescriptions ruling will cost millions – The European Court of Justice ruled that men are entitled to free prescriptions at 60, the same age as women. The Health Ministry said the Government must comply with the ruling, which will cost £30 million in the first year in lost charges from Britain's 1.4 million men aged 60 – 64, and £10 million which may be claimed back for charges already paid. (Newspaper cutting)

24th October 1995 Tuesday

43, Winchester Way, Ashby-de-la-Zouch, the newly acquired home of Steven & his fiancée Jane, has now been transformed into a magnificent residence. You would hardly believe it is the same house. It now boasts the very best new double-glazed windows & doors; & the inside is truly beautiful, with mirrored wardrobes, new carpets, exquisite tiles in the bathroom, & a lovely big kitchen.

Lamming, Brian, of Bringhurst, devoted husband of Judith, passed peacefully away on October 22nd 1995, after a long illness borne with great dignity, aged 67 years. Funeral service at Bringhurst Parish Church, on Friday, October 27th, at 2p.m. followed by interment. Further inquiries and flowers to J. Stamp and Sons, Funeral Directors, Market Harborough. Tel. (01858) 462524.

Brian Lamming

26th October 1995 Thursday

"Sold for £100, a brass lamp, brass jam kettle, brass saucepan, brass candlestick, mahogany bed-table".
That was in September 1982. Now I have sold the old gate-leg table, a small antique table & old china tea service which have all been in the house with me all my life. I sold them to 'Corner Cottage Antiques', Market Place, Market Bosworth for a total of £240.

28th October 1995 Saturday

"The Hewes – Life & Times of a Leicestershire Family". Cousin Miles is now engrossed in the compilation of a little book about our more interesting forebears. As in September 1993, he & I have spent more absorbing hours in Coalville Library delving into the very earliest editions of the Coalville Times which date from 1893. It is fascinating reading the news of 100 years ago.

A Ravenstone man is tracing his ancestors' footsteps for his forthcoming book on his family's history. Miles Wilson has been researching the book – The Hewes: Life and Times of a Leicestershire Family from 1774 – for four years and it will be on sale next year. (Newspaper cutting)   (See 24th March 1997)

30th October 1995 Monday

Like Pulcinella, I went very early yesterday morning, quite alone, to the deserted churchyard at Bringhurst to see the newly dug grave of Brian Lamming.
I read the message on a beautiful wreath: - "To Brian. Thank you for all the years of loving me. L.Y.F.E. I'll join you later. Judy xxxxx"
As the Provost said (2nd Oct. 1977) ".... tucked away in the most beautiful Leicestershire Countryside".

1st November 1995 Wednesday

"We will remember them" – The solemn remembrance of all the faithful departed means simply that we re-member them – that is, we acknowledge them as members of God's family, as alive to God as all those still here on earth. In our Christian Creed we say, "I believe in .... the Communion of Saints; the forgiveness of sins; the Resurrection of the body & the life everlasting. Amen".

3rd November 1995 Friday

"Great oaks from little acorns grow". Fifteen years ago I had a little oak tree, only 4 inches high (10 centimetres). Now it is a fine tree whose branches almost span the width of my narrow garden. After an exceptionally hot summer, all the oak trees have produced a bumper crop of acorns & my oak has dropped very nearly 1,500 acorns! Enough for a forest.

5th November 1995 Sunday

"Please to remember the fifth of November" – Katherine Sullivan absolutely loves fireworks, so each year now for several years we have been to 'the biggest & best display in the district' – bonfire & fireworks, Calke Park – Calke Abbey.
This year Katherine (91) & I (64) were taken to Calke Abbey by Cousin Miles (49).It really was the best display ever, & all beneath the full moon.
Bonfire & fireworks, Calke Park, Ticknall, by kind permission of the National Trust, is jointly organised by Ashby Rotary Club & Ashby Round Table. With over £4,000 of fireworks, it is superbly managed. The grounds themselves form a natural amphitheatre. People come in their thousands (£5 per car load) and everyone enjoys a grandstand view.

9th November 1995 Thursday

"County Emergency Planning – Volunteers Evening". Cousin Miles is Ravenstone's volunteer to be contacted in the event of a local disaster. He invited me to accompany him & Gwen to County Hall, where the County Council's Emergency Planning Officer showed a video of 'The Lockerbie Air Disaster' to illustrate just what needed to be done in an emergency. 36,000 people fly daily over Leicestershire.

11ᵗʰ November 1995 Saturday
Auction Appeal –Coalville Community Hospital League of Friends are holding an auction today.
Organisers are asking for donations for the auction – they need around 100 items in all. The proceeds will be going to the hospital.
(Newspaper cutting)

Over a hundred items were auctioned & over £500 was raised for Coalville Hospital, including my contribution, viz: Electrolux table-top freezer, purchased August 1991 made £21. Guitar, purchased September 1974 made £11. Picture from Donkey Sanctuary, 1983, made £10.

15ᵗʰ November 1995 Wednesday
Muslims in Leicester were warned a year ago that taking part in the National Lottery was forbidden by the Koran. Imam Salim Bharat, of the Masjid Noor Mosque, said that any form of gambling was impermissible for the 11,600 city Muslims. In fact it was impermissible throughout the whole world of Islam. Imagine the problem then when a Muslim won the jackpot!

19ᵗʰ November 1995 Sunday
Christmas card to, "His Holiness Pope John Paul II, Apostolic Palace, 00120 Vatican City".
Katherine, aged 91, asked me to find a very special card for her to send to the Pope. I chose a beautiful card with a picture of, "Statue of Our Lady & Child at St. Peter's Grange, Prinknash Abbey, Glos."
Katherine sends the Pope 'get well' cards when he is ill, as well as Christmas cards.

21ˢᵗ November 1995 Tuesday
Having recently sold the old heavy gate-leg table, I advertised for a 'Dining table on wheels'. However, none was forthcoming & I have now acquired another gate-leg table, not so heavy & more manageable, from 'Breedon Antiques', Breedon-on-the-Hill.

Collier, Kenneth Raymond, of Ashby Road, Donisthorpe, beloved brother of Dennis, dear brother-in-law, uncle and great-uncle, passed peacefully but suddenly away in Burton Hospital, on Tuesday November 21ˢᵗ 1995, aged 75 years. Funeral service will be held at St. Michael and All Angel's Church, Ravenstone, on Wednesday November 29ᵗʰ at 11.00a.m. prior to cremation at Bretby.

22ⁿᵈ November 1995 Wednesday
Today is the feast day of Cecilia, the patron saint of music, singers and poets.

23ʳᵈ November 1995 Thursday
Prime Minister John Major launched the National Lottery last November at 6.30a.m. There was a party & firework display at the Tower of London before tickets went on sale at 7.00a.m. John Major bought £5 worth of tickets & chose 29 – 3 – 43 – 13 – 11 & 10. (His birth

date followed by 13, plus his past & present addresses, viz. No. 11 Downing Street & No. 10 Downing Street.

25ᵗʰ November 1995 Saturday
The Princess of Wales – the would-be "Queen of Hearts". Having lived apart from the Prince of Wales for the past 3 years, Princess Diana this week poured out her innermost hopes & fears in a television hour-long interview. She did not expect ever to become Queen, but would like to be "Queen of peoples' hearts". However, psycho-analysts liken her to Narcissus & his excessive self-love.

Sir, Should your former Editor, Lord Rees-Mogg, really wish to understand Princess Diana's behaviour and interpret her aims, he should begin by reading Elizabeth Zetzel's account of 'the so-called good hysteric' (International Journal of Psycho Analysis, 1961) which clearly sets out the enormous narcissism and destructiveness of this type of character.
(Newspaper cutting)

27ᵗʰ November 1995 Monday
The new A46, Leicester Western bypass is now open. The 8 mile long, stretch of road cost £36 million & goes from the M1 (junction 21a) just north of Leicester Forest East, as far as the A46 at Syston, crossing the A50 at Groby & the A6 near Birstall. It has 8 under-bridges, 11 over-bridges, 4 underpasses and even includes one tunnel for badgers.

The closure of Carlton Hayes Hospital is just weeks away. *After nearly 90 years, the former Leicestershire and Rutland County Lunatic Asylum, at Narborough, is to be razed to the ground.*

29ᵗʰ November 1995 Wednesday
"The Settlement of 1559" – this established the Protestant Church as the official Church in England & drove the Church of Rome underground. This week the Queen was applauded loudly as she walked up the nave of the Roman Catholic Westminster Cathedral to join the congregation of 1,500 in an ecumenical service, the first reigning monarch at a Roman Catholic service since then.

1ˢᵗ December 1995 Friday
H.M.S.O. Her Majesty's Stationery Office soon will be no more. Like everything else, it is to be privatised. It was in May 1985 that I became 'Stationery Co-ordinator' at work & learned to appreciate H.M.S.O.
It was lovely in 1986 when H.M.S.O. celebrated its bi-centenary. "H.M.S.O. is proud of its record & achievements over the past 200 years. We look forward to the next 200 years of service ...."

3ʳᵈ December 1995 Sunday
Elizabeth Hewes married G. H. Woolley at Ravenstone Church exactly 100 years ago today.
This we learned from reading the old 'Coalville Times' in Coalville library. She was my grandfather's sister, known as Auntie Lizzie. Cousin Audrey, her daughter, gave me the china tea service which was a wedding present to Auntie Lizzie (see 20ᵗʰ September 1975).
According to the Coalville Times the Rector gave six

serviettes.

All the wedding presents in 1895 were recorded: - Household linen, Mrs Hewes; Coal hod, Mr & Mrs W G Hewes; Biscuit barrel, Mr & Mrs G H Hewes; Rocking chair, Mr T Hewes; Lamp, Mr H Hewes; White damask tablecloth & half dozen serviettes, Revd, G Vandeleur; & numerous others.

So why, do you suppose, did cousin Audrey think the Rector gave a tea service?

Tyrrell, Charles Henry, (Charlie), of Blackwood, Coalville. The loved father of Jeannette and Keith, the loving grandfather of Tracy, Gemma and Gary, passed peacefully but suddenly away on the 6th December, 1995, aged 72 years. The funeral service will be held at St. David's Church, Broom Leys, Coalville, on Wednesday 13th December at 11 a.m.

(See 21st December 1992)

7th December 1995 Thursday

In 1897 a man was in court accused of being drunk & disorderly. He said he was only following the teaching of the Bible & showed the court the Book of Proverbs, Chapter 31. "Give strong drink unto him that is ready to perish & wine unto those that be of heavy hearts. Let him drink & forget his poverty & remember his misery no more". Case was dismissed.

8th December 1995 Friday

A bumper audience tuned in to watch Raquel and Curly tie the knot in the 35th anniversary edition of Coronation Street.

9th December 1995 Saturday

Mr Ellis, Chief Gas Examiner, who proposed marriage to me in April 1985, died this month, aged 70.
I joined half a dozen older members of staff – Mr Plant, Gilbert, Paul Clark, John Cranfield, Veronica, Catherine & Jan, to attend the funeral at Clipston Parish Church. How sad to see his widow, so lonely & forlorn; an outsider, not accepted by his children.

11th December 1995 Monday

"Rosemary Pauline West, on each of the ten counts of murder of which you have been unanimously convicted by the jury, the sentence is one of life imprisonment. If attention is paid to what I think, you will never be released. Take her down". So said Mr Justice Mantell, to Britain's most prolific serial killer, who lived at 25 Cromwell Street, Gloucester.
"The house of horrors" – 25 Cromwell Street, was where Rosemary Pauline West & her husband Frederick West lured unsuspecting girls to their death – students Lucy Partington & Thérèse Siegenthaler; 17 year old Alison Chambers; Lynda Gough; Carole Cooper; Juanita Mott & 15 year old Shirley Hubbard; even her daughter Heather, 16; stepdaughter Charmaine, 8; & Shirley Robinson, 18.

13th December 1995 Wednesday

Civil Service Retirement Fellowship meeting & an interesting talk from local Fire Officer Bill Wells. Apart from a 20 minute video, we were told lots of true life incidents & given plenty of advice. I was intrigued to learn that part of British Telecom's multi-billion pound

'digital technology' meant that dialling '999' immediately gives them your complete address.

The £10 Christmas bonus paid to pensioners since 1972 will remain unchanged, the Government announced in a written reply. Labour had called for it to be increased. To keep pace with inflation rate, the payment would need to be £69.33p.

15th December 1995 Friday

From a small photograph of Grandma Hewes, given to me 40 years ago – Christmas 1955, by Aunt Dos, & taken long before that (Grandma Hewes died in 1931), I have now acquired a beautiful enlargement. Stephen Bloomfield specialises in bringing old photos to life. So now my dad's photo (see 6th August 1984) enhances the Middle Room & grandma's enhances the Front Room.

17th December 1995 Sunday

"Improving Management in Government" – (See 10th August 1988).
"Executive functions of Government, as distinct from Policy Advice should be carried out by units known as 'Agencies'.". Now, 7 years later, there are more than a hundred such agencies. The Government hopes to move 75% of all the work done by Whitehall into agencies, whereby certain responsibilities are delegated to managers.

19th December 1995 Tuesday

The Gas Act 1995 makes provision for the introduction of competition into the domestic gas market. The Licensing Directorate of OFGAS will be responsible for awarding and monitoring licences to new companies supplying, transporting and shipping gas. (Newspaper cutting)
The Gas Act 1995! How well I knew the Gas Act 1948 when Nationalisation created the Gas Council & 12 Gas Boards. How well I knew the Gas Act 1972 when the Gas Council became the British Gas Corporation. And how directly I was involved with the Gas Act 1986 (see August 26th 1986).
But I know nothing of the Gas Act 1995.

21st December 1995 Thursday

From my love, by post, a Christmas card - "For the One I Love", containing two £10 notes.
"Sending a wish that your Christmas will be –
as wonderfully happy as you have made me!"
With all my love at Christmas.
All my love for ever, John xxxxx.

23rd December 1995 Saturday

Newspaper cutting of cartoon of small boy in Santa's grotto, sitting on Santa's knee saying, "What do I what? You mean you didn't get my fax?"

Father Christmas today is no longer the Santa Claus who comes with his reindeer – Dasher, Dancer, Prancer, Vixen, Comet, Cupid, Donder and Blitzen. He no longer comes down the chimney. Fairy tales have no place in this high speed, high tech world.

Oadby & Wigston Borough Council
wish you all a happy Christmas

A muli-cultural sign has been put up in Oadby town centre to recognise the variety of religious festivals throughout the year. The Festive Greeting sign will be put up in The Parade at various times throughout the year to celebrate Christmas, Hanukkah, Diwali, Eid and the birthday of Guru Nanak.

25th December 1995 Monday

And a new baby next door for Christmas. Declan Elliott, son of Wayne & Tina who were married 3rd August 1991, is the first baby at No. 29 Leicester Road, since Sydney Hayes over 60 years ago. Declan was born on 12th December; & Wayne the proud father, was only too pleased to show Enid & me all over the house, including the newly decorated nursery.

27th December 1995 Wednesday

What a lovely Christmas we have had this year. Again I had Bunting staying with me. Cousin Isobel was staying with Miles & his lady-love Gwen, & we were able to join up with them on several occasions – sometimes with the addition of Pat & Evelyn, or with Katherine (aged 91), & always with full recognition of our illustrious forebears.

29th December 1995 Friday

"Glenholm", which Miles decided to re-name "Ravenstone House" earlier this year, as part of his inflated ego, is still "Glenholm". For all his big talk, he still has his mother Isobel to reckon with. She actually owns the house. She has known it since the foundation stone was laid. It has always been "Glenholm", & she has decreed that it remain so.

31st December 1995 Sunday

On this day 1695 – The window tax was imposed in Britain, resulting in many being bricked up.

"How soon we change from one generation to another" – as I said of Madge in March 1984, so now I see Bunting. It seems but yesterday (August 1948) when Bunting & I took Michael, aged 18 months, for a walk in his push-chair. Like Madge, you would not believe that she is the same person.

* * *

The Cat's Eye – How does it Work?

The cat's eye gets its name from its construction, which copies the feline form. The eye of a real cat contains a special layer – the tapetum – that reflects light which shines into it at night. The same principle is applied in the road version. Each rubber pad contains two lenses. Light from headlamps enters the cat's eye and passes through a spherical lens, then travels on to hit the mirrored rear surface at the back of the lens. The light is bounced back, and the alignment of the rear mirrored surface and shape of the lens ensure the light goes back the way it has come – towards the driver. The cat's eye is set in a rubber pad to absorb the shock of being repeatedly run over, and into the road surface in a cast-iron base. As the cat's eye is run over, it sinks into its base and the front of the lens is wiped clean. On motorways, cat's eyes have coloured lenses, with amber indicating the right-hand edge of the road, red marking the left-hand edge, and green separating slip roads from motorways. White studs separate the lanes. Contrary to myth, the inventor of the cat's eye, Yorkshireman Percy Shaw, died a wealthy man as a result of his invention. Mr Shaw, from Halifax, came up with the idea in 1934 because he had difficulty driving safely at night. He said he used to follow the glint thrown back from his headlights by the old tramlines between Halifax and Booth, and decided to invent something new when the tramlines were taken up.

Jim Callaghan, later the Prime Minister, was responsible for introducing cat's eyes along the middle of the nation's roads in 1947, when he was a junior transport minister. He said later that he believed it was one of the most valuable contributions he had made to the nation's well-being.

* * *

The Seven Liberal Arts

In mediaeval education, there were 7 subjects : -
The Trivium (3) & Quadrivium (4)

The Trivium: - Grammar; Rhetoric; Logic

Quadrivium:- Arithmetic; Geometry; Astronomy; Music

The Trivium consisted of Latin grammar, rhetoric (the art of public speaking and letter writing) & logic (the art of reasoning).
The more advanced Quadrivium covered the four branches of mathematics.

* * *

1996

1st January 1996 Monday

Ravenstone Church is launching out on a new 'Planned Giving' scheme.

A letter from the Rector, the Reverend Kerry Emmett, urges all regular members of the congregation to sign on the dotted line, "I promise pay Ravenstone PCC the sum of .... per week" (for 4 years)

"Our budgeted expenditure in 1996 is likely to be at least £17,000, and probably more".

The Times on the Internet – The Times is available from today on the Internet, the worldwide system of interlinked computers. Our pages can be found on http:// www.the-times.co.uk

(Newspaper cutting)

3rd January 1996 Wednesday

Prize from ERNIE! Bond No. 14HN 330885.

Dear Bondholder, Congratulations. One of your Premium Bonds has won a prize ....

Yours Simcerely, Dan Monaghan, Director of Operations. "Pay Miss E. Hewes Fifty Pounds Only".

Dan Monaghan, Director of Operations, is a new name & a new job title, replacing Alan McGill, Controller, who sounded more matey, adding "Good luck in future draws".

5th January 1996 Friday

The so-called 'Gas Bubble' which could cost British Gas £1 billion is the result of long-term contracts agreed long ago when British Gas was the one & only customer buying gas from the North Sea gas producers, & promised to take the gas at a fixed price. Now with all & sundry buying gas, British Gas is having to pay for more gas than it needs.

Gas bill: British Gas will begin talks on the gas bubble which could cost the company £1 billion. The excess gas which the company is contracted to buy would have been needed if the gas market had not been opened up.The contracts have left British Gas heavily exposed to buying gas at high costs, while the price at which it can sell the fuel on has plunged. (newspaper cutting)

Since March 1994 British Gas has been sub-divided into 4 separate business units: -

British Gas Supply – selling, billing, meter reading.

British Gas Retail – showrooms, known as Energy Centres.

British Gas Service – installation & servicing of gas heating.

British Gas Transco – storage & transport of gas.

If there is a gas escape, you call British Gas Transco.

Thirty million people will hand the taxman a total of £5.5 billion in unnecessary tax each year, or an average of £180 each, because they are not using their allowances and do not understand the tax regime, according to a report published yesterday.

9th January 1996 Tuesday

If 100 years is a 'centenary' what is 150 years? At Mount St. Bernard's Abbey, I asked Father Paul, thinking he might know as it was mentioned in connection with the Abbey celebrating its anniversary 1835 – 1985. Search as I could, the word eluded me. Father Paul, with the help of another learned monk, found the word for me, 'sesqui-centenary'.

A stampede of tens of thousands of learner drivers desperate to take their tests before the summer has been triggered by the Government's announcement that they will have to sit a written examination from July 1st.

(Newspaper cutting)

11th January 1996 Thursday

Yesterday, 10th January, would have been Bunting & Mostyn's Golden Wedding, but without Mostyn, Bunting had nothing to celebrate. And today, being the anniversary of my dad's death, reminded Bunting of others she had loved & lost. Even now, at the age of 80, she misses her dad, & she misses the mother she hardly knew, who died when she was 3.

13th January 1996 Saturday

Sam Land, now aged 82, is such a sad lonely old man without his beloved Florence, who died exactly a year ago today. They were a devoted couple, with one child only – Brian, who now visits his dad every day & does all he can for him. Sam's daughter-in-law Jean sends his dinner & Susan, his grand-daughter, also helps to keep the home fire's burning.

15th January 1996 Monday

The new assistant Bishop of Leicester was officially instituted at a special service on Sunday. The Right Rev Bill Down took part in a service of commissioning and installation at Leicester Cathedral attended by a host of civic dignitaries. The assistant bishop, who was previously priest in charge of Humberstone, was also installed as an Honorary Canon of the Cathedral. His new role will be to support the Bishop of Leicester, the Right Rev Dr Thomas Butler, by taking confirmation services and helping in the ordination of priests and deacons. He will also deputise for the bishop from time to time. (Newspaper cutting)

17th January 1996 Wednesday

Reynolds, Joyce Cynthia, passed peacefully away at home on January 17th 1996, aged 75 years. Much loved wife of the late George, devoted mother to Stuart and Keith, mother-in-law to Angela and loving grandma to Neil. Funeral service to take place at Ravenstone Church on Tuesday, January 23rd at 1p.m. followed by interment in the churchyard. All flowers welcome, further inquiries and flowers to The Coalville Co-operative Funeral Service, Stuart House, 128 London Road, Coalville. Tel. (01530) 836703.

Remember George, aged 62, who used to work for Mr. Prew ...? George died on 4th December 1980 & his widow Joyce has now died.

Cocky & George worked together for Mr. Prew, & it was through this that I became closely acquainted with George & Joyce.

19th January 1996 Friday

Mount St. Bernard's Abbey Annual Ecumenical Service this week was sheer joy. Katherine (aged 91) & I (aged 64) loved being in this holy place, sharing 'Ecumenical Vespers' with the monks.

The first hymn began, "Praise we our God with joy & gladness never ending; Angels & saints with us, their grateful voices blending". The reading from 'Colossians' moved me deeply.

'Let the word of Christ dwell in you richly in all wisdom'.

21st January 1996 Sunday

New commandments for schools. God gave us 'Commandments' (See 1st September 1991)

Children today have very little religious education, either at home or at school & are now to be offered a modern ten commandments in the school curriculum. Ten suggested commandments are, "Honesty; respect for others; politeness; a sense of fair play; forgiveness; punctuality; non-violent behaviour; patience; faithfulness; self-disipline".

23rd January 1996 Tuesday

British Gas has now lost most of the commercial & industrial market & now, under the Gas Act 1995, is to lose much of the domestic gas market. Starting with Devon, Cornwall & Somerset, new firms such as Sweb Gas will be supplying homes with gas.

When British Gas was offered for sale in December 1986, its statutory monopoly made it the only available supplier to British homes and businesses. But it also had obligations, written into its licence to operate, to maintain supplies no matter how cold the weather became, or how much household consumption soared in response. Britisg Gas says that to meet those obligations "we entered into many agreements for the purchase of gas on the basis of anticipated minimum annual contract quantities. If demand falls below these minimums we are required to pay for the gas whether it is taken or not. Thses 'take or pay' contracts were appropriate, and indeed necessary, to meet our legal obligations under our licence to supply". *(Newspaper cutting)*

British Gas will shortly announce a link with HFC, the American-owned bank, in preparation for a move into financial services. The joint venture, to be named Golden Eagle, is with British Gas's trading arm. A spokesman said, "We're looking at the possibility of making available a range of financial products and services". *(Newspaper cutting)*

The Gas Act 1995 makes provision for the introduction of 'competition' into the domestic gas market. With effect from 1st February this year, British Gas will lose its monopoly over the supply of gas to households. It will be a gradual transition, starting in the South West, & covering the whole country by January 1st 1999. Suppliers will have 'Gas Shippers Licence'.

27th January 1996 Saturday

"Civil Service Retirement Fellowship" this month was a belated Christmas party held at the home of Jack & Muriel Harding, who live at 103 Castle Rock Drive, Coalville. Enid joined us & was made very welcome. As usual we all took something in the way of refreshments, plus a wrapped gift. I was pleased my 'Sultana Loaf Cake' was a success.

29th January 1996 Monday

Ravenstone Church was closed for services yesterday because there was no heating. How lovely then to have 'Songs of Praise' in the dear little chapel belonging to the Alms Houses. We sang 'the old hundredth hymn' (based on Psalm 100) "All People that on Earth do Dwell", & other hymns based on specific bible readings, which were read before the hymn, giving added depth to their meaning.

31st January 1996 Wednesday

Captain Charles Hazlitt Upham, the New Zealander who won the Victoria Cross in 1941 & again in 1942, was the only fighting soldier to win two Victoria Crosses. Although three men have won double V.C.s, the other two were medical officers who won their medals for rescuing wounded men under fire. Captain Upham won his first V.C. while serving in Crete & his second in the Western Desert.

2nd February 1996 Friday

Candlemas! Every February 2nd we remember most especially the "Nunc Dimittis", words engraved in our hearts since childhood & repeated every time we attend a church service:-

"Lord, now lettest thou thy servant depart in peace, according to thy word. For mine eyes have seen thy salvation, which thou hast prepared before the face of all people, to be **a light** ...." hence the candles.

4th February 1996 Septuagesima Sunday

"Countess Maritza" is this year's choice for Coalville Amateurs. Last Tuesday I joined the team assembled at Peter Jacques' house for the allocation of tickets. I was in my element again, acting on behalf of the Treasurer, Wendy Miles, who was away on business. Pat & I, currently House Manager & Assistant, have decided to 'retire' at the next A.G.M.

6th February 1996 Tuesday

"Alumni Officer – De Montfort University". Cousin Miles has now clinched this exciting new job, communicating with some 27,000 former students & helping them keep in touch through their own magazine "Network". He will work in Leicester, but deal also with De Montfort University's other centres at Bedford, Lincoln & Milton Keynes. He started this new job yesterday.

"Network" the magazine of the De Montfort University Association, has an Editor (Miles), Production/Art Editor, Subeditor, Designer, Staff Writer, Editorial Assistant & is published by the University's Alumni Association.

9th February 1996 Friday

The IRA's statememt – "It is with great reluctance that the leadership of Oglaigh na hEireann (IRA) announces that the complete cessation of military operations will end at 6p.m. on February 9th, this evening."

(Newspaper cutting)

10th February 1996 Saturday

Cousin Miles could not have landed a better job than Alumni Officer, External Relations, Portland Building, De Montfort University, The Gateway, Leicester.

From humble beginnings in the 1870s, to a 'Polytechnic' in 1969, & ultimately De Montfort University in 1992, it has everything you could wish for & unlimited opportunities.

De Montfort University's Alumni Association was started in 1991, with a membership of 300. Leicester's 2 campuses have since gained the new purpose-built Kents Hill Campus at Milton Keynes; the 2 campuses at Bedford; & 4 campuses at Lincoln, increasing membership to 27,000. Last year, the 2nd Annual Alumni Association reunion was held at the House of Lords.

14th February 1996 Wednesday

"On Valentine's Day I'm hoping that in your heart there'll be

a special feeling equal to the happiness that you bring to me"

To the girl who is always in my heart, & I will never stop loving. Xxxxxxxx

16th February 1996 Friday

Bomb ends IRA ceasefire - A huge bomb exploded on London's Isle of Dogs last Friday evening, 9th February, as thousands of office workers were making their way home. The blast at the South Quay Docklands Light Railway Station, near Canary Wharf Tower, followed a chilling warning from the IRA that, "with great reluctance" the ceasefire that began on 31st August 1994 would end at 6p.m.

18th February 1996 Sunday

The Chinese New Year is not always on the same date. It is the day of the first new moon after the sun enters the constellation of Aquarius, which puts it between January 20th & February 19th each year. Festivities in Leicester begin tomorrow & go on for 15 days. There are about 5,000 Chinese people now in Leicester ready to greet this new year – the Year of the Rat.

Buddha called all the animals in the kingdom together for a New Year meeting but only 12 turned up. He gave each animal a year of its own, so the Chinese Zodiac repeats itself every 12 years.

(Newspaper cutting)

21st February 1996 Ash Wednesday

Jeanne Calment, who was born 21st February 1875, has now reached her 121st birthday!   (See 21st Feb 1995)

(Madame Calment, the world's oldest person, died 4th August 1997, in Arles, aged 122, from an unspecified cause)

22nd February 1996 Thursday

Civil Service Retirement Fellowship meeting & an interesting talk with coloured slides given by Des Starbuck on his 3 in 1 American holiday in Florida.

First we went to the coastal resort of Clearwater, near St. Petersburg, where pelicans abounded; then to Disneyworld, Orlando, where he stayed for a week, & we saw almost everything there; finally to Cape

Canaveral to see enormous space rockets.

23rd February 1996 Friday

Tyrrell, Annette, three years since you were so tragically taken. Remembered today and every day. So much heartache remains. Your memory is our greatest treasure. Loved too much for us ever to forget. Your loving brother Peter.

Hello Nett Nett, I'm your new little niece that you never got to know. But I'll learn all about you as I get big and grow. Lots of hugs and kisses. Baby Carris Annette.

(Newspaper cuttings)

24th February 1996 Saturday

Privatisation of British Rail is causing havoc at the moment, as 25 lines are now at different stages of being sold off. Some are already in the private sector, some are still in the public sector & some are on the brink of being sold. The London, Tilbury & Southend line (LTS Rail) was off to the worst start & everything stalled after allegations of ticket fraud.

Greenwich wins – *The battle to host the Millennium Exhibition in 2000 has been won by Greenwich, London, to the fury of rival bidders. (Newspaper cutting)*

26th February 1996 Monday

The former Bishop of Leicester, the Rt. Revd. Dr. Richard Rutt, was ordained along with the retired Bishop of Dorchester, Dr. Conrad Meyer, on 8th June 1995 at Buckfast Abbey, Devon, as a Roman Catholic priest. He works as a 'retired priest'. The Roman Catholic Church decided to admit married former Anglican clergy to the priesthood under certain circumstances.

28th February 1996 Wednesday

Department of Social Security – Benefits Agency – about the general increases in benefits.

"This is to tell you that from 8th April 1996 the amount of your benefit will go up to £70.99p a week.

Basic Pension £61.15p. Additional Pension £43.19p. Less Contracted-out deductions £34.94p. Plus Graduated Pension £1.59p." Total increase of approx. £17 per month.

Princess agrees to divorce – The Princess of Wales last night announced she had agreed to a divorce and given up her right to be called Her Royal Highness.

The agreement formally to end the marriage was made at a meeting between the Prince and Princess of Wales at her office at St. James's Palace late yesterday afternoon.

A spokesman for the Princess said, "The Princess of Wales will be known as Diana, Princess of Wales."   (newspaper cutting)

1st March 1996 Friday

Leicestershire's three Universities are – Leicester University, De Montfort University and Loughborough University. Now that cousin Miles is Alumni Officer at De Montfort University, I am much more aware of its activities.

Massive budget cuts are being faced by all three universities in Leicestershire for the coming financial year.

Leicester's budget for the next financial year has fallen from £33 million to £32.1m, De Montfort's from £44m to

£42.9m and Loughborough's from £31.3m to £30.4m.
(Newspaper cutting)

3rd March 1996 Sunday

M.R.S.A. – Methicillin Resistant Staphylococcus Aureus, i.e. S.A. which can resist being healed by methicillin, is what Elaine had in Leicester Royal Infirmary, this time last year. The resistance of bacteria to antibiotics is one of the most serious global health threats facing us today. Bacteria are driven by an instinct to survive & are learning how to fight back & not surrender to antibiotics.

The miracle mould – The discovery of antibiotics was one of the most crucial medical developments of the 20th Century. The breakthrough came in 1929 with Sir Alexander Fleming's work with penicillin. Produced by a mould, he found it could tackle a wide range of bacteria and, even in large doses, was not toxic. Since then, many other antibiotics have been developed. They work in two ways. The first is by preventing bacteria growing, giving the body's immune system time to overcome the infection. The second is by causing the bacteria's cell walls to disintegrate which causes it to take in water, expand and burst. Doctors have used antibiotics to treat a huge range of scourges, including tuberculosis, bacterial forms of meningitis and pneumonia, gangrene, and gonorrhoea. Other antibacterial drugs are available and, unlike antibiotics, are produced synthetically. *(Newspaper cutting)*

5th March 1996 Tuesday

"Countess Maritza", with its haunting Hungarian gypsy music & gorgeous costumes, ia a lovely 'finale' for brother Pat, after 50 glorious years with Coalville Amateurs. Our magnificent 'front of house' team is somewhat diminished this year, as not everyone can be there every night. Our once splendid blue sashes have seen better days & this year have been replaced by new red ones.

Glorious music and gipsy fire put passion and colour into Ian Pratley's dashing production of Countess Maritza for Coalville Amateur Operatic Society. And a splendidly turned out front-of-house team did the honours both before and after the performance with skill and panache.
(Newspaper cutting)

Signs of new growth – Signs marking the edge of the National Forest are being put up across the county in the first phase of a campaign to raise awareness of the giant tree-planting scheme in Leicestershire. Signs at entry points along major routes were first to be installed. New village signs will follow as part of the Highway Authority's ongoing replacement programme.
A £30,000 Rural Development Commission grant has helped launch the project, and almost a million of the planned 30 million trees have already been planted. Mr Simon George, chief marketing officer at the National Forest, said, "The idea of the signs is to raise the profile of the National Forest and to mark local community identity." The National Forest aims to provide almost a third tree cover over 200 square miles of Leicestershire.
(Newspaper cutting)

7th March 1996 Thursday

Joanne celebrates her 22nd birthday today. You would never believe she was the same pretty little girl I once knew. The fashion of young women today can best be described as deplorable. Joanne, overweight, & dressed in volumimous skirts down to her ankles, looks more like a Bohemian, with awful chunky boots & shapeless sloppy tops, which so many others also wear.

9th March 1996 Saturday

A third baby for Karen was born in Bedford yesterday. Andrew David is brother to Lewis, born January 1994, & Suzannah born November 1991.
Murdo & Debbie are expecting their second baby later this year. Their first baby, Murd the 3rd, born December 1994, is a lively little tough guy.

More than a third of the babies delivered in England and Wales last year – 33.9 per cent – were born outside wedlock *(Newspaper cutting)*

On this day in 1796 – Napoleon Bonaparte married Josephine, the widow of the Cicomte de Beauharnais.

11th March 1996 Monday

For the 3rd consecutive year, we have held a raffle during the interval of our Coalville Amateurs' production & have made a handsome profit.
A notable omission this year was the playing of the National Anthem. It was always a moving experience to stand in the foyer of the theatre, perfectly still, as we listened to the National Anthem being played. Today it has little respect.

13th March 1996 Wednesday

"Countess Maritza" has been a resounding success for Coalville Amateurs. Sixteen young children, who alternated in teams of eight each performance, plus a talented troupe of young dancers, added to its appeal. The massacre of 16 young children in Dunblane today shocked us all. As when Cocky married Joan, I expected the world to stop, so in Dunblane birds continued to sing merrily.

Massacre of the children – Sixteen young children and their teacher were murdered yesterday by a gunman who walked into their school and opened fire as they played in the gym. Another 12 were injured in the massacre which devastated the tiny Scottish cathedral city of Dunblane and left the nation numbed in disbelief.
(newspaper cutting)

17th March 1996 Sunday

Thought for the day – He that believeth on the Son hath everlasting life; and he that believeth not the Son shall not see life; but the wrath of God abideth on him.
(newspaper cutting)

"He that believeth on the Son **hath** everlasting life" – How my dad would have appreciated this 'thought for the day'. Of the many accounts handed down to me about my dad, one involves this very text. When he was a young soldier, he acquired the nick-name 'Hath' after he had spoken about this text, stressing '**hath** everlasting life' – not '**will have**' but hath it even now.

19th March 1996 Tuesday
Nelson Mandela, now aged 77, spent 27 years of his life in prison, supporting the cause of the underprivileged people of South Africa. How deeply moved I was in February 1990 to see him walk hand in hand with his wife Winnie, whom he had married in 1958, when he was 41 & she was 25.

But it transpired that she had another lover, a young lawyer named Dali Mpofu.

Divorce for Mandela – A South African judge officially ended one of the world's best known marriages, granting President Mandela a divorce from Winnie. (Newspaper cutting)

21st March 1996 Thursday
Elizabeth Hewes – No 811 013 027 0 012 has received her 4th Council Tax Demand Notice, with 25% discount (omly one resident in the property). In 1993 I paid £250, in 1994 £278, in 1995 £297 & this year is £313. Most of this goes to County Council services.

The odds on winning a prize on the Premium Bonds have lengthened. National Savings yesterday bowed to Treasury pressure to cut the number of prize payouts after falls in interest rates. From May 1st for the first time, there will be a set total of 350,000 prizes a month. The odds of winning any prize in the May draw will be about 17,200 – 1, compared with 15,000 – 1 now. Changes in the prize structure will mean fewer smaller £50 and £100 prizes. *(Newspaper cutting)*

23rd March 1996 Saturday
"The National Grid, the electricity transmission system for England & wales, previously owned by the regional electricity companies, was floated on the stock market in December 1995. As a result of this flotation, our domestic customers will receive a one-off discount of £50 – 56p."
This, together with a *'one-off discount of £6'* from East Midlands Electricity has reduced my bill this quarter to 52p.
Legoland clicks into action – Britain's new Legoland opens next Friday – and you'll be turned away when the park reaches its 12,000 capacity, no matter how far you've travelled. So it's best to book in advance. The 150-acre site, on the Windsor to Bracknell road, Berkshire, has 17 rides, from a traditional carousel and ferris wheel to self-drive children's cars and a canoe ride which climaxes with a plunge down a flume. Other attractions (21 in all) include a politically correct circus (no animals), magic theatre, gold-panning area, puppet theatre and a cathedral to Lego, where fans can build dinosaurs, houses, cars and people. A Lego version of Tower Bridge, using 100,000 pieces, took 500 man hours to build.
Prebook – adults £14, children £11. On the gate prices £15 and children £12.
(Newspaper cutting)

27th March 1996 Wednesday
Old romantic Hewsie chose to join the Heart of England Building Society in November 1989, purely for its heart. In 1993 it merged with Cheltenham & Gloucester Building Society who then joined the Lloyds Bank Group. Cash incentives were offered to eligible members & thanks to the money left to me by Aunt Dos, my account gained £3,000.

29th March 1996 Friday
Whatever would Ole Kirk Christiansen, who founded LEGO as a cottage industry in 1932, think of the latest high-tech Legoland Themepark opening today in the old Windsor Safari Park? He would recognise the colourful small plastic bricks built up into the most fantastic creations, but would marvel at their intricate movements, all made possible by computer control, which visitors can learn to use.

Legoland at Billen in Denmark - The Danes are so impressed with the computerised educational system that they're going to introduce it in Billen. It will also be included at the Legoland being built an California.
(Newspaper cutting)

31st March 1996 Palm Sunday
The new Office for National Statistics (ONS) will open tomorrow when the Central Statistical Office (CSO) which was set up by Winston Churchill in 1941 (wartime) in order to harness the economy to the war effort, merges with the Office of Population Censuses & Surveys. The new office will, for the first time, create a single institution which will give a complete statistical picture of social & economic life in Britain.

3rd April 1996 Wednesday
Civil Service Retirement Fellowship – Leicestershire & South Lincolnshire Branch No.76 – held their Annual General Meeting this year the Carillon Rooms, Ashby Square, Loughborough (the Masonic Hall). I sat beside Mrs Renie Martin at a buffet lunch, after which the guest of honour at the AGM was the CSRF Chairman, Peter Jones from head office, who presented certificates of merit.

4th April 1996 Maundy Thursday
"Steve & Jane request the pleasure of the company of Auntie Betty on the occasion of their marriage at the Register Office, Coalville, on Saturday 6th July 1996 at 12 noon, followed by a celebration lunch at the Fallen Knight Hotel, Ashby-de-la-Zouch"
Steven & Jane were engaged on Christmas Day 1992 & set up home together two years ago.

6th April 1996 Saturday
New "Technology Colleges" are now on the increase. In the late 1980s the Government decided to create brand new Technology Colleges funded from private industry. Private industry was not altogether forthcoming & another scheme was devised whereby existing upper schools raise £100,000 from private sponsers & the Government then adds £100,000. Leicestershire now has one at Uppingham & one at Oadby.
The idea of the Technology College scheme is to boost scientific and technological skills at selected schools across Britain.
(newspaper cutting)

8th April 1996 Easter Monday
The old cherry tree in the Hollies orchard, which every

year at May-time showered me with confetti, today came under the woodman's axe.(See 4th May 1991). I have known this tree all my life & well remember Grandpa Hewes chasing off the children who climbed the tree & scrumped his fruit. It was such a lovely tree to climb, with lower branches within reach & well away from the house.

10th April 1996 Wednesday

"Coalville Town Centre – Environmental Improvements" – Gwen & I (Miles' lady-love) attended a lively meeting hosted by Coalville Town Forum, in which plans for traffic-calming & such-like in Coalville town centre were considered. The major problem is too much traffic/traffic congestion. Short of knocking down the whole town & starting again, it seems an impossible task, but work is to begin this year.

12th April 1996 Friday

Coalville's two former adjacent pubs overlooking the clock tower "The Royal Oak" & "The Greyhound" have recently been merged into one by Banks' Brewery. A competition to name the new pub was won by Philip Paget who chose "The Pick 'n' Shovel" in recognition of the old coal-mining days. The first pint was pulled by local girl Karen Smithies, England Ladies cricket captain.

16th April 1996 Tuesday

Today marks the 250th Anniversary of the Battle of Culloden on 16th April 1746, when Bonnie Prince Charlie, the Roman Catholic heir to the British throne, failed to re-claim the crown from the Protestants. Later that year he made his escape 'over the sea to Skye' dressed as an Irish servant girl & returned to France an unhappy exile, who felt he should have been Charles III.

17th April 1996 Wednesday

Divorce today for the Yorks – The Duke and Duchess of York will today be granted a 'quickie' divorce to end their ten-year marriage, it was announced in a joint statement by their solicitors last night.The couple's case will be heard in the Family Division of the High Court at Somerset House, London, this morning, and a decree absolute is expected by the end of May.

(Newspaper cutting)

18th April 1996 Thursday

Lesley Hale & I just happened to meet up together at Snibston Discovery Park where there was an exhibition & video telling you all about the Whitwick Colliery disaster which took place in the early hours of 19th April 1898, and which resulted in the loss of 35 lives. The men were suffocated by carbon monoxide poisoning after fire broke out.

20th April 1996 Saturday

29 Leicester Road, Ravenstone, £37,950 to include fitted carpets & some curtains. This is the house next door for sale. Wayne & Tina have lived next door to me since they were married in August 1991, when Tina wept at leaving her family home. They are now returning to live near to her mother at Peggs Green. Declan, their 4 month old baby son is absolutely gorgeous.

22nd April 1996 Monday

The 16th London Marathon yesterday took place on the 70th birthday of Her Majesty Queen Elizabeth II. The winner for the 3rd consecutive year was Dionicio Céron of Mexico. In splendid isolation, ahead of all the others, he reached the winning line in the Mall.

They are the hardiest and most unyielding runners of all. They number 42 and they have completed every London marathon since the first race in 1981. In recognition of their physical and mental durability, these athletes have been given a permanent entry in the event for the rest of their lives, provided, of course, that they do not miss a year.　　　　　　　　　　*(Newspaper cutting)*

24th April 1996 Wednesday

"Dear Miss Hewes, I thought you might like to know that your local Peugeot dealership has changed ownership. Formerly known as Parkin & Jones, it is now Forest Road Garage. I would like you to know that basically the staff have not changed & that as far as we are concerned it is business as usual"

John Haynes, Dealer Principal.

26th April 1996 Friday

Katherine's birthday – 92 today & still going strong. Her friend Megan Cross, aged 70, was paying her a call when Gwen & I popped in to wish her 'Happy Birthday'. As always, Katherine held centre court, regaling us with non-stop tales of her fascinating life. She also lay on the carpet on her back, pedalling high in the air, to show us how she exercises daily in her bath.

28th April 1996 Sunday

It was thanks to my Aunt Dos that I first applied for my job in 1948 at the Motor Licence Office. She saw it advertised in the Leicester Mercury under the heading 'Public Appointments', which I did not even know meant job vacancies.

I was thus able to benefit from a good pension scheme when I retired from work at 60. Women born after 5th April 1955 cannot now retire until 65.

30th April 1996 Tuesday

From the Office of H. M. Paymaster General – "Further increase on pension due from 8th April 1996".

New Rate = £7155.55p a year, i.e. £596.30p a month less tax of £128.60p = £467.70p, payable each month. This together with the state pension for all old age pensioners, £283.96p every four weeks, gives me a monthly income now of £751.66p, about £188 per week.

2nd May 1996 Thursday

The Hubble space telescope will acquire a high-resolution spectograph & camera next year to study two stars similar in size, age & temperature to the sun, in the hope of discovering a planet akin to planet Earth. The two stars are only 15 light years away from us – a short distance on cosmic scales. Even more advanced instruments are planned in 1999, 2002 & 2005.

4th May 1996 Saturday

It was on 4th May 1970 that Mum's Aunt Mary died & with the money she left to Mum we were able to have the telephone installed, have the old fireplace in the middle room taken out & a new one fitted, & acquire an elegant table-lamp with a pretty pink shade. After 25 years service, the lampshade has now 'had it' & has needed replacing.

6th May 1996 Monday
Cousin Miles took an extended lunch break to give me a conducted tour of De Montfort University's amazing complex of buildings. We saw, in the basement of Hawthorn Building, the arches of the old Abbey Church; & the magnificent new Queens Building.

Student call – The call has gone out for former students of De Montfort University to come forward. The university's alumni officer, Mr Miles Wilson, is looking to extend the database of former students with new details. Mr Wilson said, "I am building up a comprehensive database of as many famous – or infamous – people as I can to ensure we keep in touch with them through the Alumni Office."Anyone who can help can contact the office on (0116) 255 1551.

(Newspaper cutting)

8th May 1996 Wednesday
American astronomers, using the world's largest optical telescope in Hawaii, have discovered the most distant galaxy yet, about 14 billion light years from the Earth. Dr. Thomas Barlow, one of the team, said, " This is the highest red-shift (the amount by which its light is shifted towards the red end of the spectrum) galaxy that we've detected – the closest to the beginning of the universe."

The Big Bang theory has been vindicated by a new study which shows that the universe is about 15 billion years old.

(Newspaper cutting)

10th May 1996 Friday
Landseer's four magnificent bronze lions in Trafalgar Square, London, cast in 1867, are having what is thought to be their first thorough wash and brush up in well over a century. Each of the 20 foot bronzes is having 3 weeks of treatment under scaffolding, & the operation is costing the Department of National Heritage £25,000. Tourists will then be allowed to climb on them again.

12th May 1996 Sunday
The 69th Annual Bluebell Service – Katherine aged 92 & I, together with Toffee her black curly-haired dachshund, enjoyed once more the Bluebell Service in the idyllic setting of Swithland Woods. After the service we strolled through the woods, while the birds sang their hearts out without a care in the world.

14th May 1996 Tuesday
In April 1987, Sotheby's, Geneva, auctioned the Duchess of Windsor's jewels & made over £30 million, when bids reached up to 885 times estimate. Now the same thing has happened again in New York for a memento of Jackie Onassis, including her engagement ring, sold for £1.75 million.
New York: The auction of Jacqueline Kennedy Onassis memorabilia raised $34.5 million. (£22.8 million)

16th May 1996 Thursday (Ascension Day)
The W.R.V.S. has been completely restructured over the past few years, following the Woodfield Report in 1991. From John o'Groats to Lands End, the country has been split up into 6 great 'Divisions' – Scotland, Wales, North West, South West. North East & South East. We belong to the North East Division, sub-divided into new area offices. The W.R.V.S. Diamond Jubilee will be in 1998.

The now famous W.R.V.S. is the largest active voluntary service in the United Kingdom, with more than 140,000 members. It was formed as the Women's Voluntary Service in 1938, to help local authorities prepare for civilian care in the event of war.

(Nerwspaper cutting)

18th May 1996 Saturday
Birthday card to – His Holiness Pope John Paul II, Apostolic Palace, 00120, Vatican City, has been duly sent by Katherine, aged 92. The card which I found for her was "The Light of the World" by Holman Hunt. Today the Pope is celebrating his 76th birthday. He is Poland's most famous son, formerly Karol Wojtyla, & earlier this month was made an honorary citizen of Warsaw.

20th May 1996 Monday
Civil Service Retirement Fellowship Meeting. Remember Muriel Harding who gave an interesting talk on Calligraphy (17th March 1994) & an equally interesting talk on Poetry (18th October 1995)? Well, today she brought an amazing selection of books & samples of yet more of her absorbing interests:- craftwork, crochet, tapestry, applique, tatting, quilting & intricate paper cut-outs.

22nd May 1996 Wednesday
Manchester United 1 Liverpool 0. This year saw the 115th F.A.Cup Final when Manchester United clinched a historic second double, repeating their 1994 achievement by winning both the League & the Cup. Manager Alex Ferguson said, "This is beyond my wildest dreams. When we won the Double two years ago it was so fantastic I would have been very happy to go to heaven then."

24th May 1996 Friday
"Let me know the things you like to do" said my get-up-and-go American pen-friend who was ready to welcome me like a long lost bosom friend. I wrote a cautious letter:- "..... I am always reluctant to stay in anyone else's home & this has made me unpopular with several of my own relations. Having lived for so long on my own, I like plenty of breathing space." She did not write again. (See 25th May 1995)
If you really don't want to do something say no.

(newspaper cutting)

26th May 1996 Whit Sunday
And yet again the glorious message of Whitsunday came to us again in Holy Scripture, Hymns & Prayers, even within the limits of "Songs of Praise". Our four readings fitted beautifully into the general theme developed in & around the hymns: 1) Ezekiel, Chapter 37, 1 – 14;
2) Acts of the Apostles, Chapter 2;
3) I Corinthians, Chapter 12; 4) Galatians 5, 16 – 26.

28th May 1996 Tuesday

"The Hiram Key" is the title of a new book which claims that Jesus was a Freemason.

Freemasonry originated with the building of King Solomon's Temple 3,000 years ago & Jesus was supposedly a leading figure in the Essene community at Qumran. The Passion narratives of the New Testament could date from resurrection rituals of ancient Egypt & ritually denoted re-birth into a brotherhood.

30th May 1996 Thursday

On 1st April 1974, the dear little County of Rutland & the proud City of Leicester were swallowed up in the new enlarged Leicestershire County Council. With effect from 1st April 1997, they will be free once more to run their own affairs. They are now two of the country's 13 'shadow councils', included in this month's local elections. (Independents, Liberal Democrats, Conservatives & Labour)

1st June 1996 Saturday

House for sale next door – sold in record time & new neighbours now installed. Mervyn Talbott & Margaret in their early forties, plus one 13 year old daughter. Mervyn has been married before & is the father of five. Margaret has been married before & is the mother of three. They are all out much of the time – both at work & always on the go.

3rd June 1996 Monday

Leicester City, by the skin of their teeth, are now back again in the Premier Division.

Chairman Martin George & manager Martin O'Neill are predicting that this time "We will stay up".

But, you never know with Leicester. The only way to stay up is by paying astronomical amounts of money to procure the best players of the day.

5th June 1996 Wednesday

"Dear Customer, George & I are hanging up our paperbags for the last time on 10th June after having the business for nearly 35 years .... The business is being taken over by a young local couple Neil & Glynis North. We ourselves are not moving far away & will be living in a bungalow in Ashland Drive. Best wishes, George & Jean Broadhurst." (Ravenstone's newsagents).

6th June 1996 Thursday

Monty returns – A statue of Field Marshal Montgomery was dedicated by Prince Michael of Kent at Colleville – Montgomery, France, to commemorate the 52nd anniversary of D-Day. (Newspaper cutting)

7th June 1996 Friday

Ravenstone Parish Church Summer Fair this year was held in the grounds of Ravenstone Hospital (the Alms Houses) on an idyllic summer's day. What a delightful setting beside the 14th Century church, with birdsong interspersed with music from a local brass band. Jim Bailiss & I were fully occupied selling & folding raffle tickets all afternoon. Overall, the fair raised £900.

9th June 1996 Sunday

John Paul II has made an emotional plea for an end to the artificial production of human embryos. He has sent a message to the world's scientists, doctors and law-makers asking them to halt the trade. His appeal came this week during an address to a joint assembly of two conferences being held at the Vatican.

The Pope said, "One cannot see a morally-licit solution to the human destiny of the thousands and thousands of frozen embryos which are and remain always the holders of essential rights and therefore must be juridically protected as humans."

He insisted that the inviolable rights of the human person from the moment of conception until natural death must be extended legally to human embryos.

"I appeal to the consciences of leaders in the scientific world, especially doctors, to stop the production of human embryos," he said.

"I address myself also to all law-makers and ask that they make themselves guardians of the inalienable rights which the thousands of frozen embryos intrinsically acquired at the moment of fertilisation."

(Newspaper cutting)

11th June 1996 Tuesday

Coalville Amateur Operatic Society AGM this year saw brother Pat, aged 77, relinquishing his role as House Manager, & I at the same time relinquishing my role as Assistant House Manager. We were pleased to hand over the roles to Mick Hunt & Margaret Tyler.

Pat was presented with a certificate & gold bar in recognition of his 50 years with the Society. I am still acting as Auditor.

13th June 1996 Thursday

A new pair of Italian design 'Samco' sun-glasses by Mazzucchelli £15.50p with CR39 lenses, conforming to British Standard 2724 (1987); conforming also to one of those European Directives, 89/686/EEC.

"CR 39 is a high tech material that was first used in the helmet visors of the Apollo astronauts for its clarity, strength & stability in extreme conditions", from Masons, Coalville.

15th June 1996 Saturday

Brother Pat, aged 77, has suffered a slight stroke, very similar to that suffered by Mary Moore in 1987. He lost partial use of his left side. The doctor advised him to rest & said he should soon be back to normal, but nevertheless, it has been an anxious time for all concerned. Evelyn is not in the best of health, with ulcerated legs; and his devoted dog Honey will not readily walk with anyone else.

If a clot blocks an artery to the heart it causes coronary heart disease and if it blocks a channel to the brain it results in a stroke.

Blood pressure tends to rise as the patient ages and the walls of the arteries become less elastic. The blood pressure reading, a measurement of the pressure within the arteries, should be under 140/90.

A 160/95 reading would cause anxiety, although random testing shows that 5% of men and women over 65 have blood pressures greater than 200/100.

The risk of a stroke rises after the diastolic blood pressure, the lower reading obtained when the heart is at rest, rises above 95, very steeply once it is over 105. The stroke rate increases by a factor of four when the diastolic reading rises from 105 to 110.

(newspaper cuttings)

16th June 1996 Sunday
The Planet on Sunday, June 16, 1996. No. 1
(New Sunday Newspaper) (See 16th June 1997)

17th June 1996 Monday
It is 25 years since Enid & I enjoyed a lovely holiday at Tenby in Pembrokeshire.
"Do go if ever you have the opportunity ...." thus I wrote in my diary exactly 25 years ago today.
We have always maintained a soft spot in our hearts for the beautiful county of Pembrokeshire & this year once more have chosen Tenby for our holiday, hoping to spend a week there commencing Wed. 17th July.

18th June 1996 Tuesday
Thirteen people were still in hospital today after Saturday's IRA bomb in Manchester which caused £100 million damage.

(newspaper cutting)

19th June 1996 Wednesday
OFGAS - Office of Gas Supply – this is our office at Wigston since 1st April this year.
"John Plant cordially invites you to join him for drinks & a buffet to celebrate his retirement, in the Conference Room on Friday 21st June, between 1p.m. & 3p.m." I called in at the office & was amazed at the transformation. Complete refurbishment, with no expense spared.
OFGAS, the regulatory body which makes sure that suppliers of gas, principally British Gas but increasingly private suppliers, do not overcharge their customers, is itself able to spend money like rain. Apart from total refurbishment in OFGAS colours, blue & grey, its all change in the type of work, with choice of early retirement & excessive redundancy payouts.

23rd June 1996 Sunday
Coleorton Hall, dating from 1807, owned originally by the Beaumont family & taken over by British Coal as an administrative base for its Midland pits in 1947, is now up for sale, as part of the continuing privatisation of British Coal.

The beautiful shrine of Medjugorje in Bosnia-Herzegovina has been visited by many eminent Roman Catholics, but this summer it can expect three more in the substantial and tuneful form of the three tenors – all of whom are themselves Catholics.
Pavarotti, Domingo and Carreras have agreed to sing there in July to mark the 15th anniversary of the first visions of the Virgin Mary. The concert, to be transmitted across the world by satellite, will tell the story of the shrine since 1981, when six children claimed that the Virgin Mary had appeared.

(newspaper cutting)

25th June 1996 Tuesday
Gas Examining & Gas Meter Examining, which were once our main concern, are no longer the concern of government. Modern technology can take care of all that. Veronica, our last remaining full time gas

examiner, has accepted early retirement. Only Jan, on a much lower salary, & prospects of a relatively low pension, & now aged 61, is not seeking early retirement.

27th June 1996 Thursday
JOIDES = The U K - based Joint Oceanogrophic Institutions for Deep Earth Sampling.
Their specially equipped ship "Joides Resolution" has been drilling off the coast of South Carolina, within the area of the infamous Bermuda Triangle, to obtain cores from layers of rock with pore spaces containing gas hydrates which give off methane as pressure is released.
The "Joides Resolution" was built in the late 1970s & is a floating scientific research centre with seven decks of laboratory facilities. By drilling off the coast of South Carolina it is hoped to tap the world's biggest source of natural gas, & maybe shed light on the Bermuda Triangle mystery.
Hydrates are found beneath all the oceans, but here are the most concentrated formations.

30th June 1996 Sunday
A new historical group is being set up in Ravenstone in order to compile a detailed account of the village in time for the new Millennium.
Interested villagers met for the first time on Tuesday night June 25th at the Pavilion, Ravenslea.

(newspaper cutting)

1st July 1996 Monday
New driving theory test begins today, which means that learner drivers must now sit a written test as well as the practical. The theory test, lasting about 40 minutes, consists of approximately 30 multiple choice questions on topics such as vehicle handling, knowledge of road signs, regulations & First Aid, plus other things such as driver perception & decision making.

The Rev Tom Ringland, Curate, Polegate (Chichester): to be Priest-in-charge, Christ Church, Coalville with St Peter, Bardon Hill.

(Newspaper cutting)

3rd July 1996 Wednesday
Forthcoming Marriages JARMAN Steven.
Nan is delighted to announce the wedding of a much loved grandson to "his Jane" on July 6th 1996.

Side by side may you always stay;
As much in love as you are today;
Side by side may you gladly see;
Your dreams become reality;
Side by side may you go through life;
Always happy as man and wife.

Lots of love, Nan & John
(newspaper cutting)

Mary Blue's firstborn, Steven, brought up by his Nan, Janie Jarman, when Mary Blue ran away to Scotland & now equally at home with either of his parents, is to be married on Saturday.
It is almost 6 years exactly since his sister Karen was married to her beloved Graham.

7th July 1996 Sunday
A lovely summer's day yesterday for the wedding of

Steven & Jane, who issued invitations in their own name. The bride was not 'given away' by her father as this is not included in a Registry Office ceremony. However, her father & mother were both there, as was Steven's father with his three wives, the jovial benefactor who paid for a splendid reception.

9th July 1996 Tuesday
Tinkering with the atomic clock.
I note on the inside front cover of The MagAZine (issue 307) the most interesting phenomenon of the Countdown 2000 clock in Dublin. Many readers will have noticed that the countdown (by exact seconds) is not to the millennium, but to 1st January 2000. The grand millennial misconception has been noted several times on your letters page of late. This is perhaps understandable, as everyone will celebrate a year early when the zeroes go up. But worse is to come. This clock cannot give the exact countdown in seconds to the false millennium. As an astronomer, I can say with certainty that it will have to be reset by a few seconds after 1st July 1999.

The earth's rotation is slowing down due to tidal friction, and the uniform "atomic" time scale must be retarded from time to time to keep pace with the earth's solar day. This is done by adding one whole, exact second at the start of the New Year, and if necessary also to the first second of July.

It will not be known until July 1999 exactly how many "intercalary" seconds have come between now and then, and the clock will have to be reset.   Dr Paul M Muller, Lauzerte, France.

(newspaper cutting)   (See July 9th 1994)

11th July 1996 Thursday
Your Tax Code. "Everyone under 65 is eligible for a personal allowance of £3,765." (the amount of pay or occupational pension from which tax will not be deducted). For me, you then deduct £3,691, being the amount of "state pension", which makes £74 only tax free. Hence my Tax Code L7 (L denoting under 65). This year (age 65 – 74), a totally new Tax Code elevates me to 121P.

MPs came under fire today after voting themselves a bumper 26% pay rise – nearly nine times the rate of inflation.

13th July 1996 Saturday
My birthday tomorrow – 65.
Cocky telephoned from Lancaster to say 'Happy Birthday'& sent me £20 in his birthday card.
Enid took me out to lunch on Thursday; & Pat & Evelyn are taking me out to lunch tomorrow.

Question: Why are people supposed to have seven years bad luck if they break a mirror?
The early Etruscans, the pre-Roman civilisation in Italy, believed someone who looked in a mirror saw a twin self. The other self was like a soul trapped in the mirror and any object which held something as valuable as a soul had to be protected. The Romans inherited this concept and added to it their own belief that each living thing began a new life every seven years. Thus, it was considered that a soul was harmed for seven years if a mirror was damaged. While mirrors were made of

polished stone or metal, this problem wasn't too serious. But when, in the 14th century, Italian glassmakers started to develop glass mirrors, the old superstition became more significant and the idea began that breaking a mirror brought seven years bad luck.

Only six per cent of over-65s are spinsters.
Only six per cent of Britain's females aged over 65 are 'old maids' *(newspaper cutting)*

15th July 1996 Monday
Sunday lunch for my birthday yesterday was at Sunnyside Garden Centre, Ibstock, where we have been regularly for the past 12 months. It turned out to be a gathering of 9 round the table, as we were joined by Mary Blue, Sharon & Jim, Jim's mother, plus another regular, James Hodson, organist at several churches & chapels in the area, & another acquaintance Trevelyn Mellor.

17th July 1996 Wednesday
Pembrokeshire here we come! Enid & I have chosen "Heywood Mount Hotel", Heywood Lane, Tenby, for our holiday, commencing today & due home next Wednesday 24th July.
"This beautiful refurbished gentleman's residence is set in one acre of land now transformed into a country style hotel". Just take the A478 into Tenby & follow the signs to 'Wild Life Park'.

19th July 1996 Friday
Thoroughly enjoying our 2nd holiday in Tenby. It was interesting to see the hotel on the Esplanade where we last stayed 25 years ago. The imposing great walls & ancient fortifications bear witness to its vulnerability to attack in days gone by. But oh what a pretty place it is & how lovely to be here at the peak of 'Tenby in Bloom' season.

21st July 1996 Sunday
"I would like to greet & welcome you in the name of our small community of Cistercian monks. We hope that we can share with you the peace that we try hard to establish in our own hearts, & in the hearts of all we meet" – A word of welcome to Caldey Island from the Abbott. It was on the Feast of the Epiphany, 6th January 1929, that the Cistercians officially took over ownership of the island.

23rd July 1996 Tuesday
"Just take the A478 into Tenby & follow the signs to 'Wild Life Park'. Thus we were instructed how to find our hotel. Yesterday we followed the signs right into the Wild Life Park & spent a leisurely day there. And now we come to the end of our sun-kissed holiday. We certainly saw Tenby at its very best, shimmering sea in the morning sun, & all the comforts of a good hotel.

25th July 1996 Thursday
The Reverend Michael David Webb, Vicar of St. James, Snibston, in his efforts to boost Church attendance, introduced a 'Praise Service' in the nearby Community Centre – once every 2 months – an informal short, service consisting of modern songs, as well as the 'old favourites', chosen by those attending. This included a

'Two Minute Witness Talk' & a lively joyful gathering.

27th July 1996 Saturday

"How to Build a Human Being" – Ten years ago, in July 1986, I told you that American biologists were working on the Human Genome Project (HGP) & had managed to decipher 2% of the 3.5 billion letters of the DNA alphabet. To complete the project in 10 years would take 3,000 people. They expect to achieve their goal by the year 2003.

The biggest map yet produced showing the position of 16,000 human genes has gone onto the Internet, where it can be consulted by anybody. The hunt goes on for the rest of the 80,000 to 100,000 genes that make up the entire human blueprint, or genome. The gene maps are found at www.ncbi.nlm.nih.gov/SCIENCE96

(newspaper cutting)

"The Genetic Revolution" a book written by Dr. Patrick Dixon, describes the Human Genome Project (HGP) as 'deeply disturbing'. The awesome power of this technology will alter life itself & could bring evil as well as good. Doctors are worried that the project will focus on producing designer babies, born not by the will of God, but by the will of man.

"He came unto his own, & his own received him not. But as many as received him, to them gave he power to become the sons of God, even to them that believe on his name; which were born, not of blood, nor of the will of man, but of God." (The Gospel according to Saint John, Chapter I, verses 11 – 13).

1st August 1996 Thursday

P – reg

2nd August 1996 Friday

Big Brother is watching us all - Leicester's new Closed Circuit Television cameras are now in place in an attempt to cut down the level of crime in the city centre. Costing £250,000 & £30,000 a year to maintain, 22 very high up cameras have been positioned at busy junctions in the city, & all are on 360° mounts to allow control room operators to follow suspects. They link up with others further afield.

Hillingdon Hospital's refusal to accept patients aged 75 referred by their doctors illustrates the problems facing the National Health Service.

(newspaper cutting)

4th August 1996 Sunday

Debra Hickin, who wrote me a lovely letter of appreciation when I retired as Sunday School teacher .... "*Theresa & myself thank you very much for what you have done for us & we have learnt a lot .....*" was married yesterday at Ravenstone Church. It was June 1983 when I retired as Sunday School teacher & always found Debra a delightful child to teach.

6th August 1996 Tuesday

August 6th is the Feast of the Transfiguration of our Lord, when his 3 disciples Peter, James & John saw him in glory, radiant with dazzling light.

August 6th 1945 was the day the atomic bomb was dropped on Hiroshima, when the nuclear explosion created its own horrendous dazzling light.

What a strange irony that these two events are recalled on one & the same day.   (See 6th August 1995)

8th August 1996 Thursday

"Cable TV could be coming to the Coalville area next year!"

The space age technology is set to power its way into thousands of local homes and businesses as the road to the superhighway opens up for Coalville folk. Diamond Cable Communications has the franchise for the Coalville area. The company uses high-tech fibre optic cables which are as thin as a human hair.

10th August 1996 Saturday

Lloyds TSB - Two of the biggest banks in the country, Lloyds & Trustee Savings Bank (TSB) merged last December to form Lloyds TSB. The two organisations dealt originally with totally different sorts of banking clients. Lloyds was far more upmarket than TSB with a much bigger base of corporate customers. Eventually there will be great changes for staff & customers alike, & lots of job losses.

12th August 1996 Monday

The 'Glorious Twelfth'

Samuel David Benedict Chatto is the latest baby for the Royal Family, born on 28th July this year. He is 14th in line to the throne, the son of Lady Sarah Chatto, née Lady Sarah Armstrong-Jones. Lady Sarah is the daughter of Princess Margaret & grand-daughter of King George VI. The baby's father, Daniel Chatto, has no title, so the baby is simply 'Master Samuel'.

14th August 1996 Wednesday

"P" registered cars have been selling like hot cakes. Favourite so far is P1GGY.

From 1st August this year to 31st July 1997, all new cars carry the prefix "P". The annual stampede to show off your new car is likely to stop when a new system comes into being. It is proposed splitting the year into quarters with 2 letters & 4 numbers each year, e.g. Prefix R1, R2, S1, S2 (Q is for Kit Cars).

16th August 1996 Friday

Cousin Isobel tomorrow celebrates her 80th birthday at home in Colchester. Her 'mercurial' son Miles & his lady-love Gwen, who have lived together in concubinage since November 1992, at Glenholm, Ravenstone, are spending a long weekend with Isobel. They have left the key to Glenholm with me, to draw the curtains at night etc. to make it look as though they are there.

18th August 1996 Friday

Jesus said, "I proceeded forth & came from God" (John 8, 42). Twenty years ago today I told you about the depth of meaning of these words, as spelled out in the Nicene Creed of the Holy Communion Service .... 'being of one substance with the Father'. How inspiring to hear the confirmation or our Creed spoken to us, as it were, directly from the mouth of our Lord himself.

20th August 1996 Tuesday

In the year of youth, preparing for the Millennium, 'The

Monastic Way' a monastic experience weekend for single Catholic men aged 18 – 30. A chance to take part in monastic prayer and work and to learn about the role and value of monasticism in the Church, to be held at Pluscarden Abbey from August 30 to September 2. Anyone interested should contact Fr. Benedict Hardy O.S.B. Pluscarden Abbey, Elgin, Moray, IV30 3UA.

(newspaper cutting)

Our recent visit to the Abbey Church on Caldey Island made us wonder how much longer the Monasteries would survive. All the monks there seemed to be elderly.

The new Globe theatre in London, home of William Shakespeare, opened for business on 20 August after a gap of 350 years, close to the original site on the banks of the Thames. *(newspaper cutting)*

22nd August 1996 Thursday
"The Last Plantagenet" – This is Leicester's new pub in Granby Street, formerly Maples furniture store, which has been converted by London-based pub operator Wetherspoons at a cost of £880,000. It will not have any juke box, piped music or pool tables. The pub's name refers to King Richard III, the last Plantagenet King, who died on Bosworth Field, 22nd August 1485.

24th August 1996 Saturday
Following last year's exceptionally dry summer, Severn Trent Water has launched a multi-million pound extra water scheme. Out of a £150 million programme to reduce leakage, find new resources & improve supplies, £6 million is for bringing up to seven million gallons of water a day into the network via a new 9 mile main from Anglian Water's Wing treatment works to Whatborough, East Midlands.

Some of the tallest people in Britain are taking their annual short break this Bank Holiday weekend at an hotel in the centre of Bristol. The average height of the 60 members from the Tall Persons Club of Great Britain is 6ft 6in. Among the guests is Chris Greener who, at 7ft 6in, is the tallest man in Britain.

26th August 1996 Monday
Civil Service Retirement Fellowship Meeting & an informal talk given by our Chairman Terry Watson about his most weird & wonderful experiences as a forensic scientist. He held us all spellbound as he recalled the highlights of a career which ran like an Agatha Christie thriller, solving crimes which included headless bodies, decaying corpses, & other murders.

Mother Teresa's heir – Mother Teresa handed over control of the worldwide Missionaries of Charity to Sister Nirmala, 63, a former Hindu from a high-caste Brahmin family. *(newspaper cutting)*

28th August 1996 Wednesday
"Let the flowers die" – These were the sad headlines exactly 20 years ago when Britain faced its worst drought for 250 years. "Dig up lawn; save water" were the headlines earlier this year when Severn Trent produced a leaflet aimed at gardners called Sowing the Seeds of Water Conservation, suggesting that we save water by digging up the lawns & paving them over.

The Prince & Princess of Wales, Charles & Diana, married 29th July 1981, divorced 28th August 1996.

30th August 1996 Friday
"And when Elisha was come into the house behold, the child was dead ......" II Kings, Chapter 4.
Earlier this month this story of Elisha & the dead boy he brought back to life again was read at Evensong at Ravenstone Church. In front of me sat Margaret Young whose only child David died so tragically in August 1994, & oh how I felt for her.

31st August 1996 Saturday
Traders are convinced tomorrow will be the start of regular Sunday trading in Leicester. Around 150 shops throughout the city centre will be opening their doors for the first time on a Sunday – and hopes are high it will prove a success.

(Newspaper cutting)

1st September 1996 Sunday
"A major distraction during Evensong at Ravenstone Church was a swarm of bees" – thus I wrote in my diary in September 1976, when my beloved Provost, the Very Reverend John Hughes came to preach on the 25th anniversary of his ordination to the priesthood. These bees in the stonework are still with us, making us sometimes use the Hospital Chapel.

There are no plans for Leicester Market to open on Sundays in the foreseeable future, officials have said.

(newspaper cutting)

3rd September 1996 Tuesday
With money from my retirement 'lump sum' I chose to spend £2,000 on Premium Bonds in 1991.
Over a period of 5 years, this has netted 7 small prizes, mostly @ £50. Year by year, the chances of winning have lengthened, & now the odds are about 17,000 – 1. Now, I have acquired a further £1,000 worth of Bonds, in the hope of winning one of the higher value prizes.

National Savings has announced that an extra £2 million will be distributed in Premium Bond prizes from November, with a greater number of prizes in the £100 to £50,000 range to be won. *(newspaper cutting)*

5th September 1996 Thursday
Mr Ellis, Chief Gas Examiner, who proposed marriage to me in April 1985 & who died 9 months ago after a long illness, has left his second wife Veronica all alone in the world, with little or no support from his children.
I told you in September 1987, when I first met her that I liked her very much. She & I are the same age & have now struck up a bond of friendship.

7th September 1996 Saturday
Holders of the Victoria Cross & George Cross had their £100 per year pension increased last year to £1,300. That figure was based on inflation over the 40 years since it was fixed originally at £100. However, long before that, it was known for the widow of a man who had won a posthumous VC to receive a pension of £100 a year from 'Her Majesty's Civil List'.

9th September 1996 Monday
"Jim Reason & Sharon MacLeod
request the pleasure of the company of Betty
at our marriage on 19th October 1996 at
Oakham Register Office at 1.00 p.m. and afterwards at
Melton Mowbray Working Mens' Club"

Sharon's first marriage to Darren lasted only 2½ years. Darren re-married on 17th August this year, just two months before Sharon.

11th September 1996 Wednesday
Heritage Open Days – London's Open House '96, a celebration of London's architecture, takes place next weekend, 14 & 15 September. Again I tried to book in advance for a guided tour of the Mansion House, (this year tel. 0171 332 3425). And again the same reply, "We are fully booked".
Hardly surprising when there are only 4 tours, 25 persons per tour.

13th September 1996 Friday
In London's Open House '96, highlights include the opening of the recently refurbished Marble Arch, at the north-east corner of Hyde Park. The Marble Arch was erected originally as a grand entrance to Buckingham Palace in 1828 to mark Wellington's victories at Trafalgar & Waterloo. When a large east wing was added to Buckingham Palace, the arch was moved to its present site.

15th September 1996 Sunday
Mary Blue & I had another lovely day in London enjoying its 'Open House '96'. This year we were so pleased to discover the delights of the Barbican Centre, to see inside Guildhall, climb the 311 steps of the Monument, & absorb the atmosphere of the City of London, after a rare glimpse inside Marble Arch. We wanted the buildings to stay open later.

17th September 1996 Tuesday
"Why, by interweaving our destiny with that of any part of Europe, entangle our peace and prosperity in the toils of European ambition, rivalship, interest, humour or caprice?" George Washington (1732 – 1799)
Farewell Address – 17th September 1796.

18th September 1996 Wednesday
Land, John Thomas, late of Hall Farm, Ravenstone, passed peacefully away at the Leicester General Hospital, on September 18th 1996, aged 84 years.
Much loved husband of the late Doris May, devoted father to John, father-in-law to Joyce, loving grandfather to Sarah and David. Funeral service to take place at Ravenstone Church on Thursday September 26th at 10 a.m.

(newspaper cutting)

19th September 1996 Thursday
"Mining Memorial" – Plans to erect a mining memorial in Coalville are gathering momentum with quarry giants ARC offering to donate a three or four tonne piece of Whitwick granite as a base for the statue of a working miner.
It will be a tribute to all those who lost their lives while working in the Leicestershire pits, & is scheduled for unveiling in April 1998.

21st September 1996 Saturday
Tony Blair, leader of the Labour Party since May 1994, has written a book, "New Britain – my vision of a young country". I thought of St. Paul in Athens. (Acts 17 – 21). The latest advertisement now on display & devised by the Tory party, in their attempt to discredit Labour's young dynamic leader Tony Blair, shows him with the red eyes of the devil looking through a torn off strip across his eyes with the slogan, "New Labour, New Danger". It is a sad sign of our times that politicians now stoop to such depths to win votes.

25th September 1996 Wednesday
Leicestershire live on the Internet!
Leicester Mercury launches on to the World Wide Web. Visit the Mercury's new Gateway to Leicestershire.
http://www.leicestermercury.co.uk
Monday 23rd September 1996 marked the official launch of the Gateway to Leicestershire site, developed in conjunction with ICL, De Montfort University & De Montfort Expertise.

27th September 1996 Friday
"On Your Golden Jubilee" – And yet another card from Katherine to Pope John Paul II, ready to be dispatched later in the year. All Saints Day, 1st November, is the Golden Jubilee of his ordination to the priesthood, after years of secret study hidden in the residence of Cracow's Archbishop Sapieha, when Poland was under German domination, & 6 million Jews were killed.

29th September 1996 Sunday
"O everlasting God, who hast ordained & constituted the services of angels & men in a wonderful order ...."

Political correctness does not allow such a thing to be mentioned.
What about women? You can't mention men today unless you add 'and women'.
There are some who object to "Our Father" & say "Our Father & Mother".

Staffordshire: Council officials in Staffordshire have banned the use of the words 'dinner lady', 'workmen' and 'postmen'. The county council has voted to replace dinner ladies with midday supervisors, lollipop ladies with crossing patrol attendants and ban manpower because of its male-dominated image as part of an equal opportunities drive.

(newspaper cutting)

3rd October 1996 Thursday
Kirby, Peter. Passed across the threshold of Eternity on March 19th 1996. A dearly loved brother, brother-in-law and uncle. Funeral details from Co-operative Funeral Services, London Road, Coalville. Donations please to Intensive Therapy Unit, Leicester General Hospital.
Coalville Amateur Operatic Society lost another member of the front of house team in the death of Peter Kirby, shortly after our show "Countess Maritza".

A bachelor in his 50s, with only one brother Michael, he was a lonely soul, whose chief delight was being 'front of house'.

5th October 1996 Saturday

Enid is 69 years old tomorrow. After half a century of smoking cigarettes she cannot chase around like she used to do. She still manages to look after her large garden & cut all the hedges which border the garden on all sides.

7th October 1996 Monday

8th Annual Service of Thanksgiving for All Creatures Great & Small. Katherine (aged 92), Toffee the dog & I attended this service again at St. Andrews, Jarrom Street, Leicester, where the preacher was the Revd. Glynn Richerby, Vicar of St. James the Greater, Leicester. He brought a dove & gave an inspiring sermon on the Holy Spirit 'descending like a dove'.

(See Matthew, Chapter 3: 16 – 17)

9th October 1996 Wednesday

Labour's new dynamic leader, Tony Blair, spoke at this year's Labour conference at Blackpool, like some latter-day prophet.

He offered Britain a five-year contract under which he would lead it into a new age of achievement & end '17 years of Tory hurt'. "Come home to Labour", he said, making 10 vows for his first term of government – he expects to win the next election.

These are Tony Blair's 10 vows: - More of public income to be spent on education, less of public income to go on welfare; more spending on patients, less on NHS bureaucracy; cut long-term unemployment & halve youth unemployment; halve the time it takes young offenders to come to court; contain government borrowing & inflation; keep tax promises; smaller primary schools; devolution for Scotland, Wales & English regions; new constructive relationship with Europe.

13th October 1996 Sunday

"Everything is so big" – So observed Mary Blue last year, while savouring the delights of America.

Now in Las Vegas, the 112-storey monster, like a tall elongated cooling tower of a power station, has been officially opened. It is called the Stratosphere Tower & from the roof level is a 160ft inverse bungee jump (The Big Shot) which shoots victims up 16 storeys in 2.3 seconds.

The Stratosphere Tower is described as a one thousand, one hundred & forty-nine foot concrete syringe. Costing $550 million, i.e. £367 million, it is dubbed "the eighth blunder of the world". It is the brainchild of Bob Stupak who would have liked it to be twice as high. Apart from the bungee jump, it is home to a hotel, three aerial wedding chapels & a roller-coaster.

17th October 1996 Thursday

"Is it nothing to you, all ye that pass by?" (from the Lamentations of Jeremiah, Chapter I : 12)

The Queen unveiled this memorial at Westminster Abbey to the millions of civilians who have suffered & died from the inhumanity of the 20th century.

The Dean wanted a memorial to civilian victims as a counterpoint to the Tomb of the Unknown Warrior.

19th October 1996 Saturday

Sharon, aged 27, today married Jim, aged 43.

It seems but yesterday that Sharon married Darren (15th June 1991). Again it was a wedding with a distinct Scottish flavour. Murdo the 2nd & Murdo the 3rd (now 22 months old) each looked resplendent in their kilts.

Scott, newly engaged to Miranda, was there & also Murdo the first, complete with his 3 wives, Mary Blue being 2nd wife.

21st October 1996 Monday

We meet our teacher of 58 years ago! Whilst delivering meals on wheels at Coleorton, Enid & I encountered Miss Knight, teacher at Snibston County Primary School from 1937 – 1966, & now a lively, vivacious 84 year old. She told us that she kept in touch with numerous old scholars & had already written 60 Christmas cards in readiness for the Christmas season.

23rd October 1996 Wednesday

Heinz '57 varieties' – It was 100 years ago, in October 1896, that Henry John Heinz, owner of a fast-expanding pickled food business, thought up his '57 varieties' advertising slogan & it is still going strong.

My dad likened the fast-expanding Hewes progeny in Ravenstone to this '57 varieties'.

However, Enid & I are the only 2 now left.

25th October 1996 Friday

Gas pipeline go-ahead – Construction began yesterday on the Interconnector gas pipeline that will link Britain with continental Europe. The £460 million project will carry up to 20 billion cubic metres of natural gas a year from the terminal at Bacton, Norfolk, to Zeebrugge. About 8.5 billion cubic metres a year will flow in the opposite direction. Partners in the Interconnector consortium are British Gas, BP, National Power, Elf Aquitaine of France, Russia's Gazprom, Distrigas of Belgium, Ruhrgas of Germany and Amerada Hess of America. (newspaper cutting)

29th October 1996 Tuesday

A Ravenstone man is tracing his ancestors' footsteps for his forthcoming book on his family's history. Miles Wilson has been researching the book – The Hewes: Life and Times of a Leicestershire Family from 1774 – for four years and it will be on sale next year.

(newspaper cutting)

"The Hewes – Life and Times of a Leicestershire Family". As with so many other grandiose schemes, dreamed up by cousin Miles, his book on the Hewes family never reached fruition.

This year he has devoted all his energy into his demanding job as Alumni Officer at the University. He leaves home at 6.30am each day & is in bed by 9pm.

(See 24th March 1997)

31st October 1996 Thursday

"And say not of those who are slain in the Way of Allah, "They are dead". Nay, they are living, though ye perceive it not". (The Koran Sura 2, verse 154).

"Think not of those who are slain in Allah's way as

dead. Nay, they live, finding their sustenance in the presence of their Lord. They rejoice in the bounty provided by Allah". (Sura 3 verse 169).

1st November 1996 Friday
On this day in 1956 Premium Bonds went on sale in Britain for the first time.

2nd November 1996 Saturday
Channel 5 – Britain's new TV channel!
Britain's 5th major terrestrial TV channel will begin broadcasting early next year, alongside BBC1,
BBC2, ITV and Channel 4. Like ITV & Channel 4, Britain's 5th channel will be free to watch. We are notified in advance that "The Retuners are Coming". This is primarily for retuning video recorders & satellite decoders.

4th November 1996 Monday
Savings shortfall – National savings, which holds £57 billion on behalf of 30 million people, has an unexplained shortfall of £50 million, according to a report by the head of the National Audit Office.
(newspaper cutting)
Thirty million people, including me, give a total of £57 billion to the Government's three offices manned by National Savings at Blackpool (Lytham), Durham & Glasgow, and the auditors discover a shortfall of £50 million!
"This is a matter of concern", says the Treasury, the department which oversees National Savings.

6th November 1996 Wednesday
We're off to explore Mars! Three unmanned spacecraft are being launched this month. Aboard America's spacecraft "Pathfinder" is an unmanned roving vehicle, known as "Sojourner", due to land on Mars next summer. It was built at NASA's Jet Propulsion Laboratory (JPL) in California.

7th November 1996 Thursday
The Queen has been pleased to appoint the Right Reverend Jonathan Bailey, Bishop of Derby, to be Clerk of the Closet to Her Majesty in succession to the Right Reverend John Waine, retired. The appointment to date from November 7th, 1996.
(newspaper cutting)

8th November 1996 Friday
This year's "Preacher of the Year" is Father William Anderson, a Roman Catholic priest from Aberdeen. His sermon on humility was based on Psalm 51 : 17.
I thought of St. Augustine who being asked, "What is the first thing in religion?" replied, "Humility". "And what is the second?" "Humility" "And what is the third?" "Humility". (See 13th July 1971)

9th November 1996 Saturday
Tomorrow, in many churches, the famous words of Laurence Binyon will be recited :
They shall not grow old, as we that are left grow old;
Age shall not weary them, nor the years condemn.
At the going down of the sun and in the morning
We will remember them.

10th November 1996 Sunday
Katherine taught English to the young David René James Rothschild who was born in 1942. (See 7th November 1990)
Now, aged 54, David de Rothschild, head of the Paris-based Rothschild & Campagnie Banque, has been appointed by his cousin Sir Evelyn Rothschild as head of the global committee to co-ordinate Rothschild worldwide banking.

12th November 1996 Tuesday
"Ee By Gum, Lord!" by Dr. Arnold Kellett, is a new publication of the Gospels in broad Yorkshire dialect. Dr. Kellett says the robust Yorkshire speech is the equivalent of how the "northerners" of Galilee must have sounded.
According to the Bible Society, the Bible has been published in 349 out of the world's 6,000 languages and the New Testament in 841. This is the first in Yorkshire dialect.
(newspaper cutting)
Pill, Reverend Hugh Godfrey Reginald, dearly loved husband of Peggy, treasured father of Wendy and Diane, much loved grandpa of Danielle and Dominic, sadly missed father-in-law to John and Bob, passed peacefully away in the Leicester General Hospital, on Tuesday November 12th 1996, aged 71 years. Safe in God's hands and forever in our hearts. The funeral service will take place at Hugglescote Parish Church on Wednesday, November 20th at 11.30a.m., prior to cremation at Loughborough Crematorium.

Godfrey Pill, who was ordained as priest on 30th September 1990, when he was aged 65, was shortly afterwards too ill with diabetes to continue his work as a priest. How well I remember his excellent sermons in earlier years when he preached as a lay reader at Ravenstone, especially his masterpiece on 10th December 1989 – the Story of Job.

16th November 1996 Saturday
Leicester Cathedral Newsletter, Issue Number 264, covering August/September 1996, was the last "Newsletter".
Now we have the new Cathedral Quarterly, Volume 1. No. 1. Thankfully we still have interesting news from the Provost (Derek Hole). He is one of only 12 Provosts in England's 42 Cathedrals & now there is talk of sweeping reforms to call them deans.
The Cathedrals of England have never had to be fully accountable for the last 900 years, going back even before the Norman Conquest. But moves are afoot to make each Cathedral have a new 'council' above those involved in the day to day running of the Cathedral. Deans & chapters will then cease to be governed only by ancient cathedral statutes.

Tunnel may be disrupted for months – Channel Tunnel services could be disrupted for months after the train fire on Monday night, which left a scene of devastation in the Folkestone-bound tunnel. (newspaper cutting)

20th November 1996 Wednesday
Tintoretto's "Susannah Bathing", painted in 1555-56 is now in Kunsthistorisches Museum, Vienna. If you

would like to read the story of Susannah, it is contained in "The History of Susannah", which is one of the Books of the Apocrypha.

Only very rarely will you find a Bible which includes the Apocrypha (14 books) inserted between the Books of the Old & New Testament.

Religious book shops sometimes sell "The Apocrypha" on its own.

22nd November 1996 Friday

The National Lottery is as popular today as when it was first launched in November 1994. Each week people are paying out approximately £30 million in the hope of hitting the jackpot. The best chance of winning is by being in a syndicate. My weak effort of £1 per month for 20 months achieved absolutely nothing, so I have stopped buying tickets since my 65th birthday.

24th November 1996 Sunday

Narcissus fell in love with himself when he saw his beautiful reflection in a clear fountain, with water like silver. In vain he tried to embrace this lovely creature, until he pined away & lost his colour, his vigour, & the beauty which once charmed the love-lorn wood nymph, Echo. And so he died.

His last words were, "Alas! Alas!", & Echo, who stayed ever near him, replied, "Alas!"

The Queen yesterday issued a royal warrant removing the name of Diana, Princess of Wales, from the prayers for the Royal Family in Church of England services. The Queen is Supreme Governor of the Church.

(newspaper cutting)

26th November 1996 Tuesday

"Welcome to your Alumni Association – I would like to say a very warm welcome to you all from the De Montfort University Alumni Association & introduce both myself & our latest publication "In Touch".

So writes cousin Miles in the first edition of the new magazine, 'Autumn – Winter 1996', replacing the former "Network" magazine, & now included in the University's business magazine.

Cousin Miles introduces himself as Alumni Officer thus, *"I started at the university in February of this year after a varied career in broadcasting, promotions & public relations.*

I feel that I have joined De Montfort University at an exciting time with plenty of changes taking place in the Alumni Association Office ... Don't forget the Fourth Annual Alumni Re-union, 3rd October 1997".

30th November 1996 Saturday

H.M.S.O. Her Majesty's Stationery Office was a stationery office par excellence. How I loved perusing the H.M.S.O. catalogues. Everything a government office ever needed, from the Prime Minister down to the humblest messenger. Who but H.M.S.O. knew exactly which desk size distinguished a deputy from an under-secretary, & who else had such distinctive crested paper? (See 1st December 1995 and 1997)

2nd December 1996 Monday

Chancellor Kenneth Clarke reminded me of Nathan Rothschild (1777-1836) with his short & stocky frame & huge girth, as he presented this year's budget. He looked just like Nathan, standing in profile, as he told us that cigarettes would go up in price (20 Players up from £3.08p to £3.23p), car tax would go up from £140 to £145, & basic rate tax would be cut by 1p to 23p.

There was never anyone quite like Nathan Rothschild. He was the brains behind the family fortunes. He had a prodigious memory & not only did he help to regulate the English exchange rate day by day, but he could keep in mind the fluctuating rates throughout Europe & their relations to one another.

"Who is that?" people asked. "The King of the Jews," was the reply, or "The Jew of the Kings."

Next week the Archbishop of Canterbury will be in Rome to visit Pope John Paul II.

They will pray together in the church from which St. Augustine, the first Archbishop of Canterbury, set out on his mission to make the Angles angels! (newspaper cutting)

4th December 1996 Wednesday

"Waste paper collections" – Letter from North West Leicestershire District Council, Environmental Health Department, "We are pleased to inform you that you will soon be able to recycle all your old newspapers & magazines with a new Household Collection Scheme. This service will be provided by Cheshire Recycling Ltd. .... Thank you for your support in this initiative."

6th December 1996 Friday

Veronica (widow of Mr Ellis, former Chief Gas Examiner) met me off the train at Market Harborough, & took me in her car to Clipston Churchyard to show me the little plaque in the garden of remembrance in memory of Mr Ellis, which she attends with fresh flowers every week.

Then to the Bulls Head, Clipston, for an excellent lunch, & finally back to the station for the 4 p.m. train.

8th December 1996 Sunday

One year later & what happened to the first wedding anniversary of Raquel & Curly in Britain's top soap opera, 'Coronation Street'?

Answer: - "Raquel, like star landlady Bet (see 16th October 1995) has chosen to retire from her role & seek pastures new. According to the storyline Raquel, played by Sarah Lancashire, has developed her career as a beauty therapist & accepted a job in Kuala Lumpur.

12th December 1996 Thursday

Society for the Blind – A thank you evening at the Marlene Reid Centre, Coalville.

David Scott, himself blind, who is head of Sound Services for the "Talking Newspaper", based in Leicester & covering the whole county, came to Coalville with a few colleagues to meet us on our home territory & chat informally to us.

I am in Team C, with Derek Palmer, Mrs Joan Elliott & Mrs Betty Middleton.

14th December 1996 Saturday

Centenarian helps out –Ravenstone Parish Church is holding its annual Christmas Fair on Saturday this week at 2.30pm. The event will be opened by Mr Harrison, Ravenstone's only 100-year-old resident.(newspaper cutting)

Mr Douglas Clement Harrison, who was born on 26th November 1896, lives with his daughter-in-law, the former Jean Carter.
He has outlived his 3 sons, but has eight grandchildren, 16 great-grandchildren & 15 great-great-grandchildren. He opened our Christmas Fair, where I once again helped with the raffle (since 1992).

16th December 1996 Monday

"Next Steps" – Improving Management in Government, was instigated in 1988 by Robin Ibbs. Subsequent to this came "The 1995 Next Steps Review", published at the beginning of this year, which shows clearly that "Management in Government" is improving. The majority of 'agencies' dealing with the executive functions of Government are a success. One definite failure has been the Child Support Agency.
The Child Support Agency (CSA) was in trouble right from the beginning. The idea was for the father of every baby born to contribute towards its upkeep. With so many unmarried mothers & second families, some fathers were driven to despair & committed suicide. It was impossible to track down many fathers, but some were pursued relentlessly, sometimes erroneously.

CSA pays £100 to innocent fathers.

Men claim their lives have been ruined by receiving a maintenance inquiry form identifying them as the father of a stranger's child. Mr Mitchell said the £100 was compensation for "upset and inconvenience."

A part-time independent complaints examiner will be appointed at an annual cost of £1 million to cope with the 32,000 parents a year aggrieved by the agency's performance. (newspaper cuttings)

20th December 1996 Friday

From my love by post, a Christmas Card "For the One I Love", containing a £20 note.
"Christmas is a season of warm remembrance."
"There are many things that make the season something very special, but it's your love that makes it wonderful for me. Happy Christmas with all my love."
Merry Christmas darling. All my love for ever.
John xxxx xx

22nd December 1996 Sunday

How I enjoyed the Royal Institution Annual Christmas Lecture to Young People, given by Professor Carl Sagan in January 1978.
How sad to read that he has now died from a bone marrow disease, myelodysplasia. He died on Friday 20th December 1996.

(See January 1978)

Seattle: Carl Sagan, 62, the Pulitzer Prize-winning astronomer and storyteller who extolled the grandeur and mystery of the universe in lectures, books and on television, has died of pneumonia at a cancer research centre in Seattle. He had been suffering from preleukaemia syndrome, a bone marrow disease.

(newspaper cutting)

24th December 1996 Tuesday

When baby Declan was born last December, it was the first time I had heard the name. Now I learn that St. Declan was one of those early Celtic saints who established a church & monastry at Ardmore, on the coast of County Waterford, & became its first bishop.

26th December 1996 Thursday

Bunting & I are again together for Christmas. This evening we were at Glenholm with Miles, Gwen & Isobel, where Miles, in his role as Alumni Officer at De Montfort University, was able to show us a most interesting video taken last July of the mass graduation ceremony at Buckingham Palace, when 8 universities conferred honours on Nelson Mandela.

Lady Helen Taylor, daughter of the Duke and Duchess of Kent, gave birth to a son on Boxing Day, St James's Palace announced. The boy, who is 26th in succession, has been named Cassius Edward. (see12th August 1994)
(newspaper cutting)

29th December 1996 Sunday

Almighty God, who hast given us thy only-begotten Son to take our nature upon him, and as at this time to be born of a pure Virgin; Grant that we being regenerate, and made thy children by adoption and grace, may daily be renewed by thy Holy Spirit; through the same our Lord Jesus Christ, who liveth and reigneth with thee and the same Spirit, ever one God, world without end. Amen.

At Ravenstone Church on the first Sunday after Christmas, the Collect for the day was fully expounded. The Son of God became the Son of Man, that the sons of men might become the sons of God. As man was created first in the form of flesh & blood, now, through Christ we are all regenerated into flesh & Spirit.

30th December 1996 Monday

Next year marks the 1,400th anniversary of the death of St. Columba on Iona & the arrival of St. Augustine at Canterbury.
Earlier this year at Newcastle-upon-Tyne, two mail trains were re-named St. Columba & St. Augustine. Christianity was brought to Britain in a two-pronged attack from north & south.

* * *

Not to be outdone by Virginia Bottomely and the Millennium Commission, far-sighted party organisers are laying their own foundations for New Year's Eve 1999. The Albert Hall has been booked since 1975, the Savoy has enough bookings to fill it twice over, and revellers are already beginning to stake their place in Claridge's. Madame Tussaud's and the QE2 are taken, and an order for 5,000 bottles of vintage champagne has fuelled rumours that stocks could run out.

(newspaper cutting)

Aids deaths totalled 1.5 million in 1996. (World Health Organisation)   (newspaper cutting)

Commercialism has turned Mothering Sunday into Mother's Day. The culprit was an unwitting American.
(newspaper cutting)

The 4th Sunday in Lent is Mothering Sunday

The origins of Mothering Sunday are obscure, but by the Middle Ages it was the day on which the daughter churches honoured the Mother Church and visited it in procession with banners, an honour transferred after the Reformation to the mother of the family.

By the 17th century Mothering Sunday had evolved into a holiday for young people in domestic service to return home to see their mothers, bearing spring flowers picked on their way, & to visit the church where they were baptised.

Mothering Sunday has also been called Wafering Sunday, & Furmety or Frumenty Sunday. These names refer to the wafer cakes offered to mothers & a cross between a soup & a pudding of hulled wheat, milk & cinnamon which should not, according to custom, be eaten until some wise saying has been uttered, preferably a proverb of King Solomon.

Today's celebrations, the gaudy gifts & tasteless trinkets, are largely the responsibility of Anna Jarvis, a deeply religious woman whose devotion to her mother spawned more than even she intended.

In 1907 she founded the American Mother's Day Movement, suggesting that those with mothers alive should wear pink carnations & those whose mothers were dead should wear white ones.

This led to wild price fluctuations, first in flowers & then in novelty gifts. When she raised her voice against the increasing commercialisation of the day, she was drowned out by the salesmen.

* * *

1997

2nd January 1997 Thursday
Poor Bunting, who for the 5th consecutive year has spent Christmas & New Year with me at Ravenstone, again dreads returning to the solitude of her home in Stafford. As before, she blossomed into her old familiar self while recalling the early years of her life; but sadly her memory of recent events is so very poor, that she feels lost in today's world.

4th January 1997 Saturday
In 1967, we celebrated the 40th anniversary of the re-hallowing of our Diocese & Cathedral. Now it is the 70th anniversary & also the 1,600th anniversary of the death of St. Martin.

6th January 1997 Monday
The Reverend Kerry Emmett, who was inducted as Rector of Ravenstone in May 1989, has now taken on the extra mantle of Rural Dean, 'a clergyman who, under the Bishop, has the special care & inspection of the clergy in certain parishes', in this case Akeley South, one of 13 deaneries in the Diocese of Leicester. (See 25th February 1992)
The present Bishop of Leicester is the Rt. Revd. Dr. Thomas Butler.

Hardy, Horace, of Ravenstone, passed peacefully away on January 7th, 1997, aged 75 years.
(See 13th August 1995)

8th January 1997 Wednesday
British Gas decided that the best way to survive was to split itself into 2 parts. The first is British Gas Energy (BGE) covering its gas supply business, selling gas to families & businesses; plus its service business; plus the lucrative Morecambe gas fields; plus its troublesome 'take or pay contracts'. The second is Transco International, the pipeline system & overseas work.
Transco International is worth a lot more than British Gas Energy, having at its core ownership of Britain's £18 billion gas pipeline system, & expects to earn profits of around £700 million a year from fees from 'shippers' (all the different suppliers of gas, including British Gas Energy).
It should go from strength to strength even though B.G.E. may well sink.

12th January 1997 Sunday
Highgrove House in Gloucestershire is the country home of Charles, Prince of Wales, where Camilla Parker Bowles now stays three or four times a week & runs the domestic side of the house. She & the Prince are very discreet in their relationship & are not photographed together.

Camilla gets own bedroom – *Prince Charles has allocated a bedroom at his country home to mistress Camilla Parker Bowles and ordered staff to address her as "m'lady", it was claimed today.*
(newspaper cutting)

14th January 1997 Tuesday
Donald Wesson, 9 Swannington Road, Ravenstone, is now on the list of people receiving 'Meals on Wheels'. Enid & I were the first to visit him with a hot meal & were shocked to find anyone living in such squalor. As soon as he opened the door the stench met you. He himself looked gaunt & haggard, alone & unloved in this world. Long ago, he & I were children together at Snibston School.

Wesson, Donald, late of Ravenstone, dearly loved brother of Elsie and brother-in-law to Geoff and much loved uncle of Paul and Lynne, passed away peacefully in Glenfield General Hospital on September 3rd 1997, aged 66 years.
(newspaper cutting)

16th January 1997 Thursday
Prize from ERNIE! Bond No. 14HN 331722.
Dear Bondholder, Congratulations, one of your Premium Bonds has won a prize ..... Yours Sincerely, Dan Monaghan, Director of Operations.
"Pay Miss E Hewes One Hundred Pounds Only."
A welcome win for the new year – the last time I won £100 was in 1992. My latest £1,000 worth of bonds have not yet won anything.

18th January 1997 Saturday
"Civil Service Retirement Fellowship" this month, exactly as last year (see 27th January) was a belated Christmas Party, held at the home of Jack & Muriel Harding, 103, Castle Rock Drive, Coalville. Again we all took something in the way of refreshments, plus a wrapped gift. My 'Sultana Loaf Cake' sliced & buttered, looked good & went down well.

20th January 1997 Monday
"Carousel", which we last performed in 1966, is this year's choice again for Coalville Amateurs. I was pleased to be asked once more to join the old regulars assembled at Peter Jacques' house for ticket allocation. Vincent Hardy, the oldest of the 'oldies', has now been a member of the Society for a record 60 years! Enid this year reaches her 50th year with the Society.

22nd January 1997 Wednesday
The lovely old Royal Yacht Britannia, launched by the Queen in 1953, is now at the start of her 7- month swansong voyage, calling at Malta, Egypt, Yemen, the United Arab Emirates, Pakistan, India, Thailand, Malaysia, Japan & South Korea, before arriving in Hong Kong on 23rd June, ready for Britain's handing over Hong Kong to the Chinese.
Farewell Britannia – The Royal Yacht Britannia embarks on her last voyage today. Her final duty will be to preside over the closing of another chapter in the history of the British Empire – the handing over of Hong Kong to China.
(newspaper cutting)

24th January 1997 Friday
Digital Television! (computerised form of transmitting signals & messages, rather than simply by means of radio waves). We are now being prepared for digital technology which will bring a vast expansion of choice

for television viewers, & which hopefully will be introduced next year. Going digital is the most important development for television since the introduction of colour, we are told.

Digital technology will give the viewer the choice of 200 or so film, entertainment, sport and speciality channels and will eventually make interactive services such as video-on-demand and home banking possible.

In three years, you'll be thinking to yourself – "What was analogue television?" (newspaper cutting)

26th January 1997 Sunday

Gas competition delayed – One-and-a-half million gas customers face a longer wait before they can shop around for their gas supplies. The delayed extension of gas competition, announced yesterday by Ofgas, was made to give British Gas more time to adapt its systems. Dorset and the old county of Avon will get competitive supplies in household gas from February 10th, while Kent and East and West Sussex should benefit after March 7th. The two dates are about a month later than anticipated. (newspaper cutting)

Belfast landmark: Belfast celebrates the opening of the Waterfront Hall, a new £32 million concert venue that has transformed the city. (newspaper cutting)

28th January 1997 Tuesday

"Mountain Landscape". On Cocky's 67th birthday I paid £75 for a beautiful picture 24″ x 20″, which I saw in a shop in Coalville & which now has pride of place in my elegant front room, refurbished 15 months ago.

For more than a year I have been looking for a suitable picture & now the room is complete, just as the middle room has "Morning Glory", bought for my 50th birthday.

Captain Mark Phillips, the former husband of the Princess Royal, is to marry Sandy Pflueger, a former member of the US equestrian team, in Hawaii this weekend. (newspaper cutting)

30th January 1997 Thursday

Ravenstone Church was closed again last Sunday because the heating system had failed; & once more we had 'Songs of Praise' in the dear little 'Hospital Chapel'. The little Chapel was filled to overflowing with members of two recently bereaved families swelling the numbers. As on 18th December 1988 I literally saw myriads of angels coming to earth, so again I saw 'angels descending' as we sang 'Blessed assurance.'

Happy birthday: Nearly everyone in a packed Wigmore Hall stayed to the end of a six-hour musical marathon to celebrate the 200th anniversary of the birth of Franz Schubert. (newspaper cutting)

1st February 1997 Saturday

Gamble, Hilda May, formerly of Albion Street, South Wigston, passed peacefully away on January 22nd, aged 99 years. Will be sadly missed by her family and friends. Funeral service and cremation at Loughborough Crematorium on Friday, January 31st at 10.45am. All inquiries Gilliver's Funeral Directors.

Gamble, Hilda May, late of 31B, Preston Drive, Newbold Verdon, Leics., formerly of 3, Albion Street, Sth Wigston, Leicester. Retired Corsetiere, who died on January 22nd 1997. All particulars to Harvey Ingram Owston, 20 New Walk, Leicester LE1 6TX. (Ref: B/AJC) before June 6th 1997. Executors: Mrs Jean Elizabeth Rootham, Mr Leslie Rootham.

Yesterday we attended the funeral of Hilda (née Moore), sister of Auntie Doris who died in July 1993. A lovely service with no hymns but deeply reverent, including time for meditation to organ music, and moving quotations from the scriptures and from 'Pilgrim's Progress' which the vicar knew by heart.

"Fear not; I am the first & the last; I am he that liveth & was dead; & behold, I am alive for evermore, Amen; & have the keys of hell & of death. Write the things which thou hast seen & the things which are & the things which shall be hereafter" Revelation I, 17-19.

As the sun streamed down from the high window on to me at Hilda's funeral service, I felt caught up in heaven's glory.

"The Lord make his face shine upon thee, & be gracious unto thee; the Lord lift up his countenance upon thee, & give thee peace" Numbers 6: 25-26.

And so we said farewell to Hilda; & all gathered then at the home of her grand-daughter Maureen, at Barn Farm, Odstone. It was nice to see Hilda's daughter Pat (aged 64) and her lovely family, Maureen, Richard & David & partners.

As we left Barn Farm, Odstone, home of Mr & Mrs Sam Brown & sons Ben & Joshua, we said goodbye to Sam & Maureen, Richard & Karen, David & Nickie; and then Ken Stocks (see 6th September 1995) took me to Hugglescote churchyard to show me the family grave of Uncle Sketch and Auntie Patty, incorporating Auntie Doris, her daughter Maureen and next her sister Hilda.

David Sketchley Moore & his wife Martha Hannah, parents of Doris & Hilda, kept a farm in Dennis Street, Hugglescote. This was "Uncle Sketch" (he and my grand-dad Tom Sketchley were cousins) who let Hugglescote Church have one of his fields as a burial ground, reserving for himself at the same time the choicest burial plot, & here they all now lie, safely gathered in.

Lord Lloyd-Webber – The life barony conferred upon Sir Andrew Lloyd Webber has been gazetted by the name, style and title of Baron Lloyd-Webber, of Sydmonton, in the County of Hampshire.
(newspaper cutting)

11th February 1997 Tuesday

Ecolabel, a green & blue flowerlike symbol, has been introduced to help consumers choose products which are less harmful to the environment. If a product has this label you know that it meets the European Union Environmental Award criteria.

13th February 1997 Ash Wednesday

The Millennium Bug, which is likely to cause chaos in the computer world, is the result of a space-saving measure used by programmers to indicate the year on early computer systems. They substituted two digits for four, as a result of which the computer assumes that all *dates refer to the 20th century. 00 will mean 1900.*

Three examples of millennium mayhem ....
To celebrate the new year, a man from Leicester rings his friend in New York at midnight. It's still 1999 in America so the computer will register a call from 00 to 99 – therefore the man from Leicester will be asked to pay for a 99-year-long telephone call.
Computers that calculate age will record that most people have yet to be born. For instance if I was born in 1971, it will subtract 71 from 00 and discover that I am minus 71, instead of 25 years old.
People who collect benefits based on age could be in for a pleasant or a nasty surprise depending on whether the mistake is in their favour.

The problem has arisen because computer systems typically store dates as YYMMDD.

Users should also beware February 29th 2000 meltdown: years divisible by 100 are not leap years whereas those divisible by 400 are. Does the computer know this?

(newspaper cuttings)

14th February 1997 Friday
"Valentine's Day is a day set apart for thinking of those who are dear to your heart,
Those who are special & wonderful too, so of course its a day for remembering you.
Happy Valentine's Day.
You will always be my Valentine.
All my love, guess who? xxxxxxxx

17th february 1997 Monday
"Bishops Reflections in Lent" – During Lent we again have a series of talks at Leicester Cathedral. Leicester's Assistant Bishop William Down, who has travelled the world in his work with 'Missions to Seamen', gave a resume of the Anglican Church worldwide. Although the Church is on the decline in this country, in such places as Africa the Church is growing.

19th February 1997 Wednesday
The Year of the Ox - February 7th this year marked the start of the Chinese New Year.
The 12-year cycle is – Tiger, Rabbit, Dragon, Snake, Horse, Sheep, Monkey, Chicken, Dog, Pig, Rat, Ox. In Leicester we have a Chinese community of 3,500.

On this day in 1897 – The Women's Institute was founded at Stoney Creek, Ontario, by a Mrs Hoodless.

21st February 1997 Friday
Flying Bishops! The Church of England now has a third 'Flying Bishop', appointed to minister to opponents of women priests. The Right Revd. Edwin Barnes has become the Bishop Suffragan of Richborough. Recently he was invited to preach at St. Salvador's Church in Dundee, but the Bishop of Edinburgh said, "We want no flying Bishops here in Scotland."

23rd February 1997 Sunday
"Bishops Reflections in Lent" – The Right Revd. Dr. Thomas Butler spoke to us about 'Morals for a New Millennium'.
As we sail into uncharted waters in a rapidly changing world, who is our neighbour? 'Thou shalt love thy neighbour as thyself'. No longer the old steadfast rural community, we must consider not only our worldwide fellow men, but future generations – so I thought of you.

Lord-Lieutenant for Rutland – Air Chief Marshal Sir Thomas (Jock) Kennedy to be Lord-Lieutenant for Rutland on the formation of that county on April 1st.

(newspaper cutting)

25th February 1997 Tuesday
Privatisation of British Rail did eventually solve the problem of the London, Tilbury & Southend Line (LTS) known as the 'misery line'. The £54 million a year passenger franchise was awarded to Prism Rail for 15 years. Prism was founded in 1994 by eleven bus managers who at one time worked for the state-owned National Bus Company until they were privatised. They hope to have a fleet of new trains.

President Weizman of Israel yesterday ruled out any possibility of pardoning Mordechai Vanunu, saying the former nuclear technician was a spy who had damaged his country's security.

(newspaper cutting)

27th February 1997 Thursday
From the Royal Docks in east London to Tilbury in Essex on the north bank of the Thames, & from Greenwich via Ebbsfleet to Sheerness on the south bank, has long been the worst part of London's landscape – a place where London placed its power stations, dumped its rubbish & sited its grimy industries. But the new Thames Gateway Initiative plans to change all that.

46% of pensioners rely solely on the State Pension (currently £61.15 for a single person)

(newspaper cutting)

1st March 1997 Saturday
Department of Social Security – Benefits Agency – About the general increases in benefits.
"This is to tell you that from 7th April 1997 the amount of your benefit will go up to £73.09p a week.
Basic Pension £62.45p. Additional Pension £44.10p, less Contracted-Out deductions £35.08p, plus Graduated Pension £1.62p."
Total increase of approx. £9 per month.

2nd March 1997 Sunday
"Bishops Reflections in Lent" – Leicester's Assistant Bishop, William Down reflected on 'Church Unity'. He gave us a consolidated history of Christianity & spoke of Christ's last great prayer, "Holy Father, keep through thine own name those whom thou hast given me, that they mat be one, as we are." (John 17 : 11)
We, however, are anything but one. From the very beginning we have agreed to differ.

6th March 1997 Thursday
"Carousel", which we gave in 1966, is again Coalville Amateurs' chosen production for this year & once more I am caught up in the magic of the production, albeit a minor 'Front of House' role. Mick Hunt, the new House

655

Manager, & his Assistant Margaret Tyler, are very well organised and we each have a rota of duties alternating between 'Steward', 'Programme Seller' and various others.

Gas: One in eight gas customers in Kent and Sussex have contracted to switch their supplier away from British Gas before competition officially starts today.

(newspaper cutting)

8th March 1997 Saturday

Joanne yesterday celebrated her 23rd birthday, still happily ensconced in her love nest with Glenn & their lively 2½ year old son Dale. Joanne is now 4 months pregnant again; & being on a tight financial rein is moving house this weekend. The rent on her Coalville house (owned by the Council) is rather high, so they are moving in for a while with Glenn's father at Swannington.

10th March 1997 Monday

"Bishops Reflections in Lent" – The Rt. Revd. Dr. Thomas Butler, Bishop of Leicester since August 1991, & recently appointed Member of the House of Lords, spoke to us about 'The Church & the Establishment' giving us a first hand account of how a Bishop in the Church of England is appointed via the Prime Minister & the monarch. He told us of his own experiences moving in such elevated circles.

12th March 1997 Wednesday

As in September 1992, cousin Miles had immersed himself so fully in his mother's family history that his wife Sarah packed her bags & left him, so now his lady-love Gwen, who has co-habited with him for the last 4 years, has likewise packed her bags & left him, after suffering similar neglect as cousin Miles immersed himself in his father's family history & in his full time job.

*EU Transport ministers, meeting in Brussels on Tuesday, agreed to extend the European **summertime** directive until the year 2001.*

(newspaper cutting)

14th March 1997 Friday

"Carousel" has proved to be a resounding success & a lovely 'finale' for cousin Enid now ending her front of house duties after 50 years with Coalville Amateurs.

A week of birdsong & spring sunshine by day & the joy of the theatre by night made even our President Roy Hunt wax lyrical. He composed his closing speech, thanking everyone involved, entirely in rhyme.

16th March 1997 Sunday

Four British marriages in seven end in divorce, compared with an EU average of one in three.

(newspaper cutting)

What a sad state of affairs when 4 in 7 British marriages now end in divorce. This figure has escalated over recent years. It was exactly 12 years ago today, on March 16th 1985, that I told you 'according to figures just published, one in four marriages today are ending on the rocks." When I was a child it was almost unknown to contemplate divorce.

18th March 1997 Tuesday

"Bishops Reflections in Lent" – The Rt. Revd. Dr. Thomas Butler, Bishop of Leicester, chose for his final reflection in Lent the Holy places connected with the Church. He spoke of the awesome wonder of our great Cathedrals, especially when you are in such a place all alone. The high altar, being the holiest of holy places, he loved to see all the people walking up to receive Holy Communion.

20th March 1997 Thursday

London Open House, West Hill House, 6 Swains Lane, London N6 6QU

Dear Open House Participant ..... This year London Open House will be held on the weekend 20th & 21st September. .... If you subscribe to the Open House Broadsheet, you will automatically receive an Open House '97 Directory in August. As a subscriber to Open House Broadsheet, you will have preferential booking rights & will receice advance information of buildings which require pre-booking.

(See 11th September 1996)

22nd March 1997 Saturday

Elizabeth Hewes – No. 811 013 027 0 012 has received her 5th Council Tax Demand Notice, with 25% discount. Each year it goes up, starting in 1993 at £250, it is now £350. An accompanying letter explains why North West Leicestershire District Council has to ask for more money – Grant from the Government is down, so 'our local residents have to pay more, as Government pays less."

24th March 1997 Monday

Self-assessment starts in earnest in April, when the first new-style tax returns for 1996-97 go out to nine million people who are either self-employed or who have income that has not yet been taxed. (newspaper cutting)

"You will not be liable for UK tax if you can convince the Inland Revenue that you are not ordinarily resident" Guess who comes into this category? Cousin Miles! He now boasts an Irish passport. Having abandoned his interest in the 'Hewes' family tree, he has concentrated his efforts on his father's ancestry & hey presto! He is now Miles Wilson from Ireland.

26th March 1997 Wednesday

TESSAs – Tax Exempt Savings Accounts, were introduced a few years ago to encourage the nation to save. You can put up to £9,000 in a Tessa over 5 years & receive the income from your investment tax free if you leave the money untouched for 5 years. You deposit £3,000 in the first year, £1,800 in the second, third & fourth, leaving £600 for the fifth year.

On Tuesday EU foreign ministers gathered in Rome to celebrate the 40th anniversary of the signing of the Treaty of Rome.

(newspaper cutting)

28th March 1997 Good Friday

Tomorrow I shall be 24,000 days old, & to mark this

occasion there is a comet in the heavens at present, which we can actually see (not like Comet Komoutek, heralded as the biggest & brightest comet ever recorded in 1973, which came & went unseen, as did also Halley's Comet in 1986).

However Hale-Bopp Comet, here for another month, is doing its best to outshine the stars.

It is believed that the comet last appeared in the solar system about 4,000 years ago before being 'discovered' by Alan Hale and Thomas Bopp in 1985.

(newspaper cutting)

30th March 1997 Easter Sunday

♥ **Cocky & Joan today celebrate their Ruby Wedding Anniversary** ♥

Channel 5 begins broadcasting.   *(newspaper cutting)*

1st April 1997 Tuesday
Rutland County – Mum & I visited Oakham, in Rutland at the end of March 1974, when under Local Government reorganisation, the dear little County of Rutland lost its proud status as a County in its own right & became Rutland District Council, as part of Leicestershire. How lovely today that both Rutland County Council & the proud City of Leicester have regained their independence.

2nd April 1997 Wednesday
City Cash Crisis – On 1st April 1974, we saw the proud City of Leicester & the County of Rutland swallowed up in one overall County of Leicester. Now, with effect from 1st April 1997, they have regained 'unitary' status. However, the Government has the whip hand & is allowing Leicester City £261 million when it needs £278 million.

Leicester City Cash Crisis amounts to £17 million. Drastic action is proposed.

Closing one home for the elderly = £500,000. Close St. Margaret's Baths. Close some community education centres. Close some hostels for the homeless. All this results in job losses for many people, who in turn threaten strike action. One option is to raise money through more taxation, but that is another problem.

7th April 1997 Monday
Cousin Miles has reaped the reward of his commitment to his job as Alumni Officer.

With effect from 1st April this year he transferred from 'External Relations' in the university's 'Portland Building' to the 'Development Office' in the university's 'Gateway House', into a newly created Development & Alumni Services Office, where, as a founder member, he can spread his wings even farther.

Delayed National is a grand success *– Twenty thousand punters allowed into Aintree without paying cheered as Lord Gyllene, ridden by Tony Dobbin, a Roman Catholic from Northern Ireland, won the 150th Grand National by 25 lengths. The race had been abandoned after IRA two bomb scares on Saturday.*

(newspaper cutting)

9th April 1997 Wednesday
The Oriana is now bringing the last British expatriate civil servants & their families to Britain from Hong Kong, prior to its handover to China at the end of June this year. Those on board this luxury liner are enjoying a perk from Empire days under which Her Majesty's Overseas Civil Service could return to Britain by sea when their assignment overseas ended.

11th April 1997 Friday
"Coalville Town Centre: Environmental Improvements" – Phase one of Coalville's improvement programme, funded by the Government's Single Regeneration Budget, is now completed – traffic calming measures in Ashby Road at 3 junctions: Ravenstone Road, Snibston Discovery Park & the civic amenity site; plus improvements in that area. The second phase, later this year, will improve Belvoir Road.

13th April 1997 Sunday
http://www.royal.gov.uk The Queen has now joined the Internet. Access to the royal web site gives 35 million subscribers worldwide 150 pages on the British monarchy, including a history of royal palaces, an explanation of the Queen's role in the British constitution, royal finances, forthcoming royal engagements & biographies of members of the Royal Family.

15th April 1997 Tuesday
Ffyona Campbell began her walk round the world aged 16 in 1983 and finished eleven years later, aged 27, in 1994. She walked 19,586 miles. She is the 4th person to complete the trip, but she is the first woman. She started at John o' Groats & finished at John o' Groats.

As you can see, there was much of the world, notably Asia, which she never touched.

The world has a circumference of 24,902 miles, so there is still a long way to go. But with so much of the surface covered by water, it is not so easy to walk round the world.

Saint Etheria (or Egeria) is the patron saint of walkers. She walked from the western shores of Europe to the Holy Land in the 4th century A.D. using the Bible as her only form of map.

17th April 1997 Thursday
Cousin Miles & his lady-love Gwen parted company on 6th March, i.e. 6 weeks ago.

In no time at all he had a new lady-love, Michelle, who seems to be a perfect match for him.

He, like Hiawatha, a youth with flaunting feathers, is now happy to follow in her wake, as she whisks him away to Paradise. Already they are engaged to be married & their Wedding Day is 2nd May.

19th April 1997 Saturday
Lesley Hale is now 70 years old – she was born on 10th February 1927. She is one of three local historians writing a book called 'Banded Together' about the Whitwick Colliery Disaster 1898.

Lesley Hale *is an active member of many local organisations and makes a significant contribution to the activities of the Whitwick Historical Group and the*

Swannington Heritage Trust. She acts as the chief researcher to the award winning publication 'Swannington Now and Then' and this is her first book. Miss Hale is the daughter of Lord Hale of Oldham and Dorothy Latham of Measham. Born in 1927 she was educated at Snibston and Griffydam primary schools and Loughborough High School and read law at the University of Birmingham before practising as a solicitor. She returned to Leicestershire in 1987 and took up residence in her grandparent's house, The Grove, Swannington. (newspaper cutting)

21st April 1997 Monday

The 17th London Marathon this year was most exciting as it was such a close-run thing. In the women's race, Liz McColgan of Great Britain came second to Joyce Chepchumba of Kenya, running almost side by side & beaten by one second. In the men's race likewise, only two seconds separated the winner, Antonio Pinto of Portugal & Stefano Baldini of Italy.

23rd April 1997 Wednesday

Computer takes cheque and game – World chess champion Garry Kasparov, the 34 year-old Russian Grandmaster, was devastated when he was beaten by 'Deep Blue' the IBM supercomputer. The machine, which can calculate 200 million positions a second, is the first computer to triumph over a reigning world champion in a classical chess match. The team of computer scientists & a grandmaster consultant collected the winner's prize of £435,000.

25th April 1997 Friday

How lovely to meet up again with my former workmate Reevsie, now the proud grandmother of baby Oliver, born 28th November last year.

We had lunch together at Fenwick's in Leicester, & as in July 1991, she brought me up to date on all her family news. A family rift has now alienated her from her twin sisters, but she is looking forward to retirement, having worked up until now.

27th April 1997 Sunday

Katherine's birthday yesterday – now aged 93, she is still an avid reader, with memories of 20 years spent in India as crystal clear as ever.

She loaned me her latest library book 'The Maharajahs' (see 26th April 1988) which gave me a much better understanding of the history of India than I had before, through the magnificent era of the Mogul Empire, up to & beyond "British India".

Babur, the first Mogul ruler in India, was a descendant of Genghis Khan. He swept away the Afghan overlords of northern India in 1526, occupied Delhi & Agra & began to build the Mogul Empire which flourished for two centuries. It was Shah Jehan, the 5th Mogul Emperor, who built the Taj Mahal as a tomb for his wife who died in childbirth. It was fully completed in 1653.

When the Mogul Empire disintegrated in the early 1700s, the British had begun to trade with India & gradually gained a foothold, signing treaties with various princes until they became the new masters, exerting their power & influence; until in 1857 the people mutinied. After much death & destruction, calm was restored by a Royal proclamation, & the Maharajahs thrived.

3rd May 1997 Saturday

"Is this a blue moon?"

No! This is Neptune as revealed by the Hubble space telescope.

Like Jupiter, Saturn & Uranus, it is a gas planet. Methane gas & red light make it blue.

(See 26th August 1989)

While the Earth's weather is driven by the condensation and evaporation of water, on Jupiter there are three chemicals, phosphine, water vapour and ammonia, which can evaporate and condense, making for a much more complex climate.

(newspaper cutting)

5th May 1997 Monday

Remember Pioneer 10 - the spacecraft launched on 2nd March 1972, arriving at Jupiter in December 1973 (see 2nd December 1973), which left 'the solar system' in June 1983 to travel possibly for ever among the stars? (see 12th & 14th June 1983)

Well, it is still in touch nearly 7 billion miles away and it takes 9 hours for the signals to reach Earth. It is now 66 astronomical units from Earth (one AU is the distance between Earth & Sun), but it is still in our solar system.

Pioneer 10 has taught us that our solar system reaches further than we imagined in 1983. As the spacecraft gets further & further from the Sun, there must eventually come a point when radiation from outside will exceed that from the Sun, marking the true boundary of the solar system – the Heliopause. Pioneer 10 is not yet there. We guess it is only halfway.

8th May 1997 Ascension Day

Thursday: EU institutions remain closed for Ascension Day

Friday: EU institutions close down for Robert Schuman remembrance day.

Saturday: EU institutions open their doors to the public. (newspaper cutting)

9th May 1997 Friday

The General Election on 1st May this year resulted in a landslide victory for 'New Labour' after 18 years of Tory rule.

It is hard to believe that it is only since the State Opening of Parliament in November 1989, that we have actually seen M.P.s in Parliament on TV, & it has been most amazing to see them all seemingly in the wrong place, having changed sides.

11th May 1997 Sunday

The 70th Bluebell Service – Katherine aged 93 & I, together with Toffee the dog, once more enjoyed the Bluebell Service in Swithland Woods. The Address was given by the Rt. Revd. Thomas Butler, Bishop of Leicester, who mentioned Toffee, the curly haired dog who wags his tail each time the drummer beats his drum. His owner should get him a drum kit, he suggested.

13th May 1997 Tuesday

New Labour & a totally new look Parliament. Out of Labour's 418 M.P.s, a record number of 101 are women, many of them having benefited from the party's women-only shortlist policy before it was ruled illegal 18 months ago; but many others have been selected since then.

The Tories have just 13 women on the Opposition benches. They & others make a total of 120.

15th May 1997 Thursday

Diana, Princess of Wales, has asked Christie's, the auctioneers, to hold an auction on 25th June this year in New York for her collection of ball gowns & expensive dresses – proceeds to be donated to the Royal Marsden Hospital Cancer Fund & the Aids Crisis Trust.

Catalogues are now on sale at £1,500 each. There are 250 leather-bound catalogues, each signed by the Princess & selling well.

17th May 1997 Saturday

Katherine Sullivan had many an admirer in her young days, including Peter Gwyn who taught her to love the music of Sibelius; and Chris Birdwood, son of Field Marshall Lord Birdwood, the Commander-in-Chief, India. Yesterday in the 'Times' obituaries was Vere Lady Birdwood, who died on 1st May, aged 87. She married Chris Birdwood in 1931. The marriage was dissolved in 1954. (see 2nd July 2000)

18th May Whit Sunday

All change Congo – In the space of a weekend, everything has changed. The country known as Zaire since 1971 is now the Democratic Republic of Congo. (See 28th October 1971)   (newspaper cutting) (Zaire is pronounced Zie – Ear).

19th May 1997 Monday

"BBC Songs of Praise at Gardeners' Question Time 50th Birthday Party 4pm-5pm Sunday 1st June, New National
        Forest, Moira, Near Ashby-de-la-Zouch.
    Music from the Desford Colliery Brass Band."

All churches in the area, including Ravenstone, have been invited to join in with the singing. I volunteered to sing in the choir. There will be choir rehearsals on 28th May & at mid-day on 1st June.

21st May 1997 Wednesday

The House of Commons wonders what has hit it. It never envisaged an influx of so many young vibrant ambitious M.P.s ready to turn the world upside down & do away with old medieval customs. Ruth Kelly, former Bank of England economist, aged 29 and heavily pregnant, does not like the cramped division lobbies. She and others think it is high time the Commons had electronic voting.

23rd May 1997 Friday

F A Cup Final – Chelsea 2 Middlesbrough 0

In 1994, Chelsea were well & truly beaten in the F A Cup Final by mighty Manchester United.

But this year they had no trouble beating Middlesbrough 2 – 0. Roberto Di Matteo scored the first goal within 42 seconds, an all time record – the fastest goal in an F A Cup Final.

25th May 1997 Trinity Sunday

Another thought for our 3 in 1 God was the triple temptation of Jesus (Matthew, Chapter 4).

Then was Jesus led up of the Spirit into the wilderness to be tempted of the devil, "If thou be the Son of God,

command that these stones be made bread; cast thyself down, for it is written, He shall give his angels charge concerning thee; worship me."

27th May 1997 Tuesday

Newly weds cousin Miles & Michele are still on Cloud Nine having recently returned from honeymoon in Naples & the Isle of Capri.

You never saw such a transformation as Glenholm is now undergoing as Michele introduces her own tastes & embellishments upstairs and downstairs & in the garden. No longer solely Miles dominated; Michele is everywhere, including a plate – Villa S. Michele, Capri.

29th May 1997 Thursday

Britain's biggest cycle park has opened in Leicester – in the basement of the Town Hall. It has enough space to park 140 bikes, with potential to expand. It has showers, toilet facilities, lockers etc; plus a bike equipment shop & a cycle repair service. This cycle park has cost £110,000 to set up, with £66,000 from the Department of Transport's Cycle Challenge Fund. So, 'On yer bike!'

31st May 1997 Saturday

In September last year I entrusted a further £1,000 to ERNIE, which so far has lain completely dormant. Each bond now has a one-in-19,000 chance of winning, but a few years ago it was 11,000 to one. (See 21st March 1994)

Bond prize lift – The number of Premium Bond prizes rises from 350,000 a month to about 430,000 from tomorrow, the fortieth anniversary of the first draw. Each bond now has a one-in-19,000 chance of sharing in a prize fund of £32 million.

(Newspaper cutting)

The new cathedral library at Hereford built to incorporate the medieval Chained Library, the cathedral archive and the priceless Mappa Mundi has been named as building of the year.   *(Newspaper cutting)*

2nd June 1997 Monday

It was on 2nd June 1968, Whit Sunday, that Mary Blue's baby, Steven, was Christened. Now, Steven has a darling baby of his own, Adam Steven, born on 5th April this year & a re-incarnation of Steven. Mary Blue's family is expanding rapidly. Murdo & Debbie now have a second baby, Kirstin Elizabeth, born 2nd May this year. Sharon has 2 step-children – Total 8 grand-children.

3rd June 1997 Tuesday

Gordon Brown is to keep the tradition of carrying the Budget statement to the House of Commons in a battered red box, first used by William Gladstone in 1860.

(Newspaper cutting)

4th June 1997 Wednesday

Pope John Paul II now aged 77 & looking very frail, & shaking with Parkinson's disease, is now on an eleven day pilgrimage to Poland, his beloved homeland. He said, "Every return to Poland is like a return under the roof of the parental home, where every object reminds me of what is closest & dearest." I was reminded of St. Paul's last visit to Ephesus. (Acts, Chapter 20).

"There will never be a Pope like him again," said

Genowesa Glica, a woman who camped overnight for the papal Mass at Legnica in south-western Poland. "I wanted to see him because it may be the last time." (Newspaper cutting)

York House, St James's Palace
June 4: The Duke of York this morning unveiled statues of Field Marshal Montgomery and a World War II soldier at a ceremony held at the D-Day Museum, Southsea, Portsmouth, and was received by Her Majesty's Lord-Lieutenant of Hampshire.
(Newspaper cutting)

6th June 1997 Friday
Fosse Park South, the 9½ acre site adjacent to Fosse Park, is now almost up & running with seven new attractive shops: - Currys, DFS, Maples, Carpet Depot, PC World, Harveys, & one still empty. The whole development has now been sold for £52 million to London-based Pillar Property Investments. This is considered to be a prime site, so near to the motorway intersection.

Buckingham Palace
June 7: The Duke of York, Earl of Inverness, today visited Inverness and was received by Her Majesty's Lord-Lieutenant (the Lord Gray of Contin).
(Newspaper cutting)

8th June 1997 Sunday
Deanery Service! Now that our Rector is Rural Dean, we found ourselves at the annual deanery service, held this year at St. Andrew's, Thringstone.
"The service is the occasion of Thringstone's annual 'Well Dressing' & the preacher is the Ven. Ian Stokes, Archdeacon of Loughborough."
There was no service this evening at Ravenstone, nor at any other of the churches in our deanery.

10th June 1997 Tuesday
Enid & I have chosen Canterbury for our holiday this year, being the 1,400th anniversary of the arrival of St. Augustine, sent by Pope Gregory the Great to re-establish Christianity in Southern England.
Together with St. Ambrose & St. Jerome, they became the early doctors of the Church (western tradition). John Chrysostom, Basil the Great, Gregory of Nazianzen & Athanasius = Eastern.

12th June 1997 Thursday
Coalville Amateur Operatic Society AGM this year saw Adam Markillie, leading man in our last three shows, take on the mantle of producer, assuring us all of his ability to produce a better show than ever seen before, & of his commitment for many years to come. Also a new Treasurer, Ann Day, taking over from Wendy Miles.
Our next show is 'Fiddler on the Roof', a repeat of our 1975 show.

Notice is hereby given that in 1998 the date for observance of The Queen's Birthday, at home and abroad, will be Saturday, June 13.
The Queen has been pleased to appoint the Viscount Brookeborough to be a Lord in Waiting to Her Majesty.
(Newspaper cutting)

14th June 1997 Saturday
Enid & I are now halfway through our week's holiday in Canterbury – Wednesday to Wednesday. We prefer this arrangement to travelling in the weekend traffic.
We love Canterbury which is so rich in history, has such quaint old buildings, & at the same time has all the latest Departmental Stores. The Cathedral is truly wonderful & dominates the skyline from all directions.

16th June 1997 Monday
"The Planet on Sunday" launched this time last year, closed down within a few days of issue No.1, because Clifford Hards, the Midlands entrepreneur who funded it, did not like its content.
I bought the one & only issue & decided not to buy it again. Apart from its content, the quality of the print was poor, with only one item of interest, by astronomer Patrick Moore.

18th June 1997 Wednesday
In Canterbury we have seen the oldest churches in England, most especially the Church of Saint Martin. What a welcome! As we approached the wide-open West Door up the gentle steps of the pathway, we could see inside the whole length of the Church up to the Altar. Here we attended a 'Taizé' Service, sitting in the Chancel. Here Queen Berta went to pray in 597A.D.
The religious Taizé community was founded during the Second World War by monks sheltering Jews in the French village of Taizé, near Dijon. Their message of spirituality without religious pressure has proved to be very popular & thousands of people now make a pilgrimage to Taizé every year. There were 70,000 celebrating the New Year in Stuttgart with the Taizé community.

22nd June 1997 Sunday
"In my Father's house are many mansions ..... I go to prepare a place for you. And if I go & prepare a place for you, I will come again, & receive you unto myself; that where I am, there ye may be also." (John 14: 2 – 3)
These oft repeated words, which we know so well, have now been updated to: - "In my Father's house are many rooms ......" The Rector of Ravenstone, the Revd. Kerry Emmett, spoke on this text.
"In my Father's house are many rooms ....." As the Rector of Ravenstone likened heaven to a hotel where Jesus had prepared a room for us & then escorted us there himself, provided we had booked in, I thought of the sermon we heard in February 1975, when our life was likened to a conducted tour on holiday, with Jesus as our courier, "Let us go on holiday with Jesus, to the promised land of heaven."

***£2m dress sale** – Dresses given by Diana, Princess of Wales, for auction in New York, raised $3.26 million (nearly £2 million) for the Aids Crisis Trust and the Royal Marsden Hospital Cancer Fund.*
(Newspaper cutting)

26th June 1997 Thursday
Britain's top 12 companies – from BT to Pilkington – cut their workforces by an average 44% between 1990 and 1995, a rate of attrition that is not dissimilar to what is happening in the rest of Europe, from Olivetti to

Daimler-Benz. These imposed changes have overturned the traditional work model where individuals could, for most of this century, expect to have only one, or possibly two, employers during their working life. At today's rate, European workers have an average of around six different paymasters, which means that continuous service with any one employer averages only about seven years. These movements, intended to improve efficiency, have also been a cost-cutting and staff-reduction exercise. In many cases it has been an opportunity to displace the older generation of employees. The combined effects of corporate downsizing and jobs change, like insecurity and unemployment, have been among the most important influences on people's lives in the past five years.

(Newspaper cutting)

Technology now does much of the work in the service industries previously done by clerical staff. Tens of thousands of people in their fifties have been laid off and forced to take early retirement. The experience of older people is of less value than the more youthful quick-fix thinking brought about by computer technology. This concentration of young people in state-of-the-art offices where technology is king has left the older generation way behind and jobless.

(Newspaper cutting)

28th June 1997 Saturday
Digital TV revolution speeds up (see 24th January 1997). Europe's digital broadcasting revolution moved forward this week with the award in Britain of the franchise for the world's first terrestrial digital TV services. On 23rd June, the Independent Television Commission, the TV regulator, gave British Digital Broadcasting (BDB), jointly owned by Carlton Communications & Granada TV, its franchise.

Belvoir Castle will close on Saturday June 28 for the first time in 30 years, for the wedding reception of the Duke of Rutland's daughter Lady Teresa Manners.

(Newspaper cutting)

Lady Theresa Manners, daughter of the Duke of Rutland and Dr John Chipman, director of the International Institute for Strategic Studies, were married at Bottesford Church, near the family home of Belvoir Castle.

(Newspaper cutting)

30th June 1997 Monday
Ravenstone Local History Group, formed last year in readiness for the Millennium, produced an interesting "1997 Village Calendar", depicting some old village landmarks: - Wesleyan Chapel, now demolished; Snibston Grange, now demolished; the original Ravenstone House, now demolished; Main Street, circa 1900; Church Lane, circa 1900; Darby & Joan outing, 1950.

2nd July 1997 Wednesday
A train made of bricks. The place to see this 130 foot long train, made from 185,000 bricks and weighing 1,500 tons, is Darlington. Unveiled last week, it was commissioned by Morrison's supermarket & was designed by 42 year old David Mach. It was put together by a team of 100, including engineers, architects & bricklayers. To David Mach it is akin to the Pyramids.

The Rev Jeffrey Hall, Rector, Anstey: to be Team Rector, Hugglescote with Donington, Ellistown and Snibston (Leicester).

4th July 1997 Friday
New Budget case – The Chancellor, Gordon Brown, is to ditch the battered 137-year-old Gladstonian Budget case today in favour of a new red Budget box made by apprentices at Rosyth Royal Dockyard.

(Newspaper cutting)

New Labour! New Chancellor! New Budget! And despite what you see recorded on 3rd June, a new red Budget case. Our last Budget was shortly before Christmas last year when car tax went up to £145. Now it is £150. Cigarettes went up to £3.23. Now they are £3.42. But more than anything else, the new Chancellor intends to help the long-term unemployed, & give money to education & health.

New Chancellor, Gordon Brown (now referred to as 'Capability Brown') has managed to come up with a new one-off windfall tax on the excess profits of the privatised utilities, such as electricity, water, gas etc. to give him £4.8 billion! It is estimated that the utilities have made £50 billion in profits since they became privatised & all their board members are 'Fat Cats'.

In 1994 the boards of National Power, PowerGen and National Grid took home £5.3 million in pay. It was frankly astonishing and by the summer of 1995 the fat cat phenomenon became a pariah that threatened to erupt into a full riot at the heated annual general meeting of British Gas.   (Newspaper cutting)

8th July 1997 Tuesday
On 7th July 1990, Karen married her beloved Graham. Now Karen & Graham have separated & Karen is bringing up their three children on her own – Suzannah, born 21st November 1991, Lewis, born on Cocky's 64th birthday, 28th January 1994, & Andrew, born 8th March 1996.

Karen is but one of Britain's million lone parents bringing up their children on income support.

10th July 1997 Thursday
New Labour is considering a new Bill in the autumn to outlaw the hunting with dogs of foxes, deer, mink & hares. One hundred thousand rural workers & hunt supporters from all over the country gathered today in Hyde Park to voice their complaints & defend their lifestyle.

Peasants' revolt – The biggest throng of country folk ever marshalled in Britain is marching on London. Their aim: to protest against plans to ban fox-hunting. (Newspaper cutting)

12th July 1997 Saturday
Six years of retirement & how I love being an O.A.P. – Old Age Pensioner (& yet still young at heart). British oldies would like a different name tag, such as SWELs –

Seniors with energetic lifestyles; Elderados, Elder retired ageless doyens of society; Bats – Born-again teenagers; Owls – Older, wiser, learned souls; Yippies – young at heart independent previously employed enjoying themselves.

14th July 1997 Monday
Sixty six today (2 x 3 x 11).
Cocky telephoned from Lancaster to say 'Happy Birthday' & sent me £20 in his birthday card.
Pat & Evelyn gave me a 'fine hand-crafted figurine' – Equus, a fine black horse on its own wooden base, which looks very good beside the pink wall of the front room; & Mary Blue managed to find a birthday card which had printed on the front 'For You Betty'.

16th July 1997 Wednesday
A new passport! As in February 1975, I was the proud owner of my first passport, so now I am the proud owner of my second passport (as yet with no destination fixed).
"Your new passport is a product of the latest computer technology. It also shares a common format with the passports of other member states of the European Community."

18th July 1997 Friday
Nelson Mandela, President of the Republic of South Africa, today celebrates his 79th birthday. Released from prison in February 1990, he then walked hand in hand with his wife Winnie, whom he had married in 1958. Sadly they were divorced in 1996 (see 19th March 1996). Now he has a new lady-love, Mrs Graca Machel, aged 51, widow of Samora Machel, former president of Mozambique.

Clarence House, July 19: Queen Elizabeth the Queen Mother, Lord Warden of the Cinque Ports, gave a Reception for the Confederation of the Cinque Ports at Walmer Castle this evening. *(Newspaper cutting)*

20th July 1997 Sunday
Lilian Dunkley, "doyenne of city theatre scene" has died aged 91. Her married name was Mrs Malcolm Skillington & I knew her from having singing lessons with her in the early 1950s. She was leading lady in many productions, including Coalville Amateurs.

22nd July 1997 Tuesday
"Now we have seen Mars in close-up" – So I wrote 21st July 1976, when America's Viking spacecraft landed. Now we are learning more and more about Mars & its sky blue pink sky following the landing of America's latest spacecraft 'Pathfinder'. Over the next eight years, another nine flights to Mars are planned, culminating in a craft returning with samples to Earth.

24th July 1997 Thursday
National Space Science Centre!
Leicester is proud to be the venue of a proposed National Space Science Centre, including a research centre, (the first NASA-backed Challenger Learning Centre outside America offering simulated space flights) an exhibition centre explaining the achievements & potential future of space exploration & a planetarium – linked with Leicester University.

26th July 1997 Saturday
"By the year 2020, women could give birth at 60 ....." (See 26th November 1980)
This has already happened. First there was 62 year-old Signora Della Corte in 1994 & now we hear of a 63 year-old Philippine-American in California. This can only be achieved by artificially using donor eggs. The uterus can still perform when treated with the appropriate hormones, oestrogens & progestogens.

Surely the previous record still stands as Sarah, wife of Abraham, who bore him a son when she was in her nineties? (Genesis, xvii, 17 and xxi, 1-4)
(Newspaper cutting)

28th July 1997 Monday
"The pleasure of your company is requested at the wedding (church blessing) of Trevelyn Mellor & James Hodson at St. James, Snibston on 6th September 1997 at 12 noon & afterwards at the Church Hall."
These are our regular dinner-table companions each Sunday at Sunnyside Garden Centre, Ibstock – James, widower, Trevelyn, divorcée, together with Pat, Evelyn, Mary Blue & me.

30th July 1997 Wednesday
How very sad to see listed in 'The Times' column after column of 2,200 names, including 40 Britons, who were victims of the Holocaust in World War II, & whose wealth estimated to be now worth £4 billion, lies dormant in Swiss banks. At last, after 50 years, the Swiss Bankers' Association (SBA) has dropped its policy of secrecy & is trying to trace families or survivors of the Holocaust.

1st August 1997 Friday
The first R-registration cars were being driven out of showrooms today in what could be the last ever August rush. Expected Government changes are likely to result in new numbers being introduced twice a year, March & September, to end the 1st August scramble after 30 years. I can remember in 1967 I bought a new scooter KAY 7E. The 'E' suffix ran only from Jan – 31st July.

3rd August 1997 Sunday
Our well-beloved Bishop, the Rt. Rev. John Mort, became Leicester's Assistant Bishop in 1972. He retired from the post in 1988, but continued to work as honorary Assistant Bishop. Now he has died – last Wednesday, aged 82, & his funeral will be at Old Woodhouse, where he will be buried.

5th August 1997 Tuesday
Queen Elizabeth, the Queen Mother, is now 97 & still undertaking official Royal engagements. She is Warden of the Cinque Ports – the five ancient ports lying opposite to France: - Sandwich, Dover, Hythe, Romney and Hastings. On her 95th birthday, English Heritage commissioned a new garden at Walmer Castle between Sandwich & Dover in her honour. It is open to the public.
Dover, Hastings, Hythe, Romney and Sandwich. These towns made up Edward I's Federation of Cinque Ports, a navy constructed in 1050 to protect our south coast.
(Newspaper cutting)

7th August 1997 Thursday

On 7th August 1967, I took delivery of my very first car – second-hand 'Mini' FBT 638D, having been knocked off my scooter a few days earlier.

In 1973 I had my first new car KAY 7L.

Then PNR 867R (1976), UBC 783X (1982), E479 EAY (1987), K49 PUT (1992).

Thirty years ago, a car tax disc cost £15. By 1970 it was £25, & with this year's budget, £150.

9th August 1997 Saturday

"That's where you were born," said Ken Shaw, pointing to where my grand-dad Sketchley's farm once stood. "Oh, no," I corrected him, "I was born where I live now, 27 Leicester Road, Ravenstone."

"You were born at the farm," he said, "and my mother was the mid-wife. I remember them coming to our house & saying Mary (that was your mother) was about to give birth. Come quick to the farm."

11th August 1997 Monday

All change in the world of banking! One after another, Building Societies are joining the world of banking. As you know, my Cheltenham & Gloucester Building Society joined the Lloyds Bank Group & my account gained £3,000. (Ref: 27th March 1996). As more & more Building Societies & Insurance Companies change from 'mutual' to publicly owned institutions, the overall payout to customers has reached £33.6 billion.

13th August 1997 Wednesday

"My mission is to pacify Ireland" so said Prime Minister Gladstone in 1868. (See 8th August 1993). His mission failed as did others before & others ever since. Now we have New Labour & a new Secretary of State for Northern Ireland, Dr Marjorie (Mo) Mowlam, who has given her all to pacify Ireland; but once the Marching Season started (July to September), all hell broke out once more.

15th August 1997 Friday

To Joanne, a baby daughter Shannon Louise, born this morning shortly after 1 a.m. in Leicester Royal Infirmary. At 6 p.m. when Shannon was less than one day old, she was in her pram at my back door with Joanne, Joanne's mum Sue, & Joanne's son Dale, now nearly three. She holds the record as the youngest visitor who has ever popped round to see me.

Today is the Anniversary of the Birthday of the Princess Royal. (Newspaper cutting)

17th August 1997 Sunday

House Raid

A house on Leicester Road in Ravenstone has been targeted by burglars who stole a Sanyo radio-cassette, a packet of Benson & Hedges cigarettes, a packet of Condor tobacco and a purse with £27.

(Newspaper cutting)

"A house on Leicester Road in Ravenstone" targeted by burglars, was in fact a bungalow next door to me – Aunt Dos's bungalow, occupied now by Mr & Mrs Taylor & their adult son Peter, who were asleep in bed when access was gained through a window.

19th August 1997 Tuesday

An Orange Order parade in Garvaghy Road celebrated the Protestant victory at The Battle of the Boyne in 1690. The parade had 2,000 Orangemen from 32 lodges which make up Portadown District. The lodges are known as LOL (Loyal Orange Lodge) remembering William of Orange.

21st August 1997 Thursday

Coal mining in the beautiful Vale of Belvoir was vehemently opposed when it was given approval for the go-ahead in January 1984. But the Asfordby coal mine was developed at exorbitant cost & after various set-backs, finally started operating in 1995 under 'R J B Mining' – Richard Budge being Chief Executive. Now the pit is to close, beaten by Mother Nature's layers of volcanic rock.

23rd August 1997 Saturday

The lovely old Royal Yacht Britannia, launched by the Queen in 1953, was thought to have embarked on her last voyage earlier this year (see 22 January 1997). However, New Labour has decreed a new £50 million refit to give Britannia a further 30 year extension of life. The Government plans to raise the money from private industry.

25th August 1997 Monday

This summer turned into a scorcher for the month of August only. But it was the humidity combined with the heat which made it like a continual sauna, day and night. Consequently we have learned more about the T.H.I. the Temperature-Humidity Index. The higher the relative humidity to the air temperature, the higher the apparent temperature. So high has the relative humidity been that heavy dews come each morning.

For example, when the air temperature is 84F and the relative humidity is 40% the apparent temperature decreases to 83F. However, if the air temperature is 84F but the relative humidity is 80% the apparent temperature increases to 94F. The effects are more spectacular the higher the air temperature. With an air temperature of 94F and relative humidity at 80% the apparent temperature is 129F.

(Newspaper cutting)

27th August 1997 Wednesday

Mother Teresa celebrates her 87th birthday today. Now very frail, it is her wish when she dies to be buried in a room at Mother House, the Calcutta headquarters of her Missionaries of Charity order. Mother House is one of two Christian centres in the city where prayers are held non-stop. It is her wish to be interred where there is never ceasing prayer.

29th August 1997 Friday

Brother Pat's birthday! 79 today, or as he says, "I am now in my 80th year."

I find it quite amazing to see all the people I once knew as the younger generation now transformed into the older generation. Almost all the previous older generation have now died and it is a completely different scenario.

As I wrote in December 1982, I seem to be more like an onlooker and a recorder.

31st August 1997 Sunday

Coalville Technical College yesterday changed its name to Stephenson College, Coalville (to commemorate George Stephenson, railway pioneer, who created Snibston Colliery in the early 1830s). The change is so that other college campuses in Moira & Ashby will not have the word 'Coalville' in their title. They will be Stephenson College, Heart of the National Forest Training Centre; and Stephenson College, Ashby.

September 1st 1997 Monday

Diana, Princess of Wales, died yesterday after a car crash in Paris aged 36. She was born at Park House, Sandringham, on July 1st 1961. (Newspaper cutting)

September 2nd 1997 Tuesday

Diana, Princess of Wales, has been killed in a horrendous car crash and it seems that the whole world is weeping. From all corners of the globe comes the cry, "Alas," and she is hailed, "Queen of Hearts."

4th September 1997 Thursday

Never have we seen such a massive outpouring of public grief as people everywhere pour out their love for their beloved Princess, now acknowledged as the People's Princess. Her coffin lies privately in the Chapel Royal, within St. James' Palace, until Saturday 6th September, when her funeral will be held at Westminster Abbey, prior to interment with her ancestors at Great Brington.

Island will be final resting place

The Princess will be buried on an island surrounded by an ornamental lake, 100 yards from the ancestral family home at Althorp, rather than in the Spencer family chapel. The decision was made because of fears that interment at the chapel in Great Brington would have overwhelmed the Northamptonshire village with visitors for years to come. (Newspaper cutting)

6th September 1997 Saturday

Mother Teresa, a saint of our time, died yesterday. Diana, Princess of Wales who loved her dearly, died tragically last Sunday & her funeral is today.

Mother Teresa, Roman Catholic missionary and Nobel Peace Prize winner, died yesterday, aged 87. She was born in Skopje (then in Albania) on August 27th 1910.

(Newspaper cutting)

8th September 1997 Monday

William Bees V.C. served in the Boer War (1899-1902) & was awarded the Victoria Cross for his outstanding bravery in 1901.

Born at Loughborough in 1872, he later moved to Coalville, where he died in 1938. Thousands of people lined the streets of Coalville to pay their last respects to the local hero, and his grave in Coalville's London Road Cemetery (at the far end) continues to be honoured.

10th September 1997 Wednesday

"A complete cessation of military operations"

"How long for?" people wonder.

That was 3 years ago. It lasted until February 1996 when a huge bomb exploded on London's Isle of Dogs & the old troubles re-surfaced.

Now we have another supposed ceasefire which came

into force on 20th July 1997.

"How long for?" we wonder.

12th September 1997 Friday

Heritage Open Days – And yet again I tried to book in advance for a guided tour of the Mansion House (this year tel: 0171 332 3320). This year however, I subscribed to the Open House monthly broadsheet to qualify for priority advance booking and to my great delight was granted 2 tickets. The excitement was as great as that in March 1974 when I had tickets for Trooping the Colour.

14th September 1997 Sunday

"Please ring the bell on arrival."

This is the printed instruction on my beautiful ticket of admission to the Mansion House, private residence of the Right Honourable the Lord Mayor of London, open to the public next weekend.

Mary Blue and I each have identical tickets, each with our name printed, admitting the named bearer only.

"Please arrive 10 minutes before the 3-15 p.m. tour."

16th September 1997 Tuesday

Prince Henry of Wales yesterday celebrated his 13th birthday, with the tragic death of his mother Diana, Princess of Wales, still uppermost in all our minds. What a sad day for this young prince named Henry Charles Albert David & known as Prince Harry. What beautiful pictures we have of him snuggling up to his mother & enfolded in her love.

18th September 1997 Thursday

"Our entry wall was taken down."

Thus I recorded in my diary in September 1960, when Aunt Dos was living next door in her bungalow & preferred an open aspect, which I have enjoyed for the past 37 years. Now, following the burglary next door, Mr & Mrs Taylor have erected a five foot high lattice fence to keep out any further would-be burglars.

20th September 1997 Saturday

Mary Blue & I had a wonderful day in London enjoying our 3rd 'London Open House' day.

First we visited the ultra-modern ITN headquarters in Grays Inn Road, then the ancient College of Arms in Queen Victoria Street; on then to the sumptuous marble interiors of Vintners Place in Upper Thames Street; the NatWest Bank head office; the magnificent Mansion House and finally the re-furbished Foreign Office.

22nd September 1997 Monday

Coalville & Ashby's main road, the A50, has had a name change to the A511. A 16-mile stretch of the A50 from Junction 22 of the M1 at Markfield to Hatton near Burton-on-Trent is to become the A511.

The name change is because the Derby southern by-pass is now open & will be known as the A50. Heavy lorries can travel on the A50 from Leicester & connect to it via the M1.

24th September 1997 Wednesday

"Michael and his angels fought against the dragon"
Revelation 12 : 7

The war in heaven between Michael and his angels and

the forces of evil, represented by the dragon, is a spiritual warfare between the uniting and transforming principle of sacrificial love, and the divisive and destructive anarchy whose allure is a specious and deceitful freedom. To believe in angels is to believe that human beings are not the only personal order created by God, and that God acts towards us through these intermediaries, the agents of his love and his transforming grace.

(Newspaper cutting)

26th September 1997 Friday
On 25th September 1897, one hundred years ago, my grandfather bought part of a field called "Little Nook" for £267-7s-6d. He bought 2 acres, one rood and eighteen perches. On this land he built "The Hollies" for himself and several other houses, including the house and home where I have lived all my life, thanks entirely to the guiding hand of Providence.

25th September 1897
Abstract of the Title of George Harry Hewes to a piece of land site at Snibstone in the Parish of Ravenstone with Snibstone in the County of Leicester.
By Indre of this date made between John German of Ashby-de-la-Zouch in the County of Leicester Estate Agent of the one part and George Harry Hewes of Coalville in the County of Leicester Architect of the other part.
Reciting that the said John German was seised of the pieces of land for an estate of inheritance in fee simple in possession free from incumbrances and he had agreed to sell the same to the said George Harry Hewes for the sum of two hundred and sixty seven pounds, seven shillings and sixpence.
The said John German conveyed unto the said G. H. Hewes all those two pieces of land containing two thousand six hundred and sixty two and two thousand nine hundred and eighty eight square yards respectively site at Snibstone in the Parish of Ravenstone with Snibstone in the said County of Leicester forming part of a field of land called 'Little Nook' stated to contain two acres one rood and eighteen perches or thereabouts and formerly in the occupation of John Neal then of the said John German and then of William Hardy.

28th September 1997 Sunday
"Ye are the salt of the earth ....." Matthew 5 : 13.
The Rector of Ravenstone, the Revd Kerry Emmett, gave a thought-provoking sermon on the many & varied uses and qualities of salt. I had always considered salt as a pinch of salt to add to the flavour of a meal; but we were reminded that salt was the greatest preserver, long before refrigeration. Salt also melts the icy grip of winter.

30th September 1997 Tuesday
The New Revised Standard Version (N.R.S.V.) of the Bible has been rejected by the Vatican for use in liturgical & catechetical texts because it is a propagandist version which mirrors the feminist ideology. It is not a faithful rendering of the original Hebrew and Greek texts. The word 'man' has been removed altogether. 'Fishers of men' (Luke 5: 10) becomes 'Fishers of people'.

2nd October 1997 Thursday
Only in 1995 did I discover the merits of the golfing world's Ryder Cup (see Journal 23rd September 1995). Held once every 2 years, this year we saw America beaten by Europe at Valderrama in Spain. Coverage by terrestrial TV was minimal, while BSkyB provided non-stop cover.

4th October 1997 Saturday
'Parkin & Jones' have been my garage since October 1970. Now I am a privileged customer & have been given one of their latest 'customer privilege cards' (dating from 5th August this year). "To put the seal on a job well done, your vehicle will always be washed before it is returned – 5% discount on services for the first year, 10% the second, 15% after 2 years."

6th October 1997 Monday
Enid's birthday today – three score years and ten. Now a septuagenarian, she will shortly be great-aunt to Alison's baby (and I will be great-auntie cuz).
Enid is especially close to her younger brother David, his wife Irene & their only child, Alison. She has virtually no contact with her elder sister Margaret, so it came as something of a shock when Margaret rang her on her birthday.

8th October 1997 Wednesday
Baby Adam, son of Steven and Jane, and grandson of Mary Blue, is a beautiful bonny, baby now six months old. Watching him with his mother, who absolutely adores him, I am reminded of Grandma Hewes who wrote to her sister in February 1886, describing her own beautiful bonny baby, her little pet Freddy, whom she likewise adored & for whom she was making a new set of pinafores.

10th October 1997 Friday
Ninth Annual Service of Thanksgiving for all creatures great & small was held last Sunday at Saint Andrews, Jarrom Street, Leicester. Again Katherine, now aged 93, Toffee the dog & I attended this service where the preacher was the Venerable Ian Stanes, Archdeacon of Loughborough. He told us the true story of Bobby of Greyfriars, Edinburgh, the most faithful of little dogs.

12th October 1997 Sunday
'Paradise Found' – A picture postcard from Michael & Josie in Barbados who are having another lovely holiday there, visiting old friends & feeling as much at home there as in England. So much so that they are actually building a house there in this idyllic part of the British Commonwealth, 4,000 miles across the Atlantic, where people from Britain first settled in 1627.

14th October 1997 Tuesday
Roberts portable radio R757 – Sound for Generations – by appointment to H.M. Queen Elizabeth II, by appointment to H.M. Queen Elizabeth, the Queen Mother, by appointment to H.R.H. the Prince of Wales. Paid £80 for this rather special 3-band portable radio from G. W. Cowling Ltd. 26 Belvoir Street, Leicester. How I love listening to the radio – it is my bedside companion.

16th October 1997 Thursday

'Coronation Street' like everything else today is changing out of all recognition of its old self. Long established characters are either leaving of their own accord or being written out in an attempt to keep Coronation Street fresh and at the top of the ratings. According to producer Brian Park, more racy storylines are proving a massive hit with the viewers. I think he is wrong.

18th October 1997 Saturday

Coronation Street's latest new characters are a problem family, the Battersbys. Both mother and father, Janice & Les have been in prison & the children are prone to shop-lifting & playing truant. They have a clapped-out car & ghetto-blasters & try to sell stolen goods to others in the street. They are producer Brian Park's idea of 'an exciting injection of fresh blood into the Street.'

20th October 1997 Monday

Civil Service Retirement Fellowship meeting & a most interesting talk by Wendy Greene on the history of jewellery. Before mankind ever wore clothes, he bedecked himself with animal teeth and tusks. Then came the discovery of gold, silver & precious stones to adorn temples & holy shrines. Henry VIII bedecked himself with jewels from the wealthy churches he destroyed & so on up to the present day.
Wendy Greene, Handmade Fashion Jewellery,
94, Maplewell Road, Woodhouse Eaves,
Loughborough, Leics. LE12 8RA England. (01509) 890403

22nd October 1997 Wednesday

Leicester City Football Club is to be floated on the Stock Market on Friday 24th October.
The club has been valued at £24million & anyone can apply for a minimum of 400 shares worth 110p each, i.e. £440. Leicester will join the Alternative Investment Market, which is less regulated than the main stock market, through a deal with Soccer Investments, who thereby offer City £10 million.

24th October 1997 Friday

Leicester City plc is run jointly by Leicester City & Soccer Investments (the shell company floated recently with the sole intention of taking over a Premiership side. It will exchange 31 of its shares for each Leicester share). Club chairman Tom Smeaton becomes Chief Executive of the board of directors of Leicester City plc. Sir Rodney Walker, chairman of Soccer Investments is non-executive chairman.

26th October 1997 Sunday

"We've won the Forest" proclaimed the Leicester Mercury in October 1990.
"History is Planted" it said in December that year as the first sapling, a tiny oak, was planted.
So how is it progressing?
This old coalfield covering about 200 square miles (500 sq. kilometres) is scheduled to be 30% covered by trees within 50 years. With nearly a million trees planted, plus 6% already there, it is now 7%.

30th October 1997 Thursday

Hardy, Thomas Vincent of Coalville passed away suddenly at home October 22nd 1997, aged 82 years. Beloved husband of Ivy. A much loved father and grandpa. The funeral service will take place at Ebeneezer Baptist Church, Coalville on Wednesday, October 29th at 12 noon, followed by interment in Hugglescote Cemetery.

The funeral yesterday of Vincent Hardy, the one and only Hon. Life Member of Coalville Amateur Operatic Society, was truly memorable.
Peter Jacques, who himself has been with the society for more than 50 years, spoke beautifully of their long association, recalling Vincent's many roles on stage from pre-war days until this year's 'Carousel'.
We all sang, 'You'll never walk alone'.

1st November 1997 Saturday

'Farewell Britannia' we were told in January. Along came New Labour on May 1st and in August we were told 'Britannia granted costly reprieve'. Now this bright idea has been scrapped & we are beginning to mistrust much of what New Labour says. Chancellor of the Exchequer, Gordon Brown was to keep the old battered red box for Budget Day (3rd June 1997), but on Budget Day he had a new one.

3rd November 1997 Monday

More than 19,000 new trees have been planted across Leicestershire in the past year as part of a plan to form a 200 square mile forest in the Midlands.
(Newspaper cutting)
My darling oak tree had to go. Sadly, my narrow garden could not contain so great a tree & I called on the services of Coleorton Tree Surgeons who removed it completely, leaving no trace at all. How sad to see so fine a tree brought low, its lovely leafy branches in their autumn glory, hauled into the waiting trailer, ready for dispatch, and away to a bonfire.

Since November 1st, domestic gas users in Scotland and northern England have been free to select the company supplying their gas.
(Newspaper cutting)

5th November 1997 Wednesday

"Talking Newspapers" Joan Elliott, Derrick Palmer and I were photographed recently by the Coalville Times photographer as we prepared to record for the blind. We formed our team five years ago. Now our photograph is in the newspaper.

7th November 1997 Friday

Diana, Princess of Wales, who died so tragically on 31st August this year, would often consult soothsayers & spiritual gurus for advice & guidance.
Not long before her death she and her new love Dodi Fayed had flown to Derbyshire specially to visit psychic Rita Rogers.
Maybe she had some premonition of what was about to happen, like the troubled King Saul.
(I Samuel, Chap. 28)

Crawshaw, William Michael Clifton, 4th Baron of Whatton, Leicestershire, on Friday November 7th in hospital after a short illness. Much loved brother of Mary, David and Johnny. Private funeral for family, the village and very close friends at All Saints Church, Long Whatton on Friday, November 14th at 2.30p.m.

(Newspaper cutting)

9th November 1997 Sunday
Bernard Daws, a retired teacher, who has been a valued lay reader at Ravenstone Church for the last 7 years, has now 'hung up his robes' & we have bid him a fond farewell.

As I told you on 12th May 1994, "A Church Service made up only of hymn singing is to me like a 5 course meal stripped of all but the sweet course." Bernard provided a 5 course meal.

11th November 1997 Tuesday
Ravenstone Local History Group invited all the oldies of the village, including Pat, Evelyn, Enid & me, to an afternoon tea & an afternoon of reminiscences of life & times in yesteryear Ravenstone. We had a lovely afternoon looking at old photos, watching old slides on a big screen, & recalling by-gone days. The group is hoping to produce a book for the millennium, covering the 20th century.

15th November 1997 Saturday
Rugby Union - Tigers 90 Glasgow 19
Good old Leicester! One area where we do excel is on the Rugby field. On our way to the European Cup quarter-finals, we scored the biggest total by any other side in the tournament, an amazing 90. This included the highest number of tries (14) and the highest number of points scored by one player (35). This does however indicate what a poor team Glasgow has.

17th November 1997 Monday
The mystery of the Stock Exchange became a little clearer to me when Big Bang Two, the new electronic trading system, known as Sets, was unveiled recently at the London Stock Exchange, completing the process begun in 1986 when floor trading was abolished in favour of computerised market makers in the UK's original Big Bang. This further step is only for FTSE 100 companies, the top hundred.

Q. What is the new trading system?
A. The system is called Sets, the Stock Exchange Electronic Trading System.

Bull – *A bull is an investor who buys into the market because he thinks shares will go up, thus creating a bull market.*

Bear – *A bear chases prices down by selling shares in the belief that prices are going to fall. A falling market is a bear market.*

FTSE – *The Financial Times Stock Exchange 100 – to give it its full title – measures the top 100 stocks on the London Stock Exchange ranked by total value of their shares (market capitalisation). This is worked out by multiplying the share price by the amount of shares on the market. There is also a FTSE 250 and a FTSE 350.*

FTSE's value tops £1 trillion – *The value of companies in the FTSE 100 stock market index has risen above £1 trillion (£1,000 billion) for the first time. It follows a wave of takeover bids.*

(Newspaper cuttings)

19th November 1997 Wednesday
Whatever would Nathan Mayer Rothschild have thought of this latest computerised trading system that matches buyers with sellers and does away with the middleman? The new system sees the market move from a quote-driven to an order-driven system. Under the quote-driven system, the price was decided by market makers (middle men).

Nathan, who died in 1836, was like a computer.

20th November 1997 Thursday
Royal Golden Wedding - The Queen and Prince Philip celebrate 50 years of marriage today.

23rd November 1997 Sunday
The National Lottery goes from strength to strength. On Wednesday, 5th February this year we had the first midweek lottery draw in addition to the regular Saturday night draw & this is now a regular event. 'Camelot', the consortium which runs the lottery is to be congratulated on its efficiency.

Fraudsters have no chance, as the computer knows exactly where and when tickets are sold.

£6bn on lottery. National: *sales for the National Lottery have reached £6 billion – more than a pound for every member of the human race.*

(Newspaper cutting)

25th November 1997 Tuesday
Marks & Spencer in Gallowtree Gate, Leicester has now expanded to reach out at the back into the Haymarket Towers shopping complex. The £15 million expansion includes a new food hall which will be the biggest operated by Marks & Spencer in the East Midlands, & will open from 8 a.m. to 8 p.m. The unveiling took place yesterday. The extension is part of the former Lewis's store.

27th November 1997 Thursday
Humphrey the cat was a stray when in 1989, he decided to settle in at No. 10 Downing Street. Everybody knows & loves Humphrey; everybody that is, except new Prime Minister Tony Blair & his family. Eleven year old Humphrey has now been given a transfer & moved elsewhere.

29th November 1997 Saturday
In May 1965 I became a Friend of Leicester Cathedral. In August 1992 I became a Friend of the Settle-Carlisle Line. In September 1993 I became a Friend of St. George's, Windsor. Now, from the Friends of Shakespeare's Globe, comes the following acknowledgement, "We are delighted to welcome you to the Friends of Shakespeare's Globe & have pleasure in enclosing your membership card and first mailing."

1st December 1997 Monday
H.M.S.O. had to go because it was not making a profit. In 1995 it lost £45 million! It now operates under the name 'The Stationery Office', having been privatised

last year. To make it a profitable business it has been streamlined from 14 to 4 divisions: Printing, Publishing, Business Supplies, and Facilities Management! It is based in Norwich.

2nd December 1997 Tuesday
St Paul's Cathedral, rebuilt by Sir Christopher Wren, was opened on this day in 1697.

3rd December 1997 Wednesday
There was never anyone quite like Nathan Rothschild, 1777 – 1836. He was the brains behind the family fortunes. He had a prodigious memory & not only did he help to regulate the English exchange rate day by day, but he could keep in mind the fluctuating rates throughout Europe & their relations to one another. "Who is that?" people asked.
"The King of the Jews," was the reply, or "The Jew of the Kings."

Photographs will be included on driving licences from next summer, the Government announced last night. The scheme, ordered by the European Union, will be phased in and will not affect licence holders immediately.
(Newspaper cutting)

5th December 1997 Friday
On 1st May this year we had a General Election & a new Government. We therefore had an unusual 'July' Budget & a new Chancellor Gordon Brown.
We expect the next Budget to be in March next year, but we have been given our first 'Draft Budget' namely a 'Pre-Budget Report', aimed at ending some of the secrecy surrounding the real thing, yet not revealing too many details.

7th December 1997 Sunday
Everybody knows where Diana, Princess of Wales, is buried – on an island surrounded by an ornamental lake in the grounds of Althorp House, Northamptonshire. (See 5th September 1997)
Now I learn from Sam Land, aged 83, a retired farmer, with Northamptonshire connections, that in fact, the body of Diana was placed, as originally intended, in the family vault inside the parish church at Great Brington.

9th December 1997 Tuesday
The Government is planning to introduce a sixth 'good cause' which will drain money from the existing five causes.
(Newspaper cutting)
New Labour & 26 new Bills to deal with, including: - Lottery – new funds for education & health. Such has been the success of the National Lottery, launched 3 years ago to help five worthy causes (see 16th November 1994) that the Government now sees itself as a sixth good cause & has decided to create a New Opportunities Fund, which in effect will put £1 billion a year into its coffers.

11th December 1997 Thursday
"The House of Horrors", 25 Cromwell Street, Gloucester, where Frederick & Rosemary West murdered & buried their victims was demolished eventually by the council, brick by brick & the whole

lot, bricks, rubble & masonry ground to dust. All the wood was burned to ashes so that no trace of it whatsoever should remain.
Gloucester tried to erase forever evidence of its house of horrors by removing it completely from Cromwell Street. After full consultation with the victims' families and the neighbours, it was agreed to have a 150ft long walkway – no plaque & no seating. There is now a block-paved walkway, unveiled on 14th July 1997.

12th December 1997 Friday
New union created - The biggest union for civil servants will be created in the new year, promising to improve services to its members. The 260,000-strong Public and Commercial Services union (PCS), which has been formed through the merger of the PTC and CPSA unions, aims to be more 'member centred' and has promised that the rank and file will have the final say on major decisions such as pay.
(Newspaper cutting)

13th December 1997 Saturday
Society for the Blind – another get together at the Marlene Reid Centre, Coalville, where those who read for the 'Talking Newspaper' were joined by others who run groups and organise outings for isolated elderly blind people in the Coalville & Ashby catchment areas. Director Philip Parkinson spoke to us all as we sat round one big table, & each spoke in turn of their particular role.

15th December 1997 Monday
Struggle over Onassis fortune – Lussy-sur-Morges: - Thierry Roussel, fourth husband of the late Christina Onassis, says he fears for the well-being of his daughter Athina, heir to the $3 billion (£1.8 billion) Onassis fortune. Disclosure of an alleged plot to kidnap the 12-year-old has thrown light on a bitter legal battle pitting M Roussel against Stelios Papadimitriou, president of the Onassis Foundation, and three other Greek trustees of Christina's will who are managing the estate until Athina reaches 18. (Reuters).
(Newspaper cutting)

This is Athina, now aged 12, poor little rich girl, torn between two conflicting cultures and families, all because she alone is left so burdensome a fortune.
(See also 15th December 2000)

16th December 1997 Tuesday
At the gleaming new Getty Centre in Los Angeles, which opens today, you can see dozens of important artworks never exhibited before.
(Newspaper cutting)

17th December 1997 Wednesday
Aristotle Socrates Onassis, possibly the richest man in the world when he died 15th March 1975, was the grandfather whom Athina never knew.
Having lost his son & heir in a plane crash, he left the bulk of his fortune to his daughter's son, not then conceived, nor ever conceived. His daughter Christina died in November 1988, aged 37, leaving a 3-year-old daughter (now 12) to inherit the fortune.

19th December 1997 Friday

We've done it! That was the message today from organisers of Macmillan's Green Ribbon Appeal as the magnificent fund-raising effort reached its £1.2 million target.

Macmillan's Green Ribbon Appeal was launched in April 1995 to add £1.2 million to £11 million of Government NHS funding for a new cancer centre at Leicester Royal Infirmary. The centre will include two 19-bed wards, new chemotherapy and radiotherapy suites; combined inpatient and day-care facilities for 22 patients in haematology; facilities for pain management; a theatre suite; and a hostel for overnight stay for radiotherapy patients who have difficulty attending for treatment. The centre will be called the Osborne Building, named after Osborne House on the Isle of Wight, country home of Queen Victoria, and in keeping with the naming of all infirmary buildings after royal residences.

(Newspaper cutting)

21st December 1997 Sunday

From my love by post, a Christmas card "Because You're the One I Love", containing £25.

"Thanks for all you do to make our life together so special".

Our life together is entirely in our hearts and minds. As I told you in July 1988, "We share the same thoughts and can communicate involuntarily, by telepathy, as if our hearts are linked in some way by a 'heart telephone'."

23rd December 1997 Tuesday

To Aunty Cuz, from Alison, Simon & Eleanor. My first Christmas card from Eleanor Mary, born on 17th November this year. It was Christmas 1967 when Alison, then one day old, sent her first Christmas card.

My first Christmas card also from Adam Steven, born on 5th April this year, included in the card from Steve, Jane & Adam. Steven, Mary Blue's firstborn was born 28th December 1967.

25th December 1997 Thursday

After attending 'Family Eucharist' at 9.30am in the Collegiate Church of St Mary, Stafford, I then stayed with Bunting in her home until 2.30pm, arriving home before dark. Poor Bunting is in such a sorry state, she does not know whether it is day or night, winter or summer. All the curtains were closed when I arrived & I let myself in with a key hidden outside. Bunting, looking quite wild, sat on the settee.

27th December 1997 Saturday

Christmas Day lunch with Bunting at Stafford; Boxing Day lunch with Mary Blue, Scott & Miranda, Pat & Evelyn, at Pat's home in Hugglescote. Later in the day, Pat, Evelyn, Mary Blue & I joined James Hodson & his new wife Trevelyn for tea & the evening at their home in Ibstock. Cousin Miles & his new wife Michele are spending Christmas in a hotel in Derbyshire.

29th December 1997 Monday

The wedding of Ffion Jenkins to William Hague, leader of Her Majesty's Opposition.

On Friday, 19th December this year, Tory leader William Hague married his Welsh fiancée Ffion Jenkins in the crypt chapel at the Palace of Westminster. He, being a proud Yorkshire man, wore a white rose buttonhole. The service was conducted in both English & Welsh. It was when William Hague was Secretary of Sate for Wales that they met.

31st December 1997 Wednesday

As we approach the third Millennium, we find ourselves leaving the machine era for the cyberspace age. America has produced a blue-print entitled, 'Framework for Global Electronic Commerce'. Electronic transactions account for £150 billion of the annual global economy at present. By the year 2005 it could be £2 trillion. Work will leave the office for cyberspace.

* * *

Rhyme for remembering the Kings & Queens of England in correct order.

Willy, Willy, Harry, Steve;
Harry, Dick, John, Harry Three;
One, Two, Three Neds, Richard Two;
Henry Four, Five, Six – then who?
Edwards, Four, Five, Dick the Bad,
Harries Twain and Ned the Lad.
Mary, Bessie, James the Vain, Charles One, Two, then James again.
William and Mary, Anna Gloria,
Four Georges, William & Victoria.
Edward the Seventh & George the Fifth.
Edward the Eighth & George the Sixth.
Now we have Elizabeth......

Question: Can anyone complete the Cockney alphabet which begins A for 'orses, B for mutton, C for th' Highlanders, etc.?

There are many versions of the 'Cockney alferbet' found all over the world. However the most popular seems to be –

A for 'orses, B for mutton. C for th'Highlanders, D for rential, E for brick, F for vescence, G for police, H for retirement, I for Novello, J for orange, K for teria, l for leather, M for size, N for lope, O for the wings of a dove, P for a whistle, Q for a bus, R for Mo, S for Williams, T for two, U for me, V for La France, W for a fiver, X for breakfast, Y for mistress, Z for breezes

Other versions include – C for yourself, C for miles, D for dumb, E for Adam, G for whizz, I for Lutin, I for the engine, K for rancis, N for eggs, O for the garden wall, P for relief, P for a penny, Q for billiards, Q for a song, Q for the pictures, Q for rations, R for crown, S for Rantzen, U for got my birthday, U for missum, V for Espana, V for Zapata, V for victory, W for the kitty, X for cougar, Y for husband, Y for not, Y for golf, Y for goodness sake, Z for miles, etc.

David Evans, Orpington, Kent

This wasn't so much a Cockney alphabet as a comic one broadcast in the late thirties by the comedy duo Clapham and Dwyer. I've never forgotten it.   Bert Gordon,
West Drayton, Middx.

1998

1st January 1998 Thursday
1998! This is the Triple 666 year.
But we seem to be heading for major problems in the world of computers not only next year with the advent of European Monetary Union (EMU) when Britain will be excluded, while at the same time businesses with chains overseas will be partly included; but nearer & nearer looms the new millennium, when all the computers might simply give up.

New driving licences will have to carry the holder's photograph from next summer, the Government has announced.
The change will bring the UK into line with Europe and follows an EU directive. (Newspaper cutting)

3rd January 1998 Saturday
"Be at the Heart of the Millennium – 728 Days to go"
The Leicester Mercury has decided to give us all a 2 year-long countdown to the Millennium. It certainly is a very special event, a once in a thousand years occasion.

5th January 1998 Monday
Today I met Gwen in Leicester, merely by chance. Having co-habited with cousin Miles for 4 years & then simply walking out on him 10 months ago, she brought me up to date on her new lifestyle, living in a bungalow at 14 Slade Place, Eyres Monsell, off Sturdee Road, Leicester.
I brought her up to date on cousin Miles & his whirlwind romance with Michele. Gwen had no idea that Miles was now married.

7th January 1998 Wednesday
A new washing machine. On what would have been Brian Lamming's 70th birthday, I took delivery of a new Electronic 1050 de Luxe Model 9605 Hotpoint top loader. This is my 2nd washing machine; it replaces the first Hotpoint 1509 top loader which has given me more than 20 years excellent service. Purchased for £104 in August 1977, it is replaced by one now costing £550.

9th January 1998 Friday
You never know what British Gas will do next. No sooner did we have the split into British Gas Energy (B.G.E.) & Transco International, than the next thing we knew was the demerger giving us
BG plc, an updated version of Transco International and Centrica, an updated version of British Gas Energy.

11th January 1998 Sunday
I always felt it was grossly unfair to plunge British Gas into £1 billion debt, when privatisation left it in a dire dilemma, as shown 5th January 1996. The problem rested eventually with Centrica, who in compensation was given the Morecambe field.

Centrica, the gas business that includes British Gas, yesterday declared that its expensive take-or-pay obligations to buy high-priced gas were now back under control after agreeing to pay Conoco, Elf and Total a total of £365 million. (Newspaper cutting)

13th January 1998 Tuesday
Having worked with scientists dealing with gas & oil measurement from 1978 to 1991, I knew that the Morecambe gas field was the jewel in the crown of British Gas's exploration arm, with its 3 trillion m^3 reserves of gas. Finding so much gas in Morecambe Bay helped keep Britain afloat financially. In our laboratories at work we constantly monitored the many fluctuating components of the gas.

15th January 1998 Thursday
Woodings, Ethel Mabel of Ravenstone, passed peacefully away at The Rowans Nursing Home on 3rd January 1998. Dearly loved Mother of Margaret and Keith, dear mother-in-law of Peter and Brenda and a proud Grandma of Andrew, John and the late David. Funeral service at Ravenstone ParishChurch on Wednesday 14th January at 12 noon followed by Cremation at Loughborough. No flowers by request but donations in her memory if desired may be made to Ravenstone Church Restoration Fund, c/o Mr S. Land, 54, Leicester Road, Ravenstone.

Mabel Woodings has died, aged 85. A stalwart member of RavenstoneChurch for many years, her funeral yesterday was well attended. Her daughter Margaret was particularly sad, having lost her own son David in August 1994, the lovely lad mentioned in this diary August 30th 1994.

16th January 1998 Friday
Dolman, John Joseph, passed suddenly away at Glenfield General Hospital on January 16th 1998, aged 78 years, devoted husband to Lynda, dearly loved father to Anne. Funeral service to take place at Ravenstone Church on Friday January 23rd at 1p.m. followed by interment at Ravenstone Churchyard. (Newspaper cutting)

17th January 1998 Saturday
Visited Gwen in her new little home, a bungalow at 14 Slade Place, Eyres Monsell, very near to where I worked at the Department of Energy from 1978 1991. After 4 years with cousin Miles, where she spent most of the time in the kitchen and was never truly loved, she finally broke away, declared herself homeless, and was granted a council bungalow where she is at last completely 'at home'.

19th January 1998 Monday
Well done Centrica! The section of dear old British Gas left with a £1 billion problem of take-or-pay for gas, once the gas industry was privatised. Now it has managed to re-negotiate contracts with the major oil companies, albeit at a total cost of £1 billion. Having recently paid Conoco, Elf and Total £365 million, & earlier made new deals with BP & Mobil, now with Chevron, it is there.

21st January 1998 Wednesday
When the children of Israel chose to ignore God's commandments, the Lord spoke to them through his prophets, 'Behold, I am bringing such evil upon Jerusalem & Judah, that whosoever heareth of it, both his ears shall tingle ...... I will wipe Jerusalem as a man

wipeth a dish, wiping it & turning it upside down.' I think of II Kings 21: 13 when I wash & dry the dishes.

23rd January 1998 Friday
Digital television! For a start we will need a Set-Top Box (STB). First will be Satellite company BSkyB; next will be digital cable TV; thirdly will be the terrestrial broadcasters – the BBC & ITV companies, becoming British Digital Broadcasting (BDB). Eventually STBs will be inbuilt.
Scheduled launch of DVB-S (digital satellite TV): Spring 1998. Scheduled launch of DVB-T (digital terrestrial TV): 1998

25th January 1998 Sunday
British Sky Broadcasting (BSkyB), a consortium in which News International, owners of 'The Times', has a 40% stake, has decided to get together with Cable & Wireless Communications in order to co-ordinate their digital plans. They have now agreed to launch their services on the same day & are preparing an enormous joint marketing & promotional campaign right now.

27th January 1998 Tuesday
'Civil Service Retirement Fellowship' this month, for the 3rd consecutive year, was a belated Christmas party, held this time at the home of Terry Watson, Chairman of the Coalville Group, 16 Coverdale, Whitwick.
There were about 30 assembled, each providing something towards the refreshments, plus a wrapped gift. We met at 12.30 p.m. & began to disperse while it was still light at 4 p.m.

29th January 1998 Thursday
Nottingham's pantomime this year was Cinderella. Katherine (aged 93) & I (aged 66) enjoyed this excellent performance where the ugly sisters were almost as funny as those I saw at Hinckley in 1983. The costumes were out of this world; it truly was a fairy tale par excellence. While Joanne outgrew the magic of fairy tales at the age of 9, Katherine aged 93 is as young at heart as ever she was.

31st January 1998 Saturday
'Talking Newspaper – Recording Workshop' Together with other readers from different parts of the county, I attended this recording workshop at the Royal Leicestershire Rutland & Wycliffe Society for the Blind, Resources Centre, Gedding Road, Leicester, where we were introduced to the latest Pressure Zone Microphone (PZM) & saw how the recordings are processed by 'Sound Services'.

2nd February 1998 Monday
"Don't fence me in." All my life I have lived at 27 Leicester Road, Ravenstone, a plot of land 18 feet wide and 198 feet long (6 yards by 66 yards).
Over the years two bungalows & a house have been built on the other side of the 198 feet long 'Hollies' wall. Now it is proposed to build five houses on the other side of the 18 feet wide wall at the far end of the garden, once land-locked.

4th February 1998 Wednesday
"Fiddler on the Roof" (a repeat of 1975) is this year's

choice for Coalville Amateurs. Again I was pleased to be asked to join the old regulars assembled at the home of Peter Jacques for ticket allocation.
Stalwart Vincent Hardy who died last October was replaced by choreographer Dawn Cox, joining Peter & Vera Jacques, Olive Meakin, George Taylor, Ann Day, Basil Newbold & me.

6th February 1998 Friday
"Alumni Officer – De Montfort University"
True to form, cousin Miles, the mercurial Miles Wilson, is now seeking 'early retirement' from his full time job at the University & reverting to his playboy image, dabbling in this, that and the other, including helping his new dynamic wife Michele in her lucrative business, supplying sandwiches & light snacks to local quarry workers.

8th February 1998 Septuagesima Sunday
Jan from the office retired on her 63rd birthday last month. Thirty members of staff & twenty retired members of staff (including me) had a lovely get-together at the Firs, Wigston from 12 noon – 3 p.m. in our own 'private party' room, with buffet & tables of varying sizes to choose from. Others due to retire in the next few years were all looking forward to their own retirement.

Walkers Crisps are celebrating their 50th birthday this year. *(Newspaper cutting)*

10th February 1998 Tuesday
The Further & Higher Education Act of 1992 allowed 41 polytechnics & colleges to re-title themselves as universities. This more or less doubled the number of universities in Britain – total number is now 97. The sprawling university network costs more than £6 billion a year to run, i.e. one fifth of the nation's education budget. However, the standard of education prior to university has declined.

12th February 1998 Thursday
Portcullis House, the new parliamentary building designed by Sir Michael Hopkins, just across the road from Big Ben, is due for completion early in 2001. The major work up to now has been laying the firm foundations reaching far below ground. Now, at last, the official 'foundation stone' has been unveiled (3rd February) by Betty Boothroyd, Speaker of the House of Commons.

14th February 1998 Saturday
"For my Valentine with love"
You are my Valentine for ever.
xxxxx

15th February 1998 Sexagesima Sunday
The Angel of the North was today dominating the North East skyline as Britain's largest statue.

Unhappy anniversary. Saturday marked the ninth anniversary of the fatwa decreed by Iran on Salman Rushdie.
(Newspaper cuttings)

16th February 1998 Monday

Statutory off road notification will apply to all licensed vehicles from 31st January 1998.

The Driver & Vehicle Licensing Agency (DVLA) is reminding us all of the latest legislation when we receive a vehicle tax reminder from DVLA Swansea. Either we renew the vehicle tax or declare the vehicle to be off the road by using the new Statutory Off Road Notification (SORN) section of the V11 form. This is an attempt to identify the vast number of car tax dodgers.

18th February 1998 Wednesday

Adelaide Hunter Hoodless, founder of the Women's Institute, had been invited to speak at the local 'Farmers' Institute' in Stoney Creek. (See 19th February 1997) Her address that evening was so inspirational that the women present decided to form a 'Women's Institute'. Last year, being the centenary, the bells at Loughborough Carillon rang for 15 minutes, playing a selection of appropriate tunes.

Queen Mother home – Looking remarkably spry and apparently walking with only slight difficulty, Queen Elizabeth the Queen Mother left hospital after her second hip replacement operation.

(Newspaper cutting)

22nd February 1998 Quinquagesima Sunday

Apart from having an impact wisdom tooth extracted in hospital in April 1962, my teeth have lasted very well. I needed to have one out in 1950 & another out in 1954. Last Sunday my teeth let me know that all was not well, and on Tuesday 17th February, I had the top back molar (right) extracted. Such is the advancement in dental surgery today, that the tooth was out before I so much as knew it.

24th February 1998 Shrove Tuesday

A meeting was held today at Ashby Baptist Church, where a representative from County Hall's Social Services introduced us all to a formidable 10 page form called a Daily Delivery Return (DDR), which in future must be completed each time we deliver meals on wheels. The meeting ended in uproar, as 'volunteers' refused to be dictated to by County Hall with all its bureaucracy.

25th February 1998 Ash Wednesday

Princess Margaret suffers stroke – Princess Margaret was undergoing tests at a hospital in Barbados last night after suffering a mild stroke while on holiday in the Caribbean. Buckingham Palace said that the Queen's younger sister was in a stable condition and had suffered no serious paralysis.

(Newspaper cutting)

26th February 1998 Thursday

Ebbsfleet, now a sandbank off the Kent coast, is destined to become a house built on a rock. A whole new town of over 3,000 houses is planned, as well as a large area of new commercial development. The £3 billion Channel Tunnel rail link to St. Pancras will include a station at Ebbsfleet, being close to the M25 and the A2 and an attractive connection for residents of north Kent.

28th February 1998 Saturday

Diana, Princess of Wales, died last year on 31st August 1997. For the past 6 months she has continued to feature in the newspapers almost every day. In death she is absolutely idolised, & it seems that her adoring followers will never tire of reading her life story.

The annual budget of the Department of Social Services is £91 billion. It costs every worker £15 per working day. Fraud is estimated to cost £3 billion a year.

Graduated retirement benefit: If you were an employee between April 1961 and April 1975, and earned more than £9 a week, you will have paid graduated NI contributions. These will provide you with a graduated pension benefit.   *(Newspaper cuttings)*

1st March 1998 Sunday

Pensions & Overseas Benefits Directorate – Benefits Agency – About the general increase in benefits.

"This is to tell you that from 6th April 1998 the amount of your benefit will go up to £76.79p a week. Basic Pension £64.70p. Additional Pension £45.69p, less Contracted-Out Deduction £35.28p, plus Graduated Pension £1.68p making a total increase of approximately £15 per month."

3rd March 1998 Tuesday

£10,000 per year. This was my salary in September 1987, rising to £12,000 by the time I retired from work in July 1991. However, 'net pay' was much less than 'salary' when all the necessary deductions had been made. Now, my combined Civil Service Pension & Old Age Pension, with minimum deductions, once more reach £10,000 per year – a modest but most welcome income.

"Research suggests that a pensioner of 65 and above needs at least £150 per week for a modest, though adequate, lifestyle, which means generating at least £7,800 pa after tax from his pensions and assets."   *(newspaper cutting)*

5th March 1998 Thursday

'Fiddler on the Roof' which we gave in 1975 is again Coalville Amateurs' chosen production for this year & as ever I am thrilled by the magic of the stage & love being part of the team. In 1975, I was assistant prompter & sometimes could not see the words of the libretto because of tears in my eyes. Still the story moves a new generation to tears, including me.

7th March 1998 Saturday

'Fiddler on the Roof' is proving to be very successful. Directed by Adam Markillie of Leicester, who assured us at the AGM (see 12 June last year) that he could produce a better show than ever seen before, the result has been most satisfactory. Brian Gadsby shines in the lead as Tevye, the poor milkman, supported on & off stage by a fully co-ordinated team, ranging in age from 5 to 75.

9th March 1998 Monday

Huge Angel Statue – the Angel of the North, erected last month on a windswept hillside beside the A1 overlooking Gateshead, is Britain's biggest sculpture. Costing £800,000, it is designed to withstand winds of

100 miles per hour. The 60foot steel construction, with the wingspan of a jumbo jet is not my idea of an angel & many people consider it to be a waste of money, likely to cause an accident.

11th March 1998 Wednesday

"OFGAS – Workshop Technician Vacancy" This advert in the Leicester Mercury reminded me of the time when Maurice, the messenger at work, upset Stuart, the craftsman in the workshop & like a judge, I sat & listened to both sides of the story (25 February 1985). Maurice, Stuart & I have long since left work, but the workshop now needs a technician.

13th March 1998 Friday

Following the massacre of the children of Dunblane by a lone gunman on 13th March 1996, the Government called for a ban on all handguns of more than .22 calibre. By the deadline of 1st October 1997, 160,000 were handed in to the police for destruction. Only guns kept at licensed gun-clubs remained despite strong objections from law-abiding gun owners who opposed the ban.

17th March 1998 Tuesday

"When I was a child it was almost unknown to contemplate divorce" (ref: 16th March 1997)
Why? One important factor is that we were a much less mobile society. There was a more stable base on which to build one's life. Fifty years ago many people lived within easy reach of parents, brothers, sisters, aunts & uncles, which created a pressure to conform.

Church news – the Right Rev Thomas Frederick Butler, Bishop of Leicester, to be Bishop of Southwark in succession to the Right Rev Robert Kerr Williamson who resigned on January 31st.

19th March 1998 Thursday

"Winter Fuel Payment – This winter & next, the Government is giving pensioners a total of £400 million in winter fuel payments in an unprecedented exercise to help with your fuel bills. £20 is due if you are the only person in your household entitled to help with your fuel bills. Otherwise the amount due is £10 to each pensioner. £20 will be credited to your bank in the next few days."

21st March 1998 Saturday

Elizabeth Hewes – No 811 013 027 0 012 has received her 6th Council Tax Demand Notice, £384.54p. An accompanying letter explains that the new Government is committed to sticking to its predecessor's plans for the first two years to maintain Economic Stability. Hence the grant from the Government continues its downward spiral. However, our Council's quest for increased Efficiency & Effectiveness goes on.

23rd March 1998 Monday

Cardinal Basil Hume, called from Abbot to Archbishop in March 1976, is now facing retirement & the rare opportunity for a Roman Catholic to move to the House of Lords. However, he insists, 'I have no ambition to be Lord Hume. I want to be buried in my monastic habit, not ermine. If I went to the Lords I would have to be Lord Hume, not a Lord Spiritual.' (As Anglican Bishop)

'Called from Abbott to Archbishop – not to dominate, but to animate.'
This was Cardinal Basil Hume in March 1976. If ever there was a man who climbed the ladder of humility as directed in the Rule of St Benedict, it is Cardinal Hume. He once said that as a monk & a housemaster, he came to realise that each boy in his care had at least one gift that surpassed his own. 'Each person is able to do something I cannot do,' he said. We learn from one another.

27th March 1998 Friday

"The heavens themselves blaze forth the death of princes." Last year comet Hale-Bopp was seen in the heavens prior to the death of Diana, Princess of Wales.
If ever anyone left this world in a blaze of glory it was Diana, who launched a thousand times ten thousand tributes. I recalled the first impression she made in February 1981, loving riches and her own glory.

Even Shakespeare's Julius Caesar contains evidence of the prophetic nature of comets, "When beggars die, then are no comets seen. The heavens themselves blaze forth the death of princes."
(Newspaper cutting)

29th March 1998 Sunday

Cardinal Basil Hume celebrated his 75th birthday on 2nd March this year. It is the age for a Roman Catholic Bishop to retire. At the beginning of February, in accordance with the code of Canon Law, he tendered his resignation, but this was not accepted by the Pope. Cardinal Hume therefore remains in post as the very popular Archbishop of Westminster.

Papal sign – Hints from the Vatican suggest that Archbishop Patrick Kelly of Liverpool will succeed Cardinal Basil Hume as leader of British Catholics when the Cardinal retires as Archbishop of Westminster. Hume, 75, has been 'persuaded' to see in the millennium. *(Newspaper cutting)*

31st March 1998 Tuesday

Civil Service Retirement Fellowship, Leicestershire & South Lincolnshire Branch No 76, Coalville Group:
"Meetings are usually held in the Coalville library on the third Wednesday each month at 2 p.m." Now we are to have a change of venue & next month's meeting (15th April) will be held at Thringstone Community Centre, with better facilities.

1st April 1998 Wednesday

Donaldson, Edward George of Donington Le Heath, passed peacefully away at home on April 1st 1998, aged 85 years. Beloved husband of Molly, devoted father and grandfather. Funeral service to take place at Hugglescote Church on Thursday April 9th at 11.45 a.m. followed by cremation at Loughborough Crematorium.
(See 31st January 1994)

3rd April 1998 Friday

Are you up to the Church Challenge? That's the question being asked by the Ravenstone Parish Church Restoration Club. The club is issuing the Church Challenge to anyone who wishes to help raise vital cash for the restoration of Ravenstone Parish Church and any team of six people can take on the task.

The challenge is to raise a minimum amount of £250 for the restoration fund for Ravenstone Parish Church between the beginning of June and the end of August this year.

Teams are free to choose exactly how they raise the money and events can vary from one big fundraiser to several smaller ideas. All the money raised from the challenge will go towards helping to restore the roof at the church and whichever team succeeds in raising the most sponsorship will be awarded with a trophy.

For more details and an entry form please contact David Winterton on (01530) 831827.   (Newspaper cutting)

4th April 1998 Saturday

More & more couples are choosing a Civil Wedding in preference to a Church Wedding now that the choice of venues has been extended. Favourites in Leicestershire include Rothley Court, Beaumanor Hall, Burleigh Court, Donington Manor, Prestwold Hall, Yew Lodge Hotel, Quorn Grange Hotel, Kegworth Hotel, the Priest House at Castle Donington and Quorn Country Hotel.

6th April 1998 Monday

Adam yesterday celebrated his first birthday in style surrounded by his devoted parents, grandparents & great-grandparents. I joined Pat & Evelyn, Mary Blue, Janie Jarman (Adam's great-grandma) & her partner John, plus Adam's maternal grandparents for a birthday bonanza. Adam's parents, Steven & Jane gave us their latest news that they are expecting another baby this year, in November.

8th April 1998 Wednesday

"Don't let Michael put me in a home," pleaded Bunting four years ago. Sadly, it was no longer possible for Bunting to cope without being cared for day & night and on 22nd January this year she was admitted to an exclusive new purpose-built Nursing Home, 'Maple Court', Rotherwood Drive, Rowley Park, Stafford, ST17 9AF. Telephone - 01785 245556, not far from the railway station.

10th April 1998 Good Friday

"Do I know you?" asked Bunting when I last visited her at Maple Court Nursing Home. I thought of King Lear addressing his daughter Cordelia, "Methinks I should know you, yet I am doubtful."

Oh, how very, very sad to see Bunting in such a hopeless state. Her only joy in life is being asked to sing. Deep in her subconscious mind are stored beautiful songs of long ago which once she sang.

12th April 1998 Easter Sunday

Evelyn reached her 80th birthday on 23rd March.

To mark the occasion Mary Blue organised a family luncheon get-together at the Fallen Knight, Ashby-de-la-Zouch on Mothering Sunday, attended by 15 of us: - Pat, Evelyn, Mary Blue, Steven, Jane, Karen, Scott, Sharon, Jim, Carly, Sam, Jim's mother, James, Trevelyn and me. Evelyn said it reminded her of, "Dear Octopus" whose tentacles embraced all the family.

14th April 1998 Tuesday

'Cheat' walks out – Ffyona Campbell, *the first woman to walk the world, will be removed from the Guinness Book of Records after admitting that she cheated.*

Ms Campbell discloses that her ten-year marathon went adrift between Indianapolis and Fort Summer on the American leg. Pregnant and physically unable to complete the required 25 miles a day to keep up to schedule, she hitched lifts in her back-up truck, walking only the last few miles into towns where press conferences were being held. She eventually returned to walking within the rules after an abortion.

(Newspaper cutting) See 15th April 1997.

16th April 1998 Thursday

In 1974 British Coal announced that 500 million tonnes of coal lay hidden beneath the beautiful Vale of Belvoir. The Duke of Rutland, who lived at Belvoir Castle, led the vociferous outcry at the idea of coal-mining in the Vale. Eventually, a compromise was struck & the coal-mine was sited at Asfordby in order to tunnel underground to the coal. However, volcanic rock barred the way and the mine is now closed.

18th April 1998 Saturday

A £20,000 bronze statue of a miner will be unveiled tomorrow, "This memorial is dedicated to the miners of Leicestershire who gave their lives winning the coal."

During the past 35 years the face of the coal industry – which was once so prevalent in North West Leicestershire and across the border in South Derbyshire – has not so much changed as disappeared.

Merrylees – Sunk 1941 – Merged with Desford in 1966.
Nailstone – Sunk 1865 – Merged with Bagworth in 1967.
Lount – Sunk 1924 – Closed 1968.
Snibston – Sunk 1832 – Closed 1983.
Desford – Sunk 1901 – Closed 1984.
Rawdon – Sunk 1821 – Merged with Donisthorpe in 1985.
South Leicester – Sunk 1825 – Closed 1986.
Whitwick – Sunk 1820 – Closed 1986.
Measham – Sunk 1850 – Closed 1986.
Ellistown – Sunk 1874 – Merged with Bagworth in 1986, closed 1989.
Cadley Hill – Sunk 1860 – Closed 1988.
Bagworth – Sunk 1857 – Closed 1991.

(Newspaper cuttings)

20th April 1998 Monday

Mervyn Talbott & Margaret, my next door neighbours for the past two years, have lived together as man and wife without actually being married until now. Last Thursday, 16th April, they were married at Coalville Register Office, followed by a get-together at the Plough Inn, Ravenstone. Apart from keeping pigeons, which can be a nuisance, they are good quiet neighbours, day and night.

22nd April 1998 Wednesday

The Gas Act 1995 made provision for the introduction of 'competition' into the domestic gas market. With effect from 1st February 1996, British Gas lost its monopoly over the supply of gas to households. It has been a gradual transition starting in the South West (see January 25th 1996) and due to cover the whole country by 1st January next year. Leicestershire is in stage 4, operative from 24th April 1998.

From April 24th gas consumers in Leicestershire can switch suppliers. There are currently 19 companies that are licensed to sell in the new market.

(Newspaper cutting)

24th April 1998 Friday
During the Reformation – the great religious revolution of the 16th century – most medieval lecterns were jettisoned. Norwich Cathedral's beautiful pelican lectern is one which managed to survive. It is thought to date from 1450.

Medieval lecterns survive at Merton and Corpus Christi Colleges, Oxford; at Eaton, at King's and Christ's Colleges, Cambridge; at St George's Chapel, Windsor; at Exeter, Norwich and Peterborough Cathedrals; and at King's Lynn, Yeovil, Southampton, Lowestoft, Coventry, Oundle, Bristol and Newcastle.

The majority of the survivors are more likely to be of English, probably East Anglian, manufacture than, as once thought, Flemish. They are rare and priceless survivors from the great age of English ecclesiastical art. *(Newspaper cutting)*

26th April 1998 Sunday
Katherine's birthday – 94 today and wondering what day of the week she was born. What day was 26th April 1904? Thanks to the wonderful 'Twentieth Century Calendar' spanning the whole century from 1901 to 2000, I had only to look at Calendar No 13 in my earlier 'five year' diaries for the answer. This leap year calendar, identical to 1932, 1960 and 1988, told us it was a Tuesday.

30th April 1998 Thursday
From 'Paymaster' – an Eds & Hogg Robinson Company no longer Her Majesty's Paymaster General. "With effect from 6th April 1988, new rate = £7,481.63p a year, i.e. £623.47p a month, less tax £109.58p = £513 payable each month." This together with the State Pension £307.16p every 4 weeks, gives me a monthly income of £845.77p, about £195 per week. Tax code = 122P. Tax prefix = 500.

2nd May 1998 Saturday
"Whitaker's Almanack" that excellent reference book which I bought as a reminder of life as it was in 1991, the year I retired from work, is also an on-going reference to 'an amazing variety of subjects' including (like my 5 year diaries) 'calendar for any year' spanning 1770 to 2025. (Page 120) All this is covered by 14 different calendars forming an intricate pattern of sequence.

4th May 1998 Monday
Pioneer 10, no longer justifies the cost of keeping in touch. It is now so far away that its signals hardly register, and the American space agency NASA has therefore severed contact with it.

However, it goes merrily on its way, even though it may not meet another landmark for 30,000 years. It might then reach the star Ross 248 in the constellation of Andromeda. It does carry with it greetings from Planet Earth.

6th May 1998 Wednesday
Pioneer 10 carries a plaque designed by the astronomer Carl Sagan (see 22nd December 1996), in case it should ever fall into the hands of another civilisation. The gold-plated plaque contains diagrams of a man and a woman and a celestial map in an effort to help aliens to work out where the spacecraft originated. No doubt, in another 30,000 years, the plaque will be out of date.

8th May 1998 Friday
"Cosmos" is a £2 million super computer at Cambridge University which could finally unravel the secrets of the universe, from its creation to the present day. It is the largest Origin 2000 computer in Britain, and is run by the UK Computational Cosmology Consortium, who hope to 'push back' our understanding of the first fractions of a second after the Big Bang and unravel its mysteries.

10th May 1998 Sunday
Katherine and I enjoyed once more the Bluebell Service in Swithland Woods. Toffee, her beloved dog, now ailing and elderly, stayed at home. The address was given by the Revd Joanna Ray, Diocesan Chaplain among Deaf People and we sat beside a group of deaf people. It was fascinating following the sign language for all the stirring hymns and the chorus, 'With the cross of Jesus going on before.'

12th May 1998 Tuesday
His Holiness Pope John Paul II will be celebrating his 78th birthday on 18th May, so again Katherine sends him a birthday card, chosen by me and duly despatched. Whether he ever receives these beautiful cards, I do not know, but they are formally acknowledged.

14th May 1998 Thursday
A letter from Kensington Palace, signed Colin Tebbutt, MVO, to the Lord Mayor of Leicester, acknowledges safe receipt of Tributes of Condolence signed by the people of Leicester (including me) following the death of Diana, Princess of Wales, on 31st August last year.

"Your tributes are currently being stored here at Kensington Palace and in the near future will be forwarded to Althorp Park, the Spencer family home."

16th May 1998 Saturday
The Times – On Saturday, January 1st 1785, John Walter, the founder of The Times, wrote in the first issue of his experimental broadsheet: "A News-Paper ought to be the Register of the times, and the faithful recorder of every species of intelligence; it ought not to be engrossed by any particular object, but, like a well covered table, it should contain something suited to every palate." *(Newspaper cutting)*

How I love reading 'The Times', the faithful recorder and register of the times. John Walter, the founder, was a man after my own heart. Since I retired from work in 1991, I have learned such a lot from The Times.

October 1st 1966 – Lord Thomson of Fleet became the

fourth owner of The Times. *The family of the founder (1785) John Walter owned it for 124 years; Lord Northcliffe for 15, the Astors for 46.*

Lord Thomson died in 1976 and in 1981 his son sold the paper to Rupert Murdoch.

Rupert Murdoch who runs 'The Times' does all he possibly can to increase its circulation, aiming to beat the market leader, The Daily Telegraph, whose sales exceed a million each day. He began with a vengeance in 1993 by cutting the price and running at a loss, while sales slowly rose from 400,000 to nearly 800,000. The idea being that once you hook a reader (like me), they stay with you.

'The Times' moved recently into new offices on the other side of Pennington Street, London E1.

This new building was 'blessed' by the local Rector, the Revd Craig, progressing from the reception desk through all the different sections and departments and finally reaching the conference room where he gave his address. His prayer ended, 'Let your Holy Angels dwell here to guard and preserve in peace all who work here.'

22nd May 1998 Friday

Arsenal 2: Newcastle 0. Two years ago Manchester United clinched a historic second double, repeating their 1994 achievement by winning both the League & the Cup. Now Arsenal, known as The Gunners, have also clinched a historic second double, first achieved in 1971. Double Winners – 1889 Preston North End, 1897 Aston Villa, 1961 Tottenham Hotspur, 1971 Arsenal, 1986 Liverpool, 1994 Manchester United, 1996 Manchester United, 1998 Arsenal.

24th May 1998 Sunday

'Philip's World Factbook' – What a wonderful book I discovered in Leicester's Map Shop yesterday. Only £8.99p it gives a brief résumé of every country in the world, giving the historical background and excellent maps. It shows the flag and also explains what the flag means. How the world has changed since I left school. This is a snapshot of the closing 20th century.

26th May 1998 Tuesday

Visited Bunting at Maple Court Nursing Home, Stafford, where after four months of life in a totally alien environment, she had no spirit left in her. She knows when she is hungry or thirsty and apparently takes other people's food and drink at the table. She seeks constant attention and is very disruptive unless sedated. Whatever would my dad think, who knew her and loved her as a lovely young girl?

28th May 1998 Thursday

Broadhurst, *Jean (nee Willars) formerly of Ravenstone, passed peacefully away on May 18th 1998, aged 71years. Loving wife of George and much loved mother of Lynette and Tony, dearest grandma of Stephanie and Warren. The funeral service will be held at Ravenstone Parish Church on Thursday May 28th at 11.30a.m prior to interment in the churchyard. No flowers by request, but donations in lieu if desired, for LOROS will be accepted by the Midlands Co-operative Service, 128 London Road, Coalville. Tel. 01530 836703.*

Jean, our Newsagent since 1961, who less than two years ago informed us that she and George were hanging up their paper bags for the last time on 10th June 1996, has now sadly died of cancer. Never deserting their paper shop to go on holiday, her retirement was short-lived.

30th May 1998 Saturday

Cornwall here we come! Enid & I are preparing for our summer holiday in Falmouth. We are hoping to travel in Enid's car, starting on Tuesday 2nd June, staying overnight en route at the Bendene Hotel, Exeter & then from Wednesday 3rd June for one week at the Gyllyngvase House Hotel, Falmouth. On the return journey we will stay overnight near Alison in Bristol.

1st June 1998 Monday

Mary Blue's family is still growing. Both Debbie and Jane are pregnant again, which should increase the number of grandchildren from 8 to 10.

According to my recently acquired 'Philip's World Factbook' the total population of the United Kingdom (England, Scotland, Wales and Northern Ireland) is now 58,306,000.

In my lifetime the world population has grown from 2 billion to 5¼ billion.

3rd June 1998 Wednesday

Enid & I are now ensconced in the Gyllyngvase House Hotel, Gyllyngvase Road, Falmouth for a seven night stay, after spending last night at the Bendene Hotel, Richmond Road, Exeter, to break the 300 mile car journey from Ravenstone. We would have preferred to be in Falmouth next month to see the arrival of 100 Tall Ships for the Cutty Sark Tall Ships' Race.

5th June 1998 Friday

"Dear Customer" – Ravenstone's get-up-and-make-a-big-profit Newsagents, Neil & Glynis North, informed us by letter on 26th September 1997 (the day that Glynis celebrated her 40th birthday) that delivery charges for newspapers would increase to:- 5p daily per household morning papers Monday – Saturday, 3p daily Leicester Mercury, 6p daily Sunday papers. Plus 12p for collection of payment!

7th June 1998 Trinity Sunday

Another thought for our 3 in 1 God comes from the European Centre for Nuclear Research near Geneva, where scientists attempt to recreate in miniature the conditions of the Big Bang, the fireball that existed one trillionth of a second after the creation of the Universe, when everything condensed into the three great basics: - electrons, protons and neutrons.

9th June 1998 Tuesday

No wonder Ravenstone's newsagents Neil & Glynis North have packed in the business. After only 18 months, they were only too pleased to hand over the responsibility for delivering newspapers to the Mercury News Shop, Coalville, who deliver the Mercury free of charge.

On this day in 1898 – China grants Britain a 99-year lease on Hong Kong.

11th June 1998 Thursday

Coalville Amateur Operatic Society AGM this year saw Internal Auditor Hewsie (appointed 1992) relinquish this minor role, as I approach 50 years membership with the Society. It was announced that next year's show will be 'The Card', a repeat of our 1984 production.

Several offices remain vacant – Electrician – Prompter – Props – Rehearsal Pianist. Peter Jacques remains the one driving force.

13th June 1998 Saturday

How we loved Cornwall where we felt so very much at home. It was a joy for me to take my early morning walk from the hotel, past all the little boats at anchor in the great harbour (one of the finest natural harbours in the world) and on to the Prince of Wales pier. Although we enquired about accommodation for the Tall Ships' Race, everywhere was fully booked.

15th June 1998 Monday

The new £2 coin came into circulation today. About 50 million have been initially produced by the Royal Mint. The coin's milled edge bears the inscription, "Standing on the shoulders of giants."

17th June 1998 Wednesday

On 17th June 1982, my darling mum died & almost immediately a Prince was born – Prince William will be celebrating his 16th birthday on 21st June. As Prince William, year by year, celebrates another birthday, it is a reminder of how long ago my mum died. Prince William will have the distinction of celebrating his 18th birthday – his coming of age – in that special year 2000.

19th June 1998 Friday

Although the Gas Act 1995 provided for the introduction of competition into the domestic gas market & people now can choose from a whole variety of companies that are now licensed to sell gas, I have chosen to stay with British Gas Home Energy, not only to supply me with gas but also with electricity – a composite gas & electricity bill.

20th June 1998 Saturday

On this day June 20th 1975 Lord Lucan disappeared after the murder of his children's nanny in November 1974. Police believe he killed her in mistake for his wife in the darkness of the basement at 46 Lower Belgrave Street. Scotland Yard still receives tips of alleged sightings of the peer.

(Newspaper cutting – See 29th October 1999)

21st June 1998 Sunday

Prince William is 16 years old today. He is now six feet tall, taking after his mother Diana, Princess of Wales, while his father Charles, Prince of Wales is not so tall. Prince William starts his 4th academic year at Eton in September, where he is making excellent progress. Following the untimely death of Diana last August, Prince William is taking over her role as the nation's 'pin-up'.

23rd June 1998 Tuesday

"The trouble with us is, our light has gone out!"
I thought immediately of Dr Coggan's brilliant Ashe

lecture which I heard at Ashby-de-la-Zouch in October 1974, when for the first time this week the pilot light on my gas boiler went out & I had to learn how to get it going again. Fortunately Cocky rang & was able to tell me over the phone exactly what I needed to do.

25th June 1998 Thursday

Visited Bunting & found her still heavily sedated, but nevertheless aware that I was there with her.
"Is it Betty? Is it really Betty?" I motored there via Rugely where I had an early lunch at the 'Little Chef' & a little walk around the town, arriving at Maple Court Nursing Home, Stafford shortly after 1.00 p.m. I called to see Bunting's house, now sold and being re-decorated.

27th June 1998 Saturday

Digital TV is either 'terrestrial' or by 'satellite'. France was first in Europe to offer digital satellite, for the favoured few, while digital terrestrial is a mass market. The use of digital broadcasting technologies provides crystal clear images & compact-disc quality sound & will eventually replace traditional analogue transmission (by radio waves).

29th June 1998 Monday

The Management Appreciation Course which I attended in June 1975 convinced me that I would never make a manager. Today, you need to be more than a manager, you need to be an HR Manager, a Director of Human Resources, developing HR structures, generating HR programmes, implementing HR practices, translating HR infrastructure into strategic solutions & managing them. Phew!

Boots the Chemists *– Turning flat-earth thinking into rounded, real world solutions is what we're about. Its uncharted territory, sure, but we believe that great things are just over the horizon. What we've done is to put our HR function at the heart of out business – where it's really needed.* (Newspaper cutting)

1st July 1998 Wednesday

The government is doing its best to get all the unemployed people into work. The problem today is that there are fewer and fewer unskilled jobs. People therefore need continual training & it is proposed to have a University for Industry. Already the 2 government departments of Education & Employment have merged to create a 'seamless process' for developing Human Resources.

3rd July 1998 Friday

"My wife thinks I am completely mad & lots of other people do as well but I find it very moving & uplifting. The more I read, the more I learn." So says David Bathhurst, aged 38, a magistrates' clerk in Chichester who after 6 years has learned the four Gospels by heart.
I had a similar response when I chose to record the Gospels (see 22nd January 1966) when I bought my tape recorder.

5th July 1998 Sunday

NHS 1948 – 1998 "From lawyers' bills & doctors' pills, good Lord, deliver us."
This saying was handed down from my granddad

Sketchley, who died in 1937, long before we had the benefits of the National Health Service (NHS) founded by Aneurin Bevan on 5th July 1948, exactly fifty years ago today. Aneurin (Nye) Bevan was the Minister of Health who had the courage to launch the scheme.

7th July 1998 Tuesday

Bunting – this song-bird is the ortolon or bunting. It is a Eurasian garden & field bird which is seen in France in the summer before it migrates in the autumn to North Africa & the Middle East. Thousands are trapped each year as they fly across southwest France each autumn & then eaten as a delicacy.

9th July 1998 Thursday

541 days to go. Less than 18 months now to the year 2000.

Britain's biggest bonanza will be the Millennium Experience now being created at Greenwich; plus the Millennium Bridge, a pedestrian bridge across the Thames from St Pauls.

11th July 1998 Saturday

"360° Feedback" This is the latest form of Staff Reporting for people at work. As if it is not bad enough being reported on all the time by those supposedly above you, you now have to evaluate your own strengths & weaknesses, & also be judged by those supposedly beneath you. No wonder so many are choosing early retirement. See what St Paul says, 1 Corinthians, Chapters 12 and 13.

13th July 1998 Monday

Tomorrow is indeed my birth day – born on a Tuesday. Cocky telephoned from Lancaster to say 'Happy Birthday' & sent me £20 in his birthday card.

At Ravenstone Church we have three people with a birthday on 14th July: - Church Warden Alan Roulston, bachelor; Jean Harrison, widow; and old maid Hewsie. Alan therefore invited Jean & me to a meal out together tomorrow evening.

15th July 1998 Wednesday

Just as Lewis William was born on Cocky's birthday, 28th January 1994, making Mary Blue a grandmother twice over at the age of 49, so now, on my birthday 14th July 1998, Freya Lauren is born, the 3rd child of Murdo & Debbie, Mary Blue's 9th grandchild, i.e. four natural grandchildren plus five step-grandchildren. In Norse mythology Freya was the goddess of beauty and love.

17th July 1998 Friday

Cartoon of tramp selling matches from a tray with a notice saying 'ex-revenue man forced to start own business' saying to passer-by, 'I was made redundant by self-assessment'. *(Newspaper cutting)*

"360° Feedback" This is what might befall you, if you fail to give yourself a good staff report.

In AD 65, Petronius Arbiter, the Roman Governor of Bithynia, committed suicide. He could not tolerate the demoralisation caused by re-organisation.

Funeral for tsar *– Patriarch Alexei II, the head of the Russian Orthodox Church, refused to take part, fearing* *a split among his followers over the authenticity of the tsar's bones.* *(Newspaper cutting)*

19th July 1998 Sunday

New double-sided bookcase for Ravenstone Church. At our 6p.m. Service of Holy Communion, the Rector, the Revd Kerry Emmett, dedicated a very fine new double-sided bookcase, presented to the church by affluent John Land in memory of his parents, John Thomas Land (Tom Land) who died in September 1996 & Doris Land who died in July 1993.

A new stamp was issued by the French postal service to commemorate France's World Cup victory.

23rd July 1998 Thursday

Nelson Mandela, President of South Africa, celebrated his 80th birthday last Saturday by marrying 52 year old Graça Machel; widow of Samora Machel, Mozambique's founding president. It is a union that has bound two of the continent's most celebrated political families. Their friendship dates back to 1986 when Mandela in prison wrote to her expressing his condolences when her husband died.

25th July 1998 Saturday

The Reverend Michael David Webb, Vicar of St James, Snibston, has now moved to pastures new after serving 5 years in the parish. He will be replaced by the Reverend Ronald Whittingham as Team Vicar of Hugglescote, with Donington, Ellistown & Snibston. Currently Vicar of Honley with Brockholes, in the Diocese of Wakefield, the Revd Whittingham is expected next January.

27th July 1998 Monday

"How to Build a Human Being" According to Professor Ian Stewart, a Warwick University mathematician, DNA without mathematics is irrelevant to the question of what is life. He believes the secret lies in Fibonacci Numbers, sequence in which each number is derived from adding the previous two numbers, such as 1, 2, 3, 5, 8, 13, 21, 34, 55, 89, etc. (Leonardo Fibonacci 1170 – 1230)

29th July 1998 Wednesday

"Civil Service Retirement Fellowship" this month was a get-together at the home of our chairman, Terry Watson & his wife Audrey, at 16 Coverdale, Whitwick, where it was warm enough to sit out in their lovely garden. Their grandson had shown interest in joining the Civil Service & when asked which particular Department he had in mind, he said, "Retired Civil Servants."

31st July 1998 Friday

The 'S' registration marks the last of the annual rush for new car numbers commencing 1st August. Henceforward there will be two new prefixes a year, starting with 'T' in March next year followed by 'V' in September. As always the Driver & Vehicle Licensing Agency (DVLA) is selling the choicest numbers, having increased the price from £250 a set to £400: S1MON, S1NDY, etc.

2nd August 1998 Sunday

A new guide to treating people with dementia has been launched following concerns that powerful sedative drugs are being over-used. Age Concern published the guide called Drugs and Dementia which outlines good practice in a bid to offer reassurance and information to people in care homes, their families and staff. Research shows that up to 24% of people in care homes may be on powerful anti-psychotic sedatives such as Largactil or Melleril, also known as neuroleptics.

(Newspaper cutting)

Poor old Bunting is certainly under heavy sedation at Maple Court Nursing Home, Stafford. I try to visit her once a month and she usually drops off to sleep. The Nursing Home has now started to issue a little leaflet "The Maple News" – first edition July 1998.

4th August 1998 Tuesday
A picture in the newspaper shows Queen Elizabeth the Queen Mother on her 98th birthday meeting the thousands of people who assemble each year on her birthday in front of Clarence House. Children line up to give her flowers and the guards band march past playing, 'Happy Birthday.'

6th August 1998 Thursday
A newspaper picture shows Cecil John Rhodes (1853 – 1902), British entrepreneur and statesman, who amassed a fortune in diamonds and gold in southern Africa. Rhodesia was named after Cecil Rhodes, before reverting to its African name Zimbabwe in 1980. His bones are no longer welcome in Zimbabwe and are to be dug up.

8th August 1998 Saturday
Digital Satellite, Digital Cable, Digital Terrestrial. Digital televisions are already gaining ground in Europe and the Government in Britain plans to turn off analogue transmission some time in the next decade. Cable laying is now taking place in Ravenstone, while regulators in Brussels are anxious to prevent any one giant monopoly. We can choose between ON Digital and Sky Digital.

10th August 1998 Monday
Mutuality, as regards a Building Society is one owned not by shareholders, but by its savers and borrowers. Next year there is to be a new individual savings account, known as 'ISA' which the Government hopes will encourage more and more people to save money. At the moment only half the adult population of Britain has any savings at all and many are too poor to save.

More troubles for the Government's new savings account? Having discovered that the Isa means 'god' or 'father' in Estonian, I now learn that the new account may also have a special meaning to Muslims. Isa means 'Jesus' in Arabic. Newspaper cutting)

12th August 1998 Wednesday
Brother Pat will be celebrating his 80th birthday on 29th August this year.
I have received a formal written invitation: -
Pat's 80th Birthday Buffet Celebration
Date – Saturday 29th August. Time - 5 p.m. – 8 p.m.
Place – St James Community Centre, Highfields Street, Coalville.
RSVP by 18th August to - Mrs Evelyn Hewes, 3 Totnes Close, Hugglescote.

14th August 1998 Friday
Toffee, the pampered Dachshund, loved by Katherine beyond all measure, died on Tuesday this week.
As when her beloved Alison died in February 1990, Katherine again is absolutely heartbroken. For several hours she sat with her dead dog brushing his long hair, combing him and spraying him with perfume, until he looked quite perfect, reminding me of St Matthew, Chapter 26, verses 7 – 12.

15th August 1998 Saturday
Today is the Anniversary of the Birthday of The Princess Royal. *(Newspaper cutting)*

16th August 1998 Sunday
Following a full page spread in the Coalville Times, extolling his virtues, cousin Miles is ready for lift-off again as a disc jockey. **"Re-creating the days when he rode the waves for Radio Caroline and played the clubs and videotheques in Europe."**
Needless to say, Radio Caroline was an illegal pirate radio station which went off the air in 1980.

Former radio Caroline disc jockey Miles Wilson has come out of retirement to start up a singles night aimed at the over-thirty-fives.
"There is nothing in the Midlands like this," he explained, "It is something desperately needed in Coalville for people who may be single, divorced or separated." *(Newspaper cutting)*

18th August 1998 Tuesday
"Miles & Michele are pleased to announce the opening of the Mi Amigo Singles Club to be held at the Odd House Inn, Snarestone every Wednesday 8 – 11 pm. Automatic complimentary membership to Mi Amigo Supper Club members."
The Mi Amigo Supper Club has been launched simultaneously by Miles & Michele offering jolly outings and activities, such as 'Skittles' or 'Supper Cruise on the Ashby Canal'.

20th August 1998 Thursday
B Sky B = British Sky Broadcasting. It is 40% owned by News International, owner of The Times. Profits will be somewhat reduced over the next 2 years due to the high cost of investing in its new digital satellite service. However, with a turnover of £1.43 billion it can easily afford to launch its 110 television channels and 50 audio channels on 1st October and even offer free digital installation, costing £80 a time.

22nd August 1998 Saturday
Meet Co-op Member 633513 710010083279, now that Coalville Co-op Food store has been selected by Midlands Co-op to trial the re-introduction of the Dividend which was part of the British way of life for over 100 years before it was scrapped in 1969. Your till receipt automatically prints your name and card number listing your 'dividend this visit' plus 'current dividend total'.

24th August 1998 Monday
"Mum has chosen a magnolia bush, so we are hoping anon to lead everybody up the garden path."

This was recorded in my diary in 1974 and by now you would expect the magnolia tree to be the pride and joy of the garden. But over the years it has been more of a problem than a joy, flowering briefly in May and growing into a tangle of branches. I have therefore chopped it down.

26th August 1998 Wednesday

"With Visa's Delta Card, I'm an Ex-Chequer." This was the entry in my diary on 26th August 1993. Now we have progressed to 'iris-recognition technology' as cash machines dispense money at the blink of an eye. The first such machine (the first of its type in the world) came into use on 23rd April this year at a branch of the Nationwide Building Society in Swindon, Wiltshire.

28th August 1998 Friday

The 'I have a dream' speech of Martin Luther King belongs to the American public, not his family, a judge has ruled in a blow for the relatives of the assassinated civil rights leader. The family, which claimed that it owned the copyright, argued that CBS television infringed the copyright when it reproduced the speech in a documentary series. The speech, which Dr King wrote at night in a Washington hotel overlooking the Mall before delivering it on August 28th 1963 to 200,000 people in front of the Lincoln Memorial, ranks as one of the most powerful pieces of oratory in American history. He called on everyone to share his vision of a country where the colour of someone's skin did not determine his future. (Newspaper cutting)

30th August 1998 Sunday

Brother Pat celebrated his 80th birthday yesterday in style. We had a lovely big family get-together at St James Church Hall. There were all his grand-children and great-grand-children, about a dozen cousins and about a dozen close friends. Bunting's son Michael and Josie came from Stafford; Bunting's son Julian and Shirley came from Worcester; only Bunting was missing.

1st September 1998 Tuesday

For a year and a day devotees of Diana, Princess of Wales, have mourned for her, encouraged by the tabloids and magazines which endlessly re-tell her story. But now, as in the poem "The Unquiet Grave" the twelvemonth and a day being up, we are gently asked to let her Rest in Peace.
"Oh, who sits weeping on my grave and will not let me sleep?" (An ancient ballad - anon.)

3rd September 1998 Thursday

Bishop of Southwark! On 18th March this year, it was announced that the Rt. Revd. Thomas Frederick Butler, Bishop of Leicester, was to be Bishop of Southwark. It was in September 1991 that I had the privilege of attending his Enthronement in Leicester Cathedral. Now I am delighted to have a ticket for his Enthronement at Southwark Cathedral on 12th September 1998.

5th September 1998 Saturday

Leicester Cathedral tomorrow says farewell to Bishop Thomas, the Rt. Revd. Dr. Thomas Butler. Holding the fort is the Bishop Commissary (deputy) the Rt. Revd.

Bill Down who says, "It has been really great to work with Tom and I shall miss him very much." Similarly, the Archdeacon of Leicester, the Ven. Michael Edson says, "We will miss him a lot. He will be a hard act to follow."

7th September 1998 Monday

A secret garden! No. 58, London Road, Coalville, a terraced house known as Scotland Villas, is empty following the death of 92 year-old Agnes Blower. Betty Stiles, who lives next door at No. 60, has a key and when I called to see her recently she took me through the empty house into the garden. Never have I seen such a completely overgrown garden. A forest of trees had taken over.

9th September 1998 Wednesday

Peace in Ireland seemed assured when the people themselves voted overwhelmingly for peace only four months ago in May. All hopes of peace were shattered last month when a 500 pound bomb exploded in Omagh claiming at least 28 lives. Now Sinn Fein leader Gerry Adams has urged all armed groups to stop immediately. "Violence must be for all of us now a thing of the past, over, done with and gone."

11th September 1998 Friday

The Real IRA group that bombed Omagh last month, have declared a total cease-fire. This now leaves only Continuity IRA (CIRA) as the last paramilitary organisation in Ireland still technically at war, and street-level thuggery is still rampant.
"As a result of intense consultation that has taken place over recent weeks, and in accordance with the constitution of Oglaigh na hEireann (the Real IRA), the volunteers of Oglaigh na hEireann have determined a complete cessation of all military activity. This cessation will take effect from midnight, September 7th." (Newspaper cutting)

13th September 1998 Sunday

What a wonderful experience yesterday for me to share in the Enthronement of the Rt. Revd. Father in God, Thomas Frederick Butler as Ninth Bishop of Southwark, at the Cathedral and Collegiate Church of St. Saviour & St. Mary Overie, Southwark. This was a once in a lifetime experience for me to see one and the same man twice Enthroned as Bishop. (In 1991 and in 1998).

15th September 1998 Tuesday

Prince Harry has now joined his elder brother Prince William at Eton. Prince William is now into his 4th year at Eaton and is doing very well indeed. He recently achieved 12 GCSE passes, three of them at A grade. Prince Harry is not thought to be as academically brilliant as William, but was delighted to pass his Common Entrance exam. He joins his brother in Manor House, housemaster Andrew Gailey.

17th September 1998 Thursday

"Shafts of the Glory of God can touch us in any context at any moment ......" (See 19th June 1994)
Such a moment came at 7 a.m. on Tuesday this week when, during my morning walk, I walked towards the glory of the sunrise. Turning to look behind me I saw a

complete perfect rainbow in a clear pale blue sky, holding the whole of Ravenstone in its embrace.

19th September 1998 Saturday

For our 4th 'London Open House' day, Mary Blue & I were blessed with a glorious day of blue skies & sunshine. We spent the morning visiting Greenwich for a close-up inspection of the Millennium Dome, now nearing completion, & an interesting talk on its progress. In the afternoon we visited two government buildings in Whitehall; the Ministry of Defence and the Foreign Office.

21st September 1998 Monday

The three-way marriage of the Telephone, Computer and Television gave birth to the Internet. The second birth will be Digital Television. It is predicted that by the time these two offspring reach maturity, the entire Western economy will have been changed. My latest book, 'The Internet for Beginners' makes fascinating reading. Now I know that http = hypertext transfer protocol.

Ravenstone with Snibston Parish Council is to erect a new oak seat in memory of a resident of Ravenstone who died earlier this year.
John Dolman used to be seen regularly sitting on a seat near to where he lived on Hospital Road, Ravenstone, until it was broken beyond repair by vandals last year. Three children from Ravenstone Primary School, Hannah and Ruth Moulton and Samantha Heap requested that a new seat should be placed following the death in January of this year of John Dolman who was a well respected member of the community, having worked as a farmer in Snibston and regularly contributed to the parish council meetings. He was also a member of the millennium group.
The new oak seat which will bear a plaque written by the girls saying, 'In loving memory of Mr John Dolman' will be placed with a short ceremony. It takes place on September 26th at 12 noon. *(Newspaper cutting)*

23rd September 1998 Wednesday

One for the ladies – The season in Venice opens with an exhibition of Europe's most famous lover, Casanova.
(Newspaper cutting)
Any man who is known for his amorous adventures and success with women is called a 'Casanova'. The original Casanova was Giovanni Giacomo Casanova, born in 1725 and a great adventurer, soldier, spy, writer, ecclesiastic & much more besides. Sometimes very rich, sometimes penniless, in 1760 he fled from his creditors and assumed the name Chevalier de Seingalt until his death in 1798.

25th September 1998 Friday

Casanova: the myth lives on in Venice - Giovanni Giacomo Casanova, born in Venice in 1725, died in Bohemia (the present day Czech Republic) in 1798, is being remembered particularly in Venice this year, the 200th anniversary of his death.
Reading his life story, he reminds me of cousin Miles – larger than life, his autobiography, 'History of Man' in 12 volumes, tells of all his amazing adventures in life.

26th September 1998 Saturday

Rushdie picks up the scent of 'freedom' – the author Salman Rushdie said last night that he hoped his decade-long ordeal of being protected from possible assassination could soon be over after Britain and Iran achieved a breakthrough yesterday on Ayatollah Khomeini's religious death sentence. Asked what the move meant to him, Mr Rushdie said, 'It means everything; it means freedom.' *(Newspaper cutting)*
(See 21st February 1990)

27th September 1998 Sunday

"It is a covenant of salt for ever before the Lord unto thee and to thy seed with thee" (Numbers 18-19)
Thus God made a covenant with Aaron of the tribe of Levi, when the Levites were singled out of the twelve tribes of Israel to perform the office of priests. Note that Jesus, our great High Priest, being a priest after the order of Melchizedek, belonged to the tribe of Judah.

29th September 1998 Tuesday

In praise of salt! The more I learn about salt, the more I appreciate its worth. Recently I learned that salt was vital for preserving food, long before the days of deep freeze and refrigeration; so much so that the Roman soldiers would sometimes be paid in salt rather than money. Salarium would be money given to soldiers to buy salt (hence the word salary) and 'worth one's salt'.

3rd October 1998 Saturday

Although Britain and Iran have decided to smoke the pipe of peace for the mutual benefit of them both, there are still murmurings of disaffection beneath the surface. The two countries are to resume diplomatic relations and will exchange ambassadors for the first time since 1989, but Salman Rushdie, author of 'The Satanic Verses', is by no means a free man & still hated by many Muslims.

5th October 1998 Monday

Thought for the day: Seek him that maketh the seven stars and Orion, and turneth the shadow of death into the morning, and maketh the day dark with night; that calleth for the waters of the sea, and poureth them out upon the face of the earth. The Lord is his name. Amos 5, v 8, King James Bible.

7th October 1998 Wednesday

Mohamed Al Fayed, the Egyptian-born chairman of Harrods and father of Dodi, who died in the company of Princess Diana in August last year, has tried repeatedly to secure British citizenship, but has always been denied a British passport. Now he has decided to be a Scotsman, since Scotland is about to have its own Parliament; he is thinking of applying for a Scottish passport.

9th October 1998 Friday

Mohamed Al Fayed bought a tumble-down castle in the Highlands of Scotland, north of Inverness and just north of Cromarty Firth. He paid £60,000 for Balnagown Castle and then spent £3 million transforming it into one of the most luxurious homes in Scotland. He owns the 60,000 acre Balnagown estate in Easter Ross.
When Scotland gains independence, residents will qualify for citizenship.

11th October 1998 Sunday
Deposit your money safely offshore and receive tax-free 10.75% interest in U.S. dollars.
Absolutely no taxes withheld. Your account is guaranteed to be completely confidential. Your name and country of residence will not be disclosed to anyone. You earn a fixed rate for the full term of your deposit. Trust Department available.
The Excelsior Bank, Central Bank Building, Bridgetown, Barbados.   *(Newspaper cutting)*

13th October 1998 Tuesday
So delighted was I with the Roberts Portable Radio which I bought last year, that I have now purchased another exactly the same, but with a red trim instead of grey. While one is set constantly for Radio Leicester, the other is set for Radio 4 (FM). This makes my little old portable radio, a Grundig City-boy almost redundant, apart from bath time.

15th October 1998 Thursday
New Bishop – Canon Michael Alan Houghton, Vicar of Folkestone St Peter in the Canterbury diocese, has been appointed to the Suffragan See of Ebbsfleet (same diocese) in succession to the Right Revd John Richards, who is retiring.   *(Newspaper cutting)*

A replacement Flying Bishop (see February 20th 1994). The Church of England has two provinces, York and Canterbury. The Flying Bishops are officially Provincial Episcopal Visitors, one for the Province of York, one for the eastern half and one for the western half (See of Ebbsfleet) of Canterbury.

17th October 1998 Saturday
The 1998 Nobel Peace Prize was yesterday awarded jointly to David Trimble, the Ulster Unionist leader, who is now the Province's First Minister (=Prime Minister) and John Hume the SDLP leader (Social Democratic and Labour Party). Their efforts have ended 30 years of conflict in Northern Ireland, but the fact remains that paramilitary groups are still fully armed and refuse to give up their guns.
Nobel is too soon, Trimble warns   (Newspaper cutting)

19th October 1998 Monday
"Started work at Leicester" This was the entry in my diary on 18th October 1948, exactly 50 years ago yesterday. How well I remember my first day of work at Leicestershire County Council's Motor Licence Office. I walked up to the counter where Mr Hollier was cashier. He said, 'We open at 10 o'clock.' I told him I had come to work there, but hardly expected it to be for the next 30 years!

21st October 1998 Wednesday
Prize from ERNIE! Bond No.14HN 330845
Dear Bondholder, Congratulations, one of your Premium Bonds has won a prize.... Yours Sincerely, Dan Monaghan, Operational Services Director. "Pay Miss E. Hewes Fifty Pounds only"
It is almost two years since my last win, when on average I could expect a win once a year. Still nothing from my last investment   (See 3rd September 1996).

Winning bonds are selected by Ernie (not a computer but an electronic random number indicator). Investment is from £100 to £20,000. Each bond has a one in 19,000 chance of winning a prize in any draw. Those who have the maximum holding should, on average, win 12 prizes a year.   *(Newspaper cutting)*

23rd October 1998 Friday
"Joined up thinking" - The new dynamic Labour Government under the leadership of Tony Blair is committed to revitalising Local Government, including our North West Leicestershire District Council. Instead of having Councillors on either the Leisure Committee or on the Housing Committee, or a whole range of others, they will cut straight across these traditional boundaries and work corporately.

25th October 1998 Sunday
"Joined up thinking" in N.W. Leicestershire District Council will consist of Community Services – things like leisure, housing, planning, environment & economic development; Community Values – quality of life issues such as safer communities, anti-poverty work, community health, environmental management and rural issues; Community Development – the business community, the voluntary sector, parish councils and tenants associations, etc. "Services – Values – Development"

26th October 1998 Monday
Deadline for Armageddon?
Apocalypse could be just 30 years away. Astronomers have identified an asteroid a mile across on a near-collision course with Earth. On October 26th 2028 at 6.30pm GMT, XF11 will pass within 30,000 miles of Earth – a hair's breadth in astronomical terms. The chance of an actual collision is small, but one is not out of the question.   *(Newspaper cutting)*

28th October 1998 Wednesday
"New Pope chosen – John XXIII"
This was 40 years ago in 1958. He was aged 77 when he became Pope and had kept a diary from the age of 14. The last entry in his diary was written 6 months before his death in 1963. But his was no ordinary diary – no ordinary journal. It was the Journal of a Soul, revealing his intimate spiritual thoughts from the immaturity of adolescence to the Papacy itself.

29th October 1998 Thursday
Like Pulcinella, 3 years ago, I went very early, quite alone, to the deserted churchyard at Bringhurst to see the newly dug grave of Brian Lamming. Earlier this year, on 25th January, I went similarly to the deserted churchyard at Ravenstone to see the newly dug grave of John Dolman and to read the message on a beautiful wreath: - 'My dearest John. With love for ever Lynda xx'.

31st October 1998 Saturday
An out of the blue letter from 'Whitehall' to say ".... I look forward to welcoming you as an investor with Whitehall" prompted me to draw out £10,000 from the Cheltenham & Gloucester Building Society & become a 'Founder Investor' in one of their new unit trusts which will be managed by Jupiter Asset Management Ltd.

With the world economy in crisis 'now is the time to invest'.

Unit trust: An 'open-ended' investment fund that can accept any amount of investors' money on an on-going basis, investing it in a wide range of shares, fixed-interest securities and property. The fund is divided into units which rise and fall in value in line with the value of the underlying assets. *(Newspaper cutting)*

Fear of a meltdown in world stock markets and a decline into 1930s-style economic depression has pushed the world's leading finance ministers into making an unprecedentedly strong call for an urgent and coordinated response. Ministers are anxious that their deliberations should give a positive message to stock markets after a week of plunging prices. The Group of Seven industrialised nations, which met in Washington at the weekend, urged each continent to play a part in promoting economic growth. *(Newspaper cutting)*

2nd November 1998 Monday
Diageo, formed through the merger of Guinness and Grand Metropolitan, has an annual turnover of around £14 billion! The name Guinness continues in one of Diageo's four world class businesses.
Cocky's daughter Yvonne is Finance Director at the Guinness brewery at Park Royal in West London, which is to become the centrepiece of a new £350 million business park development.

Guinness and Grand Metropolitan have dropped the name GMG Brands for their new merger company and confused their Latin with their Greek in the process by naming their new corporation Diageo.

Diageo, based on the Latin for 'day' and the Greek for 'world'. *(Newspaper cuttings)*

4th November 1998 Wednesday
'Are you up to the challenge?' This was the question posed by Ravenstone Church Restoration Club to any group of people who felt they could raise £250 for the restoration of the church (see 3rd April 1998).

Raunston Ladies agreed to make 35 kneelers, if 35 people would each pay them £30 and thereby raised £350 for the church. The kneelers will be dedicated on 15th November.

Note by Mary Blue – Surely this is a mistake and Betty meant £10 each? If so, it was an extremely rare thing for her to make an error – I have only spotted 2 or 3 in the whole of the diaries!

6th November 1998 Friday
A picture cut out of the paper shows Europa, one of Jupiter's moons. Scientists think the surface of Europa is littered with Epsom salts (magnesium sulphate) and also washing soda or bath salts (sodium carbonate). There are oceans of liquid water, covered with an icy crust, partly pure ice, but mostly salts.

7th November 1998 Saturday
420 days to go

8th November 1998 Sunday
The end of an era for G. H. Hewes & Sons. All my life, the sign of G. H. Hewes & Sons has been displayed outside the Marlborough Square office in Coalville where at one time my dad worked as an 'Estate Agent & Auctioneer'.
Enid's brother David is the last of the line to have worked there and now this month he celebrates his 65th birthday and is retiring.

10th November 1998 Tuesday
Go-ahead for houses. A small housing development has been given the green light for land in Ravenstone. North West Leicestershire District Council's Planning Committee has approved plans for the erection of six houses on a site in Wash Lane currently occupied by a house and three commercial buildings. *(Newspaper cutting)*

This refers to part of a field of land called "Little Nook", bought by my grandfather George Harry Hewes on 25th September 1897 and subsequently forming a small land-locked area belonging to his newly built home, "The Hollies".
Earlier this year (see February 2nd) the land was sold for the purpose of building five houses – now updated to six houses.

12th November 1998 Thursday
The digital revolution has begun. First off the launch pad was Sky Digital on 1st October this year offering 140 channels by satellite dish. ON digital will be next, a digital terrestrial channel (DTT) not requiring a satellite dish and offering 30 channels of which 12 will be 'primary' channels costing £10 per month & the rest will be 'premium' channels – one for £11 per month, two for £15, three for £18.

14th November 1998 Saturday
ON digital is a giant venture between Carlton Communications and Granada Group, while B Sky B, the satellite television group is 40% owned by News International, owner of 'The Times'.
ON digital channels will include premium channels from Sky such as Sky Sports & Sky Movies & some completely new channels from the BBC, ITV & Channel 4, such as BBC Choice, News 24 & Channel 4's Film Four.

18th November 1998 Wednesday
And 50 years rolled by and the "Coalville Times" printed a school photograph taken in 1948, my last year at Coalville Grammar School. What a surprise to see ourselves again as we used to be. This photo of the whole school belonged to John Saunders.

21st November 1998 Saturday
Tintoretto's **'Susannah Bathing'**, painted in 1555-56 is now in Kunsthistorisches Museum, Vienna.

22nd November 1998 Sunday
The Rt. Revd Timothy Stevens is to be the new Bishop of Leicester & will take up his position next summer. Born in 1946, he became Archdeacon of West Ham in 1991 & is now a West Ham fan.

He has a wife named Wendi & two children.

24th November 1998 Tuesday

'Are you up to the challenge?' Such was the overall response to Ravenstone Church Restoration Club's appeal (the brain-child of Church Warden David Winterton) that £4,000 has been raised this year in one form or another. The biggest fund-raiser was a Village Fun Day held on the recreation ground in August with music & competitions; this alone raised £2,500.

26th November 1998 Thursday

Benjamin Terence Jarman, weighing in at 7lbs 13½ozs was born on Tuesday this week, the second son of Steven & Jane, and 10th grandchild of Mary Blue (the 5th natural grandchild-see 15th July 1998). Steven & Jane recently moved to a new house at 8 Hailebury Avenue, Ashby-de-la-Zouch, a larger house to accommodate their growing family and expanding lifestyle.

28th November 1998 Saturday

£900 raised for church – *The Ravenstone parish church Christmas fair held on November 28th raised £900 for the on-going work of the church. The fair was a tremendous success for a variety of stalls and side shows. A big thank you to all who helped and supported in any way.* *(Newspaper cutting)*

Ravenstone Church is well blessed at the moment with a goodly band of supporters, both inside as pillars & outside acting as buttresses.

30th November 1998 Monday

A picture in the paper of a double decker bus entitled, 'New colours for Arriva'.
These are the new colours for Midland Fox buses – renamed Arriva. Over the next three years, all 350 Arriva buses will make the change to the new company livery of aquamarine and stone colours. Last year the Cowie Group, the company behind Midland Fox, changed its name to Arriva. Now all the buses are to follow suit by adopting the name and changing to the smart new livery. *(Newspaper cutting)*
(Formerly Midland Red)

2nd December 1998 Wednesday

The main motivation to the Treasury for changing the Budget back to March appears to be found in the timing of the increases in road fuel duty. The change in the timing of the Budget has enabled the Treasury to impose two full year increases in road fuel duties – one in July 1997 and one in March 1998 – during the 16-month period November 1996 to March 1998. According to Treasury figures, this will permanently increase the tax take by around £1 billion per annum, raising the same extra annual revenue as an increase in the basic rate of income tax by around ½p in the pound.
(Newspaper cutting)

New Labour swept into office on 1st May 1997 & new Chancellor of the Exchequer, Gordon Brown, presented a mini-Budget in July of that year, followed by a full-blown Budget on 17th March this year. This simple shift provided £1 billion per annum extra tax.

4th December 1998 Friday

Businessman found in lake" – this sad news on the front page of this week's Coalville Times begins:
'The body of an elderly man recovered from a lake in Heather has been named as George Raymond Wildgoose from Station Road in Ibstock. The 68 year old man was found underwater on Monday.'
How well I remember this 'elderly man' as a schoolboy in my class at Coalville Grammar School.

Wildgoose, George Raymond (Ray). Tragically taken away from us on November 30th 1998 aged 68 years. Devoted husband to Doris, dearly loved father to Ian and Michael. Much loved father-in-law to Beverley and Jane. Adored granddad to all his six grandchildren. (Newspaper cutting)

6th December 1998 Sunday

Veronica, like my American pen friend, has broken off relations with me. Last year, on 6th June, the 10th Anniversary of her marriage to Mr Ellis, I rang her, only to be told it was not a convenient time & she would ring me back. She never did. I rather suspect she looked upon me as a contender for the affections of Mr Ellis, & therefore broke off diplomatic relations.

8th December 1998 Tuesday

The National Lottery New Opportunities Fund purloined by the Government 12 months ago as a 6th good cause, is to help schoolchildren in Coalville. A new study support centre at Greenhill Youth and Community Centre is part of a national initiative known as Homework Help Clubs, where children unable to do their homework properly because of noise, can work quietly.

After 2001, this fund will also receive all the money which currently goes to the Millennium Commission – making it the largest recipient of the lottery's munificence. The fund's purpose is 'to provide direct support for a range of education, environment and public health projects', investing in activities such as lifelong learning and 'cancer prevention, treatment and care'. *(Newspaper cutting)*

12th December 1998 Saturday

"To His Holiness our dear Pope John Paul, praying you keep healthy & well, From Katherine Sullivan."
The Pope's Christmas card from Katherine, aged 94, has once more been duly despatched. She chose a painting by Correggio, 'The Virgin Adoring', purchased from the shop at Mount St Bernard's Abbey, Whitwick.
Katherine is beginning to feel her great age, but managing very well.

The Pope has said he would like to climb Mount Sinai with Jewish and Muslim leaders in the year 2000 to' *mark the reconciliation of the world's three great monotheistic faiths'.* *(Newspaper cutting)*

14th December 1998 Monday

TV channel launch - A firework display on the River Thames in London at 7 pm last Monday, 7th December, marked the arrival of ITV2, the first new channel for ITV since 1955. This new channel is billed as a general entertainment channel aimed at a slightly younger audience than ITV. It will be a free, national channel available on digital terrestrial & existing cable services.

16th December 1998 Wednesday
Curtis/Goodall/Kouroushi/Parker/Thompson
Groby Stamford Arms Football Club.
Groby Parish Council, members and staff, wish to express their deepest sympathy to the families, friends and members of the Club in their time of grief. The young men so tragically lost will be sadly missed and mourned by the entire village.   *(newspaper cutting)*

Five friends were killed & 15 others were injured on the A42 near Measham on Monday evening, 7th December, when an articulated lorry crashed into the back of their minibus. They had set off from the Stamford Arms pub in Groby on their soccer team's Christmas outing to Tamworth.

18th December 1998 Friday
Meals on Wheels! For exactly seven years Enid & I have been on the 'Meals on Wheels' rota, delivering meals to the house-bound in Ravenstone, Swannington & Coleorton. Now we have written to say we wish to 'retire' from this service because Enid is so bronchial & short of breath it has become a burden to her. Sadly, there are few volunteer replacements.
Women's Royal Voluntary Service, in Ashby, which delivers around 650 meals each month to the elderly, disabled and house-bound, needs more recruits.
   (Newspaper cutting)

20th December 1998 Sunday
From my love by post a Christmas card, 'For Someone Very Special' containing a £20 note.
   "Merry Christmas darling.
   Love you for ever, John xxxx"
Cocky & I have loved each other for more than fifty years – long enough for us to be celebrating our Golden Wedding, but here I am on the shelf, while Cocky has become a loving husband, father & grandfather elsewhere.

OAP festive gift should be £115 – *OAPs will this month collect their £10 Christmas bonus, first introduced in 1972. I have recently read that if this bonus had kept in line with inflation it would now be worth £115.45p.*
   (Newspaper cutting)

22nd December 1998 Tuesday
David Taylor M.P. – This is our Labour M.P. elected on 1st May 1997. Known as our 'ubiquitous' local M.P., he certainly makes his presence felt, here, there & everywhere in the locality. Evelyn is proud of the fact that she taught him as a child at Heather School & we all feel that we know him personally.

25th December 1998 Friday
I joined Pat, Evelyn, Mary Blue & Scott for Christmas Day lunch with Sharon & Jim in the sumptuous surroundings of their lovely home at Melton Mowbray. Jim's children, Carly & Sam had lunch elsewhere with their mum, but returned home for tea.
We watched on cine-film their latest exotic holiday in Florida's Disney World – out of this world.

26th December 1998 Saturday
Preliminary Announcement
A superb development of six individual detached three/ four bedroomed bungalows Constructed by NHBC registered builder. Situated in a sought after location Available now for reservation.
  John German 10530 412824   *(newspaper cutting)*

This is the one-time Hollies Field, sold to my grandfather by John German n 1897 & now for sale again as "The Croft".

'The Croft' is the name proposed by the Parish Council for the new development off Wash Lane as this is the historical name of this site.   *(Newspaper cutting)*

28th December 1998 Monday
"Saint John, Apostle & Evangelist" – How lovely to have a sermon at Ravenstone Church last night devoted entirely to St. John, the disciple whom Jesus loved (see John 13 : 23). The Revd Kerry Emmett, Rector of Ravenstone spoke of St John, author of the Gospel, plus three Epistles. His written words conclude, 'This is the disciple which testifieth of these things and wrote these things ....'

30th December 1998 Wednesday
Seven pips! The year will end tomorrow with a seventh pip added to the time signals emitted by the National Physical Laboratory's Rugby transmitter (see July 9th 1994). This will be the 22nd leap-second since we learned how to calculate time to the accuracy of two billionths of a second a day, bearing in mind the inaccuracy of the Earth's rotation by ½ a second per year.

31st December 1998 Thursday

366 days to go

* * *

1999

1st January 1999 Friday
For the past ten years people have been booking hotel rooms in Cornwall in order to see a total eclipse of the sun on 11ᵗʰ August at 11.11a.m. in this year 1999. The last total eclipse of the sun in Britain was in 1927 and the next will be in 2046.

2ⁿᵈ January 1999 Saturday
Manners, Charles John Robert, 10ᵗʰ Duke of Rutland CBE, DL died January 2ⁿᵈ 1999 at Belvoir Castle.
(Newspaper cutting)

Charles John Robert Manners, 10ᵗʰ Duke of Rutland, CBE, died on January 3ʳᵈ aged 79. He was born on May 28ᵗʰ 1919. *(Newspaper cutting)*

3ʳᵈ January 1999 Sunday
Keeping a diary from schooldays onwards has been a great joy to me. One of my jobs as Branch Liaison Officer in the Department of Energy was the annual distribution of diaries supplied to all office staff. Now the office diary is being overtaken by the computer, by networked diaries that can be co-ordinated and updated.

4ᵗʰ January 1999 Monday

362 days to go

5ᵗʰ January 1999 Tuesday
On-Board Information: www.on-board-info.com
The Economist: www.economist.co.uk
Letts: www.letts.co.uk *(Newspaper cutting)*
On-Board Information sells its Diary Companion, a pair of floppy disks crammed with 4,000 dates and events worldwide. The Economist also provides On-Board Information; and diary publishers Letts are on the network.

6ᵗʰ January 1999 Wednesday
Sandringham House – January 6: It is with the greatest pleasure that the Queen and the Duke of Edinburgh announce the betrothal of their beloved son the Prince Edward to Miss Sophie Rhys-Jones, daughter of Mr and Mrs Christopher Rhys-Jones. *(Newspaper cutting)*

7ᵗʰ January 1999 Thursday
"Winter Fuel Payment" – Last winter the Government offered to give pensioners financial help with their fuel bills, for two consecutive years (see 19ᵗʰ March 1998). Last year I received a welcome £20 and now again this year '£20 will be credited to your bank account in the next few days.'

9ᵗʰ January 1999 Saturday
Cousin Isobel, mother of Miles, died yesterday, aged 82. She collapsed with a stroke shortly before Christmas and lay all night alone in her lovely home at Colchester, before being taken to hospital where she died.
So many people have died since Christmas, that there is a nation-wide waiting list for funerals. Isobel's will be on 26ᵗʰ January.

11ᵗʰ January 1999 Monday
Evensong at Ravenstone Church yesterday took us into new realms with our 1999 Church Lectionary, and a lesson and a sermon based on the First Chapter of the Epistle to the Hebrews. It was my pleasure and privilege to read this lovely 'Lesson' followed by an excellent sermon by the Revd Kerry Emmett.

13ᵗʰ January 1999 Wednesday
"The Card" is this year's choice for Coalville Amateur's (a repeat of 1984). Again I was pleased to be asked to join the old regulars who assemble at the home of Peter Jacques for ticket allocation.
The chosen date for this is 26ᵗʰ January, the very same date as Isobel's funeral in Colchester, which I hope to attend with Lesley.

15ᵗʰ January 1999 Friday
Cousin Isobel & cousin Don (who died in February 1988) were brother & sister, children of my Uncle Fred. Isobel had two sons, Miles and Murray. Don had three children, Peter (who died in June 1992, aged 50), Lesley and Susan. Lesley is hoping to drive to Colchester for Isobel's funeral with me as passenger.

17ᵗʰ January 1999 Sunday
Birmingham's pantomime this year was Cinderella. Katherine (aged 94) and I (aged 67) joined a bus-load of retirees & were picked up at Ravenstone Institute. Such is the sign of the times that we went to a Sunday performance, where a packed theatre seemed oblivious to the fact that it was the Sabbath Day. Monday is their day off.

19ᵗʰ January 1999 Tuesday
Mount St Bernard's Abbey Annual Ecumenical Service this week was once again sheer joy. Katherine & I sat with two monks to the right of me & also two monks to the left of Katherine. At the end of the service it was raining heavily & we were all allowed to walk with the monks through their quarters for refreshments.

21ˢᵗ January 1999 Thursday
My brother Rob died in June 1951, aged 17.
He was born on 21ˢᵗ January 1934 and if he had lived until now, today would be his 65ᵗʰ birthday. Today he would be officially entitled to his old age pension. As it is, he will be forever young; never more than a teen-ager, while 'we that are left grow old'.

23ʳᵈ January 1999 Saturday
"Civil Service Retirement Fellowship" this month for the 4ᵗʰ consecutive year was a belated Christmas Party, held at Thringstone Community Centre, where we have been holding our monthly meetings since last April. There were about 30 assembled & the Centre itself was able to supply all the crockery & excellent kitchen facilities.

25ᵗʰ January 1999 Monday
Hinckley's pantomime this year was 'The Pied Piper of Hamelin'. Enid & I joined a bus load from Ravenstone, organised from Coalville by Dawn Cox, whose father-in-law Fred Cox died last week.
There is no doubt about it; the Hinckley pantomimes are

so good we enjoy them more than those at Nottingham or Birmingham.

27th January 1999 Wednesday

Isobel's funeral took place at 11.45am yesterday at Colchester Crematorium. Lesley and I joined about 30 people for an impressive service where, like at Hilda's funeral in January 1997, the sun streamed down from the high window on to me & once again I felt caught up in heaven's glory.

I met Mile's brother Murray.

Isobel's lovely home was at 8 Welshwood Park Road, Colchester – a select area on the outskirts of town, where all her neighbours knew and loved her. Following the funeral, Isobel's family, friends & neighbours gathered at the Sun Hotel, Dedham for refreshments.

Dedham was home to England's painter – Constable.

31st January 1999 Sunday

The Rector of Ravenstone, the Revd Kerry Emmett, his wife Tricia and two daughters Elizabeth (now aged 18) and Caris (now aged 16) have been in Ravenstone for 10 years. When they arrived in 1989, Caris was known by the name Nesta. She is an adopted daughter and decided she did not like her name. She preferred 'Caris'.

2nd February 1999 Tuesday

'Dear Miss Hewes, I am sorry to learn that you have retired from WRVS' Meals-on-Wheels service.

Your loyal service over the years has been greatly appreciated and I am sure that you will be missed by the people you have served ..... I hope you will remain a member of WRVS.'

4th February 1999 Thursday

Leicester Cathedral Quarterly arrived by post, covering February, March & April, and much to my surprise & delight included a letter I had written to Canon Banks quoting from Cathedral Newsletter No. 26 from March 1966.

331 days to go

6th February 1999 Saturday

"The First GB Coin of the New Millennium. First dual dated coin 1999 – 2000. Reserve before 28th February 1999. £5 for £5. Issue date November 1999." Ordered this coin - nine months in advance.

8th February 1999 Monday

"Ravenstone Court" – This is the latest name chosen for Ravenstone Almshouses, known more recently as Ravenstone Hospital. The trustees have agreed to change the name and it will begin first as "Ravenstone Court (The Almshouses)". When we have all become familiar with the new name, then "The Almshouses" will go.

10th February 1999 Wednesday

"The Hewes: Life & Times of a Leicestershire Family" – This was the book which cousin Miles was supposed to have produced in 1996 and which never reached fruition (see 29th October 1996).

However, he offered to speak to Coalville's Historical Society this evening on "The Hewes Family".

I went to the meeting, but the speaker never arrived.

12th February 1999 Friday

Cousin Miles, with his mind full of his wife Michele's birthday today, plus his commitment to his regular Wednesday night at his 'Amigo Club' simply forgot all about his talk scheduled for 10th February.

However, like President Clinton of America, the come-back kid, today acquitted of Impeachment, Miles is to come back in April.

14th February 1999 Sunday

"For the one I love on Valentine's Day, a message from the heart"

"You stole my heart, you broke my heart, and then we drifted apart. But now's the day for me to say you are always in my heart. Always love you xxxx."

16th February 1999 Shrove Tuesday

"Times readers give £100,000 for bridge." The Central American Republic of Honduras was devastated last year when Hurricane Mitch completely destroyed 98 bridges. From all over the world came offers of help. I am pleased to be associated with the new vital bridge over the Amarateca River, north of Tegucigalpa.

18th February 1999 Thursday

The new Bishop of Leicester, the Rt. Revd Timothy Stevens, is to be enthroned at Leicester Cathedral on Saturday 19th June. He says, "The Church is promoting 'The New Start' complex. A new start with God, a new start at home and a new start for the world's poor."

20th February 1999 Saturday

Humphrey the cat who made himself at home at 10 Downing Street (see 27th November 1997) was named after Sir Humphrey Appleby, a fictitious character in the popular television series, 'Yes Minister'. Sir Humphrey, played by actor Nigel Hawthorne, was a devious Permanent Secretary. Now knighted, the actor himself is Sir Nigel.

22nd February 1999 Monday

Civil Service Retirement Fellowship meeting and an interesting talk with coloured slides showing a selection of holiday slides taken by Mr Congrave on his holidays in the old Yugoslavia, now Slovenia, Croatia and various beautiful islands on the shores of the Adriatic. What a lovely selection of pictures we saw.

24th February 1999 Wednesday

From 'Friends of the Settle-Carlisle Line' comes the Quarterly Magazine No 75, using the latest 'Mailsort' technology. (M Royal Mail Postage Paid Bradford 679) (FoSCL Magazine Mailing)

'M' is for Mailsort 3, meaning that the packet will be delivered within a certain timescale; their licence number is Bradford 679 & they pre-sort their mail into different postcode areas.

'Mailsort' saves the Royal Mail a lot of work & qualifies the sender for a considerable discount.

The country is divided up into 1,400 Direct Selection postcode groups and the FoSCL sends out 300 mailbags containing 3,336 packets.

Each member has been allocated a selection code. I am 406.

28ᵗʰ February 1999 Sunday

Civil Service Club, 13-15 Great Scotland Yard, London SW1A 2HJ Tel 0171 930 4881

Meet Elizabeth Hewes, Member No 29451 of the Civil Service Club, which I joined this month in order to have somewhere in London for food & drink & an overnight stay.

1ˢᵗ March 1999 Monday

Dear Miss Hewes, As you may have heard, Lloyds Bank has joined forces with TSB (Trustees Savings Bank). From Monday 22ⁿᵈ March, the Lloyds Bank branch in Oadby (my bank) will provide banking facilities for both Lloyds & TSB. It will be Lloyds TSB.

March 1ˢᵗ sees the introduction of the new twice-yearly number plate system. After 31 years the traditional number plate prefix change on August 1ˢᵗ is coming to an end following a campaign led by the Retail Motor Industry Federation.   (Newspaper cutting)

***T- reg** – the new letter is the first step in the overhaul of the traditional car registration system, which will switch to a continental-style regional identification system by 2001.   (Newspaper cutting)*

3ʳᵈ March 1999 Wednesday

"The Card" is Coalville Amateurs' chosen production for this year & this is opening night.

The 'oldies' assembled once more in their humble role as 'Front of House'. House Manager Mick Hunt, with his assistant Margaret Tyler and 8 supporters: Don, Basil, Barry, Olive, Chris, Barbara, Ann and me.

5ᵗʰ March 1999 Friday

"The Croft" Wash Lane, Ravenstone is the former field bordering the end of my garden.

Now proclaimed as: *"An exclusive development of six detached bungalows under construction in this popular village, set within private cul-de-sac location, prices starting from £135,950."*

Now a hive of activity with one already with its roof on.

7ᵗʰ March 1999 Sunday

***Simpson,** John Colston, of Loughborough (late Coalville), passed away suddenly on March 4ᵗʰ 1999 aged 64 years. Devoted husband and best friend of Ruth, much loved and loving father of Andrew and Genevieve, Christopher and Carol, Carolyn and Justin. Will be greatly missed by us all, but always in our thoughts.*

John Simpson appears in Coalville Amateurs' programme, year by year, as 'Follow Spot'. Standing at the back of the theatre, behind his spotlight directed at the stage, he collapsed and died last Thursday evening.

9ᵗʰ March 1999 Tuesday

Budget 99 - Chancellor of the Exchequer, Gordon Brown (Labour) continues to make a favourable impression as he manages like magic to please a whole cross-section of the people in his latest Budget. Pensioners are guaranteed at least £78 per week. The winter fuel allowance of £20 will go up to £100 for elderly households.

11ᵗʰ March 1999 Thursday

We've been together now for 50 years! That is Coalville Amateur Operatic Society and I.

My contribution now is only minimal, mostly during the performance itself as programme seller / raffle ticket seller. Nevertheless, it is lovely to belong & be swept along with all the drama, both on stage & behind the scenes.

12ᵗʰ March 1999 Friday

295 days to go

13ᵗʰ March 1999 Saturday

Last night of Coalville Amateurs' "The Card". This is the day we all have tea together after the matinee. President Roy Hunt this year was assisted by Joan Dillow in the final presentation of bouquets (his wife Molly who usually has this privilege was ill at home with flu). Joan has been with the society since 1945.

15ᵗʰ March 1999 Monday

Whitehall Fund Managers Limited - Having entrusted £10,000 to one of Whitehall's new unit trusts, the 'Times' financial adviser suggests you should have at least 25% of your portfolio invested in Europe. Of the 20 top performing unit trusts over the past 5 years, almost half are European.

17ᵗʰ March 1999 Wednesday

Stay tuned and you could win a baby – A television event aimed at creating millennium babies has been attacked by church and family groups for devaluing human life. March 17ᵗʰ has been identified as the best date to begin efforts for conceiving a child born on January 1ˢᵗ 2000, and ITV is planning *Birth Race 2000* – an evening of 'sex-orientated programming to get the nation in the mood'.

19ᵗʰ March 1999 Friday

Le bébé d'Evelyn est une grand-mere.

Her 10 grand-children are Steven's Adam and Ben, Karen's Suzannah, Lewis and Andrew, Murdo's Murdo, Kirstin and Freya, Sharon's step-children Sam and Carly. Sharon, like Murdo, is Mary Blue's step-child. Sam and Carly are therefore grand-children of a different family tree.

21ˢᵗ March 1999 Sunday

" ...... and in sin did my mother conceive me." Psalm 51, verse 5.

The Rector of Ravenstone, the Revd Kerry Emmett, said that this meant that from the moment of conception we all are one in Adam. By one man sin entered the world and death by sin: by one sinless man, Jesus Christ, we gain life eternal.   (Romans, Chapter 5)

22ⁿᵈ March 1999 Monday

Ernie Wise, 73, who with Eric Morecambe became one of Britain's most popular comedians, died yesterday in a Berkshire hospital two months after a heart bypass.
*   (Newspaper cutting)*

23ʳᵈ March 1999 Tuesday

"West Leicestershire Care & Repair provides wide

ranging advice & practical assistance with home repairs & improvements for older people".

With one leaking shed roof & one back yard all cracked up and in dire need of attention, subsequent to the filling of two wells in 1988, I contacted "Care & Repair" for assistance.

25th March 1999 Thursday

"This is to tell you that from 12th April 1999 the amount of your benefit will go up to £80.14p a week." (Currently £76. 79p) The basic pension goes up from £64.70p to £66.75p making a welcome increase of £13.40p every 4 weeks, when adding the additional pensions accrued since 1978.

27th March 1999 Saturday

Scott, aged 25, son of Mary Blue, is now in Australia. He flew there on Monday and is hoping to stay until early next year. He and Miranda became engaged in 1996, but sadly their relationship has finished. He has friends in Brisbane and is hoping to find a job there. Pat has asked to see him back for the Diamond Wedding next year.

29th March 1999 Monday

Elizabeth Hewes – No. 811 013 027 0 012 has received her 7th Council Tax Demand Notice, with 25% discount (only one resident in the property).

As ever, it goes up and up and up in price. Starting in 1993, I paid £250, 1994 - £278, 1995 - £297, 1996 – £313, 1997 - £350, 1998 - £384 and this year it is £411.18p.

30th March 1999 Tuesday

277 days to go

31st March 1999 Wednesday

Civil Service Retirement Fellowship meeting & a most interesting 'chat' by Mrs Veasey, a local lady who leads a full life and can talk non-stop about any of her many experiences. Today she spoke of a holiday in the American state of Vermont on the Canadian border. Here you find 'Martha's Vineyard', favoured by rich Americans.

2nd April 1999 Good Friday

"Now leave him alone". At our Good Friday service in Ravenstone Church, 2pm – 3pm, the Rector expounded on this new version of 'let be'.   (Matthew 27: 49)

Income from any source in the current tax year below £4,195 is not liable to income tax. Income tax at the lower rate, currently 20%, is payable on the next £4,300. Between this amount and £27,100, basic-rate tax is payable at 23%. Higher rate tax of 40% is payable on income above this figure. The personal allowance is higher for those over 65 and rises again after age 75. For those between 65 and 74, the personal allowance is £5,410. For those aged 75 and over it is £5,600. As well as personal allowances, there is a married couple's allowance of £1,900. This too is age-related. After 65 it rises to £4,305 and after 75 there is an extra £40 allowance. The tax savings rate for basic-rate taxpayers is 20%.

For each pensioner between 65 and 74, this allowance will increase from £5,410 to £5,720 from April 6th 1999. For pensioners over 75, the allowance rises from £5,600 to £5,980.

(Newspaper cuttings)

4th April 1999 Easter Sunday

"Abba Pater" – Songs, Chants and Prayers set to music with the voice of His Holiness Pope John Paul II is the latest compact disc released this Easter.

6th April 1999 Tuesday

"The Croft" Wash Lane, Ravenstone.

A picture in the paper gives a clearer idea of what I can see developing at the end of my garden. All six bungalows have their foundations laid. First, No.1 was built to roof level and next No.2. Beyond No.6 is my 18ft. wide garden wall to be screened from view.

8th April 1999 Thursday

"Joined up Thinking" (see 23rd & 25th October 1998) is causing widespread concern amongst staff at N.W. Leicestershire District Council at Coalville. Two senior officers are to become redundant.

The Chief Executive stays with three new directors in charge of i) resources, ii) environment, development & regeneration and iii) community & social well-being.

10th April 1999 Saturday

"Coalville Town Centre: Environmental Improvements"
It was three years ago today that Gwen & I attended a lively meeting in connection with traffic calming in Coalville.

Phase 1, Ashby Road, has been completed and causes great frustration to motorists.

Phase 2, Belvoir Road, Memorial Square and Marlborough Square is now about to cause more frustration.

12th April 1999 Monday

"Coalville Town Centre"
The sign you are not likely to see on the outskirts of town is, 'Welcome to Coalville'.

In fact, Coalville Councillor Barrie Hall actually said, 'The whole point of this scheme is to calm the traffic down and put people off coming into town by car unless they absolutely have to.'   (See June 14th 2000)

On this day in 1945: Franklin Delano Roosevelt, 32nd American president, died.   (Newspaper cutting)

14th April 1999 Wednesday

Reevsie, my former workmate, and I, again had lunch together at Fenwick's in Leicester. We last met in April 1997 and had two years of news to catch up with. Reevsie's mother died 18 months ago and left a will for her broken family which is causing much anguish since it was not signed in strict accordance with the law.

16th April 1999 Friday

Ravenstone Youth Club: - Launch Date, Thursday 15th April 1999. Venue: - Ravenstone Pavilion.

8 – 11 years 6.00 – 7.30pm. 11 – 18 years 7.30 – 9.00pm. then every Thursday evening.

Activities include Pool, Music, Computer, Tuck-shop, Games.

18th April 1999 Sunday

Again, at Evensong, I enjoyed reading an entirely new 'Lesson' from the Book of Lamentations, Chapter 3, 19 – 33: - "It is of the Lord's mercies that we are not consumed, because his compassions fail not. They are new every morning; great is thy faithfulness."
We sang the hymns, 'New Every Morning .... ' and 'Great is Thy Faithfulness'.

19th April 1999 Monday

257 days to go

20th April 1999 Tuesday

Cousin Miles, the come-back kid, has now given his speech to the Coalville Historical Society on 'The Hewes Family'. I was there in the spell-bound audience enjoying the antics of our once thriving get-up-and-go family, now almost defunct. Gleaned almost entirely from the Coalville Times of old, it was an excellent speech.

22nd April 1999 Thursday

"Celebrating New Organ" – Hazel Hudson, daughter of my Snibston School headmaster, Albert Henry Hudson, recently made a generous donation to St James Church Snibston of a magnificent new electronic organ. Enid and I attended the musical evening at St James Church and were enthralled at her musical talent.

24th April 1999 Saturday

What a lovely house Steven & Jane have bought at 8 Hailebury Avenue, Ashby-de-la-Zouch.
I saw it for the first time on Easter Monday (5th April) when Mary Blue, Pat, Evelyn & I called to see Adam celebrating his 2nd birthday.
How they have progressed since their first tiny rented flat on The Green.   (March 1994)

26th April 1999 Monday

Burnham, *Patricia Mary of Newbold Verdon, formerly of Odstone, passed away on April 20th aged 66 years. A beloved mother and granny. Funeral service at Shackerstone Parish Church on Monday April 26th at 11.30 am prior to interment*

Burnham, *Patricia Mary.*
Love, kindness, smiles and contentment. Your special qualities mum, that were so admired. You were one of life's true inspirations. Those we love don't go away; they walk beside us every day. And you will never be forgotten. Love always – Maureen, Richard, David, Sam, Karen, Nicky, Ben, Max, Josh and Annabel.

How very sad to learn of the death of Pat, aged 66, whose mother Hilda died 22nd January 1997, aged 99. (Mum's cousin)

28th April 1999 Wednesday

Catherine Wells who was an Executive Officer together with me at the Department of Energy, now changed to OFGAS, held her retirement party today at 'The Kaffir', Cambridge Road, Whetstone.
What a glorious day we had. The sun shone and we were able to sit out of doors. It was lovely to be made so welcome by staff both old and new.

30th April 1999 Friday

Hitler's influence still holds sway today. As he was hell-bent on the annihilation of the Jews, today we have President Milosevic of Yugoslavia similarly inclined towards Albanians in Kosovo.
In England we have 'Combat 18' stirring up trouble. 18 = AH, the initials of Adolf Hitler.

In 1995, the U.S. Office of Technological Assessment submitted a report to a Senate sub-committee identifying 17 countries believed to possess biological weapons. These were: Libya, North Korea, South Korea, Iraq, Taiwan, Syria, Israel, Iran, China, Egypt, Vietnam, Laos, Cuba, Bulgaria, India, South Africa and Russia. More have joined the list since.
(Newspaper cutting)

2nd May 1999 Sunday

How sad to see for sale the lovely home of George Merrill and his wife Marjorie (my friend and former next door neighbour in childhood). Only four weeks ago on Easter Sunday I was there for morning coffee. George, no longer well enough to care for his beloved garden, was reluctant to leave. A £145,000 home.
The sale of 9 Ashby Road offers house-hunters the chance to buy a three-bedroomed detached home in Ravenstone.
(Newspaper cutting with photograph of house)

3rd May 1999 Monday

243 days to go

4th May 1999 Tuesday

London has ambitious plans for its first directly elected mayor. A splendid office, like a huge fencing mask is to be the centre of a 13 acre riverside development, close to Tower Bridge.

Londoners get date for mayor – Londoners will vote for their first Mayor on May 4th 2000, the Government announced. John Prescott, the Deputy Prime Minister, named the date when he opened the second reading debate on the Greater London Authority Bill. He said, however, that regional assemblies would not come into being before the next General Election.
(Newspaper cutting)

6th May 1999 Thursday

So unpopular was the Conservative Government when the last local Council election was held four years ago, that 'New Labour' absolutely swept the board. Our Tory Councillor, Nigel Smith, who lives at Ravenstone Hall, was knocked off his perch by Labour's Mrs Abbott. She polled 561 votes then and once again she has beaten him.

Ravenstone *(1 seat)*
Helen Mary Abbott (Lab) 534,
Nigel Smith (Con) 397 Lab hold.   *(Newspaper cutting)*

8th May 1999 Saturday

'Songs of Praise' at Ravenstone Church is still held once

a month. It is now 5 years since the Rector, the Revd Kerry Emmett, invited people, not only to choose a hymn, but also to give a testimony, saying what their religion or the hymn means to them.

The only person so far to give such a testimony, is the Rector.

9th May 1999 Rogation Sunday

The 72nd Bluebell Service - How lovely to be in Swithland Woods again for the Annual Bluebell Service. The Address this year was given by the Revd Howard Ketton, Minister of Quorn Baptist Church. He paused for a short silence to enable us all to experience the peace of the woods and the Peace of God, while still the birds sang.

11th May 1999 Tuesday

The gold price was sent plummeting last week from already depleted levels as the Treasury announced plans to sell more than half its reserves – reducing its pile from 715 tonnes to 300 tonnes 'over the medium term'. The first auction of 125 tonnes is due by March 2000.

(Newspaper cutting)

12th May 1999 Wednesday

Scotland has its own Parliament for the first time in almost 300 years. The election for this new Scottish Parliament was held on 6th May this year. The First Minister (equivalent of Prime Minister) is Donald Dewar. As was proudly announced, "The Scottish Parliament, which was adjourned on 25th May 1707, is hereby reconvened."

14th May 1999 Friday

Cricketers from all over the world are here in Britain for the Cricket World Cup. Today sees the opening match between England and Sri Lanka at Lords. Each match lasts only one day. Twelve teams are competing: the final is on 20th June.

16th May 1999 Sunday

And another new lesson from the 1999 Church Lectionary, followed by an excellent sermon from our visiting preacher, Mrs C Willett, based on Zechariah 4: 1 – 10.

Never under-estimate 'small things'. God reassures the people of the 70 year long captivity that their temple will rise again. "Not by might, nor by power, but by my spirit," saith the Lord.

17th May 1999 Monday

Palace of Holyroodhouse: The Rt. Hon Donald Dewar, MP, MSP, was received by The Queen upon his appointment as First Minister of the Scottish Executive.

(Newspaper cutting)

18th May 1999 Tuesday

The Pope's 79th birthday and from Katherine, 95, a birthday card to His Holiness Pope John Paul II, Apostolic Palace, 00120, Vatican City.

Also for Cardinal Hume, Archbishop of Westminster, now gravely ill with cancer, a beautiful card to His Eminence Cardinal Basil Hume, Archbishop's House, Westminster, London, SW1P 1QJ.

20th May 1999 Thursday

The Croft, Wash Lane, Ravenstone – The 6 bungalows being built at the end of my garden are well on the way to completion. As you can see, Plot 1 has been sold and the last one, No.6 which is nearest to my garden wall, will look the same as No.1 in reverse (imagine my wall behind the garage). An added bonus for me has been my wall built up to 7 feet. (*Photograph in the paper*)

22nd May 1999 Saturday

Viscount Linley, son of Princess Margaret, and his wife, the former Serena Stanhope were married on 8th October 1993 at St Margaret's Church, Westminster. They are looking forward to the birth of their baby next month.

24th May 1999 Monday

Manchester United 2 Newcastle 0

Manchester United won both the League and the Cup in 1994. Two years later they did it again and now this year they have clinched a historic third double. Later this week they play Munich in the European Cup Final.

26th May 1999 Wednesday

Manchester United triumph – The European Cup Final resulted in a win for Manchester United who beat Bayern Munich 2 – 1.They have thus secured a unique treble in English football: the Premiership, the FA Cup and the European Cup. Their euphoria knew no bounds after this triumph.

28th May 1999 Friday

Ravenstone House, Leicester Road, Ravenstone
* Traditional detached residence occupying a prominent position having oil fired central heating
* Porch, reception, hallway
* Lounge with feature fireplace
* Separate dining room with feature fireplace
* Day room off, breakfast room
* Well fitted kitchen with b.i. appliances
* 1st floor – 3 good sized bedrooms
* Bathroom with full suite
* Externally – gardens to front of property, good sized rear gardens having patio area and lawns, flower beds, vehicular access to rear leading to extensive car standing space, £124,950   *(Newspaper cutting)*

"Ravenstone House" for sale.

This is in fact "Glenholm" bequeathed to cousin Miles in his mother Isobel's will. Isobel died on 8th January this year. She knew the house from its very foundation (see 29th December 1995). To Isobel it was "Glenholm" and would be so long as it was hers. But for mercurial Miles it is a £125,000 windfall.

30th May 1999 Trinity Sunday

Another thought for our 3 in 1 God is that Christ is Prophet, Priest and King.

'A prophet mighty in deed and word before God & all the people.' Luke 24: 19.

'Consider the Apostle and High Priest of our profession, Christ Jesus.' Hebrews 3: 1.

'The King of Kings and Lord of Lords.' I Timothy 6: 15.

31st May 1999 Monday

God 'our Mother' – The Right Rev Tim Stevens defended

his decision to pray to God as 'our Mother' at the service for his enthronement as Bishop of Leicester next month. (Newspaper cutting)

1st June 1999 Tuesday

Premium Bonds are selling like hot cakes. There are 185,000 people who hold the maximum number allowed £20,000. I have opted for £3,000. In this month's draw there are 516,666 prizes including five £100,000, nine £50,000 and 485,000 £50 prizes. Sales have rocketed since the million pound prize.

3rd June 1999 Thursday

"Dear Miss Hewes, On 28th June 1999, Lloyds and TSB will become one bank. So I am writing to welcome you to your new bank – Lloyds TSB. Thank you very much for banking with us.

Yours sincerely, Peter Ellwood, Chief Executive.

5th June 1999 Saturday

Ashburner, Jan. Happy memories of a wonderful friend and neighbour. Thanks for everything, will miss you so much. Love Edith and Family.

Ashburner, Janet, passed away suddenly in LOROS on June 2nd 1999, aged 64 years. Will be sadly missed by brother Mike, sister-in-law and rest of family.
The funeral will take place Thursday, June 10th at St Marys Church, Knighton 2,15pm, followed by cremation at Gilroes at 3pm. Donations in lieu of flowers to LOROS please, all other inquiries to Midlands Co-operative Funeral Service, Tudor House, 511 Welford Road. Tel. 270 3111.

What a shock to read of Jan's death, after the lovely get-together we had for her retirement party from work only 14 months ago.
Jan, who lived alone, died at LOROS - Leicestershire Organisation for the Relief Of Suffering.

7th June 1999 Monday

Midlands Asian TV (MATV Channel 6) was officially opened on 27th May this year. It is a Leicester based local station consisting almost entirely of Leicestershire news, and aimed very much at Asian audiences. It has a restricted broadcast area: the frequency is UHF Channel 68 (top of the scale), from the Waltham transmitter.

Millennium shutdown – Britain is set for an 11-day millennium shut down with the Government being warned that most people would not be at work from Friday December 24th to Monday January 3rd inclusively. (Newspaper cutting)

9th June 1999 Wednesday

Ravenstone Parish Church Summer Fair was held indoors last Saturday, due to inclement weather.
Keith Woodings (Mabel's baby, referred to 3rd & 9th June 1945) was the opener. Again I enjoyed sitting at the Prize Draw table with Church Warden Jim Bailiss, a role I first took on at our Annual Christmas Fair in 1992.

11th June 1999 Friday

Jan's funeral yesterday at St Mary Magdalen Church,

Knighton, Leicester, was a beautiful service in Memory and Thanksgiving for the life of Janet H. Ashburner.
Jan was a regular church attender and there was a goodly congregation of church people, office colleagues and relatives from Somerset. Afterwards we had a get-together in the Church Hall.

12th June 1999 Saturday

203 days to go

13th June 1999 Sunday

Gas Central Heating at Ravenstone Church! How lovely to have a new central heating system at church, thanks very much to the fund raising efforts over the past 5 years of our excellent Church Warden, David Winterton. Also, the great nave is being re-roofed at a cost exceeding £30,000.
Future restoration projects include new windows and re-wiring of the building.

15th June 1999 Tuesday

Prize from Ernie! Bond No. 14HN 331170
Dear Bondholder, Congratulations, one of your Premium Bonds has won a prize ..... Yours sincerely,
Christopher Moxey, Commercial Director.
"Pay Miss E. Hewes Fifty Pounds only".
This is my 10th win since I invested £2,000 in July 1991, when I retired from work. (8 @ £50 and 2 @ £100).

16th June 1999 Wednesday

Screaming Lord Sutch, leader of the Official Monster Raving Loony Party, was found hanged on June 16th, he was 58. He was born on November 12th 1940.
(Newspaper cutting)

17th June 1999 Thursday

Cricket World Cup – In the semi-finals Pakistan beat New Zealand by 9 wickets. Australia tied with South Africa – the most exciting match I have ever watched. No such excitement in the final when Australia easily beat Pakistan.

Wednesday, Old Trafford: Pakistan v New Zealand
Thursday, Edgbaston: Australia v South Africa
The greatest game does not get more exciting than this. After goodness knows how many twists and turns and despite another ferocious piece of hitting at the death by Lance Klusener, a desperate run-out in the final over left South Africa one run short of the 214 they needed to win their World Cup semi-final outright. The match was tied, but Australia went through to the final against Pakistan on Sunday because they finished higher than South Africa at the end of the Super Six stage.

19th June 1999 Saturday

Twelve months ago I chose to have a composite gas & electricity bill from British Gas, but so far have continued to receive electricity bills from East Midlands Electricity. Now I am informed by British Gas that, 'We will start supplying you with electricity from 25th June 1999.'

British Gas, which has 1.5 million electricity customers, said that further restructuring of the electricity industry was required. Distribution and supply needed to be separated and the electricity pool trading arrangements reformed. *(Newspaper cutting)*

21st June 1999 Monday

The Enthronement of the new Bishop of Leicester, the Right Reverend Timothy Stevens, on 19th June this year, included the following prayer. The new Bishop first heard the prayer at last summer's Lambeth Conference, spoken by the Bishop of the Church of South India, showing the transcendent nature of God.

Awakening to the Presence of God

By your word, O light of this whole universe,
we live, move and have our being.
As you have illuminated the hearts of
people at many times in the past,
we pray, eternal God, for your awakening within us.
From delusion to truth, and unto your righteous way.
Lead us, Source of all, our Father and our Mother.
From darkness to light and into your gracious will.
Lead us, O Christ, our Friend and our Brother.
From death to eternal life and into your infinite joy.
Lead us, Divine Spirit, enlivening Power within, for we seek your awakening touch.

23rd June 1999 Wednesday

Enid & I have chosen Salisbury for our holiday this year & have booked for one week commencing today & ending Wednesday 30th June.
'The beautiful medieval City of Salisbury cannot fail to delight the discerning visitor. The Cathedral with its spire, the tallest in England, is famous the world over.'

24th June 1999 Thursday

Lloyds TSB deal – the big financial deal that everyone has been predicting for so long finally materialised yesterday when Lloyds TSB, the UK's biggest retail bank, raided its savings account to pay £7 billion for Scottish Widows, the UK's fifth-biggest life insurance company. *(Newspaper cutting)*

25th June 1999 Friday

Cardinal Basil Hume, Roman Catholic Archbishop of Westminster since 1976, has died.
Like my mum, he died on 17th June. Like my mum, he died aged 76.
Called from Abbott to Archbishop, he chose to be buried in his monastic habit in his Cathedral.

27th June 1999 Sunday

Halfway through our holiday at Salisbury, Enid & I spent the day at Romsey, visiting 'Broadlands' the magnificent stately home of Lord Mountbatten who was murdered in Ireland by the IRA, 20 years ago. At 6.30pm we attended Evensong at Romsey Abbey, Hampshire's largest parish church, where Lord Mountbatten now lies.

28th June 1999 Monday

Centrica, owner of British Gas, is to buy the Automobile Association for £1.1 billion, triggering £240 windfalls for AA members, the company announced today
(Newspaper cutting)

29th June 1999 Tuesday

Today, the last full day of our holiday, it decided to rain all day long. We visited Wilton House, only 3 miles from Salisbury & acknowledged as one of the Treasure Houses of England. Set in 21 acres of landscaped parkland, we lingered long inside the house, but missed the pleasure of walking through the gardens.

1st July 1999 Thursday

Arrived home yesterday from holiday to find my leaking shed roof repaired by Mr Boam from Whitwick – cost £73.50p, which I was only too pleased to pay after 6 months of problems with water ingress. Also, the last bungalow at The Croft, Wash Lane, at the end of my garden, now possessed its skeletal roof.

2nd July 1999 Friday

Boy for Linleys – Viscount Linley's wife, Serena, gave birth to a boy at the Portland Hospital in Central London on Thursday. The baby, weighing 6lb 1oz, is their first child and is 13th in line to the Throne. He has not yet been named. *(Newspaper cutting)*

3rd July 1999 Saturday

Picture postcard showing Surfers Paradise, Gold Coast, Australia from Mary Blue, on holiday for three weeks visiting Scott, 'Having a lovely time and seeing so many wonderful sights ....'
Scott went to Australia in March this year and is hoping to stay there for a year.

5th July 1999 Monday

Ursula Hall, whom I know so well for her long association with Coalville Amateurs, has been a widow since December 1992, when her beloved husband died. Ursula, now in her mid-60s, has taken up residence at Ravenstone Court (Almshouses) and it was lovely to have her with us last night at church.

7th July 1999 Wednesday

Bunting's birthday, 84 today. How sad that Bunting is not even aware that it is her birthday. Suffering from Alzheimer's disease, the dreadful illness which affects the brain & causes dementia, it is ironic that Alois Alzheimer, the German neurologist (1864 – 1915) died in 1915, the year that Bunting was born.

9th July 1999 Friday

Cousin Miles & Michele, who were married in May 1997, are now ready for off. Less than a year ago, they launched their Mi Amigo Supper Club and Singles Club, "something desperately needed in Coalville". Now they are hoping to live in Malta, where they have chosen an apartment overlooking Mellieha Bay, to the north.
Michele loves the sun. Her idea of Paradise is a sun-drenched land; and both she and Miles have fallen in love with Malta, after spending several holidays there and getting to know quite a few of the locals.
How long Miles will be content within the confines of so small an island remains to be seen. He has a boat, 'Mi Amigo'.

10th July 1999 Saturday

Queen Elizabeth the Queen Mother, Lord Warden of the Cinque Ports, gave a reception for the Confederation of

the Cinque Ports at Walmer Castle this evening.
(Newspaper cutting)

12th July 1999 Monday

173 days to go

13th July 1999 Tuesday

My birthday tomorrow – 68: Cocky telephoned from Lancaster to say, 'Happy Birthday' and sent me £20 in his birthday card.

Alan Roulston, Churchwarden at Ravenstone Church, whose birthday is the same as mine, is taking me for a meal on the Master Cutler 'in the splendour of a First Class railway journey of a bygone railway age.'

14th July 1999 Wednesday

Sixty-Eighth Birthday

As life runs on, the road grows strange
With faces new, and near the end
The milestones into headstones change,
'Neath every one a friend.

J. R. Lowell

James Russell Lowell, the American poet who wrote "Sixty-Eighth Birthday" was born in Massachusetts on 22nd February 1819 and died in August 1891.

He and my good friend Longfellow were fellow poets. When Lowell's beloved wife died in 1853, Longfellow wrote his exquisite poem, 'The Two Angels', in ever loving memory.

The name of J. R. Lowell's house was 'Elmwood'. Longfellow wrote a poem, 'The Herons of Elmwood', which shows what a wonderful friend he was to J. R. Lowell.

Similarly, Lowell wrote a poem, 'To H. W. L., on his birthday, 27th February 1867' which shows how much he loved and admired Longfellow.

18th July 1999 Sunday

All hope lost for JFK Jr – Hope of finding John F. Kennedy Jr alive was all but abandoned last night as the US Coast Guard combed the seas off Massachusetts for the wreckage of his aircraft and America struggled to come to terms with the death of yet another member of America's ill-fated Kennedy family.
(Newspaper cutting)

21st July 1999 Wednesday

John F. Kennedy Jr., born 25th November 1960, was the son of President John F. Kennedy of America who was assassinated in Dallas, Texas on 22nd November 1963.

Last Friday, 16th July, John F. Kennedy, Jr., together with his wife and her sister, died when the aircraft he was piloting crashed into the sea. Tomorrow they will be buried at sea.

22nd July 1999 Thursday

Kennedy's burial at sea at 9 am EDT (1400 BST)

23rd July 1999 Friday

Average earnings now exceed £20,000 a year. My combined Civil Service Pension and Old Age Pension is now £10,630.32p. Without my Civil Service Pension, now £6,463.32p, I would be in a poor state. It seems today that people are very rich or very poor, and yet the vast majority, if at all possible, will own a motor car.

£20,000 is 'average' – Average earnings have soared to £20,700 a year, according to a new report today, after the £20,000 barrier was breached for the first time last year.
(Newspaper cutting)

24th July 1999 Saturday

A major £875,000 facelift in the heart of Leicester's shopping precinct is officially launched today. Humberstone Gate has been transformed from a busy, bus-clogged road into a paved pedestrian plaza.
(Newspaper cutting)

25th July 1999 Sunday

"You are invited to Sharon's Birthday Party at 7.30 pm on 20th August at Melton Mowbray Working Men's Club." Sharon, who married Jim Reason in October 1996, celebrates her 30th birthday on 23rd August (same birthday as my mum). As I am hoping to visit 'The Globe' on 21st August, I declined this invitation.

27th July 1999 Tuesday

Every Tuesday afternoon, I take Katherine shopping in Coalville for her groceries, etc. Today we were able for the first time to park with her newly acquired 'Orange Badge', issued to the old and infirm for parking in the choicest parking spaces. Cousin Enid also has an 'Orange Badge' on account of her breathlessness.

29th July 1999 Thursday

Wreck found – Johannesburg:
The wreck of the SS Waratah, a British passenger ship that sunk with 211 people on board off the South African coast in 1909, has been found, expedition leaders said.

The ship that fell down a hole: a great maritime mystery solved.
(Newspaper cuttings)

Found at last! This is the ship which apparently sailed off the earth. (See 28th June 1966 and 27th June 1994)

That which was lost, is found. The 16,000 ton liner Waratah did not sail off the earth, was not sucked down by a gas blow-out beneath the depths of the ocean, but was the victim of treacherous seas along the east coast of South Africa, where the powerful Agulhas current sweeps south and collides with south-westerly gales.

2nd August 1999 Monday

A coffee evening in the grounds of Ravenstone Court (The Almshouses), 6.30pm to 8pm., was well attended and gave Enid & me the opportunity to see Ursula's newly acquired flat, No 21, which overlooks the garden of 'The Chaplain's House'. Also recently ensconced here at No 10 is Sally Springthorpe.

4th August 1999 Wednesday

The Queen Mother's 99th birthday.

Only one week to go to the total eclipse of the Sun, which will cross briefly the tip of Cornwall & Devon on its way Eastwards via the English Channel through Europe to India.

I have chosen to spend 3 nights in Southampton, August 9th – 11th, hoping to experience this once-in-a-lifetime phenomenon.

5ᵗʰ August 1999 Thursday

Lord of the Plinth – *Sir John Mortimer, the playwright and author, has been asked by the Government to end the 150-year-old dispute over what should grace the empty plinth in London's Trafalgar Square.*
The 75-year-old creator of Rumpole of the Bailey, who called his new role 'Lord of the Plinth', is to lead an advisory panel that will invite suggestions from the public. The plinth has been vacant since the square was built by Charles Barry in 1841. Plans for a statue of King William IV on horseback were scrapped through lack of funds.

6ᵗʰ August 1999 Friday

Peter Jacques and his wife Vera (née Walker) both stalwart members of Coalville Amateur Operatic Society, who first met at Coalville Grammar School, today celebrate their Golden Wedding. They both look younger than their years, and have many interests and friends.

8ᵗʰ August 1999 Sunday

From far & wide people are making their way to Cornwall to see next Wednesday's total eclipse of the Sun. This eclipse of the Sun, according to astrologers, is exceptional because of the way it forms the fourth corner of a rare cosmic cross: Sun/Moon (N) Saturn (E) Uranus (S) Mars (W) with Earth centre.

10ᵗʰ August 1999 Tuesday

I am now in Southampton, where I have booked 3 nights accommodation (Mon, Tues, Wed) at Lodge Road Travelodge, hoping to experience something of the Solar Eclipse tomorrow morning. Had a lovely day today exploring Southampton, especially walking the old city walls with a Blue Badge Guide, starting at 10.30 am.

12ᵗʰ August 1999 Thursday

I chose to experience the Solar Eclipse at Stonehenge & joined the 'Stonehenge Tour' which runs daily from Salisbury railway station (a bus tour). It was estimated that 10,000 people assembled at Stonehenge for the Solar Eclipse, but there was ample room for us all beneath the vast open sky on this special day.

14ᵗʰ August 1999 Saturday

Home again after my mini-holiday in Southampton, and a memorable day seeing and feeling the chill of the Solar Eclipse at Stonehenge.
Home to find new neighbours living at White Lodge, the other side of my garden wall, where once was the tennis court at 'The Hollies' – a young family with two boys.

16ᵗʰ August 1999 Monday

I have now accepted the quote from D. Boam, Professional Builders, 9c, Silver Street, Whitwick: Total £880 (plus 5% for 'Care & Repair') to 'Break up cracked concrete; reduce level; lay hardcore; shutter for & lay 75mm concrete' on my poor old back yard. Work is due to start early in September.
Care and Repair West Leicestershire has had a demanding and productive year in its work of advertising and assisting elderly people in privately owned housing. Its annual report lays emphasis on the development of fresh partnerships and working closely with other organisations. Another positive achievement has been the raising of sufficient funds to keep the popular handyperson service going for three years.
                                          (Newspaper cutting)

18ᵗʰ August 1999 Wednesday

Final Electricity Account from East Midlands Electricity, as I next pay my electricity bill to British Gas. PowerGen is one of the UK's principle generating companies, approximately 20%.

19ᵗʰ August 1999 Thursday

135 days to go

20ᵗʰ August 1999 Friday

When Baptized: - 20ᵗʰ August 1931 (Thursday) Elizabeth Hewes, Number 651, Abode – Snibston.
Baptism solemnized in the Parish of St Mary's, Snibston by J. Duncan C. Wallace, Vicar of Snibston, in the County of Leicester.
According to Pope John Paul II, people should celebrate the day of baptism, as one celebrates a birthday.

When Christians are baptised they are plunged into the life of Christ, and that is why the word 'christening', if we hear it right as 'Christ-ening', points us so powerfully to the heart of what baptism, and Christian life, is about. It is both a birth and a death, a dying and a rising with Christ, and a being born again by water and the living Spirit of God.   *(Newspaper cuttings)*

The Didache, one of the oldest Christian writings, tells us that from the moment of baptism 'the living water bubbles away within us' as John Wesley knew when he sang of Christ, 'Thou of life the fountain art, freely let me taste of Thee, Spring thou up within my heart, Rise to all eternity.'

22ⁿᵈ August 1999 Sunday

"Mr & Mrs M. R. J. Wilson, P.O.Box 42, St Paul's Bay, Malta, SPB 01."
Miles & Michele are due to move to their new home in Malta on 12ᵗʰ September. They were there for a week earlier this month and on 15ᵗʰ August, the Feast of the Assumption of the Blessed Virgin Mary, shared in the fireworks and fiesta.

24ᵗʰ August 1999 Tuesday

"Jesus wants me for a moonbeam – were you one of these little moonbeams?"
This was the question posed recently by the Coalville Times when it showed a very old photograph taken around 1912 – 1914. I thought the twin girls could well be my mum and her sister Elizabeth, born in 1905. Elizabeth died in 1915.

26ᵗʰ August 1999 Thursday

Calcutta is now to be known as Kolkata. India is now ridding itself of its old British Empire image which it knew from 1858 to 1947. Already Bombay has changed to Mumbai, Madras has changed to Chennai. We still think of Sri Lanka as Ceylon (it changed as long ago as 1972).

27th August 1999 Friday

127 days to go

28th August 1999 Saturday
Ravenstone, Leicester Road, Detached 3 bed double fronted traditional style character property, oil fired central heating, lounge, dining room, breakfast room, furnished to high standard, gardens to front and rear, available early September. £625 pcm
(Newspaper cutting)
This is Glenholm, for sale for three months at £124,950. Advertised as 'Ravenstone House' by cousin Miles, and still not sold. Now it is offered 'To Let' £625 pcm. Nobody seems willing to pay so much money.

30th August 1999 Monday
140 Pay & Display parking meters are now installed on the streets of Leicester, ready to operate from 1st September. No more early morning free parking, as these operate from 7.30am to 6pm. Seven parking attendants, as distinct from Traffic Wardens, will enforce the parking rules. The council contracted a company called Sureway for this.

1st September 1999 Wednesday
We are galloping through the changes in Registration Numbers for car number plates since we reached the 'S' prefix on 1st August 1998. This changed to 'T' on 1st March 1999 (there never is 'U')
Now it is 'V'. This format will end on 31st August 2001.

The DVLA's Sale of Marks, including select registrations and the classic collection, has made almost £250 million for the Treasury and 500,000 have been sold since 1989, when the scheme started.
(Newspaper cutting)

3rd September 1999 Friday
Today we are remembering 3rd September 1939; the day war broke out, 60 years ago. A formal declaration of war was broadcast on the wireless at 11.00am, long before we had television.
My poor mum had been widowed in January 1939 and left with two young children. Long years of hardship were to follow.

3 September 1999: Judge Hervé Stephan's official report concludes that the Princess and Dodi Fayed were killed because their driver took a mixture of alcohol and anti-depressant drugs. Unqualified to drive the heavy limousine, he had been at the wheel because of decisions taken by Dodi Fayed. *(Newspaper cutting)*

5th September 1999 Sunday
The Diana Report – Judge Hervé Stephan led the two-year inquiry into the death of Diana, Princess of Wales, who was killed on 31st August 1997.
It has been the longest road crash investigation in French history and cost an estimated £6 million. The final dossier runs to more than 50,000 pages. The driver Henri Paul was also killed.

7th September 1999 Tuesday
The full text of the report into the death of Diana,

Princess of Wales, was reported in 'The Times'. The cause of Diana's death was a wound to the upper left pulmonary vein, together with a rupture to the pericardium (the sac around the heart). Although she suffered serious intra-thoracic lesions, she did not die instantly.

9th September 1999 Thursday
The Diana Report – It was late evening (11.25 GMT) on Saturday 30th August 1997 that the black Mercedes, type S280, registration number 680 LTV 75, driven by Henri Paul, deputy security manager at the Ritz Hotel in Paris, crashed. Only one passenger, Trevor Rees Jones, a bodyguard, survived. He suffered serious face injuries.

Death in the Tunnel *– Saturday, 11.20 GMT - Diana and Dodi Fayed leave Ritz in car accompanied by chauffeur and bodyguard.*
11.25 GMT car crashes – After a high-speed chase involving paparazzi the car crashed, killing Dodi Fayed and the driver. The Princess died later in hospital.
(Newspaper cutting of Paris map)

11th September 1999 Saturday
"Dear Miss Hewes, We're sorry to see from our records that you no longer take your electricity supply from us but thought you'd like to know that East Midlands Electricity is now part of the PowerGen Group .... we'd love you to come back."   Robert Sharp

13th September 1999 Monday
"If your wiring is reaching its Jubilee, don't rejoice – re-wire."
In 1977, when H. M. Queen Elizabeth II celebrated the Silver Jubilee of 'sitting on the throne for 25 years' (see 14th June 1977) Mum & I chose to have our house re-wired. Work began in September 1977. This week Enid is having No 50, Leicester Road, Ravenstone re-wired.

15th September 1999 Wednesday
Enid has had one almighty clear-out of books which have cluttered up the cupboards for 50 years or more. She offered me an old battered book, dropping to bits, 'The Canterbury Tales' by Geoffrey Chaucer – a new text with illustrative notes. I was introduced to Chaucer at school and find this book fascinating.

17th September 1999 Friday
Branson, Barry, died suddenly on September 7th 1999. Funeral service to be held at St Gabriel's Parish Church on Friday September 17th at 11.00am, followed by burial at Gilroes Cemetery. All Barry's friends are welcome at the funeral. All flowers and further inquiries to Ginns and Gutteridge Funeral Directors of Leicester.

Branson, Baz. A very funny man and a true friend who touched everyone with his great sense of humour and his sincerity. I remember when I wasn't well, Barry came visiting with a bag of sweets, jigsaws, colouring books and crayons and made me laugh so much I nearly broke my stitches.

Branson, Baz, always a funny day when you were on the same job as us, never done any work for laughing. The job won't be the same. God bless. From all at Transbuild.

***Branson**, Baz. Farewell old mate. We had some great times, you will be greatly missed. God must have wanted a joker up there with him, he took the best.*

***Branson**, Barry (Baz). This town has lost a character, one of the funniest men I ever knew. Goodbye my friend. - Tallo. (Newspaper cuttings)*

These are but a sample of more than 200 tributes in the Leicester Mercury to Barry Branson, whose funeral is today. Not since Annette Tyrell died in February 1993 (see 29th October 1994) have so many tributes been paid to one person. I never knew either of them personally.

Hundreds of people crowded into a Leicester church to pay their last respects to Barry Branson. Barry, also known as 'Barmy Baz', died suddenly last week aged 49, and his funeral at St Gabriel's Church on Gipsy Lane was a measure of a man who touched many people's lives with his boundless humour. (Newspaper cutting)

19th September 1999 Sunday
London Open House '99 - Mary Blue & I had another wonderful day in London yesterday enjoying our 5th 'London Open House' day. As I told you in September 1995, this is part of Europe's Heritage Days and is organised in this country by the Civic Trust, with funding from the Dept. of National Heritage.

Mary Blue & I visited five buildings this year:
1) The Scottish Office, Dover House, 66 Whitehall.
2) The Crown Estate Office, 16 Carlton Terrace (responsible for Crown property).
3) The Civic Trust, next door at No 17.
4) London Transport Headquarters at 55 Broadway.
5) Department for Culture, Media and Sport, Cockspur Street.

The Department for Culture, Media & Sport is New Labour's re-naming of the former Department of National Heritage (heri in Latin means yesterday, and New Labour looks for ever forward). However, this ultra-modern department provides the money for the Civic Trust (which is a charity) to organise such things as 'Open House Day'.

25th September 1999 Saturday
The Very Revd Derek Hole, Provost of Leicester since April 1992, retired this week, aged 66. He finishes his term of office at the end of November but is enjoying a 3 months sabbatical until then, during which good old Canon Michael Banks is holding the fort.
The Cathedral has launched a £2 million Millennium Appeal.

27th September 1999 Monday
Leicester Cathedral's Millennium Appeal is an ambitious project for the future of the Cathedral.
£2 million is required for proper facilities for the visitors, including a refectory, shop and meeting place, besides upgrading the interior of the Cathedral. The organ also needs attention, as does the central heating system.

29th September 1999 Wednesday
Christ Church, Coalville, 8th Gala Concert – This is an annual event organised entirely by Peter Jacques. He puts on a concert of singers & musicians who perform free of charge – proceeds for various charities. His contact with several Amateur Operatic Societies as Musical Director is a great help. He then contacts 200 'regulars' for the audience.

1st October 1999 Friday
"You are invited to join Mr Keith Lewin at the Grand Hotel, South Wigston, on 20th October 1999 for a buffet & drinks to celebrate his forthcoming retirement."
Keith Lewin was employed as a handyman (or to be politically correct – handyperson) where I worked at Wigston. It was my job to interview him.
(See 26th November 1984)

3rd October 1999 Sunday
Picture postcard from Miles & Michele, now living in Malta. '........ have settled in our new home and it is paradise. Just had lunch on our balcony with the blue 'Med' below ......'
(Glenholm is let with effect from 8th October for 12 months.)

5th October 1999 Tuesday
Enid celebrates her 72nd birthday tomorrow. We have arranged to spend the day visiting two National Trust properties. 1) Belton House, Belton, near Grantham, acclaimed as the perfect English country house, in 600 acres of parkland. 2) Woolsthorpe Manor, not far from Belton House – birthplace of Isaac Newton.

7th October 1999 Thursday
How fortunate Enid and I were yesterday to have such a lovely sunny day for our outing to Belton House & Woolsthorpe Manor. Nevertheless, we were fully aware of the dreadful rail disaster which occurred on Tuesday this week not far from Paddington Station, London: the worst for many years.

***90 feared dead in rail crash** – By lunchtime the death toll had risen to six, then it was eight. By teatime, when those commuters should have been returning home, it reached 26. Last night there were reports of at least another 60 victims in one carriage that was virtually destroyed when two trains crashed near Paddington Station in the morning rush-hour. (Newspaper cutting)*

9th October 1999 Saturday
London's wheel to rise today – The first attempt on Friday 10th September this year to lift London's 1,600 tonne Millennium Wheel to its upright position failed. This weekend a second attempt is made and is a great success, bringing much applause.

11th October 1999 Monday
On 11th October 1986, I showed you Patrick Magee, then aged 35, given life imprisonment for planting a bomb and killing 4 people, injuring 32, at the Annual Tory Conference in 1984.

He is now a free man, granted early release in June this year.

13th October 1999 Wednesday

The United Nations declared this week that the world's population has now reached six billion.

It is, of course, impossible to know when the six billion mark is reached. The U.S. Census Bureau gave the date as 19th July this year. It all depends on the methods used for estimating population.

15th October 1999 Friday

The Old Wesleyan Chapel, Swannington

A magnificent conversion of an Edwardian Chapel providing accommodation centred around a spacious split level living area. Property has been restored by craftsmen, retaining a wealth of original features, views to open countryside. Entrance vestibule, sitting room, dining area, study area, kitchen, utility, breakfast room with original pews. Cloakroom/WC, 2 ground floor bedrooms, 2 bathrooms. Spiral staircase leads to 1st floor master suite of bedroom, en-suite, living area, second staircase. Externally – grounds will be fully landscaped with a block paved drive leading to new double garage with WC, spacious studio room over.

(Newspaper cutting)

Here is the former Methodist Church at Swannington, wonderfully converted into a lovely home and now for sale (price not revealed). It was in July last year that we attended 'A Final Service of Remembrance & Thankfulness' where we were reminded that God was not dead & all was not lost.

16th October 1999 Saturday

77 days to go

The Croft, Wash Lane, Ravenstone

An exclusive development of six detached bungalows under construction. Popular village location set back in private cul de sac location. Built by NHBC registered builder RJH Building Construction Ltd to a very high specification. 2/3 bedroom bungalows with ensuite, uPVC double glazed cottage style windows, gas central heating, single and double garages and many other extras included. Prices start from £135,950.

(Newspaper cutting)

19th October 1999 Tuesday

Snibston Gardens, Coalville – George Merrill and his wife Marjorie are now happily ensconced in their gorgeous new home with this lovely address, "Snibston Gardens" (See 2nd May 1999).

I called to see them and found George only too pleased to have finally made the break from his dear old home.

21st October 1999 Thursday

In praise of trees - As we approach the new millennium, we are reminded that at least 100 British trees are more than 1,000 years old.

The great hurricane of October 1987 destroyed 15 million of our trees in one night, but still we have one or two yew trees more than 3,000 years old.

The Woodland Trust has £10 million of lottery money to create 250 'community woods'. The Conservation Foundation and the Church of England are collaborating in a scheme to plant a new yew in every parish. *(Newspaper cutting)*

Yews for remembrance

From Professor David Bellamy, President of The Conservation Foundation

Sir, Richard Morrison, in his interesting article on the cultural importance of trees (Times 3, October 15th), mentions the planting of yew trees in many parishes across Britain by the Conservation Foundation and the Church of England.

There are 7,000 such parishes. Each has been given a cutting taken from yews that were growing here in Britain before Christ was born.

So this is set to be one of the largest and most down-to-earth celebrations of, not the millennium, but of what the world is really celebrating – the cultural heritage of the bi-millennium: 2,000 years since the birth of Christ.

Yours faithfully, David J. Bellamy, President, The Conservation Foundation,

1 Kensington Gore, SW7 2AR
conserve@gn.apc.org
October 18th

23rd October 1999 Saturday

Keith Lewin's retirement get-together on Wednesday this week at the Grand Hotel, South Wigston, gave me the opportunity to catch up with all the latest changes since I retired from work in July 1991. The Office is in the process of becoming part of OFGEM (Gas & Electricity regulation), so major upheaval.

25th October 1999 Monday

(19p stamp stuck in diary) This is one of Royal Mail's Millennium stamps. It shows Robert the Bruce who had himself crowned King of Scotland at Scone in 1306. The venerated Stone of Scone had been captured by Edward I in 1296.

27th October 1999 Wednesday

The AA under Centrica's ownership – "Pay Miss E. Hewes £248.56p."

A very welcome cheque from Centrica to every member of the AA – this amount is based on the total purchase price for the AA of £1.1 billion divided by the number of eligible members. (See 28th June 1999)

The cheque is for the amount due to you from redeemable shares in the AA.

29th October 1999 Friday

Lucan is dead – official.

"Be it known that the Right Honourable Richard John Bingham, Seventh Earl of Lucan, of 72a Elizabeth Street, London SW1, died on or since the 8th day of November 1974."

The Earl of Lucan, missing since the murder of his children's nanny on 7th November 1974, has now been officially declared dead. (See 20th June 1998)

Lucan has not been seen since the night of November 7th 1974, when Sandra Rivett was bludgeoned to death with a lead pipe by an 'intruder' at the family home in

Belgravia. When his wife went to investigate, the man attacked her. She ran, covered in blood, to a nearby pub to raise the alarm. Police believe Lord Lucan had intended to murder her and killed the nanny by mistake.

The Earl of Lucan committed suicide in the Channel after fleeing Britain in 1974, according to his best friend, John Aspinall. The casino owner and conservationist, said that he believed that Lord Lucan's bones were lying '250ft under the Channel'. The claim is unlikely, however, to bring to an end the worldwide search for the peer, wanted for the murder of his children's nanny, Sandra Rivett, in 1974. Scotland Yard said yesterday that the file would remain open. Mr Aspinall, 73, was speaking for the first time about the peer's disappearance since he was interviewed by the police in 1974. He told The Sunday Telegraph: "He (Lord Lucan) tied a stone around his body and scuttled the powerboat he kept at Newhaven and down he went. I think it's a very brave thing."

Mr Aspinall said that he had no doubt his friend had bludgeoned his children's nanny to death after mistaking her for his wife. He added: "He reckoned that if he wasn't around any more, there'd always be a question mark over his guilt, which would be good for his children."   *(Newspaper cuttings)*

30th October 1999 Saturday

63 days to go

31st October 1999 Sunday
Millennium fever is very much in evidence at the moment. This evening at church I acquired the Millennium Plate, depicting a scene of Main Street, Ravenstone, circa 1925 and indicating 1000 – 2000 A.D. I also have a cock-eyed little Millennium Bear, known to me as Cock-Eye, Millennium mugs and a Millennium brooch.

2nd November 1999 Tuesday
One replacement back yard. The work which was due to start early in September, started in effect late in October, when the rainy season and autumn falling leaves created havoc.
From 'Care & Repair' I receive a brusque request for payment £924 – "Following completion & inspection of the work done, I am now anxious to pay the contractor."

4th November 1999 Thursday
The right of hereditary peers to sit and vote in the House of Lords is almost over. Only 42 hereditary Tory peers have a temporary reprieve, plus 50 others of various sorts. The number of Tory peers at present is 470, out of an overall total of 640.

If the first Earl of Suffolk had not noticed a suspicious chap called Guy Fawkes loitering in the cellars of Parliament, the House of Lords would have been destroyed on November 5th 1605.
Tomorrow, exactly 394 years later, the 21st Earl will be thrown out of the Lords when he succumbs to new Labour's own constitutional fireworks. Tony Blair will succeed where the Catholic mercenary failed when those peers failing to win a reprieve lose their last chance to

stay in the Lords.   *(Newspaper cutting)*

Sculpture idea is welcomed
Ideas for the fantastic new sculpture on Ravenstone village green have been welcomed by residents and councillors.
Artist Phil Townsend gave a presentation about his plans for the millennium centrepiece which has been designed to reflect the village's rich history and exciting future. It will take pride of place on the village green which is being created in Leicester Road.
The statue will be made out of embossed stone with an aluminium archway which will depict two ravens making a nest. The design will be cut out of the metal so a beautiful shadow will appear on the ground when the sun shines through. The two stone columns will be made into triangle shapes and staggered so that people driving in each direction will be able to see the two decorative features holding up the arch. On each side of the stone a different design will be carved into it to depict scenes in the village.
One of the views, which portrayed the village's mining history, was a picture of Snibston Discovery Park which used to be a working mine.
It is hoped granite sets will be able to be put in around the feature making sure the surrounding area is in keeping with the scene.
All the councillors agreed it was very good and were looking forward to it going up in the village. The idea behind the sculpture came from the Ravenstone Millennium Steering Group which over the past four years has helped to raise a fantastic total in excess of £13,000 to fund the project.
(Newspaper cutting)

6th November 1999 Saturday
"The Isles" is the latest book by Norman Davies about the British Isles, telling you that all its history which we learn at school is nothing more than the Roman Conquest (of England), and then 1066 and all that concerning England, Ireland, Scotland and Wales count for very little. No wonder we English have a distorted view of our country.

8th November 1999 Monday
"Monday in The Times – start reading The Isles"
Norman Davies, author of 'The Isles' thinks that the U.K. was a concept cobbled together to unite the Scots and English in the task of winning a global empire. When the empire fell apart, it left us in a vacuum. He predicts the break-up of the United Kingdom, maybe before its 300th birthday in 2007.

10th November 1999 Wednesday
"Personal finance will be on the school curriculum in September 2000" – Not only did we learn history at school, as though England was the centre of the universe, we learned absolutely nothing about personal finance. Next year the Personal Finance Education Group (PFEG) is to help children understand finance.

12th November 1999 Friday
Gustav Aronsohn, Rector of Ravenstone from 1960 to 1965, while I was Sunday school teacher, was a Dutchman. I remember how appalled he was when he

asked the Sunday school children what they knew about Napoleon. We all knew nothing. I certainly learned more in later life about Napoleon than I did at school.

13th November 1999 Saturday

Leicestershire's hereditary peers expressed their sadness yesterday as they lost their centuries-old right to sit in the House of Lords. They are among 650 hereditaries who have been stripped of their right to vote on British laws. A rump of 92 has been allowed to stay on in the transitional second chamber.

(Newspaper cutting)

14th November 1999 Sunday

And now, at the age of 68, I learn why I belong to England, to Great Britain, and at the same time to the United Kingdom, thanks to "The Isles" written by Norman Davies.
The complicated history of the Isles –
The High Kingship of Ireland, to AD 1169
The Ancient British tribal principalities, to circa AD 70
Independent 'Pictland', to the 9th century AD
Roman Britannia, AD 43 – circa AD 410
The independent British/Welsh principalities, from the 5th century to 1283, including Cornwall, Cumbria and Strathclyde
The Anglo-Saxon kingdoms, from the 5th to 10th centuries
The Kingdom of the Scots, from the 9th century to 1651, and 1660 – 1707
The Kingdom of England, from the 10th century to 1536, together with its dependencies including the Channel Islands, the Isle of Man, the Welsh March and English-occupied Wales and Ireland.
The Kingdom of England and Wales, 1536 – 1649, 1660 – 1707
The Kingdom of Ireland, 1541 – 1649, 1660 – 1800
The Commonwealth and Free State of England, Wales and Ireland, 1649 – 1654
The Commonwealth of Great Britain and Ireland, alias the First British Republic, 1654 – 1660
The Kingdom of Great Britain, 1707 – 1800
The United Kingdom of Great Britain and Ireland, 1801 – 1922
The Irish Free State, later Eire then the Republic of Ireland, since 1922
The United Kingdom of Great Britain and Northern Ireland, since 1922

15th November 1999 Monday

47 days to go

16th November 1999 Tuesday

"Dear Collector, The eve of the Millennium is only a few weeks away and it is with great pleasure I enclose your £5 Millennium circulation coin – a worthwhile memento to keep."
Received by post from The Crown Collections Ltd. P.O. Box 229, Tunbridge Wells, the Millennium coin I ordered earlier.   (See 6th February 1999).

18th November 1999 Thursday

"Ravenstone with Snibston – a celebration of 2,000 years of village life"

This is a book produced by Ravenstone Local History Group for the Millennium. Like Snibston School Diary which I was given to read in October 1982, it has a good sprinkling of members of the Hewes family, including Bunting as a singer in 1940.

20th November 1999 Saturday

Coalville Library is one of thousands across the country which has teamed up with the BBC to teach us all how to use the Internet. I have now had a go at using the 'mouse' and hope to complete four hourly lessons.

Folk given internet taster offer – Get Webwise! That's the message from staff at Coalville Library where folk are being invited to take part in some free internet taster sessions.   (Newspaper cutting)

The Internet is fast becoming a part of everyday life as we move into the new millennium, so if you don't want to be left behind book your session now.

(Newspaper cutting)

In June 1997, 100,000 people had Internet access. By December last year that figure had risen to more than 10.6 million.   (Newspaper cutting)

22nd November 1999 Monday

Church of England Sunday attendance has fallen below a million. Trying to count attendance at church is almost impossible. No two weeks record the same people. Some attend every week, some never, and some occasionally. Certainly I have seen numbers dwindle in my lifetime, but we have a stalwart nucleus.

Attendances under a million – Attendances at Church of England services on Sundays have fallen below one million for the first time, according to reports published today.   (Newspaper cutting)

24th November 1999 Wednesday

The George Cross, awarded "for acts of the greatest heroism or of the most conspicuous courage in circumstances of extreme danger" was instituted by Georg VI in 1940 – the highest civilian award for gallantry. There have been 151 individual recipients, plus 2 collective recipients: The People of Malta and now the R.U.C.

RUC awarded the George Cross – The Queen delighted Unionists but angered republicans by awarding the George Cross to the Royal Ulster Constabulary.

(Newspaper cutting)

The Citation – The text of the citation for the RUC's George Cross reads –
"For the past 30 years the RUC has been both the bulwark against, and the main target of, a sustained and brutal terrorist campaign. The force has suffered heavily in protecting both sides of the community from danger – 302 officers have been killed in the line of duty and thousands more injured, many seriously. Many officers have been ostracised by their own community and others have been forced to leave their homes in the face of threat to them or their families. As Northern Ireland reaches a turning point in its political development this

award is made to recognise the collective courage and dedication to duty of all those who have served in the RUC and who have accepted the danger and stress this has brought to them and to their families."

(Newspaper cutting)

25th November 1999 Thursday

Plans by Ravenstone with Snibston Parish Council to floodlight the parish church in Ravenstone for the millennium are well under way with the contractor set to start work next week. The parish council has been putting aside money each year to mark the millennium in Ravenstone and decided on the floodlighting project. Electrician Roger West, from the village, will be carrying out the work. The separate Ravenstone Millennium Group has also arranged for a village marker to be erected as part of the village's millennium celebrations. *(Newspaper cutting)*

26th November 1999 Friday

Earlier this month I said to Ursula, who now regularly attends services in the Chapel attached to Ravenstone Alms Houses, how I would love to see this dear little Chapel restored to its former glory. Now it seems about to happen. (See Travel Journal 1997, June 13th)

New look for chapel – A listed building in Ravenstone could soon be given a new look for the millennium if plans to carry out repairs are given the go ahead. A. R. Argyle of Burton on Trent has applied to North West Leicestershire District Council to carry out internal and external repair work to Ravenstone Chapel. The Chapel on Hospital Lane is a listed building which is looked after by the Ravenstone Hospital Charity Trust.

(Newspaper cutting)

28th November 1999 - The First Sunday of Advent

Advent Sunday heralds the beginning of the Church Year. More than any other Advent Sunday I have known, this was undoubtedly the most special of all, leading us into the 3rd Millennium of Christianity.
At Ravenstone Church we had 'Songs of Praise' including a 'reading' from Haggai 2: 1 – 9, which I had the privilege to read.

30th November 1999 Tuesday

There I was learning how to get web-wise, when, out of the blue, a photographer appeared and took this photograph. *(Photo of Betty in Coalville Times entitled 'Elizabeth Hewes surfs the internet')*

Local folk are now learning how to get wise on the web thanks to a new Internet teaching session.
Coalville Library on High Street now offers free Internet lessons, showing people how to surf the net in a friendly and supportive environment. The taster sessions are part of the BBC's 'Webwise' programme which aims to get more people using the Internet. And the hour long session will teach you everything you need to know about using the web, from how to log on to searching the many pages.
If you fancy learning how to use the Internet telephone Coalville Library on 01530 835951 to arrange a suitable time and date. *(Newspaper cutting)*

1st December 1999 Wednesday

31 days to go

2nd December 1999 Thursday

"The Signpost" is a new composite Church Magazine for the United Benefice of Hugglescote, Snibston and Ellistown. Pat and Evelyn belong to St James Church, Snibston. James Hodson and his wife Trevelyn, whom I meet every Sunday for lunch with Pat, Evelyn and Mary Blue, have launched the magazine and I paid £3 for one year.

3rd December 1999 Friday

A little more daylight was shed on the mystery of monarchy yesterday with the first televising of a royal investiture at Buckingham Palace. (Newspaper cutting)

4th December 1999 Saturday

"Christingle" services were brought to England from the Moravian Church by the Children's Society in 1968. Ravenstone Church is one of many which have supported the Children's Society by distributing Christingle boxes at this time of year. All this is about to change now that lesbians and gays are to be considered as adoptive parents.

Dozens of churches are to withhold their annual December donations to the Church of England Children's Society after it lifted its ban on homosexuals and lesbians adopting and fostering children..

(Newspaper cutting)

6th December 1999 Monday

"After careful consideration Ravenstone Church P.C.C. has decided that the Children's Society's change of policy, whereby gays and lesbians are to be considered as adoptive/foster parents, is contrary to our understanding of Christian teaching. If this policy is not reversed by Christingle 2000, we will have to reconsider supporting the Society."

8th December 1999 Wednesday

"God save the Queen and God help the Consort" (See 16th February 1986). I was reminded of the banners of welcome for the Queen in Nepal as 'The Times Charity Appeal 2000' appeals to readers to donate their time, skills and money to Save the Children and Help the Aged.

A third of all children in Britain, some 4.5 million, now live in poverty and 1.5 million older people have to rely on state benefits for their income. (Newspaper cutting)

10th December 1999 Friday

"Winter Fuel Payment – We are sending out winter fuel payments again this year to help make sure that pensioners do not worry about turning up their heating when it is cold. The amount has gone up to £100 and a payment of £100 will be paid into your bank in the next few days."
(Previously £20, see 19th March 1998).

11th December 1999 Saturday

Village gets in festive mood – Festive folk in Ravenstone

will be celebrating a double switch-on of lights on Saturday December 11ᵗʰ. At 6pm the new floodlights at Ravenstone Parish Church will be turned on for the first time. The lights are the millennium project of the Ravenstone with Snibston Parish Council.
Then at 6.30pm locals will be heading to the Christmas tree in Main Street for the official switch on of the Christmas lights and carol singing. Everyone is welcome. *(Newspaper cutting)*

12ᵗʰ December 1999 Sunday
H.M.S.O. Her Majesty's stationery Office was privatised 3 years ago and is now made up of four independent businesses: Security Printing, Government Publishing, Banner Office Supplies and largest of the four, Document Management, newly named Tactica, all due for sell-off.

The Stationery Office (TSO), the privatised former HMSO, has demerged into four operational companies as a precursor to separate flotations or sell-offs which will net big profits for its chairman, Rupert Pennant-Rea, and Electra Fleming, the City financiers.
(Newspaper cutting)

14ᵗʰ December 1999 Tuesday
"Dear Miss Hewes, I know that PowerGen no longer supplies your electricity. One reason you changed could be that you were under the impression you would save money. A significant number of British Gas customers would actually have lower bills if they took both electricity and gas from PowerGen ...... we'd love to have you back."

16ᵗʰ December 1999 Thursday
Viscount and Lady Linley (see 22ⁿᵈ May 1999) became the proud parents of a baby son on 1ˢᵗ July. Earlier this month the baby was christened in the Queen's Chapel, St James Palace. He has been given the splendid name: Charles Patrick Inigo Armstrong Jones.

18ᵗʰ December 1999 Saturday
(Photograph stuck in diary) This is Mr Douglas Clement Harrison who opened our Christmas Fair in 1996, having celebrated his 100ᵗʰ birthday on 26ᵗʰ November that year. As you can see he is still going strong, aged 103, and able to get out and about, well looked after by his family.

Church profit – the Christmas Fair held for Ravenstone parish church saw a wide variety of stalls, sideshows and goods available. Although numbers attending were down on last year, those who came spent very generously and approximately £800 will have been raised. *(Newspaper cutting)*

Greenwich to be e-time centre – The status of Greenwich as the home of time is to be assured under a scheme to make the London site the global timekeeper for the Internet. Greenwich Electronic Time – known as GeT – will act as a standard. *(Newspaper cutting)*

20ᵗʰ December 1999 Monday
From my love by post a Christmas card for the end of this Millennium, having been in love with each other for

more than 50 years.
"You're so very special and you deserve a Christmas that's special too.
Happy Christmas darling. All my love John xxxx"
Also a £20 note which bought me "2000 Years of Prayer".

21ˢᵗ December 1999 Tuesday

11 days to go

22ⁿᵈ December 1999 Wednesday
Last year I enjoyed Christmas Day with Pat, Evelyn, Mary Blue and Scott at the lovely home of Sharon and Jim in Melton Mowbray. Apart from Scott who is at present living in Australia, we have all been invited again this year to Sharon and Jim's home for Christmas Day and to James and Trevelyn's home for Boxing Day.

24ᵗʰ December 1999 Friday
Today I am 25,000 days old!! Tomorrow is Christmas Day and I hope to take early morning Holy Communion (9.00am) at little St Mary's, Snibston. I was there for Holy Communion at Easter.
This truly is a momentous time, as we celebrate our Lord's 2,000ᵗʰ birthday. (Albeit somewhat miscalculated).

26ᵗʰ December 1999 Sunday
The 20ᵗʰ century is drawing to its close. The Pope (John Paul II) has declared that next year, the year 2000, will be the Jubilee Year culminating at the Feast of the Epiphany, 6ᵗʰ January 2001.
Epiphany is the day we remember the arrival of the wise men bringing gifts to the Christ-child: gold, frankincense and myrrh.

An article in the 'Daily Telegraph' stated that the government had recently admitted in a House of Commons statement that we were celebrating the 'Millennium' a year early. *(Newspaper cutting)*

It should be obvious that until the year 2000 has finished, the 20ᵗʰ Century cannot possibly be over, and, therefore, the new 21ˢᵗ Century will begin on January 1ˢᵗ 2001, and so, of course, does the third 'Millennium'.
(Newspaper cutting)

28ᵗʰ December 1999 Tuesday
"2000 Years of Prayer", my Christmas present from Cocky, is a wonderful book which I came across quite by chance on my last visit to the shop at Mount St Bernard's Abbey, Whitwick.
Not only does it give you the greatest prayers over all that time, but traces the background of those who lived and often died for Christ.

30ᵗʰ December 1999 Thursday
Was there ever a prayer to God like that for George Herbert (1593 – 1633)? A brilliant scholar who chose to live as a country parson. He wrote such beautiful hymns: - "The God of love my shepherd is", "Teach me my God and King" etc. Those who knew and loved him prayed during his final illness, for him to be restored to them 'our dear brother'.

31ˢᵗ December 1999 Friday

The global population will reach 8.9billion in 2050, up from 6 billion now. (Newspaper cutting)

Into a New Millennium
Jubilee year ahead

* * *

Question: Why do we call a man Mr irrespective of his marital status, but differentiate between women with Miss or Mrs?

This custom arises from the indisputable fact that men don't bear children. For many years, society required a method of ascertaining the father of any given child to preserve the rights of inheritance. The mother had to make a formal declaration of the identity of her child's father. Since this doesn't seem to be so important now, it is considered proper for a married woman to retain her father's surname and continue to be called Miss if she wishes. (Newspaper cutting)

* * *

Many people think that Doctor Johnson wrote the first English dictionary, but in fact, that honour goes to Robert Cawdrey, who published a list of 2,500 'hard and unusual English words' in 1604.
Johnson's dictionary of 1755 was a much larger undertaking, its 45,000 words collected by a team of seven over six years. However, the most ambitious dictionary must be that which became known as the Oxford English Dictionary. The first edition, completed in 1927, contained 414,825 words and had taken 70 years to compile. (Newspaper cutting)

* * *

2000

1st January 2000 Saturday

New Millennium

As we move into the new millennium, the Age of Pisces gives way to the Age of Aquarius.

2nd January 2000 Sunday

And so we greet the long expected New Year: a new century, a new millennium. We tiptoe tentatively into the vast Third Millennium which stretches far, far away beyond our horizon.

It was the Reverend Gustav Aronsohn who reminded us in January 1961 of the words, "I said to the man who stood at the gate of the year."

4th January 2000 Tuesday

"I said to the man who stood at the gate of the year, 'Give me a light that I may tread safely into the unknown' and he replied, 'Go out into the darkness and put your hand into the hand of God. That shall be to you better than light and safer than a known way.'

(Quoted by King George VI at Christmas 1939)

According to a study by the Credit Card Research Group last year, more than a third of the UK population – 16.5 million people – have some form of unsecured debt. The average person owes more than £6,300 through personal loans, credit cards and hire purchase. As a nation, we owe about £105.3 billion.

(Newspaper cutting)

During Jubilee Year Pope John Paul will beatify John XXIII and people from six other countries – including Ireland.   *(Newspaper cutting)*

6th January 2000 Epiphany

Epiphany is the day we remember the wise men from the east who came with gifts for the Christ child. (St Matthew, Chapter 2).

This year, the most unlikely wise men from the east (rulers of the former Soviet republics, Russia, Ukraine, Belarus, Moldova and Georgia) came to Bethlehem to mark the Orthodox Christmas.

7th January 2000 Friday

St James's Palace January 7: the Prince of Wales, Member, today gave a Lunch for the Saints and Sinners Club of London.   *(Newspaper cutting)*

8th January 2000 Saturday

Film star Elizabeth Taylor has been 'knighted' in the New Year's Honours List and is now Dame Elizabeth Taylor. She will be celebrating her 68th birthday next month and is honoured for her tremendous support for charities.

10th January 2000 Monday

Yesterday we changed our venue for Sunday lunch. For the past five years, Pat, Evelyn, James, Trevelyn, Mary Blue and I have enjoyed our Sunday lunch at Sunnyside Garden Centre, Ibstock.

The chef, Richard, has now moved to Lakeside Lodge Tea Room Restaurant, Moira and we have followed him there.

12th January 2000 Wednesday

Picture postcard from Miles & Michele (see 3rd October 1999) to say that a gas fire plus cylinder had blown up in their home in Malta.

"Absolute devastation from fire and smoke damage. All disco gear saved and we survived. Three weeks later the apartment has been completely refurbished."

14th January 2000 Friday

A phone call from Bunting's son Michael, to say that he and Josie are off once more to Barbados, where they will be staying in their newly built home, now furnished and all theirs. They now have two homes, one in Stafford and one in Barbados. They will be in Barbados for several months and miss Pat's Diamond Wedding.

16th January 2000 Sunday

Land, Samuel, passed peacefully away in Glenfield Hospital on January 15th aged 86 years. Loving husband of the late Florence and much loved father of Brian. Loving father-in-law of Jean, and devoted grandfather and great-grandfather of Susan, Jade, Lauren. The funeral will take place at Ravenstone Church on Monday January 31st at 10.00am followed by interment in churchyard. Family flowers only, donations if so desired to Ravenstone Church c/o Reverend Kerry Emmett. Further inquiries to Midlands Co-operative Funeral Service, 128 London Road, Coalville LE67 3JD

On 13th January 1995, Florence Land died. Now almost five years to the day later (15th January 2000) her devoted husband Sam has died. So many people have died recently that Sam's funeral cannot take place until 31st January.

17th January 2000 Monday

The first wedding has taken place at the new County Hall Register Office Suite.

Anjali Pattni and Sailesh Rajnikant, of Narborough Road, Leicester, were the first couple to tie the knot in the new suite.   *(Newspaper cutting)*

18th January 2000 Tuesday

Mount St Bernard's Abbey Ecumenical Service this week included members from the Russian Orthodox Church. The service was by invitation only, primarily for local clergy and their wives. Katherine & I therefore missed out on what would have been a very special service.

20th January 2000 Thursday

Pat & Evelyn are looking forward to their Diamond Wedding on 16th March this year. Already Mary Blue has been in touch with Buckingham Palace to arrange for a greetings card from H.M. the Queen.

Scott, who is now living in Australia, is returning to England in order to be here for this special anniversary.

22nd January 2000 Saturday

"Civil Service Retirement Fellowship" this month for the 5th consecutive year was a belated Christmas Party, held across the road from Thringstone Community Centre, at the Chapel assembly room. There were about 40 assembled, including non-Civil Servants, all friends and associates of our well-known leader, Terry Watson.

24th January 2000 Monday

Concordia Theatre, Stockwell Head, Hinckley – The Pantomime Company presents Cinderella.

Hinckley's pantomime "Cinderella" was as always a sheer delight. Devised and produced to perfection by John Hill. Costumes by John Hill. Scenic design, a joy to behold, by Roy Johnson; plus star performers and dancers.

26th January 2000 Wednesday

Enid's niece Alison today gave birth to her 2nd baby, Jessica Frances, a sister for Eleanor Mary, born 17th November 1997. So for the 2nd time I am great-auntie-cuz.

Bunting's younger son Julian celebrates his 50th birthday on 30th January and then celebrates his Silver Wedding Anniversary on 31st May.

28th January 2000 Friday
Happy Birthday ♥
To my ain wee darling – now 70

Cocky woke with this thought: - "The days of our years are threescore years and ten" (Psalm 90).

Mr Harrison, aged 103, Ravenstone's oldest resident, died on Cocky's 70th birthday, well over five score years.

***Harrison**, Douglas Clement, of Ravenstone, passed peacefully away at Coalville Community Hospital on January 28th 2000 at the age of 103 years.*

Funeral service and cremation at Loughborough Crematorium on Monday February 7th at 1.15pm.

Villager dies aged 103

30th January 2000 Sunday

In 1945 on this date, the snow lay deep on the ground. Thankfully, today, the winters in this country are milder, due no doubt to global warming. The long term effects of global warming, however, spell disaster.

This week the contraceptive pill celebrates its 39th birthday. On January 30th 1961 the Pill became licensed for general use. (Newspaper cutting)

1st February 2000 Tuesday

Ravenstone Church was filled yesterday for the funeral of Sam Land, Church Warden and Church Treasurer for many years.

The two hymns were the favourites of his beloved wife Florence who died five years ago. "Great is Thy Faithfulness, O God my Father" and "Blessed Assurance, Jesus is Mine".

3rd February 2000 Thursday

The Rt. Revd Cormac Murphy-O'Connor, aged 67, Roman Catholic Bishop of Arundel & Brighton is to succeed the late Cardinal Basil Hume as Archbishop of Westminster. He expects to be created a cardinal during this year.

5th February 2000 Saturday

From 16th January 1944 to 5th February 1944, my poor old Mum spent three weeks recuperating at the home of her cousin Madge at Willoughby-on-the-Wolds, having been at death's door with pneumonia. Rob & I, then aged 10 and 12, stayed in Ravenstone at the home of a good neighbour, Mrs Dalby, whose teenage son John died 5th May 1944.

7th February 2000 Monday

Peter Mould, now aged 55, who has been living at Holme Lodge Cheshire Home, West Bridgford, for the last 6 or 7 years, is hoping to return to the Cheshire Home at Edinburgh. This evening I had an unexpected telephone from his friend Ruth Spalton, Manor Farm, Isley Walton, to say he was in hospital in Nottingham.

9th February 2000 Wednesday

Ofgas, our office at Wigston since April 1996, is now ofgem (the Office of Gas & Electricity Markets)

"You are invited to join Mr Edward Ludlow at the Firs Inn on Tuesday 29th February 2000 for drinks and a finger buffet to celebrate his forthcoming retirement. The celebration will start at 12.00 and finish at 14.30."

11th February 2000 Friday

"Pat & Evelyn Hewes request the pleasure of the company of Betty on the occasion of their 60th Wedding Anniversary on Sunday March 19th (Mary Blue's birthday). Time: 6.00 for 6.30 pm at the Lakeside Lodge, Shortheath Road, Moira. R.S.V.P. to 3 Totnes Close, Hugglescote."

13th February 2000 Sunday

"Today & always, Valentine, its you I'm dreaming of – For you fill my heart with happiness and fill my life with love. To my Valentine, All my love for ever. xxxxx."

The Royal Mail is expecting to deliver an estimated 12.25 million valentine cards. (Newspaper cutting)

15th February 2000 Tuesday

Miss E Hewes, Your tax code for the year 2000 – 01 is 149P (P = those aged 65 – 74).

Personal Allowance = £5,720. Take away State Pension / State Benefits which total £4,228 and your tax free amount for the year is £1,492, making your tax code 149P. (Tax code last year was 124P)

17th February 2000 Thursday

The Revd Canon Vivienne Frances Faull, aged 44, is to replace the Very Revd Derek Hole as Provost of Leicester Cathedral. She is expected to take up her post in the summer. Her husband is vice-provost and canon pastor of Coventry Cathedral.

Historic appointment - The Church of England's first woman provost is set to be appointed to Leicester Cathedral, in the shape of the Rev Canon Vivienne Frances Faull. (Newspaper cutting)

19th February 2000 Saturday

Prize from ERNIE!

At last, the £1,000 Premium Bonds 62AS 382001 – 383000 which I purchased in July 1996 have produced a winner. Bond No 62AS 382848 has won £50. I was beginning to wonder how much longer they would lie dormant. I would like to buy another £2,000 worth.

21st February 2000 Monday

Her Majesty The Queen Mother is Patron of the Civil Service Retirement Fellowship. Now aged 99, her birthday on 4th August this year will be very special. At our February meeting we each had the opportunity to sign a special headed sheet of paper from our branch to form eventually greetings from the whole country.

23rd February 2000 Wednesday

From "Friends of the Settle-Carlisle Line" comes a most interesting Quarterly Magazine – No 79.
The large bus company 'Arriva', with interests nationwide, has offered £35 million for M.T.L., the parent company of Settle-Carlisle franchise holders 'Northern Spirit'. Arriva buses operate all over the land, next will be trains.

25th February 2000 Friday

"Friends of the Settle-Carlisle Line" Magazine No 79.
How I enjoyed reading the account of train buff David Mathias who spent much of November 1999 watching the re-laying of the track on various chunks of the Settle-Carlisle Line. His account was so good; I felt that I had actually watched it myself.

27th February 2000 Sunday

"Dear Betty, Thank you for your donation of £20 which you gave to our church in memory of the late Sam Land. Sam was a great stalwart of St Michael's, serving for many years as churchwarden, treasurer....... The donations received with thanks totalled £300, a fitting memorial for a much loved member of St Michael's. Yours in Christ, Kerry – Revd Kerry C. Emmett."

29th February 2000 Tuesday

In July 1991 I invested £2,000 in Premium Bonds; in July 1996, I invested a further £1,000: now on this auspicious date, a once in 400 years leap year ending '00', I invested another £2,000, making a total of £5,000. Considering that a new car costs well over this, it can soon gain or lose.

29th February 1600: Europe enjoys the last leap year to be held in a year ending '00'. The next date for this quadricentennial event will be 29th February 2000.
(Newspaper cutting)

2nd March 2000 Thursday

On 30th November 1989 I opened an account with the Heart of England ♥ Building Society, purely for its heart. On 2nd October 1993 it was swallowed up by Cheltenham & Gloucester Building Society. The Cheltenham & Gloucester is now closing its Coalville branch on 31st March this year. I decided to transfer my £2,000 account into Premium Bonds.

4th March 2000 Saturday

Ted Ludlow's retirement get-together last Tuesday at 'The Firs' was in the very same room where Jan held her retirement only two years ago.
From far and near they came for Ted's retirement, he being Chief Gas Meter Examiner with contacts nationwide. Once more the 'oldies' enjoyed meeting up together again.

6th March 2000 Monday

'Charlie Girl' is Coalville Amateurs chosen production for this year (1st March – 11th March), a repeat of our 1989 production when we first transferred from the Miners' Welfare Centre to the King Edward VII Community College. Although not a Box Office success, it is proving to be a lovely show & I am thrilled as always to be in the midst.

8th March 2000 Ash Wednesday

Peter Jacques, Musical Director, Hon Chairman and mainstay of Coalville Amateur Operatic Society, is the only one who keeps it going when others fall by the wayside. House Manager Mick Hunt, with his assistant Margaret Tyler, has eleven supporters this year: Joan, Ann, Olive, Barbara, Chris, Hilda and me, plus Don, Alan, Basil and Brian.

10th March 2000 Friday

Charlie Girl – Every year during the week of Coalville Amateurs show, several people repeatedly celebrate their birthday, including Betty Leader (in charge of drinks during the interval) who this year on 6th March celebrated her 70th birthday; and Dawn Cox (née Henn) choreographer, who celebrates her 50th birthday tomorrow (the last night) 11th March.

12th March 2000 Sunday

Dawn Cox, choreographer at Coalville Amateurs for many years, was presented as usual with a bouquet on stage by President Roy Hunt in front of the full company. He told the audience that it was Dawn's 50th birthday, the orchestra struck up 'Happy Birthday to you' and she was serenaded by a mighty chorus of good singers.

14th March 2000 Tuesday

Knight, Florence Mabel. Formerly of Coleorton and Ravenstone. Passed peacefully away at Park Manor Nursing Home on March 3rd 2000, aged 87 years. Will be fondly remembered by family and friends. Funeral service and cremation to take place on Monday March 13th 3.30 pm at Gilroes Crematorium. Family flowers only. Donations for Park Manor Nursing Home Residents Fund may be sent to Midlands Co-operative Funeral Service, Stuart House, 128 London Road, Coalville. Enquiries to Shirley Arnold.

This is Miss Knight, my teacher at Snibstone County Primary School when I was aged about seven to eight.
Enid and I met her by chance in October 1996, when we were delivering Meals on Wheels at Coleorton. She was then a lively, vivacious, 84 year-old, still driving a car.

16th March 2000 Thursday

Hewes – Roberts
Pat and Evelyn
On 16th March 1940 at Marlborough Square, Coalville
Congratulations and love from all the family

(Diamond Anniversary)   (Newspaper cutting)

19th March 2000 Sunday
Pat & Evelyn's Diamond Wedding was a lovely family get-together, where Mary Blue, their only daughter, was in the midst of her five offspring, including Scott, home from Australia as promised, but hoping to return soon to his new fiancée Sheridan.
A Celebration Card from Her Majesty the Queen was the icing on the cake.

20th March 2000 Monday
From the moment of conception we all are one in Adam (See 21st March 1999).
Psalm 139 also teaches us the importance God bestows on us from the time of conception: -
"...... thou hast covered me in my mother's womb".
"...... My substance was not hid from thee, when I was made in secret and curiously wrought ....."
(See 26th October 2000)

22nd March 2000 Wednesday
"Thine eyes did see my substance, yet being unperfect; and in thy book all members were written, which in continuance were fashioned, when as yet there was none of them" Psalm 139: verse 16.
Just as Psalm 139 teaches us the importance God bestows on our embryonic state, so also the Koran repeats this same theme.

Drought caused the American side of the Niagara Falls to run short of water on this day in 1903
(Newspaper cutting)

24th March 2000 Friday
"This is to tell you that from 10th April 2000 the amount of your benefit will go up to £81.35p a week"
(Currently £80.14p) The Basic Pension goes up from £66.75p to £67.50p, which is only 75p for pensioners with no other means of income. There has been a public outcry over this.

26th March 2000 Sunday
Stocks, Ken passed away suddenly on March 17th aged 78 years. A much loved father of Graham and Roger, their wives Susannah and Christine, grandfather of James and George and very dear friend of Dorothy. Funeral service at Loughborough Crematorium on Thursday March 23rd at 2 pm. Flowers or donations for The British Heart Foundation may be sent to Stevens Goodburn Funeral Service, 33 Scalford Road, Melton Mowbray. Tel. (01664 481201).

This is Ken Stocks, married for almost 50 years to Maureen, daughter of 'Auntie Doris'.
Maureen died on 12th June 1995, only 11 days short of her Golden Wedding.
In August 1995, Ken wined and dined me, but I saw no more of him until Pat Gamble's funeral in April 1999.

28th March 2000 Tuesday
Elizabeth Hewes – No 811 013 027 0 012 has received her 8th 'Council Tax Bill' formerly 'Council Tax Demand Notice', for 27 Leicester Road, Ravenstone. "Band A" property, originally valued at up to £40,000. (This is the cheapest band) Council Tax is £582.15p, less 25% as sole occupant: £436.61p.

30th March 2000 Thursday
The funeral last week of Ken Stocks gave me the opportunity to make contact again with my mum's side of the family. We sang Isaac Watts' hymn, "O God our help in ages past" bringing back memories of Southampton where the tune is played every day by the Civic Centre clock. We had a get-together after the funeral at Cotes Mill.

1st April 2000 Saturday
It is the season of Lent, the sad time of the church calendar before Good Friday, when we remember Christ crucified. Always during Lent we used to sing "The Story of the Cross" (see 11th March 1945 when Doreen Carter and her father were the soloists).
Doreen is in the choir this year, preparing to sing again "The Story of the Cross".

3rd April 2000 Monday
Duke 'is in love' - The Duke of York (Prince Andrew) aged 40, who married Sarah Ferguson in 1986 and divorced in 1996, is reported today to be 'head over heels' in love with an Australian-born public relations girl. He is said to have fallen for blonde Emma Gibbs soon after his 40th birthday on 19th February this year. He is a very handsome prince.

7th April 2000 Friday
Ravenstone – Det 3 bed double fronted traditional style character property, OFCH, lounge, dining rm, brkfst rm, furnished to a high standard, gardens to frnt & rr, available short, £595 pcm. *(Newspaper cutting)*

"Glenholm" now has new lessees, while Miles, the absentee landlord, is only too pleased to receive this extra income. Nobody seems to tend the front garden and slowly the shrubs are taking over and hiding the windows.

By 2003 you will have to compile a seller's pack if you want to put your home on the market. Under the proposals, sellers will have to spend up to £700 on a pack before they can begin to market their home. The packs will include title documents, searches, surveys and a draft contract. At present, the buyer is expected to commission surveys and searches but the Government wants the seller to pay for these essentials upfront.
(Newspaper cutting)

9th April 2000 Sunday
Today, the 5th Sunday in Lent, otherwise called Passion Sunday, Ravenstone Church rejoiced to hear again "The Story of the Cross". This was my request included on the list of requests for 'Songs of Praise'. I provided the Rector with the words and music and we all sang in unison – not perfect, but a noble effort.

11th April 2000 Tuesday
Southampton, here I come! Last year I spent three nights at the Travelodge in Southampton (9th -11th August) and learned to know and love this great city. Now I am preparing to spend another three nights at the Travelodge (14th – 16th April) hoping to see the Tall Ships as they prepare to sail the Atlantic in the "Tall Ships 2000 Race".

13th April 2000 Thursday
"Top civic award for caring Jane" – this refers to Janie Jarman, mother of Terry Jarman who married Mary Blue in April 1965. A photograph in the Leicester Mercury shows Janie being presented with a framed "Civic Award for 1999" by the Mayor of Ashby. Janie, a former nurse, was honoured for her work with Arthritis Care.

15th April 2000 Saturday
Here I am in Southampton, enjoying the full carnival atmosphere down by the dockside – Dock Gate No 4, with the high & mighty Tall Ships before they set sail tomorrow in the "Tall Ships 2000 Race" circumnavigating the Atlantic. Today happens to be the anniversary of the sinking of the Titanic in 1912, which sailed from Southampton.

17th April 2000 Monday
Yesterday, the 20th London Marathon took place, while I was enjoying a long weekend in Southampton for the start of the Tall Ships Race.
Antonio Pinto of Portugal won in 2 hours 6 minutes and 36 seconds, a course record.

19th April 2000 Wednesday
Mr & Mrs J. T. Stevenson (Bunting's son Julian) request the pleasure of the company of Miss B. Hewes on the occasion of the marriage of their daughter Katherine Louise to Mr Simon Lilley at All Saints Church, Shelsley Beauchamp on Saturday 10th June 2000 at 12 noon, followed by reception at Stone Manor Hotel, Stone, Near Kidderminster.

21st April 2000 Good Friday
Phone numbers are changing 22nd April:
00 International Codes
01 Existing Area Codes
02 New Area Codes
03 Reserved for Area Code
04 Reserved for Future Use
05 Reserved for Future Use
06 Reserved for Future Use
07 Mobile, Pagers & Personal Numbering
08 Freephone & Special Rate Services
09 Premium Rate Services
"These changes will prevent the UK numbering system from running out of numbers."

Have you heard this before?
The last major change on 16th April 1995 was planned to last 'several generations'.

23rd April 2000 Easter Sunday
St George's Day this year falls on Easter Sunday. It is also Shakespeare's birthday, born at Stratford-on-Avon 1564. He died at Stratford-on-Avon on this day 1616.

25th April 2000 Tuesday
Notification from "Paymaster" of a slight increase in salary payable each month from £538.61p to £545.71p. Also Tax Code changed in recent Budget to 155P. Combined with the State Pension, my monthly income is now about £898: annual income £10,778. Also from the Paymaster, his first Civil Service Pensions Newsletter.

27th April 2000 Thursday
Land, *Brian Samuel of Main Street, Ravenstone, passed suddenly away at home on April 21st 2000 aged 58 years. Loving husband of Jean and much loved dad of Sue and John. Also devoted granddad of Jade and Lauren. Funeral service will take place at St Michael's Church, Ravenstone on Friday May 5th 2000 at 10.00 am followed by interment in the churchyard. Family flowers only please donations if so desired to Ravenstone Church. Further inquiries to David Tivey, Midlands Co-operative Funeral Services, Stuart House, 128 London Road, Coalville LE67 3JD*

The unexpected death of Brian Land, only three months after his father Sam, has stunned the village of Ravenstone.
How well I remember his wedding in April 1964, when Ravenstone Church was filled to overflowing.

29th April 2000 Saturday
Brian Land was a fine figure of a man, who looked the picture of health. Brought up as a farmer's son, he had a good outdoor complexion and spent many hours caring for his dad's garden across the road from my house. He was one of the few left who addressed me as 'Bet' and will be sadly missed.

1st May 2000 Monday
Goodbye Magnolia. In 1974 Mum chose a magnolia for the garden. Over the years it grew into a tangle of branches and in August 1998 I chopped it down. Now at last I have managed to dig up the roots.
Phew! What a job!

3rd May 2000 Wednesday
"The Miracle Maker" is the latest film on the life of Jesus. I enjoyed seeing this animated feature film made with foot high latex model figures, but so very life-like thanks to the latest computer technology and the voices of great actors. It was a moving story told through the eyes of a child, the little daughter of Jairus.

5th May 2000 Friday
Brian Land's funeral today filled Ravenstone Church to absolute maximum capacity with people standing in the belfry and in every aisle. I doubt whether the church had ever been so packed before. Apart from his large family, the police were there (he was a Special Constable), the farming community, work colleagues, friends and villagers.

7th May 2000 Sunday
What is a Priest? (See 12th September 1990)
My good friend, Canon Michael Banks of Leicester Cathedral, who has been acting provost since the departure of the Revd Derek Hole, says of our new lady provost, "I do not think she is a priest, but I am sure she thinks she is a priest."

9th May 2000 Tuesday
What is a Priest?
The Catechism of the Catholic Church, which we received in its English translation in 1994, is a large book consisting of nearly 700 pages. Section 2 covers the seven sacraments of the Church, including the

Sacrament of Holy Orders. Here you learn what is a Priest.

11th May 2000 Thursday

Phone call from Malta!

Cousin Miles who went to live in Malta last September rang me to ask the exact date of death of cousin Don and of Uncle Fred. He needs to know in connection with winding up his mother Isobel's estate.

Thanks to my diaries I was able to tell him 15th February 1988 and 4th November 1965.

13th May 2000 Saturday

Bob Brewin of Ravenstone's Local History Group wanted to know the exact date of the Olde Tyme Music Hall which was held at Ravenstone Institute. He was in possession of a group photo which included Aunt Dos and me. Again, thanks to my diaries, I was able to tell him 20th April 1968.

15th May 2000 Monday

The Times is voted Newspaper of the Year
                                        (Newspaper cutting)

On 1st January 1785, John Walter, founder of 'The Times' wrote in the first issue: "A News-Paper, like a well covered table, should contain something suited to every palate."(Ref: - 16th May 1998)

Well done, John Walter!

17th May 2000 Wednesday

Prize from ERNIE!

Unlike the £1,000 Premium Bonds which lay dormant for over 3 years, my latest £2,000 Premium Bonds, invested on that unique date, 29th February 2000, have borne fruit almost immediately.

M HQ 888 on the envelope heralded the news: - 'Pay Miss E. Hewes One Hundred Pounds Only'.

19th May 2000 Friday

His Holiness Pope John Paul II yesterday celebrated his 80th birthday. From Katherine, now aged 96, a birthday card winged its way to the Apostolic Palace, 00120, Vatican City. The Pope is by no means in the best of health but is determined to carry out a full programme in this great Jubilee Year.

The Pope has Parkinson's disease, but the Vatican denied that he may retire. He once joked, "Who would I hand my resignation to?
                                        (Newspaper cutting)

21st May 2000 Sunday

An attempt to assassinate Pope John Paul II on 13th May 1981 left him with serious injuries. The date was particularly significant, being the anniversary of the supposed appearance of the Blessed Virgin Mary to three shepherd children at Fatima in 1917. The Pope believes that he was saved by 'Our Lady of Fatima' and went there last week.

22nd May 2000 Monday

Dame Barbara Cartland, DBE, romantic novelist, was born on July 9th 1901.
She died yesterday, aged 98.   *(Newspaper cutting)*

23rd May 2000 Tuesday

Chelsea - 1 Aston Villa - 0. This year was a historic occasion as the FA Cup Final took place at Wembley Stadium for the last time with the famous twin towers dominating the scene. Built in 1923, those famous landmarks are soon to be demolished to make way for a new 21st century stadium.

25th May 2000 Thursday

Leicester Cathedral's £2 million Millennium Appeal (see 27th September 1999) is doing wonderfully well. Already it has topped the £1 million mark, in the form of cash donations and pledges of gifts in kind in respect of the building of the Visitor Centre and the structural work at 21 St Martins, which is to be the Cathedral Centre.

27th May 2000 Saturday

Azalea Pontica! This exquisitely perfumed plant has now been in my garden for seven years, but not being cared for by a very good gardener, i.e. me, it almost met the same fate as the poor old magnolia. At last, this year, it has burst into bloom.

29th May 2000 Monday

Notification from 'Paymaster' to update the recent update (recorded 25th April 2000). Tax code changed again from 155P to 156P. This increases monthly salary from £545.71p to £547.22p.

31st May 2000 Wednesday

Queen Elizabeth the Queen Mother, now almost 100 years old, is still carrying out official engagements – see below. Carlton House Terrace overlooks the Mall at the Admiralty Arch end.

Mary Blue and I discovered Carlton House Terrace last September during London's 'Open House' and went inside Numbers 16 and 17.

1st June 2000 Ascension Day

Clarence House: June 1st: Queen Elizabeth the Queen Mother today honoured the President of the Royal Society (Sir Aaron Klug) with her presence at Luncheon at 6 Carlton House Terrace. The Lady Margaret Colville and Sir Alastair Aird were in attendance.
                                        (Newspaper cutting)

2nd June 2000 Friday

Ravenstone Church's Summer Fair (tomorrow) sees the Rector, the Revd. Kerry Emmett, in the stocks being pelted with wet sponges, 20p for 3, or a bucket full of water £1 a go.

Jim Bailiss and I have now relinquished our role at the Prize Draw Table, a twice yearly job which I first took on at Christmas 1992.

Summer Fair
Saturday 3 June 2.30pm
Ravenstone Court (The Almshouses)
Stalls   Sideshows   Prize Draw
Refreshments   Rector in the Stocks!

4th June 2000 Sunday

Goodbye Magnolia and welcome pretty little manageable-sized shrubs and bedding plants to make the garden a picture of delight. Dwarf Rhododendrons and Pieris, planted three years ago, add welcome splashes of colour together with a new Dwarf Rhododendron this year and two low growing evergreen Azaleas with pink flowers.

6th June 2000 Tuesday
Coalville Amateur Operatic Society AGM saw most of the old stalwarts holding the fort. New-comer Adam Markillie, appointed producer at our 1997 AGM, who assured us of his commitment for many years to come, quit after two years as producer. Our next show, in March 2001, is to be "The King and I".

8th June 2000 Thursday
The Princess Royal today unveiled a new bronze portrait bust of Queen Elizabeth the Queen Mother at a service for the Friends of St Paul's in St Paul's Cathedral, London. The bust was paid for by the Friends of St Paul's.

Clarence House: June 8: Queen Elizabeth the Queen Mother was present this evening at a Festival Service for the Friends of St Paul's which was held in St Paul's Cathedral. (Newspaper cutting)

10th June 2000 Saturday
Final-salary schemes are widely regarded as the pinnacle of pensions planning. But such schemes are being regularly shut to new entrants, who are instead offered a money purchase plan. Members of money purchase plans contribute to their fund, which is invested on the stock market.

At retirement, the accumulated fund is used to buy an annuity from an insurance company. This provides an income until death. With a final-salary scheme the risk is all on the employer, whereas members of money purchase schemes shoulder the risk themselves.

The difference in retirement income between the two schemes can be considerable. A 25-year-old joining a final-salary scheme and remaining with the same employer until retirement at 65 would receive a pension of two thirds of final salary. Even with five different employers, all with final-salary schemes, the retired person could expect an income of half his or her final salary.

But a member of a money purchase scheme contributing 12% of salary from the age of 25 to 65 would receive a pension of 41% of salary at retirement.

Starting a pension late, or failing to make adequate contributions, can have devastating effects on a money purchase pension. Paying 5% of earnings over 40 years will produce a pension of just 17% of final salary. If the same contributions are delayed until the age of 35, the retirement income will fall to a miserly 11%.

The situation worsens considerably for the 59% of people planning to retire at the age of 60 or earlier. In a money purchase scheme, contributing 12% of earnings from the age of 25 will produce a pension of only 30% of salary for those retiring at 60. Contributions of 5% over the same period will mean eking out retirement with just 13% of salary. (Newspaper cutting)

12th June 2000 Monday
"Final salary schemes are widely regarded as the pinnacle of pensions planning" (See 10th June)
An article in 'The Times Weekend Money News'

spelled out in detail the new 'Money Purchase Plan' which people at work in future can expect.
How thankful I am for my Civil Service Pension, which is a God-send to me.

14th June 2000 Wednesday
"If pedestrians can't cross the road safely then they shouldn't be out on their own."
Another example of Coalville's Council members, this time from the Highways Department. Motorists and pedestrians alike complain in vain at the problems they face daily, while the Council 'improve' Memorial Square and drive everybody mad (See 12 April 1999).

18th June 2000 Trinity Sunday
W471 MRY is Enid's spanking new Ford Fiesta car, replacing her old F905 NFP, been going strong since 1988. My first ride in the new car this weekend was to the Flower Festival combining an exhibition by the Coalville 150 Group of 'Old Coalville' at Ebenezer Baptist Church, where I saw the Baptismal Pool.

22nd June 2000 Thursday
Enid and I have chosen the Gresham Hotel, 120 The Esplanade, Weymouth, Dorset, for our holiday this year and I have booked for one week commencing Saturday 1st July.
Overlooking Weymouth Bay this little **promontory** of coastline ends at Portland Bill. King George III came to Weymouth and is still remembered here.

24th June 2000 Midsummer Day
'Blue Peter' is an excellent TV programme for children which I enjoy watching from 5 pm to 5.30 pm each Monday, Wednesday and Friday. Presented by two energetic young men and two lively ladies, we now say farewell to lovely Katy Hill and welcome Liz Barker.

26th June 2000 Monday
Fashion store group C & A with over a hundred stores in the U K and 577 branches in 12 European countries, which has been going strong since 1841, is to close all its U K stores. Owned by the Brenninkmeijer family, it began with the Brenninkmeijer brothers Clemens and August (C & A) in Holland, but has now been hit by the difficult U K market.

28th June 2000 Wednesday
"The new public square that you are creating around Coalville clock tower looks most impressive."
So says Mike Gwilliam, director of the Civic Trust, whose H.Q. at No. 17 Carlton House Terrace, London, I visited last September. All the upheaval in Coalville is funded from the Single Regeneration Budget, a Government fund when the coal pits closed.

30th June 2000 Friday
Weymouth here we come!
From Ravenstone to Weymouth is approximately 215 miles, much of the journey being on the M5, down as far as Taunton, and then bearing southeast towards Yeovil, Dorchester and Weymouth. The A354 from Dorchester to Weymouth comes down to the Esplanade where our hotel, the Gresham, is at No. 120.

2ⁿᵈ July 2000 Sunday

Chris Birdwood, who became Lord Birdwood on the death of his father in 1951, fell in love with my 96 year-old friend Katherine when they both lived in India.

He divorced his wife Vere Lady Birdwood in 1954 (see 17th May 1997). In 1954 he married again and died in 1962, aged 62.

On 28th June 2000, his widow No. 2 died aged 87.

The Dowager Lady Birdwood, political activist, was born in Winnipeg, Canada, on May 18th 1913.
She died on June 28th aged 87. (Newspaper cutting)

4ᵗʰ July 2000 Tuesday

The Dowager Lady Birdwood who died last week, 2ⁿᵈ wife of Lord Birdwood, assumed the title of Dowager Baroness somewhat against the family's wishes, since she was not the mother of the heir.

Her stepson Mark became Lord Birdwood but she was never acknowledged as a true member of the family.

6ᵗʰ July 2000 Thursday

Enid and I are now enjoying our holiday in Weymouth. Since our arrival last Saturday, we have done such a lot of interesting things. On Sunday we were in Dorchester where we attended Festival Evensong at St Peter's Church. On Monday we were on the 'Isle' of Portland and yesterday we explored Weymouth more fully.

8ᵗʰ July 2000 Saturday

Enid and I returned home today from our holiday in Weymouth. How we loved the whole area of Dorset which we managed to visit. The scenery was truly beautiful and it was lovely to have a 'seaside' holiday, with a very good hotel on the sea front, looking out across the broad sweep of the bay and distant cliffs.

10ᵗʰ July 2000 Monday

The Queen Mother's 100th birthday on 4th August this year is being celebrated by several events in advance. Tomorrow is a service of thanksgiving in St Paul's Cathedral. On 19th July is a great pageant, besides THE day 4th August.

The Queen Mother was born Lady Elizabeth Angela Marguerite Bowes-Lyon at her parents' home in Grosvenor Gardens, London, in 1900.
The Queen Mother's father was Lord Glamis, later 14th Earl of Strathmore and Kinghorne, descended from the Royal House of Scotland, whose family seat was Glamis Castle. (Newspaper cuttings)

11ᵗʰ July 2000 Tuesday

The Right Rev Lord Runcie, MC, PC, Archbishop of Canterbury, 1980-91, was born on October 2ⁿᵈ 1921. He died on July 11th aged 78. (Newspaper cutting)

12ᵗʰ July 2000 Wednesday

"For me the Commons has never been just a career. It's my life." So said Miss Betty Boothroyd in July 1992 when she became the 155th Speaker of the House of Commons – our first woman Speaker.

Now, aged 70, she has decided to retire from the Speaker's Chair and also resign as Labour M.P. for West Bromwich West.

14ᵗʰ July 2000 Friday

My birthday!

69 today, which means I am now in my 70th year.

From Cocky a beautiful card with pink ribbon and pink roses proclaiming "You're so special to me – Happy Birthday – with lots of love. May today be as special as you are all year."

Enclosing £20, Cocky added: "Happy Birthday darling. Love you forever, John. xxxx xxx xx"

16ᵗʰ July 2000 Sunday

The collect for today, the fourth Sunday after Trinity, reminds us once more 'so to pass through things temporal that we finally lose not the things eternal'. As children at Sunday school we learned each week the Collect for the Day.

The fourth Sunday after Trinity
The Collect
O God, the protector of all that trust in thee, without whom nothing is strong, nothing is holy:
Increase and multiply upon us thy mercy; that, thou being our ruler and guide, we may so pass through things temporal, that we finally lose not the things eternal: Grant this, O heavenly Father, for Jesus Christ's sake our Lord. Amen. (Newspaper cutting)

18ᵗʰ July 2000 Tuesday

From Fenwick's of Leicester I have now purchased an 'Old Charm' oak hall chest, £239, which comes with a **lifetime guarantee**. Like the dear little oak table I bought in May 1991 for £35, I expect it will live on from century to century, unlike much of the 'here today, gone tomorrow' rubbish of today.

(Note by Mary Blue – I learned from Betty, in February 2001, that she had planned to finish writing her diary at the end of 2001 and that she had purchased this oak chest especially for the diaries safe keeping. She wanted them to be passed on as far into the future as possible.)

19ᵗʰ July 2000 Wednesday

The huge sums needed for an adequate retirement income reflect the poor value of annuities, an insurance policy that pays a predetermined income for the rest of the holder's life. Annuity rates – which are based on the yields of gilts (government debt) – have almost halved over the past decade, as inflation has been tamed and interest rates have tumbled. Nevertheless, you are compelled to buy an annuity on retirement, unless you belong to a defined-benefit scheme where the value of your pension is tied to your final salary and the length of your service. (Newspaper cutting)

Clarence House: July 19: Queen Elizabeth the Queen Mother, accompanied by the Prince of Wales, was present this afternoon at a One Hundredth Birthday Tribute on Horse Guards by the Armed Services and Civilian Organisations with which Her Majesty is associated. (Newspaper cutting)

20ᵗʰ July 2000 Thursday

Yesterday's pageant in Horse Guards Parade, London, to honour the 100th birthday of Queen Elizabeth the Queen Mother (4th August) was a joyous occasion for all who participated or watched, especially for the Queen Mother.

22nd July 2000 Saturday
Peter Mould, who celebrated his 56th birthday on 30th June this year, has transferred from the psychiatric ward of Nottingham's Queen's Medical Hospital to Landmere Nursing Home, Wilford, six miles south of Nottingham, which is primarily for people with dementia. He has been at low ebb lately.

24th July 2000 Monday
Visited Peter Mould at Landmere Nursing Home, Ruddington Lane, Wilford, a spacious home purpose-built for confused elderly people who wander around non-stop, lost in their own little world. How sad for Peter to be in such a place. Apparently he is heavily drugged, having been difficult to control.

26th July 2000 Wednesday
Concorde crash – Concorde, the world's only supersonic passenger aircraft, came into service in 1976. Jointly designed and financed by the British and French aviation industries, it is our pride and joy. British Airways have seven Concordes and Air France, who had six, now have only five, following a heart-breaking crash yesterday.

28th July 2000 Friday
The French Concorde 001 had its first test flight on 2nd March 1969.
"Without doubt, Concorde died on Tuesday 25th July 2000, aged 31."
Thus said the French newspaper, Le Figaro. On television we have seen the scenes of utter devastation following Concorde's tragic end, whilst overhead on high, the lark continues to sing.

30th July 2000 Sunday
New Choir Robes (blue) dedicated at Ravenstone Church. What a come-down. Money donated to Ravenstone Church in memory of Brian Land has been used to buy new Choir Robes. No-one seemed to know or care that Ravenstone Church has the special privilege of wearing the royal red robes.

1st August 2000 Tuesday
A Coffee Evening in the grounds of Ravenstone Court, 6.30 pm to 8 pm, and advertised in the Coalville Echo as a 'Coffee morning at Arms House, Hospital Lane, between 6.30 -8 pm' was again well attended. Ursula, having lived here now for 12 months, is well and truly settled in, sings in Ravenstone Church Choir, and truly belongs.

3rd August 2000 Thursday
As the Queen Mother looks forward to her 100th birthday tomorrow, Labour's Chancellor of the Exchequer, 49 year-old Gordon Brown today marries 36 year-old Sarah Macaulay.

4th August 2000 Friday

100th Birthday

5th August 2000 Saturday
"We have come to the unanimous decision that there should be a rotating exhibition of modern sculpture on the plinth." So said Sir John Mortimer, 'Lord of the Plinth' and his advisory panel after one year's deliberation. (See 5th August 1999) In July 1999 we saw "Ecce Homo". In March 2000 we saw "Regardless of History". Next will be "Inverted Plinth".

7th August 2000 Monday
Coalville-born James Hunt, now aged 57 and living in Northamptonshire, is to become a judge in September when he will be sworn in at the House of Lords. I remember him as a child – his mother called him Jimbo. His brother is Roy Hunt.

9th August 2000 Wednesday
Roy Hunt, brother of James Hunt, is President of Coalville Amateur Operatic Society.
James Hunt is one of three brothers. In 1968 he was called to the Bar and became a deputy circuit judge in 1979. He became a Crown Court recorder in 1982 and a QC in 1987. By 1995 he was a deputy High Court Judge and now he is to be a High Court Judge.

11th August 2000 Friday
C & A, the fashion store group which is gradually closing down and soon will be no more, is known affectionately as "Coats and 'ats". I chose to spend the £20 which Cocky sent for my birthday on a little black 'at from C & A.

13th August 2000 Sunday
Evensong at Ravenstone at 6 pm was in the Chapel at Ravenstone Court, while the church was being decorated and cleaned inside. I was one of the lesson readers this evening and experienced for the first time reading at a portable lectern in the chapel.
The lesson was Hebrews Chapter 12: - "Whom the Lord loveth, he chasteneth."

15th August 2000 Tuesday
"Begin Computing in your Retirement" – Today I signed on for a 12 weeks **free** course, commencing Tuesday 19th September, 4.00 – 6.00 pm at Ibstock Community College, prompted by their glossy Community Programme 2000 – 2001, through my letter-box.

17th August 2000 Thursday
Last Saturday, 12th August, a Russian nuclear submarine 'The Kursk' with 118 men on board sank to the bottom of the sea in the icy waters north of Norway in the Barents Sea, following a mysterious explosion on board. Frantic efforts to rescue the men trapped inside have been attempted day after day without success.

19th August 2000 Saturday
The Kursk – Named after the city of Kursk, 270 miles south of Moscow, Russia's newest nuclear submarine can carry 24 nuclear anti-ship missiles.
Now it lies helpless at the bottom of the sea, some 108 metres down. The Russians have tried in vain to save the men inside and today a British rescue is attempted.

21st August 2000 Monday
British and Norwegian deep-sea divers finally gain entry through the rescue hatch in the stern of the Kursk and find the whole boat completely flooded, entombing all 118 submariners. Hundreds of grieving relatives gather on the seashore and are inconsolable; some refusing to believe it is true.

Princess Margaret celebrates her 70th birthday today.
(Newspaper cutting)

23rd August 2000 Wednesday
August 23rd 1905 was the day my mum was born. Today she would be aged 95. My friend Katherine is now 96, but is beginning to feel her great age, although still fiercely independent.

25th August 2000 Friday
Two prizes from ERNIE! Would you believe it? Two £50 prizes arrived by post together.
Bond No. 20 CG 674033 and also Bond No. 20 CG 674857 – both purchased this year on that unique date 29th February 2000. Never been known before.

27th August 2000 Sunday
Sally Springthorpe, stalwart of Ravenstone Church for many years, now aged 83, is now in Coalville Hospital having fallen and broken her hip. I have volunteered to take over her role as Parish Magazine distributor to some dozen readers resident on Leicester Road. Enid has offered to share the job.

29th August 2000 Tuesday
'Money Receiver' from the sale of the Ravenstone Parish Magazine was one of the little jobs I had with effect from 30th December 1974. Sally was even then distributing the magazine to Leicester Road. In this here-today, gone-tomorrow age, people are on the move a lot more, but Sally remains one true constant.

31st August 2000 Thursday
"Statue was by one of country's leading sculptors" – This was the heading given by the Coalville Times to a letter to the Editor which I wrote in response to one written last week - "Statue should be in new square" from S. Leawood, Coalville. I agreed with S. Leawood that our statue deserved better recognition.

2nd September 2000 Saturday
St Michael & All Angels Church, Ravenstone 'Restoration Club' monthly draw was launched 7 years ago in September 1993. We each pay £12 per year and hope one day perhaps to win a prize. Half the money is for the Church and half for prize money – maximum £50 per month. At last this July after paying in £84, I won a prize - £15.

4th September 2000 Monday
On a truly beautiful sunny day, Pat and I motored to Stafford arriving at Maple Court Nursing Home at 11.15 am where Michael joined us to visit poor old Bunting, weary and worn and sad.
Michael informed us that today would have been Mostyn's 85th birthday. Bunting is now very weak and unable to stand, but is eating well.

6th September 2000 Wednesday
"Our Seventh Year" – The annual 'thank you letter' from Church Warden David Winterton keeps us up to date on all that our 'Restoration Group' is achieving at Ravenstone: - Church totally re-wired: new spot-lights in Chancel: new glass light shades in the Nave: Nave roof timbers painted: At long last we are going to have a toilet!

8th September 2000 Friday
Brooks, *Priscilla (Cilla), much loved mother of Jacqui and John, grandma of Jon and Becky, passed away at the Glenfield Hospital September 8th 2000 aged 80 years. No more pain mum united at last with dad.*
Funeral service to take place at Ravenstone Church on Friday September 15th at 10 am followed by interment at Ravenstone Churchyard, family flowers only please by request, but donations if so desired to Breast Care Unit Glenfield Hospital, further inquiries and donations to Midlands Co-operative Funeral Service, Stuart House, 128 London Road, Coalville. Tel. 01530 836703.
All inquiries to Lee Cooper.

Cilla was a regular attender at Ravenstone Church on Sunday evenings. For the last few years I have given her a lift to and from church from her home in Ravenslea. She developed breast cancer early this year.

10th September 2000 Sunday
Mrs June Barras, who at one time was a Sunday school teacher with me and others at Ravenstone, is now a qualified Lay Reader based at Broomleys Church, Coalville and who now sometimes takes Evensong here at Ravenstone. She was a great help in 1976 during our Diocesan Jubilee Year: she made the splendid banners in our pageant.

12th September 2000 Tuesday
The Harvest Moon, the full moon nearest the autumnal equinox, will be for Leicester's Chinese community a Moon Festival this evening. The Chinese Moon Festival falls on the 15th day of the 8th lunar month of the Chinese calendar (see 18th February 1996), the day the moon is at its greatest distance from the earth and brightest.

14th September 2000 Thursday
Dental Surgeons, Baines & Henry, Gray, Garland & Gupta, Private & NHS
'Baines & Henry', 3 Rutland Street, Leicester, have been my dentist for about 50 years, after I started work in Leicester at 14 Friar Lane. In 1968, Mr Garland joined the practice and has been my dentist until now he is retiring, aged 60, and I transfer to Mr Gray.

16th September 2000 Saturday
Sydney, Australia, is hosting the Olympic Games for the next two weeks.
Yesterday we watched on television the 4-hour long spectacular opening ceremony which started at
9 am our time – 7 pm Sydney time.

18th September 2000 Monday
The first of our 12 lessons "Begin Computing in Retirement" sees 12 of us oldies being addressed by an enthusiastic young computer 'whiz' assuring us that pen

and paper will soon be a thing of the past.

I know most of the people in the class, including Bernard Daws, Val Duncombe, Dr. Torrance, Ken Willars and his wife Betty.

22nd September 2000 Friday
London Open House 2000: Mary Blue and I visited six buildings this year:

Royal Courts of Justice, the Strand

Australia House, the Strand

BBC Bush House

Canada House, Trafalgar Square

Marlborough House, Pall Mall (our favourite)

Chatham House, named after William Pitt the Elder (Earl of Chatham), St James Square.

24th September 2000 Sunday
Harvest Thanksgiving Service, 3.00 pm at little St Mary's Snibston.

I scrubbed and cleaned my dad's gravestone and also my granddad Sketchley's immediately behind and took flowers for them both. A day of torrential rain, but a lovely service attended by the faithful few. I sat with Marjorie and Sybil Hayes.

26th September 2000 Tuesday
Collier, Dennis, (Former landlord of Kings Arms, Ravenstone) Be-loved husband of Norma, much loved father of Angie and Chris, father-in-law of Dave and Janice, treasured uncle of Ivor and Caroline, granddad of Andrew, Ben, Hannah, William and devoted pets Bessie and Mack, all of whom he lived for. Passed away peacefully at Queen's Hospital, Burton on Monday September 18th 2000, aged 73 years. His funeral service will be held at St Michael and All Angels Church, Ravenstone on Monday September 25th at 10.45 am, followed by cremation at Bretby at 12 noon. All flowers and enquiries to A E Grice Funeral Service, 4 Derby Road, Ashby, Leics. LE65 2HE Tel. 01530 412229.

This is Dennis Collier, born in Ravenstone and stalwart of Ravenstone Church until he moved to Coleorton in November 1966.

He features in my first 5-year diary which began 1st January 1964 : -

'After the midnight service Dennis Collier rang the three bells all by himself.'

28th September 2000 Thursday
"Don't fence me in," I said on 2nd February 1998, as my house became surrounded by new homes.

The lovely wide-open spaces we once knew in Ravenstone are fast disappearing as ever more houses are built.

Go-ahead given for estate plan – District planners in North West Leicestershire have given the go-ahead for a 47-dwelling housing estate to be built in Ravenstone. David Wilson Homes had applied for permission to build the new estate on land off Heather Lane once earmarked as a potential site for a new village school. As part of the planning permission conditions, the company have promised to create a village green, provide affordable housing and carry out a significant amount of National Forest tree planting. Ravenstone Parish Council is also to be consulted about the village green as part of the agreement (Newspaper cutting)

30th September 2000 Saturday
The second of our 12 lessons "Begin Computing in Retirement" showed us all the inner parts of the computer taken out and re-assembled, to explain what lives where and what it is there to do. We saw first the Mother Board to which everything connects by a myriad of electric cables. Our teacher Dean literally built us a computer.

2nd October 2000 Monday
Dental Surgery - 1950: 1954: 1998: and now one more of my good teeth have been extracted.

Having said my fond farewell to Mr Garland my dentist only three weeks ago, prior to his forthcoming retirement, I developed a painful abscess and the tooth is now out. Fortunately the tooth has not left a noticeable gap.

4th October 2000 Wednesday
The 3rd of our 12 lessons "Begin Computing in Retirement" saw 12 of us seated at 12 computers while Dean Portsmouth, our teacher, showed us how to start using Microsoft Windows '95.

As we became more adept at controlling the 'mouse' I struggled with his instruction to write 'click', until it dawned on me that he said, "Right click."

6th October 2000 Friday
Mini panto – A Harvest Supper will be held on Friday October 6th at 6.30 pm in Ravenstone Village Institute. The supper will be followed by an auction of produce and a mini pantomime. (Newspaper cutting)

Ravenstone's mini panto was a hilarious school scene of unruly girls. Mr Willie Wackem (Keith Reynolds) was the teacher. The Chaplain was the Rector, the Revd Kerry Emmett, and I was delighted to be the School Secretary. (See 12th October 2000)

8th October 2000 Sunday
(Photo in paper of house for sale)

Here we go again. This is Glenholm, first offered for sale by cousin Miles as Ravenstone House @ £125,000 (See 28th May 1999). Subsequently 'Let' for 12 months, it is now for sale again @ £130,000.

10th October 2000 Tuesday
There I was on Leicester Station when this magnificent train passed slowly by and stopped with the rear carriages right in front of me. Never in my life had I seen the famous Orient-Express. It was going to Inverness via Lancaster.

Cocky, like me, quite by chance, saw this train pass by.

12th October 2000 Thursday
Leicester Mercury, Village Voice, Ravenstone, Patricia Emmett 01530 839802

Harvest hilarity – *naughty schoolgirls and inadequate teachers brought the house down in the mini-panto which was performed as part of Ravenstone's harvest supper. The script for the popular panto was loosely based on St Trinians. It was an opportunity for the 100*

people in the audience, a chance to see the characters in the cast as they have never been seen before. Already the organisers are being asked to include something similar in the programme next year.
A delicious supper was swerved by the Raunston Ladies' group before an auction of goods and the drawing of a raffle. *(Newspaper cutting)*
(See 6th October 2000)

14th October 2000 Saturday
The 4th of our 12 lessons "Begin Computing in Retirement" saw us again seated at 12 computers, continuing our lesson in Word Processing. We delved deeper into the mysteries of all the mystic signs and symbols, getting a drop-down menu and learning how to type 'bold', 'italic' and 'underlined' and real fancy typing.

16th October 2000 Monday
"Coronation Street", the popular soap-opera on television, which two years ago introduced the rough Battersbys into the storyline to add more spice to the street life, continues its downward spiral. New raunchy characters replace old favourites. Sarah Lou is pregnant, aged 13, and now we have a male stripper on board.

18th October 2000 Wednesday, St Luke's Day
The 5th of our 12 lessons "Begin Computing in Retirement" gave us an introduction to 'spreadsheets'.
This was a lesson on how to keep your accounts up-to-date. We became familiar with the plus, minus, multiply and division keys on the keyboard and watched our figures add themselves up, etc. We had our own floppy disc to save our work.

20th October 2000 Friday
Civil Service Retirement Fellowship AGM for our Branch No. 76, covering Leicestershire, Rutland and South Lincolnshire, hosted this year by Coalville Group and held at Thringstone Chapel Assembly Room. I was pleased to meet up again with Gilbert Paul-Clark, who worked at the Department of Energy, and is now with the Leicester Group.

22nd October 2000 Sunday
"Yews Farm, Snibston"
How lovely that my mum should have come to live at Snibston when she was 7 years old and have come to 'Yews Farm'. Prior to that she lived at Willoughby-on-the-Wolds. *(See 21st October 1999)*

24th October 2000 Tuesday
Half term at Ibstock Community College, so we have to wait until 31st October for our 6th lesson "Begin Computing in Retirement".
The more I learn about computing the more I see how closely it relates to Chapter 13 in the Book of Revelation. The computer already controls most things in today's world.

26th October 2000 Thursday
Church Times – Statistics prompt abortion prayer
Sir, - The Government's last yearly figures for abortion in the UK were the highest ever. They reached 199,826: 187,402 in England and Wales, and 12,424 in Scotland.

That is 16,600 a month; 3,800 a week; more than 500 every day. One pregnancy in five in the UK now ends in abortion.
A national day of prayer about abortion will be held on Friday 27th October, the anniversary of the passing of the 1967 Abortion Act. A free prayer pack can be had from Image (Christians caring for the image of God from conception to death) at the address below.
Stuart Cunliffe, Prayer Co-ordinator, Image, P.O.Box 51, Hyde, Cheshire, SK14 1PY *(Newspaper cutting)*
(See 20th and 22nd March 2000)

30th October 2000 Monday
The DVLA (Driver & Vehicle Licensing Agency) continues to make a mint selling cherished car numbers. In 1986 it held back numbers 1 – 20 when 'D' prefix numbers were issued. These numbers are available for purchase from today. Already D 1 SCO has been sold at auction for £10,000.
DVLA Telesales Hotline is 0870 6000 142.

1st November 2000 Wednesday
The 6th of our 12 lessons "Begin Computing in Retirement" continued our introduction to spreadsheets. Again we used our own floppy disc, adding to what we had 'saved' on Lesson 5.
We learned how to zoom along the top line January to December, entering our own figures: -
Price: Amount: Total: for our annual accounts.

3rd November 2000 Friday
(Photograph of a house cut from newspaper)
Ravenstone, Main Street: A super opp to purchase this listed building within Ravenstone, sit in the cons area. 4 bedrms, lnge, sep din rm, kit, conserve, beams to the ceiling, util, bathrm, gdns to the rr.
The prop rich in char with many trad style features.
£116,950 *(Newspaper cutting)*

Brian Land who died in April this year lived here with his wife Jean.
Jean has now bought herself a more manageable modern home in the village & is selling this house, the oldest in Ravenstone, built 1641.

5th November 2000 Sunday
At Ravenstone Church this evening we were reminded again by the preacher of the Gunpowder Plot on 5th November 1605, when an attempt was made to blow up King James I of England. His persecution of the Catholics resulted in many plots being formed against him. His oppression of the Puritans was almost as bad.
Please to remember the Fifth of November,
Gunpowder Treason and Plot
We know no reason why gunpowder treason
Should ever be forgot *(Newspaper cutting)*

7th November 2000 Tuesday
The 7th of our 12 lessons "Begin Computing in Retirement" took us back to Word Processing.
We needed to prove to the College that we had indeed learned something, by our printouts.

9th November 2000 Thursday
Auction at hospital – A grand auction is being prepared

by friends to raise funds for Coalville hospital.

(Newspaper cutting)

In November 1995, I contributed one Electrolux table-top freezer, one guitar & one large picture from the Donkey Sanctuary towards Coalville Hospital's auction. This year I gave them my large mirror 3ft by 4ft. A record total of £705 was made.

11th November 2000 Saturday

The complicated history of the British Isles explains why the Sinn Fein Youth of today in the Republic of Ireland refuse to be associated with the wearing of a poppy. They of course remember their 1916 Easter Rising rather than the 1914-18 World War. Freedom for them came in 1922.

13th November 2000 Monday

Civil Service Retirement Fellowship Meeting & an interesting talk by one of our own members, a jovial lady in her mid 60s, Pat Jessop, who also belongs to Ashby Ivanhoe Garden Club.

She explained what they did at their meetings & told us about some of the truly beautiful gardens they have visited both near & far.

15th November 2000 Wednesday

The 8th of our 12 lessons "Begin Computing in Retirement" and a longer piece of written work to type out, amend, add bits in, take bits out, etc. This sorted out the wheat from the chaff. The touch typists were well away; others struggled to get to the end: I was somewhere mid-way; but slowly we are beginning to improve.

17th November 2000 Friday

TV Licence renewal now due - Up & up & up goes the price of the TV licence. Last year I paid £101, licence valid until 30th November. This year I pay £104; licence valid until 30th November 2001. However, with effect from 1st November this year, if you are aged over 75 you are eligible for a FREE licence. My TV licence No. 0783449963 remains constant year after year.

19th November 2000 Sunday

"Christianity 2000" – This evening I attended an excellent special service at St James Church, Snibston, which explained in a nutshell how Christianity has evolved over the last 2000 years.

Our friend James was organist, a fine choir made up of about 15 of the best local singers led the singing, & there were three readers.

21st November 2000 Tuesday

The 9th of our 12 lessons "Begin Computing in Retirement", & more practice at changing single-line spacing to double-line spacing, changing text alignments from left aligned to justify both margins, then move both margins in by 10 characters, '1 inch' by typing 2.54 (centimetres) in the left & right box & other various tricks.

24th November 2000 Friday

In the last two months Britain has experienced some of the worst rain and flooding since records began 300 years ago.

Can there be anything left of money put by for a rainy day? *(Newspaper cuttings)*

25th November 2000 Saturday

Our computer course at Ibstock Community College comes under the jurisdiction of Stephenson College, Coalville, which in turn offers examinations offered by the Royal Society of Arts (RSA) including a Certificate in Computer Literacy & Information Technology (CLAIT), a structured course for beginners.

27th November 2000 Monday

The 10th of our 12 lessons "Begin Computing in Retirement" & more practice at manipulating text. Most of our 12 members, including me, have been persuaded to continue with our studies until next summer with the next stage of learning known as CLAIT.

29th November 2000 Wednesday

My 4 hourly lessons trying to 'surf the internet' at Coalville library last year culminated in a Certificate of Achievement, although in fact I achieved very little.

"This is to certify that Elizabeth Hewes has started getting Webwise & has achieved an understanding of sending e-mails, navigating the World Wide Web & searching the Web."

1st December 2000 Friday

Dean Portsmouth, the young computer whiz who is our teacher at "Begin Computing in Retirement", is a great devotee of the Internet.

In October this year he launched his own new company "Futurenet Solutions Ltd.", which designs websites & is a prelude to the opening of Coalville's first cyber café: www.futurenet-solutions.com

3rd December 2000 Sunday

Common Worship has arrived! *(Newspaper cutting)*

I was brought up at Church with the 16th & 17th century language of the Book of Common Prayer. These are the words of our Church services engraved on my heart. Twenty years ago this was updated by the Alternative Service Book 1980 (ASB). Today on this Advent Sunday, out goes the ASB & in comes "Common Worship".

The Book of Common Prayer of 1662 remains in lawful use in the Church of England. The demise of the ASB and its replacement by Common Worship does not affect the status of the Prayer Book at all.

Parishes continue to be free to use it exclusively or to have a mixture of Prayer Book and newer services.

(Newspaper cutting)

5th December 2000 Tuesday

Chronic Obstructive Pulmonary Disease (COPD).

This is what caused Enid to be so bronchial & short of breath in December 1998 that we gave up delivering Meals on Wheels. This illness is the result of a lifetime of smoking. It was fashionable to smoke when we were young & many women our age now have COPD.

6th December 2000 Wednesday

BETHLEHEM, the traditional birthplace of Jesus, will not hold Christmas celebrations this year because of the

continued Israeli-Palestinian fighting.

(Newspaper cutting)

7th December 2000 Thursday

The 11th of our 12 lessons "Begin Computing in Retirement" & my cleverest effort so far. With guidance & help from the teacher I was able to print out a page of tabulated columns of figures beneath a central heading. Also I produced a 'Front Cover' with my chosen icon image to enhance the final printout.

9th December 2000 Saturday

"Winter Fuel Payment – we are sending out Winter Fuel Payments again this year to help meet the costs of your heating this winter. This winter the payment is £200 & a payment of £200 will be paid into your bank or building society account in the next few days."

A sop to all pensioners after their 75p. (See 24th March 2000.)

Coronation Street – The 40th anniversary.

(Newspaper cutting)

11th December 2000 Monday

"Handyperson Scheme Invoice" Client No. N1961: HP ref. no. HpN759. Invoice No. 1111.

Clean out gutters – provide & fix 2 airbricks at top of capped off chimney. Total cost £21.

Please make cheque payable to Care & Repair (West Leics. Ltd.)

This bargain most useful job was done by Richard Stones, handyman.

13th December 2000 Wednesday

The last of our 12 lessons "Begin Computing in Retirement" & an introduction to navigating the World Wide Web & searching the Web. First we clicked into Internet Explorer, Microsoft's browser, & browsed for a while in that. Then we used www.yahoo.com (yahoo is a search engine) & there before us was all the world's knowledge.

15th December 2000 Friday

(Photograph cut out of newspaper) This is Athina Roussel, heir to the Onassis fortune, now aged 15 (See 15th December 1997). Still the battle rages between the Greeks & her French father Thierry Roussel who is not bringing her up as an undiluted Greek.

17th December 2000 Sunday

Civil Naming Ceremonies (rather than Christenings) are now on offer.

Today sees the first such ceremony in Britain. Tamara Geraldine Ebel Cliffe, nine-week old daughter of John Ebel & Tracy Cliffe, has been officially named in a non-religious service in the de luxe Rookery Hall Country House Hotel in Worleston, approved by Cheshire County Council.

19th December 2000 Tuesday

From my love by post a Christmas card: -

"You're Special to Me" – "I think the World of You"

"Although I may not show it, I hope you know it's true,
You're very special to me and I think the world of you.
Have a Merry Christmas."

Happy Christmas darling. All my love John xxxx.
Also enclosed a £20 note.

21st December 2000 Thursday

My first Christmas card from Australia 'Love Scott & Sheridan' happily sharing life together down under.

Pat, Evelyn, Mary Blue & I have been invited for the 3rd consecutive year to share Christmas Day with Sharon & Jim.

23rd December 2000 Saturday

And from Miles & Michele in Malta, a Christmas card to say: -

"Life is great: Malta is perfect: Mi Amigo Roadshow now well established. Six nights a week!"

Victor Borge, comic pianist, was born in Copenhagen on January 3rd 1909. He died in Galeston, Connecticut, on December 23rd aged 91.

25th December 2000 Monday

After 9am Holy Communion at little St Mary's Snibston, Mary Blue picked me up at 11.15am where together with Pat, Evelyn & Honey the dog, she kindly drove us to Sharon & Jim's lovely home at Melton Mowbray for a lovely Christmas Day, before bringing us all safely home again in the evening.

27th December 2000 Wednesday

Yesterday, Boxing Day, Pat, Evelyn, Mary Blue & I spent a jolly evening with James & Trevelyn at their home in Ibstock.

Arriving at 4pm we watched on TV Rossini's fairy tale comic opera Cinderella until 5.30pm. After tea we watched on TV 'Oklahoma' & then played a new game 'Who Wants to be a Millionaire?'

29th December 2000 Friday

With £20 from Cocky for Christmas, I have chosen the very latest book "A Thousand Years of the English Parish" by Anthea Jones.

Beautifully illustrated with many of this country's finest old churches, it traces the overall background of our parish churches before & after the turbulent mid 16th century.

31st December 2000 Sunday

How lovely to end this very special year 2000 on a Sunday, with our first Holy Communion using the new 'Common Worship' Order One, which was virtually unchanged. We sang the moving hymn: - "Lord, for the years your love has kept & guided, urged & inspired us, cheered us on our way, sought us & saved us ...."

* * *

The Babylonians were the first to find fun in figures. They were obsessed with astronomical observations, and are responsible for basing all such data on the number 60: hence 360 degrees, 60 seconds to a minute and 60 minutes to the hour.

But it was the Pythagoreans who really worshipped mathematics as a godlike art. They gave numbers human attributes: one was unity, two was male, three female and five (male + female) was marriage.

They particularly liked the number 10, the sum of 1 + 2 + 3 + 4.   *(newspaper cutting)*

Domesday Book – 1086

The greatest single achievement of William the Conqueror was his making of Domesday Book in 1086, a year before he died.

This survey of the land, county by county, was done with such thoroughness that the Anglo-Saxon Chronicle commented with pardonable exaggeration that there was not one ox nor one cow nor one pig which was left off the record.

Such detailed and consistent information was achieved by requiring jurors representing each hundred to answer a battery of questions in connection with three different dates: - when Edward the Confessor was alive (1065), when William the Conqueror granted the estate (depending on when that was), and at present (1086).

Such an unprecedented & searching inquisition gave the book its name "Domesday", because it reminded the natives of Doomsday that last Judgement when Christ in majesty would judge the living & the dead. The questions included information about the dead – the Anglo-Saxon landowners who had been killed or died since 1065.

This was to serve as a final judgement about every disputed property.

The fact that Domesday Book was 20 years after the Conquest of 1066, suggests that William the Conqueror needed such a survey because the redistribution of lands had been somewhat chaotic.

* * *

The 26 characters in the modern English alphabet go back 2,700 years. From the same ancestral roots – traceable to Syria & the Near East – also come the Hebrew & Arabic scripts.

Today's Western European alphabet is derived from classical Greek, by way of Etruscan & Latin, as is the Cyrillic alphabet which spread throughout Orthodox Eastern Europe & Russia in the Middle Ages.

The Greek alphabet was the first to add vowels, an innovation never adopted in Hebrew or Arabic. Today's modern Greek order was officially adopted in 403 BC. The Romans dropped Z, which was then the seventh letter, & invented G in 312 BC to replace it. When they later conquered Greece, they found that they could not spell Greek words so they added Y & brought back Z, putting them both at the end of the alphabet. As the alphabet of the Roman Church, it spread across Western Europe.

The letter W was invented by Norman French scholars in the 12th century to transcribe Saxon words rather than using the Saxon 'wyn'. The English name – double-u, rather than double-v, – is explained by the fact that the two letters U and V were not properly differentiated, like I and J, until the 17th century. The first alphabet, the North Semitic, was acrophonic; that means it used a picture symbol of an object to represent the initial syllable or sound of the name of the object.

* * *

2001

1st January 2001 Monday
Unwell: Princess Margaret (Newspaper cutting)
Like Princess Margaret, now aged 70, I face the year 2001 feeling unwell. I am presently on anti-biotics to kill bacteria in my inner parts & feel constant discomfort & loss of appetite.
Poor Princess Margaret was confined to her bed over the Christmas period. Like her, I am to have an internal examination.

3rd January 2001 Wednesday
CLAIT (Computer Literacy & Information Technology) which culminates in a Certificate, is the course which I was persuaded to sign up for last November. The course begins next week on 9th January & continues until July. However, feeling unwell as I am at present, I have now cancelled my name from this course.

5th January 2001 Friday
Katherine, aged 96, is also unwell at the moment. Having spent Christmas & the New Year with her friends Rosemary & George at Milton Keynes, she arrived home yesterday feeling unwell & the doctor came to see her. He arranged for her to go immediately into Coalville Hospital for observation, suspecting a slight stroke.

7th January 2001 Sunday
Services at Ravenstone, rota for readers:
D Winterton & B Hewes
Evensong at 4pm should have included me reading the Lesson, but I was not well enough to attend. I had informed the Rector last week of this likelihood & asked if he would arrange for my name to be removed from the list of lesson readers, a privilege I have enjoyed since September 1971.

9th January 2001 Tuesday
"To every thing there is a season, & a time to every purpose under the heaven ..... a time to keep, and a time to cast away" (Ecclesiastes, Chapter 3).
Twenty years ago, in the January sales, I bought a beautiful gilt-edged mirror which I recently 'cast away'. Approaching my 70th birthday, I am gradually shedding items too large to handle.

11th January 2001 Thursday
"Oh, by the way, I have some news for you."
So said Scott to Mary Blue, as she finished speaking to him on the telephone, "You are going to be a granny again."
Scott & his Australian fiancée Sheridan are expecting a baby in August. Sheridan & her family are delighted, while Mary Blue is still almost incredulous.

13th January 2001 Saturday
"Please attend the Endoscopy Unit at 12.45pm on Saturday 13th January 2001 for Flexible Sigmoidoscopy at Glenfield Hospital. Consultant: J. S. de Caestecker, Speciality: Gastroenterology".
This is the internal examination I am to have today. Flexible Sigmoidoscopy is an examination of the lower bowel with a special camera.

15th January 2001 Monday
How I appreciated the wonderful support of Mary Blue on Saturday when I attended the Endoscopy Unit at Glenfield Hospital. She took me there at 11.30am & brought me home at 5.30pm. There was a lot of waiting about & she was able to go home in between times. I was very thankful when it was all over.

17th January 2001 Wednesday
"The King & I" is this year's choice for Coalville Amateurs, & again I was pleased to be asked to join the regulars this evening for allocation of tickets at Peter Jacques' house.
This year I have had to decline this invitation as I am not well enough to take up my accustomed seat for booking.

19th January 2001 Friday
Prize from ERNIE! The welcome postmark HQ 888 heralded a prize from ERNIE.
"Pay Miss E. Hewes One Hundred Pounds Only": - Bond No. 14 HN 330710.
Last year I had a record £250 total prize money from ERNIE: - £50 in February; £100 in May; and a rare double £50, received on the same day in August.

21st January 2001 Sunday
Tomorrow is the centenary of the death of Queen Victoria, our longest reigning monarch.
I am reminded of the day in August 1973, when I met a man who, when he was a child, spoke to Queen Victoria. The man was 'Bomb', Aunt Dos' friend. The Queen asked him what he would do when grown up. "Be a soldier, ma'am."

23rd January 2001 Tuesday
The Family Tree!
Graham Stocks (grandson of Auntie Doris) wrote to me a fortnight ago to say that he is progressing with his family tree which includes my mum's side of the family – the Baileys & the Sketchleys.
He is in touch with David Bailey, son of mum's cousin Eric. Today I received a letter from David Bailey (Devon).

25th January 2001 Thursday
Like Graham Stocks, David Bailey is now actively involved in his family history & this is how they have made contact with each other.
All in the middle of their searchings they find Tom Sketchley, my grand-dad & Ann Eliza Bailey, my grand-ma whom I never knew. They each can now tell me more about them.

27th January 2001 Saturday
Pope announces new cardinals – the Roman Catholic Archbishop of Westminster, the Most Revd Cormac Murphy-O'Connor, has been made a cardinal by the Pope. The Archbishop was one of 37 new cardinals appointed on Sunday. The College of Cardinals will be responsible foe electing a successor to the current Pope.
(Newspaper cutting)

28th January 2001 Sunday

Note by Mary Blue –Together with my Mum & Dad (referred to in the diaries as brother Pat & Evelyn) I picked Betty up in my car to go for Sunday lunch as usual at Lakeside Lodge in Moira, where we always shared a table with Trevelyn & James Hodson. When we arrived Betty declared she wasn't hungry and wanted to stay in the car while we had lunch. For the past few weeks she had been eating less & less and this had become a matter of great concern to me.

After lunch I took her home and stayed with her because she was continually being sick and was obviously very ill. I rang the emergency doctor who came quite quickly and on examining Betty said she must go into hospital. We had to wait for the hospital to telephone us when a bed was available, which they did later that evening.

As I helped Betty to pack a bag she included a notebook and pen saying she needed to carry on with her diary. She explained that she was in the habit of writing notes in a 'rough book' and then every few days she would pick out salient points from her notes and write up her diary.

The following diary entries are taken from this rough book in their entirety......

Admitted to Assessment Ward 16, Glenfield Hospital, after contacting Emergency Doctor – non-stop sickness. Mary Blue took me. Arrived at 10.15pm & Mary stayed with me until 1.30am while I was tested thoroughly from top to toe. Put on a saline drip & no food or water for 24 hrs.

29th January 2001 Monday

In bed all day feeling weak & dehydrated. A second saline drip plus a tube up my nose into stomach to clear the sickness. An unexpected visit from Rector & also Gwen in afternoon.

George Watson, aged 92, also admitted to Ward 16 (the Assessment Ward, busy all night long).

At mid-day I transferred to Ward 29 (the stomach ward). In the evening Mary Blue came & stayed with me a nice long time. I was sick once even with tube up my nose directing sickness directly into bag (like a catheter bag). The sickness tube was then 'aspirated' (like a syringe action to get sick flowing).

30th January 2001 Tuesday

Dr Duthie brought 9 students to ask me what I was in hospital for & particularly to look at my hands & learn what the hands can tell them.

10.30 am - Wheeled down to ground floor for ultrasound scan of bloated stomach. Smeared with gel & slowly checked all round. Brought back to Ward 29 by a trolley porter born in Ravenstone.

11.00 am - Visited by Dr Guy, on behalf of Dr Robinson. He told me I had fluid on my left lung & also in my stomach. I was next to have some fluid siphoned off my stomach to reduce bloating.

11.45 am – An unexpected brief visit from Debbie, bringing me a Get Well Wish Card & Jasmine plant. (Murdo & children were waiting in the car park).

12.15 pm – Two student doctors (Indian girl & English girl) came to ask me about my being in hospital & what was being done to help me.

12.30 pm – Got to know the visitors of Madge (sister of Jabez Rowell) aged 85, in next bed from Melbourne Street, Coalville. She had a stroke last week. (Marion Ayers)

2.00 pm – Blood pressure taken.

2.15 pm – Two more young lady trainee doctors (one Indian, one English) due to take exams shortly came to interview me. One asked me copious questions. The other performed on me as a doctor would, pressing my stomach & tapping to hear where the fluid was etc. They also wanted to look at my hands.

2.45 pm – 500ml of fluid siphoned out of my bloated stomach.

3.00 pm – Pat, Evelyn & Mary arrived & stayed until 4.45pm. While they were here the Hospital Chaplain came to see me. After about 10 minutes his mobile phone rang & he was called away.

Pat told me that Richard had finished serving meals at Lakeside Lodge; next Sunday he will be chef at Maynards, Bagworth.

31st January 2001 Wednesday

Woke feeling very weak, having been allowed nothing to eat or drink since I came to hospital last Sunday evening. (NBM = nil by mouth) Sustained only by saline & glucose drip.

An unexpected delivery by post to my bedside. Get Well Card from David & Sheila Winterton.

11.30 am – 30ml of fluid removed from my left lung (via my back).

2.00 pm – Another lovely surprise. Afternoon visit by James, Trevelyn, Pat & Evelyn.

4.30 pm – Very mild enema.

6.00 pm - 8.45 pm - Welcome visit of Mary Blue. Feeling much better this evening. Allowed to drink first sips of water.

1st February 2001 Thursday

After drinking nothing for several days, today I am given a great container of milk-like fluid (barium) to drink in readiness for going into the scanner.

9.30am – Taken by wheelchair to the C T Examination room to go slice by slice through the scanner. My problem of excessive sickness seems to stem from my OMENTUM. (An omen in the tum?)

12 noon – Visited by Mary Blue, Karen & Suzannah. Suzannah had been to Leicester hospital & also supported a 'bag' attached to her leg. (Bladder & kidney problems all her young life, now aged 9).

The Chaplain called again while they were here (Tim Gurney).

I am now to be weighed daily. Today 62.2 kilos (9 stone 11lbs) (mostly fluid).

A quiet visitor-less afternoon & then an early evening visit from Steven until 7.15pm. He was en route home from work.

2nd February 2001 Friday
Diagnosis of Cancer

Now well & truly battered & bruised with daily 'taking of blood' plus intravenous drip & one thing or another. Still feeling weak. Today's weight = 63.1 kilos, which means ever more bloating of whole torso.

11.00 am – Postal delivery to my bedside. "Hope you get well soon" from Jim & Mary Bailiss.

"Thinking of You" from Mary & George.

12 noon – A posse of doctors round my bed & <u>I was told that I had cancer</u> which had spread from the outer covering of the bowel to the tangled inner covering & was therefore incurable. The Doctor who told me this was Dr de Caestecker (sounded like Dr Elastic). His son is in Coronation Street, playing the part of Mike Baldwin's long lost 12 year-old son.

Afternoon visit from Enid. Mary Blue saw Enid briefly. Their paths crossed at 5pm. Mary Blue stayed until 8.30pm.

3rd February 2001 Saturday

Getting weaker & weaker. Still being sick. Had injections to try & control sickness.

9.00 am – A lovely bed bath & clean clothes. Mary brought me a pretty new pink nightie last night.

12 noon – A nurse washed my lank & languid hair, in the hospital bathroom.

Weight today 63.2 kilos. Afternoon visit by Steven & Jane who left the children in Mary's care.

Evening visit 6 pm - 9 pm by Mary Blue, whom I entrusted with my affairs.

4th February 2001 Sunday

Today's weight 64.2 kilos

3.00 pm - Murdo visited & stayed until 4 pm.

3.30 pm – Pat, Evelyn & Mary came & stayed until 5 pm.

6 pm – 8 pm - My good friend Reevsie visited me, during which time I was sick twice. She stuck to me throughout my sickness.

5th February 2001 Monday

Weight today 64.8 kilos

11.00 am – Post to my bedside. A Get Well Wish from Lesley plus a card from Olive & Derek Meakin.

1.30 pm – Too feeble to walk to the toilet, Nurse Lorna took me in a commode chair & helped me sit at the wash basin to clean my teeth.

3 pm – 5 pm – Visit by Enid, during which time the Rector, Kerry Emmett, joined us for a jovial afternoon. I was not feeling sick while they were here. Also visited by therapist who stressed the importance of keeping mobile. Too long lying in bed would soon waste the leg muscles.

5 pm – I was provided with a ripple mattress to prevent bed sores.

5.45 pm – Mary Blue arrived followed shortly afterwards by Sharon who had arrived from Thailand yesterday.

6th February 2001 Tuesday

9.00 am – Enema.

Made an appointment for Trim, Shampoo & Set for tomorrow.

Weight now 65.9 kilos.

My medication now includes steroids & various other tablets & medicine, which succeeded in curbing my sickness overnight.

12 noon to 1.30 pm – Visited by Janie and John, followed immediately by David Winterton and Alan Roulston (the two Ravenstone Church Wardens) who stayed until 3.30 pm in time to see the arrival of Pat, Evelyn, Mary Blue and Gwen.

7.00 pm – Visited for an hour by Eileen, Doug & Peter who met my good friend Reevsie when she arrived at 8.00 pm! She helped me walk to the toilet & saw me safely tucked up in bed by 9.15 pm.

How I appreciated having 12 different visitors in one day.

7th February 2001 Wednesday

Weight now 67 kilos.

Enema 9.00 am.

11.00 am – To the hospital hairdressers (a big improvement on my hairdressers at Coalville) for a £12.50p trim and blow-wave. Felt much better for this.

Social Services brought me "Welfare Rights Service – Briefing Note", a 12 page dossier dealing with the financing of care. How opportune that Trevelyn, Pat & Evelyn visited from 2.00 pm to

3.15 pm to wade through the small print which this entailed.

4.00 pm - I was attached to another feed (2 feeds now into my right wrist – extra dextrazone).

Received by post a 'Get Well Soon' card from Ivy Hardy.

Evening spent with Mary Blue preparing for meeting with Dr Simon the Oncologist tomorrow at Leicester Royal Infirmary at 3.00 pm.

8th February 2001 Thursday

Three cards by post; one from David and Irene, one from Joyce and George Dixon and one from Ravenstone P.C.C. members, who held their meeting this week –

The Rector, Kerry Emmett, Jean Underwood (Treasurer), Ruth Simpson, M. Jones, Daphne Robinson, David Winterton (Church Warden), Alan Roulston (Church Warden), Ian Freestone and Joanne Freestone.

3.00 pm – Arrived escorted by nurse at Osborne Building, Leicester Royal Infirmary, to see Oncologist Dr Simon – good old Mary Blue was already there, having spent nearly an hour queuing to get into the car park.

After being examined it was decided to operate within 24 hours to remove the obstruction which is causing my sickness. Mary Blue then left and I was cared for by Nurse Hannah who had accompanied me from Glenfield. Much to my surprise I saw Doreen Smith from Ravenstone who was amazed and delighted to see me, having tried in vain to get in touch with me for several weeks.

And so to Balmoral, from Osborne, via Windsor, to an en suite room all to myself, in preparation for tomorrow's surgery, wearing oxygen mask all night long. Mary Blue brought my belongings from Glenfield Hospital at closing time (7.30pm) but they let her stay until 9.00 pm.

Written from Balmoral by Mary Blue for Betty, 8th February 2001.

9th February 2001 Friday

2.00 am – Rudely awakened to be wheeled off to a lower floor for chest & stomach x-ray which entailed a long wait, sitting in a wheelchair.

7.30 am – Visit from Mr Hemmingway the top surgeon who, together with the oncologist Dr Simon, would be performing my operation.

I was attached to numerous electrodes and then taken down to theatre at 8.30 am after being asked to sign a consent form from a prostrate position (almost impossible). First an epidural was administered into my spine to ensure no pain, afterwards followed by the anaesthetic which was sprayed liberally all over my face, and so to oblivion...................

Next thing I knew it was 5 pm and at 6 pm I arrived on S.A.U. Ward 21, the silent recovery room, in 'Willow Bay' and welcome arrival of Mary Blue. (S.A.U. = Surgical Assessment Unit)

7.15 pm – Disc jockey from Leicester's Radio Fox arrived asking for our musical requests.

I chose "The Chorus of the Hebrew Slaves" by Verdi from "Nabucco" (which means Nebuchadnezzar), or alternatively "March of the Siamese Children" from "The King & I".

With help from Mary Blue following detailed instructions on screen I was delighted to hear _both_ of these played for me! (At 8.00 pm).

Then a brief phone call to brother Pat using bedside phone.

At 9.00 pm Mary Blue left me feeling relaxed and free from pain in my corner bed with a wonderful view from this 6th floor elevation of the whole of Leicester lit up by night. I was provided with a 'morphine' pain-relief button which helped to give me a good night's restful sleep.

10th February 2001 Saturday

Transferred from my 'nil by mouth' routine to sips of water, the first for almost 2 weeks.

A welcome afternoon visit by Mary Blue who kindly wrote my journal.

Joan Elliot from our 'Reading for the Blind' group phoned and Mary was able to speak to her.

I was transferred to the opposite corner of the room where, in daylight, nearby Leicester City Football ground could be seen.

This was the evening when Jane Jarman's John was given a surprise 80th birthday party. Had I been well, I would have joined the family gathering for this party at Hood Park, Ashby-de-la-Zouch. Again I had the comfort of a 'morphine' pain relief button to help give me another restful sleep. Room 21 is the recovery room, where strict silence has to be maintained. No place for shouting across the room to other patients.

11th February 2001 Sunday

11.30 am – Visit from hospital Chaplain who came to offer me Holy Communion, which I did not take as I was only allowed to sip water.

4.00 pm – Pat, Evelyn & Mary Blue arrived. All is silent in this recovery room. Everyone whispers & there is no place for frivolity under the watchful eye of doctors & nurses. Mary Blue clipped my nails nice & short & silently, using Pat's clippers, before they all crept silently away.

12th February 2001 Monday

9.00 am – Still have the reassurance of my 'morphine' pain relief press button which lasts for a few hours. I have a urine catheter attached since my operation. My gash bloodies my vest & pretty nightie. I change therefore into an open back hospital nightie ready for the next progression to 'walking in agony' to the loo several times to relieve constipation. I am encouraged to drink as much milk as possible to divert sickness to its internal proper place rather than always being sick. I have about 25 silver clips holding my stomach gash into place from midriff to lower abdomen.

Meanwhile, back at the Ranch, Mary Blue is arranging a family consultation with Mr Hemmingway, the top surgeon, for the latest bulletin. (This will be next Thursday)

For the 3rd consecutive Monday, the Revd Kerry Emmett discovers where I am & pays me an afternoon visit. (29th January, Glenfield Hospital, Ward 29: 5th February, Glenfield Hospital, Ward 29: Today, 12th February, Leicester Royal Infirmary, silent recovery ward on 6th floor, Ward 21.)

I now have a 'Patient & Visitor Information' leaflet, showing the layout of Leicester Royal Infirmary. Ward 21 is in the Accident & Emergency part of the Balmoral Building & patients are coming & going day & night with broken arms or legs or post operatives.

From my penthouse on the 6th floor I look across to Havelock Street as it winds round towards Aylestone Road & then on to the prison.

6.00 pm – Tried to swallow soluble paracetamol and was immediately sick at which point good old Bluey arrived and saved the day.

7.00 pm – Sharon & Jim arrived and I was sick for the 2nd time today, having been assured by the doctor that it had been adequately kept under control.

13th February 2001 Tuesday

Unlucky for some, the 13th February.

9.00 am – A lovely bed bath & still allowed the assurance of my 'morphine' pain relief press button connected to my drip from a square black box.

I ask for a straw to try & get rid of my milk drink – seems a bit easier to swallow like that.

11.00 am – Harassed yet again by flippin' MacMillan Nurse. Also take a laborious tentative walk for a few yards & back again.

1.00 pm – An unexpected visit from Enid who brought me the wonderful card created specially for me "Thinking of you Betty" "You are Special to us all at C.A.O.S." & signed by over 40 members of this year's "The King & I". Also a "Get Well" card from Dorth and Doreen Smith (Dorth has known me since I was a little baby down at my grand-dad's farm).

I received a delivery through the post from Derrick Palmer & his wife Peggy. They had earlier written to me at Glenfield Hospital, only to discover that I had since transferred to Leicester Royal Infirmary. I have received nothing from Glenfield since I transferred to L.R.I.

1.15 pm – Visited by Gwen, who had learned of my whereabouts from Doug Taylor. She offered to visit Enid at Ravenstone next Saturday, but Enid was having none of that.

Like me, Enid does not wish to entertain people at home non-stop, when we would rather be gadding about choosing our own particular interests.

14th February 2001 Wednesday
Valentine's Day

10.00 am – Lady Doctor Waterhouse called to see me & enquire about my sickness.

Receive first of my post at L.R.I. re-directed from Glenfield:

Card from Rosemary & George Howard.

Original card from Derrick & Peggy Palmer. (Please send to Surgical Assessment Unit L.R.I.)

Card from Joan Elliott (Reading for the Blind)

Card from Lesley Sear

Card from Lesley & Bill Hale

I have a lovely water bed (sideways) which is better than the one at Glenfield.

I try to eat my first 'food' but cannot eat much; in fact a complete failure.

At 1.00 pm I transfer from my bedside chair into bed for the removal of the Epidural put into my back prior to my operation.

At 1.15 pm I am sick.

At 1.30 pm the Epidural is removed & I stay in bed.

3.00 pm - Peter Jacques visited until 4.00 pm when he witnessed me having projectile sickness.

6.00 pm – Mary Blue arrived and at 7.45 pm more projectile sickness.

To bed with 'morphine' drip & sick again at 6.00 am.

15ᵗʰ February 2001 Thursday

10.15 am – Mary Blue has an appointment with Mr Hemmingway, the top surgeon here, to update her on my condition. Meanwhile, the doctors on their early morning round tell me NOT to attempt eating 'food' and stick to warm milk. Had a lovely bed bath.

10.30 am – Mary Blue arrived at my bedside after seeing Mr Hemmingway, the top surgeon, in his office at 10.00 am. She is now convinced that I should try the 'chemotherapy' treatment as it will shrink the cancer down and enable me to eat normally. If I can eat & drink, then the swelling in my legs will go down. Lack of protein causes them to swell, so it is a vicious cycle.

Mary Blue received in the post a note from David Bailey in Devon to whom she had written to tell of my cancer. He enclosed 'Just a Note' – 'Handmade with Love' from June & David Bailey. (Son of Eric Bailey, my mother's cousin from Willoughby-on-the-Wolds)

1.00 pm – Oncologist Dr Simon calls to see me for a friendly chat & to tell me about the proposed Chemotherapy due next week.

2.00 pm – Postal Delivery "Thinking of you always – you are a very special person" from Joan Dillow & family.

3.00 pm – Projectile sickness yet again during process of drinking warm milk. Advised to stop drinking milk & take sips of water.

5.00 pm – Returned to bed for more comfort.

9.00 pm – Sick again – only slightly. Due for injection to curb sickness when night staff come on – to try & persuade my inside not to feel sick.

As the night dragged on & on I was sick so many times I knew the injection to curb sickness had been of no use at all.

16ᵗʰ February 2001 Friday

As it has now been assessed by Dr Simon that I am to have chemotherapy early next week, I shall soon be transferred from Ward 21 to another part of L.R.I.

11.00 am – Lesley Hale phoned to enquire whether it was alright to visit today. I said, 'Yes'.

1.00 pm – Mary Blue called in to see me after having her hair coloured & after shopping in Leicester.

2.00 pm – Lesley Hale visited me for an hour, briefly meeting Mary Blue whom she did not know, their paths having never crossed before.

1.00 pm – Have (Metaglocerene? albumen?) Metoclopramide drip fixed to supply me with more nutrients, (like egg white). This is up until 5.15pm.

6.30 pm – Very sick again. Took ½ hour to get me cleaned up, during which time my good friend Reevsie arrived to be told I was 'temporarily *disposed*'. She waited long & patiently to see me & stayed with me until 8 pm.

10.30 pm – Sick again.

12 midnight – Sick again. Fitted then with all night drip of Metoclopramide to attack my sickness with a vengeance. The urge to be sick & the urge not to be sick were then in battle.

17ᵗʰ February 2001 Saturday

High drama during the early hours of the morning as a dozen nurses rushed urgently to attend to poor old Margaret struggling to breathe. They brought the oxygen cylinder & frantically administered to her. Doctors then appeared equally urgently, but in the end she died & was removed from the ward.

12 noon – I finally 'got up' & was washed.

1.00 pm – Mary Blue arrived; she had received a letter from Graham Stocks of Quorn (Auntie Doris's grandson) to ask whether I would like a visit from Graham, Susannah and baby George.

I said leave it for a while to see how I feel next week. She also brought from Sharon a copy of 'Desiderata' which includes, 'You are a child of the Universe, no less than the trees and the stars'.

2.00 pm – Already football fans are arriving for the Cup Match between Leicester City and Bristol City and we can hear their loudspeakers.

3.00 pm – Kick off – Leicester City v Bristol City (Final score, Leicester won 3 - 0)

3.30 pm – Postal delivery from Coalville's C.S.R.F. (Civil Service Retirement Fellowship) signed by members at the recent meeting. Also Card from cousin Rita, co-incidentally here in hospital with a broken leg, but due home shortly. (Now in Langham Ward)

5.00 pm – Sickness returned again.

5.30 pm – An unexpected visit from Murdo, who said he called to see me this morning at 8.00 am but I was asleep & he did not like to wake me.

6.00 pm to bed.

10.30 pm Slightly sick despite 2ⁿᵈ 24 hour drip feed into my side of Metoclophomide.

18ᵗʰ February 2001 Sunday

10.00 am – A lovely bed bath.

3.30 pm – Pat, Evelyn and Mary Blue visited until 5.00 pm.

4.45 pm – Lynda Durcan popped in with a card from Lynda, Michael, Rosie, Frances, Bernadette and Ci........ ?

8.00 pm Sick yet again.

19ᵗʰ February 2001 Monday

4.00 am – Sick again. The doctor came to see me & decided to alter the amount of fluid in the drip. That seemed to help.

8.00 am – A lovely proper bath, complete with hoist chair & my hair washed.

12 noon – Sick again.

1.00 pm – Welcome visit of Enid. She managed to escape before Gwen arrived at 2.00 pm. Almost immediately I was asked to try & stand up & walk, but I could not even manage to stand up on my over-bloated legs. Most welcome arrival in the post of 2 envelopes bearing the postmark Barbados – cards from Julian & Michael, together there.

6.00 pm – Mary Blue arrived and found me tucked up in bed trying to drink my hot chocolate – which hopefully would not make me sick, as milk has been doing previously.

20th February 2001 Tuesday

Being encouraged today to drink and drink and drink. Also tried my first attempt at food, ice cream for lunch and again for tea.

Not made at all comfortable in bed and was therefore sick again at 5.00 pm.

3.30 pm – Visited by Revd Kerry Emmett, Rector of Ravenstone, who fortunately arrived after I had been seated comfortably in my chair.

5.00 pm – Was put back into bed and was sick.

6.00 pm – Welcome visit by Steven when I was still in discomfort in bed.

Written for Betty by Steven.

21st February 2001 Wednesday

From Balmoral to Osborne, having been promised the first vacant bed – but still being sick.

5.00 pm – Sick.

6.00 pm – Sick, when Mary Blue arrived.

6.30 pm – Welcome arrival of Lesley Sear.

22nd February 2001 Thursday

Oncology East L.R.I. – Encouraged to drink, drink, drink – more and more and more.

After drinking hot chocolate at breakfast time I was sick. After drinking hot chocolate again for elevenses I was sick.

12.30 – Mary Blue arrived.

Betty wrote her last notes on February 19th and from then on dictated them.

23rd February 2001 Friday

No more sickness! Nil by mouth since last night.

pm – I had to sign to give my consent to an Endoscopy whilst lying down! Given slight sedation whilst a camera went down my throat to investigate the unseen blockage. Taken by porter named Baz (whose breath smelt of smoke) to Windsor Building over the bridge.

2 cards by post – one from Marianne – one from Margaret Moore, formerly of Ravenstone and her husband Derek Grundy; now both belong to Broom Leys Church.

3.00 pm – Leicester City kick-off. Leicester v Sunderland, Leicester won 2 – 0.

5.30 pm – Mary Blue arrived. Betty was feeling drowsy and wearing an oxygen mask and being drip-fed.

Written from Oncology East L.R.I. for Betty by Mary Blue.

24th February 2001 Saturday

Steven & Jane attempted to visit, but just could not park

- either in the hospital car park or anywhere else – so gave up and went home after an hour. This was due to both Leicester Tigers (rugby) and Leicester City (football) playing this afternoon at home. A notice in the main entrance does indicate to whom any complaints should be made.

Mary Blue arrived approximately 5.45 pm and stayed until 8.00 pm. Betty still on saline drip and nil by mouth; feeling weak and using oxygen. Slept very little but only a little sickness.

25th February 2001 Sunday

Late riser! At 11.00 am.

1.00 pm – Like Henry VIII in full armour I was hoisted from my bedside chair to land on my bed – but I was not sitting as straight up as I would have liked because I'm too bendy in the middle.

3.25 pm – Welcome arrival of Pat, Evelyn and Mary Blue, who brought two letters – one from Inland Revenue and one from the Cathedral.

26th February 2001 Monday

1.00 pm – Enid visited.

3.00 pm – Kerry Emmett, Rector of Ravenstone, visited.

6.00 pm – Mary Blue visited.

7.00 pm – Sharon visited.

Doctors wanted to start Chemotherapy by means of an intravenous drip – but were unable to insert a cannula into a vein because I am too swollen. They will review the situation tomorrow.

27th February 2001 Tuesday

Pancake Day!

Just as Cleopatra of the Nile, in the days of Anthony and Julius Caesar, luxuriated in the gorgeous waters of the Nile to bathe – so today at 3 pm I had the luxury of a Jacuzzi bath – absolutely wonderful – sheer bliss!

Lesley visited, followed shortly afterwards by Reevsie. Gwen also visited.

28th February 2001 Wednesday

Two cards delivered – one from Civil Service Retirement Fellowship group, one from Harry and Mary Baxter.

Every time any medication is given I am asked my date of birth as a double check that they have the right medicine for the right person. Tonight I answered 14th July 1931 when they brought my injection and the nurse observed that my star sign is 'Cancer'. How ironic!

1st March 2001 Thursday

Very helpless – extensive care given!

2nd March 2001 Friday

Drinking a lot rather than eating – always thirsty.

Mary Blue came 1.00 pm to 3.00 pm.

3rd March 2001 Saturday

Mary Blue arrived early because Leicester City are playing Liverpool this afternoon.

After I had eaten my lunch (apple and date crumble and custard) Mary Blue fetched me an orange ice lolly.

Later I was transferred to Room 7 – a private room where I am to be isolated because I have an infection – M.R.S.A. (Methicillin-resistant Staphylococcus aureus)

Leicester won 2 – 0!

4ᵗʰ March 2001 Sunday
Still in isolation. Pat, Evelyn and Mary Blue visited in the afternoon at 3.30 pm.

5ᵗʰ March 2001 Monday
Room 7 – Still isolated with M.R.S.A. Enid visited at dinner time. Mary Blue visited at 6.30 pm.
Today a 'Hickman Line' was put into my chest just below my shoulder (collar bone) and I am going to have an x-ray to ensure it is in the correct place in a vein leading to my heart (this is very important). Then I can be fed through it – either with vitamins or chemotherapy, or both – in the next few days. Meanwhile I am being injected with antibiotics.

6ᵗʰ March 2001 Tuesday
Still in isolation.

7ᵗʰ March 2001 Wednesday
Syringe driver came out and I was sick. Tube put up nose into stomach and aspirated to empty stomach. Syringe driver and anti-sickness drug re-given.
Evening – two drip bags into Hickman Line. One to feed me and one is chemotherapy. Next chemotherapy dose due in three weeks time. Mary Blue came.

8ᵗʰ March 2001 Thursday
Slightly better; Mary Blue came 12.30 pm.

9ᵗʰ March 2001 Friday
Feeling much worse and sick. Mary Blue came 1.00 pm.

Note by Mary Blue – The hospital rang me very early on Saturday 10ᵗʰ March to say I ought to come. I rang my dad (Betty's brother Pat) and he wanted to come as well. I fetched him in my car from Hugglescote and together we went to L.R.I.
Betty died at 7.00 am just before we arrived.

* * *

During my many conversations with Betty while she was in hospital she told me of her diary.
I was aware that she kept a diary which she had begun in 1944 - the year I was born. My mum used to tease me and my dad about it, keeping us in line by saying, 'Watch out – or you'll be in the diary!'

When she was diagnosed with cancer Betty told me that she had planned to finish her diaries at the end of 2001 in any case, and she asked me to finish writing them for her. She told me where they were and that she had bought an oak chest for them to be stored in safely. (See 18ᵗʰ July 2000)
I was to keep them and make sure they were passed on as far into the future as possible. I was told I could begin reading them and I was amazed at their neatness. Each day of the five-year diaries had just six lines to be

written on and each entry filled these lines exactly, leaving no space at the end. I mentioned this to Betty and she said achieving this was 'a work of art' which she had perfected over many years. She was especially pleased if the six lines could be completely filled with just one sentence! She also said they had to be written with a fountain pen – her Parker pen – because ink from a ball-point fades over time. Feeling very nervous at being charged with this task and not wanting to spoil the last diary with my not-so-neat handwriting, I decided to transcribe the whole lot and put them onto a compact disc. It has been a labour of love that has taken me seven years on and off; but I think this will ensure they go on into the future even if one of my descendants should decide to chuck them on a bonfire one day!

Intending to complete her diary and finish at the end of 2001, Betty had filled some dates in advance with pertinent entries – so I will write, right to the end, that which she had planned......

2ⁿᵈ April 2001 Monday
On this day in history in 1801: Nelson put his telescope to his blind eye at the Battle of Copenhagen, and so did not see the signal from Admiral Parker to cease fighting. He continued the action until the Danish fleet were totally subdued.   *(Newspaper cutting)*

14ᵗʰ July 2001 Saturday
From my Septuagenarian heights, I..........(See Psalm 90)
                         (Note on loose scrap of paper)

By the time someone is 70 there are hosts of medical hazards which can confront them.   (Newspaper cutting)

Epigram on his 70ᵗʰ Birthday

The world is wide in time & tide,
And God is guide, then – do not hurry.
That man is blest who does his best
And leaves the rest, then – do not worry.
                         Charles F. Deems.

16ᵗʰ November 2001 Friday
Margaret of Scotland, Queen, Wife, Mother, 1093.
Today is the feast day of St. Margaret, born to Prince Edward, the exiled son of King Edmund Ironside, who preceded King Canute. Born in 1045, she enjoyed life as a teenager at the English court of Edward the Confessor. When William the Conqueror came in 1066, she fled to Scotland, married Malcolm III of Scotland & died in 1093.

27ᵗʰ November 2001 Tuesday
On this day in 1701: Anders Celsius, Swedish astronomer who created the centigrade temperature scale, was born in Upsala. He originally used boiling point of water as 0 and freezing point as 100 – this order was later reversed.   *(Newspaper cutting)*

24ᵗʰ December 2001 Monday
As the Good Book says (The Glorious Quran) Sura 9: 72: "Allah hath promised to believers, men & women,

gardens under which rivers flow, to dwell therein, and beautiful mansions in gardens of everlasting bliss. But the greatest bliss is the good pleasure of Allah. That is the supreme felicity."

26th December 2001 Wednesday

So Farewell! For I am going –
On a long and distant journey.
But my books I leave behind me,
Listen to their words of wisdom,
Listen to the truth they tell you.

28th December 2001 Friday

"God and Sons" – Peacemakers.

Blessed are the peacemakers; for they shall be called the children of God. Be therefore a peacemaker. Be perfect, be of good comfort, be of one mind, live in peace. And the God of peace be with you.

30th December 2001 Sunday

"Pure religion and undefiled before God and the Father is this, to visit the fatherless and widows in their affliction, and to keep himself unspotted from the world."

Find this verse in the Bible and find wisdom.

31st December 2001 Monday

I thank God for the Buddha's inspiration:
"Now may every living being, young or old, weak or strong, living near or far, known or unknown, living or departed or yet unborn, may every living thing be full of bliss."   *(Newspaper cutting)*

* * *

Extracts from Snibston Parish Magazine, September 1931.

The Glory of Life

The Glory of Life is to love,
Not to be loved,
To give, not to get,
To serve, not to be served,
To be a strong hand in the dark to another
In the time of need,
To be a cup of strength to any soul
In a crisis of weakness.
This is to know the Glory of Life.

Baptisms
August 20: Elizabeth, daughter of Reginald Arthur & Mary Hewes.

* * *

The Fullness of Time

On a rusty iron throne
Past the furthest star of space
I saw Satan sit alone,
Old and haggard was his face;
For his work was done and he
Rested in eternity.

And to him from out the sun
Came his father and his friend
Saying, now the work is done
Enmity is at an end:
And he guided Satan to
Paradises that he knew.

Gabriel without a frown,
Uriel without a spear,
Raphael came singing down
Welcoming their ancient peer,
And they seated him beside
One who had been crucified.

James Stephens

Thought for the day:
Surely goodness and mercy shall follow me all the days of my life: and I will dwell in the house of the Lord for ever. Psalm 23 v9, King James Bible.
(Newspaper cutting)

* * *

Hewes, Elizabeth (Betty) of Ravenstone, passed peacefully away at Leicester Royal Infirmary on March 10th 2001 aged 69 years.
Daughter of the late Reginald Arthur and Mary Hewes, dearly loved sister of Bunting, Pat and the late Robin, aunt to Mary, Michael and Julian.
The funeral service will take place at St. Michaels Church, Ravenstone on Tuesday March 20th at 2.15 pm followed by cremation at Loughborough Crematorium. No flowers by request and donations in lieu if so desired for Ravenstone Church Restoration Fund, c/o the Co-operative Funeral Service, Stuart House, 128 London Road, Coalville.   *(Newspaper cutting)*

* * *